Gleim Publications, Inc. offers five university-level study systems:

Auditing & Systems Exam Questions and Explanations with Test Prep CD-Rom
Business Law/Legal Studies Exam Questions and Explanations with Test Prep CD-Rom
Federal Tax Exam Questions and Explanations with Test Prep CD-Rom
Financial Accounting Exam Questions and Explanations with Test Prep CD-Rom
Cost/Managerial Accounting Exam Questions and Explanations with Test Prep CD-Rom

The following is a list of Gleim examination review systems:

CIA Review: Part I, Internal Audit Role in Governance, Risk, and Control
CIA Review: Part II, Conducting the Internal Audit Engagement
CIA Review: Part III, Business Analysis and Information Technology
CIA Review: Part IV, Business Management Skills

CMA Review: Part 1, Business Analysis
CMA Review: Part 2, Management Accounting and Reporting
CMA Review: Part 3, Strategic Management
CMA Review: Part 4, Business Applications

CPA Review: Financial
CPA Review: Auditing
CPA Review: Business
CPA Review: Regulation

EA Review: Part 1, Individuals
EA Review: Part 2, Businesses
EA Review: Part 3, Representation, Practice, and Procedures

W9-AHB-604

An order form is provided at the back of this book, or contact us at www.gleim.com or (800) 874-5346.

Groundwood Paper and Highlighters — All Gleim books are printed on high-quality groundwood paper. We recommend you use a non-bleed-through (dry) highlighter (e.g., the Avery *Glidestick*™ – ask for it at your local office supply store) when highlighting items within these books.

Visit our Internet site (www.gleim.com) for the latest updates and information on all of our products.

REVIEWERS AND CONTRIBUTORS

Garrett W. Gleim, B.S., CPA (not in public practice), is a graduate of The Wharton School at the University of Pennsylvania. Mr. Gleim coordinated the production staff, reviewed the manuscript, and provided production assistance throughout the project.

Grady M. Irwin, J.D., is a graduate of the University of Florida College of Law, and he has taught in the University of Florida College of Business. Mr. Irwin provided substantial editorial assistance throughout the project.

John F. Rebstock, B.S.A., is a graduate of the Fisher School of Accounting at the University of Florida. He has passed the CPA and CIA exams. Mr. Rebstock reviewed portions of the manuscript.

Stewart B. White, B.M., *Cum Laude*, University of Richmond, B.S., Virginia Commonwealth University, has passed the CPA and CISA exams and has worked in the fields of retail management, financial audit, IT audit, COBOL programming, and data warehouse management.

Scott Lawton, B.S., is a graduate of Brigham Young University-Idaho and Utah Valley State College. He has been employed by the Utah State Tax Commission.

A PERSONAL THANKS

This manual would not have been possible without the extraordinary effort and dedication of Kyle Cadwallader, Julie Cutlip, Mumbi Ngugi, Eileen Nickl, and Teresa Soard, who typed the entire manuscript and all revisions, and drafted and laid out the diagrams and illustrations in this book.

The authors also appreciate the production and editorial assistance of Jacob Brunny, Katie Goodrich, James Harvin, Jean Marzullo, Shane Rapp, Victoria Rodriguez, Joanne Strong, Laura Ter Keurst, and Martha Willis.

The authors also appreciate the critical reading assistance of Lisa Arsenault, Brooke Aveni, Ellen Buhl, Corrine Contento, Margaret Curtis, Ellie Gonzales, Holly Johnson, Jennifer Stein, and Jeremy Wright.

Finally, we appreciate the encouragement, support, and tolerance of our families throughout this project.

2008 EDITION

CPA REVIEW

Business

by

Irvin N. Gleim, Ph.D., CPA, CIA, CMA, CFM

with the assistance of
Grady M. Irwin, J.D.

The AICPA formal title of this section is *Business Environment and Concepts*, and the AICPA acronym is BEC.

ABOUT THE AUTHOR

Irvin N. Gleim is Professor Emeritus in the Fisher School of Accounting at the University of Florida and is a member of the American Accounting Association, Academy of Legal Studies in Business, American Institute of Certified Public Accountants, Association of Government Accountants, Florida Institute of Certified Public Accountants, The Institute of Internal Auditors, and the Institute of Management Accountants. He has had articles published in the *Journal of Accountancy*, *The Accounting Review*, and *The American Business Law Journal* and is author/coauthor of numerous accounting books, aviation books, and CPE courses.

iv

Gleim Publications, Inc.
P.O. Box 12848
University Station
Gainesville, Florida 32604
(800) 87-GLEIM or (800) 874-5346
(352) 375-0772
FAX: (352) 375-6940
Internet: www.gleim.com
Email: admin@gleim.com

This is the first printing of the 2008 edition of *CPA Review: Business*. Please email update@gleim.com with **CPA BEC 2008-1** included in the subject or text. You will receive our current update as a reply. Updates are available until the next edition is published.

EXAMPLE:

To:	update@gleim.com
From:	*your email address*
Subject:	CPA BEC 2008-1

ISSN: 1547-8084

ISBN: 978-1-58194-615-4 *CPA Review: Auditing*
ISBN: 978-1-58194-618-5 *CPA Review: Regulation*
ISBN: 978-1-58194-617-8 *CPA Review: Financial*
ISBN: 978-1-58194-616-1 *CPA Review: Business*
ISBN: 978-1-58194-647-5 *CPA Review: A System for Success*

ACKNOWLEDGMENTS

Material from *Uniform Certified Public Accountant Examination Questions and Unofficial Answers*, Copyright © 1974-2007 by the American Institute of Certified Public Accountants, Inc., is reprinted and/or adapted with permission. Visit the AICPA web page at www.aicpa.org or call (212) 596-6200 for more information.

The author is indebted to the Institute of Certified Management Accountants for permission to use problem materials from past CMA examinations. Questions and unofficial answers from the Certified Management Accountant Examinations, copyright by the Institute of Certified Management Accountants, are reprinted and/or adapted with permission.

The author is grateful for permission to reproduce Certified Internal Auditor Examination Questions, Copyright © 1991-1995 by The Institute of Internal Auditors, Inc.

This publication was printed and bound by Corley Printing Company, St. Louis, MO, a registered ISO-9002 company. More information about Corley Printing Company is available at www.corleyprinting.com or by calling (314) 739-3777.

TABLE OF CONTENTS

PREFACE FOR CPA CANDIDATES

The purpose of this Gleim *CPA Review* study book is to help YOU prepare to pass the Business Environment and Concepts section (referred to throughout the rest of this text as BEC) of the CPA examination. Our overriding consideration is to provide an inexpensive, effective, and easy-to-use study program. This book

1. Explains how to optimize your grade by focusing on the BEC section of the CPA exam.
2. Defines the subject matter tested on the BEC section of the CPA exam.
3. Outlines all of the subject matter tested on the BEC section in 20 easy-to-use study units.
4. Presents multiple-choice questions from recent CPA examinations to prepare you for business questions in future CPA exams. Our answer explanations are presented to the immediate right of each question for your convenience. Two bookmarks are provided at the back of this book. Use a bookmark to cover our answer explanations as you study the questions.

The outline format, the spacing, and the question and answer formats in this book are designed to facilitate readability, learning, understanding, and success on the CPA exam. Our most successful candidates use the Gleim CPA Complete System,* which includes books, *Test Prep* CD-Rom, audio CDs, *Gleim Online*, and a Personal Counselor; or a group study CPA review program. (Check our website for live courses we recommend.) This review book and all Gleim *CPA Review* materials are compatible with other CPA review materials and courses that follow the AICPA Content Specification Outlines.

To maximize the efficiency and effectiveness of your CPA review program, begin by **studying** (not merely reading) *CPA Review: A System for Success*. It has been carefully organized and written to provide important information to assist you in passing the CPA examination.

Thank you for your interest in the new Gleim *CPA Review* materials. We deeply appreciate the thousands of letters and suggestions received from CIA, CMA, EA, and CPA candidates during the past 4 decades. Please send your suggestions, comments, and corrections concerning this review book. The last page has been designed to help you note corrections and suggestions during your study process. Please tear it out and mail it to us with your comments immediately after you take the CPA exam. We will respond to each letter on an individual basis.

Good Luck on the Exam,

Irvin N. Gleim

December 2007

*Call (800) 874-5346 to order.

OPTIMIZING YOUR BUSINESS SCORE

This introduction is a summary of Gleim's *CPA Review: A System for Success*, an 80-page booklet containing a detailed discussion of the steps to exam success. *CPA Review: A System for Success* is a necessity for all CPA candidates. It should be studied at least twice: at the start of a candidate's study program and again 1 or 2 weeks before taking the CPA exam. It is a separate booklet, so you do not have to carry it with you when you use this book, *CPA Review: Business*.

BEC is scheduled for 2-1/2 hours (150 minutes).

AICPA title:	Business Environment and Concepts
AICPA acronym:	BEC
Gleim title:	Business
Question format:	90 multiple-choice questions in 3 testlets of 30 questions each
Areas covered:	I. (20%) Business Structure
	II. (10%) Economic Concepts
	III. (20%) Financial Management
	IV. (25%) Information Technology
	V. (25%) Planning and Measurement

OVERVIEW OF BUSINESS

This section of the CPA exam covers the knowledge of general business environment and business concepts that candidates need to know in order to understand the underlying business reasons for (and accounting implications of) transactions, as well as the skills needed to apply such knowledge in performing financial statement audit and attestation engagements and other functions normally performed by CPAs that affect the public interest. Content covered in this section includes knowledge of business structure; economic concepts essential to obtaining an understanding of an entity's operations, business, and industry; financial management; information technology; and planning and measurement.

The AICPA suggests reviewing current textbooks and business periodicals that cover business law, managerial accounting, management, finance, economics, accounting information systems, management information systems, and budgeting and measurement for business. Our outlines and answer explanations are based on these and other important resources, and organized into meaningful, easy-to-use, common-sense study units to facilitate your exam preparation via the *Gleim Knowledge Transfer System*.

AICPA CONTENT SPECIFICATION OUTLINES (CSOs)

The AICPA has indicated that the content specification outlines have several purposes, including:

1. *Ensure consistent coverage of subject matter from one examination to the next.*

2. *Provide guidance to those who are responsible for preparing the examination in order to ensure a balanced examination.*

3. *Assist candidates in preparing for the examination by indicating subjects that may be covered by the examination.*

4. *Alert accounting educators about the subject matter considered necessary to prepare for the examination.*

Below and on the following page are the AICPA BEC CSOs and corresponding Gleim study units.

<table>
<tr><td colspan="2" align="center">AICPA CONTENT SPECIFICATION OUTLINES</td><td align="center">GLEIM STUDY UNITS</td></tr>
<tr><td colspan="2">Business Environment and Concepts</td><td></td></tr>
<tr><td>I.</td><td>Business structure (20%)</td><td>I. BUSINESS STRUCTURE</td></tr>
<tr><td>A.</td><td>Advantages, implications, and constraints of legal structures for business</td><td>1. Proprietorships and General Partnerships</td></tr>
<tr><td></td><td>1. Sole proprietorships and general and limited partnerships</td><td></td></tr>
<tr><td></td><td>2. Limited liability companies (LLC), limited liability partnership (LLP), and joint ventures</td><td>2. Noncorporate Limited Liability Entities</td></tr>
<tr><td></td><td>3. Subchapter C and subchapter S corporations</td><td>3. Corporations: Formation, Powers, and Financing</td></tr>
<tr><td>B.</td><td>Formation, operation, and termination of businesses</td><td></td></tr>
<tr><td>C.</td><td>Financial structure, capitalization, profit and loss allocation, and distributions</td><td>4. Corporations: Governance and Fundamental Changes</td></tr>
<tr><td>D.</td><td>Rights, duties, legal obligations, and authority of owners and management (directors, officers, stockholders, partners, and other owners)</td><td></td></tr>
<tr><td>II.</td><td>Economic concepts essential to obtaining an understanding of an entity's business and industry (10%)</td><td>II. ECONOMIC CONCEPTS</td></tr>
<tr><td>A.</td><td>Business cycles and reasons for business fluctuations</td><td>5. Microeconomics</td></tr>
<tr><td>B.</td><td>Economic measures and reasons for changes in the economy, such as inflation, deflation, and interest rate changes</td><td>6. Macroeconomics</td></tr>
<tr><td>C.</td><td>Market influences on business strategies, including selling, supply chain, and customer management strategies</td><td>7. International Trade</td></tr>
<tr><td>D.</td><td>Implications to business of dealings in foreign currencies, hedging, and exchange rate fluctuations</td><td></td></tr>
<tr><td>III.</td><td>Financial management (20%)</td><td>III. FINANCIAL MANAGEMENT</td></tr>
<tr><td>A.</td><td>Financial modeling, including such factors as financial indexes, taxes and opportunity costs, and models, such as economic value added, cash flow, net present value, discounted payback, and internal rate of return</td><td>8. Working Capital Policy and Management</td></tr>
<tr><td></td><td>1. Objectives
2. Techniques
3. Limitations</td><td>9. Long-Term Capital Financing

10. Risk Management and Profitability</td></tr>
<tr><td>B.</td><td>Strategies for short-term and long-term financing options, including cost of capital and derivatives</td><td></td></tr>
<tr><td>C.</td><td>Financial statement and business implications of liquid asset management</td><td></td></tr>
<tr><td></td><td>1. Management of cash and cash equivalents, accounts receivable, accounts payable, and inventories</td><td></td></tr>
<tr><td></td><td>2. Characteristics and financial statement and business implications of loan rates (fixed vs. variable) and loan covenants</td><td></td></tr>
</table>

AICPA CONTENT SPECIFICATION OUTLINES	GLEIM STUDY UNITS

IV. Information technology (IT) implications in the business environment (25%)

A. Role of business information systems

   1. Reporting concepts and systems
   2. Transaction processing systems
   3. Management reporting systems
   4. Risks

B. Roles and responsibilities within the IT function

   1. Roles and responsibilities of database/network/Web administrators, computer operators, librarians, systems programmers, and applications programmers

   2. Appropriate segregation of duties

C. IT fundamentals

   1. Hardware and software, networks, and data structure, analysis, and application, including operating systems, security, file organization, types of data files, and database management systems

   2. Systems operation, including transaction processing modes, such as batch, online, real-time, and distributed processing, and application processing phases, such as data capture; edit routines; master file maintenance; reporting, accounting, control, and management; query, audit trail, and ad hoc reports; and transaction flow

D. Disaster recovery and business continuity, including data backup and data recovery procedures, alternate processing facilities (hot sites), and threats and risk management

E. Financial statement and business implications of electronic commerce, including electronic fund transfers, point of sale transactions, Internet-based transactions, and electronic data interchange

V. Planning and measurement (25%)

A. Planning and budgeting

   1. Planning techniques, including strategic and operational planning
   2. Forecasting and projection techniques
   3. Budgeting and budget variance analysis

B. Performance measures

   1. Organization performance measures, including financial and nonfinancial scorecards

   2. Benchmarking, including quality control principles, best practices, and benchmarking techniques

C. Cost measurement

   1. Cost measurement concepts (standard, joint product, and by-product costing)

   2. Accumulating and assigning costs (job order, process, and activity-based costing)

   3. Factors affecting production costs

IV. INFORMATION TECHNOLOGY

11. Information Technology I
12. Information Technology II
13. Information Technology III
14. Information Technology IV
15. Information Technology V

V. PLANNING

16. Planning and Budgeting
17. Business Performance
18. Cost Behavior and Definitions
19. Product Costing and Related Topics
20. Standard Costs and Variance Analysis

A SYSTEM FOR SUCCESS

To ensure your success on the BEC section of the CPA examination, you should focus on the following steps:

1. **Understand the exam, including coverage, content, format, administration, and grading.**

    a. The better you understand the examination process from beginning to end, the better you will be able to perform.

    b. Study Gleim's *CPA Review: A System for Success*. Please be sure you have a current copy of this useful booklet. (*CPA Review: A System for Success* is also available online at www.gleim.com/accounting/cpa/systemforsuccess.php.)

2. **Learn and understand the subject matter tested.** The AICPA's CSOs for the BEC section, along with the questions that have appeared in recent CPA examinations and the suggestions from recent CPA candidates,* are the basis for the study outlines that are presented in each of the 20 study units that make up this book. You will also learn and understand the BEC material tested on the CPA exam by answering numerous multiple-choice questions from recent CPA exams. Multiple-choice questions with the answer explanations to the immediate right of each question are a major component of each study unit.

3. **Practice answering recent exam questions to perfect your question-answering techniques.** Answering recent exam questions helps you understand the standards to which you will be held. This motivates you to learn and understand while studying (rather than reading) the outlines in each of the 20 study units.

    a. Question-answering techniques are suggested for multiple-choice questions in Study Unit 4 of *CPA Review: A System for Success*.

    b. Our **CPA Test Prep** CD-Rom contains thousands of additional multiple-choice questions that are not offered in our books. Additionally, the software has many useful features, including documentation of your performance and the ability to simulate the CBT (computer-based testing) exam environment.

    c. Our **CPA Gleim Online** is a powerful Internet-based program that allows CPA candidates to learn in an interactive environment and provides feedback to candidates to encourage learning. It includes simulation (constructive response) questions in Prometric's format. All *CPA Gleim Online* candidates have access to a Personal Counselor, who helps candidates organize study plans that work with their busy schedules.

4. **Plan exam execution.** Anticipate the exam environment and prepare yourself with a plan: When to arrive? How to dress? What exam supplies to bring? How many questions and what format? Order of answering questions? How much time to spend on each question? See Study Unit 7 in *CPA Review: A System for Success*.

    a. Expect the unexpected and adjust! Remember, your sole objective when taking an examination is to maximize your score. CPA exam grading is curved, and you must outperform your peers.

5. **Be in control.** Develop confidence and ensure success with a controlled preparation program followed by confident execution during the examination.

---

*Please complete the form on pages 705 and 706 IMMEDIATELY after you take the CPA exam so we can adapt to changes in the exam. Our approach has been approved by the AICPA.

HOW TO STUDY A STUDY UNIT USING GLEIM'S COMPLETE SYSTEM

To ensure that you are using your time effectively, we recommend that you follow the steps listed below when using all of the materials together (books, CD-Rom, audios, and Gleim Online):

1. (25-30 minutes) In the Gleim Online course, complete Multiple-Choice Quiz #1 in 20-25 minutes (excluding the review session). It is expected that your scores will be lower on the first quiz than on subsequent quizzes.

    a. Immediately following the quiz, you will be prompted to review the questions you marked and/or answered incorrectly. For each question, analyze and understand why you answered it incorrectly. This step is an essential learning activity.

2. (15-30 minutes) Use the online audiovisual presentation for an overview of the study unit. The Gleim *CPA Review Audios* can be substituted for audiovisual presentations and can be used while driving to work, exercising, etc.

3. (30-45 minutes) Complete the 30-question True/False quiz. It is interactive and most effective if used prior to studying the Knowledge Transfer Outline.

4. (60 minutes) Study the Knowledge Transfer Outline, specifically the troublesome areas identified from the multiple-choice questions in the Gleim Online course. The Knowledge Transfer Outline can be studied either online or from the books.

5. (25-30 minutes) Complete Multiple-Choice Quiz #2 in the Gleim Online course.

    a. Immediately following the quiz, you will be prompted to review the questions you marked and/or answered incorrectly. For each question, analyze and understand why you answered it incorrectly. This step is an essential learning activity.

6. (40-50 minutes) Complete at least two 20-question quizzes while in Test Mode from the *CPA Test Prep* CD-Rom. Continue taking 20-question quizzes until you approach your desired proficiency level, e.g., 75%+.

7. (50 minutes, plus 10 minutes for review) Complete a simulation in the Gleim Online course. (This only applies to AUD, FAR, and REG since there are no simulations in BEC.)

When following these steps, you will complete all 20 study units in about 70-80 hours. Then spend about 10-20 hours using the *CPA Test Prep* CD-Rom to create customized tests for the problem areas that you identified. To review the entire section before the exam, use the *CPA Test Prep* CD-Rom to create 20-question quizzes that draw questions from all 20 study units. Continue taking 20-question quizzes until you approach your desired proficiency level, e.g., 75%+.

CPA GLEIM ONLINE

Gleim's *CPA Gleim Online* is a versatile, interactive, self-study review program delivered via the Internet. With *CPA Gleim Online*, Gleim guarantees that you will pass the CPA exam on your first sitting. It is divided into four courses (one for each section of the CPA exam).

Each course is broken down into 20 individual, manageable study units. Completion time per study unit will vary from 1-5 hours. Each study unit in the course contains an audiovisual presentation, 30 true/false study questions, 10-20 pages of Knowledge Transfer Outlines, and two 20-question multiple-choice quizzes. Simulation questions are also included with each study unit in AUD, FAR, and REG.

Gleim's *CPA Gleim Online* provides you with a Personal Counselor, a real person who will provide support to ensure your competitive edge. *CPA Gleim Online* is a great way to get confidence as you prepare with Gleim. This confidence will continue during and after the exam.

GLEIM BOOKS AND TEST PREP CD-ROM

Twenty-question tests in the *CPA Test Prep* CD-Rom will help you to focus on your weaker areas. Make it a game: How much can you improve?

Our *CPA Test Prep* forces you to commit to your answer choice before looking at answer explanations; thus, you are preparing under true exam conditions. For each study unit, it also keeps track of your time and performance history, both of which are available in either a table or graphical format.

Simplify the exam preparation process by following our suggested steps listed below. DO NOT omit the step in which you diagnose the reasons for answering questions incorrectly; i.e., learn from your mistakes while studying so you avoid making similar mistakes on the CPA exam.

1. In test mode, answer a 20-question diagnostic quiz from each study unit before studying any other information.

2. Study the Knowledge Transfer Outline for the corresponding study unit in your Gleim book. Place special emphasis on the weaker areas that you identified with the initial diagnostic quiz in Step 1.

3. Take two or three 20-question quizzes in test mode after you have studied the Knowledge Transfer Outline.

4. Immediately following the quiz, you will be prompted to review the questions you marked and/or answered incorrectly. For each question, analyze and understand why you answered it incorrectly. This step is an essential learning activity.

5. Continue this process until you approach a predetermined proficiency level, e.g., 75%+.

6. Modify this process to suit your individual learning process.

   a. Learning from questions you answer incorrectly is very important. Each question you answer incorrectly is an **opportunity** to avoid missing actual test questions on your CPA exam. Thus, you should carefully study the answer explanations provided until you understand why the original answer you chose is wrong, as well as why the correct answer indicated is correct. This learning technique is clearly the difference between passing and failing for many CPA candidates.

   b. Also, you **must** determine why you answered questions incorrectly and learn how to avoid the same error in the future. Reasons for missing questions include:

      1) Misreading the requirement (stem)
      2) Not understanding what is required
      3) Making a math error
      4) Applying the wrong rule or concept
      5) Being distracted by one or more of the answers
      6) Incorrectly eliminating answers from consideration
      7) Not having any knowledge of the topic tested
      8) Employing bad intuition (WHY?) when guessing

   c. It is also important to verify that you answered correctly for the right reasons. Otherwise, if the material is tested on the CPA exam in a different manner, you may not answer it correctly.

   d. It is imperative that you complete your predetermined number of study units per week so you can review your progress and realize how attainable a comprehensive CPA review program is when using Gleim's Complete System. Remember to meet or beat your schedule to give yourself confidence.

GLEIM AUDIO REVIEWS

Gleim *CPA Review* audios provide a 15- to 40-minute overview of the outline for each study unit in the *CPA Review* book. The purpose is to get candidates "started" so they can relate to the questions they will answer before reading the study outlines in each study unit.

The audios are short and to the point, as is the entire **Gleim System for Success**. We are working to get you through the CPA exam with minimum time, cost, and frustration. You can listen to an informative discussion about the CPA exam and hear a sample of an audio review (The Equity Method) on our website at www.gleim.com/accounting/demos.

MULTIPLE-CHOICE QUESTION-ANSWERING TECHNIQUE

Expect 3 testlets of 30 multiple-choice questions each on the BEC section with a 150-minute time allocation. See Study Unit 4 in *CPA Review: A System for Success* for additional discussion of how to maximize your score on multiple-choice questions.

1. **Budget your time.** We make this point with emphasis. Just as you would fill up your gas tank prior to reaching empty, so too would you finish your exam before time expires.

   a. Here is our suggested time allocation for BEC:

	Minutes	Start Time	
Testlet 1 (MC)	45	2 hours	30 minutes
Testlet 2 (MC)	45	1 hour	45 minutes
Testlet 3 (MC)	45	1 hour	0 minutes
***Extra time	15	0 hour	15 minutes

   b. Before beginning your first testlet of multiple-choice questions, prepare a Gleim Time Management Sheet as recommended in Study Unit 7 of *CPA Review: A System for Success*.

   c. As you work through the individual items, monitor your time. In BEC, we suggest 45 minutes for each testlet of 30 questions. If you answer five items in 7 minutes, you are fine, but if you spend 10 minutes on five items, you need to speed up.

   ***Remember to allocate your budgeted "extra time," as needed, to each testlet. Your goal is to answer all of the items and achieve the maximum score possible.

2. **Answer the questions in consecutive order.**

   a. Do **not** agonize over any one item. Stay within your time budget.

   b. Mark any questions you are unsure of and return to them later as time allows.

   1) Once you have selected either the Continue or Quit option, you will no longer be able to review/change any answers in the testlet completed.

   c. Never leave a multiple-choice question unanswered. Make your best guess in the time allowed. Remember that your score is based on the number of correct responses. An educated guess is inherently better than a blank answer.

3. **For each multiple-choice question:**

   a. **Ignore the answer choices.** Do not allow the answer choices to affect your reading of the item stem (the part of the question that precedes the answer choices).

      1) If four answer choices are presented, three of them are incorrect. These choices are called **distractors** for good reason. Often, distractors are written to appear correct at first glance.

   b. **Read the question** carefully to determine the precise requirement.

      1) Focusing on what is required enables you to ignore extraneous information and to proceed directly to determining the correct answer.

         a) Be especially careful to note when the requirement is an **exception**; e.g., "Which of the following is **not** valid acceptance of an offer?"

      2) By adhering to these steps, you know what is required and which are the relevant facts.

   c. **Determine the correct answer** before reading the answer choices.

      1) However, some multiple-choice items are structured so that the answer cannot be determined from the question alone.

   d. **Read the answer choices carefully.**

      1) Even if answer (A) appears to be the correct choice, do **not** skip the remaining answer choices. Answer (B), (C), or (D) may be even better.

      2) Treat each answer choice as a true/false question as you analyze it.

   e. **Click on the best answer.**

      1) If you are uncertain, guess intelligently. Improve on your 25% chance of getting the correct answer with blind guessing.

      2) For many multiple-choice questions, two answer choices can be eliminated with minimal effort. This can reduce the risk of random guessing and increase your chances of success.

4. After you have answered all the items in a testlet, and <u>before</u> you select either the Continue or Quit option, go back to the questions you marked and reconsider your answer choices.

5. **If you don't know the answer,**

   a. Again, guess; but make it an educated guess, which means select the best possible answer. First, rule out answers that you think are incorrect. Second, speculate on what the AICPA is looking for and/or the rationale behind the question. Third, select the best answer or guess between equally appealing answers. Your first guess is usually the most intuitive. If you cannot make an educated guess, read the item and each answer and pick the best or most intuitive answer. It's just a guess!

   b. Make sure you accomplish this step within your predetermined time budget per testlet.

GLEIM BEC STUDY UNIT LISTING

Also see the Business Review Checklist presented on pages 681 and 682 and the AICPA's Content Specification Outlines on pages 2 and 3.

USER INQUIRIES (TECHNICAL ASSISTANCE) AND CUSTOMER SERVICE PROCEDURES

Technical questions about our materials should be sent to us via <u>mail</u>, <u>email</u>, or <u>fax</u>. The appropriate author, consultant, or staff member will give your correspondence thorough consideration and a prompt response.

Questions concerning orders, prices, shipments, or payments will be handled via telephone, mail, email, Internet, or fax by our competent and courteous customer service staff.

For Test Prep CD-Rom technical support, you may use our automated technical support service at www.gleim.com/support, email us at support@gleim.com, or call us at (800) 874-5346.

CONTROL: HOW TO BE IN

Remember, you must be in control to be successful during exam preparation and execution. Perhaps more importantly, control can also contribute greatly to your personal and other professional goals. Control is the process whereby you

1. Develop expectations, standards, budgets, and plans.
2. Undertake activity, production, study, and learning.
3. Measure the activity, production, output, and knowledge.
4. Compare actual activity with what was expected or budgeted.
5. Modify the activity to better achieve the expected or desired outcome.
6. Revise expectations and standards in light of actual experience.
7. Continue the process.

Exercising control will ultimately develop the confidence you need to outperform 2 out of 3 CPA candidates and PASS the CPA exam! Obtain our *CPA Review: A System for Success* booklet for a more detailed discussion of control and other exam tactics.

STUDY UNIT ONE
PROPRIETORSHIPS AND GENERAL PARTNERSHIPS

(13 pages of outline)

The most basic and common form of business organization is the **sole proprietorship**. It consists of one individual who may be engaged in any kind of business. A sole proprietorship is ordinarily a small enterprise. Because it is not distinct from its owner, it is not a separate legal entity.

A **partnership** is an association of two or more persons carrying on a business as co-owners for profit. Unlike a sole proprietorship, a partnership is often treated as an entity distinct from its owners. For example, the UCC and bankruptcy law adopt the separate entity view. However, a partnership was traditionally regarded as a form of agency involving the individual partners. This study unit addresses the form of partnership that may be created without statutory formalities: the **general partnership**.

1.1 SOLE PROPRIETORSHIPS

1. **Formation.** Of all business organizations, the sole proprietorship is the easiest and cheapest to create. Most filing, registration, and attorneys' fees are avoided.

    a. It is formed at the will of the proprietor.
    b. Formation is subject to only a few legal requirements, for example, local zoning and licensing laws. States rarely require licensing.

        1) However, a proprietor doing business under a fictitious name is usually required to make a d/b/a or **"doing business as"** filing under state law. This kind of statute also applies to partnerships.

2. **Capitalization.** A major weakness of a sole proprietorship is that it cannot raise equity capital other than the personal resources of the proprietor.

    a. Consequently, **debt financing** may be necessary to obtain working capital or to expand the enterprise.

        1) Sources of loans are banks and the federal government's **Small Business Administration (SBA)**.
        2) If **equity financing** is desired, e.g., by bringing in a partner or issuing ownership interests, the form of the business organization will change.

3. **Profits and losses.** The proprietor has the advantage of receiving all profits. (S)he has the disadvantage of **unlimited personal liability** for all losses and debts.

    a. The personal assets of the proprietor are therefore at risk.

4. **Taxation.** The proprietor and the proprietorship are not distinct entities, so the income/loss of the business is reported by the proprietor.

    a. The proprietor receives the tax benefits of all business deductions and losses.
    b. Other tax advantages are the need to file only one return and the avoidance of the double taxation that corporate earnings are subject to.
    c. A self-employed person may make contributions to a retirement plan [such as a SEP IRA, SIMPLE 401(k), or self-employed 401(k)]. Plan earnings are exempt from tax until withdrawn.

5. **Operation.** The sole proprietorship is the most flexible of all business organizations. The proprietor has authority to make all management decisions without answering to other executives, directors, or owners.

    a. Thus, control and accountability are completely centralized.

    b. A disadvantage is that a sole proprietorship may lack the expertise and the checks and balances relative to the decision-making process that are found in more complex organizations.

    c. An advantage is that a sole proprietorship ordinarily can do business in any state without having to file, register, or otherwise qualify to do business in that state.

        1) The **Internet** allows a sole proprietorship to conduct business nationally or even internationally.

6. **Termination.** The duration of the sole proprietorship is at the proprietor's discretion.

    a. The interest of the proprietor may be transferred during his/her life, but the sole proprietorship is then dissolved.

        1) An advantage of a sole proprietorship is that a change in control of the enterprise can occur only with the proprietor's consent.

        2) A transfer of interest often is accompanied by the proprietor's signing of a **noncompetition agreement**.

    b. The sole proprietorship is automatically terminated upon the proprietor's death.

    c. Accordingly, lack of **continuity of existence** is a disadvantage of this form of organization.

7. Stop and review! You have completed the outline for this subunit. Study multiple-choice questions 1 and 2 on page 24.

1.2 GENERAL PARTNERSHIPS

1. **Definition.** According to the **Revised Uniform Partnership Act (RUPA)**, a partnership is "an association of two or more persons to carry on as co-owners a business for profit."

    a. The **general partnership** is the oldest, simplest, and most common form of business organization other than the sole proprietorship.

        1) It differs from other partnerships in that **each partner** has **unlimited personal liability** for all losses and debts of the business. This distinction is a major disadvantage of the general partnership.

        2) Each partner has consented to being both a principal and an agent of the partnership. A **principal** is a person who permits or directs another to act on his/her behalf. An **agent** is a person who agrees to act on the principal's behalf.

            a) An agent has **actual or apparent authority** to take actions that obligate the partnership. Thus, the personal liability incurred by one partner **as a principal** may result from conduct of another partner **as an agent**.

               i) Such liability may arise without the partner's fault, authorization, or knowledge.

    b.   An issue with many accounting and auditing implications is whether a partnership is an **entity separate from its owners**.

        1)   A partnership is **an entity distinct from** the partners (owners).

            a)   The assets of a partnership are treated as those of the business unit.
            b)   Title to real property may be acquired in the partnership name.
            c)   Each partner is considered a fiduciary of the partnership.
            d)   Each partner is considered an agent of the partnership.
            e)   The partnership may sue and be sued in its own name.

                i)   Thus, a judgment against the partnership is not a judgment against a partner.

        2)   However, in other ways, a partnership is treated as an **aggregate** of the individual partners.

            a)   The duration of a partnership is limited by, for example, the will or the lives of the partners. Thus, it lacks continuity of existence.
            b)   No person can become a partner without consent of all the partners.

                i)   A transferee of a partnership interest, unlike a transferee of shares in a corporation, does not become an owner.

            c)   Debts of a partnership are ultimately the debts of the individual partners.
            d)   A partnership is not subject to regular federal income tax.

    c.   The partnership may be **for a term**. The partners may specify the duration of the partnership to be for a specific term or until the completion of a specific project.

        1)   The partnership may be **at will**. The partners have not agreed to remain partners until the end of a definite term or the completion of a specific undertaking. The partnership can be dissolved at any time by any partner by giving notice of his/her express will to withdraw as a partner.

        2)   Hence, the **going-concern assumption** may be inappropriate for a partnership.

2. **Formation.**

    a.   An advantage of the general partnership is that it can be created without any formalities. No filings are required, and the existence of the partnership may arise from a written or oral agreement.

        1)   An agreement also may be implied by the conduct of the parties.

        2)   If the partnership is to exist for a definite period exceeding one year, the **statute of frauds** requires the partnership agreement to be in writing. However, an agreement to transfer real estate, not an agreement to form a partnership to deal in real estate, must be written.

        3)   **Fictitious name statutes** have been enacted in most states for the protection of creditors. Registration permits creditors to discover the persons liable for the debts of the enterprise. The creation and operation of a partnership is little affected by the requirement because a partnership need not adopt a name, although use of a name may help to distinguish a partnership action from that of a partner. Moreover, the use of a name does not necessarily indicate the existence of a partnership or that a named person is a member of the firm.

    b.   Another advantage is that the partners may by **contract** establish the relationships among themselves and between themselves and the partnership.

        1)   The law recognizes the supremacy of the **partnership agreement** in most situations. The RUPA is therefore largely a series of default rules that govern matters not addressed by the partners in their agreement.

2) Nevertheless, the partnership agreement cannot

    a) Unreasonably restrict access to books and records,
    b) Eliminate the duty of loyalty or the obligation of good faith and fair dealing,
    c) Unreasonably reduce the duty of care,
    d) Vary the power to dissociate,
    e) Waive or vary the right to seek court expulsion of another partner,
    f) Vary the law applying to a limited liability partnership,
    g) Vary the right to dissolution and winding up, or
    h) Restrict third-party rights.

c. **Intent.** If the elements of a partnership are present, it is formed even if the parties do not intend to be partners. But, a partnership is not formed if an element is missing even if the parties intend to be partners.

    1) Consequently, parties may disagree about whether their business arrangement is a partnership, especially in the absence of a written agreement.

d. A partnership is an **association of persons**.

    1) Any person who has the **legal capacity** to enter into a contract may enter into a partnership agreement. **Persons** include individuals, partnerships, corporations, estates, trusts, joint ventures, and other associations. Under the RUPA, persons include any legal or commercial entity.

e. A partnership must carry on a **business**. A business is any trade, occupation, or profession.

f. Each of the parties must be a **co-owner**. They must share **profits and losses** and **management authority** (unless they agree otherwise).

g. To form a partnership, the co-owners also must intend that their business make a **profit** even if no profit is earned. Thus, religious, patriotic, and educational organizations that are not for profit are not considered partnerships.

    1) **Profit sharing** by itself does not necessarily signify the existence of a partnership. A person who receives a share of the profits of a business is generally **presumed** to be a partner. This presumption is overcome if the receipt is merely as payment of, or for, any of the following:

        a) Debt or interest on a loan

        b) Compensation to an employee or independent contractor

        c) Rent to a landlord

        d) A health or retirement benefit to the beneficiary or a representative of a deceased or retired partner

        e) Purchase of goodwill of a business or of other property

    2) A **joint interest** in (co-ownership of) property or the **sharing of gross returns** does not by itself establish a partnership.

h. A **partnership by estoppel** may be recognized when an actual partnership does not exist. The duties and liabilities of a partner sometimes may be imposed on a nonpartner (a **purported partner**). A purported partner has represented him/herself as a partner or has consented to such a representation. Moreover, the purported partner is assumed to be an agent of persons who have consented to the representation.

    1) A third party who has reasonably relied on the representation and suffered harm as a result may assert the existence of a partnership. The purported partner then will be prevented (estopped) from denying the existence of a partnership.

2) For example, Lawyer A falsely represented to Client that Lawyer A and Lawyer B were partners. Client, in reasonable reliance on this statement, sought legal services from Lawyer B. Because these services were performed without due care, Client suffered harm. Lawyer A (as well as Lawyer B) was liable as a partner despite the absence of an actual partnership.

3. **Capitalization.** A general partnership is advantageous relative to a sole proprietorship because two or more persons may contribute cash, property, or services to the business.

     a. Combining resources may improve the credit standing of the business.
     b. However, a general partnership cannot raise equity capital by selling shares.
     c. The partnership agreement should state the nature and amounts of initial and subsequent **contributions** by partners. It should also address whether

         1) Withdrawals are restricted and
         2) Individual partner capital, income, and drawing accounts are to be maintained.

     d. A person may become a partner by contributing cash, property, or services.

4. **Profits, losses, distributions, and the partnership interest.**

     a. The **right to share in profits**, unless otherwise agreed, allows each partner to have an equal share in partnership profits regardless of differences in the amount of contributions. Also, unless agreed otherwise, each partner must contribute in proportion to his/her share of the profits toward any **losses** of the partnership.

     b. A partner also has the **right to distributions**. A distribution is a transfer of partnership property from the partnership to a partner. A distribution may take various forms:

         1) A share of profits;
         2) Compensation for services;
         3) Reimbursement for payments made, and indemnification for liabilities incurred, in the ordinary course of business or to preserve the business or its property; and
         4) Reimbursement for advances (loans) in excess of agreed capital contributions.

             a) The payments made and liabilities incurred are **loans** that accrue interest.

     c. The **right to compensation for services** is in essence the right to receive a share of the profits. A partner is not entitled to be paid for services rendered for the partnership except winding up its business. However, a partnership agreement often does provide for additional compensation.

     d. A **partner's transferable interest** consists of a partner's share of partnership profits and losses and the right to receive distributions.

         1) Partners may sell, pledge, or otherwise **transfer (assign)** their interests to the partnership, another partner, or a third party without loss of the rights, duties, and liabilities of a partner (except the interest transferred). Thus, neither dissociation nor dissolution occurs. Moreover, unless all the other partners agree to accept the assignee as a new partner, the assignee does not become a partner in the firm. Without partner status, an assignee has no liability for partnership obligations.
         2) The ability to transfer the financial interest in the firm but not ownership status is a disadvantage of a partnership. For example, a partner cannot, during his/her life or through inheritance, transfer ownership to a family member.

    3)   When a partner dies, his/her partnership interest is considered part of the **estate**. The interest is personal property and may be inherited according to the provisions of the deceased partner's will. Heirs of the partnership interest are assignees, not partners.

        a)   The estate does not become a partner.

        b)   Many partnership agreements provide that the surviving partners or the partnership itself will have a right of first refusal to purchase the interest.

            i)   A partnership agreement may incorporate a provision to fund the purchase of the interest using life insurance proceeds.

        c)   The estate is responsible for the partner's allocated share of any partnership liabilities. These liabilities may include post-dissociation contracts entered into with third parties who reasonably believe that the dissociated person is still a partner.

    4)   A creditor who has obtained a judgment against a partner may attach the partner's transferable interest in the partnership only by securing a charging order from a proper court. A **charging order** is a lien on the transferable interest.

        a)   The court may order foreclosure of the interest at any time. After the order, the debtor partner's interest is sold at a judicial sale. Before the sale, the debtor, the other partners, or the partnership itself may redeem the interest by paying the debt. The **purchaser** does not become a partner unless all partners consent.

  5. **Taxation.** A principal advantage of a partnership is that it is not a taxable entity. However, it must file an annual informational return on **Form 1065**.

    a.   The partnership's profit/loss is **passed through** to the partners, who report their shares of that profit/loss on their personal income tax returns.

    b.   A partner may make contributions to the partnership's 401(k) plan.

  6. **Rights of partners.** The rights, duties, and powers between and among partners are largely defined by the law of **agency**. However, partners may agree to limit rights to which individual partners may otherwise be entitled by law. Nevertheless, neither the partners nor the partnership can modify obligations to third parties imposed by law.

    a.   Each partner has a **right to equal participation in management** of the partnership.

        1)   The general rule for ordinary matters is majority rule.

        2)   Issues not ordinarily connected with day-to-day partnership business (such as amending a partnership agreement or admitting a new partner) require a unanimous decision.

        3)   Different classes of partners may be formed with different management rights.

        4)   A disadvantage of a partnership is that a decision-making deadlock may develop when partners have equal management rights.

        5)   Partnership agreements commonly restrict management rights to a few partners or even one partner.

    b.   A partner's **right of access to partnership information** is the right to access, inspect, and copy the partnership books and records, if any. They must be maintained at the partnership's chief executive office.

        1)   Each partner and the partnership must provide a partner with information "reasonably required for the proper exercise of the partner's rights and duties" under the partnership agreement or the RUPA.

            a)   A reasonable demand for any other information about the partnership also must be honored.

    c.   The **right to use or possess partnership property** may only be exercised on behalf of the partnership. The RUPA states, "Property acquired by a partnership is property of the partnership and not of the partners individually."

        1)   Property is partnership property when it is acquired **in the name of the partnership**. It is also deemed to be partnership property when it is acquired **in the name of a partner**, provided that the instrument of transfer indicates the existence of a partnership.

        2)   Furthermore, property purchased with **partnership assets** is presumed to be partnership property.

        3)   Partners do not own any specific partnership property directly or individually. It is owned by the partnership as a legal entity.

            a)   Likewise, the creditors and heirs of an individual partner have no right to specific partnership property. A partner's interest in specific partnership property is a joint right of possession for partnership purposes only. The partner's interest in a specific item of such property is not transferable and cannot be attached by personal creditors or passed through a deceased partner's estate.

            b)   Whether property belongs to the partnership or a partner also determines who has the power to transfer it, who receives the proceeds (or bears the loss) from its disposal, and how it will be disposed of upon termination of the firm.

    d.   The **right to choose associates** means that no partner may be forced to accept any person as a partner. The RUPA states, "A person may become a partner only with the consent of all of the partners."

        1)   When a partner transfers his/her interest to another, the purchaser or other transferee is entitled only to receive the share of profits and losses and the right to distributions allocated to the interest (s)he has acquired.

    e.   The RUPA provides a broad **right to maintain an action against the partnership or other partners**, with or without an **accounting** as to partnership business, for any form of relief available from a court.

        1)   Suit may be brought to enforce rights under the partnership agreement or the RUPA or to protect interests arising independently of the partnership.

        2)   The RUPA also allows the partnership to sue a partner for breaching the partnership agreement or violating a duty to the partnership.

    f.   Each partner is assumed to have an **account** that is credited with his/her contributions made and share of profits, and debited for distributions received and share of losses.

7.   **Duties of partners.** A partner has the actual or apparent authority under the principles of agency law to take actions that impose personal liability on the other partners without their knowledge and consent. Hence, a partner is in a **fiduciary position**, i.e., a position involving trust and confidence. (S)he has a duty to act primarily for the benefit of the other partners in partnership affairs.

    a.   Duties imposed upon partners include the **fiduciary duties** of loyalty and care. The **duty of loyalty** is limited to

        1)   Not competing with the partnership;

        2)   Not dealing with the partnership in the conduct or winding up of the partnership business as (or for) a party with an adverse interest; and

        3)   Accounting to the partnership and holding for it in trust any benefit resulting from

            a)   The conduct or winding up of the partnership business or
            b)   The use of partnership property.

                i)   Accordingly, a partner cannot for personal gain exploit a partnership opportunity or secretly use partnership assets.

  b.   The **duty of care** in the conduct or winding up of the partnership business is not to engage in knowing violations of the law, intentional wrongdoing, gross negligence, or reckless behavior.

  c.   A partner also has an obligation of **good faith and fair dealing**.

        1)   A partner therefore must be honest in fact and meet reasonable (objective) standards of fair dealing.

  d.   However, no duty is violated solely because a partner acts in his/her own interest.

  e.   A partner may lend money to, or otherwise do business with, the partnership on the same basis as a nonpartner.

8.   **Powers of partners.** The powers granted to each partner are governed by law and by the specific terms contained in the partnership agreement.

  a.   A partner's status grants him/her **apparent authority** to act as an **agent** of the partnership in any legal transaction that is apparently for "carrying on in the ordinary course the partnership business or business of the kind carried on by the partnership" (business that is normal for the partnership or for a similar partnership).

        1)   Apparent authority is derived from words or actions of the principal (the partnership) that reasonably induce a third party to rely on the agent's (partner's) authority. The partnership is bound even if the partner had no actual authority in the matter unless the third party knew or had received notification of the lack of actual authority.

        2)   However, if a partner acts **without actual or apparent authority**, neither the partnership nor the other partners are bound by the act unless the other partners **ratify** the transaction.

        3)   The RUPA provides for filing a **statement of partnership authority** that may give notice of limitations on the authority of a partner.

            a)   A **statement of denial** also may be filed by a person named in a statement of authority. It states the fact denied, e.g., partner authority or status.

            b)   The extent of authority described in the statement of authority may be relied upon by a person dealing with a partner if that person gives value in a transaction without knowledge to the contrary (assuming no other filing cancels the authority).

            c)   A stronger safeguard against unauthorized transfers is provided for real property. If the filing limits a partner's authority to transfer the partnership's **real property**, and filing is in the public **real property records**, any person is assumed to know of the limitation.

                i)   Except for real property filings and filed statements of dissociation or dissolution, a nonpartner is not assumed to know of a limitation on authority solely because of a filing.

  b.   **Transfer of Partnership Property**

        1)   Subject to a filed statement of authority, property **in the name of the partnership** may be transferred by any partner in the partnership name.

        2)   Property **in the name of a partner(s)** or **in the name of another person(s)** may be transferred by the named person(s).

3) **Recovery** of partnership property requires the partnership to prove that

a) The transferor partner(s) had no authority (actual or apparent), and

b) The transferee for value had notice of these facts.

9. **Liabilities of partners.** The liability of a partner and the partnership is founded on the principles of agency. A partner acts as both a principal and an agent for the partnership. Thus, a general partner is liable as a principal for actions of employees within the course and scope of employment by the partnership.

a. (S)he also acts as an agent for the co-partners. When an actual partner appears to a third party to be carrying on the business of a partnership in the usual manner or when a partner is authorized by the other partners to take an unusual action, (s)he has the power to obligate the partnership and the co-partners.

1) Accordingly, a partnership is liable for loss or injury caused by the **actionable conduct** (torts and other wrongful acts or omissions) of any partner while the partner is acting within the ordinary course of the partnership business or with its authority. Examples are malpractice, other negligence, fraud, and misappropriation of customer assets.

b. Each general partner normally has **joint and several liability** for any partnership obligation. Thus, partners are individually liable for the full amount of a partnership obligation and also liable as a group. Joint and several liability allows either joint suits or separate actions (and separate judgments) at the plaintiff's option.

1) If a creditor obtains a judgment against a partner based on a claim against the partnership, the partner will **not be liable unless** (a) the partnership is in bankruptcy; (b) attempts to use judicial process to collect from the partnership are unsuccessful; (c) the court rules that partnership assets are clearly insufficient, exhaustion of its assets is unduly burdensome, or equity will be served by permitting suit against the partner; (d) the partner agrees that the creditor need not exhaust partnership assets; or (e) the partner is independently liable.

c. A partner may obligate the partnership and partners by **contract** when (1) specifically authorized by the partnership agreement, (2) apparently carrying on partnership business in the usual manner, or (3) acting with the actual or implicit consent of the other partners.

1) When partners agree to limit the authority of a partner to act for the partnership, a third party who has no notice of the limitation is not bound.

d. **Admission** into an existing partnership results in liability for partnership obligations. However, a new partner is liable for preadmission obligations of the partnership only to **the extent of his/her investment**. An incoming partner may expressly or implicitly assume personal liability for existing partnership debt, and (s)he has unlimited liability for partnership obligations arising after admission.

e. **Criminal liability** is not ordinarily imposed on partners as a result of a co-partner's criminal conduct unless they were involved.

f. A **partner's knowledge or receipt of notice** of a fact relating to the partnership is attributed to the partnership.

g. A **withdrawing partner** remains liable for debts of the partnership incurred before withdrawal unless the creditors agree otherwise.

1) Termination of the partnership also does not discharge any partner's obligations to third parties.

10. **Termination of partnerships.** The process to end a partnership may be governed by the partnership agreement. If it is not, the RUPA provides a scheme that consists of dissociation, dissolution, winding up (also known as liquidation), and termination.

a. **Dissociation** is the legal effect of a partner's ceasing to be associated in carrying on the business of the partnership. A partner has the power (if not the right) to dissociate at any time, subject to payment of damages if the dissociation is wrongful.

1) The partner's management rights (except with regard to winding up) terminate.

2) After dissociation, the business either continues after purchase of the dissociated partner's interest, or dissolution begins.

3) The dissociation of a partner terminates the **duty not to compete**. The other aspects of the **duties of loyalty and care** continue only with regard to predissociation matters unless the partner participates in winding up.

4) Dissociation results from

   a) Notice to the partnership of a partner's express will to withdraw;

   b) An event stipulated in the agreement;

   c) **Expulsion** of a partner under the terms of the **partnership agreement**;

   d) **Expulsion** by a **unanimous vote** of the other partners on the grounds that the partnership business cannot legally be conducted with that partner, the partner is a dissolving corporation or partnership, the partner has transferred substantially all of his/her interest, or the partner's interest is subject to a changing order;

   e) A **court order** on the grounds of a material breach of the partnership agreement or a duty, misconduct materially affecting the business, or conduct making continuation of the business with the partner impracticable (e.g., a deadlock between partners);

   f) Incapacity;

   g) Death;

   h) Insolvency; and

   i) Distribution by a trust or estate of its entire transferable interest.

5) The partnership is not necessarily dissolved by dissociation unless it occurs by **express will** of the partner.

6) A **statement of dissociation** may be filed by the partnership or a dissociated partner. It is deemed to provide notice of dissociation 90 days after filing.

   a) Such notice terminates the partner's apparent authority and his/her liability for the partnership's post-dissociation obligations.

   b) Without this statement or some other form of notice, the dissociated partner will have apparent authority for 2 years to bind the partnership to contracts with third parties who reasonably believe the person is a partner.

   c) A dissociated partner remains liable to creditors for **predissociation obligations** even if the other partners agreed to assume the debts.

   d) A dissociated partner also may be liable on **post-dissociation contracts** for up to 2 years if third parties reasonably believe that (s)he is still a partner. Thus, a dissociated partner has an obvious motive for filing a statement of dissociation.

7) If the business is not wound up, the partnership must **purchase the dissociated partner's interest**. The price is determined based on a hypothetical sale of the partnership at the dissociation date.

    a) The buyout price is the amount of the distribution receivable by the partner if the partnership were sold for the greater of

        i) Liquidation value or
        ii) The sales value of the entire going concern without the partner.

    b) The buyout price is offset by damages for wrongful dissociation and other amounts owed to the partnership.

8) The dissociation provision assures greater **continuity** of partnerships and supports the view that a partnership is to be treated, whenever possible, as an **entity**.

b. **Dissolution and winding up** is the alternative to dissociation and continuation of the partnership. However, although dissolution changes the working relationships of the partners, it is distinct from winding up.

1) In a partnership at will, dissolution results from notice of a partner's **express will to withdraw**. It also results from

    a) In a partnership for a **definite term or specific undertaking**,

        i) Expiration of the term or completion of the undertaking
        ii) Unanimous agreement of the partners
        iii) Wrongful dissociation or death of a partner, unless a majority in interest of the other partners agree to continue

    b) An event designated in the partnership agreement as causing winding up

    c) Illegality of the business

    d) On application of a partner, a **judicial determination** of

        i) Frustration of the economic purpose of the partnership
        ii) Impracticability of doing business with a particular partner
        iii) Impracticability of doing business under the partnership agreement

    e) A judicial determination made at the request of a transferee of a transferable interest that **winding up is equitable**

2) A partnership continues until the **winding up** of partnership affairs is complete. All partners are entitled to participate in the winding up (liquidation) process except a partner who has wrongfully dissociated.

    a) However, before winding up is complete, the partners (excluding a wrongfully dissociated partner) may **unanimously agree to continue the business** as if dissolution had not occurred.

        i) This provision furnishes another opportunity to compensate for the continuity (going-concern) problems faced by partnerships.

3) The **actual authority** of a partner to act on behalf of the partnership terminates upon dissolution except as necessary to wind up partnership affairs.

4) **Apparent authority** of a partner may continue to exist throughout the winding up process unless notice of the dissolution has been communicated to the other party to the transaction.

5) The **fiduciary duties** of the partners also remain in effect with the exception of the duty not to compete, which ceases to exist after dissolution.

6) A **statement of dissolution** may be filed by any partner who has not wrongfully dissociated. It is deemed to provide notice to nonpartners 90 days after the filing regarding dissolution and the limitation of the partners' authority.

c.   **Winding up** is the administrative process of settling partnership affairs, including the use of partnership assets and any required contributions by partners to pay creditors.

1)   The RUPA states that the person winding up may

a)   Continue the business as a going concern for a reasonable time,
b)   Take judicial actions,
c)   Settle and close the business,
d)   Dispose of and transfer property,
e)   Discharge liabilities,
f)   Distribute assets,
g)   Settle disputes by mediation or arbitration, and
h)   Perform other necessary acts.

2)   Creditors are paid in full before any distributions are made to partners. However, **partners who are creditors** share equally with nonpartner creditors under the RUPA. In practice, because partners are liable for all partnership debts, partnership creditors are paid first.

3)   After payment of creditors, any surplus is paid **in cash** to the partners. A partner has no right to a **distribution in kind**. A partner also need not accept a distribution in kind.

4)   To settle **partnership accounts** with credit balances, each partner receives a **distribution** equal to the excess of credits over debits to his/her account. Thus, no distinction is made between distributions of capital and of profits.

a)   Profits and losses from liquidation of assets are credits and debits, respectively.

b)   Prior credits to an account include contributions made and the partner's share of profits.

c)   Prior debits include distributions received and the share of losses.

5)   If a partner's account has a debit balance, the partner is liable to **contribute** the amount of the balance.

a)   If a partner does not make a required contribution, the other partners must pay the difference in the same proportion in which they share losses.

b)   A partner making an excess contribution may recover the excess from the other partners.

c)   Moreover, the representative of creditors of the partnership or of a partner (e.g., a trustee in bankruptcy) may enforce the obligation to contribute to the partnership.

d)   One effect of these rules is that the priority rules for unsecured partnership creditors and individual partners' unsecured creditors are consistent with the federal **Bankruptcy Code**. Thus, unsecured partnership creditors

i)   Have priority in partnership assets and

ii)   Share equally with creditors of partners in the partners' separate assets.

11.   Stop and review! You have completed the outline for this subunit. Study multiple-choice questions 3 through 37 beginning on page 24.

1.3 JOINT VENTURES

1. **Definition.** A joint venture is an easily formed business structure common in international commerce. It is an association to accomplish a specific business purpose or objective and is often organized for a single transaction.

    a. A joint venture is not a partnership because it does not **carry on a business**.

    b. However, most rules governing general partnerships apply to joint ventures, including those relating to formation.

    c. A disadvantage of the joint venture is that it **lacks continuity of existence**.

        1) Moreover, the interests in the enterprise are **not readily transferable**.

    d. The rights and duties of **joint venturers** are generally governed by the RUPA.

        1) A joint venturer, like a partner, has a right of access to information.

        2) Joint venturers owe each other the same **fiduciary duties** as partners.

        3) The most significant difference between joint venturers and partners is that joint venturers typically have **less implied and apparent authority** to bind their associates due to the limited scope of the joint venture.

            a) Thus, an advantage is that no joint venture is liable for similar activities of other joint ventures outside the scope of the venture.

        4) Each joint venturer is **personally liable** for debts of the venture.

        5) Each joint venturer is liable for negligence of another acting within the scope and course of the business of the venture.

        6) Joint ventures are treated as partnerships (nontaxable entities) for **federal income tax** purposes. Hence, joint ventures have the advantage of avoiding double taxation.

        7) Barring a contrary agreement, joint venturers share **profits and losses** equally.

        8) Joint venturers may be sued.

            a) The joint venture is usually not a legal entity and therefore **cannot be sued**.

        9) **Antitrust laws** apply to joint venturers who are competitors.

            a) However, less stringent rules are applied to international joint ventures.

        10) **Not-for-profit entities** cannot be joint ventures. The limited objective of a joint venture necessarily includes earning a **profit**.

2. Stop and review! You have completed the outline for this subunit. Study multiple-choice questions 38 through 40 beginning on page 35.

QUESTIONS

1.1 Sole Proprietorships

1. The formation of a sole proprietorship

    A. Requires registration with the federal government's Small Business Administration.

    B. Requires a formal "doing business as" filing under state law if the proprietor will be conducting business under a fictitious name.

    C. Requires formal registration in each state the proprietor plans to do business in.

    D. Is not as easy and inexpensive to form as an S corporation.

Answer (B) is correct. *(Publisher, adapted)*
REQUIRED: The characteristic of the formation of a sole proprietorship.
DISCUSSION: A proprietor doing business under a fictitious name is usually required to make a d/b/a or "doing business as" filing under state law. On the other hand, the formation of a sole proprietorship is subject to only a few legal requirements, such as local zoning and licensing. In this respect, the sole proprietorship is the easiest and least expensive to create of all the business organizations.
    Answer (A) is incorrect because the Small Business Administration (SBA) is a source of loans for sole proprietorships. No formal registration is required with the SBA. Answer (C) is incorrect because a sole proprietorship may conduct business in any state without having to file, register, or otherwise qualify to do business in that state. Answer (D) is incorrect because, of all business organizations, the sole proprietorship is the easiest and least expensive to create.

2. Which of the following is not a characteristic of both a sole proprietorship and a general partnership?

    A. Equity capital may not be raised by selling shares of the business.

    B. The business's profits and losses are passed through to the owner(s).

    C. The death of an owner causes the termination of the business.

    D. A "doing business as" filing is usually required if the owner(s) will conduct business under a fictitious name.

Answer (C) is correct. *(Publisher, adapted)*
REQUIRED: The characteristic not common to a sole proprietorship and a general partnership.
DISCUSSION: In a sole proprietorship, the death of the proprietor causes the automatic termination of the business. However, the death of a general partner results in dissociation, not the termination of the partnership.
    Answer (A) is incorrect because neither the proprietors nor general partners may sell shares of the business to raise additional equity capital. Answer (B) is incorrect because both a sole proprietorship and a general partnership act as pass-through entities for the taxation of the business income. Answer (D) is incorrect because similar statutes exist requiring both proprietors and partners to make "doing business as" filings if conducting business under a fictitious name.

1.2 General Partnerships

3. Partners have a fiduciary relationship with each other. Accordingly, a partner

    A. May engage in a business that competes with the partnership if it is operated with his/her own resources.

    B. May take advantage of a business opportunity within the scope of the partnership enterprise if the partnership agreement will terminate before the benefit will be received.

    C. Must exercise a degree of care and skill as a professional.

    D. May not earn a secret profit in dealings with the partnership or partners.

Answer (D) is correct. *(Publisher, adapted)*
REQUIRED: The true statement about the duties owed by partners to each other.
DISCUSSION: A partner is an agent of the partnership and the other partners and thus owes fiduciary duties of loyalty and due care. A partner also has an obligation of good faith and fair dealing. In dealings with the partnership or other partners, a partner may not earn a secret profit. (S)he must account to the partnership and hold as trustee for it any benefit derived in the conduct or winding up of the partnership business or from use of partnership property (including appropriation of a partnership opportunity).
    Answer (A) is incorrect because a partner's duty of loyalty precludes competition with the partnership. Answer (B) is incorrect because a partner's duty of loyalty precludes competition with the partnership. Answer (C) is incorrect because a partner's duty of care to the partnership and other partners is limited to refraining from gross negligence, reckless conduct, intentional misconduct, or knowing violation of the law. (S)he is not liable for ordinary negligence to fellow partners if his/her honest errors of judgment are not intended and do not result in personal benefit.

4. A general partnership must

- A. Pay federal income tax.
- B. Have two or more partners.
- C. Have written articles of partnership.
- D. Provide for apportionment of liability for partnership debts.

Answer (B) is correct. *(CPA, adapted)*
REQUIRED: The essential element of a general partnership.
DISCUSSION: A partnership is an association of two or more persons conducting a business that they co-own for profit. Absent association by agreement of at least two persons as partners, there is no partnership.
Answer (A) is incorrect because a partnership is not subject to regular federal income tax. Answer (C) is incorrect because a general partnership may be formed orally. Answer (D) is incorrect because a general partnership agreement need not provide for apportionment of liability for partnership debts. General partners have joint and several liability for partnership debts.

5. Generally, under the Revised Uniform Partnership Act, a partnership has which of the following characteristics?

	Unlimited Duration	Obligation for Payment of Federal Income Tax
A.	Yes	Yes
B.	Yes	No
C.	No	Yes
D.	No	No

Answer (D) is correct. *(CPA, adapted)*
REQUIRED: The characteristic(s), if any, of a partnership.
DISCUSSION: A partnership is an association of two or more persons to carry on a business as co-owners for profit. For federal income tax purposes, it is a flow-through entity. Thus, partnership income (loss) is reported on the owners' tax returns, but the partnership itself does not pay taxes. Moreover, one of the distinguishing characteristics of the partnership form of business is its lack of continuity of life.

6. When parties intend to create a partnership that will be recognized under the Revised Uniform Partnership Act, they must agree to

	Conduct a Business for Profit	Share Gross Receipts From a Business
A.	Yes	Yes
B.	Yes	No
C.	No	Yes
D.	No	No

Answer (B) is correct. *(CPA, adapted)*
REQUIRED: The item(s), if any, that must be agreed to when parties intend to create a partnership under the RUPA.
DISCUSSION: A partnership is an association of two or more persons conducting a business, which they co-own, for profit. Thus, partners must objectively intend that their business make a profit, even if no profit is earned. Each of the parties must be a co-owner; i.e., they share profits and losses of the venture and management authority (unless they agree otherwise).
Answer (A) is incorrect because the partnership agreement may specify that gross receipts are not shared. Answer (C) is incorrect because partners must intend that their business make a profit, but partners do not have to agree to share gross receipts. Answer (D) is incorrect because partners must intend that their business make a profit.

7. Which of the following statements about the form of a general partnership agreement is true?

- A. It must be in writing if the partnership is to last for longer than 1 year.
- B. It must be in writing if partnership profits would not be equally divided.
- C. It must be in writing if any partner contributes more than $500 in capital.
- D. It could not be oral if the partnership would deal in real estate.

Answer (A) is correct. *(CPA, adapted)*
REQUIRED: The true statement regarding whether a general partnership agreement must be in writing.
DISCUSSION: Most oral agreements to enter into a partnership are valid. If the partnership agreement is for a definite period in excess of 1 year, however, the majority of states require that the partnership agreement be in writing to be enforceable. If the statute of frauds is not complied with, a partnership at will results.
Answer (B) is incorrect because a choice by the partners to divide profits unequally has no impact on whether the partnership agreement must be written. Answer (C) is incorrect because there is no threshold on contributions beyond which a written agreement is required. Answer (D) is incorrect because a partnership agreement to enter into the real estate business does not involve the transfer of real estate and therefore does not need to be in writing.

8. In a general partnership, which of the following acts must be approved by all the partners?

A. Dissolution of the partnership.

B. Admission of a partner.

C. Authorization of a partnership capital expenditure.

D. Conveyance of real property owned by the partnership.

Answer (B) is correct. *(CPA, adapted)*
REQUIRED: The act that requires partner approval.
DISCUSSION: The right to choose associates means that no partner may be forced to accept any person as a partner. The RUPA states, "A person may become a partner only with the consent of all of the partners." When a partner transfers his/her interest to another, the purchaser or other transferee is entitled only to receive the share of profits and losses and the right to distributions allocated to the interest (s)he has acquired.
Answer (A) is incorrect because the dissolution of the partnership may result from notice of any partner's express will to withdraw. Answer (C) is incorrect because a partner's status grants at least apparent authority to act as an agent of the partnership in any legal transaction that is apparently for "carrying on in the ordinary course the partnership business or business of the kind carried on by the partnership" (business that is normal for the partnership or for a similar partnership). Answer (D) is incorrect because, subject to a filed statement of authority, property in the name of the partnership may be transferred by any partner in the partnership name.

9. Under the Revised Uniform Partnership Act, which of the following have the right to inspect partnership books and records?

A. Employees.

B. Former partners.

C. Inactive partners.

D. Transferees of partners' interests.

Answer (C) is correct. *(CPA, adapted)*
REQUIRED: The parties with a right to inspect partnership books and records.
DISCUSSION: The RUPA states that the partnership must provide a partner with information "reasonably required for the proper exercise of the partner's right and duties," including access to the partnership books and records. No distinction is made between active and inactive partners.
Answer (A) is incorrect because the RUPA creates no obligation of the partnership to provide employees with access to the partnership's books and records. Answer (B) is incorrect because former partners do not have the rights of partners. Answer (D) is incorrect because transferees of partners' interests are not entitled to (partner) ownership status and therefore do not have the rights of partners.

10. A partner's interest in specific partnership property is

	Assignable to the Partner's Individual Creditors	Subject to Attachment by the Partner's Individual Creditors
A.	Yes	Yes
B.	Yes	No
C.	No	Yes
D.	No	No

Answer (D) is correct. *(CPA, adapted)*
REQUIRED: The nature of a partner's interest in specific partnership property.
DISCUSSION: A partner may assign his/her interest in the partnership, but is not allowed to assign rights in specific partnership property. A partner's individual creditors may not attach partnership property, but may charge a partner's interest in the partnership. Only a claim against the entire partnership allows specific partnership property to be attached.
Answer (A) is incorrect because a partner's interest in specific partnership property cannot be assigned to or attached by a partner's individual creditors. Answer (B) is incorrect because a partner's interest in specific partnership property also cannot be assigned to a partner's individual creditors. Answer (C) is incorrect because a partner's interest in specific partnership property also cannot be attached by a partner's individual creditors.

11. When a party deals with a partner who lacks actual or apparent authority, a general partnership will be bound by the resulting contract if the other partners

	Ratify the Contract	Amend the Partnership Agreement
A.	Yes	Yes
B.	Yes	No
C.	No	Yes
D.	No	No

Answer (B) is correct. *(CPA, adapted)*
REQUIRED: The act(s), if any, that bind a partnership to an unauthorized contract.
DISCUSSION: A general partnership is bound on a contract made by a partner acting within the scope of his/her actual authority (either express or implied) or by the apparent authority a third party reasonably believes an agent has. A partnership also may be liable on an unauthorized contract by ratification. Ratification is approval after the fact of an unauthorized act and binds the partnership as if the partner had been initially authorized. Ratification may be express or implied from conduct of the principal. However, amending the partnership agreement alone would not imply ratification.

12. The apparent authority of a partner to bind the partnership in dealing with third parties

- A. Will be effectively limited by a formal resolution of the partners of which third parties are unaware.
- B. Will be effectively limited by the filing of a statement of partnership authority.
- C. Would permit a partner to submit a claim against the partnership to arbitration.
- D. Must be derived from the express powers and purposes contained in the partnership agreement.

Answer (B) is correct. *(CPA, adapted)*
REQUIRED: The true statement concerning apparent authority of a partner.
DISCUSSION: Each partner in a general partnership is an agent of the partnership. The partners may not limit partnership liability to third parties by agreement among the partners alone. But apparent authority is effectively limited to the extent a third party knows of limitations imposed on a partner's authority. The RUPA provides for filing of a statement of authority that may give notice of limitations on the authority of a partner.
Answer (A) is incorrect because the scope of apparent authority is limited by the filing of a statement of authority in accordance with RUPA. Answer (C) is incorrect because the scope of apparent authority is limited to "carrying on in the ordinary course the partnership business or business of the kind carried on by the partnership." Thus, actual authority most likely is required to bind the partnership to arbitration. Answer (D) is incorrect because apparent authority is derived from words or actions of the principal (the partnership) that reasonably induce a third party to rely on the agent's (partner's) authority. The partnership is bound even if the partner had no actual authority in the matter unless the third party knew or had received notification of the lack of actual authority.

13. Eller, Fort, and Owens do business as Venture Associates, a general partnership. Trent Corp. brought a breach of contract suit against Venture and Eller individually. Trent won the suit and filed a judgment against both Venture and Eller. Venture then entered bankruptcy. Under the RUPA, Trent will generally be able to collect the judgment in full from

- A. Partnership assets but not partner personal assets.
- B. The personal assets of Eller, Fort, and Owens.
- C. Eller's personal assets only after partnership assets are exhausted.
- D. Eller's personal assets.

Answer (D) is correct. *(CPA, adapted)*
REQUIRED: The assets from which a judgment against a partnership and a specific partner may be collected.
DISCUSSION: The RUPA provides that partners are jointly and severally liable for all obligations of the partnership (RUPA Section 306), including those arising out of a contract. The keys to the question are that (1) Trent sued both the partnership and one partner, (2) that partner can be held individually liable for the entire amount of a partnership obligation (joint and several liability), and (3) only parties who are judgment debtors can be held liable. Because Trent won the lawsuit against Venture and Eller, either Venture or Eller or both are liable for the judgment amount. Thus, the collection of the judgment will come from the partnership, Eller, or both. In this scenario, the partnership is in bankruptcy. When a plaintiff wins a judgment against a defendant in bankruptcy, the plaintiff typically collects very little, if any, of the judgment. Accordingly, Trent's judgment against the partnership will be subordinated to the claims of secured creditors and creditors with priority. As a result, Trent will likely seek to recover the full judgment from Eller's personal assets, given that Eller was a co-defendant in the lawsuit. Furthermore, because Venture is in bankruptcy, Section 307 of the RUPA provides that Trent need not seek a writ of execution against (compel collection of the judgment amount from) Venture before proceeding against Eller's personal assets.
Answer (A) is incorrect because Trent may collect in full from Eller. Answer (B) is incorrect because Fort and Owens must be judgment debtors to be held liable by Trent. Answer (C) is incorrect because Trent need not exhaust the partnership assets. Venture is in bankruptcy.

14. Fil and Breed are 50% partners in F&B Cars, a used-car dealership. F&B maintains an average used-car inventory worth $150,000. On January 5, National Bank obtained a $30,000 judgment against Fil and Fil's child on a loan that Fil had cosigned and on which Fil's child had defaulted. National sued F&B to be allowed to attach $30,000 worth of cars as part of Fil's interest in F&B's inventory. Will National prevail in its suit?

A. No, because the judgment was not against the partnership.

B. No, because attachment of the cars would dissolve the partnership by operation of law.

C. Yes, because National had a valid judgment against Fil.

D. Yes, because Fil's interest in the partnership inventory is an asset owned by Fil.

Answer (A) is correct. *(CPA, adapted)*
REQUIRED: The result of a suit by a partner's creditor against the partnership to collect a judgment on a defaulted loan cosigned by the partner for a relative.
DISCUSSION: National will not prevail. Fil was not acting as a partner, that is, within the ordinary course of the partnership business or with the partnership's authority, when cosigning the child's loan. Furthermore, the partnership was not a party to the suit that resulted in a judgment against the partner and the child. The judgment creditor has no right to specific partnership property. The partner's interest in property is not transferable and cannot be attached. Instead, a judgment creditor may attach the partner's transferable interest in the partnership by securing a charging order from a proper court. A charging order is a lien on the transferable interest. The court may order foreclosure of the interest at any time. After the order, the debtor partner's interest is sold at a judicial sale. Before the sale, the debtor, the other partners, or the partnership itself may redeem the interest by paying the debt.
Answer (B) is incorrect because dissolution of a partnership is not caused by a lawsuit to collect a debt owed by a partner. Answer (C) is incorrect because the plaintiff has no judgment against the partnership. Answer (D) is incorrect because the Revised Uniform Partnership Act states, "property acquired by a partnership is property of the partnership and not of the partners individually."

15. Which of the following statements is(are) usually true regarding general partners' liability?

I. All general partners are jointly and severally liable for partnership torts.

II. All general partners are liable only for those partnership obligations they actually authorized.

A. I only.

B. II only.

C. Both I and II.

D. Neither I nor II.

Answer (A) is correct. *(CPA, adapted)*
REQUIRED: The true statement(s), if any, about general partners' liability.
DISCUSSION: Partners are jointly and severally liable for the torts committed by another partner who acted within the ordinary course of the partnership business or with the authorization of the other partners. Joint and several liability means that all of the partners are liable, but a third party may hold any partner liable for the entire amount. Because a general partner is an agent of the business, (s)he has apparent authority to bind the partnership to contracts with third parties formed while carrying on the partnership business in the usual way.

16. Which of the following statements is true regarding the apparent authority of a partner to bind the partnership in dealings with third parties? Under the RUPA, the apparent authority

A. Must be derived from the express powers and purposes contained in the partnership agreement.

B. Will be effectively limited by a formal resolution of the partners of which third parties are unaware.

C. May allow a partner to bind the partnership to representations made in connection with the sale of goods.

D. Would permit a partner to submit a claim against the partnership to arbitration.

Answer (C) is correct. *(CPA, adapted)*
REQUIRED: The liability of a partnership based on a partner's apparent authority.
DISCUSSION: The RUPA provides that the act of a partner for the apparent purpose of carrying on the partnership business or business of the kind carried on by the partnership binds the partnership unless the person with whom (s)he is dealing knows the acting partner lacks actual authority, for example, because of the partnership's filing of a statement of authority. Courts interpret this language as establishing the apparent authority of partners to take actions that are usual for partnerships. These actions include buying and selling goods and making representations in connection with the sale. The apparent authority of a general partner is substantial.
Answer (A) is incorrect because apparent authority is not derived from the partnership agreement. Answer (B) is incorrect because apparent authority is not effectively limited by a resolution of the partners of which third parties are unaware. Answer (D) is incorrect because acts outside the ordinary course of partnership business require the consent of all partners.

17. Under the Revised Uniform Partnership Act (RUPA), which of the following statements concerning the powers and duties of partners in a general partnership is(are) true?

I. Each partner is an agent of every other partner and acts as both a principal and an agent in any business transaction within the scope of the partnership agreement.

II. Each partner is subject to joint and several liability on partnership debts and contracts.

    A. I only.

    B. II only.

    C. Both I and II.

    D. Neither I nor II.

Answer (C) is correct. *(CPA, adapted)*
  REQUIRED: The true statement(s), if any, about the powers and duties of general partners.
  DISCUSSION: Under the RUPA, a general partnership is primarily an agency relationship. Each partner is an agent of every other partner and acts as both a principal and an agent in any business transaction within the actual or apparent scope of the partnership. Application of this principle of agency law results in joint and several liability of the partners for the partnership's debts and contracts. The RUPA provides that all partners are jointly and severally liable for all obligations of the partnership unless agreed otherwise by the claimant or provided by state law.

18. If no provisions are made in an agreement, a general partnership allocates profits and losses based on the

    A. Value of actual contributions made by each partner.

    B. Number of partners.

    C. Number of hours each partner worked in the partnership during the year.

    D. Number of years each partner belonged to the partnership.

Answer (B) is correct. *(CPA, adapted)*
  REQUIRED: The default method of allocating general partnership profits and losses.
  DISCUSSION: Under the Revised Uniform Partnership Act, the partnership agreement, to the extent it allocates partnership profits and losses among partners, governs. Absent agreement, each partner is entitled to an equal share of profits and must contribute toward losses in the same proportion (s)he is entitled to share in profits.

19. Berry, Drake, and Flanigan are partners in a general partnership. The partners made capital contributions as follows: Berry, $150,000; Drake, $100,000; and Flanigan, $50,000. Drake made a loan of $50,000 to the partnership. The partnership agreement specifies that Flanigan will receive a 50% share of profits and that Drake and Berry each will receive a 25% share of profits. Under the Revised Uniform Partnership Act and in the absence of any partnership agreement to the contrary, which of the following statements is correct regarding the sharing of losses?

    A. The partners will share equally in any partnership losses.

    B. The partners will share in losses on a pro rata basis according to the capital contributions.

    C. The partners will share in losses on a pro rata basis according to the capital contributions and loans made to the partnership.

    D. The partners will share in losses according to the allocation of profits specified in the partnership agreement.

Answer (D) is correct. *(CPA, adapted)*
  REQUIRED: The partners' profit-sharing arrangement.
  DISCUSSION: Unless the partners agree otherwise, the RUPA provides for equal sharing of the partnership's profits. Also, unless otherwise agreed, each partner must contribute in proportion to his/her share of the profits toward any losses of the partnership. Thus, Flanigan, Drake, and Berry will be responsible for 50%, 25%, and 25%, respectively, of the partnership's losses.
  Answer (A) is incorrect because, if the partnership agreement provides for an unequal sharing of profits and is silent about sharing of losses, the partners will not share equally in losses. Answer (B) is incorrect because the partnership agreement regarding profits controls the sharing of losses. Answer (C) is incorrect because, given that the partnership agreement regarding profits does not mention capital contributions and loans, these factors will not determine the sharing of losses.

20. Gillie, Taft, and Dall are partners in an architectural firm. The partnership agreement is silent about the payment of salaries and the division of profits and losses. Gillie works full-time in the firm, and Taft and Dall each work half-time. Taft invested $120,000 in the firm, and Gillie and Dall invested $60,000 each. Dall is responsible for bringing in 50% of the business, and Gillie and Taft 25% each. How should profits of $120,000 for the year be divided?

	Gillie	Taft	Dall
A.	$60,000	$30,000	$30,000
B.	$40,000	$40,000	$40,000
C.	$30,000	$60,000	$30,000
D.	$30,000	$30,000	$60,000

Answer (B) is correct. *(CPA, adapted)*
REQUIRED: The division of partnership profits when the partnership agreement is silent about salaries and the division of profits and losses.
DISCUSSION: Partners are not entitled to compensation for their actions, skill, and time applied on behalf of the partnership, except when such an arrangement is explicitly provided for in the partnership agreement. The partnership agreement is silent on this point, so salaries are not paid to the partners. Profits and losses may be divided among the partners according to any formula stipulated in the partnership agreement. In the absence of such a stipulation, partners share equally in the profits. Thus, each partner will receive $40,000.

21. Cobb, Inc., a partner in TLC Partnership, assigns its partnership interest to Bean, who is not made a partner. After the assignment, Bean may assert the rights to

I. Participation in the management of TLC.
II. Cobb's share of TLC's partnership profits.

A. I only.

B. II only.

C. I and II.

D. Neither I nor II.

Answer (B) is correct. *(CPA, adapted)*
REQUIRED: The right(s), if any, of an assignee of a partnership interest.
DISCUSSION: Partnership rights may be assigned without the dissolution of the partnership. The assignee is entitled only to the profits the assignor would normally receive. The assignee does not automatically become a partner and would not have the right to participate in managing the business or to inspect the books and records of the partnership. The assigning partner remains a partner with all the duties and other rights of a partner.

22. The partnership agreement for Owen Associates, a general partnership, provided that profits be paid to the partners in the ratio of their financial contribution to the partnership. Moore contributed $10,000, Noon contributed $30,000, and Kale contributed $50,000. For the year ended December 31, Owen had losses of $180,000. What amount of the losses should be allocated to Kale?

A. $20,000

B. $60,000

C. $90,000

D. $100,000

Answer (D) is correct. *(CPA, adapted)*
REQUIRED: The partner's share of partnership loss.
DISCUSSION: The partnership agreement specifies that profits are to be allocated based on financial contributions. The RUPA provides that, unless otherwise agreed, losses are allocated in the same manner as profits. Hence, Kale will be allocated losses of $100,000 {$180,000 × [$50,000 ÷ ($10,000 + $30,000 + $50,000)]}.
Answer (A) is incorrect because $20,000 equals Moore's share of the losses. Answer (B) is incorrect because $60,000 is Noon's share of the losses. Answer (C) is incorrect because $90,000 is the sum of the contributions.

23. Which of the following statements best describes the effect of the assignment of an interest in a general partnership?

A. The assignee becomes a partner.

B. The assignee is responsible for a proportionate share of past and future partnership debts.

C. The assignment automatically dissolves the partnership.

D. The assignment transfers the assignor's interest in partnership profits and losses and the right to distributions.

Answer (D) is correct. *(CPA, adapted)*
REQUIRED: The effect of assignment of an interest in a partnership.
DISCUSSION: A partner's transferable interest in the partnership consists of the partner's share of profits and losses and the right to distributions. It may be assigned without the dissolution of the partnership. The assignee does not automatically become a partner and would not have the right to participate in managing the business or to inspect the books and records of the partnership.
Answer (A) is incorrect because admission as a partner requires approval by all partners. Answer (B) is incorrect because the assignee has no liability for partnership debts unless (s)he becomes a partner. Answer (C) is incorrect because an assignment does not dissolve the partnership.

24. Laura Lark, a partner in DSJ, a general partnership, wishes to withdraw from the partnership and sell Lark's interest to Ward. All of the other partners in DSJ have agreed to admit Ward as a partner and to hold Lark harmless for the past, present, and future liabilities of DSJ. As a result of Lark's withdrawal and Ward's admission, Ward

A. Acquired only the right to receive Ward's share of DSJ profits.

B. Has the right to participate in DSJ's management.

C. Is personally liable for partnership liabilities arising before and after being admitted as a partner.

D. Must contribute cash or property to DSJ to be admitted with full partnership rights.

Answer (B) is correct. *(CPA, adapted)*
REQUIRED: The rights and obligations of a newly admitted partner.
DISCUSSION: The other partners agreed to admit Ward as a partner. Accordingly, Ward is vested with all partnership rights, duties, and powers, including the right to participate in management.
Answer (A) is incorrect because Lark's assignment of her interest to Ward was approved by the other partners, and Ward was admitted as a partner. Ward succeeds fully to Lark's interest in the partnership, not just the right to share in profits. Answer (C) is incorrect because, when a new partner is admitted, (s)he is usually subject to any partnership liabilities arising before admission. However, satisfaction of such liability is limited to the investment in the partnership unless the incoming party assumes personal liability. Answer (D) is incorrect because a partner may be admitted to a partnership without a contribution of cash or property.

25. Unless the partnership agreement prohibits it, a partner in a general partnership may validly assign rights to

	Partnership Property	Partnership Distributions
A.	Yes	Yes
B.	Yes	No
C.	No	Yes
D.	No	No

Answer (C) is correct. *(CPA, adapted)*
REQUIRED: The assignability of a partner's right to specific partnership property or distributions.
DISCUSSION: Partnership property is owned by the partnership and not by the individual partners. A partner has no interest in partnership property, which can be assigned or otherwise transferred. A partner may assign his/her interest in the partnership but is not allowed to assign rights in specific partnership property. However, unless the partnership agreement prohibits it, a partner in a general partnership may validly assign rights to his/her share of partnership distributions.

26. Dawn was properly admitted as a partner in the ABC Partnership after purchasing Jim's partnership interest. Jim immediately withdrew. The partnership agreement states that the partnership will continue on the withdrawal or admission of a partner. Unless the partners otherwise agree,

A. Dawn's personal liability for existing partnership debts will be limited to Dawn's interest in partnership property.

B. Jim will automatically be released from personal liability for partnership debts incurred before Dawn's admission.

C. Jim will be permitted to recover from the other partners the full amount that Jim paid on account of partnership debts incurred before Dawn's admission.

D. Dawn will be subjected to unlimited personal liability for partnership debts incurred before being admitted.

Answer (A) is correct. *(CPA, adapted)*
REQUIRED: The effect on partnership liabilities of admitting a new partner.
DISCUSSION: As a new partner, Dawn's liability for previously existing partnership debts is limited to the amount of her capital contribution, which is Dawn's interest in partnership property.
Answer (B) is incorrect because, absent a novation, a withdrawing partner remains liable for debts incurred prior to withdrawal. Answer (C) is incorrect because Jim is liable for his share of debts incurred while he was a partner and would only be permitted to recover amounts he paid in excess of his share. Answer (D) is incorrect because Dawn's liability is limited to her capital contribution.

27. The partners of College Assoc., a general partnership, decided to dissolve the partnership and agreed that none of the partners would continue to use the partnership name. Which of the following events will occur on dissolution of the partnership?

	Each Partner's Existing Liability Would Be Discharged	Each Partner's Apparent Authority Would Continue
A.	Yes	Yes
B.	Yes	No
C.	No	Yes
D.	No	No

Answer (C) is correct. *(CPA, adapted)*
REQUIRED: The liability and authority of partners upon dissolution.
DISCUSSION: Dissolution can occur by an agreement of the partners to end the partnership. Although actual authority to act on behalf of the partnership ceases at dissolution, apparent authority to conduct business in the usual way continues until notice is given to third parties or the partnership business winds up. A partner's liability for the existing obligations of the partnership does not cease when the partnership is terminated. The unilateral act of the partners cannot discharge obligations to third parties.

28. Park and Graham entered into a written partnership agreement to operate a retail store. Their agreement was silent as to the duration of the partnership or its purposes. Which of the following statements is true?

A. Park may dissociate from the partnership at any time.

B. Unless Graham consents to a dissolution, Park must apply to a court and obtain a decree ordering the dissolution.

C. Park may dissolve the partnership by any reasonable means.

D. Park may dissolve the partnership only after notice of the proposed dissolution is given to all partnership creditors.

Answer (A) is correct. *(CPA, adapted)*
REQUIRED: The extent of a partner's right to dissociate and dissolve a partnership.
DISCUSSION: A partner has the power (if not the right) to dissociate at any time. The partnership may not be dissolved by dissociation of a partner unless it is by notice of the express will of that partner to withdraw. A statement of dissociation may be filed by the partnership or dissociating partner. Within 90 days after filing, notice of dissociation terminates the partner's apparent authority and post-dissociation obligations.
Answer (B) is incorrect because, in a partnership at will, Park may dissolve the partnership by giving notice of express will to withdraw. Answer (C) is incorrect because, in a partnership at will, Park may not dissolve the partnership unilaterally without judicial intervention unless (s)he gives notice to the partnership of his/her express will to withdraw. Answer (D) is incorrect because Park may dissolve the partnership by giving notice to the partnership of his/her express will to withdraw.

29. Wind, who has been a partner in the PLW general partnership for four years, decides to withdraw from the partnership despite a written partnership agreement that states, "No partner may withdraw for a period of five years." Under the Revised Uniform Partnership Act (RUPA), what is the result of Wind's withdrawal?

A. Wind's withdrawal causes a dissolution of the partnership by operation of law.

B. Wind's withdrawal has no bearing on the continued operation of the partnership by the remaining partners.

C. Wind's withdrawal is not effective until Wind obtains a court-ordered decree of dissolution.

D. Wind's withdrawal causes dissociation from the partnership despite being in violation of the partnership agreement.

Answer (D) is correct. *(CPA, adapted)*
REQUIRED: The result of an early withdrawal from a partnership.
DISCUSSION: Under the RUPA, a partnership is considered an entity substantially separate from its partners. A partner has the power (if not the right) to dissociate at any time. However, if the partner wrongfully dissociates from the partnership, (s)he is liable for any resulting damages to the other partners. After dissociation, the business either continues after purchase of the dissociated partner's interest or dissolution begins.
Answer (A) is incorrect because a partnership is not dissolved by operation of law under RUPA when a partner withdraws. Such a dissolution results from such events as the illegality of the business and certain judicial determinations. Answer (B) is incorrect because Wind will remain liable to creditors for predissociation obligations and any post-dissociation contracts for up to 2 years unless (s)he files a statement of dissociation. Answer (C) is incorrect because a court-ordered decree is not needed for the withdrawal to be effective. The partner may withdraw by notice to the partnership of an express will to withdraw.

30. When the Revised Uniform Partnership Act applies and there is no general partnership agreement, which of the following events, if any, occur(s) when a partner dies?

	The Partner Is Dissociated	The Deceased Partner's Estate Is Free From Any Partnership Liability
A.	Yes	Yes
B.	Yes	No
C.	No	Yes
D.	No	No

Answer (B) is correct. *(CPA, adapted)*
REQUIRED: The effect of a partner's death on a general partnership.
DISCUSSION: Under the RUPA, the death of a partner results in dissociation of the partner but not automatic dissolution of the partnership. Other events (e.g., incapacity, insolvency, or expulsion by a unanimous vote of the other partners or under the terms of the partnership agreement) also cause dissociation. However, the only form of dissociation that dissolves the partnership is dissociation by notice of an express will to withdraw. When a partner dies, the partnership interest becomes part of the deceased partner's estate. Moreover, the estate is responsible for the partner's allocated share of any partnership liabilities. These liabilities may include post-dissociation contracts entered into with third parties who reasonably believe that the dissociated person is still a partner.

31. A parent and children currently own and operate a farm as equal partners. Under the Revised Uniform Partnership Act, what effect would the death of the parent have on the partnership?

A. The estate of the deceased partner automatically becomes a partner.

B. The surviving partners could continue the partnership.

C. The partnership would be dissolved and wound up.

D. A partnership agreement could not have governed the continuation of the partnership.

Answer (B) is correct. *(CPA, adapted)*
REQUIRED: The transfer of a partnership interest upon the death of a partner.
DISCUSSION: The death of a partner results in the dissociation of that partner from the partnership, not dissolution of the partnership. The remaining partners may choose to continue the partnership. The estate still has an interest in the partnership, but the beneficiaries of the estate do not become partners without the unanimous consent of the existing partners.
Answer (A) is incorrect because the surviving partners would have to consent to the estate becoming a partner. Otherwise, the estate has only an equity interest in the partnership. Answer (C) is incorrect because the death of a partner results in dissociation of the partner, not dissolution of the partnership. Answer (D) is incorrect because the partnership may have granted the existing partners the preemptive right to purchase the partnership interest from the estate.

32. X, Y, and Z have capital balances of $30,000, $15,000, and $5,000, respectively, in the XYZ Partnership. The general partnership agreement is silent as to the manner in which partnership losses are to be allocated but does provide that partnership profits are to be allocated as follows: 40% to X, 25% to Y, and 35% to Z. The partners have decided to dissolve and liquidate the partnership. After paying all creditors, the amount available for distribution will be $20,000. X, Y, and Z are individually solvent. Z will

A. Receive $7,000.

B. Receive $12,000.

C. Personally have to contribute an additional $5,500.

D. Personally have to contribute an additional $5,000.

Answer (C) is correct. *(CPA, adapted)*
REQUIRED: The distribution of partnership assets after dissolution and liquidation.
DISCUSSION: Upon termination, a partnership must first pay all creditors, including partners who are creditors, and then distribute the remaining assets to the partners. In this case, $20,000 is available for distribution. However, the total of capital contributions is $50,000, and a $30,000 loss must be allocated among the partners. When the partnership agreement does not specify otherwise, losses are allocated in the same ratio as profits. Thus, Z is properly allocated 35% of the loss, or $10,500 ($30,000 × 35%). Z's capital contribution of $5,000 is less than Z's share of the loss. Hence, Z must contribute an additional $5,500 to the partnership.
Answer (A) is incorrect because it allocates 35% of the amount available for distribution without regard to the capital contributions of the partners. Answer (B) is incorrect because, if partnership assets are insufficient to return any partner's capital contribution, each partner is obligated to contribute cash to enable it. Answer (D) is incorrect because the obligation to contribute cash to permit return of capital is allocated to partners in the same proportion as is a partnership loss.

33. Under the RUPA, unless otherwise provided in a general partnership agreement, which of the following statements is true when a partner dies?

	The Deceased Partner's Executor Would Automatically Become a Partner	The Deceased Partner's Estate Would Be Free from Any Partnership Liabilities	The Partnership Would Be Dissolved Automatically
A.	Yes	Yes	Yes
B.	Yes	No	No
C.	No	Yes	No
D.	No	No	No

Answer (D) is correct. *(CPA, adapted)*
REQUIRED: The effect of a partner's death.
DISCUSSION: Under the RUPA, the death of a partner results in dissociation, not automatic dissolution. In many instances, dissociation will result in a buyout of the dissociated partner's interest and a continuation of the partnership rather than a winding up. The partnership interest becomes part of the deceased partner's estate. However, neither the executor nor the successor to the partnership interest automatically becomes a partner unless the other partners agree. The estate is responsible for the partner's allocated share of any partnership liabilities.

34. D, E, F, and G formed a general partnership. Their written partnership agreement provides that the profits will be divided so that D will receive 40%; E, 30%; F, 20%; and G, 10%. There is no provision for allocating losses. At the end of its first year, the partnership has losses of $200,000. Before allocating losses, the partners' capital account balances are D, $120,000; E, $100,000; F, $75,000; and G, $11,000. G refuses to make any further contributions to the partnership. Ignore the effects of federal partnership tax law. After losses are allocated to the partners' capital accounts and all liabilities are paid, the partnership's sole asset is $106,000 in cash. How much will E receive on dissolution of the partnership?

A. $29,500
B. $35,333
C. $37,000
D. $40,000

Answer (C) is correct. *(CPA, adapted)*
REQUIRED: The share of assets received by a partner on dissolution.
DISCUSSION: Absent agreement, the loss is allocated in the same proportion as profits (D, $80,000; E, $60,000; F, $40,000; G, $20,000). G's excess over his/her capital account balance ($9,000) must be allocated to the other partners in the same ratio as that for sharing profits (4:3:2). Thus, $4,000 is allocated to D, $3,000 to E, and $2,000 to F. The $106,000 is allocated in full to the balance of partnership capital accounts (D, $36,000; E, $37,000; F, $33,000).

35. Under the Revised Uniform Partnership Act, which of the following statements is(are) correct regarding the effect of the assignment of an interest in a general partnership?

I. The assignee is personally responsible for the assigning partner's share of past and future partnership debts.

II. The assignee is entitled to the assigning partner's interest in partnership profits and surplus on dissolution of the partnership.

A. I only.
B. II only.
C. Both I and II.
D. Neither I nor II.

Answer (B) is correct. *(CPA, adapted)*
REQUIRED: The true statement(s), if any, about assignment of an interest in a general partnership.
DISCUSSION: A partner's transferable interest consists of a partner's share of partnership profits and losses and the right to receive distributions. Partners may sell or otherwise transfer (assign) their interests to the partnership, another partner, or a third party without loss of the rights and duties of a partner (except the interest transferred). Moreover, unless all the other partners agree to accept the assignee as a new partner, the assignee does not become a partner in the firm. Without partnership status, the assignee has no obligation for partnership debts.

36. What term is used to describe a partnership without a specified duration?

A. A perpetual partnership.

B. A partnership by estoppel.

C. An indefinite partnership.

D. A partnership at will.

Answer (D) is correct. *(CPA, adapted)*
REQUIRED: The partnership without a specified duration.
DISCUSSION: A partnership at will is one "in which the partners have not agreed to remain partners until the expiration of a definite term or the completion of a particular undertaking" (RUPA).
Answer (A) is incorrect because the term "a perpetual partnership" is not used in the RUPA or the common law. Answer (B) is incorrect because a partnership by estoppel may be recognized when an actual partnership does not exist. For example, the duties and liabilities of a partner may be imposed on a nonpartner (a purported partner) who has represented him/herself as a partner or has consented to such a representation. A third party who has reasonably relied on the representation and suffered harm as a result may assert the existence of a partnership. The purported partner then will be prevented (estopped) from denying the existence of a partnership. Answer (C) is incorrect because the term "an indefinite partnership" is not used in the RUPA or in the common law.

37. Smith and James were partners in S and J Partnership. The partnership agreement stated that all profits and losses were allocated 60% to Smith and 40% to James. The partners decided to terminate and wind up the partnership. The following was the balance sheet for S and J on the day of the windup:

Cash	$40,000
Accounts receivable	12,000
Property and equipment	38,000
Total assets	$90,000
Accounts payable	$24,000
Smith, capital	30,000
James, capital	36,000
Total liabilities and capital	$90,000

Of the total accounts receivable, $10,000 was collected, and the remainder was written off as bad debt. All liabilities of S and J were paid by the partnership. The property and equipment are sold for $32,000. Under the Revised Uniform Partnership Act, what amount of cash was distributed to Smith?

A. $25,200

B. $26,000

C. $30,000

D. $34,800

Answer (A) is correct. *(CPA, adapted)*
REQUIRED: The cash distributed to Smith.
DISCUSSION: During the winding up process, all assets of the entity are sold, the creditors are paid, any remaining assets are distributed, and the entity is dissolved. The loss on accounts receivable is $2,000 ($12,000 – $10,000 collected). The loss on property and equipment is $6,000 ($38,000 – $32,000 collected). Thus, the partnership must recognize $8,000 in losses. After paying the creditors, the total cash to be distributed is $58,000 ($40,000 + $10,000 – $24,000 + $32,000). Accordingly, the amount distributed to Smith is $25,200 [$30,000 capital – ($8,000 loss × 60%)]. The amount distributed to James is $32,800 [$36,000 capital – ($8,000 loss × 40%)].
Answer (B) is incorrect because Smith is allocated 60% of the loss. Answer (C) is incorrect because $30,000 is the balance of Smith's capital before winding up. Answer (D) is incorrect because Smith does not receive 60% of the $58,000 in cash distributable to the partners.

1.3 Joint Ventures

38. A joint venture is

A. An association limited to no more than two persons in business for profit.

B. An enterprise of numerous co-owners in a nonprofit undertaking.

C. A corporate enterprise for a single undertaking of limited duration.

D. An association of persons engaged as co-owners in a single undertaking for profit.

Answer (D) is correct. *(CPA, adapted)*
REQUIRED: The definition of a joint venture.
DISCUSSION: A joint venture is similar to a partnership, but it does not carry on a business. The joint venture is an association of persons to undertake a specific business project for profit.
Answer (A) is incorrect because the association is not limited to two persons, and the venture involves only a specific project, not a business. Answer (B) is incorrect because a joint venture is undertaken for profit. Answer (C) is incorrect because a corporation formed for a single undertaking is governed by corporate, not partnership, law.

39. The most significant distinction between a general partner and a joint venturer is that

A. A joint venturer is personally liable for debts of the entity.

B. A joint venturer has less apparent authority.

C. Only a partner has a right to an accounting.

D. Neither is liable for taxes on entity profits.

Answer (B) is correct. *(Publisher, adapted)*
REQUIRED: The most significant distinction between a general partner and a joint venturer.
DISCUSSION: The most significant difference between joint venturers and partners is that joint venturers typically have less implied and apparent authority to bind their associates due to the limited scope of the joint venture. Thus, an advantage of the joint venture is that no joint venture is liable for similar activities of other joint ventures outside the scope of the venture.
Answer (A) is incorrect because both are personally liable for entity debts. Answer (C) is incorrect because both have a right to an accounting. Answer (D) is incorrect because the income and expenses of general partnerships and joint venturers are passed through to the owners.

40. Leslie, Kelly, and Blair wanted to form a business. Which of the following business entities does **not** require the filing of organization documents with the state?

A. Limited partnership.

B. Joint venture.

C. Limited liability company.

D. Subchapter S corporation.

Answer (B) is correct. *(CPA, adapted)*
REQUIRED: The business entity created without a statutory filing.
DISCUSSION: A joint venture is an association to accomplish a specific business purpose or objective. It has the advantage of ease of formation and is often organized for a single transaction. No state statute requires a filing to create a joint venture.
Answer (A) is incorrect because a limited partnership is required by the RULPA to file a written certificate of limited partnership as a public record with the appropriate secretary of state. Answer (C) is incorrect because a limited liability company must file written articles of organization. Answer (D) is incorrect because a subchapter S corporation must file articles of incorporation with the state.

Use Gleim's **CPA Test Prep** for interactive testing with over 2,000 additional multiple-choice questions!

STUDY UNIT TWO
NONCORPORATE LIMITED LIABILITY ENTITIES

(11 pages of outline)

The fundamental types of business structures for multiple-owner enterprises are the general partnership and the corporation. The most significant advantage of the **general partnership** is that it is a **pass-through entity** for tax purposes. Its most significant drawback is that the partners have **unlimited personal liability** for all partnership debts and losses. In contrast, a **corporation** provides its owners with limited liability, but its earnings are subject to double taxation.

Accordingly, additional business structures have emerged that combine the tax advantages of the general partnership with the liability limitations of the corporation. The three major noncorporate hybrid structures are discussed in this study unit. They are the limited partnership, the limited liability partnership (LLP), and the limited liability company (LLC). A corporate hybrid structure, the S corporation, is discussed in Study Unit 3.

2.1 LIMITED PARTNERSHIPS

1. **Definition.** A **limited partnership** has characteristics of both a general partnership and a corporation. It facilitates investments by those who want a financial interest in a commercial venture but who do not want a management interest or unlimited liability.

   a. The limited partnership is a separate legal entity.

   b. It is a partnership formed by two or more persons under a state statute. These statutes are based on the **Revised Uniform Limited Partnership Act (RULPA)**. A limited partnership has one or more general partners and one or more limited partners.

      1) The term **person** includes a natural person, general partnership, limited partnership, trust, estate, association, or corporation.

      2) A **general partner** assumes management of the partnership and has full personal liability for debts of the partnership.

         a) In the majority of states, a general partner may be another partnership or a corporation.

      3) A **limited partner** is an investor who makes a contribution of cash or other property to the partnership in exchange for an interest in the partnership and is

         a) Not personally liable for partnership debts

            i) The limited partner's exposure to partnership liabilities is limited to his/her contributions to the partnership.

         b) Not active in management of the partnership
         c) Not automatically an agent of the partnership

      4) A person can be both a general partner and a limited partner with the rights and liabilities of each.

         a) These interests are separately accounted for by the limited partnership.
         b) A limited partner is not entitled to become a general partner.

2. **Formation.** Compared with the general partnership, the limited partnership has the disadvantage of requiring significant legal formalities for its creation.

 a. The RULPA requires that a written **certificate of limited partnership** (a document similar to a corporation's articles of incorporation) be filed as a public record with the secretary of state of the state in which it is organized. The certificate gives potential creditors **notice** of the limited liability of the limited partners.

   1) If a certificate is not filed, the organization is treated as a general partnership.
   2) A **certificate of amendment** may be filed for "any proper purpose" determined by the general partners. A certificate of amendment also must be filed within 30 days after certain fundamental changes:
      a) Admission of a general partner
      b) Withdrawal of a general partner
      c) Continuation of the business after an **event of withdrawal of a general partner** (any of various events that result in voluntary or involuntary withdrawal, such as death, dissolution of a corporate general partner, incapacity, or transfer of all of the partner's interest)
   3) A **certificate of cancelation** is filed either after dissolution and the beginning of winding up or at any time when there are no limited partners.
   4) A **limited partnership agreement**, although not legally required, is also commonly executed by the partners. The agreement sets forth the rights and duties of the general and limited partners and the terms and conditions of operation, dissolution, and termination.
      a) Absent a separate agreement, the certificate of limited partnership serves as the articles of limited partnership, and state law (the RULPA) fills in omissions in the agreement.

 b. **Content of the limited partnership certificate.** This document must be signed by all general partners. However, it need not record capital contributions and other financial information. It contains

   1) The name of the limited partnership,
   2) The address of its office,
   3) The name and address of its agent for service of process,
   4) The name and business address of each general partner (but not of each limited partner),
   5) The latest date upon which the limited partnership is to dissolve, and
   6) Any other matters the general partners determine should be included.

 c. **Date of formation.** A limited partnership comes into existence when the certificate of limited partnership is filed or at a later date specified in the certificate.

   1) **Substantial compliance** with the filing requirements suffices for creation of the limited partnership.

 d. A limited partnership may **carry on any business** that a general partnership may conduct, with statutory exceptions (e.g., banking).

 e. **Name.** To protect creditors, the name must include the words "limited partnership."

   1) The name ordinarily may not include the name of a limited partner.
   2) The name may not be deceptively similar to that of a corporation or another limited partnership doing business in the state.

 f. A limited partnership must continuously maintain an **office** in the state.

g. Certain **records** must be kept in the office.

    1) Names and addresses of the partners

    2) The certificate of limited partnership and any amendments

    3) Financial statements of the limited partnership for the last 3 years

    4) The written partnership agreement

    5) Income tax returns and reports (federal, state, and local) of the limited partnership, if any, for the last 3 years

    6) Events causing winding up if not included in the written partnership agreement

    7) Information about contributions if not included in the written partnership agreement

h. The limited partnership is required to maintain an office, keep records, and appoint an agent to ensure that the courts of the state have **jurisdiction** over the limited partnership. They constitute sufficient **minimum contacts** so that the limited partnership can be sued in the state.

i. To do business in any other state, the limited partnership must **register** as a **foreign limited partnership** with that state's secretary of state.

    1) The foreign limited partnership must make various disclosures and appoint an **agent** for service of process so that it can bring suit in the state.

    2) Registration requirements are similar for foreign limited partnerships and foreign corporations.

3. **Capitalization.** Like a general partnership, a limited partnership may be financed by the partners' **contributions** of cash, property, services, or promises to make such contributions. (But a limited partner's promise is not a legal obligation unless it is in a signed writing.)

a. An advantage of the limited partnership is that it can attract greater financing than the general partnership because of the limited liability of the limited partners.

b. A disadvantage is that a limited partner's right of withdrawal of his/her capital contribution is restricted. It may be withdrawn upon the dissolution of the partnership, at the date specified in the certificate, upon 6 months' notice in writing to all the members, or with the consent of all the members but only if all creditors are paid or sufficient assets are available for creditors.

4. **Profits, Losses, Distributions, and Assignment of Partnership Interests**

a. The written **partnership agreement** controls the sharing of profits, losses, and distributions.

    1) In the absence of such an agreement, they are shared in proportion to the **value of the partners' contributions** received (and not returned).

b. The **partnership interests** of general and limited partners are intangible personal property and are assignable. These interests are rights to share in profits and losses and to receive distributions.

    1) The **assignment of a partnership interest** does not dissolve the limited partnership or entitle the assignee to become a partner. However, although unlimited rights to assignment may enhance the ability of the firm to raise capital, restraints on assignment are often imposed by the partnership.

        a) Limited partnership interests are securities subject to registration under **federal securities laws** and regulation by the **Securities and Exchange Commission (SEC)**. If the partners wish to sell these interests under an exemption from registration, ready assignability may prevent these interests from qualifying for such an exemption. An exemption may require restrictions on resale.

  b) Ready assignability of limited partnership interests also may cause the IRS to view the partnership as a corporation for **tax purposes**.

  c) Consequently, the partnership agreement may restrict transfers.

 2) The **assignee** of a partnership interest is entitled only to receive the distributions owed to the assignor-partner.

  a) However, the assignee of a partnership interest (limited or general) may become a limited partner if

   i) All partners agree, or

   ii) The partnership agreement gives the assignor the right to **confer limited partner status** on the assignee.

    • In this case, the assignee-limited partner is subject to the known liabilities (e.g., to make contributions) of the assignor. The assignor continues to be liable for promised unpaid contributions.

 3) The interest of a limited partner is subject to a **charging order** obtained by a creditor from a court for the payment of an unpaid judgment. The effect of the order is an involuntary assignment of the limited partnership interest to the creditor or a third party.

  a) The judgment creditor does not become a limited partner as a result of obtaining a charging order.

5. **Taxation.** Like the general partnership, the limited partnership is a pass-through (nontaxable) entity. Hence, the partners report their shares of the limited partnership's taxable and deductible items on their personal returns.

 a. The limited partnership files only an **informational return**.

 b. A limited partner not only enjoys limited liability, but also avoids the double taxation to which corporate earnings are subject.

 1) The IRS considers whether a limited partnership is in substance a corporation. It evaluates factors, such as the transferability of interests and the assets and net worth of the general partners, to determine whether the limited partnership form should be disregarded for tax purposes.

  a) For example, a **publicly traded partnership** is taxed as a corporation unless at least 90% of its gross income is passive income. However, it is not taxed as a corporation if it elects to be taxed at a rate of 3.5% of its gross income from the active conduct of a trade or business.

6. **Rights of Partners**

 a. A **general partner** in a limited partnership has the same rights, duties, liabilities, and authority as a partner in a general partnership (see Study Unit 1).

 b. A **limited partner** has no authority to **participate in management and control** of the business. Such participation and control causes loss of limited-partner status even if allowed by the partnership agreement.

 1) Control means participation in daily management decisions.

 c. A limited partner has rights that protect his/her/its position as a passive investor but does not otherwise have the rights, duties (fiduciary, etc.), and liabilities of a general partner. Thus, without loss of limited liability status, a limited partner has the right to

 1) If granted by the partnership agreement, **vote** on any matter

 2) Withdraw from the partnership upon 6 months' notice or in accordance with the partnership agreement

 3) Do business with the partnership, e.g., make a secured loan to it

        4) Inspect and copy the partnership records

        5) Obtain financial information, tax returns, and, if just and reasonable, other partnership information

        6) File a **derivative suit** on behalf of the partnership

        7) Assign his/her/its partnership interest

        8) Apply for dissolution of the partnership

        9) Receive the fair value of the partnership interest upon withdrawal

        10) Invest in competing limited partnerships

  d. A limited partner is **not** considered to have **participated in management and control** of the business solely by

        1) Serving as an employee, agent, or contractor for the limited partnership or a general partner

        2) Acting as a consultant to a general partner

        3) Acting as a guarantor of an obligation of the limited partnership

        4) Requesting or attending a partners' meeting

        5) Making proposals and approving or disapproving certain matters, such as

            a) Dissolution and winding up of the limited partnership

            b) Transfer of substantially all assets

            c) Incurrence of debt not in the ordinary course of business

            d) Changing the nature of the business

            e) Admission or removal of a general or limited partner

            f) Transactions involving a general partner's conflict of interest

            g) Amendment of the partnership agreement or the certificate of limited partnership

            h) Any other matters that the partnership agreement designates as subject to the limited partners' approval

7. **Liabilities of Limited Partners**

  a. Typically, the financial risk of a limited partner who does not participate in management and control of the business is limited to the partner's investment in the partnership. But a limited partner may incur personal liability for the firm debts if

        1) No limited partnership certificate was filed.

        2) The certificate contained a false statement at the time it was filed, and a person suffered loss by relying on the statement.

            a) A general partner, but not a limited partner, will be liable if the information in the certificate becomes inaccurate subsequent to filing.

        3) (S)he knowingly permits his/her name to be used as part of the partnership name and is held out as a participant in management.

  b. Personal liability for participation in management and control is only to persons who reasonably believed the limited partner was a general partner.

  c. A person may contribute to a business in the **erroneous belief** that (s)he has become a limited partner.

        1) Such a person may avoid liability as a general partner by filing

            a) An appropriate certificate of limited partnership or an amendment, or

            b) A certificate of withdrawal from equity participation

        2) These measures are not effective to avoid liability to third parties who did business with the enterprise previous to the filing. However, the third parties must have had a good-faith belief that the person was a general partner.

8. **Termination.** A limited partnership goes through **dissolution and winding up** before it is terminated.

    a. A limited partnership can be dissolved upon any of the following events:

        1) The time or event specified in the limited partnership agreement occurs.

        2) All the partners agree, in writing, to dissolve.

        3) An **event of withdrawal** of a general partner occurs unless

            a) The written terms of the agreement provide that the business may be carried on by the remaining general partners (if any).

            b) All partners agree in writing within 90 days to continue the business and appoint one or more new general partners if necessary or desired.

        4) The limited partnership is dissolved by court order.

    b. The limited partnership is not dissolved by the bankruptcy, incapacity, or death of a limited partner.

        1) The personal representative of the estate of a deceased limited partner does not become a substituted limited partner. However, (s)he has the rights and liabilities of a limited partner for the purpose of settling the estate.

    c. After dissolution, winding up is done by a **general partner** who has not caused the dissolution. If there is no general partner to conduct the winding up, it may be performed by the limited partners or by some person designated by a court.

    d. Assets, if any, are distributed first to **creditors**, including creditors who are partners. Remaining assets are then distributed as follows, except as otherwise provided in the limited partnership agreement:

        1) To current and former partners for **distributions** previously due them and unpaid

        2) To the partners as a return of their **contributions**

        3) To the partners for their **partnership interests** in the proportions in which they share distributions

    e. The final distribution terminates the limited partnership.

9. Stop and review! You have completed the outline for this subunit. Study multiple-choice questions 1 through 16 beginning on page 47.

2.2 LIMITED LIABILITY PARTNERSHIPS (LLPs)

1. **Definition.** An LLP is essentially a general partnership with limited liability for the partners. It is a creation of state law. The LLP is a business structure that is often adopted by providers of professional services (e.g., attorneys, CPAs, and physicians) and family enterprises.

    a. Except for the filing requirements discussed on the next page, an LLP is ordinarily treated as a legal entity to the same extent as a general partnership.

2. **Formation.** A disadvantage of the LLP is that its creation and continuation require compliance with statutory provisions.

    a. For an existing partnership, changing to LLP status is equivalent to **amending the partnership agreement.** Thus, the partners must elect (often unanimously) to make the change in accordance with the agreement.

    b.   Under the RUPA, partners must register by filing a **statement of qualification** with the secretary of state to become an LLP.

        1)   An LLP, or a **foreign LLP** authorized to transact business in the state, also must file an **annual report** containing substantially the same (but updated) information as the statement of qualification (name, jurisdiction where formed, and facts sufficient for service of process).

        2)   Errors or later changes in the information in the statement of qualification have no effect on status as an LLP or the liability of partners, but failure to file an annual report may result in revocation of LLP status.

            a)   The result may be a gap in the liability shield. Nevertheless, a corrective filing within 2 years will cure the gap because it relates back to the date of revocation.

        3)   The end of an LLP's **name** must alert persons dealing with it to the existence of the liability shield (e.g., Registered Limited Liability Partnership).

        4)   All of the foregoing requirements are intended to provide clear **notice of limited liability status** to those who do business with an LLP. Creditors will adjust their assessments of creditworthiness accordingly.

3.   **Capitalization.** Like a general partnership, an LLP is financed by partner contributions and the entity's borrowings.

    a.   An advantage of an LLP is that the limitation on the personal liability of partners may attract additional capital.

4.   **Profits, losses, distributions, and assignment of LLP interests.** The rules governing these matters that apply to general partnerships ordinarily also apply to LLPs.

    a.   However, assignments of LLP interests raise the same federal securities law and tax issues as assignments of limited partnership interests. Thus, restrictions on assignment may be necessary to retain the tax advantages of the LLP.

5.   **Taxation.** Like other partnerships, an LLP is a pass-through (nontaxable) entity. Hence, the partners report on their personal returns their shares of the LLP's taxable and deductible items.

    a.   The LLP files only an **informational return**.

    b.   Consequently, all partners in an LLP not only enjoy limited liability but also avoid the double taxation to which corporate earnings are subject.

6.   The **rights, duties, and authority** of partners in an LLP are similar to those of general partners.

    a.   The **management** of an LLP is facilitated because outside parties who do business with partners have notice by public filing of the limitation on personal liability.

7.   **Liability.** The RUPA provides for a shield from personal liability for any partnership obligation (whether arising out of a contract, a tort, or otherwise) incurred while the partnership was an LLP. Unlike the limitation on liability in a limited partnership, the liability shield in an LLP protects the partners who manage the business.

    a.   The shield is created even if the partnership agreement contains an inconsistent provision just prior to the vote to become an LLP.

    b.   However, a partner who personally incurs an obligation, including liability for negligence and malpractice, in the conduct of partnership business is fully liable. The shield is provided only for liability that is imputed simply because a partner is a partner, not for liability directly incurred by the partner.

        1)   Moreover, the supervisor of a person who commits negligence or malpractice (or other wrongful act within the scope of employment) also is liable. Depending on the statute, the liability may be (a) joint and several or (b) proportionate.

c. As a condition of granting LLP status, some states require the firm to obtain **liability insurance**.

d. A **choice of law** issue arises when a **foreign LLP** (one that was formed in another state) does business in a state.

   1) Because the liability shield may vary from state to state, the RUPA provides that the law of the **state of formation** controls.

   2) The RUPA also provides that a **statement of foreign qualification** may not be denied because of differences in state law.

8. **Termination** of an LLP involves the same process (dissolution and winding up) as in a general partnership.

9. Stop and review! You have completed the outline for this subunit. Study multiple-choice questions 17 through 25 beginning on page 52.

2.3 LIMITED LIABILITY COMPANIES (LLCs)

1. **Definition.** An LLC is a noncorporate hybrid business structure that may be formed only under a **state statute**. It combines the limited liability of the corporation with the tax advantages of the general partnership.

   a. The uniform act is the **Uniform Limited Liability Company Act (ULLCA)**. However, the ULLCA has not been adopted by a majority of jurisdictions, and state laws vary. Thus, business law textbooks emphasize the common aspects of state laws and the ULLCA.

   b. Like a corporation, a limited partnership, and an LLP, an LLC is a **legal entity** separate from its owners that can be created only under state law.

      1) An LLC may enter into contracts, sue, be sued, own property in its own name, engage in other transactions in property, make donations, be a general or limited partner, and appoint agents.

      2) The owner-investors (**members**) may file **derivative suits** on behalf of the LLC, with any damages awarded by the court being paid to the LLC.

   c. Like a partnership, the LLC may have owner management, a limited duration, and restricted transfer of interests.

   d. Like the shareholders of a corporation but unlike the partner-managers of a limited partnership, the owners of an LLC who participate in management enjoy limited liability.

2. **Formation.** An LLC is formed by **one or more persons** who file **articles of organization** with the appropriate secretary of state (or the equivalent). Thus, formation is more difficult than for a sole proprietorship or a general partnership.

   a. Some states require that an LLC have at least two members, but most state statutes (and the ULLCA) permit single-member LLCs.

   b. The **name of the LLC** must indicate by words or abbreviations that it is an LLC.

   c. The articles of organization should state the LLC's name. It should also

      1) Include certain basic information, such as the names and addresses of organizers, the initial agent for service of process, and initial managers;

      2) Provide for existence

         a) For a specified **term** or
         b) **At-will**;

      3) Indicate whether management will be by owners or managers; and

      4) State whether one or more members will be liable for the LLC's obligations.

d. The members' **operating agreement**, which is not legally required and may be oral, may address matters such as

    1) Management arrangements,

    2) Voting rights (absent a contrary agreement, members, or managers in a manager-managed LLC, have equal voices),

    3) Member meetings,

    4) Profit sharing (absent a contrary agreement, statutes usually provide for equal sharing),

    5) Transfer of members' interests, and

    6) The circumstances causing dissolution.

e. The LLC comes into **existence** when the articles are filed. The filing is conclusive proof that the organizers met the conditions for creation of the LLC.

f. The LLC must at all times maintain an **agent** for service of process and an **office** in the state.

    1) These requirements are the same as for limited partnerships and corporations.

g. A **foreign LLC** must obtain a **certificate of authorization** to operate in the state.

    1) The requirements for obtaining the certificate are similar to those that must be met by a foreign LLP or a foreign corporation.

    2) However, the law of the state of formation is ordinarily followed with regard to the conditions for creation of the foreign LLC and member relations.

3. **Capitalization.** Funding of an LLC is from **members' contributions**. In the absence of an agreement to the contrary, it may consist of tangible and intangible property and services, including services to be performed.

a. The advantages of limited liability and avoidance of double taxation may attract member-investors.

b. Other advantages are that an LLC may offer multiple classes of stock, and its members may be partnerships, corporations, and nonresident aliens.

    1) An **S corporation** (covered in Study Unit 3) does not offer these benefits.

    2) Moreover, unlike an S corporation, an LLC has no limit on the number of members, can make disproportionate allocations and distributions, and can distribute appreciated property without incurring a taxable gain.

    3) A member of an LLC can contribute appreciated property in exchange for a membership interest without recognizing a taxable gain.

4. **Profits, Losses, Distributions, and Transfer of LLC Interests**

a. In the absence of a contrary agreement, profits and losses are shared equally.

    1) A member is not automatically entitled to compensation, except for winding up the enterprise.

b. The rules for distributions upon liquidation of the LLC or dissociation of a member are similar to those for partnerships (RUPA).

c. A member can transfer his/her **distributional interest**, which is essentially the member's portion of the net assets of the LLC.

    1) The member has no right in specific property of the LLC.

    2) The transfer may be involuntary, for example, via a charging order obtained by a creditor.

    3) The transfer also may be through the estate of a deceased member.

    4) A transferee does not become a member in the absence of consent of all members or a provision in their agreement.

5. **Taxation.** Members may elect to be taxed as partners, and single-member LLCs may be taxed as sole proprietors.

   a. **Taxation as a corporation** may be advantageous if reinvestment in the LLC is desired and corporate rates are lower than personal rates.

   b. Thus, an LLC has the advantage of being a pass-through entity or a taxable entity at the discretion of the member(s).

6. **Management.** An LLC is deemed to be member-managed unless the articles of organization provide otherwise.

   a. Under the ULLCA, in a **member-managed LLC**, all members have a right to participate, and most business matters are decided by the majority.

   b. In a **manager-managed LLC**, each manager has equal rights, and most business matters are decided by the manager or by a majority of the managers.

      1) Managers are selected or removed by a majority vote of the members and are fiduciaries regarding the LLC and the members. They have **duties** of loyalty, care, and good faith.

         a) The members in a member-managed LLC have the same duties.

   c. The ULLCA further provides that, in any LLC, members must **unanimously agree** about some matters, for example,

      1) Amending the operating agreement or the articles,
      2) Dissolution,
      3) Waiver of the right to have the business wound up,
      4) Merger, and
      5) Admission of new members.

   d. Members have the right to inspect books and records and to be informed about the business.

   e. If the articles vest management of the LLC in elected managers, they are **agents** of the LLC. Any one manager may therefore have the statutory authority to bind the LLC.

   f. If the articles vest management in its members, they are agents. Thus, it may be possible, depending on the statute, for any one member to incur indebtedness or otherwise contractually bind the company.

   g. Persons who conduct business as an LLC when statutory requirements for its formation have not been complied with do not have limited liability and are jointly and severally liable as partners.

7. **Liability.** A great advantage of an LLC is that the creditors of the entity ordinarily have no claim on the personal assets of the members or managers.

   a. However, the members or managers remain liable for personal misconduct (e.g., negligence or criminal behavior). Moreover, misuse of the LLC form (e.g., to commit fraud or mislead others about who is conducting the business) may cause a court to "pierce the corporate veil."

   b. Federal and state laws also may provide other avenues for reaching personal assets. For example, the IRS may proceed against an individual for a fraudulent transfer or nonpayment of trust fund taxes, and a state may hold individuals liable for not providing workers' compensation insurance.

8. **Termination.** Generally, subject to the LLC's solvency, a member is entitled to a return of his/her capital contribution upon dissolution or other specified event.

    a. An LLC will be **dissolved** upon

        1) Expiration of a specified time period or occurrence of a specified event

        2) Consent of a number or percentage of members provided in their agreement

        3) Death, retirement, resignation, expulsion, bankruptcy, or dissolution of a member, or upon the occurrence of any other event that terminates the LLC under the articles or by the required consent of remaining members

        4) **Judicial determination** of

            a) Frustration of purpose

            b) Impracticability of continuing because of a member's conduct

            c) Impracticability of continuing under the articles and operating agreement

            d) Inappropriate behavior of controlling members or managers

            e) The equitability of liquidation

    b. Liquidation results in payment of proceeds in the following order:

        1) Outside creditors

        2) Loans from members

        3) Members' capital contributions

        4) Remaining amounts equally to members

    c. If dissociation of a member does not cause dissolution, the LLC must purchase the member's interest at **fair value**.

9. Stop and review! You have completed the outline for this subunit. Study multiple-choice questions 26 through 35 beginning on page 54.

QUESTIONS

2.1 Limited Partnerships

1. A valid limited partnership

A. Cannot be treated as an "association" for federal income tax purposes.

B. May have an unlimited number of partners.

C. Is exempt from all Securities and Exchange Commission regulations.

D. Must designate in its certificate the name, address, and capital contribution of each general partner and each limited partner.

Answer (B) is correct. *(CPA, adapted)*

REQUIRED: The true statement regarding a valid limited partnership.

DISCUSSION: A valid limited partnership has no maximum limit on the number of partners (limited or general). The only requirement is that it have at least one limited and one general partner. In contrast, S corporations currently have a limit of 100 shareholders.

Answer (A) is incorrect because a partnership will be treated as an association (and taxed as a corporation) if it has more corporate than partnership attributes. Answer (C) is incorrect because a limited partnership interest is considered a security and generally subject to SEC regulations. Answer (D) is incorrect because, under the RULPA, the name and business address of each general partner (but not the other information) must be included in the certificate.

2. Which of the following statements regarding a limited partner is(are) usually true?

I. The limited partner is subject to personal liability for partnership debts.

II. The limited partner has the right to take part in the control of the partnership.

A. I and II.

B. I only.

C. II only.

D. Neither I nor II.

Answer (D) is correct. *(CPA, adapted)*

REQUIRED: The true statement(s), if any, about a limited partner.

DISCUSSION: A limited partner's liability for partnership obligations is limited to his/her capital contribution to the business, whereas a general partner has unlimited personal liability for partnership debts. The limited partner is also restricted in the right to control the partnership; (s)he is not allowed to participate in the day-to-day management of the partnership business.

3. Marshall formed a limited partnership for the purpose of engaging in the export-import business. Marshall obtained additional working capital from Franklin and Lee by selling them each a limited partnership interest. Under these circumstances, the limited partnership

   A. Will usually be treated as a taxable entity for federal income tax purposes.

   B. Will lose its status as a limited partnership if it has more than one general partner.

   C. Can limit the liability of all partners.

   D. Can exist as such only if it is formed in a state that has adopted the original or revised Uniform Limited Partnership Act or a similar statute.

Answer (D) is correct. *(CPA, adapted)*
   REQUIRED: The true statement regarding a limited partnership.
   DISCUSSION: The limited partnership is not available as a form of business organization under the common law. An organization purporting to be a limited partnership but formed in a state with no statutory authority for such a form of business organization will very likely be treated as a general partnership.
   Answer (A) is incorrect because a partnership is not a taxable entity for federal income tax purposes. Partnerships are required to file informational returns only. Answer (B) is incorrect because a limited partnership may have more than one general partner. The minimum is at least one limited and one general partner. Answer (C) is incorrect because at least one general partner must have unlimited personal liability.

4. Which of the following statements is true?

   A. Directors owe fiduciary duties to the corporation, and limited partners owe such duties to the partnership.

   B. Corporations and limited partnerships must be formed pursuant to a state statute. A copy of the organizational document must be filed with the proper state agency.

   C. Shareholders may be entitled to vote on corporate matters, whereas limited partners are prohibited from voting on partnership matters.

   D. Stock of a corporation may be subject to registration under federal securities laws, but limited partnership interests are automatically exempt from such requirements.

Answer (B) is correct. *(CPA, adapted)*
   REQUIRED: The true statement comparing corporations and limited partnerships.
   DISCUSSION: Both corporations and limited partnerships are recognized only under the authority of statutes. Common law cannot be a basis for their formation. Both require the filing with appropriate state authorities of organizational documents (articles of incorporation or certificates of limited partnership).
   Answer (A) is incorrect because limited partners are not fiduciaries and owe no such duty to the partnership. Answer (C) is incorrect because, although not allowed to participate in management, limited partners may still vote on such partnership matters as dissolution of the partnership or the removal of a general partner. Answer (D) is incorrect because limited partnership interests are subject to registration requirements.

5. Which of the following statements is true with respect to a limited partnership?

   A. A limited partner may not be an unsecured creditor of the limited partnership.

   B. A general partner may not also be a limited partner at the same time.

   C. A general partner may be a secured creditor of the limited partnership.

   D. A limited partnership can be formed with limited liability for all partners.

Answer (C) is correct. *(CPA, adapted)*
   REQUIRED: The characteristics of a limited partnership.
   DISCUSSION: A limited partner's liability is limited to his/her contributions to partnership capital. But a limited partnership must have at least one general partner with unlimited liability. A general partner may be another partnership, a corporation, or another entity. A general partner may also be a limited partner. A limited partner and the partnership may engage in transactions such as extending secured credit or property sales.
   Answer (A) is incorrect because a limited partner and the partnership may engage in such a transaction. Answer (B) is incorrect because one person may be a general and a limited partner. Answer (D) is incorrect because every limited partnership must have at least one partner with unlimited liability for obligations of the partnership.

6. A limited partner's capital contribution to the limited partnership

   A. Results in the limited partner having an intangible personal property right.

   B. Can be withdrawn at the limited partner's option at any time prior to the filing of a petition in bankruptcy against the limited partnership.

   C. Can only consist of cash or marketable securities.

   D. Must be indicated in the limited partnership's certificate.

Answer (A) is correct. *(CPA, adapted)*
   REQUIRED: The true statement regarding a limited partner's capital contribution.
   DISCUSSION: The limited partner's interest is an investment in the entity as a whole. The interest is personal property. It constitutes an intangible because the limited partner has no right to specific partnership property.
   Answer (B) is incorrect because a limited partner's right of withdrawal of his/her capital contribution is restricted. It may be withdrawn upon the dissolution of the partnership, at the date specified in the certificate, upon 6 months' notice in writing to all the members, or with the consent of all the members but only if all creditors are paid or sufficient assets are available for creditors. Answer (C) is incorrect because a limited partner's capital contribution may consist of cash, other property, or services. Answer (D) is incorrect because a limited partner's contribution need not be described in the certificate.

7. A limited partner

   A. May not withdraw his/her capital contribution absent sufficient limited-partnership property to pay all general creditors.

   B. Must not own limited-partnership interests in other competing limited partnerships.

   C. Is automatically an agent for the partnership with apparent authority to bind the limited partnership in contract.

   D. Has no liability to creditors even if (s)he takes part in the control of the business as long as (s)he is held out as being a limited partner.

Answer (A) is correct. *(CPA, adapted)*
   REQUIRED: The true statement about a limited partner.
   DISCUSSION: Outside creditors have priority over liabilities to limited partners for the return of their capital contributions. Thus, a limited partner may not withdraw his/her capital contribution if the effect is to impair the creditors' rights.
   Answer (B) is incorrect because the reason that a limited partner may own an interest in competing partnerships or compete in other ways is that (s)he does not engage in the management of the partnership. Answer (C) is incorrect because limited partners are not agents of the partnership and have no apparent or other authority to bind the partnership. Answer (D) is incorrect because a limited partner who takes part in the control of the business will become personally liable to creditors, even if held out as a limited partner.

8. Which of the following rights would a limited partner not be entitled to assert?

   A. To have a formal accounting of partnership affairs whenever the circumstances render it just and reasonable.

   B. To have the same rights as a general partner to a dissolution and winding up of the partnership.

   C. To have reasonable access to the partnership books and to inspect and copy them.

   D. To be elected as a general partner by a majority vote of the limited partners in number and amount.

Answer (D) is correct. *(CPA, adapted)*
   REQUIRED: The right that a limited partner is not entitled to assert.
   DISCUSSION: A new general partner may be admitted to a limited partnership only with the specific written consent of each and every partner (both limited and general). The limited partners therefore do not have the power to admit new general partners, and unanimous consent is needed unless the partnership agreement provides otherwise.
   Answer (A) is incorrect because a limited partner is entitled to an accounting if the circumstances are reasonable. Answer (B) is incorrect because a limited partner has the same rights as a general partner in winding up a partnership. Answer (C) is incorrect because a limited partner has a reasonable right to access books and records.

9. In general, which of the following statements is true with respect to a limited partnership?

   A. A limited partner has the right to obtain from the general partner(s) financial information and tax returns of the limited partnership.

   B. A limited partnership can be formed with limited liability for all partners.

   C. A limited partner may not also be a general partner at the same time.

   D. A limited partner may hire employees on behalf of the partnership.

Answer (A) is correct. *(CPA, adapted)*
   REQUIRED: The true statement about a limited partnership.
   DISCUSSION: Both general and limited partners have the right to inspect and copy the books of the partnership at any time. Thus, they can obtain financial information and tax returns of the limited partnership.
   Answer (B) is incorrect because, in the absence of a special statutory provision permitting the establishment of limited liability limited partnerships, a limited partnership must have at least one general partner with unlimited liability. Answer (C) is incorrect because it is possible for a person to be both a general and a limited partner in the same partnership. Answer (D) is incorrect because a limited partner is not an agent of the partnership and is not allowed to participate in day-to-day management.

10. The XYZ Limited Partnership has two general partners: Smith and Jones. A provision in the partnership agreement allows the removal of a general partner by a majority vote of the limited partners. The limited partners vote to remove Jones as a general partner. Which of the following statements is true?

A. The limited partners are now liable to third parties for partnership obligations.

B. Limited partners may vote to remove a general partner without losing their status as limited partners.

C. By voting to remove a general partner, the limited partners are presumed to exercise control of the business.

D. Limited partners may participate in management decisions without limitation if this right is provided for in the limited partnership agreement.

Answer (B) is correct. *(D.B. MacDonald)*
REQUIRED: The effect on the status of limited partners of voting for removal of a general partner.
DISCUSSION: Under Section 303 of the Revised Uniform Limited Partnership Act, a limited partner is not liable to third parties for partnership obligations as long as the limited partner does not take part "in the control of the business." The RULPA lists several activities in which a limited partner may engage without being considered "in the control of the business," among them, voting on the removal of a general partner. Excessive involvement in the management of the business may constitute taking part "in the control of the business." The result would be liability to those parties who have knowledge of the limited partner's participation in control or, if the limited partner is exercising the powers of a general partner, to all third parties.

11. Stanley Kowalski is a well-known retired movie personality who purchased a limited partnership interest in Terrific Movie Productions upon its initial syndication. Which of the following is true?

A. If Stanley permits his name to be used in connection with the business and is held out as a participant in the management of the venture, he will be liable as a general partner.

B. The sale of these limited partnership interests is not subject to SEC registration.

C. This limited partnership may be formed with the same informality as a general partnership.

D. The general partners are prohibited from also owning limited partnership interests.

Answer (A) is correct. *(CPA; adapted)*
REQUIRED: The true statement concerning a limited partnership.
DISCUSSION: A limited partner who permits his/her name to be used in the name of the partnership or in connection with the business will be liable to creditors who give credit without actual knowledge that (s)he is not a general partner. Such a limited partner will forfeit his/her limited liability because the use of his/her name may have led unsuspecting creditors to believe that (s)he was a general partner with unlimited liability.
Answer (B) is incorrect because limited partnership interests are considered to be securities and must be registered with the SEC unless an exemption applies. Answer (C) is incorrect because a limited partnership can only be formed pursuant to a statute permitting the formation and existence of limited partnerships, and such statutes require many formalities. Answer (D) is incorrect because a general partner may also be a limited partner.

12. Ms. Wall is a limited partner of the Amalgamated Limited Partnership. She is insolvent and her debts exceed her assets by $28,000. Goldsmith, one of Wall's largest creditors, is resorting to legal process to obtain the payment of Wall's debt to him. Goldsmith has obtained a charging order against Wall's limited partnership interest for the unsatisfied amount of the debt. As a result of Goldsmith's action, which of the following will happen?

A. The partnership will be dissolved.

B. Wall's partnership interest must be redeemed with partnership property.

C. Goldsmith automatically becomes a substituted limited partner.

D. Goldsmith becomes in effect an assignee of Wall's partnership interest.

Answer (D) is correct. *(CPA, adapted)*
REQUIRED: The result of a creditor obtaining a charging order against an insolvent limited partner's interest.
DISCUSSION: A charging order is a court order that has the effect of an involuntary assignment of the limited partner's interest to the judgment-creditor (or an independent third party called a receiver). The limited partner's interest may be temporarily assigned until the profits distributed pay off the debt, or it may be permanently assigned using its fair value to pay off the debt.
Answer (A) is incorrect because a limited partnership is not dissolved by the bankruptcy of a limited partner or by assignment of his/her interest. Answer (B) is incorrect because Wall's partnership interest is not required to be redeemed. Answer (C) is incorrect because an assignee of a limited partnership interest does not become a substituted limited partner unless the assignor gives the assignee that right pursuant to the limited partnership agreement, or all the members of the partnership agree.

13. Unless otherwise provided in the certificate of limited partnership, which of the following is true if Grey, one of the limited partners, dies?

A. Grey's personal representative will automatically become a substituted limited partner.

B. Grey's personal representative will have all the rights of a limited partner for the purpose of settling the estate.

C. The partnership will automatically be dissolved.

D. Grey's estate will be free from any liabilities incurred by Grey as a limited partner.

Answer (B) is correct. *(CPA, adapted)*
REQUIRED: The effect of the death of a limited partner.
DISCUSSION: The death of a limited partner does not result in dissolution of the partnership. The limited partner's estate will retain all of Grey's rights and liabilities as a limited partner, and Grey's personal representative will act as limited partner for the purpose of settling the estate.
Answer (A) is incorrect because a limited partner's personal representative is not actually made a limited partner but is only entitled to act in that capacity for purposes of settling the estate. Answer (C) is incorrect because a partnership is not automatically dissolved upon the death of a limited partner. Answer (D) is incorrect because the estate retains both the rights and liabilities that would accrue to Grey as a limited partner.

14. Absent any contrary provisions in the agreement, under which of the following circumstances will a limited partnership be dissolved?

A. A limited partner dies and his/her estate is insolvent.

B. A personal creditor of a general partner obtains a judgment against the general partner's interest in the limited partnership.

C. A general partner retires and all the remaining general partners do not consent to continue.

D. A limited partner assigns his/her partnership interest to an outsider and the purchaser becomes a substituted limited partner.

Answer (C) is correct. *(CPA, adapted)*
REQUIRED: The circumstance in which a limited partnership will be dissolved.
DISCUSSION: Retirement of a general partner will generally dissolve a limited partnership just as it would dissolve a general partnership. However, dissolution can be avoided if the business is continued by the remaining general partners either with the consent of all partners or pursuant to a stipulation in the partnership agreement.
Answer (A) is incorrect because the death of a limited partner, regardless of the solvency of the estate, does not dissolve the partnership. Answer (B) is incorrect because a judgment against the interest of a general partner is similar to an assignment of that interest, which does not dissolve the partnership. Answer (D) is incorrect because the assignment of a limited partnership interest does not dissolve the partnership. It makes no difference whether the assignee becomes a substituted limited partner.

15. Under the Revised Uniform Limited Partnership Act and in the absence of a contrary agreement by the partners, which of the following events is most likely to dissolve a limited partnership?

A. A majority vote in favor by the partners.

B. A two-thirds vote in favor by the partners.

C. A withdrawal of a majority of the limited partners.

D. Withdrawal of the only general partner.

Answer (D) is correct. *(CPA, adapted)*
REQUIRED: The event most likely to dissolve a limited partnership.
DISCUSSION: A limited partnership can be dissolved upon any of the following events: (1) the time or event specified in the limited partnership agreement occurs; (2) all the partners agree, in writing, to dissolve; (3) an event of withdrawal of the only general partner occurs; or (4) the limited partnership is dissolved by court order.
Answer (A) is incorrect because all partners must agree in writing to dissolve. Answer (B) is incorrect because all partners must agree in writing to dissolve. Answer (C) is incorrect because the withdrawal must be by the only general partner.

16. Wichita Properties is a limited partnership created in accordance with the provisions of the Uniform Limited Partnership Act. The partners have voted to dissolve and settle the partnership's accounts. Which of the following will be the last to be paid?

A. General partners for unpaid distributions.

B. Limited partners in respect to capital.

C. Limited and general partners in respect to their undistributed profits.

D. General partners in respect to capital.

Answer (C) is correct. *(CPA, adapted)*
REQUIRED: The lowest priority of distribution upon liquidation of a limited partnership.
DISCUSSION: Under the RULPA, limited and general partners are treated equally. Unless the partnership agreement provides otherwise, assets are distributed as follows:

1) Creditors (including all partner-creditors)
2) Partners for unpaid distributions (i.e., declared but not paid)
3) Partners for the return of their contributions
4) Partners for remaining assets (i.e., undistributed profits) in the proportions in which they share distributions

2.2 Limited Liability Partnerships (LLPs)

17. A limited liability partnership (LLP)

A. Starts life as a corporation.

B. Is typically adopted by providers of professional services.

C. Is ordinarily treated as a legal entity to the same extent as a corporation.

D. Offers a liability shield only for professional malpractice.

Answer (B) is correct. *(Publisher, adapted)*
REQUIRED: The true statement about an LLP.
DISCUSSION: An LLP is a general partnership that has been changed to LLP status in accordance with state law. The LLP is a business structure that is often adopted by providers of professional services (e.g., attorneys, CPAs, and physicians) and family enterprises.
Answer (A) is incorrect because an LLP is typically a general partnership that has been changed to LLP status in accordance with state law. Answer (C) is incorrect because an LLP is ordinarily treated as a legal entity to the same extent as a general partnership. Answer (D) is incorrect because early statutes provided the limitation on personal liability only for professional malpractice, but most states have now enacted LLP legislation that provides for a broad personal liability shield.

18. What is a possible disadvantage of forming an LLP as opposed to remaining a general partnership?

A. Creation and continuation require compliance with statutory provisions.

B. Partners are subject to a broad personal liability shield.

C. LLPs are pass-through entities.

D. Termination of an LLP involves the same process as in a general partnership.

Answer (A) is correct. *(Publisher, adapted)*
REQUIRED: The possible disadvantage of forming an LLP.
DISCUSSION: A disadvantage of the LLP is that its creation and continuation require compliance with statutory provisions. Hence, becoming an LLP is more complicated because the partners must amend the partnership agreement and file a statement of qualification with the secretary of state.
Answer (B) is incorrect because the personal liability shield is an advantage of the formation of an LLP. Answer (C) is incorrect because avoiding the double taxation of the corporate entity is an advantage of an LLP. Answer (D) is incorrect because the simple dissolution and winding up of a general partnership should be viewed as an advantage of the LLP formation.

19. Under the RUPA, which of the following provides notice of limited liability status to those who do business with a limited liability partnership (LLP)?

A. Filing of an annual report with the SEC.

B. The way the partnership is managed.

C. The first words of the partnership name.

D. The statement of qualification.

Answer (D) is correct. *(Publisher, adapted)*
REQUIRED: The practice that gives notice of limited liability status.
DISCUSSION: Under the RUPA, partners must register by filing a statement of qualification with the secretary of state to become an LLP. An LLP, or a foreign LLP authorized to transact business in the state, also must file an annual report containing substantially the same (but updated) information as the statement of qualification (name, jurisdiction where formed, and facts sufficient for service of process).
Answer (A) is incorrect because the annual report is filed with the state. Answer (B) is incorrect because management practice may be the same for a general partnership and a limited liability partnership. Answer (C) is incorrect because the end of an LLP's name will alert persons dealing with it to the existence of the liability shield.

20. How may an LLP be financed?

I.   Public issuance of LLP shares.
II. Partner contributions.
III. Entity borrowings.

A. I only.

B. I and III only.

C. II and III only.

D. I, II, and III.

Answer (C) is correct. *(Publisher, adapted)*
REQUIRED: The capitalization method(s) of an LLP.
DISCUSSION: Like a general partnership, an LLP is financed by partner contributions and the entity's borrowings. The personal liability shield may attract additional partners, hence greater capital contributions. LLP's shares are not publicly traded.

21. Which of the following are similarities between partners in a general partnership and partners in an LLP?

I. Rights.
II. Duties.
III. Authority.

   A. I only.

   B. I and III only.

   C. II and III only.

   D. I, II, and III.

Answer (D) is correct. *(Publisher, adapted)*
REQUIRED: The similarities between partners in an LLP and general partners.
DISCUSSION: The rights, duties, and authority of partners in an LLP are similar to those of general partners.

22. Under the RUPA, in which of the following situations will a partner in an LLP most likely be personally liable?

   A. The managing partner in the Texas office when individuals in the New York office engaged in fraudulent activities.

   B. The managing partner in the New York office when an employee in the office who was supervised by another partner engaged in fraudulent activities.

   C. The partner who personally incurs an obligation in the conduct of partnership business.

   D. A nonmanaging partner in an office where another partner committed negligence.

Answer (C) is correct. *(Publisher, adapted)*
REQUIRED: The situation in which a partner in an LLP will be liable.
DISCUSSION: A partner who personally incurs an obligation in the conduct of partnership business is fully liable. The shield is provided only for liability that is imputed simply because a partner is a partner, not for liability directly incurred by the partner.
Answer (A) is incorrect because the managing partner in the Texas office has nothing to do with fraudulent activities in the New York office. Answer (B) is incorrect because, unlike the limitation in a limited partnership, the liability shield in an LLP protects the partners who manage the business. Answer (D) is incorrect because, under the RUPA, the liability shield extends to any obligation of the LLP.

23. Which of the following partners of a limited liability partnership (LLP) may avoid personal liability when a partner commits a negligent act?

   A. All the partners.

   B. The supervisor of the negligent partner.

   C. All the partners other than the negligent partner.

   D. All the partners other than the negligent partner and his/her supervisor.

Answer (D) is correct. *(CPA, adapted)*
REQUIRED: The partner(s) not personally liable for the negligence of a partner.
DISCUSSION: Partners are not liable for a negligent act committed by another partner in a limited liability partnership. This shield is provided only for liability imputed solely because of partnership status. Thus, the negligent partner is the only partner liable. However, a partner who is an immediate supervisor is also liable for any negligent acts committed by an employee within the scope of employment.
Answer (A) is incorrect because only the partner who committed the act and his/her supervisor are liable. Answer (B) is incorrect because the negligent partner also is liable. Answer (C) is incorrect because a partner who was not (1) directly liable or (2) the supervisor of a negligent person is not liable.

24. Which of the following is a false statement about a foreign LLP?

   A. It was formed in a state different from the one in which it conducts business.

   B. It was formed in a foreign country.

   C. A choice of law issue arises when a foreign LLP does business in a state.

   D. Under the RUPA, a statement of foreign qualification may not be denied because of differences in state law.

Answer (B) is correct. *(Publisher, adapted)*
REQUIRED: The false statement about a foreign LLP.
DISCUSSION: A foreign LLP, by definition, is an LLP that was formed in a state other than the one in which it conducts business.
Answer (A) is incorrect because a foreign LLP is an entity formed in the U.S. but not in the forum state. Answer (C) is incorrect because a choice of law issue arises when a foreign LLP does business in another state. The liability shield may vary from state to state. Answer (D) is incorrect because the RUPA provides that a statement of foreign qualification may not be denied because of differences in state law.

25. Jones, Smith, and Bay wanted to form a company called JSB Co. but were unsure about which type of entity would be most beneficial based on their concerns. They all desired the opportunity to make tax-free contributions and distributions when appropriate. They wanted earnings to accumulate tax-free. They did not want to be subject to personal holding company tax and did not want double taxation of income. Bay was going to be the only individual giving management advice to the company and wanted to be a member of JSB through his current company, Channel, Inc. Which of the following would be the most appropriate business structure to meet all of their concerns?

    A. Proprietorship.

    B. S corporation.

    C. C corporation.

    D. Limited liability partnership.

Answer (D) is correct. *(CPA, adapted)*
    REQUIRED: The appropriate business structure to meet the specified needs.
    DISCUSSION: An LLP is the most beneficial business entity. Contributions to a partnership are tax-free. The earnings are taxed when they are earned, whether distributed or not, and are not subject to personal holding company tax. In addition, unlike the earnings of a C corporation, which are taxed to the corporation and to recipients of its dividends, earnings of an LLP are not subject to double taxation. Furthermore, a corporation may be a partner in an LLP but not a shareholder in an S corporation.
    Answer (A) is incorrect because a proprietorship is operated by one individual. However, two or more persons who associate to carry on as co-owners of a business for profit form a partnership unless the statutory requirements of another form of organization are met. Answer (B) is incorrect because an S corporation cannot have any corporate shareholders. Bay would be unable to operate through Channel, Inc. Answer (C) is incorrect because a C corporation's earnings are subject to double taxation and the personal company holding tax if earnings are not distributed.

2.3 Limited Liability Companies (LLCs)

26. Which of the following is false regarding an LLC?

    A. An LLC has a noncorporate hybrid business structure.

    B. An LLC may be formed only under a state statute.

    C. An LLC combines the limited liability of the corporation with the tax advantages of the general partnership.

    D. An LLC is a hybrid corporation and is taxed at corporate rates.

Answer (D) is correct. *(Publisher, adapted)*
    REQUIRED: The false statement regarding an LLC.
    DISCUSSION: Although an LLC has a hybrid structure, its profits are not taxed at corporate rates if the members elect to be taxed as partners. Its profits are generally passed through to its shareholders and taxed at their individual rates.
    Answer (A) is incorrect because an LLC has a noncorporate hybrid business structure. Answer (B) is incorrect because an LLC must be formed under a state statute. Answer (C) is incorrect because the shareholders of an LLC are entitled to limited liability, yet the entity is taxed as a partnership if the members elect to be taxed as partners.

27. An LLC may be formed when

I.   One person files articles of organization with the appropriate secretary of state.

II. Two or more persons file articles of organization with the appropriate secretary of state.

    A. I only.

    B. II only.

    C. I and II.

    D. Neither I nor II.

Answer (C) is correct. *(Publisher, adapted)*
    REQUIRED: The formation of an LLC.
    DISCUSSION: An LLC is formed by one or more persons who file articles of organization with the appropriate secretary of state. Thus, formation is more difficult than for a sole proprietorship or a general partnership.

28. An LLC's articles of organization need **not**

A. State the LLC's name.

B. Include all names of future members.

C. Provide for existence for a specified term or at-will.

D. Indicate whether management will be by owners or managers.

Answer (B) is correct. *(Publisher, adapted)*
REQUIRED: The true statement regarding an LLC's articles of organization.
DISCUSSION: An LLC's articles of organization should state the LLC's name, basic information, provide for existence, indicate the type of management, and state members' liability for the LLC's obligations. The articles of organization cannot include the names of all future members. This information is generally unknown at the time of organization.
Answer (A) is incorrect because the articles of organization must state the LLC's name. Answer (C) is incorrect because the articles of organization must provide for existence, either for a specified term or at-will. Answer (D) is incorrect because the articles of organization must indicate whether management will be by owners or managers.

29. Which of the following is a legal entity separate from its owners?

A. Limited partnership.

B. LLP.

C. LLC.

D. All of the answers are correct.

Answer (D) is correct. *(Publisher, adapted)*
REQUIRED: The entities that are legally separate from their owners.
DISCUSSION: Limited partnerships, LLPs, and LLCs are all legally separate from their owners. Such an entity may enter into contracts, sue, be sued, and own property in its own name.

30. An LLC must maintain which of the following contacts with the state where it was formed?

I.   An agent for service of process
II. An attorney for representation in lawsuits
III. An office

A. I only.

B. I and III only.

C. II and III only.

D. I, II, and III.

Answer (B) is correct. *(Publisher, adapted)*
REQUIRED: The contacts, if any, that an LLC must have with the state where it was formed.
DISCUSSION: An LLC must at all times maintain in its state of formation an agent for service of process and an office. These requirements are the same as for limited partnerships and corporations. An LLC is not required by the state to retain an attorney.

31. Which of the following capitalization characteristics are advantages of an LLC over an S corporation?

I.   An LLC offers only one class of stock.

II. An LLC has no limit on the number of members.

III. Members of the LLC may contribute appreciated property in exchange for membership interests without recognizing taxable gain.

A. I, II, and III.

B. I and II only.

C. II and III only.

D. I and III only.

Answer (C) is correct. *(Publisher, adapted)*
REQUIRED: The advantageous capitalization characteristics of an LLC.
DISCUSSION: An LLC ordinarily has a greater ability to raise capital than an S corporation. It (1) may offer more classes of stock, (2) can make disproportionate allocations and distributions, and (3) has no limit on the number of members. Moreover, its members may contribute appreciated property without recognizing taxable gain.
Answer (A) is incorrect because an LLC may offer multiple classes of stock. Answer (B) is incorrect because an LLC may offer multiple classes of stock, and its members may contribute appreciated property without recognizing taxable gain.
Answer (D) is incorrect because an LLC may offer multiple classes of stock, and an LLC has no limit on the number of members.

32. Which of the following is a false statement about the taxation of an LLC?

A. Members may elect to be taxed as partners.

B. Members may elect to be taxed as a corporation.

C. It may be advantageous for an LLC to be taxed as a corporation.

D. Single-member LLCs must be taxed as corporations.

Answer (D) is correct.   *(Publisher, adapted)*
REQUIRED: The false statement about the taxation of an LLC.
DISCUSSION: Members may elect to be taxed as partners, and single-member LLCs may be taxed as sole proprietorships. Furthermore, taxation as a corporation is an option and may be advantageous if reinvestment in the LLC is desired and corporate rates are lower than personal rates.
Answer (A) is incorrect because members may elect to be taxed as partners. Answer (B) is incorrect because members may elect to be taxed as a corporation and will usually do so when it is advantageous to them. Answer (C) is incorrect because members may choose to be taxed as either a partnership or a corporation.

33. In the absence of a member agreement, how are profits and losses shared by members of an LLC?

A. In proportion to their capital contributions.

B. Equally.

C. In proportion to their voting power.

D. In proportion to their partnership interests.

Answer (B) is correct.   *(Publisher, adapted)*
REQUIRED: The distribution of profits and losses by an LLC.
DISCUSSION: In the absence of a contrary agreement, profits and losses are shared equally in an LLC. A member is not automatically entitled to compensation, except when winding up the enterprise.

34. What is the order of payment of proceeds in the event of a liquidation of an LLC?

I. Outside creditors.
II. Members' capital contributions.
III. Loans from members.

A. I, II, III.

B. I, III, II.

C. II, III, I.

D. III, I, II.

Answer (B) is correct.   *(Publisher, adapted)*
REQUIRED: The order of payments in a liquidation of an LLC.
DISCUSSION: The following is the order of priority in the liquidation of an LLC: outside creditors, loans from members, members' capital contributions, and remaining amounts equally to members.

35. Which of the following parties generally has the most management rights?

A. Minority shareholder in a corporation listed on a national stock exchange.

B. Limited partner in a general partnership.

C. Member of a limited liability company.

D. Limited partner in a limited partnership.

Answer (C) is correct.   *(CPA, adapted)*
REQUIRED: The party that generally has the most management rights.
DISCUSSION: In a member-managed LLC, all members have a right to participate, and most business matters are decided by the majority. In a manager-managed LLC, each manager has equal rights, but managers are selected or removed by a majority vote of the members. An LLC is deemed to be member-managed unless the articles of organization state otherwise.
Answer (A) is incorrect because a minority shareholder in a public corporation generally has little or no management rights. Answer (B) is incorrect because a general partnership has no limited partners. Answer (D) is incorrect because, in a limited partnership, a limited partner has no authority to participate in management and control of the business.

Use Gleim's *CPA Test Prep* for interactive testing with over 2,000 additional multiple-choice questions!

STUDY UNIT THREE
CORPORATIONS:
FORMATION, POWERS, AND FINANCING

(14 pages of outline)

The basic forms of multiple-owner business structures are the partnership and the **corporation**. The corporation is the dominant form in which business is conducted in the United States. A corporation may be used for everything from the smallest to the largest enterprises. The fundamental characteristic that distinguishes a corporation from all other business organizations is that for all purposes it is a **separate legal entity**. Unlike a sole proprietorship or a general partnership, its rights and obligations are separate from those of its owners.

A corporation is created under state law. Although state laws vary considerably, they are all influenced by the **Model Business Corporation Act (MBCA)**, a statement of modern corporate law first published in 1933. Like all model acts, it does not become law unless adopted by the legislature of a state or incorporated into the common law. However, its purpose is to provide legislators, lawyers, and legal commissions with a basis for drafting and amending state incorporation laws. The MBCA has been amended frequently, and some of its provisions have been adopted to some degree by every state. The **Revised Model Business Corporation Act of 1984 (RMBCA)** applies to publicly held and closely held corporations and is followed in most recent textbooks. It is the basis for our outlines.

The two basic ways to acquire capital to finance a corporation are to issue equity or debt securities. **Equity** represents ownership of the corporation. Equity securities include both common and preferred stock. Shareholders, as owners, have a significantly different relationship to the issuing corporation than do its creditors. **Debt** generally represents the corporation's promise to pay interest while the debt is outstanding and to repay principal. Debt securities (e.g., bonds) may be secured, in which case a lien is granted upon specific corporate property. They also may be unsecured, in which case the debt is backed only by the general credit of the corporation.

3.1 DEFINITION

1. Unlike a sole proprietorship or a general partnership, a corporation is a legal entity created under authority of a **state statute** to carry out the purposes permitted by that statute and the articles of incorporation. The corporation is treated as a legal person with rights and obligations separate from its owners and managers.

2. Corporations are governed by **shareholders** (owners) who elect a board of directors and approve fundamental changes in the corporate structure. **Directors** establish corporate policies and elect or appoint corporate **officers** who carry out the policies in the day-to-day management of the organization.

3. Stop and review! You have completed the outline for this subunit. Study multiple-choice question 1 on page 71.

3.2 FORMATION

1. A corporation is formed under a state statute when persons, called incorporators, file **articles of incorporation** and receive a **certificate of incorporation** (a corporate charter) from the state.

2. **Classification.** Corporations are classified in a variety of ways.

    a. A **private corporation** is organized to earn profits for its owners (for-profit corporation) or for charitable, educational, social, religious, or philanthropic purposes (nonprofit corporation).

        1) A **close** (or closely held) **corporation** often has the following features:

            a) It is owned by a relatively small number of shareholders.
            b) It does not sell its stock to the public, so liquidating an investment or raising equity capital may be difficult.
            c) Its officers and directors own all the stock.
            d) Shareholders are active in management and control.
            e) Transfer of shares is often restricted.
            f) A supermajority may be required for important actions.

        2) A **publicly held corporation's** stock is sold to the public at large, generally on a nationally recognized stock exchange. Its share price quotations are regularly published.

    b. **Quasi-public corporations** owe a duty to the public because they enjoy a favored status granted by the state; e.g., a utility may enjoy monopoly status and a limited power of eminent domain. They are highly regulated.

    c. A **public corporation** is organized for public purposes related to the administration of government, e.g., an incorporated municipality. It is formed by specific legislation that defines its purpose and powers. It may be funded by local taxes.

    d. A corporation is classified as **domestic** in the state in which it is organized, i.e., where its articles of incorporation are filed. It cannot be required to incorporate in any other state.

    e. A corporation is **foreign** in every other state. A **certificate of authority** required to **do business** within the borders of another state is obtained by

        1) Filing appropriate documents with the secretary of state,
        2) Paying required fees, and
        3) Designating a resident agent.

    f. A corporation organized in another country is classified as **alien**. It must obtain a certificate of authority to do business from each host state.

    g. An **S corporation** is a close corporation whose shareholders have elected under federal law to be taxed similarly to a partnership. Hence, an S corporation does not usually pay income tax. (It should be distinguished from a **C corporation**, that is, an entity subject to the corporate income tax.) The shareholders report their proportionate shares of the entity's income, losses, deductions, and credits, regardless of whether they have received distributions. S corporation status is terminated immediately when any one of the following eligibility requirements is no longer met:

        1) The corporation may have only one class of stock.
        2) The number of shareholders is limited to 100, but family members may elect to be treated as one shareholder.
        3) The corporation must be incorporated in the U.S.

4) An S corporation should not have excessive net passive investment income.

5) Shareholders are limited to individuals, estates, qualified trusts, and certain tax-exempt entities (e.g., charitable organizations with qualified pension plans).

    a) S corporations may own 80% or more of a C corporation. However, the S corporation may not elect to file a joint tax return with its C corporation subsidiary.

        i) Dividends from the 80%-or-more owned subsidiary are not treated as passive investment income if the C corporation's income was from a trade or business.

    b) An S corporation may own a **Qualified Subchapter S Subsidiary**. A QSSS is an electing domestic corporation that qualifies as an S corporation and is wholly owned by an S corporation parent.

    c) A shareholder may own the S corporation's shares through a **limited liability company** that has elected to be taxed as a partnership. In that case, the shareholder is deemed to be a direct owner of the S corporation.

6) Nonresident aliens may not own shares.

h. **Professional corporations** (professional service associations). State statutes may allow accountants, lawyers, and other professionals to incorporate. The statutes typically restrict stock ownership to specific professionals licensed within that state.

3. Advantages of a Corporation

a. **Limited liability.** A shareholder owns a property interest in the underlying net assets of the corporation and is entitled to share in its profits, but his/her personal assets are not subject to corporate liabilities. The shareholder's exposure is limited to the investment in the corporation.

b. **Separation of ownership from management.** Shareholders have no inherent right to participate directly in management. They elect a board that sets corporate policy and appoints officers to conduct operations. A shareholder may be an officer or a director.

c. **Free transferability of interests.** Absent contractual or legal restriction, shares in a corporation may be freely transferred, e.g., by sale, gift, pledge, or inheritance.

1) A shareholder has no interest in specific corporate property. (S)he owns a proportional, intangible property interest in the entire corporation.

2) Traditionally, the shareholder's ownership interest was represented by a stock certificate. The interest was usually transferred by endorsing the certificate.

    a) **Indirect holding.** However, securities of publicly traded corporations are now customarily held indirectly so as to facilitate trading. Thus, certificates are held by a depository institution on behalf of **securities intermediaries** (brokers or banks) that represent the owners.

        i) Trades are reflected in accounting entries made by the securities intermediaries rather than in physical transfer of certificates.

d. **Perpetual life.** A corporation has perpetual existence unless the articles provide for a shorter life or it is dissolved by the state. Death, withdrawal, or addition of a shareholder, director, or officer does not end its existence.

e. **Ease of raising capital.** A corporation raises capital (to start or expand the business) by selling stock or issuing bonds. The sale of stock may be governed by state "blue sky" laws and federal securities laws.

f.   **Constitutional rights.** A corporation is a **person** for most purposes under the **U.S. Constitution**. Thus, it has the right to equal protection, due process, freedom from unreasonable searches and seizures, and freedom of speech.

1)   However, commercial speech (e.g., advertising) and political speech (e.g., political contributions) are given less protection than that afforded to the same speech by natural persons.

g.   **Transfers of property to a controlled corporation.** A transfer of assets for stock of any corporation is **tax-free** if the transferors are in control of the corporation immediately after the exchange. A person who transfers appreciated property will receive the benefit if another transferor transfers property and together they meet the control test. Property includes money.

1)   **Control** is ownership of stock possessing at least 80% of the total combined voting power of all classes of stock entitled to vote and at least 80% of the total number of shares of all other classes of stock of the corporation.

4.   **Disadvantages of a corporation.** Adopting corporate status may result in

a.   Reduced individual control of the business.

b.   Payment of taxes on corporate income and payment by the shareholders of taxes on distributions received from the corporation (unless the entity qualifies for and elects S corporation status).

c.   Substantial costs of meeting the requirements of corporate formation and operation.

d.   Hostile takeover of a publicly traded corporation.

e.   Transfer of unrestricted shares in a close corporation to unknown parties.

f.   An inability of a minority shareholder in a close corporation to liquidate his/her interest or to influence the conduct of the business.

g.   Becoming subject to state and federal regulation of securities transactions through reporting and registration requirements.

5.   **Preincorporation contracts.** A **promoter** is one who arranges for formation of the corporation. The promoter provides for the capital structure and financing of the corporation and for compliance with any relevant securities law. The promoter also may arrange for procurement of necessary personnel, services, assets, licenses, equipment, leases, etc.

a.   **Prior to incorporation**, the promoter enters into ordinary and necessary contracts required for initial operation of the business. If the contracts are executed in the promoter's name and there is no further action, the promoter is personally liable on them.

1)   The corporation is not liable because a promoter cannot be an agent of a not-yet-existing corporation. Prior to formation, a corporation cannot be principal because it has no capacity to enter into contracts or employ agents.

2)   A preincorporation contract made by promoters in the name of a corporation and on its behalf may bind the corporation if so provided by statute.

b.   A corporation may **not ratify** a preincorporation contract because no principal existed at the time of contracting. However, the corporation may adopt contracts formed by a promoter. **Adoption** is a legal substitute for ratification. It is acceptance of the assignment of rights and delegation of duties.

1)   Adoption may be implied from accepting the benefits of a contract.

2)   The contract, by its terms, may provide that the promoter is released from liability upon adoption of the contract by the corporation.

c.   A promoter may avoid liability by acquiring an **option** (assignable to the corporation) to bind the third party to a contract.

    d.   If the promoter has no liability by the terms of an agreement, and the agreement is not an option, it may be treated as a **continuing offer** until revoked or accepted by the corporation.

    e.   If the promoter, the third party, and the corporation enter into a **novation** substituting the corporation for the promoter, only the corporation is liable and the promoter is released.

    f.   Promoters owe a **fiduciary duty** to each other, to the corporation, and to stock subscribers and shareholders. This fiduciary duty requires good faith, fair dealing, and full disclosure of all material facts concerning transactions on behalf of the soon-to-be-formed corporation.

        1)   Promoters have a **duty to account** for any secret profits earned when dealing with the corporation, e.g., by a sale of their own property to the corporation.

    g.   The promoter secures potential investors using **stock subscription agreements**. Each subscriber agrees to purchase a certain amount of stock at a specified price, payable at an agreed future time. A subscription differs from an **executory contract**. The first but not the second reflects an intent that the investor become a shareholder at the time of contracting.

        1)   The subscriber (offeror) offers to enter into a contract of purchase.

        2)   Under the RMBCA, a **preincorporation subscription agreement** is irrevocable for 6 months, unless otherwise provided in the agreement or all subscribers consent to revocation. Furthermore, many statutes provide that it be written.

        3)   State law may provide that the subscriber is a shareholder when the corporation is formed or it adopts the agreement.

        4)   A **public corporation** cannot use subscriptions because of how its stock is traded and held and the requirements of the securities laws.

6.   **Incorporation** may be in any state and may be done by mail or online. Each state requires that **articles of incorporation** be filed with the secretary of state or another designated official. (A corporation may incorporate in one state but have its principal place of business or conduct its business operations in another state or states.)

    a.   **Incorporators** sign the articles. Typically, they may not be minors. Only one incorporator is required. It may be a corporation.

    b.   **Content of articles.** Under the RMBCA, they must include the

        1)   Corporation's name
        2)   Number of authorized shares of stock
        3)   Street address of the corporation's initial registered office
        4)   Name of the registered agent at that office
        5)   Name and address of each incorporator

    c.   **Date existence commences.** A corporation is first recognized as a legal entity when the articles are filed with the secretary of state (RMBCA). But, some states also may require filings in designated counties. In other states, issuance of a **certificate of incorporation** commences existence. **Filing** means state approval by

        1)   Affixing an official stamp to the documents,
        2)   Issuing a formal charter, and
        3)   Issuing a dated receipt for the filing fee.

    d.   After filing, the incorporators elect the members of the **initial board of directors** if they have not been named in the articles. They also may adopt bylaws. The incorporators then resign.

e.   The board of directors holds an **organizational meeting** to take all steps needed to complete the organizational structure. The new board

1)   Adopts **bylaws** to govern the internal management of the corporation if they were not adopted by the incorporators.

a)   The power to change bylaws is vested in the board unless specifically reserved to the shareholders in the articles.

b)   Bylaws may contain any provision for managing the business and regulating the entity's affairs that does not conflict with the law or the articles.

2)   Elects officers, typically a president, a treasurer, and a secretary.

3)   Considers other transactions appropriate for furthering the business purposes of the corporation, such as

a)   Adopting or rejecting preincorporation contracts of the promoters,

b)   Adopting the form of certificate representing shares of the company's stock,

c)   Accepting or rejecting stock subscriptions, and

d)   Complying with requirements for doing business in other states.

7.   **Defective incorporation.** A corporation incorporated in strict compliance with the applicable state statute is a **de jure corporation**.

a.   A **de facto** corporation is recognized if there was

1)   A statute under which the business could have incorporated,

2)   A good-faith but unsuccessful attempt to comply with it, and

3)   An actual or attempted exercise of corporate powers.

b.   Under the MBCA, the legal existence of a de facto corporation can be challenged only by the state, not by a creditor of the corporation.

c.   The RMBCA establishes a **conclusive presumption** that, when the articles have been filed, the corporation exists even if the filing was defective. The effect is to treat a corporation as de jure once the secretary of state has filed the articles even though a mandatory legal provision was not complied with.

1)   If the entity is so defectively formed that it does not even qualify as a de facto corporation, the RMBCA imposes liability on "all persons purporting to act on behalf of a corporation, knowing that there was no incorporation under this act." The RMBCA therefore excuses inactive parties and those not knowing of the defective incorporation.

d.   **Corporation by estoppel.** An organization that is neither a de jure nor a de facto corporation may be treated as a corporation in a suit by a third party. Thus, the organization will be prevented (estopped) from denying corporate status if

1)   The organization has represented itself as a corporation,

2)   The representation is followed by reasonable reliance and material alteration of position by a third party based on that representation,

3)   The third party demonstrates fair and equitable conduct, and

4)   Injustice can be avoided only by treating the business as a corporation.

8. **Piercing the corporate veil.** Courts disregard the separate corporate entity when the corporate form is used merely to commit wrongdoing, shield its shareholders from liability for fraud, or otherwise circumvent the law. If so, shareholder(s) are personally liable for corporate acts (as is a general partner in a partnership). A court might disregard a corporate entity if it finds

    a. The corporation is merely the alter ego of a shareholder, for example, if

        1) Assets of the corporation and the shareholder(s) are commingled,
        2) Corporate formalities are ignored, and
        3) The corporation was established for a sham purpose.

    b. Two or more enterprises are related corporations (such as a parent and its subsidiary or corporations that are under common control) and in practice do not maintain sufficiently independent existence.

    c. A corporation is inadequately capitalized to carry on its intended business.

9. **State jurisdiction.** A state may exercise personal jurisdiction (authority) over a foreign corporation, e.g., to require registration with the state or to allow **service of process** (giving valid notice to a defendant corporation) in another state. However, a state has personal jurisdiction only if the corporation has at least minimum contacts with the state.

    a. **Minimum contacts** consist of activities that are not isolated and that

        1) Are purposefully directed towards the state, e.g., advertising on radio stations heard within the state and intended to generate product demand in the state, or
        2) Place a product in the stream of interstate commerce with an expectation or intent that it will ultimately be used in the state.

    b. Thus, a **state long-arm statute** may authorize **general jurisdiction** over a foreign corporation based on an active business office or substantial activity in the state. Such activity might include maintaining inventory and records.

        1) A state may therefore validly exercise authority over a defendant corporation even when the matter in controversy has no relationship to the state except that the defendant is subject to its jurisdiction.

    c. However, mere solicitation of offers to be accepted out of state, to be delivered by interstate carrier from out of state, and to be paid for by mail is not doing business sufficient to constitute minimum contacts.

    d. State long-arm statutes also authorize jurisdiction over foreign corporations that perform isolated or single acts in the state or whose conduct directly affects the state, but only for claims arising from those acts. Examples of isolated acts are maintaining bank accounts or hiring residents of the state.

10. Stop and review! You have completed the outline for this subunit. Study multiple-choice questions 2 through 19 beginning on page 71.

3.3 POWERS OF A CORPORATION

1. Authority for corporate action derives from the **state incorporation statute** or **the articles of incorporation**. The RMBCA grants a corporation broad authority to exercise the "same powers as an individual to do all things necessary or convenient to carry out its business and affairs." Thus, it may engage in any lawful business. However, statutory corporate powers may be limited (not expanded) by the articles. The powers include the right to

   a. Sue, be sued, complain, and defend in the corporate name

   b. Exist perpetually

   c. Acquire real or personal property, or any legal or equitable interest, wherever it may be located

   d. Elect directors, appoint officers and agents, hire employees, set their compensation, and lend them money or credit

      1) Accordingly, a corporation not only may act through agents but also may be held liable for their conduct.

         a) **Respondeat superior**, or "let the master answer," is the doctrine that is the basis for a principal's (e.g., a corporation's) liability for an agent's torts (civil wrongs not arising from a break of contract, e.g., negligence). For this doctrine to apply, the wrongs must be committed within the scope of the agency.

   e. Operate within or outside the state of incorporation

   f. Engage in any transactions involving interests in, or obligations of, any other entity

   g. Make contracts, give guarantees, incur liabilities, issue debt instruments (whether or not convertible or containing options to purchase other securities), or give security interests

   h. Be a partner, promoter, manager, or associate of a partnership, joint venture, trust, or other entity

   i. Lend money, invest funds, and hold collateral

   j. Have a corporate seal

   k. Make and amend bylaws

   l. Dispose of all or part of its property by any proper means

   m. Make donations for the public welfare or for charitable, scientific, or educational purposes

   n. Pay pensions and establish profit-sharing and other benefit or incentive plans for corporate officers, directors, employees, and agents

   o. Transact any lawful business in aid of governmental policy

   p. Acquire the corporation's own shares

   q. Make payments or donations or do any other lawful act in the furtherance of the business of the corporation

2. These powers and rights are either **inherent** or **statutory powers**.

3. **Express powers** are specifically granted to a particular corporation by the articles of incorporation. They describe ownership, control, and overall operational structure.

4. **Implied powers** are necessary and appropriate to carry out express powers.

5. The doctrine of **ultra vires** states that a corporation may not act beyond the powers inherent in the corporate existence or provided in the articles of incorporation and the incorporation statutes.

   a. However, ultra vires has been largely eliminated as a defense. The RMBCA states that, with certain exceptions, "the validity of corporate action may not be challenged on the ground that the corporation lacks or lacked power to act." Those exceptions provide a cause of action in three instances in which the power to act may be questioned:

      1) A shareholder may seek an injunction to prohibit a corporation from performing an act.

      2) Corporations, directly or derivatively, may proceed against directors and officers or other corporate agents.

      3) The state attorney general may proceed against the corporation if it has continued to exceed its legal authority or obtained its articles of incorporation by fraud.

   b. Articles of incorporation authorizing **any lawful business transaction** are now common.

6. Stop and review! You have completed the outline for this subunit. Study multiple-choice questions 20 through 25 beginning on page 77.

3.4 FINANCING

1. **Debt securities.** By definition, every corporation issues or offers to issue equity securities. It may or may not issue debt securities. The greatest disadvantage of debt is that it increases risk. It must be repaid at fixed times even if the corporation is not profitable. Advantages are that (a) debt usually does not dilute shareholder control, (b) interest is tax deductible, and (c) debt holders receive no more than their claims upon liquidation.

   a. **Short-term debt financing** may consist of obtaining short-term bank credit, assigning accounts receivable, pledging some or all of the corporation's properties, and issuing short-term notes.

   b. A corporation accomplishes **long-term debt financing** primarily through issuing bonds. These debt securities represent, not ownership interests in the corporation, but a debtor-creditor relationship between the corporation and the holders.

      1) A **bond** is a negotiable security expressing the corporation's promise to pay

         a) The amount of the bond at a future date (generally principal), and
         b) Interest (typically semiannually at a fixed rate).

      2) The board of directors may issue bonds without shareholder authorization.

      3) **Secured bonds** (also called mortgage bonds) represent creditors' claims that are enforceable against specific corporate property.

         a) If the collateral is insufficient, the bondholder becomes a general unsecured creditor of the corporation for the amount of the deficiency.

      4) **Unsecured bonds** (also called **debentures**) are backed only by the general credit of the corporation. No property is pledged as security.

         a) Debenture holders are unsecured creditors and rank equally with other general creditors.

      5) **Callable bonds** are subject to a redemption privilege that permits the corporation to redeem or pay off all or part of the issue before maturity.

      6) **Convertible bonds** are convertible into shares of stock of the issuing corporation based on a formula stated on the face of the bond.

7) Most corporate bonds are **registered**. In this context, the term means that the bonds are issued to an owner whose name is stated on their face.

    a) The owner is registered in the records of the issuing corporation.

8) Corporations also may obtain financing by issuing **long-term notes** to such lenders as insurance companies and banks.

9) The greatest disadvantage of debt financing is that it increases the corporation's **risk**. Debt must be repaid at fixed times even if the entity is not profitable, but dividends on equity securities are declared only at the director's discretion. The following are advantages of debt financing:

    a) Debt securities do not usually provide voting rights and therefore do not dilute the shareholders' **control** of the corporation.

    b) Upon liquidation of a corporation, the holders of debt securities receive no more than the amount of their claims.

    c) Interest on debt is a **tax deductible** expense, but dividends on equity securities are not.

    d) **Leverage** (also called trading on the equity) results if the return on the borrowed funds differs from their cost (interest). The effect of leverage is to increase earnings (losses) when the entity is successful (unsuccessful).

10) Shareholders may make significant loans to a **thinly capitalized corporation**, that is, one with a high debt-to-equity ratio. In these circumstances, the IRS may treat the loans as equity and disallow the interest deductions.

2. **Equity securities.** Shareholders have an ownership interest in the corporation. But a share of stock does not confer title to any specific property owned by the corporation. Moreover, equity securities are not debt. Payments to shareholders (e.g., dividends) are discretionary.

    a. **Priority.** In the event of bankruptcy or liquidation, creditors, including bondholders, have first claim on corporate assets. Any surplus is distributed to the shareholders.

        1) Hence, shareholders have greater potential risks and rewards than bondholders.

    b. Most state incorporation statutes require that the **articles of incorporation** specify the number of **authorized shares** and the **classes of stock**.

        1) Authorized capital stock cannot be increased or decreased without amending the articles.

        2) The board may choose to issue all, part, or none of the authorized shares.

    c. **Consideration for shares.** Subject to state and federal securities regulation, shares may be issued for cash, property (tangible or intangible), or past services rendered.

        1) The RMBCA provides that consideration may consist "of any tangible or intangible property or benefit to the corporation, including cash, promissory notes, services performed, contracts for services to be performed, or other securities of the corporation." However, the RMBCA also provides for placing shares in escrow or making other restrictive arrangements until "the services are performed, the note is paid, or the benefits are received."

            a) The usual state statute does not permit shares to be issued for promissory notes and future services.

        2) Shares may be issued without certificates.

        3) **Watered stock** is stock not issued for full and adequate consideration.

d. Until shares of stock have been issued, they are **authorized but unissued** shares. Afterward they are **issued and outstanding** shares.

e. Any issuance of stock in violation of state corporate law is voidable (not void) at the option of the recipient shareholder.

f. **Par value**, if set by the promoters or the board, is a dollar amount below which the shares may not be initially sold without future assessment against the shareholders.

    1) However, the RMBCA has abolished the par value requirement.

g. All states do (and the articles may) authorize issuance of **no-par stock**. It is sold by the issuing corporation at any price set by the board in good faith and in the exercise of reasonable business judgment.

    1) This decision will be upheld in the absence of fraud or self-dealing.

h. **Treasury stock** is stock issued and later reacquired by the corporation. Under the RMBCA, repurchased shares are restored to **authorized but unissued** status. The shares may be held indefinitely, resold at any price set by the board in good faith, issued as a stock dividend, or retired.

    1) The corporation may not pay dividends on treasury stock, and the shares may not be voted.

i. **Common stock.** The most widely used classes of stock are common and preferred (but the RMBCA does not use these terms). Common shareholders are entitled to receive **liquidating distributions** only after all other claims have been satisfied, including those of preferred shareholders.

    1) Common shareholders are not entitled to **dividends**. A corporation may choose not to declare dividends.

    2) State statutes typically permit different classes of common stock with different rights or privileges, e.g., class A common with voting rights and class B common with no voting rights.

    3) If only one class of stock is issued, it is treated as common, and each shareholder must be treated equally.

    4) Common shareholders elect directors to the board.

j. **Preferred stock.** Preferred shareholders have an intermediate position between common shareholders and debtholders. They have the right to receive dividends at a specified rate stated on the face of the shares (before common shareholders may receive any) and the right to receive distributions before common shareholders (but after creditors) upon **liquidation** or bankruptcy. But they tend not to have voting rights or to enjoy the same level of capital gains as the common shareholders when the entity is successful.

    1) The articles must designate which shares are preferred.

    2) If a board issues preferred stock, it may establish different classes or series. Each may be assigned independent rights, dividend rates, and redemption prices.

    3) **Cumulative preferred stock** gives the holder the right to receive the stated dividend in full each year. If payment is not made in any year, the unpaid dividends accumulate and these **dividends in arrears** must be paid in full before any dividends are paid to common shareholders.

        a) A dividend may be **cumulative to the extent earned**. Hence, preferred dividends may accumulate in a given year only if the corporation had sufficient earnings to pay them.

        b) If the nature of preferred stock is unclear, most courts have ruled that preferred stock is impliedly cumulative.

4) **Participating preferred stock.** In addition to being entitled to the stated dividend before any dividend can be paid to common shareholders, the holders participate with the common shareholders in any remaining funds allocated for dividend payments.

5) **Convertible preferred stock.** Shareholders have the option to convert the stock into shares of another class (at a predetermined ratio set forth in the articles or bylaws).

   a) Moreover, some types of preferred stock may be convertible into shares of another entity.

6) **Redeemable preferred stock** is issued with the condition that it may be called (redeemed or repurchased) by the issuer at a stated price and time. Issuers may establish a **sinking fund** for redemption purposes.

   a) Preferred stock also may be redeemable at the option of the shareholder.

   b) The Securities and Exchange Commission prohibits the combining of common and preferred stock and of redeemable and nonredeemable preferred stock in financial statements.

   c) Moreover, "shareholders equity" may not include redeemable preferred stock.

   d) Accordingly, redeemable preferred stock, especially **transient preferred stock** (redeemable within a relatively short period, such as 5 to 10 years), may be akin to debt.

      i) The FASB requires that **mandatorily redeemable financial instruments (MRFI)** be accounted for as liabilities unless the redemption is required only upon the liquidation or termination of the entity. MRFIs are redeemable shares that embody an unconditional obligation to transfer assets at a fixed or determinable time or upon an event certain to occur.

k. A **stock warrant** is a certificate evidencing a **right** to purchase shares of stock at a specified price within a specified period. Thus, it is an equity security. Warrants are usually attached to other securities.

3. **Distributions.** The board of directors has discretion to determine the time and amount of dividends and other distributions. The RMBCA defines a distribution as a transfer of money or other property (but not the corporation's own shares) or an incurrence of debt to or for shareholders in respect of their shares.

   a. Persons who invest in corporate stock are motivated in part by the expectation of receiving **dividends**. The directors must declare a dividend.

      1) To ensure the corporation's financial health and growth, profits or some portion can be reinvested in the corporation.

      2) The corporation's directors determine the time and amount of dividends, if any. However, if the directors refuse to declare a dividend and they have clearly abused their discretion, a court may require payment of a dividend.

   b. All states impose the **equity insolvency test**. Thus, payment of a dividend is prohibited if, as a result, the corporation could not pay its debts as they become due in the usual course of business.

      1) The RMBCA also prohibits a distribution if the result would be that total assets are less than the sum of liabilities and liquidation preferences.

2) Moreover, it permits the board to determine the acceptability of a distribution based on either

    a) Financial statements prepared using accounting principles reasonable in the circumstances or

    b) A fair valuation or other method that is reasonable in the circumstances.

3) Profitability is not a legal condition for payment of dividends.

c. The majority of states require that dividends be paid out of earned surplus and not stated capital. However, the RMBCA and many states have abolished the concepts of stated capital and surplus because they provide no protection to investors.

1) **Stated capital** is the par value of par-value stock (or the stated value of no-par stock).

2) **Capital surplus** is the excess of the selling price over the par or stated value.

    a) Many states allow payment of dividends from capital surplus if approved by the shareholders or pursuant to the bylaws.

3) **Earned surplus** is retained earnings.

4) If a statute mandates a stated (legal) capital, the amount received for no-par stock is allocated to stated capital and capital surplus at the board's discretion.

d. A **nimble dividend** is permitted in Delaware. It may be paid out of current earnings if sufficient capital exists to pay the liquidation preference of all shares, even if the corporation has a negative surplus.

e. **Directors** who approve a dividend that violates the applicable state test have abused their discretion. They are jointly and severally liable to the corporation.

1) **Shareholders** generally must repay a dividend only if they know it is illegal.

f. The **declaration date** is the date the board of directors by vote approves a resolution to declare a dividend. The vote is irrevocable. Once declared, payment of the dividend is a **legal obligation** of the corporation.

g. The directors fix a **record date**. The registered holder on the record date is sent the payment on the payment date.

1) If the **record holder** receives payment but has transferred the stock, the corporation is not liable to the transferee provided it was unaware of the transfer. The transferee must sue the transferor for the amount.

2) Absent an agreement with the transferee to the contrary, the transferor is entitled to all dividends declared prior to the transfer.

3) However, stock traded on an organized exchange (listed stock) and purchased during the settlement period (the 4 business days prior to the record date) is **ex dividend** (without dividend) to the buyer.

4) If a record date is not set, the declaration date is treated as the record date.

h. The **payment date** is the date that the corporation will actually tender payment of the dividend to the shareholders of record.

i. **Dividends** are returns on capital investment. They are paid in cash, stock, stock rights, or other property (a dividend in kind).

1) **Liquidating dividends** are a return of, not a return on, a shareholder's capital investment.

j.   A **stock dividend** is payable in the stock of the dividend-paying corporation.

1)   The corporation generally issues new stock for this purpose.

2)   Stock dividends do not increase the equity of each shareholder because they are distributed in proportion to the shares already owned.

3)   When a stock dividend is declared, the corporation transfers the legally required amount from earned surplus (retained earnings) to stated capital. Thus, total equity is not changed.

   a)   In a state that requires maintenance of stated capital, a dividend of authorized but previously unissued shares is possible only if a transfer can be made from capital surplus or retained earnings to stated capital to cover the par or stated value of the stock issued.

4)   The dividend shares are typically of the same class as the shares entitled to the dividend and are distributed in a fixed ratio.

5)   Dividend shares may be of another class or series if authorized by the articles or a majority of outstanding shares of the same class as the proposed dividend.

6)   A stock dividend does not affect earnings and profits declared for federal income tax purposes. It also is not included in the recipient's gross income.

k.   A **stock split** is an issuance of shares for the purpose of reducing the unit value of each share. Accordingly, the par or stated value, if any, is also reduced. The ratio at which shares are exchanged is arbitrary. Shares may be split one-and-a-half-to-one, two-to-one, or in any other way.

1)   A stock split does not increase a shareholder's proportionate ownership.

2)   A stock split does not require that a corporation possess retained earnings or meet any statutory dividend requirements.

3)   In a reverse stock split, the number of shares owned is reduced in reverse proportion.

4)   When an issuance of shares intended to reduce the per-unit price exceeds more than 20-25% of the outstanding shares, the accounting rule is to treat it as a **split-up in the form of a dividend**. The amount capitalized is that required by statute (e.g., par value).

   a)   The SEC rule, which applies to publicly traded companies, requires this treatment if the issuance exceeds 25% of outstanding shares.

4.   Stop and review! You have completed the outline for this subunit. Study multiple-choice questions 26 through 42 beginning on page 79.

QUESTIONS

3.1 Definition

1. Which of the following statements is true with respect to the general structure of a corporation?

A. The corporation is treated as a legal person with rights and obligations jointly shared with its owners and managers.

B. Shareholders establish corporate policies and elect or appoint corporate officers.

C. Corporations are governed by shareholders (owners) who elect a board of directors and approve fundamental changes in the corporate structure.

D. The board of directors is responsible for carrying out the corporate policies in the day-to-day management of the organizations.

Answer (C) is correct. *(Publisher, adapted)*
REQUIRED: The general structure of a corporation.
DISCUSSION: A corporation is an entity formed under state law that is treated as a legal person, with rights and obligations separate from its owners. Shareholders hold the voting power of a corporation. This power gives them the ability to elect a board of directors and to approve fundamental changes in the corporate structure. Thus, the shareholders have the power to govern the corporation.
Answer (A) is incorrect because a corporation is considered a legal entity with rights and obligations separate from its owners and managers. Answer (B) is incorrect because directors hold the power to establish corporate policies and elect or appoint corporate officers, not shareholders. Answer (D) is incorrect because corporate officers are responsible for carrying out the policies in the day-to-day management of the organization.

3.2 Formation

2. Which of the following statements best describes an advantage of the corporate form of doing business?

A. Day-to-day management is strictly the responsibility of the directors.

B. Ownership is contractually restricted and is not transferable.

C. The operation of the business may continue indefinitely.

D. The business is free from state regulation.

Answer (C) is correct. *(CPA, adapted)*
REQUIRED: The advantage of the corporate form.
DISCUSSION: A corporation has perpetual existence unless it is given a shorter life under the articles of incorporation or is dissolved by the state. Death, withdrawal, or addition of a shareholder, director, or officer does not terminate its existence.
Answer (A) is incorrect because officers run day-to-day operations. Answer (B) is incorrect because, absent a specific contractual restriction, shares are freely transferable, e.g., by gift, sale, pledge, or inheritance. Answer (D) is incorrect because a corporation can be created only under state law.

3. Which of the following statements is true with respect to the differences and similarities between a corporation and a limited partnership?

A. Directors owe fiduciary duties to the corporation, and limited partners owe such duties to the partnership.

B. A corporation and a limited partnership may be created only under a state statute, and each must file a copy of its organizational document with the proper governmental body.

C. Shareholders may be entitled to vote on corporate matters, but limited partners are prohibited from voting on any partnership matters.

D. Stock of a corporation may be subject to registration under federal securities laws, but limited partnership interests are automatically exempt from such requirements.

Answer (B) is correct. *(CPA, adapted)*
REQUIRED: The true statement of a difference or similarity between a corporation and a limited partnership.
DISCUSSION: Common law is not a basis for formation of either a corporation or a limited partnership. Each is formed and exists only under the authority of a statute. Filing organizational documents (articles of incorporation or certificates of limited partnership) with appropriate state authorities is required for both.
Answer (A) is incorrect because limited partners are investors, not fiduciaries, and owe no such duty to the partnership. Answer (C) is incorrect because, although not allowed to participate in management, limited partners may still vote on such matters as dissolution of the partnership or the removal of a general partner. Answer (D) is incorrect because limited partnership interests are securities and are subject to registration and reporting requirements under federal securities laws.

4. Which of the following is a requirement for a small business corporation to elect S corporation status?

A. It has only one class of stock.

B. It has at least one partnership as a shareholder.

C. It has international ownership.

D. It has more than 75 shareholders.

Answer (A) is correct. *(CPA, adapted)*
REQUIRED: The requirement for S corporation status.
DISCUSSION: To elect S corporation status, a company must have only one class of stock. Among the other S corporation requirements are that the number of shareholders be limited to 100 and that the corporation be incorporated in the U.S.
Answer (B) is incorrect because a partnership may not be a shareholder. Answer (C) is incorrect because nonresident aliens may not own shares in an S corporation. Answer (D) is incorrect because an S corporation must have no more than 100 shareholders (but family members may elect to be treated as one shareholder).

5. Which of the following statements describes the same characteristic for both an S corporation and a C corporation?

A. Both corporations can have more than 100 shareholders.

B. Both corporations have the disadvantage of double taxation.

C. Shareholders can contribute property into a corporation without being taxed.

D. Shareholders can be either citizens of the United States or foreign countries.

Answer (C) is correct. *(CPA, adapted)*
REQUIRED: The common characteristic of an S corporation and a C corporation.
DISCUSSION: A transfer of assets for stock of any corporation is tax-free if the transferors are in control of the corporation immediately after the exchange. A person who transfers appreciated property will receive the benefit if another transferor transfers property and together they meet the control test. Property includes money. Control is ownership of stock possessing at least 80% of the total combined voting power of all classes of stock entitled to vote and at least 80% of the total number of shares of all other classes of stock of the corporation.
Answer (A) is incorrect because an S corporation may not have more than 100 shareholders. Answer (B) is incorrect because an S corporation is a pass-through entity. Answer (D) is incorrect because a shareholder of an S corporation may not be a nonresident alien.

6. Under the Revised Model Business Corporation Act, which of the following items of information must be included in a corporation's articles of incorporation (charter)?

A. Name and address of each preincorporation subscriber.

B. Nature and purpose of the corporation's business.

C. Name and address of the corporation's incorporator.

D. Election of either C corporation or S corporation status.

Answer (C) is correct. *(CPA, adapted)*
REQUIRED: The information included in the charter.
DISCUSSION: Under the RMBCA, the charter must include (1) the corporation's name, (2) the number of authorized shares, (3) the street address of the initial registered office, (4) the name of the registered agent at that office, and (5) the name and address of each incorporator.
Answer (A) is incorrect because incorporators, not subscribers, must be named. Answer (B) is incorrect because the nature and purpose of the corporation's business may, but is not required to, be included in the charter. Answer (D) is incorrect because an election of S corporation is a matter governed solely by U.S. federal tax law.

7. Which of the following documents would most likely contain specific rules for the management of a business corporation?

- A. Articles of incorporation.
- B. Bylaws.
- C. Certificate of authority.
- D. Shareholders' agreement.

Answer (B) is correct. *(CPA, adapted)*
REQUIRED: The document most likely containing corporate management rules.
DISCUSSION: Bylaws govern the internal structure and operation of a corporation. Initial bylaws are adopted by the incorporators or the board. They may contain any provision for managing the business and regulating the affairs of the corporate entity not in conflict with the law or the articles of incorporation.
Answer (A) is incorrect because the articles contain only basic information that must be filed with a designated state official as part of forming the corporation. Answer (C) is incorrect because a certificate of authority is required to do business in a state where the corporation is not incorporated. It is obtained from the secretary of state after paying fees and designating a resident agent. Answer (D) is incorrect because a shareholder agreement "governs the exercise of the corporate powers or the management of the business and affairs of the corporation or the relationship among the shareholders, the directors, and the corporation, and is not contrary to public policy" (RMBCA). For example, it may eliminate the board or restrict its powers. In contrast, bylaws usually address such details as methods of electing directors or the details of scheduling meetings. Also, a shareholder's agreement may be included in the bylaws.

8. Under the Revised Model Business Corporation Act, which of the following statements regarding a corporation's bylaws is(are) true?

I. A corporation's initial bylaws shall be adopted by either the incorporators or the board of directors.

II. A corporation's bylaws are contained in the articles of incorporation.

- A. I only.
- B. II only.
- C. Both I and II.
- D. Neither I nor II.

Answer (A) is correct. *(CPA, adapted)*
REQUIRED: The true statement(s), if any, regarding a corporation's bylaws.
DISCUSSION: The bylaws of a corporation are the rules and regulations that govern its internal management. The adoption of the bylaws is one of the first items of business at the organizational meeting. Under the RMBCA, either the incorporators or the board of directors may adopt the bylaws. Bylaws are independent of the articles of incorporation and do not have to be publicly filed. The articles are filed with the appropriate public official. They include the name of the corporation, the names and addresses of the incorporators, the name of the registered agent, the address of the initial registered office, and the number of authorized shares.

9. The president of a company has signed a $10 million contract with a construction company to build a new corporate office. Which of the following corporate documents sets forth the scope of authority under which this transaction is governed?

- A. Certificate of incorporation.
- B. Charter.
- C. By-laws.
- D. Proxy statement.

Answer (C) is correct. *(CPA, adapted)*
REQUIRED: The document authorizing the president's agreement for the construction of a corporate office.
DISCUSSION: By-laws of a corporation may contain any provision for managing the business and regulating the entity's affairs that does not conflict with the law or the articles of incorporation. Contracting to build a new office is within the scope of the president's authority to manage the corporation's business.
Answer (A) is incorrect because the certificate of incorporation is a document furnished by the state in which the company is incorporated. It states general facts about the corporation, such as the name of the corporation, names of the incorporators, whether it is for-profit or non-profit, etc. Answer (B) is incorrect because the charter is another name for the certificate of incorporation. Answer (D) is incorrect because proxy statements are sent to shareholders by a party soliciting their proxies (agreements to allow the party to vote on their behalf). The content of a proxy statement is regulated by the SEC. It must contain a full and accurate statement of the facts relevant to the issues to be voted on.

10. The corporate veil is most likely to be pierced and the shareholders held personally liable if

A. The corporation has elected S corporation status under the Internal Revenue Code.

B. The shareholders have commingled their personal funds with those of the corporation.

C. An ultra vires act has been committed.

D. A partnership incorporates its business solely to limit the liability of its partners.

Answer (B) is correct. *(CPA, adapted)*
REQUIRED: The factor most likely a basis for piercing the corporate veil.
DISCUSSION: If the shareholders do not treat the corporation as a separate entity, e.g., by disregarding formalities, a corporate creditor may persuade a court to ignore the corporate form and hold the shareholders personally liable. Commingling of shareholders' personal funds with those of the corporation is evidence that the corporation is merely the alter ego of the shareholders and that the corporate form is a sham.
Answer (A) is incorrect because the law expressly allows a corporation to elect S status. Answer (C) is incorrect because, to the degree an act is recognized as ultra vires, the existence of the corporation is recognized. Answer (D) is incorrect because limited liability is a major incentive for incorporation.

11. Case Corp. is incorporated in State A. Under the Revised Model Business Corporation Act, which of the following activities engaged in by Case requires that Case obtain a certificate of authority to do business in State B?

A. Maintaining bank accounts in State B.

B. Collecting corporate debts in State B.

C. Hiring employees who are residents of State B.

D. Maintaining an office in State B to conduct intrastate business.

Answer (D) is correct. *(CPA, adapted)*
REQUIRED: The interstate business activity that requires a certificate of authority.
DISCUSSION: A state may exercise authority over a foreign corporation if the corporation has at least minimum contacts with the state. The minimum contacts consist of activities that (1) are not isolated and (2) either are purposefully directed toward the state or place a product in the stream of interstate commerce with an expectation or intent that it will be used in the state. Maintaining an office in State B to conduct intrastate business creates minimum contacts with State B under this test.
Answer (A) is incorrect because maintaining bank accounts in State B is an isolated activity that does not meet the minimum contacts test. Answer (B) is incorrect because the collection of debts in State B does not by itself constitute minimum contacts in State B. For example, the debts may not have arisen from activities that involved State B. Answer (C) is incorrect because hiring employees who reside in State B is not an activity that is purposefully directed toward the state or that places a product in interstate commerce with the expectation or intent that it will be used in the state.

12. Lobo Manufacturing, Inc. is incorporated under the laws of New Mexico. Its principal place of business is in California, and it has permanent sales offices in several other states. Under the circumstances, which of the following is true?

A. California may validly demand that Lobo incorporate under the laws of the State of California.

B. Lobo must obtain a certificate of authority to transact business in California and the other states in which it does business.

C. Lobo is a foreign corporation in California, but not in the other states.

D. California may prevent Lobo from operating as a corporation if the laws of California differ regarding organization and conduct of the corporation's internal affairs.

Answer (B) is correct. *(CPA, adapted)*
REQUIRED: The true statement regarding the operations of a corporation outside the state of incorporation.
DISCUSSION: Because Lobo has its principal place of business in California, it has sufficient contact with the state to qualify as "doing business" there. A corporation doing business but not incorporated in that state is considered a foreign corporation and must obtain a certificate of authority to transact business there.
Answer (A) is incorrect because no state may require an existing corporation to incorporate under its laws simply because it is doing business within the state. Answer (C) is incorrect because Lobo is a foreign corporation in all states in which it is not incorporated. Answer (D) is incorrect because, under the Full Faith and Credit Clause of the U.S. Constitution, a corporation validly formed in one state must be recognized as a corporate entity in all other states.

13. Boyle, as a promoter of Delaney Corp., signed a 9-month contract with Austin, a CPA. Prior to the incorporation, Austin rendered accounting services pursuant to the contract. After rendering accounting services for an additional period of 6 months pursuant to the contract, Austin was discharged without cause by the board of directors of Delaney. Absent agreements to the contrary, who will be liable to Austin for breach of contract?

    A. Both Boyle and Delaney.

    B. Boyle only.

    C. Delaney only.

    D. Neither Boyle nor Delaney.

Answer (A) is correct. *(CPA, adapted)*
    REQUIRED: The liability of a corporation and a promoter on a preincorporation agreement.
    DISCUSSION: A promoter who contracts for a nonexistent corporation is personally liable on such contracts. Delaney is also liable because it impliedly adopted the contract by accepting Austin's performance.
    Answer (B) is incorrect because the corporation impliedly adopted the contract by accepting its benefits. Answer (C) is incorrect because a promoter is generally liable on preincorporation contracts. Answer (D) is incorrect because Boyle was not released and a novation did not occur. Delaney adopted the contract by implication.

14. Following the formation of a corporation, which of the following terms best describes the process by which the promoter is released from, and the corporation is made liable for, preincorporation contractual obligations?

    A. Assignment.

    B. Novation.

    C. Delegation.

    D. Accord and satisfaction.

Answer (B) is correct. *(CPA, adapted)*
    REQUIRED: The process by which a promoter is released from preincorporation obligations.
    DISCUSSION: The parties to a contract may discharge each other from performance without breaching the contract. A novation substitutes a new party (the corporation) for an original party (a promoter of that corporation). For the novation to be effective, the corporation must agree to assume the promoter's obligations, and the third party must agree to release the promoter.
    Answer (A) is incorrect because an assignment transfers an interest in a right or property. Answer (C) is incorrect because delegation of the authority to perform a duty does not release the delegator from the obligation. Answer (D) is incorrect because an accord and satisfaction is a payment by a debtor less than or different from what was owed. In exchange, the creditors who are parties to the arrangement agree to extinguish the debt.

15. An organization that is neither a de jure nor a de facto corporation has attempted to exercise corporate powers. It may be treated as a corporation if

  I. The other party demonstrates fair and equitable conduct.

  II. Injustice can be avoided only by treating the business as a corporation.

  III. A good-faith but unsuccessful effort to comply with the incorporation statute has been made.

    A. I only.

    B. I and II only.

    C. II and III only.

    D. I, II, and III.

Answer (B) is correct. *(Publisher, adapted)*
    REQUIRED: The condition(s) that must be met for an organization that is not a de jure or de facto corporation to be treated as a corporation.
    DISCUSSION: As a defendant in a suit, an organization that is neither a de jure nor a de facto corporation may be treated as a corporation by estoppel if certain conditions are met: (1) The organization has represented itself as a corporation, (2) the representation is followed by reasonable reliance and material alteration of position by the other party based on that representation, (3) the other party demonstrates fair and equitable conduct, and (4) injustice can be avoided only by treating the business as a corporation. In contrast, a de facto corporation is recognized given (1) a statute under which the business could have incorporated, (2) a good-faith but unsuccessful attempt to comply with it, and (3) an actual or attempted exercise of corporate powers.

16. Which of the following is not a characteristic usually possessed by a close (or closely held) corporation?

A. The officers and directors own all the stock.

B. It does not sell its stock to the public.

C. Transfer of shares is often restricted.

D. Shareholders are not active in management and control.

Answer (D) is correct. *(Publisher, adapted)*
REQUIRED: The feature that is not usually possessed by a close (or closely held) corporation.
DISCUSSION: A close (or closely held) corporation often has characteristics that include ownership by a relatively small number of shareholders, issuing stock that is not publicly traded, ownership of all the stock by the officers and directors, restriction on the transfer of shares, and a requirement that a supermajority be obtained for important actions. Another characteristic is that shareholders of a closely held corporation are active in management and control.

17. In which type of business entity is the entire ownership interest most freely transferable?

A. General partnership.

B. Limited partnership.

C. Corporation.

D. Limited liability company.

Answer (C) is correct. *(CPA, adapted)*
REQUIRED: The business entity in which the entire ownership interest is most freely transferable.
DISCUSSION: Simply acquiring a corporation's stock gives an individual an ownership interest. Shares can be freely bought and sold, usually without any restriction.
Answer (A) is incorrect because an ownership interest in a general partnership is not easily transferable. An interest can be assigned, but an assignee does not have the rights of a general partner. Moreover, the other partners must approve the admission of a new partner. Answer (B) is incorrect because an ownership interest in a limited partnership is not easily transferable. The partnership may impose restraints on assignability, for example, to qualify for an exemption from registration under federal securities law. Answer (D) is incorrect because an ownership interest in a limited liability company is not easily transferable. A transferee does not become a member absent consent of all members or a provision in their agreement.

18. In which type of business organization are income taxes always required to be paid by the entity on profits earned as well as by the owners upon distribution thereof?

A. General partnership.

B. Limited liability company.

C. Subchapter C corporation.

D. Subchapter S corporation.

Answer (C) is correct. *(CPA, adapted)*
REQUIRED: The business organization in which income taxes always are paid by the entity on its profits.
DISCUSSION: A Subchapter C corporation is an entity subject to the corporate income tax. Any corporation that is not a Subchapter S corporation is a Subchapter C corporation. A Subchapter S corporation is a closely held corporation that has made an election under federal law to be taxed similarly to a partnership. Hence, an S corporation does not usually pay income tax.
Answer (A) is incorrect because a general partnership is a pass-through entity that files an informational return. It avoids the double taxation to which a Subchapter C corporation is subject. Answer (B) is incorrect because an LLC's members may elect to be taxed as partners, and single-member LLCs may be taxed as sole proprietorships. Additionally, taxation as a corporation is an option. It may be advantageous if reinvestment in the LLC is desired and corporate rates are lower than personal rates. Answer (D) is incorrect because a Subchapter S corporation is a closely held corporation that has made an election under federal law to be taxed similarly to a partnership. Hence, an S corporation does not usually pay income tax.

19. An officer-shareholder of a corporation could be held personally liable for which one of the following debts?

A. Unpaid U.S. corporate income taxes.

B. A bank note signed by a shareholder in his/her capacity as president of the corporation.

C. Federal payroll taxes that were withheld from the employees' wages but never remitted to the IRS.

D. A judgment against the corporation stemming from a tort committed by a former employee.

Answer (C) is correct. *(Publisher, adapted)*
REQUIRED: The debts for which an officer-shareholder can be held personally liable.
DISCUSSION: An employer is required to withhold from an employee's salary income taxes and Social Security taxes (FICA). If an officer-shareholder is deemed to be a "responsible party" by the IRS, (s)he can be held personally liable for these taxes because they are considered to be held "in trust" for the benefit of the employee until remitted to the IRS.
Answer (A) is incorrect because personal liability is not extended to unpaid U.S. corporate income taxes. Answer (B) is incorrect because the officer-shareholder is not personally liable on the bank note if (s)he signed as an agent of the corporation. In closely held corporations, two signatures are often required, one as an agent of the corporation and one in an individual capacity. Answer (D) is incorrect because the corporation insulates owners from liability for torts of their employees.

3.3 Powers of a Corporation

20. Modern corporations wield many powers. A corporation

A. Can do anything permitted by the incorporation statute.

B. Can exercise any power as long as it is expressly conferred by statute or the articles.

C. Has the powers expressly or impliedly conferred by the bylaws.

D. Has the powers expressly or impliedly conferred by resolutions of the board.

Answer (A) is correct. *(Publisher, adapted)*
REQUIRED: The powers of a corporation.
DISCUSSION: Subject to the limitations imposed by the federal or state constitution, a state incorporation statute is the primary source of a corporation's powers. The articles of incorporation may narrow the grant of authority but cannot broaden it. The powers include not only those expressed in the statute or articles but also those implied as reasonably necessary to carry out the expressed powers and purposes.
Answer (B) is incorrect because the RMBCA grants to the corporation all powers necessary or convenient to effect its purposes. Answer (C) is incorrect because bylaws are the rules adopted by a corporation to regulate its internal affairs. Answer (D) is incorrect because the board must act within limits set by the state statute, the articles, and the bylaws.

21. Special Case, Inc. entered into a contract with Marnier Corporation. The transaction proved to be ultra vires. Which of the following parties may properly assert the ultra vires doctrine?

A. Special Case, to avoid performance.

B. A shareholder of Special Case, to enjoin the sale.

C. Marnier Corporation, to avoid performance.

D. Special Case, to rescind the consummated sale.

Answer (B) is correct. *(Publisher, adapted)*
REQUIRED: The party that may properly assert the ultra vires doctrine.
DISCUSSION: The doctrine of ultra vires states that a corporation may not act beyond the powers inherent in the corporate existence or provided in the articles of incorporation and the incorporation statutes. Ultra vires has been eliminated as a defense. The RMBCA states that, with certain exceptions, "the validity of corporate action may not be challenged on the ground that the corporation lacks or lacked power to act." Those exceptions provide a cause of action in three instances in which the power to act may be questioned: (1) A shareholder may seek an injunction, (2) corporations may proceed against directors and officers, and (3) the state attorney general may proceed against the corporation.
Answer (A) is incorrect because the parties who entered into the contract will not be allowed to avoid performance by asserting the ultra vires doctrine. Answer (C) is incorrect because the parties who entered into the contract will not be allowed to avoid performance by asserting the ultra vires doctrine. Answer (D) is incorrect because courts will not use the ultra vires doctrine to rescind a fully executed contract.

22. Powers that are specifically granted to a corporation by its articles of incorporation are

    A. Inherent powers.

    B. Statutory powers.

    C. Express powers.

    D. Implied powers.

Answer (C) is correct. *(Publisher, adapted)*
    REQUIRED: The identification of express powers.
    DISCUSSION: Authority for corporate action derives from the state incorporation statute or the articles of incorporation. Express powers are those specifically granted to a particular corporation by the articles of incorporation. They describe ownership, control, and overall operational structure.
    Answer (A) is incorrect because inherent powers are not specifically described in the articles of incorporation. Answer (B) is incorrect because statutory powers are derived from the state incorporation statute, not the articles of incorporation. Answer (D) is incorrect because implied powers are necessary and appropriate to carry out express powers, but they are not granted by the articles of incorporation.

23. All of the following are powers that a corporation possesses except the right to

    A. Acquire and dispose of real or personal property.

    B. Engage in activities beyond its implied powers.

    C. Sue and be sued in the corporate name.

    D. Engage in any transactions involving interests in, or obligations of, any other entity.

Answer (B) is correct. *(Publisher, adapted)*
    REQUIRED: The item not a power exercisable by a corporation.
    DISCUSSION: The RMBCA grants a corporation the "same powers as an individual to do all the things necessary or convenient to carry out its business and affairs. The powers include, among several other powers, the right to operate within and outside the state of incorporation." A corporation may not exceed its express or implied powers.

24. What is the doctrine under which a corporation is made liable for the torts of its employees, committed within the scope of their employment?

    A. Respondeat superior.

    B. Ultra vires.

    C. Estoppel.

    D. Ratification.

Answer (A) is correct. *(CPA, adapted)*
    REQUIRED: The doctrine making a corporation liable for the torts of its employees.
    DISCUSSION: Respondeat superior, or "let the master answer," is the doctrine that is the basis for a principal's liability for an agent's torts (civil wrongs not arising from a breach of contract, e.g., negligence). For this doctrine to apply, the wrongs must be committed within the scope of the agency.
    Answer (B) is incorrect because the doctrine of ultra vires prohibits actions beyond powers inherent in the corporation's existence, the articles of incorporation, and the incorporation statutes. Answer (C) is incorrect because a corporation by estoppel arises when an entity that is neither a de jure nor a de facto corporation is treated as a corporation in a suit by a third party. Thus, the entity will be prevented (estopped) from denying corporate status if (1) the organization has represented itself as a corporation, (2) the representation is followed by reasonable reliance and material alteration of position by a third party based on that representation, (3) the third party demonstrates fair and equitable conduct, and (4) injustice can be avoided only by treating the business as a corporation. Answer (D) is incorrect because ratification is the act of accepting and giving legal effect to an obligation that was not previously enforceable against the ratifying party. For example, a principal may ratify a contract entered into by an agent with no authority. In the corporate context, a newly formed corporation cannot ratify a preincorporation contract because no principal existed at the time of contracting. However, the new entity may adopt such a contract.

25. A corporation has the right to

I. Lend money, invest funds, and hold collateral.

II. Make contracts, give guarantees, and incur liabilities.

III. Make and amend bylaws.

A. I only.

B. I and III only.

C. II and III only.

D. I, II, and III.

Answer (D) is correct. *(Publisher, adapted)*
REQUIRED: The powers exercisable by a corporation.
DISCUSSION: A corporation is granted the same powers of an individual to do all things necessary and convenient to carry out it business and affairs. The powers include the right to lend money, invest funds, and hold collateral; the right to make and amend bylaws; and the right to make contracts, give guarantees, and incur liabilities.

3.4 Financing

26. Which of the following are corporate debt securities?

	Convertible Bonds	Debenture Bonds	Warrants
A.	Yes	Yes	Yes
B.	Yes	No	Yes
C.	Yes	Yes	No
D.	No	Yes	Yes

Answer (C) is correct. *(Publisher, adapted)*
REQUIRED: The identification of corporate debt securities.
DISCUSSION: A corporation may be financed by issuing equity and finance securities. A bond is a negotiable security that embodies the corporation's promise to pay a specified amount at a future date (plus interest). A convertible bond is a bond that is convertible into a share or shares of stock. A debenture bond is an unsecured bond, backed only by the general obligation of the corporation to pay. A stock warrant is a certificate evidencing a right to purchase shares of stock at a specified price within a specified period. Thus, it is an equity security. Warrants are usually attached to other securities.

27. Loop owns 400 shares of Fruit Corp. cumulative preferred stock. In the absence of any specific contrary provisions in Fruit's articles of incorporation, which of the following statements is true?

A. Loop is entitled to convert the 400 shares of preferred stock to a like number of shares of common stock.

B. If Fruit declares a cash dividend on its preferred stock, Loop becomes an unsecured creditor of Fruit.

C. If Fruit declares a dividend on its common stock, Loop will be entitled to participate with the common shareholders in any dividend distribution made after preferred dividends are paid.

D. Loop will be entitled to vote if dividend payments are in arrears.

Answer (B) is correct. *(Publisher, adapted)*
REQUIRED: The statement regarding cumulative preferred stock.
DISCUSSION: The holder of preferred stock must be paid the stated dividend before a common shareholder may receive any dividends. If payment of the stated dividend is not made to a cumulative preferred shareholder in any year(s), the dividends accumulate and must be paid in full prior to payment of any dividends to common shareholders. But a dividend on any stock does not become a payment obligation (debt) of the corporation until it has been declared.
Answer (A) is incorrect because cumulative preferred stock is not inherently convertible. Answer (C) is incorrect because cumulative preferred stock is not inherently participating. Answer (D) is incorrect because cumulative preferred stock is not inherently endowed with voting rights.

28. In general, which of the following statements concerning treasury stock is true?

A. A corporation may not reacquire its own stock unless specifically authorized by its articles of incorporation.

B. On issuance of new stock, a corporation has preemptive rights with regard to its treasury stock.

C. Treasury stock may be distributed as a stock dividend.

D. A corporation is entitled to receive cash dividends on its treasury stock.

Answer (C) is correct. *(Publisher, adapted)*
REQUIRED: The true statement regarding treasury stock.
DISCUSSION: Shares may be issued pro rata and without consideration to the shareholders by an action of the directors. Under the RMBCA, treasury shares have the status of authorized but unissued shares, which may be used for stock dividends.
Answer (A) is incorrect because a corporation may acquire its own shares provided it remains solvent. Answer (B) is incorrect because a corporation does not have preemptive rights regarding treasury stock. Answer (D) is incorrect because a corporation has no dividend rights with regard to its treasury stock.

29. Which of the following statements is correct regarding the declaration of a stock dividend by a corporation having only one class of par value stock?

A. A stock dividend has the same legal and practical significance as a stock split.

B. A stock dividend increases a stockholder's proportionate share of corporate ownership.

C. A stock dividend causes a decrease in the assets of the corporation.

D. A stock dividend is a corporation's ratable distribution of additional shares of stock to its stockholders.

Answer (D) is correct. *(CPA, adapted)*
REQUIRED: The true statement about the declaration of a stock dividend.
DISCUSSION: A stock dividend is payable in the stock of the dividend-paying corporation. New stock generally is issued for this purpose. A stockholder's equity in the corporation is not increased because a stock dividend does not increase the recipient's proportional ownership of the corporation.
Answer (A) is incorrect because the practical significance of a stock split is to reduce the unit value of each share. Answer (B) is incorrect because a stock dividend is distributed in proportion to shares already owned and has no effect on a stockholder's equity. Answer (C) is incorrect because a stock dividend causes a transfer from retained earnings to stated capital, not from an asset account to stated capital.

30. Bennet Corp. declared a 7% stock dividend on its common stock. The dividend

A. Must be registered with the SEC pursuant to the Securities Act of 1933.

B. Is includible in gross income of the recipient taxpayers in the year of receipt.

C. Has no effect on Bennet's earnings and profits for federal income tax purposes.

D. Requires a vote of Bennet's shareholders.

Answer (C) is correct. *(Publisher, adapted)*
REQUIRED: The true statement regarding stock dividends.
DISCUSSION: A stock dividend is a distribution of additional shares of the corporation's stock in proportion to current holdings. Total equity is not changed. The value is transferred from earned or capital surplus to stated capital. Earnings and profits is a tax account that is not changed by a stock dividend because it does not affect the corporation's economic ability to pay a cash or property dividend.
Answer (A) is incorrect because the Securities Act of 1933 does not require registration of stock issued to shareholders who hold previously issued stock. Answer (B) is incorrect because stock dividends are usually not treated as gross income for federal tax purposes. Answer (D) is incorrect because dividend policy is within the discretion of the board.

31. When does the board of directors most likely have a right to declare and pay dividends?

A. Only in years that the corporation is profitable.

B. Never out of capital surplus.

C. As a stock dividend of authorized but unissued shares given no available retained earnings or capital surplus.

D. When the corporation has both capital surplus and retained earnings.

Answer (D) is correct. *(Publisher, adapted)*
REQUIRED: The circumstance that will most likely give the right to the board of directors to declare and pay dividends.
DISCUSSION: The financial requirements of the corporation vary as to when dividends are proper. They are almost always proper if paid out of earned surplus (retained earnings). In addition, dividends are never proper if the corporation is or would become insolvent. Also, under the RMBCA's net assets test, a distribution is improper if total assets would be less than the sum of total liabilities and amounts payable to holders of preferential rights upon dissolution.
Answer (A) is incorrect because dividends may be paid out of prior years' earned surplus even if there are no current earnings. Answer (B) is incorrect because many states permit the payment of dividends out of capital surplus with approval of the shareholders or pursuant to the bylaws. Answer (C) is incorrect because, in a state that requires maintenance of stated capital, a dividend of authorized but previously unissued shares is possible only if a transfer can be made from capital surplus or retained earnings to stated capital to cover the par or stated value of the stock issued.

32. Which of the following statements illustrates a disadvantage of debt financing for a corporation?

A. Interest on debt is a tax deductible expense.

B. Debt must be repaid at fixed times, even if the entity is not profitable.

C. Upon liquidation of a corporation, the holders of debt securities receive no more than the amount of their claims.

D. Debt securities do not usually provide voting rights and therefore do not dilute the shareholder's control of the corporation.

Answer (B) is correct. *(Publisher, adapted)*
REQUIRED: The disadvantage of debt financing for a corporation.
DISCUSSION: A corporation may choose to obtain some of the financing of its operations by issuing debt securities. These instruments, usually in the form of bonds or notes, represent an obligation of the corporation to repay the holder within a stated amount of time, accompanied by interest. The greatest disadvantage of debt financing is that it increases the risk of the corporation. Debt must be repaid at fixed times even if the entity is not profitable.

33. All of the following distributions to shareholders are considered asset or capital distributions except

A. Liquidating dividends.

B. Stock splits.

C. Property distributions.

D. Cash dividends.

Answer (B) is correct. *(Publisher, adapted)*
REQUIRED: The type of distribution to a shareholder that is considered an asset or capital distribution.
DISCUSSION: A stock split is not a distribution. The amount of earned or capital surplus or stated capital does not change. The value of each share changes, but not the shareholder's proportionate ownership interest. Under the RMBCA, a distribution is "a direct or indirect transfer of money or other property (except its own shares) or incurrence of indebtedness by a corporation to or for the benefit of its shareholders in respect of any of its shares."
Answer (A) is incorrect because liquidating dividends are returns of capital in the form of money or other property. Answer (C) is incorrect because a distribution to shareholders of noncash property might constitute a dividend or return of capital. Answer (D) is incorrect because dividends are returns on capital. They are usually distributed in the form of money or property from corporate assets.

34. The owner of cumulative preferred stock has the right to

A. Convert preferred stock into common stock.

B. A residual share in profits after a fixed dividend has been paid to both common and preferred shareholders.

C. The carryover of fixed dividends to subsequent periods from years in which they were not paid.

D. Receive the par value of their shares but not unpaid dividends before common shareholders receive anything in liquidation.

Answer (C) is correct. *(Publisher, adapted)*
REQUIRED: The rights of a cumulative preferred stock owner.
DISCUSSION: Normally, a preferred shareholder is entitled to a fixed dividend that must be paid before dividends are received by the common shareholders. If the preferred stock is cumulative, any dividends not paid in preceding years will be carried over and must be paid before the common shareholders may receive anything. Under case law, preferred stock dividends are impliedly cumulative unless stated otherwise, but the RMBCA suggests that whether stock is cumulative or noncumulative should be included in the articles.
Answer (A) is incorrect because the right of cumulation does not apply to conversion of one class of security into another. Conversion rights, rates, or price are set out in the articles of incorporation. Answer (B) is incorrect because participating preferred stock receives a residual share in profits after a fixed dividend has been paid to both common and preferred shareholders. Answer (D) is incorrect because the liquidation preference of cumulative preferred shareholders extends both to the par value of their shares and to unpaid dividends.

35. Which of the following statements concerning treasury stock is true?

A. Cash dividends paid on treasury stock are transferred to stated capital.

B. A corporation may not purchase more than 20% of its total authorized shares of stock unless specifically authorized by its articles of incorporation.

C. Treasury stock may not be used for a stock dividend.

D. Treasury stock may be resold at a price less than par value.

Answer (D) is correct. *(Publisher, adapted)*
REQUIRED: The true statement regarding treasury stock.
DISCUSSION: Treasury stock is stock that was issued and later reacquired by the issuing corporation. Treasury stock may be held, resold, retired, or used for a stock dividend. If resold, the price set by the board of directors in good faith may be less than par value. Treasury stock is not voted and does not receive dividends. The RMBCA does not use the term "treasury stock," and it treats reacquired shares as authorized but unissued.
Answer (A) is incorrect because no dividends are paid on treasury stock. Answer (B) is incorrect because the articles customarily have no such limitation on purchase of treasury stock. Answer (C) is incorrect because treasury stock may be held, resold, retired, or used for stock dividends.

36. Shares of stock without par value may be issued for such consideration (in dollars) as may be fixed by a corporation's

    A. Creditors.

    B. Officers.

    C. Board of directors.

    D. Minority shareholders.

Answer (C) is correct. *(Publisher, adapted)*
REQUIRED: The party that determines the issue value for stock without par value.
DISCUSSION: The board of directors has authority to fix the amount of consideration to be received for the issuance of no-par stock, as well as all other stock. The board is obligated to act in good faith (without fraud) and to exercise reasonable business judgment. Capital surplus (additional paid-in capital) arises not only from receipt of amounts in excess of any par value but also from an allocation of amounts received for no-par shares or from a reappraisal of certain assets. The RMBCA and many states have abolished the concepts of par value, stated capital, and capital surplus. However, the RMBCA allows a company to elect to establish a par value.
Answer (A) is incorrect because creditors have no management rights. Answer (B) is incorrect because officers manage day-to-day business and do not have the right to fix the amount of consideration to be received for the issuance of no-par stock. Answer (D) is incorrect because minority shareholders only vote to elect directors and approve fundamental corporate changes. They have no other management rights.

37. Runco Corp. plans to issue more stock. What is the most likely mechanism for limiting the number of shares that it may issue?

    A. Its bylaws.

    B. Its articles of incorporation.

    C. Its surplus.

    D. There is no limit if no-par stock is issued.

Answer (B) is correct. *(Publisher, adapted)*
REQUIRED: The mechanism that limits the number of shares issued by a corporation.
DISCUSSION: Shares are outstanding if they are authorized and issued to shareholders but have not been reacquired by the corporation. Authorized shares are those permitted by the articles of incorporation to be issued. Issued shares are those actually issued, including shares reacquired by the corporation. Treasury shares are authorized and issued, but not outstanding. (The RMBCA, however, abolishes treasury shares. It treats reacquired shares as authorized but unissued. Thus, if a state has adopted this provision, the accounting for reacquired shares does not follow the traditional method.)
Answer (A) is incorrect because the corporation's bylaws contain details of corporate administration and internal operating procedures. They do not contain any directives regarding issuance of stock. Answer (C) is incorrect because the number of surplus shares is not related to how many total shares a corporation is allowed to issue. Answer (D) is incorrect because there is a limit, regardless of whether no-par stock is issued.

38. Under traditional rules, the consideration received by a corporation when issuing shares of stock must constitute stated capital to the extent of the par value of the shares, and any excess will constitute

    A. Treasury shares.

    B. Earned surplus.

    C. Restricted surplus.

    D. Capital surplus.

Answer (D) is correct. *(Publisher, adapted)*
REQUIRED: The definition of capital surplus.
DISCUSSION: Under traditional rules, when stock with a par value is issued, consideration equal to the par value is allocated to stated capital. Consideration in excess of the par value constitutes capital surplus (additional paid-in capital).
Answer (A) is incorrect because treasury shares are originally issued by the corporation and then repurchased by the corporation. Answer (B) is incorrect because earned surplus (retained earnings) consists of earnings of the corporation that have been retained. Answer (C) is incorrect because restricted surplus is either earned surplus or capital surplus that is restricted in its use, e.g., to repay bonds.

39. Assuming no agreement on the matter between the buyer and seller of stock, who is entitled to a declared dividend?

A. If the stock is listed on a stock exchange, the buyer if the purchase was 6 days before the record date.

B. If the stock is not listed on a stock exchange, the seller if the purchase was between the ex dividend and record dates.

C. If the stock is listed on a stock exchange, the buyer if the purchase was after the record date.

D. If the stock is not listed on a stock exchange, the shareholder of record at the ex dividend date.

Answer (A) is correct. *(Publisher, adapted)*
REQUIRED: The party that is entitled to a declared dividend when no agreement is present.
DISCUSSION: When the dividend is declared, the board sets a date of record. The corporation will have no liability to third parties if it pays the dividend to the recorded shareholders at that date. Between the transferor and transferee of shares, their contractual agreement controls disposition of the dividend. In the absence of an agreement, the transferor receives the dividend if the transfer occurred after the record date. But if the stock is listed on a stock exchange, the transferor is entitled to the dividend if the transfer occurred after the ex dividend date (4 business days before the record date). Accordingly, a buyer who buys the stock 6 days prior to the record date has a right to the dividend.
Answer (B) is incorrect because, if the stock is not listed, the ex dividend date is not relevant. A transferee before the record date is entitled to the dividend. Answer (C) is incorrect because, whether or not the stock is listed, the transferor has a right to the dividend if the transfer is after the record date. Answer (D) is incorrect because, if the stock is not listed, the ex dividend date is not relevant. A transferee before the record date is entitled to the dividend.

40. Which of the following is the most accurate statement regarding preferred shareholders?

A. They incur more risk than common shareholders.

B. They incur less risk than bondholders.

C. They have less opportunity for benefiting from the growth of the corporation than common shareholders.

D. They have a stronger position upon dissolution than bondholders or common shareholders.

Answer (C) is correct. *(Publisher, adapted)*
REQUIRED: The accurate statement about preferred shareholders.
DISCUSSION: Preferred stock offers a fixed return, whereas common stock dividends may grow as the firm prospers. Preferred stock is also frequently redeemable for a fixed price at the corporation's option. Thus, common shareholders are more likely to benefit from appreciation of the value of their shares. Preferred shareholders, however, may have participation or conversion rights that offset these disadvantages.
Answer (A) is incorrect because preferred stock has preferences regarding both dividends and dissolution. Answer (B) is incorrect because bonds pay a return regardless of dividends. Bondholders are creditors with priority of payment over all shareholders in dissolution. Answer (D) is incorrect because creditors, including bondholders, are paid before shareholders when the corporation is liquidated.

41. When no-par shares are issued in a corporation, the value that must be allocated to capital surplus as distinct from stated capital is

A. The carrying amount of the shares.

B. The fair market value of the shares.

C. The entire amount of the consideration received.

D. Any portion of the proceeds so directed by the board of directors.

Answer (D) is correct. *(Publisher, adapted)*
REQUIRED: The appropriate value to be allocated to capital surplus upon the issuance of no-par value stock.
DISCUSSION: If the state statute requires that the corporation maintain a stated or legal capital account and if no-par shares are issued, the entire consideration received for the shares must be allocated to the stated capital account of the corporation except to the extent that the directors in their discretion allocate any part of the proceeds to capital surplus. However, the RMBCA and many modern statutes have abolished the concepts of the par or stated value, stated capital, and capital surplus.

42. Which of the following statements is correct regarding both debt and common shares of a corporation?

    A. Common shares represent an ownership interest in the corporation, but debt holders do not have an ownership interest.

    B. Common shareholders and debt holders have an ownership interest in the corporation.

    C. Common shares typically have a fixed maturity date, but debt does not.

    D. Common shares have a higher priority on liquidation than debt.

Answer (A) is correct. *(CPA, adapted)*
REQUIRED: The true statement about debt and common shares.
DISCUSSION: Common shares are equity securities. Thus, they are ownership interests. In contrast, debt holders do not have ownership interests. Rather, debt holders have claims on the corporation's assets. In the event of a liquidation, the debt holders' claims must be satisfied before any distribution to common shareholders.
    Answer (B) is incorrect because debt holders do not have an ownership interest in the corporation. Answer (C) is incorrect because debt securities typically have a fixed maturity date, but common shares do not. Answer (D) is incorrect because, in the event of bankruptcy or liquidation, creditors, including bond-holders, have first claim on corporate assets.

Use Gleim's ***CPA Test Prep*** for interactive testing with over 2,000 additional multiple-choice questions!

STUDY UNIT FOUR
CORPORATIONS:
GOVERNANCE AND FUNDAMENTAL CHANGES

(17 pages of outline)

The powers of a corporation are exercised by or under the authority of its **board of directors**, who are elected by the **shareholders**. The board is the source of overall corporate policy, which is implemented by the **officers** and other employees of the corporation. The board directs the corporate business; the officers implement the board's directives by conducting day-to-day transactions.

Fundamental corporate changes are extraordinary measures that normally require shareholder approval. Examples of typical changes on which the shareholders customarily must vote are amendments to the articles of incorporation, mergers and share exchanges, a disposition of assets leaving the corporation without a significant continuing business activity, and voluntary dissolution.

4.1 GOVERNANCE

1. **Shareholders' rights.** An acquisition of stock makes a person an owner of the corporation. However, a shareholder has no direct management rights.

   a. The shareholders' primary participation in corporate policy and management is by **meeting annually and electing directors** by majority vote.

      1) By their power to remove any and all directors, shareholders indirectly control the actions of the corporation.

      2) In addition to electing directors, shareholders must approve fundamental corporate changes.

   b. **Voting rights.** The **articles of incorporation** may provide for more or less than one vote per share. It also may require a supermajority.

      1) Usually, each shareholder is entitled to one vote per share owned for each new director to be elected, i.e., **straight voting**. Election is by a **plurality**.

      2) **Cumulative voting** for directors is mandatory in some states. But the **Revised Model Business Corporation Act (RMBCA)** allows cumulative voting only if it is provided for in the articles.

         a) Cumulative voting entitles shareholders to accumulate votes. The shareholder can then either give one candidate as many votes as the number of directors to be elected, multiplied by the number of shares owned, or distribute that number of votes among as many candidates as (s)he wishes.

         b) Formula: *Number of directors to be elected × Number of shares of the shareholder = Number of votes the shareholder may allocate to any one or more candidates.*

         c) Cumulative voting allows a minority shareholder or group of them to obtain representation on the board if they own a certain minimum number of shares. It can preclude the holders of more than 50% of the voting stock from electing the entire board of directors.

d) EXAMPLE: A shareholder has 25,000 shares out of a total outstanding of 100,000, and 4 directors are to be elected. The shareholder can cast all 100,000 votes (4 × 25,000) for one director and be assured of representation no matter how the other 300,000 votes (4 × 75,000) are allocated.

   i) Under straight voting, the shareholder would be outvoted 75,000 to 25,000 for each open directorship.

3) Shareholders entitled to vote are those who are identified on a **voting list** prepared by the corporation for the purpose of giving notice of a meeting.

   a) The **record date** may not be more than 70 days prior to the meeting (RMBCA).

   b) Recording shareholders' names also is the basis for notice of meetings, payment of dividends, and distribution of reports.

4) The RMBCA permits different voting rights for different classes of shares. For example, each class may have the right to elect one director. The result is **class voting**.

   a) Thus, even a closely held corporation may have two or more classes of common shares with different voting rights.

5) The RMBCA specifically permits a **voting agreement**, a signed contract in which shareholders specify how they will vote their shares.

   a) It is specifically enforceable. The party who breaches the contract may be legally compelled to vote the shares as agreed rather than pay damages.

6) **Voting trusts.** Shareholders may transfer their shares to one or more voting trustees in exchange for voting trust certificates. The trust is **irrevocable** for the stated period. The trustees must comply with the trust agreement, which may grant them considerable discretion.

   a) The agreement must be signed by the participants.

   b) The term of a voting trust is initially limited to 10 years.

      i) Shareholders who agree in a signed writing may continue it beyond 10 years.

   c) A voting trust indenture (document) must be made public, and copies must be available for inspection at the corporate offices.

   d) Holders of the certificates, which are frequently transferable, are entitled to corporate distributions.

   e) A voting trust permits the trustees, such as creditors of a corporation in reorganization, to exercise concentrated voting power.

7) A **proxy** is an appointment by a shareholder for someone else to vote on his/her behalf. Usually, a proxy must be in writing or in an authorized electronic transmission. It is **revocable** at any time, e.g., by signing a later proxy.

   a) Under the RMBCA, a proxy is effective for no more than 11 months, unless another time period is specifically included in the appointment.

   b) A proxy is irrevocable if it is **coupled with an interest**, e.g., if the shares are collateral for a loan, subject to a buy/sell agreement, or subject to a voting agreement.

   c) An otherwise irrevocable proxy is revocable by a bona fide purchaser of the shares who has no notice of the proxy.

   d) A general proxy permits a holder to vote on all corporate proposals other than fundamental corporate changes. A limited proxy permits a holder to vote only on matters specified in the proxy.

e) Under federal securities law, a dissident shareholder may require the corporation to furnish a list of the shareholders and mail out proxy materials to those shareholders, as long as the dissident shareholder pays the cost of the mailing.

  i) A **proxy statement** is sent to a shareholder whose proxy is being solicited. Its content is requested by the SEC. It must contain a full and accurate statement of the facts relevant to the issues to be voted on.

c. **Preemptive rights** are important to owners of a close corporation. They give a shareholder an option to subscribe to a new issuance of shares in proportion to the shareholder's current interest in the corporation. Thus, they limit dilution of equity in the corporation.

  1) Almost all states recognize preemptive rights. However, preemptive rights may not exist unless they are specifically reserved in the articles of incorporation.

  2) There are substantial limitations on preemptive rights. For example, they may apply only to new issues, not to previously authorized but unissued shares, treasury shares, or shares issued in a business combination. Under the RMBCA, preemptive rights do not apply to stock issued

    a) As an incentive to officers, directors, or employees

    b) In satisfaction of conversion or option rights

    c) For something other than money

    d) Within 6 months of incorporation if the shares were authorized in the articles

  3) Publicly traded corporations sometimes issue **options** to purchase stock at a specified price. These securities are frequently given to executives as a form of incentive. Moreover, options to purchase **(call options)** or to sell **(put options)** may be created by parties other than the issuer of the underlying stock.

    a) The term **rights** is often applied to short-term options. They are issued to current shareholders, most often in connection with a preemptive right.

    b) The term **warrants** is often applied to longer-term options evidenced by certificates. They are usually attached to other securities, for example, bonds or preferred stock.

    c) The foregoing securities may be transferable and traded on stock exchanges.

d. Under the RMBCA, shareholders and their agents have a fundamental **right to inspect** the corporation's books and records that may not be limited by the articles or bylaws.

  1) Inspection must be at the corporation's principal office during regular business hours. The shareholders must give 5 business days' written notice that states the purpose of the demand and the records to be inspected. The records must be directly related to the purpose.

  2) Inspection must be in good faith and for a **proper purpose**. For example, it may involve

    a) Corporate financial condition

    b) The propriety of dividends

    c) Mismanagement of the corporation

    d) The names and addresses of other shareholders

    e) Election of directors

    f) A shareholder suit

3) An **improper purpose** is one that does not relate to the shareholder's interest in the corporation. Improper purposes include

a) Harassment of management
b) Discovery of trade secrets
c) Gaining a competitive advantage
d) Development of a mailing list for sale or similar use

4) Courts have permitted a shareholder to obtain a copy of a shareholder list, even when the only purpose was to engage in a takeover battle.

5) Shareholders have an unconditional right to inspect records, such as the articles, bylaws, minutes of shareholder meetings, and the annual report.

e. **Shareholder meetings.** Generally, shareholders may act only at a meeting.

1) **Annual meetings** are required and must be held at a time fixed in the bylaws. The purpose is to elect new directors and to conduct necessary business.

a) **Notice** of any meeting must be in writing, and defective notice or lack of notice voids action taken at the meeting.

2) Under the RMBCA, **special meetings**, e.g., to approve a merger, may be called by the board of directors, the owner(s) of at least 10% of the issued and outstanding common stock, or any other persons authorized in the articles.

a) Special meetings require written notice and a description of purpose.

3) A **quorum** must be represented in person or by proxy to conduct business. The RMBCA defines a quorum as a majority of shares outstanding.

4) The RMBCA permits shareholders to **act without a meeting** if all shareholders entitled to vote consent in writing to the action.

f. Shareholders may amend or repeal **bylaws**.

g. **Shareholder suits.** An individual shareholder may sue a corporation to preclude ultra vires acts, to recover improper dividends, to obtain a remedy for management's breach of duty, etc. A shareholder also may enforce preemptive, inspection, dividend, or other rights of shareholders. These rights may have been created by statute, the articles, the bylaws, or common law.

1) **Direct suits.** Shareholders may sue directly on their own behalf, either individually or as members of a class. In a **class action** or representative suit, the plaintiffs represent not only themselves but "all others similarly situated."

2) A shareholder also may file a **shareholder derivative suit** to recover for wrongs done to the corporation. The action is for the benefit of the corporation, and any recovery belongs to it, not to the shareholder. It is the true plaintiff.

a) A shareholder must first demand that the corporation bring suit unless it is obvious the demand would be futile; e.g., the action is against corporate officers or directors.

b) Most states require that the shareholder prove the following:

i) (S)he owned shares at the time of wrongdoing.
ii) A written demand was made on the directors.
iii) The directors refused to sue.
iv) The refusal was in bad faith.

c) For a shareholder to file a derivative suit, the RMBCA requires that 90 days have expired since the demand (unless notice of rejection has been given or irreparable harm will be done to the corporation).

    i) A derivative suit will be dismissed if independent directors or a court-appointed panel determines in good faith after reasonable inquiry that the action is not in the best interests of the corporation.

    ii) Discontinuation or settlement of a derivative suit must be approved by the court, with notice to other shareholders. These provisions discourage secret settlements and abusive suits.

d) The business judgment rule applies to the board's decision not to pursue a corporate legal claim.

e) A shareholder can generally recover reasonable litigation expenses from the corporation but no compensation for his/her time.

h. Under the RMBCA, shareholders have no right to receive **stock certificates**. Thus, any or all issued shares may be uncertificated.

i. In a **liquidation** of corporate assets, equity shareholders are paid after all other claimants.

2. **Shareholder liability.** The RMBCA states that shareholders are not personally liable for acts or debts of the corporation except by reason of their own acts. Thus, a shareholder's liability is limited to his/her capital contribution except in certain instances, for example, if the corporate veil is pierced or the corporation was defectively formed.

    a. **Stock subscription agreements.** The subscriber remains liable to the corporation for any unpaid installment balance, even if the corporation becomes insolvent or declares bankruptcy. If the subscriber dies, his/her estate may be liable for any balance due.

    b. **Par or stated value.** If authorized stock is issued with a par or stated value and is originally issued (sold) for less, the purchasing shareholder is and remains liable (to the corporation) for the deficiency.

        1) A person who subsequently purchases the stock is subject to liability if (s)he knows the stock was issued for less than par or stated value.

        2) The RMBCA has eliminated the concept of par value.

    c. **Watered stock.** If stock is not issued in exchange for full and adequate consideration and the facts indicate fraud or bad faith by the shareholders, they (and probably the directors) will be personally liable for any amount underpaid.

    d. **Illegal dividends.** A dividend paid when the corporation is **insolvent** is always illegal. State law also may require that dividends be paid only from designated accounts, that is, from retained earnings, current net profits, or any surplus. Moreover, a dividend may be illegal if it causes insolvency.

        1) A corporation generally may recover damages from a shareholder who receives a dividend or other corporate distribution only when the shareholder knows that the distribution is wrong.

        2) A shareholder may be held liable for unpaid debts of the corporation up to the amount received as an illegal dividend or distribution.

    e. A **seller of a controlling block of shares** may be liable to nonselling minority shareholders if the seller has or should have had a reasonable suspicion that the purchaser would mismanage or loot the corporation, unless investigation shows no basis for it.

        1) A court also may compel the seller of a controlling interest to distribute ratably to all shareholders any **control premium** received in excess of the fair value.

f.   **Usurpation.** If a purchaser wishes to buy the corporation's assets and the controlling shareholder proposes that the purchaser buy his/her stock instead, the controlling shareholder may be liable for usurping a corporate opportunity.

g.   A **fiduciary duty** is owed by the majority to the minority in a closely held corporation. It requires utmost good faith, loyalty, and impartiality. Accordingly, a breach of the fiduciary duty results in liability for oppressive conduct. Controlling shareholders must

1)   Not cause the corporation to purchase their shares at a price unavailable to the minority

2)   Act in good faith regarding payment of salaries and dividends

3.   **Shareholder agreements.** The RMBCA permits shareholders to change, by unanimous agreement, the provisions for corporate governance. This flexibility may allow a close corporation to function more nearly as a partnership without loss of corporate status.

a.   Thus, **RMBCA 7.32** provides for a shareholder agreement set forth in the articles, bylaws, or a separate signed agreement and **approved by all shareholders**. It "governs the exercise of the corporate powers or the management of the business and affairs of the corporation or the relationship among the shareholders, the directors, and the corporation, and is not contrary to public policy." It is valid for 10 years unless otherwise agreed. The shareholder agreement may, for example,

1)   Eliminate the board or restrict its powers;

2)   Permit dividends not in proportion to ownership;

3)   Determine who will be officers and directors, their terms of office, and how they are chosen or removed;

4)   Set voting requirements (in general or for specific issues) for actions by shareholders or directors;

5)   Establish the terms of any agreement for transfer of property or provision of services between

a)   The corporation and
b)   A shareholder, officer, director, or employee, or among any of them;

6)   Transfer authority to

a)   Exercise corporate powers,
b)   Manage the business or other affairs, or
c)   Resolve a deadlock among shareholders or directors; and

7)   Require corporate dissolution upon

a)   Request of a shareholder(s) or
b)   Occurrence of a given event.

4.   **Board of Directors**

a.   Each state has a specific requirement with respect to the **number of directors** elected to sit on the board. Many states require a minimum of three. Under the provisions of the RMBCA, a minimum of one director is usually required.

1)   However, the RMBCA permits a corporation to dispense with a board pursuant to a unanimous shareholder agreement.

b.   The **initial board** is usually appointed by the incorporators or named in the articles, and this board serves until the first meeting of the shareholders.

1)   Subsequent directors are elected by the shareholders at the annual meeting.

c.   Most publicly held corporations have two types of directors. **Inside directors** are officers and full-time employees. **Outside directors** may be unaffiliated with the corporation except for stock ownership.

    d.   Generally, a director serves a 1-year term. The articles or bylaws may provide for a longer term.

        1)   Directors on a board of nine or more are often **classified**. This arrangement permits staggering of terms by creating separate classes of directors. The members of one class will then be elected at each annual meeting.

    e.   Power authorizing the board to increase its **size** without shareholder approval may be reserved in the articles or bylaws.

    f.   Normally, a director is elected by a **plurality** (not a majority) of shareholder votes.

        1)   For example, if candidates A, B, and C receive 150, 100, and 100, respectively, of 350 possible votes, candidate A has received a plurality.

        2)   Cumulative voting may be permitted or mandatory.

    g.   **Vacancies.** Typically, if a director dies or resigns or if the size of the board has been increased, the remaining directors may elect a director(s) to fill the vacancy(ies) until the next shareholders' meeting.

    h.   In most states, shareholders may by a majority vote remove, **with or without cause**, any director or the entire board.

    i.   Statutes usually permit the **board to remove a director** who has been declared insane or convicted of a felony. Rarely would a board be permitted to remove a director for any other reason.

    j.   The RMBCA authorizes a court to issue an **order to remove a director** in a proceeding brought by or on behalf of the corporation if the court finds

        1)   The director engaged in fraudulent conduct regarding the corporation or the shareholders, intentionally harmed the corporation, or grossly abused his/her authority, and

        2)   Removal is in the best interest of the corporation.

    k.   A director ordinarily need not be a shareholder, be a resident of the state of incorporation, or meet an age requirement.

5.   **Board authority and actions.** Although directors formulate overall corporate policy, they are **neither trustees nor agents** of the corporation. A director cannot act individually.

    a.   The board establishes and implements corporate policy, including

        1)   Selection and removal of officers

        2)   Decisions about capital structure, including the consideration to be received for shares

        3)   Adding, amending, or repealing bylaws (unless this authority is reserved to the shareholders)

            a)   **Bylaws** govern the internal structure and operation of the corporation. Initial bylaws are adopted by the incorporators or the board. They may contain any provision for managing the business and regulating the entity's affairs that does not conflict with the law or the articles.

        4)   Initiation of fundamental changes

        5)   Dividends, including whether and when to declare them

        6)   Setting of management compensation

    b.   Directors owe a fiduciary duty to the corporation. Thus, express agreement is necessary to authorize **compensation**. It is common to compensate outside directors.

    c.   Directors have power to bind the corporation only when **acting as a board**.

    d.   The board may act only at a **formal meeting** or by duly executed **written consent** if authorized by statute, unless contrary to the articles or bylaws.

e. Many statutes, articles, and bylaws permit boards to act (1) by simultaneous telephone conference call, (2) by video conference, or (3) without a meeting by unanimous written consent.

f. Formal meetings are held at fixed intervals established in the bylaws.

g. **Special meetings** may be held after proper notice has been given to all directors.

   1) A director's attendance at any meeting is a **waiver of notice**, unless the director attends for the express purpose of objecting to the transaction on the grounds that the meeting is not lawfully convened.

h. **Meeting location.** Unless required by statute or bylaws, the board need not meet at the corporate offices or even in the state of incorporation. Most modern statutes allow meetings outside the U.S.

i. Actions taken by a board are expressed in **formal resolutions** adopted by a majority of the board during a meeting at which a quorum is present.

   1) Generally, a **quorum** consists of a majority of board members. A director is not allowed to vote by proxy.

j. If a formal **dissent** (by entry in the minutes) is not communicated, concurrence with the majority decision is presumed.

   1) Written dissent may be sent by registered mail to the secretary of the corporation immediately after adjournment of the meeting.

k. If permitted by the articles or bylaws, a board may delegate authority to **committees** composed of its members or corporate officers. Committee members usually have a specific skill or extensive experience in an area of concern.

   1) The RMBCA requires that committee formation and appointment of members be approved by the greater of

      a) A majority of all the directors in office when the action is taken or
      b) The number of directors required by the charter or bylaws to take action.

   2) Committees may exercise broad **powers** consistent with the limits of the resolutions by which they were established. However, they may not take extraordinary actions, e.g., issue stock, adopt bylaws, approve a matter requiring a shareholder vote, or authorize distributions.

   3) **New York Stock Exchange** rules require every listed corporation to have an **audit committee** consisting of outside directors.

l. Directors have the **right to inspect corporate books and records** so they can perform their duties.

6. **Directors' duty of care.** Directors have a **fiduciary relationship** to the corporation. They can be held personally liable for failure to be informed of matters internal to, and external but relevant to, the corporation. A director's conduct is tested objectively.

a. The **RMBCA** requires that a director discharge his/her duties

   1) In good faith
   2) In a manner (s)he reasonably believes to be in the best interests of the corporation
   3) With the care that a person in a similar position would reasonably believe appropriate under similar circumstances

b. **Reliance on others.** In exercising reasonable care, a director may rely on information, reports, opinions, and statements prepared or presented by officers or employees whom the director **reasonably believes** to be competent in the matters presented.

        1) A director may also rely on the specialized knowledge of lawyers, accountants, investment bankers, and board committees.

   c. Directors are expected to be **informed** about pertinent corporate information when giving advice. To exercise the required care, a director must

        1) Attend meetings of the board
        2) Analyze corporate financial statements
        3) Review pertinent legal opinions
        4) Become conversant with the available relevant information

7. **Directors' duty of loyalty.** Directors of a corporation owe a duty of loyalty to the corporation. For example, serving on the board of a competitor may violate this duty.

   a. **Conflicting interest transactions.** To protect the corporation against **self-dealing**, a director is required to make **full disclosure** of any financial interest (s)he may have in any transaction to which both the director and the corporation may be a party.

        1) Under the RMBCA, a transaction is not voidable merely on the grounds of a director's conflict of interest. If the transaction (a) is fair to the corporation or (b) has been approved by a majority of informed, qualified directors or holders of qualified shares after required disclosure, it is not voidable and does not result in sanctions. This rule applies even if the director was counted for the quorum and voted to approve the transaction.

           a) A transaction is **fair** if reasonable persons, bargaining at arm's-length (independently), would have entered into the transaction in the same circumstances.

           b) A **qualified director** does not have (1) a conflict of interest regarding the transaction or (2) a special relationship (familial, professional, financial, etc.) with another director who has a conflict of interest. **Shares are qualified** if they are not controlled by a person with (1) a conflict of interest or (2) a close relationship with someone who has a conflict.

           c) A contract between a director and the corporation that is neither fair nor approved by disinterested directors or shareholders may be rescinded or upheld by the corporation, and the director may be required to pay damages.

           d) Under the **Sarbanes-Oxley Act of 2002**, an issuer generally may not make **personal loans** to its directors and officers.

   b. Directors may not usurp any **corporate opportunity**. A director must give the corporation the right of first refusal.

        1) A corporate opportunity is one in which the corporation has a right, property interest, or expectancy.

        2) A corporate opportunity arises when

           a) A director becomes aware of the opportunity in his/her corporate capacity,
           b) The opportunity is within the scope of corporate activity, or
           c) Corporate capital, equipment, personnel, or facilities were used to develop the opportunity.

        3) Generally, a corporate opportunity does not exist if

           a) Action by the corporation would be beyond its powers,
           b) The corporation cannot obtain necessary financing or capital to take advantage of the opportunity, or
           c) The opportunity is rejected by a majority vote of disinterested directors.

8. Directors who approve **unlawful distributions** are personally liable to the corporation for excess distributions if they failed to comply with their duty of care.

9. Directors and officers owe a **fiduciary duty** to the corporation to (a) act in its best interests, (b) be loyal, (c) use due diligence in carrying out their responsibilities, and (d) disclose conflicts of interest. Controlling or majority shareholders owe similar duties. For example, courts will often protect the interests of **minority shareholders** by ordering the payment of dividends that were withheld in bad faith or by compelling a seller of a controlling block of shares to distribute ratably among all shareholders any "control premium" paid in excess of the fair value of the stock.

10. **Business judgment rule.** Courts avoid substituting their business judgment for that of the corporation's officers or directors.

    a. The rule protects an officer or a director from **personal liability** for honest mistakes of judgment if (s)he

        1) Acted in good faith
        2) Was not motivated by fraud, conflict of interest, or illegality
        3) Was not grossly negligent

    b. To avoid personal liability, directors and officers must

        1) Make informed decisions (educate themselves about the issues)
        2) Be free from conflicts of interest
        3) Have a rational basis to support their position

    c. Some decisions concern incumbent management's opposition to **tender offers**, i.e., offers to shareholders made by a third party to buy the shareholders' stock at a price above the market price. Directors may be liable to shareholders, i.e., the business judgment rule may not apply, if

        1) The directors make a decision to oppose a tender offer before they have carefully studied it, or
        2) Their actions indicate that they are opposing it to preserve their jobs.

    d. Most states permit corporations to **indemnify** directors and officers for expenses of litigation concerning business judgments, subject to some exceptions.

        1) The RMBCA permits the **articles** to limit the liability of directors to the corporation or shareholders. However, the limitation applies only to **money damages**. The articles may not limit liability for

            a) Intentional infliction of harm on the corporation
            b) Intentional criminal conduct
            c) Unlawful distributions
            d) Receipt of financial benefits to which a director is not entitled

        2) Usually, an officer or director who is liable to the corporation because of negligence in the performance of his/her duties is not entitled to indemnification. However, a **court** may order indemnification of an officer or director (even though found negligent) if the court determines (s)he is **fairly and reasonably** entitled to it in view of all the relevant circumstances.

11. **Officers** are elected or appointed by the board. They generally serve at the will of the board, which may remove any officer at any time. However, the board may not remove without cause an officer elected or employed by the shareholders.

    a. Typically, state statutes set a minimum number of officers, but not a maximum. Under the RMBCA, the corporation has the officers stated in the bylaws or appointed by the board pursuant to the bylaws. They need not be shareholders. One officer must be delegated responsibility for

        1) Preparing the minutes of directors' meetings
        2) Authenticating records of the corporation

    b.   Officers typically appointed are president, vice president, secretary, and treasurer. **One person may hold more than one office.** Moreover, an officer may serve as a director. Many states require that the same person not hold the offices of president and secretary simultaneously.

    c.   The officers are **agents** of the corporation. They have **express authority** conferred by the bylaws or the board. They have **implied authority** to do things that are reasonably necessary to accomplish their express duties. Courts have held that official titles confer limited **inherent authority** on officers.

        1) **President.** (S)he supervises and controls all the business and affairs of the corporation, subject to the discretion of the board.

           a) (S)he presides at board and shareholders' meetings.

           b) Traditionally, the president had no inherent authority. But the trend is that (s)he can bind the corporation in the ordinary course of its business.

        2) **General manager or chief executive officer.** The title grants broad implied authority to conduct the corporation's business.

        3) **Vice president.** (S)he traditionally performs the duties of the president if the president is unable to. A vice president has no inherent authority. But a person named vice president of a specific department, e.g., finance, has authority to transact business within the scope of that department.

        4) **Secretary.** (S)he is the custodian of the corporate seal and records.

           a) The secretary notifies participants of shareholders' and board meetings and maintains the minutes (records).

           b) The secretary maintains the stock transfer ledgers and, along with the president, signs for the issuance of stock certificates.

           c) The secretary certifies the authenticity of the president's signature and corporate records when necessary.

        5) **Treasurer.** (S)he maintains the financial accounts and records. Typically, the treasurer signs all checks and gives receipts for, and deposits money due and payable to, the corporation.

    d.   Officers, like directors, owe **fiduciary duties** to the corporation.

        1) As an agent, an officer has a duty to act within authority granted by the articles, the bylaws, and the board.

        2) Officers are subject to the same duties of care and loyalty as are directors.

        3) Likewise, absent bad faith, fraud, or breach of a fiduciary duty, the **business judgment rule** applies to officers. Like a director, the officer is protected if the management decision is informed, conflict-free, and rational.

           a) Officers may be indemnified to the extent, consistent with public policy, provided by the articles, bylaws, actions of the board, or contract.

    e.   The SEC requires issuers to provide detailed disclosures about **executive compensation** paid to the CEO, CFO, and the next three highest-paid officers: (1) base pay, (2) stock options and grants, and (3) other benefits.

12. The **Sarbanes-Oxley Act of 2002** is a response to numerous financial reporting scandals involving large public companies. It contains provisions relating to corporate governance that impose new responsibilities on public companies and their auditors. The act applies to **issuers** of publicly traded securities subject to federal securities laws.

    a.   It requires that each member of the **audit committee**, including at least one who is a **financial expert**, be an **independent** member of the issuer's **board of directors**.

        1) An independent director is not affiliated with, and receives no compensation (other than for service on the board) from, the issuer.

2) The audit committee must be directly responsible for appointing, compensating, and overseeing the work of the issuer's **public accounting firm**. This firm must **report directly** to the audit committee, not to management.

    a) This firm must be registered with the **Public Company Accounting Oversight Board (PCAOB)**, a private-sector body created to regulate the accounting profession. Violations of its rules are violations of the **Securities Exchange Act of 1934**. The PCAOB establishes auditing and related standards; inspects and investigates accounting firms; and enforces compliance with its rules, professional standards, the Sarbanes-Oxley Act, and relevant portions of securities laws.

3) Another function of the audit committee is to implement procedures for the receipt, retention, and treatment of **complaints about accounting and auditing matters**.

4) **Audit reports received by audit committees** must include

    a) All critical accounting policies and practices to be used

    b) All material alternative treatments of financial information within GAAP discussed with management

    c) Ramifications of the use of alternative disclosures and treatments

    d) The treatments preferred by the external auditors

5) **Correcting adjustments** identified by the public accountants must be disclosed in an issuer's required periodic GAAP-based reports.

    a) Annual and quarterly reports must disclose all material **off-balance-sheet transactions** and other relationships with unconsolidated entities with material current or future effects on financial condition.

6) **SEC regulations** issued under Sarbanes-Oxley generally prohibit auditors of issuers from performing certain **nonaudit services**:

    a) Appraisal and other valuation services

    b) Designing and implementing financial information systems

    c) Internal auditing or actuarial functions unless the firm reasonably concludes it will not examine such work during the financial statement audit

        i) The Federal Reserve, Federal Deposit Insurance Corporation, Comptroller of the Currency, and Office of Thrift Supervision prohibit issuers and depository institutions with $500,000,000 or more in assets from outsourcing internal auditing to external auditors.

    d) Management services

    e) Human resource services

    f) Bookkeeping if the firm also conducts an audit

    g) Expert services not pertaining to the audit

    h) Investment banking or advisory services

    i) Broker-dealer services

7) Audit firms may continue to provide conventional tax planning and other nonaudit services not listed above to audit clients if **preapproved by the audit committee**. Also, the PCAOB may grant exemptions from these prohibitions on a case-by-case basis, subject to approval by the SEC.

8) The audit committee must be **appropriately funded** by the issuer and may hire independent counsel or other advisors.

b. The **chief executive officer** and **chief financial officer** of the issuer must **certify** that the issuer's **financial statements and disclosures** "fairly present, in all material respects, the operation and financial condition of the issuer." This statement must accompany the audit report.

    1) A CEO or CFO will be liable only if (s)he **knowingly and intentionally** violates this part of the act. The maximum penalty for a violation is a fine of $500,000 and imprisonment for 5 years.

c. It is also illegal for an officer or director to exert **improper influence on the conduct of an audit** with the intent to make financial statements materially misleading.

d. If an issuer materially **restates its financial statements** as a result of material noncompliance with reporting requirements, the CEO and CFO must return to the issuer any amounts received within 12 months after the issuance or filing in the form of incentive- or equity-based compensation and profits from sale of the issuer's securities.

e. The SEC may **freeze extraordinary payments** to directors, officers, and others during an investigation of securities law violations. Also, it may prohibit anyone convicted of **securities fraud** from serving as an officer or director of a publicly traded firm.

    1) Sarbanes-Oxley created a new **25-year felony for defrauding shareholders of publicly traded companies**. This measure is a broad, generalized provision. It criminalizes the knowing or attempted execution of any scheme to defraud persons in connection with securities of issuers or to obtain their money or property in connection with the purchase or sale of securities. It gives prosecutors flexibility to protect current and future shareholders against any frauds that inventive criminals may devise.

f. Directors, officers, and 10% owners must report **transactions with the issuer** by the end of the second business day.

g. **Personal loans** to executives or directors are generally prohibited.

h. Sarbanes-Oxley prohibits the **conflict of interest** that arises when the CEO, CFO, controller, chief accounting officer, or the equivalent was employed by the company's public accountant within one year before the audit.

i. **Tampering with documents** may involve altering, destroying, or concealing accounting records, audit working papers, or other documents for the purpose of impairing their integrity or obstructing an official proceeding. Such tampering is a crime punishable by up to 20 years in prison.

j. **Internal control report.** Under **Section 404**, management must establish and document internal control and include in the annual report an assessment of **the company's internal control over financial reporting**.

    1) This report is to include

        a) A statement of management's responsibility for internal control;

        b) Management's assessment of the effectiveness of internal control as of the end of the most recent fiscal year;

        c) Identification of the framework used to evaluate the effectiveness of internal control (such as the report of the Committee of Sponsoring Organizations);

        d) Disclosure of material weaknesses and a statement about whether significant changes in controls were made after their evaluation, including any corrective actions; and

        e) A statement that the external auditor has issued an attestation report on management's assessment.

2) The issuer's auditor must attest to, and report on, management's assessment. The auditor also must express an opinion directly on the client's internal control.

3) The issuer must disclose whether it has adopted an **ethics code** for its senior financial officers and the content.

13. Stop and review! You have completed the outline for this subunit. Study multiple-choice questions 1 through 28 beginning on page 102.

4.2 FUNDAMENTAL CORPORATE CHANGES

1. Some changes affect a corporation so fundamentally they require shareholder approval. Shareholder approval of fundamental changes does **not usually require unanimity**. In some instances, minority shareholders have the **right to dissent** and recover the fair value of their shares after appraisal.

   a. Under the RMBCA, the first step is approval of the change by the **board**. All shareholders must then be **notified**, including those without voting rights regarding the matter. A majority vote of the shareholders taken at an annual or special meeting is sufficient to pass the proposal unless the articles require a greater percentage. **Voting by class** is required for share exchanges and mergers if the interests of a class are significantly affected. The articles may provide that class voting is required on other transactions.

2. **Appraisal (dissenters') rights.** Shareholders who disagree with fundamental corporate changes may be paid the fair value of their stock in cash.

   a. Under the RMBCA, **fair value** is the value immediately before the corporation acts on the proposed fundamental change. Fair value is determined using current valuation techniques without discounting for lack of marketability or minority status.

   b. The RMBCA requires that a shareholder asserting appraisal rights

      1) Not vote in favor of the transaction
      2) Make written demand before the vote that the corporation purchase his/her stock if the action is approved

   c. Under the RMBCA, the **right to dissent** covers

      1) A disposition of assets that leaves the corporation without a significant continuing business activity
      2) Mergers (including consolidations) and share exchanges
      3) Certain amendments to the articles of incorporation, for example, when the right is provided in the articles, bylaws, or a board resolution

         a) However, other statutes provide a broad right to dissent when an amendment **materially and adversely** affects shareholder rights.

   d. Most state statutes (including the RMBCA) exclude shares that are publicly traded from being subject to appraisal rights.

3. **Amendments to the articles.** Modern corporation statutes permit the articles of incorporation to be freely amended.

   a. Generally, the board adopts a resolution setting forth, in writing, the proposed amendment. The resolution then must be approved in a meeting at which a **quorum** is present, i.e., a majority of the shareholder votes entitled to be cast.

      1) Some statutes require a supermajority shareholder vote.
      2) A class of shareholders may be entitled to vote as a **class**.

   b. After shareholder approval, **articles of amendment** are filed with the secretary of state. Amendment is effective when a certificate of amendment is issued.

    c.   The RMBCA permits the board to adopt certain de minimis amendments, e.g., changing the corporation's registered agent without shareholder action, unless the articles of incorporation provide otherwise.

4.   **Sale or lease of corporate assets.** If a sale or lease of **all or substantially all** corporate assets is not in the regular course of business, approval of the board and shareholders is required if the corporation is left without a **significant continuing business activity**.

    a.   In most states, dissenting shareholders have appraisal rights.

    b.   A **mortgage or pledge** of any or all of the property and assets of a corporation, whether or not in the regular course of business, does not require shareholder approval (absent a contrary provision in the articles).

    c.   The acquirer does not ordinarily become liable for the acquiree's obligations. Exceptions are made for express or implied assumptions of liability when business is continued, when the transaction was in effect a merger or consolidation, and in certain other cases.

5.   **Merger.** A merger is the combination of all the assets of two or more corporations. In a merger, one corporation is absorbed by another corporation and ceases to exist, e.g., A + B = A. State statutes set forth specific procedures for mergers.

    a.   The shareholders of a merged corporation may receive stock or other securities issued by the surviving corporation.

    b.   Stock of the merged (acquired) corporation is canceled.

    c.   A merger requires the approval of each board and of shareholders entitled to vote for each corporation. Under the RMBCA, shareholder approval must be given at a special meeting at which a majority of votes entitled to be cast is represented. (But the articles or the board may require a greater vote or a greater number of votes to be represented.)

        1)   Other statutes require a supermajority to approve the merger.

        2)   Shareholders of each corporation must be provided a copy of the formal **plan of merger** to enable informed voting.

    d.   The surviving corporation succeeds to the rights, duties, liabilities, and assets of the merged corporation.

    e.   Shareholders of each corporation have appraisal rights.

    f.   Under the RMBCA, no shareholder approval is required in a **short-form merger**. In a short-form merger, a corporation that owns at least 90% of the outstanding shares of a subsidiary merges the subsidiary into itself.

        1)   The parent must give 10 days' notice to the subsidiary's shareholders.

        2)   Shareholders of the subsidiary have appraisal rights.

    g.   The RMBCA requires that **articles of merger** be filed with the secretary of state.

    h.   The RMBCA provisions for **share exchanges** are similar to those for mergers.

        1)   A share exchange occurs when one corporation acquires all of the shares of one or more classes or series of shares of another in exchange for shares, securities, cash, other property, etc.

        2)   A share exchange maintains the separate corporate existence of both entities.

    i.   A purchase of another corporation's stock that allows the purchasing company a controlling interest does not imply a merger of two entities. Although the purchasing company would have to prepare consolidated financial statements, the company is legally a separate entity. This transaction creates no fundamental corporate change. Thus, shareholder approval is not necessary.

6. **Consolidations.** A new corporation is formed, and the two or more consolidating corporations cease operating as separate entities, e.g., A + B = C.

   a. Otherwise, the requirements and effects of the combination are similar to those for a merger.

   b. The shareholders receive stock or other securities issued by the new corporation.

   c. The term **statutory merger** applies to combinations involving merger or consolidation.

7. **Tender offers.** A merger, consolidation, or purchase of substantially all of a corporation's assets requires approval of the board of directors of the corporation whose shares or assets are acquired. An acquiring corporation may bypass board approval by extending a tender offer of cash or shares, usually at a higher than market price, directly to shareholders to purchase a certain number of the outstanding shares.

   a. After obtaining control of the target corporation, the tender offeror may effect a merger or consolidation.

   b. Managements of target corporations have implemented diverse strategies to counter hostile tender offers. Courts apply the **business judgment rule** when such strategies are challenged. They have generally upheld the strategies. Examples of antitakeover strategies follow:

      1) **Persuasion.** Management of the target persuades target shareholders to reject an offer.

      2) **Poison pill.** A target corporation's articles, bylaws, or contracts include provisions that reduce the value of the target to potential tender offerors. For example, a valuable contract may terminate by its terms upon a specified form of change of ownership of the target.

      3) **Flip-over rights.** The charter of a target corporation provides for its shareholders to acquire in exchange for their stock a greater interest (e.g., twice the shares of stock of equivalent value) in an acquiring entity.

      4) **Flip-in rights.** Acquisition of more than a specified ownership interest (e.g., 25%) in the target corporation by a raider triggers additional rights in the stock not acquired by the raider; e.g., each share becomes entitled to two votes.

      5) **Issuing stock.** The target corporation significantly increases the amount of outstanding stock.

      6) **Reverse tender** (also called the Pac-Man defense). The target corporation makes a tender offer to acquire control of the tender offeror.

      7) **Self-tender.** The target borrows money to tender an offer to repurchase shares of itself. The defense is called **greenmail** when the target repurchases the shares from the hostile suitor at a premium.

      8) **ESOP.** An employee stock ownership plan is likely to vote the shares allocated to it against a raider who is likely to destabilize the target corporation's current structure.

      9) **White knight merger.** Target management arranges an alternative tender offer with a different acquirer that will be more favorable to incumbent management and shareholders.

      10) **Crown jewel transfer.** The target corporation sells or otherwise disposes of one or more assets that made it a desirable target.

      11) **Legal action.** A target corporation may challenge one or more aspects of a tender offer. A resulting delay increases costs to the raider and enables further defensive action.

      12) **Scorched earth.** A target firm sells off the assets or divisions that the offeror finds most attractive or acquires substantial amounts of debt that would come due if the firm were acquired in a hostile takeover. Either scenario renders the target firm less desirable to the offeror.

13) **Shark repellent.** The corporation may amend its articles or bylaws to create obstacles to a hostile takeover, for example, by requiring supermajority approval.

14) **Lobster trap.** Owners of convertible securities of the target are prohibited from converting if they already own, or would own after conversion, a specified percentage of voting stock. Thus, only the large "lobsters" are caught.

c. States regulate tender offers by statutes or administrative regulations to protect interests other than those of a would-be raider.

d. The **Williams Act of 1968** extended reporting and disclosure requirements of federal securities regulation to tender offers.

8. **Dissolution.** The RMBCA permits voluntary dissolution of a corporation that has not commenced business or issued stock by a majority vote of its incorporators or directors.

a. A corporation that has issued stock and commenced business may be **voluntarily dissolved** by a shareholder vote at a special meeting called for the purpose if the directors have adopted a resolution of dissolution. Unless the board or the articles require otherwise, a majority of the votes entitled to be cast must be represented at the meeting.

1) The corporation files **articles of dissolution** with the secretary of state to petition for voluntary dissolution. A dissolution is effective when filed.

b. The secretary of state may proceed administratively to dissolve a corporation that fails to file its annual report, pay any franchise tax or penalty, or maintain a resident agent or office in the state.

1) Typically, the secretary of state gives written notice to the corporation to correct the default or demonstrate that none exists.

c. Expiration of the period of duration stated in the articles is another basis for administrative dissolution.

d. Under the RMBCA, shareholders may seek a judicial **dissolution** if a corporate deadlock develops; if those in control have acted, are acting, or will act illegally, oppressively, or fraudulently; or if assets are being misapplied or wasted.

e. The **attorney general** may seek judicial dissolution of a corporation if it is proved that a corporation obtained its articles of incorporation by fraud or that it exceeded or abused its legal authority.

f. A **creditor** may seek judicial dissolution of an insolvent corporation if

1) The creditor has an unsatisfied judgment against the debtor, or
2) The debtor has admitted the claim in writing.

9. **Liquidation.** After dissolution, the corporate business and affairs must be wound up and liquidated.

a. The **directors** have a duty to "discharge or make reasonable provision" for **claims**. They then must distribute assets to shareholders.

b. Directors will not be liable to claimants with regard to claims barred or satisfied if they have complied with the RMBCA's statutory procedures for

1) Giving notice to known claimants,
2) Publishing notice of dissolution,
3) Requesting that other claimants present their claims, and
4) Obtaining appropriate judicial determinations, for example, of the amount of collateral needed for payment of contingent claims, claims reasonably expected to arise after dissolution, or claims not yet made.

10. Stop and review! You have completed the outline for this subunit. Study multiple-choice questions 29 through 37 beginning on page 111.

QUESTIONS

4.1 Governance

1. A shareholder's right to inspect books and records of a corporation will be properly denied if the shareholder

- A. Wants to use corporate shareholder records for a personal business.
- B. Employs an agent to inspect the books and records.
- C. Intends to commence a shareholder's derivative suit.
- D. Is investigating management misconduct.

Answer (A) is correct. *(CPA, adapted)*
REQUIRED: The basis for denying shareholder inspection of books and records.
DISCUSSION: A shareholder has a right to inspect corporate books and records. But the right must be exercised for a proper purpose and in a proper manner. Use of corporate shareholder records for a personal business is not a proper purpose because it does not concern the shareholder's interest in the corporation.
Answer (B) is incorrect because an agent may exercise the right on the shareholder's behalf. Answer (C) is incorrect because a shareholder's derivative suit is a proper purpose, except if instituted in bad faith. Answer (D) is incorrect because investigating management misconduct is a proper purpose.

2. A corporate shareholder is entitled to which of the following rights?

- A. Elect officers.
- B. Receive annual dividends.
- C. Approve dissolution.
- D. Prevent corporate borrowing.

Answer (C) is correct. *(CPA, adapted)*
REQUIRED: The right of a shareholder.
DISCUSSION: Shareholders do not have the right to manage the corporation or its business. Shareholder participation in policy and management is through exercising the right to elect directors. Shareholders also have the right to approve charter amendments, disposition of all or substantially all of the corporation's assets, mergers and consolidations, and dissolutions.
Answer (A) is incorrect because the board elects officers. Answer (B) is incorrect because a shareholder does not have a general right to receive dividends. The board determines dividend policy. Answer (D) is incorrect because determining capital structure and whether the corporation should borrow are policy and management determinations to be made according to the board's business judgment.

3. For what purpose will a shareholder of a publicly held corporation be permitted to file a shareholder derivative suit in the name of the corporation?

- A. To compel payment of a properly declared dividend.
- B. To enforce a right to inspect corporate records.
- C. To compel dissolution of the corporation.
- D. To recover damages from corporate management for an ultra vires management act.

Answer (D) is correct. *(CPA, adapted)*
REQUIRED: The basis for a shareholder derivative suit.
DISCUSSION: A derivative suit is a cause of action brought by one or more shareholders on behalf of the corporation to enforce a right belonging to the corporation. Shareholders may bring such an action when the board of directors refuses to act on the corporation's behalf. Generally, the shareholder must show (1) (s)he owned stock at the time of the wrongdoing, (2) (s)he made a demand to the corporation to bring suit or take other appropriate action, and (3) a bad faith refusal of the board of directors to pursue the corporation's interest. The recovery, if any, belongs to the corporation. An action to recover damages from corporate management for an ultra vires act is an example of a derivative suit. An ultra vires act is one beyond the limits of the corporate purposes defined in the articles of incorporation.
Answer (A) is incorrect because shareholders must sue directly on their own behalf to compel payment of a properly declared dividend. Answer (B) is incorrect because shareholders must sue directly on their own behalf to enforce a right to inspect corporate records. Answer (C) is incorrect because shareholders must sue directly on their own behalf to compel dissolution of the corporation.

4. All of the following are legal rights of shareholders in U.S. publicly traded companies except the right to

    A. Vote on major mergers and acquisitions.

    B. Receive dividends if declared.

    C. Vote on charter and bylaw changes.

    D. Vote on major management changes.

Answer (D) is correct. *(CMA, adapted)*
    REQUIRED: The item not a basic legal right of shareholders in publicly traded corporations.
    DISCUSSION: A corporation is owned by shareholders who elect a board of directors to manage the company. The board of directors then hires managers to supervise operations. Shareholders do not vote on major management changes because the powers of the board include selection and removal of officers and the setting of management compensation. Shareholders do have the right to vote on fundamental corporate changes, e.g., mergers and acquisitions, any changes in the corporate charter and bylaws, and dissolution.
    Answer (A) is incorrect because shareholders in publicly traded U.S. corporations have the right to vote on fundamental corporate changes. Answer (B) is incorrect because shareholders have the right to receive declared dividends. Answer (C) is incorrect because shareholders have the right to vote on charter and bylaw changes.

5. Shareholder voting

    A. Is required to be cumulative in all states.

    B. May usually be accomplished by oral or written proxy.

    C. May usually be by proxy, but the agency thus created is limited to a specific issue.

    D. May be by proxy, but a proxy not coupled with an interest may be revoked by the shareholder at any time.

Answer (D) is correct. *(Publisher, adapted)*
    REQUIRED: The true statement about shareholder voting.
    DISCUSSION: A proxy is a written authorization to vote another person's shares. Because it is an agency, it may be revoked at any time unless it is coupled with an interest (e.g., if the shares are subject to a voting agreement). The rule that the last proxy signed by a shareholder revokes prior proxies is a significant issue in proxy battles. A proxy is also revoked when the shareholder actually attends the meeting and votes his/her shares or when (s)he becomes incapacitated or dies.
    Answer (A) is incorrect because cumulative voting, which facilitates minority representation, is allowed but not required in most states. For example, if three directors are to be elected and a shareholder has 40 of the 100 outstanding shares, (s)he has 120 votes, which can all be cast for one director. Answer (B) is incorrect because a proxy must usually be written. Answer (C) is incorrect because proxies commonly authorize action regarding all matters presented at the shareholders' meeting.

6. Shareholders representing a majority of the voting shares of Nadier, Inc. have transferred their shares to Thomasina Trusty to hold and vote irrevocably for 10 years. Trusty has issued certificates to the shareholders and pays over to them the dividends received. The agreement

    A. Is an illegal voting trust and is void because it is against public policy.

    B. Is valid if entered into pursuant to a written voting trust agreement.

    C. Need not be filed with the corporation.

    D. May be revoked because it is in essence a proxy.

Answer (B) is correct. *(Publisher, adapted)*
    REQUIRED: The legal status of a voting trust agreement.
    DISCUSSION: The RMBCA provides that an irrevocable voting trust agreement authorizing a trustee to hold and vote shares for a period of up to 10 years (unless extended by a new agreement) is valid if written and filed with the corporation where it will be available for inspection by shareholders.
    Answer (A) is incorrect because the voting trust is a legal arrangement that has a statutory or case law basis in most states. Answer (C) is incorrect because one of the statutory requirements for a valid voting trust is that the agreement be filed with the corporation and be available for inspection. Answer (D) is incorrect because the voting trust differs substantially from a proxy. It is irrevocable for the agreed period.

7. A shareholder of a corporation

    A. Must receive stock certificates because ownership rights are intangible.

    B. Generally has a preemptive right to the extent permitted by the articles.

    C. Has an absolute right to dividends in any year when the corporation is profitable.

    D. Has no right to have his/her name recorded in the corporation's stock record book.

Answer (B) is correct. *(Publisher, adapted)*
REQUIRED: The true statement about the specific rights of a shareholder.
DISCUSSION: A preemptive right is a shareholder's right to purchase a proportionate share of a new stock issue so that his/her percentage interest in the entity can be maintained. Some statutes grant the preemptive right but allow it to be denied in the articles, while other statutes, including the RMBCA, deny the right but allow it to be granted in the articles. The articles are therefore generally determinative.
Answer (A) is incorrect because, under the RMBCA, shareholders have no right to certificates. All or any issued shares may be uncertificated. Answer (C) is incorrect because the directors have broad discretion to withhold declaration of dividends even if ample funds are available. Answer (D) is incorrect because recordation of shareholders' names in the corporate books is the basis for voting rights, notice of meetings, payment of dividends, and distribution of reports.

8. Bassel Hardheart is the majority shareholder and chairman of the board of Close Corporation. Carrie Carter and Gina Kelly are respectively a minority common shareholder and a holder of nonvoting preferred stock. Bassel has diverted corporate assets to personal use. Bassel has also caused the board to declare and pay dividends on common stock without paying preferred dividends. Under these circumstances,

    A. Carter may bring a representative action against Close Corporation based on Hardheart's diversion of assets.

    B. Kelly may bring a representative action against Close Corporation based on Hardheart's diversion of assets.

    C. Carter may bring a derivative action against the corporation for withholding the preferred dividends.

    D. Kelly may bring a representative action against the corporation for withholding the preferred dividends.

Answer (D) is correct. *(Publisher, adapted)*
REQUIRED: The appropriate legal action given certain causes of action.
DISCUSSION: Both representative and derivative suits are shareholder suits in which the plaintiff represents a class of (or all) shareholders. The representative suit (class action) is brought directly against the corporation for a wrong done by the corporation itself. The derivative action is brought on behalf of the corporation for a wrong done to the corporation. The withholding of the preferred dividends would give rise to a right of action by the preferred shareholders against the corporation. Thus, Kelly could bring a representative action as a preferred shareholder.
Answer (A) is incorrect because the diversion of corporate assets by Hardheart would be the basis for a derivative suit by Carter against Hardheart, not against the corporation. Answer (B) is incorrect because the diversion of corporate assets by Hardheart would be the basis for a derivative suit by Kelly against Hardheart, not against the corporation. Answer (C) is incorrect because the suit for withholding the preferred dividend would be a representative suit. It could not be brought by Carter because she is not a preferred shareholder.

9. The term "watered stock" typically refers to

    A. The decline in value of a share of stock following a stock split.

    B. The issuance of stock as fully paid in exchange for overvalued property or services.

    C. The issuance of stock at less than the proportionate book value of the corporation.

    D. The difference between the amount received by the corporation and the amount subscribed.

Answer (B) is correct. *(Publisher, adapted)*
REQUIRED: The statement describing watered stock.
DISCUSSION: When a corporation issues stock as fully paid but full payment has not been made, the stock is said to be "watered." This situation can arise when stock is issued in exchange for property or services that are held out to have value equivalent to the stock but that actually are substantially overvalued.
Answer (A) is incorrect because stock splits have no effect on the capitalization of the corporation. A stock split increases the number of shares without altering the proportionate ownership. Answer (C) is incorrect because the directors may fix the price at which stock will be sold; there is no "water" as long as the price is fully paid. Book value is not relevant to the issue of stock. Answer (D) is incorrect because it describes the unpaid portion of a stock subscription, which is an enforceable debt.

10. Under which of the following circumstances is a shareholder who receives an illegal dividend not obligated to repay the dividend?

   A. The shareholder was not aware the dividend was improper and the corporation was solvent at the time of payment.

   B. The shareholder was not aware the dividend was improper and the corporation insolvent at the time of payment.

   C. The shareholder was aware the dividend was improper and the corporation was solvent at the time of payment.

   D. The shareholder was aware the dividend was improper and the corporation was insolvent at the time of payment.

Answer (A) is correct. *(Publisher, adapted)*
   REQUIRED: The circumstances in which a shareholder who receives an illegal dividend need not repay it.
   DISCUSSION: A dividend paid by an insolvent corporation is always illegal. Moreover, a corporation ordinarily may recover damages from shareholders who receive a dividend or other corporate distribution when the shareholder knows that the distribution is wrong. If the shareholder was not aware the dividend payment was improper, and the corporation was solvent at the time of payment, the shareholder is not liable.
   Answer (B) is incorrect because a dividend paid by an insolvent corporation is always illegal. Answer (C) is incorrect because the shareholder ordinarily is liable if (s)he was aware that the dividend was improper. Answer (D) is incorrect because the shareholder ordinarily is liable if (s)he was aware that the dividend was improper. Moreover, a dividend paid by an insolvent corporation is always illegal.

11. Absent a specific provision in its articles of incorporation, a corporation's board of directors has the power to do all of the following except

   A. Repeal the bylaws.

   B. Declare dividends.

   C. Fix compensation of directors.

   D. Amend the articles of incorporation.

Answer (D) is correct. *(CPA, adapted)*
   REQUIRED: The limit on the board's authority.
   DISCUSSION: Authority to formulate and implement corporate policy is vested in the board, including selection of officers, determining capital structure, proposing fundamental changes, declaring dividends, and setting management compensation. Amending the articles of incorporation, however, is a power reserved for the shareholders.
   Answer (A) is incorrect because the board has authority to add, amend, or repeal bylaws to govern the corporation's internal structure and operation. Answer (B) is incorrect because the board has discretion to formulate and implement dividend policy. Answer (C) is incorrect because director compensation is fixed by the board.

12. Which of the following statements about the directors of a corporation is true?

   A. Under the Revised Model Business Corporation Act, a corporation may dispense with a board of directors in certain circumstances.

   B. Directors may serve only annual terms.

   C. Directors may be elected by the shareholders only.

   D. The number of directors may not exceed the number of shareholders.

Answer (A) is correct. *(Publisher, adapted)*
   REQUIRED: The true statement about corporate directors.
   DISCUSSION: In the absence of a shareholder agreement meeting the requirements of the RMBCA, a corporation must have a board of directors consisting of at least one individual. Some states require a minimum of three directors but permit the number of directors to equal the number of shareholders if less than three. Other states require at least three directors. Given a unanimous agreement, however, the RMBCA permits the shareholders to dispense with directors.
   Answer (B) is incorrect because, under the RMBCA, staggered multi-year terms also are allowed if the corporation has at least nine directors. Answer (C) is incorrect because the remaining directors may fill vacancies resulting from the death, removal, or resignation of directors until the next shareholders' meeting. They also may fill new positions established by amendment of the bylaws or articles. Answer (D) is incorrect because no such requirement exists.

13. A director of a corporation

   A. Must usually be a resident of the state of incorporation.

   B. Is often removable for cause by the other directors.

   C. Must ordinarily be a shareholder.

   D. Must usually be at least 21 years old.

Answer (B) is correct. *(Publisher, adapted)*
   REQUIRED: The true statement about a corporate director.
   DISCUSSION: The RMBCA allows the shareholders to remove a director with or without cause at a meeting called for that purpose. Many states permit the board to remove a director for cause, e.g., insanity or conviction of a felony, subject to shareholder review.
   Answer (A) is incorrect because residency requirements are imposed by statute in only a few states. Answer (C) is incorrect because directors ordinarily need not be shareholders.
   Answer (D) is incorrect because age requirements are imposed by statute in only a few states.

14. Which of the following corporate actions is subject to shareholder approval?

A. Election of officers.

B. Removal of officers.

C. Declaration of cash dividends.

D. Removal of directors.

Answer (D) is correct.   *(CPA, adapted)*
REQUIRED: The action that must be approved by the shareholders.
DISCUSSION: A corporation is governed by shareholders (owners) who elect the directors on the corporation's board and who approve fundamental changes in the corporate structure. Directors establish corporate policies and elect or appoint corporate officers who carry out the policies in the day-to-day management of the organization. In most states, the shareholders may by a majority vote remove, with or without cause, any director or the entire board.
Answer (A) is incorrect because the officers are elected by the directors. Answer (B) is incorrect because officers are removed by the directors. Answer (C) is incorrect because the board of directors has the discretion to determine the nature, time, and amount of dividends and other distributions.

15. Delegation of the powers of the board of directors is generally

A. Prohibited.

B. Allowed with regard to any matter upon which the board may act.

C. Prohibited except when required by an outside agency, for example, a stock exchange that requires members to have audit committees.

D. Allowed except with regard to specified important transactions.

Answer (D) is correct.   *(Publisher, adapted)*
REQUIRED: The true statement about delegation of directors' authority.
DISCUSSION: If the articles or bylaws permit, the directors may, by majority vote of the full board, delegate authority to specified directors constituting an executive or other committee. The committee may exercise all the powers of the board except with regard to significant or extraordinary transactions, such as declaring dividends, issuing stock, or amending bylaws. The committee must consist only of directors.
Answer (A) is incorrect because executive, audit, finance, and other committees are normally allowed. Answer (B) is incorrect because certain powers may not be delegated. Answer (C) is incorrect because committees are not established solely to meet requirements, such as the New York Stock Exchange's rule requiring members to establish audit committees of outside directors.

16. Iago and Des are the sole directors, officers, and shareholders of the ID Corporation, a theatrical group incorporated in Florida. They regularly hold board meetings outside of Florida or by videoconferencing. Recently, without a meeting, Des increased compensation of the directors and declared the regular dividend. Iago later filed in the minutes a signed, written consent to the actions taken. If the articles and bylaws are silent on these matters,

A. Board meetings must be held in the state of incorporation or where the corporation has its principal business and must be conducted in person.

B. The board may declare dividends but may not fix its own compensation.

C. ID is in violation of the Revised Model Business Corporation Act because it has fewer than three directors.

D. Unanimous written consent of all directors may substitute for a meeting.

Answer (D) is correct.   *(Publisher, adapted)*
REQUIRED: The true statement about the formalities required of a close corporation.
DISCUSSION: Traditionally, the board of directors could act only after a formal meeting at which a quorum was present. Under modern statutes, unanimous written consent filed in the minutes is a sufficient basis for action by the board.
Answer (A) is incorrect because board meetings may be conducted anywhere and are not required to be in person; e.g., the meetings may be held by videoconference. Answer (B) is incorrect because the board of directors may routinely declare dividends and may also fix its own compensation unless the articles provide otherwise. Answer (C) is incorrect because the RMBCA provides for a minimum of one director. Furthermore, the shareholders may unanimously agree to dispense with the board.

17. Seymore was recently invited to become a director of Buckley Industries, Inc. If Seymore accepts and becomes a director, he, along with the other directors, will not be personally liable for

   A. Lack of reasonable care.

   B. Honest errors of judgment.

   C. Declaration of a dividend that the directors know will impair legal capital.

   D. Diversion of corporate opportunities to themselves.

Answer (B) is correct. *(CPA, adapted)*
   REQUIRED: The situation in which a director will not be held personally liable.
   DISCUSSION: The directors of a corporation owe a fiduciary duty to the corporation and the shareholders. They also are expected to exercise reasonable business judgment. The law does recognize human fallibility and allows for directors to be safe from liability for honest mistakes of judgment.
   Answer (A) is incorrect because directors must discharge their duties with the care that a person in a similar position would reasonably believe appropriate under similar circumstances. Answer (C) is incorrect because directors are prohibited from declaring dividends that would violate a state statute establishing a minimum legal capital. Answer (D) is incorrect because a director may not exploit opportunities presented to him/her in his/her capacity as a director for his/her own benefit without first offering them to the corporation.

18. Laser, a privately held corporation, lent $5,000 to Mr. Jackson, a member of its board of directors. Mr. Jackson was also vice-president of operations. The board of directors, but not the shareholders, of Laser authorized the loan on the basis that the loan would benefit the corporation. The loan made to Mr. Jackson is

   A. Improper because Mr. Jackson is both a director and an employee.

   B. Improper because Mr. Jackson is an employee.

   C. Improper because Mr. Jackson is a director.

   D. Proper.

Answer (D) is correct. *(CIA, adapted)*
   REQUIRED: The propriety of a loan made by a corporation to a director-officer.
   DISCUSSION: Approval of a loan to a fellow director is not a per se violation of the director's fiduciary obligation to the corporation. Subject to that obligation and the duty to act with reasonable care, the directors may approve a loan that, in their judgment, would benefit the corporation. It would be inappropriate for Jackson to vote on the loan resolution, but his vote would not necessarily make it voidable. The shareholders need not authorize the loan. A conflicting interest transaction will not result in sanctions (e.g., damages), be enjoined, or be set aside if (1) it is fair to the corporation, or (2) it is approved after required disclosure by a majority of informed, qualified directors or of shares voted by holders of qualified shares. Qualified directors do not have a conflict of interest. Qualified shares are not controlled by a person with a conflict. (NOTE: The Sarbanes-Oxley Act of 2002 generally prohibits personal loans to executives or directors of public companies.)

19. A corporate director commits a breach of duty if

   A. The director's exercise of care and skill is minimal.

   B. A contract is awarded by the company to an organization owned by the director.

   C. An interest in property is acquired by the director without prior approval of the board.

   D. The director's action, prompted by confidential information, results in an abuse of corporate opportunity.

Answer (D) is correct. *(CIA, adapted)*
   REQUIRED: The breach of a corporate director's duty.
   DISCUSSION: Corporate directors have a fiduciary duty to provide the corporation with business opportunities that come to them in their positions as directors of the corporation. A director who personally takes such a business opportunity has breached his/her duty.
   Answer (A) is incorrect because a director is under a duty to use good business judgment, but (s)he is not responsible for the highest standard of care and skill. Moreover, a director may reasonably rely on information from competent officers, employees, and experts. Answer (B) is incorrect because a director is not prohibited from entering into a conflicting interest transaction if it is (1) fair to the corporation or (2) approved after required disclosure by a majority of disinterested directors or of shares voted by disinterested parties. Answer (C) is incorrect because a director is under no duty to report personal property investments unless they relate to corporate business.

20. Davis, a director of Active Corp., is entitled to

A. Serve on the board of a competing business.

B. Take sole advantage of a business opportunity that would benefit Active.

C. Rely on information provided by a corporate officer.

D. Unilaterally grant a corporate loan to one of Active's shareholders.

Answer (C) is correct. *(CPA, adapted)*
   REQUIRED: The action not a breach of a director's duties.
   DISCUSSION: A director is a fiduciary of the corporation and its shareholders. (S)he has duties of care and loyalty. Thus, a director must perform, without conflict or usurping an opportunity in which the corporation has an interest, with the care an ordinarily prudent person in a similar position would exercise under similar circumstances. But, in exercising good business judgment or reasonable care, a director is entitled to rely on information provided by an officer (or professional specialist) if the director reasonably believes the officer has competence in the relevant area.
   Answer (A) is incorrect because serving as a director of a competing business is a conflict of interest. Answer (B) is incorrect because usurping a business opportunity of the corporation is a breach of the director's fiduciary duty of loyalty. Answer (D) is incorrect because a director is not an agent of the corporation, and directors authorize corporate transactions by approving resolutions as a board.

21. Knox, president of Quick Corp., contracted with Tine Office Supplies, Inc. to supply Quick's stationery on customary terms and at a cost less than that charged by any other supplier. Knox later informed Quick's board of directors that Knox was a majority shareholder in Tine. Quick's contract with Tine is

A. Void because of Knox's self-dealing.

B. Void because the disclosure was made after execution of the contract.

C. Valid because of Knox's full disclosure.

D. Valid because the contract is fair to Quick.

Answer (D) is correct. *(CPA, adapted)*
   REQUIRED: The enforceability of a contract entered into by a corporate officer with an interest in the contract.
   DISCUSSION: An officer, like a director, owes fiduciary duties of care and loyalty to the corporation and its shareholders. Knox was required to disclose fully the financial interest in the transaction to which the corporation was a party. But a transaction approved by a majority of informed, disinterested directors or shareholders or that is fair to the corporation is valid, notwithstanding a conflict of interest.
   Answer (A) is incorrect because self-dealing does not render a transaction voidable if it is fair to the corporation. Answer (B) is incorrect because nondisclosure does not render a transaction voidable if it is fair to the corporation. Answer (C) is incorrect because full disclosure merely forms a basis for approval by a majority of informed, disinterested directors or shareholders.

22. Smith was an officer of CCC Corp. As an officer, the business judgment rule applied to Smith in which of the following ways?

A. Because Smith is not a director, the rule does not apply.

B. If Smith makes, in good faith, a serious but honest mistake in judgment, Smith is generally not liable to CCC for damages caused.

C. If Smith makes, in good faith, a serious but honest mistake in judgment, Smith is generally liable to CCC for damages caused, but CCC may elect to reimburse Smith for any damages Smith paid.

D. If Smith makes, in good faith, a serious but honest mistake in judgment, Smith is generally liable to CCC for damages caused, and CCC is prohibited from reimbursing Smith for any damages Smith paid.

Answer (B) is correct. *(CPA, adapted)*
   REQUIRED: The application of the business judgment rule to a corporate officer.
   DISCUSSION: Officers, like directors, owe fiduciary duties to the corporation. As an agent, an officer has a duty to act within authority granted by the articles, the bylaws, and the board. Officers are subject to the same duties of care and loyalty to the corporation as are directors. Likewise, absent bad faith, fraud, or breach of a fiduciary duty, the business judgment rule applies to officers. Like a director, the officer is insulated by the business judgment rule if the management decision is informed, conflict-free, and rational. Officers may be indemnified to the extent, consistent with public policy, provided by the articles of incorporation, bylaws, actions of the board, or contract.
   Answer (A) is incorrect because the rule applies to officers. Answer (C) is incorrect because the rule generally protects an officer from liability. Moreover, reimbursement is permissible. Answer (D) is incorrect because the rule generally protects an officer from liability. Moreover, reimbursement is permissible.

23. Under the Revised Model Business Corporation Act, which of the following statements is true regarding corporate officers of a public corporation?

    A. An officer may not simultaneously serve as a director.

    B. A corporation may be authorized to indemnify its officers for liability incurred in a suit by shareholders.

    C. Shareholders always have the right to elect a corporation's officers.

    D. An officer of a corporation is required to own at least one share of the corporation's stock.

24. Food Corp. owned a restaurant called The Ambers. The corporation's president, T.J. Jones, hired a contractor to make repairs at the restaurant, signing the contract, "T.J. Jones for The Ambers." Two invoices for restaurant repairs were paid by Food Corp. with corporate checks. Upon presenting the final invoice, the contractor was told that it would not be paid. The contractor sued Food Corp. Which of the following statements is correct regarding the liability of Food Corp.?

    A. It is not liable because Jones is liable.

    B. It is not liable because the corporation was an undisclosed principal.

    C. It is liable because Jones is not liable.

    D. It is liable because Jones had authority to make the contract.

25. Jeri Fairwell is executive vice-president and treasurer of Wonder Corporation. She was named as a party in a shareholder derivative action in connection with certain activities she engaged in as a corporate officer. In the lawsuit, she was held liable for negligence in performance of her duties. Fairwell seeks indemnity from the corporation. The board of directors would like to indemnify her, but the articles of incorporation do not contain any provisions regarding indemnification of officers and directors. Indemnification

    A. Is not permitted because the articles of incorporation do not so provide.

    B. Is permitted only if Fairwell is found not to have been grossly negligent.

    C. Cannot include attorney's fees because Fairwell was found to have been negligent.

    D. May be permitted by court order although Fairwell was found to be negligent.

Answer (B) is correct. *(CPA, adapted)*
REQUIRED: The true statement regarding corporate officers of a public corporation.
DISCUSSION: According to the RMBCA, corporations may indemnify their officers for liability incurred in a suit by shareholders, except when inconsistent with public policy, to the extent provided by the articles of incorporation, bylaws, actions of the board, or contract.
Answer (A) is incorrect because an individual may serve as both a director and an officer. Answer (C) is incorrect because a corporation's officers are appointed by the board of directors, not by shareholders. Answer (D) is incorrect because an officer of a corporation need not be a shareholder.

Answer (D) is correct. *(CPA, adapted)*
REQUIRED: The liability of a corporation to a contractor hired by its president.
DISCUSSION: The officers are agents of the corporation. They have express authority conferred by the bylaws or the board. They have implied authority to do things that are reasonably necessary to accomplish their express duties. Courts have held that official titles confer limited inherent authority on officers. The president supervises and controls all the business and affairs of the corporation, subject to the discretion of the board. Traditionally, the president had no inherent authority. But the trend is that (s)he can bind the corporation in the ordinary course of its business. Thus, Food Corp. cannot escape liability on the grounds that Jones had no authority.
Answer (A) is incorrect because the business judgment rule protects directors and officers from personal liability if they (1) act in good faith; (2) are not motivated by fraud, conflict of interest, or illegality; and (3) are not grossly negligent. The facts suggest no reason for the rule not to apply to Jones. Answer (B) is incorrect because the corporation was disclosed (i.e., the signature on the contract and the use of corporate checks). Answer (C) is incorrect because Food Corp.'s liability is not contingent upon the nonliability of Jones. An agent with actual or apparent authority may bind the principal without becoming liable.

Answer (D) is correct. *(CPA, adapted)*
REQUIRED: The true statement about indemnification of a negligent officer of a corporation.
DISCUSSION: Usually, an officer or director who is liable to the corporation because of negligence in the performance of his/her duties is not entitled to indemnification. However, a court may order indemnification of an officer or director of a corporation (even though found negligent) if the court determines (s)he is fairly and reasonably entitled to it in view of all the relevant circumstances.
Answer (A) is incorrect because indemnification is permitted unless the articles expressly prohibit it. Answer (B) is incorrect because a court may order indemnification if it determines that the officer is reasonably entitled to it in view of all the relevant circumstances, even if the officer was negligent. Answer (C) is incorrect because an officer who is entitled to indemnification may receive attorney's fees.

26. Which of the following actions is required to ensure the validity of a contract between a corporation and a director of the corporation?

    A. An independent appraiser must render to the board of directors a fairness opinion on the contract.

    B. The director must disclose the interest to the independent members of the board and refrain from voting.

    C. The shareholders must review and ratify the contact.

    D. The director must resign from the board of directors.

Answer (B) is correct.   *(CPA, adapted)*
    REQUIRED: The action to ensure the validity of a contract between a corporation and a director.
    DISCUSSION: To protect the corporation against self-dealing, a director is required to make full disclosure of any financial interest (s)he may have in any transaction to which both the director and the corporation may be a party. Under the RMBCA, a transaction is not voidable merely on the grounds of a director's conflict of interest if the transaction is fair to the corporation or has been approved by a majority of (1) informed, disinterested qualified directors or (2) holders of qualified shares. This rule applies even if the director was counted for the quorum and voted to approve the transaction. A qualified director does not have (1) a conflict of interest regarding the transaction or (2) a special relationship (familial, professional, financial, etc.) with another director who has a conflict of interest. Shares are qualified if they are not controlled by a person with (1) a conflict of interest or (2) a close relationship with someone who has a conflict. Thus, the director who contracts with the corporation cannot provide the vote that approves the contract.
    Answer (A) is incorrect because the RMBCA states no such requirement. However, shareholders who disagree with fundamental corporate changes have appraisal rights to receive the fair value of their shares. Answer (C) is incorrect because shareholder ratification is unnecessary. However, if the transaction is fair, approval by shareholders prevents it from being voided. Furthermore, unanimous shareholder approval may release the director from liability even if the transaction is unfair. Answer (D) is incorrect because resignation is not required. Self-dealing transactions are permissible in many cases.

27. Which of the following statements is true regarding the fiduciary duty?

    A. A director's fiduciary duty to the corporation may be discharged by merely disclosing his/her self-interest.

    B. A director owes a fiduciary duty to the shareholders but not to the corporation.

    C. A promoter of a corporation to be formed owes no fiduciary duty to anyone, unless the contract engaging the promoter so provides.

    D. A majority shareholder as such may owe a fiduciary duty to fellow shareholders.

Answer (D) is correct.   *(CPA, adapted)*
    REQUIRED: The fiduciary duty of directors, promoters, and shareholders.
    DISCUSSION: Directors and officers owe a fiduciary duty to the corporation to act in its best interests, to be loyal, to use due diligence in carrying out their responsibilities, and to disclose conflicts of interest. Controlling as well as majority shareholders owe similar duties. For example, courts will often protect the interests of minority shareholders by ordering the payment of dividends that were withheld in bad faith or by compelling a seller of a controlling block of shares to distribute ratably among all shareholders any "control premium" paid in excess of the fair value of the stock.
    Answer (A) is incorrect because the fiduciary duty is far more extensive. Answer (B) is incorrect because the duty is owed to the corporation, not the shareholders. Answer (C) is incorrect because a promoter owes a fiduciary duty of fair dealing, good faith, and full disclosure to subscribers, shareholders, and the corporation.

28. Shareholder action on fundamental changes in a large publicly held corporation generally requires that a meeting be convened. Under the RMBCA and unless the articles or bylaws stipulate otherwise,

    A. Holders of not less than 10% of the voting shares may call a special meeting.

    B. Action on extraordinary transactions may only be taken at the annual meeting.

    C. Notice of a special but not an annual meeting must include an agenda if extraordinary transactions are to be approved.

    D. Action on extraordinary transactions taken at special but not annual meetings is void absent notice, waiver of notice, or attendance without objection.

Answer (A) is correct.   *(Publisher, adapted)*
    REQUIRED: The true statement about shareholder meetings.
    DISCUSSION: When shareholder action is required concerning a fundamental corporate change, a meeting must be held. If the issue must be resolved before the annual meeting, a special meeting may be called by the board, by a person authorized by the bylaws (e.g., the president), or by holders of not less than 10% of the shares entitled to be voted at the meeting.
    Answer (B) is incorrect because action may also be taken at special meetings. Answer (C) is incorrect because notice must be given prior to any meeting or the action taken is void. Answer (D) is incorrect because, if extraordinary changes are to be voted on, the purposes must be stated in the notice, including that for an annual meeting.

4.2 Fundamental Corporate Changes

29. Fundamental corporate changes require shareholder approval. Under the RMBCA, which of the following is false?

A. Notice must be given to shareholders whether or not entitled to vote.

B. The articles may require a supermajority vote.

C. The board of directors usually gives prior approval to the change.

D. At least a majority of each class must approve, even though the rights of a class may not be affected.

Answer (D) is correct. *(Publisher, adapted)*
   REQUIRED: The false statement about procedures for making fundamental changes.
   DISCUSSION: Under the RMBCA, the first step is approval of the change by the board. All shareholders must then be notified, including those without voting rights regarding the matter. A majority vote of the shareholders taken at an annual or special meeting is sufficient to pass the proposal unless the articles require a greater percentage. Voting by class is required by the RMBCA for share exchanges and mergers if the interests of a class are significantly affected. The articles may provide that class voting is required on other transactions.
   Answer (A) is incorrect because all shareholders must be notified. Answer (B) is incorrect because a greater-than-majority vote may be required by the articles. Answer (C) is incorrect because approval by the directors is the initial step.

30. Which of the following statements is a general requirement for the merger of two corporations?

A. The merger plan must be approved unanimously by the shareholders of both corporations.

B. The merger plan must be approved unanimously by the boards of both corporations.

C. The absorbed corporation must amend its articles of incorporation.

D. The shareholders of both corporations must be given due notice of a special meeting, including a copy or summary of the merger plan.

Answer (D) is correct. *(CPA, adapted)*
   REQUIRED: The prerequisite to a merger.
   DISCUSSION: A corporation is merged into another when shareholders of the target corporation receive cash or shares of the surviving corporation in exchange for their shares. The target shares are canceled, and the target corporation ceases to exist. State law usually requires approval by a majority of the board and a majority of the shareholders of each corporation. A special shareholder meeting notice (stating the purpose) and a copy of the merger plan must be provided to shareholders of each corporation to permit informed voting.
   Answer (A) is incorrect because, unless state statute or the charter imposes a supermajority requirement, majority approval by shareholders is usually required. Answer (B) is incorrect because, usually, only majority approval by the boards of both corporations is required. Answer (C) is incorrect because the absorbed corporation ceases to exist.

31. Which of the following actions may be taken by a corporation's board of directors without shareholder approval?

A. Purchasing substantially all of the assets of another corporation.

B. Selling substantially all of the corporation's assets.

C. Dissolving the corporation.

D. Amending the articles of incorporation.

Answer (A) is correct. *(CPA, adapted)*
   REQUIRED: The action by a corporation's board of directors not requiring shareholder approval.
   DISCUSSION: The board of directors directly controls a corporation by establishing overall corporate policy and overseeing its implementation. In exercising their powers, board members must maintain high standards of care and loyalty but need not obtain shareholder approval except for fundamental corporate changes. Purchasing substantially all of the assets (or stock) of another corporation is a policy decision properly made by the board of directors, not a fundamental change. It does not require shareholder approval in the absence of a bylaw or special provision in the articles of incorporation.
   Answer (B) is incorrect because selling substantially all of the corporation's assets is considered a fundamental change and therefore must be voted on and approved by the shareholders. Fundamental changes are usually initiated by resolution of the board of directors urging the shareholders to approve the change. Answer (C) is incorrect because dissolving the corporation is considered a fundamental change and therefore must be voted on and approved by the shareholders. Fundamental changes are usually initiated by resolution of the board of directors urging the shareholders to approve the change. Answer (D) is incorrect because amending the articles of incorporation is considered a fundamental change and therefore must be voted on and approved by the shareholders. Fundamental changes are usually initiated by resolution of the board of directors urging the shareholders to approve the change.

32. Under the Revised Model Business Corporation Act, a merger of two public corporations usually requires all of the following except

A. A formal plan of merger.

B. An affirmative vote by the holders of a majority of each corporation's voting shares.

C. Receipt of voting stock by all shareholders of the original corporations.

D. Approval by the board of directors of each corporation.

Answer (C) is correct. *(CPA, adapted)*
REQUIRED: The item not required for a merger of two public corporations.
DISCUSSION: A corporation is merged into another when shareholders of the target corporation receive cash or shares of the surviving corporation in exchange for their shares. State law usually requires approval of the board and a majority of shareholders of each corporation, and a copy of the merger plan must be provided to the shareholders of each corporation prior to voting.

33. Which of the following statements, if any, is(are) true regarding the methods a target corporation may use to ward off a takeover attempt?

I. The target corporation may make an offer ("self-tender") to acquire stock from its own shareholders.

II. The target corporation may seek an injunction against the acquiring corporation on the grounds that the attempted takeover violates federal antitrust law.

A. I only.

B. II only.

C. Both I and II.

D. Neither I nor II.

Answer (C) is correct. *(CPA, adapted)*
REQUIRED: The true statement regarding methods a corporation may use to ward off a takeover attempt.
DISCUSSION: Managers of target corporations have implemented diverse strategies to counter hostile tender offers. Examples of antitakeover strategies include self-tender and legal action, as well as persuasion, creation of poison pills, reverse tenders, crown-jewel transfers, and white knight mergers.

34. Under the Revised Model Business Corporation Act (RMBCA), which of the following actions by a corporation would entitle a shareholder to dissent from the action and obtain payment of the fair value of his/her shares?

I. An amendment to the articles of incorporation that materially and adversely affects rights in respect of a dissenter's shares because it alters or abolishes a preferential right of the shares

II. Consummation of a plan of share exchange to which the corporation is a party as the corporation whose shares will be acquired, if the shareholder is entitled to vote on the plan

A. I only.

B. II only.

C. Both I and II.

D. Neither I nor II.

Answer (C) is correct. *(CPA, adapted)*
REQUIRED: The corporate action(s), if any, permitting a shareholder to exercise the appraisal right.
DISCUSSION: Shareholders who disagree with fundamental corporate changes may have dissenters' or appraisal rights. The corporation must pay dissenting shareholders the fair value of their stock in cash. Under the RMBCA, an existing dissenters' right may be invoked only when a shareholder has a right to vote on a fundamental change, does not vote in favor, and gives written notice of a demand for payment. Fundamental changes include an amendment to the articles that materially and adversely affects rights in respect of a dissenter's shares because it alters or abolishes a preferential right. These rights may also derive from a merger required to be voted on by the shareholders, the merger of the corporation into its parent, the sale or exchange of substantially all of the property of the corporation in a transaction not in the ordinary course of business, and consummation of a plan of share exchange to which the corporation is a party as the corporation whose shares will be acquired.

35. Acorn Corp. wants to acquire the entire business of Trend Corp. Which of the following methods of business combination will best satisfy Acorn's objectives without requiring the approval of the shareholders of either corporation?

    A. A merger of Trend into Acorn, whereby Trend shareholders receive cash or Acorn shares.

    B. A sale of all the assets of Trend, outside the regular course of business, to Acorn, for cash.

    C. An acquisition of all the shares of Trend through a compulsory share exchange for Acorn shares.

    D. A cash tender offer, whereby Acorn acquires at least 90% of Trend's shares, followed by a short-form merger of Trend into Acorn.

Answer (D) is correct. *(CPA, adapted)*
    REQUIRED: The acquisition method that does not require shareholder approval.
    DISCUSSION: A merger, consolidation, or purchase of substantially all of a corporation's assets requires approval of the board of directors of the corporation whose shares or assets are acquired. An acquiring corporation may bypass board approval by extending a cash tender offer directly to shareholders to purchase a certain number of the outstanding shares. After obtaining control of the target corporation, the tender offeror may effect a merger or consolidation.
    Answer (A) is incorrect because a merger requires the approval of shareholders. Answer (B) is incorrect because a sale of all assets requires the approval of shareholders. Answer (C) is incorrect because a compulsory share exchange requires the approval of shareholders.

36. Under the Revised Model Business Corporation Act (RMBCA), which of the following conditions is necessary for a corporation to achieve a successful voluntary dissolution?

    A. Successful application to the secretary of state in which the corporation holds its primary place of business.

    B. A recommendation of dissolution by the board of directors and approval by a majority of all shareholders entitled to vote.

    C. Approval by the board of directors of an amendment to the certificate of incorporation calling for the dissolution of the corporation.

    D. Unanimous approval of the board of directors and two-thirds vote of all shareholders entitled to vote on a resolution of voluntary dissolution.

Answer (B) is correct. *(CPA, adapted)*
    REQUIRED: The conditions necessary for a corporation to achieve a successful voluntary dissolution.
    DISCUSSION: The RMBCA permits voluntary dissolution of a corporation that has not commenced business or issued stock by a majority vote of its incorporators or directors. A corporation that has issued stock and commenced business may be voluntarily dissolved by a shareholder vote at a special meeting called for the purpose if the directors have adopted a resolution of dissolution. Unless the board or the articles of incorporation require otherwise, a majority of the votes entitled to be cast must be represented at the meeting. The dissolution is effective when filed with the secretary of state.
    Answer (A) is incorrect because the secretary of state will not process the application unless it is approved by a majority of shareholders entitled to vote. Answer (C) is incorrect because only the shareholders can amend the articles of incorporation. Answer (D) is incorrect because, under the RMBCA, shareholders must approve dissolution at a meeting at which only a majority of the shareholders entitled to vote must be represented, assuming the directors (as a condition to submitting the proposal) or the articles do not require otherwise.

37. Under the Revised Model Business Corporation Act (RMBCA), following what type of corporate acquisition does the acquiring corporation automatically become liable for all obligations of the acquired corporation?

    A. A leveraged buyout of assets.

    B. An acquisition of stock for debt securities.

    C. A cash tender offer.

    D. A merger.

Answer (D) is correct. *(CPA, adapted)*
    REQUIRED: The type of corporate acquisition in which the acquirer automatically becomes liable for all obligations of the acquired corporation.
    DISCUSSION: Under the RMBCA, when a merger becomes effective, (1) the entity designated in the plan of merger as the survivor comes into existence, (2) every entity merged ceases to exist separately, (3) the property and contract rights of the merged entities are vested in the survivor, and (4) the liabilities of the merged entities also are vested in the survivor.
    Answer (A) is incorrect because a debt-financed purchase of assets or stock does not inherently impose liability on the acquirer for the other entity's obligations. The assets essentially are security for the debt incurred in the purchase. However, the acquirer might subsequently merge with the acquiree, in which case it would become liable. Answer (B) is incorrect because a debt-financed purchase of assets or stock does not inherently impose liability on the acquirer for the other entity's obligations. The assets essentially are security for the debt incurred in the purchase. However, the acquirer might subsequently merge with the acquiree, in which case it would become liable. Answer (C) is incorrect because acquiring another entity's shares pursuant to a cash tender offer does not automatically vest the liabilities of the acquiree in the acquirer. However, the offer might include an undertaking to assume those liabilities.

Use Gleim's *CPA Test Prep* for interactive testing with over 2,000 additional multiple-choice questions!

STUDY UNIT FIVE
MICROECONOMICS

(21 pages of outline)

This study unit is the first of three study units ("Microeconomics," "Macroeconomics," and "International Trade") related to the economic environment of a business and its industry. It begins with an outline of the microeconomic concepts of supply and demand.

5.1 DEMAND, SUPPLY, AND EQUILIBRIUM

1.   **Demand -- the Buyer's Side of the Market**

   a.   **Demand** is a **schedule** of the amounts of a good or service that consumers are willing and able to purchase at various prices during a period of time.

      1)   **Quantity demanded** is the amount that will be purchased at a **specific price** during a period of time.

Demand Schedule

Price per Unit	Quantity Demanded
$10	0
$9	1
$8	2
$7	3
$6	4
$5	5
$4	6
$3	7
$2	8
$1	9
$0	10

   b.   A demand schedule can be **graphically depicted** as a relationship between the prices of a commodity (on the vertical axis) and the quantity demanded at the various prices (horizontal axis), holding other determinants of demand constant.

      1)   **The law of demand.** If all other factors are held constant (*ceteris paribus*), the price of a product and the quantity demanded are inversely (negatively) related; i.e., the higher the price, the lower the quantity demanded.

Law of Demand

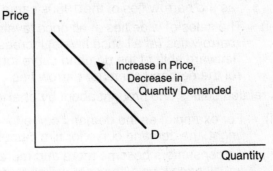

   a)   As the price of a good falls, consumers have more **buying power** (also called higher real income). They can buy more of the good with the same amount of money. This is termed the **income effect**.

b) As the price of one good falls, it becomes cheaper **relative to other goods**. Consumers will thus have a tendency to spend money on the cheaper good in preference to the more expensive one. This is termed the **substitution effect**.

2) A change in **price** results in a change in **quantity demanded**, i.e., movement along a demand curve (depicted in the graph on the previous page). A change in one of the **determinants of demand** results in a change in **demand**, i.e., a shift of the curve itself.

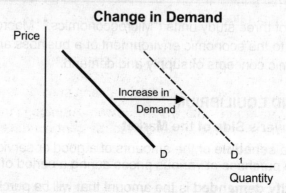

Change in Demand

c. The **determinants of demand** are <u>any factors</u> **other than price** that affect the amount of a commodity that consumers purchase.

1) Consumer incomes

a) Most goods are **normal goods**, that is, commodities for which demand is positively (directly) related to income, e.g., steak, new clothes, and airline travel.

i) As consumer incomes rise, the demand curves for normal goods shift to the right. People with more disposable income are willing to purchase more of these goods at all price levels.

b) However, a few goods are **inferior goods**, that is, commodities for which demand is negatively (inversely) related to income, e.g., potatoes, used clothing, and bus transportation.

i) As consumer incomes fall, the demand curves for inferior goods shift to the right. People whose disposable income is decreasing are willing to purchase more of these goods at all price levels.

2) Consumer taste and preference

a) When consumers' **interest in a particular product** changes, the change is reflected in a shift of the demand curve.

i) For example, the wide neckties of the 1970s fell out of favor with men as the narrow ties of the 1980s came into fashion.

ii) The sales of wide ties at all price levels fell off and the sales of narrow ties (at all price levels) increased. This was depicted as a leftward shift of the demand curve for wide ties and a rightward shift of the demand curve for narrow ties.

b) A related shift is one brought about by **changing technology**.

i) For example, as the demand curve for digital cameras shifts to the right, the demand curve for film cameras shifts to the left.

ii) As consumers become more and more enamored of digital cameras at all price levels, they are willing to buy ever fewer film cameras (no matter how low the price).

3) Prices of related goods

    a) If a **price increase** in A results in an **increase in demand** for B, A and B are said to be **substitutes**. For example, when beef prices rise, the demand for chicken increases.

    b) If a **price increase** in A results in a **decrease in demand** for B, A and B are said to be **complements**. For example, if the price of bread increases, the demand for jelly decreases.

    c) This phenomenon is referred to as cross-elasticity of demand, described under item 1.b. in Subunit 2.

4) Consumer expectations

    a) Consumers **anticipating a price increase** for a given product in the near future will buy more of that product in the hopes of avoiding the higher price, driving the current demand curve to the right.

    b) Consumers **anticipating lower incomes** in the near future will forgo planned purchases, driving the current demand curve for those products to the left.

5) Consumer demographics

    a) **Changes in population size** are reflected in demand shifts. For example, a larger population will demand more of everything at every price level, reflected in a rightward movement of demand curves.

    b) In addition, **changes within a population** bring about changes in demand. For example, as the number of older citizens increases, the demand curve for elder-care services shifts to the right and the demand curve for baby products shifts to the left.

2. **Supply -- the Seller's Side of the Market**

    a. **Supply** is a **schedule** of the amounts of a good that producers are willing and able to offer to the market at various prices during a specified period of time.

        1) **Quantity supplied** is the amount that will be offered at a **specific price** during a period of time.

    b. A supply schedule can be **graphically depicted** as a relationship between the prices of a commodity (on the vertical axis) and the quantity offered at the various prices (horizontal axis), holding other determinants of supply constant.

        1) **The law of supply.** If all other factors are held constant (*ceteris paribus*), the price of a product and the quantity supplied are directly (positively) related; i.e., the higher the price, the greater the quantity supplied.

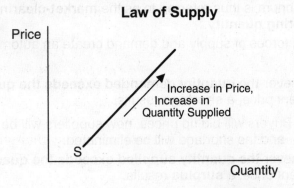

Law of Supply

        2) A change in **price** results in a change in **quantity supplied**, i.e., movement along a supply curve (depicted in the graph above). A change in **one of the determinants of supply** results in a change in **supply**, i.e., a shift of the curve itself.

Change in Supply

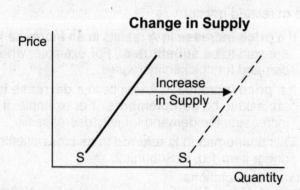

c.   The **determinants of supply** are any factors **other than price** that affect the amount of a commodity that producers offer.

1)   Costs of inputs
2)   Change in efficiency of the production process, e.g., newer technology
3)   Expectations about price changes
4)   Passage of time
5)   Taxes and subsidies

3.   **Market demand** is the sum of the individual demand curves of all buyers in the market. **Market supply** is the sum of the individual supply curves of all sellers in the market.

a.   **Market equilibrium** is the combination of price and quantity at which the market demand and market supply curves intersect.

Market Equilibrium

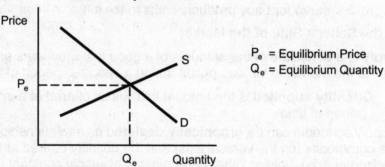

P_e = Equilibrium Price
Q_e = Equilibrium Quantity

b.   At the point of intersection of the supply and demand curves, anyone wishing to purchase economic goods at the **market price** can do so, and anyone offering the goods can sell everything they bring to market.

1)   Equilibrium is thus referred to as the **market-clearing price** and the **market-clearing quantity**.

c.   The market forces of supply and demand create an automatic, efficient **rationing system**.

1)   Whenever **the quantity demanded exceeds the quantity supplied** at the current price, a **shortage** results.

a)   Buyers will bid up prices, new suppliers will be induced to enter the market, and the shortage will be eliminated.

2)   Whenever **the quantity supplied exceeds the quantity demanded** at the current price, a **surplus** results.

a)   Sellers will cut prices, suppliers will exit the market, and the surplus will be eliminated.

d. **The effects on equilibrium of shifts** in the supply and demand schedules:

	Demand increase	Demand constant	Demand decrease
Supply increase	P_e unknown Q_e up	P_e down Q_e up	P_e up Q_e unknown
Supply constant	P_e up Q_e up	– –	P_e down Q_e down
Supply decrease	P_e up Q_e unknown	P_e up Q_e down	P_e unknown Q_e up

4. Explicit vs. Implicit Costs

  a. **Explicit costs** are those requiring actual cash disbursements. For this reason, they are sometimes called out-of-pocket or outlay costs.

  1) **Explicit costs are accounting costs**; that is, they are recognized in a concern's formal accounting records.

  2) For example, an entrepreneur opening a gift shop has to make certain cash disbursements to get the business up and running.

Inventory	$50,000
Display cases	9,000
Rent	4,000
Utilities	1,000
Total explicit costs	**$64,000**

  b. **Implicit costs** are those costs not recognized in a concern's formal accounting records.

  1) **Implicit costs are opportunity costs**, i.e., the maximum benefit forgone by using a scarce resource for a given purpose and not for the next-best alternative.

  2) To measure the true economic success or failure of the venture, the entrepreneur in the above example must tally up more than just the explicit costs that can easily be found in the accounting records.

  a) The entrepreneur's opportunity costs are the most important implicit costs. (S)he could have simply gone to work for another company rather than open the gift shop.

  b) The money put into startup costs could have been invested in financial instruments.

  c) A **normal profit** is a **crucial implicit cost**. In this example, the normal profit is the income that the entrepreneur could have earned applying his/her skill to another venture.

Salary forgone	$35,000
Investment income forgone	3,600
Entrepreneurial income forgone	10,000
Total implicit costs	**$48,600**

  c. **Economic costs are total costs.**

  1) The true hurdle for an economic decision is whether the revenues from the venture will cover all costs, both explicit and implicit.

Economic costs = Total costs
= Explicit costs + Implicit costs
= $64,000 + $48,600
= **$112,600**

5.   Accounting vs. Economic Profit

    a.   **Accounting profits** are earned when the (book) income of an organization exceeds the (book) expenses.

        1)   After the first year of operation, the gift shop owner made a tidy accounting profit.

Sales revenue	$100,000
Explicit costs	(64,000)
Accounting profit	**$ 36,000**

    b.   **Economic profits** are a significantly higher hurdle. They are not earned until the organization's income exceeds not only costs as recorded in the accounting records but the firm's implicit costs as well. Economic profit is also called **pure profit**.

        1)   Once total costs are taken into account, a different picture emerges.

Accounting profit	$ 36,000
Implicit costs	(48,600)
Economic loss	**$(12,600)**

6.   Stop and review! You have completed the outline for this subunit. Study multiple-choice questions 1 through 12 beginning on page 136.

5.2 ELASTICITY

1.   **Elasticity of Demand**

    a.   **Price elasticity of demand** (E_d) measures the sensitivity of the quantity demanded of a product to a change in its price.

$$E_d = \frac{Percentage\ change\ in\ quantity\ demanded}{Percentage\ change\ in\ price}$$

        1)   Elasticity describes the reaction to a change in price **from one level to another**. Thus, the most accurate way of calculating elasticity is the **arc method**, which measures elasticity across a **range**.

$$E_d = \frac{\%\ \Delta\ Q}{\%\ \Delta\ P} = \frac{(Q_1 - Q_2) \div [(Q_1 + Q_2) \div 2]}{(P_1 - P_2) \div [(P_1 + P_2) \div 2]}$$

           a)   Both numerator and denominator percentages can be calculated as "the change over the midpoint."

        2)   For a demand schedule obeying the **law of demand** (downward sloping), the elasticity coefficient (E) is **negative**. However, when interpreting E_d, the **absolute value** is ordinarily used.

Price Elasticity of Demand

Quantity Demanded	Delta Q	(Q1+Q2) /2	Numerator Delta Q over Midpoint	Price	Delta P	(P1+P2) /2	Denominator Delta P over Midpoint	Equals Price Elasticity	Range Price Decreasing	Price Increasing
0	–	–	–	$10	–	–	–	–	–	–
1	1	0.5	200.00%	$9	$1	$9.50	10.53%	19.000	$10 to $9	$10 to $11
2	1	1.5	66.67%	$8	$1	$8.50	11.76%	5.667	$9 to $8	$9 to $10
3	1	2.5	40.00%	$7	$1	$7.50	13.33%	3.000	$8 to $7	$8 to $9
4	1	3.5	28.57%	$6	$1	$6.50	15.38%	1.857	$7 to $6	$7 to $8
5	1	4.5	22.22%	$5	$1	$5.50	18.18%	1.222	$6 to $5	$6 to $7
6	1	5.5	18.18%	$4	$1	$4.50	22.22%	0.818	$5 to $4	$5 to $6
7	1	6.5	15.38%	$3	$1	$3.50	28.57%	0.538	$4 to $3	$4 to $5
8	1	7.5	13.33%	$2	$1	$2.50	40.00%	0.333	$3 to $2	$3 to $4
9	1	8.5	11.76%	$1	$1	$1.50	66.67%	0.176	$2 to $1	$2 to $3
10	1	9.5	10.53%	$0	$1	$0.50	200.00%	0.053	$1 to $0	$1 to $2

a)   These relationships can be depicted graphically as follows:

Price Elasticity of Demand

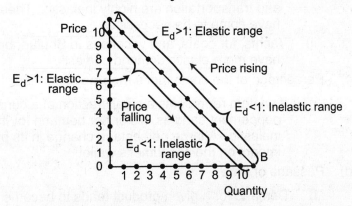

3)   When the demand elasticity coefficient is

a)   **Greater than one**, demand is in a **relatively elastic** range. A small change in price results in a large change in quantity demanded.

b)   **Equal to one**, demand has **unitary elasticity** (usually a very limited range). A single-unit change in price brings about a single-unit change in quantity demanded.

c)   **Less than one**, demand is in a **relatively inelastic** range. A large change in price results in a small change in quantity demanded.

d)   **Infinite**, demand is **perfectly elastic** (depicted as a horizontal line).

i)   In pure competition, the number of firms is so great that one firm cannot influence the market price. The demand curve faced by a single seller in such a market is perfectly elastic (although the demand curve for the market as a whole has the normal downward slope).

ii) EXAMPLE: Consumers will buy a farmer's total output of soybeans at the market price but will buy none at a slightly higher price. Moreover, the farmer cannot sell below the market price without incurring losses.

e)   **Equal to zero**, demand is **perfectly inelastic** (depicted as a vertical line).

i)   Some consumers' need for a certain product is so high that they will pay whatever price the market sets. The number of these consumers is limited and the amount they desire is relatively fixed.

ii) EXAMPLE: Addiction to illegal drugs tends to result in demand that is unresponsive to price changes. In this example, existing buyers (addicts) will not be driven out of the market by a rise in price, and no new buyers will be induced to enter the market by a reduction in price.

4)   **Factors affecting the price elasticity of demand** are

a)   Availability of **substitutes**

i)   The demand for food taken as a whole is extremely inelastic, but the demand curves for individual foods are highly elastic. Consumers can shift their purchases from one food to another with ease.

b) **Centrality** to the consumer's existence

i)   An individual consumer's demand for food, shelter, clothing, utilities, and transportation are highly inelastic. These goods and services have come to be necessities.

ii) Yachts, fur coats, and vacations to Bhutan, being luxuries, tend to have more elastic demand curves.

c) Percentage of the consumer's **income** expended

i)   If an item represents a small fraction of a consumer's income, e.g., peppermint candies, his or her demand for it will tend to be inelastic. A large percentage change in its price will not have much impact on the consumer's wallet.

d) Passage of **time**

i)   Demand for a given product tends to become more elastic as time passes because consumers are able to find substitutes.

ii) The classic example is gasoline. Drivers have short-term commitments that require the consumption of a certain amount of fuel. With the passage of time, however, they may find more efficient travel routes and purchase vehicles that get better mileage.

5) Price elasticity of demand is useful for a firm wondering how a **change in the price** of a product will **affect total revenue** from that product.

Effect on Total Revenue

	Elastic Range	Unitary Elasticity	Inelastic Range
Price increase	Decrease	No change	Increase
Price decrease	Increase	No change	Decrease

b. **Cross-elasticity of demand** measures the percentage change in demand for one good given a percentage change in the price of another good.

1) Cross-elasticity of demand mathematically depicts the **substitution effect**. When a price decreases, new buyers will enter the market. The good will be cheaper relative to other goods and is substituted for them.

2) The cross-elasticity coefficient (E_{xy}) is found by using the following equation:

$$E_{xy} = \frac{\%\,\Delta\,Q_x}{\%\,\Delta\,P_y} = \frac{\text{Percentage change in quantity demanded of good } X}{\text{Percentage change in price of good } Y}$$

3) If the coefficient is

a) **Positive**, the two goods are **substitutes** [see the example in item c.4)]. Substitutability is directly correlated with the magnitude of the positive coefficient.

b) **Negative**, the two goods are **complements**. Complementarity is directly correlated with the magnitude of the negative coefficient.

c) **Zero**, or near zero, the two goods are unrelated.

4) EXAMPLE: The price of orange soda increases 20%, and the demand for root beer increases 10%. Accordingly, orange soda and root beer are substitutes.

$$E_{xy} = \frac{10\%}{20\%} > 0$$

5) Cross-elasticity of demand can be used to define a market and to determine an appropriate marketing strategy. In addition, the information can be used to determine what and how much to produce.

    c. **Income elasticity of demand** measures the percentage change in quantity demanded given a percentage change in income.

        1) Income elasticity of demand mathematically depicts the **income effect**. When a price decreases, individuals have more buying power and will buy more of the product.

        2) The income elasticity (E_I) is found using the following equation:

$$E_I = \frac{\%\ \Delta Q}{\%\ \Delta I} = \frac{Percentage\ change\ in\ quantity\ demanded}{Percentage\ change\ in\ income}$$

        3) If the coefficient is

           a) **Greater than zero**, the good is considered a **normal good**, also called a superior good. If income rises, consumption of the good rises.

           b) **Less than zero**, the good is considered an **inferior good**. If income rises, consumption of the good decreases.

        4) EXAMPLE: Income increases by 20%, and the demand for diamonds increases by 15%. Diamonds are normal goods. As people earn more, they purchase more diamonds.

$$E_I = \frac{15\%}{20\%} > 0$$

2. **Elasticity of Supply**

    a. **Price elasticity of supply** (E_s) measures the sensitivity of the quantity supplied of a product to a change in its price.

$$E_s = \frac{Percentage\ change\ in\ quantity\ supplied}{Percentage\ change\ in\ price}$$

        1) The same formula used in the calculation of price elasticity of demand (the arc method) is used to calculate the price elasticity of supply (see item 2. in Subunit 1).

        2) When the supply elasticity coefficient is

           a) Greater than one, supply is in a **relatively elastic** range. A small change in price results in a large change in quantity supplied.

           b) Equal to one, supply has **unitary elasticity** (usually a very limited range). A single-unit change in price brings about a single-unit change in quantity supplied.

           c) Less than one, supply is in a **relatively inelastic** range. A large change in price results in a small change in quantity supplied.

           d) Infinite, supply is **perfectly elastic** (depicted as a horizontal line).

              i) A perfectly elastic supply curve exists only in theory. The costs of inputs and fixed investments in property, plant, and equipment prevent a supplier from charging a single price for the whole range of possible quantities.

           e) Equal to zero, supply is **perfectly inelastic** (depicted as a vertical line).

              i) A perfectly inelastic supply curve indicates that, in the very short run, a seller cannot change the quantity supplied.

              ii) EXAMPLE: A farmer offering a perishable good with no means of storage must sell the entire crop regardless of the price buyers offer. The farmer cannot offer a larger quantity because the harvest has ended for the season.

3) **Factors affecting the price elasticity of supply** are

a) Cost and feasibility of storage

i) EXAMPLE: A high cost of storage results in low elasticity because, as the price of carrying a good increases, the tendency to hold that good decreases.

b) Characteristics of the production process

i) EXAMPLE: The price elasticity of supply of a joint product may be affected by the demand for the other joint products.

c) Time

i) EXAMPLE: Production of goods, i.e., the ability to supply them, becomes more elastic with time.

b. **Price and total revenue** always move in the same direction regardless of the price elasticity of supply.

3. Review of Terms

Term	Elasticity	Description
A. Price elasticity of demand (supply)		
Perfectly or completely inelastic	Zero	Quantity demanded (supplied) does not change as price changes
Inelastic	Greater than zero, less than one	Quantity demanded (supplied) changes by a smaller percentage than price.
Unit elasticity	One	Quantity demanded (supplied) changes by exactly the same percentages as price.
Perfectly, completely, or infinitely elastic	Infinity	Purchasers (sellers) are prepared to buy (sell) at some price and none at an even higher (lower) price.
B. Income elasticity of demand		
Inferior good	Negative	Quantity demanded decreases as income increases.
Normal good	Positive	Quantity demanded increases as income increases:
Income-inelastic	Less than one	Less than in proportion to income increase
Income-elastic	Greater than one	More than in proportion to income increase
C. Cross elasticity of demand		
Substitute goods	Positive	Price increase of a substitute leads to an increase in quantity demanded (and less quantity demanded of the substitute).
Complementary goods	Negative	Price increase of a complement leads to a decrease in quantity demanded (and less quantity demanded of the complement).

4. Stop and review! You have completed the outline for this subunit. Study multiple-choice questions 13 through 18 beginning on page 139.

5.3 MARKET STRUCTURES

1.   Pure Competition

     a.   **Defining Characteristics**

          1)   **A very large number** of buyers and sellers act independently.

               a)   Examples are the stock market and agricultural markets.

          2)   The **product is homogeneous** or standardized.

               a)   Thus, the product of one firm is a **perfect substitute** for that of any other firm.

               b)   The only basis for competition is **price**.

          3)   Each firm produces an immaterial amount of the industry's total output and thus **cannot influence the market price**.

          4)   **No barriers to entry or exit** from the market exist.

          5)   Every firm has **perfect information**.

     b.   Pure competition **exists only in theory**. However, the model is useful for understanding basic economic concepts. It also provides a standard of comparison for real-world markets.

     c.   As with any normal good, the **demand curve** for the product of an industry in perfect competition is **downward sloping** (if the industry as a whole expects to increase sales, it must lower price).

          1)   However, since each **individual firm** can satisfy only a small part of the demand facing the industry, its demand curve is **perfectly elastic (horizontal)**.

Pure Competition

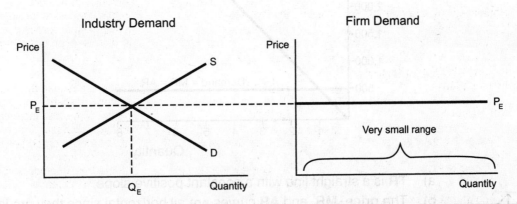

          a)   The tiny segment of the industry's demand curve occupied by each individual firm is necessarily at the point of **market equilibrium**.

          b)   Firms in perfect competition are therefore called **price takers** because they must sell at the market price.

2) The firm's perfectly elastic demand curve means that **marginal revenue equals average revenue equals market price**.

Output	Unit Price (Average Revenue)	Total Revenue	Marginal Revenue
1	$500	$ 500	$500
2	500	1,000	500
3	500	1,500	500
4	500	2,000	500
5	500	2,500	500
6	500	3,000	500
7	500	3,500	500
8	500	4,000	500

3) The following graph depicts the relationships among **total revenue (TR)**, **average revenue (AR)**, and **marginal revenue (MR)** for a firm in pure competition.

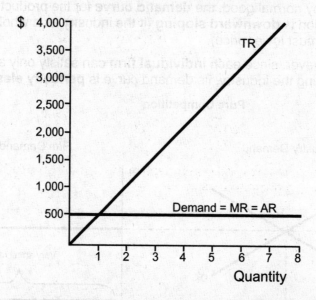

Revenue Relationships for
a Purely Competitive Firm

a) **TR** is a straight line with a constant positive slope.

b) The **price, MR**, and **AR** curves are all horizontal since they are identical to the perfectly inelastic demand curve **(Price = MR = AR)**.

d. **Short-Run Profit Maximization**

1) In the short run, a firm should produce **(continue to operate)** when it can

a) Earn a profit or

b) Incur a loss smaller than fixed costs.

i) In the short run, **operating at a loss** may be preferable to shutting down. This option is indicated when revenues cover all variable costs and some fixed costs (costs incurred even if the firm shuts down).

2) If the firm decides to produce, it must next decide how much (the **level of output**). The output level chosen should **maximize profits or minimize losses** in the short run.

    a) Short-run profit maximization is achieved when the **excess of total revenue (TR) over total cost (TC)** is largest.

        i) **Losses are minimized** when the excess of TC over TR is smallest and the excess is less than total fixed costs (so that at least some fixed costs are covered).

3) A second method applied to short-run production decisions is to **compare marginal revenue (MR) and marginal cost (MC)**.

    a) **For all market structures**, a firm that does not shut down should **produce the level of output at which MR = MC**.

        i) **As long as the next unit of output adds more in revenue** (MR) than in cost (MC), the firm will increase total profit or decrease total losses.

        ii) For a purely competitive firm, price = MC is the same as MR = MC.

Output	Average Variable Cost	Average Total Cost	Price = Marginal Revenue	Total Cost	Marginal Cost
1	$800	$1,800	$960	$1,800	$ 800
2	750	1,250	960	2,500	700
3	700	1,033	960	3,100	600
4	650	900	960	3,600	500
5	640	860	960	4,200	600
6	680	847	960	5,080	880
7	720	863	960	6,040	960 ✳
8	770	895	960	7,160	1,120

    b) The following graph depicts the **short-run profit-maximizing quantity** for a price taker.

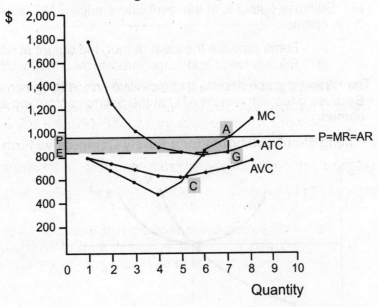

Price Taking for a Purely Competitive Firm

        i) Being in a purely competitive industry, the firm has no choice but to find its price along the horizontal MR curve.

ii)   The profit-maximizing quantity to produce is found at the point where the MC curve crosses MR (following the short-run profit maximizing rule MR = MC).

iii) Point A reveals a quantity of 7 units. This is confirmed by consulting the table and verifying that, at an output of 7, MR = MC.

c) The firm's **short-run supply curve** (points representing output at different prices) consists of the **MC curve above where it crosses average variable cost**.

i)   Below the intersection of MC and AVC (point C), the firm **will not operate** (it is not covering its fixed costs below this level).

4) The **short-run equilibrium price for the industry** is at the intersection of the market demand curve and the market supply curve.

a) This price establishes the **short-run equilibrium price for the firm**.

b) Thus, price = MR is a given. The firm's output is based on the given price and its MC (supply) curve.

e. **Long-Run Profit Maximization**

1) In the preceding graph, the firm was earning an **economic profit** in the short run.

a) In the long run, the **entry of new firms** will eliminate economic profits by driving down the market price as the supply curve shifts to the right.

i)   If firms are incurring **losses**, some will leave the industry. The resulting leftward shift of the supply curve will increase the market price.

2) The standard theory assumes that all firms are **equally efficient**. Thus, the minimum **average total cost (ATC)** is the same for all firms.

a) When the entry of new firms or the departure of old firms causes price to equal minimum ATC, firms earn **normal profits** only.

i)   If **more efficient producers** with lower ATC curves enter the market, they will earn economic profits in the long run.

b) Because output is at the level where price = MC, allocation of resources is optimal.

i)   Firms produce the ideal output, the output at which ATC is lowest.
ii) Price is lower and output greater than in any other market structure.

3) The following graph depicts a competitive firm in **long-run equilibrium**. Because price = minimum ATC at the optimal output, no economic profit is earned.

Long-Run Equilibrium for a Purely Competitive Firm

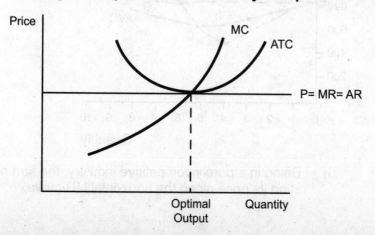

2. Pure Monopoly

   a. **Defining Characteristics**

      1) The industry consists of **one firm**.

      2) The product has **no close substitutes**.

      3) The firm can **strongly influence price** because it is the sole supplier of the product. Economists commonly use two terms to describe a monopolist's pricing behavior:

         a) **Price maker** draws attention to the monopolist's power to set price as high as it likes, unconstrained by competition.

         b) **Price searcher**, on the other hand, implies that the monopolistic firm will not simply set prices arbitrarily high but will seek the price that maximizes its profits (explained in item b. below).

      4) **Entry** by other firms is **completely blocked** in a pure monopoly.

      5) A **natural monopoly** exists when economic or technical conditions permit only one efficient supplier.

         a) Very large operations are needed to achieve low unit costs and prices (economies of scale are great).

         b) Thus, the long-term average cost of meeting demand is minimized when the industry has one firm. Examples are utilities, such as electricity and gas distribution.

   b. The **demand curve** facing a monopolist is **downward sloping** because, as with any normal good, the monopolistic firm can only sell more product by lowering price.

      1) However, unlike a competitive firm, which faces only a very small portion of the whole industry's demand curve, the **monopolistic firm's demand curve is the entire industry's demand curve**.

         a) Thus a monopolist's **marginal revenue continuously decreases** as it raises output. Past the point where MR = $0, the monopolist's total revenue begins to decrease.

Output	Unit Price (Average Revenue)	Total Revenue	Marginal Revenue
1	$960	$ 960	$960
2	910	1,820	860
3	860	2,580	760
4	810	3,240	660
5	760	3,800	560
6	710	4,260	460
7	660	4,620	360
8	610	4,880	260
9	560	5,040	160
10	510	5,100	60
11	460	5,060	(40)
12	410	4,920	(140)

2) The following graph depicts the relationships between output and revenue for a pure monopoly:

**Demand and Total Revenue
for a Pure Monopoly**

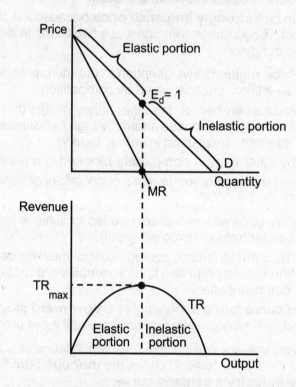

a) In the **elastic portion** of the demand curve, **TR increases** with every cut in price.

b) At the point of **unitary elasticity, TR is maximized**. This is also the point where **MR = $0**.

c) In the **inelastic portion** of the demand curve, **TR decreases** with every cut in price.

c. Revenue maximization, however, is irrelevant to a monopolist. The rational choice is to **maximize profits**.

1) As discussed in Subunit 1, the **competitive firm** must accept the market price and adjust its output accordingly, seeking the level which just covers its average total costs.

a) This results in a competitive firm earning **no long-term profits**.

2) The **monopolist**, on the other hand, has the power to set output at the level where profits are maximized, that is, where **MR = MC**.

a) The corresponding **price** is found with reference to the (downward-sloping) demand curve.

i) Note that monopoly does NOT result in the highest possible price, nor does the monopolist produce at the lowest ATC.

ii) Note also that a monopolist has no supply curve. This is because its price-setting power means it is not subject to the same sensitivities in price changes as firms in competition.

Monopoly Profits

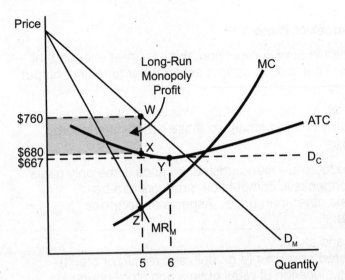

W= profit-maximizing price/quantity for a monopolist
X= profit-maximizing average total cost for a monopolist
Y= lowest point of average total cost
Z= profit-maximizing quantity for a monopolist (MR=MC)

D_c = demand curve for competitive firm

D_M= demand curve for pure monopolist

MR_M = marginal revenue curve for pure monopolist

b) The shaded area represents the firm's **excess profits** stemming from its monopoly power.

c) Note that the monopolist can set price no higher without sacrificing profit. This is the essence of **price searching**.

3) The schedule below is the table on which the above graph is based:

Price Searching for a Monopolist

Output	Unit Price (Average Revenue)	Total Revenue	Marginal Revenue	Average Total Cost	Total Cost	Marginal Cost	Profit/ (Loss)
1	$960	$ 960	$960	$1,800	$ 1,800	$ 800	$ (840)
2	910	1,820	860	1,200	2,400	600	(580)
3	860	2,580	760	933	2,800	400	(220)
4	810	3,240	660	750	3,000	200	240
5	760	3,800	560	680	3,400	400	400 ✳
6	710	4,260	460	✳ 667	4,000	600 ✳	260
7	660	4,620	360	686	4,800	800	(180)
8	610	4,880	260	725	5,800	1,000	(920)
9	560	5,040	160	778	7,000	1,200	(1,960)
10	510	5,100	60	840	8,400	1,400	(3,300)
11	460	5,060	(40)	909	10,000	1,600	(4,940)
12	410	4,920	(140)	983	11,800	1,800	(6,880)

a) A key point is that, when the monopolist lowers price to increase sales, the price must be reduced for all units. Thus, **Price = AR**.

b) If price falls below AVC, the firm will cease operations (the shutdown case).

d. **Economic Consequences of Monopoly**

1) Given sufficiently low costs and adequate demand, a monopolist earns an **economic profit in the long run** (if the cost structure is high enough, even a monopoly can lose money).

a) Because the firm is restricting the level of output to the profit-maximizing level, consumers have **fewer goods and pay higher prices** than under pure competition.

2) Because **price exceeds MC**, resources are **underallocated**.

a) Allocation is efficient when price is reduced to MC, the value of what is forgone by society to make the product.

3.   Monopolistic Competition

    a.   **Defining Characteristics**

        1)   The industry has a **large number of firms**.

            a)   The number is fewer than in pure competition, but it is great enough that firms **cannot collude**. That is, they cannot act together to restrict output and fix the price.

                i)   Consequently, firms act independently. The effect of a competitor's actions on its many rivals is small, so these actions are ignored.

        2)   **Products are differentiated.**

            a)   In pure competition, products are standardized, so price is the only basis for competition. In monopolistic competition, products can be differentiated on a basis other than price. Aspects of **nonprice differentiation** include:

                i)   **Quality**, brands, and styles
                ii)   Availability of **related services** (e.g., delivery, repair, or credit)
                iii)   **Accessibility** (e.g., location of retail outlets and store hours)

            b)   When a firm engages in product differentiation, its goals are to

                i)   **Shift its demand curve to the right** and
                ii)   **Make demand less elastic.**

                  •   The idea is to create a mini-monopoly in one's own product, summed up by the old phrase "only Cadillac makes a Cadillac."

            c)   A firm has **some price control**. Product differentiation allows the firm to charge a higher price up to a point.

        3)   **Few barriers** to entry and exit exist.

            a)   Since firms tend not to be large, **great economies of scale do not exist**.
            b)   The **cost of product differentiation** is the most significant barrier to entry.

                i)   Some existing firms may have patents, trademarks, trade names, and other intangible assets. These increase the difficulty of success for a new firm.

        4)   **Advertising** is crucial.

            a)   Customers must be informed of the nonprice ways in which the firm's product is differentiated from its substitutes.

    b.   To **maximize profits** (or minimize losses) in the short run or long run, a firm in monopolistic competition produces at the level of output at which **MR = MC**.

        1)   **Just as for a monopolist**, the MR curve is negatively sloped and lies below the demand curve.

        2)   In monopolistic competition, a firm has **competitors** offering **substitute products**.

            a)   The demand curve is **less negatively sloped than the curve for a pure monopoly** (i.e., more elastic; see the graph on the next page).

                i)   Thus, a small price increase results in a relatively large decrease in quantity demanded, especially if the product is not differentiated.

            b)   The profit-maximizing quantity is found where MR = MC.

                i)   Since the price corresponding to the this level of output exceeds the price found on the ATC curve, the firm will **earn economic profits in the short run**.

Short-Run Profits in Monopolistic Competition

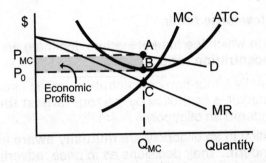

A = profit-maximizing price/quantity
B = lowest point on ATC
C = profit-maximizing quantity (MR = MC)

3) In the **long run**, a firm in monopolistic competition tends to earn only a **normal profit**.

   a) Attracted by excess short-run profits, **competitors enter the market**.

   b) More substitutes are now available to consumers, driving the **demand curve to the left**, eventually moving it so far that it is just tangent to the ATC curve.

      i) The excess profits that originally attracted new entrants are now gone.

   c) Firms may cut price (further squeezing profits) or increase advertising (driving the ATC curve up) in an attempt to gain market share at the expense of competitors. **Short-run losses** ensue.

   d) **Unprofitable firms exit the market**, reducing the number of substitutes and allowing the demand curve to move back to the right.

      i) Price will settle at equilibrium where demand is tangent to ATC. The **long-run tendency** is thus merely to **break even**.

Long-Run Equilibrium in Monopolistic Competition

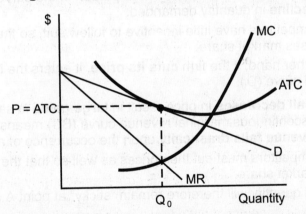

4) As with pure monopoly, **price exceeds MC** and **underallocation** of resources results. Monopolistic competition shares three other aspects with pure monopoly:

   a) Price exceeds the lowest point of ATC. Thus, **production is inefficient** and firms are too small.

   b) **Price is higher and output lower** than in pure competition.

   c) If price falls below AVC, the firm will cease operations (the shutdown case).

4.   Oligopoly

   a.   **Defining Characteristics**

      1)   The industry has **few large firms**.

         a)   The degree to which the market leaders dominate an industry is measured by the **concentration ratio**.

            i)   Frequently a four-firm concentration ratio is used. If **40% or more** of the market is controlled by the **four largest firms**, that industry is considered an oligopoly.

         b)   Firms operating in an oligopoly are **mutually aware** and **mutually interdependent**. Their decisions as to price, advertising, etc., are to a very large extent dependent on the actions of the other firms.

      2)   **Products** can be **differentiated** (e.g., autos) **or standardized** (e.g., steel).

      3)   **Prices** tend to be **rigid** (sticky) because of the interdependence among firms.

         a)   An oligopoly must often confront **cyclical or seasonal fluctuations** in the quantity demanded. Price rigidity makes it difficult for oligopolists to maintain sales levels by reducing price when the demand curve shifts to the left or by increasing sales and output when demand increases.

      4)   **Entry is difficult** because of barriers that can be

         a)   Natural, e.g., an absolute cost advantage, or

         b)   Created, e.g., ongoing advertising or ownership of patents.

   b.   The price rigidity normally found in oligopolistic markets can be explained in part by the **kinked demand curve** theory. The essence of the theory is that firms will follow along with a price decrease by a competitor but not a price increase (see the graph on the next page).

      1)   If price and quantity for the industry are at P and Q, a firm that **raises its price** will move into the **elastic portion** of the demand curve (D_E).

         a)   A **small increase** in price in this portion of the curve leads to a **large decline** in quantity demanded.

         b)   Competitors have little incentive to follow suit, so the price-raising firm loses market share.

      2)   On the other hand, if the firm **cuts its price**, it enters the **inelastic portion** of the demand curve (D_I).

         a)   **Small decreases** in price result in **large gains** in sales. However, the discontinuous marginal revenue curve (BC) means that **marginal revenue falls drastically** upon the occurrence of a small price cut.

         b)   Competitors must cut their prices as well so that the first firm gains no market share.

      3)   Price and quantity will therefore remain "sticky" at point A on the demand curve.

Kinked Demand for an Oligopoly

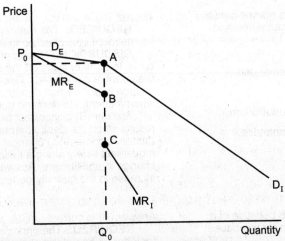

4) To avoid the hazards of the kinked demand curve, **price leadership** is typically employed in oligopolistic industries.

  a) Under price leadership, **price changes are announced** first by a major firm in the industry. Once the industry leader has spoken, other firms match the price charged by the leader.

c. A **cartel** arises when a group of oligopolistic firms join together for price-fixing purposes. This practice is illegal except in international markets.

  1) For example, the international diamond cartel DeBeers has successfully maintained the market price of diamonds for many years by incorporating into the cartel almost all major diamond-producing sources.

  2) A cartel is a **collusive oligopoly**. Its effects are similar to those of a monopoly. Each firm will restrict output, charge a higher (collusive or agreed-to) price, and earn the maximum profit.

    a) Thus, each firm in effect becomes a monopolist, but only because it is colluding with other members of the cartel.

d. A **group boycott** also can affect demand and prices. A boycott is a concerted effort to avoid doing business with a particular supplier.

5. Stop and review! You have completed the outline for this subunit. Study multiple-choice questions 19 through 29 beginning on page 141.

QUESTIONS

5.1 Demand, Supply, and Equilibrium

1. A movement from one point on a normal demand schedule to a second point (on the same demand curve) at a lower price, is

   A. An increase in the quantity demanded.

   B. A shift in the demand curve.

   C. A change in demand-supply equilibrium.

   D. A decrease in the quantity demanded.

Answer (A) is correct. *(CIA, adapted)*
   REQUIRED: The nature of a movement from one point on a normal demand schedule to a second point at a lower price.
   DISCUSSION: Movement from one point on a demand curve to another point on the same demand curve is a change in the quantity demanded. This change is solely the result of a change in price when demand is fixed. The curve itself shifts when a change in demand occurs.
   Answer (B) is incorrect because a shift in the demand curve results when the determinants of demand other than price (tastes, income, etc.) change. Answer (C) is incorrect because a movement solely along a fixed demand curve is not by itself a change in equilibrium. Answer (D) is incorrect because an increase in the quantity demanded will occur at the lower price.

2. The demand for machinery drops because of a drop in the cost of labor. The reason for this cause and effect relationship is the law of

   A. Diminishing returns.

   B. Substitution.

   C. Complementary resources.

   D. Competing resources.

Answer (B) is correct. *(CIA, adapted)*
   REQUIRED: The principle explaining a decreased demand for labor given a decreased cost of labor.
   DISCUSSION: The substitution effect occurs when a product becomes less costly relative to the alternatives. Because labor can be substituted for machinery, a decline in the price of labor will increase the amount of labor demanded and decrease the demand for machinery. Thus, when two resources are substitutes, the price of one and the demand for the other are directly correlated.
   Answer (A) is incorrect because, according to the law of diminishing returns, the average product will ultimately fall as increasing amounts of a given variable input are combined with a fixed amount of complementary inputs. Answer (C) is incorrect because a decrease in the cost of a resource will cause the demand for a complementary resource to increase. Answer (D) is incorrect because the phrase "competing resources" is not meaningful in this context.

3.

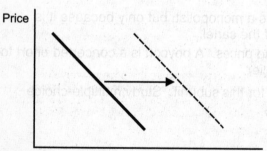

The situation depicted in the graph above could be caused by

   A. A price cut by all producers.

   B. A price hike by all producers.

   C. A rise in the country's population.

   D. An improvement in manufacturers' productivity.

Answer (C) is correct. *(Publisher, adapted)*
   REQUIRED: The cause of the situation.
   DISCUSSION: A downward-sloping curve relating price to quantity depicts the demand schedule for a normal good. When a country's population grows, producers can sell more of their products at every price level. This is depicted as a rightward shift in the demand curve.
   Answer (A) is incorrect because a price cut by all producers would be depicted as a downward movement along a fixed curve. Answer (B) is incorrect because a price hike by all producers would be depicted as an upward movement along a fixed curve. Answer (D) is incorrect because an improvement in manufacturers' productivity would be depicted by a shift in the (upward-sloping) supply curve, not the (downward-sloping) demand curve.

4. Factors such as changes in consumers' tastes, the prices of related goods, and consumer expectations all are examples of

- A. A change in the quantity demanded.
- B. A change in the quantity supplied.
- C. Nonprice determinants of supply.
- D. Nonprice determinants of demand.

Answer (D) is correct. *(CIA, adapted)*
REQUIRED: The proper characterization of changes in consumers' tastes, the prices of related goods, and consumer expectations.
DISCUSSION: The demand schedule is a relationship between the prices of a product and the quantity demanded at each price, holding other determinants of the quantity demanded constant. A movement along an existing demand curve occurs when the price is changed. A shift in the curve itself occurs when any of the determinants other than price changes. Such shifts can be caused by a change in the tastes and preferences of consumers toward a product, for example, as a result of a successful advertising campaign, an increase in consumer income (if a product is a normal good), or changes in the prices of substitute or complementary products.
Answer (A) is incorrect because a change in the quantity demanded is a movement along a demand curve caused by a price change. Answer (B) is incorrect because demand, not supply, is at issue. Answer (C) is incorrect because demand, not supply, is at issue.

5. A decrease in the price of a complementary good will

- A. Shift the demand curve of the joint commodity to the left.
- B. Increase the price paid for a substitute good.
- C. Shift the supply curve of the joint commodity to the left.
- D. Shift the demand curve of the joint commodity to the right.

Answer (D) is correct. *(CMA, adapted)*
REQUIRED: The effect of a decrease in the price of a complementary good.
DISCUSSION: A decrease in the price of a complementary good (e.g., gasoline) will cause the demand curve of the joint commodity (e.g., automobiles) to shift to the right (increase). The lower price results in greater demand by consumers at each price level. A movement along an existing demand curve occurs when the price for the product is changed but demand is constant.
Answer (A) is incorrect because a shift to the left (a decrease in demand) would occur if the price of a complementary product increased. Answer (B) is incorrect because demand for a substitute would decrease, thereby lowering its equilibrium price. Answer (C) is incorrect because the demand curve will shift to the right, but the supply curve will not change.

6. X and Y are substitute products. If the price of product Y increases, the immediate impact on product X is that its

- A. Price will increase.
- B. Quantity demanded will increase.
- C. Quantity supplied will increase.
- D. Price, quantity demanded, and supplies will increase.

Answer (B) is correct. *(CIA, adapted)*
REQUIRED: The immediate effect on one product of an increase in the price of its substitute.
DISCUSSION: By definition, if two goods are substitutes, the price of one and the demand for the other are directly related. For example, if the price of Y increases, the quantity demanded of X will increase.
Answer (A) is incorrect because the price will remain unchanged. Answer (C) is incorrect because the change in quantity supplied will not be immediate. Answer (D) is incorrect because only quantity demanded will increase immediately.

7. X and Y are complementary products. If the price of product Y increases, the immediate impact on product X is that its

- A. Price will decrease.
- B. Quantity demanded will decrease.
- C. Quantity supplied will decrease.
- D. Price, quantity demanded, and supplies will remain unchanged.

Answer (B) is correct. *(CIA, adapted)*
REQUIRED: The immediate effect on one product of an increase in the price of its complement.
DISCUSSION: By definition, if two goods are complements, such as tennis racquets and tennis balls, an increase in the quantity demanded of one tends to increase the quantity demanded of the other. As a result, the price of one and the quantity demanded of the other are inversely related. Thus, if the price of Y increases, the quantity demanded of X will decrease.
Answer (A) is incorrect because a price increase for one product does not immediately affect the price of another product. Answer (C) is incorrect because quantity supplied will remain unchanged in the short run. Answer (D) is incorrect because quantity demanded will decrease.

8. A supply curve illustrates the relationship between

- A. Price and quantity supplied.
- B. Price and consumer tastes.
- C. Price and quantity demanded.
- D. Supply and demand.

Answer (A) is correct. *(CMA, adapted)*
REQUIRED: The relationship illustrated by a supply curve.
DISCUSSION: A supply curve illustrates the relationship between price and the quantity of a good that sellers are willing to supply. As price increases, the supply will increase.
Answer (B) is incorrect because consumer tastes are reflected by the demand curve, not the supply curve. Answer (C) is incorrect because the demand curve shows the relationship between price and quantity demanded. Answer (D) is incorrect because the supply curve shows only the supply, not the demand.

9. An increase in the market supply of beef would result in a(n)

- A. Increase in the price of beef.
- B. Decrease in the demand for beef.
- C. Increase in the price of pork.
- D. Increase in the quantity of beef demanded.

Answer (D) is correct. *(CMA, adapted)*
REQUIRED: The effect of an increase in the market supply of beef.
DISCUSSION: If demand is constant, an increase in supply should result in a lower equilibrium price. The supply curve shifts to the right; that is, more is supplied at each price. Thus, the new intersection of the supply and demand curves is at a lower point on the demand curve. The result is an increase in the quantity demanded.
Answer (A) is incorrect because the increased supply will lead to a lower price. Answer (B) is incorrect because an increase in supply increases quantity demanded, not overall demand. Answer (C) is incorrect because pork is a substitute for beef. Hence, the lower price of beef will shift demand for pork to the left, resulting in a lower equilibrium price.

10.

The graph above depicts a relationship between the price and the quantity of white bread. The movement depicted by the arrow could have resulted in

- A. A decrease in the demand for strawberry preserves.
- B. An increase in the demand for peanut butter.
- C. A decrease in the price of whole wheat bread.
- D. An increase in the price of whole wheat bread.

Answer (A) is correct. *(Publisher, adapted)*
REQUIRED: The possible result of the movement.
DISCUSSION: White bread and strawberry preserves are complementary products, meaning the price of one and the demand for the other move in opposite directions. This graph depicts an increase in the price of white bread. The result will be a decrease in the demand for all of white bread's complements (butter, jam, preserves, etc.).
Answer (B) is incorrect because white bread and peanut butter are complementary products, meaning the price of one and the demand for the other move in opposite directions. This graph depicts an increase in the price of white bread. The result will be a decrease in the demand for all of white bread's complements (butter, jam, preserves, etc.). Answer (C) is incorrect because white bread and whole wheat bread are substitutable products, meaning the price of one and the demand for the other move in the same direction. This graph depicts an increase in the price of white bread. The result will be an increase in the demand for (not a decrease in the price of) all of white bread's substitutes (whole wheat, rye, focaccia, etc.). Answer (D) is incorrect because white bread and whole wheat bread are substitutable products, meaning the price of one and the demand for the other move in the same direction. This graph depicts an increase in the price of white bread. The result will be an increase in the demand for (not the price of) all of white bread's substitutes (whole wheat, rye, focaccia, etc.).

11. The competitive model of supply and demand predicts that a surplus can arise only if there is a

A. Maximum price above the equilibrium price.

B. Minimum price below the equilibrium price.

C. Maximum price below the equilibrium price.

D. Minimum price above the equilibrium price.

Answer (D) is correct. *(CMA, adapted)*
REQUIRED: The circumstance that could lead to a product surplus.
DISCUSSION: In the competitive model of supply and demand, a surplus can never occur unless government intervenes to impose price controls. A surplus can arise if a minimum price is set that exceeds the equilibrium price. For example, if the minimum price is $5 and the equilibrium price is $4, consumers will demand fewer goods at $5 than $4, but producers will supply more goods at $5 than $4. Thus, a surplus will occur. However, at a price of $4, supply would exactly equal demand.
Answer (A) is incorrect because a maximum price in excess of the equilibrium price creates neither a surplus nor a shortage. Answer (B) is incorrect because a minimum price below the equilibrium price creates neither a surplus nor a shortage. Answer (C) is incorrect because a maximum price (such as rent controls) set lower than the equilibrium price leads to shortages. Producers will not be willing to supply as much as consumers demand.

12. If the federal government regulates a product or service in a competitive market by setting a maximum price below the equilibrium price, what is the long-run effect?

A. A surplus.

B. A shortage.

C. A decrease in demand.

D. No effect on the market.

Answer (B) is correct. *(CMA, adapted)*
REQUIRED: The effect of the government's setting a price below the equilibrium point in a competitive market.
DISCUSSION: Price fixing is the setting of mandatory or artificial prices. It often interferes with the free operation of the market. A price ceiling is a price below the equilibrium point. The result is a shortage because consumer demand will exceed supply.
Answer (A) is incorrect because a surplus arises when the price is set above the equilibrium point. Supply will exceed demand. Answer (C) is incorrect because a decrease in demand (a leftward shift in the demand curve) may result when future prices are expected to decline. However, given a price set below equilibrium, pressure on prices is upward. Answer (D) is incorrect because the price ceiling will cause shortages.

5.2 Elasticity

13. Last week, the quantity of apples demanded fell from 51,500 units per week to 48,500 units per week. If this was a result of a 10% price increase, what is the price elasticity of demand for apples?

A. 1.67

B. 1.06

C. 0.16

D. 0.60

Answer (D) is correct. *(Publisher, adapted)*
REQUIRED: The price elasticity of demand.
DISCUSSION: The price elasticity of demand is calculated by dividing the percentage change in quantity demanded by the percentage change in price. The numerator and denominator are computed as "the change over the range." Thus, the change in quantity of 3,000 units (51,500 – 48,500) divided by 100,000 (51,500 + 48,500) equals 6%. Dividing the 6% quantity decline by the 10% price increase produces an elasticity of 0.6.
Answer (A) is incorrect because 1.67 is the inverse of the elasticity. Answer (B) is incorrect because 1.06 is the result of adding the 6% quantity decline to 1. Answer (C) is incorrect because the price elasticity of demand is found by dividing the 6% quantity decline by the 10% price increase, not by adding them.

14. The difference between a normal profit and an economic profit is that an economic profit

    A. Equals total revenue minus the costs of land, labor, and capital.

    B. Is an amount in excess of the economic costs of the firm.

    C. Is an economic cost.

    D. Is the payment required to acquire and retain entrepreneurial services.

Answer (B) is correct. *(CIA, adapted)*
    REQUIRED: The difference between a normal profit and an economic profit.
    DISCUSSION: An economic profit is the excess of total revenue over the economic costs of the firm. Economic costs are the payments needed to acquire and retain productive resources, such as materials, land, labor, capital, and entrepreneurial services. A normal profit is an economic cost because it is the payment required to acquire and retain entrepreneurial services. An entrepreneur must be paid to organize the enterprise and combine the other resources needed for production.
    Answer (A) is incorrect because an economic profit is the excess of total revenue over all economic costs, not just those incurred to acquire and retain land, labor, and capital. Answer (C) is incorrect because a normal profit is an economic cost. An economic profit is not. Answer (D) is incorrect because a normal profit is the payment required to acquire and retain entrepreneurial services.

15. Under which of the following conditions is the supplier most able to influence or control buyers?

    A. When the supplier's products are not differentiated.

    B. When the supplier does not face the threat of substitute products.

    C. When the industry is controlled by a large number of companies.

    D. When the purchasing industry is an important customer to the supplying industry.

Answer (B) is correct. *(CPA, adapted)*
    REQUIRED: The circumstances in which a supplier is most likely to be most able to influence buyers.
    DISCUSSION: By definition, if two goods are substitutes, the price of one and the demand for the other are directly related. For example, if the price of Y increases, the quantity demanded of substitute X will increase. Without substitutes, demand will be inelastic, and the supplier will have greater bargaining power relative to buyers.
    Answer (A) is incorrect because lack of product differentiation increases the availability of substitutes and reduces the supplier's bargaining power. Answer (C) is incorrect because competition reduces a supplier's bargaining power. Answer (D) is incorrect because a supplier's bargaining power is lower when the purchaser is an important customer.

16. If the demand for a product is inelastic,

    A. A price decrease causes total revenue to increase.

    B. A price increase causes total revenue to increase.

    C. A price decrease leaves total revenue unchanged.

    D. A price increase leaves total revenue unchanged.

Answer (B) is correct. *(CIA, adapted)*
    REQUIRED: The true statement if demand for a product is inelastic.
    DISCUSSION: If the demand for a product is inelastic, the coefficient of price elasticity of demand (percentage change in quantity demanded $\div$ percentage change in price) is less than 1.0. The relationship between price changes and total revenue (TR) changes is TR = price $\times$ quantity. The result is that a price increase causes total revenue to increase.
    Answer (A) is incorrect because a price decrease causes total revenue to increase if demand is price elastic. Answer (C) is incorrect because a price decrease leaves total revenue unchanged if demand has unitary price elasticity. Answer (D) is incorrect because a price increase leaves total revenue unchanged if demand has unitary price elasticity.

17. The local video store's business increased by 12% after the movie theater raised its prices from $6.50 to $7.00. Thus, relative to movie theater admissions, videos are

    A. Substitute goods.

    B. Superior goods.

    C. Complementary goods.

    D. Public goods.

Answer (A) is correct. *(CMA, adapted)*
    REQUIRED: The type of goods for which sales increase when the price of another good is raised.
    DISCUSSION: The increase in prices at the movie theater caused consumers to demand fewer movies at the theater and more movies at the video store (where prices were unchanged). Thus, cross-elasticity of demand existed because the percentage change in quantity demanded of videos was correlated with the percentage change in the price of movie theater tickets. The correlation was positive, so the goods are substitutes.
    Answer (B) is incorrect because superior (normal) goods are defined as those for which demand is positively correlated with income. Answer (C) is incorrect because sales of a complementary good are negatively correlated with changes in the price of its complement. For example, sales of tennis balls decrease with an increase in tennis racquet prices. Answer (D) is incorrect because public goods are characterized by the difficulty of excluding individuals from their benefits. Examples are national defense and public parks.

18. All of the following are complementary goods except

    A. Margarine and butter.

    B. Cameras and rolls of film.

    C. VCRs and video cassettes.

    D. Razors and razor blades.

Answer (A) is correct. *(CMA, adapted)*
  REQUIRED: The pair that does not represent complementary goods.
  DISCUSSION: Goods or services are complements if the price change of one has an inverse relationship to the demand for the other. For example, when the price of one good increases, the demand for a complementary good decreases. Margarine and butter, however, are substitutes and their relationship is direct. When the price of one good increases, demand for a substitute good also increases.
  Answer (B) is incorrect because cameras and rolls of film are examples of complementary products. For instance, when the price of cameras decreases, people take more pictures and the demand for rolls of film increases. Answer (C) is incorrect because VCRs and video cassettes are examples of complementary products. A decrease in the price of VCRs will result in increased demand of video cassettes. Answer (D) is incorrect because razors and razor blades are examples of complementary products. A decrease in the price of razors will result in increased demand for razor blades.

5.3 Market Structures

19. The individual purely competitive firm faces a demand schedule that is

    A. Perfectly inelastic.

    B. Relatively inelastic.

    C. Perfectly elastic.

    D. Relatively elastic.

Answer (C) is correct. *(Publisher, adapted)*
  REQUIRED: The type of demand curve faced by a firm operating under perfect competition.
  DISCUSSION: The demand curve faced by a firm operating under perfect competition is perfectly elastic (horizontal) because the firm is a price taker. It must sell at the market price. If the firm tries to increase its price, demand will drop to zero.
  Answer (A) is incorrect because, if the firm raises prices, its total revenues will decrease, not increase. Answer (B) is incorrect because, if the firm raises prices, its total revenues will decrease, not increase. Answer (D) is incorrect because the firm must sell at the market price. If the firm tries to increase its price, demand will drop to zero.

20. In the short run in perfect competition, a firm maximizes profit by producing the rate of output at which the price is equal to

    A. Total cost.

    B. Total variable cost.

    C. Average fixed costs.

    D. Marginal cost.

Answer (D) is correct. *(CMA, adapted)*
  REQUIRED: The profit-maximizing price in the short run in perfect competition.
  DISCUSSION: A firm should increase production until the marginal revenue equals marginal cost. In the short run, this is the same as saying the firm will increase production until marginal cost equals price. The result is the short-run maximization of profits. As long as selling price exceeds marginal cost, a firm should continue producing. In the short run in perfect competition, the market price equals marginal revenue because no firm can affect price by its production decisions.
  Answer (A) is incorrect because there would be no profit when selling price and total costs are the same. Answer (B) is incorrect because equating selling price to total variable costs leaves nothing to cover fixed costs. Answer (C) is incorrect because using only average fixed costs ignores variable costs, which increase in total with every unit produced.

21. When markets are perfectly competitive, consumers

- A. Are able to avoid the problem of diminishing returns.
- B. Have goods and services produced at the lowest cost in the long run.
- C. Do not receive any consumer surplus unless producers choose to overproduce.
- D. Must search for the lowest price for the products they buy.

Answer (B) is correct. *(CMA, adapted)*
REQUIRED: The true statement about consumers in perfectly competitive markets.
DISCUSSION: Pure competition is characterized by a large number of buyers and sellers acting independently, homogeneous or standardized products, free entry into and exit of firms from the market, perfect information, no control over prices, and no nonprice competition. Because price equals marginal cost, allocation of resources is optimal. Firms produce the ideal output, the output at which average cost is lowest. Price is lower and output greater than in any other market structure.
Answer (A) is incorrect because diminishing returns can exist in any market structure. Answer (C) is incorrect because in pure competition, the optimal output is produced. Because resource allocation is ideal, no over- or underproduction occurs, and consumer surplus (the difference between what consumers are willing to pay and what they actually pay) is nonexistent. Answer (D) is incorrect because all suppliers will charge the market price, given perfect information.

22. Which one of the following statements concerning pure monopolies is true?

- A. The demand curve of a monopolist is perfectly elastic.
- B. The price at which a monopolist maximizes its profit is where price equals both marginal cost and marginal revenue.
- C. A monopolist's marginal revenue curve lies below its demand curve.
- D. For a monopolist, there is a unique relationship between the price and the quantity supplied.

Answer (C) is correct. *(CMA, adapted)*
REQUIRED: The true statement concerning pure monopolies.
DISCUSSION: In a pure monopoly, the marginal revenue curve is negatively (downwardly) sloped. The reason is that the demand curve faced by the monopolist is also negatively sloped; that is, price must decrease to increase sales. However, a price cut to increase sales applies not only to the incremental units but also to all other units. Each additional unit adds its price minus the sum of the reductions on preceding units to total revenue. Thus, marginal revenue (change in total revenue) declines as output rises, and the marginal revenue curve will lie below the demand curve. If marginal revenue equaled the price change, the marginal revenue and demand curves would be the same.
Answer (A) is incorrect because the demand curve in pure competition is perfectly elastic. Answer (B) is incorrect because a monopolist's profit is maximized when price exceeds marginal revenue and marginal cost. Answer (D) is incorrect because a monopolist has no supply curve. Because a monopolist equates marginal revenue and marginal cost, but marginal revenue is not price, different demand curves may result in different prices at the same output level. Thus, price and quantity supplied do not have a unique relationship.

23. When compared with firms in perfectly competitive markets, monopolists ordinarily

- A. Use more advertising to increase sales.
- B. Charge a higher price and produce a higher rate of output.
- C. Use more capital and less labor to avoid problems with workers.
- D. Charge a higher price and produce a lower rate of output.

Answer (D) is correct. *(CMA, adapted)*
REQUIRED: The true statement about monopolists.
DISCUSSION: Competitive markets are preferable to other types of markets, such as monopolies, because price is lower and output greater. Firms in all market structures should increase production until marginal revenue (MR) equals marginal cost (MC). For a competitive firm, MR equals price at all output levels because the firm is a price taker. However, a monopolist must reduce price to raise sales, so its MR curve will decline with output. Assuming no difference between the MC curves of the purely competitive firm and the monopolist, the latter's downward-sloping MR curve will intersect the MC curve at a lower output level than that for a competitive firm. This lower output level corresponds to a higher point (a higher price) on the demand curve.
Answer (A) is incorrect because only goodwill advertising is likely to be used. The monopolist will already be maximizing its profits because it has no competitors. Answer (B) is incorrect because monopolists produce a lower rate of output than in a competitive market. Answer (C) is incorrect because the blend of capital and labor is not a consideration exclusive to the monopolist.

24. All of the following are characteristics of monopolistic competition except that

   A. The firms sell a homogeneous product.

   B. The firms tend not to recognize the reaction of competitors when determining prices.

   C. Individual firms have some control over the price of the product.

   D. The consumer demand curve is highly elastic.

Answer (A) is correct. *(CMA, adapted)*
   REQUIRED: The item not a characteristic of monopolistic competition.
   DISCUSSION: Monopolistic competition assumes a large number of firms with differentiated (heterogeneous) products, and relatively easy entry into the market. Sellers have some price control because of product differentiation. Monopolistic competition is characterized by nonprice competition, such as advertising, service after the sale, and emphasis on trademark quality. In the short run, firms equate marginal revenue and marginal cost. In the long run, firms tend to earn normal (not economic) profits, and price exceeds marginal cost, resulting in an underallocation of resources. Firms produce less than the ideal output, and the industry is populated by too many firms that are too small in size. Price is higher and output less than in pure competition.
   Answer (B) is incorrect because responses to competitors' actions are unnecessary if products are sufficiently differentiated to make price competition meaningless. Answer (C) is incorrect because product differentiation permits some price control. Answer (D) is incorrect because the availability of close substitutes makes the product demand curve elastic.

25. A good example of monopolistic competition is the

   A. Agriculture market.

   B. Fast food industry.

   C. Steel industry.

   D. Auto industry.

Answer (B) is correct. *(CMA, adapted)*
   REQUIRED: The industry that is a good example of monopolistic competition.
   DISCUSSION: Monopolistic competition is best represented by the fast food industry. Many firms are in competition, but the products are differentiated.
   Answer (A) is incorrect because agriculture is closer to pure competition. Many producers sell an undifferentiated product. Answer (C) is incorrect because the steel industry has few firms and is best characterized as an oligopoly. Moreover, its products tend to be standardized. Answer (D) is incorrect because the auto industry is oligopolistic. Few producers exist because of the difficulty of entering the market.

26. The following graph depicts the marginal cost (MC), marginal revenue (MR), demand, and average total cost (ATC) curves of a firm in a monopolistically competitive industry:

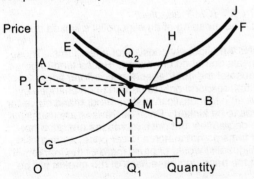

If the firm is producing the optimal output, it is most likely

   A. Incurring a loss in the short run if its average total cost curve is IJ.

   B. Earning profits in the long run if its average total cost curve is IJ.

   C. Earning an economic profit if its average total cost curve is EF.

   D. Incurring a loss in the short run if its average total cost curve is EF.

Answer (A) is correct. *(Publisher, adapted)*
   REQUIRED: The profit (loss) position of a monopolistic competitor.
   DISCUSSION: AB is a typical demand curve of a monopolistic competitor. It is negatively sloped but is more elastic (less sloped) than that of a pure monopoly. CD is the MR curve because it is negatively sloped and below the demand curve. GH is the MC curve, and its intersection with the MR curve at point M establishes the optimal output (Q_1) and the price (P_1), which correspond to point N on the demand curve AB. Consequently, EF and IJ must be ATC curves because they have negative slopes above the MC curve and positive slopes below it. They also intersect the MC curve at their minima. If the firm's ATC curve is IJ, it is incurring a short-run loss because ATC at the optimal output exceeds the price. The loss equals output times the excess of ATC over price. This loss is a short run loss because in the long run a firm will most likely shut down when ATC exceeds price.
   Answer (B) is incorrect because the firm is incurring a loss. Answer (C) is incorrect because, when the ATC curve is tangent to the demand curve at the optimal output, the firm is earning a normal, not an economic, profit. The firm is breaking even, which is the long-run tendency for a monopolistic competitor. Answer (D) is incorrect because, when the ATC curve is tangent to the demand curve at the optimal output, the firm is earning a normal, not an economic, profit. The firm is breaking even, which is the long-run tendency for a monopolistic competitor.

27. A natural monopoly exists because

    A. The firm owns natural resources.

    B. The firm holds patents.

    C. Economic and technical conditions permit only one efficient supplier.

    D. The government is the only supplier.

Answer (C) is correct. *(CMA, adapted)*
REQUIRED: The reason a natural monopoly exists.
DISCUSSION: A natural monopoly exists because economic and technical conditions exist in the industry or economy that permit only one efficient supplier in a locale. A natural monopoly exists when economies of scale are very great, that is, when very large-scale operations are required to achieve low unit costs and prices. In a natural monopoly, the unit cost (the long-term average cost) of meeting the entire demand is minimized when the industry consists of one firm. Thus, competition would be undesirable because the presence of two or more firms would prevent the realization of the necessary economies of scale.
Answer (A) is incorrect because the ownership of natural resources is not a necessary factor in the existence of a natural monopoly. Answer (B) is incorrect because the ownership of patents is not a necessary factor in the existence of a natural monopoly. Answer (D) is incorrect because the government is typically not the supplier when a natural monopoly exists.

28. The distinguishing characteristic of oligopolistic markets is

    A. A single seller of a homogeneous product with no close substitute.

    B. A single seller of a heterogeneous product with no close substitute.

    C. Lack of entry and exit barriers in the industry.

    D. Mutual interdependence of firm pricing and output decisions.

Answer (D) is correct. *(CMA, adapted)*
REQUIRED: The distinguishing characteristic of oligopolistic markets.
DISCUSSION: The oligopoly model is much less specific than the other market structures, but there are typically few firms in the industry. Thus, the decisions of rival firms do not go unnoticed. Products can be either differentiated or standardized. Prices tend to be rigid (sticky) because of the interdependence among firms. Entry is difficult because of either natural or created barriers. Price leadership is typical in oligopolistic industries. Under price leadership, price changes are announced first by a major firm. Once the industry leader has spoken, other firms in the industry match the price charged by the leader. The mutual interdependence of the firms influences both pricing and output decisions.
Answer (A) is incorrect because oligopolies contain several firms; a single seller is characteristic of a monopoly. Answer (B) is incorrect because oligopolies contain several firms; a single seller is characteristic of a monopoly. Answer (C) is incorrect because oligopolies are typified by barriers to entry; that is the reason the industry has only a few firms.

29. An oligopolist faces a "kinked" demand curve. This terminology indicates that

    A. When an oligopolist lowers its price, the other firms in the oligopoly will match the price reduction, but if the oligopolist raises its price, the other firms will ignore the price change.

    B. An oligopolist faces a non-linear demand for its product, and price changes will have little effect on demand for that product.

    C. An oligopolist can sell its product at any price, but after the "saturation point," another oligopolist will lower its price and, therefore, shift the demand curve to the left.

    D. Consumers have no effect on the demand curve, and an oligopolist can shape the curve to optimize its own efficiency.

Answer (A) is correct. *(CMA, adapted)*
REQUIRED: The meaning of an oligopolist's kinked demand curve.
DISCUSSION: An oligopoly consists of a few firms. Thus, the decisions of rivals do not go unnoticed. Prices tend to be rigid (sticky) because of the interdependence among firms. Because competitors respond only to certain price changes by one of the firms in an oligopolistic industry, the demand curve for an oligopolist tends to be kinked. Price decreases are usually matched by price decreases, but price increases are often not followed. If other firms do not match a lower price, a price decrease by an oligopolist would capture more of the market. If other firms match the price decrease, less of the market will be captured.
Answer (B) is incorrect because price changes will have an effect on demand for an oligopolist's product. Answer (C) is incorrect because an oligopolist must essentially match the price of other firms in the industry. Answer (D) is incorrect because an oligopolist cannot shape its demand curve.

Use Gleim's ***CPA Test Prep*** for interactive testing with over 2,000 additional multiple-choice questions!

STUDY UNIT SIX
MACROECONOMICS

(26 pages of outline)

This study unit is the second of three related to the economic environment of a business and its industry. **Macroeconomics** is the study of the **three interrelated aspects** of any economy taken as a whole: inflation, unemployment, and growth.

In the process of attempting to describe (and manage) these factors, macroeconomists require measurements of an economy's performance. **National income accounting** is the subdiscipline concerned with calculating these measures, such as gross domestic product and national income.

Over time, macroeconomists have noted that economic growth in capitalistic economies has not been constant but has been punctuated by distinct **cycles** of expansion and contraction.

Classical economic theory maintains that the free market contains **self-correcting mechanisms** that eventually rein in the forces of inflation and unemployment to reestablish aggregate equilibrium.

The worldwide **Great Depression** of the 1930s, however, brought that theory profoundly into question. Prices, employment, and output stayed bottomed out year after year. The supposed self-correcting mechanisms of the free market never seemed to kick in. Observing this situation, English economist **John Maynard Keynes** (1883–1946, pronounced "kaynz") theorized that if **pessimism** were deep enough among businesspeople, they would never feel the sense of confidence about the future necessary to invest in the productive capacity that would get the economy booming again.

To Keynes, the answer lay in **government intervention**, the subject of Subunits 4 and 5. **Fiscal policy** refers to government purchasing goods and services in the marketplace (creating the demand that private business can then supply). **Monetary policy** refers to the setting of interest rates and managing the supply of money which businesses can deploy to purchase productive capacity. These practices are, to this day, termed **Keynesian economics**.

After the Second World War ended, the large numbers of discharged servicemen returning to the United States were expected to cause a disastrous spike in unemployment. In response, Congress passed the **Employment Act of 1946**, in which the federal government assumed responsibility for full employment, price stability, and economic growth. This was a triumph for Keynesian economics.

6.1 THREE PRINCIPAL ISSUES IN MACROECONOMICS

1. **Inflation**

   a. Inflation is a **sustained increase in the general level of prices**. The reported rate of inflation is therefore an **average** of the increase across all prices in the economy. This simple definition is not sufficient to fully understand inflation's impact, however.

      1) The **value of** any unit of **money** (e.g., the U.S. dollar) is measured by how many goods and services can be acquired in exchange for it. This is referred to as money's **purchasing power**.

      2) If the rate of inflation for all goods and services were the average, consumers would be able to buy less and less with each dollar -- their **purchasing power would steadily be eroded**. There are two main reasons why this is not the case, however:

         a) The prices of individual goods and services rise and fall at different rates.
         b) Wages generally rise in step with inflation.

      3) Thus, **mild, steady inflation does not usually erode purchasing power**. High or unpredictable inflation, on the other hand, can be very disruptive of economic activity.

   b. The **rate of inflation** is stated in **percentage terms**, calculated using a price index.

      1) A **price index** is a measure of the price of a market basket of goods and services in one year compared with the price in a designated base year. By definition, the **index for the base year is 100**.

         a) The **rate of inflation** is calculated by comparing the change in the two years' indexes.

         $$\frac{Current\text{-}year\ price\ index\ -\ Prior\text{-}year\ price\ index}{Prior\text{-}year\ price\ index}$$

         b) For example, if the market basket in Year 3 was 10% higher than the base year and in Year 4 was 15% higher, the inflation rate for Year 4 is:

         $$\frac{115\ -\ 110}{110} = 4.55\%$$

         c) The most commonly used index is the Consumer Price Index [see item 2.c.1) in Subunit 2].

   c. The distinction between nominal income and real income is crucial for understanding the effects of inflation.

      1) **Nominal income** is the **amount in money** received by a consumer as wages, interest, rent, and profits. For example, a systems analyst might have an annual salary, and therefore a nominal income, of $64,000.

      2) **Real income** is the **purchasing power** of the income received, regardless of how it is denominated. Purchasing power relates directly to the consumer's standard of living.

      3) **Real income shrinks when nominal income does not keep pace with inflation.**

   d. **Macroeconomic Effects of Inflation**

      1) Inflation **arbitrarily redistributes wealth**. This redistribution reflects neither the workings of the free market nor the government's attempt to intervene.

      2) When inflation is **unexpected**, it can cause economic chaos.

      3) The **efficiency** of business relationships is **reduced**. Such efficiency relies on stable pricing.

4) **Usury laws** place arbitrary, nonmarket-determined caps on nominal interest rates, regardless of the real interest rate. A ceiling is placed on the price of money, choking off the available supply of lendable funds.

e. **Two Types of Inflation**

1) **Demand-pull inflation** is generated by **demand outpacing the supply of goods** to satisfy it.

   a) Since the economy cannot produce enough to keep up with demand, the prices of existing goods are bid up. This kind of inflation is depicted by the phrase, **"Too many dollars chasing too few goods."**

   b) In a modern economy, demand-pull inflation arises when the economy approaches **full employment** and **demand continues to increase.**

2) **Cost-push inflation** is generated by **increased per-unit production costs**, which are passed on to consumers in the form of higher prices.

   a) Increases in raw materials costs are the principal cause, particularly when they come about suddenly in the form of a **supply shock**.

      i) The most prominent example is the first OPEC oil embargo of 1973–74, in response to the United States, Western Europe, and Japan taking the side of Israel in the "October War."

   b) Cost-push inflation tends to be **self-limiting**.

      i) With input prices increasing, output is driven down and unemployment is driven up. As lower output and higher unemployment set in, the economy falls into recession and further price increases are no longer possible.

2. **Unemployment**

a. The **unemployment rate** is stated in percentage terms. Controversies swirl around the derivation of both the numerator and denominator.

$$\frac{Number\ of\ unemployed}{Size\ of\ labor\ force} \times 100$$

1) The unemployment rate is published by the **U.S. Bureau of Labor Statistics**. The Bureau samples American households each month.

   a) The first group **excluded from the denominator** consists of those who are (1) under the age of 16 or (2) incarcerated or institutionalized.

   b) The second group **excluded from the denominator** consists of those classified as **not in the labor force**.

      i) Among the people counted in this group are homemakers, full-time students, and retirees.

      ii) Also included in this group are **discouraged workers**, a major bone of contention when discussing the official unemployment rate. These are the unemployed who are able to work but are **not actively seeking work**.

   c) Among those who **remain in the denominator**, no distinction is made between **full- and part-time workers**. They are all considered equally employed.

   d) The **numerator** consists of those who are willing and able to work and who are **seeking employment**.

2) The official statistics can be **distorted** by

   a) Discouraged workers who falsely claim to be seeking work

   b) Those employed in the underground economy

b. **Three Types of Unemployment**

1) **Frictional unemployment** is the amount of unemployment caused by the normal workings of the labor market.

a) This group can include those moving to another city, those ceasing work temporarily to pursue further education and training, and those who are simply between jobs.

b) This definition acknowledges that a "normal" amount of unemployment exists at any given time in a dynamic economy.

2) **Structural unemployment** results when the composition of the workforce doesn't match the need. It is the result of changes in consumer demand, technology, and geographical location.

a) As consumers' desires shift, certain skills become obsolete. As horse racing, once the biggest sport in the United States, lost popularity, jockeys and grooms became less employable.

b) The computer revolution has drastically changed the skills required for many jobs and completely eliminated others.

c) As automakers shifted production from the (unionized) Rust Belt to the (nonunionized) Sun Belt, workers in the old cities of the midwest were laid off.

3) **Cyclical unemployment** is directly related to the level of an economy's output. For this reason, it is sometimes called **deficient-demand unemployment**.

a) As consumers slow their spending, firms cut back production and lay off workers.

b) The Great Depression was a period of low prices, low demand, and extremely low industrial output. During the worst of this period (ca. 1933), as much as 25% of the American labor force was out of work.

c. **"Full" Employment**

1) The **natural rate of unemployment** consists of frictional and structural unemployment combined.

a) Economists consider the economy to be at **full employment** when all unemployed workers fall into only these two categories.

b) The rate varies over time because of demographic and institutional changes in the economy.

2) The **economy's potential output** is the real (i.e., inflation-adjusted) domestic output that could be achieved if the economy sustained full employment.

a) This concept illustrates the importance of providing all interested workers with productive jobs.

d. **Macroeconomic Effects of Unemployment**

1) **Lost value to the economy** is the primary economic cost of unemployment. The goods not produced and services not provided by idle workers can never be regained.

a) This loss is called the **GDP gap** (GDP, or gross domestic product, is a measure of national output; see item 1. in Subunit 2).

b) **Okun's law**, proposed in the early 1960s by American economist Arthur Okun (1928–1980), states that for each **1% excess** of actual unemployment over the natural rate, a **2%–3% GDP gap** results.

2) The **burdens of unemployment are spread unequally** among groups of workers.

    a) Blue-collar workers are more often impacted than white-collar workers. Similarly, lower-skilled workers experience higher rates of unemployment than those with larger skillsets.

    b) The young and ethnic minorities tend to be unemployed more often. However, unemployment rates for men and women are roughly the same.

3) Unemployment has **social costs**, including loss of skills, personal and family stress, violence and other crime, and social upheaval.

e. **The Trade-Off Between Inflation and Unemployment**

1) In the late 1960s, New Zealand economist A.W. Phillips (1914–1975) proposed a graph similar to the one presented below as depicting a predictable trade-off between wages and the unemployment rate.

    a) The curve was later adapted by macroeconomists to depict a trade-off between inflation and unemployment and was named the **Phillips Curve**.

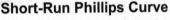

Short-Run Phillips Curve

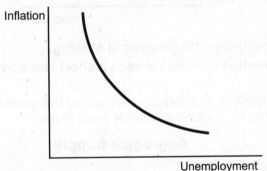

2) The Phillips Curve was held to be a sound description of macroeconomic reality until the petroleum supply shocks of 1973–74 and 1979–80.

    a) Until that time, inflation had been **from the demand side**. With total output and prices increasing together, job creation kept pace with demand. The Phillips Curve appeared to supply a set of options from which macroeconomists could choose to **"fine-tune" the economy**.

    b) The drastic jumps in the price of (and slashing in the supply of) oil experienced in the 70s, however, imposed inflation **from the supply side**. Stagflation, a general rise in prices accompanied by a fall in overall output, arose.

3) Thus, when an economy is experiencing **demand-side inflation**, high inflation is compensated for by an improvement in the unemployment rate. The Phillips Curve depicts this phenomenon in the **short-run**.

    a) When an economy is experiencing **supply-side inflation**, by contrast, the problems of high inflation are compounded by an increase in unemployment.

3.   **Aggregate demand and supply.** Just as individual firms face supply and demand curves, an economy as a whole can be described by using the same graphical tools.

   a.   **Aggregate demand** is a schedule reflecting all the goods and services that consumers are willing and able to buy at various price levels. The curve thus reflects the relationship between the **price level and real GDP**.

Aggregate Demand

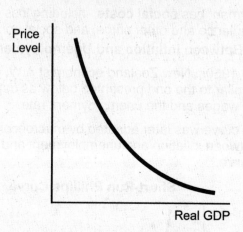

   1)   Aggregate demand is **downward sloping**.
   2)   **No distinction** is made between a **short-run and long-run** aggregate demand curve.

   b.   **Aggregate supply** is a schedule reflecting all the goods and services an economy is willing and able to produce at various price levels.

Aggregate Supply

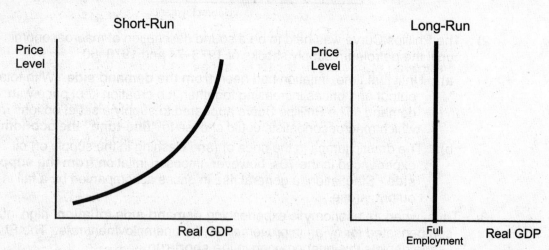

   1)   Over the short run, wages and other input prices may take quite some time to adjust to the changes in other price levels. The firm can produce more in the short term and earn excess profits.

      a)   Thus, the **short-run aggregate supply curve is upward sloping**.

2)   In the long run, wages and other input prices adjust to match changes in other price levels, and excess profits earned in the short-term are squeezed out.

    a)   Thus, the **long-run aggregate supply curve is a vertical line** extending up from the point of full-employment GDP on the x axis.

3)   The distinction between the short-run and long-run aggregate supply curves is captured in the aphorism **"All costs are variable in the long run."**

4.   **Economic Growth**

   a.   An economy is in equilibrium where the aggregate demand and aggregate supply curves intersect. **Economic growth** takes place when both curves are driven to the right. Both the level of output and the price level increase.

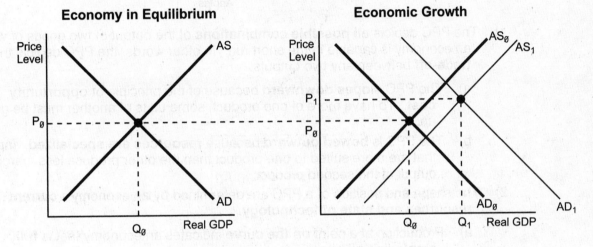

1)   Growth is a **major macroeconomic goal** because when an economy grows

    a)   Workers earn higher real wages and have access to a richer variety, and greater quantity, of goods and services are made available. This is the essence of a **rising standard of living**.

2)   Growth can be achieved not only by increased resource inputs but also by **improved efficiency in the use** of those resources. This is termed productivity.

    a)   **Productivity** is usually measured by **worker productivity**, that is, the total real GDP produced during the year divided by the total number of hours worked in the economy. The more a worker can produce in an hour of work, the more productive (s)he is.

    b)   Productivity consists of **three factors**:

       i)   **Amount of capital.** The more an economy has invested in plant and machinery, the higher its productivity will be.

       ii)   **State of technology.** The more technologically advanced an economy's plant and machinery are, the higher its productivity will be.

       iii)   **Workforce competence.** The more educated and trained an economy's workers are, the higher its productivity will be.

b.   Another way to understand growth is with a **production possibilities curve (PPC)**.

Production Possibilities Curve

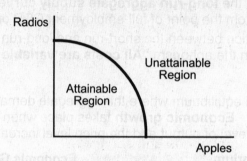

1)   The PPC depicts **all possible combinations** of the output of two goods of which an economy is capable in the short run. In other words, the PPC depicts the **trade-off** between any two outputs.

   a)   The PPC **slopes downward** because of the principle of **opportunity cost**. To have more of one product, some units of another must be given up.

   b)   The PPC is **bowed outward** because **resources are specialized**. Inputs that are more suited to one product than the other produce less marginal output of the second product.

2)   The shape and position of a PPC are determined by an economy's **current resources and state of technology**.

   a)   Production at a point **on the curve** indicates an economy that is **fully employing** all its resources.

      i)   All resources are in use and no additional output can be produced in the short run. An increase in aggregate demand will serve to drive inflation.

   b)   Production at a point **within the curve** indicates a failure to achieve full employment and full production.

   c)   Production at a point **outside the curve** is only possible by incurring a **trade deficit**, i.e., importing more than the country exports.

3)   In the **long run**, the curve can be **shifted outward with economic growth**.

c.   **Policies for Economic Growth**

1)   **Demand-side policies.** In modern economies, actors in a free market are not the only parties to the determination of aggregate demand.

   a)   The **government** can deploy the tools of fiscal policy and monetary policy to either **stimulate or suppress demand** (depending on whether a recessionary or inflationary environment looms, respectively).

      i)   To **encourage economic growth**, stimulative policies are required.

2)   **Supply-side policies.** The government can also implement policies to increase the country's **stock of investment capital**. Businesses use this capital to increase their productive capacity, thereby **stimulating aggregate supply**.

5.   Stop and review! You have completed the outline for this subunit. Study multiple-choice questions 1 through 10 beginning on page 170.

6.2 DOMESTIC OUTPUT, NATIONAL INCOME, AND PRICE LEVELS

1. **Measuring an Economy's Output**

   a. In the United States, the **Bureau of Economic Analysis** (BEA, an agency of the Department of Commerce) is responsible for compiling the National Income and Product Accounts (NIPA). These can be found at www.bea.gov.

   b. **Gross domestic product (GDP)** is the principal measure of national economic performance.

      1) GDP is

         a) The **total market value**
         b) Of **all final goods and services**
         c) Produced **within the boundaries of the U.S.**
         d) By **domestic- or foreign-owned sources**
         e) During a **specified period of time** (usually a year)

      2) GDP is calculated **without regard to the ownership** of productive resources.

         a) Thus, the value of the output of a U.S.-owned factory abroad is excluded, but the output of a foreign-owned factory in the U.S. is included.

         b) This is in contrast to **gross national product (GNP)**, which is the total market value of all final goods and services produced by U.S.-owned sources, no matter where located.

            i) In early 1992, the BEA changed the focus of its national income reporting from GNP to GDP to more closely parallel the reporting of other countries.

   c. There are **two approaches** to the measurement of GDP.

      1) The **expenditures approach** is the simpler of the two. It calculates GDP as the sum of all expenditures in the economy.

         Expenditures Approach

	In Billions
Consumption by households	$6,000
Investment by businesses	1,200
Government purchases	2,020
Net exports	(400)
Gross domestic product	**$8,820**

         GICE

      2) The **income approach** is much more complex because it measures each category of the economy's output. The income approach yields two important **intermediate measures**.

         a) **National income (NI)** is all income **generated by American-owned resources**, no matter where located. By far the largest component is employee compensation.

            Income Approach

		In Billions
Wages		$5,000
Rents		100
Interest		500
Profits:		
Proprietors' income	$500	
Corporate income taxes	100	
Distributed corp. profits (dividends)	500	
Undistributed corp. profits (retained earnings)	100	
Total profits (retained earnings)		1,200
National income		**$6,800**

b) **Net domestic product (NDP)** measures income **generated in the U.S.**, no matter who owns the resources that generated it. Two components are added to national income to arrive at this figure:

   i) Indirect business taxes (sales taxes, excise taxes, etc.) that are collected by businesses and passed on to some level of government, and

   ii) Net foreign-factor income, which is the excess of income generated in the U.S. from foreign-owned resources over income generated in other countries from U.S.-owned resources.

		In Billions
National income		$6,800
Indirect business taxes		500
Foreign-factor income:		
U.S. income from foreign-owned resources	$30	
Foreign income from U.S.-owned resources	(10)	
Net foreign-factor income		20
Net domestic product		$7,320

c) **Gross domestic product (GDP)** is arrived at by adding back to net national product the **capital stock that was consumed** in the process of generating the income.

   i) Even though it is merely an accounting convention and not an exact engineering measurement, **depreciation** is considered to be the amount of **capital stock consumed** during a period.

	In Billions
Net domestic product	$7,320
Depreciation	1,500
Gross domestic product	$8,820

d) **Alternative calculations** can be derived by working backwards through the formulas:

   i) **NDP** = GDP – depreciation
   ii) **NI** = NDP – Net foreign-factor income – indirect business taxes

3) **Two Other Income Measures**

   a) **Personal income (PI)** is all income **received by individuals**, whether earned or unearned.

   b) **Disposable income (DI)** is the income of **individuals after taxes** have been taken out.

      i) Disposable income is divided between (a) consumption and interest payments and (b) savings.

	In Billions
National income	$6,800
Social Security contributions	(600)
Corporate income taxes	(100)
Undistributed corporate profits	(100)
Transfer payments	1,400
Personal income	$7,400
Personal taxes	(1,600)
Disposable income	$5,800

    d.   **GDP as a Measure of a Country's Prosperity**

        1)   **Real per capita GDP** is the easiest way to measure the improvement in a country's **standard of living**.

            a)   If **real GDP** (i.e., adjusted for inflation) rises at a faster rate than the population, the country is experiencing a rising standard of living.

    e.   **Challenges Inherent in the Calculation of GDP**

        1)   Calculating GDP requires aggregating an **enormous amount of data**, some of which, from privately held companies for instance, may be difficult to acquire.

            a)   GDP includes both goods and services, and the **value placed on services** can sometimes be highly subjective.

        2)   GDP is a monetary measure; therefore, **comparing GDP over time** requires adjustment for changes in the price level (see "Nominal GDP" and "Real GDP" under item 2. below).

    f.   **Limitations of GDP**

        1)   GDP includes **only final goods and services**. Much economic activity involves the trading of **intermediate goods**, such as when a tire company buys rubber.

            a)   The exchange of intermediate goods is not captured in GDP since that would involve **double counting** some goods.

        2)   Increases in GDP often involve **environmental damage** such as noise, congestion, or pollution.

            a)   Also, some economic activity takes place as a result of **disasters**. Following a hurricane, home improvement stores experience a boom in sales. While this benefit is reflected in GDP, the devastating financial loss of the customers is not included in the calculation.

        3)   A huge amount of economic activity in **developing countries** takes place in the **underground economy**. None of this is captured in GDP.

            a)   This affects the calculation of GDP in developed nations as well, since such activities as **housework** and **cash-basis lawncare** are left out of the calculation.

        4)   GDP includes **only goods produced**; if the goods are **not sold** until a later period, GDP does not capture this.

        5)   The value placed by consumers on **leisure time** is not included in GDP.

2.   **Price Level Accounting**

    a.   **Nominal GDP.** The basic GDP calculation involves adding the total market value of all final goods and services in **current dollars**.

        1)   This is clearly unsatisfactory when trying to compare the output of one year with that of another, since the general price level is constantly fluctuating.

    b.   **Real GDP.** To facilitate year-to-year comparisons, nominal GDP is adjusted for changes in the general price level so it can be reported in **constant dollars**.

$$Real\ GDP = \frac{Nominal\ GDP}{Price\ index}$$

c.   **Choice of Price Index**

1)   The **consumer price index (CPI)** is the most common price index for adjusting nominal GDP.

a)   The CPI measures inflation by a **monthly pricing** of items on a **typical household shopping list**.

$$CPI = \frac{Cost\ of\ market\ basket\ in\ current\ year}{Cost\ of\ market\ basket\ in\ base\ year} \times 100$$

2)   The **GDP deflator** is a far more comprehensive price index and is for that reason preferred by some economists.

a)   Where the CPI focuses only on the goods consumed by typical households, the GDP deflator includes **every item produced in the economy**.

3.   **Leading Economic Indicators**

a.   Economists use **leading indicators** to help them **forecast future economic trends** (by the same token, lagging indicators report past economic activity).

1)   The best-known set of leading indicators is that prepared by **The Conference Board**, a private research group with more than 2,700 corporate and other members worldwide.

2)   The Conference Board's **index of leading indicators** consists of 10 measures.

b.   A change in either of the following indicators suggests a future change in real GDP in the **same direction**:

1)   The average workweek for manufacturing workers
2)   New orders for consumer goods
3)   New orders for nondefense capital goods
4)   Building permits for houses
5)   Stock prices
6)   The money supply
7)   The spread between short- and long-term interest rates
8)   Consumer expectations

c.   A change in either of the following indicators suggests a future change in real GDP in the **opposite direction**:

1)   Initial claims for unemployment insurance (more people out of work indicates slowing business activity)

2)   Vendor performance (because vendors have more time on their hands and are carrying high levels of inventory)

4.   Stop and review! You have completed the outline for this subunit. Study multiple-choice questions 11 through 18 beginning on page 173.

6.3 BUSINESS CYCLES

1. Over the **very long run**, growth in capitalistic economies has not been steady. The overall trend of growth is periodically interrupted by **periods of instability**.

    a. This tendency toward instability within the context of overall growth is termed the **business cycle** and can be depicted by the following graph:

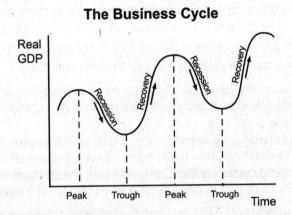

The Business Cycle

1) At a **peak**, the economy is

    a) At or near full employment, and

    b) At or near maximum output for the current level of resources and technology.

        i) In other words, the economy is **booming**.

2) During a **recession**, income, output, and employment fall. This period must last **at least six months** to be recognized as such.

    a) In an attempt by businesses to hold on to profits, **prices may not fall** even as wages do.

        i) If the recession is severe enough, prices will fall and the phase will be considered a **depression**.

3) In a **trough**, economic activity reaches its lowest ebb.

4) During a **recovery**, output and employment rise. Eventually, the price level rises also.

    b. **Possible Causes**

1) When **consumer confidence declines**, i.e., when consumers become pessimistic about the future, they spend less. Unsold inventory starts to pile up. Businesses respond by cutting back production and laying off workers.

2) The **introduction of major innovations**, such as railroads, airplanes, and computers, can have a destabilizing effect on an economy.

3) A **miscalculation in fiscal or monetary policy** by the government may be sufficient to induce a recession or a boom.

2. Stop and review! You have completed the outline for this subunit. Study multiple-choice questions 19 and 20 beginning on page 175.

6.4 FISCAL POLICY

1. **Definition**

   a. Even in capitalistic countries, **government** plays a very large role in the workings of the economy.

      1) The first major area in which government participates is called **fiscal policy**, that is, the government as one of the players in the marketplace, taking in revenues (taxes) and making purchases (the annual budget).

      2) The other major area is called monetary policy and is discussed in Subunit 5.

   b. Fiscal policies can be discretionary or nondiscretionary.

      1) **Discretionary** fiscal policy involves spending that is under the control of individuals within the government, such as contracting for new weapons systems.

      2) **Nondiscretionary** fiscal policy is that which is enacted in law. Certain outlays, e.g., Social Security, must be made regardless of their consequences or source of funding because the Congress has made them a legal requirement. No individual or group can choose to withhold (or increase) these expenditures.

2. **Gross domestic product (GDP)** is a comprehensive measure of an economy's output during a given period of time.

   a. The simplest way to calculate GDP is simply as **the sum of all spending**, public and private, in the economy over the course of the year. This is known as the **expenditures approach**.

      1) The expenditures approach classifies spending into **four broad categories**.

   b. **Consumer spending (C).** This is by far the largest component of GDP, and its most important determinant is **personal incomes**.

      1) Changes in incomes do not affect GDP dollar-for-dollar, however. For every additional dollar consumers receive in income, some portion is spent and the remainder is siphoned off into savings.

      2) These phenomena are known as the **marginal propensity to consume (MPC)** and the **marginal propensity to save (MPS)**.

         a) For example, if, taken as a whole, consumers in an economy spend 80% of each new unit of income they receive, the MPC for that economy is .80, and the MPS is .20 (1.0 − .80).

   c. **Investment spending (I).** While not as large a component of GDP as consumer spending, business investment is by far the most **volatile** component. This is because investment reflects the level of businesses' **optimism** about future demand, and business optimism is subject to wide and sudden variations.

   d. **Government spending (G).** Government's component of total spending consists of

      1) Outlays for **goods and services** that are consumed by the government, and

      2) Outlays for long-lived **public infrastructure assets**, such as schools, bridges, and military bases.

         a) Transfer payments are not included since they will be spent on final goods and services by consumers.

   e. **Net exports (NX).** GDP attempts to capture all spending on American-made goods, no matter who purchases them.

f. The following schedule is an example of the expenditures approach to calculating GDP:

	In Billions	Legend
Consumption by households	$6,000	C
Investment by businesses	1,200	I
Government purchases	2,020	G
Net exports	(400)	NX
Equilibrium GDP	**$8,820**	**C + I + G + NX**

1) These functions can be depicted graphically as follows:

Aggregate Expenditures and Equilibrium GDP

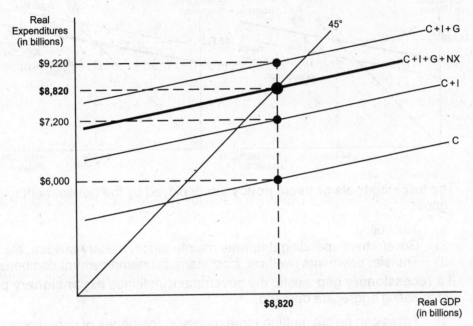

2) The **slope of the consumption function is the marginal propensity to consume** [see item 2.b.2) on the previous page].

3. By definition, **total expenditures equal real GDP**.

a. Thus, **demand-side equilibrium** is at any point on the **45° line** (along which the values on the x and y axes are equal).

b. A **shift** in any of the four expenditure functions causes **equilibrium GDP to rise or fall**.

1) **Consumer spending (C).** If consumers increase their spending, for example, because they expect incomes to rise or because taxes have been lowered, the consumption function shifts up, reflecting a rise in national output.

2) **Investment spending (I).** If businesses increase their spending on productive facilities, for example, because a new generation of technology is available or because real interest rates have fallen, the investment function shifts up, reflecting a rise in national output.

3) **Government spending (G).** If government increases its spending, for example, because of a military buildup, the government function shifts up, reflecting a rise in national output.

4) **Net exports (NX).** If American firms sell more products overseas, the net exports function shifts up, reflecting a rise in national output. If exports eventually exceed imports, this will become a positive number.

c.   In the previous example, the economy is in equilibrium at an output-and-consumption level of $8.82 trillion.

   1)   If the **current level** of output and spending is **less than** the amount of which the economy is capable at full employment of all its resources, the actual aggregate expenditures curve rests below the full-employment curve. The distance between the two is a **recessionary gap**.

   2)   If the **current level** of output and spending **exceeds** the full-employment level, the actual aggregate expenditures curve rests above the full-employment curve. The distance between the two is an **inflationary gap**.

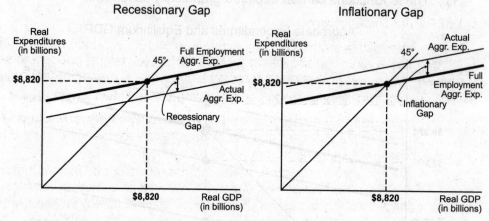

d.   The following **tools of fiscal policy** are deployed by the government to close these gaps:

   1)   Tax policy
   2)   Government spending (highway maintenance, military buildup, etc.)
   3)   Transfer payments (welfare, food stamps, unemployment compensation, etc.)

e.   If a **recessionary gap** exists, the government institutes **expansionary policies**, stimulating aggregate demand.

   1)   Taxes can be cut, putting more money in the hands of consumers.
   2)   Government can increase its spending, generating demand for goods and services from the private sector.
   3)   Transfer payments can be increased, putting more money in the hands of consumers.

f.   If an **inflationary gap** exists, the government institutes **contractionary policies**, suppressing aggregate demand.

   1)   Taxes can be increased, giving consumers less disposable income.
   2)   Government can cut its spending, reducing demand for goods and services from the private sector.
   3)   Transfer payments can be decreased, giving consumers less disposable income.

4.   **Multiplier effect.** When the government increases its own spending or encourages business investment, the **effect** of each new dollar injected into the economy is **greater than one**.

   a.   When a dollar enters the economy, it is one person's income. When that person spends it, it becomes another person's income, and so forth.

   b.   As money "ricochets" through the economy, then, it has a **cumulative effect** greater than the single amount. (Likewise, when a dollar is removed from the cycle, it has an impact greater than that of removing a single dollar.)

c.   With **each round of earning and spending**, the effect of the dollar diminishes. This effect can be greatly simplified in algebraic form as follows:

$$Multiplier = \frac{1}{MPS}$$

   1)   For example, if the MPC is .80 and expenditures increase by $100 million, the increase in equilibrium GDP is $500 million [$100,000,000 × (1.0 ÷ .20)].

d.   As stated on the previous page, the multiplier is only applicable to changes in the **investment (I) and government (G)** expenditure functions. These amounts are injected directly into the economy.

5.   **Effects of Public Expenditure**

a.   **Public expenditure** is the **G** function in the aggregate expenditures model (see item 2. in this subunit). By purchasing (or curtailing purchase of) goods and services from the private sector, government can play a large role in managing aggregate demand.

b.   Public goods and private goods can be distinguished in two ways:

   1)   **Private goods** are characterized by **exclusivity of consumption**. One consumer's enjoyment of a strawberry milkshake means that no other consumer can have the benefit of the same shake.

   2)   **Public goods**, on the other hand, are characterized by **indivisibility of consumption**. All citizens enjoy the benefits of nuclear submarine patrols and public parks, no matter the level of their contribution to these benefits.

c.   Governments are the major (often the only) purchasers of public goods. For example, the federal government is the only consumer of tanks and fighter planes. This has two implications:

   1)   **Income is redistributed** to defense contractors.

   2)   Since a multi-player marketplace is not at work, **resources may not be allocated** as efficiently as possible.

   3)   The relationship of government spending to consumer spending can be graphically illustrated with a production possibilities curve as shown below.

Private vs. Public Goods

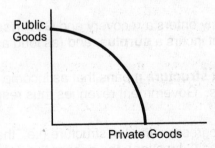

6. **Budget Deficits and Surpluses**

    a. Keynesian theory calls for expansionary fiscal policy during times of recession (to stimulate aggregate demand) and contractionary policy during boom times (to prevent inflation).

        1) **Expansionary policy**, involving increased spending, tax cuts, or both, causes government to incur a **budget deficit**, i.e., the government is spending more than it takes in.

        2) **Contractionary policy**, involving decreased spending, tax hikes, or both, causes government to incur a **budget surplus**, i.e., the government is taking in more than it spends.

    b. The government can avail itself of **two methods for financing a budget deficit**:

        1) **Borrowing.** The government can sell debt instruments such as Treasury bonds and notes to citizens and to foreigners.

        2) **Printing money.** The government can simply order that more paper currency be created.

    c. Both methods of financing a deficit carry **risks**.

        1) **Borrowing** can lead to the **crowding-out effect**. Government debt securities compete in the marketplace for investors. This puts upward pressure on interest rates, inevitably leading to the inability of some private sellers of debt to find financing for their ventures.

        2) **Printing money** tends to devalue the currency ("too many dollars chasing too few goods"), leading to **inflation**.

7. **Progressive Taxation** as a **Built-in Stabilizer**

    a. The progressive rate structure of the Federal tax code constitutes an automatic macroeconomic stabilizer.

        1) The amount of government spending for a period is enacted into law. Congress sets the tax rate structure to approximate the amount of revenue needed to cover the mandated level of spending.

        2) If the economy enters a recession and **GDP falls**, tax revenues also fall. Thus, government inevitably incurs a **deficit**, creating a **stimulus to aggregate demand**.

        3) If the economy enters a recovery and **GDP rises**, tax revenues also rise. Government incurs a **surplus**, and (as long as it isn't spent) **inflation is prevented**.

    b. A **progressive tax structure** means that as income increases, the taxpayer is subject to higher tax rates. Government revenues thus respond in proportion to the desired effect.

        1) The more progressive the tax structure (i.e., the steeper the T function is with respect to the G function), the deeper the deficit is when GDP falls and the greater the government's contribution to economic stimulus.

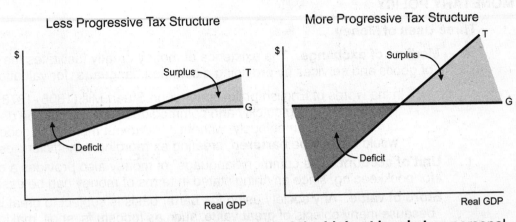

2) For example, in 1993, **Congress raised the highest bracket** on personal income taxes and increased the rate for corporate taxes.

   a) This "stretching out" of tax rates on the high end made the tax system **more progressive**, reflected by an increase in the slope of the T function.

   b) In the latter part of the decade, the U.S. economy entered a boom phase. The **increased progressivity** of the tax structure resulted in a budget surplus, allowing the boom to proceed **without sparking inflation**.

8. **Cyclical vs. structural deficits.** The budget deficit is the **sum** of the cyclical deficit and the structural deficit.

   a. A **cyclical deficit** is one that results from **economic downturns** and not from government action.

      1) As illustrated above, when real GDP falls, tax revenues decrease because of the progressive tax system.

   b. A **structural deficit** is the deficit that **would exist at full employment** if there was no downturn in the economy.

      1) In other words, a structural deficit results from government action, i.e., discretionary fiscal policy.

9. **Timing Issues**

   a. **Recognition lag** is the time it takes for macroeconomists to recognize that a recession (or inflation) is occurring.

   b. **Administrative lag** is the time it takes for the government to act on macroeconomic changes.

   c. **Operational lag** is the time it takes for the changes implemented by the government to take effect; also called **response lag**.

10. Stop and review! You have completed the outline for this subunit. Study multiple-choice questions 21 through 25 beginning on page 176.

6.5 MONETARY POLICY

1. **Three Uses of Money**

    a. **Medium of exchange.** The existence of money greatly facilitates the free exchange of goods and services by providing a common "language" for valuation.

    1) In the words of English philosopher John Stuart Mill (1806–1873), money "is a machine for doing quickly and commodiously what would be done, though less quickly and commodiously, without it." Without money, all goods and services would have to be **bartered**, creating extraordinary inefficiencies.

    b. **Unit of account.** The common "language" of money also provides a convenient basis for bookkeeping, since anything stated in terms of money can be easily compared.

    c. **Store of value.** Any society using the barter basis is subject to great inefficiencies, because many objects of great value, such as foodstuffs, spoil, making them worthless. The value of a unit of money is determined by the quantity of goods and services it can be exchanged for.

2. **The Demand for Money**

    a. When money is **borrowed**, the debtor pays the lender back an amount in addition to the sum that was borrowed.

    1) This amount is called **"interest"** and is, in effect, the **"price" of the loan.**

    a) The rate of interest on a given loan is stated in terms of a **percentage** of the face amount of the loan.

    2) The two major **determinants of the interest rate** on a loan are

    a) Overall economic conditions as reflected in the prime rate [see item 7.d.3) in this subunit], and

    b) The creditworthiness of the borrower.

    b. The **total demand for money** has two components:

    1) **Transactions demand** reflects money's role as a medium of exchange.

    a) When economic activity increases, people need more money to carry out transactions. As **nominal GDP rises**, then, the transactions demand for money **rises**.

    b) For simplicity, it is assumed that the transactions demand for money is determined **entirely** by GDP and not by the interest rate.

    2) **Asset demand** reflects money's role as a store of value.

    a) People have an incentive to hold money since it is the most liquid and least risky of assets.

    b) However, holding money entails an opportunity cost. If money is held in a savings account, it earns less than it would if it were invested in a money-making venture. If it is held outside a financial institution altogether, it earns no return at all.

c)   When rates of return are high, people are more and more likely to place their money in venture projects rather than leave it in the bank. Thus, as **interest rates rise**, the asset demand for money **falls**.

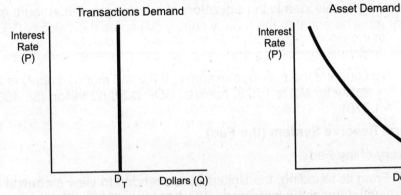

3)   **The total demand for money**, then, is simply the sum of the transactions demand curve and the asset demand curve.

4)   **Money market equilibrium** is attained at the rate where the demand and supply curves intersect. When rates are too low, a surplus of money results; when rates are too high, a shortage results.

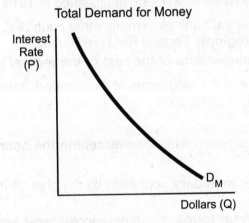

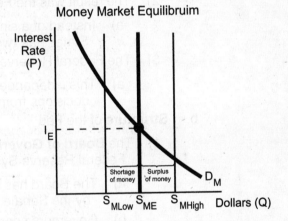

3.   **The Supply of Money**

a.   The Federal Reserve System tracks and reports the **amount of money in circulation**.

1)   The three most widely used metrics are **M1, M2,** and **M3**. M1 includes only the most liquid forms of money. Each successive category includes less and less liquid forms.

2)   The following is a hypothetical money supply calculation for an economy the approximate size of that of the U.S.:

	In Billions
Currency (paper money + coins)	$600
Checking accounts	700
M1 money supply	**$1,300**
Savings accounts, including money market accounts	2,900
Small time deposits (< $100,000)	1,400
Money market mutual funds	800
M2 money supply	**$6,400**
Large time deposits (>= $100,000)	2,200
M3 money supply	**$8,600**

4. **The Velocity of Money**

    a.   The **velocity** of money is the **number of times** the average dollar is **spent in a single year**.

    b.   A corollary of this idea is the **equation of exchange**: the amount expended during a year must be equal to the money supply (M) times the velocity (V).

$$Nominal\ GDP = M \times V$$

        1)   To continue the previous example, if the M2 money supply is $6.4 trillion and the velocity for M2 is 1.378, nominal GDP is $8.82 trillion ($6,400,000,000,000 × 1.378).

5. **The Federal Reserve System (the Fed)**

    a.   **History** of the Fed

        1)   From its founding, the United States tended to view a **central bank** as an anti-democratic institution. The **banking panics** of the late 1800s and early 1900s, however, convinced Congress that such an institution was needed for **stability**.

            a)   A bank panic, also called a **"run,"** occurs when depositors demand to withdraw more cash than the bank has on hand on a given day.

        2)   The result was the Federal Reserve System, established in **1913**.

            a)   Instead of a single central bank as in many other countries, the United States has **twelve regional** Federal Reserve Banks.

        3)   The Federal Reserve is **independent of the rest of the federal government**.

            a)   This independence, and the long terms of its members, insulate the Fed's decisions from political pressures.

    b.   **Structure** of the Fed

        1)   The **Board of Governors** is responsible for **overseeing the operations** of the Federal Reserve System.

            a)   The Board has **seven members** appointed by the president and confirmed by the Senate.

            b)   Governors serve **14-year terms**, and their appointments are staggered. The chair and vice-chair are appointed for 4-year terms by the president and confirmed by the Senate.

        2)   The **Federal Open Market Committee (FOMC)** is responsible for **administering monetary policy**.

            a)   The FOMC consists of **12 members**:

                i)   The seven members of the Board of Governors,

                ii)   The president of the Federal Reserve Bank of New York, and

                iii)   Four presidents from the 11 other Reserve Banks, selected on a rotating basis for a 1-year term.

            b)   The FOMC **meets eight times per year** at the Federal Reserve's headquarters in Washington, DC.

            c)   It is in the role of presiding officer over the FOMC that the chair of the Federal Reserve is the **most powerful central banker** in the world. The financial world hung on every word of every public pronouncement during the chairmanship of **Alan Greenspan** (served 1987–2006).

c. **Roles** of the Fed

    1) **Open market operations.** The Federal Reserve's most important function is the management of the nation's money supply by trading government debt securities (see item 7.b. on the next page).

    2) **Setting reserve requirements.** The Fed can also affect the money supply by changing the percentage of deposits that banks must keep on hand (see item 6.b. below).

    3) **Serving as the bankers' bank.** The Fed serves the same purpose for the nation's banks that banks do for the general public; that is, the Fed loans funds to, and accepts deposits from, commercial financial institutions.

    4) **Overseeing check collection.** The Fed coordinates the clearing of checks written against the nation's checking accounts.

    5) **Issuing currency.** The paper money used in the U.S. (and, to a great extent, the world) economy is distributed by the twelve regional banks. Each bill is marked with a letter code indicating its Federal Reserve Bank of origin (A = Boston, E = Richmond, I = Minneapolis, etc.).

    6) **Serving as fiscal agent for the U.S. government.** The enormous amounts of money collected and spent by the United States Treasury pass through the Federal Reserve System.

    7) **Examining banks.** The Fed assesses individual banks as to profitability and conformity with laws and regulations.

6. **Banks and the Creation of Money**

    a. A review of the example M1 **money supply** calculation in item 3.a.2) on page 165 reminds us that **paper money and coins** (collectively referred to as currency) make up **less than half** the total.

        1) How can there be double the amount of money in the economy than there is currency to represent it?

            a) The answer is that the U.S. Bureau of Engraving and Printing does not create all the money there is. In addition to the federal government, **banks create money**.

        2) For example, a bank customer deposits $1,000 and the bank then loans out $800 of it.

            a) The depositor has a statement showing that (s)he has a claim on $1,000 of cash and the borrower has $800 of cash in his/her hand.

            b) $1,800 now exists where there was only $1,000 previously. The **bank has just created** $800.

    b. **Fractional reserve banking** is the practice of prohibiting banks from lending out all the money they receive on deposit.

        1) The **reserve ratio** is the percentage of each dollar deposited that a bank is required to either (a) keep on hand in its vault or (b) deposit with the Federal Reserve Bank in its district.

            a) The bare minimum that must be held by law is called **required reserves**. As of October 2006, the Fed requires banks with checking account balances between $8.5 million and $45.8 million to keep 3% on hand.

                i) Anything held by the bank above this amount (that is not loaned out) is termed **excess reserves**.

    b)   Fractional reserves are obviously not sufficient to prevent a bank's collapse in the event of a run (that purpose is fulfilled by the Federal Deposit Insurance Corporation).

        i)   The **real purpose** of required reserves is to provide the Fed with another tool for **controlling the money supply** (see item 7.c. on the next page).

    c.   The amount of money banks potentially can create can be approximated by using the **monetary multiplier**.

$$\text{Monetary multiplier} = \frac{1}{\text{Required reserve ratio}}$$

        1)   For example, if the Fed required reserves of 4% on all deposits, a bank with $10 million on deposit would be able to create $250 million of new money [$10,000,000 × (1.0 ÷ .04)].

        2)   Because the multiplier is an inverse, it clearly shows that the **money supply will grow as required reserves are lowered**.

7.   **Goals and Tools of Monetary Policy**

    a.   The Fed attempts to balance the goals of gradual, steady **economic growth** and **price stability** (manageable inflation).

        1)   The Fed has **three tools of monetary policy** at its disposal to achieve these goals:

            a)   Open-market operations,
            b)   The required reserve ratio, and
            c)   The discount rate.

    b.   **Open-market operations** are the Fed's most valuable tool. The Fed can choose a range of potential impacts from large to small, and the effect is immediate.

        1)   **U.S. Treasury securities** are traded on the open market. The Fed can either purchase them from, or sell them to, commercial banks.

            a)   When the Fed wishes to **loosen** the money supply, it **purchases** Treasury securities.

            b)   When the Fed wishes to **tighten** the money supply, it **sells** Treasury securities.

        2)   The **Federal funds rate** is the rate **banks charge each other** for overnight loans.

            a)   Banks with excess reserves do not have to leave these funds idle. They can lend them on a short-term basis to banks that are in danger of dipping below the required reserve ratio.

            b)   When the Fed **buys** Treasury securities, the Federal funds rate **falls**. When the Fed **sells** Treasury securities, the Federal funds rate **rises**.

        3)   This chain of cause and effect is summarized in the following table:

To Loosen Money Supply	To Tighten Money Supply
1. FOMC sees **recession** looming	1. FOMC fears **inflation** heating up
2. Fed **buys government securities** on the open market	2. Fed **sells government securities** on the open market
3. Fed **credits cash to reserve accounts** of banks selling securities	3. Fed **decreases cash in reserve accounts** of banks buying securities
4. Increase in supply of cash **creates excess reserves;** banks now willing to lend	4. Decrease in supply of cash **reduces excess reserves;** banks unable to lend
5. Greater availability of cash for overnight loan causes **decline in Federal funds rate**	5. Lower availability of cash for overnight loan causes **increase in Federal funds rate**

   c.   **Changes in the required reserve ratio** are used less frequently. Requiring banks to leave more funds in (noninterest-bearing) reserve accounts has a dramatic effect on profits.

      1)   When the Fed wishes to **loosen** the money supply, it **lowers** the required reserve ratio.

         a)   If banks have to keep less money on hand, they have more available to lend out.

      2)   When the Fed wishes to **tighten** the money supply, it **raises** the required reserve ratio.

         a)   If banks have to keep more money on hand, they have less available to lend out.

   d.   The **discount rate** has come to **reflect, rather than enact, changes** the Fed wishes to make. The discount rate is the rate Federal Reserve banks charge to commercial banks that need loans.

      1)   After the Fed has **put money into the economy** by buying Treasury securities, the market reacts by lowering interest rates (since money is now easier to come by).

         a)   The Fed then **lowers** the discount rate to match the interest rate action of the market.

      2)   After the Fed has **taken money out of the economy** by selling Treasury securities, the market reacts by raising interest rates (since money is now harder to come by).

         a)   The Fed then **raises** the discount rate to match the interest rate action of the market.

      3)   The discount rate must be contrasted with the **prime rate**, which is determined by commercial banks with regard to their most creditworthy customers and is thus not under the direct control of the Fed.

8. **Weaknesses of Monetary Policy**

   a.   The same **recognition lag** and **operational lag** (see item 9. in Subunit 4) that plague attempts to use fiscal policy also affect the use of monetary policy.

      1)   Recognition lag is the time it takes for macroeconomists to recognize that a recession (or inflation) is occurring, and operational lag (also called response lag) is the time it takes for the changes implemented by the government to take effect.

    2) Administrative lag, on the other hand, is not the same obstacle to carrying out monetary policy that it is to the execution of fiscal policy. Whereas the changes necessary to enact fiscal policy must pass through an elaborate legislative process, the Fed can act immediately on open-market operations decided on by the FOMC.

  b. **Changes in velocity** may work counter to the Fed's intentions. If the money supply is loosened and interest rates fall, consumers are less willing to invest their cash and the rate of investment falls.

  c. The theory of **cyclical asymmetry** holds that a tight monetary policy is effective but a loose policy is less so.

    1) Reducing the money supply by locking up reserves and selling on the open market unquestionably takes cash out of the economy.

    2) On the other hand, simply loosening the money supply may not lead to increased spending. Other factors, such as banks' concerns about liquidity or high consumer debt loads, may forestall the intended round of anti-recessionary spending.

9. Stop and review! You have completed the outline for this subunit. Study multiple-choice questions 26 through 36 beginning on page 177.

QUESTIONS

6.1 Three Principal Issues in Macroeconomics

1. The value of money

  A. Varies directly with the tax rates.

  B. Varies directly with government spending.

  C. Varies directly with investment.

  D. Varies inversely with the general level of prices.

Answer (D) is correct. *(CMA, adapted)*
  REQUIRED: The correct statement about the value of money.
  DISCUSSION: Part of the value of money comes from its usefulness as a store of value or wealth. As prices rise, the purchasing power of a stock of money held diminishes. Accordingly, the value of money and the general level of prices must be inversely related.
  Answer (A) is incorrect because tax rates do not directly influence the value of money. Tax rates might indirectly affect the value of money through their possible influence on the general level of prices. Answer (B) is incorrect because government spending does not directly influence the value of money. Government spending may indirectly affect the value of money by influencing the general level of prices. Answer (C) is incorrect because investment does not directly influence the value of money. Investment might indirectly affect the value of money through its possible influence on the general level of prices.

2. Rising inflation

  A. Increases the price level, which benefits those who are entitled to receive specific amounts of money.

  B. Enhances the positive relationship between the price level and the purchasing power of a unit of money.

  C. Will not affect contracts that include the indexing of payments.

  D. Increases the price level, which is negatively related to the purchasing power of a unit of money.

Answer (D) is correct. *(CMA, adapted)*
  REQUIRED: The true statement about a period of rising inflation.
  DISCUSSION: Inflation increases the price level, which means that a static supply of dollars will purchase fewer goods. In other words, the purchasing power of money declines as the price level increases.
  Answer (A) is incorrect because an increased price level hurts those who are entitled to receive specific amounts of money. Fixed amounts will purchase less than before. Answer (B) is incorrect because the price level and the purchasing power of money have an inverse relationship. Answer (C) is incorrect because rising inflation activates the indexing provision of contracts indexed for inflation. However, payments made under such a provision may reflect a purchasing power loss because of inefficiencies in the adjustment mechanism.

3. Which of the following indicators is used by the federal government to measure inflation?

- A. Dow Jones index.
- B. Consumer price index.
- C. Consumer confidence index.
- D. Corporate profits.

Answer (B) is correct. *(CPA, adapted)*
REQUIRED: The government measure for inflation.
DISCUSSION: The CPI measures inflation by a monthly pricing of items on a typical household shopping list. The current index uses a base year as a reference point. The price in the current year of a market basket of goods and services is determined relative to the same basket for the base year.
Answer (A) is incorrect because the Dow Jones Industrial Average is based on the share prices of 30 blue-chip stocks listed on the New York Stock Exchange. It is the most widely cited indicator of stock market performance. Answer (C) is incorrect because consumer confidence measures the confidence that the public has in the performance of the economy. It is a key determinant of the aggregate demand curve and the source of business-cycle instability. Answer (D) is incorrect because corporate profits measure how profitable one or a group of corporations are. They do not accurately reflect inflation.

4. Chihuahua Bank is willing to lend a business firm $1 million at an annual real and nominal interest rate of 10%. What is the annual interest rate Chihuahua Bank will charge the business firm if instead the rate of inflation is anticipated to be 6%?

- A. 4%
- B. 6%
- C. 10%
- D. 16%

Answer (D) is correct. *(Publisher, adapted)*
REQUIRED: The interest rate a bank will charge at a given rate of inflation.
DISCUSSION: If Chihuahua Bank requires a real return of 10%, a 6% inflation rate will increase the rate charged to 16%.
Answer (A) is incorrect because 4% is the real rate given a 10% nominal rate and a 6% inflation premium. The rate of inflation increases the rate charged. Answer (B) is incorrect because 6% is the rate of inflation. Answer (C) is incorrect because 10% is the rate given zero inflation.

5. If nominal income increases <List A> the price level, real income will <List B>.

	List A	List B
A.	Faster than	Rise
B.	Slower than	Rise
C.	At the same rate as	Fall
D.	At the same rate as	Rise

Answer (A) is correct. *(CIA, adapted)*
REQUIRED: The relationship of changes in nominal and real income.
DISCUSSION: The percentage change in real income is the difference between the percentage change in nominal income and the percentage change in the price level. If nominal income increases more than the price level, real income also increases.

6. The rate of unemployment caused by changes in the composition of employment opportunities over time is referred to as the

- A. Frictional unemployment rate.
- B. Cyclical unemployment rate.
- C. Structural unemployment rate.
- D. Full employment unemployment rate.

Answer (C) is correct. *(CIA, adapted)*
REQUIRED: The rate of unemployment caused by changes in the composition of employment opportunities over time.
DISCUSSION: Economists define full employment as occurring when cyclical unemployment is zero. Hence, the natural rate of unemployment (the full employment unemployment rate) equals the sum of structural and frictional unemployment. Cyclical unemployment is caused by insufficient aggregate demand. Frictional unemployment occurs when both jobs and the workers qualified to fill them are available. This definition acknowledges that there will be changing of jobs, temporary layoffs, etc. Structural unemployment exists when aggregate demand is sufficient to provide full employment, but the distribution of the demand does not correspond precisely to the composition of the labor force. This form of unemployment arises when the required job skills or the geographic distribution of jobs changes.
Answer (A) is incorrect because frictional unemployment results from imperfections in the labor market. Answer (B) is incorrect because cyclical unemployment is caused by a deficiency of aggregate spending. Answer (D) is incorrect because the full employment unemployment rate is the sum of frictional and structural unemployment.

7. A nation's unemployment rate increased from 4% to 6%. The economic cost of this increase in unemployment can be described as the amount by which

A. Actual gross domestic product falls short of potential gross domestic product.

B. Aggregate expenditures fall short of the full-employment level of net domestic product.

C. Aggregate spending exceeds the full-employment level of net domestic product.

D. Merchandise imports exceed exports.

Answer (A) is correct. *(CIA, adapted)*
    REQUIRED: The economic cost of an increase in unemployment.
    DISCUSSION: In macroeconomic terms, the cost of unemployment is lost production. This lost output is measured in terms of the GDP gap, that is, the difference between actual and potential GDP. According to Okun's Law, a 2.5% GDP gap results from every 1% excess of the actual unemployment rate over the natural rate.

8. In national income terms, aggregate demand is

A. Demand for money by the community in a period of full employment.

B. Total expenditure on capital goods by entrepreneurs during a period of full employment.

C. Demand that is needed if a country's economy is to operate at optimum level and the level of investment is to be raised.

D. Total expenditure on consumer goods and investment, including government and foreign expenditure, during a given period.

Answer (D) is correct. *(CMA, adapted)*
    REQUIRED: The definition of aggregate demand.
    DISCUSSION: Aggregate demand reflects the real domestic output at each possible price level. This is an inverse relationship, so the curve slopes downward. As the price level falls, real purchasing power increases, interest rates decline, and foreign purchases increase. The determinants of aggregate demand are changes in consumer spending, investment, government spending, and net exports.
    Answer (A) is incorrect because the demand for money is excluded. Answer (B) is incorrect because aggregate demand includes all expenditures. Answer (C) is incorrect because the definition does not depend upon an optimum level.

9. An improvement in technology that in turn leads to improved worker productivity would most likely result in

A. A shift to the right in the supply curve and a lowering of the price of the output.

B. A shift to the left in the supply curve and a lowering of the price of the output.

C. An increase in the price of the output if demand is unchanged.

D. Wage increases.

Answer (A) is correct. *(CMA, adapted)*
    REQUIRED: The result of improved technology and improved worker productivity.
    DISCUSSION: Enhanced technology and worker productivity would cause the supply curve to shift to the right where it would intersect with the demand curve at a lower price level. The shift is caused by the producer's ability to lower costs and produce more at a given market price.
    Answer (B) is incorrect because the increased productivity would cause a rightward shift in the supply curve. Answer (C) is incorrect because the rightward shift would result in an intersection with the demand curve at a lower price. Answer (D) is incorrect because the effect on wages cannot be determined from the information given.

10. Which of the following statements is correct if there is an increase in the resources available within an economy?

A. More goods and services will be produced in the economy.

B. The economy will be capable of producing more goods and services.

C. The standard of living in the economy will rise.

D. The technological efficiency of the economy will improve.

Answer (B) is correct. *(CPA, adapted)*
    REQUIRED: The effect of increased resources available within the economy.
    DISCUSSION: The production possibilities curve (PPC) is used to analyze the current production in an economy and the possibility for economic growth. If society produces on the curve, more of a product cannot be produced unless society begins producing less of another product. However, an increase in the resources available in the economy causes an outward shift of the curve. If demand is sufficient and society can employ the resources, more goods and services will be produced as it moves toward the curve.
    Answer (A) is incorrect because more goods and services may not be produced if there is no increase in demand. Answer (C) is incorrect because an increase in resources will not cause an increase in the standard of living if resources are not employed or the additional output is not consumed within the society. Answer (D) is incorrect because improved technological efficiency comes about from advances in technology, not an increase in resources.

6.2 Domestic Output, National Income, and Price Levels

11. Which of the following is not included in the gross domestic product (GDP)?

    A. Purchase of a new home.

    B. An automotive worker's wages.

    C. A doctor's fee.

    D. Purchase of common stock.

Answer (D) is correct. *(CMA, adapted)*
    REQUIRED: The transaction not included in GDP.
    DISCUSSION: GDP is the value of all final goods and services produced in the U.S., whether by domestic or foreign-owned sources, during a specified period. A common stock purchase is not a new good or service. It is instead a claim to ownership of property that already exists.
    Answer (A) is incorrect because a new home is a productive good and is included in GDP. Answer (B) is incorrect because the services of an autoworker are productive and are part of GDP. Answer (C) is incorrect because the doctor's services were produced during the year. His/her fee is part of GDP.

12. All of the following are components of the formula used to calculate gross domestic product except

    A. Household income.

    B. Foreign net export spending.

    C. Government spending.

    D. Gross investment.

Answer (A) is correct. *(CPA, adapted)*
    REQUIRED: The item not a component of GDP.
    DISCUSSION: GDP is the value of all final goods and services produced in the U.S., whether by domestic or foreign-owned sources, during a specified period. Under the expenditure approach, GDP is the sum of (1) personal consumption expenditures, (2) gross private domestic investment, (3) government purchases (consumption and investment), and (4) net exports. Household income is not an element of GDP calculated using either the income or the expenditure approach. Moreover, the value of homemakers' work is excluded.

13. Gross domestic product includes which of the following measures?

    A. The size of a population that must share a given output within one year.

    B. The negative externalities of the production process of a nation within one year.

    C. The total monetary value of all final goods and services produced within a nation in one year.

    D. The total monetary value of goods and services including barter transactions within a nation in one year.

Answer (C) is correct. *(CPA, adapted)*
    REQUIRED: The measure included in GDP.
    DISCUSSION: Gross domestic product (GDP) is the principal measure of national economic performance. It is the total market value of all final goods and services produced within the boundaries of a nation, whether by domestic or foreign-owned sources, during a specified period of time (usually a year). GDP is calculated without regard to the ownership of productive resources. Thus, the value of the output of a U.S.-owned factory abroad is excluded, but the output of a foreign-owned factory in the U.S. is included.
    Answer (A) is incorrect because GDP is not adjusted for changes in the population, which change per capita income. Answer (B) is incorrect because negative externalities (spillovers) are costs, such as pollution, that are imposed on third parties. Hence, they are excluded from GDP. Answer (D) is incorrect because, to avoid double counting in the computation of GDP, the value added to each good or service at each stage of production over the period must be summed. Alternatively, the total market value of all final goods and services may be added.

Questions 14 through 16 are based on the following information. The following data is based on a private economy model and therefore ignores government expenditures and taxes.

Real GDP	Consumption and Investment	Net Exports
$500	$512	$4
520	528	4
540	544	4
560	560	4
580	576	4
600	592	4
620	608	4
640	624	4

14. The real gross domestic product has an equilibrium of

A. $560

B. $580

C. $600

D. $640

Answer (B) is correct. *(Publisher, adapted)*
REQUIRED: The equilibrium gross domestic product.
DISCUSSION: The equilibrium GDP occurs when consumption, investment, and net exports total the real GDP. This occurs only when GDP equals $580.
Answer (A) is incorrect because consumption and investment ($560), when added to exports ($4), exceeds $560. Answer (C) is incorrect because $600 exceeds the combination of consumption, investment, and net exports. Answer (D) is incorrect because $640 exceeds the $628 combination of consumption, investment, and net exports.

15. What is the equilibrium real GDP if net exports are increased by $4 at each level of GDP?

A. $520

B. $580

C. $600

D. $620

Answer (C) is correct. *(Publisher, adapted)*
REQUIRED: The equilibrium real GDP if net exports increase by a constant amount at each GDP level.
DISCUSSION: Equilibrium occurs when the combination of consumption, investment, and net exports equals GDP. If exports are $8 and consumption and investment combined equal $592, equilibrium will be at $600.

16. If the marginal propensity to consume (MPC) is 0.4, a $20 increase in net exports will cause an increase in equilibrium real GDP of

A. $30

B. $33.40

C. $50

D. $100

Answer (B) is correct. *(Publisher, adapted)*
REQUIRED: The increase in equilibrium real GDP resulting from an increase in net exports given the MPC.
DISCUSSION: A change in consumption, investment, or net exports results in a multiplied change in equilibrium GDP. This multiplier phenomenon occurs because the initial change in spending has a multiplier effect. The formula for the multiplier is 1 divided by the MPS (marginal propensity to save). The MPS is 1 minus the MPC (1 − .4 = .6). Thus, the multiplier is 1.67 (1 ÷ 0.6). An increase in net exports of $20 results in a $33.40 increase in real GDP (1.67 × $20).
Answer (A) is incorrect because $40 implies a multiplier of 1.5 rather than 1.67. Answer (C) is incorrect because $50 results from using the MPC of 0.4 rather than an MPS of .6. Answer (D) is incorrect because an increase of $100 can occur only if the multiplier is 5.

17. When the addition to capital goods in an economy exceeds the capital consumption allowance, the economy has experienced

    A. Negative net investment.

    B. Equilibrium investment.

    C. Positive gross investment.

    D. Positive net investment.

Answer (D) is correct. *(CMA, adapted)*
    REQUIRED: The condition in which the addition to capital goods exceeds the capital consumption allowance.
    DISCUSSION: When the addition to capital goods exceeds the depreciation on existing capital goods, positive net investment occurs. In national income accounting, depreciation is the capital consumption allowance. This allowance is deducted from GDP to arrive at national income.
    Answer (A) is incorrect because a negative net investment would occur when depreciation exceeded the additions to the capital stock. Answer (B) is incorrect because equilibrium investment is the investment when national income is at equilibrium. Answer (C) is incorrect because gross investment is the total addition to capital stock.

18. Under the income approach, gross domestic product (GDP) is measured as

    A. Depreciation charges and indirect business taxes + Wages + Rents + Interest + Profits − Net American income earned abroad.

    B. Wages + Rents + Interest + Profits.

    C. Depreciation charges and indirect business taxes + Wages + Rents − Interest + Profits.

    D. Wages + Rents + Interest − Profits + Net American income earned abroad.

Answer (A) is correct. *(CIA, adapted)*
    REQUIRED: The income approach to measuring GDP.
    DISCUSSION: GDP is the total value of goods and services produced within the boundaries of the United States. It may be measured using an expenditures approach or an income approach. Under the income approach, GDP equals all income derived from the production of the year's output, with an adjustment for net U.S. income earned abroad. Two types of nonincome charges or allocations must be added to incomes (wages, rents, interest, and profits). Depreciation reflects the consumption of fixed capital during the period. It is the part of the year's receipts that must be allocated to replace the machinery, plant, etc., used up in the production of GDP. Indirect business taxes, such as sales, excise, and property taxes, are treated by businesses as a cost of production and form part of the total price of goods and services. Thus, they are not paid as wages, rents, interest, and profits. Accordingly, GDP may be measured as the sum of consumption of fixed capital, indirect business taxes, wages, rents, interest, and profits (proprietors' income, corporate taxes, dividends, and undistributed corporate profits), with an adjustment for net U.S. income earned abroad.
    Answer (B) is incorrect because nonincome charges and net U.S. income earned abroad must also be included in the calculation. Answer (C) is incorrect because interest income is added, not subtracted. Also, net U.S. income earned abroad must be considered. Answer (D) is incorrect because profits are added, not subtracted. Also, nonincome charges must be included in the calculation.

6.3 Business Cycles

19. During the recessionary phase of a business cycle,

    A. The purchasing power of money is likely to decline rapidly.

    B. The natural rate of unemployment will increase dramatically.

    C. Potential national income will exceed actual national income.

    D. Actual national income will exceed potential national income.

Answer (C) is correct. *(CMA, adapted)*
    REQUIRED: The effect of the recessionary phase.
    DISCUSSION: During the recessionary phase, economic activities and employment levels contract and society's resources are underused. Thus, potential national income will exceed actual national income.
    Answer (A) is incorrect because, technically, the purchasing power of money is unrelated to the concept of recession; purchasing power relates to inflation. However, demand-pull inflation is unlikely during a recession. Answer (B) is incorrect because the natural rate of unemployment, which results from the normal workings of the labor market, remains unchanged. Any increase in unemployment will be cyclical, i.e., the amount caused by inadequate aggregate demand. Answer (D) is incorrect because potential income will be greater than actual national income given the existence of idle capacity.

20. Which of the following segments of the economy will be least affected by the business cycle?

    A. Commercial construction industry.

    B. Machinery and equipment industry.

    C. Residential construction industry.

    D. Healthcare industry.

Answer (D) is correct. *(CPA, adapted)*
REQUIRED: The segment of the economy least affected by the business cycle.
DISCUSSION: Business cycles are periodic changes in output, usually with changes in price and employment levels. For example, recessions result because prices are low relative to costs of production. However, healthcare is less affected than most segments. Aggregate demand for its products and services remains steady even in a recession.
Answer (A) is incorrect because commercial construction is more strongly affected than healthcare by the business cycle. The aggregate demand for such products has greater variability. Answer (B) is incorrect because the machinery and equipment industry is more strongly affected than healthcare by the business cycle. The aggregate demand for such products has greater variability. Answer (C) is incorrect because residential construction is more strongly affected than healthcare by the business cycle. The aggregate demand for such products has greater variability.

6.4 Fiscal Policy

21. A consumer has the following consumption patterns at different income levels:

Level of Income	Consumption
$250	$130
$300	$160
$350	$190

At an income level of $300, this consumer has a marginal propensity to consume of <List A> and an average propensity to save of <List B>.

	List A	List B
A.	0.40	0.47
B.	0.40	0.53
C.	0.60	0.47
D.	0.60	0.53

Answer (C) is correct. *(CIA, adapted)*
REQUIRED: The marginal propensity to consume and average propensity to save at a given income level.
DISCUSSION: The marginal propensity to consume is the increase in consumption divided by the increase in income. Thus, it equals [($160 – $130) ÷ ($300 – $250)], or .60. The average propensity to save equals the difference between income and consumption, divided by level of income. Thus, it equals [($300 – $160) ÷ $300], or .47.
Answer (A) is incorrect because the marginal propensity to save is .4. Answer (B) is incorrect because the marginal propensity to save is .4, and the average propensity to consume is .53. Answer (D) is incorrect because the average propensity to consume is .53.

22. If personal consumption expenditures increase from $720 billion to $760 billion when disposable income increases from $900 billion to $950 billion, the marginal propensity to consume equals

    A. 0.20

    B. 0.40

    C. 0.60

    D. 0.80

Answer (D) is correct. *(Publisher, adapted)*
REQUIRED: The marginal propensity to consume given increases in personal expenditures and disposable income.
DISCUSSION: The marginal propensity to consume is the change in consumption divided by the change in income. The change in consumption is $40 billion, and the change in income is $50 billion. Hence, the marginal propensity to consume equals .8 ($40 billion ÷ $50 billion).

23. Government transfer payments

    A. Reallocate the consumption of goods and services to the public sector.

    B. Increase aggregate demand for private sector goods and services.

    C. Reallocate the consumption of goods and services in the private sector.

    D. Decrease aggregate demand for private sector goods and services.

Answer (C) is correct. *(CMA, adapted)*
    REQUIRED: The true statement about government transfer payments.
    DISCUSSION: Government expenditures, such as those for welfare and Social Security, are not actual expenditures on goods or services. Instead, they are transfers of money from the government to households in the form of a negative tax designed to redistribute income. Through taxation and transfer payments, income redistribution is effected and consumption in the private sector will be reallocated.
    Answer (A) is incorrect because the reallocation is not to the public sector. Individuals in the private sector will decide how the money will be spent. Answer (B) is incorrect because transfer payments do not increase demand, per se. Answer (D) is incorrect because transfer payments do not decrease aggregate demand.

24. The federal budget deficit is the

    A. Total accumulation of the federal government's surpluses and deficits.

    B. Excess of state, local, and federal spending over their revenues.

    C. Amount by which the federal government's expenditures exceed its revenues in a given year.

    D. Amount by which liabilities exceed assets on the federal government's balance sheet.

Answer (C) is correct. *(CMA, adapted)*
    REQUIRED: The definition of the federal budget deficit.
    DISCUSSION: The federal budget deficit is the amount by which the federal government's expenditures (transfers and purchases) exceed its revenues (tax collections) in a given year.
    Answer (A) is incorrect because the concept of a budget deficit refers to a single period of time; it is not an accumulation. Answer (B) is incorrect because state and local deficits are not included in the federal budget deficit. Answer (D) is incorrect because the federal budget deficit is a flow concept relating to a single period of time; it is not a balance sheet concept.

25. Government borrowing to finance large deficits increases the demand for lendable funds and

    A. Increases the supply of lendable funds.

    B. Exerts downward pressure on interest rates.

    C. Has no impact on interest rates.

    D. Puts upward pressure on interest rates.

Answer (D) is correct. *(CMA, adapted)*
    REQUIRED: The true statement about government borrowing to finance large deficits.
    DISCUSSION: When the government borrows money, it enters into the same market as private business and competes for funds. The added demand will drive the interest rate higher. This activity produces the crowding-out effect. The result is reduced corporate borrowing and investment.
    Answer (A) is incorrect because the supply of lendable funds is unaffected by government borrowing. Only the demand is affected. Answer (B) is incorrect because the increased demand for funds increases interest rates. Answer (C) is incorrect because increased demands for funds does have an impact on interest rates.

6.5 Monetary Policy

26. The narrow definition of money supply, M1, consists of

    A. Currency and demand deposits.

    B. Currency, demand deposits, other checkable deposits, and travelers' checks.

    C. Currency, demand deposits, and small time deposits.

    D. Currency, demand deposits, small time deposits, and money market mutual fund balances.

Answer (B) is correct. *(CMA, adapted)*
    REQUIRED: The narrow definition of money supply.
    DISCUSSION: The narrow definition of money supply includes coins, currency, and checking account deposits (including travelers' checks).
    Answer (A) is incorrect because it omits travelers' checks. Answer (C) is incorrect because it includes small time deposits. Answer (D) is incorrect because the broader definition adds small time deposits (e.g., CDs of low values owned by individuals) and money market funds.

27. All of the following are functions of the Federal Reserve System except

A. Acting as a lender of last resort to the business community.

B. Accepting deposits of, and making loans to, commercial banks.

C. Supplying the economy with paper money in the form of Federal Reserve notes.

D. Providing for the collection of checks.

Answer (A) is correct.   *(CMA, adapted)*

REQUIRED: The item not a function of the Federal Reserve System.

DISCUSSION: The Fed lends only to its member banks, not to the business community.

Answer (B) is incorrect because accepting deposits of, and making loans to, commercial banks is a legitimate function of the Federal Reserve System. Answer (C) is incorrect because supplying the economy with paper money in the form of Federal Reserve notes is a legitimate function of the Federal Reserve System. Answer (D) is incorrect because providing for the collection of checks is a legitimate function of the Federal Reserve System.

28. The creation of deposit money by U.S. commercial banks increases the

A. Real wealth of the United States.

B. Real U.S. national income.

C. U.S. money supply.

D. Purchasing power of the U.S. dollar.

Answer (C) is correct.   *(CMA, adapted)*

REQUIRED: The effect of the creation of deposit money by U.S. commercial banks.

DISCUSSION: As money is deposited with banks, the banks lend the money to qualified customers. Banks may only lend a certain percentage of their funds because of the reserve requirement. The more funds they have, the more they can lend. Thus, as the amount of money deposited increases, the amount and number of loans and the money supply increase.

Answer (A) is incorrect because real wealth is not directly affected by the creation of deposit money. Answer (B) is incorrect because national income is not directly affected by the creation of deposit money. Answer (D) is incorrect because the purchasing power of the dollar (amount of goods that can be bought with a dollar) may well be decreased by the expansion of the money supply.

29. The Federal Reserve System's reserve ratio is

A. The specified percentage of a commercial bank's deposit liabilities that must be deposited in the central bank.

B. The rate that the central bank charges for loans granted to commercial banks.

C. The ratio of excess reserves to legal reserves that are deposited in the central bank.

D. The specified percentage of a commercial bank's demand deposits to total liabilities.

Answer (A) is correct.   *(CMA, adapted)*

REQUIRED: The definition of the reserve ratio.

DISCUSSION: The reserve ratio is the percentage of the customer deposits that banks must deposit with the Fed. These deposits are required by law to ensure the soundness of the bank and also serve as a tool for monetary policy, i.e., changes in the reserve ratio affect the money supply.

Answer (B) is incorrect because it refers to the discount rate: the amount that the Fed charges for loans granted to commercial banks. Answer (C) is incorrect because excess reserves is a term referring to amounts in excess of the reserve ratio. Answer (D) is incorrect because specific percentage is a term referring to amounts in excess of the reserve ratio.

30. Given a deposit expansion model in which the required reserve ratio is 12.5%, a $100,000 purchase of government securities by the Federal Reserve will result in a maximum increase (decrease) in the money supply of

A. $(87,500)

B. $12,500

C. $87,500

D. $800,000

Answer (D) is correct.   *(Publisher, adapted)*

REQUIRED: The maximum change in the money supply given a purchase of securities and a specified reserve ratio.

DISCUSSION: This purchase of government securities provides $100,000 of excess reserves for member banks. The maximum effect of this transaction, that is, assuming no leakage of money except for required reserves, is to expand demand deposits (and the money supply) by an amount equal to the excess reserves times the money multiplier (1.0 ÷ the reserve ratio). Accordingly, the increase in the money supply is $800,000 [$100,000 × (1.0 ÷ .125)].

Answer (A) is incorrect because the money supply must increase when the Federal Reserve purchases government securities. Answer (B) is incorrect because $12,500 equals 12.5% of the increase in excess reserves. Answer (C) is incorrect because $87,500 equals the increase in excess reserves minus 12.5%.

31. Assume an economy in which the marginal propensity to consume is 90%. Given an increase in government spending of $100, equilibrium gross domestic product will increase by

A. $100

B. $90

C. $190

D. $1,000

Answer (D) is correct. *(Publisher, adapted)*
REQUIRED: The increase in equilibrium GDP given the marginal propensity to consume.
DISCUSSION: The multiplier effect applies. Dividing the $100 additional spending by the marginal propensity to save (10%) results in an increase in equilibrium GDP of $1,000.

32. Economists and economic policy makers are interested in the multiplier effect because the multiplier explains why

A. A small change in investment can have a much larger impact on gross domestic product.

B. Consumption is always a multiple of savings.

C. The money supply increases when deposits in the banking system increase.

D. The velocity of money is less than one.

Answer (A) is correct. *(CMA, adapted)*
REQUIRED: The reason economists are interested in the multiplier effect.
DISCUSSION: The multiplier effect is the increase in GDP that occurs as a result of a change in investment. A given investment can result in a much larger increase in GDP because the investment is spent several times. The multiplier is the reciprocal of the marginal propensity to save.
Answer (B) is incorrect because the consumption function relates disposable income, the marginal propensity to consume, and the amount of consumption at zero income. Answer (C) is incorrect because the multiplier is not concerned with monetary policy. Answer (D) is incorrect because the velocity of money is the ratio of nominal GDP to the money supply. It is greater than one in the U.S. economy.

33. To address the problem of a recession, the Federal Reserve Bank most likely would take which of the following actions?

A. Lower the discount rate it charges to banks for loans.

B. Sell U.S. government bonds in open-market transactions.

C. Increase the federal funds rate charged by banks when they borrow from one another.

D. Increase the level of funds a bank is legally required to hold in reserve.

Answer (A) is correct. *(CPA, adapted)*
REQUIRED: The most likely Fed action to address a recession.
DISCUSSION: The Fed may lower the discount rate it charges to banks for loans to encourage borrowing. The effect is to increase the money supply because money is created when banks lend their excess reserves (reserves greater than the amount legally required to be held). A lower discount rate means that banks may lend more when borrowing from the Fed is less costly. Expanding the money supply is anti-recessionary because money needed for investment and growth will be cheaper.
Answer (B) is incorrect because the Fed may sell U.S. government bonds in open-market transactions to reduce the money supply and slow economic growth. Answer (C) is incorrect because the Fed may increase the federal funds rate charged by banks when they borrow from each other to reduce the money supply and slow economic growth. A higher federal funds rate encourages banks to lend less. Answer (D) is incorrect because increasing the reserve requirement decreases the supply of lendable funds and slows growth.

34. Which of the following actions is the acknowledged preventive measure for a period of deflation?

A. Increasing interest rates.

B. Increasing the money supply.

C. Decreasing interest rates.

D. Decreasing the money supply.

Answer (B) is correct. *(CPA, adapted)*
REQUIRED: The means of preventing deflation.
DISCUSSION: Deflation is a decrease in the general price level. Its causes and effects are the opposite of those of inflation. Deflation reflects an excess aggregate supply of goods and services. The purchasing power of the nation's currency increases and interest rates decrease. However, because prices are generally lower, incomes also are lower. Thus, increasing the money supply is a preventive measure for deflation because it decreases the purchasing power of a unit of the currency.
Answer (A) is incorrect because increasing interest rates is a preventive measure for inflation. Answer (C) is incorrect because the ultimate purpose of decreasing interest rates is to increase the money supply to combat recession and possibly deflation. Answer (D) is incorrect because decreasing the money supply is a preventive measure for inflation.

35. The discount rate of the Federal Reserve System is

A. The specified percentage of a commercial bank's deposit liabilities that must be deposited in the central bank.

B. The rate that the central bank charges for loans granted to commercial banks.

C. The rate that commercial banks charge for loans granted to the public.

D. The ratio of excess reserves to legal reserves that are deposited in the central bank.

Answer (B) is correct. *(CMA, adapted)*
REQUIRED: The definition of the discount rate.
DISCUSSION: The discount rate is the amount the central bank charges when making loans to member banks.
Answer (A) is incorrect because it refers to the reserve ratio. Answer (C) is incorrect because the rate that commercial banks charge for loans to the general public is usually scaled upward from the prime rate, which is the rate charged to the most creditworthy customers. Answer (D) is incorrect because the rate described is nonsensical.

36. One problem with using monetary policy to stabilize business cycles is the time it takes for economists to recognize that a recession is occurring. This is known as the:

A. Operational lag.

B. Recognition lag.

C. Administrative lag.

D. Keynesian lag.

Answer (B) is correct. *(Publisher, adapted)*
REQUIRED: The term for the time it takes for economists to recognize that a recession is occurring.
DISCUSSION: A recognition lag is the term for the time it takes economists to recognize that a recession is occurring. As a result, monetary policy cannot be implemented as early as might be necessary.
Answer (A) is incorrect because operational lag is the time it takes for implemented monetary policy changes to make an impact on the economy. Answer (C) is incorrect because administrative lag is the time it takes for the Fed to act once the economists have identified that a recession is occurring. Answer (D) is incorrect because Keynesian lag is a nonsense term.

Use Gleim's **CPA Test Prep** for interactive testing with over 2,000 additional multiple-choice questions!

STUDY UNIT SEVEN
INTERNATIONAL TRADE

(14 pages of outline)

This study unit is the last of three related to the economic environment of a business and its industry. The primary emphasis of this study unit is on how international trade affects the economy and individual firms.

7.1 ADVANTAGES OF INTERNATIONAL TRADE

1.   The laws of supply and demand affect imports and exports in the same way that they affect domestic goods. For example, a cutback in petroleum production in a single Middle Eastern country can raise the world price of oil.

   a.   The term **net exports** refers to the amount of a country's exports minus its imports. Conversely, a nation can have **net imports** if its imports exceed its exports.

2.   **Terms of trade (the exchange ratio)** is the ratio of a country's export price index to its import price index, multiplied by 100.

   a.   EXAMPLE: A simple illustration uses two countries and two products.

      1)   Kenya's entire exports for the year consist of $800,000 worth of coffee to Spain, and Spain's entire exports consist of $1,000,000 worth of concrete to Kenya.

      2)   Kenya's terms of trade are thus 80 [($800,000 ÷ $1,000,000) × 100]. Spain's terms of trade are 125 [($1,000,000 ÷ $800,000) × 100].

   b.   When the ratio falls, a country is said to have deteriorating terms of trade. When the ratio is less than 100, the country is an overall loser in terms of world trade.

3.   **Countries vary greatly in their efficiency** in producing certain goods because of the immobility of resources. This variation can be largely attributed to differences from country to country in the following five factors:

   a.   Climatic and geographical conditions
   b.   Human capacities
   c.   Supply and type of capital accumulation
   d.   Proportions of resources
   e.   Political and social climates

4.   Given these differences, it is clear that countries can **mutually benefit from trade**.

   a.   The greatest advantage from trade is obtained **when each nation specializes** in producing what it can produce most efficiently or, more precisely, least inefficiently.

      1)   If nations specialize and then exchange with others, **more is produced and consumed** than if each nation tries to be self-sufficient.

   b.   We know that specialization of labor is beneficial for individuals; the same principle applies to nations.

5.   The explanatory mechanism for this phenomenon is **comparative advantage**, a term coined by the English economist David Ricardo (1772-1823). This principle is based on **relative opportunity costs**.

    a.   EXAMPLE: The following table displays the comparative costs of production for two countries and products. Assume the two countries produce and consume only these two products and that labor is the only input.

	U.S.	Japan
Food (1 bushel)	1 hour	2 hours
Cars (1 car)	1.5 hours	1 hour

        1)   If the two countries specialize, **both will be better off**. There will be an increase in total output if the U.S. uses its resources to grow food and Japan uses its resources to produce cars (given a fixed amount of inputs).

            a)   Total output will be maximized when each nation specializes in the products in which it has the **lower opportunity cost**, that is, a comparative advantage.

        2)   The U.S. has an opportunity cost for 1 bushel of food of 2/3 of a car (1 ÷ 1.5). The Japanese opportunity cost for 1 bushel of food is 2 cars (2 ÷ 1).

        3)   At the same time, the U.S. opportunity cost for 1 car is 1.5 bushels of food (1.5 ÷ 1). The Japanese opportunity cost for 1 car is .5 of a bushel of food (1 ÷ 2).

        4)   Accordingly, the U.S. has the lower opportunity cost for food production (2/3 car to 2 cars) and the Japanese have the lower opportunity cost for car production (.5 bushels to 1.5 bushels).

            a)   For 100,000 units of labor input, the U.S. economy can produce either 100,000 bushels of food or 66,667 cars. If the labor input is divided equally, however, the U.S. economy can produce 50,000 bushels of food and 33,333 cars.

            b)   At the same time, if the Japanese economy divides its efforts equally, input of 100,000 units of labor can produce 25,000 bushels of food and 50,000 cars.

            c)   In the absence of world trade, therefore, the two economies together can produce 75,000 bushels of food (50,000 + 25,000) and 83,333 cars (33,333 + 50,000).

        5)   But if each country concentrates on the product in which it has a comparative advantage, the total production will be 100,000 bushels of food (all produced in the U.S.) and 100,000 cars (all produced in Japan).

b.   This phenomenon can be represented graphically by plotting the production possibilities curves for the two countries:

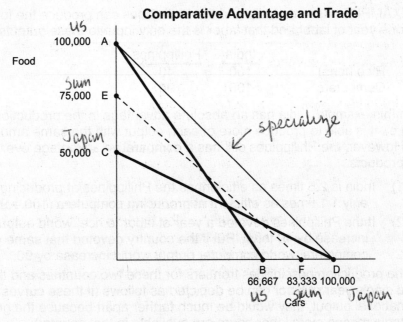

Comparative Advantage and Trade

1)   The individual production possibilities frontier for the U.S. is line AB and that for Japan is line CD. If both countries devote half of their resources to each product and there is no international trade, total production will be along line EF.

2)   However, if the two countries specialize and engage in trade, the new production possibilities curve is line AD, which is superior to any of the other curves.

c.   In this example, the U.S. has an **absolute** advantage with respect to food production (because the price of food is lower in the U.S.), and Japan has an absolute advantage in car production.

1)   Along with its absolute advantage, the U.S. has a **comparative** advantage in food production [because its opportunity cost for food production (cars forgone) is lower than Japan's]. Similarly, Japan has a comparative advantage in car production because Japan's opportunity cost for car production (food forgone) is lower.

2)   Thus, each country has both an absolute and a comparative advantage in a particular product.

3)   **Comparative advantage** is initially a comparison of costs in one country. It determines what that country produces most efficiently. The result of this analysis is a determination of opportunity costs. Thus, no matter what the costs may be elsewhere, the U.S. will always have a comparative advantage in the production of food rather than cars. Similarly, Japan has a comparative advantage in the production of cars as opposed to food.

4)   **Absolute advantage** compares the costs of inputs between countries. Thus, a given country might have an absolute advantage with respect to every product compared with a specific other country.

5)   In the previous example, Japan would continue to have a comparative advantage with respect to cars even if its costs were 1.6. In that case, the U.S. would have an absolute advantage (1.5 is less than 1.6). Nevertheless, trade is still beneficial because the opportunity costs of car production are 1.5 bushels of food in the U.S. but only 0.8 bushels of food in Japan. Only if both countries have identical opportunity costs would trade not be beneficial.

6. The principle of comparative advantage is so powerful, it even applies when one country has an **absolute advantage in both products**.

    a. EXAMPLE: Assume India and the Philippines can produce the following products with one year of labor and that labor is the only input to these outputs:

	India	Philippines
Rice (tons)	100	40
Computers	100	90

    b. In this example, India has an absolute advantage in the production of **both** products, i.e., it is able to produce more of each output with the same amount of input. However, the Philippines still has a comparative advantage over India in one of the products.

        1) India is 2.5 times as efficient as the Philippines at producing rice (100 ÷ 40), but only 1.1 times as efficient at producing computers (100 ÷ 90).

        2) If the Philippines devoted a year of labor to rice, world output of rice would only increase by 40 tons. But if the country devoted that same year of labor to computers, world computer output would increase by 90.

    c. The production possibilities frontiers for these two countries and these two products for a single year of labor can be depicted as follows (if these curves were for total national output, they would be much farther apart because the greater population of India means more labor hours are available in that country):

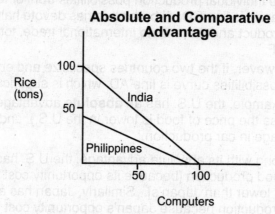

Absolute and Comparative Advantage

        1) The slope of India's curve is 1 (100 ÷ 100), meaning that India gains one computer by trading off one ton of rice. However, the slope of the Philippines' curve is only .44 (40 ÷ 90), meaning that the Philippines only has to trade off .44 tons of rice to gain one computer.

        2) Thus, the Philippines' comparative advantage stems from the fact that its **opportunity cost is lower** than that of India for computers with respect to rice.

    d. If the two countries specialize and engage in trade, the world has more of both food and computers. Thus, specialization and trade **enhance world output without changing total inputs**.

        1) Moreover, the greater abundance of affordable goods means that workers in **both countries** experience higher real wages.

7. A nation will **export** goods in which it has a **comparative advantage** and **import** goods in which it has a **comparative disadvantage**.

    a. Developing countries exporting primarily raw materials are dependent on vibrant economies in developed (importing) countries.

    b. Even when one country is technologically superior in all industries, one of the industries will go out of business when free trade takes place.

        1) Therefore, **technological superiority is no guarantee** of continuing operation in a case of free trade. A country must have a comparative advantage in the production of a good, not necessarily an absolute advantage, to guarantee continuing production when free trade exists.

        2) Thus, the superior technology in developed countries is no indication that developing countries cannot compete in international trade.

    c. A high-wage country with a comparative advantage for a product will see that product survive even though the laborers in the developing country have lower wages.

        1) Thus, a **knowledge of wage rates is not sufficient information** to determine which country's industry would decline under free trade. In other words, a domestic industry may not decline simply because foreign firms pay their workers lower wages.

    d. If a country has only two factors of production (labor and capital) and a relative abundance of capital, it will tend to export capital-intensive goods and import labor-intensive goods. Thus, factors of production and the varying efficiency in producing goods determine which products a country will export and import.

        1) Capital-intensive goods are those requiring a high level of investment, e.g., oil refining.

        2) Labor-intensive goods are those requiring a high level of labor, e.g., manufacture of fashion clothes.

    e. For nations to receive the full advantages of international specialization and exchange, free trade must be allowed among **all** countries.

        1) Trade barriers cause resources to be **misallocated** in the country that established the barrier because inputs are used to produce products that could be produced more economically in other countries.

        2) As a result, products that could be efficiently produced in that country are not produced. In the other countries where the product was originally being produced economically, there is an oversupply of the product and the domestic price is driven down, resulting in efficient producers going out of business.

8. Stop and review! You have completed the outline for this subunit. Study multiple-choice questions 1 through 9 beginning on page 195.

7.2 TRADE BARRIERS

1. Even though individuals (on the whole) are best off under free trade, **governments** often establish policies designed to **interfere** in the workings of the marketplace.

    a. In fact, until economists such as Adam Smith and David Ricardo gave life to the free-trade movement in the late 18th and early 19th centuries, it was the **policy** of governments around the world to **actively impede trade**.

    b. The belief was that exports were to be promoted and imports discouraged in all cases because exports led people in other countries to owe domestic producers money. This theory went by the name of **mercantilism**. Certain aspects of mercantilism survive in modern protectionist practices.

2. **Protectionism** is any measure taken by a government to protect domestic producers. Protectionism takes many forms.

    a. **Tariffs** are consumption taxes designed to restrict imports, e.g., a tax on German beer. Governments raise tariffs to discourage consumption of imported products.

        1) The agreements reached during the Uruguay Round (1986-1994) of negotiations specified the rules for levying antidumping tariffs. Most cases hinge on the definition of "cost."

        2) In the U.S., the Secretary of the Treasury must first determine that a class of foreign merchandise is being sold in the U.S. at less than its fair value.

    b. **Import quotas** set fixed limits on different products, e.g., French wine.

        1) In the short run, import quotas will help a country's balance of payments position by increasing domestic employment, but the prices of the products produced will also increase.

        2) An **embargo** is a total ban on some kinds of imports. It is an extreme form of the import quota.

    c. **Domestic content rules** require that at least a portion of any imported product be constructed from parts manufactured in the importing nation.

        1) This rule is sometimes used by capital-intensive nations. Parts can be produced using idle capacity and then sent to a labor-intensive country for final assembly.

    d. **Voluntary export restrictions** are agreements entered into by exporters to reduce the number of products made available in a foreign country in an attempt to avoid official sanctions.

        1) These restrictions can be counterproductive. Because the supply of the product desired by consumers in the importing country is held artificially low, the exporter sometimes can charge a price high enough to earn profits greater than normal.

    e. A **trigger price mechanism** automatically imposes a tariff barrier against unfairly cheap imports by levying a duty (tariff) on all imports below a particular reference price (the price that "triggers" the tariff).

    f. **Antidumping rules** prevent foreign producers from "dumping" excess goods on the domestic market at less than cost to squeeze out competitors and gain control of the market.

    g. **Exchange controls** limit foreign currency transactions and set exchange rates. The purpose is to limit the ability of a firm selling in a country to repatriate its earnings.

    h. **Export subsidies** are payments by the government to producers in certain industries in an attempt to increase exports.

        1) A government may impose "countervailing duties" on imported goods if those goods were produced in a foreign country with the aid of a governmental subsidy.

i. **Special tax benefits to exporters** are an indirect form of export subsidy. The best U.S. examples were Foreign Sales Corporations (FSCs). They were entities located in U.S. possessions or in countries with tax information exchange agreements with the U.S. FSCs received an exemption of about 15% of qualified export income. However, after the World Trade Organization (WTO) ruled them to be illegal, the legislation creating them was repealed.

j. The **Export Trading Company Act of 1982** permits competitors to form export trading companies without regard to U.S. antitrust legislation.

k. Certain exports may require **licenses**. For example, sales of technology with military applications are limited by western nations that are members of the Coordinating Committee for Multilateral Export Controls. The related U.S. legislation is the Export Administration Act of 1979.

3. The **economic effects of tariffs and quotas** can be summarized as follows:

   a. **Workers** are shifted from relatively efficient export industries into **less efficient** protected industries. **Real wages decline** as a result, as does total world output.

   b. Under a **tariff**, the excess paid by the customer for an imported good goes into **government coffers** where it can be spent on domestic concerns.

      1) Under a **quota**, prices are also driven up (by the induced shortage), but the excess goes to the **exporter** in the foreign country.

   c. A **tariff** is laid on all importers equally; thus, the more efficient ones will still be able to set their **prices lower** than the less efficient ones.

      1) An import **quota**, on the other hand, does not affect foreign importers equally and import licenses can be assigned as much for **political favoritism** as on any other grounds.

4. A major reason for trade restrictions is that the costs of competition are direct and concentrated (people lose jobs and firms go out of business), but benefits of unrestricted trade are less noticeable and occur in the future (lower prices, higher wages, more jobs in export industries).

   a. Special-interest groups are strong and well organized, and they lobby effectively, getting legislation passed that is harmful to free trade.

   b. **Economic integration** is the joining of the markets from two or more nations into a free-trade zone. Examples of economic blocs of trading nations are the European Union and the North American Free Trade Agreement (NAFTA). Generally, the trading bloc provides trading incentives to member nations and discriminates against nonmember nations.

5. Stop and review! You have completed the outline for this subunit. Study multiple-choice questions 10 through 17 beginning on page 199.

7.3) FOREIGN CURRENCY RATES AND MARKETS

1. For international trade to occur, the two currencies involved must be easily converted at some prevailing exchange rate. The **exchange rate** is the price of one country's currency in terms of another country's currency.

   a. Currency appreciates when it can buy more units of another currency.

   b. Currency depreciates when it can purchase fewer units of another currency.

   c. In other words, depreciation in country A's currency is an appreciation of the currency of country B.

2.   **Exchange Rate Determination**

a.   Equilibrium exchange rates in floating markets are determined by the supply of, and demand for, the currencies.

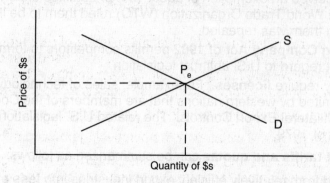

The equilibrium rate of P_e will prevail in the market. No surplus (or deficit) occurs at P_e.

1)   Demand for currencies comes from international trade in goods and services, investor global trading (e.g., an American buys a French stock or bond), and international corporate activity.

2)   Supply of currencies comes from reversing these transactions.

b.   **Fixed exchange rates** are set by some outside force (e.g., the government). One traditional method of establishing rates is to require that currencies be convertible to specified amounts of gold.

1)   An exchange rate set too high (in foreign currency units per dollar) tends to create a deficit U.S. balance of payments. This deficit must be financed by drawing down foreign reserves or by borrowing from the central banks of the foreign countries. This effect is short-term because, at some time, the country will deplete its foreign reserves.

   a)   A major reason for a country's devaluation is to improve its balance of payments.

   b)   As an alternative to drawing down its reserves, a country might change its trade policies or implement exchange controls or exchange rationing. Many developing countries use currency exchange rationing to avoid a deficit balance of payments.

2)   An exchange rate set too low (in foreign currency units per dollar) tends to create a surplus U.S. balance of payments. In this case, surplus reserves build up. At some time, the country will not want any greater reserve balances and will have to raise the value of its currency.

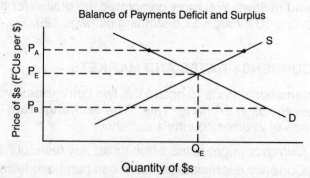

Balance of Payments Deficit and Surplus

3)   At exchange rate A (P_A foreign currency units per dollar), a greater quantity of dollars is supplied by U.S. interests than demanded by foreign interests (i.e., U.S. imports exceed exports). The result is a trade deficit. At exchange rate B, a smaller quantity of dollars is supplied by U.S. interests than demanded by foreign interests (i.e., U.S. exports exceed imports). The result is a trade surplus.

   c.   A **managed float** is the current method of exchange rate determination.

      1)   Supply and demand forces primarily guide exchange rates.

      2)   During periods of extreme fluctuation in the value of a nation's currency, intervention by governments or central banks may occur to maintain fairly stable exchange rates.

      3)   Floating rates permit adjustments to eliminate balance of payments deficits or surpluses. For example, if the U.S. has a deficit in its trade with country X, the U.S. dollar will depreciate relative to country X's currency. This adjustment should decrease imports from, and increase exports to, country X.

3.   Floating exchange rates may fluctuate differently in the long, medium, and short term.

   a.   **Long-term exchange rates** are dictated by the purchasing-power parity theorem.

      1)   In the long run, real prices should be the same worldwide (net of government taxes or trade barriers and transportation costs) for a given good. Exchange rates will adjust until purchasing-power parity is achieved. In other words, relative price levels determine exchange rates. In the real world, exchange rates do not perfectly reflect purchasing-power parity, but relative price levels are clearly important determinants of those rates.

   b.   **Medium-term exchange rates** are dictated by the economic activity in a country.

      1)   When the U.S. is in a recession, spending on imports (as well as domestic goods) will decrease. This reduced spending on imports shifts the supply curve for dollars to the left, causing the equilibrium value of the dollar to increase (assuming the demand for dollars is constant); that is, at any given exchange rate, the supply to foreigners is less.

      2)   If more goods are exported because of an increased preference for U.S. goods, the demand curve for dollars shifts to the right, causing upward pressure on the value of the dollar.

      3)   An increase in imports or a decrease in exports will have effects opposite to those described in b.1) above.

   c.   **Short-term exchange rates** are dictated by **interest rates**. Big corporations and banks invest their large reserves of cash where the real interest rate is highest. A rise in the real interest rate in a country will lead to an appreciation of the currency because it will be demanded for investment at the higher real interest rate, thereby shifting the demand curve to the right (outward).

      1)   The reverse holds true for a decline in real interest rates because that currency will be sold as investors move their money out of the country.

      2)   However, the interplay of interest rates and inflation must also be considered. Inflation of a currency relative to a second currency causes the first currency to depreciate relative to the second. Moreover, nominal interest rates increase when inflation rates are expected to increase. The effect on exchange rates of inflation reflected in nominal interest rates is expressed by the **interest-rate parity theorem**. The ratio of the current forward and spot exchange rates (expressed in units of foreign currency per dollar) equals the ratio of one plus the current nominal foreign rate to one plus the current nominal domestic rate.

$$\frac{\textit{Forward exchange rate}}{\textit{Spot exchange rate}} = \frac{1 + \textit{Foreign interest rate}}{1 + \textit{Domestic interest rate}}$$

       For example, if the current nominal foreign interest rate increases, the forward rate in terms of units of the foreign currency per dollar will increase. Hence, that currency will trade at a discount in the forward market.

4.   **Effective Interest Rate on a Foreign Currency Loan**

a.   EXAMPLE: A U.S. company takes out a one-year, 12,000,000 peso loan at 6.5% to pay a Mexican supplier. After a year, the U.S. company repays the loan with interest but, in the meantime, the peso has experienced a slight appreciation. Thus, the company's effective rate on the loan is higher than the stated rate, calculated as follows:

		Times: Conversion Rate	Equals: Equivalent USD
Amount borrowed	12,000,000 Pesos	0.0921496	$1,105,795
Times: stated rate	6.5%		
Equals: interest charged	780,000 Pesos		
Total repayment	12,780,000 Pesos	0.0940000	1,201,320
Difference			$ 95,525

Effective rate:
Difference ÷ amount borrowed = ($95,525 ÷ $1,105,795)   **8.64%**

5.   **Interaction in Foreign Currency Markets**

a.   The **spot rate** is the exchange rate paid for immediate delivery of a currency.

b.   The **forward exchange rate** is the future price of the currency.

1)   If the forward rate in foreign currency units per dollar is greater than the spot rate, the dollar is selling at a premium.

2)   If the spot rate in foreign currency units per dollar is greater than the forward rate, the dollar is selling at a discount.

3)   The annual effect in the forward market equals

$$\frac{Forward\ market\ rate\ (FC)\ -\ Spot\ rate\ (FC)}{Spot\ rate\ (FC)} \times \begin{array}{c} Number\ of\ forward \\ periods\ in\ a\ year \end{array}$$

a)   FC means that the amount is denominated in foreign currency.

b)   For example, if there is a 1% premium in a 30-day forward market, the annual premium is 12%.

c.   The **discount or premium** is related to the difference between the nominal interest rates paid by foreign and domestic banks (differences in interest rates are largely related to differences in expected inflation).

1)   When the foreign nominal interest rate is lower than the domestic nominal rate, the forward foreign currency sells at a premium. If this were not true, investors would borrow at the lower interest rate, invest at the higher rate, and buy a forward contract for the principal and interest.

2)   If the foreign nominal rate exceeds the domestic nominal rate, the forward foreign currency sells at a discount.

d.   A foreign currency will depreciate or appreciate relative to the dollar at a rate equivalent to the amount by which its inflation rate exceeds or is less than the dollar's inflation rate (everything else constant).

1)   EXAMPLE: If the inflation rate in U.K. is 12% and the inflation rate in the U.S. is 10%, the dollar should appreciate by 2%.

e.   Borrowing in a country with the lowest nominal rate may result in an exchange rate loss if the borrower's currency depreciates relative to the lender's.

1)   Foreign currency exchange rates equalize inflation rates.

6. **Avoidance of Exchange Rate Risk in Foreign Currency Markets**

   a. The firm may **hedge** its risk by purchasing or selling forward exchange contracts.

      1) A firm may buy or sell forward contracts to cover liabilities or receivables, respectively, denominated in a foreign currency.

      2) Any gain or loss on the foreign payables or receivables because of changes in exchange rates is offset by the loss or gain on the forward contract.

   b. The firm may choose to **minimize receivables and liabilities** denominated in foreign currencies.

   c. Maintaining a monetary **balance between receivables and payables** denominated in a particular foreign currency avoids a net receivable or net liability position in that currency. Monetary items are those with fixed cash flows.

      1) A firm may attempt to achieve a net monetary debtor (creditor) position in countries with currencies expected to depreciate (appreciate).

      2) Large multinational corporations have established multinational netting centers as special departments to attempt to achieve balance between foreign receivables and payables.

         a) They also enter into foreign currency futures contracts when necessary to achieve balance.

   d. Another means of managing exchange rate risk is by the use of **trigger pricing**. Under trigger pricing, foreign funds are supplied at an indexed price but with an option to convert to a futures-based fixed price when a specified basis differential exists between the two prices.

   e. A firm may seek to minimize its exchange-rate risk by diversification. If it has transactions in both strong and weak currencies, the effects of changes in rates may be offsetting.

   f. A **speculative forward contract** does not hedge any exposure to foreign currency fluctuations; it creates the exposure.

7. **Analysis of Foreign Investments**

   a. A company planning a foreign investment can either purchase the stock of a foreign corporation or make a **direct foreign investment**. A direct foreign investment involves buying equipment and buildings for a new company.

      1) The advantages of a direct foreign investment include

         a) Lower taxes in the foreign nation
         b) Annual depreciation allowances for the amount invested
         c) Access to foreign capital sources

      2) Disadvantages include

         a) Bureaucratic hurdles (e.g., documentation, licensing) required specifically of foreign investors

         b) Risk of expropriation or loss to violent change of government

         c) Local laws designed to protect domestic firms

         d) Limitations on remittances to investor country

   b. Relevant cash flows are the dividends and possible future sales price of the investment paid to the investor. To this extent, traditional capital budgeting techniques can be used.

    c.   **Cost of capital** for foreign projects is higher because of

        1)   Exchange-rate risk

        2)   Sovereignty (or political) risk arising from possible expropriation (or other restrictions), with net losses to the parent company

        3)   Laws requiring financing from certain sources, such as majority ownership of foreign subsidiaries by locals

        4)   The risk that contentious tax issues may arise

    d.   Foreign operations are more difficult to manage than domestic operations.

8.   Foreign investments are funded by

    a.   Parent company resources

    b.   Common stock sales in the foreign country

    c.   Bond sales in the foreign country

    d.   Borrowing in world financial markets

9.   Stop and review! You have completed the outline for this subunit. Study multiple-choice questions 18 through 38 beginning on page 202.

7.4 BALANCE OF PAYMENTS

1.   The balance of payments is an economic measure that includes all international payments made by one nation to another, including those for imports, exports, investments, unilateral transfers, and capital movements. The principal accounts are the current account and the **capital account**.

    a.   The **current account** records

        1)   Exports (credits) and imports (debits) of goods

            a)   The **balance of trade** is the difference between total exports and total imports of goods.

            b)   A **trade deficit** occurs when a country imports more goods than it exports.

        2)   Exports (credits) and imports (debits) of services

            a)   The **balance on goods and services** is the difference between total exports and total imports of goods and services.

        3)   Interest and dividends received on investments abroad (credits) and interest and dividends paid on foreign investments in the U.S. (debits)

        4)   Net unilateral transfers, e.g., foreign aid, pension payments, and remittance to relatives (credits or debits, depending on whether the flow is into or out of the U.S., respectively)

        5)   The balance on the current account

    b.   The **capital account** records capital flows resulting from the purchase and sale of fixed or financial assets.

        1)   Inflows of foreign capital (credits) are effectively exports of stocks and bonds and therefore result in inflows of foreign currencies.

        2)   Outflows of capital (debits) use up supplies of foreign currencies.

        3)   A capital account surplus therefore indicates that inflows exceeded outflows.

    c.   The **balance of payments deficit or surplus** is the net of the current and capital account balances.

d.   The **official reserves account** records transactions involving the central bank and its official reserve assets, such as gold and foreign currency.

1)   Also among a central bank's reserves are **special drawing rights** (SDRs). They are accounting entries established by the **International Monetary Fund**. The IMF is a banking organization that helps to manage international transactions by holding currency reserves and making loans to central banks.

a)   Another important international financial institution is the **World Bank**, established to provide credit for development purposes to underdeveloped countries.

e.   EXAMPLE (in billions):

Current account:		
Exports of goods	$1,272	
Imports of goods	(1,996)	
Balance of trade		**$(724)**
Exports of services	$ 380	
Imports of services	(322)	58
Balance on goods and services		**$(666)**
Net investment income		1
Net transfers		(83)
Balance on current account		**$(748)**
Capital account:		
Capital inflows	$1,293	
Capital outflows	(1,216)	
Balance on capital account		77
Balance of payments		**$(671)**
Official reserves account		671
Net		**$ 0**

f.   The references to debits and credits treat the balance of payments account as if it were a revenue or expense account. In other words, a debit is similar to an expense in that it is unfavorable for the country's balance of payments position.

1)   EXAMPLE: A debit (such as an import) is undesirable because it contributes to an unfavorable balance of payments. The U.S. has an unfavorable balance of payments when payments by the U.S. to foreign countries exceed the payments made from foreign countries to the U.S. It is also unfavorable because foreign currency reserves held by the U.S. must be given up to correct the imbalance.

2)   A credit in the balance of payments account is desirable (exports, for instance) because foreigners will be paying more to the U.S. than the U.S. is paying out. Thus, the foreign currency reserves available to the U.S. increase.

g.   In addition to decreasing the reserves of foreign currencies held by the U.S., an unfavorable balance of payments can also affect the domestic economy.

1)   EXAMPLE: An excess of imports can cause an unfavorable balance of payments. At the same time, consumers may not be buying domestic products, which may result in domestic layoffs and production cutbacks. These in turn will mean less investment opportunity domestically, and investors will begin sending their investment dollars overseas. The flow of capital overseas compounds the balance of payments problem because investing in a foreign country is essentially the same as importing a product (i.e., the investor is importing foreign stocks and bonds).

2) Steps to correct an unfavorable balance of payments:

  a) Establish **import quotas**.

    i) One country's unfavorable balance of payments may be caused by another nation's import quotas. For example, if the U.S. has a continuing unfavorable balance of payments with Japan, it might be possible to encourage Japan to remove the trade barriers set up to keep U.S. electronics products out. The removal of Japan's trade restrictions would help the U.S. balance of payments (but might result in an unfavorable balance of payments for Japan).

  b) Provide **export incentives**.

    i) EXAMPLE: The tax law provisions for Domestic International Sales Corporations (DISCs) and Foreign Sales Corporations (FSCs) permitted exporters to postpone or avoid income taxes on export-related income as long as that income is reinvested in export-related assets. Provisions for FSCs were enacted in 1985 to replace DISCs because the latter were criticized as illegal export subsidiaries. FSCs were ruled illegal by the WTO, and the FSC rules were repealed as of September 30, 2000.

  c) **Develop substitutes** for products currently being imported.

    i) EXAMPLE: The U.S. has tried to develop substitutes for or local sources of oil.

3) An automatic correction results when a debtor nation's monetary unit declines relative to that of a creditor nation. For example, the huge U.S. trade deficit with China is attributable in part to the artificially low valuation of the yuan that results from its being pegged to the U.S. dollar.

h. A balance of payments deficit (imbalance) must be equalized by shipments of goods or reductions in reserves.

  1) Gifts and grants also are used.

i. In the 1980s, the U.S. became the nation with the largest foreign debt. The reasons include the following:

  1) Federal budget deficits financed by foreigners
  2) Growth in the economy that attracted foreign investors
  3) High real interest rates
  4) A strengthened dollar in the early 1980s that encouraged imports
  5) The shift from a manufacturing to a service economy
  6) A decrease in exports of agricultural goods

j. The following are the actual or potential effects of the U.S.'s debt:

  1) An increase in the percentage of the GDP used for debt service
  2) Reduced reserves leading to a devalued dollar, inflation, and increased exports
  3) A decline in net imports and improvement in the trade balance
  4) Increased savings as a result of economic uncertainty
  5) Increased pressure for trade protectionism
  6) Potentially high interest rates to curtail inflation and tighten the money supply, with the consequent incentive for foreign investment

2. Stop and review! You have completed the outline for this subunit. Study multiple-choice questions 39 through 44 beginning on page 207.

QUESTIONS

7.1 Advantages of International Trade

1. One of the major consequences of international trade between nations is

   A. Higher prices for consumers.

   B. A decreased variety of consumer products.

   C. The possibility for total world output to increase.

   D. Reduced competition for businesses.

Answer (C) is correct. *(CMA, adapted)*
   REQUIRED: The major consequence of international trade.
   DISCUSSION: Under the concept of comparative advantage, total world output will be maximized when each nation specializes in the products in which it has the lowest opportunity costs, that is, a comparative advantage. When nations specialize in what they produce most efficiently and then exchange with others, more is produced and consumed than if each nation tries to be self-sufficient. Specialization is beneficial for individuals. The same principle applies to nations.
   Answer (A) is incorrect because prices will be lower and greater quantities will be available with international trade. Answer (B) is incorrect because variety will be increased by international trade. Answer (D) is incorrect because competition will be increased when more producers are in the market.

2.

Curves ABC and DEF on the graph represent production possibility curves for a nation. If point E on curve DEF represents the current combination of goods #1 and #2 consumed by that nation, the nation can reach point B on curve ABC by

   A. Discovering more or better resources.

   B. Discovering improved production techniques.

   C. Incurring a trade deficit.

   D. Incurring a trade surplus.

Answer (D) is correct. *(CIA, adapted)*
   REQUIRED: The method by which a nation can change its production possibilities curve.
   DISCUSSION: If a nation's exports are greater than its imports, the combination of goods consumed will be less than the combination produced. Hence, the production possibilities curve will shift inward, for example, to point B on curve ABC.
   Answer (A) is incorrect because the discovery of more or better resources causes an outward shift of the production possibilities curve. Answer (B) is incorrect because the discovery of improved production techniques causes an outward shift of the production possibilities curve. Answer (C) is incorrect because incurring a trade deficit results in consumption of a combination of goods outside the current production possibilities curve.

3. Which one of the following statements concerning international trade and protection is true?

   A. Protection is necessary in order to keep U.S. money in the U.S.

   B. When two nations trade, one must gain while the other must lose.

   C. The U.S. cannot compete with nations whose labor costs are lower.

   D. U.S. imports raise living standards in the U.S.

Answer (D) is correct. *(CMA, adapted)*
   REQUIRED: The true statement about international trade and protection.
   DISCUSSION: Imports can raise the standard of living because more goods are available to consumers. Tariffs, quotas, and other trade restraints are undesirable because free trade will maximize the total benefit to consumers worldwide (under the concept of comparative advantage).
   Answer (A) is incorrect because U.S. investment abroad has proven to be beneficial. Answer (B) is incorrect because both nations should benefit from international trade. Under the concept of comparative advantage, no country will be worse off through international trade. Answer (C) is incorrect because the U.S. has other advantages not possessed by countries with low labor costs.

4. Holland produces 90 million cases of soda and 20 million pounds of cheese. To increase production of cheese to 30 million pounds, it must sacrifice 30 million cases of soda. Iceland produces 65 million cases of soda and 65 million pounds of cheese, but to produce 75 million pounds of cheese, it must sacrifice 10 million cases of soda. It can be concluded that

A. Holland has an absolute advantage in both soda and cheese production.

B. Iceland has an absolute advantage in soda production, and Holland has an absolute advantage in cheese production.

C. Iceland has an absolute advantage in both soda and cheese production.

D. Holland has a comparative advantage in soda production, and Iceland has an absolute advantage in cheese production.

Answer (D) is correct. *(Publisher, adapted)*
REQUIRED: The true statement with respect to comparative and absolute advantage.
DISCUSSION: A comparative advantage analysis compares costs of multiple products within countries and then determines which country has the lowest opportunity cost. Absolute advantage compares the costs of inputs between countries. In Holland, the cost of 10 million pounds of cheese is 30 million cases of soda, or a 1-to-3 ratio. In Iceland, the cost of 10 million pounds of cheese is 10 million cases of soda, or a 1-to-1 ratio. Thus, Iceland has an absolute advantage in cheese production because it can produce cheese less expensively than Holland. Furthermore, Holland has a comparative advantage in soda production. It must forgo 1/3 pound of cheese per case of soda produced, whereas Iceland must forgo 1 pound.
Answer (A) is incorrect because Iceland has the absolute advantage with respect to cheese. Answer (B) is incorrect because Holland has the absolute advantage in soda production. Answer (C) is incorrect because Holland has the absolute advantage with respect to soda.

Questions 5 and 6 are based on the following information. Two countries, the U.S. and Japan, each have 100,000 days of labor available each year. That labor can be used to produce the following three products: food, cars, and wine. Labor is the only input required for production. The relative costs to produce each of these products is as follows (in days):

	U.S.	Japan
Food	1	2
Cars	1.5	1
Wine	3	4

5. How many cars will the entire economy produce if no international trade occurred, and the U.S. and Japan divided their available labor resources equally among the three products?

A. 33,333

B. 55,555

C. 66,667

D. 100,000

Answer (B) is correct. *(Publisher, adapted)*
REQUIRED: The number of cars produced given no international trade and equal division of labor resources among the three products in each country.
DISCUSSION: If the 100,000 days of resources are divided equally, 33,333 days will be available for each product in each country. Because food costs 1 day of labor in the U.S., that country could produce 33,333 units of food. Similarly, 22,222 units of cars could be produced with 33,333 available days. These and other outputs are shown in the following table:

	U.S.	Japan	Total
Food	33,333	16,667	50,000
Cars	22,222	33,333	55,555
Wine	11,111	8,333	19,444

Thus, with no international trade, 55,555 cars will be produced.
Answer (A) is incorrect because 33,333 is the number of days available for each product in each country. Answer (C) is incorrect because 66,667 is the total number of days available to produce cars in both countries. Answer (D) is incorrect because 100,000 is the total number of days available to each country.

6. If international trade occurs and the U.S. and Japan each specialize in producing what it can produce most efficiently,

    A. The U.S. should specialize in both food and wine.

    B. The U.S. should specialize in food and Japan in wine.

    C. Japan should specialize in both food and wine.

    D. Japan should specialize in food and the U.S. in wine.

Answer (A) is correct. *(Publisher, adapted)*

REQUIRED: The countries that should specialize in food and wine given international trade.

DISCUSSION: The U.S. has an absolute advantage and a comparative advantage (the latter involving a lower opportunity cost measured in output of cars) with respect to food and wine, so it should specialize in both. Of course, in a three-product economy, it might not be possible for one country to specialize in something to the exclusion of the other products. For example, if the U.S. specialized in food and wine, and Japan specialized in cars, the result would be as follows:

	U.S.	Japan	Total
Food	50,000	0	50,000
Cars	0	100,000	100,000
Wine	16,667	0	16,667

The outputs are an equal amount of food, nearly twice as many cars, but less wine. It is possible that consumers may want more cars and less wine, but that is not certain. Thus, Japan would have to produce some wine even though it has no comparative advantage. For example, to equal the wine output that existed in the absence of trade, Japan would have to reduce the labor devoted to cars to produce 2,777 units of wine. The following is the revised table of outputs:

	U.S.	Japan	Total
Food	50,000	0	50,000
Cars	0	88,892	88,892
Wine	16,667	2,777	19,444

This combination (only one of many possibilities) results in the same amount of food and wine as without trade, but far more cars (88,892 versus 55,555). Accordingly, international trade is a benefit for everyone because the U.S. is allowed to specialize in those products in which it has a comparative advantage, and Japan produces all of the world's cars, the product in which it has a comparative advantage.

Answer (B) is incorrect because Japan should specialize in car production. Answer (C) is incorrect because Japan should specialize in car production. Answer (D) is incorrect because the U.S. has a comparative and absolute advantage in producing food.

Questions 7 through 9 are based on the following information.

One Unit of Resources Can Produce

	Soybeans (tons)	Chips (units)
Taiwan	6	1,500
United States	12	1,800

7. If there were free trade between Taiwan and the United States, which one of the following statements is true?

A. Only the United States will gain from free trade.

B. The United States would specialize in the production of both chips and soybeans.

C. The United States will export chips to Taiwan.

D. Taiwan will specialize in the production of chips.

Answer (D) is correct. *(CMA, adapted)*
REQUIRED: The true statement about free trade between the two countries.
DISCUSSION: Countries should specialize in the production and export of products for which they have a comparative advantage. They should import those products for which they do not have a comparative advantage. Taiwan's opportunity cost for 1 ton of soybeans is 250 units of chips (1,500 ÷ 6). The U.S.'s opportunity cost for 1 ton of soybeans is 150 units of chips (1,800 ÷ 12). Thus, the U.S. should produce soybeans because it has the lower opportunity cost. Taiwan's opportunity cost for 1 unit of chips is .004 ton of soybeans (6 ÷ 1,500). The U.S.'s opportunity cost for 1 unit of chips is .007 ton of soybeans (12 ÷ 1,800). Taiwan should specialize in the production of chips because it has the lower opportunity cost.
Answer (A) is incorrect because both countries will benefit from free trade. Specialization results in the optimal total output. Answer (B) is incorrect because the U.S. will specialize in the production of soybeans. Answer (C) is incorrect because Taiwan will produce chips and export them to the U.S.

8. In trade between Taiwan and the United States,

A. Taiwan has an absolute advantage in producing soybeans.

B. The United States has a comparative advantage in producing soybeans.

C. Taiwan has a comparative advantage in producing soybeans.

D. The United States has a comparative advantage in producing chips.

Answer (B) is correct. *(CMA, adapted)*
REQUIRED: The true statement about comparative and absolute advantage in a two-country, two-product model.
DISCUSSION: Given two countries and two products, each country will always have a comparative advantage with respect to one of the products. Each country may or may not have an absolute advantage. In this case, the U.S. has an absolute advantage with respect to both products because with one unit of resources it can produce more soybeans (12 to 6) and more chips (1,800 to 1,500) than Taiwan. Comparatively, the U.S. has an advantage with respect to soybeans. Comparative advantage is measured by determining which product can be manufactured more cheaply (for the lower opportunity cost) in comparison with the other country. For 1 ton of soybeans, the U.S. opportunity cost is 150 units (1,800 ÷ 12) of chips. The opportunity cost for Taiwan is 250 units (1,500 ÷ 6) of chips.
Answer (A) is incorrect because Taiwan does not have an absolute advantage with respect to either product. Answer (C) is incorrect because the U.S. has the comparative advantage in the production of soybeans. Answer (D) is incorrect because Taiwan has the comparative advantage in the production of chips.

9. Assuming free trade between the United States and Taiwan, the relative prices of soybeans and chips will be

A. Exactly 1 ton of soybeans for 250 chips.

B. Between 150 to 250 chips for 1 ton of soybeans.

C. Between 1.2 to 2.0 tons of soybeans for 100 chips.

D. Exactly 1 ton of soybeans for 120 chips.

Answer (B) is correct. *(CMA, adapted)*
   REQUIRED: The relative prices of two products assuming free trade.
   DISCUSSION: Taiwan's opportunity cost for 1 ton of soybeans is 250 units of chips. The U.S.'s opportunity cost for 1 ton of soybeans is 150 units of chips (1,800 ÷ 12). Thus, the U.S. should produce soybeans because it has the lower opportunity cost. The lowest price that the U.S. should charge is 150 units of chips per ton of soybeans. Charging a lower price is disadvantageous given that the U.S. can produce 150 units of chips by forgoing 1 ton of soybeans. Moreover, Taiwan should not pay more than 250 units of chips for imported soybeans because they could be made domestically for that price. Consequently, the trading price must be between 150 and 250 units of chips per ton of soybeans if trade is to be advantageous.
   Answer (A) is incorrect because 1 ton of soybeans for 250 chips is the opportunity cost for Taiwan. Answer (C) is incorrect because the lowest price the U.S. should charge is 150 units of chips per ton of soybeans, and the maximum price that Taiwan should pay is 250 units of chips per ton of soybeans. Answer (D) is incorrect because the lowest price that the U.S. should charge is 150 units of chips per ton of soybeans. Taiwan should not pay more than 250 units of chips per ton of soybeans.

7.2 Trade Barriers

10. Which of the following is a tariff?

A. Licensing requirements.

B. Consumption taxes on imported goods.

C. Unreasonable standards pertaining to product quality and safety.

D. Domestic content rules.

Answer (B) is correct. *(CIA, adapted)*
   REQUIRED: The example of a tariff.
   DISCUSSION: Tariffs are excise taxes on imported goods imposed either to generate revenue or protect domestic producers. Thus, consumption taxes on imported goods are tariffs.
   Answer (A) is incorrect because licensing requirements limit exports, e.g., of militarily sensitive technology. Answer (C) is incorrect because unreasonable standards pertaining to product quality and safety are nontariff trade barriers. Answer (D) is incorrect because domestic content rules require that a portion of an imported good be made in the importing country.

11. Which of the following is a direct effect of imposing a protective tariff on an imported product?

A. Lower domestic prices on the imported item.

B. Lower domestic consumption of the item.

C. Reduced domestic production of the item.

D. Higher sales revenues for foreign producers of the item.

Answer (B) is correct. *(CIA, adapted)*
   REQUIRED: The direct effect of imposing a protective tariff on an imported product.
   DISCUSSION: A protective tariff adds to the purchase price of imported goods. If an imported good's sales price is higher than a comparable, less expensive domestic good, consumers will purchase the domestic good. Thus, the direct effect of imposing a protective tariff on an imported good is lower domestic consumption of the imported product.
   Answer (A) is incorrect because a protective tariff can only increase the domestic price of the imported item. Answer (C) is incorrect because, as the imported item's domestic price increases, demand for domestic goods will increase. Thus, domestic production will increase, not decrease. Answer (D) is incorrect because, as the imported item's domestic price increases, demand for the item decreases. Lower sales revenues will result.

12. Many domestic industries, such as cars and textiles, are partially protected from foreign competition by a system of import tariffs and import quotas. A major effect of such tariffs and quotas is to

- A. Raise the domestic price of internationally produced cars and textiles.
- B. Lower the domestic price of internationally produced cars and textiles.
- C. Increase the volume of international trade in cars and textiles.
- D. Reduce employment in the car and textile industries in the short run.

13. Which one of the following groups would be the primary beneficiary of a tariff?

- A. Domestic producers of export goods.
- B. Domestic producers of goods protected by the tariff.
- C. Domestic consumers of goods protected by the tariff.
- D. Foreign producers of goods protected by the tariff.

14. In trade discussions between the United States and Japanese governments, if Japan voluntarily agrees to restrict automobile exports, which one of the following is true?

- A. This restriction has no effect on the price paid by the consumer.
- B. The United States government gains from these restrictions.
- C. Profit margins for Japanese auto manufacturers have increased.
- D. Under this agreement, the Japanese have an incentive to export less expensive cars to the United States.

Answer (A) is correct. *(CMA, adapted)*
REQUIRED: The major effect of import tariffs and import quotas on cars and textiles.
DISCUSSION: Import tariffs and quotas cause the prices of goods to increase. Tariffs directly increase the prices paid by consumers. Quotas decrease supply and therefore indirectly raise the price. At the same time, resources will shift from relatively efficient export industries to less efficient protected industries. Prices will rise as resources are misallocated to high-cost producers.
Answer (B) is incorrect because prices will increase. Answer (C) is incorrect because the volume of trade will decline as less efficient domestic producers remain in or enter the market. Total worldwide real output will also decline. Answer (D) is incorrect because employment in the protected industries will increase in the short run, but total employment may not be affected.

Answer (B) is correct. *(CMA, adapted)*
REQUIRED: The primary beneficiaries of a tariff.
DISCUSSION: Despite the advantages of free trade, nations often levy tariffs to discourage the importation of certain products. A tariff is a tax on imports intended to protect a domestic producer from foreign competition. For instance, a tariff on imported autos benefits U.S. auto manufacturers because it is an additional cost imposed on U.S. consumers of imported products. The disadvantages of the tariff are that it may protect an inefficient domestic producer and increase prices paid by domestic consumers.
Answer (A) is incorrect because domestic producers of export goods are not benefited. They may also be harmed by retaliatory tariffs. Answer (C) is incorrect because domestic consumers must pay higher prices for imported goods. Answer (D) is incorrect because the foreign producers will be forced to bear an additional cost.

Answer (C) is correct. *(CMA, adapted)*
REQUIRED: The true statement about Japan's voluntary agreement to restrict automobile exports to the United States.
DISCUSSION: A voluntary agreement to restrict exports to the United States forestalls possible trade restrictions. Such an agreement is more likely if Japan's domestic profit margins are sufficiently high that its dependence on exports to the U.S. has been reduced.
Answer (A) is incorrect because this restriction increases the price to U.S. consumers. The reduced supply may not be matched by reduced demand. Answer (B) is incorrect because the government will not directly benefit from the restriction on auto imports from Japan. The restriction benefits U.S. manufacturers and helps equalize the balance of payments. Answer (D) is incorrect because Japan will want to export more expensive cars to the U.S. The higher-priced cars will have higher margins of profit.

15. The graph depicts the domestic supply of and demand for a product that is also sold in the domestic market by foreign producers. The domestic producers are protected by a tariff of the amount P_t minus P_w. P_t is the domestic price including the tariff, and P_w is the world price for the product. The effect of the tariff is to

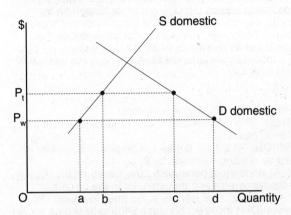

A. Reduce the domestic price from OP_w to OP_t.

B. Reduce foreign sales in the domestic market from ac to bc.

C. Increase domestic production from Ob to Oc.

D. Increase domestic production from Oa to Ob.

Answer (D) is correct. *(CIA, adapted)*
REQUIRED: The effect of a tariff.
DISCUSSION: Without the tariff, domestic production is determined by the intersection of the P_w line with the domestic supply curve at the quantity Oa. Domestic production increases from Oa to Ob as a result of the introduction of the tariff. Supply intersects the P_t line at a higher price and at a greater domestic quantity, Ob.
Answer (A) is incorrect because the inclusion of the tariff increases the domestic price. Answer (B) is incorrect because foreign sales in the domestic market decline from ad to bc. Answer (C) is incorrect because domestic production increases from Oa to Ob.

16. The creation of a regional economic bloc of trading nations, such as the European Union (EU),

A. Discourages foreign investment by nonmember multinational companies.

B. Encourages trade between the member nations and nonmember nations.

C. Requires the adoption of a common monetary unit.

D. Discriminates economically against nonmember nations.

Answer (D) is correct. *(CMA, adapted)*
REQUIRED: The effect of the creation of a regional economic bloc of trading nations.
DISCUSSION: A trading bloc provides trading incentives to member nations and discriminates against nonmember nations. For example, the European Union calls for abolition of internal tariffs and import quotas, free movement of capital and labor within the market, and implementation of common policies for the member nations. However, the EU also imposed a common system of tariffs on goods of nonmember nations.
Answer (A) is incorrect because foreign investment may be welcomed under the appropriate conditions. Answer (B) is incorrect because the EU provides incentives to trade with other members, not nonmembers. Answer (C) is incorrect because currencies are not affected by bloc membership.

17. Which of the following measures create the most restrictive barrier to exporting to a country?

A. Tariffs.

B. Quotas.

C. Embargoes.

D. Exchange controls.

Answer (C) is correct. *(CIA, adapted)*
REQUIRED: The most restrictive barriers to exports to a country.
DISCUSSION: An embargo is a total ban on some kinds of imports. It is an extreme form of quota. Embargoes totally prohibit the exporting firm from selling in that country and are the most restrictive type of import/export law.
Answer (A) is incorrect because a tariff is a tax levied by a foreign government against certain imported products. The tariff reduces profitability or competitiveness in the foreign market but does not prevent the firm from exporting to that country.
Answer (B) is incorrect because a quota is a limit on the amount of goods that an importing country will accept in certain product categories. The effect of a quota is to restrict the quantity the firm can export to that country but not to prevent the firm from selling in that market. Answer (D) is incorrect because exchange controls limit the amount of foreign currency that can be exchanged or the exchange rates. These controls limit the ability of a firm selling in the country to repatriate its export earnings but do not prevent the firm from selling in that market.

7.3 Foreign Currency Rates and Markets

18. The most widely used currency in international business today is the

    A. United States dollar.

    B. Euro.

    C. Japanese yen.

    D. Swiss franc.

Answer (A) is correct. *(CMA, adapted)*
    REQUIRED: The most widely used currency in international business.
    DISCUSSION: The U.S. dollar is the most widely used currency in international markets today. It is considered much more stable than any of the third-world currencies. Thus, many third-world countries rely on the U.S. dollar for foreign trade.
    Answer (B) is incorrect because the Euro is not as heavily used as the U.S. dollar. Answer (C) is incorrect because the Japanese yen is not as heavily used as the U.S. dollar. Answer (D) is incorrect because the Swiss franc is not as heavily used as the U.S. dollar.

19. If the U.S. dollar-peso exchange rate is $1 for 9 pesos, a product priced at 45 pesos will cost a U.S. consumer

    A. $.20

    B. $5

    C. $45

    D. $405

Answer (B) is correct. *(Publisher, adapted)*
    REQUIRED: The price in dollars of a product for which the price is quoted in pesos.
    DISCUSSION: At a 1-for-9 rate, the price in U.S. dollars is $5, calculated by dividing 45 pesos by 9.
    Answer (A) is incorrect because $.20 is based on an inversion of the numerator and denominator in the calculation. Answer (C) is incorrect because $45 is the price in pesos, not dollars. Answer (D) is incorrect because $405 is based on multiplying 45 and 9.

20. If a U.S. firm can buy £20,000 for $100,000, the rate of exchange for the pound is

    A. $.20

    B. $5

    C. $20

    D. $50

Answer (B) is correct. *(Publisher, adapted)*
    REQUIRED: The rate of exchange.
    DISCUSSION: Dividing $100,000 by £20,000 produces an exchange rate of $5 to the pound.

21. An overvalued foreign currency exchange rate

    A. Represents a tax on exports and a subsidy to imports.

    B. Represents a subsidy to exports and a tax on imports.

    C. Has an effect on capital flows but no effect on trade flows.

    D. Has no effect on capital flows but does affect trade flows.

Answer (A) is correct. *(CMA, adapted)*
    REQUIRED: The effect of an overvalued exchange rate.
    DISCUSSION: An overvalued exchange rate is a tax on exports because they will be overvalued in terms of the foreign currency. For example, if the true value of $1 is 5 foreign currency units (FCUs) but the exchange rate is $1 to 6 FCUs, the cost of goods priced in dollars will include a 20% tax for holders of FCUs. It is also a subsidy to imports because the overly high exchange rate causes the price of foreign goods and services to be undervalued. In the same example, $1 will buy 6 FCUs' worth of imports instead of 5, a 20% subsidy.
    Answer (B) is incorrect because devaluation taxes imports and subsidizes exports. Answer (C) is incorrect because trade flows will be affected. Answer (D) is incorrect because capital flows will be affected.

22. Exchange rates are determined by

    A. Each industrial country's government.

    B. The International Monetary Fund.

    C. Supply and demand in the foreign currency market.

    D. Exporters and importers of manufactured goods.

Answer (C) is correct. *(CMA, adapted)*
    REQUIRED: The factor that determines foreign exchange rates.
    DISCUSSION: Although currencies can be supported by various means for short periods, the primary determinant of exchange rates is the supply of and demand for the various currencies. Under current international agreements, exchange rates are allowed to "float." During periods of extreme fluctuations, however, governments and control banks may intervene to maintain stability in the market.
    Answer (A) is incorrect because governments have only temporary influence, if any, on the setting of exchange rates. Answer (B) is incorrect because the International Monetary Fund has only temporary influence, if any, on the setting of exchange rates. Answer (D) is incorrect because they have only temporary influence, if any, on the setting of exchange rates.

23. A U.S. company invested $100,000 in Canada for one year at 10%. The Canadian dollar was selling at a spot rate of $.65 when the investment was made and $.70 when the investment matured. What was the approximate yield on this investment?

A. 2.14%

B. 7.69%

C. 10.00%

D. 18.46%

Answer (D) is correct. *(Publisher, adapted)*
REQUIRED: The yield on a foreign investment given a change in spot rates.
DISCUSSION: The investment in terms of Canadian dollars was $153,846.15 ($100,000 U.S. dollars ÷ .65). A 10% return increases that amount to $169,230.76 in Canadian dollars. Converting $169,230.76 in Canadian dollars to U.S. dollars (by multiplying by .7) results in $118,461.53 in U.S. dollars. Dividing the $18,461.53 (118,461.53 – 100,000) by the $100,000 original investment results in a return of 18.46%.
Answer (A) is incorrect because 2.14% is based on a reversal of the beginning and ending spot rates. Answer (B) is incorrect because 7.69% is based only on the change in spot rates–not the 10% return. Answer (C) is incorrect because the nominal return must be adjusted for the change in spot prices.

24. Two countries have flexible exchange rate systems and an active trading relationship. If incomes <List A> in country 1, everything else being equal, then the currency of country 1 will tend to <List B> relative to the currency of country 2.

	List A	List B
A.	Rise	Remain constant
B.	Fall	Depreciate
C.	Rise	Depreciate
D.	Remain constant	Appreciate

Answer (C) is correct. *(CIA, adapted)*
REQUIRED: The effect of a change in incomes in one nation on its currency.
DISCUSSION: If incomes in country 1 rise, consumers in country 1 will increase their imports from country 2. The resulting increase in the supply of currency 1 will result in a tendency for it to depreciate relative to the currency of country 2.
Answer (A) is incorrect because, if incomes in country 1 rise, the result will be a tendency for it to devalue relative to the currency of country 2. Answer (B) is incorrect because, if incomes in country 1 fall, consumers in country 1 will reduce their imports. The resulting decrease in the supply of currency 1 will result in a tendency for it to appreciate relative to the currency of country 2. Answer (D) is incorrect because, if incomes in country 1 remain constant, the currency of country 1 will not tend to appreciate or depreciate relative to the currency of country 2.

25. The purchasing-power parity exchange rate

A. Is a fixed (pegged) exchange rate.

B. Is always equal to the market exchange rate.

C. Results in undervalued currencies of countries that are net importers.

D. Holds constant the relative price levels in two countries when measured in a common currency.

Answer (D) is correct. *(CMA, adapted)*
REQUIRED: The definition of purchasing-power parity exchange rate.
DISCUSSION: The purchasing-power parity theorem states that, in the long run, the real price of a good in country A will equal the price of the same good in country B when the prices are expressed in a common currency and converted at the current exchange rate (adjustments for tariffs, taxes, or transportation cost may need to be made).
Answer (A) is incorrect because purchasing-power parity is achieved through floating exchange rates. Answer (B) is incorrect because the purchasing-power parity exchange rate is a long-run measure, but the market rate may reflect short-term or medium-term conditions. Answer (C) is incorrect because purchasing-power parity does not affect valuation.

26. What is the effect on prices of U.S. imports and exports when the dollar depreciates?

A. Import prices and export prices will decrease.

B. Import prices will decrease and export prices will increase.

C. Import prices will increase and export prices will decrease.

D. Import prices and export prices will increase.

Answer (C) is correct. *(CPA, adapted)*
REQUIRED: The effect on imports and exports of a depreciated dollar.
DISCUSSION: When the U.S. dollar depreciates, U.S. products become cheaper for foreign countries to purchase. A depreciated dollar acts as a subsidy to exports by decreasing their price. However, the opposite is true for imports. When the dollar depreciates, imports become more costly because it buys less of the foreign currency. Thus, a depreciated dollar increases the price to import goods to the U.S.

27. If consumers in Japan decide they would like to increase their purchases of consumer products made in the United States, in foreign currency markets there will be a tendency for

- A. The supply of dollars to increase.
- B. The supply of dollars to decrease.
- C. The Japanese yen to appreciate relative to the U.S. dollar.
- D. The demand for dollars to increase.

Answer (D) is correct. *(CMA, adapted)*
REQUIRED: The effect of decisions by Japanese consumers to increase their purchases of U.S. products.
DISCUSSION: The increase in demand for U.S. products will increase the demand for the dollars necessary to pay for those products.
Answer (A) is incorrect because the demand for dollars, not the supply, will be affected by the decision to purchase additional U.S. products. Answer (B) is incorrect because the supply is not affected. The demand may increase. Answer (C) is incorrect because the dollar should appreciate relative to the yen owing to the increased demand for dollars.

28. Debt-servicing problems of less developed countries that primarily sell raw materials to the United States are eased by

- A. A recession in the United States with declines in interest rates.
- B. An expanding U.S. economy with stable money supply growth.
- C. An expansion of the lending authority of the World Bank.
- D. A significant increase in the level of U.S. tariffs.

Answer (B) is correct. *(CMA, adapted)*
REQUIRED: The means of easing debt-servicing problems of less developed countries.
DISCUSSION: An expanding U.S. economy results in greater demand for raw materials from these countries. Also, because the money supply and interest rates are inversely proportional (when the money supply is rising, interest rates are falling), less developed nations can borrow again at lower rates. Moreover, if the money supply is rising, inflation might increase and U.S. dollars will become cheaper, thereby easing the burden of foreign debtors with obligations payable in dollars.
Answer (A) is incorrect because a recession results in less U.S. demand for raw materials from abroad and a reduction in funds available to the underdeveloped nations to pay debts. Answer (C) is incorrect because an expansion of lending authority can only increase the debt outstanding and make it less possible for less developed countries to service their debts. Answer (D) is incorrect because tariffs reduce exports to the U.S. and thus the funds available for debt service.

29. One U.S. dollar is being quoted at 120 Japanese yen on the spot market and at 123 Japanese yen on the 90-day forward market; hence, the annual effect in the forward market is that the

- A. U.S. dollar is at a premium of 10%.
- B. U.S. dollar is at a premium of 2.5%.
- C. U.S. dollar is at a discount of 10%.
- D. U.S. dollar is at a premium of 0.025%.

Answer (A) is correct. *(CMA, adapted)*
REQUIRED: The annual effect in the forward market of the difference between the current (spot) rate and the 90-day rate.
DISCUSSION: The price difference of three yen is a difference of 2 1/2% (3 ÷ 120) for 90 days. Annualizing this difference (multiplying by 4) produces an annual premium of 10%. Because the 90-day price of the dollar is higher than the current price, it is said that the dollar is at a premium on the 90-day forward market.
Answer (B) is incorrect because 2.5% is the premium for 90 days. Answer (C) is incorrect because the effect is a 10% premium, not discount. Answer (D) is incorrect because the 90-day effect is a 2.5% or 0.025 premium.

30. The spot rate of a foreign currency unit (FCU) is $.90. If the spot rate one year from now is $.85, the FCU will have

- A. Appreciated by 5.56%.
- B. Depreciated by 5.56%.
- C. Appreciated by 5.88%.
- D. Depreciated by 5.88%.

Answer (B) is correct. *(Publisher, adapted)*
REQUIRED: The appreciation or depreciation due to a change in spot rates.
DISCUSSION: Currently, the FCU sells for $.90. In a year, the price will drop to $.85. At $.90, a person can purchase 100 FCUs for $90. Next year, the same 100 FCUs will cost $85, meaning the FCU will be less valuable (in terms of dollars). Thus, the value of the FCU will depreciate against the dollar. The amount of the decline of $5, divided by the original price of $90, will result in a 5.56% depreciation.
Answer (A) is incorrect because the FCU will depreciate rather than appreciate. Answer (C) is incorrect because the FCU will depreciate and the denominator for the calculation should be .85, not .20. Answer (D) is incorrect because it uses .85 in the denominator instead of .90.

31. Assuming that the real rate of interest is the same in both countries, if country A has a higher nominal interest rate than country B, the currency of country A will likely be selling at a

A. Forward discount relative to the currency of country B.

B. Forward premium relative to the currency of country B.

C. Spot discount relative to the currency of country B.

D. Spot premium relative to the currency of country B.

Answer (A) is correct. *(CIA, adapted)*
REQUIRED: The effect of a higher nominal interest rate.
DISCUSSION: If the real rates of interest are equal, the country with the higher nominal interest rate is expected to experience a higher rate of inflation. A higher rate of inflation is associated with a devaluing currency, so the currency of the country with the higher nominal interest rate will likely be selling at a forward discount. The spot relationship between the two currencies cannot be determined from the information given.

32. If the annual U.S. inflation rate is expected to be 5% while the Japanese yen is expected to depreciate against the U.S. dollar by 10%, a Japanese firm importing from its U.S. parent can expect its yen costs for these imports to

A. Decrease by about 10%.

B. Decrease by about 5%.

C. Increase by about 5%.

D. Increase by about 16.6%.

Answer (D) is correct. *(CMA, adapted)*
REQUIRED: The combined effect of inflation and currency depreciation.
DISCUSSION: Assuming the original exchange rate is $1 to 2,000 yen and that U.S. inflation is 5%, the cost in yen to purchase what once cost $1 will now be 2,100 yen (2,000 × 1.05). However, if the yen also depreciates by 10%, that is, if the yen is expected to be worth 90% of its current value against the dollar, the exchange rate before inflation will be $1 to 2,222 yen (2,000 ÷ .9). At this rate, 2,333 yen (2,222 × 1.05) will be required to purchase $1. Yen costs will thus increase by over 16.6% (333 ÷ 2,000).

33. An American importer of English clothing has contracted to pay an amount fixed in British pounds three months from now. If the importer worries that the U.S. dollar may depreciate sharply against the British pound in the interim, it would be well advised to

A. Buy pounds in the forward exchange market.

B. Sell pounds in the forward exchange market.

C. Buy dollars in the futures market.

D. Sell dollars in the futures market.

Answer (A) is correct. *(CMA, adapted)*
REQUIRED: The action to hedge a liability denominated in a foreign currency.
DISCUSSION: The American importer should buy pounds now. If the dollar depreciates against the pound in the next 90 days, the gain on the forward exchange contract would offset the loss from having to pay more dollars to satisfy the liability.
Answer (B) is incorrect because selling pounds would compound the risk of loss for someone who has incurred a liability. However, it would be an appropriate hedge of a receivable denominated in pounds. Answer (C) is incorrect because the importer needs pounds, not dollars. Answer (D) is incorrect because, although buying pounds might be equivalent to selling dollars for pounds, this is not the best answer. This choice does not state what is received for the dollars.

34. Consider a world consisting of only two countries, Canada and Avalon. The Canadian currency is the Canadian dollar ($) and the Avalonian currency is the ACU. Inflation in Canada in 1 year was 5% and in Avalon 10%. Which one of the following statements about the Canadian exchange rate (rounded) during that year will be true?

A. Inflation has no effect on the exchange rates.

B. The Canadian dollar will appreciate by 5%.

C. The Canadian dollar will depreciate by 5%.

D. The Canadian dollar will depreciate by 15%.

Answer (B) is correct. *(CMA, adapted)*
REQUIRED: The true statement about the exchange rate of a currency given domestic and foreign inflation.
DISCUSSION: Because Avalon has experienced the greater inflation, its currency should depreciate in relation to Canada's. For example, if Canada trades 100 units of a product to Avalon for a preinflation price of $100 (the domestic price in Canada), and Avalon pays with 10,000 units of an Avalonian product that sells domestically for 10,000 preinflation ACUs, the exchange rate without regard to inflation is 100 ACUs per $1 (10,000 ACUs ÷ $100). Allowing for the inflation, the 100 units of the Canadian product would sell for $105. The 10,000 units of the Avalonian product would sell for 11,000 ACUs. Thus, the new exchange rate will be 104.76 ACUs per $1 (11,000 ACUs ÷ $105), and the price of the Canadian dollar will increase by 4.76% (rounded to 5%).
Answer (A) is incorrect because inflation affects exchange rates by diminishing a currency's purchasing power. Answer (C) is incorrect because the Canadian currency will appreciate relative to Avalon. Canadian inflation was lower. Answer (D) is incorrect because the Canadian dollar will appreciate, and the appreciation is approximately 5%.

35. A company manufactures goods in Esland for sale to consumers in Woostland. Currently, the economy of Esland is booming and imports are rising rapidly. Woostland is experiencing an economic recession, and its imports are declining. How will the Esland currency, $E, react with respect to the Woostland currency, $W?

A. The $E will remain constant with respect to the $W.

B. The $E will increase with respect to the $W.

C. The $E will decline with respect to the $W.

D. Changes in imports and exports will not affect currency changes.

Answer (C) is correct. *(CPA, adapted)*
REQUIRED: The effect on the exchange rate for the currencies of a nation in a recession and a nation in an expansion.
DISCUSSION: If the growth of a country's national income is more rapid than other countries' national income, its currency is likely to depreciate. A country's imports vary directly with its level of income. As income rises in Esland, Esland consumers purchase more domestic and foreign goods. The greater demand for foreign goods causes a demand for the foreign currency. When demand increases for the foreign currency, its price increases, and Esland's currency depreciates as a result.
Answer (A) is incorrect because $E will depreciate against $W. Answer (B) is incorrect because the rise in imports will cause $E to depreciate. Answer (D) is incorrect because imports and exports have a substantial effect on currency exchange rates.

36. A company has a foreign-currency-denominated trade payable, due in 60 days. In order to eliminate the foreign currency exchange-rate risk associated with the payable, the company could

A. Sell foreign currency forward today.

B. Wait 60 days and pay the invoice by purchasing foreign currency in the spot market at that time.

C. Buy foreign currency forward today.

D. Borrow foreign currency today, convert it to domestic currency on the spot market, and invest the funds in a domestic bank deposit until the invoice payment date.

Answer (C) is correct. *(CIA, adapted)*
REQUIRED: The means of eliminating exchange-rate risk.
DISCUSSION: The company can arrange to purchase the foreign currency today rather than in 60 days by buying the currency in the forward market. This hedging transaction will eliminate the exchange-rate risk associated with the trade payable.
Answer (A) is incorrect because a forward market sale of foreign currency is appropriate to hedge a receivable denominated in a foreign currency. Answer (B) is incorrect because waiting to buy the currency in 60 days does not eliminate the risk of an adverse exchange-rate movement. Answer (D) is incorrect because this strategy would be comparable to a future sale of the foreign currency at a rate known today, which would not provide the currency needed to pay the invoice. However, the opposite strategy would be an effective money market hedge. If the company converted domestic currency to foreign currency in the spot market today and invested in a foreign bank deposit or treasury bill, it could then use the proceeds from the foreign investment to pay the invoice in 60 days.

37. Which one of the following did not contribute to the high value of the U.S. dollar during the 1980s?

A. Relatively high, real interest rates.

B. A large demand for U.S. dollars.

C. U.S. demand for foreign goods.

D. A stable U.S. government and currency.

Answer (C) is correct. *(CMA, adapted)*
REQUIRED: The event that did not contribute to the high value of the U.S. dollar during the 1980s.
DISCUSSION: Many factors influence the value of a country's currency on the international market. These factors include interest rate differentials, inflation differentials, balance of trade, balance of payments, and stability of governments. However, a demand by Americans for more foreign goods would drive down the price of the dollar because of the resulting increased demand for foreign currencies.
Answer (A) is incorrect because, in the 1980s, high real interest rates made investments in the U.S. more attractive. Thus, demand for U.S. dollars increased. Answer (B) is incorrect because a large demand for dollars drives up the price of dollars relative to other currencies. Answer (D) is incorrect because the stability of the U.S. government and its currency made the dollar a secure store of value in the eyes of many foreigners; these foreigners therefore acquired dollars to hold as a safeguard against inflation in their own countries.

38. If the annual U.S. inflation rate is expected to be 3%, and the Ptomanian TCU is expected to depreciate against the U.S. dollar by 12%, a Ptomanian firm importing from its U.S. parent can expect the costs of imports denominated in TCUs to

    A. Decrease by about 12%.

    B. Decrease by about 5%.

    C. Increase by about 3%.

    D. Increase by about 17%.

Answer (D) is correct. *(Publisher, adapted)*
    REQUIRED: The effect on prices of imports given depreciation of the importing country's currency relative to the exporting country's currency.
    DISCUSSION: Assuming the original exchange rate is $1 to 2 TCUs and that U.S. inflation is 3%, the cost in TCUs to purchase what once cost $1 will now be 2.06 TCUs (2 × 1.03). However, if the TCU also depreciates by 12%, that is, if the TCU is expected to be worth 88% of its current value, the exchange rate (before inflation) will be $1 to 2.2727 (2 ÷ .88) TCUs. At this rate, 2.3409 TCUs (2.2727 × 1.03) will be required to purchase $1. Costs in TCUs will therefore increase by just over 17% (.3409 ÷ 2.00).
    Answer (A) is incorrect because prices paid by the Ptomanian buyer will increase. It must adjust payments in TCUs upward for both U.S. inflation and Ptomanian monetary depreciation. Answer (B) is incorrect because prices paid by the Ptomanian buyer will increase. It must adjust payments in TCUs upward for both U.S. inflation and Ptomanian monetary depreciation. Answer (C) is incorrect because prices will increase by 3% simply as a result of inflation. This answer disregards the effect of the currency depreciation.

7.4 Balance of Payments

39. In relation to the balance of trade, all international transactions involving the purchase or sale of physical products between domestic and foreign countries are reflected in

    A. The balance of the capital account.

    B. Official reserves held by the central banks.

    C. The official financing account.

    D. The trade balance in the current account.

Answer (D) is correct. *(CMA, adapted)*
    REQUIRED: The correct account.
    DISCUSSION: The balance of payments represents all international payments made by one nation to another, including those for imports, exports, investments, unilateral transfers, such as pensions and gifts, and capital movements. The principal accounts are the current account and the capital account. The current account includes a net trade balance in goods, net investment receipts or payments, net receipts or payments for services, and the balance of unilateral transfers.
    Answer (A) is incorrect because the capital account includes capital movements only; the direction of capital movements is influenced by the prevailing interest rates in each nation. Answer (B) is incorrect because official reserves are assets held by central banks and are not necessarily related to current transactions. Answer (C) is incorrect because this is a nonsense answer.

40. Which one of the following items represents a credit in the U.S. balance of payment accounts?

    A. U.S. imports of crude oil.

    B. Expenditures of American tourists abroad.

    C. Earnings belonging to foreign businesses that have U.S. plants.

    D. Loans to Americans by foreigners.

Answer (D) is correct. *(CMA, adapted)*
    REQUIRED: The item that represents a credit in the U.S. balance of payments accounts.
    DISCUSSION: Basically, exports of goods and services are credited to the U.S. balance of payments accounts and imports are debited. Similarly, capital movements may be debited or credited. For example, transfers of capital from foreigners to Americans, such as loans, are credits in the accounts. In effect, these loans constitute exports of debt instruments and increase the supply of foreign exchange available for the U.S.
    Answer (A) is incorrect because imports are debited. Answer (B) is incorrect because expenditures of American tourists abroad are treated as imports and are therefore debited. Answer (C) is incorrect because earnings of foreigners represent outflows of foreign exchange and are debited.

41. If a country has a freely floating exchange rate system and is experiencing an appreciation in the external value of its currency, it has

A. A current account deficit and a capital account surplus.

B. A current account surplus and a capital account deficit.

C. Shrinking official reserves.

D. No balance of payments surplus or deficit after short-run exchange-rate adjustments are complete.

Answer (D) is correct. *(CIA, adapted)*
REQUIRED: The effect of an appreciation in the external value of a country's currency given floating exchange rates.
DISCUSSION: In a freely floating exchange-rate system, exchange rates automatically adjust so as to eliminate balance of payments surpluses or deficits. For example, if U.S. demand for country X's currency increases, the result is a U.S. deficit at the existing exchange rate because demand now exceeds the supply of X's currency at that rate. However, the system of floating exchange rates allows the change in the relative strength of the currencies to be reflected in their exchange rate. The appreciation of X's currency against the U.S. dollar, that is, the increase in the amount of U.S. dollars exchangeable for a unit of X's currency, makes U.S. products cheaper to buyers in country X. Furthermore, X's products are more expensive to U.S. buyers. Consequently, U.S. imports will fall, U.S. exports will rise, and the balance of payments deficit will decrease.

42. The dominant reason countries devalue their currencies is to

A. Improve the balance of payments.

B. Discourage exports without having to impose controls.

C. Curb inflation by increasing imports.

D. Slow what is regarded as too rapid an accumulation of international reserves.

Answer (A) is correct. *(CMA, adapted)*
REQUIRED: The dominant reason countries devalue their currencies.
DISCUSSION: Currency devaluations result in a change in the balance of payments. A devaluation means that other currencies will buy more of the devaluing nation's currency, and the prices of goods denominated in the devalued currency are therefore less expensive. A devaluation usually results in an increase in exports, a decrease in imports (caused by higher relative input prices), and an improved balance of trade.
Answer (B) is incorrect because a devaluation will encourage exports. Answer (C) is incorrect because a devaluation will discourage imports and may encourage domestic inflation. Foreign goods will be more expensive. Answer (D) is incorrect because devaluation most likely occurs when a country is losing its reserves.

43. When analyzing a country's balance of payments accounts, the

A. "Current account" refers only to merchandise exports and imports.

B. "Current account" and "trade balance" are the same.

C. "Capital account" refers to the transactions related to the international movement of financial capital.

D. Country will be in financial jeopardy unless each component in the balance of payments accounts balances at the end of the year.

Answer (C) is correct. *(CMA, adapted)*
REQUIRED: The true statement about a country's balance of payments accounts.
DISCUSSION: The balance of payments accounts include all international payments made by one nation to another, including capital movements, imports, exports, and unilateral transfers. The capital account records the net of all cross-border exchanges of capital assets and financial instruments.
Answer (A) is incorrect because the current account also includes exports and imports of services, interest and dividends payments, and nonreciprocal transfers (foreign aid, transmittals to relatives, etc. Answer (B) is incorrect because the trade balance concerns goods only. Answer (D) is incorrect because the various components are never in balance. In reality, the important consideration is the total, and that is more of a long-run than an annual problem.

44. The following transactions were noted for an economy whose currency is denominated in pesetas (Pta).

	Amount in Pesetas
Imports of goods	20,300
Exports of goods	15,760
Domestic long-term investment in foreign countries	6,300
Investment by foreigners in the country	1,400
Interest payments on foreign loans	3,700
Gifts received from abroad	1,240

For this economy, the

A. Current account has a surplus of Pta 7,000.

B. Capital account has a surplus of Pta 4,000.

C. Capital account has a deficit of Pta 7,700.

D. Current account has a deficit of Pta 7,000.

Answer (D) is correct. *(CMA, adapted)*
   REQUIRED: The deficit or surplus in the current or capital account.
   DISCUSSION: The balance of trade is the balance of imports and exports of goods. The current account also considers trade in services (none for this economy), unilateral transfers (e.g., gifts), and investment receipts and payments. It does not include capital transactions. Thus, investments by foreigners in the domestic economy and investments made in foreign countries will not be included in the current account. These transactions will be reflected in the capital account. The capital account will therefore have a deficit of 4,900 (6,300 – 1,400) pesetas because investment in foreign countries is greater than investment by foreigners. The current account will have a deficit of 7,000 pesetas (15,760 – 20,300 + 1,240 – 3,700).
   Answer (A) is incorrect because the current account has a deficit, not a surplus, of Pta 7,000. Answer (B) is incorrect because investment by foreigners should be deducted from, not added to, domestic investment in foreign countries. Furthermore, interest payments on foreign loans affect the current, not the capital account, and the capital account has a trade deficit, not a surplus. Answer (C) is incorrect because investment by foreigners should be deducted from, not added to, domestic investment in foreign countries.

Use Gleim's *CPA Test Prep* for interactive testing with over 2,000 additional multiple-choice questions!

210   Notes

STUDY UNIT EIGHT
WORKING CAPITAL POLICY AND MANAGEMENT

(17 pages of outline)

This study unit addresses the management of the firm's current assets and its short-term financing options. Longer-term financing and investing issues are discussed in the next study unit.

8.1 FINANCIAL MANAGEMENT

1. The **primary objective of the firm** is to maximize the shareholders' wealth in the long term. This can be accomplished by paying dividends or increasing the price per share of common stock.

2. The market price of the stock is the result of the firm's investment and financing decisions within the context of legal and ethical bounds, including those relating to

   a. Product safety
   b. Minority hiring
   c. Pollution control
   d. Fair competition
   e. Fair advertising

3. Other objectives of the firm are less beneficial to shareholders than wealth maximization.

   a. **Profit maximization** sometimes may be inconsistent with the maximization of shareholder wealth. For example,

      1) Investing in high-risk projects may increase profits, but the increase may not be commensurate with the additional risk borne by the firm.
      2) Increasing equity investment (resulting in a lower return on equity) will lower EPS and the stock price.
      3) Delaying needed maintenance may increase accounting profits, but damage to capital may more than offset this increase in short-term profit.

   b. **Sales maximization** is a nonoptimal objective since it may not result in increased profits.

      1) A firm wants to increase sales only when the marginal revenue from the sale is greater than (or equal to) the marginal cost of the sale. Only in this case, i.e., when an additional sale is profitable, is shareholders' wealth maximized.

   c. **Social responsibility** is an important issue, but if it were the only objective of the firm, the firm's existence would be short.

      1) However, some mutual funds invest only in socially responsible firms. Consequently, social responsibility can increase the demand for a corporation's stocks and bonds and thus increase shareholder wealth.

4. Management's **investment decisions** are geared to obtaining a proper mix of productive assets, such as machinery and other capital assets. It must then obtain **financing** of these assets at the optimal cost of capital, thereby maximizing shareholders' wealth.

5.   The investing and financing decisions are not independent.

    a.   The amount and **composition of assets** are directly related to the amount and composition of financing.

    b.   Given current and expected industry and overall economic conditions, the resulting mix of assets, liabilities, and capital determines the **business risk**. The business risk then affects the discount rate when investors value the company. Discount rates are discussed in Study Unit 9, but the effects of financial management on the value of the firm are integral to this study unit.

        1)   Business risk is not completely controllable by management. There are also many "outside" **(exogenous)** variables, such as:

            a)   Technological developments

            b)   Weather

            c)   National fiscal policies

            d)   National monetary policies

            e)   International relations and their effect on particular industries

            f)   Competitors' actions (may not be exogenous if they are affected by the company's decisions)

6.   **Tax strategy** is an important part of financial management.

    a.   **Taxes** (federal, state, local, and foreign) are an important consideration of financial management because they are frequently 25% to 50% of all costs. They include income, use, excise, property, legal document, payroll, and others.

        1)   Thus, governmental services (national defense, fire, police, etc.) are an important and costly factor of production.

    b.   **Tax planning** is the heart of tax strategy.

        1)   **Investment tax credits** have at times provided direct reduction of taxes when assets were purchased for use in the business.

            a)   The net effect is to decrease the cost of the asset.

            b)   The amount of the credit and limitations on the tax credit on used equipment affect investment decisions.

        2)   **Accelerated depreciation** is permitted on many types of business assets.

            a)   Accordingly, in the early periods of an asset's life, depreciation is higher, taxable income is lower, and the rate of return on investment is higher.

        3)   **Corporate capital gains** are taxed at regular rates.

        4)   **Special loss carryforward and carryback rules** permit businesses to deduct net operating losses incurred in one period against income earned in other periods.

        5)   A **dividends received deduction** makes tax free 70% to 100% (based on stock ownership percentage) of dividends received by one corporation from investments in the stock of another.

            a)   The DRD prevents or reduces double taxation.

        6)   **Interest** is a tax-deductible expense of the debtor.

            a)   But dividends on common or preferred stock are not deductible by the issuer.

7. **Working capital finance** concerns the optimal level, mix, and use of current assets and the means used to acquire them, notably current liabilities. The objective is to minimize the cost of maintaining liquidity (i.e., money in the bank) while guarding against the possibility of technical insolvency.

    a. From a financial analyst's perspective, **working capital equals current assets**. Its components include cash, marketable securities, receivables, and inventory. From the accounting perspective, working capital equals current assets minus current liabilities.

       1) **Assets** are current if they are reasonably expected to be realized in cash or sold or consumed during the normal operating cycle of the business.

       2) **Current liabilities** include trade accounts payable, taxes payable, unearned revenues, other accrued operating costs, short-term debt, and the currently due component of long-term debt. Liabilities are current if their liquidation will require the use of current assets or the incurrence of other current liabilities.

    b. A firm that adopts a **conservative policy** seeks to minimize liquidity risk by increasing working capital. The result is that it forgoes the potentially higher returns available from using the additional working capital to acquire long-term assets.

       1) An **aggressive policy** reduces the current ratio (and liquidity) and accepts a higher risk of short-term cash flow problems in an effort to increase profitability.

       2) To maximize working capital, the firm should delay paying accounts payable and establish credit policies that encourage customers to pay collectibles quickly.

    c. **Permanent working capital** is a concept reflecting the observation that a firm always maintains a minimum level of current assets. **Temporary working capital**, however, fluctuates seasonally.

       1) Hence, permanent working capital is akin to the firm's fixed assets and should increase as the firm grows. It differs in that the items included in working capital turn over relatively rapidly although their minimum total is maintained or increased over the long term.

8. Stop and review! You have completed the outline for this subunit. Study multiple-choice questions 1 through 3 on page 228.

8.2 CASH MANAGEMENT

1. **Cash management** is an integral part of financial management. In general, a company attempts to delay payments for purchases and accelerate collections on credit sales because the firm can then stretch its financial resources further.

2. In addition to maximizing the utility of cash, a company normally minimizes its liquid cash on hand because of the opportunity cost of holding rather than investing cash.

    a. In Study Unit 10, we will explain in detail the reasons why a company attempts to minimize the amount of liquid cash. At this point, it is important to understand that a company typically only wants to have enough cash on hand to pay its obligations with a margin of safety.

3. The first step in managing a company's cash flows is the **cash budget**. It details projected receipts and disbursements, preferably with a view to planning the **synchronization of inflows and outflows**.

    a. Cash receipts are based on projected sales and credit terms, estimated collection percentages, and estimated purchases and payment terms.

    b. Projected cash outflows are based on the budgeted level of sales.

    c.   Budgets must be for a specified period of time, and the units of time must be short enough to ensure that all cash payments can be made.

        1)   The cash budget takes into account the **cash flow/cash conversion cycle**, which is the length of time from disbursement for inventory purchases to the receipt of cash from the sale of the inventory.

        2)   While the budget is for a specific period of time, cash budgeting is an ongoing, cumulative activity that is re-evaluated constantly to ensure all objectives are being met.

    d.   The cash flow/cash conversion cycle is the length of time from when a company pays for inventory purchases to when it receives cash from the sale of the inventory.

4.   For a cash budget to be successful, a company needs to estimate how much cash it needs on hand. A company needs to maintain cash for the following reasons:

    a.   As a **medium of exchange**. Cash is still needed for some business transactions.

    b.   As a **precautionary measure**. Cash or a money-market fund can be held for emergencies. Normally, investment in high-grade, short-term securities is a better alternative to holding cash, but these securities are classified as cash under GAAP.

    c.   For **speculation**. Cash may be held to take advantage of bargain-purchase opportunities. However, for this purpose, short-term, highly liquid securities are preferable.

    d.   As a **compensating balance** in exchange for a bank's services or loans (see item 7. on the next page).

5.   The cash budget also examines **cash collections**. Sound financial management requires that cash collections be expedited.

    a.   Invoices should be mailed promptly.

    b.   Credit terms must be competitive but geared to encourage prompt payment.

        1)   Cash discounts (sales discounts) are a means of accelerating cash collection by rewarding customers for early payment.

            a)   EXAMPLE: Items are commonly sold with terms of 2/10, n/30 (i.e., 2% discount if payment made within 10 days, entire balance due in 30 days).

    c.   A **lockbox system** may be used to expedite the receipt of funds. A firm maintains mailboxes, often in numerous locations around the country, to which customers send payments.

        1)   A bank checks these mailboxes several times a day, and funds received are immediately deposited to the firm's account without first being processed by its accounting system. This practice hastens availability of the funds.

        2)   In addition, having several lockboxes throughout the country reduces the time a payment is in the postal system.

    d.   **Transfer of monies by wire** expedites cash management. A **wire transfer** is any electronic funds transfer by means of a two-way system, for example, the Federal Reserve Wire Transfer System (Fedwire).

    e.   **Electronic funds transfer (EFT)** and customer debit cards expedite cash inflows. With the recent widespread growth of **electronic commerce** (the buying and selling of products and services over the Internet) by individuals, the use of EFT has mushroomed. Entities such as PayPal enable individuals to transfer funds to each other at little or no cost.

    f.   **Automated clearing house (ACH)** is an electronic network that facilitates the reading of data among banks.

g. Under the **Check Clearing for the 21st Century Act**, financial institutions may convert paper checks to electronic images (**substitute checks** that are legal copies of the originals). The paper checks may then be destroyed.

   1) The effect of the conversion will be to expedite check clearing. Consequently, cash collections and disbursements will be credited or debited, respectively, to the firm's accounts more quickly.

6. If the firm is able to slow cash disbursements without increasing costs, the firm can increase available cash on hand.

   a. Payment beyond normal credit terms, however, creates vendor ill will and may incur interest charges. If these interest charges are higher than alternative lending choices, this practice will not maximize shareholder wealth and should be avoided.

   b. Payments should be made within **discount periods** if the cost of not taking a discount exceeds the firm's cost of capital. The cost of not taking a discount (not considering compounding effects) is approximately

   1)
   $$\frac{360}{(Total\ pay\ period - Discount\ period)} \times \frac{Discount\ \%}{(100\% - Discount\ \%)}$$

   2) For example, 2/10, net 30 results in the following calculation:
   $$\frac{360}{30 - 10} \times \frac{2}{100 - 2} = \frac{360}{20} \times \frac{2}{98} = 36.7\%\ annualized\ interest$$

   c. Payment by **draft** (a three-party instrument in which the drawer orders the drawee to pay money to the payee) is a means of slowing cash outflows.

   1) A check is the most common draft. **Check float** arises from the delay between an expenditure or receipt by check and the clearing of the check.

      a) The effect is an interest-free loan to the payor.

      b) Accordingly, firms attempt to maximize **disbursements float** (the period from when checks are written to when they are deducted from the bank balance) and minimize **collections float**, which consists of the sum of the time checks are in the mail, internal processing time, and the time required for clearing through the banking system.

7. The cash budget also must take into account cash required to be kept on deposit with banks to satisfy compensating balances.

   a. A **compensating balance** is one required to be kept on deposit at a bank when a borrower executes a loan agreement.

   b. Whenever compensating balances are negotiated, use of average rather than absolute compensating balances frees most of the compensating balance for use as a contingency fund.

   1) An average compensating balance provides a firm with **overdraft protection** for the days when cash demands are greatest and deposits fail to materialize. An absolute compensating balance is inflexible, establishing a minimum below which the balance cannot dip without penalty.

   2) The effective interest rate on loans requiring compensating balances equals total adjusted interest cost divided by total adjusted principal.

      a)
      $$\frac{Total\ interest\ cost}{Total\ principal}$$

      b) Total principal is reduced by the account's ordinary balance, and total interest cost is reduced by the amount of interest that the company would earn on its ordinary balance.

8.   Firms are also able to arrange **zero-balance checking accounts (ZBAs)**. These accounts allow the firm to slow disbursements and increase cash balances.

    a.   The account balance is maintained at zero until a check is presented. The resulting overdraft is covered by a transfer from a master (parent) account earning interest.

        1)   The disadvantages are that the bank may charge a fee for this service and the amount needed in the master account still needs to be estimated.

9.   The amount of **cash on hand** should be determined by cost-benefit analysis. Since the objective of financial management is to maximize shareholder wealth, minimizing the cost of holding cash and maximizing the returns on investing cash are paramount.

    a.   The reduction in average cash times the interest rate (cost of capital or investment yield rate) is the benefit.

    b.   Costs of having insufficient cash include incremental personnel cost, lost discounts, and lost vendor goodwill.

    c.   Whenever possible, a firm's excess cash should be placed in an investment with a high return and little risk.

    d.   A firm with excessive cash might tend to be an attractive takeover target.

10.   Stop and review! You have completed the outline for this subunit. Study multiple-choice questions 4 through 26 beginning on page 228.

8.3 MARKETABLE SECURITIES MANAGEMENT

1.   Because firms seek investments with a high return and little risk, short-term marketable securities (e.g., T-bills and CDs) are sometimes held as substitutes for cash. They also can be held as temporary investments. Examples of short-term marketable securities are listed below.

    a.   **Treasury bills** are short-term government debt securities guaranteed explicitly by the U.S. government and exempt from state and local taxation. They are sold on a discount basis.

        1)   **Default risk** is the possibility that a bond issuer will default on a payable. Government loans such as T-bills and Treasury notes are considered to have the least amount of risk because they are backed by the full faith and credit of the U.S. Federal government.

            a)   Obligations of federal agencies are not guaranteed by the U.S. government but only by the agency itself.

        2)   **Event risk** is the risk that an unfavorable event (e.g., a leveraged buyout, recapitalization of company, or devaluation of a government's currency) will occur that increases default risk. Event risk is greater for long-term than for short-term securities.

    b.   **Certificates of deposit** are a form of savings deposit that cannot be withdrawn before maturity without a high penalty. However, negotiable CDs are traded under the regulation of the Federal Reserve System.

    c.   **Money-market accounts** are similar to checking accounts but pay higher interest.

    d.   **High-grade commercial paper** consists of unsecured, short-term notes issued by large companies that are very good credit risks. Commercial paper may yield a higher return than CDs. It is riskier because of a lack of FDIC insurance.

2. **Interest-rate risk** is the risk of interest rates changing after the purchase of a marketable security. This risk arises because interest rates greatly affect the price of securities. The reasons behind this are explained in more detail in Study Unit 10.

   a. Therefore, interest-rate risk is minimized with short-term securities. Their shorter lives make them less subject to fluctuations in value from changes in the general level of interest rates.

3. **Changes in the general price level** (usually inflationary) alter the purchasing power of payments on investments (principal and interest). Therefore, the general price level affects the value of securities.

4. The degree of **marketability** of a security determines its **liquidity**, that is, the ability to resell at the quoted market price.

5. The firm's **tax position** is an important consideration. For example, a firm with net loss carryforwards may prefer a higher-yielding taxable security to a tax-exempt municipal bond.

6. Short-term marketable securities are usually chosen for reasons that make high-yield, high-risk investments unattractive. Hence, a higher return may be forgone in exchange for greater safety. Given the various options available, a company should have an **investment policy statement** to provide continuing guidance to management regarding the risk-return trade-off.

   a. Given the various options available, a company should have an **investment policy statement** to provide continuing guidance to management regarding the risk-return trade-off.

   b. Thus, speculative tactics such as **selling short** (borrowing and selling securities in the expectation that their price will decline by the time they must be replaced) and **margin trading** (borrowing from a broker to buy securities) are avoided.

7. Stop and review! You have completed the outline for this subunit. Study multiple-choice questions 27 through 29 beginning on page 236.

8.4 RECEIVABLES MANAGEMENT

1. Sound financial management requires the firm to try and accelerate the payment of receivables. However, the discounts offered to encourage a prompt payment must not raise the firm's cost of capital.

2. Another **objective** of sound financial management concerning receivables management is having an optimal amount of receivables outstanding and the optimal amount of bad debts.

   a. This balance requires a trade-off between the benefits of credit sales, such as higher revenue, and the costs of accounts receivable, e.g., collection, interest, and bad debt costs.

   b. The **optimal credit policy** does not seek merely either to maximize sales (e.g., by lowering credit standards, offering longer discount periods, or charging lower interest) or to minimize default risk.

   c. Thus, a firm should extend credit until the marginal benefit (profit) is zero (considering opportunity costs of alternative investments).

3. Credit terms, collection policies, etc., are frequently determined by **competitors**. A firm must match such inducements to make sales.

4. Firms often use a statistical technique called **credit scoring** to determine whether to extend credit to a specific customer.

   a. Credit scoring assigns numerical values to the elements of credit worthiness, e.g., income, length of time employed in the same job, occupation, and home ownership.

5. Receivables management seeks to maximize the **accounts receivable turnover ratio**, that is, to shorten the average time receivables are held.

   a. Accounts receivable turnover ratio = Net credit sales ÷ Average accounts receivable.

   b. The average collection period is the average number of days it takes for a receivable to be collected.

   c. A common analytical tool is an **aging schedule** developed from an accounts receivable ledger. It stratifies the accounts depending on time outstanding.

6. The following are different types of credit instruments used in receivables management:

   a. An **invoice** is a bill issued by a firm that has provided goods or services to a customer. It includes the prices, terms, and types of goods. In asset-based lending (such as factoring), an invoice means an account receivable.

   b. A **promissory note** is a two-party negotiable instrument that contains an unconditional promise to pay a fixed sum of money at a definite time.

   c. A **conditional sales contract** is a financing method often used by sellers of equipment. The buyer receives possession and use of the goods. The seller initially receives a promissory note but retains title until the installment debt is paid. Retention of title facilitates repossession.

7. Other tools of credit such as bank charge cards should be evaluated as an alternative to charge accounts.

   a. Banks charge a fee equal to 3% to 5% of charge sales.

   b. Charge tickets can be deposited at a bank in the same way as customer checks and money is instantly available to the seller.

8. Stop and review! You have completed the outline for this subunit. Study multiple-choice questions 30 through 36 beginning on page 237.

8.5 SHORT-TERM CREDIT

1. **Short-term credit** is debt scheduled to be repaid within 1 year. It often involves a lower interest rate and is more readily available than long-term credit.

   a. Firms utilize short-term credit because often the cost of short-term financing (i.e., the interest rate) is less than the firm's cost of capital.

   b. For example, it may be more advantageous for a firm to invest its cash in new machinery in Year 1 and borrow any necessary monies to satisfy working capital (e.g., the firm may need to pay a supplier for raw materials before the firm's customer pays for the manufactured widget) in Years 2, 3, etc. Thus, in this example, the new machine's benefits outweigh the cost of interest.

2. **Trade credit** is a type of short-term credit provided by suppliers. It is **spontaneous financing** because it arises automatically as part of the purchase transaction. The terms of payment are set by suppliers.

   a. **Accrued expenses** are another source of spontaneous financing. Accruals such as salaries, wages, interest, dividends, and taxes also represent an interest-free method of financing because no interest accumulates until the due date; examples include payday for workers and the quarterly time set for payment of federal income taxes. Accruals have the additional advantage of fluctuating directly with operating activity, satisfying the matching principle.

3. **Commercial banks** offer many types of short-term credit, too. All of the types of short-term credit below will be shown on the balance sheet of the borrower as a note payable to the commercial bank lender.

    a. **Note maturity** is usually in less than a year, which requires the firm to roll over the debt frequently if needed. The **promissory note** states the terms of the loan and repayment policy.

    b. **Compensating balances.** Banks may require a borrower to keep a certain percentage of the face amount of the loan in his/her account, which raises the real rate of interest to the borrower.

    c. A **line of credit** is the maximum amount that a bank agrees to lend the borrower in a certain period.

        1) EXAMPLE: On January 1, a bank official tells Firm X that it may borrow up to $100,000 in the coming year. A **revolving line of credit** allows the amount borrowed to be repaid and then borrowed again.

        2) A line of credit is the most practical form of financing for most small retail businesses.

    d. **Letters of credit** are widely used in domestic and international trade and are intended primarily to facilitate the purchase and sale of goods. A letter of credit is a definite undertaking by an issuer (such as a bank) to a beneficiary (such as a seller) at the request of an applicant (such as a buyer who is a customer of the bank) to honor a presentation of documents by payment or delivery of an item of value. The function of the letter of credit is to finance the movement of goods in commerce and to ensure that the seller will be paid.

        1) A letter of credit is separate from the **underlying contract** between the applicant (buyer) and the beneficiary (seller). The issuer (bank) is required to look only to the terms of the letter of credit, not to the contractual obligations between the parties (buyer and seller).

        2) The issuer of a letter of credit is dealing in documents and not in contract performance. When the documents (a document of title, invoice, and insurance policy) are duly presented and comply with the conditions specified in the letter of credit, the issuer is obligated to pay the letter of credit.

            a) The traditional letter of credit provides assurance to the seller of prompt payment upon compliance with the conditions specified in the letter of credit (typically, mere presentation of the documents). A letter of credit simply involves the exchange of documents and money through intermediaries with a better guarantee of payment than without the intermediaries.

        3) A nontraditional use of a letter of credit obligates the issuer to pay only in the event of **default** by the applicant. Such a use of a letter of credit is referred to as a **standby** or **guaranteed letter of credit**. Under a standby letter of credit, the issuer receives no documents of title, that is, nothing of value other than the promise by the applicant to reimburse the issuer for any expenditure made under the letter.

e. **Cost of Bank Loans**

   1) **Regular (simple) interest** (principal and interest paid at maturity)

       a) $$\frac{Interest}{Borrowed\ amount}$$

   2) **Discounted interest** (interest paid in advance)

       a) $$\frac{Interest}{Borrowed\ amount\ -\ Interest}$$

   3) **Installment (add-on) interest** (principal plus interest equals the sum of installments)

       a) $$\frac{Interest}{Average\ borrowed\ amount}$$

f. The **prime interest rate** is the rate charged by commercial banks to their best (the largest and financially strongest) business customers. It is traditionally the lowest rate charged by banks.

4. **Commercial paper** consists of short-term, unsecured notes payable issued in large denominations ($100,000 or more) by large corporations with high credit ratings to other corporations and institutional investors, such as pension funds, banks, and insurance companies. Maturities of commercial paper are at most 270 days. No general secondary market exists for commercial paper. Commercial paper is a lower-cost source of funds than bank loans. It is usually issued at below the prime rate.

   a. Advantages

      1) Provides broad and efficient distribution
      2) Provides a great amount of funds (at a given cost)
      3) Avoids costly financing arrangements

   b. Disadvantages

      1) Impersonal market
      2) Total amount of funds available limited to the excess liquidity of big corporations

5. **Factoring.** A factor purchases accounts receivable and assumes the risk of collection. The firm involved receives money immediately to reinvest in new inventories. The financing cost is usually high – about two points or more above prime, plus a fee for collection.

   a. Credit cards act like factoring because the credit card company pays the store immediately, less approximately 2% of the charge. The credit card company then assumes the credit card user's debt, and the credit card holder pays the credit card company, not the store, for the purchase.

   b. A firm that uses a factor can eliminate its credit department and accounts receivable staff.

   c. Bad debts are eliminated.

   d. These reductions in costs can more than offset the fee charged by the factor.

   e. The factor can often operate more efficiently than its clients because of the specialized nature of its service.

   f. Before the advent of computers, factoring was often considered a last-resort source of financing, used only when bankruptcy was imminent. However, the factor's computerization of receivables means it can operate a receivables department more economically than most small manufacturers. Factoring is no longer viewed as an undesirable source of financing.

g. EXAMPLE: A typical question concerns the cost to the firm of a proposed factoring agreement. Assume a factor charges a 2% fee plus an interest rate of 18% on all monies advanced. Monthly sales are $100,000, and the factor advances 90% of the receivables submitted after deducting the 2% fee and the interest. Credit terms are net 60 days. What is the cost of this arrangement?

Amount of receivables submitted	$100,000
Minus: 10% reserve	(10,000)
Minus: 2% factor's fee	(2,000)
Amount accruing to the firm	$ 88,000
Minus: 18% interest for 60 days (on $88,000)	(2,640)
Amount to be received immediately	$ 85,360

1) The firm will also receive the $10,000 reserve at the end of the 60-day period if it has not been absorbed by sales returns and allowances. Thus, the total cost to the firm to factor the sales for the month is $4,640 ($2,000 factor's fee + interest of $2,640). Assuming that the factor has approved the customers' credit in advance, the seller will not absorb any bad debts.

2) The previously listed costs should be compared with the cost of operating a credit department, collection department, the cost of potential bad debt, and the cost of borrowing monies otherwise advanced by the factor. Sound financial management requires that the benefits outweigh the costs; therefore, if factoring is to be used, it should be more beneficial than having a credit department and accounts receivable staff.

6. Other Types of Short-Term Funding

a. **Bankers' acceptances** are drafts drawn, by a nonfinancial firm, on deposits at a bank. The acceptance by the bank is a guarantee of payment at maturity. These are often used by importers and exporters and as a money-market fund investment.

b. **Repurchase agreements** involve sales by a dealer in government securities who agrees to repurchase at a given time for a specific price. Maturities may be very short-term. This arrangement is essentially a secured loan.

c. Loans secured by receivables (**pledging** receivables). A bank will often lend up to 80% of outstanding receivables.

d. **Money-market mutual funds** invest in portfolios of short-term securities.

e. **Warehouse financing** uses inventory as security for the loan. A third party, a public warehouse for example, holds the collateral and serves as the creditor's agent, and the creditor receives the **terminal warehouse receipts** evidencing its rights in the collateral. A **field warehouse** is established when the warehouser takes possession of the inventory on the debtor's property. The inventory is released (often from a fenced-in area) as needed for sale. Warehouse receipts may be negotiable or nonnegotiable. A nonnegotiable receipt is issued to a named party, e.g., the lender, and does not state that the goods are deliverable to bearer or to the order of a named person. A negotiable warehouse receipt meets all of the requirements of the Uniform Commercial Code for negotiability and is transferable by endorsement.

f. **Trust receipts** are used in inventory financing. The creditor purchases and holds title to the inventory. The debtor is considered a trustee for purposes of selling the inventory and bears the risk of loss.

g. **Agency securities** are issued by government agencies (not the Treasury), such as the Federal Home Loan Banks and other agencies that provide credit to farmers, home buyers, etc. An example is the Federal National Mortgage Association (Fannie Mae), which issues mortgage-backed securities. Agency securities may be long- or short-term.

h. **Treasury bills** are short-term U.S. government obligations issued by the Treasury at a discount from their face value. A T-bill is highly liquid and nearly free of risk, and it is often held as a cash substitute.

i. **Treasury notes and bonds** are long-term investments, but issues near maturity are effectively short-term securities with high liquidity.

j. **State and local governments** issue short-term securities exempt from taxation.

k. **Eurodollars** are time deposits of U.S. dollars in banks located abroad.

l. **Chattel mortgages** are loans secured by movable personal property (e.g., equipment or livestock).

m. **Floating liens** attach to property, such as inventory, the composition of which is constantly changing.

7. Stop and review! You have completed the outline for this subunit. Study multiple-choice questions 37 through 45 beginning on page 240.

8.6 INVENTORY AND SUPPLY CHAIN MANAGEMENT

1. Sound financial management treats **inventory management** similar to cash management. Therefore, the firm should attempt to minimize the costs associated with holding inventory.

   a. A firm carries inventories because of the difficulty in predicting the amount, timing, and location of supply and demand. Thus, one purpose of **inventory control** is to determine the optimal level of inventory necessary to **minimize costs**.

   b. Inventory management, which is a major component of financial management, concerns the effective and efficient acquisition, use, and distribution of inventory.

   c. Although traditional inventory management minimizes inventory and the related holding costs, and modern just-in-time methods may seek to eliminate it altogether, some firms may still use inventory as a hedge against inflation as well as a guarantee of future availability.

2. One method of minimizing inventory costs is transferring them to suppliers or customers.

   a. If a manufacturer knows exactly when materials will be needed, orders can be placed so that materials arrive no earlier than when they are required.

      1) This practice relies on a supplier who takes the responsibility for storing the needed inventory and shipping it to arrive on time.

      2) Suppliers are more willing to provide this service when they have many competitors.

   b. Customers sometimes carry large quantities of inventory when given special quantity discounts or extended credit terms.

   c. If customers are willing to accept long lead times, inventory can be manufactured to order, avoiding the need to store large quantities.

      1) Lead time is the amount of time between when the order for materials is placed and the materials are received.

   d. Although these measures can reduce inventory carrying costs, additional costs might be incurred by adopting them. Shortage (stockout) costs may be incurred when an item is out of stock. These include the lost contribution margin on sales, customer ill will, and production interruptions.

   e. Inventory policies should consider the types of costs and any limitations the firm may have, such as storage space.

      1) Constraints also may be imposed by suppliers.

      2) The cost of maintaining inventory records also should be considered.

3.   Inventory and Ordering Terms

    a.   **Ordering costs** include all costs of placing and receiving orders.

    b.   **Carrying costs** include rent, insurance, taxes, security, depreciation, and opportunity cost (i.e., the cost incurred by investing in inventory rather than making an income-earning investment).

        1)   Carrying costs also may include a charge for spoilage of perishable items or for obsolescence.

    c.   **Reorder points, safety stock, and stockout cost**

        1)   The cost of holding safety stock and the cost of stockouts should be minimized.

            a)   Safety stock is the amount of extra stock that is kept to guard against stockouts. It is the inventory level at the time of reordering minus the expected usage while the new goods are in transit.

            b)   The problem may be diagrammed as follows:

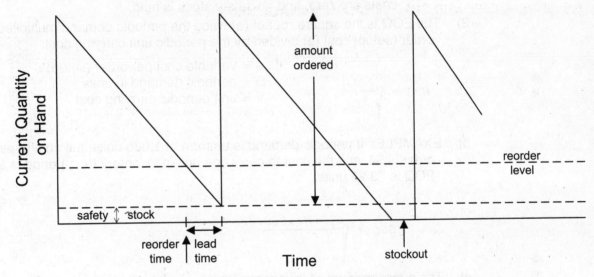

                i)   The economic order quantity (EOQ) determines order size.

                ii)   The reorder point is the intersection of the reorder level and the downward-sloping total inventory line that allows sufficient lead time for an order to be placed and received.

            c)   The total expected cost of safety stock equals the sum of the expected annual stockout cost and the expected annual carrying cost. Annual expected stockout cost equals the cost per occurrence, times the probability of a stockout per cycle, times the number of cycles. Annual expected carrying cost of a safety stock equals the unit carrying cost times the number of units.

4.   **Economic Order Quantity (EOQ)**

    a.   **Inventory models** are quantitative models designed to control inventory costs by determining the optimal time to place an order (or begin production) and the optimal order quantity (production run).

        1)   The timing of an order can be periodic (placing an order every X days) or perpetual (placing an order whenever the inventory declines to X units).

            a)   **Periodic order systems** place minimal emphasis on record keeping. However, a risk of substantial overstock or understock may arise unless inventories are checked for assurance that the model is still appropriate.

  b) **Perpetual systems** detect an inventory decline to the reorder point by entering every withdrawal on a perpetual record that shows the balance.

  c) Physical inventories should be taken to reconcile records and verify models in either a periodic or a perpetual system.

 b. The **basic EOQ model** minimizes the sum of ordering (setup) and carrying costs.

  1) The following are the characteristics of this model:

   a) It is a periodic model.

   b) Demand is known and uniform throughout the period.

   c) The fixed costs of ordering are eliminated when the total cost equation is differentiated to arrive at the EOQ.

   d) Cost per order (setup) and unit carrying cost are constant.

    i) Thus, the model is based on variable costs.

   e) Full replenishment occurs instantly when the last item is used, stockout costs are zero, and no safety stock is held.

  2) The EOQ is the square root of (a) twice the periodic demand multiplied by the order (setup) cost (b) divided by the periodic unit carrying cost.

$$EOQ = \sqrt{\frac{2aD}{k}}$$

    If: a = variable cost per order (setup)
      D = periodic demand in units
      k = unit periodic carrying cost

  3) EXAMPLE: If periodic demand is uniform at 1,000 units, the cost to place an order is $4, and the cost to carry one unit in inventory for a period is $2, the EOQ is 63.25 units.

$$EOQ = \sqrt{\frac{2(\$4)(1,000)}{\$2}} = 63.25 \ units$$

  4) The **average level of inventory** for this model will be one-half of the EOQ. The formula shows that the EOQ varies directly with demand and order (setup) costs, but inversely with carrying costs. Therefore, if demand quadruples, the EOQ will only double because of the square root.

  5) The EOQ results from differentiating the total cost with regard to order (production) quantity. The EOQ formula is the result of a differential equation. Therefore, it is based on variable costs. This means that order (setup) cost and unit carrying cost are in the equation, but all fixed costs are eliminated.

   a) EOQ is the minimum point on the total cost curve. In terms of microeconomics (Study Unit 5), it can be conceptualized as the intersection of the variable carrying cost and the variable ordering cost curves.

 c. Variations of the EOQ model are numerous.

  1) The effects of quantity discounts can be considered by using trial and error. The optimal order quantity is the one giving the lowest periodic total cost.

  2) Lead time is accounted for by simply placing orders in advance. If back ordering is acceptable to customers, it can also be incorporated into the model.

  3) The limitations of the EOQ model are its restrictive assumptions, especially that of constant demand. But it can be combined with probability concepts to form an effective perpetual system.

5. One method available to minimize inventory costs, which helps maximize shareholder wealth, is the implementation of a **just-in-time (JIT) inventory model**. Firms have traditionally built parts and components for subsequent operations on a preset schedule. Such a schedule provides a cushion of inventory so that the next operation will always have parts to work with – a just-in-case method.

    a. In contrast, JIT limits output to the demand of the subsequent operation. Reductions in inventory levels result in less money invested in idle assets; reduction of storage space requirements; and lower inventory taxes, pilferage, and obsolescence risks.

        1) High inventory levels often mask production problems because defective parts can be overlooked when plenty of good parts are available. If only enough parts are made for the subsequent operation, however, any defects will immediately halt production.

        2) The focus of quality control under JIT shifts from the discovery of defective parts to the prevention of quality problems, so zero machine breakdowns (achieved through preventive maintenance) and zero defects are ultimate goals. Higher quality and lower inventory go together.

    b. JIT is a reaction to the trends of global competition and rapid technological progress that have resulted in shorter product life-cycles and greater consumer demand for product diversity.

        1) Objectives are higher productivity, reduced order and carrying costs, faster and cheaper setups, shorter manufacturing cycle times, better due date performance, improved quality, and more flexible processes. The ultimate objectives are increased competitiveness and higher profits.

    c. JIT systems are based on a manufacturing philosophy popularized by the Japanese that combines purchasing, production, and inventory control. Minimization of inventory is a goal because many inventory-related activities are viewed as nonvalue-added. Indeed, carrying inventory is regarded as a symptom of correctable problems, such as poor quality, long cycle times, and lack of coordination with suppliers.

    d. However, JIT also encompasses changes in the production process itself. JIT is a pull system; items are pulled through production by current demand, not pushed through by anticipated demand. Thus, one operation produces only what is needed by the next operation, and components and raw materials arrive just in time to be used. To implement this approach and to eliminate waste of materials, labor, factory space, and machine usage, the factory is reorganized to permit what is often called lean production.

        1) Plant layout in a JIT-lean production environment is not arranged by functional department or process but by manufacturing cells (work cells). Cells are sets of machines, often grouped in semicircles, that produce a given product or product type.

            a) Each worker in a cell must be able to operate all machines and perform support tasks, such as setup activities, preventive maintenance, movement of work-in-process within the cell, and quality inspection.

            b) In contrast, in a pull system, workers might often be idle if they are not multi-skilled. On the other hand, JIT systems reduce or eliminate central support departments, space is saved, fewer and smaller factories may be required, and materials and tools are brought close to the point of use. Manufacturing cycle time and setup time are also reduced. As a result, on-time delivery performance and response to changes in markets are enhanced, and production of customized goods in small lots becomes feasible.

c) A cellular organization requires workers to operate as effective teams, so employee empowerment is crucial in a JIT-lean production system. Greater participation by employees is needed to achieve continuous improvement and zero defects goals. They may have the power to stop production to correct a problem, be consulted about changes in processes, or become involved in hiring co-workers. Thus, managers in such a system usually play more of a facilitating role than a support role.

e. The Japanese term **kanban** and JIT have often been confused. JIT is the total system of purchasing, production, and inventory control. Kanban is one of the many elements in the JIT system as it is used in Japan. Kanban means ticket. Tickets (also described as cards or markers) control the flow of production or parts so that they are produced or obtained in the needed amounts at the needed times.

1) A basic kanban system includes a withdrawal kanban that states the quantity that a later process should withdraw from its predecessor and a production kanban that states the output of the preceding process. A vendor kanban tells a vendor what, how much, where, and when to deliver.

2) Many firms have not been comfortable with controlling production using tickets on the production floor. Computerized information systems have been used for many years, and these firms have been reluctant to give up their computers in favor of the essentially manual kanban system. Instead, they have integrated their existing systems, which are complex computerized planning systems, with the JIT system.

f. Another feature of the lower inventory levels in a JIT system is elimination of the need for several traditional internal controls. Frequent receipt of deliveries from suppliers often means less need for a sophisticated inventory control system and for control personnel.

1) JIT also may eliminate central receiving areas, hard copy receiving reports, and storage areas. A central warehouse is not needed because deliveries are made by suppliers directly to the area of production.

2) The quality of parts provided by suppliers is verified by use of statistical controls rather than inspection of incoming goods. Storage, counting, and inspecting are eliminated in an effort to perform only value-added work.

g. In a JIT system, the dependability of suppliers is crucial. Firms that adopt JIT systems therefore develop close relationships with a few carefully chosen suppliers who are extensively involved in the buyer's processes.

1) Long-term contracts are typically negotiated to reduce order costs. Indeed, some major retailers have agreed to continuous replenishment arrangements whereby a supplier with superior demand-forecasting ability essentially tells the buyer when and how much to reorder.

2) Buyer-supplier relationships are further facilitated by electronic data interchange, a technology that allows the supplier access to the buyer's online inventory management system. Thus, electronic messages replace paper documents (purchase orders and sales invoices), and the production schedules and deliveries of the parties can be more readily coordinated.

h. A concept closely related to JIT is **continuous replenishment of products (CRP)**. In a CRP system, such as Wal-Mart's, inventory management is the supplier's responsibility. When customers pay for goods at checkout, point-of-sale (POS) devices note bar codes and send automatic purchase orders to a central computer. The orders from all stores are then collected and retransmitted to the supplier. Thus, purchases are adjusted to demand with great speed.

6. **Increasing systems integration** has been the trend in inventory and manufacturing control.

    a. **Materials requirements planning (MRP)** was the earliest tool for inventory management. MRP is an integrated computer-based information system designed to plan and control raw materials used in a production setting.

        1) MRP is a **push-through system** because production is activated by forecasts of demand, not actual customer needs.

        2) MRP is also a **dependent-demand system**. It assumes that the forecasted demand for materials is typically dependent upon some other factor, which can be programmed into the computer, e.g., the demand for the completed product. The timing of deliveries is vital to avoid production delays.

            a) EXAMPLE: An auto manufacturer need only tell a computer how many autos of each type are to be manufactured. The MRP system determines how many of every component part will be needed. The computer will generate a complete list of every part and component needed.

        3) MRP, in effect, creates schedules of when items of inventory will be needed in the production departments. If parts are not in stock, the computer will automatically generate a purchase order on the proper date (considering lead times) so that deliveries will arrive on time.

    b. **Manufacturing resource planning (MRP II)** is a closed-loop computerized manufacturing system that integrates all facets of a manufacturing business, including production, sales, inventories, schedules, and cash flows.

        1) The same system is used for both financial reporting and management of operations (both use the same transactions and numbers).

        2) MRP II uses a **master production schedule (MPS)**, which is a statement of the anticipated manufacturing schedule for selected items for selected periods.

            a) MRP also uses the MPS. Thus, MRP is a component of an MRP II system.

    c. **Enterprise resource planning (ERP)** is the latest phase in the development of computerized systems for managing organizational resources. ERP **integrates information systems across the enterprise**.

        1) ERP **connects all operations** within the organization: personnel, financial accounting, production, marketing, distribution, etc.

        2) ERP also connects the organization with its **suppliers and customers**.

7. Stop and review! You have completed the outline for this subunit. Study multiple-choice questions 46 through 79 beginning on page 242.

QUESTIONS

8.1 Financial Management

1. Net working capital is the difference between

   A. Current assets and current liabilities.

   B. Fixed assets and fixed liabilities.

   C. Total assets and total liabilities.

   D. Shareholders' investment and cash.

Answer (A) is correct. *(CMA, adapted)*
   REQUIRED: The definition of net working capital.
   DISCUSSION: Net working capital is defined as the difference between current assets and current liabilities. Working capital is a measure of short-term solvency.
   Answer (B) is incorrect because working capital refers to the difference between current assets and current liabilities; fixed assets are not a component. Answer (C) is incorrect because total assets and total liabilities are not components of working capital; only current items are included. Answer (D) is incorrect because shareholders' equity is not a component of working capital; only current items are included in the concept of working capital.

2. Determining the appropriate level of working capital for a firm requires

   A. Changing the capital structure and dividend policy of the firm.

   B. Maintaining short-term debt at the lowest possible level because it is generally more expensive than long-term debt.

   C. Offsetting the benefit of current assets and current liabilities against the probability of technical insolvency.

   D. Maintaining a high proportion of liquid assets to total assets in order to maximize the return on total investments.

Answer (C) is correct. *(CMA, adapted)*
   REQUIRED: The requirement for determining the appropriate level of working capital.
   DISCUSSION: Working capital finance concerns the determination of the optimal level, mix, and use of current assets and current liabilities. The objective is to minimize the cost of maintaining liquidity, while guarding against the possibility of technical insolvency. Technical insolvency is defined as the inability to pay debts as they come due.
   Answer (A) is incorrect because capital structure and dividends relate to capital structure finance, not working capital finance. Answer (B) is incorrect because short-term debt is usually less expensive than long-term debt. Answer (D) is incorrect because liquid assets do not ordinarily earn high returns relative to long-term assets, so holding the former will not maximize the return on total assets.

3. All of the following statements in regard to working capital are true except

   A. Current liabilities are an important source of financing for many small firms.

   B. Profitability varies inversely with liquidity.

   C. The hedging approach to financing involves matching maturities of debt with specific financing needs.

   D. Financing permanent inventory buildup with long-term debt is an example of an aggressive working capital policy.

Answer (D) is correct. *(CMA, adapted)*
   REQUIRED: The false statement about working capital.
   DISCUSSION: Financing permanent inventory buildup, which is essentially a long-term investment, with long-term debt is a moderate or conservative working capital policy. An aggressive policy uses short-term, relatively low-cost debt to finance the inventory buildup. It focuses on high profitability potential, despite high risk and low liquidity. An aggressive policy reduces the current ratio and accepts a higher risk of short-term lack of liquidity. Financing inventory with long-term debt increases the current ratio and accepts higher borrowing costs in exchange for greater liquidity and lower risk.
   Answer (A) is incorrect because current liabilities, e.g., trade credit, is a major source of funds for small firms. Answer (B) is incorrect because liquid investments tend to have low returns. Answer (C) is incorrect because matching of asset and liability maturities is a moderate policy that minimizes risk. The expectation is that cash flows from the assets will be available to meet obligations for the liabilities.

8.2 Cash Management

4. The most direct way to prepare a cash budget for a manufacturing firm is to include

   A. Projected sales, credit terms, and net income.

   B. Projected net income, depreciation, and goodwill amortization.

   C. Projected purchases, percentages of purchases paid, and net income.

   D. Projected sales and purchases, percentages of collections, and terms of payments.

Answer (D) is correct. *(CMA, adapted)*
   REQUIRED: The most direct way of preparing a cash budget for a manufacturing firm.
   DISCUSSION: The most direct way of preparing a cash budget requires incorporation of sales projections and credit terms, collection percentages, estimated purchases and payment terms, and other cash receipts and disbursements. In other words, preparation of the cash budget requires consideration of both inflows and outflows.
   Answer (A) is incorrect because net income includes noncash elements, e.g., goodwill amortization and depreciation. Answer (B) is incorrect because depreciation and amortization are noncash elements. Answer (C) is incorrect because collection percentages must be considered, and net income includes noncash elements.

5. RLF Corporation had income before taxes of $60,000 for the year. Included in this amount were depreciation of $5,000, a charge of $6,000 for the amortization of bond discounts, and $4,000 for interest expense. The estimated cash flow for the period is

A. $60,000

B. $66,000

C. $49,000

D. $71,000

Answer (D) is correct. *(CMA, adapted)*
REQUIRED: The estimated cash flow for the period.
DISCUSSION: To determine cash flow for the period, all noncash expenses should be added back to net income. Adding the $5,000 of depreciation and the $6,000 of discount amortization to the $60,000 of net income produces a cash flow of $71,000.
Answer (A) is incorrect because the cash flow for the period is greater than net income given noncash expenses in the form of depreciation and bond discount amortization. Answer (B) is incorrect because $66,000 does not reflect the noncash expense for depreciation. Answer (C) is incorrect because the $5,000 of depreciation and the $6,000 for amortization should be added back to, not subtracted from, income.

6. Shown below is a forecast of sales for Cooper Inc. for the first 4 months of the year (all amounts are in thousands of dollars).

	January	February	March	April
Cash sales	$ 15	$ 24	$18	$14
Sales on credit	100	120	90	70

On average, 50% of credit sales are paid for in the month of sale, 30% in the month following the sale, and the remainder is paid 2 months after the month of sale. Assuming there are no bad debts, the expected cash inflow for Cooper in March is

A. $138,000

B. $122,000

C. $119,000

D. $108,000

Answer (C) is correct. *(CMA, adapted)*
REQUIRED: The expected cash inflows for March.
DISCUSSION: Cash inflows for March consist of 50% of March credit sales (50% × $90 = $45), plus 30% of February credit sales (30% × $120 = $36), plus 20% of January credit sales (20% × $100 = $20), plus cash sales for March of $18. Consequently, total collections equal $119,000.
Answer (A) is incorrect because $138,000 equals the sum of February credit sales and March cash sales. Answer (B) is incorrect because $122,000 equals 50% of January credit sales, 30% of February credit sales, 20% of March credit sales, and 100% of March cash sales. Answer (D) is incorrect because $108,000 is the total sales for March, not the total cash collections for March.

7. The treasury analyst for Garth Manufacturing has estimated the cash flows for the first half of next year (ignoring any short-term borrowings) as follows.

	Cash (millions)	
	Inflows	Outflows
January	$2	$1
February	2	4
March	2	5
April	2	3
May	4	2
June	5	3

Garth has a line of credit of up to $4 million on which it pays interest monthly at a rate of 1% of the amount utilized. Garth is expected to have a cash balance of $2 million on January 1 and no amount utilized on its line of credit. Assuming all cash flows occur at the end of the month, approximately how much will Garth pay in interest during the first half of the year?

A. Zero.

B. $60,000

C. $60,702

D. $80,000

Answer (C) is correct. *(CMA, adapted)*
REQUIRED: The interest expense for six months.
DISCUSSION: The sum of the beginning balance and inflows exceeds the outflows for the first 2 months. At the end of March, however, Garth must use $2,000,000 of its line of credit ($2,000,000 beginning balance + $6,000,000 inflows − $10,000,000 outflows). Thus, interest for April is $20,000 (1% × $2,000,000). The net cash outflow for April (ignoring short-term borrowings) is $1,000,000 of an additional $1,000,000 of the line of credit. However, the $20,000 of interest for April must also be paid, so the amount of the line of credit used in May is $3,020,000 ($2,000,000 + $1,000,000 + $20,000). Interest for May is therefore $30,200 (1% × $3,020,000). Given the net cash inflow for May of $2,000,000 (again ignoring short-term borrowings) and the borrowing of $30,200 to pay the interest for May, the amount of the line of credit used in June is $1,050,200. Interest in June is $10,502 (1% × $1,050,200), and total interest is $60,702 ($20,000 + $30,200 + $10,502).
Answer (A) is incorrect because interest must be paid monthly when the credit line is used in April, May, and June. Answer (B) is incorrect because interest must be added to the line of credit. Answer (D) is incorrect because the company would repay the credit line at the end of months with a positive cash flow.

8. Cleveland Masks and Costumes Inc. (CMC) has a majority of its customers located in the states of California and Nevada. Keystone National Bank, a major west coast bank, has agreed to provide a lockbox system to CMC at a fixed fee of $50,000 per year and a variable fee of $0.50 for each payment processed by the bank. On average, CMC receives 50 payments per day, each averaging $20,000. With the lockbox system, the company's collection float will decrease by 2 days. The annual interest rate on money market securities is 6%. Assuming a 365-day year, if CMC uses the lockbox system, what is the net benefit to the company?

A. $59,125

B. $60,875

C. $50,000

D. $120,000

Answer (B) is correct.   *(CMA, adapted)*
   REQUIRED: The net benefit to the company if a lockbox system is adopted.
   DISCUSSION: If payments are collected 2 days earlier, the company can earn $120,000 ($20,000 × 50 payments per day × 2 days × .06) at a cost of $59,125 [$50,000 + (50 payments × 365 days × $.50)], a gain of $60,875.
   Answer (A) is incorrect because $59,125 is the annual lockbox cost. Answer (C) is incorrect because $50,000 is the annual fixed fee. Answer (D) is incorrect because $120,000 is the annual savings without regard to costs.

9. Newman Products has received proposals from several banks to establish a lockbox system to speed up receipts. Newman receives an average of 700 checks per day averaging $1,800 each, and its cost of short-term funds is 7% per year. Assuming that all proposals will produce equivalent processing results and using a 360-day year, which one of the following proposals is optimal for Newman?

A. A $0.50 fee per check.

B. A flat fee of $125,000 per year.

C. A fee of 0.03% of the amount collected.

D. A compensating balance of $1,750,000.

Answer (D) is correct.   *(CMA, adapted)*
   REQUIRED: The optimal fee structure for a lockbox system.
   DISCUSSION: Multiplying 700 checks times 360 days results in a total of 252,000 checks per year. Accordingly, under the proposal of a $0.50 fee per check, total annual cost is $126,000 ($.50 × 252,000), which is less desirable than the $125,000 per year flat fee. Given that the annual collections equal $453,600,000 ($1,800 × 700 × 360), the proposal of a fee of 0.03% of the amount collected is also less desirable because the annual fee would be $136,080 (.03% × $453,600,000). The best option is therefore to maintain a compensating balance of $1,750,000 when the cost of funds is 7%, resulting in a total cost of $122,500 (.07 × $1,750,000).
   Answer (A) is incorrect because the annual cost is $126,000. Answer (B) is incorrect because the annual cost is $125,000. Answer (C) is incorrect because the annual cost is $136,080.

10. If the average age of inventory is 60 days, the average age of the accounts payable is 35 days, and the average age of accounts receivable is 45 days, the number of days in the cash flow cycle is

A. 140 days.

B. 95 days.

C. 70 days.

D. 105 days.

Answer (C) is correct.   *(Publisher, adapted)*
   REQUIRED: The length of the cash flow cycle.
   DISCUSSION: The cash flow cycle begins when the firm pays for merchandise it has purchased and ends when the firm receives cash from the sale of the merchandise. Inventory is held for an average of 60 days prior to sale, but the average age of accounts payable is 35 days. Consequently, the average time between outlay and sale is 25 days. Receivables are collected an average of 45 days after sale, so the length of the cash flow cycle is 70 days (25 + 45).
   Answer (A) is incorrect because the age of payables should be deducted from the sum of the other items. Answer (B) is incorrect because the payables are not added to the inventory period. They are deducted. Answer (D) is incorrect because 105 days equals the sum of the inventory cycle and the receivables cycle.

Questions 11 and 12 are based on the following information.

CyberAge Outlet, a relatively new store, is a cafe that offers customers the opportunity to browse the Internet or play computer games at their tables while they drink coffee. The customer pays a fee based on the amount of time spent signed on to the computer. The store also sells books, T-shirts, and computer accessories. CyberAge has been paying all of its bills on the last day of the payment period, thus forfeiting all supplier discounts.

Shown below are data on CyberAge's two major vendors, including average monthly purchases and credit terms.

Vendor	Average Monthly Purchases	Credit Terms
Web Master	$25,000	2/10, net 30
Softidee	50,000	5/10, net 90

11. Assuming a 360-day year and that CyberAge continues paying on the last day of the credit period, the company's weighted-average annual interest rate for trade credit (ignoring the effects of compounding) for these two vendors is

A. 27.0%

B. 25.2%

C. 28.0%

D. 30.2%

Answer (B) is correct. *(CMA, adapted)*
REQUIRED: The weighted-average annual interest rate.
DISCUSSION: If the company pays Web Master within 10 days, it will save $500 (2% × $25,000). Thus, the company is effectively paying $500 to retain $24,500 ($25,000 – $500) for 20 days (30 – 10). The annualized interest rate on this borrowing is 36.7346% [($500 ÷ $24,500) × (360 days ÷ 20 days)]. Similarly, the company is, in effect, paying Softidee $2,500 (5% × $50,000) to hold $47,500 ($50,000 – $2,500) for 80 days (90 – 10). The annualized rate on this borrowing is 23.6842% [($2,500 ÷ $47,500) × (360 days ÷ 80 days)]. The average amount borrowed from Web Master is $16,333.33 [1 month × $24,500 × (20 days ÷ 30 days)], and the average amount borrowed from Softidee is $126,666.67 [3 months × $47,500 × (80 days ÷ 90 days)]. Thus, the weighted average of these two rates based on average borrowings is 25.2% {[36.7346% × $16,333.33) + (23.6842% × $126,666.67)] ÷ ($16,333.33 + $126,666.67)}. This calculation, however, understates the true cost of not taking the discount because it does not consider the effects of compounding.
Answer (A) is incorrect because 27.0% is based on weights of $25,000 and $50,000. Answer (C) is incorrect because 28.0% is based on weights of $24,500 and $47,500. Answer (D) is incorrect because 30.2% is an unweighted average of the two interest rates.

12. Should CyberAge use trade credit and continue paying at the end of the credit period?

A. Yes, if the cost of alternative short-term financing is less.

B. Yes, if the firm's weighted-average cost of capital is equal to its weighted-average cost of trade credit.

C. No, if the cost of alternative long-term financing is greater.

D. Yes, if the cost of alternative short-term financing is greater.

Answer (D) is correct. *(CMA, adapted)*
REQUIRED: The true statement about the decision to use trade credit and pay at the end of the credit period.
DISCUSSION: The company is currently obtaining trade credit from its suppliers and paying at the end of the credit period. This policy should be continued if trade credit is the only source of financing, or if other sources are available only at a higher rate.
Answer (A) is incorrect because the company should continue the current practice unless alternative short-term financing is available at a lower rate. Answer (B) is incorrect because the weighted-average cost of capital is usually a concern in capital budgeting and is not as important in the decision process as the marginal cost of capital. Furthermore, trade credit is just one element in the firm's financing structure. An optimal mix of financing sources may require that trade credit be obtained at less than the weighted-average cost of capital. Answer (C) is incorrect because the company should maintain its current practice if the cost of alternative long-term financing is higher.

13. DLF is a retail mail order firm that currently uses a central collection system that requires all checks to be sent to its Boston headquarters. An average of 6 days is required for mailed checks to be received, 3 days for DLF to process them, and 2 days for the checks to clear through its bank. A proposed lockbox system would reduce the mailing and processing time to 2 days and the check clearing time to 1 day. DLF has an average daily collection of $150,000. If DLF adopts the lockbox system, its average cash balance will increase by

A. $1,200,000

B. $750,000

C. $600,000

D. $450,000

Answer (A) is correct. *(Publisher, adapted)*
REQUIRED: The average increase in cash after the adoption of a lockbox system.
DISCUSSION: Checks are currently tied up for 11 days (6 for mailing, 3 for processing, and 2 for clearing). If that period were reduced to 3 days, DLF's cash balance would increase by $1,200,000 (8 days × $150,000 per day).
Answer (B) is incorrect because the decrease is 8 days, not 5. Answer (C) is incorrect because $600,000 represents only a 4-day savings. Answer (D) is incorrect because the lockbox system will result in an additional 8 days of savings, not 3.

14. Troy Toys is a retailer operating in several cities. The individual store managers deposit daily collections at a local bank in a non-interest bearing checking account. Twice per week, the local bank issues a depository transfer check (DTC) to the central bank at headquarters. The controller of the company is considering using a wire transfer instead. The additional cost of each transfer would be $25; collections would be accelerated by 2 days; and the annual interest rate paid by the central bank is 7.2% (0.02% per day). At what amount of dollars transferred would it be economically feasible to use a wire transfer instead of the DTC? Assume a 350-day year.

A. It would never be economically feasible.

B. $125,000 or above.

C. Any amount greater than $173.

D. Any amount greater than $62,500.

Answer (D) is correct. *(CMA, adapted)*
REQUIRED: The amount at which wire transfers are preferable.
DISCUSSION: Given a $25 fee and an interest rate of 0.02% per day for 2 days, the breakeven amount is $62,500 [$25 transfer fee ÷ (2 × .02% interest rate)]. Thus, the interest earned on a transfer of any amount greater than $62,500 would exceed the $25 fee.
Answer (A) is incorrect because the $25 transfer fee is covered by the interest on $62,500 for 2 days. Answer (B) is incorrect because $125,000 is required if collections are accelerated by only one day. Answer (C) is incorrect because the interest on $173 for 2 days is less than $.07.

15. A company obtained a short-term bank loan of $250,000 at an annual interest rate of 6%. As a condition of the loan, the company is required to maintain a compensating balance of $50,000 in its checking account. The company's checking account earns interest at an annual rate of 2%. Ordinarily, the company maintains a balance of $25,000 in its checking account for transaction purposes. What is the effective interest rate of the loan?

A. 6.44%

B. 7.00%

C. 5.80%

D. 6.66%

Answer (A) is correct. *(CMA, adapted)*
REQUIRED: The effective interest rate on a loan that requires a compensating balance of $25,000 above the company's normal working balance.
DISCUSSION: The $50,000 compensating balance requirement is partially satisfied by the company's practice of maintaining a $25,000 balance for transaction purposes. Thus, only $25,000 of the loan will not be available for current use, leaving $225,000 of the loan usable. At 6% interest, the $250,000 loan would require an interest payment of $15,000 per year. This is partially offset by the 2% interest earned on the $25,000 incremental balance, or $500. Subtracting the $500 interest earned from the $15,000 of expense results in net interest expense of $14,500 for the use of $225,000 in funds. Dividing $14,500 by $225,000 produces an effective interest rate of 6.44%.
Answer (B) is incorrect because 7.00% fails to consider that the $25,000 currently being maintained counts toward the compensating balance requirement. Answer (C) is incorrect because 5.8% fails to consider the compensating balance requirement. Answer (D) is incorrect because 6.66% fails to consider the interest earned on the incremental balance being carried.

16. A compensating balance

   A. Compensates a financial institution for services rendered by providing it with deposits of funds.

   B. Is used to compensate for possible losses on a marketable securities portfolio.

   C. Is a level of inventory held to compensate for variations in usage rate and lead time.

   D. Is the amount of prepaid interest on a loan.

Answer (A) is correct. *(CMA, adapted)*
   REQUIRED: The true statement about compensating balances.
   DISCUSSION: Banks sometimes require a borrower to keep a certain percentage of the face amount of a loan in a noninterest-bearing checking account. This requirement raises the effective rate of interest paid by the borrower. This greater rate compensates a bank for services provided and results in greater profitability for the financial institution. Funds kept as a compensating balance can often be withdrawn if a certain average balance is maintained.
   Answer (B) is incorrect because, in financial accounting, a valuation allowance is used to reflect losses on marketable securities. Answer (C) is incorrect because safety stock is held for this purpose. Answer (D) is incorrect because interest deducted in advance is discount interest.

17. A firm has daily cash receipts of $300,000. A bank has offered to provide a lockbox service that will reduce the collection time by 3 days. The bank requires a monthly fee of $2,000 for providing this service. If money market rates are expected to average 6% during the year, the additional annual income (loss) of using the lockbox service is

   A. ($24,000)

   B. $12,000

   C. $30,000

   D. $54,000

Answer (C) is correct. *(Publisher, adapted)*
   REQUIRED: The amount a company will gain or lose by hiring a bank lockbox service to process cash collections.
   DISCUSSION: Because collections will be accelerated by 3 days at a rate of $300,000 per day, the company will have an additional $900,000 to invest. At a rate of 6%, the interest earned will be $54,000 per year. However, the bank will charge $24,000 (12 months × $2,000 per month) for its services. Thus, the firm will increase its income by $30,000 ($54,000 − $24,000).
   Answer (A) is incorrect because ($24,000) ignores the additional interest revenue from investing the increased funds. Answer (B) is incorrect because $12,000 is based on 2 days of accelerated inflows rather than 3. Answer (D) is incorrect because $54,000 ignores the $24,000 bank service charge.

18. A company uses the following formula in determining its optimal level of cash.

$$C^* = \sqrt{\frac{2bT}{i}}$$

If: b = fixed cost per transaction
   i = interest rate on marketable securities
   T = total demand for cash over a period of time

This formula is a modification of the economic order quantity (EOQ) formula used for inventory management. Assume that the fixed cost of selling marketable securities is $10 per transaction and the interest rate on marketable securities is 6% per year. The company estimates that it will make cash payments of $12,000 over a one-month period. What is the average cash balance (rounded to the nearest dollar)?

   A. $1,000

   B. $2,000

   C. $3,464

   D. $6,928

Answer (C) is correct. *(CMA, adapted)*
   REQUIRED: The average cash balance.
   DISCUSSION: The EOQ for inventory is a function of ordering cost per order, inventory demand, and carrying cost. In the cash model, the fixed cost per sale of securities is equivalent to the ordering cost, the demand for cash is similar to the demand for inventory, and the interest rate is effectively the cost of carrying a dollar of cash for the period. Substituting in the formula yields an optimal cash balance of about $6,928. Thus, the average cash balance is $3,464 ($6,928 ÷ 2).

$$\sqrt{\frac{2bT}{i}} = \sqrt{\frac{2 \times \$10 \times \$12,000}{6\% \div 12 \text{ months}}} = \sqrt{\frac{\$240,000}{.005}} = \$6,928$$

   Answer (A) is incorrect because $1,000 results from using 24% in the denominator. Answer (B) is incorrect because $2,000 results from using 6% in the denominator. Answer (D) is incorrect because $6,928 is the optimal cash balance.

19. The high cost of short-term financing has recently caused a company to reevaluate the terms of credit it extends to its customers. The current policy is 1/10, net 60. If customers can borrow at the prime rate, at what prime rate must the company change its terms of credit in order to avoid an undesirable extension in its collection of receivables?

A. 2%

B. 5%

C. 7%

D. 8%

Answer (D) is correct. *(Publisher, adapted)*
REQUIRED: The prime rate at which a vendor must change its terms to avoid an undesirable extension in the collection of its receivables.
DISCUSSION: Terms of 1/10, net 60 mean that a buyer can save 1% of the purchase price by paying 50 days early. In essence, not taking the discount results in the buyer's borrowing 99% of the invoice price for 50 days at a total interest charge of 1% of the invoice price. Because a year has 7.3 50-day periods (365 ÷ 50), the credit terms 1/10, net 60 yield an effective annualized interest charge of approximately 7.37% [(1% ÷ 99%) × 7.3]. If the prime rate were higher than 7.37%, the buyer would prefer to borrow from the vendor (i.e., not pay within the discount period) rather than from a bank. Consequently, an 8% prime rate could cause the vendor's receivables to increase.

20. Clauson Inc. grants credit terms of 1/15, net 30 and projects gross sales for next year of $2,000,000. The credit manager estimates that 40% of their customers pay on the discount date, 40% on the net due date, and 20% pay 15 days after the net due date. Assuming uniform sales and a 360-day year, what is the projected days' sales outstanding (rounded to the nearest whole day)?

A. 20 days.

B. 24 days.

C. 27 days.

D. 30 days.

Answer (C) is correct. *(CMA, adapted)*
REQUIRED: The projected days' sales outstanding.
DISCUSSION: Given that 40% of sales will be collected on the 15th day, 40% on the 30th day, and 20% on the 45th day, the days' sales outstanding can be determined by weighting the collection period for each group of receivables by its collection percentage. Hence, the projected days' sales outstanding equal 27 days [(40% × 15) + (40% × 30) + (20% × 45)].
Answer (A) is incorrect because average receivables are outstanding for much more than 20 days. Answer (B) is incorrect because 24 days assumes 40% of receivables are collected after 15 days and 60% after 30 days. Answer (D) is incorrect because more receivables are collected on the 15th day than on the 45th day; thus, the average must be less than 30 days.

Questions 21 through 23 are based on the following information. Morton Company needs to pay a supplier's invoice of $60,000 and wants to take a cash discount of 2/10, net 40. The firm can borrow the money for 30 days at 11% per annum with a 9% compensating balance. Assume a 360-day year.

---

21. The amount Morton Company must borrow to pay the supplier within the discount period and cover the compensating balance is

A. $60,000

B. $65,934

C. $64,615

D. $58,800

Answer (C) is correct. *(Publisher, adapted)*
REQUIRED: The amount the company must borrow to pay the supplier within the discount period and cover the compensating balance requirement.
DISCUSSION: The company will need $58,800 ($60,000 × 98%) to pay the invoice. In addition, it will need a compensating balance equal to 9% of the loan. The equation is

$$Loan = \$58,800 + .09 \; Loan$$

Thus, the loan amount needed is $64,615 ($58,800 ÷ .91).
Answer (A) is incorrect because $60,000 is the invoice amount. Answer (B) is incorrect because $65,934 assumes the amount paid to the supplier is $60,000. Answer (D) is incorrect because $58,800 is the amount to be paid to the supplier.

22. Assuming Morton Company borrows the money on the last day of the discount period and repays it 30 days later, the effective interest rate on the loan is

A. 11%

B. 10%

C. 12.09%

D. 9.90%

Answer (C) is correct. *(Publisher, adapted)*
REQUIRED: The effective interest rate when a company borrows to take a discount when the terms are 2/10, net 40.
DISCUSSION: The company will need $58,800 ($60,000 × 98%) to pay the invoice. In addition, it will need a compensating balance equal to 9% of the loan. The equation is

$$Loan = \$58,800 + 0.09 \; Loan$$

Thus, the loan amount needed is $64,615 ($58,800 ÷ .91). The interest at 11% annually on a 30-day loan of $64,615 is $592.30 [$64,615 × 11% × (30 ÷ 360)]. However, the company has access to only $58,800. The interest expense on usable funds is therefore at an annual rate of 12.09% [($592.30 ÷ $58,800) × 12 months].

23. If Morton fails to take the discount and pays on the 40th day, what effective rate of annual interest is it paying the vendor?

A. 2%

B. 24%

C. 24.49%

D. 36.73%

Answer (C) is correct. *(Publisher, adapted)*
REQUIRED: The effective interest rate paid when a discount of 2/10, net 40 is not taken.
DISCUSSION: By failing to take the discount, the company is essentially borrowing $58,800 for 30 days. Thus, at a cost of $1,200, the company acquires the use of $58,800, resulting in a rate of 2.04081% ($1,200 ÷ $58,800) for 30 days. Assuming a 360-day year, the effective annual rate is 24.489% [2.04081% × (360 days ÷ 30 days)].
Answer (A) is incorrect because 2% is the discount rate for a 30-day period. Answer (B) is incorrect because 24% assumes that the available funds equal $60,000. Answer (D) is incorrect because 36.73% assumes a 20-day discount period.

Questions 24 and 25 are based on the following information. JH Company has a 10% cost of borrowing and incurs fixed costs of $500 for obtaining a loan. It has stable, predictable cash flows, and the estimated total amount of net new cash needed for transactions for the year is $175,000. The company does not hold safety stocks of cash.

---

24. When the average cash balance of JH Company is higher, the <List A> the cash balance is <List B>.

	List A	List B
A.	Opportunity cost of holding	Higher
B.	Total transactions costs associated with obtaining	Higher
C.	Opportunity cost of holding	Lower
D.	Total costs of holding	Lower

Answer (A) is correct. *(CIA, adapted)*
REQUIRED: The effect of a higher cash balance.
DISCUSSION: Opportunity cost is the forgone benefit, that is, the benefit from the next best alternative use of a resource. The opportunity cost of holding cash balances is calculated by multiplying the average cash balance by the opportunity cost rate (the return on the best alternative use of the cash). The opportunity cost of holding cash balances is higher if the average cash balance is higher.
Answer (B) is incorrect because, if other factors are constant, a higher average cash balance requires fewer replenishing transactions. Hence, the total transactions costs associated with obtaining cash balances for the period are lower. Answer (C) is incorrect because the opportunity cost of holding a higher cash balance is higher. Answer (D) is incorrect because the total costs of holding cash equal the sum of the opportunity costs and transaction costs. Accordingly, the company should determine the optimal average cash balance that minimizes total holding costs. Whether total costs are lower when the average balance is higher depends on whether it is below, at, or above the optimal average balance for the company.

---

25. If the average cash balance for JH Company during the year is $20,916.50, the opportunity cost of holding cash for the year will be

A. $2,091.65

B. $4,183.30

C. $8,750.00

D. $17,500.00

Answer (A) is correct. *(CIA, adapted)*
REQUIRED: The opportunity cost of holding cash.
DISCUSSION: The opportunity cost of holding cash balances for the year equals the average cash balance multiplied by the opportunity cost rate, or $2,091.65 ($20,916.50 × 10%).
Answer (B) is incorrect because $4,183.30 results if twice the average cash balance is used in calculating the opportunity cost. Answer (C) is incorrect because $8,750.00 results if half the total cash requirement for the year is used in calculating the opportunity cost. Answer (D) is incorrect because $17,500.00 results if the total cash required for the year is used in calculating the opportunity cost.

26. A company plans to tighten its credit policy. The new policy will decrease the average number of days in collection from 75 to 50 days and will reduce the ratio of credit sales to total revenue from 70% to 60%. The company estimates that projected sales will be 5% less if the proposed new credit policy is implemented. If projected sales for the coming year are $50 million, what is the dollar impact on accounts receivable of this proposed change in credit policy assuming a 360-day year?

    A. $3,817,445 decrease.

    B. $6,500,000 decrease.

    C. $3,333,334 decrease.

    D. $18,749,778 increase.

Answer (C) is correct.   *(CMA, adapted)*
    REQUIRED: The dollar impact on accounts receivable of a change in credit policy.
    DISCUSSION: If sales are $50 million, 70% of which are on credit, total credit sales will be $35 million. The receivables turnover equals 4.8 times per year (360 days ÷ 75-day collection period). Receivables turnover equals net credit sales divided by average receivables. Accordingly, average receivables equal $7,291,667 ($35,000,000 ÷ 4.8). Under the new policy, sales will be $47.5 million (95% × $50,000,000), and credit sales will be $28.5 million (60% × $47,500,000). The collection period will be reduced to 50 days, resulting in a turnover of 7.2 times per year (360 ÷ 50). The average receivables balance will therefore be $3,958,333 ($28,500,000 ÷ 7.2), a reduction of $3,333,334 ($7,291,667 − $3,958,333).

8.3 Marketable Securities Management

27. When managing cash and short-term investments, a corporate treasurer is primarily concerned with

    A. Maximizing rate of return.

    B. Minimizing taxes.

    C. Investing in Treasury bonds since they have no default risk.

    D. Liquidity and safety.

Answer (D) is correct.   *(CMA, adapted)*
    REQUIRED: The primary concern when managing cash and short-term investments.
    DISCUSSION: Cash and short-term investments are crucial to a firm's continuing success. Sufficient liquidity must be available to meet payments as they come due. At the same time, liquid assets are subject to significant control risk. Therefore, liquidity and safety are the primary concerns of the treasurer when dealing with highly liquid assets. Cash and short-term investments are held because of their ability to facilitate routine operations of the company. These assets are not held for purposes of achieving investment returns.
    Answer (A) is incorrect because most companies are not in business to earn high returns on liquid assets (i.e., they are held to facilitate operations). Answer (B) is incorrect because the holding of cash and cash-like assets is not a major factor in controlling taxes. Answer (C) is incorrect because investments in Treasury bonds do not have sufficient liquidity to serve as short-term assets.

28. All of the following are alternative marketable securities suitable for investment except

    A. U.S. Treasury bills.

    B. Eurodollars.

    C. Commercial paper.

    D. Convertible bonds.

Answer (D) is correct.   *(CMA, adapted)*
    REQUIRED: The item that is not a marketable security.
    DISCUSSION: Marketable securities are near-cash items used primarily for short-term investment. Examples include U.S. Treasury bills, Eurodollars, commercial paper, money-market mutual funds with portfolios of short-term securities, bankers' acceptances, floating rate preferred stock, and negotiable CDs of U.S. banks. A convertible bond is not a short-term investment because its maturity date is usually more than one year in the future and its price can be influenced substantially by changes in interest rates or by changes in the investee's stock price.

29. Determining the amount and timing of conversions of marketable securities to cash is a critical element of a financial manager's performance. In terms of the rate of return forgone on converted securities and the cost of such transactions, the optimal amount of cash to be raised by selling securities is

A. Inversely related to the rate of return forgone and directly related to the cost of the transaction.

B. Directly related to the rate of return forgone and directly related to the cost of the transaction.

C. Directly related to the rate of return forgone and inversely related to the cost of the transaction.

D. Inversely related to the rate of return forgone and inversely related to the cost of the transaction.

Answer (A) is correct. *(CIA, adapted)*
REQUIRED: The relationship of the optimal amount of cash to be raised by selling securities to the rate of return forgone and the cost of transactions.
DISCUSSION: The optimal amount of cash to be raised by selling securities is calculated by a formula similar to that used to determine the economic order quantity for inventory.

$$C^+ \sqrt{\frac{2(F)(T)}{k}}$$

If: C^+ = Cash to be raised
 T = Total cash needed for the period
 F = Cost of making a securities trade
 k = Opportunity cost of holding cash

The optimal amount of cash to be raised by selling securities is inversely related to the rate of return forgone (opportunity cost) and directly related to the cost of the transaction.

8.4 Receivables Management

30. The sales manager at Ryan Company feels confident that, if the credit policy at Ryan's were changed, sales would increase and, consequently, the company would utilize excess capacity. The two credit proposals being considered are as follows:

	Proposal A	Proposal B
Increase in sales	$500,000	$600,000
Contribution margin	20%	20%
Bad debt percentage	5%	5%
Increase in operating profits	$75,000	$90,000
Desired return on sales	15%	15%

Currently, payment terms are net 30. The proposed payment terms for Proposal A and Proposal B are net 45 and net 90, respectively. An analysis to compare these two proposals for the change in credit policy would include all of the following factors except the

A. Cost of funds for Ryan.

B. Current bad debt experience.

C. Impact on the current customer base of extending terms to only certain customers.

D. Bank loan covenants on days' sales outstanding.

Answer (B) is correct. *(CMA, adapted)*
REQUIRED: The factor not considered in an analysis of proposed credit policies.
DISCUSSION: All factors should be considered that differ between the two policies. Factors that do not differ, such as the current bad debt experience, are not relevant. Ryan must estimate the expected bad debt losses under each new policy.
Answer (A) is incorrect because the cost of funds is an obvious element in the analysis of any investment. Answer (C) is incorrect because the impact on the current customer base of extending terms to only certain customers is relevant. The current customers may demand the same terms. Answer (D) is incorrect because existing loan agreements may require Ryan to maintain certain ratios at stated levels. Thus, Ryan's ability to increase receivables and possible bad debt losses may be limited.

31. Jackson Distributors sells to retail stores on credit terms of 2/10, net 30. Daily sales average 150 units at a price of $300 each. Assuming that all sales are on credit and 60% of customers take the discount and pay on day 10 while the rest of the customers pay on day 30, the amount of Jackson's accounts receivable is

A. $1,350,000

B. $990,000

C. $900,000

D. $810,000

Answer (D) is correct. *(CMA, adapted)*
REQUIRED: The amount of accounts receivable for a firm with credit terms of 2/10, net 30.
DISCUSSION: The firm has daily sales of $45,000 consisting of 150 units at $300 each. For 30 days, sales total $1,350,000. Forty percent of these sales, or $540,000, will be uncollected because customers do not take their discounts. The remaining 60%, or $810,000, will be paid within the discount period. However, by the end of 30 days, only 2/3 of the $810,000 will be collected because the sales from days 21 through 30 are still within the discount period. Therefore, an additional $270,000 ($810,000 – $540,000) will still be uncollected after the 30th day, but will be subject to a discount. In total, the average receivable balance is $810,000, consisting of $540,000 on which no discount will be taken and $270,000 that will be paid within the discount period.
Answer (A) is incorrect because 60% of the sales will be paid for within the 10-day discount period. Answer (B) is incorrect because $990,000 is based on a sales total of $1,650,000 for 30 days rather than $1,350,000. Answer (C) is incorrect because $900,000 is based on a sales total of $1,500,000 for 30 days rather than $1,350,000.

32. A firm averages $4,000 in sales per day and is paid, on an average, within 30 days of the sale. After they receive their invoice, 55% of the customers pay by check, while the remaining 45% pay by credit card. Approximately how much will the company show in accounts receivable on its balance sheet on any given date?

A. $4,000

B. $120,000

C. $48,000

D. $54,000

Answer (B) is correct. *(CMA, adapted)*
REQUIRED: The average balance in accounts receivable given the average payment period and sales per day.
DISCUSSION: If sales are $4,000 per day, and customers pay in 30 days, 30 days of sales are outstanding, or $120,000. Whether customers pay by credit card or cash, collection requires 30 days.
Answer (A) is incorrect because $4,000 is only one day's sales. Answer (C) is incorrect because invoices are outstanding for 30 days, not 12 days. Answer (D) is incorrect because $54,000 is based on the 45% of collections via credit card.

33. A change in credit policy has caused an increase in sales, an increase in discounts taken, a decrease in the amount of bad debts, and a decrease in the investment in accounts receivable. Based upon this information, the company's

A. Average collection period has decreased.

B. Percentage discount offered has decreased.

C. Accounts receivable turnover has decreased.

D. Working capital has increased.

Answer (A) is correct. *(CMA, adapted)*
REQUIRED: The true statement about a change in credit policy that has resulted in greater sales and a reduction in accounts receivable.
DISCUSSION: An increase in discounts taken accompanied by declines in receivables balances and doubtful accounts all indicate that collections on the increased sales have been accelerated. Accordingly, the average collection period must have declined. The average collection period is a ratio calculated by dividing the number of days in a year (365) by the receivable turnover. Thus, the higher the turnover, the shorter the average collection period. The turnover increases when either sales (the numerator) increase, or receivables (the denominator) decrease. Accomplishing both higher sales and a lower receivables increases the turnover and results in a shorter collection period.
Answer (B) is incorrect because a decrease in the percentage discount offered provides no incentive for early payment. Answer (C) is incorrect because accounts receivable turnover (sales ÷ average receivables) has increased.
Answer (D) is incorrect because no information is given relative to working capital elements other than receivables. Both receivables and cash are elements of working capital, so an acceleration of customer payments will have no effect on working capital.

34. Best Computers believes that its collection costs could be reduced through modification of collection procedures. This action is expected to result in a lengthening of the average collection period from 28 days to 34 days; however, there will be no change in uncollectible accounts. The company's budgeted credit sales for the coming year are $27,000,000, and short-term interest rates are expected to average 8%. To make the changes in collection procedures cost beneficial, the minimum savings in collection costs (using a 360-day year) for the coming year will have to be

    A. $30,000

    B. $360,000

    C. $180,000

    D. $36,000

Answer (D) is correct. *(CMA, adapted)*
    REQUIRED: The minimum savings in collection costs that would be necessary to make the lengthened credit period beneficial.
    DISCUSSION: Given sales of $27,000,000, the average amount of daily sales must be $75,000 ($27,000,000 ÷ 360 days). The increased accounts receivable balance is therefore $450,000 (6 days × $75,000). With an additional $450,000 of capital invested in receivables, the company's interest cost will increase by $36,000 per year (8% × $450,000). Thus, the company must save at least $36,000 per year to justify the change in procedures.

35. A change in credit policy has caused an increase in sales, an increase in discounts taken, a reduction in the investment in accounts receivable, and a reduction in the number of doubtful accounts. Based upon this information, we know that

    A. Net profit has increased.

    B. The average collection period has decreased.

    C. Gross profit has declined.

    D. The size of the discount offered has decreased.

Answer (B) is correct. *(CMA, adapted)*
    REQUIRED: The true statement about a change in credit policy that has resulted in greater sales and a reduction in accounts receivable.
    DISCUSSION: An increase in discounts taken accompanied by declines in receivables balances and doubtful accounts all indicate that collections on the increased sales have been accelerated. Accordingly, the average collection period must have declined. The average collection period is a ratio calculated by dividing the number of days in a year (365) by the receivable turnover. Thus, the higher the turnover, the shorter the average collection period. The turnover increases when either sales (the numerator) increase, or receivables (the denominator) decrease. Accomplishing both higher sales and a lower receivables increases the turnover and results in a shorter collection period.
    Answer (A) is incorrect because no statement can be made with respect to net profits without knowing costs. Answer (C) is incorrect because no statement can be made with respect to gross profit without knowing costs. Answer (D) is incorrect because the discount may have been increased, which has led to quicker payments.

36. Spotech Co.'s budgeted sales and budgeted cost of sales for the coming year are $212,000,000 and $132,500,000, respectively. Short-term interest rates are expected to average 5%. If Spotech could increase inventory turnover from its current 8.0 times per year to 10.0 times per year, its expected cost savings in the current year would be

    A. $165,625

    B. $0

    C. $3,312,500

    D. $828,125

Answer (A) is correct. *(CMA, adapted)*
    REQUIRED: The expected cost savings from increasing the inventory turnover rate.
    DISCUSSION: If cost of sales is $132,500,000, and the inventory turnover rate is 8.0 times per year, the average inventory is $16,562,500 ($132,500,000 ÷ 8). If the turnover increases to 10.0 times annually, the average inventory will decline to $13,250,000 ($132,500,000 ÷ 10), a decrease of $3,312,500. At a 5% rate, reducing working capital by $3,312,500 will save the company $165,625 (.05 × $3,312,500).
    Answer (B) is incorrect because the faster turnover reduces working capital and releases funds for other uses. Answer (C) is incorrect because $3,312,500 is the decrease in average inventory. Answer (D) is incorrect because $828,125 is 5% of $16,562,500.

8.5 Short-Term Credit

37. Which one of the following provides a spontaneous source of financing for a firm?

- A. Accounts payable.
- B. Mortgage bonds.
- C. Accounts receivable.
- D. Debentures.

Answer (A) is correct. *(CMA, adapted)*
REQUIRED: The item that provides a spontaneous source of financing.
DISCUSSION: Trade credit is a spontaneous source of financing because it arises automatically as part of a purchase. Because of its ease in use, trade credit is the largest source of short-term financing for many firms both large and small.
Answer (B) is incorrect because mortgage bonds do not arise automatically as a result of a purchase transaction. Answer (C) is incorrect because the use of receivables as a financing source requires an extensive factoring arrangement and often involves the creditor's evaluation of the credit ratings of the borrower's customers. Answer (D) is incorrect because debentures do not arise automatically as a result of a purchase.

38. Assuming a 360-day year, the current price of a $100 U.S. Treasury bill due in 180 days on a 6% discount basis is

- A. $97
- B. $94
- C. $100
- D. $93

Answer (A) is correct. *(CMA, adapted)*
REQUIRED: The current price of a Treasury bill.
DISCUSSION: The 6% discount rate is multiplied times the face amount of the Treasury bill to determine the amount of interest the lender will earn. The interest on this Treasury bill is $3 (6% × .5 year × $100), thus the purchase price is $97 ($100 – $3).
Answer (B) is incorrect because the interest is for 180 days, not a full year. Answer (C) is incorrect because the purchase price will always be less than the face value when the Treasury bill is sold at a discount. Answer (D) is incorrect because the interest rate is 6% per year.

39. Commercial paper

- A. Has a maturity date greater than 1 year.
- B. Is usually sold only through investment banking dealers.
- C. Ordinarily does not have an active secondary market.
- D. Has an interest rate lower than Treasury bills.

Answer (C) is correct. *(CMA, adapted)*
REQUIRED: The true statement about commercial paper.
DISCUSSION: Commercial paper is a form of unsecured note that is sold by only the most creditworthy companies. It is issued at a discount from its face value and has a maturity period of 270 days or less. Commercial paper usually carries a low interest rate in comparison to other means of financing. SMA 4M, *Understanding Financial Instruments*, observes that no general (active) secondary market exists for commercial paper, but that "most dealers or organizations will repurchase an issue that they have sold."
Answer (A) is incorrect because commercial paper usually has a maturity date of 270 days or less to avoid securities registration requirements. Answer (B) is incorrect because commercial paper is often issued directly by the borrowing firm. Answer (D) is incorrect because interest rates must be higher than those of Treasury bills to entice investors. Commercial paper is more risky than Treasury bills.

Questions 40 through 43 are based on the following information.

The Frame Supply Company has just acquired a large account and needs to increase its working capital by $100,000. The controller of the company has identified the four sources of funds given below.

A. Pay a factor to buy the company's receivables, which average $125,000 per month and have an average collection period of 30 days. The factor will advance up to 80% of the face value of receivables at 10% and charge a fee of 2% on all receivables purchased. The controller estimates that the firm would save $24,000 in collection expenses over the year. Assume the fee and interest are not deductible in advance.

B. Borrow $110,000 from a bank at 12% interest. A 9% compensating balance would be required.

C. Issue $110,000 of 6-month commercial paper to net $100,000. (New paper would be issued every 6 months.)

D. Borrow $125,000 from a bank on a discount basis at 20%. No compensating balance would be required.

Assume a 360-day year in all of your calculations.

40. The cost of Alternative A. is

A. 10.0%

B. 12.0%

C. 13.2%

D. 16.0%

Answer (D) is correct. *(CMA, adapted)*
REQUIRED: The annual percentage cost of factoring receivables.
DISCUSSION: The factor will advance $100,000 (80% × $125,000). This amount is the average balance outstanding throughout the year. Thus, annual interest will be $10,000 (10% × $100,000). In addition, the company will pay an annual fee of $30,000 (2% × $125,000 per month × 12 months), so the total annual net cost is $16,000 ($10,000 + $30,000 − $24,000 savings). Hence, the annual cost is 16% ($16,000 ÷ $100,000 loan).
Answer (A) is incorrect because 10% is the interest rate on the amount advanced. Answer (B) is incorrect because 12% is the sum of the interest rate and the fee percentage. Answer (C) is incorrect because 13.2% is the cost of option B.

41. The cost of Alternative B. is

A. 9.0%

B. 12.0%

C. 13.2%

D. 21.0%

Answer (C) is correct. *(CMA, adapted)*
REQUIRED: The annual percentage cost of borrowing with a compensating balance requirement.
DISCUSSION: Even though the company will borrow $110,000, it will have use of only $100,100 because a 9% compensating balance, or $9,900, must be maintained at all times. Consequently, the effective annual interest rate is 13.2% [(12% × $110,000) ÷ $100,100].
Answer (A) is incorrect because 9% is the compensating balance requirement. Answer (B) is incorrect because 12% is the contract rate. Answer (D) is incorrect because 21% is the sum of the contract rate and the compensating balance requirement.

42. The cost of Alternative C. is

A. 9.1%

B. 10.0%

C. 18.2%

D. 20.0%

Answer (D) is correct. *(CMA, adapted)*
REQUIRED: The annual percentage cost of issuing commercial paper.
DISCUSSION: By issuing commercial paper, the company will receive $100,000 and repay $110,000 every six months. Thus, for the use of $100,000 in funds, the company pays $10,000 in interest each six-month period, or a total of $20,000 per year. The annual percentage rate is therefore 20% ($20,000 ÷ $100,000).
Answer (A) is incorrect because 9.1% is the 6-month rate based on the face amount of the paper. Answer (B) is incorrect because 10% is the rate for six months. Answer (C) is incorrect because 18.2% is based on the face amount of the commercial paper.

43. The cost of Alternative D. is

A. 20.0%

B. 25.0%

C. 40.0%

D. 50.0%

Answer (B) is correct. *(CMA, adapted)*
REQUIRED: The annual percentage cost of a discounted note.
DISCUSSION: The company will receive $100,000 (80% × $125,000) at an annual cost of $25,000, so the annual interest rate is 25% ($25,000 ÷ $100,000).
Answer (A) is incorrect because the effective rate must exceed the contract rate of 20%. Answer (C) is incorrect because 40% assumes no discount and a 6-month loan term. Answer (D) is incorrect because 50% assumes a 6-month loan term.

44. A firm often factors its accounts receivable. Its finance company requires a 6% reserve and charges a 1.4% commission on the amount of the receivables. The remaining amount to be advanced is further reduced by an annual interest charge of 15%. What proceeds (rounded to the nearest dollar) will the firm receive from the finance company at the time a $100,000 account due in 60 days is factored?

A. $92,600

B. $96,135

C. $90,285

D. $85,000

Answer (C) is correct. *(Publisher, adapted)*
REQUIRED: The proceeds of factoring.
DISCUSSION: The factor will withhold $6,000 (6% × $100,000) as a reserve against returns and allowances and $1,400 (1.4% × $100,000) as a commission. The remaining $92,600 will be reduced by interest at the rate of 15% annually. The interest charge should be $2,315, assuming a 360-day year [($92,600 × .15) × (60-day payment period ÷ 360 days)]. The proceeds to be received by the seller equal $90,285 ($92,600 – $2,315).
Answer (A) is incorrect because $92,600 ignores interest. Answer (B) is incorrect because $96,135 fails to deduct the 6% reserve. Answer (D) is incorrect because $85,000 assumes that the only amount withheld is a full year's interest on $100,000.

45. Management of a firm does not want to violate a working capital restriction contained in its bond indenture. If the firm's current ratio falls below 2.0 to 1, it will be in technical default. The firm's current ratio is now 2.2 to 1. If current liabilities are $200 million, the maximum new commercial paper that can be issued to finance inventory expansion is

A. $20 million.

B. $40 million.

C. $240 million.

D. $180 million.

Answer (B) is correct. *(Publisher, adapted)*
REQUIRED: The amount of commercial paper that can be issued without violating the bond indenture.
DISCUSSION: If current liabilities are $200 million and the current ratio (current assets ÷ current liabilities) is 2.2, current assets must be $440 million (2.2 × $200 million). If X amount of commercial paper is issued to finance inventory (current assets), thereby increasing both current assets and current liabilities by X, the level of current assets at which the new current ratio will be 2.0 is $480 million ($440 million + $40 million of commercial paper).

$$(\$440 + X) \div (\$200) + X) = 2.0$$
$$\$440 + X = 2(\$200 + X)$$
$$\$440 + X = \$400 + 2X$$
$$\$440 = \$400 + X$$
$$X = \$40$$

Answer (A) is incorrect because $20 million ignores the increase in current assets. This answer would be appropriate if noncurrent assets were being financed. Answer (C) is incorrect because $240 million is the amount of working capital both before and after the issuance of commercial paper. Answer (D) is incorrect because $180 million is a nonsense answer.

8.6 Inventory and Supply Chain Management

46. An example of a carrying cost is

A. Disruption of production schedules.

B. Quantity discounts lost.

C. Handling costs.

D. Spoilage.

Answer (D) is correct. *(CMA, adapted)*
REQUIRED: The inventory carrying cost.
DISCUSSION: Inventory costs fall into three categories: order or set-up costs, carrying (holding) costs, and stockout costs. Carrying costs include storage costs for inventory items plus opportunity cost (i.e., the cost incurred by investing in inventory rather than making an income-earning investment). Examples are insurance, spoilage, interest on invested capital, obsolescence, and warehousing costs.
Answer (A) is incorrect because disruption of production schedules may result from a stockout. Answer (B) is incorrect because quantity discounts lost are related to ordering costs or inventory acquisition costs. Answer (C) is incorrect because shipping and handling costs are included in acquisition costs.

47. To determine the inventory reorder point, calculations normally include the

   A. Ordering cost.

   B. Carrying cost.

   C. Average daily usage.

   D. Economic order quantity.

Answer (C) is correct. *(CPA, adapted)*
   REQUIRED: The item needed to calculate the reorder point.
   DISCUSSION: The reorder point is the amount of inventory on hand indicating that a new order should be placed. It equals the sales per unit of time multiplied by the time required to receive the new order (lead time).
   Answer (A) is incorrect because cost is not a factor in the reorder-point calculation. Answer (B) is incorrect because the carrying cost is not a factor in the reorder-point calculation. Answer (D) is incorrect because the economic order quantity determines order size and can be used to determine the number of orders per period, but it is not used to calculate the reorder point.

48. Which one of the following is not considered a carrying cost associated with inventory?

   A. Insurance costs.

   B. Cost of capital invested in the inventory.

   C. Cost of obsolescence.

   D. Shipping costs.

Answer (D) is correct. *(CMA, adapted)*
   REQUIRED: The item that is not a carrying cost of inventory.
   DISCUSSION: Carrying costs are incurred to hold inventory. Examples include such costs as warehousing, insurance, the cost of capital invested in inventories, inventory taxes, and the cost of obsolescence and spoilage. Neither shipping costs nor the initial cost of the inventory are carrying costs.

49. The ordering costs associated with inventory management include

   A. Insurance costs, purchasing costs, shipping costs, and spoilage.

   B. Obsolescence, setup costs, quantity discounts lost, and storage costs.

   C. Purchasing costs, shipping costs, setup costs, and quantity discounts lost.

   D. Shipping costs, obsolescence, setup costs, and capital invested.

Answer (C) is correct. *(CMA, adapted)*
   REQUIRED: The items included in ordering costs.
   DISCUSSION: Ordering costs are costs incurred when placing and receiving orders. Ordering costs include purchasing costs, shipping costs, setup costs for a production run, and quantity discounts lost.
   Answer (A) is incorrect because insurance costs are a carrying cost. Answer (B) is incorrect because obsolescence, spoilage, and storage costs are carrying costs. Answer (D) is incorrect because obsolescence and interest on invested capital are carrying costs.

50. The amount of inventory that a company tends to hold in stock will increase as the

   A. Sales level falls to a permanently lower level.

   B. Cost of carrying inventory decreases.

   C. Variability of sales decreases.

   D. Cost of running out of stock decreases.

Answer (B) is correct. *(CMA, adapted)*
   REQUIRED: The reason for an increase in inventory.
   DISCUSSION: Inventory management attempts to minimize the total costs of ordering, carrying inventory, and stockouts. Thus, a firm incurs carrying costs to reduce ordering and stockout costs. If the cost of carrying inventory declines, the inventory level must increase to minimize total inventory costs.

51. In inventory management, the safety stock will tend to increase if the

   A. Carrying cost increases.

   B. Cost of running out of stock decreases.

   C. Variability of the lead time increases.

   D. Variability of the usage rate decreases.

Answer (C) is correct. *(CMA, adapted)*
   REQUIRED: The factor that will cause safety stocks to increase.
   DISCUSSION: A company maintains safety stocks to protect itself against the losses caused by inventory stockouts. These can take the form of lost sales or lost production time. Safety stock is necessary because of the variability in lead time and usage rates. As the variability in lead time increases, a company will tend to carry larger safety stocks.
   Answer (A) is incorrect because an increase in inventory carrying costs makes it less economical to carry safety stocks. Thus, safety stocks will be reduced. Answer (B) is incorrect because, if the cost of stockouts declines, the incentive to carry large safety stocks is reduced. Answer (D) is incorrect because a decline in the variability of usage makes it easier to plan orders, and safety stocks will be less necessary.

52. To minimize total inventory cost, which inventory management approach places orders so that carrying costs equate most nearly to restocking costs?

A. Economic order quantity.

B. Just-in-time.

C. Materials requirements planning.

D. ABC.

Answer (A) is correct. *(CMA, adapted)*
REQUIRED: The inventory management method that equates carrying costs with restocking (ordering) costs.
DISCUSSION: The EOQ model is a deterministic model that calculates the ideal order (or production lot) quantity given specified demand, ordering or setup costs, and carrying costs. The model minimizes the sum of inventory carrying costs and either ordering (restocking) or production setup costs. This minimum is at the intersection of the total carrying cost and total ordering cost curves.
Answer (B) is incorrect because a JIT system is based on the pull of current demand by the next operation. Answer (C) is incorrect because an MRP system is a computer-based system that activates production based on demand forecasts.
Answer (D) is incorrect because ABC (activity-based costing) is a method of accumulating and assigning costs of production, not an inventory control method.

53. The Stewart Co. uses the economic order quantity (EOQ) model for inventory management. A decrease in which one of the following variables will increase the EOQ?

A. Annual sales.

B. Cost per order.

C. Safety stock level.

D. Carrying costs.

Answer (D) is correct. *(CMA, adapted)*
REQUIRED: The variable for which a decrease will lead to an increase in the economic order quantity (EOQ).
DISCUSSION: The EOQ model minimizes the total of ordering and carrying costs. The EOQ is calculated as follows:

$$\sqrt{\frac{2(Demand)(Order\ costs)}{Carrying\ costs\ per\ unit}}$$

Increases in the numerator (demand or ordering costs) will increase the EOQ, whereas decreases in demand or ordering costs will decrease the EOQ. Similarly, a decrease in the denominator (carrying costs) will increase the EOQ.
Answer (A) is incorrect because a decrease in demand (annual sales), which is in the numerator, will decrease the EOQ. Answer (B) is incorrect because a decrease in ordering costs will encourage more orders, or a decrease in the EOQ. Answer (C) is incorrect because a decrease in safety stock levels will not affect the EOQ, although it might lead to a different ordering point.

54. Edwards Manufacturing Corporation uses the standard economic order quantity (EOQ) model. If the EOQ for Product A is 200 units and Edwards maintains a 50-unit safety stock for the item, what is the average inventory of Product A?

A. 250 units.

B. 150 units.

C. 125 units.

D. 100 units.

Answer (B) is correct. *(CMA, adapted)*
REQUIRED: The average inventory of a product.
DISCUSSION: If safety stock is 50 units, the receipt of an order should increase the inventory to 250. That amount will decline to 50 just prior to the receipt of the next order. Thus, the average inventory would be the average of 250 and 50 [(250 + 50) ÷ 2], or 150 units.
Answer (A) is incorrect because 250 is the maximum inventory level. Answer (C) is incorrect because 125 units assumes an EOQ of 250 units and no safety stock. Answer (D) is incorrect because 100 units assumes no safety stock.

55. Which of the following is included in the economic order quantity formula?

	Inventory Carrying Cost	Stockout Cost
A.	Yes	No
B.	Yes	Yes
C.	No	Yes
D.	No	No

Answer (A) is correct. *(CPA, adapted)*
REQUIRED: The variable(s) in the economic order quantity formula.
DISCUSSION: The elements needed to compute the EOQ are the periodic demand (sales), cost of a production run or of placing an order, and the periodic unit carrying cost (including storage costs). The risk of obsolescence and deterioration is part of the inventory carrying cost. The stockout cost is not used in the EOQ calculation.

56. A major supplier has offered Alpha Corporation a year-end special purchase whereby Alpha could purchase 180,000 cases of sport drink at $10 per case. Alpha normally orders 30,000 cases per month at $12 per case. Alpha's cost of capital is 9%. In calculating the overall opportunity cost of this offer, the incremental cost of carrying the increased inventory will be

A. $32,400

B. $40,500

C. $64,800

D. $81,000

Answer (A) is correct. *(CMA, adapted)*
REQUIRED: The cost of carrying the increased inventory.
DISCUSSION: If Alpha makes the special purchase of 6 months of inventory (180,000 cases ÷ 30,000 cases per month), the average inventory for the 6-month period will be $900,000 [(180,000 × $10) ÷ 2]. If the special purchase is not made, the average inventory for the same period will be the average monthly inventory of $180,000 [(30,000 × $12) ÷ 2]. Accordingly, the incremental average inventory is $720,000 ($900,000 – $180,000), and the interest cost of the incremental 6-month investment is $32,400 [($720,000 × 9%) ÷ 2].
Answer (B) is incorrect because $40,500 is the result of assuming an incremental average inventory of $900,000. Answer (C) is incorrect because $64,800 is the interest cost for 12 months. Answer (D) is incorrect because $81,000 is the result of assuming an incremental average inventory of $900,000 and a 12-month period.

57. The economic order quantity formula assumes that

A. Periodic demand for the good is known.

B. Carrying costs per unit vary with quantity ordered.

C. Costs of placing an order vary with quantity ordered.

D. Purchase costs per unit differ due to quantity discounts.

Answer (A) is correct. *(CPA, adapted)*
REQUIRED: The assumption underlying the EOQ formula.
DISCUSSION: The EOQ formula is

$$EOQ = \sqrt{\frac{2aD}{k}}$$

D = demand
a = order cost
k = carrying cost

A change in unit demand will cause a change in the economic order quantity. All other values are given and assumed to be constant. The simplest form of the EOQ model is based on the assumption that demand is known and that usage is uniform throughout the period.
Answer (B) is incorrect because the model assumes that unit carrying cost is constant. Answer (C) is incorrect because the costs of placing an order are deemed to be constant. Answer (D) is incorrect because the cost of the item being purchased is assumed to be constant.

58. As a consequence of finding a more dependable supplier, Dee Co. reduced its safety stock of raw materials by 80%. What is the effect of this safety stock reduction on Dee's economic order quantity?

A. 80% decrease.

B. 64% decrease.

C. 20% increase.

D. No effect.

Answer (D) is correct. *(CPA, adapted)*
REQUIRED: The effect of the safety stock reduction on the EOQ.
DISCUSSION: The variables in the EOQ formula are periodic demand, cost per order, and the unit carrying cost for the period. Thus, safety stock does not affect the EOQ. Although the total of the carrying costs changes with the safety stock, the cost-minimizing order quantity is not affected.

59. In Belk Co.'s just-in-time production system, costs per setup were reduced from $28 to $2. In the process of reducing inventory levels, Belk found that there were fixed facility and administrative costs that previously had not been included in the carrying cost calculation. The result was an increase from $8 to $32 per unit per year. What were the effects of these changes on Belk's economic lot size and relevant costs?

	Lot Size	Relevant Costs
A.	Decrease	Increase
B.	Increase	Decrease
C.	Increase	Increase
D.	Decrease	Decrease

Answer (D) is correct. *(CPA, adapted)*
REQUIRED: The effect of a JIT production system on economic lot size and relevant costs.
DISCUSSION: The economic lot size for a production system is similar to the EOQ. For example, the cost per set-up is equivalent to the cost per order (a numerator value in the EOQ model). Hence, a reduction in the setup costs reduces the economic lot size as well as the relevant costs. The fixed facility and administrative costs, however, are not relevant. The EOQ model includes variable costs only.

60. Which changes in costs are most conducive to switching from a traditional inventory ordering system to a just-in-time ordering system?

	Cost per Purchase Order	Inventory Unit Carrying Costs
A.	Increasing	Increasing
B.	Decreasing	Increasing
C.	Decreasing	Decreasing
D.	Increasing	Decreasing

Answer (B) is correct. *(CPA, adapted)*
REQUIRED: The changes in costs most conducive to switching to a just-in-time ordering system.
DISCUSSION: A JIT system is intended to minimize inventory. Thus, if inventory carrying costs are increasing, a JIT system becomes more cost effective. Moreover, purchases are more frequent in a JIT system. Accordingly, a decreasing cost per purchase order is conducive to switching to a JIT system.

61. Which of the following is a characteristic of just-in-time (JIT) inventory management systems?

A. JIT users determine the optimal level of safety stocks.

B. JIT is applicable only to large companies.

C. JIT does not really increase overall economic efficiency because it merely shifts inventory levels further up the supply chain.

D. JIT relies heavily on good quality materials.

Answer (D) is correct. *(CIA, adapted)*
REQUIRED: The characteristic of just-in-time (JIT) inventory management systems.
DISCUSSION: Poor quality materials cause major problems in a JIT system. No safety stock is on hand to replace defective materials. Substandard materials cause major production disruptions and defeat the purpose of lowering cost and lead time while increasing product quality.
Answer (A) is incorrect because safety stocks are not held in JIT systems, the goal of which is to minimize inventory by insuring that materials arrive at the plant just in time for production. Safety stocks raise inventory levels and increase the risk of defective materials through obsolescence and potential damage during storage. Answer (B) is incorrect because many smaller firms are adopting JIT with favorable results. In fact, smaller companies may implement JIT more readily because they can more easily redefine job functions and retrain workers. Answer (C) is incorrect because the close coordination required between suppliers and customers usually leads to overall inventory reductions throughout the production-distribution chain.

62. Which of the following is not considered a cost of carrying inventory?

A. Shipping and handling.

B. Property tax.

C. Insurance.

D. Depreciation and obsolescence.

Answer (A) is correct. *(CIA, adapted)*
REQUIRED: The cost not considered a cost of carrying inventory.
DISCUSSION: Inventory shipping and handling costs are classified as ordering costs, not carrying costs. Property tax, taxes on inventory, rent, security costs, insurance, and depreciation and obsolescence are inventory carrying costs.

63. The internal auditor of a retailing company is auditing the purchasing area. To evaluate the efficiency of purchase transactions, the auditor decides to calculate the economic order quantity for a sample of the company's products. To calculate the economic order quantity, the internal auditor would need data for which of the following?

A. The volume of product sales.

B. The purchase prices of the products.

C. The fixed cost of ordering products.

D. The volume of products in inventory.

Answer (A) is correct. *(CIA, adapted)*
REQUIRED: The information needed for the economic order quantity.
DISCUSSION: The basic economic order quantity (EOQ) model minimizes the sum of order costs and carrying costs. Demand is assumed to be known and constant throughout the year. The EOQ is equal to the square root of twice annual demand multiplied by the variable cost of placing an order, divided by the unit variable carrying cost. Thus, sales volume (demand) must be known.
Answer (B) is incorrect because price is not a variable in the model. Answer (C) is incorrect because fixed costs are not included in the model. Answer (D) is incorrect because the amount of items in the inventory is not included in the model.

64. The economic order quantity for inventory is higher for an organization that has

    A. Lower annual unit sales.

    B. Higher inventory ordering costs.

    C. Higher annual carrying costs as a percentage of inventory value.

    D. A higher purchase price per unit of inventory.

Answer (B) is correct. *(CIA, adapted)*
    REQUIRED: The reason for a higher EOQ.
    DISCUSSION: The higher the ordering costs per order, the greater the EOQ. If orders are made less frequently because amounts ordered are larger, total ordering costs for the period will be lower.
    Answer (A) is incorrect because EOQ is higher for a company that has higher, not lower, annual unit sales. Greater sales means more inventory is needed. Answer (C) is incorrect because higher carrying costs will result in a lowering of order quantities so that average inventory is reduced. Answer (D) is incorrect because higher unit purchase prices will increase inventory carrying costs and reduce the EOQ.

65. An organization has an inventory order quantity of 10,000 units and a safety stock of 2,000 units. The cost per unit of inventory is $5, and the carrying cost is 10% of the average value of inventory. The annual inventory carrying cost for the organization is

    A. $3,000

    B. $3,500

    C. $5,000

    D. $6,000

Answer (B) is correct. *(CIA, adapted)*
    REQUIRED: The total annual inventory carrying cost.
    DISCUSSION: The total annual inventory carrying cost equals average inventory times the percentage carrying cost. Average inventory equals the sum of the safety stock and 50% of the EOQ. Accordingly, average inventory quantity is 7,000 units [2,000 + (50% × 10,000)], its cost is $35,000, and 10% of the cost is $3,500.
    Answer (A) is incorrect because $3,000 omits safety stock from the calculation of annual inventory carrying cost. Answer (C) is incorrect because $5,000 omits safety stock from the calculation and fails to divide the EOQ by two to calculate average inventory. Answer (D) is incorrect because $6,000 fails to divide the EOQ by two when calculating average inventory.

66. When the economic order quantity (EOQ) decision model is employed, the <List A> are being offset or balanced by the <List B>.

	List A	List B
A.	Ordering costs	Carrying costs
B.	Purchase costs	Carrying costs
C.	Purchase costs	Quality costs
D.	Ordering costs	Stockout costs

Answer (A) is correct. *(CIA, adapted)*
    REQUIRED: The true statement about cost relationships in the EOQ.
    DISCUSSION: The objective of the EOQ model is to find an optimal order quantity that balances carrying and ordering costs. Only variable costs should be considered. The EOQ is the point where the ordering cost and carrying cost curves intersect. It corresponds to the minimum point on the total inventory cost curve.
    Answer (B) is incorrect because purchase costs are not directly incorporated into the EOQ model. Answer (C) is incorrect because neither purchase costs nor quality costs are incorporated into the EOQ model. Answer (D) is incorrect because stockout costs are not directly incorporated into the EOQ model.

67. The calculation of an economic order quantity (EOQ) considers

    A. The purchasing manager's salary.

    B. A corporate charge for advertising expenses.

    C. The shipping costs to deliver the product to the customer.

    D. Capital costs.

Answer (D) is correct. *(CMA, adapted)*
    REQUIRED: The true statement about the calculation of the economic order quantity.
    DISCUSSION: The determination of the economic order quantity balances the variable costs of ordering and carrying inventory. Factors in the equation include the cost of placing an order, unit carrying cost, and annual demand in units. Carrying costs include storage costs, handling costs, insurance, property taxes, obsolescence, and the opportunity cost of investing capital in inventory. Thus, the return on capital that is forgone when it is invested in inventory should be considered.
    Answer (A) is incorrect because the purchasing manager's salary is a fixed cost. The EOQ model includes variable costs only. Answer (B) is incorrect because advertising is not an ordering or carrying cost. Answer (C) is incorrect because the cost of shipping to customers is a selling expense.

68. Companies that adopt just-in-time purchasing systems often experience

A. An increase in carrying costs.

B. A reduction in the number of suppliers.

C. A greater need for inspection of goods as the goods arrive.

D. Less need for linkage with a vendor's computerized order entry system.

Answer (B) is correct. *(CMA, adapted)*
REQUIRED: The true statement about companies that adopt just-in-time (JIT) purchasing systems.
DISCUSSION: The objective of JIT is to reduce carrying costs by eliminating inventories and increasing the deliveries made by suppliers. Ideally, shipments of raw materials are received just in time to be incorporated into the manufacturing process. The focus of quality control under JIT is the prevention of quality problems. Quality control is shifted to the supplier. JIT companies typically do not inspect incoming goods; the assumption is that receipts are of perfect quality. Suppliers are limited to those who guarantee perfect quality and prompt delivery.
Answer (A) is incorrect because carrying costs typically decline in JIT companies. Less inventory is on hand. Answer (C) is incorrect because, in a JIT system, materials are delivered directly to the production line ready for insertion in the finished product. Answer (D) is incorrect because the need for communication with the vendor is greater. Orders and deliveries must be made on short notice, sometimes several times a day.

69. A manufacturing company is attempting to implement a just-in-time (JIT) purchase policy system by negotiating with its primary suppliers to accept long-term purchase orders which result in more frequent deliveries of smaller quantities of raw materials. If the JIT purchase policy is successful in reducing the total inventory costs of the manufacturing company, which of the following combinations of cost changes would be most likely to occur?

Cost Category to Increase	Cost Category to Decrease
A. Purchasing costs	Stockout costs
B. Purchasing costs	Quality costs
C. Quality costs	Ordering costs
D. Stockout costs	Carrying costs

Answer (D) is correct. *(CIA, adapted)*
REQUIRED: The combination of cost changes.
DISCUSSION: The objective of a JIT system is to reduce carrying costs by eliminating inventories and increasing the deliveries made by suppliers. Ideally, shipments are received just in time to be incorporated into the manufacturing process. This system increases the risk of stockout costs because the inventory buffer is reduced or eliminated.
Answer (A) is incorrect because the supplier may seek a concession on the selling price that will raise purchasing costs, but the manufacturing company's stockout costs will increase. Answer (B) is incorrect because the cost of quality is not necessarily affected by a JIT system. Answer (C) is incorrect because fewer purchase orders are processed by the manufacturer, so the ordering costs are likely to decrease. However, the cost of quality is not necessarily affected by a JIT system.

70. Each stockout of a product sold by A.W. Inn Co. costs $1,750 per occurrence. The carrying cost per unit of inventory is $5 per year, and the company orders 1,500 units of product 24 times a year at a cost of $100 per order. The probability of a stockout at various levels of safety stock is

Units of Safety Stock	Probability of a Stockout
0	.50
100	.30
200	.14
300	.05
400	.01

The optimal safety stock level for the company is

A. 0 units.

B. 100 units.

C. 300 units.

D. 400 units.

Answer (D) is correct. *(CMA, adapted)*
REQUIRED: The optimal level of safety stock.
DISCUSSION: The total expected cost of safety stock equals the sum of the expected annual stockout cost and the expected annual carrying cost. Annual expected stockout cost equals the cost per occurrence ($1,750), times the probability of a stockout per cycle, times the number of cycles (24). Annual expected carrying cost of a safety stock equals the unit carrying cost ($5) times the number of units. Hence, a safety stock of 400 units has the lowest total expected cost.

Units Held	Expected Carrying Cost	Expected Stockout Cost Per Cycle	Expected Stockout Cost for 24 Cycles	Total Expected Cost
0	$ 0	$875.00	$21,000	$21,000
100	500	525.00	12,600	13,100
200	1,000	245.00	5,880	6,880
300	1,500	87.50	2,100	3,600
400	2,000	17.50	420	2,420

Answer (A) is incorrect because a safety stock of 0 units has a total expected cost of $21,000. Answer (B) is incorrect because a safety stock of 100 units has a total expected cost of $13,100. Answer (C) is incorrect because a safety stock of 300 units has a total expected cost of $3,600.

Questions 71 through 73 are based on the following information. The diagram presented below represents the economic order quantity (EOQ) model.

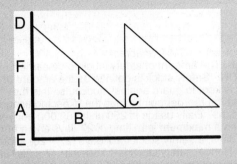

71. Which line segment represents the reorder lead time?

A. AB.

B. AE.

C. AF.

D. BC.

Answer (D) is correct. *(CMA, adapted)*
  REQUIRED: The line segment representing the reorder lead time.
  DISCUSSION: The quantity of inventory on hand is represented by the y axis and time by the x axis. The reorder lead time is represented by the line segment BC.
  Answer (A) is incorrect because AB is the time between receipt of the last order and the placing of the next order. Answer (B) is incorrect because AE is the safety stock. Answer (C) is incorrect because AF represents the quantity of inventory that will be used during the reorder lead time.

72. Which line segment identifies the quantity of safety stock maintained?

A. AB.

B. AE.

C. AC.

D. BC.

Answer (B) is correct. *(CMA, adapted)*
  REQUIRED: The line segment representing the quantity of safety stock maintained.
  DISCUSSION: Quantities of inventory are shown along the y axis. Safety stock is represented by the line AE.
  Answer (A) is incorrect because AB is the time between the receipt of the last order and the placing of the next order. Answer (C) is incorrect because AC is the time to consume the EOQ. Answer (D) is incorrect because BC is the reorder lead time.

73. Which line segment represents the length of time to consume the total quantity of materials ordered?

A. DE.

B. BC.

C. AC.

D. AE.

Answer (C) is correct. *(CMA, adapted)*
  REQUIRED: The line representing the time to consume all the materials ordered.
  DISCUSSION: Time is shown along the x axis. The line segment AC depicts the time to consume an entire order (to reduce the inventory to the safety stock).
  Answer (A) is incorrect because DE represents the total inventory on hand just after an order has been received. Answer (B) is incorrect because BC is the reorder lead time. Answer (D) is incorrect because AE is the safety stock.

Questions 74 and 75 are based on the following information. The Huron Corporation purchases 60,000 headbands per year. The average purchase lead time is 20 working days. Maximum lead time is 27 working days. The corporation works 240 days per year.

74. Huron Corporation should carry safety stock of

A. 5,000 units.

B. 6,750 units.

C. 1,750 units.

D. 250 units.

Answer (C) is correct. *(CMA, adapted)*
REQUIRED: The amount of safety stock to be carried.
DISCUSSION: Safety stock is defined as the amount of extra stock that is kept to guard against stockouts. It is the inventory level at the reorder point minus the expected usage during the lead time. Daily usage is 250 units (60,000 per year ÷ 240 days). Given a maximum lead time of 27 days and a normal lead time of 20 days, a safety stock for 7 days (27 – 20) should be maintained. Hence, safety stock is 1,750 units (7 × 250 units).
Answer (A) is incorrect because 5,000 units represents the quantity expected to be sold during the normal lead time. Answer (B) is incorrect because 6,750 units includes not only the safety stock but also the units expected to be sold during the normal lead time. Answer (D) is incorrect because 250 units is 1 day's sales.

75. If the amount of safety stock is 1,750 units and daily usage is 250 units, then Huron Corporation should reorder headbands when the quantity in inventory reaches

A. 5,000 units.

B. 6,750 units.

C. 1,750 units.

D. 5,250 units.

Answer (B) is correct. *(CMA, adapted)*
REQUIRED: When Huron should reorder.
DISCUSSION: The reorder point is the quantity on hand when an order is placed. With a 20-day normal lead time, a 7-day safety stock, and usage of 250 units per day, an order should be placed when 27 days of inventory are on hand, a total of 6,750 units (27 × 250).
Answer (A) is incorrect because 5,000 units does not allow for safety stock. Answer (C) is incorrect because 1,750 units covers only safety stock. Answer (D) is incorrect because 5,250 units includes only 1 day of safety stock.

76. Given demand in excess of capacity, no spoilage or waste, and full use of a constant number of assembly hours, the number of components needed for an assembly operation with an 80% learning curve should

I. Increase for successive periods.
II. Decrease per unit of output.

A. I only.

B. II only.

C. Both I and II.

D. Neither I nor II.

Answer (A) is correct. *(CPA, adapted)*
REQUIRED: The relationship between the number of components needed in an assembly operation and the operation's learning curve.
DISCUSSION: Learning curves reflect the increased rate at which people perform tasks as they gain experience. An 80% learning curve means that the cumulative average time required to complete a unit (or the time required to produce the last unit) declines by 20% when unit output doubles in the early stages of production. Thus, as the cumulative average time per unit (or the time to complete the last unit) declines, the number of units produced per period of time increases. As more units are produced, more components are needed for the production. The number of components per unit of output is not affected by an increase in output.
Answer (B) is incorrect because the number of components needed per unit of output produced should remain constant, assuming no spoilage or waste. Answer (C) is incorrect because the number of components needed per unit of output produced should remain constant, assuming no spoilage or waste. Answer (D) is incorrect because the number of components needed will increase for successive periods for an assembly operation with an 80% learning curve.

Questions 77 and 78 are based on the following information. Ryerson Computer Furniture Inc. (RCF) manufactures a line of office computer chairs. The annual demand for the chairs is estimated to be 5,000 units. The annual cost to hold one unit in inventory is $10 per year, and the cost to initiate a production run is $1,562.50. There are no computer chairs on hand, and the first production run will begin immediately. RCF has 250 business days per year, sales occur uniformly throughout the year, and production start-up is within one day. RCF is considering using the following formula for determining the economic order quantity (EOQ):

$$EOQ = \sqrt{\frac{2AD}{K}}$$

If: A = cost to initiate a production run per purchase order
       D = annual unit demand
       K = cost of carrying one unit per year

77. The number of production runs per year of computer chairs that would minimize the sum of carrying and setup costs for the coming year is

A. 1

B. 2

C. 4

D. 5

Answer (C) is correct. *(CMA, adapted)*
REQUIRED: The number of production runs that minimizes the sum of setup and carrying costs.
DISCUSSION: The EOQ minimizes the sum of carrying and setup costs. The EOQ is the amount at which carrying costs are equal to setup costs. Thus, plugging the data into the EOQ formula results in the following:

$$EOQ = \sqrt{\frac{2(\$1,562.50)(5,000)}{\$10}} = 1,250 \text{ units}$$

Thus, if each lot consists of 1,250 units, four production runs per year are needed to meet the 5,000-unit demand. At this level, setup costs will total $6,250 (5 × $1,250). Carrying costs will equal $6,250 (average inventory of 625 units × $10 per unit carrying cost). Accordingly, total costs are minimized at $12,500.
Answer (A) is incorrect because a single production run indicates an EOQ of 5,000 units. The carrying costs of $25,000 [$10 × ($5,000 ÷ 2)] would exceed the $1,250 of setup costs. Answer (B) is incorrect because two production runs correspond to an EOQ of 2,500 units and an average inventory of 1,250 units. The resulting $12,500 of carrying costs would exceed the $2,500 of setup costs. Answer (D) is incorrect because five production runs correspond to an EOQ of 1,000 units and an average inventory of 500 units. The resulting $5,000 of carrying costs would be less than the $6,250 of setup costs.

78. If RCF does not maintain a safety stock, the estimated total carrying costs for the computer chairs for each period of the coming year is

A. $4,000

B. $5,000

C. $6,250

D. $12,500

Answer (C) is correct. *(CMA, adapted)*
REQUIRED: The estimated total annual carrying costs assuming no safety stock is held.
DISCUSSION: The economic order quantity (EOQ) formula also may be used to determine the economic production run. Hence, the economic production run equals 1,250 units {square root of [(2 × $1,562.50 × 5,000) ÷ $10]}. Inventory will total 1,250 units at the completion of each run but will decline to zero just prior to the next run. Thus, the average inventory for the period is 625 units (1,250 ÷ 2), and the total carrying cost is $6,250 (625 units × $10).
Answer (A) is incorrect because the cost of maintaining an average inventory of 625 units is $6,250. Answer (B) is incorrect because $5,000 is based upon an EOQ of 1,000 units and an average inventory of 500 units. Answer (D) is incorrect because $12,500 is based on the maximum inventory level.

79. A manufacturing resource planning (MRP II) system

A. Performs the same back-office functions for a manufacturer as an ERP system.

B. Uses a master production schedule.

C. Lacks the forecasting and budgeting capabilities typical of an ERP system.

D. Performs the same front-office functions for a manufacturer as an ERP system.

Answer (B) is correct.   *(Publisher, adapted)*
REQUIRED: The true statement about MRP II.
DISCUSSION: Manufacturing resource planning (MRP II) continued the evolution begun with materials requirements planning (MRP). It is a closed-loop manufacturing system that integrates all facets of manufacturing, including production, sales, inventories, schedules, and cash flows. The same system is used for accounting and finance functions, which use the same transactions and numbers. MRP II uses an MPS (master production schedule), which is a statement of the anticipated manufacturing schedule for selected items for selected periods. MRP also uses the MPS. Thus, MRP is a component of an MRP II system.

Answer (A) is incorrect because an MRP II system does not integrate all the subsystems internal to the organization (back-office functions), such as human resources and customer service. Answer (C) is incorrect because MRP II includes forecasting and planning capacities for generating cash and other budgets. Answer (D) is incorrect because MRP, MRP II, and traditional ERP do not provide for front-office functions, that is, connections with customers, suppliers, owners, creditors, and strategic allies.

Use Gleim's *CPA Test Prep* for interactive testing with over 2,000 additional multiple-choice questions!

STUDY UNIT NINE
LONG-TERM CAPITAL FINANCING

(29 pages of outline)

The first subject covered in this study unit is long-term financing, which is accomplished principally by issuance of common stock and bonds. The second subunit addresses methods of optimizing the permanent capital structure of the firm, with an emphasis on the cost of the various types of capital. The third subunit discusses strategies for providing equity holders with a return on their investment through corporate distributions. The final subunit outlines various financial models for evaluating investments.

9.1 SOURCES OF LONG-TERM FINANCING

1. A firm may have long-term funding requirements that it cannot, or does not want to, meet using retained earnings. It must therefore issue equity or debt securities to obtain the necessary funding. Certain hybrid forms are also used for long-term financing, e.g., convertible securities.

2. The principal considerations when reviewing financing choices are cost, risk, and the lender's (investor's) view of the financing device.

3. **Common stock.** The common shareholders are the owners of the corporation, and their rights as owners, although reasonably uniform, depend on the laws of the state in which the firm is incorporated. Equity ownership involves risk because holders of common stock are not guaranteed a return and are last in priority in a liquidation. Equity provides the cushion for creditors if any losses occur on liquidation.

   a. **Advantages of Common Stock to the Issuer**

      1) Dividends are not fixed. They are paid from profits when available.
      2) There is no fixed maturity date for repayment of the capital.
      3) The sale of common stock increases the creditworthiness of the firm by providing more equity.
      4) Common stock is frequently more attractive to investors than debt because it grows in value with the success of the firm.

         a) The higher the common stock value, the more advantageous equity financing is over debt financing.

   b. **Disadvantages of Common Stock to the Issuer**

      1) Control (voting rights) is usually diluted as more common stock is sold.
      2) New common stock sales dilute earnings available to existing shareholders because of the greater number of shares outstanding.
      3) Underwriting costs are typically higher for common stock issues.
      4) Too much equity may raise the average cost of capital of the firm above its optimal level.
      5) Cash dividends are not deductible as an expense and thus reduce after-tax cash flows of the firm.

c.   Common shareholders ordinarily have **preemptive rights**.

1)   Preemptive rights give common shareholders the right to purchase any additional stock issuances in proportion to their current ownership.

2)   If state law or the corporate charter does not provide preemptive rights, the firm may nevertheless sell to the common shareholders in a **rights** offering. Each shareholder is issued a certificate or warrant that is an option to buy a certain number of shares at a fixed price within a given time.

a)   Until the rights are actually issued, the stock trades **rights-on**, that is, the stock and the rights are not separable. After the rights are received, the stock trades **ex-rights** because the rights can be sold separately. The price of a stock right sold rights-on is

$$\frac{P - S}{N + 1}$$

If: P = value of a share rights-on
      S = subscription price of a share
      N = number of rights needed to buy a share

d.   **Stock warrants** (certificates evidencing call options to buy stock at a given price within a certain period) may be issued to employees as compensation, or they may be issued with bonds or preferred stock.

1)   Issuance with other securities may permit the firm to pay a lower interest rate or preferred dividend. Purchasers have an opportunity to share in the growth of the firm as holders of common equity.

2)   One can **distinguish between warrants and rights** because a warrant is sometimes defined as an option having a relatively long exercise period and an exercise price greater than the market price at the time of its issuance. A right is an option with a relatively brief exercise period and an exercise price lower than the market price at the time of its issuance.

3)   Most warrants issued with other securities are **detachable**. Thus, they trade separately. When the warrant is in the money (market price exceeds the exercise price), exercise is likely when the warrants are about to expire, dividends on common stock are attractive, or the exercise price is about to increase. Absent these factors, the warrants would not be exercised. Their value on the market would be greater than their value when exercised.

4)   A virtue of warrants is that they normally generate funds when the firm is successful and most in need of new equity. A disadvantage of warrants is that exercise results in issuance of new equity and a dilution of the holdings of current shareholders.

5)   Warrants should be distinguished from the call options and put options traded in the markets that were not written by the issuer of the common stock.

e.   A stock's **par value** represents legal capital. It is an arbitrary value assigned to stock before the stock is issued. It also represents the maximum liability of a shareholder.

4.   **Preferred stock** is a hybrid of debt and equity. It has a fixed charge and increases leverage, but payment of dividends is not a legal obligation.

a.   **Advantages of Preferred Stock to the Issuer**

1)   It is a form of equity and therefore builds the creditworthiness of the firm.

2)   Control is still held by common shareholders.

3)   Superior earnings of the firm are usually still reserved for the common shareholders.

b. **Disadvantages of Preferred Stock to the Issuer**

1) Preferred stock cash dividends paid are not tax deductible. The result is a substantially greater cost relative to bonds because there is not a tax shield.

2) In periods of economic difficulty, accumulated (past) dividends may create major managerial and financial problems for the firm.

c. **Typical Provisions of Preferred Stock Issues**

1) **Par value.** Par value is the liquidation value, and a percentage of par equals the preferred dividend.

2) **Priority** in assets and earnings. If the firm goes bankrupt, the preferred shareholders have priority over common shareholders.

3) **Accumulation of dividends.** If preferred dividends in arrears are cumulative, they must be paid before any common dividends can be paid.

4) **Convertibility.** Preferred stock issues may be convertible into common stock at the option of the shareholder.

5) **Participation.** Preferred stock may participate with common in excess earnings of the firm. For example, 8% participating preferred stock might pay a dividend each year greater than 8% when the corporation is extremely profitable. But nonparticipating preferred receives no more than the stated rate.

6) **Redeemability.** Some preferred stock may be redeemed at a given time or at the option of the holder or otherwise at a time not controlled by the issuer. This feature makes preferred stock more nearly akin to debt, particularly in the case of **transient preferred stock**, which must be redeemed within a short time (e.g., 5 to 10 years). The SEC requires a separate presentation of redeemable preferred, nonredeemable preferred, and common stock.

7) **Voting rights.** These may be conferred if preferred dividends are in arrears for a stated period.

8) **Callability.** The issuer may have the right to repurchase the stock. For example, the stock may be noncallable for a stated period, after which it may be called if the issuer pays a call premium (an amount exceeding par value).

9) **Maturity.** Preferred stock may have a sinking fund that allows for the purchase of a given annual percentage of the outstanding shares.

d. Investing in preferred stock rather than bonds provides corporations a tax advantage because of the **dividends received deduction**. At least 70% of the dividends received from preferred stock may be tax deductible, but all bond interest received is taxable.

1) The dividends received deduction also applies to common stock.

2) Because of the tax advantage, nonconvertible preferred stock is held almost entirely by corporations. Individuals can earn higher yields at lower risk by purchasing bonds.

5. **Bonds** are long-term debt instruments. They are similar to term loans except that they are usually offered to the public and sold to many investors.

a. **Advantages of Bonds to the Issuer**

1) Basic control of the firm is not shared with the debtholder.

2) Cost of debt is limited. Bondholders usually do not participate in the superior earnings of the firm.

3) Ordinarily, the expected yield of bonds is lower than the cost of stock.

4) Interest paid on debt is tax deductible.

5) Debt may add substantial flexibility in the financial structure of the corporation through the use of call provisions.

b.   **Disadvantages of Bonds to the Issuer**

1)   Debt has a fixed charge. If the earnings of the firm fluctuate, the risk of insolvency is increased by the fixed interest obligation.

2)   Debt adds risk to a firm. Shareholders will consequently demand higher capitalization rates on equity earnings, which may result in a decline in the market price of stock.

3)   Debt usually has a maturity date.

4)   Debt is a long-term commitment, a factor that can affect risk profiles. Debt originally appearing to be profitable may become a burden and drive the firm into bankruptcy.

5)   Certain managerial prerogatives are usually surrendered in the contractual relationship defined in the bond indenture. For example, specific ratios may have to remain above a certain level during the term of the loan.

6)   The amount of debt financing available to the individual firm is limited. Generally accepted standards of the investment community will usually dictate a certain debt-equity ratio for a firm. Beyond this limit, the cost of debt may rise rapidly, or debt financing may not be available.

7)   Loan covenants sometimes include an **acceleration clause** that allows the lender to demand early payment of the entire balance or additional collateral under certain circumstances, such as failure to make timely payments, filing for bankruptcy, or not maintaining key ratios at a certain level.

c.   Interest paid on bonds is calculated as follows: face amount × stated interest rate

1)   Compound interest in any year may be found using the following formula: $P = C (1 + r)^t$.

2)   P is the future amount, C is the initial investment, r is the interest rate, and t is the number of years invested.

d.   The **bond indenture** is the contractual arrangement between the issuer and the bondholders. It contains restrictive covenants intended to prevent the issuer from taking actions contrary to the interests of the bondholders. A trustee, often a bank, is appointed to ensure compliance.

1)   **Call provisions** give the corporation the right to redeem bonds. If interest rates decline, the company can call high-interest bonds and replace them with low-interest bonds.

2)   Bonds are **putable** or redeemable if the holder has the right to exchange them for cash. This option is usually not activated unless the issuer takes a stated action, for example, greatly increasing its debt or being acquired by another entity.

3)   **Sinking fund** requirements provide for the firm to retire a certain portion of its bonds each year or to set aside money for repayment in the future. Such terms increase the probability of repayment for bondholders but require the use of capital by the firm.

4)   The issuer may be required to maintain its financial ratios, e.g., times-interest-earned, at specified levels.

5)   Dividends may be limited if earnings do not meet specified requirements.

6)   The amount of new bonds issued may be restricted to a percentage of bondable property (fixed assets).

7)   Bonds may be issued at a premium or discount, depending upon whether they are issued for more than their face amount (premium) or less (discount).

e. **Types of Bonds**

1) Securitization

a) **Mortgage bonds** are backed by specific assets, usually real estate.

b) **Debentures** are backed by the borrower's general credit, not by specific collateral.

c) **Collateral trust bonds** are backed by specific securities.

d) **Guaranty bonds** are guaranteed by a third party, e.g., the parent firm of the issuer.

2) Maturity Pattern

a) A **term bond** has a single maturity date at the end of its term.

b) A **serial bond** matures in stated amounts at regular intervals.

3) Ownership

a) **Registered bonds** are issued in the name of the owner. Interest payments are sent directly to the owner. When the owner sells registered bonds, the bond certificates must be surrendered and new certificates issued.

b) **Bearer bonds**, also called coupon bonds, are bearer instruments. Whoever presents the periodic interest coupons is entitled to payment.

4) Priority

a) **Subordinated debentures** and **second mortgage bonds** are junior securities with claims inferior to those of senior bonds.

5) Repayment Provisions

a) **Income bonds** pay interest contingent on the debtor's profitability.

b) Some bond indentures require the issuer to establish a **sinking fund** (a long-term investment) to set aside assets for the repayment of interest and principal. The amounts transferred plus the revenue earned on the investments provide the necessary funds.

c) **Revenue bonds** are issued by governmental units and are payable from specific revenue sources.

d) **Participating bonds** share in excess earnings of the debtor as defined in the bond indenture.

e) **Indexed bonds** (purchasing power bonds) pay interest that is indexed to a measure of general purchasing power, such as the Consumer Price Index.

6) Valuation

a) **Variable rate bonds** pay interest that is dependent on market conditions.

b) **Zero-coupon bonds** pay no interest but sell at a deep discount.

i) The need to reinvest the periodic payments from normal bonds makes their final return uncertain because future reinvestment rates are uncertain. But investors know the exact return on a zero-coupon bond. Investors might therefore be willing to pay a premium (an amount greater than the maturity amount discounted at the market rate) for them, which in turn might lead firms to issue them.

ii) The lack of interest payments means the firm faces no additional insolvency risk from the issue until it matures.

        c) **Commodity-backed bonds** are payable at prices related to a commodity such as gold.

        d) **High-yield bonds**, also called non-investment grade bonds or junk bonds, are issued to finance leveraged buyouts and mergers. Their high yields are commensurate with their high degree of risk. They also are issued by troubled firms. They exploit the large tax deductions for interest paid by entities with high debt ratios.

    7) Redemption Provisions

        a) **Callable bonds** may be repurchased by the issuer before maturity.

        b) **Redeemable bonds** may be presented for payment by the creditor prior to the maturity date. The bonds usually are redeemable only after a specified period.

        c) **Convertible bonds** may be converted into equity securities of the issuer at the option of the holder (buyer) under the conditions specified in the bond indenture.

    8) International Bonds

        a) **Foreign bonds** are denominated in the currency of the nation in which they are sold.

        b) **Eurobonds** are denominated in a currency other than that of the nation where they are sold.

           i) Foreign bonds issued in the United States and denominated in dollars must be registered with the SEC, but such extensive disclosure is not required in most European nations. Thus, an American firm may elect to issue Eurobonds denominated in dollars in a foreign nation because of the convenience of not having to comply with registration requirements.

  f. **Bond ratings** play a role in bond yields. The correlation between the bond rating (based on risk) and the interest rate that is attractive to an investor tends to be inverse. A high rating (low risk) will lead to a lower interest rate.

    1) The two largest bond rating agencies are Standard and Poor's and Moody's.

    2) **Investment-grade bonds** are the safest and receive the highest ratings. Some fiduciary organizations (such as banks and insurance companies) are only allowed to invest in investment-grade bonds.

    3) **Speculative-grade bonds** are riskier than investment-grade bonds.

    4) The bond rating agencies base their evaluations on the profitability of the issuing corporation, stability of the industry, competitive position, and the usual financial ratios.

6. **American depository receipts (ADRs)** are ownership rights in foreign corporations.

  a. Foreign stocks are deposited with a large U.S. bank, which in turn issues ADRs representing ownership in the foreign shares. The ADR shares then trade on a U.S. stock exchange, and the firm's original shares trade on a foreign stock market.

  b. ADRs permit foreign firms to increase their development of a U.S. shareholder base.

  c. Foreign firms want to participate in the U.S. equity market for a number of reasons, including a desire to increase liquidity of stocks and to raise equity capital without putting pressure on the stock price in the home market.

7. **Dividend reinvestment plans (DRPs).** Any dividends due to shareholders are automatically reinvested in shares of the same corporation's common stock. Broker's fees on such purchases of stock are either zero (the costs absorbed by the corporation) or only a few cents per shareholder because only one purchase is made and the total fee is divided among all shareholders participating.

8. **Intermediate-term financing** involves debt issues with approximate maturities of greater than 1 but fewer than 10 years. The principal types of intermediate-term financing are term loans and lease financing. Major lenders under term agreements are commercial banks, life insurance companies, and, to some extent, pension funds.

    a. **Term loans.** One possible feature of a term loan is tying the interest payable to a variable rate. This **floating rate**, usually stated as some percentage over the prime, may result in extremely high borrowing costs.

        1) This risk must be traded off against

            a) The need of the firm to obtain the loan
            b) The flexibility inherent in term borrowing
            c) The ability of the firm to borrow in the capital market
            d) Other available types of debt financing
            e) The amount of privacy desired

                i) Term loans are private contracts between private firms, but long-term debt securities usually involve the SEC and massive disclosure.

        2) Variable or floating rate loans are advantageous to lenders because they permit better matching of interest costs and revenues. The market values of these loans also tend to be more stable than those for fixed rate loans.

            a) The disadvantages include a heightened risk of default, losses of expected revenues if interest rates decline or if market rates rise above the ceiling specified in the agreement, and the difficulty of working with a more complex product.

    b. **Lease financing** must be analyzed by comparing the cost of owning to the cost of leasing. Leasing has become a major means of financing because it offers a variety of tax and other benefits. If leases are not accounted for as installment purchases, they provide off-balance-sheet financing. Thus, under an operating lease, the lessee need not record an asset or a liability, and rent expense rather than interest is recognized. The following are three principal forms of leases:

        1) A **sale-leaseback** is a financing method. A firm seeking financing sells an asset to an investor (creditor) and leases the asset back, usually on a noncancelable lease. The lease payments consist of principal and interest paid by the lessee to the lessor.

        2) **Operating leases** usually provide for financing and maintenance services.

        3) **Capital leases (or financial leases)**, which do not provide for maintenance services, are noncancelable and fully amortize the cost of the leased asset over the term of the basic lease contract; i.e., they are installment purchases.

9. **Maturity matching** (equalizing the life of an asset acquired with the debt instrument used to finance it) is an important factor in choosing the source of funds. Financing long-term assets with long-term debt allows the firm to generate sufficient cash flows from the assets to satisfy obligations as they mature.

$P = C(1+i)^t$

10. **Initial public offerings (IPOs).** A firm's first issuance of securities to the public is an IPO. The process by which a closely held corporation issues new securities to the public is called **going public**. When a firm goes public, it issues its securities on a **new issue** or **IPO market** (a primary market).

   a. **Advantages of Going Public**

   1) The ability to raise additional funds
   2) The establishment of the firm's value in the market
   3) An increase in the liquidity of the firm's stock

   b. **Disadvantages of Going Public**

   1) Costs of the reporting requirements of the SEC and other agencies
   2) Access to the firm's operating data by competing firms
   3) Access to net worth information of major shareholders
   4) Limitations on self-dealing by corporate insiders
   5) Pressure from outside shareholders for earnings growth
   6) Stock prices that do not accurately reflect the true net worth of the firm
   7) Loss of control by management as ownership is diversified
   8) Need for improved management control as operations expand
   9) Increased shareholder servicing costs

   c. To have its stock listed (have it traded on a stock exchange), the firm must apply to a stock exchange, pay a fee, and fulfill the exchange's requirements for membership. Included in the requirements for membership is disclosure of the firm's financial data.

   d. The firm's next step is to prepare and file an SEC registration statement and prospectus, unless an exemption is available.

   1) A **registration statement** is a complete disclosure to the SEC of all material information with respect to the issuance of the specific securities.

   2) A **prospectus** must be furnished to any interested investor. Its purpose is to supply sufficient facts to make an informed investment decision. The prospectus contains material information (financial and otherwise) with respect to the offering and the issuer.

   3) The entire allotment of securities ordinarily is made available for purchase on the effective date of the registration statement.

   e. In an IPO, the value of a stock is determined by an underwriter on the basis of a number of factors, including general market conditions, book value of the stock, earning potential of the firm, and the P-E ratios of competing firms. Nevertheless, such arbitrary assignments of value are rarely accurate, and a major change in stock price often occurs in the week of the IPO.

11. Stop and review! You have completed the outline for this subunit. Study multiple-choice questions 1 through 12 beginning on page 281.

9.2 OPTIMAL CAPITALIZATION AND COST OF CAPITAL

1. The **financial structure** of a firm encompasses the right-hand side of the balance sheet, which describes how the firm's assets are financed.

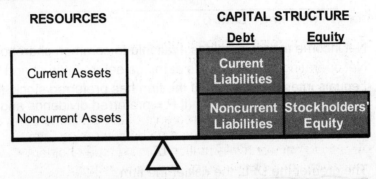

2. Capital structure is the **permanent financing** of the firm and is represented primarily by

   a. **Long-term debt**, which is the creditor interest in the firm.

      1) The firm is contractually obligated to repay debtholders. The terms of repayment (i.e., timing of interest and principal) are specified in the debt agreement.

      2) As long as the return on debt capital exceeds the amount of interest paid, the use of debt financing is advantageous to a firm. This is due to the fact that interest payments on debt are tax-deductible.

      3) Most firms renew (roll over) their long-term obligations. Thus, long-term debt is often effectively permanent.

   b. **Preferred Stock**
   c. **Common Equity**

      1) Common stock
      2) Additional paid-in capital
      3) Retained earnings

3. The following factors influence financial structure:

   a. Growth rate and stability of future sales
   b. Competitive structures in the industry
   c. Asset makeup of the individual firm
   d. Attitude of owners and management toward risk
   e. Control position of owners and management
   f. Lenders' attitudes toward the industry and a particular firm
   g. Tax considerations

4. **Leverage** is the attempt of the firm to borrow money at a stated rate with the intent to provide a greater return on the funds than the cost of borrowing them. This allows the firm's potential returns (positive and negative) to be magnified. Traditionally, firms with significant debt (i.e., leverage) enjoy higher returns on equity.

   a. Leverage, by definition, **creates financial risk**, which relates directly to the question of the cost of capital. The more leverage, the higher the financial risk, and the higher the cost of debt capital.

   b. **Earnings per share** will ordinarily be higher if debt is used to raise capital instead of equity, provided that the firm is not over-leveraged. The reason is that the cost of debt is lower than the cost of equity because interest is tax deductible. However, the prospect of higher EPS is accompanied by greater risk to the firm resulting from required interest costs, creditors' liens on the firm's assets, and the possibility of a proportionately lower EPS if sales volume fails to meet projections.

c.   The **degree of financial leverage (DFL)** is the percentage change in earnings available to common shareholders that is associated with a given percentage change in net operating income.

d.
$$DFL = \frac{\% \; \Delta \; in \; net \; income}{\% \; \Delta \; in \; net \; operating \; income} = \frac{EBIT}{EBIT \; - \; I}$$

1)   Net income means earnings available to common shareholders.

2)   Net operating income equals earnings before interest and taxes (EBIT).

3)   I equals interest expense. If the firm has preferred stock, the second formula is further modified as follows (if P = preferred dividends and T is the tax rate):

$$\frac{EBIT}{EBIT \; - \; I \; - \; [P \div (1 \; - \; T)]}$$

4)   The greater the DFL, the riskier the firm.

e.   If the return on assets exceeds the cost of debt, additional leverage is favorable.

5.   **Operating leverage** concerns the extent to which fixed costs are used in the production process. A firm with a high percentage of fixed costs is more risky than a firm in the same industry that relies more heavily on variable production costs.

a.   The **degree of operating leverage (DOL)** is the change in net operating income (EBIT) resulting from a percentage change in revenues. It measures the extent to which a firm incurs fixed rather than variable costs in operations. Thus, the greater the DOL, the greater the risk of loss when revenues decline and the greater the reward when revenues increase.

1)
$$Operating \; leverage = \frac{\% \; \Delta \; in \; net \; operating \; income}{\% \; \Delta \; in \; revenues}$$

2)   The assumption is that firms with larger investments (and greater fixed costs) will have higher contribution margins and more operating leverage. Thus, as they invest in better and more expensive equipment, their variable production costs should decrease.

a)   EXAMPLE: If revenues increase by 40% and net operating income increases by 50%, the DOL is 1.25 (50% ÷ 40%).

3)   If Q equals the number of units sold, P is unit price, V is unit variable cost, and F is fixed cost, the DOL also can be calculated by dividing total contribution margin by net operating income (total contribution margin – fixed cost). This formula is derived from the formula above, but the derivation is not given.

$$\frac{Q(P \; - \; V)}{Q(P \; - \; V) \; - \; F} = \frac{Total \; contribution \; margin \; (TCM)}{Net \; operating \; income}$$

4)   The DOL is calculated with respect to a given **base level of revenues**. The significance of the DOL is that a given percentage increase in revenues yields a percentage increase in net operating income equal to the DOL for the base revenues level times the percentage increase in revenues.

b.   The **degree of total leverage (DTL)** combines the DFL and the DOL. It equals the degree of financial leverage times the degree of operating leverage. Thus, it also equals the percentage change in net income that is associated with a given percentage change in revenues.

1)

$$DTL = DFL \times DOL = \frac{\% \; \Delta \; in \; net \; income}{\% \; \Delta \; in \; net \; operating \; income} \times \frac{\% \; \Delta \; in \; net \; operating \; income}{\% \; \Delta \; in \; revenues}$$

$$= \frac{\% \; \Delta \; in \; net \; income}{\% \; \Delta \; in \; revenues}$$

    a)   EXAMPLE: If net income increases 15% with a 5% increase in revenues, DTL is 3.0.

2)   Firms with a high degree of operating leverage do not usually employ a high degree of financial leverage and vice versa. One of the most important considerations in the use of financial leverage is operating leverage.

    a)   EXAMPLE: A firm has a highly automated production process. Because of automation, the degree of operating leverage is 2. If the firm wants a degree of total leverage not exceeding 3, it must restrict its use of debt so that the degree of financial leverage is not more than 1.5. If the firm had committed to a production process that was less automated and had a lower DOL, more debt could be employed, and the firm could have a higher degree of financial leverage.

6.   A firm's **cost of capital** is the price, in both dollar terms and opportunity cost, of raising funds.

    a.   Managers must know the firm's cost of capital when making investment (long-term funding) decisions because investments with a return higher than the cost of capital will increase the value of the firm (shareholders' wealth).

    b.   The theory underlying the cost of capital applies to new, long-term funding because long-term funds finance **long-term investments**. Long-term investment decisions are typically made using the cost of capital to discount future cash flows.

        1)   Working capital and other temporary needs are met with short-term funds. Thus, cost of capital is of less concern for short-term funding.

7.   The **weighted-average cost of capital (WACC)** weights the cost of each debt and equity component by the percentage of that component in the financial structure.

    a.   The **cost of debt** is the after-tax interest rate of the debt.

$$Interest \; rate \times (1 - Marginal \; tax \; rate)$$

        1)   The after-tax rate is used because interest paid is a tax deduction to the firm. Hence, as tax rates go up, debt becomes a more attractive financing option.

    b.   The **cost of preferred stock** includes flotation costs necessary to offer the stock to the investing public.

$$Dividend \; per \; share \div Net \; issuance \; cost \; per \; share$$

        1)   Because preferred dividends paid are not deductible by the firm, the tax rate is not taken into account.

    c.   The **cost of new external common equity** factors in the return that potential shareholders expect. It is higher than the cost of retained earnings because of stock flotation costs.

> *Dollar return demanded by investors ÷ Net issuance cost per share*

        1)   An issue of new common stock is used mostly by young, growing companies. Mature firms rarely issue new common stock to the general public because of the issue costs involved and the depressing influence a new issue can have on the stock's price.

    d.   The **cost of retained earnings** is an opportunity cost, i.e., the rate that investors can earn elsewhere on investments of comparable risk.

        1)   If the firm is not able to generate a shareholder's required rate of return, the retained earnings should be paid out in the form of dividends so that the shareholders can find their own, higher-return investments.

    e.   **Providers of equity capital** are exposed to **more risk** than are lenders because the firm is not obligated to pay them a return. Also, in case of liquidation, equity investors trail creditors in priority.

        1)   Thus, **equity financing is more expensive than debt** because equity investors require a higher return to compensate for the greater risk assumed.

    f.   EXAMPLE: Note that short-term debt is not part of a firm's capital structure.

Component	(1) Carrying Amount	(2) Interest or Dividend Rate	(3) After-Tax Rate or Expected Return	(4) Market Value	(5) Weight (Proportion of Total Market Value)	(3) × (5) Weighted-Average Cost of Capital
Bonds Payable	$ 2,000,000	8.5%	7.4%	$ 2,200,000	0.1000	0.7400%
Preferred Stock	4,000,000	14.0%	10.0%	4,600,000	0.2091	2.0909%
Common Stock	12,000,000		16.0%	14,000,000	0.6364	10.1818%
Retained Earnings	1,200,000		16.0%	1,200,000	0.0545	0.8727%
Totals	$19,200,000			$22,000,000	1.0000	13.8855%

8.   Standard financial theory provides a model for the **optimal capital structure** of every firm. This model holds that shareholder wealth-maximization results from **minimizing the weighted-average cost of capital**.

    a.   Thus, the focus of management should **not** be on **maximizing earnings per share**. EPS can be increased by taking on debt, but debt increases risk.

        1)   The optimal capital structure usually involves some debt but not 100% debt.

    b.   The relevant relationships are depicted below:

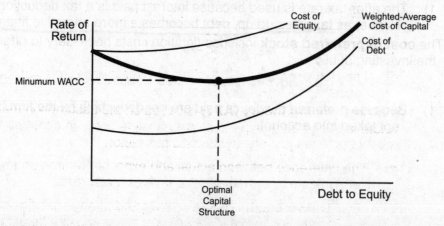

    c.   Ordinarily, firms cannot identify this optimal point precisely. Thus, they should attempt to find an optimal range for the capital structure.

d. The **required rate of return on equity capital (R)** can be estimated as follows:

1) The **capital asset pricing model (CAPM)** adds the risk-free rate (determined by government securities) to the product of the beta coefficient (a measure of the firm's risk) and the difference between the market return and the risk-free rate. Below is the basic equilibrium equation for the CAPM.

$$R = R_F + \beta(R_M - R_F)$$

a) The **market risk premium** ($R_M - R_F$) is the amount above the risk-free rate required to induce average investors to enter the market.

b) The **beta coefficient (β)** of an individual stock is the correlation between the volatility (price variation) of the stock market and the volatility of the price of the individual stock.

   i) EXAMPLE: If an individual stock rises 10% and the stock market 10%, the beta coefficient is 1.0. If the stock rises 15% and the market only 10%, beta is 1.5.

   ii) The CAPM is a model that uses just one systematic risk factor to explain the asset's return. That factor is the expected return on the market portfolio, i.e., the market-valued weighted average return for all securities available in the market.

$.12 + 1.2(.17 - .12)$

c) EXAMPLE: Assuming a beta of 1.20, a market rate of return of approximately 17%, and an expected risk-free rate of 12%, the required rate of return on equity capital is .12 + 1.20 (.17 − .12), or 18%.

d) The graph of this equation (with interest rates plotted on the vertical axis and betas on the horizontal axis) is the **security market line (SML)**. The slope of the SML equals the market risk premium, and the y-intercept is the risk-free rate.

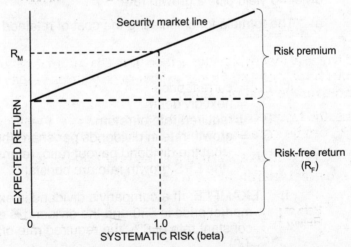

e) The **risk premium** is the difference in expected rates of return on a risky asset and a less risky asset.

2) **Arbitrage pricing theory (APT)** is based on the assumption that an asset's return is based on multiple systematic risk factors. In contrast, the CAPM is a model that uses just one systematic risk factor.

a) The difference between actual and expected returns on an asset is attributable to systematic and unsystematic risks.

   i) **Unsystematic risk** (also called company-specific risk or diversifiable risk) is specific to a particular asset and can be eliminated by sufficient diversification.

        ii)   However, **systematic risk** (also called market risk or nondiversifiable risk) affects many assets and is undiversifiable.

        iii)   Thus, investors must be paid a risk premium to compensate them for systematic (market) risk.

  b)   Accordingly, APT provides for a separate beta and a separate risk premium for each systematic risk factor identified in the model. Examples of the many potential systematic risk factors are the gross domestic product (GDP), inflation, and real interest rates. The APT for a three-factor model may be formulated as follows:

$$R = R_F + \beta_1 k_1 + \beta_2 k_2 + \beta_3 k_3$$

If: R = expected rate of return
        R_F = risk-free rate
        $\beta_{1,2,3}$ = individual factor beta coefficients
        $k_{1,2,3}$ = individual factor risk premiums

  c)   EXAMPLE: Assume R_F = 9% and

        k_1 = 2% β_1 = .6
        k_2 = 5% β_2 = .4
        k_3 = 8% β_3 = .2

Applying the above values, the expected rate of return is .09 + (.6)(.02) + (.4)(.05) + (.2)(.08), or 13.8%.

 3)   R also may be estimated by adding a percentage to the firm's long-term cost of debt. A 3% to 5% premium is frequently used.

 4)   The **dividend growth model** estimates the cost of retained earnings using the dividends per share, the expected growth rate, and the market price. To justify retention of earnings, management must expect a return at least equal to the dividend yield plus a growth rate.

  a)   The formula for calculating the cost of retained earnings is

$$R = \frac{D_1}{P_0} + G$$

If: P_0 = current price
    D_1 = next dividend
    R = required rate of return
    G = growth rate in dividends per share (but the model assumes that the dividend payout ratio, retention rate, and therefore the EPS growth rate are constant)

        i)   EXAMPLE: If a company's dividend is expected to be $4 while the market price is $50 and the dividend is expected to grow at a constant rate of 6%, the required rate of return is 14% ($4 ÷ $50 + .06).

  b)   To determine the **cost of new common stock** (external equity), the model is altered to incorporate the flotation cost. As the **flotation cost** rises, R increases accordingly.

$$R = \frac{D_1}{P_0(1 - Flotation\ cost)} + G$$

c) The dividend growth model is also used for **stock price evaluation**. The formula can be restated in terms of P_0 as follows:

$$P_0 = \frac{D_1}{R - G}$$

d) The stock price is affected by the **dividend payout ratio** because some investors may want capital gains, but others may prefer current income. Thus, investors will choose stocks that give the proper mix of capital gains and dividends.

e. A firm cannot continue to raise unlimited amounts of new funds at its historical cost of capital. At some point, the costs of servicing new sources of funding will increase a firm's cost of capital.

1) The **marginal cost of capital (MCC)** is the cost to a firm of the next dollar of new capital raised.

2) EXAMPLE: The company depicted in the schedule in item 2.f. on page 264 has determined that it requires $2,000,000 of new funding to fulfill its plans.

a) The simplest source of new funding is retained earnings, but they are insufficient. The additional $800,000 will have to come from another source.

i) If the company issues new bonds, the firm's debt-to-equity ratio will be increased, revealing the company to be a riskier investment, forcing a higher interest rate than the one on the currently outstanding bonds.

ii) If the company issues new preferred stock, the investors will demand a priority dividend.

iii) If the company issues new preferred or common stock, issue costs will be involved.

b) Clearly, the company's cost of capital will be its current marginal rate of 13.8855% for the $1,200,000 of retained earnings, but will shift to a higher marginal rate for the next dollar after that.

3) This phenomenon can be depicted as follows:

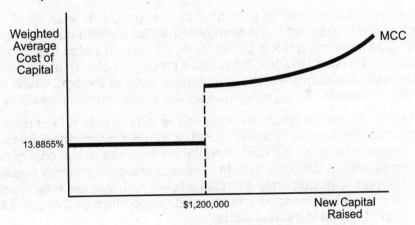

4)   The **marginal efficiency of investment** is the decrease in return on additional dollars of capital investment because the most profitable investments are made initially.

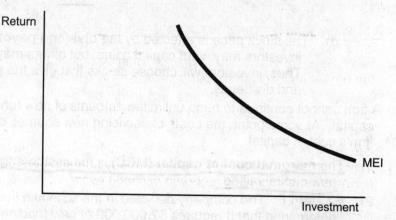

a)   Combining the MCC and MEI curves highlights the equilibrium investment level for the firm (Q*) at a particular interest rate (I) and given capital budget.

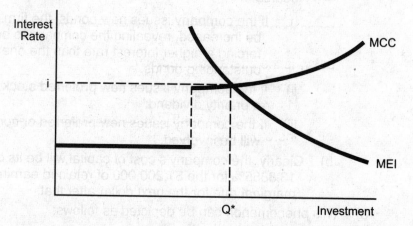

9.   The foregoing outline describes the traditional approach to analysis of capital structure. A contrary view is asserted in the **Modigliani-Miller Hypothesis**, a proposition largely responsible for winning Nobel prizes for its authors. It states that, in an efficient capital market with no tax distortions, the relative proportion of debt and equity in a corporate capitalization does not affect the total market value of the firm, which is dependent on its profitability and risk. Thus, no unique capital structure maximizes firm value.

a.   In a world with no taxes, leverage raises the required rate of return on equity by increasing the risk of equity. In other words, the weighted average cost of capital is constant because the cost of equity will increase as the cost of debt decreases. The implication is that issuing debt is not advantageous merely because its cost is low. Nevertheless, corporate financial officers and financial engineers continue to search for market inefficiencies and tax-related opportunities that can lower a corporation's cost of capital in the real world.

b.   Dividends play no role in the Modigliani-Miller analysis because the cost of capital is the same regardless of the source.

c.   The hypothesis also assumes that there are no transaction costs for selling equity or debt securities.

10.   Stop and review! You have completed the outline for this subunit. Study multiple-choice questions 13 through 28 beginning on page 285.

9.3 DIVIDEND POLICY

1. **Dividend policy** determines what portion of a corporation's net income is distributed to shareholders and what portion is retained for reinvestment.

   a. A high dividend rate means a slower rate of growth, and a high growth rate usually means a low dividend rate. A growing company keeps its profits for reinvestment in fixed assets or R&D. Therefore, growing companies pay small dividends if any. On the other hand, a high dividend correlates to a stable cash cow company.

   b. Because both a high growth rate and a high dividend rate may be desirable, the financial manager attempts to determine the balance of dividend and growth rates that maximizes the price of the firm's shares.

   c. Normally, corporations try to maintain a stable level of dividends, even though profits may fluctuate considerably, because many shareholders buy stock with the expectation of receiving a certain dividend every year. Hence, management tends not to raise dividends if the payout cannot be sustained. For example, a firm with fluctuating earnings might pay out $1 every year whether earnings per share are $10 (10% payout rate) or $1 (100% payout rate).

      1) The tendency toward stability is the basis for the **information content or signaling hypothesis**: A change in dividend policy is a signal to the market regarding management's forecast of future earnings. The firm's stock price tends to increase (decrease) if dividends are unexpectedly high (low).

      2) Another possible reason for changes in stock prices after changes in dividend policy is the **clientele effect**.

         a) Some shareholders, e.g., retired people, desire immediate income. However, other shareholders, e.g., those in the highest tax bracket, may prefer a low payout. These shareholders may not need income and therefore favor capital gains, which may be taxed at a lower rate and are deferred until shares are sold. Furthermore, taxes may be avoided altogether by the beneficiaries if the shareholder dies.

         b) In accordance with the clientele effect, a firm attracts investors that prefer its dividend policy. Changes in that policy are likely to cause investor switching due to market inefficiencies (brokers' fees, capital gains taxes).

   d. No theoretical agreement exists concerning the optimal dividend policy.

      1) Some theorists argue that capital gains are riskier than dividends and that a high dividend payout will maximize the stock price.

      2) A second position is that a low dividend payout is preferable for tax reasons.

      3) Still another position is that dividend policy is irrelevant to the firm's valuation. According to this view, espoused by Modigliani and Miller, the value of the firm is determined solely by its earning capacity and its risk. Whether earnings are paid out or retained is not important because most investors reinvest their dividends in the same or similar companies. Moreover, risk is a function of the firm's future cash flows, not its dividend payout.

2. Other factors influence a company's dividend policy.

   a. **Legal restrictions.** Dividends ordinarily cannot be paid out of paid-in capital. A corporation must have a credit balance in its retained earnings account.

   b. **Rate of growth.** A firm with a faster growth rate will have a greater need to finance that growth with retained earnings. Thus, fast-growing firms usually have lower dividend payout ratios. Shareholders hope for large future capital gains.

   c. **Cash position.** Regardless of a firm's earnings record, cash must be available before a dividend can be paid. No dividend can be declared if all of a firm's earnings are tied up in receivables and inventories.

    d.   **Restrictions in debt agreements.** Bond indentures and other debt agreements often place restrictions on the amount of dividends that a firm can declare.

    e.   **Accumulated earnings tax.** An accumulated earnings tax is assessed on a corporation if it has accumulated retained earnings beyond its reasonably expected needs. Thus, tax law indirectly penalizes shareholders who postpone paying taxes because of low dividend payouts.

    f.   Under the residual theory of dividends, the amount (residual) of earnings paid as dividends depends on the available investment opportunities and the debt-equity at which cost of capital is minimized.

3. **Important dates concerning dividends**

    a.   The **date of declaration** is the date the directors meet and formally vote to declare a dividend. On this date, the dividend becomes a liability of the corporation.

    b.   The **date of record** is the date as of which the corporation determines the shareholders who will receive the declared dividend. Essentially, the corporation closes its shareholder records on this date. Only those shareholders who own the stock on the date of record will receive the dividend. It typically falls from 2 to 6 weeks after the declaration date.

    c.   The **date of payment** is the date on which the dividend is actually paid (when the checks are sent to the investors). The payment date is usually from 2 to 4 weeks after the date of record.

    d.   The **ex-dividend date** is a date established by the stock exchanges, such as 4 business days before the date of record, because it takes three days to settle the transaction. The period between the ex-dividend date and the date of record gives the stock exchange members time to process any transactions, which is the settlement. Unlike the other dates, it is not established by the corporate board of directors.

        1)   An investor who buys a share of stock before the ex-dividend date will receive the dividend that has been previously declared.

        2)   An investor who buys the stock after the ex-dividend date (but before the date of record or payment date) will not receive the declared dividend. Instead, the individual who sold the stock will receive the dividend because (s)he owned it on the ex-dividend date.

        3)   Usually, a stock price will drop on the ex-dividend date by the amount of the dividend because the new investor will not receive it.

4. **Stock dividends and stock splits** involve issuance of additional shares to existing shareholders. Shareholders receive no actual increase in the value of their holdings. The previous holdings are simply divided into more pieces (additional shares).

    a.   A **stock dividend** is an issuance of stock and entails the transfer of a sum from the retained earnings account to a paid-in capital account.

        1)   Casual investors may believe they are receiving something of value when in essence their previous holdings are merely being divided across more shares.

        2)   Stock dividends are often used by growing companies that wish to retain earnings in the business while placating shareholders.

    b.   A **stock split** does not involve any accounting entries. Instead, the existing shares are divided into more pieces so that the market price per share will be reduced.

        1)   EXAMPLE: If a corporation has 1 million shares outstanding, each of which sells for $90, a 2-for-1 stock split will result in 2 million shares outstanding, each of which sells for $45.

        2)   **Reverse stock splits** are the exact opposite. They reduce the shares outstanding and increase the price per share.

    c.   **Advantages of issuing stock splits and dividends**

        1)   Because more shares will be outstanding, the price per share will be lower, and more small investors may purchase the company's stock. Thus, because demand for the stock is greater, the price may increase. However, EPS and book value per share will be lower.

            a)   EXAMPLE: In the previous example, the additional investors interested in the company at the lower price may drive the price up to $46 or $47, or slightly higher than the theoretical price of $45. Hence, current shareholders may benefit from the split (or dividend) after all.

        2)   A dividend or split can be a publicity gesture. Because shareholders may believe they are receiving value (and perhaps indirectly they are), they will have a better opinion of their company.

        3)   If more shares are outstanding, the number of shareholders who are usually good customers for their own firm's products will be larger.

5.   **Treasury stock** is stock that a corporation has issued and reacquired. It is usually purchased on the open market at the current market price. The effect is to distribute retained earnings to shareholders. Regular repurchases are therefore a substitute for cash dividends.

    a.   A corporation repurchases its stock to

        1)   Meet employee stock option and bonus plan requirements

        2)   Buy out a shareholder when the stock cannot be sold on the open market or when the sale would adversely affect the market price

        3)   Support the market for the stock

        4)   Reduce the size of the business

        5)   Acquire stock needed to undertake a merger

        6)   Decrease the number of shares outstanding in hopes of increasing EPS

        7)   Increase the book value per share of the remaining shares outstanding

            a)   The market value must be less than the book value.

        8)   Hold the shares until the market rises, at which time the stock will be resold

            a)   Management treats the treasury stock as an investment in the belief that the stock is undervalued.

        9)   Provide a quick and simple means of adjusting a firm's capital structure or its financial leverage

            a)   A repurchase of shares using debt financing is an even more dramatic way of quickly changing the relationship between debt and equity.

    b.   An advantage of buying treasury stock is that it decreases the likelihood of the firm's acquisition by another corporation because fewer shares are outstanding. Additionally, a treasury stock purchase can thwart a hostile takeover. If the price is above market, this practice is known as "paying greenmail."

    c.   Disadvantages of buying treasury stock include

        1)   A higher debt-equity ratio and increased financial leverage, which may increase the difficulty of obtaining loans.

        2)   Liquidity problems because cash is being paid out to shareholders.

6.   Stop and review! You have completed the outline for this subunit. Study multiple-choice questions 29 through 37 beginning on page 291.

9.4 RANKING INVESTMENT PROPOSALS

1. **Book rate of return.** A common misstep in regard to capital budgeting is the temptation to gauge the desirability of a project by using accrual accounting numbers instead of cash flows. Shareholders and financial analysts use GAAP-based numbers because they are readily available.

    a. The measure usually produced this way is called **book rate of return** or **accrual accounting rate of return**.

    $$Book\ rate\ of\ return = \frac{GAAP\ net\ income\ from\ investment}{Book\ value\ of\ investment}$$

    b. The weakness of book rate of return is that it ignores the time value of money (discussed below).

2. A dollar received in the future is worth less than a dollar received today. Thus, when analyzing capital projects, the accountant must discount the relevant cash flows using the **time value of money**.

    a. A firm's goal is for its **discount rate** to be **as low as possible**.

        1) The lower the firm's discount rate, the lower the "hurdle" the company must clear to achieve profitability. For this reason, the rate is sometimes called the **hurdle rate**.

    b. The **two most widely used rates** in capital budgeting are

        1) The firm's weighted-average cost of capital or
        2) The shareholders' opportunity cost of capital

    c. A **common pitfall** in capital budgeting is the tendency to use the company's current rate of return as the benchmark. This can lead to rejecting projects that should be accepted.

        1) EXAMPLE: A firm's current rate of return on all projects is 12%. Its shareholders' opportunity cost of capital is 10%. The company incorrectly rejects a project earning 11%.

    d. The **two principal methods** for projecting the profitability of an investment are net present value and internal rate of return.

3. The **net present value (NPV) method** expresses a project's return in **dollar terms**.

    a. NPV **nets the expected cash streams** related to a project (inflows and outflows), then discounts them at the hurdle rate, also called the **desired rate of return**.

        1) If the NPV of a project is **positive**, the project is **desirable** because it has a higher rate of return than the company's desired rate.

    b. EXAMPLE:

        1) The company discounts a series of net cash flows using a hurdle rate of 6% (its desired rate of return).

Period	Net Cash Flow	6% PV Factor	Discounted Cash Flows
Initial Investment	$(501,000)	1.00000	$(501,000)
Year 1	77,000	0.94340	72,642
Year 2	77,000	0.89000	68,530
Year 3	77,000	0.83962	64,651
Year 4	77,000	0.79209	60,991
Year 5	85,000	0.74726	63,517
Year 6	85,000	0.70496	59,922
Year 7	85,000	0.66506	56,530
Year 8	101,800	0.62741	63,870
Net Present Value			**$ 9,653**

2) Because the project has net present value > $0, it is profitable given the company's hurdle rate.

4. The **internal rate of return (IRR)** expresses a project's return in **percentage terms**.

    a. The IRR of an investment is the **discount rate** at which the investment's **NPV equals zero**. In other words, it is the rate that makes the present value of the expected cash inflows equal the present value of the expected cash outflows.

        1) If the IRR is **higher** than the company's desired rate of return, the investment is **desirable**.

    b. EXAMPLE:

        1) The discounted cash flows used in the NPV exercise on the previous page can be recalculated using a higher discount rate (a higher rate will drive down the present value) in an attempt to get the solution closer to $0.

Period	Net Cash Flow	7% PV Factor	Discounted Cash Flows
Initial Investment	$(501,000)	1.00000	$(501,000)
Year 1	77,000	0.93458	71,963
Year 2	77,000	0.87344	67,255
Year 3	77,000	0.81630	62,855
Year 4	77,000	0.76290	58,743
Year 5	85,000	0.71299	60,604
Year 6	85,000	0.66634	56,639
Year 7	85,000	0.62275	52,934
Year 8	101,800	0.58201	59,249
Net Present Value			$ (10,759)

        2) The higher hurdle rate causes the NPV to be negative. Thus, the IRR of this project is somewhere around 6.5%.

        3) Because the company's desired rate of return is 6%, the project should be accepted, the same decision that was arrived at using the net present value method.

5. **Cash Flows and Discounting**

    a. Conceptually, net present value is calculated using the following formula:

$$NPV = \frac{Cash\ Flow_0}{(1 + r)^0} + \frac{Cash\ Flow_1}{(1 + r)^1} + \frac{Cash\ Flow_2}{(1 + r)^2} + \frac{Cash\ Flow_3}{(1 + r)^3} + etc.$$

        1) The subscripts and exponents represent the discount periods. The variable r is the discount rate.

    b. Present value tables are available as a convenient way to discount cash flows.

6. **Pitfalls of IRR.** IRR used in isolation is seldom the best route to a sound capital budgeting decision.

    a. **Direction of cash flows.** When the direction of the cash flows changes, focusing simply on IRR can be misleading.

        1) EXAMPLE: Below are the net cash flows for two potential capital projects.

	Initial	Period 1
Project X	$(222,222)	$ 240,000
Project Y	222,222	(240,000)

The cash flow amounts are the same in absolute value, but the directions differ.

2) The IRR for both projects is 8%, which can be proved as follows:

Project X	Project Y

$$\frac{\$(222,222)}{1.08^0} + \frac{\$240,000}{1.08^1} = \$0 \qquad\qquad \frac{\$222,222}{1.08^0} + \frac{\$(240,000)}{1.08^1} = \$0$$

3) In choosing between the two, a decision maker might be tempted to select the project that has a cash inflow earlier and a cash outflow later.

4) Discounting the cash flows at the company's hurdle rate reveals a different picture.

Project X	Project Y

$$\frac{\$(222,222)}{1.06^0} + \frac{\$240,000}{1.06^1} = \$4,193 \qquad\qquad \frac{\$222,222}{1.06^0} + \frac{\$(240,000)}{1.06^1} = \$(4,193)$$

    a) It turns out that, given a hurdle rate of 6%, the project with the positive cash flow earlier is by far the less desirable of the two.

    b) Clearly, a decision maker can be seriously misled if (s)he uses the simple direction of the cash flows as the tiebreaker when two projects have the same IRR.

5) This effect is known as the **multiple IRR problem**. Essentially, there are **as many solutions** to the IRR formula as there are **changes in the direction** of the net cash flows.

b. **Mutually exclusive projects.** As with changing cash flow directions, focusing only on IRR when capital is limited can lead to unsound decisions.

1) EXAMPLE: Below are the cash flows for two potential capital projects.

	Initial	Period 1	IRR
Project S	$(178,571)	$200,000	12%
Project T	(300,000)	330,000	10%

2) If capital is available for only one project, using IRR alone would suggest that Project S be selected.

3) Once again, however, discounting both projects' net cash flows at the company's hurdle rate suggests a different decision.

Project S	Project T

$$\frac{\$(178,571)}{1.06^0} + \frac{\$200,000}{1.06^1} = \$10,108 \qquad\qquad \frac{\$(300,000)}{1.06^0} + \frac{\$330,000}{1.06^1} = \$11,321$$

    a) While Project S has the distinction of giving the company a higher internal rate of return, Project T is in fact preferable because it adds more to shareholder value.

c. **Varying rates of return.** A project's NPV can easily be determined using different desired rates of return for different periods. The IRR is limited to a single summary rate for the entire project.

d. **Multiple investments.** NPV amounts from different projects can be added, but IRR rates cannot. The IRR for the whole is not the sum of the IRRs for the parts.

7. **Comparing Cash Flow Patterns**

a. Often a decision maker must choose between two mutually exclusive projects, one whose **inflows are higher in the early years** but fall off drastically later and one whose **inflows are steady** throughout the project's life.

1) The **higher a firm's hurdle rate**, the more quickly a project must pay off.
2) Firms with **low hurdle rates** prefer a slow and steady payback.

b. EXAMPLE: Consider the net cash flows of these two projects:

	Initial	Year 1	Year 2	Year 3	Year 4
Project K	$(200,000)	$140,000	$100,000	–	–
Project L	(200,000)	65,000	65,000	$65,000	$65,000

1) A graphical representation of the two projects at various discount rates helps to illustrate the factors a decision maker must consider in such a situation.

NPV Profiles

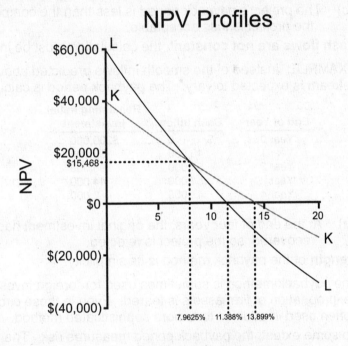

Discount Rate (%)

c. The NPV profile can be of great practical use to managers trying to make investment decisions. It gives the manager a clear insight into the following questions:

1) How sensitive is a project's profitability to changes in the discount rate?

a) At a hurdle rate of **exactly** 7.9625%, a decision maker is indifferent between the two projects. The net present value of both is $15,468 at that discount rate.

b) At hurdle rates **below** 7.9625%, the project whose **inflows last longer** into the future is the better investment (L).

c) At hurdle rates **above** 7.9625%, the project whose **inflows are "front-loaded"** is the better choice (K).

2) At what discount rates is an investment project still a profitable opportunity?

a) At any hurdle rate **above** 13.899%, Project K **loses money**. This is its IRR, i.e., the rate at which its NPV = $0 (Project L's is 11.388%).

8. The **payback period** is the **number of years** required to return the original investment; that is, the time necessary for a new asset to pay for itself. Note that **no accounting is made for the time value of money** under this method.

a. Companies using the payback method set a maximum length of time within which projects must pay for themselves to be considered acceptable.

b. **If the cash flows are constant**, the formula is

$$\text{Payback period} = \frac{\textit{Initial net investment}}{\textit{Annual expected cash flow}}$$

1) EXAMPLE: A project is being considered that will require an outlay of $200,000 immediately and will return a steady cash flow of $52,000 for the next four years. The company requires a 4-year payback period on all capital projects.

a) Payback period = $200,000 ÷ $52,000 = 3.846 years

b) The project's payback period is less than the company's maximum, and the project is thus acceptable.

c. **If the cash flows are not constant**, the calculation must be in cumulative form.

1) EXAMPLE: Instead of the smooth inflows predicted above, the project's cash stream is expected to vary. The payback period is calculated as follows:

End of Year	Cash Inflow	Remaining Initial Investment
Year 0	$ 0	$200,000
Year 1	48,000	152,000
Year 2	54,000	98,000
Year 3	54,000	44,000
Year 4	42,000	2,000

a) At the end of four years, the original investment has still not been recovered, so the project is rejected.

d. The **strength** of the payback method is its simplicity.

1) The payback method is sometimes used for foreign investments if foreign expropriation of firm assets is feared. Even in these circumstances, it is most often used in addition to a more sophisticated method.

2) To some extent, the payback period measures risk. The longer the period, the more risky the investment.

e. The payback method has two significant **weaknesses**:

1) It disregards all cash inflows after the payback cutoff date. Applying a single cutoff date to every project results in accepting many marginal projects and rejecting good ones.

2) It disregards the time value of money. Weighting all cash inflows equally ignores the fact that money has a cost.

9. The **discounted payback method** is sometimes used to overcome the second of the drawbacks inherent in the basic payback method.

    a. The net cash flows in the denominator are discounted to calculate the period required to recover the initial investment.

Period	Cash Inflow	6% PV Factor	Discounted Cash Flow	Remaining Initial Investment
Initial Investment	$ 0	1.00000	$ 0	$200,000
Year 1	48,000	0.94340	45,283	154,717
Year 2	54,000	0.89000	48,060	106,657
Year 3	54,000	0.83962	45,339	61,317
Year 4	42,000	0.79209	33,268	28,050

        1) After four years, the project is much further from paying off than under the basic method.

        2) Clearly then, this is a **more conservative** technique than the traditional payback method.

    b. The discounted payback method's advantage is that it acknowledges the time value of money.

        1) Its drawbacks are that it loses the simplicity of the basic payback method and still ignores cash flows after the arbitrary cutoff date.

10. **Other Payback Methods**

    a. The **bailout payback method** incorporates the salvage value of the asset into the calculation. It measures the length of the payback period when the periodic cash inflows are combined with the salvage value.

    b. The **payback reciprocal** (1 ÷ payback) is sometimes used as an estimate of the internal rate of return.

    c. The **breakeven time** is the period required for the discounted cumulative cash inflows on a project to equal the discounted cumulative cash outflows (usually but not always the initial cost).

        1) Thus, it is the time necessary for the present value of the discounted cash flows to equal zero. This period begins at the outset of a project, not when the initial cash outflow occurs.

        2) An alternative that results in a longer breakeven time is to consider the time required for the present value of the cumulative cash inflows to equal the present value of all the expected future cash outflows.

11. **Capital rationing** exists when a firm sets a limit on the amount of funds to be invested during a given period. In such situations, a firm cannot afford to undertake all profitable projects.

    a. Another way of stating this is that the firm cannot invest the entire amount needed to fund its theoretically optimal capital budget.

        1) Only those projects that will return the **greatest NPV** for the limited capital available in the **internal capital market** can be undertaken.

    b. **Reasons** for capital rationing include

        1) A lack of nonmonetary resources (e.g., managerial or technical personnel)

        2) A desire to control estimation bias (overly favorable projections of a project's cash flows)

        3) An unwillingness to issue new equity (e.g., because of its cost or a reluctance to reveal data in regulatory filings)

12. The **profitability index** (or excess present value index) is a method for ranking projects to ensure that limited resources are placed with the investments that will return the highest NPV.

$$\text{Profitability index} = \frac{NPV \text{ of future cash flows}}{Net\ investment}$$

a. EXAMPLE: A company has $200,000 to invest. It can therefore either invest in Project F below or in Projects G and H.

	Initial	Year 1	Year 2	Year 3	Year 4
Project F	$(200,000)	$140,000	$100,000	-	-
Project G	(100,000)	30,000	30,000	$30,000	$30,000
Project H	(100,000)	30,000	28,000	28,000	34,000

1) Discounting each project at 6% results in the following:

	NPV	NPV ÷ Net Initial Investment
Project F	$21,075	0.105
Project G	15,002	0.150
Project H	15,222	0.152

2) In an environment of capital rationing, the company can see that it should invest first in Project H, then in Project G, and, if new funding is found, last in Project F.

13. **Internal capital market** is a way of referring to the provision of funds by one division of a firm to another division. A division operating in a mature industry that generates a lot of cash can provide funding to another division that is in the cash-hungry development stage.

a. An advantage is the avoidance of stock issue costs or interest costs on new debt.

b. A disadvantage is that calling it a "market" is somewhat misleading. The dynamics of the process are more akin to centralized planning and budgeting than to the workings of a free marketplace.

14. **Linear programming** is a technique (now usually computerized) for optimizing resource allocations so as to select the most profitable or least costly way to use available resources.

a. It involves optimizing an objective function subject to the net of constraint equations.

b. For example, a linear programming application can maximize NPV for a group of projects in a capital rationing situation (expenditure constraint).

15. Comprehensive Examples

a.   EXAMPLE: Hazman Company plans to replace an old piece of equipment that is obsolete and expected to be unreliable under the stress of daily operations. The equipment is fully depreciated, and no salvage value can be realized upon its disposal. One piece of equipment being considered as a replacement will provide an annual cash savings of $7,000 before income taxes and without regard to the effect of depreciation. The equipment costs $18,000 and has an estimated useful life of 5 years. No salvage value will be used for depreciation purposes because the equipment is expected to have no value at the end of 5 years. Hazman uses the straight-line depreciation method on all equipment for both book and tax purposes. Hence, annual depreciation is $3,600. The company is subject to a 40% tax rate. Hazman's desired rate of return is 8%, so it will use the 8% column from a present value table. The company has projected the following cash flows related to the equipment:

		Annual Before-Tax Cash Flow	Annual Tax Savings (Tax)	Annual After-Tax Cash Flow	Annual After-Tax Net Income
Investment	Year 0	$(18,000)	-0-	$(18,000)	-0-
Annual cash savings	Years 1-5	7,000	$(2,800)	4,200	$ 4,200
Depreciation tax shield	Years 1-5		1,440	1,440	(2,160)
Totals				$ 5,640	$ 2,040

1)   **Net present value**   = (After-tax cash flows × Present value of an annuity)
                                        – Net investment
                                = ($5,640 × 3.993) – $21,000
                                = $22,521 – $21,000
                                = **$1,521**

2)   **Internal rate of return.** The goal is to find the discount rate that most nearly equals the net investment.

	10%	11%
After-tax cash flows	$ 5,640	$ 5,640
Times: present value factor	3.791	3.696
Net present value	$21,381	$20,845
Net initial investment	21,000	21,000
Difference	$ 381	$ (155)
Difference between NPVs	$ 536	$ 536
Ratio	71.2%	(28.8%)
Times: gap between discount rates	1%	1%
Percentage increment	0.712%	(0.288%)
Actual IRR	**10.712%**	**10.712%**

3)   **Payback period** = Net investment ÷ After-tax cash flow
                                 = $21,000 ÷ $5,640
                                 = **3.72 years**

4)   **Profitability index** = NPV of future cash flows ÷ Net investment
                                     = ($5,640 × 3.993) ÷ $21,000
                                     = $22,521 ÷ $21,000
                                     = **1.07**

b. EXAMPLE: The management of Flesher Farms is trying to decide whether to buy a new team of mules at a cost of $1,000 or a new tractor at a cost of $10,000. They will perform the same job. But because the mules require more laborers, the annual return is only $250 of net cash inflows. The tractor will return $2,000 of net cash inflows per year. The mules have a working life of 8 years and the tractor 10 years. Neither investment is expected to have a salvage value at the end of its useful life. Flesher's desired rate of return is 6%.

1) **Net Present Value**

	Mules	Tractor
Net cash inflows	$ 250	$ 2,000
Times: present value factor	6.209	7.360
Present value	1,552	14,720
Less: initial investment	(1,000)	(10,000)
Net present value	**$ 552**	**$ 4,720**

2) **Internal Rate of Return**

a) **Mules:** Initial investment ÷ Net cash inflows = $1,000 ÷ $250 = 4

   i) On the 8-year line, a factor of 4 indicates a rate of return of approximately **18.7%**.

b) **Tractor:** Initial investment ÷ Net cash inflows = $10,000 ÷ $2,000 = 5

   i) On the 10-year line, a factor of 5 indicates a rate of return of approximately **15.2%**.

3) **Payback Period**

a) **Mules:** Initial investment ÷ Net cash inflows = $1,000 ÷ $250 = **4 years**
b) **Tractor:** Initial investment ÷ Net cash inflows = $10,000 ÷ $2,000 = **5 years**

4) **Profitability Index**

a) **Mules:** Present value of cash inflows ÷ Initial investment = $1,552 ÷ $1,000
   = **1.552**

b) **Tractor:** Present value of cash inflows ÷ Initial investment = $14,720 ÷ $10,000
   = **1.472**

5) The mule investment has the higher IRR, the quicker payback, and the better profitability index.

a) However, the tractor has the better net present value. The various methods thus give different answers to the investment question.

b) Either investment will be profitable. Management may decide to let noneconomic factors influence the decision.

   i) For example, the mules will require the use of more laborers. If unemployment in the community is high, management might wish to achieve a social goal of providing more jobs.

   ii) Alternatively, a labor shortage might convince management to buy the tractor to reduce labor worries.

16. **Post-investment audits** should be conducted to serve as a control mechanism and to deter managers from proposing unprofitable investments.

    a. Actual-to-expected cash flow comparisons should be made, and unfavorable variances should be explained. The reason may be an inaccurate forecast or implementation problems.

    b. Individuals who supplied unrealistic estimates should have to explain differences. Knowing that a post-investment audit will be conducted may cause managers to provide more realistic forecasts in the future.

    c. The temptation to evaluate the outcome of a project too early must be overcome. Until all cash flows are known, the results can be misleading.

    d. Assessing the receipt of expected nonquantitative benefits is inherently difficult.

17. Stop and review! You have completed the outline for this subunit. Study multiple-choice questions 38 through 68 beginning on page 294.

QUESTIONS

9.1 Sources of Long-Term Financing

1. In general, it is more expensive for a firm to finance with equity capital than with debt capital because

  A. Long-term bonds have a maturity date and must therefore be repaid in the future.

  B. Investors are exposed to greater risk with equity capital.

  C. The interest on debt is a legal obligation.

  D. Equity capital is in greater demand than debt capital.

Answer (B) is correct. *(CMA, adapted)*
REQUIRED: The reason equity financing is more expensive than debt financing.
DISCUSSION: Providers of equity capital are exposed to more risk than are lenders because the firm is not obligated to pay them a return. Also, in case of liquidation, creditors are paid before equity investors. Thus, equity financing is more expensive than debt because equity investors require a higher return to compensate for the greater risk assumed.
Answer (A) is incorrect because the obligation to repay at a specific maturity date reduces the risk to investors and thus the required return. Answer (C) is incorrect because the existence of a legal obligation is but one reason that debt poses less risk to investors. Answer (D) is incorrect because the demand for equity capital is directly related to its greater cost to the issuer.

2. What would be the primary reason for a company to agree to a debt covenant limiting the percentage of its long-term debt?

  A. To cause the price of the company's stock to rise.

  B. To lower the company's bond rating.

  C. To reduce the risk for existing bondholders.

  D. To reduce the interest rate on the bonds being sold.

Answer (D) is correct. *(CPA, adapted)*
REQUIRED: The primary reason for a debt covenant limiting the percentage of long-term debt.
DISCUSSION: The bond indenture is the contractual arrangement between the issuer and the bondholders. It contains restrictive covenants intended to prevent the issuer from taking actions contrary to the interests of the bondholders. A trustee, often a bank, is appointed to ensure compliance. For example, the issuer may be required to (1) maintain its financial ratios, e.g., the ratio of total long-term debt to equity or times-interest-earned, at specified levels; (2) limit dividends if earnings do not meet specified requirements; or (3) restrict the amount of new bonds issued to a percentage of bondable property (fixed assets). The undertakings in the debt covenant reduce the risk for holders of the new debt and the default risk premium included in the interest rate.
Answer (A) is incorrect because the primary reason is to reduce the price of the new debt. Answer (B) is incorrect because the bond rating may rise. Answer (C) is incorrect because the risk to the new creditors is reduced.

3. The market value of a share of stock is $50, and the market value of one right prior to the ex-rights date is $2.00 after the offering is announced but while the stock is still selling rights-on. The offer to the shareholder is that it will take three rights to buy an additional share of stock at a subscription price of $40 per share. If the theoretical value of the stock when it goes ex-rights is $47.50, the shareholder

A. Does not receive any additional benefit from a rights offering.

B. Receives an additional benefit from a rights offering.

C. Merely receives a return of capital.

D. Should redeem the right and purchase the stock before the ex-rights date.

Answer (A) is correct. *(CMA, adapted)*
REQUIRED: The true statement about the effect on the value of stock when it goes ex-rights.
DISCUSSION: If R is the market value of one right when the stock is selling rights-on, P is the market value of one share of stock with rights-on, N is the number of rights necessary to purchase one share of stock, and S is the subscription price per share. The formula for determining the value of one stock right when the price of the stock is rights-on is

$$R = \frac{P - S}{N + 1}$$

Thus, the theoretical value is $2.50 per right [($50 − $40) ÷ (3 + 1)]. However, if the stock declines to $47.50 when the right is worth only $2, the original investor is worse off than before the rights issuance; i.e., the investor would have only $49.50 worth of investments. Hence, the original shareholder receives no benefit from the issuance of the rights.
    Answer (B) is incorrect because the shareholder would be worse off after the rights offering ($49.50) than before ($50). Answer (C) is incorrect because the shareholder only receives a certificate granting the right to make an additional investment. Answer (D) is incorrect because an investor cannot redeem a right before the ex-rights date, i.e., while the stock is still rights-on.

4. At the beginning of Year 1, $10,000 is invested at 8% interest, compounded annually. What amount of interest is earned for Year 2?

A. $800.00

B. $806.40

C. $864.00

D. $933.12

Answer (C) is correct. *(CPA, adapted)*
REQUIRED: The compound interest for Year 2.
DISCUSSION: Compound interest in any year may be found using the following formula: $P = C (1 + r)^t$. P is the future amount, C is the initial investment, r is the interest rate, and t is the number of years invested. This formula is only for compounding interest annually. The interest in Year 2 is the difference between the future amount for Year 2 and the future amount for Year 1. The effect in this case is to add the simple interest for Year 1 ($10,000 × 8% = $800), simple interest for Year 2 ($10,000 × 8% = $800), and Year 2 interest on Year 1 interest ($800 × 8%). The sum is $864.00.
    Answer (A) is incorrect because $800 is Year 1 interest. Answer (B) is incorrect because $806.40 is calculated using the wrong rate. Answer (D) is incorrect because $933.12 is Year 3 interest.

5. Which one of the following statements accurately compares bond financing alternatives?

A. A bond with a call provision typically has a lower yield to maturity than a similar bond without a call provision.

B. A convertible bond must be converted to common stock prior to its maturity.

C. A call provision is usually considered detrimental to the investor.

D. A sinking fund prohibits the firm from redeeming a bond issue prior to its final maturity.

Answer (C) is correct. *(CMA, adapted)*
REQUIRED: The true statement comparing bond financing alternatives.
DISCUSSION: A callable bond can be recalled by the issuer prior to maturity. A call provision is detrimental to the investor because the issuer can recall the bond when market interest rates decline. It is usually exercised only when a company wishes to refinance high-interest debt.
    Answer (A) is incorrect because callable bonds sometimes pay a slightly higher rate of interest. Investors may demand a greater return because of the uncertainty over the true maturity date. Answer (B) is incorrect because conversion is at the option of the investor. Answer (D) is incorrect because a sinking fund provision requires an issuer to retire a certain portion of its bonds each year or set aside money for repayment in the future. Such a provision increases the probability of repayment for bond-holders but does not prohibit early redemption.

6. Compared to another bond with the same risk and maturity but without a conversion feature, a convertible bond is likely to have a

    A. Higher face amount.

    B. Lower face amount.

    C. Higher coupon rate.

    D. Lower coupon rate.

Answer (D) is correct. *(CIA, adapted)*
    REQUIRED: The true statement about a convertible bond.
    DISCUSSION: Convertible bonds are convertible at the holder's option into shares of the issuer's common stock at a specified price. They have a lower coupon rate than nonconvertible bonds because they offer investors a chance for capital gains.

7. Convertible bonds and bonds issued with warrants differ in that

    A. Convertible bonds have lower coupon rates than straight bonds, but bonds issued with warrants have higher coupon rates than straight bonds.

    B. Convertible bonds have higher coupon rates than straight bonds, but bonds issued with warrants have lower coupon rates than straight bonds.

    C. Convertible bonds remain outstanding after the bondholder exercises the right to become a common shareholder, but bonds that are issued with warrants do not.

    D. Bonds that are issued with warrants remain outstanding after the bondholder exercises the right to become a common shareholder, but convertible bonds do not.

Answer (D) is correct. *(CIA, adapted)*
    REQUIRED: The difference between convertible bonds and bonds issued with warrants.
    DISCUSSION: Warrants represent options to purchase equity securities and should be separately accounted for. Because warrants are usually detachable, the bonds remain outstanding if the warrants are exercised. In contrast, convertible bonds must be surrendered when the conversion privilege is exercised. The equity feature of convertible bonds is not separately accounted for.
    Answer (A) is incorrect because bonds issued with warrants have lower coupon rates than conventional bonds. Answer (B) is incorrect because convertible bonds have lower coupon rates than conventional bonds. Answer (C) is incorrect because convertible bonds do not remain outstanding.

8. A major use of warrants in financing is to

    A. Lower the cost of debt.

    B. Avoid dilution of earnings per share.

    C. Maintain managerial control.

    D. Permit the buy-back of bonds before maturity.

Answer (A) is correct. *(CMA, adapted)*
    REQUIRED: The major use of warrants in financing.
    DISCUSSION: Warrants are long-term options that give holders the right to buy common stock in the future at a specific price. If the market price goes up, the holders of warrants will exercise their rights to buy stock at the special price. If the market price does not exceed the exercise price, the warrants will lapse. Issuers of debt sometimes attach stock purchase warrants to debt instruments as an inducement to investors. The investor then has the security of fixed-return debt plus the possibility for large gains if stock prices increase significantly. If warrants are attached, debt can sell at an interest rate slightly lower than the market rate.
    Answer (B) is incorrect because outstanding warrants dilute earnings per share. They are included in the denominator of the EPS calculation even if they have not been exercised.
Answer (C) is incorrect because warrants can, if exercised, result in a dilution of management's holdings. Answer (D) is incorrect because a call provision in a bond indenture, not the use of warrants, permits the buy-back of bonds.

9. A major difference between operating and financial leases is that

    A. Operating leases usually do not provide for maintenance but financial leases do.

    B. Operating lease contracts are written for a period that exceeds the economic life of the leased equipment.

    C. Operating leases frequently contain a cancelation clause, whereas financial leases are not cancelable.

    D. The lessee finances the assets leased for an operating lease.

Answer (C) is correct.   *(CIA, adapted)*
    REQUIRED: The major difference between operating and financial leases.
    DISCUSSION: Operating leases provide both financing and maintenance services to the lessee. An operating or service lease is usually for a term less than the economic life of the asset, and the lease payments are for an amount less than the full cost. Moreover, a cancelation clause in the agreement usually permits the lessee to return the asset before expiration of the term, for example, because of technological change. A financial lease is tantamount to a sale financed by the lessor. The payments are equal to the full cost of the asset, cancelation is not permitted, and maintenance is ordinarily not provided.
    Answer (A) is incorrect because operating leases usually provide for maintenance but financial leases do not. Answer (B) is incorrect because operating lease contracts are written for a period less than the economic life. Answer (D) is incorrect because the lessor finances the assets leased for an operating lease.

10. If a $1,000 bond sells for $1,125, which of the following statements are true?

    I. The market rate of interest is greater than the coupon rate on the bond.

    II. The coupon rate on the bond is greater than the market rate of interest.

    III. The coupon rate and the market rate are equal.

    IV. The bond sells at a premium.

    V. The bond sells at a discount.

    A. I, III, and IV.

    B. I and V.

    C. II and IV.

    D. II, IV, and V.

Answer (C) is correct.   *(CMA, adapted)*
    REQUIRED: The true statement(s) about a bond that sells at more than its face amount.
    DISCUSSION: The excess of the price over the face amount is a premium. A premium is paid because the coupon rate on the bond is greater than the market rate of interest. In other words, because the bond is paying a higher rate than other similar bonds, its price is bid up by investors.

11. Debentures are

    A. Income bonds that require interest payments only when earnings permit.

    B. Subordinated debt and rank behind convertible bonds.

    C. Bonds secured by the full faith and credit of the issuing firm.

    D. A form of lease financing similar to equipment trust certificates.

Answer (C) is correct.   *(CMA, adapted)*
    REQUIRED: The true statement about debentures.
    DISCUSSION: Debentures are unsecured bonds. Although no assets are mortgaged as security for the bonds, debentures are secured by the full faith and credit of the issuing firm. Debentures are a general obligation of the borrower. Only companies with the best credit ratings can issue debentures because only the company's credit rating and reputation secure the bonds.
    Answer (A) is incorrect because debentures must pay interest regardless of earnings levels. Answer (B) is incorrect because debentures are not subordinated except to the extent of assets mortgaged against other bond issues. Debentures are a general obligation of the borrower and rank equally with convertible bonds. Answer (D) is incorrect because debentures have nothing to do with lease financing. Debentures are not secured by assets.

12. Serial bonds are attractive to investors because

    A. All bonds in the issue mature on the same date.

    B. The yield to maturity is the same for all bonds in the issue.

    C. Investors can choose the maturity that suits their financial needs.

    D. The coupon rate on these bonds is adjusted to the maturity date.

Answer (C) is correct. *(CMA, adapted)*
    REQUIRED: The reason serial bonds are attractive to investors.
    DISCUSSION: Serial bonds have staggered maturities, that is, they mature over a period (series) of years. Thus, investors can choose the maturity date that meets their investment needs. For example, an investor who will have a child starting college in 16 years can choose bonds that mature in 16 years.
    Answer (A) is incorrect because serial bonds mature on different dates. Answer (B) is incorrect because bonds maturing on different dates may have different yields, or they may be the same. Usually, the earlier date maturities carry slightly lower yields than the later maturities. Answer (D) is incorrect because the coupon rate is the same for all bonds; only the selling price and yield differ.

9.2 Optimal Capitalization and Cost of Capital

13. The benefits of debt financing over equity financing are likely to be highest in which of the following situations?

    A. High marginal tax rates and few noninterest tax benefits.

    B. Low marginal tax rates and few noninterest tax benefits.

    C. High marginal tax rates and many noninterest tax benefits.

    D. Low marginal tax rates and many noninterest tax benefits.

Answer (A) is correct. *(CPA, adapted)*
    REQUIRED: The circumstances in which the benefits of debt financing over equity financing are likely to be highest.
    DISCUSSION: Interest paid on debt is tax deductible. Thus, debt financing decreases taxable income, and higher marginal tax rates are avoided. In contrast, dividends paid are not deductible. Consequently, they do not reduce taxable income, and higher marginal tax rates are not avoided. Moreover, when the benefits of equity financing (e.g., lack of fixed payments) are few, debt is more attractive.
    Answer (B) is incorrect because, when low marginal tax rates exist, the benefit received from any debt interest deduction is reduced. Answer (C) is incorrect because the existence of many noninterest tax benefits favors equity financing. Answer (D) is incorrect because the existence of many noninterest tax benefits favors equity financing.

14. The capital structure of a firm includes bonds with a coupon rate of 12% and an effective interest rate is 14%. The corporate tax rate is 30%. What is the firm's net cost of debt?

    A. 8.4%

    B. 9.8%

    C. 12%

    D. 14%

Answer (B) is correct. *(CPA, adapted)*
    REQUIRED: The net cost of debt.
    DISCUSSION: The firm's net cost of debt equals the interest rate times one minus the marginal tax rate [%(1 – T)] because interest is a tax deduction. In the case of bonds, the effective rate is used to determine the cost of debt, not the coupon rate (stated rate). The effective rate is the actual cost of the amount borrowed. Thus, the net cost of debt is 9.8% [14% × (100% – 30%)].
    Answer (A) is incorrect because the effective rate is used to determine the cost of debt, not the coupon rate (stated rate). Answer (C) is incorrect because 12% is the coupon rate. Answer (D) is incorrect because 14% ignores the tax effect.

Questions 15 and 16 are based on the following information. Carlisle Company currently sells 400,000 bottles of perfume each year. Each bottle costs $.84 to produce and sells for $1.00. Fixed costs are $28,000 per year. The firm has annual interest expense of $6,000, preferred stock dividends of $2,000 per year, and a 40% tax rate.

15. The degree of operating leverage for Carlisle Company is

A. 2.4

B. 1.78

C. 2.13

D. 1.2

Answer (B) is correct. *(CMA, adapted)*
REQUIRED: The degree of operating leverage.
DISCUSSION: Operating leverage is the percentage change in net operating income resulting from a percentage change in revenues. It measures how a change in volume affects profits. Firms with larger investments and greater fixed costs ordinarily have higher contribution margins and more operating leverage. The degree of operating leverage measures the extent to which fixed assets are used in the production process. A firm with a high percentage of fixed costs is more risky than a firm in the same industry that relies more on variable costs to produce. Based on a contribution margin of $.16 per unit ($1 – $.84 variable cost), the degree of operating leverage is

$$(400,000 \times \$.16) \div [(400,000 \times \$.16) - 28,000] = 1.78.$$

Answer (A) is incorrect because 2.4 is obtained by overstating the contribution margin or the fixed costs. Answer (C) is incorrect because 2.13 includes a nonoperating expense (interest) as a fixed cost. Answer (D) is incorrect because 1.2 is obtained by understating the $64,000 contribution margin or understating the $28,000 of fixed costs.

16. The degree of financial leverage for Carlisle Company is

A. 2.4

B. 1.78

C. 1.35

D. 1.2

Answer (C) is correct. *(CMA, adapted)*
REQUIRED: The degree of financial leverage.
DISCUSSION: The degree of financial leverage is the percentage change in earnings available to common shareholders that is associated with a given percentage change in net operating income. Operating income equals earnings before interest and taxes. The more financial leverage employed, the greater the degree of financial leverage and the riskier the firm. Earnings before interest and taxes equal $36,000 [$400,000 sales – ($.84 × 400,000 units) VC – $28,000 FC]. Using the formula, the calculation is as follows:

$$\frac{\$36,000}{\$36,000 - \$6,000 - (\$2,000 \div .6)} = \frac{\$36,000}{\$26,667} = 1.35$$

Answer (A) is incorrect because 2.4 is obtained by overstating the contribution margin or the fixed costs. Answer (B) is incorrect because 1.78 is the degree of operating leverage, not financial leverage. Answer (D) is incorrect because 1.2 is obtained by understating the $64,000 of contribution margin or understating the $28,000 of fixed costs.

17. Which one of the following factors might cause a firm to increase the debt in its financial structure?

A. An increase in the corporate income tax rate.

B. Increased economic uncertainty.

C. An increase in the federal funds rate.

D. An increase in the price-earnings ratio.

Answer (A) is correct. *(CMA, adapted)*
REQUIRED: The factor that might encourage a firm to increase the debt in its financial structure.
DISCUSSION: An increase in the corporate income tax rate might encourage a firm to borrow because interest on debt is tax deductible, whereas dividends are not. Accordingly, an increase in the tax rate means that the after-tax cost of debt capital will decrease. Given equal interest rates, a firm with a high tax rate will have a lower after-tax cost of debt capital than a firm with a low tax rate.
Answer (B) is incorrect because increased uncertainty encourages equity financing. Dividends do not have to be paid in bad years, but interest on debt is a fixed charge. Answer (C) is incorrect because an increase in interest rates discourages debt financing. Answer (D) is incorrect because an increase in the price-earnings ratio means that the return to shareholders (equity investors) is declining; therefore, equity capital is a more attractive financing alternative.

18. The betas and expected returns for three investments being considered by Sky, Inc. are given below.

Investment	Beta	Expected Return
A	1.4	12%
B	0.8	11%
C	1.5	13%

The return on the market is 11% and the risk-free rate is 6%. If the Capital Asset Pricing Model (CAPM) is used for calculating the required rate of return, which investments should the management of Sky make?

   A. B only.

   B. A and C only.

   C. B and C only.

   D. A, B, and C.

Answer (A) is correct. *(CMA, adapted)*
   REQUIRED: The investment(s) that should be made based on the CAPM.
   DISCUSSION: R is the required return on equity capital, R_F is the risk-free rate of return, β is the beta coefficient (a measure of the firm's risk), and R_M is the market return. The basic equation for the CAPM is

$$[R = R_F + \beta\,(R_M - R_F)]$$

Thus, the required rates of return for A, B, and C are 13% [6% + (1.4 × 5%)], 10% [6% + (.8 × 5%)], and 13.5% [6% + (1.5 × 5%)], respectively. A should be rejected (R is greater than the 12% expected return). B should be accepted (R is less than the 11% expected return). C should be rejected (R is greater than the 13% expected return).

19. The difference between the expected rate of return on a given risky investment and that on a riskless investment is the

   A. Risk premium.

   B. Coefficient of variation.

   C. Standard deviation.

   D. Beta coefficient.

Answer (A) is correct. *(CIA, adapted)*
   REQUIRED: The difference between the required rate of return on a given risky investment and that on a riskless investment with the same expected return.
   DISCUSSION: The required rate of return on equity capital in the capital asset pricing model is the risk-free rate (determined by government securities) plus the product of the market risk premium times the beta coefficient (beta measures the firm's risk). The market risk premium is the amount above the risk-free rate that will induce investment in the market. The beta coefficient of an individual stock is the correlation between the volatility (price variation) of the stock market and that of the price of the individual stock.
   Answer (B) is incorrect because the coefficient of variation is the standard deviation of an investment's returns divided by the mean return. Answer (C) is incorrect because the standard deviation is a measure of the variability of an investment's returns. Answer (D) is incorrect because the beta coefficient measures the sensitivity of the investment's returns to market volatility.

20. By using the dividend growth model, estimate the cost of equity capital for a firm with a stock price of $30.00, an estimated dividend at the end of the first year of $3.00 per share, and an expected growth rate of 10%.

   A. 21.1%

   B. 11.0%

   C. 10.0%

   D. 20.0%

Answer (D) is correct. *(CMA, adapted)*
   REQUIRED: The cost of equity capital calculated using the dividend growth model.
   DISCUSSION: The dividend growth model determines the cost of equity by adding the expected growth rate to the quotient of the next dividend and the current market price. Thus, the cost of equity capital is 20% [10% + ($3 ÷ $30)]. This model assumes that the payout ratio, the retention rate, and the earnings per share growth rate are all constant.
   Answer (A) is incorrect because the growth rate (10%) is added to the dividend yield (10%). Answer (B) is incorrect because 11.0% equals the growth rate (10%) plus 10% of the current dividend yield (10%). Answer (C) is incorrect because 10.0% is the growth rate.

Questions 21 through 23 are based on the following information.

Merrell, Inc. operates a chain of restaurants located in the Southeast. The first restaurant was opened in 1981, and the company has steadily grown to its present size of 48 restaurants. The board of directors recently approved a large-scale remodeling of the restaurants, and the company is now considering two financing alternatives.

- The first alternative consists of

  ■ Bonds that have a 9% coupon rate and will net $19.2 million after flotation costs

  ■ Preferred stock with a stated rate of 6% that will yield $4.8 million after a 4% flotation cost

  ■ Common stock that will yield $24 million after a 5% flotation cost

- The second alternative will consist of a public offering of bonds that would have an 11% coupon rate and would net $48 million after flotation costs.

Merrell's current capital structure, which is considered optimal, consists of 40% long-term debt, 10% preferred stock, and 50% common stock. The current market value of the common stock is $30 per share, and the common stock dividend during the past 12 months was $3 per share. Investors are expecting the growth rate of dividends to equal the historical rate of 6%. Merrell is subject to an effective income tax rate of 40%.

21. The after-tax cost of the common stock proposed in Merrell's first financing alternative is

A. 16.00%

B. 16.53%

C. 16.60%

D. 17.16%

Answer (D) is correct. *(CMA, adapted)*
REQUIRED: The after-tax cost of proposed common stock issuance.
DISCUSSION: Use the following calculations:

$$R = \frac{D_1}{P_0(1 - \text{Flotation})} + G = \frac{\$3.18}{\$30.00\ (.95)} + .06 = 17.16\%$$

Answer (A) is incorrect because 16% ignores the increase in dividends and flotation costs. Answer (B) is incorrect because 16.53% ignores the next dividend increasing to $3.18. Answer (C) is incorrect because 16.6% ignores the flotation costs.

22. Assuming the after-tax cost of common stock is 15%, the after-tax weighted marginal cost of capital for Merrell's first financing alternative consisting of bonds, preferred stock, and common stock is

A. 7.285%

B. 8.725%

C. 10.285%

D. 11.700%

Answer (C) is correct. *(CMA, adapted)*
REQUIRED: The weighted marginal cost of the first financing alternative.
DISCUSSION: In the calculation below, the cost of preferred stock equals the preferred dividend divided by the net issuance price. The preferred stock will yield $4,800,000 after subtracting the 4% flotation cost, so it must sell for $5,000,000 ($4,800,000 ÷ .96). The annual dividend on the preferred stock is $300,000 (6% × $5,000,000). Consequently, the cost of capital raised by issuing preferred stock is 6.25% ($300,000 dividend ÷ $4,800,000 net issuance price).

	Weight		
Bonds	40% × 9% × (1 − .4)	=	2.16%
Preferred stock	10% × 6.25%	=	.625
Common stock	50% × 15%	=	7.50
			10.285%

Flotation costs are ignored for the bonds because $20 million must be repaid at maturity date, which is not the case for preferred stock.

23. The after-tax weighted marginal cost of capital for Merrell's second financing alternative consisting solely of bonds is

A. 5.13%

B. 5.40%

C. 6.27%

D. 6.60%

Answer (D) is correct. *(CMA, adapted)*
REQUIRED: The weighted marginal cost of the second financing alternative.
DISCUSSION: The weighted marginal cost of the second financing alternative is 6.60% [11% effective interest rate × (1 − .4 effective tax rate)].
Answer (A) is incorrect because 5.13% is 5.40% reduced by the 5% stock flotation costs. Answer (B) is incorrect because 5.40% is 60% of 9%. Answer (C) is incorrect because 6.25% is 6.60% reduced by the 5% stock flotation costs.

Questions 24 through 26 are based on the following information. DQZ Telecom is considering a project for the coming year that will cost $50,000,000. DQZ plans to use the following combination of debt and equity to finance the investment:

- Issue $15,000,000 of 20-year bonds at a price of 101, with a coupon rate of 8% and flotation costs of 2% of par.
- Use $35,000,000 of funds generated from earnings.

- The equity market is expected to earn 12%. U.S. Treasury bonds are currently yielding 5%. The beta coefficient for DQZ is estimated to be .60. DQZ is subject to an effective corporate income tax rate of 40%.

24. The before-tax cost of DQZ's planned debt financing, net of flotation costs, in the first year is

A. 8.08%

B. 10.00%

C. 7.92%

D. 8.00%

Answer (A) is correct. *(CMA, adapted)*
REQUIRED: The before-tax cost of the planned debt financing, net of flotation costs.
DISCUSSION: Proceeds are $14,850,000 [(1.01 × $15,000,000) – (.02 × $15,000,000)]. The annual interest is $1,200,000 (.08 coupon rate × $15,000,000). Thus, the company is paying $1,200,000 annually for the use of $14,850,000, a rate of 8.08% ($1,200,000 ÷ $14,850,000).
Answer (B) is incorrect because 10.00% is the sum of the coupon rate and the flotation rate. Answer (C) is incorrect because 7.92% ignores the 2% flotation costs. Answer (D) is incorrect because 8.00% is the coupon rate.

25. Assume that the after-tax cost of debt is 7% and the cost of equity is 12%. Determine the weighted-average cost of capital for DQZ.

A. 10.50%

B. 8.50%

C. 9.50%

D. 6.30%

Answer (A) is correct. *(CMA, adapted)*
REQUIRED: The weighted-average cost of capital given the costs of debt and equity.
DISCUSSION: The 7% debt cost and the 12% equity cost should be weighted by the proportions of the total investment represented by each source of capital. The total project costs $50 million, of which debt is $15 million, or 30% of the total. Equity capital is the other 70%. Consequently, the weighted-average cost of capital is 10.5% [(7%)(30%) + (12%)(70%)].
Answer (B) is incorrect because 8.50% reverses the weights. Answer (C) is incorrect because 9.50% assumes debt and equity are equally weighted. Answer (D) is incorrect because the weighted-average cost cannot be less than any of its components.

26. The Capital Asset Pricing Model (CAPM) computes the expected return on a security by adding the risk-free rate of return to the incremental yield of the expected market return, which is adjusted by the company's beta. Compute DQZ's expected rate of return.

A. 9.20%

B. 12.20%

C. 7.20%

D. 12.00%

Answer (A) is correct. *(CMA, adapted)*
REQUIRED: The expected rate of return using the Capital Asset Pricing Model (CAPM).
DISCUSSION: The market return (R_M), given as 12%, minus the risk-free rate (R_F), given as 5%, is the market risk premium. It is the rate at which investors must be compensated to induce them to invest in the market. The beta coefficient (β) of an individual stock, given as 60%, is the correlation between volatility (price variation) of the stock market and the volatility of the price of the individual stock. Consequently, the expected rate of return is 9.20% [$R_F + \beta(R_M - R_F)$ = .05 + .6(.12 – .05)].
Answer (B) is incorrect because 12.20% equals the risk-free rate plus 60% of the market rate. Answer (C) is incorrect because 7.20% results from multiplying both the market rate premium and the risk-free rate by 60%. Answer (D) is incorrect because 12.00% is the market rate.

27. Brady Corporation has 6,000 shares of 5% cumulative, $100 par value preferred stock outstanding and 200,000 shares of common stock outstanding. Brady's board of directors last declared dividends for the year ended May 31, Year 1, and there were no dividends in arrears after the declaration. For the year ended May 31, Year 3, Brady had net income of $1,750,000. The board of directors is declaring a dividend for common shareholders equivalent to 20% of net income. Brady Corporation has not paid any dividends in Year 2 or Year 3. The total amount of dividends to be paid by Brady at May 31, Year 3, is

    A. $350,000

    B. $380,000

    C. $206,000

    D. $410,000

Answer (D) is correct. *(CMA, adapted)*
REQUIRED: The total amount of dividends to be paid given cumulative preferred stock.
DISCUSSION: If a company has cumulative preferred stock, all preferred dividends for the current and any unpaid prior years must be paid before any dividends can be paid on common stock. The total preferred dividends that must be paid equal $60,000 (2 years × 5% × $100 par × 6,000 shares), and the common dividend is $350,000 ($1,750,000 × 20%), for a total of $410,000.
    Answer (A) is incorrect because $350,000 is the dividend on common stock. Answer (B) is incorrect because $380,000 omits one year's ($30,000) of cumulative dividends. Answer (C) is incorrect because $206,000 is based on a flat rate of $1 per share of stock.

28. A firm's new financing will be in proportion to the market value of its current financing, shown below.

	Carrying Amount ($000 Omitted)
Long-term debt	$7,000
Preferred stock (100,000 shares)	1,000
Common stock (200,000 shares)	7,000

    The firm's bonds are currently selling at 80% of par, generating a current market yield of 9%, and the corporation has a 40% tax rate. The preferred stock is selling at its par value and pays a 6% dividend. The common stock has a current market value of $40 and is expected to pay a $1.20 per share dividend this fiscal year. Dividend growth is expected to be 10% per year, and flotation costs are negligible. The firm's weighted-average cost of capital is (round calculations to tenths of a percent)

    A. 13.0%

    B. 8.3%

    C. 9.6%

    D. 9.0%

Answer (C) is correct. *(CMA, adapted)*
REQUIRED: The weighted-average cost of capital.
DISCUSSION: The first step is to determine the after-tax cost of the long-term debt. Multiplying the current yield of 9% times one minus the tax rate (1 – .4 = .6) results in an after-tax cost of debt of 5.4% (9% × .6). The cost of the preferred stock is 6% (the annual dividend rate). The dividend growth model for measuring the cost of equity capital is a frequently used method that combines the dividend yield with the growth rate. Dividing the $1.20 dividend by the $40 market price produces a dividend yield of 3%. Adding the 3% dividend yield and the 10% growth rate gives a 13% cost of common equity capital. Once the costs of the three types of capital have been computed, the next step is to weight them according to the market values of the elements of the current capital structure. The $1,000,000 of preferred stock is selling at par. The market value of the long-term debt is 80% of carrying amount, or $5,600,000 (80% × $7,000,000). The common stock has a current market price of $8,000,000 ($40 × 200,000 shares). Thus, the weighted-average cost of capital is 9.6% ($1,402,000 ÷ $14,600,000).

Debt	.054 × $ 5,600,000 =	$ 302,400
Preferred	.06 × $ 1,000,000 =	60,000
Common	.13 × $ 8,000,000 =	1,040,000
Total	$14,600,000	$1,402,400

    Answer (A) is incorrect because 13% is the cost of equity. Answer (B) is incorrect because 8.3% is the simple average. Answer (D) is incorrect because 9% is based on carrying amounts.

9.3 Dividend Policy

29. In practice, dividends

A. Usually exhibit greater stability than earnings.

B. Fluctuate more widely than earnings.

C. Tend to be a lower percentage of earnings for mature firms.

D. Are usually set as a fixed percentage of earnings.

Answer (A) is correct. *(CMA, adapted)*
REQUIRED: The true statement about dividends and their relation to earnings.
DISCUSSION: Dividend policy determines the portion of net income distributed to stockholders. Corporations normally try to maintain a stable level of dividends, even though profits may fluctuate considerably, because many stockholders buy stock with the expectation of receiving a certain dividend every year. Thus, management tends not to raise dividends if the payout cannot be sustained. The desire for stability has led theorists to propound the information content or signaling hypothesis: A change in dividend policy is a signal to the market regarding management's forecast of future earnings. This stability often results in a stock that sells at a higher market price because stockholders perceive less risk in receiving their dividends.
Answer (B) is incorrect because most companies try to maintain stable dividends. Answer (C) is incorrect because mature firms have less need of earnings to reinvest for expansion; thus, they tend to pay a higher percentage of earnings as dividends. Answer (D) is incorrect because dividend payout ratios normally fluctuate with earnings to maintain stable dividends.

30. Treating dividends as an active policy strategy assumes that

A. Dividends provide information to the market.

B. Dividends are irrelevant.

C. Dividend payments should be made to common shareholders first.

D. Dividends are costly, and the firm should retain earnings and issue stock dividends.

Answer (A) is correct. *(CMA, adapted)*
REQUIRED: The assumption made when dividends are treated as an active policy strategy.
DISCUSSION: Stock prices often move in the same direction as dividends. Moreover, companies dislike cutting dividends. They tend not to raise dividends unless anticipated future earnings will be sufficient to sustain the higher payout. Thus, some theorists have proposed the information content or signaling hypothesis. According to this view, a change in dividend policy is a signal to the market regarding management's forecast of future earnings. Consequently, the relation of stock price changes to changes in dividends reflects not an investor preference for dividends over capital gains but rather the effect of the information conveyed.
Answer (B) is incorrect because an active dividend policy suggests management assumes that dividends are relevant to investors. Answer (C) is incorrect because preferred shareholders always receive their dividends ahead of common shareholders. Answer (D) is incorrect because an active dividend policy recognizes that investors want dividends.

31. Normally, corporations try to maintain

A. A steady level of dividends.

B. A rapidly increasing level of dividends.

C. A declining rate of dividends.

D. A fluctuating level of dividends.

Answer (A) is correct. *(Publisher, adapted)*
REQUIRED: The best practice for dividend policy.
DISCUSSION: Normally, corporations try to maintain a stable level of dividends, even though profits and losses may fluctuate considerably. The purpose is to meet the expectations of shareholders, especially those who bought stock to receive a regular payout.
Answer (B) is incorrect because, although increasing dividends may excite investors, it would hurt the growth of the company. Answer (C) is incorrect because many shareholders will buy stock with the expectation of receiving a level of dividends and will be disappointed with decreasing dividends. Answer (D) is incorrect because fluctuating dividends will not match shareholder expectations.

32. A company following a residual dividend payout policy will pay higher dividends when, everything else equal, it has

A. Less attractive investment opportunities.

B. Lower earnings available for reinvestment.

C. A lower targeted debt-to-equity ratio.

D. A lower opportunity cost of retained earnings.

Answer (A) is correct. *(CIA, adapted)*
REQUIRED: The circumstances in which a residual dividend payout policy results in higher dividends.
DISCUSSION: Under the residual theory of dividends, the firm prefers to pay dividends when investment opportunities are poor and internal financing would move the firm away from its ideal capital structure. Thus, a company with less attractive investment opportunities will have a lower optimal capital budget. Under a residual dividend policy, a lower optimal capital budget will result in a higher dividend payout ratio, other factors being constant.
Answer (B) is incorrect because, when lower earnings are available for reinvestment, any level of capital expenditures will require, other factors being constant, a greater proportion of available internal funds. The dividend payout ratio will then be lower, not higher, under a residual payout policy. Answer (C) is incorrect because the lower the debt-to-equity ratio, the higher the proportion of new investments financed with equity. Under a residual dividend payout policy, the result will be a lower, not a higher, dividend payout as more internally available funds are retained for reinvestment. Answer (D) is incorrect because the lower the opportunity cost of funds, the lower the discount rate used to evaluate capital projects and the more attractive the investment opportunities. Under a residual payout policy, more internally generated funds will be required to finance the optimal capital budget, and the dividend payout will be lower, not higher.

33. Residco, Inc. expects net income of $800,000 for the next fiscal year. Its targeted and current capital structure is 40% debt and 60% common equity. The director of capital budgeting has determined that the optimal capital spending for next year is $1.2 million. If Residco follows a strict residual dividend policy, what is the expected dividend payout ratio for next year?

A. 90.0%

B. 66.7%

C. 40.0%

D. 10.0%

Answer (D) is correct. *(CMA, adapted)*
REQUIRED: The expected dividend payout ratio assuming a strict residual dividend policy.
DISCUSSION: Under the residual theory of dividends, the residual of earnings paid as dividends depends on the available investments and the debt-equity ratio at which cost of capital is minimized. The rational investor should prefer reinvestment of retained earnings when the return exceeds what the investor could earn on investments of equal risk. However, the firm may prefer to pay dividends when investment returns are poor and the internal equity financing would move the firm away from its ideal capital structure. If Residco wants to maintain its current structure, 60% of investments should be financed from equity. Hence, it needs $720,000 ($1,200,000 × 60%) of equity funds, leaving $80,000 of net income ($800,000 NI – $720,000) available for dividends. The dividend payout ratio is therefore 10% ($80,000 ÷ $800,000 NI).
Answer (A) is incorrect because 90% is the reinvestment ratio. Answer (B) is incorrect because 66.7% is the ratio between earnings and investment. Answer (C) is incorrect because 40% is the ratio of debt in the ideal capital structure.

34. The purchase of treasury stock with a firm's surplus cash

A. Increases a firm's assets.

B. Increases a firm's financial leverage.

C. Increases a firm's interest coverage ratio.

D. Dilutes a firm's earnings per share.

Answer (B) is correct. *(CMA, adapted)*
REQUIRED: The true statement about a purchase of treasury stock.
DISCUSSION: A purchase of treasury stock involves a decrease in assets (usually cash) and a corresponding decrease in shareholders' equity. Thus, equity is reduced and the debt-to-equity ratio and financial leverage increase.
Answer (A) is incorrect because assets decrease when treasury stock is purchased. Answer (C) is incorrect because a firm's interest coverage ratio is unaffected. Earnings, interest expense, and taxes will all be the same regardless of the transaction. Answer (D) is incorrect because the purchase of treasury stock is antidilutive; the same earnings will be spread over fewer shares. Some firms purchase treasury stock for this reason.

35. A stock dividend

A. Increases the debt-to-equity ratio of a firm.

B. Decreases future earnings per share.

C. Decreases the size of the firm.

D. Increases shareholders' wealth.

Answer (B) is correct. *(CMA, adapted)*
REQUIRED: The true statement about a stock dividend.
DISCUSSION: A stock dividend is a transfer of equity from retained earnings to paid-in capital. The debit is to retained earnings and the credits are to common stock and additional paid-in capital. More shares are outstanding following the stock dividend, but every shareholder maintains the same percentage of ownership. In effect, a stock dividend divides the pie (the corporation) into more pieces, but the pie is still the same size. Hence, a corporation will have a lower EPS and a lower book value per share following a stock dividend, but every shareholder will be just as well off as previously.

36. Treating dividends as the residual part of a financing decision assumes that

A. Earnings should be retained and reinvested as long as profitable projects are available.

B. Dividends are important to shareholders, and any earnings left over after paying dividends should be invested in high-return assets.

C. Dividend payments should be consistent.

D. Dividends are relevant to a financing decision.

Answer (A) is correct. *(CMA, adapted)*
REQUIRED: The assumption made when dividends are treated as a residual part of a financing decision.
DISCUSSION: According to the residual theory of dividends, the amount (residual) of earnings paid as dividends depends on the available investment opportunities and the debt-equity ratio at which cost of capital is minimized. The rational investor should prefer reinvestment of retained earnings when the return exceeds what the investor could earn on investments of equal risk. However, the firm may prefer to pay dividends when investment opportunities are poor and the use of internal equity financing would move the firm away from its ideal capital structure.
Answer (B) is incorrect because a residual theory assumes that investors want the company to reinvest earnings in worthwhile projects, not pay dividends. Answer (C) is incorrect because dividend payments will not be consistent under a residual theory. The corporation will pay dividends only when internal investment options are unacceptable. Answer (D) is incorrect because dividends would not be important to a financing decision under the residual theory.

37. When a company desires to increase the market value per share of common stock, the company will implement

A. The sale of treasury stock.

B. A reverse stock split.

C. The sale of preferred stock.

D. A stock split.

Answer (B) is correct. *(CMA, adapted)*
REQUIRED: The transaction that increases the market value per share of common stock.
DISCUSSION: A reverse stock split decreases the number of shares outstanding, which increases the market price per share. A reverse stock split may be desirable when a stock is selling at such a low price that management is concerned that investors will avoid the stock because it has an undesirable image.
Answer (A) is incorrect because a sale of treasury stock increases the supply of shares and could lead to a decline in market price. Answer (C) is incorrect because a sale of preferred stock will take dollars out of investors' hands, thereby reducing funds available to invest in common stock; therefore, market price per share of common stock will not increase. Answer (D) is incorrect because a stock split increases the shares issued and outstanding. The market price per share is likely to decline as a result.

9.4 Ranking Investment Proposals

Questions 38 through 41 are based on the following information. Tam Co. is negotiating to purchase equipment that would cost $100,000, with the expectation that $20,000 per year could be saved in after-tax cash costs if the equipment were acquired. The equipment's estimated useful life is 10 years, with no residual value, and would be depreciated by the straight-line method. Tam's predetermined minimum desired rate of return is 12%. Present value of an annuity of $1 at 12% for 10 periods is 5.65. Present value of $1 due in 10 periods at 12% is .322.

38. Net present value to Tam Co. is

    A. $5,760

    B. $6,440

    C. $12,200

    D. $13,000

Answer (D) is correct. *(CPA, adapted)*
    REQUIRED: The net present value.
    DISCUSSION: NPV value is computed by deducting the initial cost of the investment from the present value of the future net cash inflows. The initial cost is $100,000. The present value of the future net cash inflows is $113,000 ($20,000 × 5.65 ordinary annuity factor). The NPV is $13,000 ($113,000 – $100,000).
    Answer (A) is incorrect because $5,760 is $12,200 minus $6,440. Answer (B) is incorrect because $6,440 is the present value of the after-tax savings in year 10. Answer (C) is incorrect because $12,200 is the present value of $100,000 due in ten years minus expected annual after-tax savings.

39. Payback period to Tam Co. is

    A. 4.0 years.

    B. 4.4 years.

    C. 4.5 years.

    D. 5.0 years.

Answer (D) is correct. *(CPA, adapted)*
    REQUIRED: The payback period.
    DISCUSSION: The payback period is the time required for the cumulative net cash inflows to equal the initial investment. Given a constant annual net cash inflow, the payback period equals the cost of the net investment divided by the average expected annual cash flows. Thus, the payback period is 5.0 years ($100,000 cost ÷ $20,000 expected annual cash savings).

40. Accrual accounting rate of return based on initial investment to Tam Co. is

    A. 30%

    B. 20%

    C. 12%

    D. 10%

Answer (D) is correct. *(CPA, adapted)*
    REQUIRED: The accrual accounting rate of return.
    DISCUSSION: The accounting rate of return is a capital budgeting technique that ignores the time value of money. It is calculated by dividing the increase in accounting net income by the required initial investment. The required initial investment is $100,000. The expected annual after-tax cash savings is $20,000. However, given an additional annual depreciation expense of $10,000 ($100,000 ÷ 10), the net income is increased by only $10,000 ($20,000 cash savings – $10,000 depreciation expense). Thus, the accrual accounting rate of return is 10% ($10,000 ÷ $100,000).
    Answer (A) is incorrect because 30% adds depreciation expense to net income rather than subtracting it from the cost savings. Answer (B) is incorrect because 20% excludes the effect of depreciation expense. Answer (C) is incorrect because 12% is Tam's minimum desired rate of return.

41. In estimating the internal rate of return, the factors in the table of present values of an annuity should be taken from the columns with entries closest to

    A. 0.65

    B. 1.30

    C. 5.00

    D. 5.65

Answer (C) is correct. *(CPA, adapted)*
    REQUIRED: The interest factor corresponding to IRR.
    DISCUSSION: The IRR is the discount rate at which the NPV is zero. The factor for the present value of an annuity that equates the present value of the future cash flows with the initial cost of the investment is 5.00 ($100,000 ÷ $20,000). In the standard table of interest factors for the present value of an ordinary annuity, the column with an entry closest to 5.00 in the row for 10 periods is 15%.
    Answer (A) is incorrect because 0.65 yields an NPV of $(87,000). Answer (B) is incorrect because 1.30 yields an NPV of $(74,000). Answer (D) is incorrect because 5.65 yields a positive NPV of $13,000.

42. Neu Co. is considering the purchase of an investment that has a positive net present value based on Neu's 12% hurdle rate. The internal rate of return would be

A. 0

B. 12%

C. > 12%

D. < 12%

Answer (C) is correct. *(CPA, adapted)*
REQUIRED: The IRR assuming an NPV based on a 12% hurdle rate.
DISCUSSION: The IRR is an interest rate (r) which is computed by equalizing the present value of future cash flows and the cost of the investment. The IRR can be found by trial and error using arbitrarily selected r's until an NPV of zero is obtained. As long as r is greater than the NPV's hurdle rate (k), the NPV must be positive (greater than zero). Because Neu has a positive NPV based on a 12% k, the IRR must be greater than 12%.
Answer (A) is incorrect because 0 is the NPV when r is not greater than k. Answer (B) is incorrect because 12% is the hurdle rate that the positive NPV is based on. Answer (D) is incorrect because the IRR will be greater than k.

43. Major Corp. is considering the purchase of a new machine for $5,000 that will have an estimated useful life of 5 years and no salvage value. The machine will increase Major's after-tax cash flow by $2,000 annually for 5 years. Major uses the straight-line method of depreciation and has an incremental borrowing rate of 10%. The present value factors for 10% are as follows:

Ordinary annuity with five payments   3.79
Annuity due for five payments   4.17

Using the payback method, how many years will it take to pay back Major's initial investment in the machine?

A. 2.50

B. 5.00

C. 7.58

D. 8.34

Answer (A) is correct. *(CPA, adapted)*
REQUIRED: The payback period.
DISCUSSION: The payback period is the number of years it takes for a new asset to pay for itself. The payback period is calculated by dividing the cost of the net investment by the periodic constant expected cash flow. Time value of money is ignored. Thus, the payback period is 2.50 ($5,000 net investment ÷ $2,000 after-tax cash flow).
Answer (B) is incorrect because 5.00 is the estimated useful life of the machine. Answer (C) is incorrect because 7.58 is the present value of the five payments, assuming an ordinary annuity, divided by the machine's annual straight-line depreciation. Answer (D) is incorrect because 8.34 is the present value of the five payments, assuming an annuity due, divided by the machine's annual straight-line depreciation.

44. The capital budgeting technique known as internal rate of return uses

	Cash Flow over Entire Life of Project	Time Value of Money
A.	Yes	No
B.	Yes	Yes
C.	No	Yes
D.	No	No

Answer (B) is correct. *(CPA, adapted)*
REQUIRED: The matter considered by the internal rate of return (IRR) technique.
DISCUSSION: The IRR is a capital budgeting technique that equalizes the present value of future cash flows with the initial cost of the investment. It incorporates the time value of money by determining the compound interest rate of an investment.
Answer (A) is incorrect because the technique incorporates the time value of money. Answer (C) is incorrect because the present value of future cash flows equals the initial cost of the investment. Answer (D) is incorrect because the time value of money is incorporated by computing the project's present value of future cash flows.

45. Doro Co. is considering the purchase of a $100,000 machine that is expected to result in a decrease of $25,000 per year in cash expenses after taxes. This machine, which has no residual value, has an estimated useful life of 10 years and will be depreciated on a straight-line basis. For this machine, the accounting rate of return based on initial investment would be

A. 10%

B. 15%

C. 25%

D. 35%

Answer (B) is correct. *(CPA, adapted)*
REQUIRED: The accounting rate of return based on initial investment.
DISCUSSION: The ARR is based on the accrual method and does not discount future cash flows. Accordingly, the ARR equals the decrease in annual cash expenses after taxes minus annual depreciation, divided by the initial investment. Annual straight-line depreciation is $10,000 [($100,000 cost − $0 salvage value) ÷ 10 years].

$$ARR = \frac{\$25,000 - \$10,000}{\$100,000} = 15\%$$

Answer (A) is incorrect because 10% is the depreciation rate per year. Answer (C) is incorrect because depreciation must be deducted from the $25,000 of cash expenses. Answer (D) is incorrect because depreciation must be deducted from, not added to, the $25,000 of cash expenses.

46. Which of the following statements is true regarding the payback method?

A. It does not consider the time value of money.

B. It is the time required to recover the investment and earn a profit.

C. It is a measure of how profitable one investment project is compared with another.

D. The salvage value of old equipment is ignored in the event of equipment replacement.

Answer (A) is correct. *(CPA, adapted)*
REQUIRED: The true statement about the payback method.
DISCUSSION: Payback is the number of years required to complete the return of the original investment, i.e., the time it takes for a new asset to pay for itself. This measure is computed by dividing the initial net investment by the periodic constant expected after-tax cash flow to be generated. If periodic cash flows are not constant, the calculation must be cumulative. Payback is easy to calculate, but it ignores cash flows received after the payback period, and it does not account for the time value of money.
Answer (B) is incorrect because the payback period is the investment recovery period. Answer (C) is incorrect because the net present value method is a measure of how profitable one investment project is compared with another. Answer (D) is incorrect because salvage value is a cash inflow that should be considered in calculating the payback period.

47. Division A is considering a project that will earn a rate of return which is greater than the imputed interest charge for invested capital, but less than the division's historical return on invested capital. Division B is considering a project that will earn a rate of return which is greater than the division's historical return on invested capital, but less than the imputed interest charge for invested capital. If the objective is to maximize residual income, should these divisions accept or reject their projects?

	A	B
A.	Accept	Reject
B.	Reject	Accept
C.	Reject	Reject
D.	Accept	Accept

Answer (A) is correct. *(CPA, adapted)*
REQUIRED: The acceptance or rejection of projects if the objective is to maximize residual income.
DISCUSSION: Division B's project does not maximize residual income.
Answer (B) is incorrect because Division A's project, not Division B's project, maximizes residual income. Answer (C) is incorrect because Division A's project maximizes residual income. Answer (D) is incorrect because residual income is the excess of the return on an investment over a targeted amount equal to an imputed interest charge on invested capital. A project's residual income is the project's rate of return minus the imputed interest on its invested capital. Because the rate of return on Division A's project is greater than the imputed interest charge, its residual income will be positive or maximized. Because the rate of return on Division B's project is less than the imputed interest charge, its residual income will be negative or not maximized. Thus, because the objective is to maximize residual income, Division A's project should be accepted while Division B's project should be rejected.

48. Oak Co. bought a machine that will depreciate on the straight-line basis over an estimated useful life of 7 years. The machine has no salvage value. Oak expects the machine to generate after-tax net cash inflows from operations of $110,000 in each of the 7 years. Oak's minimum rate of return is 12%. Information on present value factors is as follows:

Present value of $1 at 12% at the
  end of 7 periods   .452
Present value of an ordinary annuity
  of $1 at 12% for 7 periods   4.564

Assuming a positive net present value of $12,000, what was the cost of the machine?

A. $485,200

B. $490,040

C. $502,040

D. $514,040

Answer (B) is correct. *(CPA, adapted)*
REQUIRED: The cost of a machine given NPV data.
DISCUSSION: NPV is broadly defined as the excess of the present values of the estimated net cash inflows over the net cost of the investment. It uses the time value of money when discounting the cash flow over the life of the project. Given no salvage value, the present value of the after-tax net cash inflows is $502,040 ($110,000 annual after-tax net cash inflow for 7 periods × 4.564 PV of an ordinary annuity at 12% for 7 periods). Thus, the cost of the machine was $490,040 ($502,040 – $12,000 NPV).
Answer (A) is incorrect because $485,200 equals 4.52 times $110,000, minus $12,000. Answer (C) is incorrect because $502,040 equals the present value of the series of after-tax net cash inflows over a 7-year period. Answer (D) is incorrect because $514,040 results from adding the NPV to, not subtracting it from, the present value of the series of after-tax net cash inflows over a 7-year period.

49. The capital budgeting technique known as the accounting rate of return uses

	Revenue over Life of Project	Depreciation Expense
A.	No	Yes
B.	No	No
C.	Yes	No
D.	Yes	Yes

Answer (D) is correct. *(CPA, adapted)*
REQUIRED: The matters considered by the accounting rate of return technique.
DISCUSSION: The accounting rate of return is a capital budgeting technique. It is calculated by dividing the increase in accounting net income by the required investment. Because the numerator is the increase in accounting net income, revenues and expenses, including depreciation, over the life of the project are incorporated. However, this technique ignores the time value of money.

50. The capital budgeting technique known as the payback period uses

	Depreciation Expense	Time Value of Money
A.	No	No
B.	No	Yes
C.	Yes	Yes
D.	Yes	No

Answer (A) is correct. *(CPA, adapted)*
REQUIRED: The matters considered by the payback capital budgeting technique.
DISCUSSION: The strength of the payback method is its simplicity. The payback period is the time required for net cash inflows to equal the cost of the initial investment. Thus, except to the extent it is included in the determination of the cash flow related to taxes, depreciation is ignored in the payback calculation because it is a noncash expense. Moreover, the amount considered in the tax calculation is the depreciation allowed for tax purposes, not the depreciation expense recognized in the financial statements. Another disadvantage is that the payback method provides no measure of profitability because it ignores the time value of money and the effects of cash flows after the payback period.

51. The capital budgeting technique known as net present value uses

	Cash Flow over Life of Project	Time Value of Money
A.	No	Yes
B.	No	No
C.	Yes	No
D.	Yes	Yes

Answer (D) is correct. *(CPA, adapted)*
REQUIRED: The matters considered by the net present value technique.
DISCUSSION: The net present value method is a capital budgeting technique. It recognizes the time value of money by discounting the after-tax cash flows over a project's life using the company's minimum desired rate of return.

52. A project's net present value, ignoring income tax considerations, is normally affected by the

A. Proceeds from the sale of the asset to be replaced.

B. Carrying amount of the asset to be replaced by the project.

C. Amount of annual depreciation on the asset to be replaced.

D. Amount of annual depreciation on fixed assets used directly on the project.

Answer (A) is correct. *(CPA, adapted)*
REQUIRED: The matter affecting net present value.
DISCUSSION: To compute a project's net present value, the initial investment is subtracted from the present value of the after-tax cash flows. The proceeds from the sale of the asset to be replaced reduces the initial investment.
Answer (B) is incorrect because the carrying amount of the asset to be replaced affects the gain or loss on the sale. Answer (C) is incorrect because the amount of annual depreciation on the asset to be replaced affects the carrying value. Answer (D) is incorrect because annual depreciation of other assets, even if used directly, does not affect the project's net present value.

53. Which of the following capital budgeting techniques implicitly assumes that the cash flows are reinvested at the company's minimum required rate of return?

	Net Present Value	Internal Rate of Return
A.	Yes	Yes
B.	Yes	No
C.	No	Yes
D.	No	No

Answer (B) is correct. *(CPA, adapted)*
REQUIRED: The technique that assumes reinvestment at the minimum required rate of return.
DISCUSSION: The net present value method recognizes the time value of money by discounting the after-tax cash flows over a project's life using the company's minimum required rate of return. Reinvestment is also assumed to be at this rate. The internal rate of return (IRR) is the interest rate at which the net present value is zero. Reinvestment is assumed to be at the IRR.

54. The discount rate (hurdle rate of return) must be determined in advance for the

A. Payback period method.

B. Time-adjusted rate of return method.

C. Net present value method.

D. Internal rate of return method.

Answer (C) is correct. *(CPA, adapted)*
REQUIRED: The capital budgeting technique that determines the discount rate in advance.
DISCUSSION: The net present value method discounts the after-tax cash flows over a project's life. Because these cash flows are discounted, the discount rate must be determined in advance.

55. Which of the following characteristics represent an advantage of the internal rate of return technique over the accounting rate of return technique in evaluating a project?

I.   Recognition of the project's salvage value
II. Emphasis on cash flows
III. Recognition of the time value of money

A. I only.

B. I and II.

C. II and III.

D. I, II, and III.

Answer (C) is correct. *(CPA, adapted)*
REQUIRED: The advantage(s) of the IRR technique over the accounting rate of return technique.
DISCUSSION: The IRR is the interest rate that equalizes the present value of future cash flows with the initial cost of the investment. The accounting rate of return is calculated by dividing the increase in accounting net income by the required investment. However, it ignores the time value of money and does not emphasize cash flows.

56. How are the following used in the calculation of the internal rate of return of a proposed project? Ignore income tax considerations.

	Residual Sales Value of Project	Depreciation Expense
A.	Exclude	Include
B.	Include	Include
C.	Exclude	Exclude
D.	Include	Exclude

Answer (D) is correct. *(CPA, adapted)*
REQUIRED: The item(s) included in the calculation of the internal rate of return.
DISCUSSION: The IRR is the discount rate at which the NPV of a project is zero. The residual sales (salvage) value of a project is a future cash flow that should be discounted to determine its present value. Hence, this value must be included in the calculation of the IRR. The depreciation expense recognized in the financial statements is a noncash item and is therefore excluded. However, the depreciation allowed for tax purposes affects the cash flow for income taxes.

57. Polo Co. requires higher rates of return for projects with a life span greater than 5 years. Projects extending beyond 5 years must earn a higher specified rate of return. Which of the following capital budgeting techniques can readily accommodate this requirement?

	Internal Rate of Return	Net Present Value
A.	Yes	No
B.	No	Yes
C.	No	No
D.	Yes	Yes

Answer (D) is correct. *(CPA, adapted)*
REQUIRED: The capital budgeting technique(s) that can accommodate a higher desired rate of return for longer projects.
DISCUSSION: The IRR is the discount rate at which the NPV is zero. The NPV is the excess of the present value of the expected future net cash inflows over the cost of the investment. The calculation of the NPV (and therefore the IRR) can be readily adjusted for an increase in the desired return by changing the discount rate.
Answer (A) is incorrect because net present value can readily accommodate changing rates of return. Answer (B) is incorrect because IRR can readily accommodate changing rates of return. Answer (C) is incorrect because both NPV and IRR can readily accommodate changing rates of return.

58. For the next 2 years, a lease is estimated to have an operating net cash inflow of $7,500 per annum, before adjusting for $5,000 per annum tax-basis lease amortization, and a 40% tax rate. The present value of an ordinary annuity of $1 per year at 10% for 2 years is $1.74. What is the lease's after-tax present value using a 10% discount factor?

A. $2,610

B. $4,350

C. $9,570

D. $11,310

Answer (D) is correct. *(CPA, adapted)*
REQUIRED: The after-tax present value of a lease.
DISCUSSION: The annual net cash inflow is $7,500 minus taxes paid. Given a $5,000 tax shield, annual taxes paid equal $1,000 [($7,500 – $5,000) × 40%]. Thus, the present value of the after-tax cash flows for 2 years is $11,310 [($7,500 – $1,000) × 1.74].
Answer (A) is incorrect because $2,610 equals 1.74 times $1,500. Answer (B) is incorrect because $4,350 equals 1.74 times $2,500. Answer (C) is incorrect because $9,570 equals 1.74 times $5,500.

59. Pole Co. is investing in a machine with a 3-year life. The machine is expected to reduce annual cash operating costs by $30,000 in each of the first 2 years and by $20,000 in year 3. Present values of an annuity of $1 at 14% are

Period 1	0.88
2	1.65
3	2.32

Using a 14% cost of capital, what is the present value of these future savings?

A. $59,600

B. $60,800

C. $62,900

D. $69,500

Answer (C) is correct. *(CPA, adapted)*
REQUIRED: The present value of an investment.
DISCUSSION: The cost reductions constitute two annuities: a 3-year annuity of $20,000 per year and a 2-year annuity of $10,000 per year. Using a 14% cost of capital and ignoring tax effects, the present value of a $20,000 annuity discounted over a 3-year period is $46,400 ($20,000 × 2.32). The present value of the incremental $10,000 amounts in the first 2 years is $16,500 ($10,000 × 1.65). Hence, the total present value of the future savings is $62,900.
Answer (A) is incorrect because $59,600 equals the present value of a 3-year annuity for $30,000, minus $10,000. Answer (B) is incorrect because the present value of the future savings is $62,900. Answer (D) is incorrect because $69,500 equals the present value of a 2-year annuity for $30,000, plus $20,000.

60. Para Co. is reviewing the following data relating to an energy-saving investment proposal:

Cost	$50,000
Residual value at the end of 5 years	10,000
Present value of an annuity of 1 at 12% for 5 years	3.60
Present value of 1 due in 5 years at 12%	0.57

What would be the annual savings needed to make the investment realize a 12% yield?

A. $10,624

B. $11,111

C. $12,306

D. $13,889

Answer (C) is correct. *(CPA, adapted)*
REQUIRED: The annual savings needed to make the investment realize a specified yield.
DISCUSSION: The annual savings is the periodic amount of an ordinary annuity for five periods discounted at 12%. The present value of this annuity equals the cost minus the present value of the residual value, or $44,300 [$50,000 – ($10,000 × .57 PV of $1 due in 5 years at 12%)]. Accordingly, the annual savings is $12,306 ($44,300 ÷ 3.60 present value of an annuity of 1 at 12% for 5 years).
Answer (A) is incorrect because $10,624 results from using an annuity factor of 4.17 (3.60 + .57). Answer (B) is incorrect because $11,111 results from failing to discount the residual value. Answer (D) is incorrect because $13,889 assumes no residual value.

Questions 61 through 63 are based on the following information. Maloney Company uses a 12% hurdle rate for all capital expenditures and has done the following analysis for four projects for the upcoming year:

	Project 1	Project 2	Project 3	Project 4
Initial outlay	$4,960,000	$5,440,000	$4,000,000	$5,960,000
Annual net cash inflows				
Year 1	1,600,000	1,900,000	1,300,000	2,000,000
Year 2	1,900,000	2,500,000	1,400,000	2,700,000
Year 3	1,800,000	1,800,000	1,600,000	1,800,000
Year 4	1,600,000	1,200,000	800,000	1,300,000
Net present value	281,280	293,240	(75,960)	85,520
Profitability Index	106%	105%	98%	101%
Internal rate of return	14%	15%	11%	13%

61. Which project(s) should Maloney undertake during the upcoming year assuming it has no budget restrictions?

A. All of the projects.

B. Projects 1, 2, and 3.

C. Projects 1, 2, and 4.

D. Projects 1 and 2.

Answer (C) is correct. *(Publisher, adapted)*
REQUIRED: The project(s) that should be undertaken given no capital rationing.
DISCUSSION: A firm using the net present value (NPV) method should undertake all projects with positive NPVs that are not mutually exclusive. Given that Projects 1, 2, and 4 have positive NPVs, those projects should be undertaken. Furthermore, a firm using the internal rate of return (IRR) as a decision rule ordinarily chooses projects with a return greater than the cost of capital. Given a 12% cost of capital, Projects 1, 2, and 4 should be chosen using an IRR criterion if they are not mutually exclusive. Use of the profitability index yields a similar decision because a project with an index greater than 100% should be undertaken.
Answer (A) is incorrect because one of the projects should not be undertaken. Answer (B) is incorrect because Project 3 has a negative NPV but Project 4 does not. Answer (D) is incorrect because Project 4 has a positive NPV and should be undertaken.

62. Which projects should Maloney undertake during the upcoming year if it has only $12,000,000 of investment funds available?

A. Projects 1 and 3.

B. Projects 1, 2, and 4.

C. Projects 1 and 4.

D. Projects 1 and 2.

Answer (D) is correct. *(Publisher, adapted)*
REQUIRED: The project(s) that should be undertaken given a capital rationing limitation of $12,000,000.
DISCUSSION: With only $12,000,000 available and each project costing $4,000,000 or more, no more than two projects can be undertaken. Accordingly, Projects 1 and 2 should be selected because they have the greatest NPVs and profitability indexes.
Answer (A) is incorrect because Project 3 has a negative NPV. Answer (B) is incorrect because choosing three projects violates the $12,000,000 limitation. Answer (C) is incorrect because the combined NPV of Projects 1 and 4 is less than the combined NPV of Projects 1 and 2.

63. Which project(s) should Maloney undertake during the upcoming year if it has only $6,000,000 of funds available?

A. Project 3.

B. Projects 1 and 2.

C. Project 1.

D. Project 2.

Answer (C) is correct. *(Publisher, adapted)*
REQUIRED: The project(s) that should be undertaken given a capital rationing limitation of $6,000,000.
DISCUSSION: With only $6,000,000 available and each project costing $4,000,000 or more, no more than one project can be undertaken. Project 1 should be chosen because it has a positive NPV and the highest profitability index. The high profitability index means that the firm will achieve the highest NPV per dollar of investment with Project 1. The profitability index facilitates comparison of different-sized investments.
Answer (A) is incorrect because Project 3 has a negative NPV and should not be selected regardless of the capital available. Answer (B) is incorrect because selecting two projects violates the $6,000,000 limitation on funds. Answer (D) is incorrect because, despite having the highest NPV, Project 2 has a lower profitability index than Project 1. Consequently, Project 1 offers the greater return per dollar of investment.

64. Harvey Co. is evaluating a capital investment proposal for a new machine. The investment proposal shows the following information:

Initial cost	$500,000
Life	10 years
Annual net cash flows	$200,000
Salvage value	$100,000

If acquired, the machine will be depreciated using the straight-line method. The payback period for this investment is

A. 3.125 years.

B. 2.67 years.

C. 2.5 years.

D. 2 years.

Answer (C) is correct. *(CPA, adapted)*
REQUIRED: The payback period.
DISCUSSION: Payback is the number of years required to complete the return of the original investment, i.e., the time it takes for a new asset to pay for itself. This measure is computed by dividing the initial net investment by the periodic constant expected after-tax net cash inflow to be generated. If periodic cash flows are not constant, the calculation must be in cumulative form. Thus, the payback period is 2.5 years.
Answer (A) is incorrect because 3.125 years results from subtracting annual depreciation from annual net cash inflows. Answer (B) is incorrect because 2.67 years is a nonsense answer. Answer (D) is incorrect because 2 years results from subtracting the salvage value from the initial cost.

65. In considering the payback period for three projects, Fly Corp. gathered the following data about cash flows:

Cash Flows by Year

	Year 1	Year 2	Year 3	Year 4	Year 5
Project A	$(10,000)	$ 3,000	$ 3,000	$ 3,000	$ 3,000
Project B	(25,000)	15,000	15,000	(10,000)	15,000
Project C	(10,000)	5,000	5,000		

Which of the projects will achieve payback within three years?

A. Projects A, B, and C.

B. Projects B and C.

C. Project B only.

D. Projects A and C.

Answer (B) is correct. *(CPA, adapted)*
REQUIRED: The project(s) having a payback within three years.
DISCUSSION: Payback is the number of years required to complete the return of the original investment, i.e., the time it takes for a new asset to pay for itself. This measure is computed by dividing the initial net investment by the periodic constant expected after-tax net cash inflow to be generated. If periodic cash flows are not constant, the calculation must be in cumulative form. For B, the initial net investment is $25,000, and the total of periodic cash inflows for Years 2 and 3 is $30,000. For C, the initial net investment is $10,000, and the total of periodic cash inflows for Years 2 and 3 is $10,000.
Answer (A) is incorrect because, for Projects A, B, and C, the initial net investment of $10,000 is less than the total of periodic cash inflows for Years 2 and 3 of $6,000. Answer (C) is incorrect because the payback for Project B is also within three years. Answer (D) is incorrect because, for Projects A, B, and C, the initial net investment of $10,000 is less than the total of periodic cash inflows for Years 2 and 3 of $6,000.

66. A multiperiod project has a positive net present value. Which of the following statements is correct regarding its required rate of return?

A. Less than the company's weighted average cost of capital.

B. Less than the project's internal rate of return.

C. Greater than the company's weighted average cost of capital.

D. Greater than the project's internal rate of return.

Answer (B) is correct. *(CPA, adapted)*
REQUIRED: The true statement about the required rate of return for a multiperiod project with a positive NPV.
DISCUSSION: The internal rate of return is the discount rate at which NPV is zero. Thus, a discount rate (required rate of return) at which the NPV is positive is lower than the IRR.
Answer (A) is incorrect because the weighted-average cost of capital is frequently the entity's required rate of return. Answer (C) is incorrect because the weighted-average cost of capital is frequently the entity's required rate of return. Answer (D) is incorrect because, if the entity's required rate of return is greater than the project's internal rate of return, the NPV is negative.

67. The internal rate of return (IRR) is the

A. Hurdle rate.

B. Rate of interest for which the net present value is greater than 1.0.

C. Rate of interest for which the net present value is equal to zero.

D. Rate of return generated from the operational cash flows.

Answer (C) is correct. *(CMA, adapted)*
REQUIRED: The true statement about the internal rate of return (IRR).
DISCUSSION: The IRR is the interest rate at which the present value of the expected future cash inflows is equal to the present value of the cash outflows for a project. Thus, the IRR is the interest rate that will produce a net present value (NPV) equal to zero. The IRR method assumes that the cash flows will be reinvested at the internal rate of return.
Answer (A) is incorrect because the hurdle rate is a concept used to calculate the NPV of a project; it is determined by management prior to the analysis. Answer (B) is incorrect because the IRR is the rate of interest at which the NPV is zero. Answer (D) is incorrect because the IRR is a means of evaluating potential investment projects.

68. The profitability index is a variation on which of the following capital budgeting models?

A. Internal rate of return.

B. Economic value-added.

C. Net present value.

D. Discounted payback.

Answer (C) is correct. *(CPA, adapted)*

REQUIRED: The capital budgeting method related to the profitability index.

DISCUSSION: The profitability or excess present value index is the ratio of the present value of the future net cash inflows to the present value of the initial net investment. The weighted-average cost of capital is frequently specified. These amounts are the same ones used in the calculation of the net present value. This variation of the net present value method facilitates comparison of different-sized investments.

Answer (A) is incorrect because internal rate of return (IRR) is an interest rate computed such that the net present value of the investment is zero. Hence, the present value of the expected cash outflows equals the present value of the expected cash inflows. Answer (B) is incorrect because EVA may be treated as a type of residual income, that is, income minus some required amount of return on the investment in the reporting entity. However, under the residual income method, the cost of capital may be an arbitrary hurdle rate. In contrast, EVA is based on the calculated weighted-average cost of capital. Answer (D) is incorrect because the discounted (present value) payback method uses discounted cash flows in the denominator to calculate the period required to recover the initial investment. This is a more conservative technique than the traditional payback method.

Use Gleim's *CPA Test Prep* for interactive testing with over 2,000 additional multiple-choice questions!

STUDY UNIT TEN
RISK MANAGEMENT AND PROFITABILITY

(21 pages of outline)

This study unit covers certain aspects of the management of financial risk other than those that can be minimized by the purchase of insurance. Following a brief identification of particular types of risk in the first subunit, the second subunit describes some basic measures of risk. The third subunit addresses portfolio theory, one of the most basic concepts in finance. The fourth subunit discusses treatment of derivatives, another fundamental (and well-publicized) subject. Subunits five and six deal with ratios and how they can affect financing decisions. The AICPA seems to be asking conceptual questions concerning ratios in BEC. Thus, it is not likely that you will be asked to calculate a ratio.

10.1 TYPES OF RISK

1. **Risk** is the possibility of an unfavorable event. **Investment risk** is analyzed in terms of the probability that the actual return will be lower than the expected return. The concepts of probability distributions and expected value are basic to risk management.

   a. The risk of a security may be considered in isolation or from the perspective of its inclusion in a portfolio of assets chosen to minimize the riskiness of the whole.

2. **Specific Types of Risks**

   a. **Interest-rate risk** is the risk of fluctuations in the value of an asset due to changes in interest rates. In general, it is greater the longer the maturity of the asset.

      1) One component of interest-rate risk is **price risk**. Thus, the value of bonds declines when interest rates increase.

      2) A second component of interest-rate risk is **reinvestment-rate risk**. If interest rates decline, lower returns will be available for reinvestment of interest and principal payments received.

      3) **Immunization** is protection against interest-rate risk by holding assets and liabilities such that the product of (a) the value of the assets and their duration equals the product of (b) the value of the liabilities and their duration.

   b. **Purchasing-power risk** is the risk that a general rise in the price level will reduce what can be purchased with a fixed sum of money. Accordingly, required returns include an inflation premium.

   c. **Default risk** is the risk that a borrower will be unable to repay debt. Hence, the higher the default risk, the higher the return required by an investor.

   d. **Market risk** is the risk that changes in price will result from changes that affect all firms. Prices of all securities, even the values of portfolios, are correlated to some degree with broad swings in the economy. Market risk is also known as systematic risk or nondiversifiable risk.

   e. **Nonmarket risk** or **company-specific risk** is the risk that is influenced by an individual firm's policies and decisions. Nonmarket risk is diversifiable because it is firm-specific. Thus, it is also known as diversifiable or unsystematic risk.

    f.   **Portfolio risk** is the risk remaining after allowing for the risk-reducing effects of combining securities into a portfolio.

    g.   **Stand-alone risk** is the risk of a single asset, whereas market risk is its risk if it is held in a large portfolio of diversified securities.

    h.   **Liquidity risk** is the possibility that an asset cannot be sold on short notice for its market value. If an asset must be sold at a deep discount, it is said to have a substantial amount of liquidity risk.

    i.   **Business risk** (or **operations risk**) is the risk of fluctuations in earnings before interest and taxes or in operating income when the firm uses no debt. It is the risk inherent in its operations that excludes **financial risk**, which is the risk to the shareholders from the use of financial leverage. Business risk depends on factors such as demand variability, sales price variability, input price variability, and amount of operating leverage.

    j.   **Exchange-rate risk** is the risk that a foreign currency transaction will be negatively exposed to fluctuations in exchange rates.

    k.   **Commodities risk** includes many possibilities, for example, that an entire investment may be lost, that it may be impossible to liquidate a position under certain market conditions, that spread positions may not be less risky than simple long or short positions, that the use of leverage can lead to large losses, and that managed commodity accounts are subject to substantial management fees. A thorough knowledge of the market is necessary to be able to manage commodities risk.

    l.   **Political risk** is the probability of loss from actions of governments, such as from changes in tax laws or environmental regulations or from expropriation of assets.

    m.   **Total risk** is the risk of a single asset. It includes diversifiable and undiversifiable risk.

3.   Stop and review! You have completed the outline for this subunit. Study multiple-choice questions 1 through 3 on page 324.

10.2 RISK MEASUREMENT

1.   **Probability** provides a method for mathematically expressing doubt or assurance about the occurrence of a chance event. There are two types of probability -- objective and subjective. They differ in how they are calculated.

    a.   **Objective probabilities** are calculated from either logic or actual experience. For example, when rolling a six-sided die, logic indicates that the probability for each outcome (a given face turned upward) is about .167, assuming that each face is equally likely to be turned upward. An estimate of this probability can be objectively determined by rolling the die many times and counting how often each face is turned upward.

    b.   **Subjective probabilities** are estimates, based on personal judgment, of the likelihood of future events. In finance, subjective probability can indicate the degree of confidence a person has that a certain outcome will occur, e.g., the future performance of a stock.

2.   A **probability distribution** is the set of all possible outcomes of a decision, with a probability assigned to each outcome. For example, a simple probability distribution might be defined for the possible returns on a stock investment. A different return could be estimated for each of a limited number of possible states of the economy, and a probability could be determined for each state. Such a probability distribution is **discrete** because the outcomes are limited.

a.   A **continuous distribution** is one for which the outcomes are theoretically infinite. The normal distribution is the best-known continuous distribution. The **normal distribution** has a symmetrical, bell-shaped curve centered about the mean.

1)   Normal distributions have the following fixed relationships concerning the area under the curve and the distance from the mean.

Distance in Standard Deviations	Area under the Curve
1.0	68%
2.0	95.5%
3.0	99.7%

2)   EXAMPLE:

a)   A certain species of pine tree has an average adult height of 20 feet, with each standard deviation representing 1 foot.

b)   We can conclude that 68% of all trees in this species will reach a height between 19 and 21 feet (1 standard deviation), 95.5% will be between 18 and 22 feet (2 standard deviations), and 99.7% will be between 17 and 23 feet (3 standard deviations).

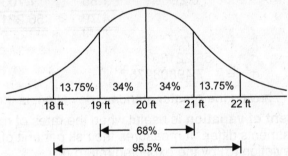

3.   The **expected rate of return** on an investment is determined using an expected value calculation. It is an average of the outcomes weighted according to their probabilities. Consequently, the expected rate of return is the mean of the probability distribution of the possible outcomes. If k_i is the return from the ith possible outcome and if p_i is its probability, the expected return ($\hat{k}$) may be expressed as

$$\hat{k} = \sum_{i=1}^{n} k_i\, p_i$$

a.   This is an intimidating formula, but it simply means that you multiply each expected outcome by its probability and then add the products to get the expected value.

1)   For example, if the value of a grape could be $3, $4, or $5, the expected value is

$$(1/3)(3) + (1/3)(4) + (1/3)(5) = 4$$

b.   The greater the standard deviation of the expected return, the riskier the investment because the less certainty of the outcome. A large standard deviation implies that the range of possible returns is wide, i.e., the probability distribution is broadly dispersed. Conversely, the smaller the standard deviation, the tighter the probability distribution and the lower the risk because of the higher confidence of the outcome.

c.   The **standard deviation** gives an exact value for the tightness of the distribution and, therefore, the riskiness of the investment. The standard deviation (σ) is the square root of the **variance**. If k_i is the return from the ith outcome, p_i is its probability, and $\hat{k}$ is the expected (mean) return, the variance (σ^2) can be calculated as follows:

$$\sigma^2 = \sum_{i=1}^{n} (k_i - \hat{k})^2 p_i$$

1)   EXAMPLE:

Stock X

Return (k_i)	Probability (p_i)	$k_i \times p_i$	$(k_i - \hat{k})^2 p_i$
4.5	0.25	1.125	4.6764063
−5.2	0.25	−1.30	7.2226563
6.3	0.25	1.575	9.3789063
−4.9	0.25	−1.225	6.4389063
		0.175	27.716875

$$\hat{k} = 0.175$$
$$\sigma^2 = 27.716875$$
$$\sigma = 5.264681852$$

Stock Y

Return (k_i)	Probability (p_i)	$k_i \times p_i$	$(k_i - \hat{k})^2 p_i$
10.2	0.25	2.55	7.317025
−8.07	0.25	−2.0175	41.3449
9.63	0.25	2.4075	5.8564
7.4	0.25	1.85	1.703025
		4.79	56.22135

$$\hat{k} = 4.79$$
$$\sigma^2 = 56.22135$$
$$\sigma = 7.498089757$$

Stock Y, having the greater standard deviation, is the riskier investment.

d.   The **coefficient of variation** is useful when the rates of return and standard deviations of two investments differ. It measures the risk per unit of return because it divides the standard deviation (σ) by the expected return ($\hat{k}$).

$$Coefficient\ of\ variation = \frac{\sigma}{\hat{k}}$$

1)   EXAMPLE:

Stock X

$$\sigma \div \hat{k} = 5.264681852 \div 0.175$$
$$= 30.0839$$

Stock Y

$$\sigma \div \hat{k} = 7.498089757 \div 4.79$$
$$= 1.5654$$

Thus, when compared on a per-unit-of-return basis, Stock X is far riskier.

4.   Whether the expected return on an investment is sufficient to entice an investor depends on its risk, the risks and returns of alternative investments, and the investor's attitude toward risk.

a.   Most serious investors are **risk averse**. They have a diminishing marginal utility for risk. The utility of a gain for serious investors is less than the disutility of a loss of the same amount.

b.   A **risk-neutral** investor adopts an expected value approach because (s)he regards the utility of a gain as equal to the disutility of a loss of the same amount. Thus, a risk-neutral investor has a purely rational attitude toward risk.

c.   A **risk-seeking** investor has an optimistic attitude toward risk. (S)he regards the utility of a gain as exceeding the disutility of a loss of the same amount.

5. **Portfolios.** The previous sections apply to investments in individual securities. When a portfolio is held, however, additional considerations apply. Risk and return should be evaluated for the entire portfolio, not for individual assets.

    a. The expected return on a portfolio is the weighted average of the returns on the individual securities.

    b. However, the risk of the portfolio is usually not an average of the standard deviations of the particular securities. Thanks to the diversification effect, combining securities results in a portfolio risk that is less than the average of the standard deviations because the returns are imperfectly correlated.

        1) The **correlation coefficient (r)** has a range from 1.0 to –1.0. It measures the degree to which any two variables, e.g., two stocks in a portfolio, are related. Perfect positive correlation (1.0) means that the two variables always move together, and perfect negative correlation (–1.0) means that the two variables always move in the opposite direction.

            a) Given perfect positive correlation, risk for a two-stock portfolio with equal investments in each stock would be the same as that for the individual assets because they move exactly the same.

            b) Given perfect negative correlation, risk would in theory be eliminated.

        2) In practice, securities are usually positively but imperfectly correlated. The normal range for the correlation of two randomly selected stocks is .50 to .70. The result is a reduction in, but not an elimination of, risk.

    c. The measurement of the standard deviation of a portfolio's returns is based on the same formula as that for a single security.

        1) An important measurement used in portfolio analysis is the **covariance**. It measures the volatility of returns together with their correlation with the returns of other securities. In other words, covariance explains how much two stocks move together.

            a) The computation of covariance will not be required on the CPA exam, but the candidate should understand the concept.

        2) The **correlation coefficient (r)** mentioned earlier is calculated to facilitate comparisons of covariances. It standardizes the covariance by dividing by the product of the standard deviations of the two assets. Moreover, if r_{xy}, σ_x, and σ_y are known, the covariance can be determined.

            $$r_{xy} = \frac{COV_{XY}}{\sigma_X \; \sigma_Y}$$

            a) EXAMPLE: The following is based on the data from the previous Stock X and Stock Y examples:

            $COV_{xy} = 27.23$
            $\sigma_x = 5.264681852$
            $\sigma_y = 7.498089757$
            $r_{xy} = 27.23 \div (5.26 \times 7.5)$
            $\quad\;\; = 0.69$

            b) Covariance will always be given. If a question asks for a covariance, it can be found using this formula and solving for the unknown variable.

6. Stop and review! You have completed the outline for this subunit. Study multiple-choice questions 4 through 10 beginning on page 325.

10.3 PORTFOLIO MANAGEMENT

1.   An investor wants to maximize expected return and minimize risk when choosing a portfolio. A feasible portfolio that offers the highest expected return for a given risk or the least risk for a given expected return is an **efficient portfolio**.

2.   An **optimal portfolio** is a portfolio that is selected from the efficient set of portfolios; it is tangent to the investor's highest indifference curve.

   a.   An **indifference curve** represents combinations of portfolios having equal utility to a particular investor. Given that risk and returns are plotted on the horizontal and vertical axes, respectively, and that the investor is risk averse, the curve has an increasingly positive slope. It is positively sloped because as risk increases, the additional required return per unit of additional risk also increases. The steeper the slope of an indifference curve, the more risk-averse an investor is. The higher the curve, the greater is the investor's level of utility of expected return.

      1)   In the diagram below, A, B, C, D, and E are indifference curves. A represents the highest level of utility and E the lowest. On a given curve, each point represents the same total utility to a risk-averse investor. For example, points 1, 2, and 3 are different combinations of risk and return that yield the same utility. The investor is indifferent as to which combination is chosen.

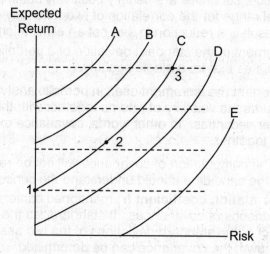

3.   Two important decisions are involved in managing a firm's portfolio:

   a.   The amount of money to invest
   b.   The securities in which to invest

4.   The investment in securities should be based on **expected net cash flows** and **cash flow uncertainty evaluations**.

   a.   Arranging a portfolio so that the maturity of funds will coincide with the need for funds will maximize the average return on the portfolio and provide increased flexibility.

      1)   **Maturity matching** ensures that securities will not have to be sold unexpectedly.

   b.   If its cash flows are relatively uncertain, a security's marketability and market risk are important factors to be considered. Transaction costs are also a consideration.

      1)   Higher yield, long-term securities provide less certainty.

   c.   When cash flows are relatively certain, the maturity date is a paramount concern.

5. **Financial instruments.** Financial managers may select from a wide range of financial instruments in which to invest and with which to raise money.

    a. Ranked from the lowest rate of return to the highest, the following is a short list of widely available long-term financial instruments:

        1) U.S. Treasury bonds
        2) First mortgage bonds
        3) Second mortgage bonds
        4) Subordinated debentures
        5) Income bonds
        6) Preferred stock
        7) Convertible preferred stock
        8) Common stock

    b. These instruments also are ranked according to the level of risk of the security backing them. An unsecured financial instrument is much riskier than a secured instrument. Thus, the riskier asset earns a higher rate of return. Mortgage bonds are secured by assets, but common stock is completely unsecured. Accordingly, common stock will earn a higher rate of return than mortgage bonds.

    c. Short-term financial instruments increase the liquidity of an entity.

6. **Risk Management**

    a. **Portfolio theory** concerns the composition of an investment portfolio that is efficient in balancing the risk and rate of return of the portfolio. **Diversification** reduces risk.

        1) **Asset allocation** is a key concept in financial planning and money management. It is the process of dividing investments among different kinds of assets, such as stocks, bonds, real estate, and cash, to optimize the risk-reward tradeoff based on specific situations and goals. The rationale is that the returns on different types of assets are not perfectly positively correlated. Asset allocation is especially useful for such institutional investors as pension fund managers, who have a duty to invest with prudence.

        2) The goal is to create a theoretically efficient portfolio that is also the firm's optimal portfolio.

    b. The **expected rate of return of a portfolio** is the weighted average of the expected returns of the individual assets in the portfolio.

    c. The **variability (risk) of a portfolio's return** is determined by the correlation of the returns of individual portfolio assets.

        1) To the extent the returns are not perfectly positively correlated, variability is decreased.

        2) In principle, **diversifiable risk** should continue to decrease as the number of different securities held increases. However, in practice, the benefits of diversification become extremely small when more than 30 to 40 different securities are held.

        3) **Portfolio insurance** is a strategy of hedging a stock portfolio against market risk by purchasing and selling derivatives, such as stock index futures and options.

d. **Firm-specific (investee-specific) risk** or **unsystematic risk** is associated with a specific firm's (investee's) operations: new products, patents, acquisitions, competitors, activities, etc.

1) This risk can be largely eliminated by proper diversification of investments.

2) The **relevant risk of an individual security** held in a portfolio is its contribution to the overall risk of the portfolio.

3) When much of a security's risk can be eliminated by diversification, its relevant risk is low.

e. The risk of an individual security that is unaffected by diversification is **market** or **systematic risk** and is measured by the **beta coefficient**.

1) The capital asset pricing model (CAPM) equation is

$$R_{return} = R_f + \beta (M - R_f)$$

a) R_f equals the risk-free interest.
b) M equals the market return rate.

2)
$$\beta = \frac{R_{return} - R_f}{M - R_f} = \frac{COV_{market\ \&\ security}}{\sigma^2_{market}}$$

3) According to the CAPM, **beta measures the volatility** of the returns of a security relative to the returns on the **market portfolio** (a portfolio of all securities).

a) An average-risk stock has a beta of 1.0 because its returns are perfectly positively correlated with those on the market portfolio. For example, if the market return increases by 20%, the return on the security increases by 20%.

b) A beta of less than 1.0 means that the security is less volatile than the market; e.g., if the market return increases by 20% and the security's return increases by 10%, the security has a beta of .5.

c) A beta over 1.0 indicates a volatile security; e.g., if the return increases 30% when the market return increases by 15%, the security has a beta of 2.0.

4) The word **beta** is derived from the equation for regressing the return of an individual security (the dependent variable) to the overall market return. The beta coefficient is the **slope of the regression line**.

5) Beta is the best measure of the risk of an individual security held in a diversified portfolio because it determines how the security affects the risk of the portfolio.

a) The **beta of a portfolio** is the weighted average of the betas of the individual securities. For example, adding high-beta securities to a portfolio tends to increase its risk.

f. The **value-at-risk (VAR) model** uses statistical analysis of historical market trends and volatilities to estimate the likelihood that a given portfolio's losses will exceed a certain amount. It is preferable to sensitivity analysis because it states the probability (stated at a specified confidence level) that a given change in a variable (e.g., a foreign currency exchange rate or an interest rate) will result in a given loss. Simulation and variance-covariance methods are among the techniques used to calculate VAR, sometimes called the maximum normal loss.

7. Stop and review! You have completed the outline for this subunit. Study multiple-choice questions 11 through 18 beginning on page 327.

10.4 DERIVATIVE FINANCIAL INSTRUMENTS

1. A **derivative** is defined informally as an investment transaction in which the buyer purchases the right to a potential gain with a commitment for a potential loss. It is a wager on whether the value of something will go up or down. The purpose of the transaction is either to speculate (incur risk) or to hedge (avoid risk).

   a. Thus, a derivative is an executory contract that results in cash flow between two **counterparties** based on the change in some other indicator of value. Examples of these indicators include prices of financial instruments, such as common shares or government bonds; currency exchange rates; interest rates; commodity prices; or indexes, such as the S&P 500 or the Dow Jones Industrial Average.

   b. Derivative instruments (derivatives) should be contrasted with financial instruments, which include cash, accounts receivable, notes receivable, bonds, preferred shares, common shares, etc.

2. Options and futures are derivative securities. They are not claims on business assets, such as those represented by equity securities. Instead, they are contracts by parties who agree to buy, sell, or exchange assets, such as stocks, commodities, or bonds, at a specified price in the future.

   a. An **American option** is a contractual arrangement that gives the owner the right to buy or sell an asset at a fixed price at any moment in time before or on a specified date. A **European option** differs from an American option because it is exercisable only at the expiration date.

   b. Exercising the option is the act of buying or selling **the underlying**. The underlying is the technical term for the asset to be bought, sold, or traded under the terms of the option. For example, the underlying for a stock option on IBM stock is IBM stock.

   c. An option is a right of the owner or holder of the option. The seller has sold the rights.

   d. The **exercise or striking price** is the price at which the owner can purchase or sell the asset underlying the option contract. The **option price**, also called **option premium**, is the amount paid to acquire an option.

      1) The **bid-ask spread** is the difference between what a buyer is willing to bid and what a seller is asking.

   e. An option usually has an expiration date after which it can no longer be exercised.

   f. The longer the time before its expiration, the more valuable the option. The reason is the increased time available for the asset's price to rise or fall.

3. There are two types of options: calls and puts.

   a. A **call option** is the most common type of option. It gives the owner the right to purchase the underlying asset at a fixed price. Thus, it represents a **long position** because the owner gains from a price increase in the underlying. The profit is the difference between the price paid and the value at the closing date, minus the brokerage fee.

      1) Call options usually involve common stock as the underlying asset; however, any type of asset may underlie an option such as a stock index.

      2) If the value of the asset underlying a call option is less than the exercise price of the option, the option is "out-of-the-money," or not worth exercising. If the value of the asset underlying the option is greater than the exercise price, it is "in-the-money" and can earn the owner a profit. If the value of the asset is at the strike price, the option is at-the-money.

      3) A call option's expiration value equals the excess of the current price of the asset over the exercise price. If the exercise price exceeds the current price, the option is worthless.

4) **Net gain or loss on a call option**

    a) For the purchaser (long position), the gain or loss is the following:
[(Market price – Exercise price) × (# of shares)] – Amount paid for option

    b) For the seller (short position), the loss or gain is the following:
[(Exercise price – Market price) × (# of shares)] + Amount option sold for

    c) The call option will not be exercised unless the market price is greater than the exercise price. The seller profits only when

        i) The option is not exercised, and

        ii) The price paid for the option exceeds the difference between the exercise price and the market price.

    d) EXAMPLE: If the exercise price is $100, the market price is $105, and 100 options were sold for $3 each, the purchaser has a gain of $200 {[($105 – $100) × 100 options] – ($3 × 100 options)}. The seller has a loss of $200 {[($100 – $105) × 100 options] + ($3 × 100 options)}.

b. A **put option** gives the owner the right to sell the underlying asset for a fixed price. It represents a **short position** because the owner benefits from a price decrease.

    1) If the value of the asset underlying a put option is greater than the option's exercise price, the put option is worthless or "out-of-the-money."

    2) If the value of the asset underlying the put option is less than the option's exercise price, the put is "in-the-money." Therefore, the option has **intrinsic value**, which is the difference between the exercise price and the market price of the underlying security.

    3) Put options also may be referred to as "at-the-money" and "out-of-the-money," just like call options.

    4) A put option's expiration value equals either zero or the excess of the exercise price over the current market price.

    5) **Net gain or loss on a put option**

        a) For the purchaser (long position), the gain or loss is the following:
[(Exercise price – Market price) × (# of shares)] – Amount paid for option

        b) For the seller (short position), the loss or gain is the following:
[(Market price – Exercise price) × (# of shares)] + Amount option sold for

        c) The put option will not be exercised unless the exercise price is greater than the market price. The seller profits only when

            i) The option is not exercised, and

            ii) The price paid for the option exceeds the difference between the market price and the exercise price.

        d) EXAMPLE: If the exercise price is $105, the market price is $100, and 100 options were sold for $3 each, the purchaser has a gain of $200 {[($105 – $100) × 100 options] – ($3 × 100 options)}. The seller has a loss of $200 {[($100 – $105) × 100 options] + ($3 × 100 options)}.

4. While there are two types of options, the method in which they are used can be referred to as a type of option.

    a. A **covered option** is one that is written against stock held in the option writer's portfolio.

    b. A **naked (uncovered) option** is one that does not have the backing of stock.

    c. In other words, put and call options can be referred to as naked options if the holder is not using the options as a hedge because (s)he does not own the underlying.

5. Stock options also can be named after the underlying. Again, there are still only puts and calls.

    a. A **stock option** is an option to buy a specific stock at some future time.

    b. An **index option** is an option whose underlying security is an index. If exercised, settlement is made by cash payment because physical delivery is not possible.

    c. **Long-term equity anticipation securities (LEAPS)** are examples of long-term stock options or index options, with expiration dates up to three years away.

    d. **Foreign currency options** give the holder the right to buy a specific foreign currency at a designated exchange rate.

6. **Put-call parity.** For European options, given market equilibrium for all relevant prices (no arbitrage possibilities), equal exercise prices for the put and the call, and the same expiration date, the put-call parity theorem states that a fixed relationship applies to the market values of the put and call options on a security.

    Call price – put price = Underlying price – PV of exercise price

7. The value of a call option is based on its exercise price, its expiration date, the price of the underlying asset, the variability of that asset, and the risk-free interest rate. The well-known **Black-Scholes option-pricing model** uses these factors.

    a. The CPA exam may ask questions concerning the volatility of the stock or market and the effect it has on the price of a call or a put.

        1) Volatility (i.e., variances of daily trading prices) and interest rates vary directly with the prices of puts and calls.

8. A **forward contract** is an agreement negotiated between two parties for the purchase and sale of a stated amount of a commodity, foreign currency, or financial instrument at a stated price, with delivery or settlement at a stated future date. Forward contracts are usually specifically negotiated agreements and are not traded on regulated exchanges. Thus, the parties are subject to default risk (i.e., that the other party will not perform).

9. A **futures contract** is a specific kind of **forward contract**, which is simply an executory contract. A futures contract is a definite agreement that allows a trader to purchase or sell an asset at a fixed price during a specific future month. Futures contracts for agricultural commodities, metals, oil, and financial assets are traded on numerous exchanges.

    a. One characteristic of a futures contract is that it may be highly leveraged. The initial **margin** paid may be a very small percentage of the price. Thus, the risk of either gain or loss to a speculator may be great.

    b. A futures contract differs from a forward contract in part because it is traded on an exchange and it is standardized. The result is a liquid market in futures that permits buyers and sellers to net out their positions. For example, a party who has sold a contract can net out his/her position by buying a futures contract.

    c. Another distinguishing feature of futures contracts is that their prices are **marked to market** every day at the close of the day to each person's account. Thus, the market price is posted at the close of business each day. A mark-to-market provision minimizes a futures contract's chance of default because profits and losses on the contracts must be received or paid each day through a clearinghouse. This requirement of **daily settlement** minimizes default and is necessary because futures contracts are sold on margin (i.e., they are highly leveraged).

d. A futures contract is entered into as either a speculation or a hedge. A financial manager can protect a firm against adverse changes in prices and interest rates by hedging in the futures market. **Hedging** is the process of using offsetting commitments to minimize or avoid the impact of adverse price movements.

    1) **Long hedges** are futures contracts that are purchased to protect against price increases.

    2) **Short hedges** are futures contracts that are sold to protect against price declines.

    3) EXAMPLE: In the commodities market, a firm might have a contract with a farmer to buy soybeans at a future date. The price is agreed upon as the current price. The firm would lose money if the soybean prices declined before the beans were delivered. To avoid any loss (or gain), the firm could sell soybeans in the future at today's price. If the price of soybeans does decline before the delivery date, it will lose money on the beans bought from the farmer, but it will gain money on the beans sold through the futures contract by buying cheap beans in the future to cover the delivery.

        a) Because commodities can be bought and sold **on margin**, considerable leverage is involved. This high degree of leverage is most beneficial to the speculator who is looking for large returns and is willing to bear the risk to get them. For hedgers, however, the small margin requirement is useful only because the risk can be hedged without tying up a large amount of cash.

e. **Swaps** are contracts to hedge risk by exchanging cash flows. The simplest form, sometimes called a **plain vanilla swap**, is an exchange of interest rates without any change in the initial debt arrangement.

    1) In an **interest-rate swap**, one firm exchanges its fixed interest payments for a series of payments based on a floating rate. Such contracts are highly customized. If a firm has debt with fixed charges, but its revenues fluctuate with interest rates, it may prefer to swap for cash outflows based on a floating rate. The advantage is that revenues and the amounts of debt service will then move in the same direction, and interest-rate risk will be reduced.

    2) A **currency swap** is an exchange of an obligation to pay out cash flows denominated in one currency for an obligation to pay in another. For example, a U.S. firm with revenues in euros has to pay suppliers and workers in dollars, not euros. To minimize exchange-rate risk, it might agree to exchange euros for dollars held by a firm that needs euros. The exchange rate will be an average of the rates expected over the life of the agreement.

    3) A **swaption** is an option on a swap, usually on an interest-rate swap, that provides the holder with the right to enter into a swap at a specified future date at specified terms (freestanding option on a swap) or to extend or terminate the life of an existing swap (embedded option on a swap).

f. **Arbitrage** is the simultaneous purchase and sale of identical or equivalent financial instruments or commodity futures to benefit from a discrepancy in their price relationship. This sometimes involves selling in one market while simultaneously buying in another market.

g. **Program trading**, also known as index arbitrage or computer-assisted trading, exploits the price discrepancies between indexes of stocks and futures contracts by using sophisticated computer models to hedge positions and trade instantaneously. Program trading arose with the advent of telecommunication technology that permits transactions in different markets to be monitored simultaneously.

h.   Interest rate caps, floors, and collars.

   1)   An **interest rate cap** is an option that limits the risk of interest rate increases. If interest rates rise above a certain level, the cap holder receives the excess of the actual interest rate over a designated interest rate (the strike or cap rate) based on the notional principal amount. The cap holder's loss is limited to the premium paid to the cap writer. The cap writer has unlimited risk from potential increases in interest rates above the specified rate.

   2)   An **interest rate floor** is an option that limits the risk of interest rate decreases. If rates fall below a specified level, the floor holder receives cash payments equal to the excess of a designated rate (the strike or floor rate) over the actual rate based on the notional principal amount. The buyer pays the writer a premium to receive this right, and the floor writer faces significant risk from potential decreases in rates below the specified rate.

   3)   A **collar** is an option that combines the strategies of a cap and a floor. The buyer acquires a cap and writes a floor. The writer writes a cap and buys a floor. Collars fix the rate a variable-rate lender will receive or a borrower will pay between the cap and floor rate levels. Collars help reduce the cost of buying outright a cap or floor. Because a borrower or lender is usually only interested in protecting against movements in interest rates in one direction, the premium received for writing a cap or floor serves to reduce the cost of the cap or floor purchased.

10.   Stop and review! You have completed the outline for this subunit. Study multiple-choice questions 19 through 35 beginning on page 330.

10.5 RATIOS

1.   **Liquidity ratios** measure the relationship of a firm's liquid assets to current liabilities. Thus, such ratios provide information about the short-term viability of the business, i.e., the firm's ability to pay its current obligations and to continue operations.

   a.   The **current ratio** (working capital ratio) equals current assets divided by current liabilities and is the most common measure of near-term solvency.

      1) $$\frac{Current\ assets}{Current\ liabilities}$$

      2)   A low ratio indicates a possible solvency problem. An overly high ratio indicates that management may not be investing idle assets productively.

      3)   The general principle is that the current ratio should be proportional to the operating cycle. Thus, a shorter cycle may justify a lower ratio.

   b.   A conservative version of the current ratio is the **acid test** or **quick ratio**, which divides the quick assets (cash, cash equivalents, net receivables, and marketable securities) by current liabilities.

      1) $$\frac{Cash + Cash\ equivalents + Net\ receivables + Marketable\ securities}{Current\ liabilities}$$

      2)   This ratio measures the firm's ability to pay its short-term debts from its most liquid assets and avoids the problem of inventory valuation.

c. **Free cash flow** is an analytical measure of financial flexibility. It is the cash from operations remaining after subtracting amounts that must be paid to sustain the current level of productive capacity. The elements subtracted, however, vary in practice.

   1) Most models subtract all **capital expenditures** to arrive at free cash flow. But some authorities treat capital expenditures to increase capacity as discretionary items and do not subtract them.

   2) Some models also subtract **interest, dividends,** and **taxes** to arrive at free cash flow because these amounts may be viewed as nondiscretionary.

2. **Leverage ratios** measure the firm's use of debt to finance assets and operations. Financial leverage **(trading on the equity)** is advantageous when earnings from borrowed funds exceed borrowing costs. However, risk increases as interest rates increase and returns decrease. Accordingly, as leverage increases, both the risk that the firm may not be able to meet its maturing obligations and the risk borne by creditors increase. Nevertheless, interest is tax deductible, so leverage increases the firm's return when it is profitable. Furthermore, debt financing permits the owners to retain control.

   a. **Solvency** is a firm's financial ability to survive in the long term by paying its long-term obligations. It is contrasted with **liquidity**, the ability to pay short-term obligations.

   b. The key ingredients of solvency are capital structure and earning power.

      1) **Capital structure** includes the firm's sources of financing, whether long-term or short-term, of its assets. Capital structure consists of equity and debt.

         a) **Equity** is the ownership interest in the firm. It represents permanent capital that cannot be withdrawn at the discretion of the owner, and its return is uncertain, ordinarily with no designated pattern of payment (e.g., dividends). Thus, equity is sometimes called the risk capital of the firm.

         b) **Debt** is the creditor interest in the firm. It must be repaid according to a designated pattern (e.g., interest and principal payments for long-term debt). The greater the debt burden, the greater the fixed payments and the greater the risk. However, when the return on debt capital exceeds interest paid, borrowing improves earnings. Moreover, the interest on debt, unlike the payments to owners (dividends), is tax deductible.

      2) **Earning power** is the capacity of the firm's operations to produce cash inflows. A predictably stable pattern of earnings is the optimal source of funds for payment of long-term debt and other fixed charges. Furthermore, it enhances the firm's credit standing, allowing it to borrow on favorable terms when its cash balance is low.

   c. The **total debt ratio** equals total liabilities divided by total assets (total capital).

      1) $$\frac{\text{Total liabilities}}{\text{Total assets (capital)}}$$

      The total debt ratio measures the percentage of funds provided by creditors. It determines long-term debt-payment ability and the degree to which creditors are protected from the firm's insolvency. Hence, creditors prefer this ratio to be low as a cushion against losses.

   d. The **total debt-to-equity ratio** equals total debt divided by total equity.

      1) $$\frac{\text{Total liabilities}}{\text{Equity}}$$

      2) It compares the resources provided by creditors with resources provided by shareholders.

e.   The **times-interest-earned ratio** (interest coverage ratio) equals earnings before interest and taxes (EBIT), divided by interest.

1) $$\dfrac{EBIT}{Interest\ expense}$$

2)   This ratio is an income statement approach to evaluating debt-payment ability. It indicates the margin of safety for payment of fixed interest charges, so a consistently high ratio is desirable.

3)   Interest is tax deductible. Hence, interest and tax must be added to net income to determine the amount available to pay interest.

f.   The **operating cash flow to total debt ratio** equals the net cash provided by operations divided by total debt.

1) $$\dfrac{Operating\ cash\ flow}{Total\ debt}$$

2)   A high ratio is desirable. Moreover, the most conservative approach is to include all debt items in the denominator.

g.   The **asset coverage ratio** measures the extent to which a firm's assets cover its debt obligations.

1) $$\dfrac{Total\ tangible\ assets}{Total\ liabilities}$$

3.   **Asset management ratios** measure the firm's use of assets to generate revenue and income. Thus, they also relate to liquidity.

a.   The **inventory turnover ratio** equals cost of sales divided by average inventory.

1) $$\dfrac{Cost\ of\ sales}{Average\ inventory}$$

2)   A high turnover implies that the firm does not hold excessive stocks of inventories that are unproductive and that lessen the firm's profitability.

3)   A high turnover also implies that the inventory is truly marketable and does not contain obsolete goods.

b.   The **number of days of inventory** (days' sales in average inventory) equals the number of days in the year divided by the inventory turnover ratio.

1) $$\dfrac{365,\ 360,\ or\ 300}{Inventory\ turnover\ ratio}$$

2)   This ratio measures the average number of days that inventory is held before sale. Thus, it reflects the efficiency of inventory management.

c.   The **receivables turnover ratio** equals net credit sales divided by average accounts receivable. (However, net sales is often used because credit sales data may be unavailable.)

1) $$\dfrac{Net\ credit\ sales}{Average\ accounts\ receivable}$$

2)   This ratio measures the efficiency of accounts receivable collection.

3)   A high turnover is preferable.

d.   The **number of days of receivables** (days' sales in average receivables, also called the average collection period) equals the number of days in the period divided by the receivables turnover ratio.

1) $$\frac{365,\ 360,\ or\ 300}{Receivables\ turnover\ ratio}$$

2)   This ratio is the average number of days to collect a receivable.

3)   The number of days of receivables should be compared with the firm's credit terms to determine whether the average customer is paying within the credit period.

4)   The **operating cycle** (conversion period) of an enterprise may be estimated by adding the number of days' sales in average inventory to the number of days' sales in average receivables.

e.   The **total assets turnover ratio** equals net sales divided by average total assets.

1) $$\frac{Net\ sales}{Average\ total\ assets}$$

2)   This ratio measures the level of capital investment relative to sales volume.

3)   For all turnover ratios, high turnover is preferable because it implies effective use of assets to generate sales.

4)   Certain assets, for example, investments, do not relate to net sales. Their inclusion decreases the ratio.

f.   The **plowback ratio** is the percentage of net income available for reinvestment.

1) $$\frac{Amount\ available\ for\ reinvestment}{Net\ income}$$

2)   A high rate means less external financing.

4.   **Cost management ratios** measure how well a firm controls its costs. However, they may be difficult for an external analyst to determine because firms conceal their detailed cost data from competitors.

a.   The **gross margin** (gross profit percentage) equals net sales minus cost of sales, divided by net sales.

1) $$\frac{Net\ sales\ -\ Cost\ of\ sales}{Net\ sales}$$

2)   A high gross margin implies effective cost control. This ratio measures how much can be spent for such items as marketing, R&D, and administrative costs while still reaching targeted net income.

5.   **Profitability ratios** measure earnings relative to some base, for example, productive assets, sales, or capital.

a.   Increased profits benefit owners not only because they make additional funds available for dividend payments but also because they may result in appreciation of a corporate entity's stock price.

b.   Profits also provide a cushion for debt coverage. Hence, profitability ratios are used by investors, creditors, and others to evaluate management's stewardship of the firm's assets.

c.   These ratios are based on accounting profits, which may differ from economic profits. **Economic profits** include all explicit and implicit revenues and costs (including the cost of capital). **Accounting profits** include only the explicit revenues and costs of a single firm. **Social profits** deduct the external factors (e.g., pollution), which impact parties other than the firm and its customers.

d. The **profit margin on sales** equals net income divided by net sales.

1) $$\frac{\text{Net income after interest and taxes}}{\text{Net sales}}$$

2) The numerator may also be stated in terms of the net income available to common shareholders.

3) Another form of the ratio excludes nonrecurring items from the numerator, e.g., unusual or infrequent items, discontinued operations, extraordinary items, and effects of accounting changes. The result is sometimes called the **net profit margin**. This adjustment may be made for any ratio that includes net income.

   a) Still other numerator refinements are to exclude equity-based earnings and items in the other income and other expense categories.

e. The **return on investment** or **ROI** (also called **return on total assets** or **return on invested capital**) may be defined in many ways, for example, as net income divided by average total assets.

1) $$\frac{\text{Net income after interest and taxes}}{\text{Average total assets}}$$

2) The numerator may be defined in various ways. One possibility is net income available to common shareholders, which subtracts preferred dividends. Another numerator adjustment is to add back a minority interest in the income of a consolidated subsidiary when invested capital is defined to include the minority interest. Still another numerator adjustment is to add back interest expense when invested capital equals total debt plus equity capital. A final example is the **basic earning power ratio**, which divides EBIT by average total assets. This ratio enhances comparability of firms with different capital structures and tax planning strategies.

3) The denominator also may be defined in many ways, for example, to include only operating assets. Investments, intangible assets, and the other asset category are excluded. Other potential definitions of the investment base include (a) adjustments to eliminate unproductive assets (e.g., idle plant), intangible assets, or accumulated depreciation; (b) excluding current liabilities to emphasize long-term capital; (c) excluding debt and preferred stock to arrive at equity capital; and (d) stating invested capital at market value.

4) This ratio tells investors whether management is using invested funds wisely. It also provides a profitability measure relating both to the income statement and the balance sheet that can be adjusted to reflect the contributions of creditors or equity providers. Other uses of this ratio are in forecasting earnings, planning, budgeting, and control.

f. The **return on common equity** equals the net income available to common shareholders divided by their average equity.

1) $$\frac{\text{Net income after interest and taxes} - \text{Preferred dividends}}{\text{Average common equity}}$$

2) The average common equity includes total equity minus the preferred shareholders' capital and any minority interest.

3) This ratio and the next one measure the return on the carrying amount of equity.

4) A variation of the return on common equity is the **marginal return on common equity** (change in net income ÷ change in common equity).

g. The **return on total equity** equals net income minus dividends on redeemable preferred stock, divided by average total equity.

1) $$\frac{\text{Net income after interest and taxes } - \text{ Dividends on redeemable preferred stock}}{\text{Average total equity}}$$

2) **Redeemable preferred stock** is usually considered to be equivalent to debt. Indeed, the SEC requires it to be reported separately from other equity.

6. A concept similar to residual income, but often applied at the overall firm level as well as at the departmental level, is that of **economic value added**, or **EVA**. It is a registered trademark of Stern Stewart & Co., which developed the concept.

a. Although many refinements and adjustments are possible, basic EVA equals net operating profit after taxes (NOPAT) minus the capital charge or total cost of capital.

1) **NOPAT** is profit before interest and taxes minus an amount of taxes that is calculated on the assumption that the firm has no debt or financial assets. This assumption is made to improve the comparability of EVA calculations. Otherwise, firms with different debt structures could have the same operating performance but different net incomes.

2) The capital charge equals the after-tax weighted-average cost of capital (calculated based on fair values of debt and equity) times the investment base or capital employed (fixed assets plus net working capital, or total assets minus current liabilities).

b. Investors earn a real profit only after capital costs have been deducted.

c. Investors can easily earn the average stock market return by investing in an index fund; thus, they are no better off investing in an individual stock unless they can earn more than the average cost of capital. EVA measures this excess return.

1) The cost of capital (required rate of return) is based on the after-tax weighted-average cost of debt as well as equity capital.

2) The capital charge is a real cost, but the traditional income statement does not include a deduction for the costs of equity capital because it is an opportunity cost. EVA is considered an improvement over traditional income measures because it does include a deduction for the costs of all forms of capital.

d. The real profit (economic profit) to investors is the profit after deducting the capital charge.

e. A company generates a positive result only after it has earned more than the average return for a company in its risk class.

f. For internal purposes, EVA is a better measure of profitability than ROI because a manager with a high ROI would be reluctant to invest in a new project with a lower ROI than is currently being earned, even though that return might be higher than the cost of capital. Thus, including a capital charge on departmental income statements helps managers to make decisions that will benefit the company.

g. EXAMPLE: A company with $100,000 in equity capital (stated at fair value) and $100,000 in 8% debt (also at fair value) had $50,000 in operating income before taxes and interest. Assume also that $200,000 equals capital employed. The combined state and federal tax rate is 40%. If that company's weighted-average after-tax cost of capital is 14%, the EVA is $2,000, calculated as follows:

Operating income before interest and tax	$50,000
Minus taxes ($50,000 × 40%)	(20,000)
After-tax operating income	$30,000
Capital charge ($200,000 × 14%)	(28,000)
EVA	$ 2,000

1) The company's traditional income statement reports income of $25,200, calculated as follows:

Operating income before interest and tax	$50,000
Minus interest ($100,000 × 8%)	(8,000)
Taxable income	42,000
Income taxes ($42,000 × 40%)	(16,800)
Net income after taxes	$25,200

2) Initially, a 25.2% return on equity ($25,200 of net income ÷ $100,000 of equity capital) seems favorable, but what is the cost of that equity capital? Given equal amounts of debt and equity, the cost of the equity capital must be 23.2% because the after-tax weighted-average cost of capital was 14%, and the after-tax cost of debt capital was 4.8% [8% × (1.0 − 40% tax rate)] [14% = (8% + X) ÷ 2]. Thus, $23,200 of the $25,200 of net income is nothing more than the opportunity cost of equity capital. The $2,000 of EVA is the only portion of earnings that has created value for the shareholders. Accordingly, if income after taxes had been only $19,000 (a 19% return on equity), shareholder value would have been reduced because the cost of equity capital would have exceeded the return.

h. Some studies have shown a direct correlation between EVA and increases in stock prices. Simply having a continuing stream of income is not enough; that income must exceed the cost of capital for a stock to rise significantly in the stock market.

i. Although most companies adopt EVA for purposes of internal reporting and for calculating bonuses, some are publishing the results in the corporate annual reports. For example, Eli Lilly reports EVA in the Financial Highlights section of the annual report.

j. EVA may be treated as a type of **residual income**, that is, income minus some required amount of return on the investment in the reporting entity. However, under the residual income method, the cost of capital may be an arbitrary hurdle rate. In contrast, EVA is based on the calculated weighted-average cost of capital. Both methods can be traced to the work of the economist David Ricardo, who in the mid-1800s used the term **super normal rent** to describe EVA.

k. One aspect that makes EVA so popular is that it uses dollars instead of percentages to measure changes. For example, it is much more appealing to report that the company generated $1 million in shareholder value than to say that the ROI increased from 10% to 15%.

7. **Growth ratios** measure the changes in the economic status of a firm over a period of years. Firms compare their growth in sales, operating income, net income, EPS, and dividends per share with the results of competitors and the economy as a whole.

a. The most accurate analysis adjusts nominal growth rates for **price level changes** to determine real growth rates. Other aspects of **earnings quality** should be addressed before relying on earnings-based measures. For example, income based on FIFO inventory valuation may not be as meaningful as income from a LIFO-based inventory valuation. Similarly, the impact on income from using straight-line depreciation or an accelerated method should be evaluated.

b. **Cash flow per share** equals net cash provided by operations minus preferred dividends, divided by common shares outstanding.

1) $$\frac{Cash\ provided\ by\ operations\ -\ Preferred\ dividends}{Common\ shares\ outstanding}$$

2) This ratio is a better indicator of short-term capacity to make capital outlays and dividend payments than EPS. However, it is not a substitute for EPS as a measure of profitability. Hence, the FASB has stated that cash flow per share is not to be reported in the financial statements.

c. The **dividend payout ratio** equals dividends per common share divided by EPS.

    1) $\dfrac{Cash\ dividends\ per\ common\ share}{EPS}$

    2) Firms develop dividend policies based on recurring earnings because they usually prefer a stable pattern of dividends.

    3) The appropriate ratio depends on the firm's unique circumstances, including shareholder preferences regarding dividend income and capital gains. The general principle, however, is that growth companies have a low payout.

8. **Valuation ratios** are broad performance measures. They reflect the basic principle that corporate management's ultimate goal is to maximize shareholder value reflected in the price of the firm's stock.

a. **Book value per share** equals the amount of net assets available to the shareholders of a given type of stock divided by the number of those shares outstanding.

    1) $\dfrac{Equity}{Shares\ outstanding}$

    2) When a company has preferred as well as common stock outstanding, the computation of book value per common share must consider potential claims by preferred shareholders, such as whether the preferred stock is cumulative and in arrears or participating. It must also consider whether the call price (or possibly the liquidation value) exceeds the carrying amount of the preferred stock.

    3) Book value per share is ordinarily based on historical cost expressed in nominal dollars. Accordingly, it may be misleading because book values ordinarily differ materially from fair values.

b. The book value per share is used to calculate the **market-to-book ratio** (price-to-book ratio).

    1) $\dfrac{Market\ price\ per\ share}{Book\ value\ per\ share}$

    2) Well-managed firms should sell at high multiples of their book value, which reflects historical cost.

c. The **price-to-earnings (P-E) ratio** equals the market price per share of common stock divided by EPS.

    1) $\dfrac{Market\ price}{EPS}$

    2) Growth companies are likely to have high P-E ratios. A high ratio may also indicate that the firm is relatively high risk or that its choice of accounting methods results in a conservative EPS.

    3) Because of the widespread use of the P-E ratio and other measures, the relationship between accounting data and stock prices is crucial. Thus, managers have an incentive to "manage earnings," sometimes by fraudulent means.

9. Stop and review! You have completed the outline for this subunit. Study multiple-choice questions 36 through 71 beginning on page 335.

10.6 LIMITATIONS OF RATIO ANALYSIS

1.   Although ratio analysis provides useful information pertaining to the efficiency of operations and the stability of financial conditions, it has inherent limitations.

   a.   Development of ratios for comparison with **industry averages** is more useful for firms that operate within a particular industry than for conglomerates (firms that operate in a variety of industries).

   b.   **Inflation** misstates a firm's balance sheet and income statement because of the effects on fixed assets and depreciation, inventory costs, long-term debt, and profitability.

   c.   Ratio analysis may be affected by **seasonal factors**. For example, inventory and receivables may vary widely, and year-end balances may not reflect the averages for the period.

   d.   A firm's management has an incentive to **window dress** financial statements to improve results.

   e.   **Comparability** of financial statement amounts and the ratios derived from them is impaired if different firms choose different accounting policies. Also, changes in a firm's own accounting policies may create some distortion in the comparison of the results over a period of years.

   f.   Misleading conclusions may result if **improper comparisons** are selected.

   g.   Whether a certain level of a ratio is favorable depends on the **underlying circumstances**. For example, a high quick ratio indicates high liquidity, but it may also imply that excessive cash is being held.

   h.   Different ratios may yield opposite conclusions about a firm's financial health. Thus, the net effects of a set of ratios should be analyzed.

   i.   **Industry averages** may include data from capital-intensive and labor-intensive firms. They also may include data from firms with far different leverage policies.

      1)   Some industry averages may be based on **small samples**.

   j.   **Different sources** of information may compute ratios differently.

   k.   Some data may be presented either before or after **taxes**.

   l.   Comparability among firms may be impaired if they have **different fiscal years**.

   m.   The **geographical locations** of firms may affect comparability because of differences in labor markets, price levels, governmental regulation, taxation, and other factors.

   n.   **Size differentials** among firms affect comparability because of differences in access to and cost of capital, economies of scale, and width of market.

2.   **Asset composition** addresses how liquid a company wants to be. A conservative company, or one with a low level of inventory, may prefer to hold highly liquid assets. A competitor might prefer a less-liquid composition.

3.   Stop and review! You have completed the outline for this subunit. Study multiple-choice questions 72 and 73 on page 344.

QUESTIONS

10.1 Types of Risk

1. The type of risk that is not diversifiable and even affects the value of a portfolio is

- A. Purchasing-power risk.
- B. Market risk.
- C. Nonmarket risk.
- D. Interest-rate risk.

Answer (B) is correct. *(Publisher, adapted)*

REQUIRED: The term for the type of risk that is not diversifiable.

DISCUSSION: Prices of all stocks, even the values of portfolios, are correlated to some degree with broad swings in the stock market. Market risk is the risk that changes in a stock's price will result from changes in the stock market as a whole. Market risk is commonly referred to as nondiversifiable risk.

Answer (A) is incorrect because purchasing-power risk is the risk that a general rise in the price level will reduce the quantity of goods that can be purchased with a fixed sum of money. Answer (C) is incorrect because nonmarket risk is the risk that is influenced by an individual firm's policies and decisions. Nonmarket risk is diversifiable because it is specific to each firm. Answer (D) is incorrect because interest-rate risk is the risk that the value of an asset will fluctuate due to changes in the interest rate.

2. Which of the following are components of interest-rate risk?

- A. Purchasing-power risk and default risk.
- B. Price risk and market risk.
- C. Portfolio risk and reinvestment-rate risk.
- D. Price risk and reinvestment-rate risk.

Answer (D) is correct. *(Publisher, adapted)*

REQUIRED: The components of interest-rate risk.

DISCUSSION: Interest-rate risk is the risk of fluctuations in the value of an asset due to changes in interest rates. One component of interest-rate risk is price risk, for example, the risk of a decline in the value of bonds as interest rates increase. Reinvestment-rate risk is another component of interest-rate risk. If interest rates decline, lower returns will be available for reinvestment of interest and principal payments received.

Answer (A) is incorrect because purchasing-power risk concerns inflation, and default risk concerns nonpayment by the debtor. Answer (B) is incorrect because market risk concerns price changes in the overall securities markets. Answer (C) is incorrect because portfolio risk is the risk remaining in a portfolio after diversifying investments.

3. O & B Company, a U.S. corporation, is in possession of accounts receivable from its European sales that are denominated in euros. To what type of risk is the company exposed?

- A. Liquidity risk.
- B. Business risk.
- C. Exchange-rate risk.
- D. Price risk.

Answer (C) is correct. *(Publisher, adapted)*

REQUIRED: The risk to which a business is exposed when accounts receivable are denominated in a foreign currency.

DISCUSSION: Exchange-rate risk is the risk that a foreign currency transaction will be negatively exposed to fluctuations in exchange rates. Because O & B Company sells goods to European customers and records accounts receivable denominated in euros, O & B Company is exposed to exchange-rate risk.

Answer (A) is incorrect because liquidity risk is the possibility that an asset cannot be sold on short notice for its market value. Answer (B) is incorrect because business risk is the risk of fluctuations in earnings before interest and taxes or in operating income when the firm uses no debt. Answer (D) is incorrect because price risk is a component of interest-rate risk.

10.2 Risk Measurement

4. An asset with high risk will have a(n)

   A. Low expected return.

   B. Lower price than an asset with low risk.

   C. Increasing expected rate of return.

   D. High standard deviation of returns.

Answer (D) is correct. *(Publisher, adapted)*
   REQUIRED: The characteristic of an asset with high risk.
   DISCUSSION: The greater the standard deviation of the expected return, the riskier the investment. A large standard deviation implies that the range of possible returns is wide; i.e., the probability distribution is broadly dispersed. Conversely, the smaller the standard deviation, the tighter the probability distribution and the lower the risk.
   Answer (A) is incorrect because an asset with high risk will have a high expected return to compensate for the additional risk. Answer (B) is incorrect because an asset with high risk will not necessarily have a lower price than an asset with low risk. For example, two bond issues with different risk levels might be sold at the same price but have different interest rates. Answer (C) is incorrect because an expected rate of return by definition is a constant expected return.

5. The expected rate of return for the stock of Corn Enterprises is 20%, with a standard deviation of 15%. The expected rate of return for the stock of Oat Associates is 10%, with a standard deviation of 9%. The riskier stock is

   A. Corn because its return is higher.

   B. Corn because its standard deviation is higher.

   C. Oat because its standard deviation is higher.

   D. Oat because its coefficient of variation is higher.

Answer (D) is correct. *(CMA, adapted)*
   REQUIRED: The riskier stock.
   DISCUSSION: The standard deviation is a measure of the degree of compactness of the values in a population. It is a measure of dispersion. The standard deviation is found by taking the square root of the quotient of the sum of the squared deviations from the mean, divided by the number of items in the population. Corn has a mean return of 20% and a standard deviation of 15%. Hence, it is not as risky as Oat, which has a standard deviation of 9% relative to a mean of only 10%. The coefficient of variation (standard deviation ÷ expected return) is much higher for Oat (.09 ÷ .10 = .9) than for Corn (.15 ÷ .20 = .75).
   Answer (A) is incorrect because the existence of a higher return is not necessarily indicative of high risk. Answer (B) is incorrect because the higher standard deviation must be viewed relative to the mean of the population. Answer (C) is incorrect because Oat does not have the higher standard deviation.

6. If the covariance of stock A with stock B is –.0076, then what is the covariance of stock B with stock A?

   A. +.0076

   B. –.0076

   C. Greater than +.0076.

   D. Less than –.0076.

Answer (B) is correct. *(Publisher, adapted)*
   REQUIRED: The covariance of two stocks.
   DISCUSSION: The covariance measures the volatility of returns together with their correlation with the returns of other securities. It is calculated using the following equation:

$$COV(XY) = \sum_{i=1}^{n}(k_{xi} - \hat{k}_x)(k_{yi} - \hat{k}_y)p_i$$

The covariance of two stocks is the same regardless of which stock is compared with the other.

Questions 7 through 9 are based on the following information.

Techspace has been a successful stock over the past few years despite its riskiness. The state of the economy has a tremendous effect on the expected returns for Techspace as shown in the next column:

Probability	State of the Economy	Techspace Returns
.05	Depression	−45%
.15	Recession	−10%
.20	Minimal Slowdown	5%
.40	Stable	10%
.15	Expansion	30%
.05	Significant Expansion	35%

7. What is the expected rate of return on Techspace stock?

A. 7.5%

B. 15%

C. 35%

D. 25%

Answer (A) is correct. *(Publisher, adapted)*
REQUIRED: The expected rate of return on a stock given probabilities for different situations and corresponding returns.
DISCUSSION: The expected rate of return on an investment is determined using an expected value calculation. It is an average of the outcomes weighted according to their probabilities. For Techspace, the average is determined by multiplying each probability by the corresponding return for each state of the economy and then calculating the sum of the products. Thus, the expected rate of return is 7.5% [.05(−.45) + .15(−.10) + .2(.05) + .4(.10) + .15(.30) + .05(.35)].
Answer (B) is incorrect because 15% adds positive products instead of negative products for the first two states. Answer (C) is incorrect because 35% is the sum of the returns (assuming all are positive) minus 1. Answer (D) is incorrect because 25% is the sum of the returns.

8. The variance of Techspace returns is

A. .1735

B. .0301

C. .075

D. .2738

Answer (B) is correct. *(Publisher, adapted)*
REQUIRED: The variance on a stock given probabilities for different situations and corresponding returns.
DISCUSSION: The variance (σ^2) is calculated using the equation

$$\sigma^2 = \sum_{i=1}^{n}(k_i - \hat{k})^2 p_i$$

If: k_i is the return for the ith outcome, $\hat{k}$ is the expected return, and p_i is the probability of the ith outcome, then

$$\hat{k} = \sum_{i=1}^{n} k_i p_i \quad \text{or} \quad .05(-.45) + .15(-.10) + .2(.05)$$

$$+ .4(.10) + .15(.30) + .05(.35) = .075$$

$$\sigma^2 = .05(-.45 - .075)^2 + .15(-.1 - .075)^2$$
$$+ .2(.05 - .075)^2 + .4(.1 - .075)^2 + .15(.30 - .075)^2$$
$$+ .05(.35 - .075)^2 = .0301$$

Answer (A) is incorrect because .1735 is the standard deviation of Techspace returns. Answer (C) is incorrect because .075 is the expected return. Answer (D) is incorrect because .2738 is the square root of the expected return.

9. The standard deviation of Techspace returns is

A. 7.5%

B. 17.35%

C. 3.01%

D. None of the answers are correct.

Answer (B) is correct. *(Publisher, adapted)*
REQUIRED: The standard deviation of Techspace returns.
DISCUSSION: The standard deviation (σ) gives an exact value for the tightness of the distribution and the riskiness of the investment. It is calculated by taking the square root of the variance. Given that the variance is .0301, the standard deviation is .1735, or 17.35%.
Answer (A) is incorrect because 7.5% is the expected return. Answer (C) is incorrect because 3.01% is the variance. Answer (D) is incorrect because the standard deviation is 17.35%.

10. A U.S. company currently has domestic operations only. It is considering an equal-size investment in either Canada or Britain. The data on expected rate of return and the risk associated with each of these proposed investments are given below.

Proposed Investment	Mean Return	Standard Deviation
British Investment	22%	10%
Canadian Investment	28%	15%

The mean return on the company's current (domestic only) business is 20%, with a standard deviation of 15%. Using the above data and the correlation coefficients, the company calculated the following portfolio risk and return (based on a ratio of 50% U.S. domestic operations and 50% international operations).

Investments	Mean Return	Standard Deviation
U.S. and Britain	21%	3%
U.S. and Canada	24%	15%

The company plans to select the optimal combination of countries based on risk and return for the domestic and international investments taken together. Based on the above data, which one of the following alternatives provides the best risk adjusted return to the firm?

A. Undertake the British investment.

B. Undertake the Canadian investment.

C. Do not undertake either investment.

D. Unable to determine based on data given.

Answer (A) is correct. *(CMA, adapted)*
REQUIRED: The option that provides the best risk adjusted return to the firm.
DISCUSSION: The coefficient of variation is useful when the rates of return and standard deviations of two investments differ. It measures the risk per unit of return because it divides the standard deviation (σ) by the expected return ($\hat{k}$).

$$Coefficient\ of\ variation\ =\ \frac{\sigma}{\hat{k}}$$

The investment in the U.S. and Britain has a coefficient of variation of .143 (3% ÷ 21%), whereas the investment in the U.S. and Canada has a coefficient of variation of .625 (15% ÷ 24%). Accordingly, the company should undertake the British investment because it has substantially less risk per unit of return.
Answer (B) is incorrect because the Canadian investment is significantly riskier per unit of return. Answer (C) is incorrect because the option of not investing in either venture has a higher coefficient of variation than either venture. Answer (D) is incorrect because coefficients of variation can be determined for all options based on the data given.

10.3 Portfolio Management

11. A measure that describes the risk of an investment project relative to other investments in general is the

A. Coefficient of variation.

B. Beta coefficient.

C. Standard deviation.

D. Expected return.

Answer (B) is correct. *(CIA, adapted)*
REQUIRED: The measure of the risk of an investment relative to investments in general.
DISCUSSION: The required rate of return on equity capital in the capital asset pricing model is the risk-free rate (determined by government securities), plus the product of the market risk premium times the beta coefficient (beta measures the firm's risk). The market risk premium is the amount above the risk-free rate that will induce investment in the market. The beta coefficient of an individual stock is the correlation between the volatility (price variation) of the stock market and that of the price of the individual stock. For example, if an individual stock goes up 15% and the market only 10%, beta is 1.5.
Answer (A) is incorrect because the coefficient of variation compares risk with expected return (standard deviation ÷ expected return). Answer (C) is incorrect because standard deviation measures dispersion (risk) of project returns. Answer (D) is incorrect because expected return does not describe risk.

12. Which of the following classes of securities are listed in order from lowest risk/opportunity for return to highest risk/opportunity for return?

A. U.S. Treasury bonds; corporate first mortgage bonds; corporate income bonds; preferred stock.

B. Corporate income bonds; corporate mortgage bonds; convertible preferred stock; subordinated debentures.

C. Common stock; corporate first mortgage bonds; corporate second mortgage bonds; corporate income bonds.

D. Preferred stock; common stock; corporate mortgage bonds; corporate debentures.

Answer (A) is correct. *(CIA, adapted)*
REQUIRED: The correct listing of classes of securities from lowest to highest risk/opportunity for return.
DISCUSSION: The general principle is that risk and return are directly correlated. U.S. Treasury securities are backed by the full faith and credit of the federal government and are therefore the least risky form of investment. However, their return is correspondingly lower. Corporate first mortgage bonds are less risky than income bonds or stock because they are secured by specific property. In the event of default, the bondholders can have the property sold to satisfy their claims. Holders of first mortgages have rights paramount to those of any other parties, such as holders of second mortgages. Income bonds pay interest only in the event the corporation earns income. Thus, holders of income bonds have less risk than stockholders because meeting the condition makes payment of interest mandatory. Preferred stockholders receive dividends only if they are declared, and the directors usually have complete discretion in this matter. Also, stockholders have claims junior to those of debtholders if the enterprise is liquidated.
Answer (B) is incorrect because a debenture is long-term debt that is not secured (collateralized) by specific property. Subordinated debentures have a claim on the debtor's assets that may be satisfied only after senior debt has been paid in full. Debentures of either kind are therefore more risky than mortgage bonds. Answer (C) is incorrect because an income bond pays interest only if the debtor earns it. Such bonds are also more risky than secured debt. Answer (D) is incorrect because unsecured debt is riskier than a mortgage bond.

13. From the viewpoint of the investor, which of the following securities provides the least risk?

A. Mortgage bond.

B. Subordinated debenture.

C. Income bond.

D. Debentures.

Answer (A) is correct. *(CIA, adapted)*
REQUIRED: The least risky security from the viewpoint of the investor.
DISCUSSION: A mortgage bond is secured with specific fixed assets, usually real property. Thus, under the rights granted in the bond indenture, creditors will be able to receive payments from liquidation of the property in case of default. In a bankruptcy proceeding, these amounts are paid before any transfers are made to other creditors, including those preferences. Hence, mortgage bonds are less risky than the others listed.
Answer (B) is incorrect because a debenture is long-term debt that is not secured (collateralized) by specific property. Subordinated debentures have a claim on the debtor's assets that may be satisfied only after senior debt has been paid in full. Debentures of either kind are therefore more risky than mortgage bonds. Answer (C) is incorrect because an income bond pays interest only if the debtor earns it. Such bonds are also more risky than secured debt. Answer (D) is incorrect because unsecured debt is riskier than a mortgage bond.

14. The best example of a marketable security with minimal risk would be

A. Municipal bonds.

B. The common stock of a AAA rated company.

C. The commercial paper of a AAA rated company.

D. Stock options of a AAA rated company.

Answer (C) is correct. *(CMA, adapted)*
REQUIRED: The best example of a marketable security with minimal risk.
DISCUSSION: Of the choices given, the commercial paper of a top-rated (most creditworthy) company has the least risk. Commercial paper is preferable to stock or stock options because the latter represent only a residual equity in a corporation. Commercial paper is debt and thus has priority over stockholders' claims. Also, commercial paper is a very short-term investment. The maximum maturity allowed without SEC registration is 270 days. However, it can be sold only to sophisticated investors without registration.
Answer (A) is incorrect because municipal bonds are rarely considered marketable securities in that they constitute long-term debt. Answer (B) is incorrect because common stock does not have as high a priority in company assets as commercial paper or other debt. Answer (D) is incorrect because stock options do not have as high a priority in company assets as commercial paper or other debt.

15. The marketable securities with the least amount of default risk are

  A. Federal government agency securities.

  B. U.S. Treasury securities.

  C. Repurchase agreements.

  D. Commercial paper.

Answer (B) is correct. *(CMA, adapted)*
REQUIRED: The marketable securities with the least default risk.
DISCUSSION: The marketable securities with the lowest default risk are those issued by the federal government because they are backed by the full faith and credit of the U.S. agency securities are issued by agencies and corporations created by the federal government, such as the Federal Housing Administration. They are backed by a secondary promise from the government.
  Answer (A) is incorrect because securities issued by a federal agency are first backed by that agency and secondarily by the U.S. government. Answer (C) is incorrect because repurchase agreements could become worthless if the organization agreeing to make the repurchase goes bankrupt. Answer (D) is incorrect because commercial paper is unsecured.

16. Based on the following information about stock price increases and decreases, make an estimate of the stock's beta: Month 1 = Stock +1.5%, Market +1.1%; Month 2 = Stock +2.0%, Market +1.4%; Month 3 = Stock –2.5%, Market –2.0%.

  A. Beta is greater than 1.0.

  B. Beta is less than 1.0.

  C. Beta equals 1.0.

  D. There is no consistent pattern of returns.

Answer (A) is correct. *(Publisher, adapted)*
REQUIRED: The true statement about the stock's beta.
DISCUSSION: Beta measures the volatility of the return of a security relative to the returns on the market portfolio. In each case, the stock price increase or decrease was a greater percentage than the market. Thus, the beta (stock change over market change) is greater than 1.0.
  Answer (B) is incorrect because the beta is greater than one when the stock price changes at a greater rate than the market. Answer (C) is incorrect because the stock change is not the same as the market change. Answer (D) is incorrect because there is a consistent pattern. The stock change is greater than the market change.

17. A company holds the following stock portfolio:

Stock	% of Total Portfolio	Beta Coefficient
W	20%	.8
X	40%	.6
Y	30%	1.0
Z	10%	2.0

The beta of the portfolio is

  A. 2.0

  B. 1.1

  C. .9

  D. .8

Answer (C) is correct. *(Publisher, adapted)*
REQUIRED: The beta of the portfolio.
DISCUSSION: Beta is the best measure of the risk of an individual security held in a diversified portfolio because it determines how the security affects the risk of the portfolio. The beta of a portfolio is the weighted average of the betas of the individual securities. For example, adding high-beta securities to a portfolio tends to increase its risk. Hence, the beta of the portfolio is .9 [(.8 × .2) + (.6 × .4) + (1.0 × .3) + (2.0 × .1)].
  Answer (A) is incorrect because 2.0 is the highest beta. Answer (B) is incorrect because 1.1 is a simple average of the betas. Answer (D) is incorrect because .8 is the lowest beta.

18. A feasible portfolio that offers the highest expected return for a given risk or the least risk for a given expected return is a(n)

  A. Optimal portfolio.

  B. Desirable portfolio.

  C. Efficient portfolio.

  D. Effective portfolio.

Answer (C) is correct. *(Publisher, adapted)*
REQUIRED: The term for a portfolio that offers the highest expected return for a given risk.
DISCUSSION: A feasible portfolio that offers the highest expected return for a given risk or the least risk for a given expected return is called an efficient portfolio.
  Answer (A) is incorrect because an optimal portfolio is a portfolio selected from the efficient set of portfolios because it is tangent to the investor's highest indifference curve. Answer (B) is incorrect because a desirable portfolio is a nonsense term. Answer (D) is incorrect because an effective portfolio is a nonsense term.

10.4 Derivative Financial Instruments

19. A company has recently purchased some stock of a competitor as part of a long-term plan to acquire the competitor. However, it is somewhat concerned that the market price of this stock could decrease over the short run. The company could hedge against the possible decline in the stock's market price by

A. Purchasing a call option on that stock.

B. Purchasing a put option on that stock.

C. Selling a put option on that stock.

D. Obtaining a warrant option on that stock.

Answer (B) is correct. *(CIA, adapted)*
REQUIRED: The means of hedging against the possible decline in the stock's market price.
DISCUSSION: A put option is the right to sell stock at a given price within a certain period. If the market price falls, the put option may allow the sale of stock at a price above market, and the profit of the option holder will be the difference between the price stated in the put option and the market price, minus the cost of the option, commissions, and taxes. The company that issues the stock has nothing to do with put (and call) options.
Answer (A) is incorrect because a call option is the right to purchase shares at a given price within a specified period. Answer (C) is incorrect because selling a put option could force the company to purchase additional stock if the option is exercised. Answer (D) is incorrect because a warrant gives the holder a right to purchase stock from the issuer at a given price (it is usually distributed along with debt).

20. When a firm finances each asset with a financial instrument of the same approximate maturity as the life of the asset, it is applying

A. Working capital management.

B. Return maximization.

C. Financial leverage.

D. A hedging approach.

Answer (D) is correct. *(CMA, adapted)*
REQUIRED: The technique used when a firm finances a specific asset with a financial instrument having the same approximate maturity as the life of the asset.
DISCUSSION: Maturity matching, or equalizing the life of an asset and the debt instrument used to finance that asset, is a hedging approach. The basic concept is that the firm has the entire life of the asset to recover the amount invested before having to pay the lender.
Answer (A) is incorrect because working capital management is short-term asset management. Answer (B) is incorrect because return maximization is more aggressive than maturity matching. It entails using the lowest cost forms of financing. Answer (C) is incorrect because financial leverage is the relationship between debt and equity financing.

21. If a call option is "out-of-the-money,"

A. The option has expired.

B. The value of the underlying asset is less than the exercise price.

C. The option no longer exists.

D. The option has become a put option.

Answer (B) is correct. *(Publisher, adapted)*
REQUIRED: The meaning of a call option's being "out-of-the-money."
DISCUSSION: When the value of the asset underlying a call option is less than the exercise price of the option, the option is "out-of-the-money."
Answer (A) is incorrect because an out-of-the-money option may not have expired. Answer (C) is incorrect because the option does exist; it is just not worth exercising. Answer (D) is incorrect because call options do not change into put options.

22. The type of option that does not have the backing of stock is called a(n)

A. Covered option.

B. Unsecured option.

C. Naked option.

D. Put option.

Answer (C) is correct. *(Publisher, adapted)*
REQUIRED: The type of option that does not have the backing of stock.
DISCUSSION: A naked or uncovered option is a call option that does not have the backing of stock. Thus, the option writer will have to purchase the underlying stock if the call option is exercised.
Answer (A) is incorrect because a covered option is one that is written against stock held in the option writer's portfolio. Answer (B) is incorrect because an unsecured option is a nonsense term. Answer (D) is incorrect because a put option is an option that gives the owner the right to sell the underlying asset for a fixed price.

23. A contractual arrangement that gives the owner the right to buy or sell an asset at a fixed price at any moment in time before or on a specified date is a(n)

 A. European option.

 B. Foreign option.

 C. Future option.

 D. American option.

Answer (D) is correct. *(Publisher, adapted)*
 REQUIRED: The type of option that can be exercised at any time before or on a specified date.
 DISCUSSION: An American option is a contractual arrangement that gives the owner the right to buy or sell an asset at a fixed price at any moment in time before or on a specified date.
 Answer (A) is incorrect because a European option is exercisable only at the expiration date. Answer (B) is incorrect because a foreign option is a nonsense term. Answer (C) is incorrect because, although an option can be exercised in the future, it is not called a future option.

24. The use of derivatives to either hedge or speculate results in

 A. Increased risk regardless of motive.

 B. Decreased risk regardless of motive.

 C. Offset risk when hedging and increased risk when speculating.

 D. Offset risk when speculating and increased risk when hedging.

Answer (C) is correct. *(Publisher, adapted)*
 REQUIRED: The effects of hedging and speculation on risk.
 DISCUSSION: Derivatives, including options and futures, are contracts between the parties who contract. Unlike stocks and bonds, they are not claims on business assets. A futures contract is entered into as either a speculation or a hedge. Speculation involves the assumption of risk in the hope of gaining from price movements. Hedging is the process of using offsetting commitments to minimize or avoid the impact of adverse price movements.
 Answer (A) is incorrect because hedging decreases risk by using offsetting commitments that avoid the impact of adverse price movements. Answer (B) is incorrect because speculation involves the assumption of risk in the hope of gaining from price movements. Answer (D) is incorrect because speculating increases risk while hedging offsets risk.

25. A forward contract involves

 A. A commitment today to purchase a product on a specific future date at a price to be determined some time in the future.

 B. A commitment today to purchase a product some time during the current day at its present price.

 C. A commitment today to purchase a product on a specific future date at a price determined today.

 D. A commitment today to purchase a product only when its price increases above its current exercise price.

Answer (C) is correct. *(Publisher, adapted)*
 REQUIRED: The terms of a forward contract.
 DISCUSSION: A forward contract is an executory contract in which the parties involved agree to the terms of a purchase and a sale, but performance is deferred. Accordingly, a forward contract involves a commitment today to purchase a product on a specific future date at a price determined today.
 Answer (A) is incorrect because the price of a future contract is determined on the day of commitment, not some time in the future. Answer (B) is incorrect because performance is deferred in a future contract, and the price of the product is not necessarily its present price. The price can be any price determined on the day of commitment. Answer (D) is incorrect because a forward contract is a firm commitment to purchase a product. It is not based on a contingency. Also, a forward contract does not involve an exercise price (exercise price is in an option contract).

26. An automobile company's use of the futures market to set the price of steel to protect a profit against price increases is an example of

 A. A short hedge.

 B. A long hedge.

 C. Selling futures to protect the company from loss.

 D. Selling futures to protect against price declines.

Answer (B) is correct. *(Publisher, adapted)*
 REQUIRED: The example of the use of the futures market to protect a profit.
 DISCUSSION: A change in prices can be minimized or avoided by hedging. Hedging is the process of using offsetting commitments to minimize or avoid the impact of adverse price movements. The automobile company desires to stabilize the price of steel so that its cost to the company will not rise and reduce profits. Accordingly, it uses the futures market to create a long hedge, which is a futures contract that is purchased to protect against price increases.
 Answer (A) is incorrect because a short hedge is a futures contract that is sold to protect against price declines. The company wishes to protect itself against price increases. Answer (C) is incorrect because the company needs to purchase futures to protect itself from loss, not sell futures. Selling futures protects against price declines. Answer (D) is incorrect because selling futures to protect against price declines is a short hedge. The company wants to protect itself against price increases.

27. If a corporation holds a forward contract for the delivery of U.S. Treasury bonds in 6 months and, during those 6 months, interest rates decline, at the end of the 6 months the value of the forward contract will have

   A. Decreased.

   B. Increased.

   C. Remained constant.

   D. Any of the answers may be correct, depending on the extent of the decline in interest rates.

Answer (B) is correct. *(Publisher, adapted)*
   REQUIRED: The effect of an interest rate decline on the value of a forward contract.
   DISCUSSION: Interest rate futures contracts involve risk-free bonds, such as U.S. Treasury bonds. When interest rates decrease over the period of a forward contract, the value of the bonds and the forward contract increase.
   Answer (A) is incorrect because the value of the forward contract will increase when interest rates decrease. Answer (C) is incorrect because the value of the forward contract will not remain constant if interest rates decline. Answer (D) is incorrect because any decline in interest rates increases the value of the bonds.

28. A firm is planning to issue a callable bond with an 8% coupon rate and 10 years to maturity. A straight bond with a similar rate is priced at $1,000. If the value of the issuer's call option is estimated to be $50, what is the value of the callable bond?

   A. $1,000

   B. $950

   C. $1,050

   D. $900

Answer (B) is correct. *(Publisher, adapted)*
   REQUIRED: The value of a callable bond.
   DISCUSSION: A callable bond is not as valuable to an investor as a straight bond. Thus, the $50 call option is subtracted from the $1,000 value of a straight bond to arrive at a $950 value for the callable bond.

29. How much must the stock be worth at expiration for a call holder to break even if the exercise price is $60 and the call premium was $3?

   A. $57.00

   B. $60.00

   C. $61.50

   D. $63.00

Answer (D) is correct. *(Publisher, adapted)*
   REQUIRED: The value of a stock at expiration allowing the option holder to break even.
   DISCUSSION: Because the call premium is $3, the stock price must be at least $63 ($60 exercise price + $3 call premium).
   Answer (A) is incorrect because $57 is the result of deducting the call premium from the exercise price. Answer (B) is incorrect because $60 is the result of failing to consider the impact of the call premium. Answer (C) is incorrect because the full call premium must be added to the exercise price.

30. A company wishes to price a call option written on a nondividend-paying stock. The current stock price is $50, the exercise price is $48, its present value is $26.48, the risk-free interest rate is 5.0%, the option expires in 1 year, and the cumulative probabilities used to calculate the present values of the final stock price and the exercise price are .65 and .58, respectively. According to the Black-Scholes Option Pricing Model, the current value of the call option is

   A. $6.02

   B. $4.66

   C. $4.02

   D. $2.00

Answer (A) is correct. *(Publisher, adapted)*
   REQUIRED: The current value of the call option according to the Black-Scholes Option Pricing Model.
   DISCUSSION: The basic formula is

$$C = SN(d_1) - Ee^{(-rt)}N(d_2)$$

$$d_1 = \frac{In(S/E) + [r + (\sigma^2 \div 2)]t}{\sigma \sqrt{t}}$$

$$d_2 = d_1 - \sigma \sqrt{t}$$

   If C is the current value of a call option with time t in years until expiration, S is the current stock price, $N(d_1)$ is the cumulative probability that a deviation less than d_1 will occur in a standardized normal distribution [$N(d_i)$ is an area to the left of d under the curve for the standard normal distribution], and $Ee^{(-rt)}$ $N(d_2)$ is approximated by the present value of the exercise price, the current value of the call option is

   C = ($50 × .65) – $26.48
      = $32.50 – $26.48
      = $6.02

   Answer (B) is incorrect because $4.66 results from omitting the term $e^{(-rt)}$ from the equation. Answer (C) is incorrect because $4.02 equals the estimated call price minus the difference between the current stock price and the exercise price. Answer (D) is incorrect because $2.00 is the difference between the current stock price and the exercise price.

31. Assume that the value of a share of QQ Company common stock at the expiration date is either $30 or $45. The difference in the net payoff on the portfolio because of a difference in the stock price at the maturity date is

A. $10.00

B. $7.50

C. $5.00

D. $0

32. Assuming the present value of the exercise price is $36 and the value of the call is $4.50, the value of the put in accordance with the put-call parity theorem to AA Company is

A. $4.50

B. $4.00

C. $.50

D. $0

Answer (D) is correct. *(Publisher, adapted)*
REQUIRED: The difference in the net payoff on the portfolio because of a difference in the stock price at the maturity date.
DISCUSSION: If the stock price at the maturity date is $30, AA Company will have a share of stock worth $30 and a put option worth $10 ($40 exercise price – $30 stock price). The call option will be worthless. Hence, the net payoff is $40 ($30 + $10). If the stock price at the maturity date is $45, the share of stock will be worth $45, the put will be worthless, and the loss on the call will be $5 ($45 – $40). Thus, the net payoff will be $40 ($45 – $5). Consequently, the difference in the net payoff on the portfolio because of a difference in the stock price at the maturity date is $0 ($40 – $40).

Answer (C) is correct. *(Publisher, adapted)*
REQUIRED: The value of the put in accordance with the put-call parity theorem.
DISCUSSION: For European options, given market equilibrium for all relevant prices (no arbitrage possibilities), equal exercise prices for the put and the call, and the same expiration date, the put-call parity theorem states that a fixed relationship applies to the market values of the put and call options on a security. For example, a strategy of selling one call option, buying one share of the stock, and buying one put option should result in a risk-free return. The gain (loss) from the stock and the put should equal the gain (loss) on the call. If V_S is the value of the stock, V_P is the value of the put, V_C is the value of the call, and PV_E is the present value of the exercise price (the time interval is the time to expiration), the formula for put-call parity may be stated as follows:

$$V_S + V_P - V_C = PV_E$$

Accordingly, the value of the put is $.50 ($36 + $4.50 – $40). Answer (A) is incorrect because $4.50 is the value of the call. Answer (B) is incorrect because $4.00 is the difference between the exercise price and its present value. Answer (D) is incorrect because the put has a value of $.50.

33. Herbert Corporation was a party to the following transactions during November and December Year 1. Which of these transactions is most likely to be defined as a derivative?

A. Purchased 1,000 shares of common stock of a public corporation based on the assumption that the stock will increase in value.

B. Purchased a term life insurance policy on the company's chief executive officer to protect the company from the effects of an untimely demise of this officer.

C. Agreed to cosign the note of its 100%-owned subsidiary to protect the lender from the possibility that the subsidiary might default on the loan.

D. Based on its forecasted need to purchase 300,000 bushels of wheat in 3 months, entered into a 3-month forward contract to purchase 300,000 bushels of wheat to protect itself from changes in wheat prices during the period.

Answer (D) is correct.   *(Publisher, adapted)*
REQUIRED: The transaction resulting in an investment in a derivative instrument.
DISCUSSION: A derivative is a financial instrument or other contract that (1) has (a) one or more underlyings and (b) one or more notional amounts or payment provisions, or both; (2) requires either no initial net investment or an immaterial net investment; and (3) requires or permits net settlement. An underlying may be a specified interest rate, security price, commodity price, foreign exchange rate, index of prices or rates, or other variable. A notional amount is a number of currency units, shares, bushels, pounds, or other units specified. Settlement of a derivative is based on the interaction of the notional amount and the underlying.
Answer (A) is incorrect because it involves a net investment equal to the fair value of the stock. Answer (B) is incorrect because insuring the CEO's life is a transaction based on an identifiable event. Answer (C) is incorrect because cosigning a subsidiary's note is a transaction based on an identifiable event.

34. An American importer expects to pay a British supplier 500,000 British pounds in three months. Which of the following hedges is best for the importer to fix the price in dollars?

A. Buying British pound call options.

B. Buying British pound put options.

C. Selling British pound put options.

D. Selling British pound call options.

Answer (A) is correct.   *(CPA, adapted)*
REQUIRED: The best hedge of an expected payment in British pounds.
DISCUSSION: Hedging is the process of using offsetting commitments to minimize or avoid the effect of adverse price movements. The risk to be hedged is that the exchange rate stated in dollars per pound will increase. Accordingly, the importer should buy call options for 500,000 British pounds that can be exercised in three months. A call option is the most common type of option. It gives the owner the right to purchase the underlying asset at a fixed price. Thus, it represents a long position because the option owner gains from a price increase. The profit is the difference between the price paid (the exercise price) and the higher price at the closing date, minus the brokerage fee. The approximate effect is to limit the price of pounds paid by the importer to the exercise price. If the price decreases, the option is "out of the money" and is not exercised.
Answer (B) is incorrect because a put option gives the owner the right to sell the underlying asset for a fixed price. It represents a short position because the owner benefits from a price decrease. Accordingly, buying British pound put options serves to hedge a future receipt (not payment) of pounds. Answer (C) is incorrect because selling British pound put options allows the buyer to hedge the risk of holding pounds. Answer (D) is incorrect because selling British pound call options allows the buyer to hedge the risk of an expected purchase of pounds.

35. Which of the following ratios is appropriate for the evaluation of accounts receivable?

A. Days' sales outstanding.

B. Return on total assets.

C. Collection to debt ratio.

D. Current ratio.

Answer (A) is correct.   *(CPA, adapted)*
REQUIRED: The ratio appropriate for the evaluation of accounts receivable.
DISCUSSION: Days' sales outstanding (DSO) is a measure of the average number of days that a company takes to collect revenue after a sale has been made. The DSO is the number of days in the period (e.g., 300, 360, or 365) divided by the accounts receivable turnover (net credit sales ÷ average accounts receivable).
Answer (B) is incorrect because return on total assets is a measure of how effectively a company uses its assets or invested funds. Answer (C) is incorrect because the collection to debt ratio is not a measure of accounts receivable. Answer (D) is incorrect because the current ratio is a measure of liquidity.

10.5 Ratios

36. Amicable Wireless, Inc. offers credit terms of 2/10, net 30 for its customers. Sixty percent of Amicable's customers take the 2% discount and pay on day 10. The remainder of Amicable's customers pay on day 30. How many days' sales are in Amicable's accounts receivable?

- A. 6
- B. 12
- C. 18
- D. 20

Answer (C) is correct. *(CPA, adapted)*
REQUIRED: The days' sales in accounts receivable.
DISCUSSION: The number of days of receivables (days' sales in average receivables, also called the average collection period) ordinarily is defined as the number of days in the period divided by the receivables turnover ratio. However, the information given allows an alternative expected value calculation. If 60% of the customers pay on day 10 and 40% pay on day 30, the total amount of days' sales that are in accounts receivable is 18 [(60% × 10 days) + (40% × 30 days)].
Answer (A) is incorrect because 6 days equals 60% of 10 days. Answer (B) is incorrect because 12 days equals 40% of 30 days. Answer (D) is incorrect because 20 days equals 30 days – 10 days.

37. What is the primary disadvantage of using return on investment (ROI) rather than residual income (RI) to evaluate the performance of investment center managers?

- A. ROI is a percentage, while RI is a dollar amount.
- B. ROI may lead to rejecting projects that yield positive cash flows.
- C. ROI does not necessarily reflect the company's cost of capital.
- D. ROI does not reflect all economic gains.

Answer (B) is correct. *(CPA, adapted)*
REQUIRED: The primary disadvantage of using ROI rather than RI to evaluate investment center performance.
DISCUSSION: Return on investment or ROI (also called return on assets or return on invested capital) may be defined in many ways, for example, as net income divided by average total assets. By comparison, residual income (RI) is an amount of income minus an imputed charge for the opportunity cost of capital employed (also stated as required ROI). An ROI performance measure motivates managers to accept projects that generate the highest percentage returns relative to other projects. Consequently, managers may reject projects with lower percentage returns that nevertheless yield amounts of cash flows in excess of required ROI. RI does not have this disadvantage because it leads to accepting such projects.
Answer (A) is incorrect because expressing ROI as a percentage is not in itself a primary disadvantage. For example, RI is based on an imputed ROI. Answer (C) is incorrect because ROI may reflect the company's cost of capital. For example, using net income as the numerator takes into account interest expense from debt incurred to purchase assets. Answer (D) is incorrect because failing to use an income measure that reflects all economic gains also is a possible disadvantage of RI.

38. A company has two divisions. Division A has operating income of $500 and total assets of $1,000. Division B has operating income of $400 and total assets of $1,600. The required rate of return for the company is 10%. The company's residual income would be which of the following amounts?

- A. $0
- B. $260
- C. $640
- D. $900

Answer (C) is correct. *(CPA, adapted)*
REQUIRED: The residual income.
DISCUSSION: Residual income is the excess of the return on an investment over a targeted amount equal to an imputed interest charge on invested capital. The company's total operating income is $900 ($500 + $400), and its total assets are $2,600 ($1,000 + $1,600). Accordingly, the required return is $260 ($2,600 × 10%), and the residual income is $640 ($900 – $260).
Answer (A) is incorrect because operating income exceeds residual income. Answer (B) is incorrect because $260 is the required return. Answer (D) is incorrect because $900 is operating income.

39. What type of ratio is earnings per share?

- A. Growth ratio.
- B. Activity ratio.
- C. Liquidity ratio.
- D. Leverage ratio.

Answer (A) is correct. *(Publisher, adapted)*
REQUIRED: The proper classification of EPS.
DISCUSSION: EPS is a growth ratio. It measures the changes in the economic status of a firm over a period of years on a per share basis.
Answer (B) is incorrect because activity ratios measure management's efficiency in using specific resources. Answer (C) is incorrect because liquidity ratios indicate the ability of a company to meet short-term obligations. Answer (D) is incorrect because leverage or equity ratios concern the relationship of debt to equity and the impact of debt on profitability and risk.

40. Which one of the following inventory cost flow assumptions will result in a higher inventory turnover ratio in an inflationary economy?

A. FIFO.

B. LIFO.

C. Weighted average.

D. Specific identification.

Answer (B) is correct. *(CMA, adapted)*
REQUIRED: The cost flow assumption that will result in a higher inventory turnover ratio in an inflationary economy.
DISCUSSION: The inventory turnover ratio equals the cost of goods sold divided by the average inventory. LIFO assumes that the last goods purchased are the first goods sold and that the oldest goods purchased remain in inventory. The result is a higher cost of goods sold and a lower average inventory than under other inventory cost flow assumptions if prices are rising. Because cost of goods sold (the numerator) will be higher and average inventory (the denominator) will be lower than under other inventory cost flow assumptions, LIFO produces the highest inventory turnover ratio.

41. Return on investment may be calculated by multiplying total asset turnover by

A. Average collection period.

B. Profit margin.

C. Debt ratio.

D. Fixed-charge coverage..

Answer (B) is correct. *(CIA, adapted)*
REQUIRED: The method of calculating return on investment.
DISCUSSION: Return on investment is equal to profit divided by the average total assets. Asset turnover is equal to net sales divided by average total assets. Profit margin is equal to the profit divided by net sales. Thus, multiplying the asset turnover by the profit margin results in the cancelation of net sales from both ratios, leaving a ratio composed of profit in the numerator and average total assets in the denominator, which equals return on investment.

42. Return on investment (ROI) is a term often used to express income earned on capital invested in a business unit. A firm's ROI is increased if

A. Sales increase by the same dollar amount as expenses and total assets.

B. Sales remain the same and expenses are reduced by the same dollar amount that total assets increase.

C. Sales decrease by the same dollar amount that expenses increase.

D. Net profit margin on sales increases by the same percentage as total assets.

Answer (B) is correct. *(CMA, adapted)*
REQUIRED: The change that will increase a firm's ROI.
DISCUSSION: If equal amounts are added to the numerator and denominator of a fraction that is less than one, the ratio will increase. Assuming that the ROI (net income ÷ total assets) is less than one, keeping sales constant while reducing expenses and increasing total assets by equal amounts will increase the ROI because the increase in net income equals the increase in total assets.
Answer (A) is incorrect because increasing sales and expenses by the same amount does not change net income (sales – expenses). Increasing the denominator without increasing the numerator reduces the ratio. Answer (C) is incorrect because decreasing the numerator without changing the denominator reduces the ratio. Answer (D) is incorrect because equal percentage changes in its elements neither increase nor decrease the ratio.

43. Minon, Inc. purchased a long-term asset on the last day of the current year. What are the effects of this purchase on return on investment and residual income?

	Return on Investment	Residual Income
A.	Increase	Increase
B.	Decrease	Decrease
C.	Increase	Decrease
D.	Decrease	Increase

Answer (B) is correct. *(CPA, adapted)*
REQUIRED: The effect of a long-term asset purchase on ROI and residual income.
DISCUSSION: ROI equals net income divided by average total assets. A purchase of a long-term asset on the last day of the fiscal year has little or no effect on net income but increases average total assets. Thus, it decreases ROI. Residual income is income minus some required return on the investment in the reporting entity. Given no change in net income or the required rate of return, an increase in the investment decreases residual income.
Answer (A) is incorrect because ROI and residual income decrease. Answer (C) is incorrect because ROI decreases. Answer (D) is incorrect because residual income decreases.

44. Vested, Inc. made some changes in operations and provided the following information:

	Year 2	Year 3
Operating revenues	$ 900,000	$1,100,000
Operating expenses	650,000	700,000
Operating assets	1,200,000	2,000,000

What percentage represents the return on investment for Year 3?

A. 22.5%

B. 10%

C. 20.83%

D. 25%

Answer (D) is correct. *(CPA, adapted)*
REQUIRED: The ROI.
DISCUSSION: Based on the given data, ROI must equal operating income divided by an investment defined as average operating assets. Consequently, ROI is ($1,100,000 operating revenues – $700,000 operating expenses) ÷ {[($2,000,000 + $1,200,000) ÷ 2] average operating assets} = 25%.
Answer (A) is incorrect because 22.5% is based on Year 2 expenses. Answer (B) is incorrect because 10% is based on Year 2 revenues. Answer (C) is incorrect because 20.83% is the ROI for Year 2.

45. Assume that a firm's debt ratio is currently 50%. It plans to purchase fixed assets either by using borrowed funds for the purchase or by entering into an operating lease. The firm's debt ratio as measured by the balance sheet will

A. Increase whether the assets are purchased or leased.

B. Increase if the assets are purchased, and remain unchanged if the assets are leased.

C. Increase if the assets are purchased, and decrease if the assets are leased.

D. Remain unchanged whether the assets are purchased or leased.

Answer (B) is correct. *(CIA, adapted)*
REQUIRED: The effect on the debt ratio of the acquisition of fixed assets.
DISCUSSION: Under an operating lease, the lessee records neither a lease asset nor a lease liability on the balance sheet. The ratio of debt to total assets is therefore unchanged if this method of financing is used. In contrast, borrowing results in equal increases of both debt and total assets. The debt ratio is equal to the amount of debt divided by total assets. Given that the ratio of debt to total assets is currently 50% (less than 1.0), increasing both the debt (numerator) and the total assets (denominator) by an equal amount will increase the ratio.

46. Which one of the following statements about the price-to-earnings (P-E) ratio is true?

A. A company with high growth opportunities ordinarily has a high P-E ratio.

B. A P-E ratio has more meaning when a firm has losses than when it has profits.

C. A P-E ratio has more meaning when a firm has abnormally low profits in relation to its asset base.

D. A P-E ratio expresses the relationship between a firm's market price and its net sales.

Answer (A) is correct. *(CMA, adapted)*
REQUIRED: The true statement about the P-E ratio.
DISCUSSION: A company with high growth opportunities typically has a high P-E ratio because investors are willing to pay a price for the stock higher than that justified by current earnings. In effect, they are trading current earnings for potential future earnings.
Answer (B) is incorrect because a P-E ratio cannot be computed when a firm has losses. Answer (C) is incorrect because a firm with abnormally low profits could have an extremely high, and thus meaningless, P-E ratio. Answer (D) is incorrect because the P-E ratio expresses the relationship between market price and a firm's EPS.

47. If the ratio of total liabilities to equity increases, a ratio that must also increase is

A. Times interest earned.

B. Total liabilities to total assets.

C. Return on equity.

D. The current ratio.

Answer (B) is correct. *(CMA, adapted)*
REQUIRED: The ratio that will increase if the ratio of total liabilities to equity increases.
DISCUSSION: Because total assets will be the same as the sum of liabilities and equity, an increase in the liabilities to equity ratio will simultaneously increase the liabilities to assets ratio.
Answer (A) is incorrect because no determination can be made of the effect on interest coverage without knowing the amounts of income and interest expense. Answer (C) is incorrect because the return on shareholders' equity may be increased or decreased as a result of an increase in the liabilities to equity ratio. Answer (D) is incorrect because the current ratio equals current assets divided by current liabilities, and additional information is necessary to determine whether it would be affected. For example, an increase in current liabilities from short-term borrowing would increase the liabilities to equity ratio but decrease the current ratio.

Questions 48 through 52 are based on the following information.

The data presented to the right show actual figures for selected accounts of McKeon Company for the fiscal year ended May 31, Year 2, and selected budget figures for the Year 3 fiscal year. McKeon's controller is in the process of reviewing the Year 3 budget and calculating some key ratios based on the budget. McKeon Company monitors yield or return ratios using the average financial position of the company. (Round all calculations to three decimal places if necessary.)

	5/31/Yr 3	5/31/Yr 2
Current assets	$210,000	$180,000
Noncurrent assets	275,000	255,000
Current liabilities	78,000	85,000
Long-term debt	75,000	30,000
Common stock ($30 par value)	300,000	300,000
Retained earnings	32,000	20,000

Year 3 Operations

Sales*	$350,000
Cost of goods sold	160,000
Interest expense	3,000
Income taxes (40% rate)	48,000
Dividends declared and paid in Year 3	60,000
Administrative expense	67,000

Current Assets

	5/31/Yr 3	5/31/Yr 2
Cash	$ 20,000	$10,000
Accounts receivable	100,000	70,000
Inventory	70,000	80,000
Other	20,000	20,000

*All sales are credit sales.

---

48. McKeon Company's debt-to-total-asset ratio for Year 3 is

A. 0.371

B. 0.315

C. 0.273

D. 0.237

Answer (B) is correct. *(CMA, adapted)*
REQUIRED: The debt-to-total-asset ratio.
DISCUSSION: The debt-to-total-asset ratio is equal to the total debt at year-end divided by total assets at year-end. Total debt at year-end is $153,000 ($78,000 current liabilities + $75,000 long-term debt). Total assets equal $485,000 ($210,000 current assets + $275,000 noncurrent assets). Thus, the debt-to-total-asset ratio is 0.315 ($153,000 ÷ $485,000)
Answer (A) is incorrect because 0.371 is the current ratio. Answer (C) is incorrect because 0.273 is noncurrent liabilities divided by noncurrent assets, a nonsense ratio. Answer (D) is incorrect because 0.237 is the debt-to-total-asset ratio for Year 1.

---

49. The Year 3 accounts receivable turnover for McKeon Company is

A. 2.235

B. 3.500

C. 5.000

D. 4.118

Answer (D) is correct. *(CMA, adapted)*
REQUIRED: The accounts receivable turnover.
DISCUSSION: The accounts receivable turnover is equal to the total credit sales divided by the average balance in accounts receivable. The average accounts receivable is equal to $85,000 [($70,000 beginning balance + $100,000 ending balance) ÷ 2]. The accounts receivable turnover is therefore equal to 4.118 ($350,000 credit sales ÷ $85,000 average receivables).
Answer (A) is incorrect because 2.235 is gross profit (sales – cost of goods sold) divided by average inventory. Answer (B) is incorrect because 3.500 is credit sales divided by ending accounts receivable. Answer (C) is incorrect because 5.000 is credit sales divided by beginning accounts receivable.

---

50. Using a 365-day year, McKeon's inventory turnover is

A. 171 days.

B. 160 days.

C. 183 days.

D. 78 days.

Answer (A) is correct. *(CMA, adapted)*
REQUIRED: The inventory turnover in terms of days.
DISCUSSION: Inventory turnover in terms of days is determined by dividing 365 by the inventory turnover ratio. The inventory turnover ratio is equal to the $160,000 cost of goods sold divided by the $75,000 average balance in inventory [($80,000 beginning balance + $70,000 ending balance) ÷ 2]. Hence, the inventory turnover ratio is 2.133 times per year. Dividing 365 by 2.133 results in an inventory turnover of 171 days.
Answer (B) is incorrect because 160 days is calculated using ending inventory. Answer (C) is incorrect because 183 days is calculated using beginning inventory. Answer (D) is incorrect because 78 days is calculated using sales instead of cost of goods sold.

51. McKeon Company's total asset turnover for Year 3 is

A. 0.805
B. 0.761
C. 0.722
D. 0.348

Answer (B) is correct. *(CMA, adapted)*
REQUIRED: The total asset turnover.
DISCUSSION: Total asset turnover is equal to $350,000 sales divided by average total assets. The amount of average total assets is equal to the average of beginning total assets of $435,000 ($180,000 current assets + $255,000 noncurrent assets) and ending total assets of $485,000 ($210,000 current assets + $275,000 noncurrent assets). The total asset turnover is therefore equal to .761 ($350,000 ÷ $460,000).
Answer (A) is incorrect because 0.805 is sales divided by beginning total assets. Answer (C) is incorrect because 0.722 is sales divided by ending total assets. Answer (D) is incorrect because 0.348 is cost of goods sold divided by average total assets.

52. The Year 3 return on assets for McKeon Company is

A. 0.761
B. 0.148
C. 0.157
D. 0.166

Answer (C) is correct. *(CMA, adapted)*
REQUIRED: The return on assets.
DISCUSSION: Return on assets is equal to net income divided by average total assets. As indicated below, net income is equal to $72,000. As determined in the previous question, average total assets is equal to $460,000. Hence, return on assets is 15.7% ($72,000 ÷ $460,000).

Sales	$ 350,000
Cost of goods sold	(160,000)
Interest expense	(3,000)
Taxes	(48,000)
Administrative expense	(67,000)
Net income	$ 72,000

Answer (A) is incorrect because 0.761 uses sales instead of net income. Answer (B) is incorrect because 0.148 uses ending total assets instead of average total assets. Answer (D) is incorrect because 0.166 uses beginning total assets instead of average total assets.

53. Miller and Rogers Partnership has $3 million in total assets, $1.65 million in equity, and a $500,000 capital budget. To maintain the same debt-equity ratio, how much debt should be incurred?

A. $50,000
B. $225,000
C. $275,000
D. $450,000

Answer (B) is correct. *(Publisher, adapted)*
REQUIRED: The portion of the capital budget that should be debt-financed to maintain the debt-equity ratio.
DISCUSSION: The debt-equity ratio is $1,350,000 to $1,650,000, or .81818 to 1.0. Thus, divide the amount of capital available ($500,000) by 1.81818 to determine the amount of new investment that should be financed by equity capital. The amount to be financed by equity capital equals $275,000. Thus, the remaining $225,000 would come from debt-financing.
Answer (A) is incorrect because $50,000 is not based on the present debt-equity ratio of 1.35 to 1.65. Answer (C) is incorrect because $275,000 is the amount needed in equity financing. Answer (D) is incorrect because $450,000 is not based on the present debt-equity ratio.

54. If Dorsey, Inc. had accounts receivable of $650 and $612 at the end of each of the last two years, and revenue for last year was $3,070, what is the average collection period?

A. 68 days.
B. 72 days.
C. 75 days.
D. 77 days.

Answer (C) is correct. *(Publisher, adapted)*
REQUIRED: The average collection period.
DISCUSSION: The average receivables are $631 [($612 + 650) ÷ 2]. Dividing $3,070 of sales by $631 results in a turnover of 4.86529 times. Dividing 365 days by 4.86529 results in an average collection period of 75 days.
Answer (A) is incorrect because 68 days is based on the wrong turnover rate. Answer (B) is incorrect because 72 days is based on $612 instead of $631 of average receivables. Answer (D) is incorrect because 77 days is based on average receivables of $650 rather than $631.

55. If Biba Partnership has a capital budget of $1 million, a plowback ratio of 40%, and net income of $750,000, how much external funding is needed?

    A. $250,000

    B. $400,000

    C. $550,000

    D. $700,000

Answer (D) is correct. *(Publisher, adapted)*
    REQUIRED: The amount of external financing needed.
    DISCUSSION: Given a plowback ratio of 40%, $300,000 (40% × $750,000 net income) is available for reinvestment. Thus, $700,000 ($1,000,000 – $300,000) of external funds must be raised.
    Answer (A) is incorrect because $250,000 is based on the assumption that all net income is available for reinvestment. Answer (B) is incorrect because $400,000 is based on the assumption that the plowback ratio applies to the capital budget. Answer (C) is incorrect because $550,000 results from using a 60% plowback ratio.

Questions 56 through 61 are based on the following information. Depoole Company is a manufacturer of industrial products and employs a calendar year for financial reporting purposes. Assume that total quick assets exceeded total current liabilities both before and after each transaction described. Further assume that Depoole has positive profits during the year and a credit balance throughout the year in its retained earnings account.

---

56. Payment by Depoole of a trade account payable of $64,500 will

    A. Increase Depoole's current ratio, but the quick ratio will not be affected.

    B. Increase Depoole's quick ratio, but the current ratio will not be affected.

    C. Increase both the current and quick ratios for Depoole.

    D. Decrease both the current and quick ratios for Depoole.

Answer (C) is correct. *(CMA, adapted)*
    REQUIRED: The effect of paying a trade account payable on the current and quick ratios.
    DISCUSSION: Given that the quick assets exceed current liabilities, both the current and quick ratios exceed one because the numerator of the current ratio includes other current assets in addition to the quick assets of cash, net accounts receivable, and short-term marketable securities. An equal reduction in the numerator and the denominator, such as a payment of a trade payable, will cause each ratio to increase.

---

57. The purchase by Depoole of raw materials for $85,000 on open account will

    A. Increase Depoole's current ratio.

    B. Decrease Depoole's current ratio.

    C. Increase Depoole's net working capital.

    D. Decrease Depoole's net working capital.

Answer (B) is correct. *(CMA, adapted)*
    REQUIRED: The effect of a credit purchase of raw materials on the current ratio and/or working capital.
    DISCUSSION: The purchase increases both the numerator and denominator of the current ratio by adding inventory to the numerator and payables to the denominator. Because the ratio before the purchase was greater than one, the ratio is decreased. The purchase of raw materials on account has no effect on working capital (current assets and current liabilities change by the same amount).

---

58. The collection by Depoole of a current accounts receivable of $29,000 will

    A. Increase Depoole's current ratio.

    B. Decrease Depoole's current ratio and the quick ratio.

    C. Increase Depoole's quick ratio.

    D. Not affect Depoole's current or quick ratios.

Answer (D) is correct. *(CMA, adapted)*
    REQUIRED: The effect of collection of a current account receivable on the current and/or quick ratios.
    DISCUSSION: Collecting current accounts receivable has no effect on either the current ratio or the quick ratio because current assets, quick assets, and current liabilities are unchanged by the collection.

59. Obsolete inventory of $125,000 was written off by Depoole during the year. This transaction

A. Decreased Depoole's quick ratio.

B. Increased Depoole's quick ratio.

C. Increased Depoole's net working capital.

D. Decreased Depoole's current ratio.

Answer (D) is correct. *(CMA, adapted)*
REQUIRED: The effect of writing off obsolete inventory.
DISCUSSION: Writing off obsolete inventory reduced current assets, but not quick assets (cash, receivables, and marketable securities). Thus, the current ratio was reduced the quick ratio was unaffected, and working capital was decreased.

60. The issuance by Depoole of new shares in a five-for-one split of Depoole's common stock

A. Decreases the book value per share of common stock.

B. Increases the book value per share of common stock.

C. Increases total equity.

D. Decreases total equity.

Answer (A) is correct. *(CMA, adapted)*
REQUIRED: The effect of a five-for-one split of common stock.
DISCUSSION: Given that five times as many shares of stock are outstanding, the book value per share of common stock is one-fifth of the former value after the split. The stock split does not change the amount of equity.

61. The issuance by Depoole of serial bonds in exchange for an office building, with the first installment of the bonds due late this year,

A. Decreases Depoole's net working capital.

B. Decreases Depoole's current ratio.

C. Decreases Depoole's quick ratio.

D. Affects all of the answers as indicated.

Answer (D) is correct. *(CMA, adapted)*
REQUIRED: The effect of issuing serial bonds with the first installment due late this year.
DISCUSSION: The first installment is a current liability, so the amount of current liabilities increases with no corresponding increase in current assets. The effect is to decrease working capital, the current ratio, and the quick ratio.
Answer (A) is incorrect because the bond issuance also decreases the current ratio and the quick ratio. Answer (B) is incorrect because the bond issuance also decreases net working capital and the quick ratio. Answer (C) is incorrect because the bond issuance also decreases net working capital and the current ratio.

62. When compared with a debt-to-assets ratio, a debt-to-equity ratio is

A. About the same as the debt-to-assets ratio.

B. Higher than the debt-to-assets ratio.

C. Lower than the debt-to-assets ratio.

D. Unrelated to the debt-to-assets ratio.

Answer (B) is correct. *(CMA, adapted)*
REQUIRED: The true statement comparing the debt-to-equity and debt-to-assets ratios.
DISCUSSION: Because debt plus equity equals assets, a debt-to-equity ratio has a lower denominator than a debt-to-assets ratio. Thus, the debt-to-equity ratio is higher than the debt-to-assets ratio.
Answer (A) is incorrect because the ratios are always different unless either debt or equity equals zero. Answer (C) is incorrect because the lower denominator in the debt-to-equity ratio means that it will always be higher than the debt-to-assets ratio. Answer (D) is incorrect because the two ratios are related. They always move in the same direction.

63. A measure of long-term debt-paying ability is a firm's

A. Length of the operating cycle.

B. Return on assets.

C. Inventory turnover.

D. Times interest earned.

Answer (D) is correct. *(CMA, adapted)*
REQUIRED: The measure of long-term debt-paying ability.
DISCUSSION: The times-interest-earned ratio is one measure of a firm's ability to pay its debt obligations out of current earnings. This ratio equals earnings before interest and taxes divided by interest expense.
Answer (A) is incorrect because the length of the operating cycle does not affect long-term debt-paying ability. By definition, long-term means longer than the normal operating cycle. Answer (B) is incorrect because return on assets measures only how well management uses the assets that are available. It does not compare the return with debt service costs. Answer (C) is incorrect because inventory turnover is a measure of how well a company is managing one of its assets.

64. The days' sales-in-receivables ratio will be understated if the firm

A. Uses a natural business year for its accounting period.

B. Uses a calendar year for its accounting period.

C. Uses average receivables.

D. Does not use average receivables.

Answer (A) is correct.   *(CMA, adapted)*
   REQUIRED: The reason the days' sales-in-receivables ratio will be understated.
   DISCUSSION: The days' sales-in-receivables ratio equals the days in the year divided by the receivables turnover ratio (sales ÷ average receivables). Days' sales may also be computed based only on ending receivables. In either case, use of the natural business year tends to understate the ratio because receivables will usually be at a low point at the beginning and end of the natural year.

65. To determine the operating cycle for a retail department store, which one of the following pairs of items is needed?

A. Days' sales in accounts receivable and average merchandise inventory.

B. Cash turnover and net sales.

C. Accounts receivable turnover and inventory turnover.

D. Asset turnover and return on sales.

Answer (C) is correct.   *(CMA, adapted)*
   REQUIRED: The pair of items needed to determine the operating cycle for a retailer.
   DISCUSSION: The operating cycle is the time needed to turn cash into inventory, inventory into receivables, and receivables back into cash. For a retailer, it is the time from purchase of inventory to collection of cash. Thus, the operating cycle of a retailer is equal to the sum of the number of days' sales in inventory and the number of days' sales in receivables. Inventory turnover equals cost of goods sold divided by average inventory. The days' sales in inventory equals 365 (or another period chosen by the analyst) divided by the inventory turnover. Accounts receivable turnover equals net credit sales divided by average receivables. The days' sales in receivables equals 365 (or other number) divided by the accounts receivable turnover.
   Answer (A) is incorrect because cost of sales must be known to calculate days' sales in inventory. Answer (B) is incorrect because cash turnover and net sales are insufficient to permit determination of the operating cycle. Answer (D) is incorrect because asset turnover and return on sales are insufficient to permit determination of the operating cycle.

66. Accounts receivable turnover will normally decrease as a result of

A. The write-off of an uncollectible account (assume the use of the allowance for doubtful accounts method).

B. A significant sales volume decrease near the end of the accounting period.

C. An increase in cash sales in proportion to credit sales.

D. A change in credit policy to lengthen the period for cash discounts.

Answer (D) is correct.   *(CMA, adapted)*
   REQUIRED: The event that will cause the accounts receivable turnover to decrease.
   DISCUSSION: The accounts receivable turnover equals net credit sales divided by average receivables. Hence, it will decrease if a firm lengthens the credit period or the discount period because the denominator will increase as receivables are held for longer times.
   Answer (A) is incorrect because write-offs do not reduce net receivables (gross receivables – the allowance) and will not affect the receivables balance and therefore the turnover ratio if an allowance system is used. Answer (B) is incorrect because a decline in sales near the end of the period signifies fewer credit sales and receivables, and the effect of reducing the numerator and denominator by equal amounts is to increase the ratio if the fraction is greater than 1.0. Answer (C) is incorrect because an increase in cash sales with no diminution of credit sales will not affect receivables.

67. If a firm is profitable and is effectively using leverage, which one of the following ratios is likely to be the largest?

A. Return on total assets.

B. Return on operating assets.

C. Return on common equity.

D. Return on total shareholders' equity.

Answer (C) is correct.   *(CMA, adapted)*
   REQUIRED: The ratio that is likely to be largest if a profitable firm is effectively using leverage.
   DISCUSSION: The purpose of leverage is to use creditor capital to earn income for shareholders. If the return on the resources provided by creditors or preferred shareholders exceeds the cost (interest or fixed dividends), leverage is used effectively, and the return to common equity will be higher than the other measures. The reason is that common equity provides a smaller proportion of the investment than in an unleveraged firm.

Question 68 is based on the following information.

Selected data from Ostrander Corporation's financial statements for the years indicated are presented in thousands.

	Year 2 Operations
Net sales	$4,175
Cost of goods sold	2,880
Interest expense	50
Income tax	120
Gain on disposal of a segment (net of tax)	210
Net income	385

	December 31	
	Year 2	Year 1
Cash	$ 32	$ 28
Trading securities	169	172
Accounts receivable (net)	210	204
Merchandise inventory	440	420
Tangible fixed assets	480	440
Total assets	1,397	1,320
Current liabilities	370	368
Total liabilities	790	750
Common stock outstanding	226	210
Retained earnings	381	360

68. The number of times interest was earned for Ostrander Corporation for Year 2 is

A. 57 times.

B. 7.70 times.

C. 3.50 times.

D. 6.90 times.

Answer (D) is correct. *(CMA, adapted)*
REQUIRED: The number of times interest was earned.
DISCUSSION: The interest coverage ratio (times-interest-earned ratio) is computed by dividing net income from operations before taxes and interest by interest expense. Net income of $385, minus the disposal gain of $210, is added to income taxes of $120 and interest expense of $50 to produce a ratio numerator of $345. Dividing $345 by $50 results in an interest coverage of 6.90 times.
Answer (A) is incorrect because .57 is the debt ratio. Answer (B) is incorrect because 7.70 times is based on net income from operations after taxes and interest. Answer (C) is incorrect because 3.50 times results from not adding interest and taxes to net income after the gain on disposal is subtracted.

69. Economic value added (EVA) is a measure of managerial performance. EVA equals

A. Net income after interest and taxes – (the weighted-average cost of capital × total assets).

B. [Earnings before interest and taxes × (1.0 – the tax rate)] – [the weighted-average cost of capital × (total assets – current liabilities)].

C. Earnings before interest and taxes – residual income.

D. After-tax operating income – interest on debt – dividends paid.

Answer (B) is correct. *(Publisher, adapted)*
REQUIRED: The definition of EVA.
DISCUSSION: Economic value added (EVA) is a more specific version of residual income. It equals after-tax operating income [earnings before interest and taxes × (1.0 – the tax rate)] minus the product of the after-tax weighted-average cost of capital and an investment base equal to total assets minus current liabilities. EVA represents the business unit's true economic profit primarily because a charge for the cost of equity capital is implicit in the cost of capital. The cost of equity is an opportunity cost, that is, the return that could have been obtained on the best alternative investment of similar risk. Hence, the EVA measures the marginal benefit obtained by using resources in a particular way. It is useful for determining whether a segment of a business is increasing shareholder value.
Answer (A) is incorrect because interest should not be subtracted twice. The WACC includes interest. Answer (C) is incorrect because EVA is a specific way of calculating residual income. Answer (D) is incorrect because the EVA calculation subtracts an opportunity cost of equity capital, not an actual cost.

70. Zig Corp. provides the following information:

Pretax operating profit	$ 300,000,000
Tax rate	40%
Capital used to generate profits 50% debt, 50% equity	$1,200,000,000
Cost of equity	15%
Cost of debt	5%

What of the following represents Zig's year-end economic value-added amount?

A. $0

B. $72,000,000

C. $120,000,000

D. $180,000,000

Answer (B) is correct. *(CPA, adapted)*
REQUIRED: The EVA.
DISCUSSION: EVA equals after-tax operating income minus the product of the after-tax weighted-average cost of capital and an investment base equal to total assets minus current liabilities. Given an investment base of $1,200,000,000 (50% debt, 50% equity), EVA is $72,000,000 {[$300,000,000 × (1.0 – .4)] – (.15 × $600,000,000) – (0.05 × (1 – 0.4) × $600,000,000}.
Answer (A) is incorrect because $0 assumes a 60% tax rate. Answer (C) is incorrect because $120,000,000 is the capital charge. Answer (D) is incorrect because $180,000,000 is the net operating profit after taxes.

71. Valecon Co. reported the following information for the year just ended:

	Segment A	Segment B	Segment C
Pre-tax operating income	$ 4,000,000	$ 2,000,000	$3,000,000
Current assets	4,000,000	3,000,000	4,000,000
Long-term assets	16,000,000	13,000,000	8,000,000
Current liabilities	2,000,000	1,000,000	1,500,000

If the applicable income tax rate and after-tax weighted-average cost of capital for each segment are 30% and 10%, respectively, the segment with the highest economic value added (EVA) is

A. Segment A.

B. Segment B.

C. Segment C.

D. Not determinable from this information.

Answer (C) is correct. *(Publisher, adapted)*
REQUIRED: The segment with the highest economic value added.
DISCUSSION: EVA equals after-tax operating income minus the product of the after-tax weighted-average cost of capital and an investment base equal to total assets minus current liabilities. Thus, the EVA for Segment C is $1,050,000 {[$3,000,000 × (1.0 – .3)] – [.10 × ($4,000,000 + $8,000,000 – $1,500,000)]}.
Answer (A) is incorrect because the EVA for Segment A is $1,000,000. Answer (B) is incorrect because the EVA for Segment B is – $100,000. Answer (D) is incorrect because the EVAs are determinable.

10.6 Limitations of Ratio Analysis

72. Which of the following is not a limitation of ratio analysis affecting comparability among firms?

A. Different accounting policies.

B. Different fiscal years.

C. Different sources of information.

D. All of the choices are limitations of ratio analysis.

Answer (D) is correct. *(Publisher, adapted)*
REQUIRED: The factor that is not a limitation of ratio analysis affecting comparability among firms.
DISCUSSION: Ratio analysis provides useful information regarding the efficiency of operations and the stability of financial condition. Nevertheless, it has several inherent limitations, such as firms using different accounting policies, different fiscal years, and different sources of information. Each of these factors impairs the comparability of financial statement amounts and the ratios derived from them.

73. Which of the following is not a limitation of ratio analysis?

A. Much of accounting data is subject to estimation.

B. Failure to use weighted averages may distort data.

C. Liquidity cannot be analyzed.

D. Effects of inflation misstate financial statement data.

Answer (C) is correct. *(Publisher, adapted)*
REQUIRED: The factor that is not a limitation of ratio analysis.
DISCUSSION: Ratio analysis is an analytical method that facilitates comparison among different companies by providing useful information pertaining to the efficiency of operation and the stability of financial condition. Liquidity may be analyzed with ratios such as the current ratio and the acid test.

Use Gleim's *CPA Test Prep* for interactive testing with over 2,000 additional multiple-choice questions!

STUDY UNIT ELEVEN
INFORMATION TECHNOLOGY I

(14 pages of outline)

This study unit is the first of five covering information technology (IT). Business information today is largely produced through the use of computer-based systems. A CPA, as a provider of a portion of this information, is involved with these systems in three roles:

1.   Designer -- as a consultant in the development of systems
2.   Auditor -- as an evaluator of the quality of the system's output, composition, and security
3.   User -- as a recipient of the systems' output and as a source of input for decision making

Accordingly, a CPA must understand IT before (s)he can design, audit, or use computer-based systems. In particular, a CPA must understand how the use of specific systems affects the risks associated with the unique nature and characteristics of IT.

11.1 ROLE OF BUSINESS INFORMATION SYSTEMS

1.   A **business information system** is any combination of people, procedures, and computing equipment employed to pursue a business objective (business in this context means any organization that needs data to carry out its mission: publicly held corporation, institution of higher education, not-for-profit, etc.).

    a.   The first generation of business information systems served the finance and accounting functions, since computing lends itself so readily to quantitative tasks.

    b.   Business information systems have evolved to serve the needs of **users at all levels** of the organizational hierarchy, and even, with the advent of fast telecommunications, **users outside the organization.**

    c.   **Stakeholders** in business information systems are those who affect, or are affected by, the output of the information system. They have an interest in the system's effective and efficient functioning.

        1)   Hence, they include users such as managers, employees, IT personnel, suppliers, and customers.

    d.   Any information system performs **four major tasks:**

        1)   **Input.** The system must acquire (capture) data from within or outside of the entity.

        2)   **Transformation.** Raw materials (data) are converted into knowledge useful for decision making (information).

        3)   **Output.** The ultimate purpose of the system is communication of results to internal or external users.

        4)   **Storage.** Before, during, and after processing, data must be temporarily or permanently stored, for example, in files or databases.

5) EXAMPLE: All four tasks can be identified in the following description:

A firm collects sales and expense data in its automated accounting system. At year-end, adjusting and closing entries are added to the system, and the data are processed into a special format, from which the annual report is produced. The firm owns a number of high-speed, high-capacity hard drives on which all of its transactions and formatted financial statements are kept.

e. Business information systems can be classified by their **level of complexity**.

2. **Transaction Processing System (TPS)**

a. A transaction is a **single, discrete event** that can be captured by an information system.

1) Examples include the movement of raw materials from storage to production, the taking of a reservation, the recording of a new employee's personal data, or the sale of a piece of merchandise.

b. A TPS therefore captures the **fundamental data** that reflect the economic life of an organization.

3. **Management Information System (MIS)**

a. A MIS typically receives **input from a TPS**, aggregates it, then reports it in a format useful by **middle management** in running the business. For this reason, MISs are often classified by function or activity:

1) **Accounting:** general ledger, accounts receivable, accounts payable, fixed asset management, tax accounting

2) **Finance:** capital budgeting, operational budgeting, cash management

3) **Manufacturing:** production planning, cost control, quality control

4) **Logistics:** inventory management, transportation planning

5) **Marketing:** sales analysis, forecasting

6) **Human resources:** projecting payroll, projecting benefits obligations, employment-level planning, employee evaluation tracking.

b. These single-function systems, often called **stovepipe systems** because of their limited focus, are gradually being replaced by **integrated systems** that link multiple business activities across the enterprise.

4. **Data Warehouse**

a. A data warehouse is a **central database** for transaction-level data from more than one of the organization's TPSs. Data warehouses are very large and require that the transaction records be converted to a standard format.

1) The ability of the data warehouse to relate data from multiple systems makes it a very powerful tool for ad hoc queries.

2) The data warehouse can also be accessed using analytical and graphics tools, a technique called **online analytical processing (OLAP)**.

a) An important component of OLAP is **drill-down analysis**, in which the user is first presented with the data at an aggregate level and then can display successive levels of detail for a given date, region, product, etc., until finally reaching the original transactions.

3) A data warehouse is strictly a query-and-reporting system. It is not used to carry on the enterprise's routine operations.

a) In other words, a data warehouse does not take the place of a TPS. Rather, a data warehouse gets its input from the various TPSs in the organization.

         b)   A data warehouse is optimized for data retrieval and reporting. A TPS is optimized for data entry.

    b.   **A data mart** is a subset of an enterprise-wide data warehouse.

         1)   A data mart is designed primarily to address a specific function or department's needs, whereas a data warehouse is generally meant to address the needs of the entire enterprise.

    c.   A data warehouse enables **data mining**, i.e., the search for unexpected relationships between data.

         1)   The classic example of the use of data mining was the discovery by convenience stores that diapers and beer often appeared on the same sales transaction in the late evening.

         2)   Special software and a large amount of processing power are needed for effective data mining.

5.   **Decision Support System (DSS)**

    a.   A DSS is an **interactive** system that is useful in solving **structured and semistructured problems**, that is, those requiring a management decision maker to exercise his or her insight and judgment.

         1)   This latter point requires emphasis: a DSS **does not automate a decision**. It examines the relevant data and presents a manager with choices between alternative courses of action.

    b.   A DSS has **three basic components**: the database, the model, and the dialog.

         1)   The **database** consists of the raw data that are relevant to the decision. In this context, a data warehouse (see item 4. on the previous page) is very useful. The data can come from both within and outside of the organization.

         2)   The **model** is the set of equations, comparisons, graphs, conditions, assumptions, etc., into which the data will be fed.

         3)   The **dialog** is the user interface which allows the user to specify the appropriate model and the particular set of data to which the model should be applied.

    c.   EXAMPLE: A manufacturer wishes to improve its inventory management.

         1)   The firm creates a database of the past five years of inventory and purchasing history, along with projections for future production, transportation costs, and forecasts of the prices of raw materials.

         2)   The firm creates a model containing the formula for economic order quantity, an algorithm for calculating safety stock, and graphs of inventory levels over time.

         3)   The firm creates a dialog screen allowing the decision maker to specify time periods, particular products, and the variables for displaying on graphs.

    d.   A **group DSS** aids in the collaborative solution of unstructured problems. Users in separate areas of the organization can specify parameters pertinent to their functions.

6.   **Expert System (ES)**

    a.   An expert system is an interactive system that attempts to imitate the reasoning of a human expert in a given field. It is useful for addressing unstructured problems when there is a local shortage of human experts.

    b.   An expert system, like a decision support system, has three components:

         1)   The **knowledge database** consists of facts and the relationships among those facts.

         2)   The **inference engine** is often a series of if/then decisions.

         3)   The **dialog** allows the user to input data relevant to the current problem, which are then filtered through the inference engine and used to query the knowledge database. A suggested optimal solution is returned to the user.

c.   The knowledge base and inference engine are relevant to a limited domain of human expertise. The inference procedures use symbolic processing based on heuristics rather than algorithms.

1)   A heuristic procedure is an exploratory problem-solving technique that uses self-education methods, e.g., the evaluation of feedback, to improve performance. These systems are often very interactive and provide explanations of their problem-solving behavior.

d.   EXAMPLE: A physician in a remote area inputs a patient's unfamiliar symptoms into an expert system. The system then asks him/her a series of questions. Unseen by the doctor, each question results from a series of if/then conditions. Once the system has gathered answers to all the relevant questions, it references the knowledge database and delivers a conclusion.

e.   Experimental work is being done with expert systems in taxation, financial accounting, managerial accounting, and auditing.

7.   **Artificial Intelligence (AI)**

a.   Even more sophisticated than expert systems is computer software designed to **perceive, reason, and understand**.

1)   Expert systems work through a series of if/then questions, in which every operation has exactly two possible outcomes (yes/no, on/off, true/false, one/zero).

a)   Human reasoning, on the other hand, is extremely complex, based on deduction, induction, intuition, emotion, and biochemistry, resulting in a range of possible outcomes.

2)   AI attempts to **imitate human decision making**, which hinges on this combination of knowledge and intuition (i.e., remembering relationships between variables based on experience).

3)   The advantage of AI in a business environment is that, relative to human experts, they

a)   Can work 24 hours a day

b)   Will not become ill, die, or be hired away

c)   Are extremely fast processors of data, especially if numerous rules (procedures) must be evaluated

b.   **Fuzzy logic systems** are a form of artificial intelligence that deal with imprecise data and problems that have many solutions.

1)   Fuzzy logic, a departure from classical two-valued sets and logic, uses soft linguistic system variables (e.g., large, hot, or tall) and a continuous range of truth values rather than strict binary (true or false) decisions and assignments.

2)   Fuzzy rule-based systems apply these methods to solve many types of real-world problems, especially when a system is difficult to model, when it is controlled by a human operator or expert, or when ambiguity or vagueness is common.

3)   Fuzzy set theory allows objects to belong partly to multiple sets. Fuzzy logic is useful for describing **the vagueness of things in the real world**, where belonging to a set is really a matter of degree.

a)   Fuzzy logic is particularly useful in **the design of industrial controls**, in data retrieval, and in systems in which the user is not intimately familiar with all the data. It is also useful when absolute accuracy is costly or judgments of value must be synthesized from multiple inputs.

        b)   Fuzzy logic has emerged as a profitable tool for the controlling of subway systems and complex industrial processes, as well as for household and entertainment electronics, diagnostic systems, and other expert systems.

    4)   The key benefits of a fuzzy design are a simplified and reduced development cycle, ease of implementation, and more user-friendly and efficient performance.

  c.   **Other AI topics** include the following:

    1)   Neural networks are a collection of processing elements working together to process information much like the human brain, including learning from previous situations and generalizing concepts.

    2)   Case-based reasoning systems use a process similar to that used by humans to learn from previous, similar experiences.

    3)   Rule-based expert systems function on the basis of set rules to arrive at an answer. These cannot be changed by the system itself. They must be changed by an outside source (i.e., the computer programmer).

    4)   Intelligent agents are programs that apply a built-in or learned knowledge base to execute a specific, repetitive, and predictable task, for example, showing a computer user how to perform a task or searching websites for particular financial information.

8. **Business Intelligence (BI)**

  a.   Business intelligence is what gives upper management the information it needs to know where the organization is and how to steer it in the intended direction. BI gives an executive immediate information about an organization's critical success factors.

    1)   BI has replaced the older executive support system and executive information system models.

  b.   BI tools display information about the organization as bar graphs, pie charts, columnar reports, or any other format considered appropriate to upper management's decision making. These displays are sometimes grouped by a particular executive's needs into what is termed a **digital dashboard**.

    1)   Stock price trend, sales by region and date, on-time delivery performance, instantaneous cash balances, and profitability by customer are possible metrics to be included.

  c.   BI tools use data both from within and outside the organization.

9. **Enterprise Resource Planning (ERP)**

  a.   ERP is the latest phase in the development of computerized systems for managing organizational resources. ERP is intended to integrate enterprise-wide information systems by creating one database linked to all of an organization's applications.

    1)   At its most comprehensive, ERP subsumes materials requirements planning (MRP), manufacturing resource planning (MRP II), supply chain management (SCM), and customer relationship management (CRM).

    b.   In the **traditional ERP system**, subsystems share data and coordinate their activities. Thus, if marketing receives an order, it can quickly verify that inventory is sufficient to notify shipping to process the order.

        1)   Otherwise, production is notified to manufacture more of the product, with a consequent automatic adjustment of output schedules.

        2)   If materials are inadequate for this purpose, the system will issue a purchase order.

        3)   If more labor is needed, human resources will be instructed to reassign or hire employees.

        4)   The foregoing business processes (and others) should interact seamlessly in an ERP system. Moreover, the current generation of ERP software also provides the capability for smooth (and instant) interaction with the business processes of external parties.

    c.   The subsystems in a traditional ERP system are internal to the organization. Hence, they are often called **back-office** functions. The information produced is principally (but not exclusively) intended for internal use by the organization's managers.

    d.   The **current generation** of ERP software (**ERP II**) has added **front-office** functions. These connect the organization with customers, suppliers, owners, creditors, and strategic allies (e.g., the members of a trading community or other business association).

        1)   An ERP II system's integration with the firm's back-office functions enables supply-chain management, customer relationship management, and partner relationship management.

    e.   Because ERP software is costly and complex, it is usually installed only by the largest enterprises, but mid-size organizations are increasingly likely to buy ERP software.

        1)   Major ERP packages include R/3 from SAP AG and Oracle e-Business Suite, PeopleSoft, and JD Edwards EnterpriseOne, all from Oracle Corp.

    f.   The disadvantages of ERP are its extent and complexity, which make implementation difficult and costly.

10. **Office Automation Systems (OASs)**

    a.   The familiar word processing, spreadsheet, digital document storage, and desktop publishing applications of most office workers are part of any organization's information systems environment.

11. The tremendous variety of forms that information systems can take and the diverse needs of users have led to the concept of **information resources management (IRM)**, which takes a global view of the information holdings and needs of an organization.

    a.   This view is promoted by the Information Resources Management Association of Hershey, PA (http://www.irma-international.org/).

12. **Financial reporting** systems generate information for use primarily by external parties, such as investors, regulators, and creditors. External financial reporting is commonly in the form of financial statements (balance sheet, income statement, and statement of cash flows). Thus, financial reporting is often backward looking.

    a.   Internal financial reporting is also useful for management decision making, especially with regard to profitability and cost control.

b. An organization's financial accounting system processes transactional inputs stated in monetary terms. The traditional audit trail permits the tracking of these inputs as they flow through the system.

   1) The audit trail reflects the accounting cycle, which starts with initial entry of transactions and culminates with external reporting. The following is the general form of the accounting cycle:

      a) Entry of source data and filing of documentation, which may be paperless in modern systems

      b) Making entries in general and special journals

      c) Posting entries to accounts in the general and subsidiary ledgers

      d) Preparing a trial balance

      e) Preparing financial statements or other financial information to be reported

   2) Processing is performed electronically, with journals and ledgers maintained on magnetic disks or other storage media.

   3) Reports and other analyses can be generated quickly and at any time by the computer system.

   4) An audit trail permits the vouching of balances and other amounts in reports back through the system to the source data or the tracing of source data through the system to an amount in a report.

   5) Because computer processing may leave no hard-copy audit trail, systems should be designed to record transactions and balances before and after processing.

13. **Management reporting** has an internal focus on planning, control, and decision making that is primarily forward looking.

   a. It involves nonfinancial as well as financial data that may be reported in flexible formats on a nonroutine basis.

   b. Management reports are directed toward internal users, so they need not conform with GAAP.

   c. One major element of a management reporting system is cost accounting, which applies to an organization's purchasing, production, distribution, and marketing functions. Regardless of the nature of the organization (manufacturing, service, governmental, or nonprofit), the emphasis of its cost accounting system is ultimately on the value added by its activities.

   d. Another major element of a management reporting system is budgeting, a planning and managerial control tool. Budgets may have short-term (e.g., up to a fiscal year), intermediate (e.g., 2 to 5 years), and strategic (e.g., 5 to 10 years) horizons.

14. Stop and review! You have completed the outline for this subunit. Study multiple-choice questions 1 through 17 beginning on page 358.

11.2 RISKS ASSOCIATED WITH BUSINESS INFORMATION SYSTEMS

1. The **goals** of a business information system are the same regardless of whether it is manual or computer-based. The **risks**, on the other hand, can be quite different.

    a. **System availability.** The ability to make use of any computer-based system is dependent on

        1) An uninterrupted flow of electricity
        2) Protection of computer hardware from environmental hazards (e.g., fire and water)
        3) Protection of software and data files from unauthorized alteration
        4) Preservation of functioning communications channels between devices

    b. **Volatile transaction trails.** In any computer-based environment, a complete trail useful for audit purposes might exist for only a short time or in only computer-readable form. In online and real-time systems, data are entered directly into the computer, eliminating portions of the audit trail provided by source documents.

    c. **Decreased human involvement.** Because employees who enter transactions may never see the "final results," the potential for detecting errors is reduced. Also, output from a computer system often carries a mystique of infallibility, reducing the incentive of system users to closely examine reports and transaction logs.

    d. **Uniform processing of transactions.** Computer processing uniformly subjects like transactions to the same processing instructions, therefore virtually eliminating clerical error. Thus, it permits consistent application of predefined business rules and the performance of complex calculations in high volume.

        1) However, programming errors (or other similar systematic errors in either the hardware or software) will result in all like transactions being processed incorrectly.

    e. **Unauthorized access.** When accounting records were kept in pen-and-ink format, physical access to them was the only way to carry out an alteration. Once they are computer-based, however, access can be carried out from multiple terminals throughout the organization or from anywhere in the world by determined "hackers" using the Internet.

        1) Security measures, such as firewalls and user id-and-password combinations, are thus vital to maintaining security over data in an automated environment.

    f. **Data vulnerability.** Destruction of a few hardware devices or units of storage media could have disastrous consequences if they contain the only copies of crucial data files or application programs.

        1) For this reason, it is vital that an organization's computer files be duplicated and stored offsite periodically.

    g. **Reduced segregation of duties.** Many functions once performed by separate individuals may be combined in an automated environment.

        1) For example, receiving cash, issuing a receipt to the payor, preparing the deposit slip, and preparing the journal entry may once have been performed by separate individuals. In a computer-based system, the receipt, deposit slip, and journal entry may be automatically generated by the computer. If the same employee who receives the cash is also responsible for entering the relevant data into the system, the potential for error or fraud is increased.

h. **Reduced individual authorization of transactions.** Certain transactions may be initiated automatically by a computer-based system. This is becoming ever more widespread as an increasing number of business processes become automated.

    1) For example, an ERP system at a manufacturing concern (see item 9. in Subunit 11.1) may automatically generate a purchase order when raw materials inventory reaches a certain level. If the company shares an EDI system with the vendor (see Subunit 15.2), the purchase order may be sent to the vendor electronically without any human intervention.

    2) This reduced level of oversight for individual transactions requires careful coding to ensure that computer programs accurately reflect management's goals for business processes.

i. **Specialized knowledge.** From the beginning of the computer era in the 1950s, the ability to operate computer-based systems has depended on a high level of specialization and training among computer professionals.

    1) Even as computing has become more "democratized" by the prevalence of personal computers and the Internet, organizations require groups of employees dedicated to keeping their automated systems running.

    2) Attracting and retaining employees with the necessary skillsets can be time-consuming and expensive. This situation has led to the practice of **outsourcing**, the hiring of an outside firm to take over all or part of an organization's computer operations.

        a) Advantages of outsourcing include, in addition to greater expertise, superior service quality, avoidance of changes in the organization's IT infrastructure, cost predictability, the freeing of human and financial capital, and avoidance of fixed costs.

        b) Risks of outsourcing include the inflexibility of the relationship, the loss of control, the vulnerability of important information, and often dependency on a single vendor.

2. Stop and review! You have completed the outline for this subunit. Study multiple-choice questions 18 through 27 beginning on page 364.

11.3 ROLES AND RESPONSIBILITIES WITHIN THE IT FUNCTION

1. **Typical IT Personnel**

    a. **Database administrators (DBAs)** are responsible for developing and maintaining the organization's databases and for establishing controls to protect their integrity.

    b. **Network technicians** maintain the bridges, hubs, routers, switches, cabling, and other devices that interconnect the organization's computers. They are also responsible for maintaining the organization's connection to other networks, such as the Internet.

    c. The **webmaster** is responsible for the content of the organization's website. (S)he works closely with programmers and network technicians to ensure that the appropriate content is displayed and that the site is reliably available to users.

    d. **Computer (console) operators** are responsible for the moment-to-moment running of the organization's medium- and large-scale computers, i.e., servers and mainframes.

        1) Computers in this size range, unlike desktop computers, require 24-hour monitoring. Operators respond to messages received from the system by consulting run manuals that detail the steps for processing.

    e. **Librarians** maintain control over and accountability for documentation, programs, and data storage media.

f.   **Systems programmers** maintain and fine-tune the operating systems on the organization's medium- and large-scale computers. The operating system is the core software that performs three of a computer's four basic tasks, namely input, output, and storage (the transformation task is generally handled by application software; see item 2.a. in Subunit 12.2).

g.   **Applications programmers** design, write, test, and document computer programs according to specifications provided by the end users.

1)   These duties are often combined with those of systems analysts. A **systems analyst** uses his/her detailed knowledge of the organization's databases and applications programs to determine how an application should be designed to best serve the users' needs.

h.   **Help desk** personnel log problems reported by users, resolve minor difficulties, and forward more difficult problems to the appropriate person, such as a database administrator or the webmaster. Help desk personnel are often called on to resolve such issues as desktop computers crashing or problems with email.

2.   **Segregation of Duties within the IT Function**

a.   **Information security.** Information systems pervade every part of a modern organization's operations. Therefore, the area of security over information systems is a distinct function within the larger IT function. The **chief information security officer** is responsible for formulating and enforcing a formal information security policy for all employees and outside parties, such as EDI partners, who have access to the organization's systems.

1)   Such a policy should, among other things, inform all those with access to the organization's systems that the organization's hardware, software, and network connections are purely for the benefit of the organization and not to be used for personal reasons.

2)   In addition, the IT security function is responsible for ensuring that persons both inside and outside the organization can only gain access to those programs and data elements which are appropriate for their job duties. This requires that the IT security officer and his/her subordinates are well trained in the use of the organization's security software.

b.   **Systems development and maintenance.** Users within the organization are constantly requesting the creation of new systems to help manage business processes and changes and enhancements to existing systems.

1)   **Systems analysts and applications programmers** are responsible for designing, building, and maintaining the organization's applications. Analysts and programmers should never be able to make changes directly to programs that are used in "live" production. A separate processing area devoted to development and testing should be set up and dedicated to the use of analysts and programmers.

2)   In addition, analysts and programmers should never have access to live production data; the data used to test new or altered programs should be stored in the separate development area along with the programs.

c.   **Computer operations.** Console operators are responsible only for the smooth running of the organization's medium- and large-scale computers, i.e., the scheduling of jobs and production of output.

1)   **Operators** should therefore have no access to make changes to applications programs. Ideally, computer operators should have no programming knowledge or access to documentation not strictly necessary for their work ("ignorance is a good internal control").

2) **Librarians** are responsible for "checking out" applications programs to analysts and programmers for modification and testing and for ensuring that the properly tested version gets "checked in" to production. Ideally, they too should have no programming knowledge.

d. **Data administration.** The totality of an organization's data is an extremely valuable asset. Hardware can be replaced for a price, but each organization's data bundle is unique and is indispensable to carrying on business. In large organizations, the task of organizing and storing data is often divided into two subfunctions.

1) **Data administrators** determine how the organization's data should be stored and what relationships among the data best achieve the organization's business objectives.

a) Confusingly, this function is also called database analyst.

2) **Database administrators (DBAs)** keep the organization's databases running efficiently.

a) Every database is a unique combination of

i)   The relationships among the data (the schema),
ii) The database management system (the software), and
iii) The equipment on which the database is stored (the hardware).

b) Keeping a complex database "tuned" is a demanding task requiring a great deal of technical knowledge.

3) Depending on the size of the organization, the functions of data administrator and database administrator are often combined in a single job.

a) Because they have unfettered access to the organization's production data, employees in these functions should have no access to the application programs that process the data.

e. **End users.** In an organizational sense, the **"owners"** of data are the end user departments; the accounting function is responsible for the accuracy of accounting data, the marketing function is responsible for the accuracy of marketing data, etc. The IT function is merely the **custodian** of the data.

1) User departments should be able to access and alter only the data pertaining to their job duties; e.g., credit managers should not be able to alter accounts payable data. End users should never be able to access the code underlying applications programs.

3. Stop and review! You have completed the outline for this subunit. Study multiple-choice questions 28 through 31 beginning on page 367.

11.4 SYSTEMS DEVELOPMENT AND DESIGN

1. Developing a computer-based information system is a creative and demanding task that can and should produce economic benefits for an organization.

a. However, systems development can be a disaster, with labor and financial resources being expended with no observable return and perhaps even a system that cannot be completed.

1) Positive results are more frequently obtained if the process is **formally structured, documented, and subject to management controls**.

b. By far the the most common methodology for building new information systems is the **systems development life-cycle (SDLC) approach**.

1) The SDLC approach is highly structured and, if properly followed, can help an organization deploy maintainable, well-documented systems with the functionality that was intended.

2.   The steps in the systems development life-cycle are as follows:

    a.   The **project definition phase** includes

        1)   Preparing the project proposal
        2)   Determining project priority
        3)   Submitting the proposal for approval

    b.   A **feasibility study** consists of

        1)   An investigation of the current system
        2)   Determination of the information and processing requirements
        3)   Evaluation of the possible applications of computer data processing
        4)   Selection of the best option
        5)   An evaluation of the proposed design choice's cost effectiveness and impact on the organization

    c.   A **cost-benefit analysis** is the analysis tool to use in selecting the best system alternative.

        1)   Feasibility studies should include an analysis of the cost-benefit ratio of any system alternatives.
        2)   In many cases, the best possible system may not be cost effective.
        3)   Thus, once the decision makers have determined that two or more system alternatives are acceptable, the cost-benefit relationship should be used to select the best system for a particular application.

    d.   The **project initiation phase** includes

        1)   Promptly informing managers and employees about the project
        2)   Assembling the project team (possibly including systems analysts, programmers, accountants, and users)
        3)   Training selected personnel to improve necessary skills and enhance communication among team members
        4)   Establishing project controls (e.g., by implementing a project scheduling technique such as PERT)

    e.   **Systems analysis** is the process of learning how a system functions, determining the needs of users, and developing the logical requirements of a proposed system.

        1)   A systems analysis requires a survey of the existing system, the organization itself, and the organization's environment to determine (among other things) whether a new system is needed.
        2)   The survey results determine not only what, where, how, and by whom activities are performed but also why, how well, and whether they should be done at all.
        3)   Ascertaining the problems and informational needs of decision makers is the next step.
        4)   The **systems analyst** must consider the entity's key success variables (factors that determine its success or failure), the decisions currently being made and those that should be made, the factors important in decision making (timing, relation to other decisions, etc.), the information needed for decisions, and how well the current system makes those decisions.
        5)   Finally, the systems analysis should establish the requirements of a system that will meet user needs.

f. The process of developing specifications for the components of a system is **systems design**.

    1) Detailed systems design involves developing specifications regarding input, processing, internal controls and security measures, programs, procedures, output, and databases.

    2) The three major activities of systems design are user interface design, data design, and process design.

    3) Systems design determines how information requirements will be met.

    4) It concerns how users will interact with the system to meet their needs, how data will be organized, and the formulation of processing steps.

g. **Physical database design** depends on the existing system.

    1) New files or a new database may have to be designed.

    2) Modifying an existing database may be feasible.

    3) If the existing database provides for the new application, modification may not be necessary.

h. **Program development** entails coding programs in accordance with the specifications in the physical design phase and then testing the results.

    1) **Structured programming** divides the system's set of programs into discrete modules by functional specifications.

        a) The objective is to create modules that are independent logical units, each of which has one entry and one exit point.

        b) This reduces the complexity resulting from instructions that jump back and forth among different sections of the program (called "spaghetti code").

        c) Data sharing among modules should also be minimized.

    2) Each module can be coded by a separate team to

        a) Facilitate security, because no one group knows the complete set of programs

        b) Expedite the development process, because several programming teams can work simultaneously

        c) Facilitate maintenance, because a change or patch need only be module-specific, a less complicated procedure than fitting a patch to a complex, multifunction program

i. **Procedure development** includes writing technical manuals, forms, and other materials for all persons who will use, maintain, or otherwise work with the system.

j. **Installation and operation** are the final phases of the SDLC.

    1) Training and educating system users is important not only for proper use of the system but also to offset the resistance of users whose jobs may have been substantially changed.

    2) Acceptance testing by users of inputs, outputs, programs, and procedures is necessary to determine that the new system meets their needs.

    3) Systems conversion is the final testing and switchover.

        a) **Parallel operation** is the operation of the old and new systems simultaneously until satisfaction is obtained that the new system is operating as expected.

        b) **Pilot operation** (modular or phase-in conversion) is the conversion to the new or modified system by module or segment, e.g., one division, department, function, or branch of the company at a time. One disadvantage is the extension of the conversion time.

4) Systems follow-up or post-implementation evaluation is a subsequent review of the efficiency and effectiveness of the system after it has operated for a substantial time (e.g., 1 year).

k. **Errors** can be corrected most easily and clearly when they are found at an early stage of systems development. Their correction becomes more costly as the life cycle progresses.

l. **Systems maintenance** must be undertaken by systems analysts and applications programmers continuously throughout the life of a system.

1) Maintenance is the redesign of the system and programs to meet new needs or to correct design flaws.

2) Ideally, these changes should be made as part of a regular program of preventive maintenance.

3. Stop and review! You have completed the outline for this subunit. Study multiple-choice questions 32 through 42 beginning on page 368.

QUESTIONS

11.1 Role of Business Information Systems

1. Which of the following is a critical success factor in data mining a large data store?

A. Pattern recognition.

B. Effective search engines.

C. Image processing systems.

D. Accurate universal resource locator (URL).

Answer (A) is correct. *(CPA, adapted)*
REQUIRED: The critical success factor in data mining a large data store.
DISCUSSION: Data mining allows a user to discover hidden relationships, such as associations, sequences of events, classifications (descriptions of the groups to which the item belongs), or clusters (new groupings previously not known). Typical applications of data mining are identification of potential customers and purchasing power.
Answer (B) is incorrect because effective search engines are not relevant when the data are not on the Internet. Answer (C) is incorrect because image processing is irrelevant when the objective is to seek patterns in data. Answer (D) is incorrect because an accurate universal resource locator (URL) is not relevant when the data are not on the Internet.

2. In business information systems, the term "stakeholder" refers to which of the following parties?

A. The management team responsible for the security of the documents and data stored on the computers or networks.

B. Information technology personnel responsible for creating the documents and data stored on the computers or networks.

C. Authorized users who are granted access rights to the documents and data stored on the computers or networks.

D. Anyone in the organization who has a role in creating or using the documents and data stored on the computers or networks.

Answer (D) is correct. *(CPA, adapted)*
REQUIRED: The stakeholders in business information systems.
DISCUSSION: Stakeholders are those who affect, or are affected by, the output of the information system. They have an interest in the system's effective and efficient functioning. Hence, they include users such as managers, employees, IT personnel, suppliers, and customers.
Answer (A) is incorrect because stakeholders are not limited to the management team responsible for the security of the documents and data stored on the computers or networks. Answer (B) is incorrect because stakeholders are not limited to information technology personnel responsible for creating the documents and data stored on the computers or networks. Answer (C) is incorrect because stakeholders are not limited to authorized users who are granted access rights to the documents and data stored on the computers or networks.

3. Which group of characteristics best describes decision support systems?

    A. Programming models and interactive computer-based modeling processes.

    B. Analytical models, applications models, and interactive computer-based modeling processes.

    C. Expert systems, model-based information, electronic data interchange, and the decision maker's own insights and judgments.

    D. Analytical models, specialized databases, interactive computer-based modeling processes, and the decision maker's own insights and judgments.

Answer (D) is correct. *(CMA, adapted)*
    REQUIRED: The characteristics of decision support systems.
    DISCUSSION: A decision support system (DSS) assists middle- and upper-level managers in long-term, nonroutine, and often unstructured decision making. The system combines data, decision models, and user-friendly software to provide end users with capabilities for analysis rather than specified information flows. It is an aid to decision making, not the automation of a decision process.
    Answer (A) is incorrect because application models are used to design and construct decision support systems. They are not characteristics of decision support systems. Answer (B) is incorrect because application models are used to design and construct decision support systems. They are not characteristics of decision support systems. Answer (C) is incorrect because an expert system is a different type of information system and not a characteristic of a decision support system. Moreover, electronic data interchange provides for specific information flows.

4. Which of the following is the best example of the use of a decision support system (DSS)?

    A. A manager uses a personal-computer-based simulation model to determine whether one of the company's ships would be able to satisfy a particular delivery schedule.

    B. An auditor uses a generalized audit software package to retrieve several purchase orders for detailed vouching.

    C. A manager uses the query language feature of a database management system (DBMS) to compile a report showing customers whose average purchase exceeds $2,500.

    D. An auditor uses a personal-computer-based word processing software package to modify an internal control questionnaire for a specific audit engagement.

Answer (A) is correct. *(CIA, adapted)*
    REQUIRED: The best example of the use of a decision support system.
    DISCUSSION: A decision support system (DSS) assists middle- and upper-level managers in long-term, nonroutine, and often unstructured decision making. The system contains at least one decision model, is usually interactive, dedicated, and time-shared, but need not be real-time. It is an aid to decision making, not the automation of a decision process. The personal-computer-based simulation model is used to provide interactive problem solving (i.e., scheduling) assistance, the distinguishing feature of a DSS.
    Answer (B) is incorrect because the generalized audit software package does not provide interactive problem solving assistance in retrieving the purchase orders and thus is not a DSS. Answer (C) is incorrect because the query feature of a DBMS does not provide interactive problem solving assistance in compiling the report and thus is not a DSS. Answer (D) is incorrect because the word processing software package does not provide interactive problem solving assistance to the auditor and thus is not a DSS.

5. Business intelligence (BI) has all of the following characteristics except

    A. Focusing on obtaining strategic objectives.

    B. Giving immediate information about an organization's critical success factors.

    C. Displaying information in graphical format.

    D. Providing advice and answers to top management from a knowledge-based system.

Answer (D) is correct. *(CMA, adapted)*
    REQUIRED: The item that is not a characteristic of business intelligence (BI).
    DISCUSSION: BI serves the needs of top management for managerial control and strategic planning. BI focuses on strategic (long-range) objectives and gives immediate information about a firm's critical success factors. BI is not a program for providing top management with advice and answers from a knowledge-based (expert) system.
    Answer (A) is incorrect because BI does focus on obtaining strategic objectives. Answer (B) is incorrect because BI gives immediate information about an organization's critical (strategic) success factors. Answer (C) is incorrect because BI often displays information in graphical format.

6. The management of information systems is experiencing a transition from an emphasis on information processing to an emphasis on information resources management. Which of the following choices best describes the scope of information resources management?

    A. Computer operations, applications development, technical services, and corporate databases.

    B. Data communications, voice communications, and local area networks.

    C. External data services, word processing, and intelligent workstations.

    D. Data processing, telecommunications, and office automation.

Answer (D) is correct. *(CIA, adapted)*
REQUIRED: The best description of the scope of information resources management.
DISCUSSION: Modern information systems have evolved beyond data-based information processing to information resources management. For this purpose, information is viewed as a strategic resource, and the newer information technologies have an important role. IRM embraces at least the overlapping activities of data processing, telecommunications, and office automation.
Answer (A) is incorrect because computer operations, applications development, technical services, and corporate databases are within the traditional scope of data processing. Answer (B) is incorrect because data communications, voice communications, and local area networks are functions typically included in telecommunications. Answer (C) is incorrect because external data services, word processing, and intelligent workstations are included in office automation, which also embraces local area networks and wide area communications.

7. Which of the following are ways in which IT developments have changed business?

		Formerly	Currently
I.	Control:	Inward	Outward
II.	Business channels:	Few	Many
III.	Trademark issues:	National	Global
IV.	Business alliances:	Extensive	Limited

    A. I and IV only.

    B. II, III, and IV only.

    C. I, II, and III only.

    D. I, II, III, and IV.

Answer (C) is correct. *(Publisher, adapted)*
REQUIRED: The ways in which IT developments have changed business.
DISCUSSION: In the new electronic global business environment, brand, trademark, and intellectual property issues have global implications. Enforcing such rights on the Internet and in foreign cultures and legal systems poses obvious challenges. Moreover, IT developments, e.g., electronic commerce, means that businesses operate in an increasingly less-defined regulatory environment through multiple channels as compared with the days when sellers and customers interacted almost entirely in "bricks-and-mortar" establishments. Another feature of the new environment is outward orientation of control. Risks to partners, customers, suppliers, and allies may be risks to the organization.

8. An enterprise resource planning (ERP) system integrates the organization's computerized subsystems and may also provide links to external parties. An advantage of ERP is that

    A. The reengineering needed for its implementation should improve business processes.

    B. Customizing the software to suit the unique needs of the organization will facilitate upgrades.

    C. It can be installed by organizations of all sizes.

    D. The comprehensiveness of the system reduces resistance to change.

Answer (A) is correct. *(Publisher, adapted)*
REQUIRED: The advantage of ERP.
DISCUSSION: The benefits of ERP may significantly derive from the business process reengineering that is needed for its implementation. Using ERP software that reflects industry best practices forces the linked subunits in the organization not only to redesign and improve their processes but also to conform to one standard.
Answer (B) is incorrect because the disadvantages of ERP are its extent and complexity, which make customization of the software difficult and costly. Answer (C) is incorrect because ERP software is costly and complex. It usually is installed only by the largest enterprises. Answer (D) is incorrect because implementing an ERP system is likely to encounter significant resistance because of its comprehensiveness.

9. In a traditional ERP system, the receipt of a customer order may result in

I.   Customer tracking of the order's progress

II. Automatic replenishment of inventory by a supplier

III. Hiring or reassigning of employees

IV. Automatic adjustment of output schedules

    A. I, II, and IV only.

    B. I and III only.

    C. III and IV only.

    D. I, II, III, and IV.

Answer (C) is correct. *(Publisher, adapted)*
REQUIRED: The possible effects of receipt of a customer order by a traditional ERP system.
DISCUSSION: The traditional ERP system is one in which subsystems share data and coordinate their activities. Thus, if marketing receives an order, it can quickly verify that inventory is sufficient to notify shipping to process the order. Otherwise, production is notified to manufacture more of the product, with a consequent automatic adjustment of output schedules. If materials are inadequate for this purpose, the system will issue a purchase order. If more labor is needed, human resources will be instructed to reassign or hire employees. However, the subsystems in a traditional ERP system are internal to the organization. Hence, they are often called back-office functions. The information produced is principally (but not exclusively) intended for internal use by the organization's managers.
The current generation of ERP software (ERP II) has added front-office functions. Consequently, ERP II but not traditional ERP is capable of customer tracking of the order's progress and automatic replenishment of inventory by a supplier.

10. A principal advantage of an ERP system is

    A. Program-data dependence.

    B. Data redundancy.

    C. Separate data updating for different functions.

    D. Centralization of data.

Answer (D) is correct. *(Publisher, adapted)*
REQUIRED: The principal advantage of an ERP system
DISCUSSION: An advantage of an ERP system is the elimination of data redundancy through the use of a central database. In principle, information about an item of data is stored once, and all functions have access to it. Thus, when the item (such as a price) is updated, the change is effectively made for all functions. The result is reliability (data integrity).
Answer (A) is incorrect because an ERP system uses a central database and a database management system. A fundamental characteristic of a database is that applications are independent of the physical structure of the database. Writing programs or designing applications to use the database requires only the names of desired data items, not their locations. Answer (B) is incorrect because an ERP system eliminates data redundancy. Answer (C) is incorrect because an ERP system is characterized by one-time data updating for all organizational functions.

11. The current generation of ERP software (ERP II) has added front-office functions like

    A. Inventory control.

    B. Human resources.

    C. Purchasing.

    D. Customer service.

Answer (D) is correct. *(Publisher, adapted)*
REQUIRED: The front-office function addressed by ERP II.
DISCUSSION: The current generation of ERP software (ERP II) has added front-office functions. Customer relationship management applications in ERP II extend to customer service, finance-related matters, sales, and database creation and maintenance. Integrated data are helpful in better understanding customer needs, such as product preference or location of retail outlets. Thus, the organization may be able to optimize its sales forecasts, product line, and inventory levels.
Answer (A) is incorrect because inventory control is a back-office function. Answer (B) is incorrect because human resources is a back-office function. Answer (C) is incorrect because purchasing is a back-office function.

12. The current generation of ERP software (ERP II) may include an advanced planning and scheduling system that

    A. Determines the location of retail outlets.

    B. Connects the organization with other members of a joint venture.

    C. Controls the flow of a manufacturer's materials and components through the supply chain.

    D. Permits tracking of orders by customers.

Answer (C) is correct. *(Publisher, adapted)*
    REQUIRED: The function of an advanced planning and scheduling system.
    DISCUSSION: An advanced planning and scheduling system may be an element of a supply chain management application for a manufacturer. It controls the flow of materials and components within the chain. Schedules are created given projected costs, lead times, and inventories.
    Answer (A) is incorrect because customer relationship management applications in ERP II extend to customer service, finance-related matters, sales, and database creation and maintenance. Integrated data are helpful in better understanding customer needs, such as product preference or location of retail outlets. Answer (B) is incorrect because partner relationship management applications connect the organization not only with such partners as customers and suppliers but also with owners, creditors, and strategic allies (for example, other members of a joint venture). Answer (D) is incorrect because an advanced planning scheduling system is used by a manufacturer to control flows through the supply chain. Other software permits customers to obtain information about order availability.

13. Prudent managers will recognize the limits within which expert systems can be effectively applied. Which of the following is most suitable for an expert system?

    A. Compensate for the lack of certain technical knowledge within the organization.

    B. Help make customer-service jobs easier to perform.

    C. Automate daily managerial problem-solving.

    D. Emulate human expertise for strategic planning.

Answer (B) is correct. *(CIA, adapted)*
    REQUIRED: The most appropriate use for an expert system.
    DISCUSSION: Expert systems are systems that allow a computer to make decisions in a human way. Expert systems allow even small companies to perform activities and provide services previously only available from larger firms. The use of expert systems has helped to improve the quality of customer service in applications such as maintenance and scheduling by automating them and making them easy to perform.
    Answer (A) is incorrect because expert systems codify and apply existing knowledge, but they do not create knowledge. Answer (C) is incorrect because expert systems do best in automating lower-level clerical functions. Answer (D) is incorrect because expert systems concern problems with relatively few possible outcomes that are all known in advance.

14. The processing in expert systems is characterized by

    A. Algorithms.

    B. Deterministic procedures.

    C. Heuristics.

    D. Simulations.

Answer (C) is correct. *(CIA, adapted)*
    REQUIRED: The characteristic of processing in knowledge-based systems.
    DISCUSSION: Knowledge-based (expert) systems contain a knowledge base for a limited domain of human expertise and inference procedures for the solution of problems. They use symbolic processing based on heuristics rather than algorithms. A heuristic procedure is an exploratory problem-solving technique that uses self-education methods, e.g., the evaluation of feedback, to improve performance. These systems are often very interactive and provide explanations of their problem-solving behavior.
    Answer (A) is incorrect because algorithms are defined procedures used in typical computer programs. Answer (B) is incorrect because deterministic procedures are procedures used in computer programs that permit no uncertainty in outcomes. Answer (D) is incorrect because simulations are computer programs that permit experimentation with logical and mathematical models.

15. A bank implemented an expert system to help account representatives consolidate the bank's relationships with each customer. The expert system has

- A. A sequential control structure.
- B. Distinct input-output variables.
- C. A knowledge base.
- D. Passive data elements.

Answer (C) is correct. *(CIA, adapted)*
REQUIRED: The component of an expert system.
DISCUSSION: An expert system relies on a computer's ability to make decisions in a human way. There are three components to an expert system: a knowledge base, an inference engine, and a user interface. The knowledge base contains the rules used when making decisions.
Answer (A) is incorrect because traditional programs, e.g., in COBOL, have sequential control structures; expert systems do not. Answer (B) is incorrect because traditional programs, not expert systems, have distinct input-output variables. Answer (D) is incorrect because traditional programs, not expert systems, have passive data elements.

16. For which of the following applications would the use of a fuzzy logic system be the most appropriate artificial intelligence (AI) choice?

- A. Assigning airport gates to arriving airline flights.
- B. Forecasting demand for spare auto parts.
- C. Performing indoor climate control.
- D. Diagnosing computer hardware problems.

Answer (C) is correct. *(CIA, adapted)*
REQUIRED: The most appropriate use for fuzzy logic.
DISCUSSION: Fuzzy logic is a superset of conventional (Boolean) logic that has been extended to handle the concept of partial truth. Because they use nonspecific terms (membership functions) characterized by well-defined imprecision, fuzzy logic systems can create rules to address problems with many solutions. For example, applying fuzzy logic to indoor climate control may require defining in impressionistic terms and weighting functions such as indoor and outdoor temperature, humidity, and wind conditions. Thus, definitions (e.g., hot, warm, normal, cool, or cold, stated in temperature ranges) may overlap. The resulting rules describe actions to be taken when certain combinations of conditions exist. Fuzzy logic can be used when values are approximate or subjective, objects belong to multiple sets, membership in a set is a matter of degree, and data are incomplete or ambiguous.
Answer (A) is incorrect because assigning airport gates to arriving airline flights requires an expert system that uses precise data for quick and consistent decisions. Answer (B) is incorrect because neural networks provide the technology to undertake sophisticated forecasting and analysis. They emulate the processing patterns of the brain and therefore can learn from experience. Answer (D) is incorrect because diagnosing problems with computer hardware could be accomplished by an expert system.

17. Which of the following features is classified as part of an expert system?

- A. Use of electronic mail to route and approve purchase requisitions.
- B. Automatic obligation of budget funds as soon as an order is issued.
- C. Issuance of purchase requisition notices as soon as the on-hand balance reaches the reorder point.
- D. Automatic placement of orders with suppliers who currently offer the best combination of price, freight cost, and delivery time.

Answer (D) is correct. *(CIA, adapted)*
REQUIRED: The feature classified as part of an expert system.
DISCUSSION: The automatic placement of orders with the best combination of price, freight, and delivery time requires the maintenance of a database for all suppliers that is constantly changing as terms and conditions change. It simulates the decision process used by purchase managers.
Answer (A) is incorrect because use of electronic mail takes advantage of new software features but does not represent simulated thinking by the system. Answer (B) is incorrect because automatic obligation of funds takes advantage of the real-time capability of the system but again does not represent simulated thinking by the system. Answer (C) is incorrect because issuance of purchase requisition notices at the reorder point demonstrates a simple if/then decision but is not an example of an expert system feature.

11.2 Risks Associated with Business Information Systems

18. Which of the following is an advantage of a computer-based system for transaction processing over a manual system? A computer-based system

A. Does not require as stringent a set of internal controls.

B. Will produce a more accurate set of financial statements.

C. Will be more efficient at producing financial statements.

D. Eliminates the need to reconcile control accounts and subsidiary ledgers.

Answer (C) is correct. *(CPA, adapted)*
REQUIRED: The advantage of computer processing.
DISCUSSION: Computer processing uniformly subjects like transactions to the same processing instructions and virtually eliminates clerical error. Thus, it permits consistent application of predefined business rules and the performance of complex calculations in high volume. However, programming errors (or other similar systematic errors in either the hardware or software) will result in all like transactions being processed incorrectly when they are processed under the same conditions. Hence, computer processing of the accounting transactions reported in financial statements is more efficient than in a manual system.
Answer (A) is incorrect because many functions once performed by separate individuals may be concentrated in computer systems. Hence, an individual who has access to a computer may perform incompatible functions. As a result, other controls may be necessary to achieve the control objectives ordinarily accomplished by segregation of functions. Answer (B) is incorrect because greater accuracy is not necessarily a result of greater efficiency. Answer (D) is incorrect because reconciliations are made regardless of the processing method.

19. Which of the following is most likely a disadvantage for an entity that keeps data files prepared by personal computers rather than manually prepared files?

A. Attention is focused on the accuracy of the programming process rather than errors in individual transactions.

B. It is usually easier for unauthorized persons to access and alter the files.

C. Random error associated with processing similar transactions in different ways is usually greater.

D. It is usually more difficult to compare recorded accountability with physical count of assets.

Answer (B) is correct. *(CPA, adapted)*
REQUIRED: The disadvantage of personal-computer-prepared data files.
DISCUSSION: In a manual system, one individual is assigned responsibility for maintaining and safeguarding the records. However, in a personal computer environment, the data files may be subject to change by others without documentation or indication of who made the changes.
Answer (A) is incorrect because the focus on programming is an advantage of using the computer. A program allows transactions to be processed uniformly. Answer (C) is incorrect because an advantage of the computer is that it processes similar transactions in the same way. Answer (D) is incorrect because the method of maintaining the files is independent of the ability to compare this information in the file with the physical count of assets.

20. Which of the following risks are greater in computerized systems than in manual systems?

I. Erroneous data conversion
II. Erroneous source document preparation
III. Repetition of errors
IV. Concentration of data

A. I and II.

B. II and III.

C. I, III, and IV.

D. I, II, III, and IV.

Answer (C) is correct. *(CISA, adapted)*
REQUIRED: The risks that are greater in computerized systems than in manual systems.
DISCUSSION: Unlike a manual system, a computer system converts data to machine-readable form so that transactions can be processed. This additional step increases the risk of input error. Moreover, if an error exists in the program, systematic, repetitive errors will occur in processing transactions. Finally, data are typically stored magnetically on tapes or disks. This concentration of data increases the risk of loss from natural and other disasters. Source document preparation either precedes processing or is eliminated altogether in a computerized system. Thus, the risk of erroneous source document preparation in computerized systems is the same as or less than the equivalent risk in manual systems.

21. Your firm has recently converted its purchasing cycle from a manual process to an online computer system. Which of the following is a probable result associated with conversion to the new automatic system?

A. Processing errors are increased.

B. The firm's risk exposures are reduced.

C. Processing time is increased.

D. Traditional duties are less segregated.

Answer (D) is correct. *(CIA, adapted)*
REQUIRED: The probable result associated with conversion to the new automatic system.
DISCUSSION: In a manual system with appropriate internal control, separate individuals are responsible for authorizing transactions, recording transactions, and having custody of assets. These checks and balances prevent fraud and detect inaccurate or incomplete transactions. In a computer environment, however, this segregation of duties is not always feasible. For example, a computer may print checks, record disbursements, and generate information for reconciling the account balance.
Answer (A) is incorrect because a computer system decreases processing errors. Answer (B) is incorrect because the conversion to a new system does not reduce the number of risk exposures. Answer (C) is incorrect because processing time is decreased.

22. Matthews Corp. has changed from a system of recording time worked on clock cards to a computerized payroll system in which employees record time in and out with magnetic cards. The computer system automatically updates all payroll records. Because of this change,

A. A generalized computer audit program must be used.

B. Part of the audit trail is altered.

C. The potential for payroll-related fraud is diminished.

D. Transactions must be processed in batches.

Answer (B) is correct. *(CPA, adapted)*
REQUIRED: The effect of changing to a computerized payroll system.
DISCUSSION: In a manual payroll system, a paper trail of documents is created to provide audit evidence that controls over each step in processing are in place and functioning. One element of a computer system that differentiates it from a manual system is that a transaction trail useful for auditing purposes might exist only for a brief time or only in computer-readable form.
Answer (A) is incorrect because use of generalized audit software is only one of many ways of auditing through a computer. Answer (C) is incorrect because conversion to a computer system may increase the chance of fraud by eliminating segregation of incompatible functions and other controls. Answer (D) is incorrect because automatic updating indicates that processing is not in batch mode.

23. Which of the following statements most accurately describes the impact that automation has on the controls normally present in a manual system?

A. Transaction trails are more extensive in a computer-based system than in a manual system because a one-for-one correspondence always exists between data entry and output.

B. Responsibility for custody of information assets is more concentrated in user departments in a computer-based system than it is in a manual system.

C. Controls must be more explicit in a computer-based system because many processing points that present opportunities for human judgment in a manual system are eliminated.

D. The quality of documentation becomes less critical in a computer-based system than it is in a manual system because data records are stored in machine-readable files.

Answer (C) is correct. *(CIA, adapted)*
REQUIRED: The impact that automation has on the controls normally present in a manual system.
DISCUSSION: Using a computer does not change the basic concepts and objectives of control. However, the use of computers may modify the control techniques used. The processing of transactions may be combined with control activities previously performed separately, or control functions may be combined within the information system activity.
Answer (A) is incorrect because the audit trail is less extensive in an information system. Combining processing and controls within the system reduces documentary evidence. Answer (B) is incorrect because information assets are more likely to be under the control of the information system function. Answer (D) is incorrect because documentation is more important in an information system. Information is more likely to be stored in machine-readable form than in hard copy.

24. IT affects how transactions are initiated, recorded, processed, and reported. Thus, in a system that uses IT,

A. Controls are entirely automated.

B. Paper records, such as purchase orders and shipping documents, are retained.

C. Only discrete functions are automated.

D. Manual controls may be limited to monitoring.

Answer (D) is correct. *(Publisher, adapted)*
REQUIRED: The effect of IT.
DISCUSSION: Manual controls may be independent of IT, use IT information, or simply monitor the functioning of IT and automated controls and handle exceptions.
Answer (A) is incorrect because automated procedures use electronic records to replace paper purchase orders, invoices, shipping documents, and related accounting records. Controls in IT systems combine manual and automated controls (such as those embedded in programs). Answer (B) is incorrect because, if a system electronically initiates, records, processes, and reports transactions, paper purchase orders, invoices, shipping documents, etc., are replaced with electronic records. Answer (C) is incorrect because the use of IT may affect any of the components of the entity's operating units or business functions. Thus, IT may be part of discrete systems, for example, an accounts receivable system for a business unit or a system that controls factory equipment. However, the use of IT may be in integrated systems that support all financial reporting, operations, and compliance objectives.

25. Innovations in IT increase the importance of risk management because

A. The objective of complete security is becoming more attainable.

B. Information system security is continually subject to new threats.

C. Closed private systems have proliferated.

D. Privacy is a concern for only a very few users.

Answer (B) is correct. *(Publisher, adapted)*
REQUIRED: The reason that IT innovations increase the importance of risk management.
DISCUSSION: Senior management is responsible for identifying risks, measuring exposures, determining whether controls are in place and are effective, specifying threats to survival, and considering the costs of mitigating risks. Because information system security is continually subject to new threats, that is, to new risks and exposures, risk assessment and management must be a continual process. This process includes determining probabilities and estimating consequences so as to set priorities for allocating limited resources.
Answer (A) is incorrect because perfect security is not feasible. One reason is that system access cannot be eliminated. Answer (C) is incorrect because, although closed private systems have proliferated, risk management has become more important as a result of the need for businesses to maintain publicly accessible systems. Answer (D) is incorrect because privacy was an expectation of people everywhere before the innovations in IT that led to the globalization of e-business via the Internet. Thus, risk management has increased in importance in part because those innovations created new threats to the privacy of personal information. As such, organizations must, for example, meet statutory requirements for safeguarding the personal information of customers.

26. Which of the following characteristics distinguishes computer processing from manual processing?

A. Computer processing virtually eliminates the occurrence of computational error normally associated with manual processing.

B. Errors or fraud in computer processing will be detected soon after their occurrence.

C. The potential for systematic error is ordinarily greater in manual processing than in computerized processing.

D. Most computer systems are designed so that transaction trails useful for audit purposes do not exist.

Answer (A) is correct. *(CPA, adapted)*
REQUIRED: The feature that distinguishes computer processing from manual processing.
DISCUSSION: Computer processing uniformly subjects like transactions to the same processing instructions. A computer program defines the processing steps to accomplish a task. Once the program is written and tested appropriately, it will perform the task repetitively and without error. However, if the program contains an error, all transactions will be processed incorrectly.
Answer (B) is incorrect because, when an error does occur, for example, in input, it may not be discovered on a timely basis. Ordinarily, much less human intervention occurs once the transaction is processed. Answer (C) is incorrect because systematic (repetitive) errors will occur in computerized processing if an error exists in the program. Answer (D) is incorrect because adequately designed systems maintain transaction, console, and error logs that create useful audit trails.

27. One of the major problems in a computer system is that incompatible functions may be performed by the same individual. One compensating control is the use of

   A. Echo checks.

   B. A check digit system.

   C. Computer-generated hash totals.

   D. A computer log.

Answer (D) is correct. *(CPA, adapted)*
   REQUIRED: The control compensating for inadequate segregation of duties in a computer system.
   DISCUSSION: A computer (console) log is a record of computer and software usage usually produced by the operating system. Proper monitoring of the log is a compensating control for the lack of segregation of duties. For instance, the log should list operator interventions.
   Answer (A) is incorrect because echo checks are hardware controls used to determine if the correct message was received by an output device. Answer (B) is incorrect because a check digit system is an input control that tests identification numbers. Answer (C) is incorrect because hash totals are control totals used to check for losses or inaccuracies arising during data movement.

11.3 Roles and Responsibilities within the IT Function

28. Which of the following controls most likely could prevent computer personnel from modifying programs to bypass programmed controls?

   A. Periodic management review of computer utilization reports and systems documentation.

   B. Segregation of duties for computer programming and computer operations.

   C. Participation of user department personnel in designing and approving new systems.

   D. Physical security of computer facilities in limiting access to computer equipment.

Answer (B) is correct. *(CPA, adapted)*
   REQUIRED: The control necessary to prevent computer personnel from modifying programs to bypass controls.
   DISCUSSION: Programmers and analysts can modify programs, data files, and controls, so they should have no access to programs used to process transactions. Segregation of programming and operations is necessary to prevent unauthorized modifications of programs.
   Answer (A) is incorrect because, although periodic management review is appropriate, reports and systems documentation will not prevent or detect unauthorized modifications. Answer (C) is incorrect because user participation relates to new systems, not modification of existing systems. Answer (D) is incorrect because programmers may have access through data communications. Thus, physical security is not sufficient to prevent unauthorized modifications.

29. Which of the following areas of responsibility are normally assigned to a systems programmer in a computer system environment?

   A. Systems analysis and applications programming.

   B. Data communications hardware and software.

   C. Operating systems and compilers.

   D. Computer operations.

Answer (C) is correct. *(CPA, adapted)*
   REQUIRED: The responsibilities of systems programmers.
   DISCUSSION: Systems programmers write systems software. Systems software is usually purchased from vendors in machine or assembly language. It is necessary to facilitate the processing of application programs by the computer. It performs the fundamental tasks needed to manage computer resources, such as language translation, monitoring of data communications, job instruction, control of input and output, file management, data sorting, and access control. For example, the operating system mediates between the application programs and the computer hardware, and procedural languages may be translated into executable code (machine language) by compilers.
   Answer (A) is incorrect because systems analysts analyze and design computer systems. They should provide no programming services or have access to programs, equipment, data, or controls. Moreover, effective control should segregate systems and applications programming. Answer (B) is incorrect because systems programmers should not have access to operational hardware and software. Answer (D) is incorrect because database/network/web administrators are responsible for managing, supervising, and oversight of computer facilities.

30. Which one of the following represents a lack of internal control in a computer-based system?

A. The design and implementation is performed in accordance with management's specific authorization.

B. Any and all changes in application programs have the authorization and approval of management.

C. Provisions exist to ensure the accuracy and integrity of computer processing of all files and reports.

D. Programmers have access to change programs and data files when an error is detected.

Answer (D) is correct. *(CMA, adapted)*
REQUIRED: The example of a lack of internal control in a computer system.
DISCUSSION: A functional separation of computer activities is necessary for internal control. A programmer designs program flowcharts and writes the computer programs as required by the system. Once the program has been debugged and the documentation prepared, the programmer should have no further access to it or to data files. A librarian is responsible for permitting only computer operators, not programmers, to have access to programs.
Answer (A) is incorrect because the design and implementation should be authorized by management to maintain effective internal controls. Answer (B) is incorrect because activities that involve making changes in application programs should be authorized and approved by management to maintain effective internal controls. Answer (C) is incorrect because effective internal control ensures the reliability of records. A control group (clerk) should continuously supervise and monitor input, operations, and distribution of output.

31. A computer operator responsible for a particular job needed to know whether the job had already been run that day. The computer operator examined the

A. Console log.

B. Data control log.

C. Job queue.

D. Master run book.

Answer (A) is correct. *(CIA, adapted)*
REQUIRED: The source of information about execution of jobs.
DISCUSSION: During processing, the operating system records in the console log the activities of the computer system and the actions taken by the computer operator. It should therefore contain entries for the work performed and provide a control over operator intervention.
Answer (B) is incorrect because the data control log contains entries concerning jobs run and output distribution. However, recording is not concurrent with computer activity, and no entry may appear for some transactions already processed.
Answer (C) is incorrect because the job queue is the list of jobs waiting to be processed, not those that have been executed.
Answer (D) is incorrect because the master run book provides documentation of the system.

11.4 Systems Development and Design

32. In which of the following phases of computer system development would training occur?

A. Planning phase.

B. Analysis phase.

C. Design phase.

D. Implementation phase.

Answer (D) is correct. *(CPA, adapted)*
REQUIRED: The phase of computer system development in which training would occur.
DISCUSSION: Training occurs during the implementation (installation and operation) phase of computer system development. Training and educating users is important not only for proper use of the system, but also to offset the resistance of users whose jobs may have been substantially changed. This phase also includes acceptance testing, system conversion, and system follow-up.
Answer (A) is incorrect because training does not occur in the planning phase, which includes (1) preparing a proposal, (2) studying its feasibility, (3) determining information requirements, and (4) preparing the general design. Answer (B) is incorrect because the analysis phase is the planning phase. Answer (C) is incorrect because training does not occur in the design phase, which includes (1) developing specifications, (2) analyzing objectives and policies, (3) determining decisions to be made, and (4) determining the information required to make decisions.

33. The three major activities of systems design are

   A. User interface design, data manipulation, and output analysis.

   B. Process design, output design, and output analysis.

   C. User interface design, data design, and process design.

   D. Data design, input validation, and processing.

Answer (C) is correct. *(CMA, adapted)*
   REQUIRED: The three major activities of systems design.
   DISCUSSION: Systems design determines how information requirements will be met. It concerns how users will interact with the system to meet their needs, how data will be organized, and the formulation of processing steps.
   Answer (A) is incorrect because data manipulation is not a part of systems design; it is an operational activity that occurs after a system has been installed. Answer (B) is incorrect because output analysis occurs after a system has been installed. Answer (D) is incorrect because input validation and processing are operational activities.

34. Ordinarily, the analysis tool for the systems analyst and steering committee to use in selecting the best system alternative is

   A. Pilot testing.

   B. User selection.

   C. Decision tree analysis.

   D. Cost-benefit analysis.

Answer (D) is correct. *(CMA, adapted)*
   REQUIRED: The analysis tool to use in selecting the best system alternative.
   DISCUSSION: Feasibility studies should include an analysis of the cost-benefit ratio of any system alternatives. In many cases, the best possible system may not be cost effective. Thus, once the decision makers have determined that two or more systems alternatives are acceptable, the cost-benefit relationship should be used to select the best system for a particular application.
   Answer (A) is incorrect because pilot testing determines only whether a system works, not how efficient it is in a particular application. Answer (B) is incorrect because users may not have the necessary systems knowledge to make a decision. Answer (C) is incorrect because decision tree analysis is probably more sophisticated than is necessary in choosing between a few systems alternatives.

35. Two phases of systems planning are project definition and project initiation. All of the following are steps in the project initiation phase except

   A. Preparing the project proposal.

   B. Informing managers and employees of the project.

   C. Assembling the project team.

   D. Training selected personnel.

Answer (A) is correct. *(CMA, adapted)*
   REQUIRED: The step not a part of the project initiation phase of systems planning.
   DISCUSSION: The project initiation phase includes promptly informing managers and employees about the project, assembling the project team (possibly including systems analysts, programmers, accountants, and users), training selected personnel to improve necessary skills and enhance communication among team members, and establishing project controls (e.g., by implementing a project scheduling technique such as PERT). Preparing the project proposal is a part of the project definition phase, as are conducting feasibility studies, determining project priority, and submitting the proposal for approval.
   Answer (B) is incorrect because informing managers and employees of the project is a component of the project initiation phase. Answer (C) is incorrect because assembling the project team is a component of the project initiation phase. Answer (D) is incorrect because training selected personnel is a component of the project initiation phase.

36. The least risky strategy for converting from a manual to a computerized accounts receivable system would be a

   A. Direct conversion.

   B. Parallel conversion.

   C. Pilot conversion.

   D. Database conversion.

Answer (B) is correct. *(CMA, adapted)*
   REQUIRED: The least risky strategy for converting from a manual to a computerized accounts receivable system.
   DISCUSSION: The least risky strategy of converting from a manual to a computerized system is a parallel conversion in which the old and new systems are operated simultaneously until satisfaction is obtained that the new system is operating as expected. Slightly more risky is a pilot conversion in which the new system is introduced by module or segment.
   Answer (A) is incorrect because a direct conversion is more risky than a parallel conversion. Answer (C) is incorrect because a pilot conversion is more risky than a parallel conversion. Answer (D) is incorrect because a database conversion is more risky than a parallel conversion.

37. Workwell Company operates in several regions, with each region performing its data processing in a regional data center. The corporate management information systems (MIS) staff has developed a database management system to handle customer service and billing. The director of MIS recommended that the new system be implemented in the Southwestern Region to ascertain if the system operates in a satisfactory manner. This type of conversion is called a

- A. Parallel conversion.
- B. Direct conversion.
- C. Prototype conversion.
- D. Pilot conversion.

Answer (D) is correct. *(CMA, adapted)*
REQUIRED: The type of systems conversion process in which a new system is first implemented in one subunit of the organization.
DISCUSSION: A modular conversion approach entails switching to the new or improved system in organizational (division, region, product line, etc.) segments or system segments (accounts receivable, database, etc.). A pilot conversion is one in which the final testing and switchover are accomplished at one segment or division of the company.
Answer (A) is incorrect because parallel conversion operates the old and new systems simultaneously. Answer (B) is incorrect because direct conversion involves immediate conversion to the new system throughout the organization. Answer (C) is incorrect because a prototype conversion involves developing and putting into operation successively more refined versions of the system until sufficient information is obtained to produce a satisfactory design.

38. Errors are most costly to correct during

- A. Programming.
- B. Conceptual design.
- C. Analysis.
- D. Implementation.

Answer (D) is correct. *(CMA, adapted)*
REQUIRED: The time when errors are most costly to correct.
DISCUSSION: Errors can be corrected most easily and clearly when they are found at an early stage of systems development. Their correction becomes more costly as the life cycle progresses. Because implementation is the last stage of the process listed, errors are most costly to correct when discovered at the implementation stage.
Answer (A) is incorrect because error correction at the programming level would be less costly than at the implementation stage. Answer (B) is incorrect because error correction at the conceptual design level would be less costly than at the implementation stage. Answer (C) is incorrect because error correction at the analysis level would be less costly than at the implementation stage.

39. The process of monitoring, evaluating, and modifying a system as needed is referred to as

- A. Systems analysis.
- B. Systems feasibility study.
- C. Systems maintenance.
- D. Systems implementation.

Answer (C) is correct. *(CMA, adapted)*
REQUIRED: The term for the process of monitoring, evaluating, and modifying a system.
DISCUSSION: Systems maintenance must be undertaken by systems analysts and applications programmers continuously throughout the life of a system. Maintenance is the redesign of the system and programs to meet new needs or to correct design flaws. Ideally, these changes should be made as part of a regular program of preventive maintenance.
Answer (A) is incorrect because systems analysis is the process of determining user problems and needs, surveying the organization's present system, and analyzing the facts. Answer (B) is incorrect because a feasibility study determines whether a proposed system is technically, operationally, and economically feasible. Answer (D) is incorrect because systems implementation involves training and educating system users, testing, conversion, and follow-up.

40. The process of developing specifications for hardware, software, manpower, data resources, and information products required to develop a system is referred to as

- A. Systems analysis.
- B. Systems feasibility study.
- C. Systems maintenance.
- D. Systems design.

Answer (D) is correct. *(CMA, adapted)*
REQUIRED: The process of developing specifications for the components of a system.
DISCUSSION: Detailed systems design involves developing specifications regarding input, processing, internal controls and security measures, programs, procedures, output, and databases.
Answer (A) is incorrect because systems analysis is the process of learning how the current system functions, determining the needs of users, and developing the logical requirements of a proposed system. Answer (B) is incorrect because a feasibility study determines the technical, operational, and economic feasibility of a system. Answer (C) is incorrect because systems maintenance is the process of monitoring, evaluating, and modifying a system.

41. The process of learning how the current system functions, determining the needs of users, and developing the logical requirements of a proposed system is referred to as

    A. Systems maintenance.

    B. Systems analysis.

    C. Systems feasibility study.

    D. Systems design.

Answer (B) is correct. *(CMA, adapted)*
    REQUIRED: The term referring to the process of learning how a system functions, determining the needs of users, and developing the logical requirements of a proposed system.
    DISCUSSION: A systems analysis requires a survey of the existing system, the organization itself, and the organization's environment to determine (among other things) whether a new system is needed. The survey results determine not only what, where, how, and by whom activities are performed but also why, how well, and whether they should be done at all. Ascertaining the problems and informational needs of decision makers is the next step. The systems analyst must consider the entity's key success variables (factors that determine its success or failure), the decisions currently being made and those that should be made, the factors important in decision making (timing, relation to other decisions, etc.), the information needed for decisions, and how well the current system makes those decisions. Finally, the systems analysis should establish the requirements of a system that will meet user needs.
    Answer (A) is incorrect because maintenance is the final stage of the life cycle in that it continues throughout the life of the system; maintenance includes the redesign of the system and programs to meet new needs or to correct design flaws. Answer (C) is incorrect because the systems feasibility study does not involve the process of learning how the current system works. Answer (D) is incorrect because systems design is the process of developing a system to meet specified requirements.

42. An information system (IS) project manager is currently in the process of adding a systems analyst to the IS staff. The new systems analyst will be involved with testing the new computerized system. At which stage of the systems development life-cycle will the analyst be primarily used?

    A. Cost-benefit analysis.

    B. Requirements definition.

    C. Flowcharting.

    D. Implementation.

Answer (D) is correct. *(CMA, adapted)*
    REQUIRED: The stage of the systems development life-cycle involving testing of a new system.
    DISCUSSION: The systems development life-cycle approach is the oldest methodology applied to the development of medium or large information systems. The cycle is analytically divisible into stages: investigation, analysis, systems design, implementation, and maintenance. Testing, training, and conversion occur in the installation and operation, or implementation, stage of the life-cycle.
    Answer (A) is incorrect because cost-benefit analysis is a part of the feasibility study conducted early in the life-cycle. Answer (B) is incorrect because requirements are defined during the analysis or systems study stage. Answer (C) is incorrect because flowcharting is a necessary activity in all early stages of the life-cycle.

Use Gleim's ***CPA Test Prep*** for interactive testing with over 2,000 additional multiple-choice questions!

STUDY UNIT TWELVE
INFORMATION TECHNOLOGY II

(14 pages of outline)

This study unit is the second of five covering information technology (IT).

12.1 HARDWARE

1. **Hardware** refers to the physical devices making up a computer system. Every computer, regardless of size, has certain common components.

2. The **central processing unit (CPU)** is the "brain" of any computer. In a desktop computer, it is often referred to as the microprocessor. Larger computers, such as servers and mainframes, can have more than one CPU.

   a. The CPU coordinates all of a computer's operations. Its most important functions are to

      1) Move data from storage to main memory
      2) Execute the instructions for manipulating the data
      3) Move the results from main memory back to storage

   b. The speed of a CPU is measured by the number of instructions it can carry out per second, referred to as the clock rate.

      1) For a desktop computer CPU, the unit of measure is cycles per second, or hertz. The CPU of the original IBM Personal Computer in 1981 had a clock rate of 4.77 megahertz, or just over four and a half million cycles per second. Today, one model of the Intel Pentium 4 processor has a clock rate of 3 gigahertz, or three billion cycles per second.

      2) The speed of a mainframe CPU is usually measured in millions of instructions per second (MIPS). Some powerful current mainframe CPUs can run in the neighborhood of 20 billion instructions per second.

   c. The CPU is usually the fastest component of any computer system. The speed of the computer as a whole is almost always limited by some other component ("there's always a bottleneck somewhere").

3. **Random access memory (RAM)** is also referred to as main memory or primary storage. RAM is a holding area for data before and after processing by the CPU.

   a. The contents of RAM are "volatile," meaning RAM is emptied when the power to the computer is shut off.

   b. RAM is most often measured by its size rather than its speed. Laptop computers commonly have anywhere from half a billion to 4 billion bytes of RAM (i.e., 512 megabytes to 4 gigabytes).

4. **Read-only memory (ROM)** is permanent storage used to hold the basic low-level programs and data particular to a computer's hardware, i.e., not part of any single application.

   a. The contents of ROM are vital to operation of the hardware, and thus cannot be altered by the owner and are not affected when the power to the computer is shut off.

5. **Secondary storage devices** hold data and programs that are not currently being used by the CPU. Their key features are their large capacity and their ability to retain data after the power is shut off. Secondary storage comes in a wide variety of configurations.

    a. **Hard drives** are the most common form of secondary storage. Current laptop hard drives often hold more than 60 gigabytes (60 billion bytes) of data. Mainframe disc storage is commonly measured in terabytes, or trillions of bytes of data.

        1) Hard drives consist of a stack of rigid platters connected by a central spindle. Each platter is coated on the top and bottom with a magnetic material.

        2) As the stack of platters spins at very high speed, read/write heads pass back and forth over the surfaces of the platters. When writing, the heads arrange the magnetic particles in patterns that represent data.

        3) The heads float very close to the platter's surface, but they never touch it. If a head comes in contact with the platter or if a piece of dust gets stuck in the microscopic space between the head and the platter, the hard drive completely ceases to operate, a situation referred to as a "crash."

    b. **Optical drives** record and read data by means of a laser beam. The key distinction between optical and magnetic media is that an optical disc can be removed from the drive and inserted in another drive.

        1) The most common optical disc formats are the compact disc, or CD, which holds approximately 700 megabytes of data; and the digital versatile disc (originally called the digital video disc), or DVD, which holds about 4.7 gigabytes.

        2) Unlike magnetic discs, optical discs rotate at varying speeds.

    c. **Flash drives**, also called jump drives or thumb drives, are small, highly portable memory modules that can store a gigabyte of data or more. Unlike hard and optical drives, flash drives have no moving parts.

        1) Flash drives' high level of convenience comes from the fact that they can be plugged into and unplugged from a computer while the computer is running.

    d. Two older storage media that are still sometimes encountered are the **floppy disc**, which is slow and holds a mere 1.4 megabytes of data, and **magnetic tape**, which has a considerably higher capacity than a floppy disc but extremely slow access times.

6. **Input-output devices** are the hardware components that allow the user to input data into the computer and retrieve output.

    a. The following is a list of commonly encountered input devices:

        1) Keyboard
        2) Mouse
        3) Scanner
        4) Touch screen
        5) Magnetic ink character reader (MICR)
        6) Optical character reader (OCR)
        7) Microphone (for voice recognition)
        8) Light pen
        9) Sensor (for gauging water levels, etc.)

    b. These output devices allow the user to retrieve information from the computer:

        1) Monitor
        2) Printer
        3) Plotter
        4) Voice emulator

7. Stop and review! You have completed the outline for this subunit. Study multiple-choice questions 1 through 3 on page 387.

12.2 SOFTWARE

1. **Software** refers to the programs (i.e., sets of computer instructions) that are executed by the hardware. Software can be described from two perspectives: (a) systems vs. application software and (b) the programming language in which the software is written.

2. **Two Major Types of Software**

   a. **Systems software** performs the fundamental tasks needed to manage computer resources. The two most common pieces of systems software are

      1) The operating system, which is the "traffic cop" of any computer system (see Subunit 13.1)

      2) Utility programs, which perform basic functions that are not particular to a certain application, such as file manipulation (copying, deleting, merging, and sorting data files) and file access control

   b. **Application software** consists of programs that tell the computer what steps the user wants carried out. It may be purchased from vendors or developed internally.

      1) Examples of applications found on desktop computers include word processors, spreadsheets, graphics, and small databases.

      2) Applications found on larger computers are payroll, human resources, purchasing, accounts payable, general ledger, treasury, etc.

   c. Software is written in **languages** that are comprehensible by the computer. The following is a description of types and development of computer languages.

3. **Programming Languages**

   a. **First-generation languages** (also called machine languages) are written in binary code (a combination of ones and zeros; see Subunit 13.4) unique to each type of computer. Because they are in binary code, first generation languages are understood directly by the computer and require no translation process.

   b. **Second-generation languages** (also called assembly languages) use mnemonic symbols to represent groups of binary ones and zeros. Assembly languages must be converted to machine languages in order for the computer to understand them.

   c. **Third-generation languages** (also called procedural languages) consist of English-like words and phrases that represent multiple machine language instructions, making these languages much easier to learn. These languages must be converted to machine language in one of two ways: They are either compiled (the whole program is converted at once, then executed) or interpreted (the program is converted and executed one line at a time). Procedural languages have been deployed for decades with tremendous success. The following is a list of some of the better-known ones:

      1) COBOL (COmmon Business Oriented Language) has been enormously successful. It was designed in 1959 to be easy to read and maintain, and the standard has been extensively revised and updated over the years. Hundreds of millions of lines of COBOL are still in production.

      2) BASIC (Beginner's All-purpose Symbolic Instruction Code) was developed to teach programming but is not used in large business application processing. Visual BASIC provides a graphical user interface to develop Microsoft Windows applications from code written in BASIC.

      3) C and C++ have been very popular languages since their introduction. C++ enables the technique called object-oriented programming.

4)   Java is a high-level, object-oriented programming language developed by Sun Microsystems that, among other things, is used to write programs embedded in World Wide Web documents. It is designed to allow a user to download from a network only the data and the part of an application needed to perform a given task. When processing is complete, the data and software are erased.

a)   Thus, software is stored on the network, and the user need not be concerned about compatibility of the software with the computer platform or with upgrades and installation.

b)   Java is platform independent if each computer has a Java Virtual Machine, a program included in an operating system. It also may be incorporated into a browser. Java programs that run in a web browser are called applets, and Java programs that run on a web server are called servlets.

d.   **Fourth-generation languages** (also called problem-oriented or nonprocedural languages) provide still further simplification of programming. These interactive, English-like languages permit a nonspecialized user to describe the problem to, and receive guidance from, the computer instead of specifying a procedure.

1)   The best-known nonprocedural language is Structured Query Language (SQL), which enables the user to read, update, reorganize, and report on data contained in a relational database (see item 7. in Subunit 13.5).

2)   Generalized audit software (GAS), also known as computer-assisted audit techniques (CAAT), involves the use of computer software packages that may allow not only parallel simulation, but also a variety of other processing functions, such as extracting sample items, verifying totals, developing file statistics, and retrieving specified data fields. Audit Command Language (ACL®) and Interactive Data Extraction and Analysis (IDEA™) are the leading CAAT packages.

3)   Hypertext markup language (HTML) is the authoring software language commonly used to create and link websites. Its key features are hotlinking and graphics display.

4)   Extensible markup language (XML) is an open standard usable with many programs and platforms. Unlike HTML, XML uses codes that are extensible, not fixed, so if an industry can agree on a set of codes, software for that industry can be written by incorporating those codes. For example, XML allows the user to label the UPC (uniform product code), price, color, size, etc., of a product so that other systems will know exactly what the tag references mean.

5)   Extensible business reporting language (XBRL) is the specification developed by an AICPA-led consortium for commercial and industrial entities that report in accordance with U.S. GAAP. It is a variation of XML that is expected to decrease the costs of generating financial reports, reformulating information for different uses, and sharing business information using electronic media.

4.   Stop and review! You have completed the outline for this subunit. Study multiple-choice questions 4 through 12 beginning on page 388.

12.3 NETWORKS

1. Large **mainframe computers** dominated the electronic data processing field in its first decades.

    a. Mainframes were arranged so that all processing and data storage were done in a single, central location.

    b. Communication with the mainframe was accomplished with the use of **dumb terminals**, simple keyboard-and-monitor combinations with no processing power (i.e., no CPU) of their own.

2. The next stage in the evolution of networking was to connect computers not in different rooms of a building, but in separate buildings and eventually separate countries.

    a. This required converting the **digital signal** used internally by the computer into an **analog signal** suitable for transmission over ordinary telephone lines.

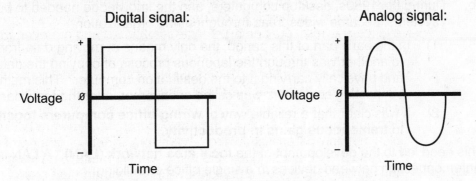

    1) This conversion is necessary because, when a digital signal travels more than about 10 feet, it starts to lose its shape and eventually resembles an analog signal. By that point, it has become completely unusable.

    b. In all-digital networks, such as LANs (see item 4. on the next page) and connections between dumb terminals and mainframes, repeaters are placed every so often to revive the digital signal and return it to its full square-wave shape.

    1) This is obviously not an option with the existing telephone network and its hundreds of thousands of miles of wire.

    2) The solution is simply to convert the computer's digital signal into an analog signal **(modulation)**, send it over the phone line, then reconvert it to a digital signal at the other end **(demodulation)**.

    3) The device that performs these conversion and reconversion functions is a **modem** (short for modulator-demodulator).

    c. The introduction of the modem allowed organizations to begin moving information between locations in purely electronic format, eliminating the need for the passage of physical documents. The potential for cost savings in this technology was obvious.

3. Improvements in technology have led to increasing **decentralization** of information processing.

    a. The mainframe-style computer was the only arrangement available in the early days of data processing. International Business Machines (now called IBM) dominated the marketplace.

    1) Mainframes are still in use at large institutions, such as governments, banks, insurance companies, and universities. However, remote connections to them are usually through desktop computers rather than through dumb terminals.

2) In the 1980s, the **minicomputer** gave organizations the ability to perform data processing without the high cost and large dedicated facilities of a mainframe. Digital Equipment Corporation (DEC) and Hewlett-Packard (HP) dominated this market.

3) As minicomputers evolved, the concept of distributed processing arose.

   a) **Distributed processing** involves the decentralization of processing tasks and data storage and assigning these functions to multiple computers, often in separate locations (see item 6. in Subunit 14.2).

   b) This allowed for a drastic reduction in the amount of communications traffic because data needed locally could reside locally.

4) In 1981, IBM introduced the **Personal Computer (PC)**. This designation quickly lost its status as a brand name and became a generic term for almost any computer smaller than a minicomputer.

b. During the 1980s, desktop computers, and the knowledge needed to build information systems, became widespread throughout the organization.

   1) In the early part of this period, the only means of moving data from one computer to another was through the laborious process of copying the data to a diskette and physically carrying it to the destination computer. This method of connecting computers was called sneakernet, after the footwear involved.

   2) It was clear that a reliable way of **wiring office computers together** would lead to **tremendous gains in productivity**.

4. This need led to the development of the **local area network (LAN)**. A LAN is any interconnection between devices in a single office or building.

   a. Very small networks with few devices can be connected using a **peer-to-peer** arrangement, where every device is connected directly to every other.

      1) Peer-to-peer networks become increasingly difficult to administer with each added device.

   b. The most cost-effective and easy-to-administer arrangement for LANs uses the client/server model.

      1) **Client/server networks** differ from peer-to-peer networks in that the devices play more specialized roles. Client processes (initiated by the individual user) request services from server processes (maintained centrally).

      2) In a client/server arrangement, **servers** are centrally located and devoted to the functions that are needed by all network users.

         a) Examples include mail servers (to handle electronic mail), application servers (to run application programs), file servers (to store databases and make user inquiries more efficient), Internet servers (to manage access to the Internet), and web servers (to host websites).

         b) Whether a device is classified as a server is not determined by its hardware configuration, but rather by the function it performs. A simple desktop computer can be a server.

      3) Technically, a **client** is any object that uses the resources of another object. Thus, a client can be either a device or a software program.

         a) In common usage, however, "client" refers to a device that requests services from a server. This understanding of the term encompasses anything from a powerful graphics workstation to a personal data assistant (PDA), such as a Palm Pilot or a Blackberry.

         b) A client device normally displays the user interface and enables data entry, queries, and the receipt of reports. Moreover, many applications, e.g., word processing and spreadsheet software, run on the client computer.

4) The key to the client/server model is that it runs processes on the platform most appropriate to that process while attempting to minimize traffic over the network. This is commonly referred to as the **three-tiered architecture** of client, application, and database.

5) Security for client-server systems may be more difficult than in a highly centralized system because of the numerous access points.

5. **Classifying networks by geographical extent and function.** The range of networking has expanded from the earliest form (two computers in the same room) to the global reach of the Internet.

   a. A **local area network (LAN)** connects devices within a single office or home or among buildings in an office park. The key aspect here is that a LAN is **owned entirely by a single organization**.

      1) The LAN is the network familiar to office workers all over the world. In its simplest conception, it can consist of a few desktop computers and a printer.

   b. A **metropolitan area network (MAN)** connects devices across an urban area, for instance, two or more office parks.

      1) This conception had limited success as a wire-based network but may make a comeback using microwaves [see item 7.d.3) on page 385].

   c. A **wide area network (WAN)** consists of a conglomerate of LANs over widely separated locations. The key aspect here is that a WAN can be either **publicly or privately owned**.

      1) WANs come in **many configurations**. In its simplest conception, it can consist of a lone desktop computer using a slow dialup line to connect to an Internet service provider.

      2) **Publicly owned** WANs, such as the public telephone system and the Internet, are available to any user with a compatible device. The assets of these networks are paid for by means other than individually imposed user fees.

         a) **Public-switched networks** use public telephone lines to carry data. This arrangement is economical, but the quality of data transmission cannot be guaranteed and security is highly questionable.

      3) **Privately owned** WANs are profit-making enterprises. They offer fast, secure data communication services to organizations that do not wish to make their own large investments in the necessary infrastructure.

         a) **Value-added networks (VANs)** are private networks that provide their customers with reliable high-speed, secure transmission of data.

            i) To compete with the Internet, these third-party networks add value by providing their customers with error detection and correction services, electronic mailbox facilities for EDI purposes, EDI translation, and security for email and data transmissions.

         b) **Virtual private networks (VPNs)** emerged as a relatively inexpensive way to solve the problem of the high cost of leased lines.

            i) A company connects each office or LAN to a local Internet service provider and routes data through the shared, low-cost public Internet.

            ii) The success of VPNs depends on the development of secure encryption products that protect data while in transit.

      c)   A **private branch exchange (PBX)** is a specialized computer used to handle telephone traffic.

          i)   A PBX can carry both voice and data and can switch digital data among computers and office equipment, e.g., printers, copiers, and fax machines. A PBX uses telephone lines, so its data transmission capacity is limited.

6.   **Equipment used in networks.** Networks consist of (a) the hardware devices being connected and (b) the medium through which the connection is made.

    a.   **Client devices.** Devices of all sizes and functions (mainframes, laptop computers, personal digital assistants, MP3 players, printers, scanners, cash registers, ATMs, etc.) can be connected to networks.

        1)   Connecting a device to a network requires a **network interface card (NIC)**. The NIC allows the device to speak that particular network's "language," that is, its protocol (see item 7. on page 382).

        2)   A development in the late 1990s called the **thin client** explicitly mimics the old mainframe-and-terminal model.

          a)   A typical thin client consists merely of a monitor, a keyboard, and a small amount of embedded memory. The key is that it has **no local hard drive**.

          b)   Essentially all **processing and data storage** is done on the **servers**. Just enough of an application is downloaded to the client to run it.

          c)   An advantage of this architecture is the large amount of IT staff time and effort saved that formerly went to configuring and troubleshooting desktop machines. A disadvantage is that there must be 100% server availability for any work to be done by users.

          d)   The thin client architecture has not met with widespread use because the cost of hard drives has continued to steadily decrease, defying predictions.

    b.   **Types of media.** The medium that connects the devices on a network can take many forms.

        1)   **Bandwidth** is the signal-carrying capacity of a transmission medium. It is a rough indication of the highest "speed" that data can attain when traveling through it.

          a)   A medium that can carry only one signal is called **baseband**. A medium that can carry multiple signals is called **broadband**.

        2)   On a **wired LAN**, the choice of cabling depends on speed requirements.

          a)   **Twisted pair** wiring is graded into categories, each of which denotes a different bandwidth. Twisted pair is fundamentally a **baseband** medium.

            i)   Twisted pair takes its name from the continuous weaving of the strands of wire around each other within the cable.

- A magnetic field is produced around any wire through which current is passed. These fields can disrupt the transmission of electrical signals, a phenomenon known as **electromagnetic interference**.
- Twisting the strands of copper around each other within a cable has the effect of canceling the magnetic fields.
- Twisted pair comes in shielded (STP) and unshielded (UTP) varieties. Shielded twisted pair carries extra protection against electromagnetic interference.

   ii) **Category 1** twisted pair is unshielded. It is usually referred to as regular telephone wire.

   iii) **Category 3** comes in both shielded and unshielded varieties and can support a higher bandwidth than Category 1.

   iv) **Category 5** also comes in both shielded and unshielded varieties and can support a higher bandwidth then Category 3.

  b) **Coaxial cable** is a commonly used medium for LANs. Coax, as it is called, is also the familiar transmission medium of cable TV.

   i) Generally, coax is necessary when **broadband** transmission is desired.

   ii) This cable design is named coaxial because one signal conductor surrounds the other, giving them a common "axis."

 3) Wired LANs depend on two basic types of **networking devices** to connect the cabling.

  a) **Hubs** are, in computing terms, very simple ("dumb") and serve only to broadcast messages to every other device on the network.

   i) The device for which the message is intended will keep it and process it. The other devices will discard it.

  b) **Bridges** improve traffic flow by dividing LANs into **segments**. Bridges are more "intelligent" than hubs.

   i) Instead of simply broadcasting messages as hubs do, bridges read the destination address and isolate the message to the segment where the destination device is located, greatly reducing unnecessary traffic on the network.

  c) Separate LANs are connected by either specialized bridges, called **remote bridges**, or by **gateways**.

 4) On a **wireless LAN**, the NIC uses an antenna instead of a cable to connect to the hub or router through the air. The differences in wireless networks are best discussed in the context of communication protocols (see item 7.d. on page 384).

 5) **WANs**, with their greater traffic requirements, need higher-capacity media.

  a) **Fiber-optic cable** consists of extremely fine threads of glass or plastic.

   i) The electrical signal is converted to **pulses of light**, which are sent through the optical medium at much higher speeds than electrical signals can travel through copper wire.

   ii) The light pulses do not travel straight down the fiber. They are deliberately aimed into the fiber at an angle with respect to the cable's insulation (called cladding).

    • This angling causes the light pulses to **continuously bounce** from one side of the fiber to the other as they travel down the length of the cable.

    • This bouncing phenomenon is an aid in separating the various signals when they arrive at the other end.

iii) Fiber optics has **two major advantages** over wire in addition to drastically greater bandwidth.

- The light pulses used in fiber optics are not subject to electromagnetic interference.
- Interception by unauthorized parties is impossible because the light pulses cannot be "tapped" as electrical signals can. Also, the cut end of an optical fiber becomes a mirror, immediately alerting the administrator that there is a problem with the cable.

b) **Microwave transmission** involves propagating electrical signals through air and space instead of through metal wire or optical fiber.

   i) **Satellite relay** involves transmitting the microwave signal to a satellite in orbit, which retransmits the signal to the destination back on Earth. This medium offers very high speeds and wide geographic coverage.

   ii) **LOS (line-of-sight) microwave** transmission is an older technology still in use in some places. It consists of beaming the signals from one tower to another from horizon to horizon.

   - Almost all long-distance voice telephone calls in the United States were transmitted by LOS microwave between the 1960s and the advent of fiber-optic cable in the 1980s.

   iii) Both satellite relay and LOS microwave systems have the advantage of not having to secure rights-of-way for the laying of physical cable over long distances.

7. **Classifying networks by protocol.** A protocol is a set of standards for message transmission among the devices on the network.

   a. **LAN Protocols**

   1) **Ethernet** has been the most successful protocol for LAN transmission. The Ethernet (capitalized because it is a trademark) design breaks up the flow of data between devices into discrete groups of data bits called "frames."

      a) ANALOGY: Ethernet follows the "polite conversation" method of communicating.

         i) Each device "listens" to the network to determine whether another conversation is taking place, that is, whether the network is busy moving another device's message.

         ii) Once the network is determined to be free of traffic, the device sends its message.

      b) Inevitably, frames collide on Ethernet networks constantly. When this happens, the two contending devices wait a random (and extremely brief) length of time, then transmit again. Eventually, both messages will hit the network at a moment when it is free.

      c) This design, while seemingly inefficient in accepting such a high number of collisions and retransmissions, has been extraordinarily successful. Over the years, Ethernet has proven to be secure, adaptable, and expandable.

2)   The **token ring** protocol originally had a much higher speed than Ethernet.

    a)   Each device is directly connected to the next device in a ring configuration. A special frame called the token is passed continuously around the ring from one device to the next.

    b)   When a device wishes to send a message, it attaches the message to the token. The token drops off the message when it arrives at the destination device.

    c)   Token ring, though heavily promoted by IBM, is expensive and difficult to expand, and its early speed advantage has been eclipsed by advances in Ethernet.

b.   **Switched Networks**

1)   As described in item 5.a. on page 379, in a **LAN**, all the devices and all the transmission media belong to **one organization**.

    a)   This single ownership of infrastructure assets plus the ability to unify all communication on a single protocol make for great **efficiency and security**.

2)   When communication must **cross organizational boundaries** or travel **beyond a limited geographical range**, this single ownership principle no longer applies. A WAN is the applicable model.

    a)   A WAN, with its hundreds of users and much greater distances, could never function using the collision-detection-and-retransmission method of Ethernet. To overcome this, the technique called **switching** is used.

3)   Switching takes two basic forms:

    a)   In **circuit switching**, a single physical pathway is established in the public telephone system, and that pathway is reserved for the full and exclusive use of the two parties for the duration of their communication.

        i)   An example is an ordinary landline telephone call or a dialup connection from a modem. This is obviously a slow and insecure alternative for data transmission.

    b)   In **packet switching**, the data bits making up a message are broken up into "packets" of predefined length. Each packet has a header containing the electronic address of the device for which the message is intended.

4)   **Switches** are the networking devices that read the address on each packet and send it along the appropriate path to its destination.

    a)   ANALOGY: The machinery for a new plant is mounted on several 18-wheelers for transport to the plant site. The trucks leave the machinery vendor's factory headed to the destination.

        i)   As each truck arrives at a traffic light, it stops while vehicles going in other directions pass through the intersection.

        ii)   As the trucks arrive at the plant site, they are unloaded and the machinery is installed.

5)   By allowing message flow from many different organizations to pass through common points, switches **spread the cost** of the WAN infrastructure.

    a)   **Frame relay** and **ATM (asynchronous transfer mode)** are examples of fast packet switched network protocols.

c. **Routed Networks**

1) **Routers** have more intelligence than hubs, bridges, or switches.

    a) Routers have **tables** stored in memory that tell them the **most efficient path** along which each packet should be sent.

    b) ANALOGY: The trucks leave the machinery vendor's factory with the same destination.

        i)   As the trucks stop at each intersection, traffic cops redirect them down different routes depending on traffic conditions.

        ii) As the trucks arrive in unknown sequence at the plant site, they are held until the machinery can be unloaded in the correct order.

2) Routing is what makes the **Internet** possible.

    a) **Transmission Control Protocol/Internet Protocol (TCP/IP)** is the suite of routing protocols that makes it possible to interconnect many thousands of devices from dozens of manufacturers all over the world through the Internet.

    b) **IP addressing** (also called dotted decimal addressing) is the heart of Internet routing. It allows any device anywhere in the world to be recognized on the Internet through the use of a standard-format IP address.

        i)   Each of the four decimal-separated elements of the IP address is a numeral between 0 and 255.

             EXAMPLE: 128.67.111.25

    c) **Dynamic host configuration protocol (DHCP)** allows tremendous flexibility on the Internet by enabling the constant reuse of IP addresses.

        i)   Routers generally have their IP addresses hardcoded when they are first installed. However, the individual client devices on most organizational networks are assigned an IP address by DHCP from a pool of available addresses every time they boot up.

d. **Wireless Networks**

1) The **Wi-Fi** family of protocols supports client devices within a radius of about 300 feet around a wireless router. This usable area is called a **hotspot**.

    a) Wi-Fi **avoids the collisions** inherent in Ethernet by constantly searching for the best frequency within its assigned range to use.

    b) Security was a problem in early incarnations of Wi-Fi. Later versions alleviated some of these concerns with encryption.

2) The **Bluetooth** standard operates over a much smaller radius than Wi-Fi, about 30 feet. This distance permits the creation of what has come to be called the **personal area network** or **PAN** (i.e., a network of devices for a single user).

    a) A prominent example is the in-ear device that allows the wearer to make telephone calls hands-free or to listen to a personal music player in wireless mode. Wireless keyboards and mice also employ the Bluetooth standard.

    b) Bluetooth is considerably slower than Wi-Fi.

3)   The **WiMax** standard uses microwaves to turn an entire city into a hotspot, reviving the old MAN model. The radius is about 10 miles and the speed is quite fast.

   a)   Providers of wired networks can bill individual customers for use of the network. However, since anyone with the right device could access a WiMax network, the initial investment in infrastructure would have to be financed through a means other than user fees, making WiMax's widespread deployment unlikely in the near future.

8.   Stop and review! You have completed the outline for this subunit. Study multiple-choice questions 13 through 23 beginning on page 390.

12.4 INTERNET AND INTRANET

1.   The **Internet** is a **network of networks** all over the world.

   a.   The Internet is descended from the original ARPANet, a product of the Defense Department's Advanced Research Projects Agency (ARPA), introduced in 1969. The idea was to have a network that could not be brought down during an enemy attack by bombing a single central location.

   1)   ARPANet connected computers at universities, corporations, and government.
   2)   In view of the growing success of the Internet, ARPANet was retired in 1990.

   b.   The Internet facilitates inexpensive communication and information transfer among computers, with gateways allowing mainframe computers to interface with personal computers.

   1)   Very high-speed Internet backbones carry signals around the world and meet at network access points.

   c.   Most Internet users obtain connections through Internet service providers (ISPs) that in turn connect either directly to a backbone or to a larger ISP with a connection to a backbone.

   1)   The topology of the backbone and its interconnections may once have resembled a spine with ribs connected along its length, but it is now almost certainly more like a fishing net wrapped around the world with many circular paths.

   d.   **TCP/IP (Transmission Control Protocol/Internet Protocol)** is a suite of communications protocols used to connect computers to the Internet. It is also built into network operating systems.

2.   The Internet was initially restricted to email and text-only documents.

   a.   In the 1980s, English computer scientist Tim Berners-Lee conceived the idea of allowing users to click on a word or phrase (a **hyperlink**) on their screens and having another document automatically be displayed.

   b.   Berners-Lee created a simple coding mechanism called **hypertext markup language (HTML)** to perform this function. He also created a set of rules called **hypertext transfer protocol (HTTP)** to allow hyperlinking across the Internet rather than on just a single computer. He then created a piece of software, called a **browser**, that allowed users to read HTML from any brand of computer. The result was the **World Wide Web** (often simply called "the Web").

   1)   As the use of HTML and its successor languages spread, it became possible to display rich graphics and streaming audio and video in addition to text.

2) **Extensible markup language (XML)** was developed by an international consortium and released in 1998 as an open standard usable with many programs and platforms.

   a) XML codes all information in such a way that a user can determine not only how it should be presented but also what it is; i.e., all computerized data may be tagged with identifiers.

   b) Unlike HTML, XML uses codes that are extensible, not fixed. Thus, if an industry can agree on a set of codes, software for that industry can be written that incorporates those codes.

c. With the explosive growth of the World Wide Web in the 1990s, whole new distribution channels opened up for businesses. Consumers can browse a vendor's catalog using the rich graphics of the Web, initiate an order, and remit payment, all from the comfort of their homes.

   1) An organization's presence on the Web is constituted in its website. The website consists of a home page (the first screen encountered by users) and subsidiary web pages (screens constructed using HTML or a similar language).

   2) Every page on the World Wide Web has a unique address, recognizable by any web-enabled device, called a **uniform resource locator (URL)**. However, just because the address is recognizable does not mean it's accessible to every user -- security is a major feature of any organization's website.

3. An **intranet** permits sharing of information throughout an organization by applying Internet connectivity standards and Web software (e.g., browsers) to the organization's internal network.

   a. An intranet addresses the connectivity problems faced by organizations that have many types of computers. It is ordinarily restricted to those within the organization and to outsiders after appropriate identification.

   b. An **extranet** consists of the linked intranets of two or more organizations, for example, of a supplier and its customers. It typically uses the public Internet as its transmission medium but requires a password for access.

4. Stop and review! You have completed the outline for this subunit. Study multiple-choice questions 24 through 28 beginning on page 393.

QUESTIONS

12.1 Hardware

1. The location in the computer where data and programs are temporarily stored during processing is the

A. Floppy disk drive.

B. Magnetic tape drive.

C. Random access memory (RAM).

D. Magnetic disk drive.

Answer (C) is correct. *(CMA, adapted)*
REQUIRED: The location in the CPU where data and programs are temporarily stored during processing.
DISCUSSION: Random access memory (RAM) holds the operating system, part or all of the application being executed, and data used by the application. It is closely connected to the CPU and is sometimes called primary storage.
Answer (A) is incorrect because a floppy disk drive is a random access storage medium for personal computers that permits long-term storage of data. Answer (B) is incorrect because a magnetic tape drive is not for temporary storage. Answer (D) is incorrect because a magnetic disk drive is a secondary storage medium for long-term storage of data.

2. The use of the magnetic disk medium for external storage

A. Allows data to be retained even when the drive is deprived of electricity.

B. Requires files to be organized and processed in sequential order.

C. Allows the system as a whole to process data faster than the CPU alone.

D. Results in slower access times than those of more mature technologies such as magnetic tape drives.

Answer (A) is correct. *(CIA, adapted)*
REQUIRED: The true statement about use of the magnetic disk medium for external storage.
DISCUSSION: The surface of a hard drive is covered with magnetic particles that are arranged by a read/write head into patterns that represent the data being stored. The nature of the magnetic particles is such that they retain their patterns after the drive has been turned off.
Answer (B) is incorrect because an advantage of disk storage is that files do not have to be organized and processed sequentially. Answer (C) is incorrect because the CPU is generally the fastest part of any computer system; hard drives are of necessity slower that CPUs. Answer (D) is incorrect because magnetic drives result in faster access times than those of older technologies such as magnetic tape.

3. In a computer system, the place where basic low-level programs are permanently stored is

A. Read only memory (ROM).

B. Magnetic disk drive.

C. Random access memory (RAM).

D. Magnetic tape drive.

Answer (A) is correct. *(CMA, adapted)*
REQUIRED: The place where parts of the operating system and language translator are stored.
DISCUSSION: ROM consists of semiconductor chips that come from the manufacturer with programs already stored in them. These chips can be read from but not written to and therefore constitute permanent storage. Start-up instructions are permanently stored in ROM in a personal computer to initiate processing and prevent users from accidentally erasing or changing the system.
Answer (B) is incorrect because a magnetic disk drive holds the operating system, application programs, and data. Answer (C) is incorrect because RAM is a temporary storage device. Answer (D) is incorrect because a magnetic tape drive is an older, slower, long-term storage device.

12.2 Software

4. XML

A. Is focused on the content of the data.

B. Has become less important as new languages on the Internet are developed.

C. Uses standardized tags.

D. Is useful to display highly unstructured data.

Answer (A) is correct. *(Publisher, adapted)*
REQUIRED: The true statement about XML.
DISCUSSION: XML (eXtensible Markup Language) is useful for putting structured data into a text file. It can be used to extract and tag information from a database for transmission and subsequent use in other applications, e.g., display on the Internet or importation into a spreadsheet.
Answer (B) is incorrect because XML has become very popular for use on the Internet. Information tagged in XML can be integrated into HTML and other presentations. Answer (C) is incorrect because XML is very flexible and allows the user to design customized (extensible) tags. Answer (D) is incorrect because the data must conform to a structure to be properly tagged.

5. Which of the following is a false statement about XBRL?

A. XBRL is freely licensed.

B. XBRL facilitates the automatic exchange of information.

C. XBRL is used primarily in the U.S.

D. XBRL is designed to work with a variety of software applications.

Answer (C) is correct. *(Publisher, adapted)*
REQUIRED: The false statement about XBRL.
DISCUSSION: XBRL (eXtensible Business Reporting Language) was developed for business and accounting applications. It is an XML-based application used to create, exchange, and analyze financial reporting information that was developed for worldwide use.
Answer (A) is incorrect because the AICPA-led consortium that developed XBRL has promoted the application as a freely licensed product. Answer (B) is incorrect because XBRL facilitates the exchange of information, for example, for reporting to the SEC. Answer (D) is incorrect because XBRL allows exchange of data across many platforms and will soon be integrated into accounting software applications and products.

6. The major justification for selecting a higher-level language over a lower-level language in computerized application programs is that higher-level languages

A. Are more machine and device independent and more easily understood.

B. Use machine resources more efficiently.

C. Have extensive access to many operating-system facilities.

D. Provide greater protection against unauthorized access to data.

Answer (A) is correct. *(CIA, adapted)*
REQUIRED: The major justification for selecting a higher-level language over a lower-level language.
DISCUSSION: Higher-level languages have certain advantages over lower-level (machine and assembler) languages. For example, higher-level languages, such as C++, COBOL, FORTRAN, and BASIC, are easier to write and understand and are therefore more human efficient. They also can be more computer independent than lower-level languages.
Answer (B) is incorrect because higher-level languages use compilers to translate source code to machine-readable object code and thus use additional computer resources. Answer (C) is incorrect because no computer language is compatible with all computer operating systems. Answer (D) is incorrect because access to data is determined by controls within application programs, not programming languages.

7. Writing computer programs in binary code would be tedious. A language allowing symbolic codes to be substituted on a one-to-one basis for binary operating codes and memory addresses is referred to as

A. Machine language.

B. Assembly language.

C. Higher level.

D. Nonprocedural.

Answer (B) is correct. *(CIA, adapted)*
REQUIRED: The language allowing symbolic codes to be substituted, on a one-to-one basis, for binary operating codes and memory addresses.
DISCUSSION: Assembly (symbolic) languages use language-like symbols to replace binary code. One assembly language instruction ordinarily corresponds to one machine language instruction. A program written in a language other than machine language is a source program. A language translator must be used to convert a source program into an object program in machine language. An assembler translates assembly language source programs into a machine language.
Answer (A) is incorrect because machine language is in binary code. Answer (C) is incorrect because each statement in a higher language is translated into multiple machine language statements. BASIC, COBOL, FORTRAN, etc., are higher-level languages. Answer (D) is incorrect because one-to-one substitution is not characteristic of problem-oriented (nonprocedural) languages.

8. BASIC, FORTRAN, and COBOL are all examples of

    A. Application programs.

    B. Machine languages.

    C. Procedural languages.

    D. Operating systems.

Answer (C) is correct. *(CIA, adapted)*

    REQUIRED: The proper classification of BASIC, FORTRAN, and COBOL.

    DISCUSSION: A procedure-oriented or higher-level language allows specification of processing steps in terms of highly aggregated operations. They are ordinarily user-friendly. Translation to an object program is performed by a compiler program. COBOL (COmmon Business Oriented Language) consists of a series of English-like statements. FORTRAN (FORmula TRANslation) is very effective for solving mathematics and engineering problems but is less so for business applications. BASIC (Beginner's All-purpose Symbolic Instruction Code) is a widely used language for personal computers but not for large business application processing.

    Answer (A) is incorrect because BASIC, FORTRAN, and COBOL are languages, not application programs. Answer (B) is incorrect because machine language is a programming language made up of instructions that a computer can directly recognize and execute. Answer (D) is incorrect because an operating system is a set of programs and routines used by the CPU to control the operations of the computer and its peripheral equipment.

9. Object-oriented programming is characterized by an emphasis on objects and the procedures performed upon them. Which of the following programming languages is most closely associated with object-oriented programming?

    A. Pascal.

    B. FORTRAN.

    C. C.

    D. C++.

Answer (D) is correct. *(Publisher, adapted)*

    REQUIRED: The programming language most closely associated with object-oriented programming.

    DISCUSSION: C++ is sometimes referred to as "C with classes." As the name implies, C is its foundation. Classes provide a means of encapsulating the objects used by the program (which ordinarily represent the program's data) into a well-organized, modular format that is easy to reuse and maintain. Through a process called inheritance, new objects can be derived from existing objects by adding new elements to the existing object design. C++ was specifically designed with these features in mind. Because code segments can be reused in other programs, the time and cost of writing software is reduced.

    Answer (A) is incorrect because Pascal traditionally emphasizes procedures rather than objects. Answer (B) is incorrect because FORTRAN traditionally emphasizes procedures rather than objects. Answer (C) is incorrect because C traditionally emphasizes procedures rather than objects.

10. Fourth-generation computer programming languages are represented by

    A. Procedure-oriented languages, which describe processing procedures.

    B. Query languages, which allow direct access to a computer database.

    C. Symbolic languages, which allow direct access to a stored database.

    D. Machine languages, which describe processing procedures.

Answer (B) is correct. *(CIA, adapted)*

    REQUIRED: The fourth-generation computer programming languages.

    DISCUSSION: Fourth-generation languages are intended to simplify programming. They are not intended to express a procedure as a specific algorithm. These interactive, English-like languages permit the user to describe the problem to and receive guidance from the computer. Query languages are most often used with databases. They permit reading and reorganization of data but not its alteration.

    Answer (A) is incorrect because procedure-oriented languages are third-generation languages that require translation into multiple machine level instructions. Answer (C) is incorrect because symbolic languages are second-generation languages. Answer (D) is incorrect because machine (first-generation) languages are far from the fourth-generation software development stage.

11. Structured Query Language (SQL) is best defined as a

   A. Programming language in which UNIX is written.

   B. Report generator used to produce customized business reports.

   C. Programming language in which many business applications are written.

   D. Data manipulation language used in conjunction with a database management system (DBMS).

Answer (D) is correct. *(Publisher, adapted)*
REQUIRED: The definition of SQL.
DISCUSSION: SQL is the most common standard data manipulation language for relational DBMSs. A data manipulation language is used for accessing and processing data from a database to satisfy requests for data and to create applications.
Answer (A) is incorrect because C is the language used in much of the UNIX operating system. Answer (B) is incorrect because a report generator has a greater emphasis on data formats, organization, and display than a query language. Answer (C) is incorrect because COBOL is the programming language in which many business applications are written.

12. A computer program processes payrolls. The program is a(n)

   A. Operating system.

   B. Application program.

   C. Report generator.

   D. Utility program.

Answer (B) is correct. *(CIA, adapted)*
REQUIRED: The term associated with a computer program used to perform a business function.
DISCUSSION: Application programs are written to solve specific user problems; that is, they perform the ultimate computer functions required by system users. Thus, a program designed to process payroll is an application program.
Answer (A) is incorrect because an operating system is a set of programs used by the CPU to control operations. Answer (C) is incorrect because a report generator is a component of a database management system that produces customized reports using data stored in the database. Answer (D) is incorrect because utility programs are standardized subroutines that can be incorporated into other programs.

12.3 Networks

13. Which of the following environmental control risks is more likely in a stand-alone personal computer environment than a mainframe environment?

   A. Copyright violations due to the use of unauthorized copies of purchased software.

   B. Unauthorized access to data.

   C. Lack of data availability due to inadequate data retention policies.

   D. All of the answers are correct.

Answer (D) is correct. *(CIA, adapted)*
REQUIRED: The environmental control risk(s) likely in a stand-alone personal computer environment.
DISCUSSION: Environmental control risks likely in a stand-alone personal computer environment include copyright violations that occur when unauthorized copies of software are made or software is installed on multiple computers. Access to application programs and related data by unauthorized persons is another concern because of lack of physical access controls, application-level controls, and other controls found in mainframe environments. Moreover, a stand-alone personal computer environment may be characterized by inadequate backup, recovery, and contingency planning that may result in an inability to re-create the system or its data.

14. Which of the following areas will usually experience an increase in risk as personal computers proliferate?

   I.   Backup and recovery
   II. Application development costs
   III. Batch updating of records
   IV. Access security
   V. Copyright violations

   A. I, II, and III.

   B. II, III, and IV.

   C. III, IV, and V.

   D. I, IV, and V.

Answer (D) is correct. *(CIA, adapted)*
REQUIRED: The areas that experience increased risk as personal computers proliferate.
DISCUSSION: Personal computer users may be unaware of the need to make frequent file back-ups or lack the expertise or hardware to do so. Personal computer use also usually results in an increase in security concerns. Another increased risk pertains to copyright violations. Making unauthorized copies of software is fairly easy and sometimes may be an informally accepted method of reducing software costs for personal computer systems.
Answer (A) is incorrect because reduced application development costs is one of the benefits of personal computers, and batch update is a characteristic of mainframes, not personal computers. Answer (B) is incorrect because reduced development costs is a benefit of personal computers, batch updating is characteristic of mainframes, and access security and copyright violations are likely to be risks associated with personal computers. Answer (C) is incorrect because batch update is a characteristic of mainframes, not personal computers.

15. Which of the following combinations form a viable configuration for an organization's client-server system?

I. Thin clients, local area network, single server

II. Fat clients, wide area network, multiple servers

III. Fat clients, connection via Internet, and single server

    A. I, II, and III.

    B. II and III only.

    C. II only.

    D. I only.

Answer (A) is correct. *(Publisher, adapted)*
REQUIRED: The viable configuration(s) for a client-server system.
DISCUSSION: The client-server network architecture takes many forms. The "fat" client has its own local long-term storage and considerable processing power, whereas the "thin" client lacks these features, having just enough memory and processing power to download and run the portions of the application(s) that it needs locally. Client-server networks can employ one or more servers, can be integrated into wide area networks, and can use the Internet.
Answer (B) is incorrect because a combination of thin clients, a local area network, and a single server is a viable configuration for a client-server system. Answer (C) is incorrect because a combination of fat clients, a wide area network, and multiple servers is not the only viable configuration for a client-server system. Answer (D) is incorrect because a combination of thin clients, a local area network, and a single server is not the only viable configuration for a client-server system.

16. A real estate brokerage firm is moving into a building that is already equipped with extensive telephone wiring. The firm is considering the installation of a digital private branch exchange (PBX) to connect computers and other office devices such as copying machines, printers, and facsimile machines. A limitation of using a PBX-based system for this network is that

    A. The firm becomes dependent on others for system maintenance.

    B. The system cannot easily handle large volumes of data.

    C. Coaxial cabling would have to be installed throughout the building.

    D. Relocating devices in the office would be difficult and expensive.

Answer (B) is correct. *(CIA, adapted)*
REQUIRED: The limitation of a PBX system.
DISCUSSION: A PBX has the advantage of using existing telephone lines and therefore not needing special wiring. Moreover, equipment can be moved without necessitating rewiring. However, because PBX-based systems use telephone wiring (most often copper wire), they cannot easily handle large volumes of data.
Answer (A) is incorrect because the firm is responsible for all maintenance of the equipment, although it could contract for service. Answer (C) is incorrect because PBXs use telephone wiring. LANs typically require their own coaxial cabling. Answer (D) is incorrect because PBX-based systems do not require rewiring when devices are moved.

17. Large organizations often have their own telecommunications networks for transmitting and receiving voice, data, and images. Very small organizations, however, are unlikely to be able to make the investment required for their own networks and are more likely to use

    A. Public switched lines.

    B. Fast-packet switches.

    C. Standard electronic mail systems.

    D. A WAN.

Answer (A) is correct. *(CIA, adapted)*
REQUIRED: The telecommunications networks likely to be used by small organizations.
DISCUSSION: Companies can use public switched lines (phone lines) on a per-transmission basis. This option is the most cost-effective way for low-volume users to conduct telecommunications.
Answer (B) is incorrect because fast-packet switches receive transmissions from various devices, break the data into packets, and route them over a network to their destination. They are typically installed by telecommunication utility companies and other large companies that have their own networks. Answer (C) is incorrect because electronic mail systems do not allow for voice transmissions. Answer (D) is incorrect because large organizations would use wide area networks.

18. Which of the following networks provides the least secure means of data transmission?

    A. Value-added.

    B. Public-switched.

    C. Local area.

    D. Private.

Answer (B) is correct. *(CIA, adapted)*
    REQUIRED: The network that provides the least secure means of data transmission.
    DISCUSSION: Public-switched networks are wide area networks that use public telephone lines. This arrangement may be the most economical, but data transmission may be of lower quality, no connection may be available, and security measures may be ineffective.
    Answer (A) is incorrect because value-added carriers provide data security and error detection and correction procedures. Answer (C) is incorrect because local area networks inherently limit data transmission exposures. Answer (D) is incorrect because private networks provide security through limited access and dedicated facilities.

19. Kelly Corporation needs an internal communication network that provides high speed communication among nodes. Which of the following is appropriate for Kelly?

    A. Wide area network (WAN).

    B. Local area network (LAN).

    C. File server.

    D. Value-added network (VAN).

Answer (B) is correct. *(Publisher, adapted)*
    REQUIRED: The network that provides the fastest communication.
    DISCUSSION: Local area networks are privately owned networks that provide high-speed communication among nodes. They are usually restricted to limited areas, such as a particular floor of an office building.
    Answer (A) is incorrect because wide area networks provide lower-speed communication, owing to them being spread out among larger areas than LANs. Answer (C) is incorrect because a file server is hardware that acts as an access control mechanism in a local area network. Answer (D) is incorrect because a VAN is a privately owned telecommunications carrier that provides capacity to outside users. It does not provide high-speed communication among nodes.

20. A national retailer required more detailed data to help stock its stores with the right products and to increase its turnover. Such data amounted to several gigabytes per day from each store. A new high-speed company-wide network was needed to transmit and analyze the data. The company wanted the features, functionality, and control of a sophisticated voice and data network without the cost of the components or the staff to maintain it. Which of the following options would be most suitable?

    A. Private wide-area network.

    B. Integrated services digital network.

    C. Value-added network.

    D. Virtual private network.

Answer (D) is correct. *(CIA, adapted)*
    REQUIRED: The network with the features of a sophisticated voice and data network without the cost.
    DISCUSSION: A virtual private network is a carrier-provided service in which the public switched network provides capabilities similar to those of dedicated private lines but at a lower cost. In effect, an unlimited number of virtual networks can be created from the single common physical network. Virtual networks are made possible by intelligent networking technology, which provides the means for routing telephone calls over the best paths without dedicated lines. Thus, the telephone carrier serves as a PBX.
    Answer (A) is incorrect because a private wide-area network is one that an individual business firm maintains for its own use. Answer (B) is incorrect because ISDN is an international standard for transmitting voice, video, and data over phone lines. Answer (C) is incorrect because a value-added network is a data-only, multipath, third-party managed network.

21. Conducting an electronic meeting among several parties at remote sites is

    A. Teleprocessing.

    B. Interactive processing.

    C. Telecommuting.

    D. Teleconferencing.

Answer (D) is correct. *(CMA, adapted)*
    REQUIRED: The process of holding an electronic meeting among several parties at remote sites.
    DISCUSSION: Conducting an electronic meeting among several parties at remote sites is teleconferencing. It can be accomplished by telephone or electronic mail group communication software. Videoconferencing permits the conferees to see each other on video screens. These practices have grown in recent years as companies have attempted to cut their travel costs.
    Answer (A) is incorrect because teleprocessing refers to connections in an online system. Answer (B) is incorrect because interactive processing allows users to converse directly with the system. It requires online processing and direct access to stored information. Answer (C) is incorrect because telecommuting refers to the practice of individuals working out of their homes by communicating with their offices via the computer.

22. A company has a very large, widely dispersed internal auditing department. Management wants to implement a computerized system to facilitate communications among auditors. The specifications require that auditors have the ability to place messages in a central electronic repository where all auditors can access them. The system should facilitate finding information on a particular topic. Which type of system would best meet these specifications?

A. Electronic data interchange (EDI).

B. Electronic bulletin board system (BBS).

C. Fax/modem software.

D. Private branch exchange (PBX).

Answer (B) is correct. *(CIA, adapted)*
REQUIRED: The best system to facilitate communications among auditors.
DISCUSSION: Bulletin board systems function as a centralized information source and message switching system for a particular interest group. Users review and leave messages for other users and communicate with other users on the system at the same time.
Answer (A) is incorrect because EDI is for the electronic transmission of business information and electronic mail, but it does not offer central repositories that store messages for many parties to read. Answer (C) is incorrect because, although fax/modem software can store images of faxes received, it does not meet the criterion of ease of access to information on a particular topic. Answer (D) is incorrect because a PBX is a telecommunications system that routes calls to particular extensions within an organization.

23. Most client-server applications operate on three-tiered architecture consisting of which of the following layers?

A. Desktop client, application, and database.

B. Desktop client, software, and hardware.

C. Desktop server, application, and database.

D. Desktop server, software, and hardware.

Answer (A) is correct. *(CPA, adapted)*
REQUIRED: The layers in a three-tiered client-server architecture.
DISCUSSION: A client-server system divides processing of an application between a client machine on a network and a server. This division depends on which tasks each is best suited to perform. User interaction is ordinarily restricted to the client part of the application. This portion normally consists of the user interface, data entry, queries, and receipt of reports. Moreover, many applications, e.g., word processing and spreadsheet software, reside on the client computer (a desktop, workstation or laptop). The server customarily manages peripheral hardware and controls access to shared databases. Thus, a client-server application must be designed as separate software components that run on different machines but appear to be one application.

12.4 Internet and Intranet

24. The firewall system that limits access to a computer by routing users to replicated websites is

A. A packet filtering system.

B. Kerberos.

C. A proxy server.

D. An authentication system.

Answer (C) is correct. *(Publisher, adapted)*
REQUIRED: The firewall system that routes users to replicated websites.
DISCUSSION: A proxy server maintains copies of websites to be accessed by specified users. Outsiders are directed there, and more important information is not available from this access point.
Answer (A) is incorrect because a packet filtering system examines each incoming IP packet. Answer (B) is incorrect because Kerberos is encryption and authentication software that uses DES encryption techniques. Answer (D) is incorrect because an authentication system verifies a user's identity and is often an application provided by a firewall system, but it is not a firewall system itself.

25. The basic purposes of an organization's internal communications network, or intranet, include all of the following except

A. Obtaining a common focus among employees.

B. Informing potential investors about company operations and financial results.

C. Aiding high-quality decision making.

D. Integrating the efforts of specialists.

Answer (B) is correct. *(CMA, adapted)*
REQUIRED: The item not one of the basic purposes of an organization's internal communications network.
DISCUSSION: An organization's internal communications network is designed to facilitate decision making, promote goal congruence among employees, integrate the efforts of all employees, and build high morale and mutual trust. Informing potential investors about company operations is a purpose of the external, not internal, communications network.
Answer (A) is incorrect because obtaining a common focus among employees is a basic purpose of an organization's internal communications network. Answer (C) is incorrect because aiding high-quality decision making is a basic purpose of an organization's internal communications network. Answer (D) is incorrect because integrating the efforts of specialists is a basic purpose of an organization's internal communications network.

26. The list of modern communication systems extends well beyond the telephone and postal service. These new systems can be distinguished by the features or capabilities they provide. Thus, features such as Answer, Edit, Forward, Send, Read, and Print indicate a system called

    A. Electronic mail.

    B. Voice store-and-forward.

    C. Desktop publishing.

    D. Digital communication.

Answer (A) is correct. *(CIA, adapted)*
    REQUIRED: The communication system that provides the listed features.
    DISCUSSION: Electronic mail is an application of office automation. It is a computer-based message system (software) that permits transfer, receipt, and storage of messages within or between computer systems via telephone lines. The "mail" consists of electronically transmitted messages. A user's "mailbox" is the storage allocated for messages. The advantages of electronic mail are high-speed transmission, reduction of message preparation costs, and the possibility of sending or reading messages at a convenient time. Moreover, electronic mail can be read wherever the recipient may be, provided (s)he has access to a terminal and a telephone link. The typical system includes the listed features as well as Compose, Delete, File, Scan, Move, Retrieve, etc.
    Answer (B) is incorrect because voice store-and-forward lacks Read and Print capability. Answer (C) is incorrect because, of the features listed, desktop publishing provides only Edit and Print capabilities. Answer (D) is incorrect because digital communication is a method of transmission.

27. The most difficult aspect of using Internet resources is

    A. Making a physical connection.

    B. Locating the best information source.

    C. Obtaining the equipment required.

    D. Getting authorization for access.

Answer (B) is correct. *(CIA, adapted)*
    REQUIRED: The most difficult aspect of using Internet resources.
    DISCUSSION: The Internet is a series of networks throughout the world that facilitates information transfer between computers. Given the vast scope of the Internet, the most difficult aspect of its use is locating the best information sources. One solution has been the development of programs, including browsers and search engines, for accessing Internet resources.
    Answer (A) is incorrect because the number of access ports is unlimited. Answer (C) is incorrect because the only requirements for accessing Internet resources are a computer, a modem, a telephone line, a service provider, and basic communications software. Answer (D) is incorrect because organizations routinely provide Internet access to their employees, and individuals can obtain access through individual subscriptions to commercial information service providers.

28. The Internet consists of a series of networks that include

    A. Gateways to allow personal computers to connect to mainframe computers.

    B. Bridges to direct messages through the optimum data path.

    C. Repeaters to physically connect separate local area networks (LANs).

    D. Routers to strengthen data signals between distant computers.

Answer (A) is correct. *(CIA, adapted)*
    REQUIRED: The composition of the Internet.
    DISCUSSION: The Internet facilitates information transfer among computers. Gateways are hardware or software products that allow translation between two different protocol families. For example, a gateway can be used to exchange messages between different email systems.
    Answer (B) is incorrect because routers are used to determine the best path for data. Answer (C) is incorrect because bridges connect LANs. Answer (D) is incorrect because repeaters strengthen signals.

Use Gleim's ***CPA Test Prep*** for interactive testing with over 2,000 additional multiple-choice questions!

STUDY UNIT THIRTEEN
INFORMATION TECHNOLOGY III

(10 pages of outline)

This study unit is the third of five covering information technology (IT).

13.1 OPERATING SYSTEMS

1. Every computer requires an **operating system**. The operating system negotiates the conversation between the computer's hardware, the application the user is running, and the data that the application is working with.

   a. With early computers, one application had to be loaded, run to completion, then unloaded before another one could be run.

   b. The first refinement to this limitation was **multiprogramming**, in which a second program could begin running while the first program was waiting for a command from the operator, or for input from a slower device such as a card reader.

   c. An important feature of the current generation of operating systems is **multitasking**, in which the operating system rapidly switches the computer's attention back and forth between programs, sometimes in a fraction of a second, giving the appearance to users of jobs running simultaneously.

   d. Multitasking should be contrasted with **multiprocessing**, in which the computer has multiple CPUs, permitting a single application to be broken up and have its parts run in parallel on the various processors, greatly speeding up completion times.

2. **z/OS** is the dominant operating system for IBM-compatible mainframes. It is the culmination of decades of mainframe operating system development by IBM.

3. For servers, popular operating systems include the following:

   a. **UNIX** was developed by programmers at Bell Labs in the 1960s and 1970s.

      1) Their motivation was to create an operating system that was portable (i.e., could be used on many brands of computer), multi-user (allow more than one person at a time to use the computer), and multi-tasking (see above). Over the years, UNIX has been greatly expanded and refined, and is considered a very robust operating system for servers.

      2) Many companies offer their own customized versions of UNIX. Two well-known variants are:

         a) Linux, which, unlike most UNIX distributions, is free (although versions of Linux with proprietary add-ons and technical support do involve some cost).

         b) Solaris, a proprietary UNIX-like operating system from Sun Microsystems. It is primarily used on high-end Sun servers and Sun workstations, though a version is available for PCs.

   b. **Windows Server** is the networking version of Microsoft's wildly popular Windows operating system for the desktop.

   c. **Novell Open Enterprise Server** is the successor to that company's once-dominant NetWare network operating system.

4.   For desktop and laptop computers, three operating systems predominate:

   a.   **Microsoft Windows** in its many variants (Windows XP, Windows ME, Windows Vista, etc.) owns the largest market share, particularly among large organizations.

   b.   **Mac OS X** (Roman numeral ten) is designed to run on desktop computers built by Apple. Apple computers are heavily favored by those in the graphics and desktop publishing fields.

   c.   **Linux** and other variants of UNIX are used for desktop computers and powerful workstations devoted to scientific and engineering functions.

5.   Early operating systems of necessity required the user to type in commands from the keyboard stroke by stroke.

   a.   An important feature of any modern desktop operating system such as Windows or OS X is the **graphical user interface (GUI)**. The essence of GUI is "point-and-click," the ability to use a mouse or touchpad to issue commands to the computer by manipulating pictorial icons on the screen.

   b.   Another characteristic of GUI is **windowing**, the ability of a computer to display more than one program on the screen at the same time. Each program has its own section of the screen, called a window.

6.   Stop and review! You have completed the outline for this subunit. Study multiple-choice questions 1 through 4 beginning on page 405.

13.2 SECURITY

1.   **Information security** encompasses not only computer hardware and software but all of an organization's information, no matter what medium it resides on. It involves far more than just user IDs and passwords.

   a.   The importance of a broad definition of information security becomes clear in light of recent incidents of firms accidentally disposing of documents containing confidential customer information with their regular trash.

   b.   Organizations have three principal **goals** for their information security programs: data confidentiality, data availability, and data integrity.

      1)   **Confidentiality** is protecting data from disclosure to unauthorized persons.

      2)   **Availability** is assuring that the organization's information systems are up and running so that employees and customers are able to access the data they need (this topic is addressed in depth in Subunit 14.4).

      3)   **Integrity** is assuring that data accurately reflect the business events underlying them and are not subject to tampering or destruction.

2.   The organization accomplishes these goals by performing the following steps:

   a.   **Identify the threats** to the organization's information, i.e., events that can potentially compromise an organization's information infrastructure.

      1)   Threats to confidentiality include the above-mentioned improper disposal of customer records; threats to availability include viruses and denial-of-service attacks; and threats to integrity include employee errors and disgruntled employee sabotage.

   b.   **Identify the risks** that these threats entail.

      1)   Risk analysis has two phases: determining the likelihood of the identified threats and the level of damage that could potentially be done should the threats materialize.

      2)   For example, an organization may conclude that, while the potential damage from sabotage is very high, its likelihood may be quite low.

    c. **Design the controls** that will compensate for the risks.

      1) Controls are designed based on the combination of likelihood and potential damage determined in the risk analysis.

      2) Controls are of three major types: physical, logical, and policy.

    d. **Incorporate the controls** into a coherent **enterprise-wide information security plan**.

      1) The plan lists the controls that will be put in place and how they will be enforced.

    e. **Policies** set forth expectations of all persons, both employees and external users, with access to the organization's systems.

      1) The single most important policy is that which governs the information resources to which individuals have access and how the level of access will be tied to their job duties.

        a) Carrying out such a policy requires the organization's systems to be able to tie data and program access to individual system IDs.

        b) One provision of the policy must be for the immediate removal of access to the system by the IDs of terminated employees.

3. The classic division of controls in information systems is between general controls and application controls.

    a. **General controls** relate to the organization's information systems environment as a whole. They include:

      1) **IT administration**

        a) A modern organization should recognize information technology as a separate function with its own set of management and technical skills. An organization that allows every functional area to acquire and administer its own systems in isolation is not serious about proper control.

        b) Treating IT as a separate functional area of the organization involves the designation of a chief information officer (CIO) or chief technology officer (CTO) and the establishment of an information systems steering committee to set a coherent direction for the organization's systems and prioritize information technology projects.

      2) **Separation of duties** within the IT function. See Subunit 11.3.

      3) Controls over **systems development**. See Subunit 11.4.

      4) **Hardware controls**

        a) Hardware controls are built into the equipment by the manufacturer. They assure the proper internal handling of data as they are moved and stored.

        b) They include parity checks, echo checks, read-after-write checks, and any other procedure built into the equipment to assure data integrity.

      5) **Physical controls** limit physical access and environmental damage to computer equipment and important documents. They include:

        a) **Access controls.** No persons except operators should be allowed unmonitored access to the computer center. This can be accomplished through the use of a guard desk, a keypad, or a magnetic card reader.

          i) The distribution of printed reports must be controlled so that unauthorized persons are not able to view data that are not connected with their job duties. This encompasses the proper disposal of documents in such a way that the disclosure of confidential customer or company data is prevented (e.g., shredding).

b) **Environmental controls.** The computer center should be equipped with a cooling and heating system to maintain a year-round constant level of temperature and humidity, and a fire-suppression system.

6) **Logical controls** are established to limit access in accordance with the principle that all persons should have access only to those elements of the organization's information systems that are necessary to perform their job duties. Logical controls have a double focus, authentication and authorization.

a) **Authentication** is the act of assuring that the person attempting to access the system is in fact who (s)he says (s)he is. The most widespread means of achieving this is through the use of **IDs and passwords**. The elements of user account management are:

i) Anyone attempting access to one of the organization's systems must supply a unique identifier (e.g., the person's name or other series of characters) and a password that is known only to that person and is not stored anywhere in the system in unencrypted format.

- Not even information security personnel should be able to view unencrypted passwords. Security personnel can change passwords, but the policy should require that the user immediately changes it to something secret.

ii) The organization's systems should force users to change their passwords periodically, e.g., every 90 days.

iii) The policy should prohibit employees from leaving their IDs and passwords written down in plain view.

b) **Authorization** is the practice of assuring that, once in the system, the user can only access those programs and data elements necessary to his/her job duties.

i) In many cases, users should be able to view the contents of some data fields but not be able to change them.

ii) An example is an accounts receivable clerk who can view customers' credit limits but cannot change them. This same clerk can, however, change a customer's outstanding balance by entering or adjusting an invoice.

iii) To extend the example, only the head of the accounts receivable department should be able to execute the program that updates the accounts receivable master balance file. An individual clerk should have no such power.

c) A **firewall** is a combination of hardware and software that separates an internal network from an external network (e.g., the Internet) and prevents passage of specific types of traffic (see Subunit 15.6).

i) Firewall systems ordinarily produce reports on organization-wide Internet use, exception reports for unusual usage patterns, and system penetration-attempt reports. These reports are very helpful as a method of continuous monitoring, or logging, of the system.

ii) A firewall alone is not an adequate defense against computer viruses. Specialized anti-virus software is a must (see Subunit 15.6).

7) Backup and contingency planning. See Subunit 14.4.

b. **Application controls** relate to specific tasks performed by each system. They should provide reasonable assurance that the recording, processing, and reporting of data are properly performed. Application controls relate to individual computerized accounting applications, for example, programmed edit controls for verifying customers' account numbers and credit limits.

1) **Input controls** provide reasonable assurance that data received for processing have been properly authorized, converted into machine-sensible form, and identified.

a) They also provide reasonable assurance that data (including data transmitted over communication lines) have not been lost, suppressed, added, duplicated, or otherwise improperly changed. Moreover, input controls relate to rejection, correction, and resubmission of data that were initially incorrect.

b) An extensive list of input controls can be found in item 2. in Subunit 14.3.

2) **Processing controls** provide reasonable assurance that processing has been performed as intended for the particular application.

a) All transactions should be processed as authorized, no authorized transactions should be omitted, and no unauthorized transactions should be added.

3) **Output controls** provide assurance that the processing result (such as account listings or displays, reports, files, invoices, or disbursement checks) is accurate and that only authorized personnel receive the output.

a) Examples of output controls can be found in item 3. in Subunit 14.3.

4. Stop and review! You have completed the outline for this subunit. Study multiple-choice questions 5 through 21 beginning on page 406.

13.3 TYPES OF DATA FILES

1. Data files can be classified as one of two main types.

a. A **master file** comes in two subtypes:

1) One type contains records that do not change very often. An example is a vendor file, containing each vendor's number, name, and address.

a) EXAMPLE: Vendor master file

vendor_num	vendor_name	address_1	city	state	zip	credit_limit	last_updated
0187634	Neyland's Nuts	101 Dandridge Av	Knoxville	TN	37915	$10,000	07/19/2002
1264428	Basic Barbecue	2224 Blossom St	Columbia	SC	29201	$50,000	06/25/2005
4552170	Bayou Bakery	10118 Florida St	Baton Rouge	LA	70801	$15,000	03/04/2006
5006321	Bulldog Barcoding	9085 Old West Point Rd	Starkville	MS	39759	$5,000	10/01/2006
8981463	Razorback Restaurant Supply	3510 West Maple St	Fayetteville	AR	72701	$20,000	07/01/2004

2) The other type of master file is one that is regularly updated to reflect ongoing activity. An example is a general ledger file, which at any given moment holds the balances of all accounts in the ledger.

a) EXAMPLE: General ledger file

account_num	account_name	balance	last_transaction_posted
A1209	Cash	$89,580.22	01/10/2008
G6573	Accounts Receivable	$72,024.57	01/10/2008
J0226	Accounts Payable	$(15,156.89)	01/10/2008
K4411	Sales	$(100,558.60)	01/10/2008
M2020	Cost of Goods Sold	$70,005.64	01/10/2008
Y3577	Administrative Expenses	$21,110.33	01/10/2008

3) A master file's **volatility** is the relative frequency with which records are added, deleted, or changed during a period.

b. A **transaction file** contains the data that reflect ongoing business activity, such as individual purchases from vendors or general journal entries.

1) EXAMPLE: Daily general journal file

transaction	transaction_date	account_num	debit	credit
GL5261904	01/10/2008	G6573	$1,001.56	$0.00
GL5261905	01/10/2008	J0226	$0.00	$(659.48)
GL5261906	01/10/2008	A1209	$898.15	$0.00
GL5261907	01/10/2008	K4411	$0.00	$(4,500.12)
GL5261908	01/10/2008	M2020	$660.48	$0.00
GL5261909	01/10/2008	Y3577	$150.75	$0.00
GL5261910	01/10/2008	R2112	$0.00	$(770.10)
GL5261911	01/10/2008	H8810	$800.80	$0.00
GL5261912	01/10/2008	Q4851	$1,378.44	$0.00

2. Transaction files and master files are constantly interacting.

a. Before an invoice can be paid, the payables transaction file must be matched against the vendor master file to see whether the vendor really exists.

b. The general ledger balance file must be updated every day by posting from the general journal transaction file.

3. Stop and review! You have completed the outline for this subunit. Study multiple-choice questions 22 through 24 on page 411.

13.4 NATURE OF BINARY DATA STORAGE

1. The digital computers in common use today store all information in **binary** format, that is, as a pattern of ones and zeros. This makes arithmetic operations and true/false decisions on the lowest level extremely straightforward.

a. A **bit** (sometimes thought of as a contraction of "binary digit") is either 0 or 1 (off or on) in binary code. Bits can be strung together to form a binary (i.e., base 2) number.

EXAMPLE of a bit:

0

b.   A **byte** is a group of bits. Each byte is used to signify a character (a number, letter of the alphabet, or symbol, such as a question mark or asterisk).

    1)   The dominant coding systems for mapping the values of binary numbers to characters are the following:

        a)   Extended Binary Coded Decimal Interchange Code (EBCDIC), which was developed by IBM for its mainframe computers and uses 8 bits to a byte.

        b)   American Standard Code for Information Interchange (ASCII), which was developed by the American National Standards Institute, is employed by most personal computers and servers, and uses 7 bits to a byte (often padded to 8).

EXAMPLE of a 7-bit ASCII byte representing the letter P:

1010000

        c)   Unicode, sponsored by the International Organization for Standards, which can use multiple bytes to represent each character, thereby enabling the deployment of special characters and all the world's alphabets.

    2)   Quantities of bytes are measured with the following units:

$$1,024 \; (2^{10}) \text{ bytes} = \textbf{1 kilobyte} = 1 \text{ KB}$$
$$1,048,576 \; (2^{20}) \text{ bytes} = \textbf{1 megabyte} = 1 \text{ MB}$$
$$1,073,741,824 \; (2^{30}) \text{ bytes} = \textbf{1 gigabyte} = 1 \text{ GB}$$
$$1,099,511,627,776 \; (2^{40}) \text{ bytes} = \textbf{1 terabyte} = 1 \text{ TB}$$

c.   A **field** is a group of bytes. The field contains a unit of data about some entity, e.g., a composer's name.

EXAMPLE of a field:

Paul Hindemith

d.   A **record** is a group of fields. All the fields contain information pertaining to an entity, e.g., an orchestral work.

EXAMPLE of a record:

Paul Hindemith	Violin Concerto	Chicago Symphony	Claudio Abbado	Josef Suk

    1)   Some field or combination of fields on each record is designated as the key. The essence of a key is that it contains enough information to uniquely identify each record, i.e., there can be no two records with the same key.

        a)   The designation of a key allows records to be sorted and managed with much greater efficiency. If all the records are sorted in the order of the key, searching for a particular one becomes much easier.

        b)   In the above example, the key is the combination of the first two fields.

            i)   The first field alone is not enough because there could be several works by each composer. The second field alone is likewise not enough since there could be many pieces with the same title.

            ii)   The combination of composer's name and title uniquely identify each piece of music.

e.   A **file** is a group of records. All the records in the file contain the same pieces of information about different occurrences, e.g., performances of several orchestral works.

EXAMPLE of a file:

Paul Hindemith	Violin Concerto	Chicago Symphony	Claudio Abbado	Josef Suk
Gustav Mahler	Das Lied von der Erde	New York Philharmonic	Leonard Bernstein	Dietrich Fischer-Dieskau
Bela Bartok	Piano Concerto No. 2	Chicago Symphony	Sir Georg Solti	Etsko Tazaki
Arnold Schoenberg	Gurrelieder	Boston Symphony	Seiji Ozawa	James McCracken
Leos Janacek	Sinfonietta	Los Angeles Philharmonic	Simon Rattle	None
Dmitri Shostakovich	Symphony No. 6	San Francisco Symphony	Kazuhiro Koizumi	None
Carl Orff	Carmina Burana	Berlin Radio Symphony	Eugen Jochum	Gundula Janowitz

2.   Stop and review! You have completed the outline for this subunit. Study multiple-choice question 25 on page 412.

13.5 FILE ORGANIZATION AND ACCESS METHODS

1.   To understand the vast improvement in performance brought about by database technology, it is helpful to review the development of file structures.

2.   The oldest file structure is the **flat file**, meaning that every record in the file has an identical layout; thus, the records can be conceived of as forming a two-dimensional pattern of rows and columns, like the table above. A telephone directory is a commonly encountered flat file.

a.   The **linked list** was the earliest means of associating the records of a flat file with each other. Each record had a pointer tacked on the end that "pointed" to the next record.

3.   **Variable-length records** represented a space-saving improvement. In the example below, a customer orders two different items on one occasion and only one item on another occasion. With variable-length records, valuable space is not taken up for the blank second item on the second order.

EXAMPLE of two variable-length records:

Record	Customer	Street	City	Order_Nbr	Part_Nbr_1	Qty_1	Price_1	Ext_1	Part_Nbr_2	Qty_2	Price_2	Ext_2
116385	Zeno's Paradox Hardware	10515 Prince Avenue	Athens, GA	19742133	A316	3	$0.35	$1.05	G457	12	$1.15	$13.80

——— (Many intervening records) ———

Record	Customer	Street	City	Order_Nbr	Part_Nbr_1	Qty_1	Price_1	Ext_1
122406	Zeno's Paradox Hardware	10515 Prince Avenue	Athens, GA	19742259	A316	4	$0.35	$1.40

a.   Some space is saved by not having empty fields representing Part Number 2 on the second order, but data redundancy has not been entirely eliminated: the customer's address is stored with both orders.

4.   While variable-length records were an improvement in terms of space, reading such files still involved the inefficient process known as **sequential access**. To find a particular record, every intervening record had to be examined and bypassed.

a.   The analogy is a cassette tape; all the intervening songs must be identified and skipped in order to find the desired song. This analogy is apt because much early data storage was on large reels of magnetic tape.

      b.   This inefficiency was overcome with the development of the **indexed** sequential access method (ISAM) by IBM.

          1)   Under this method, each file contains an extra table holding the storage location of every record (every record is said to be "indexed"). When a certain record is desired, the system consults the index table to find where the record is stored. The record can then be retrieved directly without having to examine a lot of unwanted records.

          2)   ISAM is a very powerful technique, and made the development of the relational database possible (see item 7. on the next page).

      c.   Another major improvement in efficiency came with the advent of disk drives, which can quickly seek out a given storage address. This technique is known as **direct** or **random access**.

          1)   The analogy is a phonograph record: with a cassette tape, all unwanted songs must be physically bypassed, while with a phonograph, the user can place the needle anywhere (s)he wants.

          2)   Random access is a necessity for real-time systems.

5.   The **hierarchical, or tree, database model** was the next development in file organization. Instead of the records being strung out one after the other, they form "branches" and "leaves" extending from a "root." Note that the customer's address is now stored only once.

      a.   Another feature of the tree file structure is that every "parent" record can have multiple "child" records, but each child can have only one parent.

      EXAMPLE of a tree data structure:

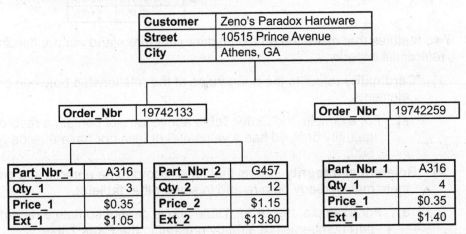

      b.   One customer has many orders, but each order can only be assigned to one customer.

          1)   The tree structure improves speed and storage efficiency for related data; for example, a parent record consisting of a customer may directly index the child records containing the customer's orders.

          2)   However, adding new records is much more difficult than with a flat file. In a flat file, a new record is simply inserted whole in the proper place. In a tree structure, the relationships between the parent and child records must be maintained.

6.   The **network database model** allowed child records to have multiple parents.

      a.   This was an attempt to make queries more efficient, but the huge number of cross-references inherent in this structure made maintenance far too complex.

7. In the **relational database model**, the elements of data "relate" to one another in a highly flexible way.

    a. What were called tables in earlier data structures are technically referred to as "relations." Likewise, a table's columns are called "attributes" and the rows are called "tuples."

    b. Each data element is stored as few times as necessary. This reduction in data redundancy is accomplished through a process called normalization.

        EXAMPLE of a relational data structure:

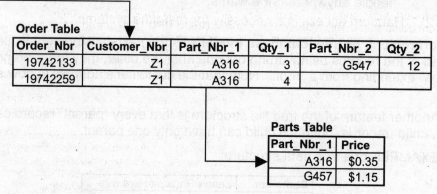

Customer Table

Customer_Nbr	Customer	Street	City
X1	Xylophones To Go	3846 N Lamar Blvd	Oxford, MS
Y1	Yellow Dog Software	1012 E Tennessee St	Tallahassee, FL
Z1	Zeno's Paradox Hardware	10515 Prince Avenue	Athens, GA

Order Table

Order_Nbr	Customer_Nbr	Part_Nbr_1	Qty_1	Part_Nbr_2	Qty_2
19742133	Z1	A316	3	G547	12
19742259	Z1	A316	4		

Parts Table

Part_Nbr_1	Price
A316	$0.35
G457	$1.15

    c. Two features that make the relational data structure stand out are cardinality and referential integrity.

        1) **Cardinality** refers to the boundaries of the relationship between certain data elements.

            a) For example, the Order Table above cannot contain a record where the quantity ordered has a value of 0 or less nor have a value greater than 500.

        2) **Referential integrity** means that for a record to be entered in a given table, there must already be a record in some other table(s).

            a) For example, the Order Table above cannot contain a record where the part number is not already present in the Parts Table.

    d. The tremendous advantage of a relational data structure is that searching for records is greatly facilitated.

        1) For example, a user can specify a customer and see all the parts that customer has ordered, or the user can specify a part and see all the customers who have ordered it. Such queries were extremely resource-intensive, if not impossible, under older data structures.

    e. A group of tables built following the principles of relational data structures is referred to as a **relational database**.

        1) If the rules of cardinality, referential integrity, etc., are not enforced, a database will no longer be relational. To aid in the exceedingly challenging task of enforcing these rules, database management systems have been developed.

8. Stop and review! You have completed the outline for this subunit. Study multiple-choice questions 26 through 34 beginning on page 412.

QUESTIONS

13.1 Operating Systems

1. A function of the operating system is to

- A. Inform the user of processor, input/output (I/O) device, or program errors.
- B. Supply prewritten programs for specific applications.
- C. Perform check-digit verification of account numbers.
- D. Access interactive information services for transactions.

Answer (A) is correct. *(CIA, adapted)*
REQUIRED: The function of the operating system.
DISCUSSION: The operating system is a form of system software that mediates between the applications programs and the computer hardware. It communicates with the operator or user in the event of processor, input/output device, or program errors.
Answer (B) is incorrect because the operating system contains a repertoire of simple commands for otherwise complicated functions but no programs for specific applications. Answer (C) is incorrect because application programs are responsible for performing check digit verification of account numbers. Answer (D) is incorrect because telecommunications software, not operating systems, access interactive information services for transactions.

2. A veterinary hospital uses a computer application program to provide client billing statements after each animal visit. Which of the following functions requires the assistance of the operating system?

- A. Retrieve each animal's file.
- B. Extract the animal owner's name from the record.
- C. Sum fees due for visit.
- D. Update remaining balance.

Answer (A) is correct. *(CIA, adapted)*
REQUIRED: The function requiring the assistance of the operating system.
DISCUSSION: Systems software in machine or assembly language is necessary to facilitate the processing of applications programs by the computer. Systems software, which is ordinarily purchased from vendors, performs such fundamental tasks as language translation, monitoring of data communications, job instruction, control of input and output, file management, sorting data, and access control.
Answer (B) is incorrect because the name is in the file. No additional input/output is required. Answer (C) is incorrect because the application program sums fees due for visits. Answer (D) is incorrect because the application program performs remaining balance updates.

3. The software that can provide multiprogramming capability is

- A. Application software.
- B. Utility software.
- C. Operating system software.
- D. Database management system software.

Answer (C) is correct. *(CIA, adapted)*
REQUIRED: The software that can provide multiprogramming capability.
DISCUSSION: In multiprogramming, the operating system processes a program until an input-output operation is required. Because input or output can be handled by peripheral hardware, the CPU can begin executing another program's instructions while output is in progress. This task is accomplished by the computer's switching among programs during processing. Operating software also can provide multiprocessing and virtual storage capabilities.
Answer (A) is incorrect because application software is designed for a specific application, but multiprogramming is a capability used for processing in general. Answer (B) is incorrect because utility software performs routine tasks, such as sorting or merging of files. Answer (D) is incorrect because database management system software allows access to stored data by providing an interface between users or programs and the stored data.

4. A characteristic of a personal computer system that displays more than one program on the screen at the same time, places each program in its own area of the screen, but permits only one program to be active, is

- A. Windowing.
- B. Distributed processing.
- C. Context switching.
- D. File extension.

Answer (A) is correct.   *(CMA, adapted)*

REQUIRED: The characteristic of a personal computer system that allows display of more than one program.

DISCUSSION: A graphical user interface is part of an operating system with which users may interact. It uses graphic icons to represent activities, programs, and files. The computer mouse is used to make selections. Windows is a graphical user interface shell initially developed by Microsoft to run in conjunction with DOS. Newer operating systems also have this feature. Thus, windowing is the characteristic that allows a computer to display more than one program on the screen at the same time. Each program has its own section of the screen, but only one program is active.

Answer (B) is incorrect because distributed processing is a means of assigning computer processing to various segments of a business, with some aspects centralized and some decentralized. Answer (C) is incorrect because context switching does not relate to the various segments on a computer screen. Answer (D) is incorrect because a file extension is a means of extending a logical collection of records.

13.2 Security

5. Which of the following is an example of how specific internal controls in a database environment may differ from controls in a nondatabase environment?

- A. Controls should exist to ensure that users have access to and can update only the data elements that they have been authorized to access.
- B. Controls over data sharing by diverse users within an entity should be the same for every user.
- C. The employee who manages the computer hardware should also develop and debug the computer programs.
- D. Controls can provide assurance that all processed transactions are authorized, but cannot verify that all authorized transactions are processed.

Answer (A) is correct.   *(CPA, adapted)*

REQUIRED: The difference between internal controls in a database environment and a nondatabase environment.

DISCUSSION: A database is a series of related files combined to eliminate unnecessary redundancy of data elements. The data dictionary states not only the meaning of a data element but also its ownership (who is responsible for its maintenance), size, format, and usage. Moreover, it states what persons, programs, reports, and functions use the data element. Thus, the issue of ownership (maintenance or updating) of, and control over access to, data elements common to many applications arises only in a database environment.

Answer (B) is incorrect because certain data should not be accessed by all individuals, and those who do have access may have different levels of authority. Thus, the controls should vary among users regardless of whether the environment includes a database. Answer (C) is incorrect because these duties should be segregated. Answer (D) is incorrect because controls can play multiple roles in a database or nondatabase environment by comparing authorized transactions with processed transactions and reporting anomalies.

6. An organization relied heavily on e-commerce for its transactions. Evidence of the organization's security awareness manual would be an example of which of the following types of controls?

- A. Preventive.
- B. Detective.
- C. Corrective.
- D. Compliance.

Answer (A) is correct.   *(CPA, adapted)*

REQUIRED: The control evidenced by a security awareness manual.

DISCUSSION: Preventive controls are measures taken in advance so that anticipated problems associated with performance of an activity will not occur. Creating a security awareness manual involves anticipating problems.

Answer (B) is incorrect because detective controls are not applied in advance. They provide post-performance feedback about whether deviations from standards have occurred. Answer (C) is incorrect because corrective controls are not applied in advance. They solve problems identified by detective controls. Answer (D) is incorrect because compliance relates to abiding by laws, regulations, contracts, etc.

7. Which of the following statements best characterizes the function of a physical access control?

A. Protects systems from the transmission of Trojan horses.

B. Provides authentication of users attempting to log into the system.

C. Separates unauthorized individuals from computer resources.

D. Minimizes the risk of incurring a power or hardware failure.

Answer (C) is correct. *(CPA, adapted)*

REQUIRED: The function of a physical access control.

DISCUSSION: Physical security controls limit physical access and protect against environmental risks and natural catastrophes, such as fire and flood. For example, keypad devices allow entry of a password or code to gain entry to a physical location or computer system. Card reader controls are based on reading information from a magnetic strip on a credit, debit, or other access card. Controls can then be applied to information about the cardholder contained on the magnetic strip.

Answer (A) is incorrect because an organization-wide network security policy that includes protections against viruses and other malicious software protects systems from the transmission of Trojan horses. Physical access control does not. Answer (B) is incorrect because logical security control (e.g., passwords and ID numbers) provides authentication of users attempting to log into the system. Answer (D) is incorrect because a disaster recovery and business continuity plan minimizes the risk of incurring a power or hardware failure. For example, it may provide for fully protected or fault-tolerant systems.

8. An auditor was examining a client's network and discovered that the users did not have any password protection. Which of the following would be the best example of the type of network password the users should have?

A. trjunpqs.

B. 34787761.

C. tr34ju78.

D. tR34ju78.

Answer (D) is correct. *(CPA, adapted)*

REQUIRED: The best network password.

DISCUSSION: tR34ju78 should be effective because it has at least eight characters consisting of random uppercase and lowercase letters and numbers. Furthermore, it does not contain words or phrases.

Answer (A) is incorrect because trjunpqs does not contain random uppercase and lowercase letters or numbers. Answer (B) is incorrect because 34787761 does not contain any letters. Answer (C) is incorrect because tr34ju78 does not contain random uppercase and lowercase letters.

9. An Internet firewall is designed to provide adequate protection against which of the following?

A. A computer virus.

B. Unauthenticated logins from outside users.

C. Insider leaking of confidential information.

D. A Trojan horse application.

Answer (B) is correct. *(Publisher, adapted)*

REQUIRED: The protection provided by an Internet firewall.

DISCUSSION: A firewall is a device that separates two networks and prevents passage of specific types of network traffic while maintaining a connection between the networks. Generally, an Internet firewall is designed to protect a system from unauthenticated logins from outside users, although it may provide several other features as well.

Answer (A) is incorrect because a firewall cannot adequately protect a system against computer viruses. Answer (C) is incorrect because industrial spies need not leak information through the firewall. A telephone or floppy disk are much more common means of sharing confidential information. Answer (D) is incorrect because, like a virus, a firewall cannot adequately protect against a Trojan horse or any other program that can be executed in the system by an internal user.

10. Which of the following is a password security problem?

A. Users are assigned passwords when accounts are created, but do not change them.

B. Users have accounts on several systems with different passwords.

C. Users copy their passwords on note paper, which is kept in their wallets.

D. Users select passwords that are not listed in any online dictionary.

Answer (A) is correct. *(CPA, adapted)*

REQUIRED: The password technique that poses a security problem.

DISCUSSION: Proper user authentication by means of a password requires password-generating procedures to assure that valid passwords are known only by the proper individuals. If passwords are assigned, users should change passwords frequently so that they are the only persons with access under those identifiers.

Answer (B) is incorrect because no security issue arises when different passwords are used for accounts on different systems. Answer (C) is incorrect because storing a password online would be a greater problem. Answer (D) is incorrect because storing a password online would be a greater problem.

11. A client who recently installed a new accounts payable system assigned employees a user identification code (UIC) and a separate password. Each UIC is a person's name, and the individual's password is the same as the UIC. Users are not required to change their passwords at initial log-in nor do passwords ever expire. Which of the following statements does not reflect a limitation of the client's computer-access control?

A. Employees can easily guess fellow employees' passwords.

B. Employees are not required to change passwords.

C. Employees can circumvent procedures to segregate duties.

D. Employees are not required to take regular vacations.

Answer (D) is correct.   *(CPA, adapted)*
REQUIRED: The item not a limitation of the client's computer-access control.
DISCUSSION: To be effective, passwords should consist of random letters, symbols, and numbers. They should not contain words or phrases which are easily guessed. Proper user authentication by means of passwords requires procedures to assure that the valid passwords generated are known only by appropriate individuals. Moreover, passwords should be changed frequently so that the maximum retention period (the period during which they may be compromised) is relatively short. However, a minimum retention period should be required so that users cannot change passwords back to their old, convenient forms. Another weakness in access control is that different passwords are not required to perform different functions, e.g., to obtain access, to read certain files, or to update certain files. Use of separate passwords is a means of segregating duties. However, the password security system is unrelated to the absence of a requirement to take vacations. Nevertheless, such requirement may be appropriate for personnel in a position to embezzle funds.
Answer (A) is incorrect because a control deficiency exists if employees can easily guess fellow employee's passwords. Answer (B) is incorrect because a control deficiency exists if employees are not required to change passwords. Answer (C) is incorrect because a control deficiency exists if employees can circumvent procedures to segregate duties.

12. A client installed the sophisticated controls using the biometric attributes of employees to authenticate user access to the computer system. This technology most likely replaced which of the following controls?

A. Use of security specialists.

B. Reasonableness tests.

C. Passwords.

D. Virus protection software.

Answer (C) is correct.   *(Publisher, adapted)*
REQUIRED: The control most likely replaced by biometric technologies.
DISCUSSION: The use of passwords is an effective control in an online system to prevent unauthorized access to computer systems. However, biometric technologies are more sophisticated and difficult to compromise.
Answer (A) is incorrect because biometric technologies do not eliminate the need for specialists who evaluate and monitor security needs. Answer (B) is incorrect because reasonableness tests are related to input controls, not access controls. Answer (D) is incorrect because virus protection software prevents damage to data in a system, not access to a system.

13. Which of the following risks can be minimized by requiring all employees accessing the information system to use passwords?

A. Collusion.

B. Data entry errors.

C. Failure of server duplicating function.

D. Firewall vulnerability.

Answer (D) is correct.   *(CPA, adapted)*
REQUIRED: The risk minimized by password use.
DISCUSSION: A firewall separates an internal network from an external network (e.g., the Internet) and prevents passage of specific types of traffic. It identifies names, Internet Protocol (IP) addresses, applications, etc., and compares them with programmed access rules. Authentication measures verify the identity of the user, thus ensuring that only the intended and authorized users gain access to the system. Most firewall systems provide authentication procedures. Access controls are the most common authentication procedures. Password use is a common access control.
Answer (A) is incorrect because collusion (e.g., improper sharing of passwords) defeats the purpose of this control. Answer (B) is incorrect because password use has no relationship to accuracy of data entry. Answer (C) is incorrect because password use has no relationship to server failure.

14. Authentication is the process by which the

    A. System verifies that the user is entitled to enter the transaction requested.

    B. System verifies the identity of the user.

    C. User identifies him/herself to the system.

    D. User indicates to the system that the transaction was processed correctly.

Answer (B) is correct. *(CISA, adapted)*

REQUIRED: The definition of authentication.

DISCUSSION: Identification is the process of uniquely distinguishing one user from all others. Authentication is the process of determining that individuals are who they say they are. For example, a password may identify but not authenticate its user if it is known by more than one individual.

Answer (A) is incorrect because authentication involves verifying the identity of the user. This process does not necessarily confirm the functions the user is authorized to perform. Answer (C) is incorrect because user identification to the system does not imply that the system has verified the identity of the user. Answer (D) is incorrect because this procedure is an application control for accuracy of the transaction.

15. Which of the following activities would most likely detect computer-related fraud?

    A. Using data encryption.

    B. Performing validity checks.

    C. Conducting fraud-awareness training.

    D. Reviewing the systems-access log.

Answer (D) is correct. *(CPA, adapted)*

REQUIRED: The activity most likely to detect computer fraud.

DISCUSSION: A system access log records all attempts to access the system. The date and time, codes used, mode of access, data involved, and interventions by operators are recorded. Thus, reviewing the systems-access log may detect improper access related to fraud.

Answer (A) is incorrect because encryption is a preventive control that codes information before transmission so that it cannot be read by someone who does not have the key. Answer (B) is incorrect because performing validity checks is a preventive control. These checks test whether transaction codes or identification numbers are authorized. Answer (C) is incorrect because conducting fraud-awareness training is a preventive control.

16. Which of the following security controls may prevent unauthorized access to sensitive data via an unattended workstation directly connected to a mainframe?

    A. Use of a screen saver.

    B. Use of passwords to identify users.

    C. Encryption of data files.

    D. Automatic log-off of inactive users.

Answer (D) is correct. *(CIA, adapted)*

REQUIRED: The control to prevent unauthorized access to data on an unattended terminal.

DISCUSSION: Automatic log-off of inactive users is a utility that disconnects a workstation from the mainframe or server after a certain amount of time. Once the workstation has been disconnected, the user must log back into the system.

Answer (A) is incorrect because a screen saver is software used to prevent the burning of an image onto the monitor's screen. Answer (B) is incorrect because the unattended workstation has likely already had the required password provided to gain access. Answer (C) is incorrect because data are only encrypted when stored in a file. While the data or file is being modified by a user, the data are not encrypted. Thus, an unattended workstation leaves data susceptible to unauthorized access.

17. An audit of the electronic data interchange (EDI) area of a banking group revealed the facts listed below. Which one indicates the need for improved internal control?

    A. Employees may only access the computer system via an ID and an encrypted password.

    B. The system employs message sequencing as a way to monitor data transmissions.

    C. Certain types of transactions may be made only at specific terminals.

    D. Branch office employees may access the mainframe with a single call via modem.

Answer (D) is correct. *(CIA, adapted)*

REQUIRED: The condition that indicates the need for improved internal control.

DISCUSSION: The system should employ automatic dial-back to prevent intrusion by unauthorized parties. This procedure accepts an incoming modem call, disconnects, and automatically dials back a prearranged number to establish a permanent connection for data transfer or inquiry.

Answer (A) is incorrect because employee access to the computer system via an ID and an encrypted password is considered acceptable. Encrypted passwords further decrease the likelihood of unauthorized access. Answer (B) is incorrect because message sequencing detects unauthorized access by numbering each message and incrementing each message by one more than the last one sent. This procedure will detect a gap or duplicate. Answer (C) is incorrect because allowing certain types of transactions (such as payroll transactions) to be made only at specific terminals minimizes the likelihood of unauthorized access.

18. Which of the following is the most effective user account management control in preventing the unauthorized use of a computer system?

    A. Management enforces a password policy that requires passwords to be 10 characters long, to be nonreusable, and to be changed weekly.

    B. An account manager is responsible for authorizing and issuing new accounts.

    C. The passwords and usernames of failed log-in attempts are logged and documented in order to cite attempted infiltration of the system.

    D. Employees are required to renew their accounts semiannually.

Answer (D) is correct. *(Publisher, adapted)*
    REQUIRED: The most effective user account management control.
    DISCUSSION: Management's network security policy should include measures to ensure that old and unused accounts are removed promptly. If employees' accounts expire semi-annually, reasonable assurance is provided that accounts in use by unauthorized employees do not exist.
    Answer (A) is incorrect because, although passwords should be changed periodically, changing a long, nonreusable password weekly encourages employees to write each new password down to remember it, a practice not considered conducive to effective control. Answer (B) is incorrect because the duties of authorization and control over assets should be separated. Answer (C) is incorrect because, although failed log-in attempts should be logged, it is considered bad practice to record the password of failed log-in attempts. Employees often mistype their passwords, and access to the log by an infiltrator could facilitate breaking into a user's account.

19. Dora Jones, an auditor for Farmington Co., noted that the Acme employees were using computers connected to Acme's network by wireless technology. On her next visit to Acme, Jones brought one of Farmington's laptop computers with a wireless network card. When she started the laptop to begin work, Jones noticed that the laptop could view several computers on Acme's network and that she had access to Acme's network files. Which of the following statements is the most likely explanation?

    A. Acme's router was improperly configured.

    B. Farmington's computer had the same administrator password as the server.

    C. Jones had been given root account access on Acme's computer.

    D. Acme was not using security on the network.

Answer (D) is correct. *(CPA, adapted)*
    REQUIRED: The fault in a network system with wireless access.
    DISCUSSION: A secure network prevents a user from having unauthorized access. Given wireless technology, anyone with wireless capacity can access the network in the absence of security. Thus, Acme's network was not protected by passwords or other security features to prevent unauthorized access.
    Answer (A) is incorrect because the router controls the forwarding of data packets along networks. It does not affect whether a user can access computers and files. Answer (B) is incorrect because the probability of having the same administrator password as the server is very remote. Answer (C) is incorrect because root access on Acme's computer would not permit Jones to access Acme's files and computers. Root account access allows a user complete access only to a particular computer, not to the network.

20. Which of the following is most likely to increase the risk of unauthorized user access?

    A. Growth in end-user development.

    B. Competitive pressures for enhanced functions in systems.

    C. Greater online access to information systems.

    D. Growing organizational reliance on information systems.

Answer (C) is correct. *(CIA, adapted)*
    REQUIRED: The factor that is most likely to increase the risk of unauthorized user access.
    DISCUSSION: An online processing system is in direct communication with the computer, giving it the capability to handle transactions as they are entered. An online system permits both immediate posting (updating) and inquiry of master files as transactions occur. Greater online access to information systems creates the risk of increased unauthorized access to systems, which can be mitigated by authenticating transactions for authorized users.
    Answer (A) is incorrect because end-user development is accomplished by authorized users. Answer (B) is incorrect because enhanced functions do not necessarily increase the number of persons who have access or weaken the controls over access. Answer (D) is incorrect because growing organizational reliance on information systems does not necessarily promote unauthorized access.

21. Management's enthusiasm for computer security tends to vary with changes in the environment, particularly the occurrence of other computer disasters. Which of the following concepts should be addressed when making a comprehensive recommendation regarding the costs and benefits of computer security?

I.   Potential loss if security is not implemented

II. Probability of occurrences

III. Cost and effectiveness of the implementation and operation of computer security

    A. I only.

    B. I and II only.

    C. III only.

    D. I, II, and III.

Answer (D) is correct. *(CIA, adapted)*
    REQUIRED: The concept(s) that should be addressed in an analysis of cost-benefit considerations.
    DISCUSSION: Potential loss is the amount of dollar damages associated with a security problem or loss of assets. Potential loss times the probability of occurrence is an estimate (expected value) of the exposure associated with lack of security. It represents a potential benefit associated with the implementation of security measures. To perform a cost-benefit analysis, the costs should be considered. Thus, all three items need to be addressed.

13.3 Types of Data Files

22. A file containing relatively long-term information used as a source of reference and periodically updated with detail is termed a

    A. Transaction file.

    B. Record layout.

    C. Master file.

    D. Dump.

Answer (C) is correct. *(Publisher, adapted)*
    REQUIRED: The file containing relatively long-term information.
    DISCUSSION: A master file containing relatively long-term information, such as an inventory file listing the part number, description, quantities on hand, quantities on order, etc., is used in a file processing run. Transactions are processed against the master file, thus periodically updating it.
    Answer (A) is incorrect because a transaction file (detail file) contains current transaction information used to update the master file, such as the number of items shipped to be removed from inventory. Answer (B) is incorrect because a record layout is a representation of the format of the records on the file. It shows the position and length of the fields in the file. The layout of every record in the file is the same. Answer (D) is incorrect because a dump is a listing of the contents of memory.

23. In a business information system, which of the following types of computer files most likely would be a master file?

    A. Inventory subsidiary.

    B. Cash disbursements.

    C. Cash receipts.

    D. Payroll transactions.

Answer (A) is correct. *(CPA, adapted)*
    REQUIRED: The file most likely to be a master file.
    DISCUSSION: A master file is permanent information that is updated for the effects of transactions. In online processing, it is immediately updated. In batch processing, transactions are accumulated in a sorted transaction file, with periodic updating to create a new master file. Thus, an inventory subsidiary account is recorded in a master file.
    Answer (B) is incorrect because cash disbursements are transactions that update the cash master file. Answer (C) is incorrect because cash receipts are transactions that update the cash master file. Answer (D) is incorrect because the master file for employee earnings and deductions is updated for payroll transactions.

24. A commonly used measure of the activity in a master file during a specified time period is

    A. Volatility.

    B. The index ratio.

    C. The frequency ratio.

    D. The volume ratio.

Answer (A) is correct. *(CMA, adapted)*
    REQUIRED: The commonly used measure of the activity in a master file.
    DISCUSSION: File volatility is the relative frequency with which records are added, deleted, or changed during a specified period.

13.4   Nature of Binary Data Storage

25. Computers understand codes that represent letters of the alphabet, numbers, or special characters. These codes require that data be converted into predefined groups of binary digits. Such chains of digits are referred to as

A. Registers.

B. ASCII code.

C. Input.

D. Bytes.

Answer (D) is correct.   *(CIA, adapted)*
REQUIRED: The term for the chains of digits that a computer is capable of understanding.
DISCUSSION: A byte is a grouping of bits required to define one unit of data, such as a letter or an integer.
Answer (A) is incorrect because a register is a location within the CPU where data and instructions are temporarily stored. Answer (B) is incorrect because ASCII (American Standard Code for Information Interchange) is the coding convention itself. Answer (C) is incorrect because input is the data placed into processing (noun) or the act of placing the data in processing (verb).

13.5   File Organization and Access Methods

26. In an inventory system on a database management system (DBMS), one stored record contains part number, part name, part color, and part weight. These individual items are called

A. Fields.

B. Stored files.

C. Bytes.

D. Occurrences.

Answer (A) is correct.   *(CIA, adapted)*
REQUIRED: The term for the data elements in a record.
DISCUSSION: A record is a collection of related data items (fields). A field (data item) is a group of characters representing one unit of information.
Answer (B) is incorrect because a file is a group or set of related records ordered to facilitate processing. Answer (C) is incorrect because a byte is a group of bits (binary digits). It represents one character. Answer (D) is incorrect because occurrences is not a meaningful term in this context.

27. The indexed sequential access method (ISAM) is an approach to file organization

A. In which each data record has a pointer field containing the address of the next record in the list.

B. In which an index of record pointers of some of the file attributes are maintained in a list.

C. That uses an algorithm to convert a record key into a storage address to assist with later retrieval.

D. In which records are stored sequentially in a direct access file and organized by a primary key stored in an index record.

Answer (D) is correct.   *(CMA, adapted)*
REQUIRED: The true statement about indexed sequential access file organization.
DISCUSSION: ISAM stores records sequentially in a direct access file that is organized by a primary key kept in an index record. It does not use pointers. A pointer is a data element attached to a record that gives the address of the next logically related record. The virtue of ISAM is that it permits sequential processing of large numbers of records while providing for occasional direct access.
Answer (A) is incorrect because a linked list is a file organization in which each data record has a pointer field containing the address of the next record in the list. Answer (B) is incorrect because ISAM does not use pointers. Answer (C) is incorrect because, in a direct file organization, a randomizing formula or hashing scheme (a transform algorithm) converts a record key into a storage address. This method permits direct access without an index.

28. In a database, there are often conditions that constrain database records. For example, a sales order cannot exist unless the corresponding customer exists. This kind of constraint is an example of

A. Normalization.

B. Entity integrity.

C. Internal schema.

D. Referential integrity.

Answer (D) is correct.   *(CIA, adapted)*
REQUIRED: The constraint exemplified by prohibiting preparation of a sales order unless it references an existing customer.
DISCUSSION: The data in a database are subject to the constraint of referential integrity. Thus, if data are collected about something, e.g., a payment voucher, all reference conditions regarding it must be met. Thus, for a voucher to exist, a vendor must also exist.
Answer (A) is incorrect because normalization is the practice of decomposing database relations to remove data field redundancies and thus reduce the likelihood of update anomalies. Answer (B) is incorrect because, in a database, entity integrity means that each item or relationship in the database is uniquely identified by a single key value. Answer (C) is incorrect because, in a database, the internal schema describes the ways the data are physically organized.

29. Of the following, the greatest advantage of a database (server) architecture is that

   A. Data redundancy can be reduced.

   B. Conversion to a database system is inexpensive and can be accomplished quickly.

   C. Multiple occurrences of data items are useful for consistency checking.

   D. Backup and recovery procedures are minimized.

Answer (A) is correct. *(CIA, adapted)*
   REQUIRED: The greatest advantage of a database architecture.
   DISCUSSION: Data organized in files and used by the organization's various application programs are collectively known as a database. In a database system, storage structures are created that render the applications programs independent of the physical or logical arrangement of the data. Each data item has a standard definition, name, and format, and related items are linked by a system of pointers. The programs therefore need only specify data items by name, not by location. A database management system handles retrieval and storage. Because separate files for different application programs are unnecessary, data redundancy can be substantially reduced.
   Answer (B) is incorrect because conversion to a database is often costly and time consuming. Answer (C) is incorrect because a traditional flat-file system, not a database, has multiple occurrences of data items. Answer (D) is incorrect because, given the absence of data redundancy and the quick propagation of data errors throughout applications, backup and recovery procedures are just as critical in a database as in a flat-file system.

30. The primary purpose of a database system is to have a single storage location for each

   A. File.

   B. Record.

   C. Database.

   D. Data item.

Answer (D) is correct. *(CIA, adapted)*
   REQUIRED: The primary purpose of a database system.
   DISCUSSION: Data organized in files and used by the organization's various applications are collectively known as a database. In a database system, storage structures are created that render the applications independent of the physical or logical arrangement of the data. Each data item has a standard definition, name, and format, and related items are linked by a system of pointers. The programs therefore only need to specify data items by name, not by location. A database management system handles retrieval and storage. Because separate files for different applications are unnecessary, data redundancy (multiple storage locations for a data item) can be substantially reduced.
   Answer (A) is incorrect because databases are not organized by file. Answer (B) is incorrect because databases are not organized by records. Answer (C) is incorrect because the database is the collective result of organizing data in this way.

31. Whenever an authorized customer initiates a transaction at an automatic teller machine, the system is required to verify the customer's identity and to update the individual's records on a real-time basis. Such a system requires

   A. Direct access files.

   B. Sequential tape files.

   C. Optically readable media.

   D. Unerasable (permanent) disk files.

Answer (A) is correct. *(CIA, adapted)*
   REQUIRED: The files or media needed in an ATM system.
   DISCUSSION: Real-time processing permits capture of transactions as they occur and prompt output. Use of random (direct) access file media is necessary in a real-time system. Random access permits data locations to be found without searching other records in the file. Magnetic disk is a random access medium.
   Answer (B) is incorrect because retrieval of information from a magnetic tape file is sequential and thus slower than from a magnetic disk. Sequential access means searching all preceding records before the desired one is located. Answer (C) is incorrect because an ATM need not use optical scanners. Answer (D) is incorrect because magnetic disk storage used in a real-time system can be written over.

32. A disk drive may be preferred to a magnetic tape drive because the disk drive

   A. Is a cheaper medium for data storage.

   B. Offers random access to data files.

   C. Can be measured in bytes per inch.

   D. Can reuse a disk, whereas a tape drive cannot reuse a tape.

Answer (B) is correct. *(CMA, adapted)*
   REQUIRED: The reason a disk storage unit may be preferred to a magnetic tape drive system.
   DISCUSSION: A disk drive stores data files by using a file name. It offers random access to these data files by retrieving the data file using the file name. A magnetic tape drive is based on obsolete technology that uses sequential access. It contains records that must be processed in order.
   Answer (A) is incorrect because a disk drive is not necessarily a cheaper medium for data storage. Answer (C) is incorrect because data are not measured in bytes per inch. Answer (D) is incorrect because a magnetic tape can be reused.

Questions 33 and 34 are based on the following information. Five brand managers in a consumer food products company met regularly to figure out what price points were being lowered by their competitors and how well coupon promotions did. The data they needed to analyze consisted of about 50 gigabytes of daily point-of-sale (POS) data from major grocery chains for each month. The brand managers are competent users of spreadsheet and database software on personal computers. They considered several alternative software options to access and manipulate data to answer their questions.

33. The brand managers' selected option is unlikely to use a hierarchical database system because

   A. A hierarchical database system requires multiple joins.

   B. Programming queries for it are too costly and time consuming.

   C. Point-of-sale data are too sensitive for routine access.

   D. Summarization of point-of-sale data would not answer the questions.

Answer (B) is correct. *(CIA, adapted)*
   REQUIRED: The reason the selected option is unlikely to use a hierarchical database system.
   DISCUSSION: A hierarchical structure is tree-like. A record is divided into segments that are connected in one-to-many relationships. Because all of the paths through the data must be prespecified, a hierarchical structure is inflexible and does not support ad hoc queries. Thus, programming queries for a hierarchical database are often costly and time consuming.
   Answer (A) is incorrect because hierarchical database systems do not have commands for joins, which are standard features in relational systems. Answer (C) is incorrect because the point-of-sale information is clearly proprietary, but brand managers must use it to manage the business. Answer (D) is incorrect because point-of-sale data contain precisely the information that, if summarized appropriately, would answer the questions.

34. The limiting factor in the brand managers' use of a relational database system to answer their ad hoc questions will most likely be

   A. Understanding what individual data records represent.

   B. Obtaining computer resources for complicated queries.

   C. Distinguishing primary and foreign keys in the data.

   D. Lack of management interest in using the results.

Answer (B) is correct. *(CIA, adapted)*
   REQUIRED: The limiting factor in the use of a relational database to answer ad hoc queries.
   DISCUSSION: The limiting factor will likely be the availability of computer resources for complicated queries about the large volume (50 gigabytes) of data. The disadvantage of relational databases is low processing efficiency. Many accesses may be needed to execute the select, join, and project commands.
   Answer (A) is incorrect because the brand managers understand the data that point-of-sale terminals capture in grocery stores. Answer (C) is incorrect because distinguishing primary and foreign keys in the data will be relatively straightforward. The brand managers are already familiar with the data. Answer (D) is incorrect because management is highly interested in the results.

Use Gleim's *CPA Test Prep* for interactive testing with over 2,000 additional multiple-choice questions!

STUDY UNIT FOURTEEN
INFORMATION TECHNOLOGY IV

(7 pages of outline)

This study unit is the fourth of five covering information technology (IT).

14.1 DATABASE MANAGEMENT SYSTEMS

1. A **database management system (DBMS)** is an integrated set of software tools superimposed on the data files that helps maintain the integrity of the underlying database.

   a. Database management systems make the maintenance of vast relational databases practical. Without the sophisticated capabilities of database management systems, enforcing the rules that make the database relational would be overwhelmingly time-consuming.

   b. A DBMS allows programmers and designers to work independently of the physical and logical structure of the database.

      1) Before the development of DBMSs, programmers and systems designers needed to consider the logical and physical structure of the database with the creation of every new application. This was extremely time-consuming and therefore expensive.

      2) With a DBMS, the physical structure of the database can be completely altered without having to change any of the programs using the data items. Thus, different users may define their own views of the data (called subschemas).

2. A particular database's design, called its **schema**, consists of the layouts of the tables and the constraints on entering new records. To a great extent, a DBMS automates the process of enforcing the schema.

   a. Two vital parts of any DBMS are as follows:

      1) A data definition language, which allows the user to specify how the tables will look and what kinds of data elements they will hold.

      2) A data manipulation language, with which the DBMS retrieves, adds, deletes, or modifies records and data elements.

      3) Both of these roles are commonly fulfilled in the current generation of database management systems by **Structured Query Language (SQL)** or one of its many variants.

   b. The **data dictionary** contains the physical and logical characteristics of every data element in a database.

      1) The data dictionary includes, for example, the name of the data element (e.g., employee name, part number), the amount of space required to store the data element (in bytes), and what kind of data is allowed in the data element (e.g., alphabetic, numeric).

      2) The data dictionary also describes the mapping of every data element to all applications where it is updated and vice versa.

      3) Thus, the data dictionary contains the size, format, usage, meaning, and ownership of every data element as well as what persons, programs, reports, and functions use the data element.

3. A DBMS can maintain a **distributed database**, meaning one that is stored in two or more physical sites.

    a. In the replication, or snapshot, technique, the DBMS duplicates the entire database and sends it to multiple locations. Changes are periodically copied and similarly distributed.

    b. In the fragmentation, or partitioning, method, specific records are stored where they are most needed. For example, a financial institution may store a particular customer's data at the branch where (s)he usually transacts his/her business. If the customer executes a transaction at another branch, the pertinent data are retrieved via communications lines.

4. A **deadly embrace**, also called a **deadlock**, can be resolved by a DBMS. This situation occurs when two transactions attempt to update a single data element simultaneously.

    a. When a deadly embrace occurs, the DBMS selects one of the transactions as the "victim" and releases the data resources it controls so that the other transaction can run to completion. The victim transaction is then restarted and permitted to run.

5. Those in the IT function responsible for dealing with the DBMS are called database administrators (see item 1.a. in Subunit 11.3).

6. Stop and review! You have completed the outline for this subunit. Study multiple-choice questions 1 through 5 beginning on page 422.

14.2 TRANSACTION PROCESSING MODES

1. **Batch processing.** In this mode, transactions are accumulated and submitted to the computer as a single "batch." In the early days of computers, this was the only way a job could be processed.

    a. In batch processing, the user cannot influence the process once the job has begun (except to ask that it be aborted completely). (S)he must wait until the job is finished running to see if any transactions in the batch were rejected and failed to post.

    b. Despite huge advances in computer technology, this accumulation of transactions for processing on a delayed basis is still widely used. It is very efficient for such applications as payroll, where large numbers of routine transactions must be processed on a regular schedule.

2. **Online processing.** In this mode, the computer processes each transaction individually as the user enters it.

    a. The user is in direct communication with the computer and gets immediate feedback on whether the transaction was accepted or not.

    b. A common example is an accounts payable system in which a payables clerk can enter each individual invoice as (s)he verifies the paperwork.

3. Many applications use **combined batch and online** modes.

    a. In such systems, users continuously enter transactions in online mode throughout the workday, collecting them in batches. The computer can then take advantage of the efficiencies of batch mode overnight when there are fewer users logged on to the system.

4. **Real-time processing.** In some systems, having the latest information available at all times is crucial to the proper functioning of the system.

    a. A thermostat is a common example, constantly monitoring the temperature in the room and engaging the heating or cooling accordingly.

    b. Online, real-time systems combine the two modes of user data entry and instant update. A common example is an airline reservation system, which is constantly updated from moment to moment and must be available all the time.

5. **Centralization.** During the early days of computer processing, computers were very large and expensive and only organizations such as large banks and governmental agencies could afford them.

    a. Of necessity, all processing and systems development were done at a single, central location. Users connected to the mainframe via "dumb terminals," i.e., simple monitor-and-keyboard combinations with no processing power of their own.

    b. Since hardware, information security, and data integrity functions were located in one office, economies of scale were achieved and controls were strong.

6. **Decentralization.** As the data processing industry evolved, computers became smaller (so-called minicomputers), and branch offices of large organizations could have their own.

    a. Each branch could store and process its data onsite, transmitting the results overnight to the mainframe at the home office. This was an early form of **distributed processing**, in which parts of an organization's computer operations could be performed in separate physical locations.

    b. In this early distributed arrangement, the home office mainframe ran its programs and the branches ran theirs. The next evolution was for a single application to be split into pieces so the parts could run on separate hardware platforms.

        1) The decision was thus no longer whether an application should run centrally or locally, but rather, which parts of the application are better performed by small local computers and which parts are better performed at some other, possibly centralized, site.

    c. Since IT functions were no longer concentrated in a single location, issues of security and training became more challenging.

7. **Client/server networks.** The key to the client/server model of distributed processing is that it runs processes on the platform most appropriate to that process while attempting to minimize traffic over the network.

    a. A "server" is centrally located and devoted to the functions that are needed by all network users.

        1) Examples include mail servers (to handle electronic mail), application servers (to run application programs), file servers (to store databases and make user inquiries more efficient), Internet servers (to manage access to the Internet), and web servers (to host websites).

        2) Whether a device is classified as a server is not determined by its hardware configuration, but rather by the function it performs. A simple desktop computer can be a server.

    b. Technically, a "client" is any object that uses the resources of another object. Thus, a client can be either a piece of hardware or a software program.

        1) In common usage, however, client generally refers to a device that requests services from a server. This use of the term encompasses anything from a Palm Pilot, to a desktop computer, to another server.

8. **Outsourcing.** Some organizations farm out all or part of their IT function to an outside provider. There are two common motivations for this practice:

    a. The outside provider offers economies of scale that are not available to the organization.

        1) For instance, the organization needs its payroll processed every two weeks and does not wish to invest in the dedicated hardware that would allow it to do that processing itself. In a case like this, the organization may keep its own IT department and simply contract with the service bureau to perform certain specified functions.

  b.   Management has decided that IT is not a core competency of the organization and that the entire IT function can be most efficiently provided by a firm specializing in providing IT services.

     1)   This arrangement is fulfilled by a facilities management organization, which provides the personnel to manage and operate the client's internal IT activity.

9.   Stop and review! You have completed the outline for this subunit. Study multiple-choice questions 6 through 16 beginning on page 424.

14.3 APPLICATION PROCESSING PHASES

1.   **Data capture.** In order to be processed, data must be entered into the system. This can be done in batch mode, by online entry (see Subunit 14.2), or even from a personal digital assistant.

2.   **Edit routines.** These are controls programmed into the software that prevent certain types of errors from ever getting into the system. They include:

  a.   Preformatting. To avoid data entry errors in online systems, a preformatted screen may be designed to look exactly like the corresponding paper document.

  b.   Field checks. Some data elements can only contain certain characters, and any transaction that attempts to use an invalid character is halted. A typical example is a Social Security Number, which is not allowed to contain letters.

  c.   Limit and range checks. Based on known limits for given information, certain entries can be rejected by the system. For example, hours worked per week cannot exceed 80 without a special override by management; date of birth cannot be any date within the last 15 years, etc.

  d.   Validity checks. In order for a transaction to be processed, some other record must already exist in another file. For example, for the system to accept a transaction requesting payment of a vendor invoice, the vendor must already have a record on the vendor master file.

  e.   Sequence checks. Processing efficiency is greatly increased when files are sorted on some designated field(s), called the "key," before operations such as matching. For instance, the accounts payable transaction file and master file should both be sorted according to vendor number before the matching operation is attempted. If the system discovers a record out of order, it may indicate that the files were not properly prepared for processing.

  f.   Self-checking digits. An algorithm is applied to, for instance, a product number and incorporated into the number.

     EXAMPLE:

     1)   A box of detergent has the product number 4187604. The last digit is actually a derived number, arrived at by applying the check-digit algorithm to the other digits.

     2)   The check digit is calculated by starting with the last position of the base product number and multiplying each successive digit to the left by 2, then by 1, then by 2, etc., and adding the results: $(0 \times 2) + (6 \times 1) + (7 \times 2) + (8 \times 1) + (1 \times 2) + (4 \times 1) = 0 + 6 + 14 + 8 + 2 + 4 = 34$. The last digit of this result becomes the check digit.

     3)   When the clerk enters 4187604 into the terminal, the system performs an immediate calculation and determines that this is a valid product number. This reduces keying errors such as dropped and transposed digits.

  g.   Zero-balance checks. The system will reject any transaction or batch thereof in which the sum of all debits and credits does not equal zero.

3. **Output controls.** These procedures are performed at the end of processing to ensure that all transactions the user expected to be processed were. They include:

   a. Error listings. All transactions rejected by the system are printed and distributed to the appropriate user department for resolution.

   b. Record counts. The total number of records processed by the system is compared to the number the user expected to be processed.

   c. Run-to-run control totals. The new financial balance should be the sum of the old balance plus the activity that was just processed.

   d. Hash totals. These are totals without a defined meaning, such as the total of employee numbers or invoice numbers.

   e. Proof account activity listing. This report shows all changes to master files. It can be sent to the appropriate user department to verify that the changes were authorized.

   f. An audit trail of all processing activity should be generated. It summarizes any or all of the totals described above.

4. **Master file maintenance.** For a description of the two subtypes of master file, see Subunit 13.3.

   a. The first subtype is only updated irregularly, for instance, when a new vendor is added or an existing one changes its mailing address.

   b. The second subtype is updated regularly, for instance, with the daily postings of journal activity.

   c. Whichever of the two subtypes is involved, the power to approve changes to a master file must be assigned in accord with a coherent organizational policy; e.g., the head of payroll cannot approve changes to the customer address file.

5. **Reporting, Accounting, Control, and Management**

   a. Reports are subsets of the organization's total set of data that are presented in such a way as to (1) reveal the organization's performance or (2) help in decision making. Reports do not necessarily have to be in paper form; they can be viewed entirely onscreen. Examples are the company's statement of income and aging of accounts receivable.

   b. No matter how powerful an organization's computing resources are, they are finite. If cost-effective, usage of the computer's resources must be measured and the allocated cost billed to the user departments who benefit from receiving IT services.

      1) Common bases for cost allocation and billing are number of CPU cycles and number of input/output operations. Special pieces of systems software track what quantity of these measures is consumed by which users.

6. **Query, Audit Trail, and Ad Hoc Reports**

   a. Online information systems are often powerful enough to allow end users to perform their own queries, i.e., to ask questions directly of the database without the assistance of IT personnel. Such querying is enabled by fourth-generation programming languages (see item 3.d. in Subunit 12.2), which are user-friendly enough to require little technical knowledge.

      1) Closely related to the concept of the query is the ad hoc report, which is a "quick-and-dirty" report drawn from one of the organization's databases that fulfills a user need but for which there is not sufficient time or resources to request formally from the IT function.

   b. An audit trail of activities is a crucial part of monitoring security over a system. The audit trail includes not only the reports described in item 3. above, but also such reports as logs of system sign-in and sign-out times to monitor who was doing what on the system.

7. Stop and review! You have completed the outline for this subunit. Study multiple-choice questions 17 through 28 beginning on page 427.

14.4 DISASTER RECOVERY AND BUSINESS CONTINUITY

1.   The information security goal of data availability (see item 1. in Subunit 13.2) is primarily the responsibility of the IT function.

    a.   **Contingency planning** is the name commonly given to this activity.

        1)   **Disaster recovery** is the process of resuming normal information processing operations after the occurrence of a major interruption.

        2)   **Business continuity** is the continuation of business by other means during the period in which computer processing is unavailable or less than normal.

    b.   Two major types of contingencies must be planned for: those in which the data center is physically available and those in which it is not.

        1)   Examples of the first type of contingency are power failure, random intrusions such as viruses, and deliberate intrusions such as hacking incidents. The organization's physical facilities are sound, but immediate action is required to keep normal processing going.

        2)   The second type of contingency is much more serious. This type is caused by disasters such as floods, fires, hurricanes, earthquakes, etc. An occurrence of this type necessitates the existence of an alternate processing facility [see item 4.c.1) on the next page].

2.   **Periodic backup and offsite rotation** of computer files is the most basic part of any disaster recovery/business continuity plan.

    a.   It is a truth seldom grasped by those who are not computer professionals that an organization's data is more valuable than its hardware. Hardware can be replaced for a price, but each organization's data bundle is unique and is indispensable to carrying on business. If it is ever destroyed, it cannot be replaced. For this reason, periodic backup and rotation are essential.

    b.   A typical backup routine involves duplicating all data files and application programs once a month. Incremental changes are then backed up and taken to the offsite location once a week. (Application files must be backed up in addition to data since programs change too.)

    c.   The offsite location must be temperature- and humidity-controlled and guarded against physical intrusion. Just as important, it must be geographically remote enough from the site of the organization's main operations that it would not be affected by the same natural disaster. It does the organization no good to have adequate backup files if the files are not accessible or have been destroyed.

    d.   In case of an interruption of normal processing, the organization's systems can be restored such that at most seven days of business information is lost. This is not an ideal situation, but it is a far cry from a complete loss of a company's files, which could essentially put it out of business.

3.   The **risk assessment** that forms the core of contingency planning involves:

    a.   Identifying and prioritizing the organization's critical applications

        1)   Not all of an organization's systems are equally important. The firm must decide which vital applications it simply cannot do business without and in what order they should be brought back into operation.

    b.   Determining the minimum recovery time frames and minimum hardware requirements

        1)   How long will it take to reinstall each critical application and what platform is required? If the interruption has been caused by an attack such as a virus or hacker, how long will it take to isolate the problem and eliminate it from the system?

c. Developing a recovery plan

　　1) Each type of contingency requires its own specific recovery procedures (see item 4. below).

4. Dealing with Specific Types of Contingencies

a. **Power failures** can be guarded against by the purchase of backup electrical generators. These can be programmed to automatically begin running as soon as a dip in the level of electric current is detected. This is a widespread practice in settings such as hospitals where 24-hour system availability is crucial.

b. Attacks such as **viruses** and denial-of-service call for a completely different response. The system must be brought down "gracefully" to halt the spread of the infection. The IT staff must be well trained in the nature of the latest virus threats to know how to isolate the damage and bring the system back to full operation.

c. The most extreme contingency is when the organization's main facility is rendered uninhabitable by **flood, fire, earthquake, etc**. It is to prepare for these cases that organizations contract for alternate processing facilities.

　　1) An **alternate processing facility** is a physical location maintained by an outside contractor for the express purpose of providing processing facilities for customers in case of disaster.

　　　　a) The recovery center, like the offsite storage location for backup files, must be far enough away that it will likely be unaffected by the same natural disaster that forced the abandonment of the main facility. Usually, companies contract for backup facilities in another city.

　　　　b) Once the determination is made that processing is no longer possible at the principal site, the backup files are retrieved from the secure storage location and taken to the recovery center.

　　　　c) Recovery centers can take many forms. Organizations determine which facility is best by calculating the tradeoff between the cost of the contract and the cost of downtime.

　　　　　　i) A hot site is a fully operational processing facility that is immediately available. A flying-start site is a hot site with the latest data and software that permit startup within a few minutes or even a few seconds.

　　　　　　ii) A warm site is a facility with limited hardware, such as communications and networking equipment, already installed but lacking the necessary servers and client terminals.

　　　　　　iii) A cold site is a shell facility lacking most infrastructure but readily available for the quick installation of hardware.

5. **Other technologies** that can assist in recovery from an interruption in processing:

a. Fault-tolerant computer systems have additional hardware and software as well as a backup power supply. A fault-tolerant computer has additional chips and disk storage. This technology is used for mission-critical applications that cannot afford to suffer downtime.

　　1) The enabling technology for fault-tolerance is the redundant array of inexpensive discs, or RAID. It is a grouping of multiple hard drives with special software that allows for data delivery along multiple paths. If one drive fails, the other discs can compensate for the loss.

b. High-availability computing is used for less-critical applications because it provides for a short recovery time rather than the elimination of recovery time.

6. Stop and review! You have completed the outline for this subunit. Study multiple-choice questions 29 through 35 beginning on page 430.

QUESTIONS

14.1 Database Management Systems

1. All of the following are methods for distributing a relational database across multiple servers except

A. Snapshot (making a copy of the database for distribution).

B. Replication (creating and maintaining replica copies at multiple locations).

C. Normalization (separating the database into logical tables for easier user processing).

D. Fragmentation (separating the database into parts and distributing where they are needed).

Answer (C) is correct.   *(CIA, adapted)*
REQUIRED: The item not a method for distributing a relational database across multiple servers.
DISCUSSION: Normalization is the term for determining how groups of data items in a relational structure are arranged in records in a database. This process relies on "normal forms," that is, conceptual definitions of data records and specified design rules. Normalization is intended to prevent inconsistent updating of data items. It is a process of breaking down a complex data structure by creating smaller, more efficient relations, thereby minimizing or eliminating the repeating groups in each relation.
Answer (A) is incorrect because the snapshot technique makes duplicates to be stored at multiple locations. Changes are periodically copied and sent to each location. If a database is small, storing multiple copies may be cheaper than retrieving records from a central site. Answer (B) is incorrect because the replication technique makes duplicates to be stored at multiple locations. Changes are periodically copied and sent to each location. If a database is small, storing multiple copies may be cheaper than retrieving records from a central site. Answer (D) is incorrect because fragmentation or partitioning stores specific records where they are most needed. For example, a financial institution may store a particular customer's data at the branch where (s)he usually transacts his/her business. If the customer executes a transaction at another branch, the pertinent data are retrieved via communications lines.

2. One advantage of a database management system (DBMS) is

A. Each organizational unit takes responsibility and control for its own data.

B. The cost of the data processing department decreases as users are now responsible for establishing their own data handing techniques.

C. A decreased vulnerability as the database management system has numerous security controls to prevent disasters.

D. The independence of the data from the application programs, which allows the programs to be developed for the user's specific needs without concern for data capture problems.

Answer (D) is correct.   *(CMA, adapted)*
REQUIRED: The advantage of a DBMS.
DISCUSSION: A fundamental characteristic of databases is that applications are independent of the database structure; when writing programs or designing applications to use the database, only the name of the desired item is necessary. Programs can be developed for the user's specific needs without concern for data capture problems. Reference can be made to the items using the data manipulation language, after which the DBMS takes care of locating and retrieving the desired items. The physical or logical structure of the database can be completely altered without having to change any of the programs using the data items. Only the schema requires alteration.
Answer (A) is incorrect because each organizational unit develops programs to use the elements of a broad database. Answer (B) is incorrect because data handling techniques are still the responsibility of the data processing department. It is the use of the data that is departmentalized. Answer (C) is incorrect because the DBMS is not necessarily safer than any other database system.

3. In a database system, locking of data helps preserve data integrity by permitting transactions to have control of all the data needed to complete the transactions. However, implementing a locking procedure could lead to

- A. Inconsistent processing.
- B. Rollback failures.
- C. Unrecoverable transactions.
- D. Deadly embraces.

Answer (D) is correct. *(CIA, adapted)*
REQUIRED: The potential disadvantage of a locking procedure.
DISCUSSION: In a distributed processing system, the data and resources a transaction may update or use should be held in their current status until the transaction is complete. A deadly embrace occurs when two transactions need the same resource at the same time. If the system does not have a method to cope with the problem efficiently, response time worsens or the system eventually fails. The system should have an algorithm for undoing the effects of one transaction and releasing the resources it controls so that the other transaction can run to completion.
Answer (A) is incorrect because inconsistent processing occurs when a transaction has different effects depending on when it is processed. Data locking ensures consistent processing. Answer (B) is incorrect because rollback failure is the inability of the software to undo the effects of a transaction that could not be run to completion. A rollback failure is not caused by data locking. However, data locking may lead to situations in which rollback is required. Answer (C) is incorrect because unrecoverable transactions are not a typical symptom of locking procedures.

4. An overall description of a database, including the names of data elements, their characteristics, and their relationship to each other, are defined by using a

- A. Data definition language.
- B. Data control language.
- C. Data manipulation language.
- D. Data command interpreter language.

Answer (A) is correct. *(CIA, adapted)*
REQUIRED: The language used to define a database.
DISCUSSION: The data definition language defines the database structure and content, especially the schema (the description of the entire database) and subschema (logical views of the database). The schema specifies characteristics such as the names of the data elements contained in the database and their relationship to each other. The subschema defines the logical data views required for applications, which limits the data elements and functions available to each application.
Answer (B) is incorrect because the data control language specifies the privileges and security rules governing database users. Answer (C) is incorrect because data manipulation language provides application programs with a means of interacting with the database to add, retrieve, modify, or delete data or relationships. Answer (D) is incorrect because data command interpreter languages are symbolic character strings used to control the current state of database management system operations.

5. To trace data through several application programs, an auditor needs to know what programs use the data, which files contain the data, and which printed reports display the data. If data exist only in a database system, the auditor could probably find all of this information in a

- A. Data dictionary.
- B. Database schema.
- C. Data encryptor.
- D. Decision table.

Answer (A) is correct. *(CIA, adapted)*
REQUIRED: The information source in a database needed to trace data through several application programs.
DISCUSSION: The data dictionary is a file (possibly manual but usually computerized) in which the records relate to specified data items. It contains definitions of data items, the list of programs used to process them, and the reports in which data are found. Only certain persons or entities are permitted to retrieve data or to modify data items. Accordingly, these access limitations are also found in the data dictionary.
Answer (B) is incorrect because the schema describes the structure of the database. Answer (C) is incorrect because an encryptor encodes data. Answer (D) is incorrect because a decision table is a type of logic diagram that presents in matrix form the decision points and related actions reflected in a computer program.

14.2 Transaction Processing Modes

6. Batch processing

   A. Is not used by most businesses because it reduces the audit trail.

   B. Allows users to inquire about groups of information contained in the system.

   C. Accumulates transaction records into groups for processing against the master file on a delayed basis.

   D. Can only be performed on a centralized basis.

Answer (C) is correct. *(CMA, adapted)*
REQUIRED: The true statement about batch processing.
DISCUSSION: Batch processing is the accumulation and grouping of transactions for processing on a delayed basis. The batch approach is suitable for applications that can be processed against the master file at intervals and involve large volumes of similar items, such as payroll, sales, inventory, and billing.
Answer (A) is incorrect because batch processing provides as much of an audit trail as any computerized operation. Answer (B) is incorrect because batch processing refers to the input of data, not inquiry. Answer (D) is incorrect because batch processing can also be performed on a decentralized basis.

7. Compared to batch processing, real-time processing has which of the following advantages?

   A. Ease of auditing.

   B. Ease of implementation.

   C. Timeliness of information.

   D. Efficiency of processing.

Answer (C) is correct. *(CPA, adapted)*
REQUIRED: The advantage of real-time processing over batch processing.
DISCUSSION: Real-time processing involves processing an input record and receiving the output soon enough to affect a current decision-making process. Thus, the emphasis is on receiving the output in a timely fashion. In comparison, the batch approach is suitable for applications that can be processed at intervals.
Answer (A) is incorrect because real-time processing is more difficult to audit. Batch processing involves uniform processing of a group of transactions at one place and time. Thus, it produces as much of an audit trail as any computer operation. Real-time processing permits immediate updating as transactions occur and access from multiple sites. Answer (B) is incorrect because real-time processing is more difficult to implement. It requires the system to have the capability to handle inquiries and update files as transactions occur. Answer (D) is incorrect because batch processing is more efficient.

8. An interactive system environment is best characterized by

   A. Data files with records arranged sequentially.

   B. The processing of groups of data at regular intervals.

   C. Sorting the transaction file before processing.

   D. The processing of data immediately on input.

Answer (D) is correct. *(CMA, adapted)*
REQUIRED: The characteristic of an interactive system environment.
DISCUSSION: In an interactive (inquiry) system, users employ interactive terminals to converse directly with the system. The system is characterized by online entry and processing, direct access, and timesharing.
Answer (A) is incorrect because an interactive system requires direct-access files. Answer (B) is incorrect because an interactive system permits immediate, online processing of single transactions. Answer (C) is incorrect because the transaction file need not be sorted before processing.

9. Information processing made possible by a network of computers dispersed throughout an organization is called

   A. Online processing.

   B. Interactive processing.

   C. Time sharing.

   D. Distributed data processing.

Answer (D) is correct. *(CMA, adapted)*
REQUIRED: The method of information processing by dispersed computers.
DISCUSSION: Distributed processing is characterized by a merger of computer and telecommunications technology. Distributed systems permit not only remote access to a computer but also the performance of local processing at local sites. The result is greater flexibility in systems design and the possibility of an optimal distribution of processing tasks.
Answer (A) is incorrect because online processing is a method of processing data that permits both immediate posting (updating) and inquiry of master files as transactions occur. Answer (B) is incorrect because interactive processing is a method of processing data immediately upon input. Answer (C) is incorrect because time sharing is the processing of a program by the CPU until an input or output operation is required. In time sharing, the CPU spends a fixed amount of time on each program.

10. A firm is considering two possible computer configurations. System I would have a mainframe computer tied to 16 time-sharing terminals. System II would have a minicomputer tied to 16 intelligent workstations. Which of these two systems could be termed a "distributed system"?

    A. System I only.

    B. System II only.

    C. Both Systems I and II.

    D. Neither System I nor II.

Answer (B) is correct. *(CIA, adapted)*
    REQUIRED: The system(s) that can be described as a distributed system.
    DISCUSSION: The advent of cheaper and smaller computers has permitted the development of a somewhat different alternative to centralization or decentralization: distributed data processing. In a distributed data processing system, the organization's processing needs are examined in their totality. The decision is not whether an application should be done centrally or locally, but rather which parts of the application are better performed by small local computers as intelligent terminals, and which parts are better performed at some other, possibly centralized, site. In essence, the best distribution of processing tasks within application areas is sought. The key distinction between decentralized and distributed systems is the interconnection among the nodes (sites) in the latter kind of network. Hence, System I is a traditional system, and System II is a distributed system.

11. Distributed computing systems provide several advantages over a centralized computer. Which of the following is not an advantage of distributed systems?

    A. Communications costs are usually lower.

    B. Alternate processing locations are available in case one site's computer is not functioning.

    C. Security measures are easier to provide.

    D. Investment in hardware is smaller for each site than for a central site.

Answer (C) is correct. *(CIA, adapted)*
    REQUIRED: The response that is not an advantage of distributed computing.
    DISCUSSION: In a distributed system, a determination is made as to which parts of an application are best performed by small computers (e.g., intelligent terminals) and which should be performed at some other, possibly centralized, site. In other words, the best distribution of processing tasks among the interconnected nodes of the system is sought. Security therefore becomes more difficult when there are more sites to secure.
    Answer (A) is incorrect because lower communications costs are an advantage of distributed computing. Answer (B) is incorrect because the availability of alternate processing locations is an advantage of distributed computing. Answer (D) is incorrect because, given smaller, less complex hardware requirements, the cost for each site would be much less than for a central site.

12. A company updates the payroll master file at the end of the week. The payroll cards are transported to the computer center for processing. The sequence of events followed by the computer center in updating its master file should be

    A. Converting to machine-readable form, batching records of transactions, validating input, updating the master.

    B. Batching records of transactions, converting to machine-readable form, validating input, updating the master.

    C. Validating input, batching records of transactions, converting to machine-readable form, updating the master.

    D. Batching records of transactions, validating input, converting to machine-readable form, updating the master.

Answer (B) is correct. *(CIA, adapted)*
    REQUIRED: The sequence of events for updating a master file.
    DISCUSSION: Batching is the collection and grouping of similar input records for processing. Information must be converted to machine language so the computer can read it. Validating input is checking the validity of account numbers, customer numbers, etc., included in the batched input records. The master file contains current or almost current records. The transaction (i.e., batch) file must be processed against the master file to bring the almost current records to a current state.
    Answer (A) is incorrect because data must be batched before it is converted. Answer (C) is incorrect because data must be batched first. Answer (D) is incorrect because data are validated by various computer checks after, not before, conversion to machine-readable form.

13. A payroll system's master file is stored on tape. The payroll is processed at night once every 2 weeks. There is relatively little file maintenance required. Which of the following is most likely to be the appropriate processing method under the circumstances?

    A. Parallel.

    B. Online, real-time.

    C. Network.

    D. Batch.

Answer (D) is correct. *(CIA, adapted)*
    REQUIRED: The appropriate processing method.
    DISCUSSION: Batch processing is the accumulation and grouping of transactions for processing on a delayed basis. The batch approach is suitable for applications that can be processed at intervals and involve large volumes of similar items, e.g., payroll, sales, inventory, and billing.
    Answer (A) is incorrect because parallel means that two or more processes are executed concurrently. Answer (B) is incorrect because online means simply that data entry is performed via a terminal to a computer, and real-time means that transactions are processed when captured. The payroll operation need not be online or real-time. Answer (C) is incorrect because a network of computers may employ any mode of processing but is most likely to be used for online, real-time applications.

14. A new purchasing system for just-in-time production requirements has been proposed. Users want access to current master file information at all times. To satisfy user needs, master file changes should be implemented with

    A. Periodic entry with subsequent batch processing.

    B. Periodic entry with immediate batch processing.

    C. Online entry with subsequent batch processing.

    D. Online entry with immediate processing.

Answer (D) is correct. *(CIA, adapted)*
    REQUIRED: The appropriate system for JIT production.
    DISCUSSION: JIT production attempts to minimize inventory by more closely coordinating deliveries of needed materials and production. Thus, inventory data must be current. Online entry with immediate (real-time) processing gives users current master file information because changes are entered and applied to the master file as they occur. However, check printing can still occur in batch mode.
    Answer (A) is incorrect because periodic entry and batch processing do not permit the immediate updating required by JIT production. Answer (B) is incorrect because periodic entry does not permit immediate updating, and "immediate batch processing" is a contradiction in terms. Answer (C) is incorrect because online entry and subsequent batch processing do not permit the immediate updating required by JIT production.

15. What type of computer processing system is characterized by data that are assembled from more than one location and records that are updated immediately?

    A. Personal computer systems.

    B. Data compression systems.

    C. Batch processing systems.

    D. Online, real-time systems.

Answer (D) is correct. *(CPA, adapted)*
    REQUIRED: The system allowing data entry from multiple locations and immediate updating.
    DISCUSSION: Real-time processing involves processing an input record and receiving the output soon enough to affect a current decision-making process. In a real-time system, the user interacts with the system to control an ongoing activity. Online indicates that the decision maker is in direct communication with the computer. Online, real-time systems usually permit access to the main computer from multiple remote terminals.
    Answer (A) is incorrect because access from multiple locations is more typical of mid-range or larger computer systems than of personal computer systems. Answer (B) is incorrect because data compression systems encode data to take up less storage space. Answer (C) is incorrect because batching of transactions requires assembly of data at one place and a delay in updating.

16. Misstatements in a batch computer system caused by incorrect programs or data may not be detected immediately because

    A. Errors in some transactions may cause rejection of other transactions in the batch.

    B. The identification of errors in input data typically is not part of the program.

    C. There are time delays in processing transactions in a batch system.

    D. The processing of transactions in a batch system is not uniform.

Answer (C) is correct. *(CPA, adapted)*
    REQUIRED: The reason errors may not be detected immediately in a batch computer system.
    DISCUSSION: Transactions in a batch computer system are grouped together, or batched, prior to processing. Batches may be processed either daily, weekly, or even monthly. Thus, considerable time may elapse between the initiation of the transaction and the discovery of an error.
    Answer (A) is incorrect because the transactions within the batch are typically not contingent upon one another. Answer (B) is incorrect because edit checks can be incorporated into batch processing environments. However, the edit checks are used to test the transactions in batches. Answer (D) is incorrect because a batch of transactions is typically processed uniformly.

14.3 Application Processing Phases

17. Which of the following is a validity check?

A. The computer ensures that a numerical amount in a record does not exceed some predetermined amount.

B. As the computer corrects errors and data are successfully resubmitted to the system, the causes of the errors are printed out.

C. The computer flags any transmission for which the control field value did not match that of an existing file record.

D. After data are entered, the computer sends certain data back to the terminal for comparison with data originally sent.

Answer (C) is correct. *(CPA, adapted)*
REQUIRED: The validity check.
DISCUSSION: Validity checks test identification numbers or transaction codes for validity by comparison with items already known to be correct or authorized. For example, a validity check may identify a transmission for which the control field value did not match a preexisting record in a file.
Answer (A) is incorrect because a limit check determines whether a numerical amount exceeds a predetermined amount. Answer (B) is incorrect because an error log or error listing identifies errors that were previously detected and subsequently corrected. Answer (D) is incorrect because closed-loop verification sends certain data back to the terminal for comparison with data originally sent by the operator.

18. A customer's order was never filled because an order entry clerk transposed the customer identification number while entering the sales transaction into the system. Which of the following controls would most likely have detected the transposition?

A. Sequence test.

B. Completeness test.

C. Validity check.

D. Limit test.

Answer (C) is correct. *(CPA, adapted)*
REQUIRED: The control that would most likely have detected the transposition.
DISCUSSION: Validity checks are tests of identification numbers or transaction codes for validity by comparison with items already known to be correct or authorized.
Answer (A) is incorrect because sequence tests determine whether records are in proper order. Answer (B) is incorrect because completeness checks of transmission of data determine whether all necessary information has been sent. Answer (D) is incorrect because limit tests are based on known limits for given information. For example, hours worked per week cannot exceed 168.

19. An employee in the receiving department keyed in a shipment from a remote terminal and inadvertently omitted the purchase order number. The best systems control to detect this error is

A. Completeness test.

B. Sequence check.

C. Reasonableness test.

D. Compatibility test.

Answer (A) is correct. *(CMA, adapted)*
REQUIRED: The control to detect the omission of a purchase order number keyed in from a remote terminal.
DISCUSSION: A completeness test checks that all data elements are entered before processing. An interactive system can be programmed to notify the user to enter the number before accepting the receiving report.
Answer (B) is incorrect because a sequence check tests for the ordering, not omission, of records. Answer (C) is incorrect because a limit or reasonableness test checks the values of data items against established limits. Answer (D) is incorrect because a compatibility test (field check) determines whether characters are appropriate to a field.

20. Which one of the following input validation routines is not likely to be appropriate in a real-time operation?

A. Sign check.

B. Reasonableness check.

C. Sequence check.

D. Redundant data check.

Answer (C) is correct. *(CMA, adapted)*
REQUIRED: The input validation routine not appropriate in a real-time operation.
DISCUSSION: The program controls listed prescreen or edit data prior to processing, but the sequence check is most likely to be used only in batch processing. A sequence check tests to determine that records are in proper order. For example, a payroll input file can be sorted into Social Security number order. A sequence check can then be performed to verify record order. This control would not apply in a real-time operation because records are not processed sequentially.
Answer (A) is incorrect because sign checks test data for the appropriate arithmetic sign. For instance, hours worked in a payroll should always be a positive number. Answer (B) is incorrect because reasonableness tests verify that amounts fall within predetermined limits. Answer (D) is incorrect because a redundancy check requires sending additional data items to serve as a check on the other transmitted data; for example, part of a customer name can be matched against the name associated with the transmitted customer number.

21. To ensure the completeness of update in an online system, separate totals are accumulated for all transactions processed throughout the day. The computer then agrees these totals to the total of items accepted for processing. This is an example of

    A. Run-to-run totals.

    B. Computer matching.

    C. Computer sequence check.

    D. One-for-one checking.

Answer (A) is correct. *(CIA, adapted)*
    REQUIRED: The procedure that compares the total of all transactions processed with the total of items accepted.
    DISCUSSION: During each program run in a series, the computer accumulates the totals of transactions that have been processed. The run-to-run check reconciles them with the totals forwarded from the previous program run. Run-to-run totals thus ensure completeness of update.
    Answer (B) is incorrect because computer matching compares transaction data with referenced fields or records. Answer (C) is incorrect because computer sequence checks identify changes or breaks in a numerical sequence. Answer (D) is incorrect because one-for-one checking usually requires manual comparisons of input with processing results.

22. An entity has the following invoices in a batch:

Invoice Number	Product	Quantity	Unit Price
201	F10	150	$ 5.00
202	G15	200	$10.00
203	H20	250	$25.00
204	K35	300	$30.00

Which of the following numbers represents the record count?

    A. 1

    B. 4

    C. 810

    D. 900

Answer (B) is correct. *(CPA, adapted)*
    REQUIRED: The record count.
    DISCUSSION: Input controls in batch computer systems are used to determine that no data are lost or added to the batch. Depending on the sophistication of a particular system, control may be accomplished by using record counts, batch totals, or hash totals. A record count establishes the number of source documents and reconciles it to the number of output records. The total number of invoices processed is an example of a record count. In this case, the record count is 4.
    Answer (A) is incorrect because 1 is the number of batches. Answer (C) is incorrect because 810 is a hash total of the invoice numbers. Answer (D) is incorrect because 900 is the total quantity of items.

23. An entity has the following invoices in a batch:

Invoice Number	Product	Quantity	Unit Price
201	F10	150	$ 5.00
202	G15	200	$10.00
203	H20	250	$25.00
204	K35	300	$30.00

Which of the following most likely represents a hash total?

    A. FGHK80

    B. 4

    C. 204

    D. 810

Answer (D) is correct. *(CPA, adapted)*
    REQUIRED: The example of a hash total.
    DISCUSSION: Input controls in batch computer systems are used to determine that no data are lost or added to the batch. Depending on the sophistication of a particular system, control may be accomplished by using record counts, batch totals, or hash totals. The hash total is a control total without a defined meaning, such as the total of employee numbers or invoice numbers, that is used to verify the completeness of data. The hash total of the invoice numbers is 810.
    Answer (A) is incorrect because a hash total is ordinarily the sum of a numeric field. Answer (B) is incorrect because 4 is a record count. Answer (C) is incorrect because 204 is an invoice number.

24. A customer intended to order 100 units of product Z96014, but incorrectly ordered nonexistent product Z96015. Which of the following controls most likely would detect this error?

    A. Check digit verification.

    B. Record count.

    C. Hash total.

    D. Redundant data check.

Answer (A) is correct. *(CPA, adapted)*
    REQUIRED: The control that would detect a nonexistent product number.
    DISCUSSION: Check digit verification is used to identify incorrect identification numbers. The digit is generated by applying an algorithm to the ID number. During input, the check digit is recomputed by applying the same algorithm to the entered ID number.
    Answer (B) is incorrect because a record count is a control total of the number of transactions in a batch. Answer (C) is incorrect because a hash total is a control total that is the sum of a field without a defined meaning. Answer (D) is incorrect because a redundant data check searches for duplicate information in a database.

25. Which of the following is an example of a validity check?

A. The computer ensures that a numerical amount in a record does not exceed some predetermined amount.

B. As the computer corrects errors and data are successfully resubmitted to the system, the causes of the errors are printed out.

C. The computer flags any transmission for which the control field value did not match that of an existing file record.

D. After data for a transaction are entered, the computer sends certain data back to the terminal for comparison with data originally sent.

Answer (C) is correct. *(CPA, adapted)*
REQUIRED: The example of a validity check.
DISCUSSION: Validity checks test identification numbers or transaction codes for validity by comparison with items already known to be correct or authorized. For example, a validity check may identify a transmission for which the control field value did not match a preexisting record in a file.
Answer (A) is incorrect because a limit check determines whether a numerical amount exceeds a predetermined amount. Answer (B) is incorrect because an error log or error listing identifies errors that were previously detected and subsequently corrected. Answer (D) is incorrect because a closed-loop verification sends certain data back to the terminal for comparison with data originally sent by the operator.

26. Able Co. uses an online sales order processing system to process its sales transactions. Able's sales data are electronically sorted and subjected to edit checks. A direct output of the edit checks most likely would be a

A. Report of all missing sales invoices.

B. File of all rejected sales transactions.

C. Printout of all user code numbers and passwords.

D. List of all voided shipping documents.

Answer (B) is correct. *(CPA, adapted)*
REQUIRED: The output of edit checks.
DISCUSSION: Edit checks test transactions prior to processing. Rejected transactions should be recorded in a file for evaluation, correction, and resubmission. Edit checks are applied to the sales transactions to test for completeness, reasonableness, validity, and other related issues prior to acceptance. A report of missing invoices, a printout of all user code numbers and passwords, and a list of all voided shipping documents are unlikely to be direct outputs of the edit routine.

27. In the accounting system of Acme Company, the amounts of cash disbursements entered at a computer terminal are transmitted to the computer, which immediately transmits the amounts back to the terminal for display on the terminal screen. This display enables the operator to

A. Establish the validity of the account number.

B. Verify the amount was entered accurately.

C. Verify the authorization of the disbursement.

D. Prevent the overpayment of the account.

Answer (B) is correct. *(CPA, adapted)*
REQUIRED: The effect of displaying the amounts entered at a terminal.
DISCUSSION: The display of the amounts entered is an input control that permits visual verification of the accuracy of the input by the operator. This is termed "closed-loop verification."
Answer (A) is incorrect because displaying the amounts entered at a terminal does not establish the validity of the account number. Answer (C) is incorrect because displaying the amounts entered at a terminal does not verify the authorization of the disbursement. Answer (D) is incorrect because displaying the amounts entered at a terminal does not prevent the overpayment of the account.

28. Which of the following input controls would prevent an incorrect state abbreviation from being accepted as legitimate data?

A. Reasonableness test.

B. Field check.

C. Digit verification check.

D. Validity check.

Answer (D) is correct. *(CPA, adapted)*
REQUIRED: The input control that will detect an incorrect abbreviation.
DISCUSSION: Validity checks are tests of identification numbers or transaction codes for validity by comparison with items already known to be correct or authorized.
Answer (A) is incorrect because reasonableness (relationship) checks consider the logical correctness of relationships among the values of data items on an input and the corresponding master file record. For example, it may be known that employee John Smith works only in departments A, C, or D. Thus, a reasonableness check could be performed to determine that the payroll record contains one of the likely department numbers. (In some texts, the term reasonableness check is defined to encompass limit checks.) Answer (B) is incorrect because field checks are tests of the characters in a field to verify that they are of an appropriate type for that field. For example, the field for a Social Security number cannot contain alphabetic characters. Answer (C) is incorrect because check digit verification is used to identify incorrect identification numbers. The digit is generated by applying an algorithm to the ID number.

14.4 Disaster Recovery and Business Continuity

29. In which of the following locations should a copy of the accounting system data backup of year-end information be stored?

A. Secure off-site location.

B. Data backup server in the network room.

C. Fireproof cabinet in the data network room.

D. Locked file cabinet in the accounting department.

Answer (A) is correct.   *(CPA, adapted)*
REQUIRED: The storage location of a copy of the accounting system data backup of year-end information.
DISCUSSION: The IT function should have a reconstruction and recovery plan that will allow it to regenerate important programs and data files. It should create backup (duplicate) copies of data files, databases, programs, and documentation. It should also store backup copies off-site and plan for auxiliary processing at another site.
Answer (B) is incorrect because the backup of year-end accounting system information should be stored off-site in a remote location. Answer (C) is incorrect because the backup of year-end accounting system information should be stored off-site in a remote location. Answer (D) is incorrect because the backup of year-end accounting system information should be stored off-site in a remote location.

30. Which of the following procedures should be included in the disaster recovery plan for an Information Technology department?

A. Replacement of personal computers for user departments.

B. Identification of critical applications.

C. Physical security of warehouse facilities.

D. Cross-training of operating personnel.

Answer (B) is correct.   *(CPA, adapted)*
REQUIRED: The disaster recovery procedure.
DISCUSSION: The IT function should have a reconstruction and recovery plan that will allow it to regenerate important programs and data files. It should create backup (duplicate) copies of data files, databases, programs, and documentation; store backup copies off-site; and plan for auxiliary processing at another site. Thus, the organization must undertake contingency planning and risk analysis. Management must determine how various processing disruptions may affect the entity. Risk analysis (1) identifies and prioritizes critical applications, (2) evaluates their organizational impact, (3) determines recovery time frames and minimum hardware platform requirements, (4) assesses insurance coverage, (5) identifies exposures and their implications, and (6) develops recovery plans.
Answer (A) is incorrect because replacement of personal computers is a procedure for upgrading computers, not disaster recovery. Answer (C) is incorrect because physical security may prevent a disaster but is not a specific recovery procedure. Answer (D) is incorrect because cross-training of operating personnel is not a specific recovery procedure.

31. An insurer has decentralized its information processing. Its regional processing centers are responsible for initiating policies, communicating with policyholders, and adjusting claims. The company has a regional center in an earthquake-prone area and is planning how to continue processing if that center, or any other single center, is unable to perform its processing. The company considered mirroring the data stored at each regional center at another center. A disadvantage of such an arrangement is

A. Lack of awareness at headquarters of the state of processing.

B. Increased cost and complexity of network traffic.

C. Interference of the mirrored data with original source data.

D. Confusion on the part of insurance agents about where customer data are stored.

Answer (B) is correct.   *(CIA, adapted)*
REQUIRED: The disadvantage of mirroring data across centers.
DISCUSSION: If data stored at one regional center are to mirror the data stored at another center, the most efficient method to ensure each center has the most current data is to transfer data across a network. Consequently, the cost of network traffic will increase dramatically. The complexity of the network will also increase as the network will need to provide a high level of security when transferring data.
Answer (A) is incorrect because headquarters can monitor the network on a real-time basis and have complete awareness of the state of processing. Answer (C) is incorrect because adequate controls will ensure that the mirrored data will not affect the source data. Answer (D) is incorrect because the location of the data is not relevant to the insurance agents. The agents will retrieve customer data through the network.

32. Which of the following best describes the primary reason that organizations develop contingency plans for their computer-based information systems operations?

    A. To ensure that they will be able to process vital transactions in the event of any type of disaster.

    B. To ensure the safety of important records.

    C. To help hold down the cost of insurance.

    D. To plan for sources of capital for recovery from any type of disaster.

Answer (A) is correct. *(CIA, adapted)*
    REQUIRED: The primary reason that organizations develop contingency plans for their IS operations.
    DISCUSSION: Many organizations have automated their operating, purchasing, receiving, and sales functions. Thus, they have developed contingency plans because continuity of operations is dependent upon the ability to properly process vital transactions in the event of a disaster.
    Answer (B) is incorrect because the safety of records is a secondary reason. Answer (C) is incorrect because the reduction of insurance costs is a secondary reason. Answer (D) is incorrect because planning for sources of capital is seldom included in disaster recovery planning.

33. In one company, the application systems must be in service 24 hours a day. The company's senior management and information systems management have worked hard to ensure that the information systems recovery plan supports the business disaster recovery plan. A crucial aspect of recovery planning for the company is ensuring that

    A. Organizational and operational changes are reflected in the recovery plans.

    B. Changes to systems are tested thoroughly before being placed into production.

    C. Management personnel can fill in for operations staff should the need arise.

    D. Capacity planning procedures accurately predict workload changes.

Answer (A) is correct. *(CIA, adapted)*
    REQUIRED: The crucial aspect of recovery planning.
    DISCUSSION: Recovery planning may be obsolete if it does not reflect organizational and operational changes. Thus, they should be regularly reviewed and updated. This process considers inadequacies in the existing plan, internal organizational changes, and changes in priorities or business directions.
    Answer (B) is incorrect because testing changes to systems thoroughly before being placed into production is not a part of recovery planning. Answer (C) is incorrect because operational staff would not be replaced by management personnel. Answer (D) is incorrect because forecasting workload changes accurately permits a company to minimize its information systems facility costs, but it is not a part of recovery planning.

34. When evaluating the downsizing of the plant materials inventory system, data center personnel considered a redundant array of inexpensive (or independent) disks (RAID) for the inventory database. One reason to use RAID is to ensure that

    A. If one drive fails, all data can still be reconstructed.

    B. All data are split evenly across pairs of drives.

    C. Before-and-after images are stored for all transactions.

    D. Write time is minimized to avoid concurrency conflicts.

Answer (A) is correct. *(CIA, adapted)*
    REQUIRED: The reason to use RAID.
    DISCUSSION: A disk array expedites data transfer and provides fault tolerance. It combines two or more drives with special controller circuitry and software to execute reads and writes as if only one disk drive existed. When files are stored on a RAID, data can be reconstructed even if one drive fails.
    Answer (B) is incorrect because splitting data evenly across pairs of drives (data striping) results in faster reads and writes but reduced reliability. The failure of one drive causes loss of all data. Answer (C) is incorrect because writing before-and-after images is a means of creating a transaction log for database transactions, which can be implemented with or without RAID. Answer (D) is incorrect because minimizing write time is not an advantage of RAID.

35. Which of the following procedures would an entity most likely include in its computer disaster recovery plan?

    A. Develop an auxiliary power supply to provide uninterrupted electricity.

    B. Store duplicate copies of critical files in a location away from the computer center.

    C. Maintain a listing of all entity passwords with the network manager.

    D. Translate data for storage purposes with a cryptographic secret code.

Answer (B) is correct. *(CPA, adapted)*
    REQUIRED: The most likely procedure to follow in a computer disaster recovery plan.
    DISCUSSION: Off-site storage of duplicate copies of critical files protects them from a fire or other disaster at the computing facility. The procedure is part of an overall disaster recovery plan.
    Answer (A) is incorrect because the use of an uninterruptible power supply assures continued processing rather than recovery from a disaster. Answer (C) is incorrect because maintaining a safeguarded copy of passwords protects against loss of passwords by personnel. Answer (D) is incorrect because encrypting stored data files protects them from unauthorized use.

STUDY UNIT FIFTEEN
INFORMATION TECHNOLOGY V

(10 pages of outline)

This study unit is the last of five covering information technology (IT). E-commerce is the purchase and sale of goods and services by electronic means. E-business is a more comprehensive term defined as all methods of conducting business electronically. E-commerce may occur via online transactions over public networks (e.g., the Internet), electronic data interchange (EDI), electronic funds transfer (EFT), and email. Moreover, even traditional point-of-sale (POS) transactions have become part of e-commerce through the use of IT methods that allow instant capture of business information.

15.1 ELECTRONIC COMMERCE

1. **E-business** is an umbrella term referring to all methods of conducting business electronically. This can include strictly internal communications as well as nonfinancial dealings with outside parties (e.g., contract negotiations).

   a. **E-commerce** is a narrower term referring to financial transactions with outside parties, e.g., the purchase and sale of goods and services.

      1) E-commerce comes in two basic varieties, business-to-business (B2B) and business-to-consumer (B2C). E-business and e-commerce are sometimes considered to be synonymous.

2. **Business-to-business commerce (B2B)** is not limited to EDI and other direct links between businesses but also involves activities within the broader electronic market.

   a. B2B involves working with vendors, distributors, and other businesses over the Internet.

   b. There are two types of B2B companies:

      1) **Vertical companies** work at all levels within an industry and mostly earn their revenues from advertising on a specialized sector or from transaction fees from the e-commerce they may host.

         a) Websites of vertical companies are the most likely to contain such community features as industry news, articles, and discussion groups.

      2) **Horizontal companies** operate across numerous industries.

         a) They provide products, goods, materials, or services that are not specific to a particular industry or company.

   c. **Benefits of B2B** include

      1) Reduced purchasing costs. Purchasing products online saves time, and electronically processing an order simplifies the ordering process.

      2) Increased market efficiency. By using the Internet, companies have easy access to price quotes from various suppliers. Buyers are more likely to get a better price, given the increased number of suppliers.

      3) Greater market intelligence. B2B provides producers with better insights into the demand levels in any given market.

4) Decreased inventory levels. Companies can make better use of their inventory and raw materials. The Internet allows companies using JIT manufacturing techniques to achieve better control of their operations, for example, by more precise coordination of delivery of raw materials. It also allows companies to use less working capital to do the same amount of work, which allows those funds to be invested elsewhere.

d. The overriding principle of online B2B is that it can make companies more efficient. Increased efficiency means lower costs, which is a goal that interests every company. Thus, the potential of B2B online commerce is enormous.

3. Because e-commerce transactions cross the boundaries of the enterprise, security is of primary concern.

   a. **Security issues** include

   1) The correct identification of the transacting parties (authentication)
   2) Determination of who may rightfully make binding agreements (authorization)
   3) Protecting the confidentiality and integrity of information
   4) Assuring the trustworthiness of listed prices and discounts
   5) Providing evidence of the transmission and receipt of documents
   6) Guarding against repudiation by the sender or recipient
   7) The proper extent of verification of payment data
   8) The best method of payment to avoid wrongdoing or disagreements
   9) Lost or duplicated transactions
   10) Determining who bears the risk of fraud

   b. **Responses to security issues** include

   1) Encryption and associated authentication methods, preferably by physically secure hardware rather than software
   2) Numerical sequencing to identify missing or false messages
   3) The capacity of the host computer to avoid downtime and repel attacks
   4) Nonrepudiation methods, such as digital certificates, which prove origination and delivery so that parties cannot disclaim responsibility for sending or receiving a message

      a) Sellers and buyers routinely provide acknowledgments and confirmations, respectively, in a website dialogue to avoid later disputes.

      b) In EDI (see Subunit 15.2), control over nonrepudiation is achieved by sequencing, encryption, and authentication.

   5) Adherence to legal requirements, such as privacy statutes
   6) Documenting trading agreements, especially the terms of trade and methods of authorization and authentication
   7) Agreements for end-to-end security and availability with providers of information services and value-added networks (see item 3.b. on page 436)
   8) Disclosure by public trading systems of their terms of business

4. Stop and review! You have completed the outline for this subunit. Study multiple-choice question 1 on page 443.

15.2 ELECTRONIC DATA INTERCHANGE (EDI)

1. **Electronic data interchange (EDI)** is the leading method of carrying on e-commerce.

    a. EDI involves the communication of data in format agreed to by the parties directly from a computer in one entity to a computer in another entity, for example, to order goods from a supplier or to transfer funds.

    b. EDI was the first step in the evolution of e-business.

        1) Successful EDI implementation begins with mapping the work processes and flows that support achievement of the organization's objectives.

        2) EDI was developed to enhance just-in-time (JIT) inventory management.

    c. **Advantages** of EDI include reduction of clerical errors, speed of transactions, and the elimination of repetitive clerical tasks, such as document preparation, processing, and mailing.

    d. **Disadvantages** of EDI include the following:

        1) Information may be insecure.

            a) Thus, end-to-end data encryption should be used to protect data during EDI.

        2) Data may be lost.

        3) Transmissions to trading partners may fail.

        4) EDI is less standardized and more costly than Internet-based commerce, which ordinarily uses XML.

            a) EDI requires programming expertise and leased telephone lines or the use of a value-added or third-party network, whereas XML is simple and easy to understand.

    e. An extension of EDI is computer-stored records, which can be less expensive than traditional physical file storage.

2. **Terms and components** of EDI include the following:

    a. Standards concern procedures to convert written documents into a standard electronic document-messaging format to facilitate EDI.

    b. Conventions are the procedures for arranging data elements in specified formats for various accounting transactions, e.g., invoices, materials releases, and advance shipment notices.

    c. A data dictionary prescribes the meaning of data elements, including specification of each transaction structure.

    d. Transmission protocols are rules used to determine how each electronic envelope is structured and processed by the communications devices.

        1) Normally, a group of accounting transactions is combined in an electronic envelope and transmitted into a communications network.

        2) Rules are required for the separation and transmission of envelopes.

3. **Methods of communication** between computers include the following:

    a. A point-to-point system requires the use of dedicated computers by all parties.

        1) Each computer must be designed to be compatible with the other(s). This system is very similar to a network within one company. Dedicated lines or modems are used.

  b. Value-added networks (VANs) are private, third-party providers of common interfaces between organizations.

    1) Subscribing to a VAN eliminates the need for one organization to establish direct computer communication with a trading partner.

    2) VANs provide translation of the sender's protocol (data configuration) to the receiver's protocol. Thus, the sender and receiver do not have to conform to the same standards, conventions, and protocols.

    3) Moreover, VANs eliminate the need for dedicated computers waiting for incoming messages.

    4) In addition, VANs store messages so companies can batch outgoing and incoming messages.

  c. An **extranet** is another means of carrying on e-commerce.

    1) Extranets rely on the established communications protocols of the Internet. Thus, the expensive, specialized equipment needed for EDI is unnecessary.

    2) **Firewalls**, special combinations of hardware and software [see item 3.a.6)c) in Subunit 13.2], provide security.

    3) The extranet approach is based on less formal agreements between the trading partners than in EDI and requires the sending firm to format the documents into the format of the receiving firm.

 4. The use of EDI has certain **implications for control**.

  a. EDI eliminates the paper documents, both internal and external, that are the traditional basis for many controls, including internal and external auditing.

  b. Moreover, an organization that has reengineered its processes to take full advantage of EDI may have eliminated even the electronic equivalents of paper documents.

    1) For example, the buyer's **point-of-sale (POS)** system may directly transmit information to the seller, which delivers on a JIT basis. Purchase orders, invoices, and receiving reports are eliminated and replaced with

      a) Evaluated receipts settlements (authorizations for automatic periodic payment);

      b) A long-term contract establishing quantities, prices, and delivery schedules;

      c) Production schedules;

      d) Advance ship notices; and

      e) Payments by EFT.

  c. Accordingly, auditors must seek new forms of evidence to support assertions about EDI transactions, whether it exists at the client organization, the trading partner, or a third party, such as a VAN.

    1) Examples of such evidence are

      a) The authorized paper purchase contract,

      b) An electronic completed production schedule image, and

      c) Internal and external evidence of evaluated receipts settlements sent to the trading partner.

    2) Auditors must evaluate digital signatures and reviews when testing controls.

    3) Auditors may need to consider other subsystems when testing a particular subsystem. Thus, production cycle evidence may be needed to test the expenditure cycle.

 5. Stop and review! You have completed the outline for this subunit. Study multiple-choice questions 2 through 12 beginning on page 443.

15.3 ELECTRONIC FUNDS TRANSFER (EFT)

1. EFT is a service provided by financial institutions worldwide that is based on electronic data interchange (EDI) technology.

    a. An EFT is a transfer of funds via an access device, i.e., an electronic terminal (e.g., ATM or POS terminal), telephone, computer, or magnetic tape (e.g., credit, debit, and check cards).

    b. EFT transaction costs are lower than for manual systems because documents and human intervention are eliminated from the transaction process. Moreover, transfer customarily requires less than a day.

    c. A typical consumer application of EFT is the **direct deposit** of payroll checks in employees' accounts or the automatic withdrawal of payments for cable and telephone bills, mortgages, etc.

2. The most important application of EFT is **check collection**. Because of the enormous volume of paper, the check-collection process has been computerized.

    a. The result has been to reduce the significance of paper checks because EFT provides means to make payments and deposit funds without manual transfer of negotiable instruments. Thus, wholesale EFTs among financial institutions and businesses (commercial transfers) are measured in the trillions of dollars.

        1) The two major systems for these "wire" or nonconsumer transfers are Fedwire (Federal Reserve wire transfer network) and CHIPS (New York Clearing House Interbank Payment System). Private systems also are operated by large banks.

3. The emergence of EFT systems offered by financial institutions created a need to refine consumer protection legislation. Hence, Congress enacted the **Electronic Fund Transfer Act of 1978 (EFTA)** to regulate electronic banking services.

    a. The primary purpose of the EFTA is to provide disclosure to consumers who use these services. EFT services include

        1) Automatic teller machines (ATMs),
        2) Point-of-sale systems (POS),
        3) Direct deposit and payment, and
        4) Payment by telephone (PBT).

    b. The EFTA applies to banks, savings and loan institutions, and credit unions. It does not cover commercial transfers.

    c. The act is implemented by the Federal Reserve through its Regulation E.

    d. The EFTA requires that the financial institution provide an easily understandable written contract explaining the system and the consumer's rights and duties. For each EFT, the financial institution must furnish a receipt for the transaction unless it is initiated by telephone. When a receipt is required, it must set forth the following:

        1) Amount involved,
        2) Date of the transaction,
        3) Type of transfer,
        4) Identity of the account,
        5) Identity of any third party from whom or to whom funds are transferred, and
        6) Location or identification of the electronic terminal involved.

    e. The EFTA also requires that the financial institution provide a statement, typically monthly, for each account accessible by EFT. The statement must set forth a record of transactions and must include

        1) The amount of fees or charges assessed for maintenance of the account,
        2) The balances of the account at the beginning and end of the period, and
        3) The address and telephone to be used in case of error.

f.   Customers have 60 days after receiving a statement to report errors. The financial institution then has 10 days after it receives a report of an error to investigate.

   1)   If an error is found, the bank has 1 day to correct it.

      a)   As an alternative, a financial institution may credit a customer's account and then have 45 days to investigate (in contrast with the 10-day limit).

g.   To protect consumers, the EFTA sets limits on liability. Consumers are liable for a maximum of $50 for unauthorized transfers.

   1)   A consumer may be liable for up to $500 if (s)he does not notify the bank within 2 business days after (s)he discovers the loss of an EFT card or personal identification number (PIN).

   2)   If the customer does not give notice within 60 days after receiving a statement showing the transfers, (s)he has unlimited liability.

4.   EFT differs from the use of **electronic money**, which may someday supplant traditional currency and coins.

a.   For example, stored-value cards (such as phone cards) are already in wide use.

b.   Smart cards contain computer chips rather than magnetized stripes. A smart card therefore can store data and security programs. It not only stores value but also authenticates transactions, such as by means of its digital signature.

   1)   A potentially important use of smart cards is to transmit funds over the Internet as part of online banking transactions. Currently, online (virtual) banks must receive most deposits in traditional ways.

c.   A disadvantage of electronic money is that most types are not covered by the insurance offered by the Federal Deposit Insurance Corporation (FDIC). Federal Reserve rules concerning EFT (Regulation E) also do not extend to electronic money.

   1)   Users of electronic money are protected by the Federal Trade Commission Act of 1914 (as amended). It empowers the FTC to protect consumers from "unfair or deceptive acts or practices in or affecting commerce."

   2)   Furthermore, common law principles, such as those pertaining to contracts and federal privacy laws, should apply.

d.   Methods other than providing a credit card number or using electronic money may be used to make electronic payments.

   1)   One such method is an online payment system (OPS), such as PayPal. A buyer makes a payment by a customary method to the OPS. The OPS then notifies the seller that payment has been made. The final step is to transfer the money to the seller's account.

   2)   Another method is the electronic wallet, which is a software application that stores credit card numbers and other personal information and is usually kept on the buyer's computer. As the buyer visits different websites, (s)he can refer to the wallet instead of providing all the information for each transaction.

5.   Stop and review! You have completed the outline for this subunit. Study multiple-choice questions 13 through 24 beginning on page 447.

15.4 POINT-OF-SALE (POS) TRANSACTIONS

1. Electronic POS systems permit **instant capture** (for example, by bar code scanning) and transmission of retail transactional information. For example, retail and grocery stores are equipped with POS terminals that allow the instant capture of sales data, resulting in realtime updating of inventory data and reporting of sales and cash collections. A POS system may

   a. Update and analyze the perpetual inventory records for each outlet

   b. Perform other accounting tasks, such as crediting revenue accounts and debiting cash, accounts receivable, and cost of goods sold

   c. Provide marketing information to

      1) Identify and respond to trends,
      2) Make sales forecasts,
      3) Determine which products are or are not in demand,
      4) Improve customer service,
      5) Target products and promotions to customers with different demographic traits,
      6) Evaluate the effects of promotions, including coupons

   d. Help control liquid assets

   e. Facilitate purchasing decisions

   f. Minimize costs

   g. Record personal and transactional information about specific customers, including tracking of warranties, deposits, rentals, progressive discounts, and special pricing

   h. Process all forms of payment, including credit cards

   i. Combine order processing and POS activities

   j. Use bar coding in association with the stocking and warehousing functions to reduce the costs of data entry, including the effects of human error

   k. Permit instant price changes

   l. Permit integration with Internet sales applications

2. Stop and review! You have completed the outline for this subunit. Study multiple-choice question 25 on page 450.

15.5 ELECTRONIC TRANSACTION SECURITY

1. **Encryption** technology is vital for the security and therefore the success of electronic commerce, especially with regard to transactions carried out over public networks.

   a. The sender's encryption program encodes the data prior to transmission. The recipient's program decodes it at the other end. Unauthorized users may be able to intercept the data but, without the encryption key, they will be unable to decode it.

      1) The machine instructions necessary to code and decode data can constitute a 20%-to-30% increase in system overhead.

   b. Two major types of encryption routine are in general use.

      1) **Private-key**, or symmetric, encryption is the less secure of the two because there is only one key. The single key must be revealed to both the sender and recipient.

      2) **Public-key**, or asymmetric, encryption is the more secure of the two. The public key used by the sender for encoding is widely known, but the related private key used by the recipient for decoding is known only to the recipient.

         a) The analogy is a post office box. The box number is known to all and anyone can send a letter to it, but only the box owner can retrieve the letters.

          b)   Since the public and private keys must form a mathematically related pair, a trusted third party is needed to issue the keys. Such a third party is called a certificate authority (CA). VeriSign is the best-known such issuer.

          c)   The most widely used public-key encryption method is RSA, named for its developers Rivest, Shamir, and Adelman.

2.   A **digital certificate** is another means of authentication used in e-commerce. The CA issues a coded electronic certificate that contains the holder's name, a copy of its public key, a serial number, and an expiration date. The certificate verifies the holder's identity.

    a.   The recipient of a coded message uses the CA's public key (available on the Internet) to decode the certificate included in the message. The recipient then determines that the certificate was issued by the CA. Moreover, the recipient can use the sender's public key and identification data to send a coded response.

    b.   Such methods might be used for transactions between sellers and buyers using credit cards. A certificate also may be used to provide assurance to customers that a website is genuine.

3.   Stop and review! You have completed the outline for this subunit. Study multiple-choice questions 26 through 32 beginning on page 451.

15.6 MALICIOUS SOFTWARE AND ATTACKS

1.   The problem of malicious software and attacks is not limited to e-commerce applications. However, it is especially important in this context because much e-commerce is conducted using publicly available systems.

    a.   Perfect security is not possible because system access cannot be eliminated without shutting down e-commerce.

    b.   Furthermore, the threats to e-commerce from malicious software and attacks are continually evolving as technology advances.

2.   **Malicious software (malware)** may exploit a known hole or weakness in an application or operating system program to evade security measures. This kind of vulnerability may have been caused by a programming error. It may also have been intentionally (but not maliciously) created to permit a programmer simple access (a back door) to the code.

    a.   Having bypassed security controls, the intruder can do immediate damage to the system or install malware.

          1)   A Trojan horse is an apparently innocent program (e.g., a spreadsheet) that includes a hidden function that may do damage when activated.

          2)   A virus is a program that copies itself from file to file. The virus may destroy data or programs. A common way of spreading a virus is by email attachments and downloads.

          3)   A worm copies itself not from file to file but from computer to computer, often very rapidly. Repeated replication overloads a system by depleting memory or overwhelming network traffic capacity.

          4)   A logic bomb is much like a Trojan horse except it activates only upon some occurrence, e.g., on a certain date.

          5)   A maliciously created back door can be used for subsequent high level access to data, computers, and networks.

          6)   Malware may create a denial of service by overwhelming a system or website with more traffic than it can handle.

              a)   In other cases, a malware infection may have little or no effects noticeable by users.

3. **Controls** to prevent or detect infection by malware are particularly significant for file servers in large networks. The following are broad control objectives:

    a. A policy should require use only of authorized software.

    b. A policy should require adherence to licensing agreements.

    c. A policy should create accountability for the persons authorized to maintain software.

    d. A policy should require safeguards when data or programs are obtained by means of external media.

    e. Antivirus software should continuously monitor the system for viruses (or worms) and eradicate them. It should also be immediately upgraded as soon as information about new threats becomes available.

    f. Software and data for critical systems should be regularly reviewed.

    g. Investigation of unauthorized files or amendments should be routine.

    h. Email attachments and downloads (and files on unauthorized media or from networks that are not secure) should be checked.

    i. Procedures should be established and responsibility assigned for coping with malware.

        1) Procedures should reflect an understanding that another organization that has transmitted malware-infected material may have done so unwittingly and may need assistance. If such events occur repeatedly, however, termination of agreements or contacts may be indicated.

        2) Procedures and policies should be documented, and employees must understand the reasons for them.

    j. Business continuity (disaster recovery) plans should be drafted, e.g., data and software backup.

    k. Information about malware should be verified and appropriate alerts given.

    l. Responsible personnel should be aware of the possibility of hoaxes, false messages intending to create fear of a malware attack. For example, a spurious email message may be received instructing users to delete supposedly compromised files.

    m. Qualified personnel should be relied upon to distinguish hoaxes from malware.

4. **Password attacks** attempt access to a system by stealing the passwords of legitimate users and then masquerading as those users.

    a. Two principal methods are used.

        1) A brute-force attack uses password-cracking software to try large numbers of letter and number combinations to access a network.

            a) A simple variation is the use of software that tries all the words in a dictionary.

        2) Passwords (and user accounts) also may be discovered by Trojan horses, IP spoofing, and packet sniffers.

            a) Spoofing is identity misrepresentation in cyberspace, for example, by using a false website to obtain information about visitors.

            b) Sniffing is use of software to eavesdrop on information sent by a user to the host computer of a website.

b. Once an attacker has access, (s)he may do anything the rightful user could have done.

 1) If the rightful user has privileged access, the attacker may create a back door to facilitate future entry despite password and status changes.

 2) The attacker also may be able to leverage the initial access to obtain greater privileges than the rightful user.

 3) If a user has the same password for multiple hosts, cracking the password for one host compromises the rest of them.

c. Effective methods of thwarting password attacks are one-time passwords and cryptographic authentication.

 1) The best standard passwords are randomly-generated 8-character or longer combinations of numbers, uppercase and lowercase letters, and special symbols.

 2) A disadvantage is that users often write down passwords that are hard to remember. However, software has been developed that encrypts passwords to be kept on a handheld computer. Thus, the user needs to know only one password.

5. A **man-in-the-middle attack** takes advantage of network packet sniffing and routing and transport protocols to access packets flowing through a network.

a. These attacks may be used to

 1) Steal data
 2) Obtain access to the network during a rightful user's active session
 3) Analyze the traffic on the network to learn about its operations and users
 4) Insert new data or modify the data being transmitted
 5) Deny service

b. Cryptography is the effective response to man-in-the-middle attacks. The encrypted data will be useless to the attacker unless it can be decrypted.

6. A **denial-of-service (DOS) attack** is an attempt to overload a system (e.g., a network or Web server) with messages so that it cannot function (a system crash).

a. A distributed DOS attack comes from multiple sources, for example, the machines of innocent parties infected by Trojan horses. When activated, these programs send messages to the target and leave the connection open.

b. A DOS may establish as many network connections as possible to exclude other users, overload primary memory, or corrupt file systems.

7. All organizations involved in electronic commerce must have an **intrusion detection system (IDS)**. The goal of an IDS is to detect breaches of an organization's information security regime before they can do damage.

a. An IDS examines user log files and patterns of traffic over the organization's network to catch suspicious activity. The IDS alerts IT personnel who can then take the appropriate action.

8. Stop and review! You have completed the outline for this subunit. Study multiple-choice questions 33 through 45 beginning on page 453.

QUESTIONS

15.1 Electronic Commerce

1. Common security issues that must be addressed with electronic commerce transactions include

A. Authentication, authorization, confidentiality, and verification.

B. Encryption, repudiation, sequencing, and downtime.

C. Disclosure, duplicate transactions, risk of fraud, and transmission protocols.

D. Prices and discounts, evidence of transmission, digital certificates, and trading agreements.

Answer (A) is correct. *(Publisher, adapted)*
REQUIRED: The security issues relevant to e-commerce.
DISCUSSION: Security issues in electronic commerce include

1) The correct identification of the transacting parties (authentication)
2) Determination of who may rightfully make binding agreements (authorization)
3) Protecting the confidentiality and integrity of information
4) Assuring the trustworthiness of listed prices and discounts
5) Providing evidence of the transmission and receipt of documents
6) Guarding against repudiation by the sender or recipient
7) The proper extent of verification of payment data
8) The best method of payment to avoid wrongdoing or disagreements
9) Lost or duplicated transactions
10) Determining who bears the risk of fraud

Answer (B) is incorrect because encryption and sequencing are responses to security issues, not issues in themselves; downtime is a global issue for all systems, not just e-commerce. Answer (C) is incorrect because disclosure of terms of business by public trading systems is a response to security issues, not a security issue in itself; transmission protocols are a component of any communication system. Answer (D) is incorrect because digital certificates and trading agreements are responses to security issues, not issues in themselves.

15.2 Electronic Data Interchange (EDI)

2. A company using EDI made it a practice to track the functional acknowledgments from trading partners and to issue warning messages if acknowledgments did not occur within a reasonable length of time. What risk was the company attempting to address by this practice?

A. Transactions that have not originated from a legitimate trading partner may be inserted into the EDI network.

B. Transmission of EDI transactions to trading partners may sometimes fail.

C. There may be disagreement between the parties as to whether the EDI transactions form a legal contract.

D. EDI data may not be accurately and completely processed by the EDI software.

Answer (B) is correct. *(CIA, adapted)*
REQUIRED: The EDI risk addressed by tracking functional acknowledgments from trading partners.
DISCUSSION: Tracking of customers' functional acknowledgments, when required, will help to ensure successful transmission of EDI transactions. Possible controls include: the provision of end-to-end acknowledgments, particularly when multiple, interconnected networks are involved; and maintenance of a tickler file of outstanding functional acknowledgments, with issuance of warnings for those that are overdue.

Answer (A) is incorrect because unauthorized access to the EDI system should be prevented by procedures that ensure the effective use of passwords, and data integrity and privacy should be maintained through the use of encryption and authentication measures. Answer (C) is incorrect because contractual issues should be resolved by the company and its trading partners before EDI is implemented. Answer (D) is incorrect because the risk that EDI data may not be completely and accurately processed is minimized by system-based controls, not by acknowledgments from trading partners.

3. The emergence of electronic data interchange (EDI) as standard operating practice increases the risk of

    A. Unauthorized third-party access to systems.

    B. Systematic programming errors.

    C. Inadequate knowledge bases.

    D. Unsuccessful system use.

Answer (A) is correct.   *(CIA, adapted)*
    REQUIRED: The risk increased by the emergence of EDI as standard operating practice.
    DISCUSSION: EDI is the communication of electronic documents directly from a computer in one entity to a computer in another entity. EDI for business documents between unrelated parties has the potential to increase the risk of unauthorized third-party access to systems because more outsiders will have access to internal systems.
    Answer (B) is incorrect because systematic programming errors are the result of misspecification of requirements or lack of correspondence between specifications and programs. Answer (C) is incorrect because inadequate knowledge bases are a function of lack of care in building them. Answer (D) is incorrect because a benefit of EDI is to improve the efficiency and effectiveness of system use.

4. Electronic data interchange (EDI) offers significant benefits to organizations, but it is not without certain major obstacles. Successful EDI implementation begins with which of the following?

    A. Mapping the work processes and flows that support the organization's goals.

    B. Purchasing new hardware for the EDI system.

    C. Selecting reliable vendors for translation and communication software.

    D. Standardizing transaction formats and data.

Answer (A) is correct.   *(CIA, adapted)*
    REQUIRED: The initial phase of EDI implementation.
    DISCUSSION: Marked benefits arise when EDI is tied to strategic efforts that alter, not mirror, previous practices. Applying EDI to an inefficient process results in continuing to do things the wrong way, only faster. Hence, the initial phase of EDI implementation includes understanding the organization's mission and an analysis of its activities as part of an integrated solution to the organization's needs.
    Answer (B) is incorrect because the prerequisite for EDI success is an understanding of the mission of the business and the processes and flows that support its goals, followed by cooperation with external partners. Purchasing new hardware is a subsequent step. Answer (C) is incorrect because, before applying EDI technology to the business, EDI must be viewed as part of an overall integrated solution to organizational requirements. Answer (D) is incorrect because EDI is not a solution by itself. Instead of considering how to transmit and receive transactions, a company must first analyze the entire process.

5. The best approach for minimizing the likelihood of EDI software incompatibilities leading to unintelligible messages is for a company and its customers to

    A. Acquire their software from the same software vendor.

    B. Agree to synchronize their updating of EDI-related software.

    C. Agree to use the same software in the same ways indefinitely.

    D. Each write their own version of the EDI-related software.

Answer (B) is correct.   *(CIA, adapted)*
    REQUIRED: The best approach for minimizing the likelihood of software incompatibilities leading to unintelligible messages.
    DISCUSSION: EDI entails the exchange of common business data converted into standard message formats. Thus, two crucial requirements are that the participants agree on transaction formats and that translation software be developed to convert messages into a form understandable by other companies. Thus, if one company changes its software, its trading partners also must do so.
    Answer (A) is incorrect because the company and its customers may obtain their EDI-related software from the same vendor but still have software incompatibility problems if they do not synchronize their installation of updated versions. Answer (C) is incorrect because, as business requirements change, it may not be possible to use the same software in the same ways indefinitely. Answer (D) is incorrect because, even if the company and its customers each write their own versions, synchronization problems will arise from updates.

6. Organizations that move to implement EDI often use value-added networks (VANs). Which of the following is not normally performed by a VAN?

A. Store electronic purchase orders of one organization to be accessed by another organization.

B. Provide common interfaces across organizations, thereby eliminating the need for one organization to establish direct computer communication with a trading partner.

C. Maintain a log of all transactions of an organization with its trading partner.

D. Provide translations from clients' computer applications to a standard protocol used for EDI communication.

Answer (D) is correct. *(CIA, adapted)*
REQUIRED: The function not performed by a VAN.
DISCUSSION: Companies must purchase their own software to translate their data to a national standard protocol for EDI purposes, either ANSI X.12 in the U.S. or UN/EDIFACT in Europe and most of the rest of the world. Once the data are in the standard format, the VAN handles all aspects of the communication. VANs are privately-owned telecommunications carriers that sell capacity to outside users. Among other things, a VAN provides a mailbox service permitting EDI messages to be sent, sorted, and held until needed in the recipient's computer system.
Answer (A) is incorrect because VANs normally provide mailbox services. Answer (B) is incorrect because VANs normally provide common communication interfaces. Answer (C) is incorrect because VANs normally provide logs of transactions.

7. Which of the following statements is true concerning the security of messages in an electronic data interchange (EDI) system?

A. When confidentiality of data is the primary risk, message authentication is the preferred control rather than encryption.

B. Encryption performed by physically secure hardware devices is more secure than encryption performed by software.

C. Message authentication in EDI systems performs the same function as segregation of duties in other information systems.

D. Security in the transaction phase of EDI systems is not necessary because problems at that level will usually be identified by the service provider.

Answer (B) is correct. *(CPA, adapted)*
REQUIRED: The true statement about the security of messages in an EDI system.
DISCUSSION: Physically secure hardware devices for performing encryption are under the direct control of the client. Software is not easily controlled because it is portable. More control is achieved with the hardware approach.
Answer (A) is incorrect because, when confidentiality is a concern, encryption and access controls should be used. Answer (C) is incorrect because authentication relates to authorization, not message security. Answer (D) is incorrect because security in the EDI transaction phase is also an issue. The transmission of information to the service provider, such as a VAN, is subject to a variety of problems, for example, interception or alteration, that may not be detected by the service provider.

8. Which of the following are essential elements of the audit trail in an electronic data interchange (EDI) system?

A. Network and sender/recipient acknowledgments.

B. Message directories and header segments.

C. Contingency and disaster recovery plans.

D. Trading partner security and mailbox codes.

Answer (A) is correct. *(CPA, adapted)*
REQUIRED: The essential element in an EDI audit trail.
DISCUSSION: An audit trail allows for the tracing of a transaction from initiation to conclusion. Network and sender/recipient acknowledgments relate to the transaction flow and provide for the tracking of transactions.
Answer (B) is incorrect because message directories and header segments provide information controlling the message, such as originating and destination stations, message type and priority level, which are part of the message and not the audit trail. Answer (C) is incorrect because, although contingency and disaster recovery plans are important controls, they do not relate to the audit trail. Answer (D) is incorrect because, although maintaining control over security and mailbox codes is an important control, it does not relate to the audit trail.

9. Which of the following statements is true concerning internal control in an electronic data interchange (EDI) system?

A. Preventive controls generally are more important than detective controls in EDI systems.

B. Control objectives for EDI systems generally are different from the objectives for other information systems.

C. Internal controls in EDI systems rarely permit control risk to be assessed at below the maximum.

D. Internal controls related to the segregation of duties generally are the most important controls in EDI systems.

Answer (A) is correct. *(CPA, adapted)*
REQUIRED: The true statement about EDI controls.
DISCUSSION: In general, preventive controls are more important than detective controls because the benefits typically outweigh the costs. In electronic processing, once a transaction is accepted, there is often little opportunity to apply detective controls. Thus, it is important to prevent errors or frauds before they happen.
Answer (B) is incorrect because the basic control objectives are the same regardless of the nature of the processing: to ensure the integrity of the information and to safeguard the assets. Answer (C) is incorrect because, to gather sufficient evidence in a sophisticated computer system, it is often necessary to rely on the controls. Control risk may be assessed at below the maximum if relevant controls are identified and tested and if the resulting evidential matter provides the degree of assurance necessary to support the assessed level of control risk. Answer (D) is incorrect because the level of segregation of duties achieved in a manual system is usually not feasible in a computer system.

10. After a company implements EDI to communicate with its customers, an appropriate control for ensuring authenticity of the electronic orders it receives is to

A. Encrypt sensitive messages such as electronic payments for raw materials received.

B. Perform reasonableness checks on quantities ordered before filling orders.

C. Verify the identity of senders and determine whether orders correspond to contract terms.

D. Acknowledge receipt of electronic payments with a confirming message.

Answer (C) is correct. *(CIA, adapted)*
REQUIRED: The control for ensuring the authenticity of the electronic orders the company receives.
DISCUSSION: An EDI system is subject not only to the usual risk exposures for computer systems but also to those arising from the potential ineffectiveness of control on the part of the trading partner and the third-party service provider. Accordingly, authentication of users and messages received is a major security concern.
Answer (A) is incorrect because encrypting sensitive messages sent is an appropriate step but does not apply to messages received. Answer (B) is incorrect because performing reasonableness checks on quantities ordered before placing orders is a control for ensuring the correctness of the company's own orders, not the authenticity of its customers' orders. Answer (D) is incorrect because acknowledging receipt of electronic payments with a confirming message is good practice but will not authenticate orders from customers.

11. Which of the following is usually a benefit of transmitting transactions in an electronic data interchange (EDI) environment?

A. A compressed business cycle with lower year-end receivables balances.

B. A reduced need to test computer controls related to sales and collections transactions.

C. An increased opportunity to apply statistical sampling techniques to account balances.

D. No need to rely on third-party service providers to ensure security.

Answer (A) is correct. *(CPA, adapted)*
REQUIRED: The benefit of EDI.
DISCUSSION: EDI transactions are typically transmitted and processed in real time. Thus, EDI compresses the business cycle by eliminating delays. The time required to receive and process an order, ship goods, and receive payment is greatly reduced compared with that of a typical manual system. Accordingly, more rapid receipt of payment minimizes receivables and improves cash flow.
Answer (B) is incorrect because use of a sophisticated processing system would increase the need to test computer controls. Answer (C) is incorrect because computer technology allows all transactions to be tested rather than just a sample. Answer (D) is incorrect because EDI often uses a VAN (value-added network) as a third-party service provider, and reliance on controls provided by the VAN may be critical.

12. If the cycle time for manual purchase orders is 25 days, composed of 4 days of preparation, 3 days in the mail, 14 days in process at the supplier, and 4 days for delivery of raw materials, the shortest possible cycle time if a company fully implemented EDI with suppliers would be

A. 21 days.

B. 18 days.

C. 4 days.

D. 1 day.

Answer (C) is correct. *(CIA, adapted)*
REQUIRED: The shortest possible time for the purchase order cycle when an EDI is implemented.
DISCUSSION: The full implementation of an EDI system will eliminate the manufacturer's preparation time for purchase orders, the days in the mail, and processing by the supplier. The only time required will be the 4 days for physical delivery. An EDI system allows for the computer-to-computer exchange of transaction documents such as purchase orders, invoices, and shipping documents. It eliminates the printing and handling of paper by one party and the input of data by the other.
Answer (A) is incorrect because a cycle time of 21 days does not include reductions possible by using EDI to eliminate mail time and supplier processing time. Answer (B) is incorrect because a cycle time of 18 days does not include reductions possible by using EDI to eliminate supplier processing time. Answer (D) is incorrect because the cycle time cannot be reduced below the delivery time of 4 days with implementation of EDI alone. More efficient transportation would be required.

15.3 Electronic Funds Transfer (EFT)

13. Which of the following is normally a benefit of using electronic funds transfer (EFT)?

A. Improvement of the audit trail for cash receipts and disbursements.

B. Creation of self-monitoring access controls.

C. Reduction of the frequency of data entry errors.

D. Off-site storage of source documents for cash transactions.

Answer (C) is correct. *(CPA, adapted)*
REQUIRED: The benefit of using EFT for international cash transactions.
DISCUSSION: The processing and transmission of electronic transactions, such as EFTs, virtually eliminates human interaction. This process not only helps eliminate errors but also allows for the rapid detection and recovery from errors when they do occur.
Answer (A) is incorrect because the audit trail is typically less apparent in an electronic environment than in a manual environment. Answer (B) is incorrect because a key control is management's establishment and monitoring of access controls. Answer (D) is incorrect because source documents are often eliminated in EFT transactions.

14. A manufacturing company that wanted to be able to place material orders more efficiently most likely would utilize which of the following?

A. Electronic check presentment.

B. Electronic data interchange (EDI).

C. Automated clearinghouse (ACH).

D. Electronic funds transfer (EFT).

Answer (B) is correct. *(CPA, adapted)*
REQUIRED: The method used for placing material orders more efficiently.
DISCUSSION: Electronic data interchange (EDI) is the communication of electronic documents directly from a computer in one entity to a computer in another entity, for example, to order goods from a supplier or to transfer funds. EDI was developed to enhance JIT (just-in-time) inventory management.
Answer (A) is incorrect because an electronic check presentment makes the payment process more efficient. Answer (C) is incorrect because automated clearinghouses (ACHs) are electronic networks that facilitate the reading of data among banks. Answer (D) is incorrect because EFT expedites cash flows.

15. Which of the following risks is not greater in an electronic funds transfer (EFT) environment than in a manual system using paper transactions?

A. Unauthorized access and activity.

B. Duplicate transaction processing.

C. High cost per transaction.

D. Inadequate backup and recovery capabilities.

Answer (C) is correct. *(CIA, adapted)*
REQUIRED: The risk not greater in an EFT environment than in a manual system using paper transactions.
DISCUSSION: EFT is a service provided by financial institutions worldwide that is based on EDI technology. EFT transaction costs are lower than for manual systems because documents and human intervention are eliminated from the transaction process.
Answer (A) is incorrect because unauthorized access and activity is a risk specific to EFT. Answer (B) is incorrect because inaccurate transaction processing (including duplication) is a risk specific to EFT. Answer (D) is incorrect because inadequate backup and recovery capabilities is a risk specific to EFT.

16. Which one of the following is not a reason for a company to use EFT with an EDI system?

A. To take advantage of the time lag associated with negotiable instruments.

B. To allow the company to negotiate discounts with EDI vendors based upon prompt payment.

C. To improve its cash management program.

D. To reduce input time and input errors.

Answer (A) is correct. *(CIA, adapted)*
REQUIRED: The item not a reason for using EFT.
DISCUSSION: The float period is the time lag between transmittal of a regular check (a negotiable instrument) and its clearance through regular banking channels. Float is eliminated by EFT.
Answer (B) is incorrect because payment schedules may be based on the time required to process invoices, prepare checks, and transmit checks. Using EFT, payment is instantaneous, and payment schedules can be based on other criteria, e.g., discounts for prompt payment. Answer (C) is incorrect because EFT allows for more effective control of payments and transfers among accounts. Answer (D) is incorrect because integration of EDI and EFT eliminates manual input of transaction data, a process that introduces errors into the accounting system.

17. Which of the following significantly encouraged the development of electronic funds transfer systems?

I. Response to competition
II. Cost containment
III. Advances in information technology
IV. Improvements in automated control techniques
V. The development of data encryption standards

A. I, II, and IV.

B. II, III, and IV.

C. II, IV, and V.

D. I, II, and III.

Answer (D) is correct. *(CIA, adapted)*
REQUIRED: The items that most significantly encouraged the development of EFTs.
DISCUSSION: Competition has been a strong motivator in the financial services industry in the development of EFT systems, which are an application of EDI. Furthermore, containing costs in a highly competitive industry can be aided by leveraging information technology. Finally, advances in information technology, especially the wide acceptance of telecommunications standards and protocols, have made EFT systems possible.
Answer (A) is incorrect because improvements in automated control techniques follow from the development of information technology, and because advances in technology contributed to the development of EFT. Answer (B) is incorrect because improvements in automated control techniques follow from the development of information technology. Answer (C) is incorrect because data encryption standards are a response to the increase in the use of telecommunications technology.

18. Which of the following represents the greatest exposure to the integrity of electronic funds transfer data transmitted from a remote terminal?

A. Poor physical access controls over the data center.

B. Network viruses.

C. Poor system documentation.

D. Leased telephone circuits.

Answer (D) is correct. *(CIA, adapted)*
REQUIRED: The greatest exposure to the integrity of EFT data transmitted from a remote terminal.
DISCUSSION: Leased telephone circuits represent a direct exposure to the risk of breached data integrity. Leased lines are public lines that can be easily identified and tapped.
Answer (A) is incorrect because poor physical access controls represent a secondary exposure for compromise of remote data communication lines. Answer (B) is incorrect because network viruses represent a secondary exposure for compromise of remote data communication lines. Answer (C) is incorrect because poor system documentation represents a secondary exposure for compromise of remote data communication lines.

19. The Electronic Fund Transfer Act (EFTA) is consumer legislation that would not apply to transactions originated through

A. Point-of-sale terminals (POS).

B. Automated tellers (ATM).

C. Machine-generated checks.

D. Transfers by telephone (or pay-by-phone).

Answer (C) is correct. *(Publisher, adapted)*
REQUIRED: The item to which the EFTA is not applicable.
DISCUSSION: An electronic fund transfer is a "transfer of funds, other than a transaction originated by check, draft, or similar paper instrument, initiated through an electronic terminal, telephonic instrument, or computer or magnetic tape so as to order, instruct, or authorize a financial institution to debit or credit an account." The EFTA does not apply to machine-generated checks (negotiable instruments regulated by UCC Articles 3 and 4).
Answer (A) is incorrect because point-of-sale devices are within the EFTA. Answer (B) is incorrect because transactions originated in automated tellers are within the EFTA. Answer (D) is incorrect because transfers by telephone are within the EFTA.

20. The EFTA requires financial institutions to provide their customers with written documentation of electronic fund transfers at various times, including all of the following except

- A. On a periodic basis, usually monthly, in the form of a statement.
- B. At the time of each use of an automated teller.
- C. At the time of each preauthorized credit to an account.
- D. At the time of contracting for EFT services.

Answer (C) is correct. *(Publisher, adapted)*
REQUIRED: The occasion not requiring the generation of written documentation of an electronic fund transfer.
DISCUSSION: An individual may arrange with a financial institution to have transfers made to his/her account. The financial institution and consumer may agree that written notification will be given only when a scheduled credit is not actually made.

21. Under the EFTA, a financial institution holding a customer's account that may be accessed by electronic means must furnish the customer with periodic statements. If the customer discovers an error, the financial institution must comply with certain procedures prescribed by the act. Which of the following is true?

- A. A customer will collect treble damages if the institution is in error.
- B. The institution may not require written notice of the error.
- C. The institution must recredit the customer's account pending an investigation.
- D. After proper notice, the institution is obligated to investigate.

Answer (D) is correct. *(Publisher, adapted)*
REQUIRED: The true statement about the error resolution procedure under the EFTA.
DISCUSSION: The customer has 60 days to give an oral or written notice of errors in its account, but the institution may require written confirmation within 10 business days of receiving an oral notice. The notice obligates the institution to investigate and report within 10 business days. Any error must be corrected within 1 business day after its discovery. Instead, the institution may temporarily recredit the account within 10 business days of receipt of notice. If it chooses this alternative, it has 45 business days from receipt of notice to complete the investigation. If it finds no error, the institution has 3 business days to mail an explanation to the customer. Failure to adhere to the prescribed procedures or a knowing and willful conclusion (despite the evidence) that the account was not erroneous permits the customer to recover treble damages.
Answer (A) is incorrect because treble damages are available only for failure to follow the rules to resolve an error. Answer (B) is incorrect because written notice may be required. Answer (C) is incorrect because the institution can investigate first if it finishes within 10 days.

22. Hannah Palindrome became aware of the loss of her automated teller card on Monday evening, March 3. The financial statements mailed to Hannah on April 1, May 1, and June 1 showed a $60 withdrawal on March 4 and a $600 withdrawal on March 9 but no other activity in the account. Assuming that the main provisions of the EFTA apply, Hannah is liable for

- A. $660 if she reports the loss on June 15.
- B. $50 if she reports the loss on May 15.
- C. $600 if she reports the loss on March 21.
- D. $50 if she reports the loss on March 19.

Answer (A) is correct. *(Publisher, adapted)*
REQUIRED: The liability of a consumer for an unauthorized electronic fund transfer.
DISCUSSION: The consumer's liability is limited to the lesser of $50 or the amount transferred without authorization prior to notifying the financial institution. If the consumer fails to notify the institution within 2 business days after learning of the loss of the means of access, his/her liability is the lesser of $500 or the amount transferred without authorization after 2 business days following discovery of the loss but prior to notification of the institution. If the consumer does not report an unauthorized transfer or error within 60 days of the transmission of a financial statement containing such a transaction or error, the consumer bears the loss. Consequently, if Hannah does not report the loss until June 15, her liability is $660.
Answer (B) is incorrect because Hannah's liability would be $500 if she reports the loss on May 15. Answer (C) is incorrect because Hannah's liability would be $500 if she reports the loss on March 21. Answer (D) is incorrect because Hannah's liability would be $50 if she reported the loss within 2 business days.

23. Under the EFTA, a financial institution will avoid liability to its customer for failure to

A. Make a transfer in the proper amount.

B. Make a timely transfer if the terminal does not have sufficient funds.

C. Credit a deposit of funds.

D. Stop payment on a preauthorized transfer when the customer has given sufficient notice.

Answer (B) is correct. *(Publisher, adapted)*
REQUIRED: The instance in which a financial institution avoids liability under the EFTA.
DISCUSSION: The institution will not be liable when the terminal lacked the cash to complete the transaction or the customer's account had insufficient funds. Except in the case of stop-payment orders, the institution also may defend by proving that an act of nature or a technical malfunction known to the customer at the time (s)he attempted the transaction caused the failure.
Answer (A) is incorrect because, in general, the financial institution is liable in damages when it fails to make a timely transfer, within the terms of the agreement with the customer, in the correct amount. Answer (C) is incorrect because the financial institution is liable when it fails to credit a deposit. Answer (D) is incorrect because the financial institution is liable when it does not stop payment of a preauthorized transfer (a transfer authorized in advance to be repeated at specified intervals).

24. Companies now can use electronic transfers to conduct regular business transactions. Which of the following terms best describes a system in which an agreement is made between two or more parties to electronically transfer purchase orders, sales orders, invoices, and/or other financial documents?

A. Electronic mail (email).

B. Electronic funds transfer (EFT).

C. Electronic data interchange (EDI).

D. Electronic data processing (EDP).

Answer (C) is correct. *(CIA, adapted)*
REQUIRED: The term best describing electronic transfer of documents.
DISCUSSION: Electronic data interchange is the electronic transfer of documents between businesses. EDI was developed to enhance just-in-time (JIT) inventory management. Advantages include speed, reduction of clerical errors, and elimination of repetitive clerical tasks and their costs.
Answer (A) is incorrect because email can send text or document files, but the term encompasses a wide range of transfers. EDI specifically applies to the system described in the question. Answer (B) is incorrect because electronic funds transfer (EFT) refers to the transfer of money. Answer (D) is incorrect because electronic data processing (EDP) is a generic term for computerized processing of transaction data within organizations.

15.4 Point-of-Sale (POS) Transactions

25. Advanced electronic point-of-sale (POS) systems allow instant capture and transmission of information for which purposes?

I. Instant updating of accounting records
II. Accumulation of marketing information
III. Tracking of information about specific customers
IV. Facilitation of warehousing

A. I and II only.

B. III and IV only.

C. I, II, and III only.

D. I, II, III, and IV.

Answer (D) is correct. *(Publisher, adapted)*
REQUIRED: The functions of an electronic POS system.
DISCUSSION: An electronic POS system may update and analyze the perpetual inventory records for each outlet. It may also perform other accounting tasks, such as crediting revenue accounts and debiting cash, accounts receivable, and cost of goods sold. Moreover, a POS system may (1) provide marketing information to identify and respond to trends; (2) make sales forecasts; (3) determine which products are in demand; (4) improve customer service; (5) target products and promotions to customers with different demographic traits; and (6) evaluate the effects of promotions, including coupons. Another function of a POS system is to record personal and transactional information about specific customers, including tracking of warranties, deposits, rentals, progressive discounts, and special pricing. Still another function is use of bar coding in association with the stocking and warehousing functions to reduce the costs of data entry, including the effects of human error.

15.5 Electronic Transaction Security

26. The use of message encryption software

A. Guarantees the secrecy of data.

B. Requires manual distribution of keys.

C. Increases system overhead.

D. Reduces the need for periodic password changes.

Answer (C) is correct. *(CIA, adapted)*
REQUIRED: The effect of message encryption software.
DISCUSSION: Encryption software uses a fixed algorithm to manipulate plaintext and an encryption key (a set of random data bits used as a starting point for application of the algorithm) to introduce variation. The machine instructions necessary to encrypt and decrypt data constitute system overhead. As a result, processing speed may be slowed.
Answer (A) is incorrect because no encryption approach absolutely guarantees the secrecy of data. Answer (B) is incorrect because keys may also be distributed electronically via secure key transporters. Answer (D) is incorrect because periodic password changes are needed. Passwords are the typical means of validating users' access to unencrypted data.

27. What is a major disadvantage to using a private key to encrypt data?

A. Both sender and receiver must have the private key before this encryption method will work.

B. The private key cannot be broken into fragments and distributed to the receiver.

C. The private key is used by the sender for encryption but not by the receiver for decryption.

D. The private key is used by the receiver for decryption but not by the sender for encryption.

Answer (A) is correct. *(CPA, adapted)*
REQUIRED: The major disadvantage of private-key encryption.
DISCUSSION: Secret-key encryption requires only a single key for each pair of parties who want to exchange coded messages. Public-key/private-key encryption requires two keys: The public key for coding messages is widely known, but the private key for decoding messages is kept secret by the recipient. Accordingly, the parties must use pairs of public and private keys. The sender searches a directory for the recipient's public key, uses it to code the message, and transmits the message to the recipient. The latter uses the related private key to decode the message. One advantage is that the message is encoded using one key and decoded using another. In contrast, private-key encryption requires both parties to know and use the secret key. A second advantage is that neither party knows the other's private key. The related public key and private key pair is issued by a certificate authority (CA), that is, a third-party fiduciary. However, the private key is issued only to one party. Thus, key management in a secret-key system is less secure because the parties must agree on, transmit, and handle the one secret key.
Answer (B) is incorrect because the private key can be transmitted in fragments. Answer (C) is incorrect because the private key is used by both parties. Answer (D) is incorrect because the private key is used by both parties.

28. The encryption technique that requires two keys, a public key that is available to anyone for encrypting messages and a private key that is known only to the recipient for decrypting messages, is

A. Rivest, Shamir, and Adelman (RSA).

B. Data encryption standard (DES).

C. Modulator-demodulator.

D. A cypher lock.

Answer (A) is correct. *(CIA, adapted)*
REQUIRED: The encryption technique requiring two keys.
DISCUSSION: RSA is an encryption standard licensed to hardware and software vendors. Public-key encryption requires management of fewer keys for a given client-server environment than does private-key encryption. However, compared with DES, RSA entails more complex computations and therefore has a higher processing overhead. RSA requires two keys: The public key for encrypting messages is widely known, but the private key for decrypting messages is kept secret by the recipient.
Answer (B) is incorrect because DES is a shared private-key method developed by the U.S. government. It encrypts data into 64-bit blocks using a 56-bit key. DES requires only a single key for each pair of parties that want to send each other encrypted messages. DES is being replaced by AES, Advanced Encryption Standard, as the method of choice by the U.S. government. Answer (C) is incorrect because a modem is used for telecommunications. Answer (D) is incorrect because a cypher lock is a physical device.

29. A digital signature is used primarily to determine that a message is

- A. Unaltered in transmission.
- B. Not intercepted en route.
- C. Received by the intended recipient.
- D. Sent to the correct address.

Answer (A) is correct.   *(CPA, adapted)*
    REQUIRED: The primary use of a digital signature.
    DISCUSSION: A public-key/private-key encryption system is used to create digital signatures (fingerprints). A digital signature is a means of authentication of an electronic document, for example, of the validity of a purchase order, acceptance of a contract, or financial information. The sender uses its private key to encode all or part of the message, and the recipient uses the sender's public key to decode it. Hence, if that key decodes the message, the sender must have written it. One variation is to send the message in both plaintext and cyphertext. If the decoded version matches the plaintext version, no alteration has occurred.
    Answer (B) is incorrect because encryption of text does not prevent its interception. Answer (C) is incorrect because encryption of text does not ensure its receipt by the intended recipient. Answer (D) is incorrect because encryption of text does not ensure that it will be sent to the correct address.

30. Which of the following IT developments poses the least risk to organizational security?

- A. Adoption of wireless technology.
- B. Use of public-key encryption.
- C. Outsourcing of the IT infrastructure.
- D. Enterprise-wide integration of functions.

Answer (B) is correct.   *(Publisher, adapted)*
    REQUIRED: The least risky IT developments.
    DISCUSSION: Modern information systems rely on encryption, for example, public-key technology, to provide crucial controls. Encryption is essential when electronic commerce is conducted over public networks, such as the Internet. It not only safeguards the integrity of the information transmitted but also furnishes a means of authenticating the parties to transactions through such means as digital signatures and certificates. Thus, the use of public-key encryption is a response to risk, not a source of risk.
    Answer (A) is incorrect because adoption of wireless technology increases the risk that communications will be intercepted. Answer (C) is incorrect because outsourcing of the IT infrastructure means that ineffective controls over the outside service provider's operations could compromise the security of the organization's information. Answer (D) is incorrect because enterprise-wide integration of functions, for example, in an ERP system with an organization-wide database, increases the difficulty of assuring the integrity of information. In an organization with discrete, closed functional subsystems, compromising one subsystem does not affect the others. In an ERP system, however, a breach of security may affect the entire organization.

31. A client communicates sensitive data across the Internet. Which of the following controls will be most effective to prevent the use of the information if it were intercepted by an unauthorized party?

- A. A firewall.
- B. An access log.
- C. Passwords.
- D. Encryption.

Answer (D) is correct.   *(Publisher, adapted)*
    REQUIRED: The most effective control for preventing the use of intercepted information.
    DISCUSSION: Encryption technology converts data into a code. Encoding data before transmission over communications lines makes it more difficult for someone with access to the transmission to understand or modify its contents.
    Answer (A) is incorrect because a firewall prevents access from specific types of traffic to an internal network. After an unauthorized user has obtained information from the site, a firewall cannot prevent its use. Answer (B) is incorrect because an access log only records attempted usage of a system. Answer (C) is incorrect because passwords prevent unauthorized users from accessing the system. If information has already been obtained, a password cannot prevent its use.

32. The primary advantage of an application firewall over a network firewall is that it

A. Is less expensive.

B. Offers easier access to applications.

C. Provides additional user authentication.

D. Is easier to install.

Answer (C) is correct. *(Publisher, adapted)*

REQUIRED: The primary advantage of an application firewall.

DISCUSSION: Application firewalls tend to be more secure than network firewalls because they offer an extra layer between the host computer and the person seeking access. A firm might prefer an application firewall if it is trying to monitor traffic on the website and the files being accessed. For someone to access a file, (s)he must provide additional authentication before the system grants access.

Answer (A) is incorrect because network firewalls are typically less expensive to install. Answer (B) is incorrect because the additional authentication required makes user access to applications more difficult. Answer (D) is incorrect because network firewalls are easier to install.

15.6 Malicious Software and Attacks

33. The best preventive measure against a computer virus is to

A. Compare software in use with authorized versions of the software.

B. Execute virus exterminator programs periodically on the system.

C. Allow only authorized software from known sources to be used on the system.

D. Prepare and test a plan for recovering from the incidence of a virus.

Answer (C) is correct. *(CIA, adapted)*

REQUIRED: The best preventive measure against a computer virus.

DISCUSSION: Preventive controls are designed to prevent errors before they occur. Detective and corrective controls attempt to identify and correct errors. Preventive controls are usually more cost beneficial than detective or corrective controls. Allowing only authorized software from known sources to be used on the system is a preventive measure. The authorized software from known sources is expected to be free of viruses.

Answer (A) is incorrect because comparing software with authorized versions is a detective control. Answer (B) is incorrect because executing virus exterminator programs is a corrective control. Answer (D) is incorrect because preparing and testing a plan for virus recovery is a corrective control.

34. Managers at a consumer products company purchased personal computer software from only recognized vendors, and prohibited employees from installing nonauthorized software on their personal computers. To minimize the likelihood of computer viruses infecting any of its systems, the company should also

A. Restore infected systems with authorized versions.

B. Recompile infected programs from source code backups.

C. Institute program change control procedures.

D. Test all new software on a stand-alone personal computer.

Answer (D) is correct. *(CIA, adapted)*

REQUIRED: The best protection against viruses.

DISCUSSION: Software from recognized sources should be tested in quarantine (for example, in a test/development machine or a stand-alone personal computer) because even vendor-supplied software may be infected with viruses. The software should be run with a vaccine program and tested for the existence of logic bombs, etc.

Answer (A) is incorrect because, if viruses infect a system, the company should restore the system with authorized software, but this procedure does not minimize the likelihood of initial infection. Answer (B) is incorrect because, if viruses infect programs that the company created, it should recompile the programs from source code backups, but this procedure does not minimize the likelihood of initial infection. Answer (C) is incorrect because instituting program change control procedures is good practice but does not minimize the likelihood of the system's being infected initially.

35. Which of the following is an indication that a computer virus is present?

A. Frequent power surges that harm computer equipment.

B. Unexplainable losses of or changes to data.

C. Inadequate backup, recovery, and contingency plans.

D. Numerous copyright violations due to unauthorized use of purchased software.

Answer (B) is correct. *(CIA, adapted)*

REQUIRED: The indicator of a computer virus.

DISCUSSION: The effects of computer viruses range from harmless messages to complete destruction of all data within the system. A symptom of a virus would be the unexplained loss of or change to data.

Answer (A) is incorrect because power surges are caused by hardware or power supply problems. Answer (C) is incorrect because inadequate back-up, recovery, and contingency plans are operating policy weaknesses. Answer (D) is incorrect because copyright violations represent policy or compliance problems.

36. Which of the following operating procedures increases an organization's exposure to computer viruses?

    A. Encryption of data files.

    B. Frequent backup of files.

    C. Downloading public-domain software from Web sites.

    D. Installing original copies of purchased software on hard disk drives.

Answer (C) is correct.   *(CIA, adapted)*
    REQUIRED: The procedure that increases exposure to viruses.
    DISCUSSION: Viruses are spread through shared data. Downloading public-domain software carries a risk that contaminated data may enter the computer.
    Answer (A) is incorrect because viruses are spread through the distribution of contaminated programs. Answer (B) is incorrect because backing up files does not increase the chances of a virus entering the computer system. Answer (D) is incorrect because original copies of purchased software on hard disk drives should be free of viruses.

37. An organization installed antivirus software on all its personal computers. The software was designed to prevent initial infections, stop replication attempts, detect infections after their occurrence, mark affected system components, and remove viruses from infected components. The major risk in relying on antivirus software is that antivirus software may

    A. Not detect certain viruses.

    B. Make software installation overly complex.

    C. Interfere with system operations.

    D. Consume too many system resources.

Answer (A) is correct.   *(CIA, adapted)*
    REQUIRED: The major risk in relying on antivirus software.
    DISCUSSION: Antivirus software designed to identify and remove known viruses is sometimes known as a vaccine. A vaccine works only for known viruses and may not be effective for variants of those viruses or new viruses.
    Answer (B) is incorrect because having antivirus software is unlikely to make software installation overly complex. Answer (C) is incorrect because antivirus software need not interfere with system operations. Its execution can be scheduled in advance so as not to interfere with running programs. Answer (D) is incorrect because antivirus software can be set to execute at times when it would not consume too many system resources, e.g., at startup.

38. What is the best course of action to take if a program takes longer than usual to load or execute?

    A. Test the system by running a different application program.

    B. Reboot the system.

    C. Run antivirus software.

    D. Back up the hard disk files to floppies.

Answer (C) is correct.   *(CIA, adapted)*
    REQUIRED: The best response if a program takes longer than usual to load or execute.
    DISCUSSION: The described condition is a symptom of a virus. Many viruses will spread and cause additional damage. Use of an appropriate antivirus program may identify and even eliminate a viral infection. Ways to minimize computer virus risk in a networked system include restricted access, regularly updated passwords, periodic testing of systems with virus detection software, and the use of antivirus software on all shareware prior to introducing it into the network.
    Answer (A) is incorrect because running a different program as a test may cause the virus to spread and do additional damage. Answer (B) is incorrect because rebooting the system may cause the virus to spread and do additional damage. Answer (D) is incorrect because backing up hard disk files may cause the virus to spread and do additional damage.

39. Six months after a disgruntled systems programmer was fired and passwords disabled, the company's mainframe computer was brought to a halt when it suddenly erased all of its own files and software. The most likely way the programmer accomplished this was by

    A. Returning to the computer center after 6 months.

    B. Planting a computer virus through the use of telephone access.

    C. Having an accomplice in the computer center.

    D. Implanting a virus in the operating system and executing it via a back door.

Answer (D) is correct.   *(CIA, adapted)*
    REQUIRED: The most likely way a programmer caused files and software to be erased.
    DISCUSSION: Viruses are a form of computer sabotage. They are programs hidden within other programs that have the capacity to duplicate themselves and infect other systems. Sharing of storage media or participation in computer networks creates exposure to viruses. Viruses may result in actions ranging from harmless pranks to erasure of files and programs. A back door is a shortcut created in an operating system that permits a programmer simple access to the system.
    Answer (A) is incorrect because the programmer would most likely be denied access to the center. Answer (B) is incorrect because the programmer would not know the necessary passwords. Answer (C) is incorrect because collusion is less likely than individual wrongdoing.

40. Because of competitive pressures to be more responsive to their customers, some organizations have connected their internal personal computer networks through a host computer to outside networks. A risk of this practice is that

   A. Viruses may gain entry to one or more company systems.

   B. Uploaded files may not be properly edited and validated.

   C. Data downloaded to the personal computers may not be sufficiently timely.

   D. Software maintenance on the personal computers may become more costly.

Answer (A) is correct. *(CIA, adapted)*
   REQUIRED: The risk of connecting internal computer networks to outside networks.
   DISCUSSION: Viruses are harmful programs that disrupt memory and processing functions and may destroy data. They spread from network to network, from infected diskettes, or from infected machines. Hence, connecting all networked personal computers through a host computer to outside networks increases the exposure of all of a company's computers to viruses.
   Answer (B) is incorrect because whether uploaded files are properly edited and validated is independent of whether external links to other networks exist. Answer (C) is incorrect because whether data downloaded to the personal computers is sufficiently timely is independent of whether external links to other networks exist. Answer (D) is incorrect because whether software maintenance on the personal computers becomes more costly is independent of whether external links to other networks exist.

41. Attacks on computer networks may take many forms. Which of the following uses the computers of innocent parties infected with Trojan horse programs?

   A. A distributed denial-of-service attack.

   B. A man-in-the-middle attack.

   C. A brute-force attack.

   D. A password-cracking attack.

Answer (A) is correct. *(Publisher, adapted)*
   REQUIRED: The attack on a network that uses the computers of innocent parties infected with Trojan horse programs.
   DISCUSSION: A denial-of-service (DOS) attack is an attempt to overload a system (e.g., a network or Web server) with false messages so that it cannot function (a system crash). A distributed DOS attack comes from multiple sources, for example, the machines of innocent parties infected by Trojan horses. When activated, these programs send messages to the target and leave the connection open. A DOS may establish as many network connections as possible to exclude other users, overload primary memory, or corrupt file systems.
   Answer (B) is incorrect because a man-in-the-middle attack takes advantage of network packet sniffing and routing and transport protocols to access packets flowing through a network. Answer (C) is incorrect because a brute-force attack uses password cracking software to try large numbers of letter and number combinations to access a network. Answer (D) is incorrect because password-cracking software accesses a network by trying many letter and number combinations.

42. Spoofing is one type of online activity used to launch malicious attacks. Spoofing is

   A. Trying large numbers of letter and number combinations to access a network.

   B. Eavesdropping on information sent by a user to the host computer of a website.

   C. Accessing packets flowing through a network.

   D. Identity misrepresentation in cyberspace.

Answer (D) is correct. *(Publisher, adapted)*
   REQUIRED: The nature of spoofing.
   DISCUSSION: Passwords, user account numbers, and other information may be stolen using techniques such as Trojan horses, IP spoofing, and packet sniffers. Spoofing is identity misrepresentation in cyberspace, for example, by using a false website to obtain information about visitors.
   Answer (A) is incorrect because a brute-force attack uses password cracking software to try large numbers of letter and number combinations to access a network. Answer (B) is incorrect because sniffing is the use of software to eavesdrop on information sent by a user to the host computer of a website. Answer (C) is incorrect because a man-in-the-middle attack takes advantage of network packet sniffing and routing and transport protocols to access packets flowing through a network.

43. An organization's computer system should have an intrusion detection system (IDS) if it has external connections. An IDS

- A. Must monitor every call on the system as it occurs.
- B. May examine only packets with certain signatures.
- C. Uses only knowledge-based detection.
- D. Uses only behavior-based detection.

Answer (B) is correct. *(Publisher, adapted)*
REQUIRED: The way in which an IDS functions.
DISCUSSION: A network IDS works by using sensors to examine packets traveling on the network. Each sensor monitors only the segment of the network to which it is attached. A packet is examined if it matches a signature. String signatures (certain strings of text) are potential signs of attack. Port signatures alert the IDS that a point subject to frequent intrusion attempts may be under attack. A header signature is a suspicious combination in a packet header.

Answer (A) is incorrect because a host IDS provides maximum protection only when the software is installed on each computer. It may operate in the following ways: The aggressive response is to monitor every call on the operating system and application as it occurs. A less effective method of preventing attacks is analysis of access log files. A host IDS may also identify questionable processes and verify the security of system files. Answer (C) is incorrect because an IDS is not limited to knowledge-based detection. Knowledge-based detection is based on information about the system's weaknesses and searches for intrusions that take advantage of them. Answer (D) is incorrect because an IDS is not limited to behavior-based detection. Behavior-based detection presumes that an attack will cause an observable anomaly. Actual and normal system behavior (a model of expected operations) are compared. A discrepancy results in an alert.

44. Which of the following is a computer program that appears to be legitimate but performs some illicit activity when it is run?

- A. Hoax virus.
- B. Web crawler.
- C. Trojan horse.
- D. Killer application.

Answer (C) is correct. *(CPA, adapted)*
REQUIRED: The apparently legitimate computer program that performs an illicit activity.
DISCUSSION: A Trojan horse is a computer program that appears friendly, for example, a game, but that actually contains an application destructive to the computer system.

Answer (A) is incorrect because a hoax virus is a false notice about the existence of a computer virus. It is usually disseminated through use of distribution lists and is sent by email or via an internal network. Answer (B) is incorrect because a web crawler (a spider or bot) is a computer program created to access and read information on websites. The results are included as entries in the index of a search engine. Answer (D) is incorrect because a killer application is one that is so useful that it may justify widespread adoption of a new technology.

45. An auditor is gaining an understanding of a client's Internet controls. Which of the following would likely be the least effective control?

- A. The client requires all users to select passwords that are not easily guessed.
- B. The client requires users to share potentially useful downloaded programs from public electronic bulletin boards with only authorized employees.
- C. The client uses a proxy server to provide information to external web-page users.
- D. The client uses a firewall system that produces reports on Internet usage patterns.

Answer (B) is correct. *(Publisher, adapted)*
REQUIRED: The least effective control for Internet security.
DISCUSSION: Sharing programs from public electronic bulletin boards with authorized employees would be a futile control. The programs are available to anyone on the public electronic bulletin board.

Answer (A) is incorrect because passwords can be an effective control against unauthorized access. Answer (C) is incorrect because a proxy server allows only certain information to be provided to external users, thereby preventing unauthorized access. Answer (D) is incorrect because firewalls separate an internal network from an external network. Reports on Internet usage patterns can help in monitoring the effectiveness of the system.

STUDY UNIT SIXTEEN
PLANNING AND BUDGETING

(34 pages of outline)

Planning is a fundamental managerial function, providing guidelines for the accomplishment of an organization's objectives. At the highest level, strategic planning is part of the strategic management process. However, development of plans, including budgets, is required for every level and function of the organization. Plans are formulated based on objectives, assumptions about the environment in which the plans will be executed, and forecasts about the outcomes and timing of future events. Planning techniques include methods used to manage complex projects.

16.1 STRATEGIC MANAGEMENT

1. Strategic management has a **long-term planning horizon**. Thus, a strategic orientation is traditionally associated with senior management. However, this orientation should pervade the organization because it encourages farsightedness by all employees. Strategic thinking also helps employees understand and implement managerial decisions. Moreover, it is consistent with the modern trend toward cooperation and teamwork and away from authoritarian managerial styles.

2. Strategic management is a process that includes the following steps:

   a. A **mission statement** should be formalized in a written document. It should define the organization's ultimate purposes. A **grand strategy** is then developed to describe how the organization's mission is to be achieved. It is based on a **situational analysis** that considers organizational **strengths and weaknesses** (a capability profile) and their interactions with environmental **opportunities and threats (SWOT)**.

      1) Speed in reacting to environmental changes, introducing new products, etc., is an important competitive advantage. To achieve it, the organization may have to reengineer its processes.

   b. **Strategic planning** formulates specific and measurable objectives, plans, policies, and budgets.

   c. **Implementation.** Strategic plans must be filtered down the organizational structure through development of plans at each lower level. This process is most likely to succeed if (1) the structure is compatible with strategic planning, (2) personnel have the necessary abilities, (3) the organizational culture is favorable or can be changed, and (4) controls exist to facilitate implementation.

   d. **Control.** Strategic controls should be established to monitor progress, isolate problems, identify invalid assumptions, and take prompt corrective action.

      1) As plans are executed at each organizational level, control measurements are made to determine whether objectives have been achieved. Thus, objectives flow down the organizational hierarchy, and control measures flow up.

2)   One category of strategic control measures relates to **external effectiveness**. The organization measures

   a)   Performance in the marketplace (market share, etc.) at the **business-unit level**

   b)   Customer satisfaction and flexibility at the **business-operating-system level**

   c)   Quality and delivery at the **departmental** or **work-center level**

3)   A second category of strategic control measures relates to **internal efficiency**. The organization measures

   a)   Financial results at the **business-unit level**

   b)   Flexibility (both an external effectiveness and internal efficiency issue) at the **business-operating-system level**

   c)   Cycle time (time to change raw materials into a finished product) and waste at the **departmental** or **work-center level**

3.   Strategic management is dependent on **forecasts** of outcomes of events, their timing, and their future values.

4.   Strategic management is facilitated when managers think synergistically. **Synergy** occurs when the combination of formerly separate elements has a greater effect than the sum of their individual effects. The following are types of synergy observed in business:

   a.   **Market synergy** arises when products or services have positive complementary effects. Shopping malls reflect this type of synergy.

   b.   **Cost synergy** results in cost reduction. It manifests itself in many ways, for example, in recycling of by-products or in the design, production, marketing, and sales of a line of products by the same enterprise.

   c.   **Technological synergy** is the transfer of technology among applications. For example, technology developed for military purposes often has civilian uses.

   d.   **Management synergy** also entails knowledge transfer. For example, a company may hire a manager with skills that it lacks.

5.   Another concept useful in analysis of industry evolution is the **product life cycle**. It has the following stages:

   a.   **Precommercialization** (product development). The strategy in this stage is to innovate by conducting R&D, marketing research, and production tests. During product development, the firm has no sales, but it has high investment costs.

   b.   The **introduction stage** is characterized by slow sales growth and lack of profits because of the high expenses of promotion and selective distribution to generate awareness of the product and encourage customers to try it. Thus, the per-customer cost is high. Competitors are few, basic versions of the product are produced, and higher-income customers (innovators) are usually targeted. Cost-plus prices are charged. They may initially be high to permit cost recovery when unit sales are low. The strategy is to infiltrate the market, plan for financing to cope with losses, build supplier relations, increase production and marketing efforts, and plan for competition.

   c.   In the **growth stage**, sales and profits increase rapidly, cost per customer decreases, customers are early adopters, new competitors enter an expanding market, new product models and features are introduced, and promotion spending declines or remains stable. The firm enters new market segments and distribution channels and attempts to build brand loyalty and achieve the maximum share of the market. Thus, prices are set to penetrate the market, distribution channels are extended, and the mass market is targeted through advertising. The strategy is to advance by these means and by achieving economies of productive scale.

    d. In the **maturity stage**, sales peak but growth declines, competitors are most numerous but may begin to decline in number, and per-customer cost is low. Profits are high for large market-share firms. For others, profits may fall because of competitive price-cutting and increased R&D spending to develop improved versions of the product. The strategy is to defend market share and maximize profits through diversification of brands and models to enter new market segments, still more intensive distribution, cost cutting, advertising and promotions to encourage brand switching, and emphasizing customer service.

       1) Some writers identify a separate stage between growth and maturity. During the **shakeout period**, the overall growth rate falls, price cutting occurs, and weaker firms leave the market.

    e. During the **decline stage**, sales and profits drop as prices are cut, and some firms leave the market. Customers include late adopters (laggards), and per-customer cost is low. Weak products and unprofitable distribution media are eliminated, and advertising budgets are pared to the level needed to retain the most loyal customers. The strategy is to withdraw by reducing production, promotion, and inventory.

    f. **Criticisms** of the PLC concept are that some stages may be hard to distinguish, and their length may vary substantially among industries. Moreover, sales growth may not follow the pattern described in a. through e., partly because the firm's strategies affect growth. Still another consideration is that industry characteristics (degree of concentration, R&D costs, advertising costs, price competition, etc.) differ among industries. Accordingly, the PLC model is not by itself adequate to analyze industry evolution.

6. Still another approach is Michael Porter's **competitive strategies** model.

    a. **Cost leadership** is the generic strategy favored by enterprises that seek competitive advantage through lower costs and that have a broad competitive scope.

    b. **Differentiation** is the generic strategy favored by enterprises that seek competitive advantage through providing a unique product and that have a broad competitive scope.

    c. **Cost focus** is the generic strategy favored by enterprises that seek competitive advantage through lower costs and that have a narrow competitive scope (a regional or smaller market).

    d. **Focused differentiation** is the generic strategy favored by enterprises that seek competitive advantage through providing a unique product and that have a narrow competitive scope (a regional or smaller market).

7. An **operations strategy** formulates a long-term plan for using enterprise resources to reach strategic objectives. The following are five operations strategies:

    a. A **cost** strategy is successful when the enterprise is the low-cost producer. However, the product (e.g., a commodity) tends to be undifferentiated in these cases, the market is often very large, and the competition tends to be intense because of the possibility of high-volume sales.

    b. A **quality** strategy involves competition based on product quality or process quality. Product quality relates to design, for example, the difference between a luxury car and a subcompact. Process quality concerns the degree of freedom from defects.

    c. A **delivery** strategy may permit an enterprise to charge a higher price when the product is consistently delivered rapidly and on time. An example company is UPS.

    d. A **flexibility** strategy entails offering many different products. This strategy also may reflect an ability to shift rapidly from one product line to another. An example company is a publisher that can write, edit, print, and distribute a book within days to exploit the public's short-term interest in a sensational event.

e.   A **service** strategy seeks to gain a competitive advantage and maximize customer value by providing services, especially post-purchase services such as warranties on automobiles and home appliances.

8.   **Customer value and satisfaction** are central concepts in formulating customer management strategies.

   a.   A marketer responds to **customer needs** by stating a **value proposition**, that is, the benefits offered to satisfy those needs. The value proposition is an attempt to affect customer **wants** (needs focused on particular satisfiers). It becomes tangible in an **offering**, which may consist of products, services, and other things that are intended to satisfy the needs of target buyers.

   1)   **Value** is an aggregate of the elements of the **customer value triad**: quality, service, and price. Value increases as quality and service increase and price decreases.

   2)   Value also may be defined as a **benefits-to-costs ratio**: the sum of functional and emotional benefits divided by the sum of monetary, time, energy, and psychic costs. The value of the offering is increased by any means that increases the ratio, such as lowering benefits by less than a decrease in costs.

   a)   A customer will be indifferent between two offerings with equal ratios.

   b)   **Customer perceived value** is an estimate of a given offering and the alternative. **Total customer value** is what a customer believes to be the financial value of the benefits of an offering. **Total customer cost** is the sum of all costs to the customer related to the offering.

   b.   **Customer satisfaction** is the relation between the offering's perceived performance and the customer's expectations. High customer satisfaction tends to create high customer loyalty that results in repurchases. However, at lower satisfaction levels, customers are more likely to switch when a superior alternative becomes available.

   1)   **Expectations** are a function of a customer's experience, marketing information, and other factors. Marketers should not raise expectations above the level at which they can be satisfied. However, some superior firms have had great success by adopting a **total customer satisfaction** approach, that is, by elevating expectations and then satisfying them.

   2)   **High customer loyalty** is an emotional as well as rational bond that develops when a firm provides high customer value. To obtain such loyalty, the firm needs to develop a value proposition that has superior competitiveness in the target market segment. Crucially, it must be supported by an effective **value delivery system**, the accumulation of all the experiences the customer has with the offering. Thus, brand value must be supported by **core business processes** that actually deliver the promised customer value.

   3)   **Customer satisfaction information** is gathered by

   a)   Complaint and suggestion systems such as websites and hotlines

   b)   Customer surveys

   c)   Lost customer analysis (e.g., exit interviews and determination of the customer loss rate)

   d)   Testing of the treatment customers receive when purchasing the firm's (or competitors') products (ghost shopping)

   4)   Customer satisfaction must be balanced against the satisfaction level of the firm's **other stakeholders** (e.g., shareholders, employees, suppliers, and retailers). Thus, raising customer satisfaction at the expense of profit or other stakeholders may not be appropriate.

      a) **High-performance business model.** According to Arthur D. Little (a consulting firm), a business should establish satisfaction objectives for **stakeholder groups**. To achieve the objectives, it must devise strategies, reengineer and coordinate its **core processes**, and appropriately allocate resources in accordance with organizational arrangements (structure, culture, etc.).

          i) The firm may retain its **core resources** and outsource the rest.

          ii) Core processes and resources are tied to **core competencies**. The competencies provide substantial customer value and therefore are sources of competitive advantage. Moreover, they have many applications and are hard for rivals to emulate.

          iii) **Distinctive capabilities** provide superiority in certain overall business functions. According to George Day, an organization should have effective market sensing, customer linking, and channel bonding capabilities.

    5) High **customer satisfaction rankings** may be an effective marketing tool. See, for example, the J.D. Powers rankings of automotive industry performance or the **American Customer Satisfaction Index** measurements applicable to national economies, industries, and sectors as well as firms.

  c. **value creation chain** consists of the activities of a firm that create customer value and incur costs. They consist of five **primary activities** and four support activities. The following is Michael E. Porter's model:

    1) **Inbound logistics** activities involve the firms' capture of materials to be processed.

    2) **Operations** activities are conversion processes.

    3) **Outbound logistics** activities include shipment of products.

    4) **Marketing and sales** activities are the promotion and sale of final products.

    5) **Service** activities provide customer service.

    6) The four **support activities** are infrastructure (e.g., administration, finance, and planning), procurement, human resources, and technology development.

  d. To sustain customer value, the firm must seek **continuous improvement** of value-creating activities. **Benchmarking** the best performance attributes of top firms and emulating their **best practices** is a key continuous improvement technique.

  e. Effective coordination of the following **core business processes** is crucial:

    1) **Market sensing** consists of obtaining, distributing, and acting upon market intelligence.

    2) **New offering realization** should be timely and efficient. It involves R&D and the launch of products, services, and other elements of offerings.

    3) **Customer acquisition** defines target markets and researches for customers.

    4) **Customer relationship management** seeks to increase the value of the customer base by developing long-term relationships with individual customers by such methods as customer service, customized (if not personalized) offerings, and choice of marketing messages and media.

    5) **Fulfillment management** relates to order processing, on-time delivery, and collection.

  f. The **value-delivery network** is another source of competitive advantage. **Partner relationship management** involves coordinating with suppliers and distributors in this network **(the supply chain)** to provide better customer value.

9. **Customer relationship management (CRM)** is an attempt to tie together three traditionally separate functions: marketing, sales, and service.

   a. CRM employs large databases and integrated information systems to link the three customer relationship functions.

      1) **Marketing** seeks out (a) unfulfilled customer needs and (b) customer groups who might be interested in the firm's existing products.

      2) **Sales** brings the products to the attention of the targeted customers and closes the sale.

      3) **Customer service** provides after-the-sale support, such as product help and account information.

   b. The firm should seek to minimize **customer churn** (customer loss) because **customer retention** through **customer satisfaction** is a key to profitability.

      1) **High customer satisfaction** means a longer relationship with the firm, repeat purchases of new offerings and upgrades, favorable word-of-mouth, and less concern about price and competitors' offerings. Moreover, the highly satisfied repeat customer is less costly than a new customer and is more likely to provide helpful feedback.

      2) **The listening process.** Accordingly, the firm should measure customer satisfaction frequently, facilitate complaints and suggestions, and act rapidly on the results.

      3) A less effective method of customer retention is to create high **switching costs**, such as loss of discounts.

   c. The firm should emphasize customer retention because the **customer base** is an important intangible asset.

      1) Loss of some customers is unavoidable. For example, a customer may cease operations.

      2) Customer retention is far less costly than customer attraction.

      3) Increasing the retention rate increases profits exponentially.

      4) The longer the customer relationship, the more profitable it is.

   d. **Analysis of customer loss** entails the following steps:

      1) Determining the retention rate

      2) Identifying causes that can be managed, such as bad products, lack of service, or uncompetitive prices

      3) Approximating the lost profit

      4) Calculating the cost of increasing the retention rate

   e. A firm should estimate **customer lifetime value**, the net present value of the cash flows (purchases – costs of acquiring, selling to, and serving the customer) related to a particular customer. This amount indicates whether a given investment in a customer is justified.

   f. **Customer equity** is the sum of the customer lifetime values for all firm customers. According to Rust, Zeithaml, and Lemon, it has certain drivers (value, brand, and relationship equity) and subdrivers. A firm must determine the subdrivers that should be improved to increase customer equity and profits.

      1) **Value equity** is an estimate of the benefits-to-cost ratio. It is based on the following subdrivers: quality, price, and convenience. Value equity is most important when products are differentiated or require a formal assessment by the buyer.

2) **Brand equity** is a subjective evaluation. Subdrivers are the customer's awareness of, and attitude toward, the brand and the customer's belief about brand ethics. Brand equity is most significant when the product is not differentiated but has emotional appeal.

3) **Relationship equity** is the likelihood that customer loyalty is not based on any appraisal of the brand's value. Subdrivers are **programs to build customer loyalty, recognition, community, and knowledge**. This driver is most significant when the supplier-customer relationship is vital or when a customer may simply be habit-bound.

g. Jill Griffin has described the process of attracting and retaining customers as follows:

1) Identifying **suspects** (all potential customers)
2) Separating **prospects** from the suspects
3) Persuading prospects to be **first-time customers**
4) Giving preferred treatment to **repeat customers** to make them clients
5) Creating a membership program to transform clients into **members**
6) Converting members into **advocates** for the firm, its products, and its services
7) Making advocates into **partners**

h. A firm may be able to **regain lost customers** more cheaply than it could attract new ones using existing information and the results of surveys and exit interviews. A firm must determine the appropriate **investment in building customer relationships**. The levels of investment depend on unit profit margins and the numbers of customers. According to Kotler, the following are the corresponding levels of relationship marketing:

1) **Basic marketing** is merely selling (low-margin, many customers).
2) **Reactive marketing** includes encouragement of customer communication (low-to-medium margin and many customers or low margin and medium number of customers).
3) **Accountable marketing** involves seller-initiated communication to ask about problems or suggestions (low margin and few customers, medium margin and medium number of customers, or high margin and many customers).
4) **Proactive marketing** involves seller-initiated communication about new products or uses of old ones (high margin and medium number of customers or medium margin and few customers).
5) **Partnership marketing** entails continuous assistance to big customers (high margin and few customers).

i. **Strengthening ties with customers** to improve customer satisfaction and retention may be accomplished in the following ways:

1) Firm-wide coordination of planning and management of the process
2) Making every business decision from customer as well as a firm perspective
3) Marketing superior offerings
4) Developing a comprehensive and accessible customer database
5) Facilitating customer communications with appropriated firm employees
6) Giving awards for employee achievement
7) Providing financial benefits, such as club memberships and frequent-buyer programs
8) Turning customers into clients through socially sensitive, personalized relationships
9) Creating structural relationships, e.g., by providing equipment, software, or EDI linkages; entering into long-term contracts; or offering bulk discounts

j. **Customer profitability analysis** determines all revenues and all costs assignable to specific customers. Kotler provides the following classification of customers:

   1) **Platinum** – most profitable (highest investment)
   2) **Gold** – profitable (high investment, with objective of converting to platinum)
   3) **Iron** – low profit but desirable (lower investment with objective of converting to gold)
   4) **Lead** – not profitable or desirable (drop or provide low investment while raising prices or lowering costs of serving)

10. Stop and review! You have completed the outline for this subunit. Study multiple-choice questions 1 through 9 beginning on page 490.

16.2 STRATEGIC PLANNING

1. Planning is the determination of **what** is to be done, and of **how, when, where,** and **by whom** it is to be done. Plans serve to direct the activities that all organizational members must undertake and successfully perform to move the organization from where it is to where it wants to be (accomplishment of its objectives).

   a. Planning must be completed before undertaking any other managerial function.

      1) **Forecasting** is the basis of planning because it projects the future.

   b. Planning establishes the **means** to reach organizational **ends** (objectives).

      1) This means-end relationship extends throughout the organizational hierarchy and ties together the parts of the organization so that the various means all focus on the same end.

      2) One organizational level's ends provide the next higher level's means.

         a) EXAMPLE: **Management by objectives (MBO)** identifies relationships between an individual's job objectives (ends) and the immediate superior's objectives (ends). Thus, the subordinate can understand how his/her job is the means by which the superior's job is accomplished. See item 16. beginning on page 469 for fuller discussion.

2. **The Planning Process**

   a. **Long-range (strategic) planning** has a horizon of 1 to 10 years or more. Such planning is difficult because of uncertainty about future events and conditions.

      1) Thus, strategic plans tend to be general and exclude operational detail.

   b. Strategic planning embodies the concerns of senior management. It is based on

      1) Identifying and specifying organizational objectives. The future course of the organization should be consistent with the purposes stated in its **mission statement**. They may include industry leadership, business diversification, addition or deletion of products or services, entry into new markets, or service to society.

      2) Evaluating the **strengths** (competitive advantages) and **weaknesses** of the organization.

      3) Assessing **risk** levels.

      4) Identifying and forecasting the effects of **external (environmental) factors** relevant to the organization. For example, market trends, changes in technology, international competition, and social change may provide opportunities, impose limitations, or represent threats.

      5) Deriving the best strategy for reaching the objectives, given the organization's strengths and weaknesses and the relevant future trends.

      6) **Capital budgeting**, a planning process for choosing and **financing** long-term projects and programs.

      7) **Capacity planning**, an element of planning closely related to capital budgeting that includes, among other things, consideration of business combinations or divestitures.

  c. Strategic plans are translated into measurable and achievable intermediate and operational plans. Thus, intermediate and operational plans must be consistent with, and contribute to achieving, strategic objectives.

      1) **Intermediate plans** (6 months to 2 years) are developed by middle management.

      2) **Operational plans** (1 week to 1 year) are developed by lower-level managers.

      3) Such plans relate to production, materials, procurement, expenses, revenues, cash flows, etc.

  d. Advances in **information technology** and reductions in its cost have increased the use of quantitative models for strategic, intermediate, and operational planning purposes.

      1) This effect is particularly evident in large organizations in which quantitative models may be used with greater statistical reliability.

  e. **Contingency planning** is based on different sets of **premises**. It stipulates different sets of actions for management based on these premises.

      1) Contingency planning allows for forecasting error.

      2) Contingency planning is more expensive than formulating a single plan, so this additional cost must be more than balanced by improved performance.

  f. The **primary general planning principle** is that the lowest possible relevant units in management should be involved in the planning process. This form of **upward communication** is important for several reasons.

      1) Lower-level managers are aware of operational details and limitations. Thus, they can contribute to the feasibility and precision of the plan with regard to their individual areas of responsibility.

      2) Plans prepared at higher levels, without the participation of the managers who will be involved in their execution, appear to be dictated to the lower-level managers, with a consequent reduction in performance.

  g. **Additional General Planning Principles**

      1) Plans should not allocate more than the known available resources.

      2) Planning must precede action.

      3) Plans must be coordinated among related functions.

      4) Plans must be flexible and recognized as subject to change.

      5) Plans should be limited to only highly probable future events; it is impossible to include every possible action and consequence.

3. **Premises** are the underlying **assumptions** about the expected environment in which the strategic plan will be carried out. Thus, the next step in planning is **premising**, or the generation of planning assumptions.

  a. Premises should be limited to those crucial to the success of the plans.

  b. Managers should ask, "What internal and external factors would influence the actions planned for this organization (division, department, program)?" Premises must be considered at all levels of the organization.

      1) Thus, capital budgeting plans should be premised on assumptions (forecasts) about economic cycles, price movements, etc.

      2) The stores department's plans might be premised on stability of parts prices or on forecasts that prices will rise.

   c. EXAMPLES:

     1) The general economy will suffer an 11% decline next year.

     2) Our closest competitor's new model will provide greater competition for potential sales.

     3) Union negotiations will result in a general wage increase of 8%.

     4) Over the next 5 years, the cost of our raw materials will increase by 30%.

     5) The elasticity of demand for the company's products is 1.2.

4. **Objectives and Goals.** The terms objectives and goals are often used interchangeably. However, some writers distinguish between overall organizational objectives and individual, departmental, or subunit goals. Other writers reverse these meanings.

   a. The determination of organizational objectives is the first step in planning.

   b. Organizations usually have multiple objectives that are often contradictory.

     1) The objective of maximizing profit and the objective of growth could be mutually exclusive within a given year. Maximizing short-term profit might hamper or preclude future growth.

     2) Conflict among an organization's objectives is common.

   c. Objectives vary with the organization's type and stage of development.

5. **Management Objectives**

   a. The primary task of management is to reach organizational objectives effectively and efficiently.

     1) **Efficiency** is maximizing the output for a given quantity of input.

     2) **Effectiveness** is the degree to which the objective or goal is accomplished.

     3) In practice, effectiveness is of prime importance, and efficiency may be secondary because trade-offs are frequently made between efficiency and effectiveness.

       a) EXAMPLE: In a hospital, efficiency is much less important than effectiveness. Reducing the night nursing staff to the theoretical minimum might increase efficiency by reducing payroll, but if even one patient dies because of inadequate care, the hospital has failed to carry out its mission effectively.

     4) Efficiency is doing things right. Effectiveness is doing the right things.

   b. Subordinate objectives of management may include

     1) Survival

     2) Growth of market influence

     3) Employee development

     4) Social responsibility

     5) Creativity

     6) Personal need satisfaction

6. Each **subunit of an organization** may have its own objectives.

   a. Subunit objectives may conflict with overall organizational objectives.

   b. Subunit objectives unite the efforts of the people in the subunit. Consequently,

     1) The people in each subunit are bound by their collective wisdom, training, and experiences. Thus, they may have tunnel vision regarding the organization's purpose.

       a) EXAMPLE: "Why doesn't anybody take the time to see our problems in production? After all, if it weren't for us, they wouldn't have anything to sell!"

2) Subunits tend to be designed to make decisions that optimize the results of each subunit, to the possible detriment of the overall organization.

    a) Decentralized profit centers are the classic illustration.

        i) EXAMPLE: A profit center that buys services from another profit center in the same organization will seek to maximize its own welfare regardless of the consequences for corporate objectives.

  c. Subunit objectives must be established to translate broad overall corporate objectives into meaningful and measurable terms for the subunit members.

7. Objectives should be

  a. **Clearly stated in specific terms.** General or poorly defined objectives are not useful for guiding the actions of managers or measuring their performance.

  b. **Easily communicated to all concerned.** The executives who determine objectives cannot have the desired impact on the organization until they successfully communicate the objectives to all from whom action is required.

  c. **Accepted by the individuals concerned.** An objective is unlikely to be attained if it is thought to be unachievable by those affected.

8. Broad objectives should be established at the top and retranslated in more specific terms as they are communicated downward in the **means-end hierarchy**.

  a. EXAMPLE:

    1) A firm has a socioeconomic purpose, such as providing food.

    2) The firm's mission is the accomplishment of its socioeconomic purpose through the production of breakfast cereal.

    3) The firm develops long-range or strategic objectives with regard to profitability, growth, or survival.

    4) A more specific overall objective might be to provide investors with an adequate return on their investment.

    5) Divisional objectives can be developed, e.g., to increase the sales of a certain kind of cereal.

    6) Departmental objectives are developed, e.g., to reduce waste in the packaging department.

    7) Low-level managers and supervisors then develop personal performance and development objectives.

9. A divergence of opinion exists regarding the determination of organizational objectives.

  a. One view is that **service** (need satisfaction for the consumer) is primary and that profit results from service.

  b. Another view is that **profit** or **return on investment (ROI)** is primary and that service results from profit.

  c. The most relevant view for a given organization is contingent upon its particular situation or environment.

    1) EXAMPLE: A fast-food company has customer service as its primary objective. It expects profits to result from the satisfaction of consumer needs. On the other hand, a private utility provides service only if a reasonable return on investment attracts the capital needed for system maintenance and expansion. For a utility, service results from profit.

10. Objectives change over time.

    a.   EXAMPLE: The 19th-century industrialist's main objectives were to make money and increase personal power. In the 21st century, social responsibility is a significant force that must be accommodated. This change is evidenced by, for example, the expanding pressures for information disclosures to outside parties, for environmental-impact studies, and for training the unemployed.

11. After objectives and premises are formulated, the next step in the planning process is the development of **policies, procedures, and rules**. These elements are necessary at all levels of the organization and overlap both in definition and in practice.

12. Intermediate and operational plans are translated into policies, procedures, and rules, which are standing plans for repetitive situations.

    a.   Policies and procedures provide **feedforward control** because they anticipate and prevent problems and provide guidance on how an activity should be performed to best ensure that an objective is achieved.

13. **Policies** are general statements that guide thinking and action in decision making.

    a.   Policies may be explicitly published by, or implied by the actions of, management.

        1)   Managers should be certain that their subordinates do not misinterpret minor or unrelated decisions as precedents for policy.

    b.   Policies indicate a preferred method for achieving objectives.

    c.   Policies define a general area within which a manager may exercise discretion.

    d.   Policies should

        1)   Involve known principles

        2)   Be consistent with higher-level policies and with those of parallel units in the organization

        3)   Be clear and comprehensive

        4)   Be workable

        5)   Be published

    e.   Difficulties arise in the administration of policies that are not properly

        1)   Formulated

        2)   Understood

        3)   Flexible

        4)   Communicated

        5)   Updated

        6)   Accepted

    f.   A strong **organizational culture** means that the organization's key values are intensely held and widely shared. Hence, the need for formal written policies is minimized.

14. **Procedures** are specific directives that define how work is to be done.

    a.   Procedures

        1)   Usually consist of a set of specific steps in chronological order

        2)   Are found at every level of the organization

        3)   Reduce the need for managerial direction of subordinates in the accomplishment of routine matters

        4)   Improve efficiency through standardization of actions

        5)   Facilitate the training of personnel

        6)   Provide coordination among different departments of the organization

    b.   Procedures should be

        1)   Balanced
        2)   Efficient in use of resources
        3)   Subject to organized control
        4)   Flexible enough to handle most normal situations
        5)   Clearly defined and easily accessible, as in procedures manuals

15. **Rules** are specific, detailed guides that restrict behavior.

    a.   Rules are the simplest plans.

    b.   A rule requires a specific action to be taken with regard to a given situation.

    c.   Rules allow no discretion or flexibility.

    d.   A procedure may contain a sequence of rules, or a rule may stand alone.

    e.   For example, "No smoking in the paint shop. Violators will be dismissed without exception."

16. **Management by Objectives (MBO)** is a behavioral, communications-oriented, responsibility approach to management and employee self-direction. It is a comprehensive management approach and therefore is relevant to **planning and control**.

    a.   MBO is based on the **Theory Y** philosophy that employees

        1)   Want to work hard if they know what is expected
        2)   Like to understand what their jobs actually entail
        3)   Are capable of self-direction and self-motivation

    b.   MBO requires

        1)   **Senior management** participation and commitment to the program. These managers must

            a)   Determine the overall direction and objectives for the organization
            b)   Communicate these effectively in operational or measurable terms
            c)   Coordinate subordinates' objectives with overall objectives
            d)   Follow up at the end of the MBO cycle period to reward performance and review problems

        2)   **Integration of objectives** for all subunits into a compatible, balanced system directed toward accomplishment of the overall objectives.

        3)   Provisions for regular periodic **reporting of performance** toward attainment of the objectives.

        4)   Free and honest **communication** between supervisor and subordinate.

        5)   A **commitment** to a Theory Y philosophy on the part of supervisors.

        6)   An **organizational climate** that encourages mutual trust and respect.

    c.   **Steps necessary to implement an MBO program** include establishing objectives and action plans (the planning steps) and periodic review and final appraisal (the control steps).

        1)   Each subordinate should define his/her job objectives and the specific actions (s)he would like to take over the next time period to help reach those job objectives.

        2)   The subordinate's objectives and activities should be reviewed within the context of the objectives at higher levels.

        3)   When the subordinate's objectives are at odds with upper-level objectives, a **coaching session** is necessary.

            a)   This process frequently represents the acid test of MBO because the supervisor must avoid dictating the subordinate's objectives if the spirit of participation is to be preserved.

     b)   If the subordinate's objectives are deemed by the supervisor to be inappropriate, and the subordinate cannot be **coached** out of them, the supervisor can either

        i)   Let the subordinate learn by failing in doing the job his/her way, or

        ii)   Overrule on this particular issue.

     c)   A commitment to Theory Y, trust in subordinates, and the supervisor's job security (the confidence to allow subordinates still more latitude) will play important roles.

     d)   The clearer the definition of job and organizational objectives and the greater the degree of trust and communication between supervisor and subordinate, the easier it is to avoid these dilemmas in implementing MBO.

   4)   The supervisor and subordinate should mutually set and agree on a realistic action plan that can be accomplished by the end of the period.

   5)   Flexibility should be maintained during the period to accommodate unforeseen changes. Thus, after developing objectives and action plans, the third step in the MBO cycle is **periodic review**.

     a)   At regular intervals, objectives should be reconsidered to determine whether they are appropriate in the light of changed circumstances. Otherwise, progress toward achievement of the established objectives should be evaluated and feedback provided.

   6)   At the end of the MBO cycle, the supervisor and subordinate should meet for a **final performance appraisal**. They should review the results, analyze and discuss differences, and use the discussion for learning and performance feedback (not for correction or discipline).

   7)   The MBO cycle should then be repeated.

17.   Stop and review! You have completed the outline for this subunit. Study multiple-choice questions 10 through 19 starting on page 493.

16.3 FORECASTING

1.   Forecasts are the basis for business plans, including budgets. They attempt to answer questions about the outcomes of events (e.g., the effect of a war involving a producer of oil on the oil market), the timing of events (e.g., when will unemployment fall), or the future value of a statistic (e.g., sales). In addition to intuition (informed judgment), many quantitative methods are useful in projecting the future from past experience.

   a.   Examples of forecasts include sales projections, inventory demand, cash flow, and future capital needs.

     1)   Most models are used in the forecasting process. They are used to make decisions that optimize future results.

     2)   The reliability of the forecast should be determined before using it. No objective method can determine the reliability of judgmental forecasts. When quantitative methods are used, however, measurement of reliability is usually possible, e.g., by calculating the standard error of the estimate.

2.   **Correlation analysis** is used to measure the strength of the linear relationship between two or more variables. Correlation between two variables can be seen by plotting their values on a single graph to form a scatter diagram.

   a.   **Scatter diagrams** may be used to demonstrate correlations. Each observation creates a dot that pairs the x and y values. If the points tend to form a straight line, correlation is high. If they form a random pattern, correlation is low. Correlation measures only linear relationships.

b.   In standard notation, the coefficient of correlation is r; the coefficient of determination is r^2.

c.   The **coefficient of correlation** measures the relative strength of the linear relationship. It has the following properties:

1)   The magnitude of r is independent of the scales of measurement of x and y.

2) $-1.0 \leq r \leq 1.0$

a)   A value of -1.0 indicates a perfectly inverse linear relationship between x and y.

b)   A value of zero indicates no linear relationship between x and y.

c)   A value of $+1.0$ indicates a direct relationship between x and y.

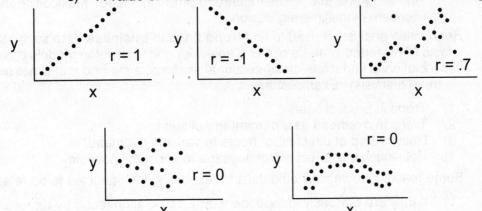

d.   The **coefficient of determination (r^2)**, or the coefficient of correlation squared, may be interpreted as the proportion of the total variation in y that is explained or accounted for by the regression equation.

1)   It is approximately equal to 1 minus the quotient of the unexplained variation divided by the total variation when the sample is large. The following is the formula:

$$r^2 = 1 - \frac{\sum (y_i - \hat{y})^2}{\sum (y_i - \bar{y})^2}$$

If: r^2 = the coefficient of determination
$\sum$ = summation
y_i = an actual data point
$\hat{y}$ = a point on the regression line calculated from the sample linear regression equation
$\bar{y}$ = the mean of the observed data points

2)   EXAMPLE: The assertion that new car sales are a function of disposable income with a coefficient of correlation of .8 is equivalent to stating that 64% ($.8^2$) of the variation of new car sales (from average new car sales) can be explained by the variation in disposable income (from average disposable income).

3)   Because r^2 increases as the number of independent variables increases, regardless of whether the additional variables are actually correlated with the dependent variable, r^2 may be adjusted (reduced) to allow for this effect. If k is the number of independent variables and n is the number of observations, the formula for adjusted r^2 is

$$r^2 - \frac{(k - 1)}{(n - k)} \times (1 - r^2)$$

3.   **Regression (least squares) analysis** extends correlation to find an equation for the linear relationship among variables. The behavior of the dependent variable is explained in terms of one or more independent variables. Thus, regression analysis determines functional relationships among quantitative variables.

   a.   **Simple regression** has one independent variable, and **multiple regression** has more than one.

      1)   EXAMPLE: A dependent variable such as sales is dependent on advertising, consumer income, availability of substitutes, and other independent variables.

      2)   **Multicollinearity** is the condition in which two or more independent variables are strongly correlated. The effect is greater uncertainty regarding the coefficient of the variables; that is, their standard errors increase. Multicollinearity is a concern in multiple regression.

   b.   Regression analysis is used to find **trend lines in business data** such as sales or costs (time series analysis or trend analysis) and to develop models based on the association of variables (cross-sectional analysis, a method that is not time related as is trend analysis). Examples are

      1)   Trend in product sales
      2)   Trend in overhead as a percentage of sales
      3)   Relationship of direct labor hours to variable overhead
      4)   Relationship of direct material usage to accounts payable

   c.   Some reasonable basis should exist for expecting the variables to be related.

      1)   If they are obviously independent, any association found by regression is mere coincidence.

      2)   Regression does not determine causality, however. Although x and y move together, the apparent relationship may be caused by some other factor.

         a)   EXAMPLE: A strong correlation exists between car-wash sales volume and sunny weather, but sales volume does not cause sunny weather.

      3)   The statistical relationships revealed by regression and correlation analysis are valid **only** for the range of the data in the sample.

   d.   The **simple regression equation** is

$$y = a + bx + e$$

      If: y = the dependent variable
            a = the y-axis intercept (the fixed cost in cost functions)
            b = the slope of the regression line (the variable portion of the total cost in cost functions)
            x = the independent variable
            e = the error term

      1)   **Assumptions of the model** are that

         a)   For each value of x, there is a distribution of values of y. The means of these distributions form a straight line. Hence, x and y are linearly related.

         b)   The error term (e) is normally distributed with a mean or expected value equal to zero.

            i)   The y-intercept (a) and the slope of the regression line (b) also have normal distributions.

    c)   Errors in successive observations are statistically independent.

        i)   Thus, the estimators are unbiased.

        ii)   **Autocorrelation (serial correlation)** occurs when the observations are not independent; in other words, later observations may be dependent on earlier ones.

    d)   The distribution of y around the regression line is constant for different values of x.

        i)   Thus, the observations are characterized by **homoscedasticity** or **constant variance**. The deviation of points from the regression line does not vary with a change in the size of the independent variable.

        ii)   Graphically, the model is represented by a series of normal distributions (subpopulations of y) around the regression line. As noted above, these subpopulations have the same variance.

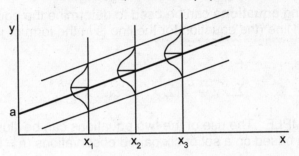

        •   **Heteroscedasticity** is the condition in which the variance of the error term is **not** constant.

    e.   From linear algebra, the **equation for a straight line** may be stated as follows:

$$y = a + bx$$

If: a = the y-axis intercept
        b = the slope of the line

    1)   Regression analysis uses the **method of least squares**, which minimizes the sum of the squares of the vertical distance between each observation point and the regression line.

    2)   EXAMPLE: Observations are collected on advertising expenditures and annual sales for a firm.

Sales ($000,000s)	Advertising ($000s)
28	71
14	31
19	50
21	60
16	35

    a)   According to the regression equation that results from using least squares computations, expected sales equal 4.2 plus .31 times the advertising expenditure.

$$y = 4.2 + .31(x)$$

b)   The observations are graphed as follows:

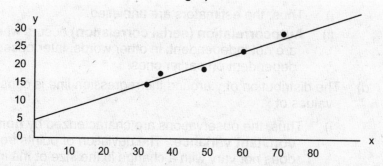

f.   Regression analysis is particularly valuable for **budgeting** and cost accounting purposes. For instance, it is almost a necessity for computing the fixed and variable portions of mixed costs for flexible budgeting.

g.   The following **equations** can be used to determine the equation for the least squares regression line (the equation for the line is in the form of $y = a + bx$):

$$\sum y = na + b(\sum x)$$

$$\sum xy = a(\sum x) + b(\sum x^2)$$

1)   EXAMPLE: The use of the two equations can be illustrated with the following data based on a set of six paired observations (n = 6):

y	x
$ 6	2
7	3
5	2
4	1
8	3
6	2
$\sum y = \$36$	$\sum x = 13$

xy	x^2
6 × 2 = 12	4
7 × 3 = 21	9
5 × 2 = 10	4
4 × 1 = 4	1
8 × 3 = 24	9
6 × 2 = 12	4
$\sum xy = 83$	$\sum x^2 = 31$

a)   Substituting into the two equations gives

$$36 = 6a + 13b$$
$$83 = 13a + 31b$$

b)   Solving simultaneously for the two unknowns,

$$1116 = 186a + 403b$$
$$1079 = 169a + 403b$$
$$37 = 17a$$

c) Thus, a = 2.176. Solving for b in the second original equation gives

$$83 = 13(2.176) + 31b$$
$$83 = 28.288 + 31b$$
$$31b = 54.712$$
$$b = 1.765$$

d) Alternative formulas that are ordinarily simpler to use are given below:

i) The slope may be expressed as

$$b = \frac{n\Sigma\, xy - \Sigma\, x\Sigma\, y}{n\Sigma\, x^2 - (\Sigma x)^2}$$

ii) The value of the y-intercept may be expressed as

$$a = \overline{y} - b(\overline{x})$$

h. The statistical significance of the **slope of the regression line** is important because, if its true value is zero, changes in the independent variable have no effect on the dependent variable.

1) Because the distribution of b is normal, the t-distribution may be used to determine whether b is significantly different from zero, that is, whether one can reject the null hypothesis that b equals zero.

a) One approach is to divide b by the standard error of the estimate of b. (The formula is not given here. The standard error is usually provided in the computer output.) If the result exceeds the critical value of t determinable from a standard table, the conclusion is that b is not zero. For example, this critical value is 2.0 for a sample of 60, 58 degrees of freedom (60 – 2 parameters of a and b estimated), and a 95% confidence level.

b) Another approach is to construct a precision interval (b ± t multiplied by the standard error of the estimate). If the interval does not contain zero, the null hypothesis may be rejected.

i) The value of t is the critical value for the given sample size, degrees of freedom, and confidence level used in the first approach.

i. The **high-low method** is used to generate a regression line by basing the equation on only the highest and lowest of a series of observations.

1) EXAMPLE: A regression equation covering electricity costs could be developed by using only the high-cost month and the low-cost month. If costs were $400 in April when production was 800 machine hours and $600 in September when production was 1,300 hours, the equation would be determined as follows:

High month	$600 for	1,300	hours
Low month	400 for	800	hours
Increase	$200	500	hours

Because costs increased $200 for 500 additional hours, the variable cost is $.40 per machine hour. For the low month, the total variable portion of that monthly cost is $320 ($.40 × 800 hours). Given that the total cost is $400 and $320 is variable, the remaining $80 must be a fixed cost. The regression equation is $y = 80 + .4x$.

2) The major criticism of the high-low method is that the high and low points may be abnormalities not representative of normal events.

4. **Time series** or **trend analysis** relies on past experience. Changes in the value of a variable (e.g., unit sales of a product) over time may have several possible components.

    a. In time series analysis, the dependent variable is regressed on time (the independent variable).

    b. The **secular trend** is the long-term change that occurs in a series. It is represented by a straight line or curve on a graph.

    c. **Seasonal variations** are common in many businesses. A variety of analysis methods includes seasonal variations in a forecasting model, but most methods make use of a seasonal index.

    d. **Cyclical fluctuations** are variations in the level of activity in business periods. Although some of these fluctuations are beyond the control of the firm, they need to be considered in forecasting. They are usually incorporated as index numbers.

    e. **Irregular** or **random variables** are any variations not included in the categories above. Business can be affected by random happenings (e.g., weather, strikes, fires, etc.).

    f. The **percentage-of-sales** method is the most widely used for sales forecasting. It adjusts the current level of sales by a specified percentage increase or decrease. This method is a form of trend analysis that is convenient and easy to apply and intuitively appealing to managers. It is also useful for developing **pro forma financial statements** by estimating items that vary directly with sales as percentages of expected sales.

        1) This method is based on the assumptions that most items directly correlate with sales and that the current levels of all assets are optimal for the current sales level.

5. **Exponential smoothing** is a technique used to level or smooth variations encountered in a forecast. This technique also adapts the forecast to changes as they occur.

    a. The simplest form of smoothing is the moving average, in which each forecast is based on a fixed number of prior observations. Exponential smoothing is similar to the moving average.

    b. Exponential means that greater weight is placed on the most recent data, with the weights of all data falling off exponentially as the data age. The selection of alpha (α), the smoothing factor, is important because a high alpha places more weight on recent data.

    c. The equation for the forecast (F) for period t + 1 is

    $$F_{t+1} = \alpha(x_t) + (1 - \alpha)F_t$$

    If: x_t = the observation for period t
    t = the most recent period
    α = the smoothing factor ($0 \leq \alpha \leq 1$)
    F_t = the forecast for period t

        1) This method weights the observation for period t by α and the forecast for period t by $(1 - \alpha)$.

6. **Learning curves** reflect the increased rate at which people perform tasks as they gain experience. The time required to perform a given task becomes progressively shorter, but this technique is applicable only to the early stages of production or of any new task.

    a. Ordinarily, the curve is expressed as a percentage of reduced time to complete a task for each doubling of cumulative production. Research has shown learning curve percentages to be approximately 80%. In other words, the time required is reduced by 20% each time cumulative production is doubled.

      1)   One common assumption made in a learning curve model is that the **cumulative average time per unit** is reduced by a certain percentage each time production doubles.

          a)   The alternative assumption is that **incremental unit time** (time to produce the last unit) is reduced when production doubles.

      2)   EXAMPLE: An 80% learning curve would result in the following performance for the lots shown, when run in sequence (top to bottom).

Cumulative Number of Tasks	Cumulative Average Minutes per Unit
100	3.0
200	2.4 (3.0 × 80%)
400	1.92 (2.4 × 80%)
800	1.536 (1.92 × 80%)
1,600	1.228 (1.536 × 80%)

  b.   **Graphical Presentation**

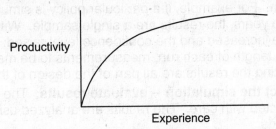

  c.   Since the average time for 100 units in the example above would be 3 minutes per unit, the total time would be 300 minutes. At an average time of 2.4 minutes for 200 units, the total time would be 480 minutes. In other words, the additional 100 units would require only 180 minutes (480 − 300), or 1.8 minutes per unit.

7.   **Simulation** is a technique for experimenting with logical and mathematical models using a computer.

  a.   Despite the power of mathematics, many problems cannot be solved by known analytical methods because of the behavior of the variables and the complexity of their interactions, e.g.,

      1)   Corporate planning models
      2)   Financial planning models
      3)   New product marketing models
      4)   Queuing system simulations
      5)   Inventory control simulations

  b.   **Experimentation** is neither new nor uncommon in business. Building a mockup of a new automobile, having one department try out new accounting procedures, and test-marketing a new product are all forms of experimentation. In effect, experimentation is organized trial and error using a model of the real world to obtain information prior to full implementation.

  c.   **Models** can be classified as either physical or abstract.

      1)   Physical models include automobile mockups, airplane models used for wind-tunnel tests, and breadboard models of electronic circuits.

      2)   Abstract models may be pictorial (architectural plans), verbal (a proposed procedure), or logical-mathematical. Experimentation with logical-mathematical models can involve many time-consuming calculations. Computers have eliminated much of this costly drudgery and have led to the growing interest in simulation for management.

d.   The **simulation procedure** has five steps.

   1)   **Define the objectives.** The objectives serve as guidelines for all that follows. The objectives may be to aid in the understanding of an existing system (e.g., an inventory system with rising costs) or to explore alternatives (e.g., the effect of investments on the firm's financial structure). A third type of objective is estimating the behavior of some new system, such as a production line.

   2)   **Formulate the model.** The variables to be included, their individual behavior, and their interrelationships must be defined in precise logical-mathematical terms. The objectives of the simulation serve as guidelines in deciding which factors are relevant.

   3)   **Validate the model.** Some assurance is needed that the results of the experiment will be realistic. This assurance requires validation of the model -- often using historical data. If the model gives results equivalent to what actually happened, the model is historically valid. Some risk remains, however, that changes could make the model invalid for the future.

   4)   **Design the experiment.** Experimentation is sampling the operation of a system. For example, if a particular policy is simulated on an inventory model for two years, the results are a single sample. With replication, the sample size can be increased and the confidence level raised. The number of runs to be made, length of each run, measurements to be made, and methods for analyzing the results are all part of the design of the experiment.

   5)   **Conduct the simulation -- evaluate results.** The simulation should be conducted with care. The results are analyzed using appropriate statistical methods.

e.   The **Monte Carlo technique** is often used in simulation to generate the individual values for a random variable. A random number generator is used to produce numbers with a uniform probability distribution (equal likelihoods of occurrence). The second step is to transform these numbers into values consistent with the desired distribution.

   1)   The performance of a quantitative model may be investigated by randomly selecting values for each of the variables in the model (based on the probability distribution of each variable) and then calculating the value of the solution. If this process is performed a large number of times, the distribution of results from the model will be obtained.

   2)   EXAMPLE: A new marketing model includes a factor for a competitor's introduction of a similar product within 1 year. Management estimates a 50% chance that this event will happen. For each simulation, this factor must be determined, perhaps by flipping a coin, or by putting two numbers in a hat and selecting one number. Random numbers between 0 and 1 could be generated. Numbers under .5 would signify introduction of a similar product; numbers over .5 would indicate the nonoccurrence of this event.

f.   The advantages of simulation are as follows:

   1)   Time can be compressed. A corporate planning model can show the results of a policy for 5 years into the future, using only minutes of computer time.

   2)   Alternative policies can be explored. With simulations, managers can ask what-if questions to explore possible policies, providing management with a powerful new planning tool.

   3)   Complex systems can be analyzed. In many cases, simulation is the only possible quantitative method for analyzing a complex system such as a production or inventory system, or the entire firm.

    g.   The limitations of simulation are as follows:

        1)   Cost. Simulation models can be costly to develop. They can be justified only if the information to be obtained is worth more than the costs to develop the model and carry out the experiment.

        2)   Risk of error. A simulation results in a prediction of how an actual system would behave. As in forecasting, the prediction may be in error.

    h.   **Sensitivity analysis.** After a problem has been formulated into any mathematical model, it may be subjected to sensitivity analysis.

        1)   A trial-and-error method may be adopted in which the sensitivity of the solution to changes in any given variable or parameter is calculated.

            a)   The risk of the project being simulated may also be estimated.

            b)   The best project may be one that is least sensitive to changes in probabilistic (uncertain) inputs.

        2)   In **linear programming** problems, sensitivity is the range within which a constraint value, such as a cost coefficient or any other variable, may be changed without changing the optimal solution. Shadow price is the synonym for sensitivity in that context.

8.   A variant of intuitive forecasting by well-informed managers is **scenario analysis** (scenario planning). This technique involves developing formal written descriptions of equally likely future alternatives (usually two to four). It is a qualitative procedure (that may reflect some quantitative input) reflecting an understanding that future events involve many variables not susceptible to quantification.

    a.   A **longitudinal scenario** concerns how future conditions will develop from current conditions.

    b.   The more common **cross-sectional scenario** describes a future state at a certain moment in time.

    c.   Scenario analysis is a long-range forecasting method (often 5 years or more) that is based on **multiple forecasts**. For example, scenarios may be written about how very favorable, normal, or unfavorable economic conditions will affect a particular market, product, or industry. This strategic planning method is beneficial because it **avoids surprise**.

9.   Well-designed **surveys** using questionnaires or interviews are often used to determine customer preferences, attitudes, and tastes. They also may be used to gather opinions from experts.

10.   The **Delphi technique** was developed by the RAND Corporation in the late 1960s as a forecasting methodology. Later, the U.S. government enhanced it as a group decision-making tool with the results of Project HINDSIGHT, which established a factual basis for the workability of Delphi. That project produced a tool in which a group of experts could reach a consensus when the decisive factors were subjective, not knowledge-based.

11.   Stop and review! You have completed the outline for this subunit. Study multiple-choice questions 20 through 37 beginning on page 496.

16.4 PROJECT MANAGEMENT

1.   Project management techniques are designed to aid the planning and control of large-scale projects having many interrelated activities.

    a.   A **project** is a temporary undertaking with specified objectives that often involves a cross-functional team and working outside customary organizational lines. Hence, interpersonal skills are at a premium in project management because a manager may not have line authority over some team members.

    b.   The **project life cycle** consists of

        1)   **Conceptualization** (setting overall objectives, budgets, and schedules)
        2)   **Planning** (obtaining resources, assigning duties, and coordinating activities)
        3)   **Execution** (monitoring, correcting, meeting expectations, and finishing the project within time and budgetary limits)

            a)   The largest amount of resources are used during this stage.

        4)   **Termination** (turning the project over to the user and redistributing project resources)

    c.   **Project management software** is available. Among other things, it should

        1)   Specify and schedule required activities
        2)   Provide the ability to do sensitivity analysis of the effects of changes in plans
        3)   Calculate a project's critical path
        4)   Establish priorities
        5)   Be able to modify or merge plans
        6)   Manage all types of project resources
        7)   Monitor progress, including adherence to time budgets for activities

    d.   **Example applications** include building construction, R&D projects, new product planning, feasibility studies, audit studies, movie production, and conversion to a new computer information system.

2.   Three of the more common scheduling techniques are Gantt or bar charts, PERT, and CPM. These techniques are suitable for any project having a target completion date and single start. **Gantt charts** or **bar charts** are simple to construct and use. To develop a Gantt chart, divide the project into logical subprojects called activities or tasks. Estimate the start and completion times for each activity. Prepare a bar chart showing each activity as a horizontal bar along a time scale.

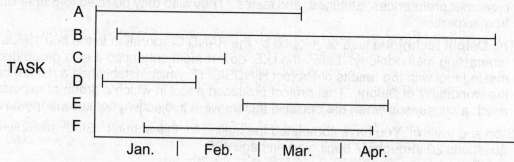

    a.   The major advantage of the Gantt chart is its simplicity. It forces the planner to think ahead and define logical activities. As the project progresses, actual completion times can be compared with planned times. Furthermore, the technique requires no special tools or mathematics and can be used on small projects as well as large ones.

    b.   The major disadvantage is that interrelationships among activities are not shown. Several special methods have been developed to show these on a Gantt chart, but they are feasible only for simple relationships.

3. **Program Evaluation and Review Technique (PERT)** was developed to aid managers in controlling large-scale, complex projects. PERT diagrams are free-form networks showing each activity as a line between events. A sequence of lines shows interrelationships among activities. PERT diagrams are more complex than Gantt charts, but they have the advantages of incorporating probabilistic time estimates and identifying the critical path.

   a. **Events** are discrete moments in time representing the start or finish of an activity. They consume no resources.

   b. **Activities** are tasks to be accomplished. They consume resources (including time) and have a duration over time.

   c. The **network diagram** is formed by

      1) The lines (activities) connected from left to right in the necessary sequence of their accomplishment. They can be marked with time lengths.

      2) Circles representing events and numbered for identification.

   d. The **critical path** is the longest path in time through the network. It is critical because, if any activity on the critical path takes longer than expected, the entire project will be delayed. Every network has at least one critical path. Some have more than one.

      1) The **mean completion time** for the critical path is the sum of the means of the activity times.

      2) The **standard deviation of the completion time** for the critical path is the square root of the sum of the variances (squares of the standard deviations) of the activity times.

         a) EXAMPLE: If the critical path has two activities, and the standard deviations of the completion times are 3 and 4, the standard deviation for the critical path is

$$\sqrt{3^2 + 4^2} = 5$$

   e. Paths that are not critical have **slack time**. One advantage of PERT is that it identifies this slack time, which represents unused resources that can be diverted to the critical path.

   f. Several techniques have been developed to include cost information in the analyses. This variation of PERT is often called **PERT-Cost**. It entails combining activities into work packages to facilitate cost control. By estimating costs for each work package, a manager can develop a budget that indicates when costs should be incurred during the project.

   g. **Activity times** can be expressed probabilistically. Computer programs are available to make the calculations and find critical paths.

   h. PERT analysis includes probabilistic estimates of activity completion times. **Three time estimates** are made -- optimistic, most likely, and pessimistic.

      1) The time estimates for an activity are assumed to approximate a beta probability distribution. In contrast with the normal distribution, this distribution has finite endpoints (the optimistic and pessimistic estimates) and is unimodal; that is, it has only one mode (the most likely time).

      2) PERT approximates the mean of the beta distribution by dividing the sum of the optimistic time, the pessimistic time, and four times the most likely time (the mode) by six.

      3) The **standard deviation** is approximated by dividing the difference between the pessimistic and optimistic times by six. The basis for the latter approximation is that various probability distributions have tails that lie about plus or minus three standard deviations from the mean. For example, 99.9% of observations in the normal distribution are expected to lie within this range.

    i.   EXAMPLE: If an activity can be completed in 6 days (optimistic time), 10 days (most likely time), or 20 days (pessimistic time), the expected duration is 11 days {[6 + (4 × 10) + 20] ÷ 6}.

        1)   Thus, the most likely time is weighted the most heavily.
        2)   The standard deviation is 2.33 [(20 − 6) ÷ 6].

    j.   EXAMPLE:

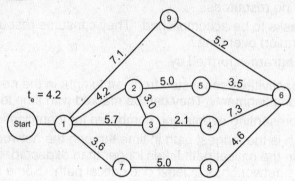

        1)   For the network above, the following are the paths and path times:

Path	Time (hours)
Start-1-9-6	16.5
Start-1-2-5-6	16.9
Start-1-2-3-4-6	20.8
Start-1-3-4-6	19.3
Start-1-7-8-6	17.4

        2)   Path Start-1-2-3-4-6 is the critical path because it has the longest time.

    k.   In the example above, path 1-3 takes only 5.7 hours, whereas the critical path events (1-2-3) take 7.2 hours. The slack time represented by path 1-3 is thus 7.2 − 5.7, or 1.5. People assigned to path 1-3 have an extra 1.5 hours to help elsewhere.

4.   The **critical path method (CPM)** was developed independently of PERT and is widely used in the construction industry. CPM may be thought of as a subset of PERT. Like PERT, it is a network technique. Unlike PERT, it uses deterministic time and cost estimates. Its advantages include cost estimates plus the concept of "crash" efforts and costs.

    a.   Activity times are estimated for normal effort and crash effort. **Crash time** is the time to complete an activity assuming that all available resources were devoted to the task (overtime, extra crew, etc.).

    b.   Activity costs are also estimated for normal and crash efforts.

    c.   These estimates allow the project manager to estimate the costs of completing the project if some of the activities are completed on a crash basis.

    d.   The **network diagram** is constructed in the same manner as PERT diagrams. Once the diagram is constructed, the critical paths are found for normal and crash times. More than one critical path may exist for each diagram.

    e.   **Crashing the network** means finding the minimum cost for completing the project in minimum time.

    f.   CPM computer programs allow updating of the solution as work proceeds.

5. **Network models** are used to solve managerial problems pertaining to project scheduling, information systems design, and transportation systems design. Networks consisting of nodes and arcs may be created to represent in graphic form problems related to transportation, assignment, and transshipment. The shortest-route, minimal spanning tree, and maximal flow problems are other applications of network models.

    a. A **shortest-route algorithm** minimizes total travel time from one site to each of the other sites in a transportation system.

    b. The **maximal flow algorithm** maximizes throughput in networks with distinct entry (source node) and exit (sink node) points. Examples of applications are highway transportation systems and oil pipelines. Flows are limited by capacities of the arcs (e.g., highways or pipes).

    c. The **minimal spanning tree algorithm** identifies the set of connecting branches having the shortest combined length. A spanning tree is a group of branches (arcs) that connects each node in the network to every other node. An example problem is the determination of the shortest telecommunications linkage among users at remote sites and a central computer.

6. Controlling **job projects** requires attention to their scope, scheduling, quality, and costs. Thus, **variance analysis** is a tool for project management.

    a. The difference between the actual cost of work performed (CWP) and the budgeted cost of work scheduled (CWS) may be analyzed in terms of two variances:

        1) The **job project-performance cost variance** is the difference between the actual CWP and the budgeted CWP. This variance may be further divided into price and efficiency variances. It measures cost overruns or underruns.

        2) The **job project-schedule cost variance** is the difference between the budgeted CWP and the budgeted CWS. It measures the extent to which the project is ahead of or behind schedule.

7. Stop and review! You have completed the outline for this subunit. Study multiple-choice questions 38 through 43 beginning on page 502.

16.5 THE BUDGETING PROCESS

1. A **budget (profit plan)** is a realistic plan for the future expressed in quantitative terms. Senior management can use a budget to plan for the future and communicate objectives to all levels of the organization, to motivate employees, to control organizational activities, and to evaluate performance.

    a. The annual budget should reflect an organization's objectives. Thus, the annual budget is usually based on a combination of financial, quantitative, and qualitative measures.

    b. The budget is a **planning** tool.

        1) Organizations that prepare budgets anticipate problems before they occur, for example, shortages of materials, merchandise, personnel, or equipment.

        2) Objectives in the form of budgets facilitate decision making.

        3) **Strategic budgeting** is a form of long-range planning based on identifying and specifying organizational objectives. The strengths and weaknesses of the organization are evaluated and risk levels are assessed. The influences of internal and external factors are forecast to derive the best strategy for reaching the organization's objectives.

            a) External factors include general economic conditions and their expected trends, governmental regulatory measures, the labor market, and the activities of competitors.

    c.   The budget is a **control** tool. A budget helps to control costs by setting cost guidelines to detect efficient or inefficient use of resources.

        1)   A manager is more likely to control **costs** if (s)he knows that all costs will be compared with the budget. A manager will be accountable if costs for which (s)he is **responsible** exceed budgeted amounts.

        2)   Budgets also reward highly effective managers. Consequently, employees should not view budgets negatively. A manager also can use a budget as a personal self-evaluation tool.

        3)   **Budgetary slack** (underestimation of probable performance) must be avoided, however, if a budget is to have its desired effects. The natural tendency of a manager is to negotiate for a less stringent measure of performance so as to avoid unfavorable variances from expectations.

        4)   For the budgetary process to serve effectively as a control function, it must be **integrated** with the accounting system and the organizational structure. Such integration enhances control by transmitting data and assigning variances to the proper organizational subunits.

    d.   The budget is a **motivational** tool. Employees are particularly motivated if they **participate** in preparing the budget. A budget must be seen as realistic by employees before it can become a good motivational tool.

        1)   Unfortunately, the budget is not always viewed in a positive manner. Some managers view a budget as a restriction.

        2)   Employees are more apt to have a positive feeling toward a budget if some degree of flexibility is allowed.

    e.   The budget is a means of **communication**. A budget can help tell employees what objectives and goals the organization is attempting to reach.

        1)   Absent an overall budget, each subunit may think the organization has different objectives.

        2)   For example, the sales department may want to keep as much inventory as possible so that no sales will be lost, but the treasurer may want to keep the inventory as low as possible so that cash need not be spent any sooner than necessary. If the budget specifies the amount of inventory, all employees can work toward the same objectives.

2.   Budgets coordinate the various activities of a firm. An overall budget, often called the **master** or **comprehensive budget**, encompasses both the operating and financial budget processes.

3.   A **budget manual** describes how a budget is to be prepared. Items usually appearing in a budget manual include a budget planning calendar and distribution instructions for all budget schedules. Instructions are important because, once a schedule is prepared, other subunits use the schedule to prepare their own budgets. Without these instructions, someone who needs a particular schedule might be overlooked.

    a.   The **budget planning calendar** is the schedule of activities for the development and adoption of the budget. It should include a list of dates indicating when specific information is to be provided to others by each information source.

    b.   The preparation of a master budget usually takes several months. For instance, many firms start the budget for the next calendar year in September, anticipating its completion by the first of December. Because all subunit budgets are based on forecasts prepared by others and the budgets of other subunits, a planning calendar is necessary to integrate the process.

4.   Stop and review! You have completed the outline for this subunit. Study multiple-choice questions 44 through 47 beginning on page 504.

16.6 THE MASTER BUDGET AND ITS COMPONENTS

1. The **master budget** encompasses the organization's operating and financial plans for a specified period (ordinarily a year). The **operating budget** is the part of the master budget that consists of the pro forma income statement and related budgets. Its emphasis is on obtaining and using resources.

2. The **sales budget** (revenues budget) presents sales in units at their projected selling prices and is usually the first budget prepared. Accordingly, accurate **sales forecasts** are crucial. A forecast considers such factors as the trends in sales, conditions in the economy and industry, activities of competitors, credit and pricing policies, marketing methods, and the existence of back orders.

   a. Given a sales estimate, the next step is to decide how much to produce or purchase.
   b. Sales are usually budgeted by product or department.
   c. The sales budget establishes targets for sales personnel.
   d. Sales volume affects production and purchasing levels, operating expenses, and cash flow.

3. The **production budget** (for a manufacturer) is based on the sales forecast, in **units**, plus or minus the desired inventory change.

   a. It is prepared for each department and used to plan when items will be produced.
   b. When the production budget has been completed, it is used in conjunction with the **ending inventory budget** to prepare three additional budgets.

      1) Direct materials usage, together with beginning inventory and targeted ending inventory data, determines the **direct materials budget**.
      2) The **direct labor budget** depends on wage rates, amounts and types of production, numbers and skill levels of employees to be hired, etc. It may also depend on employee benefits, such as employer contributions to Social Security, insurance, and pensions. Classification of **fringe benefits as direct labor cost** is theoretically sound because these benefits are a necessary part of the acquisition cost of direct labor. Nevertheless, many organizations treat such costs as overhead. Another concern is the effect of **union contracts** on wage rates and the ability to terminate workers.
      3) The **factory overhead budget** is a function of how factory overhead varies with particular cost drivers. It should distinguish between overhead items that are fixed and those that are variable.

4. The **cost of goods sold budget** reflects direct materials usage, direct labor, factory overhead, and the change in finished goods inventory.

5. Other budgets prepared during the operating budget process are those for **R&D, marketing, distribution, customer service**, and **administrative costs**. These budgets also should distinguish between fixed and variable costs. These budgets, the sales budget, and the cost of goods sold budget are needed to prepare a pro forma operating income statement.

6. The **financial budget** is the part of the master budget that includes the cash budget, capital budget, pro forma balance sheet, and pro forma statement of cash flows. Its emphasis is on obtaining the funds needed to purchase operating assets.

7. The **capital budget** is not part of the operating budget because it is not part of normal operations.

   a. It may be prepared more than a year in advance to allow time to

      1) Plan financing of major expenditures for long-term assets such as equipment, buildings, and land
      2) Receive custom orders of specialized equipment, buildings, etc.

b.   Techniques used in the capital budgeting process include net present value (NPV), internal rate of return (IRR), and payback.

1)   NPV and IRR are time-adjusted methods based on present-value tables.

8.   The **cash budget** is vital because an organization must have adequate cash at all times. Even with plenty of other assets, an organization with a temporary shortage of cash can be driven into bankruptcy. Thus, cash budgets are prepared not only for annual and quarterly periods but also for monthly and weekly periods.

a.   A cash budget projects cash flows for planning and control purposes. It helps prevent not only cash emergencies but also excessive idle cash.

b.   It cannot be prepared until the other budgets have been completed.

c.   Almost all organizations, regardless of size, prepare a cash budget.

d.   It is particularly important for organizations operating in seasonal industries.

e.   Cash budgeting facilitates planning for loans and other financing.

f.   EXAMPLE: A company had budgeted sales of $9,000 for January, $9,700 for February, and $13,950 for March. Its monthly cash budgets might appear as follows (payments of principal and interest are assumed not to be due during the quarter):

Sample Company
CASH BUDGET
For Quarter Ending March 31

	January	February	March
Beginning cash balance	$ 80	$ 20	$ 1,957
Receipts:			
Collection from sales*	6,800	9,350	11,825
Total cash available	$ 6,880	$ 9,370	$13,782
Payments:			
Purchases**	$ 3,150	$ 2,760	$ 3,960
Sales salaries	1,350	1,455	2,093
Supplies	360	388	588
Utilities	120	110	100
Administrative salaries	1,800	1,800	1,800
Advertising	80	80	80
Equipment purchases	0	820	3,000
Total payments	$ 6,860	$ 7,413	$11,591
Desired ending balance	5,000	5,000	5,000
Total required	$11,860	$12,413	$16,591
Cash available	6,880	9,370	13,782
Financing required	$ 4,980	$ 3,043	$ 2,809

*Sales are 50% cash sales and 50% on credit (net 30). Thus, 50% of each month's sales are collected in the month of the sale, and 50% are collected in the following month. For example, the February collections equaled $9,350 [($9,000 × 50%) + ($9,700 × 50%)].

**Purchase terms are net 30. Thus, purchases are paid for in the month following the purchase. The amount paid in February ($2,760) equaled the total purchases for January.

9.   The following is a summary of the **operating budget sequence** for a manufacturer that includes all elements of the value chain:

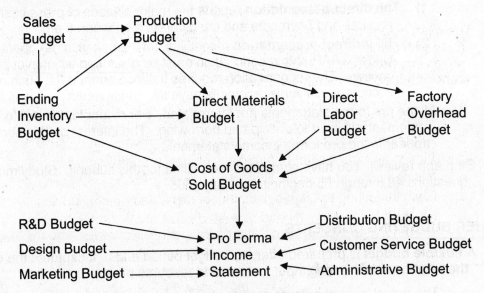

10.   The following summarizes the **financial budget sequence**:

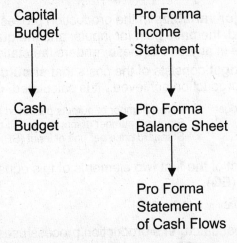

11.   Once the individual budgets are complete, budgeted financial statements can be prepared. They are often called **pro forma statements** because they are prepared before actual activities commence.

a.   The **pro forma income statement** culminates the operating budget process. It adjusts pro forma operating income for interest and taxes.

1)   It is used to decide whether the budgeted activities will result in an acceptable level of income.

b.   The **pro forma balance sheet** is prepared using the cash and capital budgets and the pro forma income statement. Thus, it and the pro forma statement of cash flows culminate the financial budget process. The pro forma balance sheet is the beginning of the period balance sheet updated for projected changes in cash, receivables, payables, inventory, etc.

1)   If the balance sheet indicates that a contractual agreement may be violated, the budgeting process must be repeated. For example, some loan agreements require that owners' equity be maintained at some percentage of total debt or that current assets be maintained at a given multiple of current liabilities.

c.   The **pro forma statement of cash flows** classifies cash flows depending on whether they are from operating, investing, or financing activities.

   1)   The **direct presentation** reports the major classes of gross cash operating receipts and payments and the difference between them.

   2)   The **indirect presentation** reconciles net income with net operating cash flow. Under GAAP, this reconciliation must be disclosed whichever presentation is chosen. The reconciliation requires balance sheet data, such as the changes in accounts receivable, accounts payable, and inventory, as well as net income.

d.   All the pro forma statements are interrelated. For example, the pro forma cash flow statement will include anticipated borrowing. The interest on this borrowing will appear in the pro forma income statement.

12.   Stop and review! You have completed the outline for this subunit. Study multiple-choice questions 48 through 55 beginning on page 505.

16.7 OTHER BUDGETING CONCEPTS

1.   A **flexible budget** is prepared after the budget period ends. It captures the **complexity of the relationships** among input, output, and resource prices.

a.   The actual level of outputs produced and prices paid for inputs rarely match those that were planned on in the static budget.

   1)   **Three major variables** in the production process are the quantity of inputs consumed, the price paid for inputs, and the quantity of outputs produced. A difference in any one of these renders the static budget less useful.

b.   The **flexible budget** consists of the costs that **should have been** incurred given the actual level of production achieved. It is calculated as follows:

Flexible budget   =   Actual number of outputs produced (AO)
                     ×   Standard number of inputs per unit of output (SI/O)
                     ×   Standard price per unit of input (SP)

   1)   The product of the first two elements of this equation make up the **"expected" quantity (EQ)**.

   Expected quantity = (AO × SI/O)

c.   EXAMPLE: A manufacturer's production process uses a single direct material, and it planned to consume 100 pounds costing $10 per pound last month. The static budget total for raw materials cost was therefore $1,000 (100 pounds × $10).

   1)   The company planned to produce 90 units of output during the month. Since 100 pounds of raw material were budgeted for this level of output, the standard input usage per unit of output was 1.1111 (100 pounds ÷ 90 outputs).

   2)   The actual level of production for the month was 94 units. The "expected" quantity of direct materials was thus 104.4434 units (94 outputs × 1.1111), and the flexible budget was $1,044 (104.4434 units × $10).

   3)   In other words, given its standard cost for raw materials, the company would have expected to spend $1,044, not $1,000, to produce 94 units of output.

2.   **Zero-base budgeting (ZBB)** is a budget and planning process in which each manager must justify his/her entire budget every year (or period). The most notable proponent of this technique in recent years has been President Jimmy Carter (1977-1980), who employed ZBB on the federal level and during his term as governor of Georgia.

a.   ZBB differs from traditional **incremental budgeting** in which the current budget is simply adjusted to allow for changes planned for the coming period. The managerial advantage of incremental budgeting is that the manager has to make less effort to justify changes in the budget.

    b.   Under ZBB, a manager must build the budget every year from a base of zero. All expenditures must be justified regardless of variance from previous years.

    c.   The **objective** is to encourage periodic reexamination of all costs in the hope that some can be reduced or eliminated.

    d.   ZBB begins with the lowest budgetary units of the entity. It requires determination of objectives, operations, and costs for **each activity** and the alternative means of carrying out that activity.

    e.   Different **levels of service (work effort)** are evaluated for each activity, measures of work and performance are established, and activities are ranked according to their importance to the entity.

    f.   For each budgetary unit, a **decision package** is prepared that describes various levels of service that may be provided, including at least one level lower than the current one. ZBB requires managers to justify each expenditure for each period and to review each cost element from a cost-benefit perspective.

3.   A **life-cycle budget** estimates a product's revenues and expenses over its entire life cycle, beginning with R&D and ending with the withdrawal of customer support. **Life-cycle budgeting**

    a.   Is intended to account for the costs at all stages of the **value chain** (R&D, design, production, marketing, distribution, and customer service). This information is important for **pricing** decisions because revenues must cover costs incurred in each stage of the value chain, not just production.

    b.   Emphasizes the relationships among costs incurred at different value-chain stages, e.g., the effect of reduced design costs on future customer-service costs.

    c.   Highlights the potential for **locking in** (designing in) future costs.

    d.   Is helpful in **target costing and pricing**.

4.   **Activity-based budgeting** focuses on the numerous activities necessary to produce and market goods and services. This approach contrasts with the traditional emphasis on functions or spending categories.

    a.   Activity-based budgeting provides greater detail, especially regarding indirect costs, because it permits the isolation of numerous cost drivers.

    b.   A cost pool is established for each activity, and a cost driver is identified for each pool.

    c.   The budgeted cost for each pool is determined by multiplying the demand for the activity by the estimated cost of a unit of the activity.

5.   A **continuous (rolling) budget** is revised on a regular (continuous) basis. Such a budget is extended for another month or quarter in accordance with new data as the current month or quarter ends. For example, if the budget is for 12 months, a budget for the next 12 months will be available continuously as each month ends.

6.   The Japanese term **kaizen** means continuous improvement, and kaizen budgeting assumes the continuous improvement of products and processes. It requires estimates of the effects of improvements and the costs of their implementation.

    a.   Kaizen budgeting is based not on the existing system but on changes yet to be made.

    b.   Budget targets cannot be reached unless those improvements occur.

7.   **Governmental budgeting** differs from private-sector budgeting. A governmental budget is not only a financial plan and a basis for evaluating performance but also an expression of public policy and a form of control having the force of law.

   a.   Thus, a governmental budget is a legal document adopted in accordance with procedures specified by applicable laws.

   b.   A governmental budget must be complied with by the administrators of the governmental unit for which the budget is prepared. By law, the administrators cannot exceed the budget without a formally approved budget amendment.

   c.   The effectiveness and efficiency of governmental efforts are difficult to measure in the absence of the profit-centered activity that characterizes business operations. Thus, the use of budgets in the **appropriation** process is crucial. **Budgetary accounts** are incorporated into the formal accounting systems of governments, and **budgetary comparison schedules** are presented as required supplementary information or in a budgetary comparison statement.

8.   Stop and review! You have completed the outline for this subunit. Study multiple-choice questions 56 through 61 beginning on page 508.

QUESTIONS

16.1 Strategic Management

1. Which of the following steps in the strategic planning process should be completed first?

A.   Translate objectives into goals.

B.   Determine actions to achieve goals.

C.   Develop performance measures.

D.   Create a mission statement.

Answer (D) is correct. *(CPA, adapted)*
REQUIRED: The first step in strategic planning.
DISCUSSION: A mission statement is a formal, written document that defines an organization's ultimate purposes in society. A grand strategy is then developed to describe how the mission is to be achieved. The next step is to formulate specific and measurable objectives, plans, policies, and budgets.
Answer (A) is incorrect because a subsequent step is to translate longer-range objectives into shorter-range objectives. However, the terms "objectives" and "goals" are defined differently by different authors. For example, "goals" might be longer-range than "objectives." Answer (B) is incorrect because determining the specific actions to achieve objectives (goals) follows defining the mission. Answer (C) is incorrect because an organization does not develop performance measures before defining its mission.

2. Strategic management includes establishment of appropriate controls. Control measurements are made to determine whether organizational objectives are being achieved. One category of strategic control measures addresses external effectiveness. A measurement relating to external effectiveness is

A.   Cycle time.

B.   Waste.

C.   Flexibility.

D.   Productivity.

Answer (C) is correct. *(Publisher, adapted)*
REQUIRED: The measure of external effectiveness.
DISCUSSION: Strategic control measures may be categorized as concerning either external effectiveness or internal efficiency. Flexibility overlaps these categories. It relates to effectiveness and efficiency. Thus, an organization must be externally flexible in responding to changing customer needs and internally flexible in reordering its structural arrangements, retraining employees, etc.

3. Development of a grand strategy involves

    A. Reengineering.

    B. Situational analysis.

    C. Budgeting.

    D. Core process redesign.

Answer (B) is correct. *(Publisher, adapted)*
    REQUIRED: The process involved in developing a grand strategy.
    DISCUSSION: Strategic management involves developing a grand strategy, strategic planning, implementation, and control. A grand strategy describes how the organization's mission is to be achieved. It is based on a situational analysis that considers organizational strengths and weaknesses (a capability profile) and their interactions with environmental opportunities and threats.
    Answer (A) is incorrect because reengineering, which entails process innovation, is a possible result of the development of a grand strategy. Answer (C) is incorrect because strategic planning may involve budgeting. However, it is a step subsequent to development of a grand strategy. Answer (D) is incorrect because core process redesign is a possible result of the development of a grand strategy.

4. In the <List A> stage of the product life cycle, <List B> tend to be highest.

	List A	List B
A.	Introduction	Sales
B.	Growth	Profits
C.	Maturity	Profits
D.	Decline	Cash flows

Answer (B) is correct. *(CIA, adapted)*
    REQUIRED: The stages in the product life cycle.
    DISCUSSION: The product life cycle consists of the product development, introduction, growth, maturity, and decline stages. In the product development stage, the company incurs investment costs but makes no sales. In the introduction stage, sales are slow because the product is being introduced, profits and cash flows are negative, and investment in marketing is high. In the growth stage, profits are at their highest, although cash flow may be negative because of high investment. In the maturity stage, sales decrease and profits level off or begin to decline. In the decline stage, sales and profits drop.
    Answer (A) is incorrect because, in the introduction stage, sales are low. Answer (C) is incorrect because, in the maturity stage, profits level off or begin to decline. Answer (D) is incorrect because, in the decline stage, sales and profits drop, and cash flows are low.

5. What operations strategy is most likely to be adopted when the product sold by an organization is a commodity and the market is very large?

    A. Flexibility strategy.

    B. Quality strategy.

    C. Service strategy.

    D. Cost strategy.

Answer (D) is correct. *(Publisher, adapted)*
    REQUIRED: The strategy most likely to be adopted when the product sold by an organization is a commodity and the market is very large.
    DISCUSSION: An operations strategy formulates a long-term plan for using enterprise resources to reach strategic objectives. A cost strategy is successful when the enterprise is the low-cost producer. However, the product (e.g., a commodity) tends to be undifferentiated in these cases, the market is often very large, and the competition tends to be intense because of the possibility of high-volume sales.
    Answer (A) is incorrect because a flexibility strategy involves offering many different products. Answer (B) is incorrect because a quality strategy involves competition based on product quality or process quality. Answer (C) is incorrect because service is not an issue in a sale of commodities.

6. Customer lifetime value for a particular customer is the

    A. Net present value of the cash flows related to a particular customer.

    B. Sum of the customer's purchases from the firm.

    C. Undiscounted amount of the net cash flows related to a particular customer.

    D. Customer equity.

Answer (A) is correct. *(Publisher, adapted)*
    REQUIRED: The measure of customer lifetime value.
    DISCUSSION: A firm should estimate customer lifetime value, the net present value of the cash flows (purchases – costs of acquiring, selling to, and serving the customer) related to a particular customer. This amount indicates whether a given investment in a customer is justified.
    Answer (B) is incorrect because the measurement of customer lifetime value also considers costs. Answer (C) is incorrect because customer lifetime value is a discounted amount. Answer (D) is incorrect because customer equity is the sum of the customer lifetime values for all of the firm's customers.

7. In Michael E. Porter's model of the value creation chain, the primary activities include

A. Logistics, operations, marketing and sales, and service.

B. Procurement, infrastructure, operations, and service.

C. Procurement, infrastructure, operations, and technology development.

D. Procurement, infrastructure, human resources, and technology development.

Answer (A) is correct. *(Publisher, adapted)*
REQUIRED: The primary activities in the value creation chain.
DISCUSSION: The model consists of primary and supporting activities. The primary activities are inbound logistics, operations, outbound logistics, marketing and sales, and service. Inbound logistics activities involve the firms' capture of materials to be processed. Operations activities are conversion processes. Outbound logistics activities include shipment of products. Marketing and sales activities are the promotion and sale of final products. Service activities provide customer service. The four support activities are infrastructure (e.g., administration, finance, and planning), procurement, human resources, and technology development.

8. Customer relationship management is best defined as

A. Coordination with members of the firm's supply chain.

B. Attracting and satisfying customers.

C. Market sensing.

D. Maximizing customer loyalty by managing customer "touchpoints."

Answer (D) is correct. *(Publisher, adapted)*
REQUIRED: The best definition of customer relationship management.
DISCUSSION: Philip Kotler defines customer relationship management as "the process of managing detailed information about individual customers and carefully managing all the customer 'touchpoints' with the aim of maximizing customer loyalty." Its purpose is to create optimal customer equity. Thus, the process involves more than merely attracting customers (through media advertising, direct mail, etc.) and satisfying them (something competitors also may do).
Answer (A) is incorrect because coordination with members of the firm's supply chain is partner relationship management. Answer (B) is incorrect because customer relationship management seeks to increase the value of the customer base by developing long-term relationships with individual customers by such methods as customer service, customized (if not personalized) offerings, and choice of marketing messages and media. Answer (C) is incorrect because market sensing consists of obtaining, distributing, and acting upon market intelligence.

9. Which relationship marketing level is appropriate for a low unit profit margin and many customers?

A. Reactive marketing.

B. Basic marketing.

C. Partnership marketing.

D. Proactive marketing.

Answer (B) is correct. *(Publisher, adapted)*
REQUIRED: The relationship marketing level appropriate for a low unit profit margin and many customers.
DISCUSSION: A firm must determine the appropriate investment in building customer relationships. The levels of investment depend on unit profit margins and the numbers of customers. Basic marketing consists only of selling (low-margin, many customers).
Answer (A) is incorrect because reactive marketing includes encouragement of customer communication (low-to-medium margin and many customers or low margin and medium number of customers). Answer (C) is incorrect because partnership marketing entails continuous assistance to big customers (high margin and few customers). Answer (D) is incorrect because proactive marketing involves seller-initiated communication about new products or uses of old ones (high margin and medium number of customers or medium margin and few customers).

16.2 Strategic Planning

10. A distinction between forecasting and planning

   A. Is not valid because they are synonyms.

   B. Arises because forecasting covers the short-term and planning does not.

   C. Is that forecasts are used in planning.

   D. Is that forecasting is a management activity whereas planning is a technical activity.

Answer (C) is correct. *(CMA, adapted)*
REQUIRED: The distinction between forecasting and planning.
DISCUSSION: Planning is the determination of what is to be done, and of how, when, where, and by whom it is to be done. Plans serve to direct the activities that all organizational members must undertake to move the organization from where it is to where it wants to be. Forecasting is the basis of planning because it projects the future. A variety of quantitative methods are used in forecasting.
Answer (A) is incorrect because forecasting is a basis for planning. Answer (B) is incorrect because both forecasting and planning may be short or long term. Answer (D) is incorrect because forecasting is probably more technical than planning. It can involve the use of a variety of mathematical models.

11. Which of the following cycles does not have accounting information recorded into the general ledger reporting system?

   A. Expenditure.

   B. Production.

   C. Planning.

   D. Revenue.

Answer (C) is correct. *(CPA, adapted)*
REQUIRED: The accounting cycle that does not have accounting information recorded in the ledger.
DISCUSSION: Planning is the determination of what is to be done and of how, when, where, and by whom it is to be done. Plans serve to direct the activities that all organizational members must undertake and successfully perform to move the organization from where it is to where it wants to be. No transactions that require recording in the general ledger take place during the planning cycle.
Answer (A) is incorrect because purchasing, receiving, cash payments, and other transactions in the expenditure cycle are recorded in the general ledger. Answer (B) is incorrect because accounting for costs, deferred costs, and property involved in the production or conversion of goods or services are recorded in the general ledger. Answer (D) is incorrect because sales, receivables, cash receipts, bad debts, and other transactions in the revenue cycle are recorded in the general ledger.

12. Strategy is a broad term that usually means the selection of overall objectives. Strategic analysis ordinarily excludes the

   A. Trends that will affect the entity's markets.

   B. Target product mix and production schedule to be maintained during the year.

   C. Forms of organizational structure that would best serve the entity.

   D. Best ways to invest in research, design, production, distribution, marketing, and administrative activities.

Answer (B) is correct. *(CMA, adapted)*
REQUIRED: The item ordinarily excluded from the process of strategic analysis.
DISCUSSION: Strategic analysis is the process of long-range planning. It includes identifying organizational objectives, evaluating the strengths and weaknesses of the organization, assessing risk levels, and forecasting the future direction and influences of factors relevant to the organization, such as market trends, changes in technology, international competition, and social change. The final step best strategy for reaching the objectives. Setting the target product mix and production schedule for the current year is not a concern of strategic analysis because it is a short-term activity.
Answer (A) is incorrect because strategic analysis includes examining marketing trends. Answer (C) is incorrect because strategic analysis evaluates organizational structure. Answer (D) is incorrect because strategic analysis includes evaluation of the best ways to invest in research, design, etc.

13. All of the following are characteristics of the strategic planning process except the

    A. Emphasis on long run.

    B. Analysis of external economic factors.

    C. Review of the attributes and behavior of the organization's competition.

    D. Analysis and review of departmental budgets.

Answer (D) is correct. *(CMA, adapted)*
    REQUIRED: The item that is not a characteristic of the strategic planning process.
    DISCUSSION: Strategic planning is the process of setting the overall organizational objectives, and involves the drafting of strategic plans. Long-range (strategic) planning is based on identifying and specifying organizational objectives, evaluating the strengths and weaknesses of the organization, assessing risk levels, forecasting the future direction and influences of factors relevant to the organization (such as market trends, changes in technology, international competition, and social change), and deriving the best strategy for reaching the objectives given the organization's strengths and weaknesses and the relevant future trends. Analyzing and reviewing departmental budgets is an aspect of operational management and not a part of strategic planning.
    Answer (A) is incorrect because emphasis on the long run is an aspect of strategic planning. Answer (B) is incorrect because analysis of external economic factors is an aspect of strategic planning. Answer (C) is incorrect because consideration of competitive factors and analysis of consumer demand are all aspects of strategic planning.

14. Policies and procedures provide guidance to management and employees. Would policies and procedures normally be found for the senior management of a multinational organization?

    A. Yes, all policies and procedures are developed by senior management.

    B. No, senior management develops policies and procedures for lower levels only.

    C. Yes, policies and procedures are used throughout an organization's ranks.

    D. No, only middle managers and below develop and use policies and procedures.

Answer (C) is correct. *(CIA, adapted)*
    REQUIRED: The reason a multinational organization may or may not have policies and procedures at the senior management level.
    DISCUSSION: Research has shown that policies and procedures are referred to by all levels of management on an as-needed basis.
    Answer (A) is incorrect because senior management develops and refers toll, policies and procedures. Answer (B) is incorrect because senior management does develop policies and procedures for their own use. Answer (D) is incorrect because senior management also develops and uses policies and procedures.

15. An organization's policies and procedures are part of its overall system of internal controls. The control function performed by policies and procedures is

    A. Feedforward control.

    B. Implementation control.

    C. Feedback control.

    D. Application control.

Answer (A) is correct. *(CIA, adapted)*
    REQUIRED: The control function of policies and procedures.
    DISCUSSION: Feedforward control anticipates and prevents problems. Policies and procedures serve as feedforward controls because they provide guidance on how an activity should be performed to best insure that an objective is achieved.
    Answer (B) is incorrect because implementation controls are controls applied during systems development. Answer (C) is incorrect because policies and procedures provide primary guidance before and during the performance of some task rather than give feedback on its accomplishment. Answer (D) is incorrect because application controls apply to specific applications, e.g., payroll or accounts payable.

16. The management of an organization has stated that two members of the same family may not be employed in the same department. Identify the component of organizational planning that is being demonstrated by management's action.

A. A strategy.
B. A policy.
C. An objective.
D. A mission statement.

Answer (B) is correct. *(CIA, adapted)*
REQUIRED: The component of organizational planning that prohibits employment of family members in the same department.
DISCUSSION: Top management establishes policies as guides to middle- and lower-management decision making. Policies are relatively broad guidelines for making routine decisions consistent with overall objectives. They channel thinking in a certain direction but allow for some managerial discretion.
Answer (A) is incorrect because a strategy is a broad, overall concept of operation. Objectives are implemented by strategies. Answer (C) is incorrect because objectives guide the organization toward accomplishment of its mission. Answer (D) is incorrect because an organization's mission is its basic task or function.

17. Formal written policies are normally recommended. However, the presence of certain conditions in an organization minimizes the need for written policies. One condition that minimizes the need for written policies is

A. A high division of labor.
B. A strong organizational culture.
C. A large span of control.
D. A strict unity of command.

Answer (B) is correct. *(CIA, adapted)*
REQUIRED: The condition minimizing the need for written policies.
DISCUSSION: If the culture is strong, the organization's key values are intensely held and widely shared. Substantial training has been expended to achieve this high degree of acceptance, minimizing the need for formal, written policies.
Answer (A) is incorrect because high specialization of labor indicates a higher need for supervision and a correspondingly strong need for formal policies and procedures. Answer (C) is incorrect because large spans of control minimize the ability of a manager to provide direct supervision. They increase the need for the indirect supervision provided by formalized policies and procedures. Answer (D) is incorrect because an organization exhibiting strict unity of command also most likely requires strict adherence to policies and procedures. Formalization of those policies and procedures promotes adherence.

18. MBO managers are most likely to believe that employees

A. Dislike their work.
B. Avoid responsibility whenever possible.
C. Work best when threatened with punishment.
D. Are self-motivated.

Answer (D) is correct. *(Publisher, adapted)*
REQUIRED: The characteristic an MBO manager attributes to employees.
DISCUSSION: MBO managers believe that employees are committed to achieving objectives, working hard to receive the rewards of achievement, and striving for self-actualization. The MBO view is that employees enjoy work, need little supervision, seek responsibility, and are imaginative problem solvers.

19. A company has a compensation system for its managers based on a management-by-objectives (MBO) approach. The essential premise of MBO is that

A. Compensation should be based on qualitative factors.
B. Employees should be concerned with routine matters, and managers should attend to exceptions.
C. Employees should participate in setting objectives.
D. Managers should establish objectives for their employees.

Answer (C) is correct. *(Publisher, adapted)*
REQUIRED: The essential premise of MBO.
DISCUSSION: The hallmark of MBO is the mutual setting of objectives by the superior and the subordinate as a basis for performance evaluation. Based on the Theory Y philosophy that employees want to work hard if they know what is expected, MBO requires top management participation and commitment to the program, integration of the objectives for all subunits into a compatible system directed toward accomplishment of overall goals, provision for regular reporting of performance, and free and honest communication between superior and subordinates. Subordinates must make careful assessments of their abilities and their interests, and managers must "coach" subordinates rather than dictate their proper goals. Both sides must maintain flexibility to accommodate unforeseen changes, and the review and analysis of results before setting the next round of goals is a vital part of the process.
Answer (A) is incorrect because MBO objectives may be set in terms of quantitative measures (such as sales dollars) or qualitative ones (such as improved service). Answer (B) is incorrect because the essence of management by exception is that employees should be concerned with routine matters, and managers should attend to exceptions. Answer (D) is incorrect because setting of objectives should be participative.

16.3 Forecasting

20. What coefficient of correlation results from the following data?

X	Y
1	10
2	8
3	6
4	4
5	2

A. 0

B. −1

C. +1

D. Cannot be determined from the data given.

Answer (B) is correct. *(CIA, adapted)*
REQUIRED: The coefficient of correlation.
DISCUSSION: The coefficient of correlation (in standard notation, r) measures the strength of the linear relationship. The magnitude of r is independent of the scales of measurement of X and Y. Its range is −1.0 to 1.0. A value of −1.0 indicates a perfectly inverse linear relationship between X and Y. A value of zero indicates no linear relationship between X and Y. A value of +1.0 indicates a perfectly direct relationship between X and Y. As X increases by 1, Y consistently decreases by 2. Hence, a perfectly inverse relationship exists, and r must be equal to −1.0.
Answer (A) is incorrect because a perfect negative correlation exists. Answer (C) is incorrect because an inverse, not a direct, relationship exists. Answer (D) is incorrect because a linear relationship exists between X and Y.

21. In regression analysis, which of the following correlation coefficients represents the strongest relationship between the independent and dependent variables?

A. 1.03

B. −.02

C. −.89

D. .75

Answer (C) is correct. *(CIA, adapted)*
REQUIRED: The correlation coefficient with the strongest relationship between independent and dependent variables.
DISCUSSION: Because the range of values is between −1.0 and 1.0, −.89 suggests a very strong inverse relationship between the independent and dependent variables. A value of −1.0 signifies a perfect inverse relationship, and a value of 1.0 signifies a perfect direct relationship.

22. Which of the following would be most impacted by the use of the percentage of sales forecasting method for budgeting purposes?

A. Accounts payable.

B. Mortgages payable.

C. Bonds payable.

D. Common stock.

Answer (A) is correct. *(CPA, adapted)*
REQUIRED: The account most affected by using the percentage of sales method for budgeting.
DISCUSSION: The percentage-of-sales method is the most widely used for sales forecasting. It adjusts the current level of sales by a specified percentage increase or decrease. This method is based on the assumptions that most items directly correlate with sales and that the current level of all assets are optimal for the current sales level. Examples of accounts that are expected to correlate directly with sales are inventory, accounts receivable, and accounts payable.
Answer (B) is incorrect because mortgages payable is less affected than accounts payable. Answer (C) is incorrect because bonds payable is less affected than accounts payable. Answer (D) is incorrect because common stock is less affected than accounts payable.

23. The letter x in the standard regression equation is best described as a(n)

A. Independent variable.

B. Dependent variable.

C. Constant coefficient.

D. Coefficient of determination.

Answer (A) is correct. *(CMA, adapted)*
REQUIRED: The meaning of the letter x in the standard regression equation.
DISCUSSION: The letter x in the standard regression equation is the independent variable. For example, in a regression to determine the total cost of production, x equals units produced.
Answer (B) is incorrect because the dependent variable is y. Answer (C) is incorrect because the constant coefficient is a. Answer (D) is incorrect because r^2 is the coefficient of determination.

24. A management accountant performs a linear regression of maintenance cost vs. production using a computer spreadsheet. The regression output shows an "intercept" value of $322,897. How should the accountant interpret this information?

A. Y has a value of $322,897 when X equals zero.

B. X has a value of $322,897 when Y equals zero.

C. The residual error of the regression is $322,897.

D. Maintenance cost has an average value of $322,897.

Answer (A) is correct. *(CPA, adapted)*
   REQUIRED: The interpretation of the intercept value in a linear regression.
   DISCUSSION: If (1) y is the dependent variable, (2) a is the y-axis intercept (the fixed cost in cost function), (3) b is the slope of the regression line (the variable cost in cost functions), (4) x is the independent variable, and (5) e is the error term, the simple regression equation is

$$y = a + bx = e$$

Thus, when production (x) is zero, the cost of maintenance (y, the dependent variable) is equal to its fixed cost.
   Answer (B) is incorrect because x is the independent variable upon which the dependent variable is regressed. Answer (C) is incorrect because the residual is the difference between a y value on the regression line and an observed y value for the same x value. Residuals are used to calculate the standard error of the estimate, a measure of dispersion analogous to the standard deviation. Answer (D) is incorrect because $322,897 is the fixed cost.

25. The internal auditor of a bank has developed a multiple regression model that has been used for a number of years to estimate the amount of interest income from commercial loans. During the current year, the auditor applies the model and discovers that the r^2 value has decreased dramatically, but the model otherwise seems to be working well. Which conclusion is justified by the change?

A. Changing to a cross-sectional regression analysis should cause r^2 to increase.

B. Regression analysis is no longer an appropriate technique to estimate interest income.

C. Some new factors, not included in the model, are causing interest income to change.

D. A linear regression analysis would increase the model's reliability.

Answer (C) is correct. *(CIA, adapted)*
   REQUIRED: The implication of the decrease in r^2.
   DISCUSSION: The coefficient of determination (r^2) is the amount of variation in the dependent variable (interest income) that is explained by the independent variables. In this case, less of the change in interest income is explained by the model. Thus, some other factor must be causing interest income to change. This change merits audit investigation.
   Answer (A) is incorrect because cross-sectional regression analysis is inappropriate. The auditor is trying to estimate changes in a single account balance over time. Answer (B) is incorrect because regression analysis may still be the most appropriate methodology to estimate interest income, but the auditor should first understand the factors that may be causing r^2 to decrease. The reason may be a systematic error in the account balance. Answer (D) is incorrect because linear regression models are simpler models, but the auditor should be searching for a systematic error in the account balance or applying a more complex model.

26. A division uses a regression in which monthly advertising expenditures are used to predict monthly product sales (both in millions of dollars). The results show a regression coefficient for the independent variable equal to 0.8. This coefficient value indicates that

A. The average monthly advertising expenditure in the sample is $800,000.

B. When monthly advertising is at its average level, product sales will be $800,000.

C. On average, every additional dollar of advertising results in $.80 of additional sales.

D. Advertising is not a good predictor of sales because the coefficient is so small.

Answer (C) is correct. *(CIA, adapted)*
   REQUIRED: The significance of the regression coefficient for the independent variable.
   DISCUSSION: The regression coefficient represents the change in the dependent variable corresponding to a unit change in the independent variable. Thus, it is the slope of the regression line.
   Answer (A) is incorrect because a regression coefficient is unrelated to the means of the variables. Answer (B) is incorrect because, to predict a specific value of sales, the value of the independent variable is multiplied by the coefficient. The product is then added to the y-intercept value. Answer (D) is incorrect because the absolute size of the coefficient bears no necessary relationship to the importance of the variable.

Questions 27 and 28 are based on the following information.

Moss Point Manufacturing recently completed and sold an order of 50 units that had costs as shown in the next column.

The company has now been requested to prepare a bid for 150 units of the same product.

Direct materials	$ 1,500
Direct labor ($8.50 × 1,000 hours)	8,500
Variable overhead ($4.00 × 1,000 hours)*	4,000
Fixed overhead **	1,400
	$15,400

* Applied on the basis of direct labor hours
** Applied at the rate of 10% of variable cost

27. If an 80% learning curve is applicable, Moss Point's total cost on this order would be estimated at

A. $26,400

B. $32,000

C. $38,000

D. $41,800

Answer (A) is correct. *(CMA, adapted)*
REQUIRED: The total cost of a new order given a learning curve percentage.
DISCUSSION: Assuming that the cumulative average-time model applies, an 80% learning curve means that the cumulative average time per unit (and labor cost, given a constant labor rate) declines by 20% when unit output doubles in the early stages of production. The first lot size was 50 units, which was produced at a total cost of $15,400 ($1,500 for materials and $13,900 for labor and overhead). Materials costs are strictly variable and should remain proportional to production. The labor ($8,500) and variable overhead ($4,000) costs (labor-related), however, will be affected by the learning curve. The average cost per lot for labor and variable overhead after 100 units have been produced should be 80% of the costs of the first lot of 50 units. Thus, the average labor and variable overhead cost per 50-unit lot will be $10,000 ($12,500 × 80%). If production doubles again (to a total production of 200 units or four lots of 50 each), the cumulative average cost for labor and variable overhead will be $8,000 per lot ($10,000 × 80%). Given four lots of 50 each, at an average cost of $8,000 per lot, the total cost for labor and variable overhead must be $32,000. Adding $6,000 for raw materials ($1,500 per 50-unit lot) gives a total variable cost of $38,000 for 200 units. Fixed overhead is 10% of total variable cost, so total cost is $41,800. The total cost for the last 150 units is $26,400 ($41,800 – $15,400).
Answer (B) is incorrect because $32,000 is the total cost for labor and variable overhead for 200 units. Answer (C) is incorrect because $38,000 is the total variable cost for 200 units. Answer (D) is incorrect because $41,800 is the total cost for 200 units.

28. If Moss Point had experienced a 70% learning curve, the bid for the 150 units would

A. Show a 30% reduction in the total direct labor hours required with no learning curve.

B. Include increased fixed overhead costs.

C. Be 10% lower than the total bid at an 80% learning curve.

D. Include 6.40 direct labor hours per unit at $8.50 per hour.

Answer (D) is correct. *(CMA, adapted)*
REQUIRED: The true statement about the bid for an incremental 150 units given a 70% learning curve effect.
DISCUSSION: The sum of the direct labor hours for the initial lot of 50 units was 1,000. A second lot of 50 would reduce the cumulative hours per lot to 700 (1,000 × 70%). A doubling to four lots would reduce the cumulative hours per lot to 490 (700 × 70%). Thus, for an output of 200 units, the total hours worked would be 1,960 (4 × 490). Subtracting the 1,000 hours required for the first 50 units from the 1,960-hour total gives 960 hours for the last 150 units. Dividing 960 hours by 150 units produces a per-unit time of 6.4 hours.
Answer (A) is incorrect because, with no learning curve effect, estimated total hours would be 4,000 instead of 1,960, a change of more than 50%. Answer (B) is incorrect because fixed costs applied per lot would decline because they are based on labor hours, which are declining. Answer (C) is incorrect because a 10% difference in learning curves does not equal a 10% difference in bids.

29. Which of the following forecasting methods relies mostly on judgment?

    A. Time series models.

    B. Econometric models.

    C. Delphi.

    D. Regression.

Answer (C) is correct. *(CPA, adapted)*

    REQUIRED: The forecasting method most reliant on judgment.

    DISCUSSION: The Delphi technique was developed by the RAND Corporation in the late 1960s as a forecasting methodology. Later, the U.S. government enhanced it as a group decision-making tool with the results of Project HINDSIGHT, which established a factual basis for the workability of Delphi. That project produced a tool in which a group of experts could reach a consensus when the decisive factors were subjective, not knowledge-based.

    Answer (A) is incorrect because time series or trend analysis relies on past experience. Changes in the value of a variable (e.g., unit sales of a product) over time may have several possible components. In time series analysis, the dependent variable is regressed on time (the independent variable). Answer (B) is incorrect because econometric models apply statistical methods to the study of economic problems and data. Answer (D) is incorrect because regression (least squares) analysis extends correlation to find an equation for the linear relationship among variables. The behavior of the dependent variable is explained in terms of one or more independent variables. Thus, regression analysis determines functional relationships among quantitative variables.

30. Cook Co.'s total costs of operating five sales offices last year were $500,000, of which $70,000 represented fixed costs. Cook has determined that total costs are significantly influenced by the number of sales offices operated. Last year's costs and number of sales offices can be used as the bases for predicting annual costs. What would be the budgeted cost for the coming year if Cook were to operate seven sales offices?

    A. $700,000

    B. $672,000

    C. $602,000

    D. $586,000

Answer (B) is correct. *(CPA, adapted)*

    REQUIRED: The budgeted costs.

    DISCUSSION: Using the formula $y = a + bx$, y is the total budgeted cost, a is the fixed costs, b is the variable cost per unit, and x is the number of budgeted sales offices. The fixed costs are $70,000, the variable cost per unit is $86,000 [($500,000 − $70,000) ÷ 5], and the number of budgeted sales offices is 7. Thus, the budgeted cost for the coming year assuming seven sales offices is $672,000 [$70,000 + ($86,000 × 7)].

    Answer (A) is incorrect because $700,000 assumes the total costs are variable. Answer (C) is incorrect because $602,000 excludes fixed costs. Answer (D) is incorrect because $586,000 is last year's total costs plus the per-unit variable cost.

31. Sago Co. uses regression analysis to develop a model for predicting overhead costs. Two different cost drivers (machine hours and direct materials weight) are under consideration as the independent variable. Relevant data were run on a computer using one of the standard regression programs, with the following results:

Machine hours	Coefficient
Y Intercept	2,500
B	5.0
$r^2 = .70$	

Direct materials weight	
Y Intercept	4,600
B	2.6
$r^2 = .50$	

Which regression equation should be used?

    A. $Y = 2,500 + 5.0x$.

    B. $Y = 2,500 + 3.5x$.

    C. $Y = 4,600 + 2.6x$.

    D. $Y = 4,600 + 1.3x$.

Answer (A) is correct. *(CPA, adapted)*

    REQUIRED: The regression equation.

    DISCUSSION: The simple regression equation is $Y = A + Bx$, given that Y is the dependent variable, A is the Y-axis intercept, B is the slope of the regression line, and x is the independent variable. To determine which cost driver to use, the coefficient of determination (r^2) is computed. The value of r^2 indicates the proportion of the total variation in Y that is explained by the regression equation. Because machine hours has a higher r^2 than direct materials weight, the coefficients for machine hours are used to predict costs. Consequently, the regression equation is $Y = 2,500 + 5.0x$.

    Answer (B) is incorrect because $Y = 2,500 + 3.5x$ incorrectly multiplies the slope by r^2. Answer (C) is incorrect because machine hours has a higher r^2 than direct materials. Answer (D) is incorrect because the machine hours coefficients should be used to predict overhead costs.

32. Which of the following may be used to estimate how inventory warehouse costs are affected by both the number of shipments and the weight of materials handled?

   A. Economic order quantity analysis.

   B. Probability analysis.

   C. Correlation analysis.

   D. Multiple regression analysis.

Answer (D) is correct. *(CPA, adapted)*
   REQUIRED: The analysis required to measure inventory warehouse costs.
   DISCUSSION: Multiple regression analysis involves the use of a linear equation. This equation consists of one dependent variable and more than one independent variable. Accordingly, estimating inventory warehouse costs involves both a dependent variable and independent variables. Hence, multiple regression should be used to estimate these costs.
   Answer (A) is incorrect because EOQ is used to determine the optimal sum of ordering and carrying costs. Answer (B) is incorrect because probability analysis assists decision making in the face of uncertainty. Answer (C) is incorrect because correlation analysis measures the strength of the linear relationship between two or more variables.

33. Box Co. uses regression analysis to estimate the functional relationship between an independent variable (cost driver) and overhead cost. Assume that the following equation is being used:

$$y = a + bx$$

What is the symbol for the independent variable?

   A. y.

   B. x.

   C. bx.

   D. a.

Answer (B) is correct. *(CPA, adapted)*
   REQUIRED: The symbol for the independent variable.
   DISCUSSION: The simple regression equation is $y = a + bx$. y is the dependent variable (overhead costs), a is the y-axis intercept (fixed costs), b is the slope of the regression line (cost driver), and x is the independent variable.
   Answer (A) is incorrect because y is the dependent variable. Answer (C) is incorrect because bx is the slope times the independent variable. Answer (D) is incorrect because a is the y-axis intercept.

34. Multiple regression differs from simple regression in that it

   A. Provides an estimated constant term.

   B. Has more dependent variables.

   C. Allows the computation of the coefficient of determination.

   D. Has more independent variables.

Answer (D) is correct. *(CPA, adapted)*
   REQUIRED: The difference between multiple and simple regression.
   DISCUSSION: Improved accuracy of forecasts may often be achieved by regressing the dependent variable on more than one independent variable. The usual multiple regression equation is linear and is in the following form when y is the dependent variable; a is the y-axis intercept; x_1, x_2, etc., are the independent variables; b_1, b_2, etc., are the coefficients of the independent variables; and e is the error term:

$$y = a + b_1x_1 + b_2x_2 + ... + e$$

   Answer (A) is incorrect because both equations have a constant y-axis intercept. Answer (B) is incorrect because both equations explain the behavior of a single dependent variable. Answer (C) is incorrect because the coefficient of determination (r^2), or the coefficient of correlation squared, may be interpreted as the proportion of the total variation in y that is explained or accounted for by the regression equation. Thus, r^2 may be calculated for both simple and multiple regressions.

35. To determine the best cost driver of warranty costs relating to glass breakage during shipments, Wymer Co. used simple linear regression analysis to study the relationship between warranty costs and each of the following variables: type of packaging, quantity shipped, type of carrier, and distance shipped. The analysis yielded the following statistics:

Independent Variable	Coefficient of Determination	Standard Error of Regression
Type of packaging	0.60	1,524
Quantity shipped	0.48	1,875
Type of carrier	0.45	2,149
Distance shipped	0.20	4,876

Based on these analyses, the best driver of warranty costs for glass breakage is

A. Type of packaging.

B. Quantity shipped.

C. Type of carrier.

D. Distance shipped.

Answer (A) is correct. *(CPA, adapted)*
REQUIRED: The best driver of warranty costs for glass breakage.
DISCUSSION: The best cost driver (independent variable) is the one that is most closely related to the incurrence of the cost. For glass breakage, the type of packaging is the best cost driver because it has the highest coefficient of determination (the proportion of the total variation of the dependent variable, or warranty costs, explained by the regression equation). The type of packaging also has the lowest standard error of regression. The lower the standard error, the better the regression (least squares) line fits the observed data, that is, the lower the dispersion between the actual and predicted values of the dependent variable (glass breakage).
Answer (B) is incorrect because quantity shipped has a lower coefficient of determination and a higher standard error of regression than type of packaging. Answer (C) is incorrect because type of carrier has a lower coefficient of determination and a higher standard error of regression than type of packaging. Answer (D) is incorrect because distance shipped has a lower coefficient of determination and a higher standard error of regression than type of packaging.

36. A vendor offered Wyatt Co. $25,000 in compensation for losses resulting from faulty raw materials. Alternatively, a lawyer offered to represent Wyatt in a lawsuit against the vendor for a $12,000 retainer and 50% of any award over $35,000. Possible court awards with their associated probabilities are as follows

Award	Probability
$75,000	0.6
$0	0.4

Compared with accepting the vendor's offer, the expected value for Wyatt to litigate the matter to a verdict provides a

A. $4,000 loss.

B. $8,000 gain.

C. $21,000 gain.

D. $38,000 gain.

Answer (A) is correct. *(CPA, adapted)*
REQUIRED: The gain or loss from litigating the matter to a verdict.
DISCUSSION: If the award is $75,000, Wyatt's net recovery is $43,000 {$75,000 – $12,000 retainer – [($75,000 – $35,000) × 50%]}. If the award is $0, Wyatt's net loss is the $12,000 retainer. The expected value is therefore $21,000 [($43,000 × .6) + (–$12,000 × .4)]. Compared with accepting the vendor's offer, litigation entails an expected loss of $4,000 ($21,000 – $25,000 settlement offer).
Answer (B) is incorrect because an $8,000 gain results if no contingent fee is charged. Answer (C) is incorrect because $21,000 is the expected value of litigating. Answer (D) is incorrect because a $38,000 gain equals $63,000 ($75,000 – $12,000) minus the vendor's $25,000 offer.

37. Which tool would most likely be used to determine the best course of action under conditions of uncertainty?

A. Cost-volume-profit analysis.

B. Expected value (EV).

C. Program evaluation and review technique (PERT).

D. Scattergraph method.

Answer (B) is correct. *(CPA, adapted)*
REQUIRED: The tool most likely to be used to determine the best course of action under conditions of uncertainty.
DISCUSSION: Expected value analysis provides a rational means for selecting the best alternative in decisions involving risk. The expected value of an alternative is found by multiplying the probability of each outcome by its payoff, and summing the products. It represents the long-term average payoff for repeated trials.
Answer (A) is incorrect because CVP analysis uses deterministic rather than probabilistic estimates of prices and costs to describe the effects of changes in prices, costs, sales mix, and production levels. Answer (C) is incorrect because PERT is a technique for controlling complex projects by developing network diagrams. It uses probabilistic time estimates. Answer (D) is incorrect because scatter diagrams may be used to demonstrate correlations. Each observation creates a dot that pairs the x and y values. The linearity and slope of these observations are related to the coefficient of correlation by the previously stated rules.

16.4 Project Management

38. When using PERT (Program Evaluation Review Technique), the expected time for an activity when given an optimistic time (a), a pessimistic time (b), and a most likely time (m) is calculated by which one of the following formulas?

A. $(b - a) \div 2$.

B. $(a + b) \div 2$.

C. $(a + 4m + b) \div 6$.

D. $(4abm) \div 6$.

Answer (C) is correct. *(CMA, adapted)*
REQUIRED: The formula for calculating the expected time for an activity when using PERT.
DISCUSSION: PERT was developed to aid managers in controlling large, complex projects. PERT analysis includes probabilistic estimates of activity completion times. Three time estimates are made: optimistic, most likely, and pessimistic. The time estimates for an activity are assumed to approximate a beta probability distribution. PERT approximates the mean of the beta distribution by dividing the sum of the optimistic time, the pessimistic time, and four times the most likely time by six.
Answer (A) is incorrect because subtracting the most likely time from the pessimistic time yields a nonsense answer. Answer (B) is incorrect because the most likely time estimate should be included in the formula. Answer (D) is incorrect because all time estimates are not weighted equally.

39. California Building Corporation uses the critical path method to monitor construction jobs. The company is currently 2 weeks behind schedule on Job #181, which is subject to a $10,500-per-week completion penalty. Path A-B-C-F-G-H-I has a normal completion time of 20 weeks, and critical path A-D-E-F-G-H-I has a normal completion time of 22 weeks. The following activities can be crashed:

Activities	Cost to Crash 1 Week	Cost to Crash 2 Weeks
BC	$ 8,000	$15,000
DE	10,000	19,600
EF	8,800	19,500

California Building desires to reduce the normal completion time of Job #181 and, at the same time, report the highest possible income for the year. California Building should crash

A. Activity BC 1 week and activity EF 1 week.

B. Activity BC 2 weeks.

C. Activity EF 2 weeks.

D. Activity DE 1 week and activity EF 1 week.

Answer (D) is correct. *(CMA, adapted)*
REQUIRED: The activity that should be crashed (speeded up at additional cost) to maximize income.
DISCUSSION: Activities that are to be crashed in a CPM problem should be ones that are on the critical (longest) path. Thus, activity BC should not be selected because it is not on the critical path. To finish activity BC 2 weeks early would not reduce the total time to complete the project. Therefore, the only feasible choices are DE and EF on the critical path. The total cost to crash DE and EF for 1 week each is $18,800 ($10,000 + $8,800), which is less than the cost to crash either activity for 2 weeks. Thus, DE and EF should be crashed for 1 week each because the total cost is less than the $21,000 ($10,500 × 2) 2-week delay penalty.

40. A PERT network has only two activities on its critical path. These activities have standard deviations of 6 and 8, respectively. The standard deviation of the project completion time is

A. 7

B. 10

C. 14

D. 48

Answer (B) is correct. *(CMA, adapted)*
REQUIRED: The standard deviation of the project completion time given the standard deviations of the activity times on the critical path.
DISCUSSION: The mean time for the critical path is simply the sum of the means of the activity times. However, the standard deviation equals the square root of the sum of the variances (squares of the standard deviations) of the times for activities on the critical path. The standard deviation of the project completion time (time for the critical path) is therefore the square root of 100 ($6^2 + 8^2$), or 10.
Answer (A) is incorrect because 7 is the average standard deviation. Answer (C) is incorrect because 14 is the sum of the standard deviations. Answer (D) is incorrect because 48 is the product of the standard deviations.

Questions 41 and 42 are based on the following information. The PERT network diagram and the corresponding activity cost chart for a manufacturing project at Networks, Inc. are presented here. The numbers in the diagram are the expected times (in days) to perform each activity in the project.

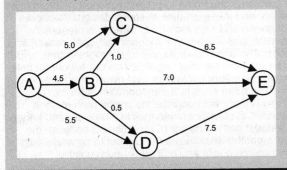

Activity	Normal Cost	Crash Time	Crash Cost
AB	$3,000	3.50 days	$4,000
AC	5,000	4.50	5,250
AD	4,000	4.00	4,750
BE	6,000	5.00	7,000
CE	8,000	5.00	9,200
DE	6,000	6.50	6,750
BC	2,500	.50	3,500
BD	2,000	.25	2,500

41. The expected time of Networks, Inc.'s critical path is

A. 12.0 days.

B. 13.0 days.

C. 11.5 days.

D. 11.0 days.

Answer (B) is correct. *(CMA, adapted)*
REQUIRED: The expected time of Networks, Inc.'s critical path.
DISCUSSION: The critical path is the longest path. The longest path in the diagram is A-D-E, which required 13 days (5.5 + 7.5) based on expected times.

42. In order to keep costs at a minimum and decrease the completion time by 1 1/2 days, Networks, Inc. should crash activity(ies)

A. AD and AB.

B. DE.

C. AD.

D. AB and CE.

Answer (A) is correct. *(CMA, adapted)*
REQUIRED: The activity(ies) that can be crashed by a specified number of days at the least cost.
DISCUSSION: The critical (longest) path is A-D-E, which has an expected time of 13 days (5.5 + 7.5). However, to decrease the project's completion time by 1.5 days, paths A-B-C-E (4.5 + 1.0 + 6.5 = 12 days) and A-B-D-E (4.5 + .5 + 7.5 = 12.5 days) as well as A-D-E must also be shortened. Hence, A-D-E must be reduced by 1.5 days, A-B-C-E by .5 day, and A-B-D-E by 1.0 day. The only way to decrease A-D-E by 1.5 days is to crash activity AD (5.5 expected time – 4.0 crash time = 1.5 days). Crashing DE results in a 1.0-day saving (7.5 – 6.5) only. Crashing AB is the efficient way to reduce both A-B-C-E and A-B-D-E by the desired amount of time because it is part of both paths. The incremental cost of crashing AB is $1,000 ($4,000 crash cost – $3,000 normal cost) to shorten the completion time by 1.0 day (4.5 – 3.5). The alternatives for decreasing both A-B-C-E and A-B-D-E are more costly.
Answer (B) is incorrect because crashing activity DE saves only 1.0 day (7.5 – 6.5) on the critical path and does not reduce the time needed for A-B-C-E. Answer (C) is incorrect because crashing AD does not reduce the time necessary to complete A-B-C-E or A-B-D-E. Answer (D) is incorrect because AB and CE are not on the critical path.

43. A shortest-route algorithm is used in network models to

    A. Identify bottlenecks in a network and hence identify the longest path.

    B. Minimize total travel time from one site to each of the other sites in a transportation system.

    C. Maximize throughput in networks with distinct entry (source node) and exit (sink node) points.

    D. Identify the set of connecting branches having the shortest combined length.

Answer (B) is correct. *(CIA, adapted)*
    REQUIRED: The purpose of a shortest-route algorithm used in network models.
    DISCUSSION: Network models are used to solve managerial problems pertaining to project scheduling, information systems design, and transportation systems design. Networks consisting of nodes and arcs may be created to represent in graphic form problems related to transportation, assignment, and transshipment. The shortest-route, minimal spanning tree, and maximal flow problems are other applications of network models. A shortest-route algorithm minimizes total travel time from one site to each of the other sites in a transportation system.
    Answer (A) is incorrect because the critical path method (CPM) is intended to identify bottlenecks in a network and hence identify the longest path. Answer (C) is incorrect because the maximal flow algorithm maximizes throughput in networks with distinct entry (source node) and exit (sink node) points. Examples of applications are highway transportation systems and oil pipelines. Flows are limited by capacities of the arcs (e.g., highways or pipes). Answer (D) is incorrect because the minimal spanning tree algorithm identifies the set of connecting branches having the shortest combined length. A spanning tree is a group of branches (arcs) that connects each node in the network to every other node. An example problem is the determination of the shortest telecommunications linkage among users at remote sites and a central computer.

16.5 The Budgeting Process

44. The budget that describes the long-term position, goals, and objectives of an entity within its environment is the

    A. Capital budget.

    B. Operating budget.

    C. Cash management budget.

    D. Strategic budget.

Answer (D) is correct. *(CMA, adapted)*
    REQUIRED: The budget that describes the long-term position and objectives of an entity.
    DISCUSSION: Strategic budgeting is a form of long-range planning based on identifying and specifying organizational goals and objectives. The strengths and weaknesses of the organization risk levels are assessed. The influences of environmental factors are forecast to derive the best strategy for reaching the organization's objectives.
    Answer (A) is incorrect because capital budgeting involves evaluating specific long-term investment decisions. Answer (B) is incorrect because the operating budget is a short-range management tool. Answer (C) is incorrect because cash management is a short-range consideration related to liquidity.

45. When budgets are used to evaluate performance and to set limits on spending, the process will often result in departments adding something "extra" to ensure the budgets will be met. This "extra" is

    A. Management by objectives.

    B. Strategic planning.

    C. Continuous budgeting.

    D. Budgetary slack.

Answer (D) is correct. *(CMA, adapted)*
    REQUIRED: The term for the extra padding that is sometimes put into budgets to make them easier to achieve.
    DISCUSSION: Budgetary slack is the term referring to the underestimation of probable performance in a budget. With slack in a budget, a manager can achieve the budget more easily. Slack must be avoided if a budget is to have its desired effects.
    Answer (A) is incorrect because management by objectives (MBO) is a behavioral, communications-oriented responsibility approach to employee self direction. Answer (B) is incorrect because strategic planning is a method of long-term planning. Answer (C) is incorrect because continuous (or rolling) budgeting is a method of extending each budget by an additional period as each period passes.

46. In an organization that plans by using comprehensive budgeting, the master budget is

- A. A compilation of all the separate operational and financial budget schedules of the organization.
- B. The booklet containing budget guidelines, policies, and forms to use in the budgeting process.
- C. The current budget updated for operations for part of the current year.
- D. A budget of a not-for-profit organization after it is approved by the appropriate authoritative body.

Answer (A) is correct. *(CMA, adapted)*
REQUIRED: The nature of the master budget.
DISCUSSION: Budgets coordinate the various activities of a firm. A company's overall budget, often called the master or comprehensive budget, encompasses both the operating and financial budget processes. Thus, all other budgets are subsets of the master budget. The operating budget is the part of the master budget that consists of the pro forma income statement and related budgets. Its emphasis is on obtaining and using resources. The financial budget is the part of the master budget that includes the cash budget, capital budget, pro forma balance sheet, and pro forma statement of cash flows. Its emphasis is on obtaining the funds needed to purchase operating assets.
Answer (B) is incorrect because the budget manual is the booklet containing budget guidelines, policies, and forms to use in the budgeting process. Answer (C) is incorrect because a continuous budget is the current budget updated for operations for part of the current year. Answer (D) is incorrect because a master budget may be prepared by a for-profit entity.

47. A budget manual, which enhances the operation of a budget system, is most likely to include

- A. A chart of accounts.
- B. Distribution instructions for budget schedules.
- C. Employee hiring policies.
- D. Documentation of the accounting system software.

Answer (B) is correct. *(CMA, adapted)*
REQUIRED: The item that will most likely be included in a budget manual.
DISCUSSION: A budget manual describes how a budget is to be prepared. Items usually included in a budget manual are a planning calendar and distribution instructions for all budget schedules. Distribution instructions are important because, once a schedule is prepared, other departments within the organization will use the schedule to prepare their own budgets. Without distribution instructions, someone who needs a particular schedule may be overlooked.
Answer (A) is incorrect because the accounting manual includes a chart of accounts. Answer (C) is incorrect because employee hiring policies are not needed for budget preparation. They are already available in the personnel manual. Answer (D) is incorrect because software documentation is not needed in the budget preparation process.

16.6 The Master Budget and its Components

48. Which of the following inputs would be most beneficial to consider when management is developing the capital budget?

- A. Supply/demand for the company's products.
- B. Current product sales prices and costs.
- C. Wage trends.
- D. Profit center equipment requests.

Answer (D) is correct. *(CPA, adapted)*
REQUIRED: The most beneficial input to the capital budget.
DISCUSSION: The capital budget is part of the financial budget, so its emphasis is on obtaining the funds needed to acquire operating assets. It may be prepared more than a year in advance to allow time to plan financing of major expenditures for such long-term assets as equipment, buildings, and land. Thus, profit center equipment requests are directly relevant to development of the capital budget.
Answer (A) is incorrect because future supply/demand for the company's products is more relevant than current supply/demand for the company's products. Furthermore, even expected unfavorable future conditions are less useful a factor than profit center requests for equipment that may be needed regardless of an economic downturn. Answer (B) is incorrect because current product sales prices and costs are less critical than future prices and costs. Answer (C) is incorrect because wage trends have an effect on a capital budget that may have less direct impact than profit center equipment requests.

49. Which one of the following items would have to be included for a company preparing a schedule of cash receipts and disbursements for Calendar Year 1?

A. A purchase order issued in December Year 1 for items to be delivered in February Year 2.

B. Dividends declared in November Year 1 to be paid in January Year 2 to shareholders of record as of December Year 1.

C. The amount of uncollectible customer accounts for Year 1.

D. The borrowing of funds from a bank on a note payable taken out in June Year 1 with an agreement to pay the principal and interest in June Year 2.

Answer (D) is correct. *(CMA, adapted)*
REQUIRED: The item included in a cash budget for Year 1.
DISCUSSION: A schedule of cash receipts and disbursements (cash budget) should include all cash inflows and outflows during the period without regard to the accrual accounting treatment of the transactions. Hence, it should include all checks written and all sources of cash, including borrowings. A borrowing from a bank in June Year 1 should appear as a cash receipt for Year 1.
Answer (A) is incorrect because the cash disbursement presumably will not occur until Year 2. Answer (B) is incorrect because the cash flow will not occur until dividends are paid in Year 2. Answer (C) is incorrect because bad debt expense is a noncash item.

50. What is the required unit production level given the following factors?

	Units
Projected sales	1,000
Beginning inventory	85
Desired ending inventory	100
Prior-year beginning inventory	200

A. 915

B. 1,015

C. 1,100

D. 1,215

Answer (B) is correct. *(CPA, adapted)*
REQUIRED: The required unit production level.
DISCUSSION: The required unit production level should be the sum of projected sales and the difference between desired ending inventory and beginning inventory. The correct unit production level is 1,015 units [1,000 units + (100 units – 85 units)].
Answer (A) is incorrect because 915 units equals 1,000 units minus 85 units. Answer (C) is incorrect because 1,100 units equals 1,000 units plus 100 units. Answer (D) is incorrect because 1,215 units equals 1,000 units + 200 units + (100 units – 85 units). The 200 units in the prior year inventory should not be used to compute the required unit production level.

51. Trumbull Company budgeted sales on account of $120,000 for July, $211,000 for August, and $198,000 for September. Collection experience indicates that 60% of the budgeted sales will be collected the month after the sale, 36% will be collected the second month, and 4% will be uncollectible. The cash receipts from accounts receivable that should be budgeted for September would be

A. $169,800

B. $147,960

C. $197,880

D. $194,760

Answer (A) is correct. *(CMA, adapted)*
REQUIRED: The budgeted cash receipts for September.
DISCUSSION: The budgeted cash collections for September are $169,800 [($120,000 July sales × 36%) + ($211,000 August sales × 60%)].
Answer (B) is incorrect because $147,960 results from reversing the percentages for July and August. Answer (C) is incorrect because $197,880 results from using the wrong months (August and September) and reversing the percentages. Answer (D) is incorrect because $194,760 assumes collections were for August and September.

52. Johnson Co. is preparing its master budget for the first quarter of next year. Budgeted sales and production for one of the company's products are as follows:

Month	Sales	Production
January	10,000	12,000
February	12,000	11,000
March	15,000	16,000

Each unit of this product requires four pounds of raw materials. Johnson's policy is to have sufficient raw materials on hand at the end of each month for 40% of the following month's production requirements. The January 1 raw materials inventory is expected to conform with this policy.

How many pounds of raw materials should Johnson budget to purchase for January?

A. 17,600

B. 46,400

C. 48,000

D. 52,000

Answer (B) is correct. *(CPA, adapted)*
REQUIRED: The materials budgeted for January.
DISCUSSION: The beginning inventory of materials equals 19,200 pounds (12,000 units to be produced in January × 4 pounds × 40%). The ending inventory equals 17,600 pounds (11,000 units to be produced in February × 4 pounds × 40%). Hence, the amount of additional materials to be purchased for production and ending inventory equals 46,400 pounds [(48,000 pounds needed for January – 19,200 pounds BI) + 17,600 EI].
Answer (A) is incorrect because 17,600 pounds equals the ending inventory for January. Answer (C) is incorrect because 48,000 pounds is the requirement for January production. Answer (D) is incorrect because 52,000 pounds is the amount to be purchased for February.

53. In the past, four direct labor hours were required to produce each unit of product Y. Material costs were $200 per unit, the direct labor rate was $20 per hour, and factory overhead was three times direct labor cost. In budgeting for next year, management is planning to outsource some manufacturing activities and to further automate others. Management estimates these plans will reduce labor hours by 25%, increase the factory overhead rate to 3.6 times direct labor costs, and increase material costs by $30 per unit. Management plans to manufacture 10,000 units. What amount should management budget for cost of goods manufactured?

A. $4,700,000

B. $5,060,000

C. $5,200,000

D. $5,980,000

Answer (B) is correct. *(CPA, adapted)*
REQUIRED: The budgeted cost of goods manufactured.
DISCUSSION: Direct labor hours per unit equal 3 [4 × (1.0 – .25]. Direct labor cost per unit equals $60 (3 × $20). Applied overhead per unit equals $216 (3.6 × $60). Unit materials cost equals $230 ($200 + $30). Accordingly, budgeted cost of goods manufactured equals $5,060,000 [10,000 units × ($60 + $216 + $230)].
Answer (A) is incorrect because $4,700,000 is based on the assumption that the overhead rate did not change. Answer (C) is incorrect because $5,200,000 is based on the original costs and rates. Answer (D) is incorrect because $5,980,000 is based on the assumption that unit labor hours will not change.

54. Mien Co. is budgeting sales of 53,000 units of product Nous for next month. The manufacture of one unit of Nous requires 4 kilos of chemical Loire. During the month, Mien plans to reduce the inventory of Loire by 50,000 kilos and increase the finished goods inventory of Nous by 6,000 units. There is no Nous work-in-process inventory. How many kilos of Loire is Mien budgeting to purchase next month?

A. 138,000

B. 162,000

C. 186,000

D. 238,000

Answer (C) is correct. *(CPA, adapted)*
REQUIRED: The number of kilos budgeted for purchase.
DISCUSSION: Projected sales of 53,000 units and a 6,000-unit increase in inventory require production of 59,000 units. Thus, 236,000 (59,000 × 4) kilos of Loire are needed for production. Mien intends to reduce the inventory of Loire by 50,000 kilos, so 186,000 (236,000 – 50,000) kilos must be purchased.
Answer (A) is incorrect because 236,000 kilos are needed [(53,000 + 6,000) × 4], and Mien intends to reduce inventory by 50,000 units, so 186,000 kilos must be purchased (236,000 – 50,000). Answer (B) is incorrect because 162,000 does not consider the 6,000-unit increase in the finished goods inventory of Nous. Answer (D) is incorrect because 236,000 kilos are needed [(53,000 + 6,000) × 4], and Mien intends to reduce inventory by 50,000 units, so 186,000 kilos must be purchased (236,000 – 50,000).

55. Rolling Wheels purchases bicycle components in the month prior to assembling them into bicycles. Assembly is scheduled one month prior to budgeted sales. Rolling pays 75% of component costs in the month of purchase and 25% of the costs in the following month. Component costs included in budgeted cost of sales are:

April	May	June	July	August
$5,000	$6,000	$7,000	$8,000	$8,000

What is Rolling's budgeted cash payments for components in May?

- A. $5,750
- B. $6,750
- C. $7,750
- D. $8,000

Answer (C) is correct.   *(CPA, adapted)*
REQUIRED: The budgeted cash payments for purchases.
DISCUSSION: The bicycle components purchased by Rolling Wheels in May will be included in bicycles sold in July. The components are purchased one month prior to assembly and assembled one month prior to sale. Rolling will pay 75% of June's $8,000 budgeted cost of sales in May and the remaining 25% in June. Moreover, 25% of June's $7,000 budgeted cost of sales is paid for in May. Consequently, Rolling's budgeted cash payments for components in May are $7,750 [($8,000 × .75) + ($7,000 × .25)].
Answer (A) is incorrect because $5,750 equals the budgeted cash payments for components in March. Answer (B) is incorrect because $6,750 equals the budgeted cash payments for components in April. Answer (D) is incorrect because $8,000 equals the budgeted cash payments for components in June.

16.7 Other Budgeting Concepts

56. A budget amount that is created using expected quantity and actual price data is known as a

- A. Continuous budget.
- B. Flexible budget.
- C. "Third" budget.
- D. Static budget.

Answer (B) is correct.   *(CMA, adapted)*
REQUIRED: The plan based on budgeted revenue and costs and actual output.
DISCUSSION: A flexible budget combines the actual quantity of outputs times the standard number of inputs per unit of output (called the expected quantity) and the standard price per unit of input.
Answer (A) is incorrect because a continuous budget is revised on a regular (continuous) basis by extending it for another month or quarter in accordance with new data as the current month or quarter ends. Answer (C) is incorrect because the "third" budget combines the actual quantity of inputs used times the standard price per unit of input. Answer (D) is incorrect because the static budget consists of the standard quantity of inputs times the standard price.

57. The basic difference between a master budget and a flexible budget is that a master budget is

- A. Prepared before the period begins while a flexible budget is prepared after it ends.
- B. Reports the costs that should have been incurred given the achieved level of production.
- C. Based on a fixed standard, whereas a flexible budget allows management latitude in meeting goals.
- D. For an entire production facility, whereas a flexible budget is applicable to single departments only.

Answer (A) is correct.   *(CPA, adapted)*
REQUIRED: The basic difference between a master budget and a flexible budget.
DISCUSSION: The static budget, prepared ahead of time, is management's best estimate about sales, production levels, and costs for the upcoming period. The flexible budget, prepared after the fact, consists of the costs that should have been incurred given the actual level of production achieved.
Answer (B) is incorrect because the budget that reports the costs that should have been incurred given the achieved level of production is the flexible budget. Answer (C) is incorrect because master budgets, not flexible budgets, recognize the organization's goals and objectives. Answer (D) is incorrect because flexible budgets can be applied at the department level or at the production facility level.

58. A flexible budget is appropriate for a

	Marketing Budget	Direct Materials Usage Budget
A.	No	No
B.	No	Yes
C.	Yes	Yes
D.	Yes	No

Answer (C) is correct.   *(CPA, adapted)*
REQUIRED: The type(s) of budget, if any, for which a flexible budget is appropriate.
DISCUSSION: A flexible budget approach is appropriate for both a materials budget and a marketing budget because each contains elements that vary with the activity level.

59. A systemized approach known as zero-base budgeting (ZBB)

A. Presents planned activities for a period of time but does not present a firm commitment.

B. Divides the activities of individual responsibility centers into a series of packages that are prioritized.

C. Classifies the budget by the prior year's activity and estimates the benefits arising from each activity.

D. Commences with the current level of spending.

Answer (B) is correct. *(CMA, adapted)*
REQUIRED: The true statement about zero-base budgeting (ZBB).
DISCUSSION: ZBB is a budgeting process in which each manager must justify a department's entire budget every year. ZBB differs from the traditional concept of budgeting in which next year's budget is largely based on the expenditures of the previous year. For each budgetary unit, ZBB prepares a decision package describing various levels of service that may be provided, including at least one level lower than the current one. Each component is evaluated from a cost-benefit perspective and then prioritized.
Answer (A) is incorrect because ZBB does represent a firm commitment. Answer (C) is incorrect because ZBB is not based on prior year's activities. Answer (D) is incorrect because ZBB starts from a base of zero.

60. The budgeting tool or process in which estimates of revenues and expenses are prepared for each product beginning with the product's research and development phase and traced through to its customer support phase is a(n)

A. Master budget.

B. Activity-based budget.

C. Zero-base budget.

D. Life-cycle budget.

Answer (D) is correct. *(CMA, adapted)*
REQUIRED: The budget tool that involves estimating a product's revenues and expenses from R&D through customer support.
DISCUSSION: A life-cycle budget estimates a product's revenues and expenses over its expected life cycle. This approach is especially useful when revenues and related costs do not occur in the same periods. It emphasizes the need to budget revenues to cover all costs, not just those for production. Hence, costs are determined for all value-chain categories: upstream (R&D, design), manufacturing, and downstream (marketing, distribution, and customer service). The result is to highlight upstream and downstream costs that often receive insufficient attention.
Answer (A) is incorrect because a master budget summarizes all of a company's budgets and plans. Answer (B) is incorrect because an activity-based budget emphasizes the costs of activities, which are the basic cost objects in activity-based costing. Answer (C) is incorrect because a zero-base budget requires each manager to justify his/her subunit's entire budget each year.

61. A continuous (rolling) budget

A. Presents planned activities for a period but does not present a firm commitment.

B. Presents the plan for only one level of activity and does not adjust to changes in the level of activity.

C. Presents the plan for a range of activity so that the plan can be adjusted for changes in activity.

D. Drops the current month or quarter and adds a future month or quarter as the current month or quarter is completed.

Answer (D) is correct. *(CMA, adapted)*
REQUIRED: The true statement about a continuous budget.
DISCUSSION: A continuous budget is one that is revised on a regular (continuous) basis. Typically, a company extends such a budget for another month or quarter in accordance with new data as the current month or quarter ends. For example, if the budget is for 12 months, a budget for the next 12 months will be available continuously as each month ends.
Answer (A) is incorrect because a continuous budget does present a firm commitment. Answer (B) is incorrect because a continuous budget can be for various levels of activity; a static budget is prepared for only one level of activity. Answer (C) is incorrect because a flexible budget presents the plan for a range of activity so that the plan can be adjusted for changes in activity.

Use Gleim's ***CPA Test Prep*** for interactive testing with over 2,000 additional multiple-choice questions!

STUDY UNIT SEVENTEEN
BUSINESS PERFORMANCE

(26 pages of outline)

This study unit concerns performance by business organizations and their subunits. A pervasive consideration is the pursuit of **quality** in all aspects of the organization's activities. Quality management has been recognized by the **International Organization for Standardization**, which has issued quality assurance standards. Another aspect of the measurement of organization performance is responsibility accounting, which encompasses the establishment of responsibility centers, common cost allocation, and transfer pricing. This study unit also addresses various issues, behavioral and otherwise, regarding performance feedback.

17.1 QUALITY CONSIDERATIONS

1. Overall, an organization must assess quality in **two fundamental areas**: process quality and product quality. **Process quality** assesses the effectiveness and efficiency of the organization's internal operations. **Product quality** focuses on the conformance of the organization's output to customer expectations.

   a. **Product quality** is best viewed from **multiple perspectives**: (1) attributes of the product (performance, serviceability, durability, etc.), (2) customer satisfaction, (3) conformity with specifications, and (4) value (relation of quality and price).

      1) One of the dimensions of quality is **conformance**, or how well a product and its components meet applicable standards. The traditional view is that conforming products are those with characteristics that lie within an acceptable specified range of values that includes a target value. This view also regards a certain percentage of defective (nonconforming) units as acceptable.

         a) The traditional view was superseded by the **zero-defects (goalpost conformance) approach**. It seeks to eliminate nonconforming output.

         b) An extension of this approach is the **robust quality (absolute quality conformance) concept**. Its goal is to reach the target value in every case. The purpose is to eliminate the hidden quality costs that occur when output varies from the target, even though the units are within specifications.

2. Management **Processes** for the Improvement of Quality

   a. **Policy deployment** is the systematic planning of corporate objectives and the detailed ways in which organizational subunits will approach the accomplishment of their related objectives. The purpose is for the objectives of the organization, its subunits, and its employees to be consistent.

   b. **Quality function deployment** ensures that customer requirements are translated into design requirements at each step in product development. It is an umbrella concept most useful in an environment in which the **Plan-Do-Check-Act (PDCA) cycle** (the Deming Wheel) is used at all levels.

      1)   PDCA is a "management by fact," or scientific-method, approach to continuous improvement. PDCA creates a process-centered environment because it involves (a) studying the current process, (b) collecting and analyzing data to identify causes of problems, (c) planning for improvement, and (d) deciding how to measure improvement (Plan).

      2)   The plan is then implemented on a small scale if possible (Do).

      3)   The next step is to determine what happened (Check).

      4)   If the experiment was successful, the plan is fully implemented (Act).

      5)   The cycle is then repeated using what was learned from the preceding cycle.

  c.   **Kaizen** is the Japanese word for the continuous pursuit of improvement in every aspect of organizational operations.

      1)   For example, a kaizen budget projects costs based on future improvements. The possibility of such improvements must be determined, and the cost of implementation and the savings must be estimated.

  d.   **Employee involvement** means training and empowering employees to harness their creativity for problem solving. Quality control circles are used to obtain input from employees and to locate the best perspective on problem solving.

  e.   **Suppliers' management** is the careful selection of suppliers and the cultivation of long-term relationships based on the consistent ability to meet mutual expectations.

  f.   **Competitive benchmarking** involves continuously evaluating the practices of the best organizations and adapting company processes to incorporate the best of these practices.

  g.   **Quality training** familiarizes all employees with the means for preventing, detecting, and eliminating nonquality. The educational processes are tailored to each group.

  h.   **Reward and recognition** for quality improvement should be group oriented. They should be based on quality measures.

3.   Several **tools for analyzing quality problems** are available.

  a.   **Statistical quality control** is a method of determining whether the shipment or production run of units lies within acceptable limits.

      1)   It is also used to determine whether production processes are out of control.

      2)   **Statistical control charts** are graphic aids for monitoring the status of any process subject to random variations.

          a)   Originally developed to control the quality of production processes, they also have applications of direct interest to the management accountant, for example, unit cost of production, direct labor hours used, ratio of actual expenses to budgeted expenses, number of calls by sales personnel, and total accounts receivable.

          b)   The chart consists of three horizontal lines plotted on a horizontal time scale.

          c)   The center line represents the average or mean value for the process being controlled.

          d)   The other two lines are the upper control limit (UCL) and the lower control limit (LCL).

          e)   The processes are measured periodically, and the values are plotted on the chart (X).

              i)   If the value falls within the control limits, no action is taken.

              ii)   If the value falls outside the limits, the process is considered out of control, and an investigation is made for possible corrective action.

f) Another advantage of the chart is that it makes trends visible.

g) EXAMPLE:

Unit Cost   X   May's results are
                                                          out of control.

$1.05   -   UCL
                              X

$1.00   _____

                  X

$0.95   -   LCL
        March   April   May

3) **P charts** are based on an attribute (acceptable/not acceptable) rather than a measure of a variable. Specifically, they show the percentage of defects in a sample.

4) **C charts** are also attribute control charts. They show defects per item.

5) An **R chart** shows the range of dispersion of a variable, such as size or weight.

6) An **X-bar chart** shows the sample mean for a variable.

b. Variations in the value of some process parameter may have several causes.

1) **Random variations** occur by chance. Present in virtually all processes, they are not correctable because they will not repeat themselves in the same manner. Excessively narrow control limits will result in many investigations of what are simply random fluctuations.

2) **Implementation deviations** occur because of human or mechanical failure to achieve target results.

3) **Measurement variations** result from errors in the measurements of actual results.

4) **Model fluctuations** can be caused by errors in the formulation of a decision model.

5) **Prediction variances** result from errors in forecasting data used in a decision model.

c. A **Pareto diagram** is a bar chart that assists managers in what is commonly called 80:20 analysis.

1) The **80:20 rule**, formulated by management theorist Joseph M. Juran, holds that 80% of all effects are the result of only 20% of all causes.

2) In the context of quality control, managers optimize their time by focusing their effort on the handful of areas from which most defects arise.

a) The independent variable, plotted on the X axis, is the factor selected by the manager as the area of interest: department, time period, geographical location, etc. The frequency of occurrence of the defect (dependent variable) is plotted on the Y axis.

b) The occurrences of the independent variable are ranked from highest to lowest, allowing the manager to see at a glance which areas are of most concern.

c)   EXAMPLE: The chief administrative officer wants to know which departments are generating the most travel vouchers that have to be returned to the submitter because of incomplete documentation.

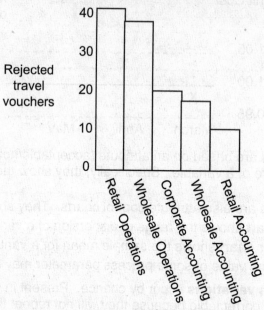

d.   A **histogram** is similar in presentation to a Pareto diagram. The major distinction is that histograms display a continuum for the independent variable.

1)   EXAMPLE: The CAO wants to know how many travel reimbursement dollars are being held up by a typical returned travel voucher.

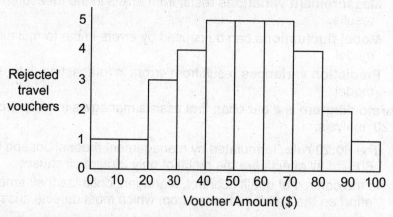

e.   A **fishbone diagram** (also called a **cause-and-effect diagram** or an **Ishikawa diagram**) is a total quality management process improvement technique that is useful in studying causation (why the actual and desired situations differ).

1)   This format organizes the analysis of causation and helps to identify possible interactions among causes.

2)   The head of the skeleton represents the statement of the problem.

3)   The principal classifications of causes are represented by lines (bones) drawn diagonally from the heavy horizontal line (the spine).

4)   Smaller horizontal lines are added in their order of probability in each classification.

5)   EXAMPLE:

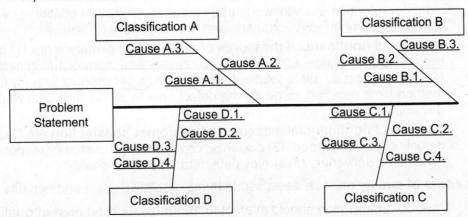

f.   The **Taguchi quality loss function** is a measure of the departure from absolute quality conformance (robust quality).

1)   It is based on the principle that quality losses occur even when items are within specified limits or tolerances. Thus, any variation from a quality target for a characteristic results in hidden quality costs.

2)   The basic formula is

$$L = k(x - T)^2$$

If: L = the quality costs per unit
k = a constant based on the entity's external failure cost experience
x = actual measure of the quality variable
T = target value of the quality variable

a)   The estimate of the constant is

$$k = c \div d^2$$

If: c = the loss at a specification limit
d = the difference between the target value and the specification limit

b)   The following is the graph of a Taguchi loss function (the quality cost at the target value is $0):

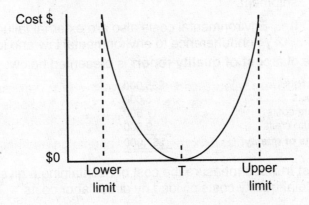

4.   **Measures** for the assessment of quality.

    a.   Customer retention is a vitally important measure of service quality. Loyal customers spend more, refer new customers, and are less costly to service.

    b.   Examples of **nonfinancial measures of internal performance** are (1) manufacturing cycle efficiency (value-added production time ÷ total manufacturing cycle time), (2) ratio of good output to total output, (3) defects per product line, (4) the half-life method (time required to reduce the defect ratio by 50%), and (5) new product development time.

    c.   Examples of **nonfinancial measures of customer satisfaction** are (1) percentage of defective goods shipped, (2) customer complaints, (3) customer response time, (4) on-time deliveries, (5) survey data, and (6) market share.

5.   The **costs of quality** must be assessed in terms of relative costs and benefits.

    a.   Thus, an organization should attempt to **minimize its total cost of quality**. Moreover, nonquantitative factors also must be considered. For example, an emphasis on quality improves competitiveness, enhances employee expertise, and generates goodwill.

    b.   Costs of quality are generally divided into two major categories and **four subcategories**:

        1)   **Conformance costs** include costs of prevention and costs of appraisal, which are financial measures of internal performance.

            a)   **Prevention** attempts to avoid defective output. These costs include (1) preventive maintenance, (2) employee training, (3) review of equipment design, and (4) evaluation of suppliers.

            b)   **Appraisal** embraces such activities as statistical quality control programs, inspection, and testing.

        2)   **Nonconformance costs** include internal failure costs (a financial measure of internal performance) and external failure costs (a financial measure of customer satisfaction).

            a)   **Internal failure** costs occur when defective products are detected before shipment. Examples are scrap, rework, tooling changes, and downtime.

            b)   The costs of **external failure**, e.g., warranty costs, product liability costs, and loss of customer goodwill, arise when problems occur after shipment.

                i)   Environmental costs also are external failure costs, e.g., fines for nonadherence to environmental law and loss of customer goodwill.

    c.   An example of a **cost of quality report** is presented below:

Prevention costs	$35,000
Appraisal costs	5,000
Internal failure costs	17,500
External failure costs	9,500
Total costs of quality	**$67,000**

    d.   **Quality cost indices** measure the cost of maintaining a given level of quality, for example, total quality costs divided by direct labor costs.

        1)   EXAMPLE: To continue the previous example, if total direct labor costs were $201,000, the quality cost index for the month was 33.3% ($67,000 ÷ $201,000).

6. **Quality and productivity** do not necessarily have an inverse relationship. The robust quality view is that improving quality and reducing costs in each category may be possible if the most efficient prevention methods are applied.

    a. For example, selection of a supplier meeting high quality standards regarding defect rates and delivery times may drive down not only failure costs, but also the prevention and appraisal costs incurred when supplier performance was less reliable.

7. **Management of time** is important to any quality improvement program.

    a. **Product development time** is a crucial factor in the competitive equation. A company that is first in the market with a new product has obvious advantages.

        1) Reducing development time is also important because product life cycles are becoming shorter.

        2) Companies need to respond quickly and flexibly to new technology, changes in consumer tastes, and competitive challenges.

    b. One financial measure of product development is **breakeven time**. It is the time from management approval of the project to the time when the cumulative present value of cash inflows equals the cumulative present value of cash outflows.

        1) The most popular method of determining breakeven time calculates the time required for the present value of the cumulative cash flows to equal zero.

            a) An alternative that results in a longer breakeven time is to consider the time required for the present value of the cumulative cash inflows to equal the present value of all the expected future cash outflows.

    c. **Customer-response time** is the delay from placement of an order to delivery of the good or service. Response time is a function of time drivers. A change in a time driver causes a change in the time required for an activity. Such changes reflect uncertainty about arrivals of customers in the queue and bottlenecks (points at which capacity is reached or exceeded).

        1) Response time consists of order receipt time (delay between the customer's placement of an order and its receipt by the production facility), manufacturing lead or cycle time (delay from the order's receipt by the production facility to its completion), and order delivery time.

        2) Manufacturing lead or cycle (throughput) time equals order waiting time plus manufacturing time.

8. Stop and review! You have completed the outline for this subunit. Study multiple-choice questions 1 through 11 beginning on page 536.

17.2 BENCHMARKING, TQM, AND THE ISO FRAMEWORK

1. **Benchmarking** is a primary tool used in quality management. It is a means of helping organizations with productivity management and business process analysis.

    a. Benchmarking involves **analysis and measurement of key outputs** against those of the best organizations. This procedure also involves identifying the underlying key actions and causes that contribute to the performance difference.

        1) **Best practices** are recognized by authorities in the field and by customers for generating outstanding results. They are generally innovative technically or in their management of human resources.

        2) Benchmarking is an ongoing process that requires quantitative and qualitative measurement of the difference between the performance of an activity and the performance by the benchmark. This entity need not be a competitor.

b. The following are **kinds of benchmarking**:

1) Competitive benchmarking studies an organization in the same industry.

2) Process (function) benchmarking studies operations of organizations with similar processes regardless of industry. Thus, the benchmark need not be a competitor or even a similar entity.

a) This method may introduce new ideas that provide a significant competitive advantage.

3) Strategic benchmarking is a search for successful competitive strategies.

4) Internal benchmarking is the application of best practices in one part of the organization to its other parts.

c. The **first phase** in the benchmarking process is to select and prioritize benchmarking projects.

1) An organization must understand its critical success factors and business environment to identify key business processes and drivers and to develop parameters defining what processes to benchmark. The criteria for selecting what to benchmark relate to the reasons for the existence of a process and its importance to the entity's mission, values, and strategy. These reasons relate in large part to satisfaction of end user or customer needs.

d. The **next phase** is to organize benchmarking teams. A team organization is appropriate. It permits an equitable division of labor, participation by those responsible for implementing changes, and inclusion of a variety of functional expertise and work experience.

1) Team members should have (a) knowledge of the function to be benchmarked, (b) respected positions in the organization, (c) good communication skills, (d) teaming skills, (e) motivation to innovate and to support cross-functional problem solving, and (f) project management skills.

2) The team must thoroughly **investigate and document the organization's internal processes**. The organization is a series of processes, not a fixed structure.

a) A process is a network of related and independent activities joined by their outputs. One way to determine the primary characteristics of a process is to trace the path a request for a product or service takes through the organization.

b) The team must develop a family of measures that are true indicators of process performance. It also must develop a process taxonomy, that is, a set of process elements, measures, and phrases that describes the process to be benchmarked.

c) The development of key indicators for performance measurement in a benchmarking context is an extension of the basic evaluative function of internal auditors. Internal auditors evaluate governance, risk management, and control processes. Evaluation requires establishment of adequate criteria by management. In the absence of these criteria, internal auditors must work with management to develop "appropriate evaluation criteria" (Performance Standard 2120.A4).

e. Researching and identifying **best-in-class performance** is often the most difficult phase. The critical steps are

1) Setting up databases,

2) Choosing information-gathering methods (internal sources, external public domain sources, and original research),

3) Formatting questionnaires (lists of questions prepared in advance), and

4) Selecting benchmarking partners.

    f.   Data analysis identifies **performance gaps**, obtains an understanding of the reasons they exist, and prioritizes the key activities that will facilitate the behavioral and process changes needed. Sophisticated statistical and other methods may be needed when the study involves many variables, testing of assumptions, or quantified results.

    g.   **Leadership** is most important in the implementation phase because the team must be able to justify its recommendations. Moreover, the process improvement teams must manage the implementation of approved changes.

2.   The emergence of the **total quality management (TQM)** concept is one of the most significant developments in managerial accounting.

    a.   TQM was developed in the mid-1940s by statistician W. Edwards Deming, who aided Japanese industry in its recovery from World War II.

    b.   The Deming Prize is awarded by the Union of Japanese Scientists and Engineers for outstanding contributions to the study or application of TQM.

3.   **TQM** recognizes that quality improvement can increase revenues and decrease costs significantly. The following are TQM's **core principles** or **critical factors**:

    a.   Emphasis on the **customer**

        1)   Satisfaction of external customers
        2)   Satisfaction of internal customers
        3)   Requirements for external suppliers
        4)   Requirements for internal suppliers

    b.   **Continuous improvement** as a never-ending process, not a destination.

    c.   **Engaging every employee** in the pursuit of total quality because avoidance of defects in products or services and satisfaction of external customers requires that all internal customers be satisfied.

4.   **TQM** is a **comprehensive approach** to quality.

    a.   It treats the pursuit of quality as a **basic organizational function** that is as important as production or marketing.

    b.   TQM is the continuous pursuit of quality in every aspect of organizational activities through a philosophy of doing it right the first time, employee training and empowerment, promotion of teamwork, improvement of processes, and attention to satisfaction of customers, both internal and external.

        1)   TQM emphasizes the supplier's relationship with the customer, identifies customer needs, and recognizes that everyone in a process is at some time a customer or supplier of someone else, either within or without the organization.

        2)   Thus, TQM begins with external customer requirements, identifies internal customer-supplier relationships and requirements, and establishes requirements for external suppliers.

        3)   Organizations tend to be vertically organized, but TQM requires strong horizontal linkages.

    c.   The management of quality is not limited to quality management staff, engineers, production personnel, etc.

        1)   The role of **management accountants** includes assisting in designing and operating quality information, measurement, and reporting systems.

            a)   In particular, they can contribute to problem solving through measuring and reporting quality costs.

5. **Implementation of TQM** cannot be accomplished by application of a formula, and the process is lengthy and difficult. The following phases are typical:

   a. Establishing an executive-level quality council of senior managers with strong involvement by the CEO.

   b. Providing quality training programs for senior managers.

   c. Conducting a quality audit to evaluate the success of the process for gathering background information to develop the strategic quality improvement plan.

      1) The quality audit also may identify the best improvement opportunities and the organization's strengths and weaknesses compared with its benchmarked competitors.

   d. Preparing a gap analysis to ascertain what is necessary to bridge the gap between the organization and the quality leaders in its industry and to establish a database for the development of the strategic quality improvement plan.

   e. Developing strategic quality improvement plans for the short and long term.

   f. Conducting employee communication and training programs.

   g. Establishing quality teams, which ensure that goods and services conform to specifications.

   h. Creating a measurement system and setting goals.

   i. Revising compensation, appraisal, and recognition systems.

   j. Reviewing and revising the entire effort periodically.

6. In 1987, the International Organization for Standardization (ISO) introduced ISO 9000, a "family" of 11 standards and technical reports that provide guidance for establishing and maintaining a **quality management system (QMS)**. The ISO's rules specify that its standards be revised every 5 years in light of technological and market developments. NOTE: ISO is not an acronym. It means equal, suggesting that entities certified under ISO 9001:2000 have equal quality.)

   a. The current standards (ISO 9000:2000) were issued in December 2000. For specific and up-to-date information, see the ISO's website (www.iso.org).

   b. The intent of the standards is to ensure the quality of the **process, not the product**. The marketplace determines whether a product is good or bad.

      1) For this reason, the ISO deems it unacceptable for phrases referring to ISO certification to appear on individual products or packaging.

   c. Only one of the standards is a certification standard.

      1) **ISO 9001:2000,** *Quality Management Systems – Requirements*, is the standard that provides a model for quality assurance programs.

      2) For this reason, "ISO 9001:2000 certified" is the only acceptable formulation. There is no such thing as "ISO 9000 certification."

      3) ISO 9000:2005 was issued recently. It applies to (a) entities implementing a QMS, (b) entities seeking assurance about products provided by suppliers, (c) users of the products, (d) everyone needing an understanding of quality terminology, (e) those who assess QMSs, (f) those who provide advice or training relative to a QMS, and (g) standard setters.

7. The following are the **objectives** of applying the standards:

   a. Achieving and continuously improving quality relative to requirements.

   b. Improving operations to meet all needs of stakeholders (interested parties).

   c. Giving confidence to employees that quality requirements are met and improvement is occurring.

   d. Giving confidence to stakeholders that quality of delivered products is achieved.

   e. Providing confidence that the quality system meets expectations.

8. QMS standards are founded on the **quality management principles** defined in ISO 9000:2000 and ISO 9004:2000, as follows:

   a. Customer focus means understanding needs, meeting requirements, and trying to surpass expectations.

   b. Leadership develops unity of purpose by maintaining an environment that permits full involvement in reaching entity objectives.

   c. Involvement of people in the fullest sense allows their abilities to be used for the entity's benefit.

   d. A process approach to managing activities and resources is the efficient way to obtain desired results.

   e. A systems approach to management integrates and aligns processes to obtain desired results more efficiently and effectively.

   f. Continual improvement of overall performance should be a permanent objective.

   g. A factual approach to decision making is based on data and information.

   h. Mutually beneficial supplier relationships increase all parties' value creation.

9. The following are the **basic requirements of a QMS**:

   a. **Key processes** affecting quality must be identified and included.

      1) A process management approach must be used. It manages the entity as a set of linked processes that are controlled for continuous improvement.

   b. **General requirements.** The entity must have a quality policy and quality goals. It also must design a QMS to control process performance. Quality goals are measurable and specific.

      1) The QMS is documented in the (a) quality policy, (b) quality manual, (c) procedures, (d) work instructions, and (e) records.

   c. **Management responsibility.** Management (1) reviews the quality policy, (2) analyzes data about QMS performance, and (3) assesses opportunities for improvement and the need for change.

      1) Management ensures that systems exist to determine and satisfy customer requirements.

   d. **Resource management.** The resources needed to improve the QMS and satisfy customer requirements must be provided.

      1) Human resources (employees) should be qualified and trained for their specific jobs.

      2) The infrastructure (physical resources needed for quality output) and the work environment should be sufficient.

   e. **Product realization processes** result in products or services received by customers. These processes must be planned and controlled. Issues are (1) means of control, (2) objectives, (3) documentation and records needed, and (4) acceptance criteria.

      1) Design and development also must be planned and controlled.

      2) Purchasing evaluates suppliers of materials and services, and the entity's materials and products must be clearly identified at all times. Moreover, customer property must be protected.

      3) Product quality must be preserved during handling, storage, and delivery.

f.   **Measurement, analysis, and improvement.** The entity must have processes for (1) inspection, (2) testing, (3) measurement, (4) analysis, and (5) improvement.

1) Thus, customer satisfaction must be measured.
2) Substandard materials and products must be controlled so that they do not reach customers.
3) Internal audits measure and monitor QMS performance.
4) All employees should use corrective and preventive action systems.
5) Work instructions must identify measuring and monitoring requirements.

10. Some companies are obtaining ISO 9000 certification because of fear that the **European Union** will require compliance with the standards in an attempt to restrict imports.

a.   The standards are not yet mandatory except among regulated products (for which health and safety are concerns), such as medical devices, telecommunications equipment, and gas appliances.
b.   Some customers demand that suppliers register.
c.   ISO 9000 registration may be a key to remaining competitive. It makes customers more comfortable with suppliers' products and services.
d.   Many companies implementing the standards uncover internal process and quality improvements as a result. ISO 9000 forces companies to share information and understand who internal customers and users are.

11. A **registrar, or external auditor**, must be selected. Registrars are usually specialists within certain Standard Industrial Classification (SIC) codes. Certification by a registrar avoids the need for each customer to audit a supplier.

a.   Following an on-site visit, the registrar, if convinced that a quality system conforms to the selected standard, issues a certificate describing the scope of the registration. Registration is usually granted for a 3-year period.
b.   Some companies have preliminary audits by official registrars.
c.   All employees are subject to being audited. They must have the ability to "say what they do" and to demonstrate that they "do what they say."

12. The ISO also has issued a set of **environmental standards** known as **ISO 14000**. These standards are comparable in purpose to ISO 9000 but concern environmental quality systems. Although they have not been as widely adopted as the ISO 9000 standards, they may become a necessity for conducting international business.

a.   ISO 14000 establishes internationally recognized standards that will diminish barriers to trade and make it easier to do business across borders.
b.   Some companies feel that adherence to ISO 14000 standards will reduce monitoring and inspection by regulatory agencies.
c.   A survey of managers found that failure to obtain ISO 14000 certification could constitute a potential nontariff trade barrier because customers will require it.
d.   At present, the main benefit of adopting ISO 14000 standards is internal. Companies learn how well their environmental management system operates relative to those of other companies.
e.   Some companies have decided to seek ISO 14000 certification because they found that ISO 9000 was beneficial.
f.   Some European countries already have environmental systems standards in place, and how these single-country standards will mesh with ISO 14000 is not clear. However, individual countries' standards are typically more strict.
g.   Some are concerned that regulators may use voluntary ISO audits or self-audits as a basis for punitive action. To allay these fears in the U.S., the Environmental Protection Agency has issued new audit guidelines that are intended to avoid such self-incrimination.

13. The scope of ISO 19011:2002 extends to (a) the principles of auditing, (b) managing audit programs, (c) conducting QMS audits and environmental management system audits, and (d) the competence of QMS and environmental management system auditors.

    a. It applies to all entities that must perform internal or external audits of QMSs or environmental management systems or manage an audit program.

    b. ISO 19011 may apply to other types of audits if due consideration is given to identifying the competencies required of the auditors.

14. ISO 10012:2003 is a generic standard. It addresses the management of measurement processes and confirmation of measuring equipment used to support compliance with required measures.

    a. It states quality management requirements of a measurement management system (MMS) that can be used as part of the overall management system.

    b. It is not to be used as a requirement for demonstrating conformance with other standards. Interested parties may agree to use ISO 10012:2003 as an input for satisfying MMS requirements in certification activities. However, other standards apply to specific elements affecting measurement results, e.g., details of measurement methods, competence of personnel, or comparisons among laboratories.

15. Stop and review! You have completed the outline for this subunit. Study multiple-choice questions 12 through 23 beginning on page 539.

17.3 RESPONSIBILITY CENTERS, COMMON COSTS, AND TRANSFER PRICING

1. Managerial performance ordinarily should be evaluated based on factors that can be influenced by the manager, such as revenues, costs, or investment. For example, a controllable cost may be defined as one directly regulated by a specific manager at a given level of production within a given time span or one that the manager can significantly influence. A well-designed responsibility accounting system establishes responsibility centers (also called **strategic business units**) for the purpose of encouraging managerial effort to attain organizational objectives, motivating managers to make decisions consistent with those objectives, and providing a basis for determining managerial compensation.

    a. A **cost center**, e.g., a maintenance department, is responsible for costs only. Hence, evaluations are related to the cost drivers of what is measured. A disadvantage of a cost center is the potential for cost shifting, for example, replacement of variable costs for which a manager is responsible with fixed costs for which (s)he is not. Another disadvantage is that long-term issues may be disregarded when the emphasis is on, for example, annual cost amounts. Yet another issue is allocation of service department costs to cost centers.

    b. A **revenue center**, e.g., a sales department, is responsible for revenues only. Thus, revenue drivers are relevant to performance measurement of revenue centers. They are factors that influence unit sales, such as changes in prices and products, customer service, marketing efforts, and delivery terms.

    c. A **profit center**, e.g., an appliance department in a retail store, is responsible for revenues and expenses. Thus, use of profit centers promotes goal congruence by (1) encouraging cooperation among organizational functions (production, marketing, and support), (2) influencing managers to think of their products or services as salable outside the firm, and (3) encouraging managers to find new ways to earn profits.

    d. An **investment center**, e.g., a branch office, is responsible for revenues, expenses, and invested capital. The advantage of an investment center is that it permits an evaluation of performance that can be compared with that of other responsibility centers or other potential investments on a return on investment basis, i.e., on the basis of the effectiveness of asset usage.

e.   **Service centers** exist primarily and sometimes solely to provide specialized support to other organizational subunits. They are usually operated as cost centers. A maintenance department is an example.

2.   **Controllability** is not an absolute basis for responsibility. For example, responsibility may be assigned based on knowledge of how a cost is incurred rather than the ability to control it directly. An assignment also may be made to influence a manager's behavior. In principle, controllability is proportionate to, but not coextensive with, responsibility.

a.   Controllability is difficult to isolate because few things are under the sole influence of one manager. Thus, separating the effects of current management's decisions from those of former management is difficult.

b.   If responsibility exceeds the extent to which a manager can influence an activity, the result may be reduced morale, a decline in managerial effort, and poor performance. Such a manager encounters greater risk because his/her success depends on uncontrollable factors. Thus, a manager in these circumstances should be compensated for the incremental risk assumed.

c.   However, if a manager is accountable solely for activities over which (s)he has extensive influence, the manager may develop too narrow a focus.

1)   For example, the manager of a cost center may make decisions based only on cost efficiency and ignore the overall effectiveness objectives of the organization. By extending the manager's responsibility to profits as well as costs, the organization may encourage desirable behavior congruent with overall objectives, such as improved coordination with marketing personnel, even though the manager still does not control revenues.

2)   A manager who does not control an activity may nevertheless be the person best informed about it. Thus, a purchasing agent may be in the best position to explain price variances even though (s)he cannot control them.

d.   Accordingly, a successful system is dependent upon the proper delegation of responsibility and the commensurate authority.

3.   **Management by objectives (MBO)** is a related concept. It is a behavioral, communications-oriented, responsibility approach to employee self-direction. Under MBO, a manager and his/her subordinates agree upon objectives and the means of attaining them. The plans that result are reflected in responsibility accounting and in the budgeting process.

4.   The purpose of a responsibility system is to motivate management performance that adheres to overall organizational objectives **(goal congruence)**.

a.   **Suboptimization** occurs when one segment takes action that is in its own best interests but is detrimental to the organization as a whole.

5.   The alignment of managerial with organizational goals requires assigning **responsibility** for activities, delegating the **authority** to perform necessary tasks, and establishing **accountability**. The result is a structure within which individual efforts can be coordinated to attain ultimate organizational goals.

a.   Larger organizations are usually divided into multiple segments, with the amount of autonomy of the divisions reflecting the degree of **decentralization**.

1)   Along with enhancing managerial morale and development, decentralization allows senior management to concentrate on a long-range focus and encourages division managers to look outside the organization to meet operational needs.

2)   Disadvantages include greater difficulty in achieving goal congruence, duplication of effort, and lack of communication among segment managers.

6. **Common costs** are the costs of products, activities, facilities, services, or operations shared by two or more cost objects.

    a. The term "joint costs" is frequently used to describe the common costs of a single process that yields two or more joint products.

7. Common costs are **indirect costs** whose allocation may be arbitrary.

    a. A direct **cause-and-effect relationship** between a common cost and the actions of the cost object to which it is allocated is desirable. Such a relationship promotes acceptance of the allocation by managers who perceive the fairness of the procedure, but identification of cause and effect may not be feasible.

    b. An alternative allocation criterion is the **benefit received**. For example, advertising costs that do not relate to particular products may increase sales of all products. Allocation based on the increase in sales by organizational subunits is likely to be accepted as equitable despite the absence of clear cause-and-effect relationships.

    c. Two specific approaches to common cost allocation are in general use.

        1) The **stand-alone method** allocates a common cost on a proportionate basis using data regarding each cost object. For example, if the common cost of providing service to customers A and B is $10,000, and the stand-alone costs of servicing customers A and B are $6,000 and $6,000, respectively, A and B should be assigned $5,000 of common costs each.

        2) The **incremental method** requires ranking the users of the cost object. The primary party is then allocated its stand-alone cost, with the secondary party receiving the balance of the common costs. In the preceding example, if customer A is deemed to be the primary user, the allocation will be $6,000 to A and $4,000 to B.

8. Cost allocation is necessary for making **economic decisions**, e.g., the price to charge for a product or whether to make or buy a part.

9. Cost allocation is also necessary for **external financial reporting** and for calculation of reimbursements, such as those involved in governmental contracting.

10. Furthermore, cost allocation serves as a **motivator**. For example, designers of products may be required to include downstream costs, such as servicing and distribution, in their cost projections to fix their attention on how their efforts affect the total costs of the company.

    a. Typically, the motivational effects of cost allocation is that it tends to encourage marketing personnel to emphasize products with large contribution margins.

11. A persistent problem in large organizations is the treatment of the costs of headquarters and other **central support costs**. Such costs are very frequently allocated.

    a. Research has shown that central support costs are allocated to departments or divisions for the following reasons:

        1) The allocation reminds managers that support costs exist and that the managers would incur these costs if their operations were independent.

        2) The allocation also reminds managers that profit center earnings must cover some amount of support costs.

        3) Departments or divisions should be motivated to use central support services appropriately.

        4) Managers who must bear the costs of central support services that they do not control may be encouraged to exert pressure on those who do. Thus, they may be able to restrain such costs indirectly.

b.   The allocation is usually based on budgeted revenue or contribution margin (CM).

1)   If allocation is based on actual sales or CM, responsibility centers that increase their sales (or CM) will be charged with increased overhead.

2)   If central support or other fixed costs are not allocated, responsibility centers might reach their revenue (or CM) goals without covering all fixed costs (which is necessary to operate in the long run).

3)   Allocation of overhead, however, is motivationally negative; central support or other fixed costs may appear noncontrollable and be unproductive.

4)   A much preferred alternative is to budget a certain amount of CM earned by each responsibility center to cover the central support costs based on negotiation. The hoped-for result is for each subunit to see itself as contributing to the success of the overall entity rather than carrying the weight (cost) of central support.

a)   Central administration can then make the decision whether to expand, divest, or close responsibility centers.

12.   Negative **behavioral effects** may arise from arbitrary cost allocations.

a.   Managers' morale may suffer when allocations depress operating results.

b.   Dysfunctional conflict may arise among managers when costs controlled by one are allocated to others.

c.   Resentment may result if cost allocation is perceived to be arbitrary or unfair. For example, an allocation on an ability-to-bear basis, such as operating income, penalizes successful managers and rewards underachievers and may therefore have a demotivating effect.

13.   **Transfer prices** are the amounts charged by one segment of an organization for goods and services it provides to another segment of the same organization. Thus, transfer pricing policy affects **performance measurement** of organizational segments.

a.   Transfer prices are used by **profit and investment centers**, but a cost center's costs are allocated to producing departments.

1)   The problem is the determination of the transfer price when one responsibility center purchases from another.

2)   In a **decentralized system**, each responsibility center theoretically may be completely separate. Thus, Division A should charge the same price to Division B as would be charged to an outside buyer. The reason for decentralization is to motivate managers, and the best interests of Division A may not be served by giving a special discount to Division B if the goods can be sold at the regular price to outside buyers. However, having A sell at a special price to B may be to the organization's advantage.

14.   A transfer price should permit a segment to operate as an independent entity and achieve its objectives while functioning in the best interests of the company. Hence, transfer pricing should motivate managers; it should encourage goal congruence and managerial effort.

a.   **Goal congruence** is agreement regarding the objectives of the organization or the segment by both supervisors and subordinates. Performance is assumed to be optimized when the parties understand that personal and segmental objectives should be consistent with those of the organization.

b.   **Managerial effort** is the extent to which a manager attempts to accomplish a goal. Managerial effort may include psychological as well as physical commitment to an objective.

c.   **Motivation** is the desire of managers to attain a specific objective (goal congruence) and the commitment to accomplish the objective (managerial effort). Managerial motivation is therefore a combination of managerial effort and goal congruence.

15. Transfer prices can be determined in a number of ways. They may be based on

    a. A **market price**, assuming that a market exists

    b. **Differential outlay cost plus opportunity cost** to the seller

        1) For example, if a good costing $4 can be sold for $10, the outlay cost is $4 and the seller's opportunity cost is $6 (given no idle capacity).

    c. **Full absorption cost**

        1) Full-cost price includes materials, labor, and full allocation of manufacturing overhead.

    d. **Cost plus** a lump sum or a markup percentage

        1) Cost may be either the standard or the actual cost. The former has the advantage of isolating variances. Actual costs give the selling division little incentive to control costs.

        2) A cost-based price ignores market prices and may not promote long-term efficiencies.

    e. **Negotiation**

        1) A negotiated price may result when organizational subunits are free to determine the prices at which they buy and sell internally. Hence, a transfer price may simply reflect the best bargain that the parties can strike between themselves. It need not be based directly on particular market or cost information. A negotiated price may be especially appropriate when market prices are subject to rapid fluctuation.

16. The choice of a transfer pricing policy (which type of transfer price to use) is normally decided by senior management. The decision will typically include consideration of the following:

    a. **Goal congruence factors.** Will the transfer price promote the objectives of the organization as a whole?

    b. **Segmental performance factors.** The segment making the transfer should be allowed to recover its incremental cost plus its opportunity cost of the transfer. The opportunity cost is the benefit forgone by not selling to an outsider.

        1) For this purpose, the transfer should be at market price.

        2) The selling manager should not lose income by selling within the company.

        3) Properly allocating revenues and expenses through appropriate transfer pricing also facilitates evaluation of the performance of the various segments.

    c. **Negotiation factors.** If the purchasing segment could purchase the product or service outside the company, it should be permitted to negotiate the transfer price.

        1) The purchasing manager should not have to incur greater costs by purchasing within the company.

    d. **Capacity factors.** Does the seller have excess capacity?

        1) If Division A has excess capacity, it should be used for producing products for Division B.

        2) If Division A is operating at full capacity and selling its products at the full market price, profitable work should not be abandoned to produce for Division B.

    e. **Cost structure factors.** What portions of production costs are variable and fixed?

        1) If Division A has excess capacity and an opportunity arises to sell to Division B at a price in excess of the variable cost, the work should be performed for Division B because a contribution to cover the fixed costs will result.

f.   **Tax factors.** Many tax issues on the interstate and international levels may arise, e.g., income taxes, sales taxes, value-added taxes, inventory and payroll taxes, and other governmental charges.

    1)   In the international context, exchange rate fluctuations, threats of expropriation, and limits on transfers of profits outside the host country are additional concerns.

17.   EXAMPLE: Division A produces a small part at a cost of $6 per unit. The regular selling price is $10 per unit. If Division B can use the part in its production, the cost to the company (as a whole) will be $6. Division B has another supplier who will sell the item to B at $9.50 per part. Division B wants to buy the $9.50 part from the outside supplier instead of the $10 part from Division A, but making the part for $6 is in the company's best interest. What amount should Division A charge Division B?

    a.   The answer is complicated by many factors. For example, if Division A has excess capacity, B should be charged a lower price. If it is operating at full capacity, B should be charged $10.

    b.   Another question to consider is what portion of Division A's costs is fixed. For example, if a competitor offered to sell the part to B at $5 each, can Division A advantageously sell to B at a price lower than $5? If Division A's $6 total cost is composed of $4 of variable costs and $2 of fixed costs, it is beneficial for all concerned for A to sell to B at a price less than $5. Even at a price of $4.01, the parts would be providing a contribution margin to cover some of A's fixed costs.

18.   **Dual pricing** is another internal price-setting alternative. For example, the seller could record the transfer to another segment at the usual market price that would be paid by an outsider. The buyer, however, would record a purchase at the variable cost of production.

    a.   Each segment's performance would be improved by the use of a dual-pricing scheme.

    b.   The organization would benefit because variable costs would be used for decision-making purposes. In a sense, variable costs would be the relevant price for decision-making purposes, but the regular market price would be used for evaluation of production divisions.

    c.   Under a dual-pricing system, the profit for the company will be less than the sum of the profits of the individual segments.

    d.   In effect, the seller is given a corporate subsidy under the dual-pricing system.

    e.   The dual-pricing system is rarely used because the incentive to control costs is reduced. The seller is assured of a high price, and the buyer is assured of an artificially low price. Thus, neither manager must exert much effort to show a profit on segmental performance reports.

19.   Stop and review! You have completed the outline for this subunit. Study multiple-choice questions 24 through 50 beginning on page 543.

17.4 THEORY OF CONSTRAINTS AND THE BALANCED SCORECARD

1.   The **theory of constraints (TOC)**, devised by Israeli physicist and business consultant Eliyahu Goldratt (b. 1948), is a system to improve human thinking about problems. It has been greatly extended to include manufacturing operations.

    a.   The basic premise of TOC as applied to business is that improving any process is best done not by trying to maximize efficiency in every part of the process, but by focusing on the **slowest part of the process**, called the **constraint**.

        1)   EXAMPLE: During the early days of the American Civil War, several units calling themselves legions were formed, consisting of combined infantry, artillery, and cavalry. This arrangement did not last because the entire unit could only maneuver as fast as the slowest part. The artillery was the constraint.

2)   Increasing the efficiency of processes that are not constraints merely creates backup in the system.

2.   The **steps in a TOC analysis** are as follows (they are described in more detail under item 3. below):

a.   **Identify** the constraint.
b.   **Determine** the most profitable product mix given the constraint.
c.   **Maximize** the flow through the constraint.
d.   **Increase** capacity at the constraint.
e.   **Redesign** the manufacturing process for greater flexibility and speed.

3.   The detailed steps in performing a TOC analysis are described below:

a.   **Identify the constraint.**

1)   The **bottleneck operation** can usually be identified as the one where work-in-process backs up the most.

2)   A more sophisticated approach is to analyze available resources (number and skill level of employees, inventory levels, time spent in other phases of the process) and determine which phase has negative slack time, i.e., the phase **without enough resources** to keep up with input.

b.   **Determine the most profitable product mix** given the constraint.

1)   A basic principle of TOC analysis is that short-term profit maximization requires maximizing the contribution margin **through the constraint**, called the **throughput margin** or throughput contribution.

a)   TOC thus helps managers to recognize that the product they should produce the most of is not necessarily the one with the highest contribution margin per unit, but the one with the **highest throughput margin per unit**; i.e., managers must make the most profitable use of the bottleneck operation.

2)   **Throughput costing**, sometimes called **supervariable costing**, recognizes **only direct materials costs** as being truly variable and thus relevant to the calculation of throughput margin. All other manufacturing costs are ignored because they are considered fixed in the short run.

Throughput margin = Sales − Direct materials

3)   To determine the most profitable use of the bottleneck operation, a manager next calculates the throughput margin **per unit of time spent in the constraint.**

a)   **Profitability is maximized** by keeping the bottleneck operation busy with the product with the highest throughput margin per unit of time.

c.   **Maximize the flow** through the constraint.

1)   **Production flow** through a constraint is managed using the **drum-buffer-rope (DBR)** system.

a)   The **drum** (i.e., the beat to which a production process marches) is the bottleneck operation. The constraint sets the pace for the entire process.

b)   The **buffer** is a minimal amount of work-in-process input to the drum that is maintained to ensure that it is always in operation.

c)   The **rope** is the sequence of activities preceding and including the bottleneck operation that must be coordinated to avoid inventory buildup.

d.   **Increase capacity** at the constraint.

   1)   In the short-run, TOC encourages a manager to make the best use of the bottleneck operation. The medium-term step for improving the process is to increase the **bottleneck operation's capacity**.

e.   **Redesign** the manufacturing process for greater flexibility and speed.

   1)   The **long-term solution** is to reengineer the entire process. The firm should take advantage of new technology, product lines requiring too much effort should be dropped, and remaining products should be redesigned to ease the manufacturing process.

      a)   **Value engineering** is useful for this purpose because it explicitly balances product cost and the needs of potential customers (product functions).

4.   **Extended Example**

a.   **Identify the constraint.**

   1)   A company makes three products: an airborne radar unit, a seagoing sonar unit, and a ground sonar unit. Under the current setup, the hours spent by each product in the two phases of the manufacturing process are as follows:

Product	Assembly	Testing
Airborne Radar	3	4
Seagoing Sonar	8	10
Ground Sonar	5	5

   2)   The company has 150 hours available every month for testing. Under the current setup, therefore, the testing phase is the constraint.

b.   **Determine the most profitable product mix** given the constraint.

   1)   The company calculates the throughput margin on each product and divides by the hours spent in testing:

	Radar	Seagoing Sonar	Ground Sonar
Price	$200,000	$600,000	$300,000
Less: Materials costs	(100,000)	(400,000)	(250,000)
Throughput margin	$100,000	$200,000	$ 50,000
Divided by: Constraint time	÷ 4	÷ 10	÷ 5
Throughput margin per hour	$ 25,000	$ 20,000	$ 10,000

   2)   The crucial factor in determining the optimal product mix is not which product is the most profitable product in terms of absolute throughput margin (the seagoing sonar), but which one generates the **highest margin per time spent** in the bottleneck operation (the radar).

   3)   To derive the most profitable product mix given finite resources, **customer demand** must be taken into account. The company has determined that it can sell 12 units of radar, 6 units of seagoing sonar, and 22 units of ground sonar per month.

4)   The **available time in the bottleneck operation** is first devoted to the product with the highest throughput margin (TM), then in descending order until the company is unable to meet demand.

a)   In the calculation below, the hours remaining after assignment to each product are the hours which can be devoted to the next product.

Product	Highest TM: Radar	2nd Highest TM: Seagoing Sonar	Lowest TM: Ground Sonar
Demand in unit	12	6	22
Hours per unit in bottleneck	× 4	× 10	× 5
Hours needed to fulfill demand	48	60	110
Hours available	150	102	42
Hours remaining	102	42	(68)

5)   Applying the principles of TOC, the company will forgo some sales of the ground sonar in favor of products that are more profitable given the current constraint.

c.   **Maximize the flow** through the bottleneck operation.

1)   The company will apply a drum-buffer-rope system to ensure that the bottleneck operation stays busy on high-TM products while keeping work-in-process inventory to a minimum.

d.   **Increase capacity** at the bottleneck operation.

1)   The company will hire and train more employees for the testing department.

e.   **Redesign the manufacturing process** for greater flexibility and speed.

1)   The company will examine its markets and new manufacturing technology to determine which products it wants to continue selling, whether to add new ones, and whether to retool the production line.

5.   A **TOC report** should present relevant performance measures for such critical success factors as throughput contribution, elimination of bottlenecks, reduction of average lead times, and number of unfilled orders.

a.   EXAMPLE: Below is a TOC report for a manufacturer of bathroom fixtures. In reviewing it, it appears that inventory levels are low for brass fixtures which provide a healthy margin. However, no immediate action may be needed because they require only a day's setup time. Also, the excess inventory in aluminum fixtures may be acceptable since they have the longest time through the bottleneck.

	Brass	Chrome	Nickel	Aluminum
Demand	Medium	Low	High	Medium
Units in unfilled orders	10	20	40	60
Average lead time in days	1	2	2	2
Price	$ 250	$ 220	$ 375	$ 400
Less: Materials costs	(180)	(165)	(310)	(280)
Throughput contribution	$ 70	$ 55	$ 65	$ 120
Divided by: Machining time in hours	÷ 4	÷ 5	÷ 4	÷ 6
Throughput contribution per hour	**$ 18**	**$ 11**	**$ 16**	**$ 20**

b.   **TOC** has a **short-term focus** based on costs of materials and product mix.

6.   Effective management control requires performance measurement and feedback. This process affects allocation of resources to organizational subunits. It also affects decisions about managers' compensation, advancement, and future assignments.

    a.   Furthermore, evaluating their performance serves to motivate managers to optimize the measures in the **performance evaluation model**. However, that model may be inconsistent with the organization's model for managerial decision making.

        1)   To achieve **goal congruence**, the models should be synchronized. For example, if senior management wishes to maximize results over the long term, subordinates should be evaluated over the long term.

        2)   Unfortunately, **information systems** seldom provide information on the outcomes of individual decisions, and senior managers may be unaware of desirable options not chosen. Moreover, performance feedback usually applies to specific responsibility centers for specific periods. The result is that use of the same criteria for decision making and managerial evaluation may be difficult.

7.   Feedback regarding managerial performance may take the form of **financial and nonfinancial measures** that may be **internally or externally generated**. Moreover, different measures have a long-term or short-term emphasis.

    a.   An example of an external financial measure is stock price.

    b.   Examples of external nonfinancial measures are market share, customer satisfaction, and delivery performance.

    c.   Examples of internal financial measures are cost variances, return on investment, residual income, return on sales, and other financial ratios.

    d.   Examples of internal nonfinancial measures are product quality, new product development time, and manufacturing lead time (cycle time).

8.   Many forms of performance feedback are based on **accounting information**. The particular measures to be chosen are dependent on a five-stage process:

    a.   Senior management must determine what measure is consistent with its **objectives**.

    b.   The **elements** of the measure must be specified; e.g., calculation of residual income requires a definition of the items to be included in investment. A manager will therefore be motivated to avoid actions that increase the investment base.

    c.   The basis for determining the **dollar values** of the elements of the measure must also be specified. For example, in a residual income calculation based on an investment base defined as total assets, present value, current cost, current disposal price, or historical cost may be the attribute used to specify the dollar value of the investment.

        1)   **Historical cost** creates comparability issues because returns on significantly depreciated assets may be higher than those on newer assets that have been acquired using inflated dollars. Thus, otherwise similarly situated managers may report different operating results. Moreover, managers may be reluctant to replace aging assets.

    d.   A standard must be established to provide a **basis for comparison**.

        1)   One issue is the difficulty of the standard.

        2)   A second issue is whether individual managers should have unique performance goals. Because different managers may face widely varying problems, establishing challenging but attainable goals tailored to individual circumstances is preferable.

    e.   The **frequency** of performance feedback depends on many factors, such as the nature of the information, its cost, the design of the accounting information system, the level of management receiving the feedback, and the usefulness of the information.

9. Organizational mechanisms for performance feedback should satisfy the behavioral criteria of **goal congruence and managerial effort**. However, they should not encroach on the desired level of autonomy granted to a subunit manager.

10. Senior management should be aware of the **limitations of accrual-accounting** measures. For example, cash-based and accrual-based measures may yield different results, so a manager may reject a project with a positive net present value because its effect on accounting income is initially negative.

11. The trend in performance evaluation is the **balanced scorecard** approach to managing the implementation of the firm's strategy. It is an accounting report that connects the firm's **critical success factors (CSFs)** determined in a strategic analysis to measurements of its performance. CSFs are financial and nonfinancial measures of the elements of firm performance that are vital to competitive advantage.

    a. A firm identifies its CSFs by means of a **SWOT analysis** that addresses internal factors (strengths and weaknesses) and external factors (opportunities and threats).

        1) The firm's greatest strengths are its **core competencies**. These are the basis for its competitive advantages and strategy.

        2) **Strengths and weaknesses** are internal resources or a lack of them, for example, technologically advanced products, a broad product mix, capable management, leadership in R&D, modern production facilities, and a strong marketing organization.

        3) **Opportunities and threats** arise from such externalities as government regulation, advances in technology, and demographic changes. They may be reflected in such competitive conditions as

            a) Raising or lowering of barriers to entry into the firm's industry by competitors

            b) Changes in the intensity of rivalry within the industry, for example, because of overcapacity or high exit barriers

            c) The relative availability of substitutes for the firm's products or services

            d) Bargaining power of customers, which tends to be greater when switching costs are low and products are not highly differentiated

            e) Bargaining power of suppliers, which tends to be higher when suppliers are few

        4) The SWOT analysis and identification of CSFs helps the firm to determine its competitive strategy.

        5) The SWOT analysis tends to highlight the basic factors of cost, quality, and the speed of product development and delivery.

    b. Once the firm has identified its CSFs, it must establish **specific measures** for each CSF that are both relevant to the success of the firm and reliably stated. Thus, the balanced scorecard varies with the strategy adopted by the firm, for example, product differentiation or cost leadership either in a broad market or a narrowly focused market (a focus strategy). These measures provide a basis for implementing the firm's **competitive strategy**.

    c. By providing measures that are nonfinancial as well as financial, long-term as well as short-term, and internal as well as external, the balanced scorecard deemphasizes short-term financial results and focuses attention on CSFs.

d.   The **development and implementation** of a comprehensive balanced scorecard requires active support and participation by senior management. This involvement will in turn assure the cooperation of lower-level managers in the identification of objectives, appropriate measures, targeted results, and methods of achieving the results.

1)   The scorecard should contain measures at the detail level to permit everyone to understand how his/her efforts affect the firm's results.

2)   The scorecard and the strategy it represents must be communicated to all managers and used as a basis for compensation decisions.

3)   The scorecard should include **lagging indicators** (such as output and financial measures) and **leading indicators** (such as many types of nonfinancial measures). The latter should be used only if they are predictors of ultimate financial performance.

4)   The scorecard should permit a determination of whether certain objectives are being achieved at the expense of others. For example, reduced spending on customer service may improve short-term financial results at a significant cost suggested by a decline in customer satisfaction measures.

e.   The following are **problems in implementation** of the balanced scorecard approach:

1)   Using too many measures, with a consequent loss of focus on CSFs

2)   Failing to evaluate personnel on nonfinancial as well as financial measures

3)   Including measures that will not have long-term financial benefits

4)   Not understanding that subjective measures (such as customer satisfaction) are imprecise

5)   Trying to achieve improvements in all areas at all times

6)   Not being aware that the hypothesized connection between nonfinancial measures and ultimate financial success may not continue to be true

f.   A typical balanced scorecard includes measures in four categories:

1)   **Financial**

a)   The **CSFs** may be sales, fair value of the firm's stock, profits, and liquidity.

b)   **Measures** may include sales, projected sales, accuracy of sales projections, new product sales, stock prices, operating earnings, earnings trend, revenue growth, gross margin percentage, cost reductions, economic value added, return on investment (or any of its variants), cash flow coverage and trends, turnover (assets, receivables, and inventory) and interest coverage.

2)   **Customer**

a)   The **CSFs** may be customer satisfaction, customer retention rate, dealer and distributor relationships, marketing and selling performance, prompt delivery, and quality.

b)   **Measures** may include returns, complaints, survey results, coverage and strength of distribution channels, market research results, training of marketing people, sales trends, market share and its trend, on-time delivery rate, service response time and effectiveness, and warranty exposure.

3)   **Internal Business Processes**

a)   The **CSFs** may be quality, productivity (an input-output relationship), flexibility of response to changing conditions, operating readiness, and safety.

          b)   **Measures** may include rate of defects, amounts of scrap and rework, returns, survey results, field service reports, warranty costs, vendor defect rate, cycle (lead) time, labor and machine efficiency, setup time, scheduling effectiveness, downtime, capacity usage, maintenance, and accidents and their results.

    4) **Learning and Growth**

          a)   The **CSFs** may be development of new products, promptness of their introduction, human resource development, morale, and competence of the workforce.

          b)   **Measures** may include new products marketed, amount of design changes, patents and copyrights registered, R&D personnel qualifications, actual versus planned shipping dates, hours of training, skill set levels attained, personnel turnover, personnel complaints and survey results, financial and operating results, technological capabilities, organizational learning, and industry leadership.

12.   EXAMPLE of a balanced scorecard.

    a.   Each **objective** is associated with one or more **measures** that permit the organization to gauge progress toward the objective.

    b.   Note that achievement of the objectives in each **perspective** makes it possible to achieve the objectives in the next higher perspective.

Financial Perspective	
Objective: Increase shareholder value	**Measures:** Increase in common stock price Reliability of dividend payment
Customer Perspective	
Objective: Increase customer satisfaction	**Measures:** Greater market share Higher customer retention rate Positive responses to surveys
Internal Business Process Perspective	
Objective: Improve product quality	**Measures:** Achievement of zero defects
Objective: Improve internal processes	**Measures:** Reduction in delivery cycle time Smaller cost variances
Learning and Growth Perspective	
Objective: Increase employee confidence	**Measures:** Number of suggestions to improve processes Positive responses to surveys
Objective: Increase employee competence	**Measures:** Attendance at internal and external training seminars

13.   The **development and implementation** of a comprehensive balanced scorecard requires active support and participation by senior management. This involvement will in turn assure the cooperation of lower-level managers in the identification of objectives, appropriate measures, targeted results, and methods of achieving the results.

    a.   The scorecard should contain measures at the detail level that permits everyone to understand how his/her efforts affect the firm's results.

    b.   The scorecard and the strategy it represents must be communicated to all managers and used as a basis for compensation decisions.

c. The following are **problems in implementation** of the balanced scorecard approach:

1) Using too many measures, with a consequent loss of focus on CSFs
2) Failing to evaluate personnel on nonfinancial as well as financial measures
3) Including measures that will not have long-term financial benefits
4) Not understanding that subjective measures (such as customer satisfaction) are imprecise
5) Trying to achieve improvements in all areas at all times
6) Not being aware that the hypothesized connection between nonfinancial measures and ultimate financial success may not continue to be true

14. Stop and review! You have completed the outline for this subunit. Study multiple-choice questions 51 through 59 beginning on page 551.

QUESTIONS

17.1 Quality Considerations

1. A traditional quality control process in manufacturing consists of mass inspection of goods only at the end of a production process. A major deficiency of the traditional control process is that

A. It is expensive to do the inspections at the end of the process.

B. It is not possible to rework defective items.

C. It is not 100% effective.

D. It does not focus on improving the entire production process.

Answer (D) is correct. *(CIA, adapted)*
REQUIRED: The major deficiency of a traditional quality control process.
DISCUSSION: The process used to produce the goods is not thoroughly reviewed and evaluated for efficiency and effectiveness. Preventing defects and increasing efficiency by improving the production process raises quality standards and decreases costs.
Answer (A) is incorrect because other quality control processes can also be expensive. Answer (B) is incorrect because reworking defective items may be possible although costly. Answer (C) is incorrect because no quality control system will be 100% effective.

2. The most important component of quality control is

A. Ensuring goods and services conform to the design specifications.

B. Satisfying upper management.

C. Conforming with ISO 9000 specifications.

D. Determining the appropriate timing of inspections.

Answer (A) is correct. *(CIA, adapted)*
REQUIRED: The most important component of quality control.
DISCUSSION: The intent of quality control is to ensure that goods and services conform to the design specifications. Whether the focus is on feedforward, feedback, or concurrent control, the emphasis is on ensuring product or service conformity.
Answer (B) is incorrect because quality control is geared towards satisfying the customer, not upper management. Answer (C) is incorrect because ensuring the conformance with ISO 9000 specifications is a component of a compliance audit, not quality control. Answer (D) is incorrect because determining the appropriate timing of inspections is only one step towards approaching quality control. Consequently, it is not the primary component of the quality control function.

3. Conformance is how well a product and its components meet applicable standards. According to the robust quality concept,

   A. A certain percentage of defective units is acceptable.

   B. Units are acceptable if their characteristics lie within an acceptable range of values.

   C. The goal is for all units to be within specifications.

   D. Every unit should reach a target value.

Answer (D) is correct. *(Publisher, adapted)*
   REQUIRED: The true statement about robust quality.
   DISCUSSION: Conformance is how well a product and its components meet applicable standards. The traditional view is that conforming products are those with characteristics that lie within an acceptable specified range of values that includes a target value. This view also regarded a certain percentage of defective (nonconforming) units as acceptable. The traditional view was superseded by the zero-defects approach that sought to eliminate all nonconforming output. An extension of this approach is the robust quality concept. Its goal is to reach the target value in every case. The reason is that hidden quality costs occur when output varies from the target even though the units are within specifications.
   Answer (A) is incorrect because the traditional view of quality treats a certain percentage of defective units as acceptable. Answer (B) is incorrect because, in the traditional view of quality, a unit is deemed to be acceptable if it is within a range of specified values. Answer (C) is incorrect because the robust quality concept is an extension of the zero-defects approach. The goal of robust quality is in every case to reach a target value, not merely a range of acceptable values.

4. According to the robust quality concept,

   A. The minimum point on the total quality cost curve occurs when conformance cost per unit equals nonconformance cost per unit.

   B. Improving quality requires tradeoffs among categories of quality costs.

   C. Beyond some point, incurrence of prevention and appraisal costs is not cost beneficial.

   D. Costs in all categories of quality costs may be reduced while improving quality.

Answer (D) is correct. *(Publisher, adapted)*
   REQUIRED: The robust quality view about quality costs.
   DISCUSSION: The optimal level of quality costs traditionally has been deemed to occur where the conformance cost curve intercepts the nonconformance cost curve, which corresponds to the minimum point on the total cost curve. Thus, beyond some point, incurrence of prevention and appraisal costs is not cost beneficial. However, the modern robust quality view is that this relationship does not always hold. Improving quality and reducing costs in each category may be possible if the most efficient prevention methods are applied. For example, selection of a supplier meeting high quality standards regarding defect rates and delivery times may drive down not only failure costs but also the prevention and appraisal costs incurred when supplier performance was less reliable.

5. Listed below are selected line items from the Cost of Quality Report for Watson Products for last month.

Category	Amount
Rework	$ 725
Equipment maintenance	1,154
Product testing	786
Product repair	695

What is Watson's total prevention and appraisal cost for last month?

   A. $786

   B. $1,154

   C. $1,940

   D. $2,665

Answer (C) is correct. *(CMA, adapted)*
   REQUIRED: The total prevention and appraisal costs.
   DISCUSSION: The costs of prevention and appraisal are conformance costs that serve as financial measures of internal performance. Prevention costs are incurred to prevent defective output. These costs include preventive maintenance, employee training, review of equipment design, and evaluation of suppliers. Appraisal costs are incurred to detect nonconforming output. They embrace such activities as statistical quality control programs, inspection, and testing. The equipment maintenance cost of $1,154 is a prevention cost. The product testing cost of $786 is an appraisal cost. Their sum is $1,940.
   Answer (A) is incorrect because $786 is the appraisal cost. Answer (B) is incorrect because $1,154 is the prevention cost. Answer (D) is incorrect because $2,665 includes rework, an internal failure cost.

6. All of the following would generally be included in a cost-of-quality report except

- A. Warranty claims.
- B. Design engineering.
- C. Supplier evaluations.
- D. Lost contribution margin.

Answer (D) is correct. *(CMA, adapted)*
REQUIRED: The item that does not normally appear in a cost-of-quality report.
DISCUSSION: A cost-of-quality report includes most costs related to quality, including the costs of external failure, internal failure, prevention, and appraisal. Lost contribution margins from poor product quality are external failure costs that normally do not appear on a cost-of-quality report because they are opportunity costs. Opportunity costs are not usually recorded by the accounting system, thereby understating the costs of poor quality. Lost contribution margins from reduced sales, market share, and sales prices are external failure costs that are also not usually included in a cost-of-quality report.
Answer (A) is incorrect because the costs of warranty claims are readily measurable external failure costs captured by the accounting system. Answer (B) is incorrect because the costs of design engineering are prevention costs that are usually included in cost-of-quality reports. Answer (C) is incorrect because the costs of supplier evaluations are prevention costs.

7. Which of the following quality costs are nonconformance costs?

- A. Systems development costs.
- B. Costs of inspecting in-process items.
- C. Environmental costs.
- D. Costs of quality circles.

Answer (C) is correct. *(Publisher, adapted)*
REQUIRED: The nonconformance costs.
DISCUSSION: Nonconformance costs include internal and external failure costs. External failure costs include environmental costs, e.g., fines for violations of environmental laws and loss of customer goodwill.
Answer (A) is incorrect because systems development costs are prevention (conformance) costs. Answer (B) is incorrect because costs of inspecting in-process items are appraisal (conformance) costs. Answer (D) is incorrect because costs of quality circles are prevention (conformance) costs.

8. In a quality control program, which of the following is(are) categorized as internal failure costs?

I.   Rework
II. Responding to customer complaints
III. Statistical quality control procedures

- A. I only.
- B. II only.
- C. III only.
- D. I, II, and III.

Answer (A) is correct. *(CPA, adapted)*
REQUIRED: The item(s) categorized as internal failure costs.
DISCUSSION: Cost accounting systems can contribute to improved product quality programs by accumulating and reporting their costs. Internal failure costs are incurred when detection of defective products occurs before shipment. Examples are scrap, rework, tooling changes, and downtime.
Answer (B) is incorrect because responding to customer complaints results in external failure costs. Answer (C) is incorrect because statistical quality control procedures result in appraisal costs. Answer (D) is incorrect because responding to customer complaints and statistical quality control procedures result in external failure costs and appraisal costs, respectively.

9. Rework costs should be regarded as a cost of quality in a manufacturing company's quality control program when they are

I. Caused by the customer
II. Caused by internal failure

- A. I only.
- B. II only.
- C. Both I and II.
- D. Neither I nor II.

Answer (B) is correct. *(CPA, adapted)*
REQUIRED: The proper classification of rework costs.
DISCUSSION: Cost accounting systems can contribute to improved product quality programs by accumulating and reporting their costs. Internal failure costs are incurred when detection of defective products occurs before shipment. Examples are scrap, rework, tooling changes, and downtime. The costs of external failure, e.g., warranty, product liability, and customer ill will, arise when problems occur after shipment.
Answer (A) is incorrect because rework results from an internal failure and therefore cannot be caused by the customer. Answer (C) is incorrect because rework results from an internal failure and therefore cannot be caused by the customer. Answer (D) is incorrect because rework costs should be regarded as costs of quality in a manufacturing company's quality control program when caused by internal failure.

10. Nonfinancial performance measures are important to engineering and operations managers in assessing the quality levels of their products. Which of the following indicators can be used to measure product quality?

I. Returns and allowances
II. Number and types of customer complaints
III. Production cycle time

   A. I and II only.

   B. I and III only.

   C. II and III only.

   D. I, II, and III.

11. Which measures would be useful in evaluating the performance of a manufacturing system?

I. Throughput time
II. Total setup time for machines/total production time
III. Number of rework units/total number of units completed

   A. I and II only.

   B. II and III only.

   C. I and III only.

   D. I, II, and III.

17.2 Benchmarking, TQM, and the ISO Framework

12. Which of the following statements regarding benchmarking is false?

   A. Benchmarking involves continuously evaluating the practices of best-in-class organization and adapting company processes to incorporate the best of these practices.

   B. Benchmarking, in practice, usually involves a company's formation of benchmarking teams.

   C. Benchmarking is an ongoing process that entails quantitative and qualitative measurement of the difference between the company's performance of an activity and the performance by the best in the world or the best in the industry.

   D. The benchmarking organization against which a firm is comparing itself must be a direct competitor.

Answer (A) is correct. *(CPA, adapted)*
  REQUIRED: The indicators of product quality.
  DISCUSSION: Nonfinancial performance measures, such as product quality, are useful for day-to-day control purposes. Examples (indicators) of nonfinancial performance measures include the following: outgoing quality level for each product line, returned merchandise, customer report card, competitive rank, and on-time delivery.

Answer (D) is correct. *(CPA, adapted)*
  REQUIRED: The measures useful in evaluating the performance of a manufacturing system.
  DISCUSSION: Throughput time is the average amount of time required to convert raw materials into finished goods ready to be shipped. Total setup time as a percentage of total production time provides valuable information for scheduling. The number of rework items as a percentage of total numbers of units completed provides efficiency and quality control data. These are all important factors in evaluating the performance of a manufacturing system.

Answer (D) is correct. *(Publisher, adapted)*
  REQUIRED: The incorrect statement about benchmarking.
  DISCUSSION: Benchmarking is an ongoing process that entails quantitative and qualitative measurement of the difference between the company's performance of an activity and the performance by a best-in-class organization. The benchmarking organization against which a firm is comparing itself need not be a direct competitor. The important consideration is that the benchmarking organization be an outstanding performer in its industry.
  Answer (A) is incorrect because benchmarking involves continuously evaluating the practices of best-in-class organization and adapting company processes to incorporate the best of these practices. Answer (B) is incorrect because benchmarking, in practice, usually involves a company's formation of benchmarking teams. Answer (C) is incorrect because benchmarking is an ongoing process that entails quantitative and qualitative measurement of the difference between the company's performance of an activity and the performance by the best in the world or the best in the industry.

13. An example of an internal nonfinancial benchmark is

A. The labor rate of comparably skilled employees at a major competitor's plant.

B. The average actual cost per pound of a specific product at the company's most efficient plant.

C. A $50,000 limit on the cost of employee training programs at each of the company's plants.

D. The percentage of customer orders delivered on time at the company's most efficient plant.

Answer (D) is correct. *(CIA, adapted)*
REQUIRED: The internal nonfinancial benchmark.
DISCUSSION: Benchmarking is a continuous evaluation of the practices of the best organizations in their class and the adaptation of processes to reflect the best of these practices. It requires analysis and measurement of key outputs against those of the best organizations. This procedure also involves identifying the underlying key actions and causes that contribute to the performance difference. The percentage of orders delivered on time at the company's most efficient plant is an example of an internal nonfinancial benchmark.
Answer (A) is incorrect because the labor rate of a competitor is a financial benchmark. Answer (B) is incorrect because the cost per pound of a product at the company's most efficient plant is a financial benchmark. Answer (C) is incorrect because the cost of a training program is a financial benchmark.

14. A company, which has many branch stores, has decided to benchmark one of its stores for the purpose of analyzing the accuracy and reliability of branch store financial reporting. Which one of the following is the most likely measure to be included in a financial benchmark?

A. High turnover of employees.

B. High level of employee participation in setting budgets.

C. High amount of bad debt write-offs.

D. High number of suppliers.

Answer (C) is correct. *(CIA, adapted)*
REQUIRED: The most likely measure to be included in a financial benchmark.
DISCUSSION: A high level of bad debt write-offs could indicate fraud, which would compromise the accuracy and reliability of financial reports. Bad debt write-offs may result from recording fictitious sales.
Answer (A) is incorrect because turnover of employees is not a financial benchmark. Answer (B) is incorrect because employee participation in setting budgets is not a financial benchmark. Answer (D) is incorrect because the number of suppliers is not a financial benchmark.

Questions 15 and 16 are based on the following information. The management and employees of We Move You, a large household goods moving company, decided to adopt total quality management (TQM) and continuous improvement (CI). They believed that, if their company became nationally known as adhering to TQM and CI, one result would be an increase in the company's profits and market share.

15. The primary reason that We Move You adopted TQM was to achieve

A. Greater customer satisfaction.

B. Reduced delivery time.

C. Reduced delivery charges.

D. Greater employee participation.

Answer (A) is correct. *(CIA, adapted)*
REQUIRED: The primary reason for adopting TQM.
DISCUSSION: TQM is an integrated system that anticipates, meets, and exceeds customers' needs, wants, and expectations.
Answer (B) is incorrect because reduced delivery time is one of many potential activities that need improvement. Answer (C) is incorrect because reduced delivery charges is just one of many potential activities that need improvement. Answer (D) is incorrect because increased employee participation is necessary to achieve TQM, but it is not the primary purpose for establishing the program.

16. Quality is achieved more economically if We Move You focuses on

A. Appraisal costs.

B. Prevention costs.

C. Internal failure costs.

D. External failure costs.

Answer (B) is correct. *(CIA, adapted)*
REQUIRED: The necessary focus for achieving quality more economically.
DISCUSSION: Prevention attempts to avoid defective output. Prevention costs include preventive maintenance, employee training, review of equipment design, and evaluation of suppliers. Prevention is less costly than detection and correction of defective output.

17. Which of the following is a characteristic of total quality management (TQM)?

   A. Management by objectives.

   B. On-the-job training by other workers.

   C. Quality by final inspection.

   D. Education and self-improvement.

Answer (D) is correct. *(CIA, adapted)*
  REQUIRED: The characteristic of TQM.
  DISCUSSION: According to management theorist W. Edwards Deming's well-known 14 points, education and self-improvement are essential. Knowledge is opportunity. Hence, continuous improvement should be everyone's primary career objective.
  Answer (A) is incorrect because one of the 14 points recommends elimination of numerical quotas. MBO causes aggressive pursuit of numerical quotas. Answer (B) is incorrect because informal learning from coworkers serves to entrench bad work habits. One of the 14 points stresses proper training of everyone. Answer (C) is incorrect because another of the 14 points states that quality by final inspection is unnecessary if quality is built in from the start.

18. Total quality management (TQM) in a manufacturing environment is best exemplified by

   A. Identifying and reworking production defects before sale.

   B. Designing the product to minimize defects.

   C. Performing inspections to isolate defects as early as possible.

   D. Making machine adjustments periodically to reduce defects.

Answer (B) is correct. *(CIA, adapted)*
  REQUIRED: The activity characteristic of TQM.
  DISCUSSION: Total quality management emphasizes quality as a basic organizational function. TQM is the continuous pursuit of quality in every aspect of organizational activities. One of the basic tenets of TQM is doing it right the first time. Thus, errors should be caught and corrected at the source, and quality should be built in (designed in) from the start.

19. One of the main reasons that implementation of a total quality management program works better through the use of teams is

   A. Teams are more efficient and help an organization reduce its staffing.

   B. Employee motivation is always higher for team members than for individual contributors.

   C. Teams are a natural vehicle for sharing ideas, which leads to process improvement.

   D. The use of teams eliminates the need for supervision, thereby allowing a company to reduce staffing.

Answer (C) is correct. *(CIA, adapted)*
  REQUIRED: The reason that implementation of a TQM program works better through the use of teams.
  DISCUSSION: TQM promotes teamwork by modifying or eliminating traditional (and rigid) vertical hierarchies and instead forming flexible groups of specialists. Quality circles, cross-functional teams, and self-managed teams are typical formats. Teams are an excellent vehicle for encouraging the sharing of ideas and removing process improvement obstacles.
  Answer (A) is incorrect because teams are often inefficient and costly. Answer (B) is incorrect because high motivation does not directly affect the process improvement that is the key to quality improvement. Answer (D) is incorrect because the use of teams with less supervision and reduced staffing may be by-products of TQM, but they are not ultimate objectives.

20. According to ISO 9000 standards, which of the following is not true?

   A. Most employees are subject to being audited.

   B. Companies may have preliminary audits by registrars.

   C. Employees must be able to competently describe their job and demonstrate they are performing it properly.

   D. Upon satisfactory completion of an on-site visit, a registrar may issue a certificate describing the scope of the registration which is valid for 3 years.

Answer (A) is correct. *(Publisher, adapted)*
  REQUIRED: The false statement regarding ISO 9000 standards.
  DISCUSSION: During an on-site visit, the registrar has the right to audit all employees if he or she decides to do so. Employees must have the ability to explain their jobs and show they are capable of performing them properly.
  Answer (B) is incorrect because some companies have preliminary audits by registrars to prepare for the official audit. Answer (C) is incorrect because employees must be able to "say what they do" and demonstrate that they "do what they say." Answer (D) is incorrect because a registrar who is convinced that a quality system conforms to the selected standard issues a certificate describing the scope of the registration. The registration is usually valid for a 3-year period.

21. Which of the following is false about the advantages of adopting ISO 9000 standards?

   A. Adoption of ISO 9000 standards may allow the company to sell products in foreign markets.

   B. ISO registration makes customers more comfortable with the supplier's products and services.

   C. ISO 9000 allows companies to understand who internal customers and users are without sharing private information.

   D. ISO registration may help companies discover internal process and quality improvements.

Answer (C) is correct. *(Publisher, adapted)*
   REQUIRED: The advantages of ISO 9000 registration.
   DISCUSSION: Market pressure is usually the main reason companies adopt ISO 9000 standards. However, many of the companies who register reengineer internal processes and achieve quality improvement as a result. ISO 9000 forces companies to share information that leads to a better understanding of who internal customers and users are.
   Answer (A) is incorrect because many foreign countries are beginning to require adoption of ISO 9000 standards as a prerequisite for a company to sell products or services in that country. Answer (B) is incorrect because many companies view ISO registration as a key to remaining competitive. ISO registration allows customers to be more comfortable with suppliers' products and services. Answer (D) is incorrect because many companies that implement ISO 9000 standards uncover internal processes and quality improvements.

22. Why have many European Union countries not adopted ISO 14000 standards?

   A. Adhering to ISO 14000 standards not will reduce monitoring and inspection by regulatory agencies.

   B. Individual European Union countries' standards are typically more strict than ISO 14000 standards.

   C. Regulators are permitted to use voluntary audits as a basis for punitive action.

   D. ISO 14000 standards will not make it easier to do business across borders.

Answer (B) is correct. *(Publisher, adapted)*
   REQUIRED: The reason European Union countries have not adopted ISO 14000 standards.
   DISCUSSION: Many European countries already have environmental systems in place. However, individual countries' standards are typically more strict than the ISO 14000 standards.
   Answer (A) is incorrect because adhering to ISO 14000 standards does not guarantee less monitoring or inspection by regulatory agencies. However, some companies cite the reduction of monitoring and inspection costs as a benefit of adopting ISO 9000 standards. Answer (C) is incorrect because many countries in the European Union have adopted measures similar to the ones in the U.S. to prevent self-incrimination during voluntary ISO audits. Answer (D) is incorrect because ISO 14000 establishes internationally recognized standards that are intended to diminish trade barriers and make it easier to do business across borders.

23. Which of the following is not required when ISO 9000 standards are adopted?

   A. Organization of a quality management system.

   B. Creation of an internal audit system.

   C. Consistent high quality products.

   D. On-site inspections by a registrar.

Answer (C) is correct. *(Publisher, adapted)*
   REQUIRED: The item not an ISO 9000 requirement.
   DISCUSSION: ISO 9000 is a set of generic standards for establishing and maintaining a quality system within a company. The standards provide no basis for judging the quality of the end product. The marketplace will make this determination. The objective of ISO 9000 standards is to ensure consistent quality, even if the quality is poor.
   Answer (A) is incorrect because one of the most important steps to adhering to ISO 9000 standards is to organize a quality management system (QMS). A QMS reflects the company's commitment to quality. Answer (B) is incorrect because internal audits assure that the company is complying with the documented QMS procedures and ISO 9000 standards. Answer (D) is incorrect because a registrar must ensure the company's quality control system conforms to the selected standard.

17.3 Responsibility Centers, Common Costs, and Transfer Pricing

24. Fairmount, Inc. uses an accounting system that charges costs to the manager who has been delegated the authority to make the decisions incurring the costs. For example, if the sales manager accepts a rush order that will result in higher than normal manufacturing costs, these additional costs are charged to the sales manager because the authority to accept or decline the rush order was given to the sales manager. This type of accounting system is known as

- A. Responsibility accounting.
- B. Functional accounting.
- C. Reciprocal allocation.
- D. Transfer price accounting.

Answer (A) is correct. *(CMA, adapted)*
REQUIRED: The system in which additional costs are charged to the manager with authority for their incurrence.
DISCUSSION: Responsibility accounting holds managers responsible for factors they directly regulate or can significantly influence. For this purpose, operations are organized into responsibility centers. Costs are classified as controllable and noncontrollable, which implies that some revenues and costs can be changed through effective management. If a manager has authority to incur costs, a responsibility accounting system will charge them to the manager's responsibility center. However, controllability is not an absolute basis for establishment of responsibility. More than one manager may be able to influence a cost, and responsibility may be assigned on the basis of knowledge about the incurrence of a cost rather than the ability to control it.

25. In responsibility accounting, a center's performance is measured by controllable costs. Controllable costs are best described as including

- A. Direct material and direct labor only.
- B. Only those costs that the manager can influence in the current time period.
- C. Only discretionary costs.
- D. Those costs about which the manager is knowledgeable and informed.

Answer (B) is correct. *(CMA, adapted)*
REQUIRED: The elements incorporated in controllable costs.
DISCUSSION: Control is the process of making certain that plans are achieving the desired objectives. A controllable cost is one that is directly regulated by a specific manager at a given level of production within a given time span or that the manager can significantly influence. For example, fixed costs are often not controllable in the short run.
Answer (A) is incorrect because many overhead costs are also controllable. Answer (C) is incorrect because controllable costs need not be discretionary. Discretionary costs are characterized by uncertainty about the relationship between input and the value of the related output; they may or may not be controllable. Answer (D) is incorrect because controllable costs are those over which a manager has control; the manager may be knowledgeable and informed about costs that (s)he cannot control.

26. A segment of an organization is referred to as a service center if it has

- A. Responsibility for developing markets and selling the output of the organization.
- B. Responsibility for combining the raw materials, direct labor, and other factors of production into a final output.
- C. Authority to make decisions affecting the major determinants of profit including the power to choose its markets and sources of supply.
- D. Authority to provide specialized support to other units within the organization.

Answer (D) is correct. *(CMA, adapted)*
REQUIRED: The definition of a service center.
DISCUSSION: A service center exists primarily and sometimes solely to provide specialized support to other units within the organization. Service centers are usually operated as cost centers.
Answer (A) is incorrect because a service center has no responsibility for developing markets or selling. Answer (B) is incorrect because a production center is engaged in manufacturing. Answer (C) is incorrect because a profit center can choose its markets and sources of supply.

27. The budgeting process that uses management by objectives and input from the individual manager is an example of the application of

- A. Flexible budgeting.
- B. Human resource management.
- C. Responsibility accounting.
- D. Capital budgeting.

Answer (C) is correct.   *(CMA, adapted)*
REQUIRED: The type of system in which the budgeting process uses MBO and input from individual managers.
DISCUSSION: Managerial performance should ideally be evaluated only on the basis of those factors controllable by the manager. Managers may control revenues, costs, or investments in resources. A well-designed responsibility accounting system establishes responsibility centers within the organization. However, controllability is not an absolute basis for establishment of responsibility. More than one manager may be able to influence a cost, and responsibility may be assigned on the basis of knowledge about the incurrence of a cost rather than the ability to control it. Management by objectives (MBO) is a related concept. It is a behavioral, communications-oriented, responsibility approach to employee self-direction. Under MBO, a manager and his/her subordinates agree upon objectives and the means of attaining them. The plans that result are reflected in responsibility accounting and in the budgeting process.
Answer (A) is incorrect because flexible budgeting is the process of preparing a series of multiple budgets for varying levels of production or sales. Answer (B) is incorrect because human resource management is the process of managing personnel. Answer (D) is incorrect because capital budgeting is a means of evaluating long-term investments.

28. Which of the following techniques would be best for evaluating the management performance of a department that is operated as a cost center?

- A. Return on assets ratio.
- B. Return on investment ratio.
- C. Payback method.
- D. Variance analysis.

Answer (D) is correct.   *(CIA, adapted)*
REQUIRED: The best method for evaluating a cost center.
DISCUSSION: A cost center is a responsibility center that is responsible for costs only. Of the alternatives given, variance analysis is the only one that can be used in a cost center. Variance analysis involves comparing actual costs with predicted or standard costs.
Answer (A) is incorrect because return on assets cannot be computed for a cost center. The manager is not responsible for revenue (return) or the assets available. Answer (B) is incorrect because return on investment cannot be computed for a cost center. The manager is not responsible for revenue (return) or the assets available. Answer (C) is incorrect because the payback method is a means of evaluating alternative investment proposals.

29. The basic purpose of a responsibility accounting system is

- A. Budgeting.
- B. Motivation.
- C. Authority.
- D. Variance analysis.

Answer (B) is correct.   *(CMA, adapted)*
REQUIRED: The basic purpose of a responsibility accounting system.
DISCUSSION: The basic purpose of a responsibility accounting system is to motivate management to perform in a manner consistent with overall company objectives. The assignment of responsibility implies that some revenues and costs can be changed through effective management. The system should have certain controls that provide for feedback reports indicating deviations from expectations. Higher-level management may focus on those deviations for either reinforcement or correction.
Answer (A) is incorrect because budgeting is an element of a responsibility accounting system, not the basic purpose. Answer (C) is incorrect because authority is an element of a responsibility accounting system, not the basic purpose. Answer (D) is incorrect because analysis of variances is an element of a responsibility accounting system, not the basic purpose.

30. Decentralized firms can delegate authority and yet retain control and monitor managers' performance by structuring the organization into responsibility centers. Which one of the following organizational segments is most like an independent business?

- A. Revenue center.
- B. Profit center.
- C. Cost center.
- D. Investment center.

Answer (D) is correct. *(CMA, adapted)*
REQUIRED: The organizational segment most like an independent business.
DISCUSSION: An investment center is the organizational type most like an independent business because it is responsible for its own revenues, costs incurred, and capital invested. The other types of centers do not incorporate all three elements.
Answer (A) is incorrect because a revenue center is responsible only for revenue generation, not for costs or capital investment. Answer (B) is incorrect because a profit center is responsible for revenues and costs but not for invested capital. Answer (C) is incorrect because a cost center is evaluated only on the basis of costs incurred. It is not responsible for revenues or invested capital.

31. Rockford Manufacturing Corporation uses a responsibility accounting system in its operations. Which one of the following items is least likely to appear in a performance report for a manager of one of Rockford's assembly lines?

- A. Direct labor.
- B. Materials.
- C. Repairs and maintenance.
- D. Depreciation on the manufacturing facility.

Answer (D) is correct. *(CMA, adapted)*
REQUIRED: The item least likely to appear on a performance report for an assembly line manager.
DISCUSSION: A well-designed responsibility accounting system establishes responsibility centers within an organization. In a responsibility accounting system, managerial performance should be evaluated only on the basis of those factors directly regulated (or at least capable of being significantly influenced) by the manager. Thus, a manager of an assembly line is responsible for direct labor, materials, repairs and maintenance, and supervisory salaries. The manager is not responsible for depreciation on the manufacturing facility. (S)he is not in a position to control or influence capital budgeting decisions.

32. Overtime conditions and pay were recently set by the personnel department. The production department has just received a request for a rush order from the sales department. The production department protests that additional overtime costs will be incurred as a result of the order. The sales department argues that the order is from an important customer. The production department processes the order. To control costs, which department should never be charged with the overtime costs generated as a result of the rush order?

- A. Personnel department.
- B. Production department.
- C. Sales department.
- D. Shared by production department and sales department.

Answer (A) is correct. *(CIA, adapted)*
REQUIRED: The department that is never charged with overtime generated by a rush order.
DISCUSSION: The sales department should be responsible for the overtime costs because it can best judge whether the additional cost of the rush order is justified. The production department also may be held responsible for the overtime costs because charging the full overtime cost to the sales department would give the production department no incentive to control these costs. However, the personnel department would never be charged with the overtime costs because it has no effect on the incurrence of production overtime.

33. Controllable revenue would be included in a performance report for a

	Profit Center	Cost Center
A.	No	No
B.	No	Yes
C.	Yes	No
D.	Yes	Yes

Answer (C) is correct. *(CPA, adapted)*
REQUIRED: The responsibility center(s), if any, that include(s) controllable revenue in a performance report.
DISCUSSION: A profit center is a segment of a company responsible for both revenues and expenses. A profit center has the authority to make decisions concerning markets (revenues) and sources of supply (costs).

34. The following is a summarized income statement of Carr Co.'s profit center No. 43 for the month just ended:

Contribution margin		$70,000
Period expenses:		
Manager's salary	$20,000	
Facility depreciation	8,000	
Corporate expense allocation	5,000	(33,000)
Profit center income		$37,000

Which of the following amounts would most likely be subject to the control of the profit center's manager?

   A. $70,000

   B. $50,000

   C. $37,000

   D. $33,000

Answer (A) is correct. *(CPA, adapted)*
   REQUIRED: The amount most likely subject to the control of the profit center's manager.
   DISCUSSION: A profit center is a segment of a company responsible for both revenues and expenses. A profit center has the authority to make decisions concerning markets (revenues) and sources of supply (costs). However, the profit center's manager does not control his/her own salary, investment, and the resulting costs (e.g., depreciation of plant assets), or expenses incurred at the corporate level. Consequently, profit center No. 43 is most likely able to control its $70,000 contribution margin (sales – variable costs) but not the other items in the summarized income statement.
   Answer (B) is incorrect because the profit center's manager does not control his/her $20,000 salary. Answer (C) is incorrect because the profit center's manager does not control the listed period expenses and therefore does not control the profit center's income. Answer (D) is incorrect because the listed period expenses ($33,000) are not controlled by the profit center.

35. The extent to which a manager can influence organizational activities is

   A. Authority.

   B. Responsibility.

   C. Accountability.

   D. Controllability.

Answer (D) is correct. *(Publisher, adapted)*
   REQUIRED: The extent to which a manager can influence organizational activities.
   DISCUSSION: Controllability may be defined as (1) the ability of a specific manager to directly regulate a cost or (2) the extent to which a manager can influence activities and related revenues, costs, or other items. In principle, controllability is proportionate to, but not coextensive with, responsibility.
   Answer (A) is incorrect because authority is the power to direct and exact performance from others. It includes the right to prescribe the means and methods by which work will be done. Answer (B) is incorrect because responsibility is the obligation to perform. Answer (C) is incorrect because accountability is the liability for failure to meet the obligation.

36. Common costs are

   A. Direct costs.

   B. Current costs.

   C. Controllable costs.

   D. Indirect costs.

Answer (D) is correct. *(Publisher, adapted)*
   REQUIRED: The nature of common costs.
   DISCUSSION: Common costs are the cost of products, activities, facilities, services, or operations shared by two or more cost objects. They are indirect costs because they cannot be traced to a particular cost object in an economically feasible manner. Hence, they must be allocated.
   Answer (A) is incorrect because direct costs can be traced to a particular cost object in an economically feasible manner. Answer (B) is incorrect because current cost is an attribute used to measure assets. Answer (C) is incorrect because controllable costs can be influenced by a particular manager.

37. Managers are most likely to accept allocations of common costs based on

   A. Cause and effect.

   B. Ability to bear.

   C. Fairness.

   D. Benefits received.

Answer (A) is correct. *(Publisher, adapted)*
   REQUIRED: The criterion most likely to result in acceptable allocations of common costs.
   DISCUSSION: The difficulty with common costs is that they are indirect costs whose allocation may be arbitrary. A direct cause-and-effect relationship between a common cost and the actions of the cost object to which it is allocated is desirable. Such a relationship promotes acceptance of the allocation by managers who perceive the fairness of the procedure, but identification of cause and effect may not be feasible.
   Answer (B) is incorrect because allocation using an ability-to-bear criterion punishes successful managers and rewards underachievers. Answer (C) is incorrect because fairness is an objective rather than a criterion. Moreover, fairness may be interpreted differently by different managers. Answer (D) is incorrect because the benefits-received criterion is preferable when a cause-effect relationship cannot be feasibly identified.

38. A large corporation allocates the costs of its headquarters staff to its decentralized divisions. The best reason for this allocation is to

A. More accurately measure divisional operating results.

B. Improve divisional managements' morale.

C. Remind divisional managers that common costs exist.

D. Discourage any use of central support services.

Answer (C) is correct. *(Publisher, adapted)*
REQUIRED: The best reason for allocating headquarters costs.
DISCUSSION: The allocation reminds managers that support costs exist and that the managers would incur these costs if their operations were independent. The allocation also reminds managers that profit center earnings must cover some amount of support costs.
Answer (A) is incorrect because an arbitrary allocation may skew operating results. Answer (B) is incorrect because the allocation may create resentment and conflict. Answer (D) is incorrect because efficient use of central support services should be encouraged.

39. Goal congruence is

A. The desire and the commitment to achieve a specific objective.

B. The sharing of objectives by supervisors and subordinates.

C. The extent to which individuals have the authority to make decisions.

D. The extent of the attempt to accomplish a specific objective.

Answer (B) is correct. *(Publisher, adapted)*
REQUIRED: The definition of goal congruence.
DISCUSSION: Goal congruence is agreement on the objectives of the organization or the segment by both supervisors and subordinates. Performance is assumed to be optimized when there is an understanding that personal and segmental objectives be consistent with those of the organization.
Answer (A) is incorrect because motivation is the desire and the commitment to achieve a specific objective. Answer (C) is incorrect because autonomy is the extent to which individuals have the authority to make decisions. Answer (D) is incorrect because managerial effort is the extent of the attempt to accomplish a specific objective.

40. Transfer pricing should encourage goal congruence and managerial effort. In a decentralized organization, it should also encourage autonomous decision making. Managerial effort is

A. The desire and the commitment to achieve a specific objective.

B. The extent to which individuals have the authority to make decisions.

C. The extent of the attempt to accomplish a specific objective.

D. The sharing of objectives between units of an organization.

Answer (C) is correct. *(Publisher, adapted)*
REQUIRED: The definition of managerial effort.
DISCUSSION: Managerial effort is the extent to which a manager attempts to accomplish an objective. Managerial effort may include psychological as well as physical commitment to an objective.
Answer (A) is incorrect because motivation is the desire and the commitment to achieve a specific objective. Answer (B) is incorrect because autonomy is the extent to which individuals have the authority to make decisions. Answer (D) is incorrect because managerial effort reflects the attempts of an individual manager or organizational unit, not those efforts shared among managers of different organization units.

41. The price that one division of a company charges another division for goods or services provided is called the

A. Market price.

B. Transfer price.

C. Outlay price.

D. Distress price.

Answer (B) is correct. *(CIA, adapted)*
REQUIRED: The price that one division of a company charges another for goods or services provided.
DISCUSSION: A transfer price is the price charged by one segment of an organization for a product or service supplied to another segment of the same organization.
Answer (A) is incorrect because market price is an approach to determine a transfer price. Answer (C) is incorrect because outlay price is an approach to determine a transfer price. Answer (D) is incorrect because distress price is an approach to determine a transfer price.

42. Spring Co. had two divisions, A and B. Division A created Product X, which could be sold on the outside market for $25 and used variable costs of $15. Division B could take Product X and apply additional variable costs of $40 to create Product Y, which could be sold for $100. Division B received a special order for a large amount of Product Y. If Division A was operating at full capacity, which of the following prices should Division A charge Division B for the Product X needed to fill the special order?

 A. $15

 B. $20

 C. $25

 D. $40

Answer (C) is correct. *(CPA, adapted)*
 REQUIRED: The transfer price charged by a division operating at full capacity.
 DISCUSSION: Division A has no idle capacity. It will forgo $25 of revenue and a $10 contribution margin ($25 – $15 variable cost) for each unit of X transferred to Division B. Consequently, the price that optimizes decision making for the company as a whole is the $25 market price (assuming all the units transferred internally could be sold externally for $25). The true unit contribution margin for Y is $35 ($100 price – $40 variable cost of Y – $15 variable cost of X – $10 unit contribution margin of X forgone).
 Answer (A) is incorrect because $15 understates the true cost to the company of transferring X internally. Answer (B) is incorrect because $20 understates the true cost to the company of transferring X internally. Answer (D) is incorrect because $40 may cause Division B to purchase X outside the company at a price higher than $25.

43. In theory, the optimal method for establishing a transfer price is

 A. Flexible budget cost.

 B. Incremental cost.

 C. Budgeted cost with or without a markup.

 D. Market price.

Answer (D) is correct. *(CMA, adapted)*
 REQUIRED: The optimal method for establishing a transfer price.
 DISCUSSION: Transfer prices are the amounts charged by one segment of an organization for goods and services it provides to another segment within the organization. Transfer prices should promote congruence of subunit goals with those of the organization, subunit autonomy, and managerial effort. Although no rule exists for determining the transfer price that meets these criteria in all situations, a starting point is to calculate the sum of the additional outlay costs and the opportunity cost to the supplier. Given no idle capacity and a competitive external market (all goods transferred internally can be sold externally), the sum of the outlay and opportunity costs will be the market price.
 Answer (A) is incorrect because using flexible budget cost as a transfer price provides no motivation to the seller to control costs and no reward for selling internally when an external market exists. Answer (B) is incorrect because using an incremental cost provides no motivation to control costs or to sell internally when an external market exists. Answer (C) is incorrect because market price is preferable to a budgeted or actual cost with or without a markup (unless the markup equals the profit earned by selling externally).

44. A limitation of transfer prices based on actual cost is that they

 A. Charge inefficiencies to the department that is transferring the goods.

 B. Can lead to suboptimal decisions for the company as a whole.

 C. Must be adjusted by some markup.

 D. Lack clarity and administrative convenience.

Answer (B) is correct. *(CIA, adapted)*
 REQUIRED: The limitation of transfer prices based on actual cost.
 DISCUSSION: The optimal transfer price of a selling division should be set at a point that will have the most desirable economic effect on the firm as a whole while at the same time continuing to motivate the management of every division to perform efficiently. Setting the transfer price based on actual costs rather than standard costs would give the selling division little incentive to control costs.
 Answer (A) is incorrect because inefficiencies are charged to the buying department. Answer (C) is incorrect because, by definition, cost-based transfer prices are not adjusted by some markup. Answer (D) is incorrect because cost-based transfer prices provide the advantages of clarity and administrative convenience.

45. Variable-cost-plus price is

A. The price on the open market.

B. The price representing the cash outflows of the supplying division plus the contribution to the supplying division from an outside sale.

C. The price usually set by an absorption-costing calculation.

D. The price set by charging for variable costs plus a lump sum or an additional markup, but less than full markup.

Answer (D) is correct. *(Publisher, adapted)*
REQUIRED: The definition of variable-cost-plus price.
DISCUSSION: The variable-cost-plus price is the price set by charging for variable cost plus either a lump sum or an additional markup but less than the full markup price. This permits top management to enter the decision process and dictate that a division transfer at variable cost plus some appropriate amount.
Answer (A) is incorrect because the price on the open market is the definition of the market price. Answer (B) is incorrect because outlay cost plus opportunity cost is the price representing the cash outflows of the supplying division plus the contribution to the supplying division from an outside sale. Answer (C) is incorrect because the full-cost price is the price usually set by an absorption-costing calculation.

46. Full-cost price is

A. The price on the open market.

B. The price representing the cash outflows of the supplying division plus the contribution to the supplying division from an outside sale.

C. The price usually set by an absorption-costing calculation.

D. The price set by charging for variable costs plus a lump sum or an additional markup, but less than full markup.

Answer (C) is correct. *(Publisher, adapted)*
REQUIRED: The definition of full-cost price.
DISCUSSION: Full-cost price is the price usually set by an absorption-costing calculation and includes materials, labor, and a full allocation of manufacturing O/H. This full-cost price may lead to dysfunctional behavior by the supplying and receiving divisions, e.g., purchasing from outside sources at a slightly lower price that is substantially above the variable costs of internal production.
Answer (A) is incorrect because the market price is the price on the open market. Answer (B) is incorrect because the outlay cost plus opportunity cost is the price representing the cash outflows of the supplying division plus the contribution to the supplying division from an outside sale. Answer (D) is incorrect because the variable-cost-plus price is the price set by charging for variable costs plus a lump sum or an additional markup, but less than full markup.

47. An appropriate transfer price between two divisions of The Stark Company can be determined from the following data:

Fabricating Division

Market price of subassembly	$50
Variable cost of subassembly	$20
Excess capacity (in units)	1,000

Assembling Division

Number of units needed	900

What is the natural bargaining range for the two divisions?

A. Between $20 and $50.

B. Between $50 and $70.

C. Any amount less than $50.

D. $50 is the only acceptable price.

Answer (A) is correct. *(CMA, adapted)*
REQUIRED: The appropriate transfer price.
DISCUSSION: An ideal transfer price should permit each division to operate independently and achieve its goals while functioning in the best interest of the overall company. Transfer prices can be determined in a number of ways, including normal market price, negotiated price, variable costs, or full absorption costs. The capacity of the Selling Division is often a determinant of the ideal transfer price. If the Fabricating Division had no excess capacity, it would charge the Assembling Division the regular market price. However, if the Fabricating Division has excess capacity of 1,000 units, negotiation is possible because any transfer price greater than the variable cost of $20 would absorb some of its fixed costs and result in increased divisional profits. Thus, any price between $20 and $50 is acceptable to the Fabricating Division. Any price under $50 is acceptable to the Assembling Division because that is the price that would be paid to an outside supplier.
Answer (B) is incorrect because the Assembling Division would not pay more than the market price of $50. Answer (C) is incorrect because Fabricating will not be willing to accept less than its variable cost of $20. Answer (D) is incorrect because Fabricating should be willing to accept any price between $20 and $50.

Questions 48 through 50 are based on the following information.

Parkside, Inc. has several divisions that operate as decentralized profit centers. Parkside's Entertainment Division manufactures video arcade equipment using the products of two of Parkside's other divisions. The Plastics Division manufactures plastic components, one type that is made exclusively for the Entertainment Division, while other less complex components are sold to outside markets. The products of the Video Cards Division are sold in a competitive market; however, one video card model is also used by the Entertainment Division.

The actual costs per unit used by the Entertainment Division are presented below.

	Plastic Components	Video Cards
Direct material	$1.25	$2.40
Direct labor	2.35	3.00
Variable overhead	1.00	1.50
Fixed overhead	.40	2.25
Total cost	$5.00	$9.15

The Plastics Division sells its commercial products at full cost plus a 25% markup and believes the proprietary plastic component made for the Entertainment Division would sell for $6.25 per unit on the open market. The market price of the video card used by the Entertainment Division is $10.98 per unit.

48. A per-unit transfer price from the Video Cards Division to the Entertainment Division at full cost, $9.15, will

A. Allow evaluation of both divisions on a competitive basis.

B. Satisfy the Video Cards Division's profit desire by allowing recovery of opportunity costs.

C. Provide no profit incentive for the Video Cards Division to control or reduce costs.

D. Encourage the Entertainment Division to purchase video cards from an outside source.

Answer (C) is correct. *(CMA, adapted)*
REQUIRED: The effect of a full-cost transfer price.
DISCUSSION: A transfer price is the amount one segment of an organization charges another segment for a product. The selling division should be allowed to recover its incremental cost plus the opportunity cost of the transfer. Hence, in a competitive market, the seller should be able to charge the market price. Using full cost as a transfer price provides no incentive to the seller to control production costs.
Answer (A) is incorrect because evaluating the seller is difficult if it can pass along all costs to the buyer. Answer (B) is incorrect because transfers at full cost do not allow for a seller's profit. Answer (D) is incorrect because a full-cost transfer is favorable to the buyer. It is lower than the market price.

49. Assume that the Entertainment Division is able to purchase a large quantity of video cards from an outside source at $8.70 per unit. The Video Cards Division, having excess capacity, agrees to lower its transfer price to $8.70 per unit. This action will

A. Optimize the profit goals of the Entertainment Division while subverting the profit goals of Parkside Inc.

B. Allow evaluation of both divisions on the same basis.

C. Subvert the profit goals of the Video Cards Division while optimizing the profit goals of the Entertainment Division.

D. Optimize the overall profit goals of Parkside Inc.

Answer (D) is correct. *(CMA, adapted)*
REQUIRED: The impact of lowering the transfer price to match an outside seller's price.
DISCUSSION: If the seller has excess capacity, it should lower its transfer price to match the outside offer. This decision optimizes the profits of the company as a whole by allowing for use of capacity that would otherwise be idle.
Answer (A) is incorrect because this action is congruent with the goals of Parkside. The use of idle capacity enhances profits. Answer (B) is incorrect because the transfer is at a loss (relative to full cost) to the seller, although the company as a whole will benefit. Answer (C) is incorrect because the buyer is indifferent as to whether to purchase internally or externally.

50. Assume that the Plastics Division has excess capacity and it has negotiated a transfer price of $5.60 per plastic component with the Entertainment Division. This price will

A. Cause the Plastics Division to reduce the number of commercial plastic components it manufactures.

B. Motivate both divisions as estimated profits are shared.

C. Encourage the Entertainment Division to seek an outside source for plastic components.

D. Demotivate the Plastics Division causing mediocre performance.

Answer (B) is correct. *(CMA, adapted)*
REQUIRED: The effect of using a negotiated transfer price that is greater than full cost but less than market price.
DISCUSSION: Given that the Plastics Division (the seller) has excess capacity, transfers within the company entail no opportunity cost. Accordingly, the transfer at the negotiated price will improve the performance measures of the transferor. Purchasing internally at below the market price also benefits the transferee, so the motivational purpose of transfer pricing is achieved. The goal congruence purpose is also achieved because the internal transaction benefits the company.
Answer (A) is incorrect because this arrangement creates no disincentive for the seller. It will make a profit on every unit transferred. Answer (C) is incorrect because the market price charged by outside sources is higher than the negotiated price. Answer (D) is incorrect because, given idle capacity, selling at any amount in excess of variable cost should motivate the seller.

17.4 Theory of Constraints and the Balanced Scorecard

51. When evaluating projects, breakeven time is best described as

A. Annual fixed costs ÷ monthly contribution margin.

B. Project investment ÷ annual net cash inflows.

C. The point at which cumulative cash inflows on a project equal total cash outflows.

D. The point at which discounted cumulative cash inflows on a project equal discounted total cash outflows.

Answer (D) is correct. *(CMA, adapted)*
REQUIRED: The definition of breakeven time.
DISCUSSION: Breakeven time evaluates the rapidity of new product development. The usual calculation determines the period beginning with project approval that is required for the discounted cumulative cash inflows to equal the discounted cumulative cash outflows. However, it may also be calculated as the point at which discounted cumulative cash inflows on a project equal discounted total cash outflows. The concept is similar to the payback period, but it is more sophisticated because it incorporates the time value of money. It also differs from the payback method because the period covered begins at the outset of a project, not when the initial cash outflow occurs.
Answer (A) is incorrect because it is related to breakeven point, not breakeven time. Answer (B) is incorrect because the payback period equals investment divided by annual undiscounted net cash inflows. Answer (C) is incorrect because the payback period is the period required for total undiscounted cash inflows to equal total undiscounted cash outflows.

52. Many forms of performance feedback are based on accounting information. For example, a divisional manager may be evaluated based on return on investment (income ÷ investment). One step in the process of developing a performance measure based on accounting information is to determine the basis for stating the measure in terms of dollars. Thus, if ROI is the chosen measure, and investment is defined as total assets, comparability issues are most likely to arise when the attribute used to calculate total assets is

A. Current cost.

B. Current disposal price.

C. Historical cost.

D. Present value.

Answer (C) is correct. *(Publisher, adapted)*
REQUIRED: The attribute most likely to create comparability problems.
DISCUSSION: Historical cost creates comparability issues because returns on significantly depreciated assets may be higher than those on newer assets that have been acquired using inflated dollars. Thus, otherwise similarly situated managers may report different operating results. Moreover, managers may be reluctant to replace aging assets. Current cost, current disposal price, and present value are attempts to remedy the theoretical deficiencies of historical cost by presenting more accurate balance sheet values.

Questions 53 and 54 are based on the following information. This information is relevant to a theory of constraints (TOC) analysis. A manufacturer that can sell all of its output produces its sole product using three operations. Each unit sells for $120, and direct materials costing $48 per unit are added at the start of the first operation. Other variable costs are immaterial. The following annual cost and capacity information is available concerning those operations:

	Operation 1	Operation 2	Operation 3
Total capacity per year	200,000 units	150,000 units	180,000 units
Total output per year	150,000 units	150,000 units	150,000 units
Fixed cost of operations (not including direct materials)	$1,200,000	$1,800,000	$2,250,000

53. Assume that additional workers are hired for the bottleneck operation to expedite setups and materials handling. The cost of the additional workers is $50,000 per year. As a result, the annual output of the bottleneck operation will increase by 500 units. The change in operating income attributable to the increase in workers is

A. $50,000

B. $36,000

C. $(14,000)

D. $(20,000)

Answer (C) is correct. *(Publisher, adapted)*
REQUIRED: The change in operating income.
DISCUSSION: Operation 2 is the bottleneck because it is functioning at its capacity. The incremental annual throughput contribution (revenues – direct materials costs) from adding workers to Operation 2 is $36,000 [500 units × ($120 unit price – $48 DM per unit)]. Because the cost of the additional workers is $50,000, the change in operating income is $(14,000).
Answer (A) is incorrect because $50,000 is the incremental cost. Answer (B) is incorrect because $36,000 is the incremental throughput contribution. Answer (D) is incorrect because $(20,000) is based on the assumption that an additional $12 per unit of fixed costs will be applied.

54. Assume that X Company offers to perform the Operation 2 function on 1,000 units at a unit price of $40, excluding direct materials cost. Also assume that Y Company offers to perform the Operation 1 function on 1,000 units at a price of $7, excluding direct materials cost. Company Y makes an alternative offer to perform the Operation 1 function on 5,000 units at a unit cost of $5 (excluding direct materials cost). Which of these mutually exclusive offers is acceptable?

A. X but not Y.

B. Y but not X.

C. X or Y.

D. Neither offer should be accepted.

Answer (A) is correct. *(Publisher, adapted)*
REQUIRED: The acceptable offer(s), if any.
DISCUSSION: X's offer should be accepted because its cost is $40,000 (1,000 units × $40), but the increase in throughput contribution is $72,000 [1,000 units × ($120 unit price – $48 DM per unit)]. X's offer effectively increases the capacity of the bottleneck operation. Y's offer should be rejected because it will result in the incurrence of additional costs with no increase in throughput contribution, given that Operation 2 is already producing at its 150,000-unit capacity.

55. Managerial performance may be measured in many ways. For example, an internal nonfinancial measure is

A. Market share.

B. Delivery performance.

C. Customer satisfaction.

D. Manufacturing lead time.

Answer (D) is correct. *(Publisher, adapted)*
REQUIRED: The internal nonfinancial measure.
DISCUSSION: Feedback regarding managerial performance may take the form of financial and nonfinancial measures that may be internally or externally generated. Moreover, different measures have a long-term or short-term emphasis. Examples of internal nonfinancial measures are product quality, new product development time, and manufacturing lead time (cycle time).
Answer (A) is incorrect because market share is an external nonfinancial measure. Answer (B) is incorrect because delivery performance is an external nonfinancial measure. Answer (C) is incorrect because customer satisfaction is an external nonfinancial measure.

56. Which of the following balanced scorecard perspectives examines a company's success in targeted market segments?

    A. Financial.

    B. Customer.

    C. Internal business process.

    D. Learning and growth.

Answer (B) is correct. *(CPA, adapted)*
    REQUIRED: The balanced scorecard perspective that examines success in targeted market segments.
    DISCUSSION: The balanced scorecard critical success factors (CSFs) for the customer perspective may include (1) customer satisfaction, (2) customer retention rate, (3) dealer and distributor relationships, (4) marketing and selling performance, (5) prompt delivery, and (6) quality. Thus, the customer perspective may use measures of sales trends, market share, and market share trends in particular market segments.
    Answer (A) is incorrect because the financial perspective addresses such CSFs as (1) sales, (2) fair value of the firm's stock, (3) profits, and (4) liquidity. Answer (C) is incorrect because the CSFs for the internal business process perspective may include (1) quality, (2) productivity, (3) flexibility of response to changing conditions, (4) operating readiness, and (5) safety. Answer (D) is incorrect because the CSFs for the learning and growth perspective may include (1) new product development, (2) promptness of introduction of new products, (3) human resource development, (4) morale, and (5) workforce competence.

57. An organization's managerial decision-making model for capital budgeting is based on the net present value of discounted cash flows. The same organization's managerial performance evaluation model is based on annual divisional return on investment. Which of the following is true?

    A. Divisional managers are likely to maximize the measures in the decision-making model.

    B. Divisional managers are likely to maximize the measures in the performance evaluation model.

    C. The manager has an incentive to accept a project with a positive net present value that initially has a negative effect on net income.

    D. The use of models with different criteria promotes goal congruence.

Answer (B) is correct. *(Publisher, adapted)*
    REQUIRED: The true statement about use of different models for decision making and managerial evaluation.
    DISCUSSION: Effective management control requires performance measurement and feedback. This process affects allocation of resources to organizational subunits. It also affects decisions about managers' compensation, advancement, and future assignments. Furthermore, evaluating their performance serves to motivate managers to optimize the measures in the performance evaluation model. However, that model may be inconsistent with the organization's model for managerial decision making.
    Answer (A) is incorrect because self-interest provides an incentive to maximize the measures used in performance evaluation. Answer (C) is incorrect because a manager evaluated on the basis of annual ROI has an interest in maximizing short-term net income, not long-term NPV. Answer (D) is incorrect because the models should be synchronized so that the goals of the organization and the manager are congruent.

58. Using the balanced scorecard approach, an organization evaluates managerial performance based on

    A. A single ultimate measure of operating results, such as residual income.

    B. Multiple financial and nonfinancial measures.

    C. Multiple nonfinancial measures only.

    D. Multiple financial measures only.

Answer (B) is correct. *(Publisher, adapted)*
    REQUIRED: The nature of the balanced scorecard approach.
    DISCUSSION: The trend in managerial performance evaluation is the balanced scorecard approach. Multiple measures of performance permit a determination as to whether a manager is achieving certain objectives at the expense of others that may be equally or more important. These measures may be financial or nonfinancial and usually include items with four perspectives: financial; customer; internal business processes; and learning, growth, and innovation.
    Answer (A) is incorrect because the balanced scorecard approach uses multiple measures. Answer (C) is incorrect because the balanced scorecard approach uses financial and nonfinancial measures. Answer (D) is incorrect because the balanced scorecard approach uses financial and nonfinancial measures.

59. On a balanced scorecard, which of the following is not a customer satisfaction measure?

A. Market share.

B. Economic value added.

C. Response time.

D. Customer retention.

Answer (B) is correct. *(Publisher, adapted)*
REQUIRED: The measure that is not an element of customer satisfaction on a balanced scorecard.
DISCUSSION: Customer satisfaction measures include market share, retention, response time, delivery performance, number of defects, and lead time. Economic value added, or EVA, is a profitability (financial) measure.

Use Gleim's **CPA Test Prep** for interactive testing with over 2,000 additional multiple-choice questions!

STUDY UNIT EIGHTEEN
COST BEHAVIOR AND DEFINITIONS

(18 pages of outline)

This is the first of three study units relating to cost measurement. This subunit contains a glossary of cost-related terms. Several of the definitions are from Statement on Management Accounting (SMA) 2A, a publication of the Institute of Management Accountants (IMA). Other topics covered include absorption vs. variable costing and cost-volume-profit analysis.

18.1 COST MEASUREMENT TERMINOLOGY

1. **Manufacturing vs. Nonmanufacturing**

   a. The **costs of manufacturing** a product can be classified as one of three types:

      1) **Direct materials (DM)** are those tangible inputs to the manufacturing process that can practicably be traced to the product, e.g., sheet metal welded together for a piece of heavy equipment.

         a) All costs of bringing raw materials to the production line, e.g., transportation-in, are included in the cost of direct materials.

      2) **Direct labor (DL)** is the cost of human labor that can practicably be traced to the product, e.g., the wages of the welder.

      3) **Manufacturing overhead (OH)** consists of all costs of manufacturing that are not direct materials or direct labor.

         a) **Indirect materials** are tangible inputs to the manufacturing process that cannot practicably be traced to the product, e.g., the welding compound used to put together a piece of heavy equipment.

         b) **Indirect labor** is the cost of human labor connected with the manufacturing process that cannot practicably be traced to the product, e.g., the wages of assembly line supervisors and janitorial staff.

         c) **Factory operating costs**, such as utilities, real estate taxes, insurance, depreciation on factory equipment, etc.

   b. Manufacturing costs are often grouped into the following classifications:

      1) **Prime cost** equals direct materials plus direct labor, i.e., those costs directly attributable to a product. (DM + DL)

      2) **Conversion cost** equals direct labor plus manufacturing overhead, i.e., the costs of converting raw materials into the finished product. (DL + OH)

   c. Operating a manufacturing concern requires the incurrence of **nonmanufacturing costs**:

      1) **Selling (marketing) costs** are those costs incurred in getting the product from the factory to the consumer, e.g., sales personnel salaries and product transportation.

      2) **Administrative expenses** are those costs incurred by a company not directly related to producing or marketing the product, e.g., executive salaries and depreciation on the headquarters building.

2.   **Product vs. Period**

a.   One of the most important classifications a managerial accountant can make is whether to capitalize costs in finished goods inventory or to expense them as incurred.

   1)   **Product costs** (also called inventoriable costs) are capitalized as part of finished goods inventory. They eventually become a **component of cost of goods sold**.

   2)   **Period costs** are expensed as incurred, i.e., they are not capitalized in finished goods inventory and are thus **excluded from cost of goods sold**.

b.   This distinction is crucial because of the required treatment of manufacturing costs for external financial reporting purposes.

   1)   **Under GAAP**, all manufacturing costs (direct materials, direct labor, variable overhead, and fixed overhead) must be treated as product costs, and all selling and administrative (S&A) costs must be treated as period costs.

      a)   This approach is called **absorption costing** (also called full costing).

   2)   For **internal reporting**, a more informative accounting treatment is often to capitalize only variable manufacturing costs as product costs, and treat all other costs (variable S&A and the fixed portion of both production and S&A expenses) as period costs.

      a)   This approach is called **variable costing** (also called direct costing).

   3)   The following table summarizes these two approaches:

	Absorption Costing (Required under GAAP)	Variable Costing (For internal reporting only)
Product Costs (Included in Cost of Goods Sold)	Variable production costs	
	Fixed production costs	
Period Costs		Fixed production costs
(Excluded from Cost of Goods Sold)	Variable S&A expenses	
	Fixed S&A expenses	

      a)   These treatments are explained more fully in item 1. in Subunit 18.3.

3.   **Direct vs. Indirect**

a.   Costs can be classified by how they are assigned to cost objects.

   1)   **Direct costs** are ones that can be associated with a particular cost object in an economically feasible way, i.e., they can be **traced** to that object.

      a)   Examples are the direct materials and direct labor inputs to a manufacturing process discussed in item 1.a. on the previous page.

   2)   **Indirect costs** are ones that cannot be associated with a particular cost object in an economically feasible way and thus must be **allocated** to that object.

      a)   Examples are the indirect materials and indirect labor inputs to a manufacturing process discussed in item 1.a.3) on the previous page.

      b)   To simplify the allocation process, indirect costs are often collected in cost pools.

         i)   A **cost pool** is an account into which a variety of similar cost elements with a common cause are accumulated.

         ii)   Manufacturing overhead is a commonly used cost pool into which various untraceable costs of the manufacturing process are accumulated prior to being allocated.

3) **Common costs** are another notable type of indirect cost. A common cost is one shared by two or more users.

   a) The key to common costs is that, since they cannot be directly traced to the users that generate the costs, they must be **allocated** using some systematic and rational basis.

   b) An example is depreciation on the headquarters building. This is a direct cost when treating the building as a whole, but it is a common cost of the departments located in the building and thus must be allocated when treating the individual departments.

4. **Fixed vs. Variable**

   a. The **relevant range** defines the limits within which per-unit variable costs remain constant and fixed costs are not changeable. It is synonymous with the **short run**.

      1) The relevant range is established by the efficiency of a company's current manufacturing plant, its agreements with labor unions and suppliers, etc.

   b. **Variable cost per unit** remains constant in the short run regardless of the level of production.

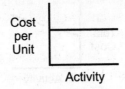

   c. **Variable costs in total**, on the other hand, vary directly and proportionally with changes in volume.

   d. EXAMPLE: A company requires one unit of direct material to be used in each finished good it produces.

Number of Units Produced	Cost per Unit	Total Cost of Units
0	$10	$0
100	$10	$1,000
1,000	$10	$10,000
5,000	$10	$50,000
10,000	$10	$100,000

   e. **Fixed costs in total** remain unchanged in the short run regardless of production level; e.g., the amount paid for an assembly line is the same even if production is halted entirely.

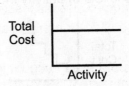

f. **Fixed cost per unit**, on the other hand, varies indirectly with the activity level.

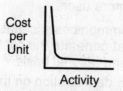

g. EXAMPLE: The historical cost of the assembly line is settled, but its cost per unit decreases as production increases.

Number of Units Produced	Cost of Assembly Line	Per Unit Cost of Assembly Line
0	$1,000,000	$1,000,000
100	$1,000,000	$10,000
1,000	$1,000,000	$1,000
5,000	$1,000,000	$200
10,000	$1,000,000	$100

h. **Mixed (semivariable) costs** combine fixed and variable elements, e.g., rental on a car that carries a flat fee per month plus an additional fee for each mile driven.

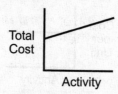

i. EXAMPLE: The company rents a piece of machinery to make its production line more efficient. The rental is $150,000 per year plus $1 for every unit produced.

Number of Units Produced	Fixed Cost of Extra Machine	Variable Cost of Extra Machine	Total Cost of Extra Machine
0	$150,000	$0	$150,000
100	$150,000	$100	$150,100
1,000	$150,000	$1,000	$151,000
5,000	$150,000	$5,000	$155,000
10,000	$150,000	$10,000	$160,000

j. Four of the five costs described above are **linear-cost functions**; i.e., they change at a constant rate (or remain unchanged) over the short run.

1) Fixed cost per unit, however, is an example of a **nonlinear-cost function**.

a) Note that fixed cost per unit has an asymptotic character with respect to the x axis, approaching it closely while never intersecting it. (It does intersect the y axis at the zero level of activity.) The function shows a high degree of variability over its range taken as a whole (see item 4.f. above).

b) Another type of nonlinear-cost function is a **step-cost function**, one that is constant over small ranges of output but increases by steps (discrete amounts) as levels of activity increase.

i) Both fixed and variable costs can display step-cost characteristics. If the steps are relatively narrow, these costs are usually treated as variable. If the steps are wide, they are more akin to fixed costs.

    k.   **Relevant Range and Marginal Cost**

        1)   **Marginal cost** is the cost incurred by a one-unit increase in the activity level of a particular cost driver.

            a)   Necessarily then, **marginal cost remains constant across the relevant range**.

        2)   Management accountants capture the concept of relevant range when they say that **"All costs are variable in the long run."**

            a)   Investment in new, more productive equipment results in higher total fixed costs but may result in lower total and per-unit variable costs.

5.   **Cost of Goods Sold and Cost of Goods Manufactured**

    a.   **Cost of goods sold** is a straightforward computation for a **retailer** because retailers have only a **single class of inventory**.

Beginning inventory	$XX,XXX
Add: purchases	X,XXX
Less: ending inventory	(X,XXX)
Cost of goods sold	**$XX,XXX**

    b.   The calculation is more complex for a **manufacturer**, because manufacturers have **three distinct classes of inventory**.

        1)   Cost of goods sold contains an additional component called **cost of goods manufactured**, analogous to the retailer's purchases account.

Beginning work-in-process inventory	$XX,XXX
Add: total manufacturing costs	X,XXX
Less: ending work-in-process inventory	(X,XXX)
Cost of goods manufactured	**$XX,XXX**

    c.   A comparison of these computations in full is as follows:

Cost of goods sold for a retailer:

Beginning inventory		$ xxx,xxx
Add: Purchases	$x,xxx,xxx	
Less: Returns and discounts	(xx,xxx)	
Net purchases	x,xxx,xxx	
Add: Freight-in	xx,xxx	x,xxx,xxx
Goods available for sale		x,xxx,xxx
Less: Ending inventory		(xxx,xxx)
Costs of goods sold		**$x,xxx,xxx**

Cost of goods sold for a manufacturer:

Beginning raw materials inventory			$ xxx,xxx
Add: Purchases		$x,xxx,xxx	
Less: Returns and discounts		(xx,xxx)	
Net purchases		x,xxx,xxx	
Add: Freight-in		xx,xxx	x,xxx,xxx
Raw materials available for use			x,xxx,xxx
Less: Ending raw materials inventory			(xxx,xxx)
Direct materials used in production			$ x,xxx,xxx
Direct labor costs			x,xxx,xxx
Total manufacturing costs for the period			**$x,xxx,xxx**
Add: Beginning work-in-process inventory			xxx,xxx
Less: Ending work-in-process inventory			(xxx,xxx)
Costs of goods manufactured			**x,xxx,xxx**
Add: Beginning finished goods inventory			xxx,xxx
Goods available for sale			**x,xxx,xxx**
Less: Ending finished goods inventory			(xxx,xxx)
Costs of goods sold			**$x,xxx,xxx**

6. **Outlay vs. Opportunity**

   a. **Outlay costs** require actual cash disbursements. They are also called **explicit, accounting**, or **out-of-pocket costs**.

      1) An example is the tuition, room, board, and books required to attend college.

   b. **Opportunity cost** is the maximum benefit forgone by using a scarce resource for a given purpose and not for the next-best alternative. It is also called **implicit cost**.

      1) An example is the wages foregone by attending college instead of working full-time.

   c. **Economic cost** is the sum of explicit and implicit costs.

   d. **Imputed costs** are those that should be involved in decision making even though no transaction has occurred that would be routinely recognized in the accounts. They may be outlay or opportunity costs.

      1) An example is the profit lost as a result of being unable to fill orders because the inventory level is too low.

7. **Relevant vs. Sunk**

   a. **Relevant costs** are those future costs that will vary depending on the action taken. All other costs are assumed to be constant and thus have no effect on (are irrelevant to) the decision.

      1) An example is tuition that must be spent to attend a fourth year of college.

   b. **Sunk costs** are costs either already paid or irrevocably committed to incur. Because they are unavoidable and will therefore not vary with the option chosen, they are not relevant to future decisions.

      1) An example is three years of tuition already spent. The previous three years of tuition make no difference in the decision to attend a fourth year.

   c. **Historical cost** is the actual (explicit) price paid for an asset. Financial accountants rely heavily on it for balance sheet reporting.

      1) Because historical cost is a sunk cost, however, management accountants often find other (implicit) costs to be more useful in decision making.

8. **Additional Cost Concepts**

   a. **Gross margin** is the intermediate figure between sales and operating income under absorption (full) costing. All manufacturing (and only manufacturing) costs, both variable and fixed, are deducted to arrive at gross margin.

      1) Only costs directly associated with manufacturing the product may be deducted.
      2) This is the only acceptable calculation under GAAP.

   b. **Contribution margin** is the intermediate figure when variable (direct) costing is used. All variable (and only variable) costs, both manufacturing and selling and administrative, are deducted to arrive at contribution margin.

      1) Contribution margin is the amount available to the firm to cover fixed costs.
      2) This calculation is often used for internal (managerial) reporting purposes.

   c. **Value-adding costs** are the costs of activities that cannot be eliminated without reducing the quality, responsiveness, or quantity of the output required by a customer or by an organization.

   d. **Incremental (differential) cost** is the difference in total cost between two decisions.

9. **Accumulating Manufacturing Costs**

    a.   **Job-order costing** is appropriate when producing products with individual characteristics or when identifiable groupings are possible.

        1) Costs are attached to specific "jobs." Each job will result in a single, identifiable end product.

        2) Examples are any industry that generates custom-built products, such as shipbuilding.

    b.   **Process costing** is used when similar products are mass produced on a continuous basis.

        1) Costs are attached to specific departments or phases of production. Examples are automobile and candy manufacturing.

        2) Since costs are attached to streams of products rather than individuals, process costing involves calculating an average cost for all units. The two widely used methods are weighted-average and first-in, first-out (FIFO).

        3) Some units remain unfinished at the end of the period. For each department to adequately account for the costs attached to its unfinished units, the units must be restated in terms of equivalent units of production (EUP).

    c.   **Activity-based costing (ABC)** attaches costs to activities rather than to physical goods.

        1) ABC is a response to the distortions of product cost information brought about by peanut-butter costing, which is the inaccurate averaging or spreading of costs like peanut butter over products or service units that use different amounts of resources.

            a) A major cause of peanut-butter costing is the significant increase in indirect costs brought about by the increasing use of technology.

        2) The difference between traditional (that is, volume-based) costing systems and ABC can be summarized as follows:

            a) Under volume-based systems, a single pool collects all indirect costs and is then allocated to production.

            b) Under ABC, by contrast, every activity that bears on the production process has its own cost pool. The costs in each pool are assigned based on a cost driver specific to the activity.

    d.   **Life-cycle costing** emphasizes the need to price products to cover all the costs incurred over the lifespan of a product, not just the costs of production.

        1) Costs incurred before production, such as R&D and product design, are referred to as upstream costs.

        2) Costs incurred after production, such as marketing and customer service, are called downstream costs.

    e.   **Operation costing** is a hybrid of job-order and process costing and is used by companies whose manufacturing processes involve some similar and some dissimilar operations.

        1) Direct materials costs are charged to specific products (as in job-order systems).

        2) Conversion costs are accumulated and a unit conversion cost for each operation is derived (as in process costing).

f. **Backflush costing** delays the assignment of costs until the goods are finished.

1) After production is finished for the period, standard costs are flushed backward through the system to assign costs to products. The result is that detailed tracking of costs is eliminated.

2) Backflush costing is best suited to companies that maintain low inventories because costs can flow directly to cost of goods sold. It is often used with just-in-time (JIT) inventory, one of the goals of which is the maintenance of low inventory levels.

10. Stop and review! You have completed the outline for this subunit. Study multiple-choice questions 1 through 31 beginning on page 573.

18.2 COST-VOLUME-PROFIT (CVP) ANALYSIS

1. **Cost-volume-profit (CVP) analysis** (also called breakeven analysis) is a tool for understanding the interaction of revenues with fixed and variable costs. It illuminates how changes in assumptions about cost behavior and the relevant ranges in which those assumptions are valid may affect the relationships among revenues, variable costs, and fixed costs at various production levels. Thus, CVP analysis allows management to discern the probable effects of changes in sales volume, sales price, product mix, etc.

2. The inherent simplifying **assumptions** of CVP analysis are as follows:

a. Cost and revenue relationships are predictable and linear. These relationships are true over the **relevant range** of activity and specified time span. For example, reductions in prices are not necessary to increase revenues, and no learning curve effect operates to reduce unit variable labor costs at higher output levels.

b. Total **variable costs** change proportionally with volume, but unit variable costs are constant over the relevant range. Raw materials and direct labor are typically variable costs.

c. Changes in inventory are insignificant in amount.

d. **Fixed costs** remain constant over the relevant range of volume, but unit fixed costs vary indirectly with volume. The classification of fixed versus variable can be affected by the time frame being considered.

e. Unit selling prices and market conditions are constant.

f. Production equals sales.

g. The **revenue (sales) mix** is constant, or the firm makes and sells only one product.

h. All costs are either fixed or variable relative to a given cost object for a given time span. The longer the time span, the more likely the cost is variable.

i. Technology and productive efficiency are constant.

j. Revenues and costs vary only with changes in physical unit volume. Hence, volume is the sole revenue driver and cost driver.

k. The breakeven point is directly related to costs and inversely related to the budgeted margin of safety and the contribution margin.

l. The time value of money is ignored.

3. The assumptions under which CVP analysis operates primarily hinge on **certainty**. However, many decisions must be made even though uncertainty exists. Assigning probabilities to the various outcomes and sensitivity ("what-if") analysis are important approaches to dealing with uncertainty.

4. **Definitions**

    a. The **breakeven point** is the level of output at which total revenues equal total expenses, that is, the point at which operating income is zero.

    b. The **margin of safety** is a measure of risk. It is the excess of budgeted revenues over breakeven revenues (or budgeted units over breakeven units).

    c. **Mixed costs (or semivariable costs)** are costs with both fixed and variable elements.

    d. The **revenue (sales) mix** is the composition of total revenues in terms of various products, i.e., the percentages of each product included in total revenues. It is maintained for all volume changes.

    e. **Sensitivity analysis** examines the effect on the outcome of not achieving the original forecast or of changing an assumption.

    f. **Unit contribution margin (UCM)** is the unit selling price minus the unit variable cost. It is the contribution from the sale of one unit to cover fixed costs (and possibly a targeted profit).

        1) It is expressed as either a percentage of the selling price **(contribution margin ratio)** or a dollar amount.

        2) The UCM is the slope of the total cost curve plotted so that volume is on the x-axis and dollar value is on the y-axis.

5. The general formula for operating income can be stated as follows:

    Operating income = Sales – Variable costs – Fixed costs

    a. The **breakeven point** can be determined by setting **operating income equal to zero** and solving the equation.

    b. EXAMPLE: A product is sold for $.60 per unit, with variable costs of $.20 per unit and fixed costs of $10,000. What is the breakeven point?

    Operating income = Sales – Variable costs – Fixed costs
    $0 = ($.60 × Q) – ($.20 × Q) – $10,000
    $.40 × Q = $10,000
    Q = 25,000 *units*

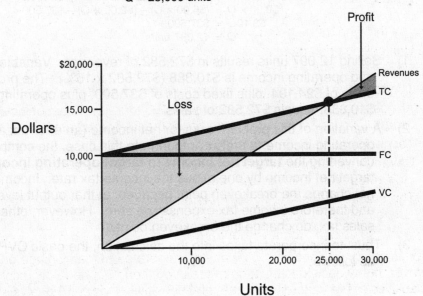

c. A simpler calculation is to divide fixed costs by the unit contribution margin (the unit contribution to coverage of fixed costs).

$$Breakeven\ point\ in\ units\ = \frac{Fixed\ costs}{UCM}$$

1) The UCM is $.40 ($.60 sales price – $.20 variable cost). Thus, to cover $10,000 of fixed costs, 25,000 units ($10,000 ÷ $.40 UCM) must be sold to break even.

d. The breakeven point in dollars can be calculated by dividing fixed costs by the contribution margin ratio {[$10,000 ÷ ($.40 ÷ $.60)] = $15,000}.

6. The **contribution income statement with per-unit amounts** is an integral part of breakeven analysis.

   EXAMPLE:

	In Total	Per Unit	Percent
Sales (40,000 units)	$ 24,000	$ 0.60	100%
Less: variable costs	(8,000)	(0.20)	(33%)
Contribution margin	$ 16,000	$ 0.40	67%
Less: fixed costs	(10,000)		
Operating income	$ 6,000		

   a. Every unit sold **contributes** a certain percentage of its sales revenue, in this case 67%, to **covering fixed costs**. Management can conclude that every unit sold in the relevant range will contribute $.40 to covering fixed costs.

   b. Once fixed costs are fully covered, all additional revenue becomes **profit**.

7. **Target operating income.** An amount of operating income, either in dollars or as a percentage of sales, is frequently required.

   a. EXAMPLE: If units are sold at $6.00 and variable costs are $2.00, how many units must be sold to realize operating income of 15% ($6.00 × .15 = $.90 per unit) before taxes, given fixed costs of $37,500?

   $$Operating\ income\ =\ Sales - Variable\ costs - Fixed\ costs$$
   $$\$0.90 \times Q\ =\ (\$6.00 \times Q) - (\$2.00 \times Q) - \$37,500$$
   $$\$3.10Q\ =\ \$37,500$$
   $$Q\ =\ 12,097\ units$$

   1) Selling 12,097 units results in $72,582 of revenues. Variable costs are $24,194, and operating income is $10,888 ($72,582 × 15%). The proof is that variable costs of $24,194, plus fixed costs of $37,500, plus operating income of $10,888, equals $72,582 of sales.

   2) A variation of this problem asks for net income (an after-tax amount) instead of operating income (a pretax amount). In this case, the computation requires converting the **target net income** to **target operating income** by dividing the target net income by one minus the income tax rate. Income tax liability does not change the breakeven point because, at that output level, operating income and therefore income tax expense are zero. However, other taxes, such as sales tax, do change the breakeven point.

   3) Thus, to incorporate taxes into the calculation, the basic CVP formula is adjusted as follows:

   $$Sales\ =\ [Target\ net\ income\ \div\ (1\ -\ tax\ rate)]\ +\ Variable\ costs\ +$$
   $$Fixed\ costs$$

4) EXAMPLE: If variable costs are $1.20, fixed costs are $10,000, and selling price is $2, and the company targets a $5,000 after-tax profit when the tax rate is 30%, the calculation is as follows:

$$\$2Q = [\$5,000 \div (1 - .3)] + \$1.20Q + \$10,000$$
$$\$.8Q = \$7,142.86 + \$10,000$$
$$\$.8Q = \$17,142.86$$
$$Q = \$17,142.86 \div .8$$
$$Q = 21,428.575 \ units$$

a) If the company plans to sell 21,428.575 units at $2 each, revenue will be $42,857.15. The following is the pro forma income statement for the target net income:

Sales (21,428.575 × $2)	$ 42,857.15
Less: variable costs (21,428.575 × $1.20)	(25,714.29)
Contribution margin	$ 17,142.86
Less: fixed costs	(10,000.00)
Operating income	$ 7,142.86
Income taxes (30%)	(2,142.86)
Net income	$ 5,000.00

8. **Multiple products (or services)** may be involved in calculating a breakeven point.

a. EXAMPLE: A and B account for 60% and 40% of total sales, respectively. The variable costs of A and B are 60% and 85% of individual product sales, respectively. What is the breakeven point, given fixed costs of $150,000?

$$S = FC + VC$$
$$S = \$150,000 + .6(.6S) + .85(.4S)$$
$$S = \$150,000 + .36S + .34S$$
$$.30S = \$150,000$$
$$S = \$500,000$$

1) In effect, the result is obtained by calculating a weighted-average contribution margin ratio (100% − 36% − 34% = 30%) and dividing it into the fixed costs to arrive at the breakeven point in sales dollars.

2) Another approach to multiproduct breakeven problems is to divide fixed costs by the UCM for a composite unit (when unit prices are known) to determine the number of composite units. The number of individual units can then be calculated based on the stated mix.

a) EXAMPLE: If 150,000 units of X and 300,000 units of Y are expected to be sold, the composite unit consists of 1 unit of X and 2 units of Y. If X and Y have UCMs of $5 and $7, respectively, the composite UCM is $19 ($5 + $7 + $7). Dividing $19 into fixed costs gives the breakeven point in composite units. The units of X and Y equal the number of composite units and twice the number of composite units, respectively.

b) In a multiple product (or service) problem, the breakeven point in total units varies with the sales mix. The BEP in units will be lower (higher) when the proportion of high (low) CM items is greater. Thus, there is no unique breakeven point in multiple-product situations. The breakeven point depends upon the specific mix of products.

9. **Choice of product.** When resources are limited, a company may produce only a single product. A breakeven analysis of the point where the same operating income or loss will result, regardless of the product selected, is calculated by setting the breakeven formulas of the individual products equal to each other.

    a. EXAMPLE: Assume a lessor can rent property to either of two lessees. One lessee offers a rental fee of $100,000 per year plus 2% of revenues. The other lessee offers $20,000 per year plus 5% of revenues. The optimal solution depends on the level of revenues. A CPA may question at what level the lessor will be indifferent. The solution is to equate the two formulas as follows:

$$\$100,000 + .02R = \$20,000 + .05R$$
$$.03R = \$80,000$$
$$R = \$80,000 \div .03$$
$$R = \$2,666,667$$

If: R = revenues

    Thus, if revenues are expected to be less than $2,666,667, the lessor would prefer the larger fixed rental of $100,000 and the smaller variable rental.

10. Sometimes CVP analysis is applied to **special orders**. This application is essentially contribution margin analysis.

    a. EXAMPLE: What is the effect of accepting a special order for 10,000 units at $8.00, given the following operating data?

Gross Approach

		Per Unit
Sales		$12.50
Less: manufacturing costs		
Variable	$6.25	
Fixed	1.75	(8.00)
Gross profit		$ 4.50
Less: selling expenses		
Variable	$1.80	
Fixed	1.45	(3.25)
Operating income		$ 1.25

    1) Because the variable cost of manufacturing is $6.25, the UCM is $1.75 ($8.00 – $6.25), and the increase in operating income resulting from accepting the special order is $17,500 (10,000 units × $1.75).

    2) The assumptions are that idle capacity is sufficient to manufacture 10,000 extra units, that sale at $8.00 per unit will not affect the price or quantity of other units sold, and that no additional selling expenses are incurred.

11. The **degree of operating leverage (DOL)** is the change in operating income (earnings before interest and taxes) resulting from a percentage change in sales. It measures the extent to which a firm incurs fixed rather than variable costs in operations.

$$Operating\ leverage = \frac{Percentage\ change\ in\ operating\ income}{Percentage\ change\ in\ sales}$$

    a. The assumption is that companies with larger investments (and greater fixed costs) will have higher contribution margins and more operating leverage.

    1) Thus, as companies invest in better and more expensive equipment, their variable production costs should decrease.

    2) EXAMPLE: If sales increase by 40% and operating income increases by 50%, the operating leverage is 1.25 (50% ÷ 40%).

b.   Given that Q equals the number of units sold, P is unit price, VC is unit variable cost, and FC is fixed cost, the DOL can also be calculated from the formula below, which equals total contribution margin divided by operating income (total contribution margin minus fixed cost). This formula is derived from the operating leverage formula on the previous page, but the derivation procedure is not given.

$$\frac{Q(P - VC)}{Q(P - VC) - FC}$$

c.   The DOL is calculated with respect to a given base level of sales. The significance of the DOL is that a given percentage increase in sales yields a percentage increase in operating income equal to the DOL for the base sales level times the percentage increase in sales.

12.   Stop and review! You have completed the outline for this subunit. Study multiple-choice questions 32 through 51 beginning on page 581.

18.3 ABSORPTION (FULL) VS. VARIABLE (DIRECT) COSTING

1.   Under **absorption costing** (sometimes called full or full absorption costing), the fixed portion of manufacturing overhead is "absorbed" into the cost of each product.

a.   **Product cost** thus includes **all manufacturing costs, both fixed and variable**.

b.   Absorption-basis cost of goods sold is subtracted from sales to arrive at gross margin.

c.   Total selling and administrative expenses (i.e., fixed and variable) are then subtracted from gross margin to arrive at operating income.

d.   This method is **required under GAAP** for external reporting purposes **and under the Internal Revenue Code** for tax purposes. The justification is that, for external reporting, product cost should include all manufacturing costs.

2.   **Variable costing** (sometimes called direct costing) is more appropriate for internal reporting.

a.   The term "direct costing" is somewhat misleading because it suggests traceability, which is not what is meant in this context. "Variable costing" is more suitable.

b.   **Product cost** includes **only variable manufacturing costs**.

c.   Variable cost of goods sold and the variable portion of selling and administrative expenses are subtracted from gross margin to arrive at **contribution margin**.

1)   This figure (sales – total variable costs) is an important element of the variable costing income statement because it is the amount available for **covering fixed costs** (fixed manufacturing and fixed selling and administrative).

2)   For this reason, some accountants call the method **contribution margin reporting**.

3)   This is an important metric internally, but it is generally irrelevant to outside financial statement users.

3.   EXAMPLE: A firm, during its first month in business, produced 100 units and sold 80 while incurring the following costs:

Direct materials	$1,000
Direct labor	2,000
Variable overhead	1,500
Manufacturing costs used in variable costing	**$4,500**
Fixed overhead	3,000
Manufacturing costs used in absorption costing	**$7,500**

a.   The impact on the financial statements from using one method over the other can be seen in these calculations:

	Manufacturing costs	Divided by: Units produced	Equals: Per-unit cost	Times: Units in ending inventory	Equals: Value of ending inventory
Absorption basis	$7,500	100	$75	20	$1,500
Variable basis	$4,500	100	$45	20	$900

b.   The per-unit selling price of the finished goods was $100, and the company incurred $200 of variable selling and administrative expenses and $600 of fixed selling and administrative expenses.

c.   The following are partial income statements prepared using the two methods:

		Absorption Costing (Required under GAAP)	Variable Costing (For Internal Reporting Only)
	Sales	$ 8,000	$ 8,000
	Beginning inventory	$ 0	$ 0
Product Costs	Plus: variable production costs	4,500 (a)	4,500 (a)
	Plus: fixed production costs	3,000 (b)	
	Goods available for sale	$7,500	$4,500
	Less: ending inventory	(1,500)	(900)
	Cost of goods sold	$(6,000)	$(3,600)
	Less: variable S&A expenses		(200) (c)
	Gross margin (abs.) / Contribution margin (var.)	**$2,000**	**$4,200**
Period Costs	Less: fixed production costs		(3,000) (b)
	Less: variable S&A expenses	(200) (c)	
	Less: fixed S&A expenses	(600) (d)	(600) (d)
	Operating income	**$1,200**	**$ 600**

d.   The $600 difference in operating income ($1,200 – $600) is the difference between the two ending inventory values ($1,500 – $900).

1)   In essence, the absorption method treats 20% of the fixed overhead costs ($3,000 × 20% = $600) as an asset because 20% of the month's production (100 available – 80 sold = 20 on hand) is still in inventory.

4.   As production and sales levels change, the two methods have varying impacts on **operating income**.

a.   When **production and sales are equal** for a period, the two methods report the **same** operating income.

1)   Total fixed costs budgeted for the period are charged to sales revenue in the period under both methods.

b. When **production and sales are not equal** for a period, the two methods report **different** operating income.

   1) ILLUSTRATION:

When production	**When production**
△ △ △ △ △ △ △	△ △ △
exceeds sales,	**is less than sales,**
△ △ △	△ △ △ △ △ △ △
ending inventory expands.	**ending inventory contracts.**
↑↑↑↑↑↑↑↑↑↑↑↑↑↑↑	↓↓↓↓↓↓
Under absorption costing, some fixed costs are still embedded in ending inventory.	**Under absorption costing,** fixed costs embedded in beginning inventory have been expensed.
Under variable costing, all fixed costs have been expensed.	**Under variable costing,** only the current period's fixed costs are expensed.
Therefore,	Therefore,
operating income is higher under <u>absorption</u> costing.	**operating income is higher under <u>variable</u> costing.**

c. Under **absorption** costing, operating income **behaves erratically** and sometimes moves in the opposite direction from sales.

   1) Under **variable** costing, operating income always moves in the **same direction as sales volume**.

   2) Operating income differences tend to be larger when calculations are made for short periods. In the long run, the two methods will report the same total operating income if sales equal production.

      a) The inequalities between production and sales are usually minor over an extended period.

      b) Production cannot continually exceed sales because an enterprise cannot produce more than it can sell in the long run.

3) **EXTENDED EXAMPLE:** A company has the following sales and cost data:

	Year 1	Year 2	Year 3
Production in units	40,000	50,000	0
Sales in units	30,000	30,000	30,000
Ending inventory in units (FIFO)	10,000	30,000	0
Unit sales price	$1.00		
Unit variable cost	$0.50		
Fixed manufacturing costs	$4,000 per year		
Variable S&A expenses	$0.03333 per unit		
Fixed S&A expenses	$1,000 per year		

Compare the three-year income statements prepared under the two methods:

Absorption Costing (Required under GAAP)				Variable Costing (For Internal Reporting Only)			
	Year 1	Year 2	Year 3		Year 1	Year 2	Year 3
Sales	**$30,000**	**$30,000**	**$30,000**	**Sales**	**$30,000**	**$30,000**	**$30,000**
Beginning inventory	$ 0	$ 6,000	$17,400	Beginning inventory	$ 0	$ 5,000	$15,000
Variable mfg. costs	20,000	25,000	0	Variable mfg. costs	20,000	25,000	0
Fixed mfg. costs	4,000	4,000	4,000				
Goods available for sale	$24,000	$35,000	$21,400	Goods avail. for sale	$20,000	$30,000	$15,000
Less: ending inventory	(6,000)	(17,400)	0	Less: ending inventory	(5,000)	(15,000)	0
Absorption CGS	**$18,000**	**$17,600**	**$21,400**	**Variable CGS**	**$15,000**	**$15,000**	**$15,000**
				Variable S&A exps.	(1,000)	(1,000)	(1,000)
Gross margin	**$12,000**	**$12,400**	**$ 8,600**	**Contribution margin**	**$14,000**	**$14,000**	**$14,000**
				Fixed mfg. costs	(4,000)	(4,000)	(4,000)
Variable S&A expenses	(1,000)	(1,000)	(1,000)				
Fixed S&A expenses	(1,000)	(1,000)	(1,000)	Fixed S&A expenses	(1,000)	(1,000)	(1,000)
Operating income	**$10,000**	**$10,400**	**$ 6,600**	**Operating income**	**$ 9,000**	**$ 9,000**	**$ 9,000**

a) Note that, assuming zero inventory at the beginning of Year 1 and at the end of Year 3, the **total operating income for the 3-year period is the same** under either costing method.

	Absorption Costing	Variable Costing
Year 1	$10,000	$ 9,000
Year 2	10,400	9,000
Year 3	6,600	9,000
3-Year Total	**$27,000**	**$27,000**

b) Absorption costing shows a higher operating income than variable costing in Years 1 and 2 because fixed overhead has been capitalized and does not get expensed until Year 3.

i) Variable costing, on the other hand, treats fixed overhead as an expense of the period in which the cost is incurred.

ii) In Year 2, despite the same cash flow, there is a $1,400 difference between the final operating income figures and an even greater difference in Year 3.

c) If fixed costs increase relative to variable costs, the differences become more dramatic (here, 50% of the selling price is variable manufacturing cost, and fixed overhead is no more than 20% of the variable manufacturing cost).

5. **Benefits of Variable Costing for Internal Purposes**

    a.   Although the use of variable costing for financial statements is controversial, most agree about its superiority for internal reporting. It is far better suited than absorption costing to the needs of management. Management requires a knowledge of cost behavior under various operating conditions. For planning and control, management is more concerned with treating fixed and variable costs separately than with calculating full costs. Full costs are usually of dubious value because they contain arbitrary allocations of fixed cost.

        1)   Under variable costing, the cost data for **profit planning and decision making** are readily available from accounting records and statements. Reference to auxiliary records and supplementary analyses is not necessary.

        2)   For example, **cost-volume-profit relationships** and the effects of changes in sales volume on operating income can easily be computed from the income statement prepared under the variable costing concept, but not from the conventional absorption cost income statement based on the same data.

        3)   **Operating income or loss** reported under variable costing has a direct relationship to sales revenue and is not affected by inventory or production variations.

        4)   Absorption cost income statements may show decreases in operating income when **sales** are rising and increases in operating income when sales are decreasing, which may be confusing to management. Attempts at explanation by means of volume variances often compound rather than clarify the confusion.

        5)   If variable costing is used, the favorable **margin between selling prices and variable cost** should provide a constant reminder of the contribution margin forgone because of lack of sales volume. A favorable margin justifies a higher production level.

        6)   The **hidden impact** of fixed costs on operating income, when they are partially included in inventory measurements under absorption costing, is emphasized by the presentation of costs on an income statement prepared under variable costing.

        7)   Proponents of variable costing maintain that **fixed manufacturing overhead** is more closely correlated to **capacity to produce** than to the production of individual units.

        8)   Production **managers cannot manipulate operating income** by producing more or fewer products than needed during a period. Under absorption costing, a production manager could increase income simply by producing more units than are currently needed for sales.

b.   Variable costing is also preferred over absorption costing for **studies of relative profitability** of products, territories, and other segments of a business. It concentrates on the contribution that each segment makes to the recovery of fixed costs that will not be altered by decisions to make and sell.

1)   **Marginal analysis** leads to **better pricing**, the principal advantage of variable costing.

2)   **Out-of-pocket expenditures** required to manufacture products conform closely with the measurements of inventory.

3)   The relationship between operating income and the major factors of selling price, sales mix, sales volume, and variable manufacturing and nonmanufacturing costs is measured in terms of a **single index of profitability**.

   a)   This profitability index, expressed as a positive amount or as a ratio, facilitates the analysis of CVP relationships, compares the effects of two or more contemplated courses of action, and aids in answering many questions that arise in profit planning.

4)   **Inventory changes** have no effect on the **breakeven computations**.

5)   Marginal analysis facilitates appraisal of **products, territories, and other business segments** without having the results hidden or obscured by allocated joint fixed costs.

6)   Questions regarding whether a particular component should be **made or bought** can be more effectively answered if only variable costs are used.

   a)   Management must consider whether to charge the product being made only with variable costs or to charge a percentage of fixed costs as well.

   b)   Management must also consider whether making the component will require additional fixed costs and a decrease in normal production.

7)   **Disinvestment** decisions are facilitated because whether a product or department is recouping its variable costs can be determined.

   a)   If the variable costs are being covered, operating a department at an apparent loss may be profitable.

8)   Management is better able to **measure performance** by organizational subunits if certain fixed costs are omitted from the statements instead of being allocated arbitrarily.

9)   Costs are guided by **sales**.

   a)   Under variable costing, **cost of goods sold** varies directly with unit sales. The influence of production on operating income is avoided.

   b)   Variable costing also eliminates having to explain **over- or under-applied fixed manufacturing overhead** to higher management.

6.   Stop and review! You have completed the outline for this subunit. Study multiple-choice questions 52 through 78 beginning on page 587.

QUESTIONS

18.1 Cost Measurement Terminology

1. Which one of the following best describes direct labor?

A. A prime cost.

B. A period cost.

C. A product cost.

D. Both a product cost and a prime cost.

Answer (D) is correct. *(CMA, adapted)*
REQUIRED: The best description of direct labor.
DISCUSSION: Direct labor is both a product cost and a prime cost. Product costs are incurred to produce units of output and are deferred to future periods to the extent that output is not sold. Prime costs are the direct cost of manufacturing, for example, direct materials and direct labor.
Answer (A) is incorrect because direct labor is also a product cost. Answer (B) is incorrect because a period cost is expensed when incurred. Direct labor cost is inventoriable. Answer (C) is incorrect because direct labor is also a prime cost.

2. Inventoriable costs

A. Include only the prime costs of manufacturing a product.

B. Include only the conversion costs of manufacturing a product.

C. Are expensed when products become part of finished goods inventory.

D. Are regarded as assets before the products are sold.

Answer (D) is correct. *(CMA, adapted)*
REQUIRED: The true statement about inventoriable costs.
DISCUSSION: Inventoriable costs, also called product costs, are capitalized as part of finished goods inventory. Contrast this treatment with that of period costs, which are expensed as they are incurred and are not capitalized as assets. Under an absorption costing system, inventoriable costs include both variable and fixed costs of production; under variable costing, inventoriable costs include only variable production costs.
Answer (A) is incorrect because overhead costs as well as prime costs (direct materials and labor) are included in inventory. Answer (B) is incorrect because materials costs are also included. Answer (C) is incorrect because inventory costs are expensed when the goods are sold, not when they are transferred to finished goods.

3. The CPA reviewed the minutes of a board of director's meeting of LQR Corp., an audit client. An order for widget handles was outsourced to SDT Corp. because LQR couldn't fill the order. By having SDT produce the order, LQR was able to realize $100,000 in sales profits that otherwise would have been lost. The outsourcing added a cost of $10,000, but LQR was ahead by $90,000 when the order was completed. Which of the following statements is correct regarding LQR's action?

A. The use of resource markets outside of LQR involves opportunity cost.

B. Accounting profit is total revenue minus explicit costs and implicit costs.

C. Implicit costs are not opportunity costs because they are internal costs.

D. Explicit costs are opportunity costs from purchasing widget handles from a resource market.

Answer (A) is correct. *(CPA, adapted)*
REQUIRED: The true statement about an outsourcing transaction.
DISCUSSION: Opportunity cost is the maximum benefit forgone by using a scarce resource for a given purpose. It is the benefit, for example, the contribution to income, provided by the best alternative use of that resource. Thus, outsourcing involves opportunity cost. The outsourcer uses resources for purposes other than filling the order and therefore forgoes the benefits it would have received.
Answer (B) is incorrect because accounting profit is based on revenues and costs that are explicitly recognized. Answer (C) is incorrect because implicit costs are the opportunity costs of the use of the entity's resources. Answer (D) is incorrect because explicit costs result when an entity makes payments to obtain the use of resources. They are not opportunity costs.

4. In cost terminology, conversion costs consist of

A. Direct and indirect labor.

B. Direct labor and direct materials.

C. Direct labor and factory overhead.

D. Indirect labor and variable factory overhead.

Answer (C) is correct. *(CMA, adapted)*
REQUIRED: The components of conversion costs.
DISCUSSION: Conversion costs consist of direct labor and manufacturing overhead. These are the costs of converting raw materials into a finished product.
Answer (A) is incorrect because all manufacturing overhead is included in conversion costs, not just indirect labor.
Answer (B) is incorrect because direct materials are not an element of conversion costs; they are a prime cost. Answer (D) is incorrect because direct labor is also an element of conversion costs.

5. Which one of the following categories of cost is most likely not considered a component of fixed factory overhead?

A. Rent.

B. Property taxes.

C. Depreciation.

D. Power.

Answer (D) is correct.   *(CMA, adapted)*
REQUIRED: The item of cost most likely not considered a component of fixed factory overhead.
DISCUSSION: A fixed cost is one that remains unchanged within the relevant range for a given period despite fluctuations in activity. Such items as rent, property taxes, depreciation, and supervisory salaries are normally fixed costs because they do not vary with changes in production. Power costs, however, are at least partially variable because they increase as usage increases.
Answer (A) is incorrect because rent is an example of fixed factory overhead. Answer (B) is incorrect because property taxes are an example of fixed factory overhead. Answer (C) is incorrect because depreciation is an example of fixed factory overhead.

6. Which of the following types of costs are prime costs?

A. Direct materials and direct labor.

B. Direct materials and overhead.

C. Direct labor and overhead.

D. Direct materials, direct labor, and overhead.

Answer (A) is correct.   *(CPA, adapted)*
REQUIRED: The prime costs.
DISCUSSION: Prime costs include a manufacturer's direct costs, for example, direct materials and direct labor. However, as technology advances allow the identification of additional direct costs, categories other than direct materials and direct labor may be considered prime costs.
Answer (B) is incorrect because overhead is an indirect cost and a conversion cost. Answer (C) is incorrect because direct labor and overhead are conversion costs. Answer (D) is incorrect because direct labor and overhead are conversion costs.

7. Fab Co. manufactures textiles. Among Fab's manufacturing costs for the month just ended were the following salaries and wages:

Loom operators	$120,000
Factory foremen	45,000
Machine mechanics	30,000

What was the amount of Fab's direct labor for the month just ended?

A. $195,000

B. $165,000

C. $150,000

D. $120,000

Answer (D) is correct.   *(CPA, adapted)*
REQUIRED: The amount of direct labor.
DISCUSSION: Direct labor costs are wages paid to labor that can feasibly be specifically identified with the production of finished goods. Because the wages of loom operators are identifiable with the production of finished goods, the $120,000 wages are a direct labor cost. However, because the salaries and wages of the factory foremen and machine mechanics are not identifiable with the production of finished goods, the $45,000 and $30,000 are not direct labor costs. Thus, $120,000 is the amount of direct labor.
Answer (A) is incorrect because $195,000 includes the wages and salaries of machine mechanics and factory foremen. Answer (B) is incorrect because $165,000 includes the salary of factory foremen. Answer (C) is incorrect because $150,000 includes the wages of machine mechanics.

8. Following are Mill Co.'s production costs for the month just ended:

Direct materials	$100,000
Direct labor	90,000
Factory overhead	4,000

What amount of costs should be traced to specific products in the production process?

A. $194,000

B. $190,000

C. $100,000

D. $90,000

Answer (B) is correct.   *(CPA, adapted)*
REQUIRED: The amount of costs traceable to specific products.
DISCUSSION: Direct materials and direct labor can feasibly be identified with the production of specific goods. Factory overhead cannot be traced to a specific product but is allocated to all products produced. Thus, the amount of costs traceable to specific products in the production process equals $190,000 ($100,000 + $90,000).
Answer (A) is incorrect because $194,000 includes factory overhead. Answer (C) is incorrect because $100,000 excludes direct labor. Answer (D) is incorrect because $90,000 excludes direct materials.

Questions 9 through 11 are based on the following information. The following amounts pertain to Arp Co.'s manufacturing operations for March:

Inventories	3/1	3/31
Direct materials	$18,000	$15,000
Work-in-process	9,000	6,000
Finished goods	27,000	36,000

Additional information for the month of March:	
Direct materials purchased	$42,000
Direct labor payroll	30,000
Direct labor rate per hour	7.50
Factory overhead rate per direct labor hour	10.00

9. For the month of March, Arp's prime costs were

A. $75,000

B. $69,000

C. $45,000

D. $39,000

Answer (A) is correct. *(CPA, adapted)*
REQUIRED: The prime cost added to production.
DISCUSSION: Prime costs consist of direct materials and direct labor. Direct labor is given as $30,000. The direct materials must be determined from the change in direct materials inventory, a decrease of $3,000 ($18,000 – $15,000), plus the $42,000 of purchases, or $45,000. Accordingly, the prime costs total $75,000 ($30,000 + $45,000).
Answer (B) is incorrect because this amount reflects an increase, not a decrease, in the direct materials inventory of $3,000. Answer (C) is incorrect because $45,000 is the amount of direct materials used. Answer (D) is incorrect because $39,000 is the amount of direct materials used assuming an increase, not a decrease, of $3,000 in the direct materials inventory.

10. For the month of March, Arp's conversion costs were

A. $30,000

B. $40,000

C. $70,000

D. $72,000

Answer (C) is correct. *(CPA, adapted)*
REQUIRED: The conversion cost added to production.
DISCUSSION: Conversion cost consists of direct labor and overhead. Direct labor is given as $30,000. Factory overhead is applied at the rate of $10.00 per direct labor hour. Given 4,000 direct labor hours ($30,000 ÷ $7.50) incurred in March, at $10.00 per hour, $40,000 of overhead was applied. Thus, the conversion costs for March total $70,000 ($30,000 + $40,000).
Answer (A) is incorrect because $30,000 is the direct labor cost. Overhead must also be added. Answer (B) is incorrect because $40,000 is the overhead applied. Direct labor payroll must also be added. Answer (D) is incorrect because $72,000 is the sum of direct materials purchased ($42,000) and direct labor ($30,000).

11. For the month of March, Arp's cost of goods manufactured was

A. $118,000

B. $115,000

C. $112,000

D. $109,000

Answer (A) is correct. *(CPA, adapted)*
REQUIRED: The cost of goods manufactured.
DISCUSSION: Cost of goods manufactured is the sum of BWIP, direct materials used, direct labor incurred, and overhead applied, minus EWIP.

BWIP (given)	$ 9,000
Direct materials	45,000
Direct labor (given)	30,000
Overhead applied	40,000
Total costs incurred	$124,000
Minus EWIP (given)	(6,000)
Cost of goods manufactured	$118,000

Answer (B) is incorrect because $115,000 is the sum of direct materials, direct labor, and overhead. Answer (C) is incorrect because it reflects the addition of EWIP ($6,000) and the subtraction of BWIP ($9,000). Answer (D) is incorrect because it omits BWIP ($9,000) from the calculation.

12. Direct materials cost is a

	Conversion Cost	Prime Cost
A.	No	No
B.	No	Yes
C.	Yes	Yes
D.	Yes	No

Answer (B) is correct. *(CPA, adapted)*
REQUIRED: The classification of direct materials cost.
DISCUSSION: Direct materials are a manufacturing cost and a prime cost. Direct materials constitute directly identifiable elements of the manufacturing costs that are inventoried. Direct materials and direct labor are also prime costs. Conversion cost consists of direct labor and factory overhead but not direct materials (the direct materials are being converted).
Answer (A) is incorrect because direct materials cost is a prime cost. Answer (C) is incorrect because direct materials cost is not a conversion cost. Answer (D) is incorrect because direct materials cost is a prime cost but not a conversion cost.

13. Direct labor cost is a

	Conversion Cost	Prime Cost
A.	No	No
B.	No	Yes
C.	Yes	Yes
D.	Yes	No

Answer (C) is correct. *(CPA, adapted)*
REQUIRED: The nature of direct labor cost.
DISCUSSION: Prime costs are direct materials and direct labor. They are the directly identifiable elements of production costs and are directly traceable to the product. Conversion costs include direct labor and factory overhead. They are the costs of converting raw materials into products.
Answer (A) is incorrect because direct labor is both a conversion cost and a prime cost. Answer (B) is incorrect because direct labor is also a conversion cost. Answer (D) is incorrect because direct labor is also a prime cost.

14. Indirect labor is a

A. Prime cost.

B. Conversion cost.

C. Period cost.

D. Nonmanufacturing cost.

Answer (B) is correct. *(CPA, adapted)*
REQUIRED: The classification of indirect labor costs.
DISCUSSION: Conversion costs include direct labor and factory overhead. Because indirect labor is included in factory overhead, indirect labor is a conversion cost.
Answer (A) is incorrect because prime costs are direct materials and direct labor. Answer (C) is incorrect because period costs are usually not identifiable with a particular product. Answer (D) is incorrect because indirect labor constitutes a manufacturing cost.

15. An example of a direct labor cost is wages paid to a

	Factory Machine Operator	Supervisor in a Factory
A.	No	No
B.	No	Yes
C.	Yes	Yes
D.	Yes	No

Answer (D) is correct. *(CPA, adapted)*
REQUIRED: An example of a direct labor cost.
DISCUSSION: Direct labor costs are wages paid to labor that can be specifically identified with the production of finished goods. Because the wages of a factory machine operator are identifiable with a finished product, the wages are a direct labor cost. Because the supervisor's salary is not identifiable with the production of finished goods, it is a part of factory overhead and not a direct labor cost.

16. Wages earned by machine operators in producing the firm's product should be categorized as

	Direct Labor	Controllable by the Machine Operators' Supervisor
A.	Yes	Yes
B.	Yes	No
C.	No	Yes
D.	No	No

Answer (A) is correct. *(CPA, adapted)*
REQUIRED: The nature of machine operators' wages.
DISCUSSION: Direct labor costs are wages paid to labor that can be specifically identified with the production of finished goods. Because machine operators' wages are identifiable with the production of finished goods, the wages should be recognized as direct labor. The supervisor controls the productivity of the machine operators. Hence, the supervisor is responsible for their wages.

17. During the month just ended, Nale Co. used $300,000 of direct materials. At month end, Nale's direct materials inventory was $50,000 more than it was at the beginning of the month. Direct material purchases during the month amounted to

A. $0

B. $250,000

C. $300,000

D. $350,000

Answer (D) is correct. *(CPA, adapted)*
REQUIRED: The amount of direct material purchases for the month.
DISCUSSION: Direct materials costs are the costs of new materials included in finished goods which can be feasibly traced to those goods. The beginning direct materials inventory plus the direct material purchases minus ending direct materials inventory equals the direct materials used. Because the direct materials inventory increased during the month, the increase can be added to the direct materials used to yield the amount of purchases. Thus, the direct materials purchases for the month amount to $350,000 ($300,000 + $50,000).
Answer (A) is incorrect because direct materials must have been purchased if materials were used and the inventory increased. Answer (B) is incorrect because $250,000 subtracts the increase in direct materials inventory. Answer (C) is incorrect because $300,000 excludes the increase in direct materials inventory.

18. As required by GAAP, the fixed portion of the semivariable cost of electricity for a manufacturing plant is a

	Period Cost	Product Cost
A.	Yes	No
B.	Yes	Yes
C.	No	Yes
D.	No	No

Answer (C) is correct. *(CPA, adapted)*
REQUIRED: The classification(s) of fixed electricity cost for a manufacturer.
DISCUSSION: A product cost is inventoried. A period cost is expensed when incurred. Electricity costs are a part of manufacturing overhead. Manufacturing overhead is a product cost, not a period cost.

19. To identify costs that relate to a specific product, an allocation base should be chosen that

A. Does not have a cause-and-effect relationship.

B. Has a cause-and-effect relationship.

C. Considers variable costs but not fixed costs.

D. Considers direct materials and direct labor but not factory overhead.

Answer (B) is correct. *(CPA, adapted)*
REQUIRED: The allocation base that best identifies costs related to a specific product.
DISCUSSION: A cost allocation base is the means by which costs are allocated. The cost allocation base is some variable (activity) that has a strong correlation with the incurrence of cost by the cost objective. For example, direct labor hours is frequently used as a cost allocation base because indirect costs are often correlated with such activity.
Answer (A) is incorrect because random allocation will not lead to useful or relevant total cost analysis. Answer (C) is incorrect because some fixed costs are product costs. Answer (D) is incorrect because factory overhead is a product cost.

20. Gram Co. develops computer programs to meet customers' special requirements. How should Gram categorize payments to employees who develop these programs?

	Direct Costs	Value-Adding Costs
A.	Yes	Yes
B.	Yes	No
C.	No	No
D.	No	Yes

Answer (A) is correct. *(CPA, adapted)*
REQUIRED: The proper categorization of costs.
DISCUSSION: Direct costs may be defined as those that can be specifically associated with a single cost object and can be assigned to it in an economically feasible manner. Wages paid to labor that can be identified with a specific finished good are direct costs. Value-adding costs may be defined as the costs of activities that cannot be eliminated without reducing the quality, responsiveness, or quantity of the output required by a customer or by an organization. Clearly, the amounts paid to programmers add value to computer programs.
Answer (B) is incorrect because the activities performed by programmers add value to computer programs. Therefore, the payments to employees who develop these programs is considered a value-adding cost. Answer (C) is incorrect because payments to programmers are both direct costs and value-adding costs of computer programs. Answer (D) is incorrect because wages paid to labor that can be identified with a specific finished good are direct costs. Therefore, payments to employees who develop computer programs is a direct cost.

21. The following information pertains to the manufacturing activities of Griss Co. during the month just ended:

Beginning work-in-process (BWIP)	$12,000
Ending work-in-process (EWIP)	10,000
Cost of goods manufactured (CGM)	97,000
Direct materials issued to production	20,000

Factory overhead is assigned at 150% of direct labor. What was the direct labor cost incurred?

A. $30,000

B. $30,800

C. $45,000

D. $50,000

Answer (A) is correct. *(CPA, adapted)*
REQUIRED: The direct labor cost.
DISCUSSION: CGM equals BWIP, plus all manufacturing costs incurred during the period (direct labor, direct materials, and factory overhead), minus EWIP. Thus, the following formula may be used to calculate direct labor:

$$\$97,000 = \$12,000 + DL + \$20,000 + 1.5DL - \$10,000$$
$$2.5DL = \$75,000$$
$$DL = \$30,000$$

Answer (B) is incorrect because $30,800 results from ignoring BWIP and EWIP. Answer (C) is incorrect because $45,000 equals factory overhead assigned. Answer (D) is incorrect because $50,000 equals $75,000 divided by 1.5.

22. Day Mail Order Co. applied the high-low method of cost estimation to customer order data for the first 4 months of the current year. What is the estimated variable order-filling cost component per order?

Month	No. of Orders	Cost
January	1,200	$ 3,120
February	1,300	3,185
March	1,800	4,320
April	1,700	3,895
	6,000	$14,520

A. $2.00

B. $2.42

C. $2.48

D. $2.50

Answer (A) is correct. *(CPA, adapted)*
REQUIRED: The estimated variable order-filling cost.
DISCUSSION: The high-low method estimates unit variable cost by dividing the difference in costs at the highest and lowest levels of activity by the differences in activity. The difference between the highest and lowest amounts of orders was 600 (1,800 − 1,200). Given a cost differential of $1,200 ($4,320 − $3,120), the estimated unit variable cost is $2.00 ($1,200 ÷ 600).
Answer (B) is incorrect because $2.42 is the total cost per unit ($14,520 ÷ 6,000). Answer (C) is incorrect because $2.48 equals the sum of the highest cost and the lowest cost ($7,440) divided by the sum of highest orders and lowest orders. Answer (D) is incorrect because $2.50 equals the average of the per-order cost of the high and low costs.

23. Clay Co. has considerable excess manufacturing capacity. A special job order's cost sheet includes the following applied manufacturing overhead costs:

Fixed costs	$21,000
Variable costs	33,000

The fixed costs include a normal $3,700 allocation for in-house design costs, although no in-house design will be done. Instead, the job will require the use of external designers costing $7,750. What is the total amount to be included in the calculation to determine the minimum acceptable price for the job?

A. $36,700

B. $40,750

C. $54,000

D. $58,050

Answer (B) is correct. *(CPA, adapted)*
REQUIRED: The total amount to be included in the calculation to determine the minimum acceptable price.
DISCUSSION: Given excess capacity, the company presumably will not incur opportunity costs if it accepts the special order. Assuming also that fixed costs will be unaffected, the incremental cost of the order (the minimum acceptable price) will be $40,750 ($33,000 VC + $7,750 cost of external design).
Answer (A) is incorrect because $36,700 equals variable costs plus the in-house design costs. Answer (C) is incorrect because $54,000 equals the fixed costs plus the variable costs. Answer (D) is incorrect because $58,050 equals the fixed costs, plus the variable costs, minus the in-house design costs, plus the external design costs.

24. When only differential manufacturing costs are taken into account for special-order pricing, an essential assumption is that

A. Manufacturing fixed and variable costs are linear.

B. Selling and administrative fixed and variable costs are linear.

C. Acceptance of the order will not affect regular sales.

D. Acceptance of the order will not cause unit selling and administrative variable costs to increase.

Answer (C) is correct. *(CPA, adapted)*
REQUIRED: The essential assumption when only differential manufacturing costs are taken into account for special-order pricing.
DISCUSSION: Granting a lower-than-normal price for a special order has potential ramifications for regular sales because other customers may demand the same price. Thus, the decision to consider only differential manufacturing costs should be based on a determination that all other costs are not relevant, that is, that these other costs do not vary with the option chosen.
Answer (A) is incorrect because manufacturing costs need not be linear. The differential analysis of a special order considers total marginal costs. Consequently, the unit variable costs and total fixed costs need not be constant, and any changes need not be in direct proportion to the measure of activity. Answer (B) is incorrect because the assumption is that selling and administrative costs are not relevant. Hence, whether they are linear is deemed to be of no concern. Answer (D) is incorrect because the assumption is that acceptance of the order will not cause total selling and administrative costs to change.

25. Buff Co. is considering replacing an old machine with a new machine. Which of the following items is economically relevant to Buff's decision? (Ignore income tax considerations.)

	Carrying Amount of Old Machine	Disposal Value of New Machine
A.	Yes	No
B.	No	Yes
C.	No	No
D.	Yes	Yes

Answer (B) is correct. *(CPA, adapted)*
REQUIRED: The relevant costs.
DISCUSSION: In a make-or-buy or replacement decision, the manager considers only the costs relevant to the investment decision. The key variable is relevant costs, not total costs. Past costs, including the book value of old equipment, are irrelevant because they are sunk costs. However, opportunity costs, disposal values of new equipment, and the fair value of an old machine are all economically relevant costs.

26. Mili Co. plans to discontinue a division with a $20,000 contribution to overhead. Overhead allocated to the division is $50,000, of which $5,000 cannot be eliminated. The effect of this discontinuance on Mili's pretax income would be an increase of

A. $5,000

B. $20,000

C. $25,000

D. $30,000

Answer (C) is correct. *(CPA, adapted)*
REQUIRED: The effect of discontinuing a division.
DISCUSSION: This disinvestment decision will eliminate $45,000 of overhead ($50,000 – $5,000) and the division's $20,000 contribution to overhead. The net effect on the company's pretax income is therefore a $25,000 increase ($45,000 – $20,000).
Answer (A) is incorrect because $5,000 is the overhead allocated to the division which cannot be eliminated. The net effect is a $25,000 increase on the company's pretax income ($45,000 overhead which can be eliminated – $20,000 contribution to overhead by the division). Answer (B) is incorrect because $20,000 is the division's contribution to overhead. Answer (D) is incorrect because the $5,000 of overhead that cannot be eliminated from the $50,000 overhead allocated to the division should be deducted.

27. A decrease in production levels within a relevant range

A. Decreases variable cost per unit.

B. Decreases total costs.

C. Increases total fixed costs.

D. Increases variable cost per unit.

Answer (B) is correct. *(CPA, adapted)*
REQUIRED: The effect on unit and total costs when production declines.
DISCUSSION: When production levels decrease within a relevant range, the total costs will decrease. Although the total fixed costs will remain constant, fixed costs per unit will increase because fewer units are available to absorb the constant amount of total fixed costs. Furthermore, total variable costs decrease assuming the unit variable costs remain constant.
Answer (A) is incorrect because variable costs per unit are assumed to remain constant. Answer (C) is incorrect because total fixed costs are assumed to remain constant. Answer (D) is incorrect because variable costs per unit are assumed to remain constant.

28. Which one of the following alternatives appropriately classifies the business application to the appropriate costing system?

	Job Costing System	Process Costing System
A.	Wallpaper manufacturer	Oil refinery
B.	Aircraft assembly	Public accounting firm
C.	Paint manufacturer	Retail banking
D.	Print shop	Beverage manufacturer

Answer (D) is correct. *(CMA, adapted)*
REQUIRED: The appropriate matching of business applications with costing systems.
DISCUSSION: A job costing system is used when products differ from one customer to the next, that is, when products are heterogeneous. A process costing system is used when similar products are mass produced on a continuous basis. A print shop, for example, would use a job costing system because each job will be unique. Each customer provides the specifications for the product desired. A beverage manufacturer, however, would use a process costing system because homogeneous units are produced continuously.
Answer (A) is incorrect because a wallpaper manufacturer would use a process costing system. Answer (B) is incorrect because a public accounting firm would use a job costing system. Answer (C) is incorrect because a paint manufacturer would use a process costing system.

29. For the year just ended, Abel Co. incurred direct costs of $500,000 based on a particular course of action during the year. If a different course of action had been taken, direct costs would have been $400,000. In addition, Abel's fixed costs were $90,000. The incremental cost was

A. $10,000
B. $90,000
C. $100,000
D. $190,000

Answer (C) is correct. *(CPA, adapted)*
REQUIRED: The incremental cost.
DISCUSSION: Incremental cost analysis is typically used in make-or-buy, special-order, and disinvestment decisions. The analysis considers only additional relevant costs, such as direct labor, direct materials, and variable overhead. Thus, Abel's incremental cost is $100,000 ($500,000 – $400,000). The fixed costs of $90,000 are not relevant.
Answer (A) is incorrect because $10,000 subtracts the fixed costs. Answer (B) is incorrect because $90,000 equals the fixed costs. Answer (D) is incorrect because $190,000 adds the fixed costs.

30. Which one of the following is correct regarding a relevant range?

A. Total variable costs will not change.
B. Total fixed costs will not change.
C. Actual fixed costs usually fall outside the relevant range.
D. The relevant range cannot be changed after being established.

Answer (B) is correct. *(CMA, adapted)*
REQUIRED: The true statement about a relevant range.
DISCUSSION: The relevant range is the range of activity over which unit variable costs and total fixed costs are constant. The incremental cost of one additional unit of production will be equal to the variable cost.
Answer (A) is incorrect because variable costs will change in total, but unit variable costs will be constant. Answer (C) is incorrect because actual fixed costs should not vary greatly from budgeted fixed costs for the relevant range. Answer (D) is incorrect because the relevant range can change whenever production activity changes; the relevant range is merely an assumption used for budgeting and control purposes.

31. Which of the following is assigned to goods that were either purchased or manufactured for resale?

A. Relevant cost.
B. Period cost.
C. Opportunity cost.
D. Product cost.

Answer (D) is correct. *(CPA, adapted)*
REQUIRED: The cost assigned to goods that were either purchased or manufactured for resale.
DISCUSSION: Product cost includes the direct materials, direct labor, and overhead allocated to units of output manufactured for resale. Product cost also may be the costs of goods purchased for resale. Moreover, product cost may be defined as the costs assigned for a given purpose, for example, the costs specified by a cost-plus contract or that are required to be reported under GAAP.
Answer (A) is incorrect because relevant costs are expected future costs that vary with the action taken. Answer (B) is incorrect because period costs are not inventoriable. They are not sufficiently identifiable with specific production. Answer (C) is incorrect because an opportunity cost is the maximum benefit forgone by using a scarce resource for a given purpose.

18.2 Cost-Volume-Profit (CVP) Analysis

32. The breakeven point in units increases when unit costs

A. Increase and sales price remains unchanged.

B. Decrease and sales price remains unchanged.

C. Remain unchanged and sales price increases.

D. Decrease and sales price increases.

Answer (A) is correct. *(CMA, adapted)*
REQUIRED: The event that causes the breakeven point in units to increase.
DISCUSSION: The breakeven point in units is calculated by dividing the fixed costs by the contribution margin per unit. If selling price is constant and costs increase, the unit contribution margin will decline, resulting in an increase of the breakeven point.
Answer (B) is incorrect because a decrease in costs will lower the breakeven point. The unit contribution margin will increase. Answer (C) is incorrect because an increase in the selling price will also increase the unit contribution margin, resulting in a lower breakeven point. Answer (D) is incorrect because both a cost decrease and a sales price increase will increase the unit contribution margin, resulting in a lower breakeven point.

33. For a profitable company, the amount by which sales can decline before losses occur is known as the

A. Sales volume variance.

B. Hurdle rate.

C. Variable sales ratio.

D. Margin of safety.

Answer (D) is correct. *(CMA, adapted)*
REQUIRED: The amount by which sales can decline before losses occur.
DISCUSSION: The margin of safety measures the amount by which sales may decline before losses occur. It equals budgeted or actual sales minus sales at the BEP. It may be stated in either units sold or sales revenue.
Answer (A) is incorrect because the sales quantity (volume) variance focuses on the firm's aggregate results. It assumes a constant product mix and an average contribution margin for the composite unit. The sales volume variance equals the budgeted average UCM calculated for the composite unit multiplied by the difference between the actual and budgeted unit sales. Answer (B) is incorrect because it is the rate of return a potential investment must earn before it is acceptable to management. Answer (C) is incorrect because it is a nonsense term.

34. Rodder, Inc. manufactures a component in a router assembly. The selling price and unit cost data for the component are as follows:

Selling price	$15
Direct materials cost	3
Direct labor cost	3
Variable overhead cost	3
Fixed manufacturing overhead cost	2
Fixed selling and administration cost	1

The company received a special one-time order for 1,000 components. Rodder has an alternative use for production capacity for the 1,000 components that would produce a contribution margin of $5,000. What amount is the lowest unit price Rodder should accept for the component?

A. $9

B. $12

C. $14

D. $24

Answer (C) is correct. *(CPA, adapted)*
REQUIRED: The lowest acceptable unit price for a special order.
DISCUSSION: The entity should apply relevant costing and contribution margin (revenue – variable cost) analysis. It presumably has two uses for the production capacity needed to make 1,000 components: (1) the special order or (2) an alternative with a unit contribution margin (UCM) of $5 ($5,000 CM ÷ 1,000 units). The fixed costs are not relevant to the choice between the two uses because they will be incurred in either case. Thus, the relevant cost is the unit variable cost ($3 *DM* + $3 *DL* + $3 *VOH* = $9). The unit price at which the entity will be indifferent between the two uses is therefore $14 ($9 unit variable cost + $5 UCM for the alternative to the special order).
Answer (A) is incorrect because $9 is the variable cost per unit. Answer (B) is incorrect because $12 is the total cost (fixed and variable) per unit. Answer (D) is incorrect because $24 equals the $9 variable cost per unit plus the $15 regular selling price per unit.

Questions 35 through 38 are based on the following information. Oradell Company sells its single product at a price of $60 per unit and incurs the following variable costs per unit of product:

Direct material	$16
Direct labor	12
Manufacturing overhead	7
Total variable manufacturing costs	$35
Selling expenses	5
Total variable costs	$40

Oradell's annual fixed costs are $880,000, and Oradell is subject to a 30% income tax rate.

35. A production and sales volume of 4,000 units of product per month would result in an annual after-tax income (loss) for Oradell Company of

A. $80,000

B. $(800,000)

C. $56,000

D. $(560,000)

Answer (C) is correct. *(CMA, adapted)*
REQUIRED: The annual after-tax income for a given sales volume.
DISCUSSION: The income statement for a volume of 48,000 units (4,000 per month × 12 months) would appear as follows.

Sales ($60/unit)	$2,880,000
Variable manufacturing ($35/unit)	(1,680,000)
Variable selling ($5/unit)	(240,000)
Contribution margin	$ 960,000
Fixed costs	(880,000)
Income before tax	$ 80,000
Tax expense (30%)	(24,000)
Net income	$ 56,000

Answer (A) is incorrect because $80,000 is the income before the tax expense of $24,000 ($80,000 × 30%). Answer (B) is incorrect because ($800,000) is the loss that would result if sales volume per year (instead of per month) were 4,000 units. Answer (D) is incorrect because a $560,000 loss would result if sales volume per year were 4,000 units, and the resulting $(800,000) loss was reduced for the tax savings of $240,000 ($800,000 × 30%).

36. The annual sales revenue required by Oradell Company in order to achieve after-tax net income of $224,000 for the year is

A. $3,600,000

B. $3,312,000

C. $1,656,000

D. $3,110,400

Answer (A) is correct. *(CMA, adapted)*
REQUIRED: The annual sales revenue needed to achieve a given after-tax net income.
DISCUSSION: The required after-tax net income of $224,000 is equal to 70% (the complement of the tax rate) of before-tax income. Thus, before-tax income must equal $320,000 ($224,000 ÷ .7), and taxes are $96,000. If sales equal $60 times X units and variable costs are $40 times X units, the following is the equation to solve for units sold (X):

$$\$60X - \$40X - \$880,000 - \$96,000 = \$224,000$$
$$\$20X = \$1,200,000$$
$$X = 60,000 \; units$$

At a unit selling price of $60, the total revenue is $3,600,000 (60,000 units × $60).
Answer (B) is incorrect because $3,312,000 is the annual sales revenue that results when the $96,000 of income tax is ignored. Answer (C) is incorrect because $1,656,000 is the annual sales revenue when the $96,000 of income tax is ignored and the sum of the fixed costs and net income ($1,104,000 = $880,000 *fixed costs* + $224,000 *net income*) is divided by the variable unit cost of $40 (instead of the contribution margin of $20). Answer (D) is incorrect because $3,110,400 is the annual sales revenue when the $96,000 of income is subtracted from (instead of added to) the $224,000.

37. The number of units of product that Oradell Company must sell annually to break even is

    A. 22,000 units.

    B. 44,000 units.

    C. 35,200 units.

    D. 30,800 units.

Answer (B) is correct. *(CMA, adapted)*
    REQUIRED: The breakeven point in units.
    DISCUSSION: The breakeven point in units equals fixed costs divided by the contribution margin per unit. At a selling price of $60 per unit and with variable costs of $40 per unit, the unit contribution margin is $20. Thus, the breakeven point is 44,000 units ($880,000 ÷ $20).
    Answer (A) is incorrect because 22,000 units is fixed costs ($880,000) divided by variable costs ($40). Answer (C) is incorrect because the contribution margin should reflect selling expenses. Answer (D) is incorrect because there are no income taxes at the breakeven point.

38. If prime costs increased by 20% and all other values remained the same, Oradell Company's contribution margin (to the nearest whole percent) would be

    A. .30

    B. .76

    C. .20

    D. .24

Answer (D) is correct. *(CMA, adapted)*
    REQUIRED: The contribution margin ratio after an increase in prime costs.
    DISCUSSION: Prime costs are direct materials and direct labor. Because these two elements totaled $28 ($16 + $12) before the increase, the new total is $33.60 ($28 × 1.2). In other words, prime costs increase by $5.60, and total variable costs increase to $45.60. Subtracting $45.60 from the $60 selling price leaves a contribution margin of $14.40. The contribution margin percentage thus becomes 24% ($14.40 ÷ $60).
    Answer (A) is incorrect because 30% is the contribution margin percentage that results from including manufacturing overhead as a prime cost. Answer (B) is incorrect because 76% is the contribution margin percentage that results from dividing total variable costs by the sales price ($45.60 ÷ 60). Answer (C) is incorrect because 20% is the contribution margin percentage that results from treating all variable costs as prime costs.

39. The breakeven point in units sold for Tierson Corporation is 44,000. If fixed costs for Tierson are equal to $880,000 annually and variable costs are $10 per unit, what is the contribution margin per unit for Tierson Corporation?

    A. $0.05

    B. $20.00

    C. $44.00

    D. $88.00

Answer (B) is correct. *(Publisher, adapted)*
    REQUIRED: The contribution margin per unit.
    DISCUSSION: The breakeven point in units is equal to the fixed costs divided by the contribution margin per unit. Thus, 44,000 = $880,000 ÷ *CM*, or CM = $20.
    Answer (A) is incorrect because $.05 results from inverting the numerator and denominator in the calculation. Answer (C) is incorrect because $44.00 results from using variable cost as part of the calculation. Answer (D) is incorrect because $88.00 results from dividing by an erroneous denominator.

40. Stuffed Animals, Inc. has decided to focus strictly on producing and selling one type of teddy bear. For the upcoming year, Stuffed Animals, Inc. hopes to make a 25% profit on sales. Fixed costs are set at $51,000, and variable costs are $9.50 per unit. If teddy bears are sold at $15 each, how many bears must be sold to meet the profit goal?

    A. 5,514

    B. 9,273

    C. 13,600

    D. 29,143

Answer (D) is correct. *(Publisher, adapted)*
    REQUIRED: The number of bears that must be sold to yield a profit equal to a specified percentage of sales.
    DISCUSSION: Sales equals the sum of fixed costs, variable costs, and total profit. The unit profit is the selling price of the good multiplied by the percentage profit that is desired. Thus,

$$\$15x = \$51,000 + \$9.50x + .25(\$15x), \text{ or}$$
$$\$15x = \$51,000 + \$13.25x, \text{ or}$$
$$\$1.75x = \$51,000, \text{ or}$$
$$x = 29,143 \text{ bears}$$

A trial-and-error approach could also be used to solve this problem by preparing an income statement for each of the four alternative production levels.
    Answer (A) is incorrect because 5,514 results from adding the profit margin to the contribution margin. Answer (B) is incorrect because 9,273 is the breakeven point. Answer (C) is incorrect because 13,600 results from using profit as the contribution margin.

41. Lake Co. has just increased its direct labor wage rates. All other budgeted costs and revenues were unchanged. How did this increase affect Lake's budgeted breakeven point and budgeted margin of safety?

	Budgeted Breakeven Point	Budgeted Margin of Safety
A.	Increase	Increase
B.	Increase	Decrease
C.	Decrease	Decrease
D.	Decrease	Increase

Answer (B) is correct.   *(CPA, adapted)*
REQUIRED: The effect on the breakeven point and margin of safety of an increase in direct labor cost.
DISCUSSION: The BEP is the sales volume at which total revenue equals total cost. The margin of safety is the excess of budgeted sales over the breakeven volume. Given that all other costs and revenues are constant, an increase in direct labor cost will increase the BEP and decrease the margin of safety.
Answer (A) is incorrect because the margin of safety will decrease. Answer (C) is incorrect because the BEP will increase. Answer (D) is incorrect because the BEP will increase and the margin of safety will decrease.

42. The following information pertains to Sisk Co.:

Sales (25,000 units)	$500,000
Direct materials and direct labor	150,000
Factory overhead:	
Variable	20,000
Fixed	35,000
Selling and general expenses:	
Variable	5,000
Fixed	30,000

Sisk's breakeven point in number of units is

A. 4,924

B. 5,000

C. 6,250

D. 9,286

Answer (B) is correct.   *(CPA, adapted)*
REQUIRED: The breakeven point in units.
DISCUSSION: The breakeven point in units is equal to the fixed costs divided by the unit contribution margin (UCM). The fixed costs are $65,000 ($35,000 + $30,000). The UCM equals unit sales price ($500,000 *sales* ÷ 25,000 *units* = $20) minus unit variable cost [($150,000 *DM and DL* + $20,000 *VOH* + $5,000 *VS&G*) ÷ 25,000 *units* = $7]. Thus, the breakeven point in units is 5,000 ($65,000 ÷ $13).
Answer (A) is incorrect because 4,924 does not include the variable selling and general expenses in the unit contribution margin calculation. Answer (C) is incorrect because 6,250 includes the unit fixed factory overhead and unit fixed selling and general expenses in the unit contribution margin. Answer (D) is incorrect because 9,286 results from using the total variable costs of $7 rather than the contribution margin of $13.

43. The following information pertains to Syl Co.:

Sales	$800,000
Variable costs	160,000
Fixed costs	40,000

What is Syl's breakeven point in sales dollars?

A. $200,000

B. $160,000

C. $50,000

D. $40,000

Answer (C) is correct.   *(CPA, adapted)*
REQUIRED: The breakeven point in sales dollars.
DISCUSSION: The breakeven point in sales dollars is the fixed costs divided by the contribution margin ratio. Variable costs equal 20% of sales ($160,000 ÷ $800,000). Hence, the contribution margin ratio is 80%, and the breakeven point in dollars is $50,000 ($40,000 FC ÷ 80%).
Answer (A) is incorrect because $200,000 is the sum of FC and VC at the $800,000 sales level. Answer (B) is incorrect because $160,000 is VC at $800,000 sales level. Answer (D) is incorrect because $40,000 is FC.

44. During Year 1, Thor Lab supplied hospitals with a comprehensive diagnostic kit for $120. At a volume of 80,000 kits, Thor had fixed costs of $1 million and a profit before income taxes of $200,000. Because of an adverse legal decision, Thor's Year 2 liability insurance increased by $1.2 million over Year 1. Assuming the volume and other costs are unchanged, what should the Year 2 price be if Thor is to make the same $200,000 profit before income taxes?

A. $120.00

B. $135.00

C. $150.00

D. $240.00

Answer (B) is correct.   *(CPA, adapted)*
REQUIRED: The price charged to earn a specified pretax profit.
DISCUSSION: Assuming the volume and other costs are unchanged, Thor wishes to earn a pretax profit of $200,000 after a $1.2 million increase in fixed costs. One approach is to treat the pretax profit as a fixed cost and to apply the formula for the breakeven unit volume (*unit volume = fixed costs ÷ unit contribution margin*). Accordingly, unit variable cost is $105 [80,000 *units* = ($1,000,000 *FC* + $200,000 *pretax profit*) ÷ ($120 *unit price for Year 1 – unit VC*)], and Year 2 unit price is $135 [80,000 *units* = ($1,000,000 *FC* + $1,200,000 *FC* + $200,000 *pretax profit*) ÷ (*Year 2 unit price* – $105)].
Answer (A) is incorrect because $120.00 was the Year 1 unit price. Answer (C) is incorrect because $150.00 assumes that the unit variable cost is $120. Answer (D) is incorrect because $240.00 assumes that the price must double, given that the sum of fixed costs and targeted profit has doubled.

45. Breakeven analysis assumes that, over the relevant range,

A. Total fixed costs are nonlinear.

B. Total costs are unchanged.

C. Unit variable costs are unchanged.

D. Unit revenues are nonlinear.

Answer (C) is correct. *(CPA, adapted)*
REQUIRED: The assumption underlying breakeven analysis.
DISCUSSION: Breakeven analysis assumes that unit selling price and unit variable costs are constant within the relevant range. It further assumes that costs and revenues are linear. Thus, total variable costs vary directly with output.
Answer (A) is incorrect because costs are linear. Answer (B) is incorrect because total costs vary with production level. Answer (D) is incorrect because revenues are linear.

46. Del Co. has fixed costs of $100,000 and breakeven sales of $800,000. What is its projected profit at $1,200,000 sales?

A. $50,000

B. $150,000

C. $200,000

D. $400,000

Answer (A) is correct. *(CPA, adapted)*
REQUIRED: The projected profit at a given sales level.
DISCUSSION: Del's variable costs are 87.5% of sales [($800,000 breakeven sales – $100,000 fixed costs) ÷ $800,000 breakeven sales]. At sales of $1,200,000, variable costs are $1,050,000 and fixed costs are $100,000. Thus, profit is $50,000 ($1,200,000 – $1,050,000 – $100,000).
Answer (B) is incorrect because $150,000 is the contribution margin. Answer (C) is incorrect because $200,000 is the profit of $50,000 plus a contribution margin of $150,000. Answer (D) is incorrect because $400,000 results from subtracting the breakeven amount from total projected sales.

47. Based on potential sales of 500 units per year, a new product has estimated traceable costs of $990,000. What is the target price to obtain a 15% profit margin on sales?

A. $2,329

B. $2,277

C. $1,980

D. $1,935

Answer (A) is correct. *(CPA, adapted)*
REQUIRED: The target price.
DISCUSSION: Costs of the product must be 85% of sales to achieve a 15% profit on sales. Hence, sales must be $1,164,706 ($990,000 ÷ .85). The price per unit is $2,329 ($1,164,706 ÷ 500).
Answer (B) is incorrect because $2,277 results from multiplying $990,000 by 1.15 and dividing by 500 units. Answer (C) is incorrect because $1,980 is the cost per unit. Answer (D) is incorrect because $1,935 is 85% of $2,277.

48. The following information is taken from Wampler Co.'s current-year contribution income statement:

Sales	$200,000
Contribution margin	120,000
Fixed costs	90,000
Income taxes	12,000

What was Wampler's margin of safety?

A. $50,000

B. $150,000

C. $168,000

D. $182,000

Answer (A) is correct. *(CPA, adapted)*
REQUIRED: The margin of safety.
DISCUSSION: The margin of safety is the excess of sales over breakeven sales. Thus, income taxes are not relevant because the margin of safety is a pretax amount. Sales are given ($200,000). Breakeven sales equal fixed costs divided by the contribution margin ratio (contribution margin ÷ sales). Hence, breakeven sales equal $150,000 [$90,000 FC ÷ ($120,000 CM ÷ $200,000 sales)], and the margin of safety is $50,000 ($200,000 sales – $150,000 BE sales).
Answer (B) is incorrect because $150,000 equals breakeven sales. Answer (C) is incorrect because breakeven sales do not equal $32,000. Answer (D) is incorrect because breakeven sales do not equal $18,000.

49. At annual sales of $900,000, the Ebo product has the following unit sales price and costs:

Sales price	$20
Prime cost	6
Manufacturing overhead	
Variable	1
Fixed	7
Selling & admin. costs	
Variable	1
Fixed	3
Total costs	18
Profit	$ 2

What is Ebo's breakeven point in units?

A. 25,000

B. 31,500

C. 37,500

D. 45,000

Answer (C) is correct.   *(CPA, adapted)*
   REQUIRED: The breakeven point in units.
   DISCUSSION: The breakeven point in units is equal to the fixed costs divided by the unit contribution margin (UCM). The fixed costs are $450,000 [(45,000 units × ($7 FOH + $3 FS&A). The UCM equals unit sales price minus unit variable cost or $12 ($20 – $6 – $1 – $1). Thus, the breakeven point in units is 37,500 ($450,000 ÷ $12).
   Answer (A) is incorrect because 25,000 does not include the prime cost in variable expenses for the calculation of the unit contribution margin. Prime cost is direct labor plus direct materials. Answer (B) is incorrect because the breakeven point is calculated by dividing fixed costs by the unit contribution margin. The unit contribution margin is the unit selling price minus the unit variable cost. Answer (D) is incorrect because dividing the fixed costs of $450,000 by the unit fixed costs of $10 ($7 FOH + $3 FS&A) does not equal the breakeven point.

50. When an organization is operating above the breakeven point, the degree or amount that sales may decline before losses are incurred is called the

A. Residual income rate.

B. Marginal rate of return.

C. Margin of safety.

D. Target (hurdle) rate of return.

Answer (C) is correct.   *(CMA, adapted)*
   REQUIRED: The rate or amount that sales may decline before losses are incurred.
   DISCUSSION: The margin of safety is the excess of budgeted revenues over breakeven revenues. It is considered in sensitivity analysis.
   Answer (A) is incorrect because residual income is the excess of earnings over an imputed charge for the given investment base. Answer (B) is incorrect because a marginal rate of return is the return on the next investment. Answer (D) is incorrect because a target or hurdle rate of return is the required rate of return. It is also known as the discount rate or the opportunity cost of capital.

51. Waldo Company produces one product. The following are the data for the current month:

Selling price per unit	$80

Variable cost per unit	
Direct materials	$21
Direct labor	10
Variable manufacturing overhead	3
Variable selling and administrative	6

Fixed costs	
Manufacturing overhead	$76,000
Selling and administrative	58,000

Units	
Beginning inventory	0
Month's production	5,000
Number sold	4,500
Ending inventory	500

The contribution margin is

A. $46,000

B. $180,000

C. $207,000

D. $226,000

Answer (B) is correct.   *(CMA, adapted)*
   REQUIRED: The contribution margin.
   DISCUSSION: The contribution margin equals sales revenue minus all variable costs. Fixed costs are subtracted from variable costs to determine operating income. Waldo's unit variable cost is $34 ($21 + $10 + $3). Thus, its contribution margin is calculated as follows:

Sales (4,500 × $80)		$ 360,000
BI	$ 0	
Variable costs (5,000 × $34)	170,000	
EI (500 × $34)	(17,000)	
Variable CGS		(153,000)
Manufacturing CM		$ 207,000
Variable S&A (4,500 × $6)		(27,000)
Contribution margin		$ 180,000

   Answer (A) is incorrect because fixed overhead and fixed selling and administrative expenses are not subtracted to determine contribution margin. Answer (C) is incorrect because the variable selling and administrative expenses must be subtracted to determine contribution margin. Answer (D) is incorrect because because total inventoriable cost per unit is $34.

18.3 Absorption (Full) vs. Variable (Direct) Costing

52. Which of the following statements is true for a firm that uses variable costing?

A. The cost of a unit of product changes because of changes in number of units manufactured.

B. Profits fluctuate with sales.

C. An idle facility variation is calculated.

D. Product costs include variable administrative costs.

Answer (B) is correct. *(CMA, adapted)*
REQUIRED: The true statement about variable costing.
DISCUSSION: In a variable costing system, only the variable costs are recorded as product costs. All fixed costs are expensed in the period incurred. Because changes in the relationship between production levels and sales levels do not cause changes in the amount of fixed manufacturing cost expensed, profits more directly follow the trends in sales.
Answer (A) is incorrect because changing unit costs based on different levels of production is a characteristic of absorption costing systems. Answer (C) is incorrect because an idle facility variation is calculated in absorption costing. Answer (D) is incorrect because neither variable nor absorption costing includes administrative costs in inventory.

53. When a firm prepares financial reports by using absorption costing,

A. Profits will always increase with increases in sales.

B. Profits will always decrease with decreases in sales.

C. Profits may decrease with increased sales even if there is no change in selling prices and costs.

D. Decreased output and constant sales result in increased profits.

Answer (C) is correct. *(CMA, adapted)*
REQUIRED: The profit relationship between output and sales under absorption costing.
DISCUSSION: In an absorption costing system, fixed overhead costs are included in inventory. When sales exceed production, more overhead is expensed under absorption costing because fixed overhead is carried over from the prior inventory. If sales exceed production, more than one period's fixed overhead is recognized as expense. Accordingly, if the increase in fixed overhead expensed is greater than the contribution margin of the increased units sold, less profit may result from an increased level of sales.
Answer (A) is incorrect because profit is a function of both sales and production, so profit may not increase with increases in sales. Answer (B) is incorrect because profit is a function of both sales and production, so profit may not decrease with decreases in sales. Answer (D) is incorrect because decreased output will increase the unit cost of items sold. Fixed overhead per unit will increase.

54. Which method of inventory costing treats direct manufacturing costs and manufacturing overhead costs, both variable and fixed, as inventoriable costs?

A. Direct costing.

B. Variable costing.

C. Absorption costing.

D. Conversion costing.

Answer (C) is correct. *(CMA, adapted)*
REQUIRED: The method of inventory costing that treats direct manufacturing costs and all factory overhead as inventoriable.
DISCUSSION: Absorption (full) costing considers all manufacturing costs to be inventoriable as product costs. These costs include variable and fixed manufacturing costs, whether direct or indirect. The alternative to absorption is known as variable (direct) costing.
Answer (A) is incorrect because direct costing does not inventory fixed factory overhead. Answer (B) is incorrect because variable costing does not inventory fixed factory overhead. Answer (D) is incorrect because conversion costs include direct labor and factory overhead but not direct materials.

55. Which one of the following statements is true regarding absorption costing and variable costing?

A. Overhead costs are treated in the same manner under both costing methods.

B. If finished goods inventory increases, absorption costing results in higher income.

C. Variable manufacturing costs are lower under variable costing.

D. Gross margins are the same under both costing methods.

Answer (B) is correct. *(CMA, adapted)*
    REQUIRED: The true statement regarding absorption costing and variable costing.
    DISCUSSION: Under variable costing, inventories are charged only with the variable costs of production. Fixed manufacturing costs are expensed as period costs. Absorption costing charges to inventory all costs of production. If finished goods inventory increases, absorption costing results in higher income because it capitalizes some fixed costs that would have been expensed under variable costing. When inventory declines, variable costing results in higher income because some fixed costs capitalized under the absorption method in prior periods are expensed in the current period.
    Answer (A) is incorrect because fixed factory overhead is treated differently under the two methods. Answer (C) is incorrect because variable costs are the same under either method. Answer (D) is incorrect because gross margins will be different. Fixed factory overhead is expensed under variable costing and capitalized under the absorption method.

56. Absorption costing and variable costing are two different methods of assigning costs to units produced. Of the cost items listed below, identify the one that is not correctly accounted for as a product cost.

		Part of Product Cost Under	
		Absorption Cost	Variable Cost
A.	Manufacturing supplies	Yes	Yes
B.	Insurance on factory	Yes	No
C.	Direct labor cost	Yes	Yes
D.	Packaging and shipping costs	Yes	Yes

Answer (D) is correct. *(CMA, adapted)*
    REQUIRED: The cost not correctly accounted for.
    DISCUSSION: Under absorption costing, all manufacturing costs, both fixed and variable, are treated as product costs. Under variable costing, only variable costs of manufacturing are inventoried as product costs. Fixed manufacturing costs are expensed as period costs. Packaging and shipping costs are not product costs under either method because they are incurred after the goods have been manufactured. Instead, they are included in selling and administrative expenses for the period.
    Answer (A) is incorrect because manufacturing supplies are variable costs inventoried under both methods. Answer (B) is incorrect because factory insurance is a fixed manufacturing cost inventoried under absorption costing but written off as a period cost under variable costing. Answer (C) is incorrect because direct labor cost is a product cost under both methods.

57. Jansen, Inc. pays bonuses to its managers based on operating income. The company uses absorption costing, and overhead is applied on the basis of direct labor hours. To increase bonuses, Jansen's managers may do all of the following except

A. Produce those products requiring the most direct labor.

B. Defer expenses such as maintenance to a future period.

C. Increase production schedules independent of customer demands.

D. Decrease production of those items requiring the most direct labor.

Answer (D) is correct. *(CMA, adapted)*
    REQUIRED: The action that will not increase bonuses based on operating income.
    DISCUSSION: Under an absorption costing system, income can be manipulated by producing more products than are sold because more fixed manufacturing overhead will be allocated to the ending inventory. When inventory increases, some fixed costs are capitalized rather than expensed. Decreasing production, however, will result in lower income because more of the fixed manufacturing overhead will be expensed.
    Answer (A) is incorrect because producing more of the products requiring the most direct labor will permit more fixed overhead to be capitalized in the inventory account. Answer (B) is incorrect because deferring expenses such as maintenance will increase income in the current period (but may result in long-range losses caused by excessive down-time). Answer (C) is incorrect because increasing production without a concurrent increase in demand applies more fixed costs to inventory.

58. At the end of a company's first year of operations, 2,000 units of inventory are on hand. Variable costs are $100 per unit, and fixed manufacturing costs are $30 per unit. The use of absorption costing, rather than variable costing, would result in a higher net income of what amount?

A. $60,000

B. $140,000

C. $200,000

D. $260,000

Answer (A) is correct. *(CPA, adapted)*
REQUIRED: The effect of using absorption costing.
DISCUSSION: Absorption costing is required under GAAP. It includes all manufacturing costs in product cost: direct materials, direct labor, and fixed as well as variable manufacturing overhead. Variable costing differs only in that it expenses fixed manufacturing overhead. Hence, given no beginning inventory, pretax net income for absorption costing purposes exceeds pretax net income for variable costing purposes by $60,000 (2,000 units in EI × $30 fixed manufacturing cost per unit). This amount is expensed using variable costing and treated as a product cost using absorption costing.
Answer (B) is incorrect because $140,000 equals total variable costs minus total fixed costs for 2,000 units. Answer (C) is incorrect because $200,000 equals total variable costs for 2,000 units. Answer (D) is incorrect because $260,000 equals total variable costs plus total fixed costs for 2,000 units.

Questions 59 and 60 are based on the following information. At the end of its fiscal year, C.G. Manufacturing recorded the data below:

Prime cost	$800,000
Variable manufacturing overhead	100,000
Fixed manufacturing overhead	160,000
Variable selling and other expenses	80,000
Fixed selling and other expenses	40,000

59. If C.G. uses variable costing, the inventoriable costs for the fiscal year are

A. $800,000

B. $900,000

C. $980,000

D. $1,060,000

Answer (B) is correct. *(CMA, adapted)*
REQUIRED: The inventoriable costs using variable costing.
DISCUSSION: The only costs capitalized are the variable costs of manufacturing. Prime costs (direct materials and direct labor) are variable.

Prime costs, direct materials, and direct labor	$800,000
Variable manufacturing overhead	100,000
Total inventoriable costs	$900,000

Answer (A) is incorrect because $800,000 equals the prime costs. Answer (C) is incorrect because $980,000 includes the variable selling and other expenses. Answer (D) is incorrect because $1,060,000 equals inventoriable costs under absorption costing.

60. Using absorption (full) costing, C.G.'s inventoriable costs are

A. $800,000

B. $900,000

C. $1,060,000

D. $1,080,000

Answer (C) is correct. *(CMA, adapted)*
REQUIRED: The inventoriable costs using absorption costing.
DISCUSSION: Absorption costing is required by GAAP. It charges all costs of production to inventories. The prime costs ($800,000), variable manufacturing overhead ($100,000), and the fixed manufacturing overhead ($160,000) are included. They total $1,060,000.
Answer (A) is incorrect because $800,000 equals prime costs. Answer (B) is incorrect because $900,000 equals inventoriable costs under variable costing. Answer (D) is incorrect because $1,060,000 includes the fixed and variable selling and other expenses.

Questions 61 and 62 are based on the following information. Osawa, Inc. planned and actually manufactured 200,000 units of its single product during its first year of operations. Variable manufacturing costs were $30 per unit of product. Planned and actual fixed manufacturing costs were $600,000, and selling and administrative costs totaled $400,000. Osawa sold 120,000 units of product at a selling price of $40 per unit.

61. Osawa's operating income using absorption (full) costing is

A. $200,000

B. $440,000

C. $600,000

D. $840,000

Answer (B) is correct. *(CMA, adapted)*
REQUIRED: The operating income under absorption costing.
DISCUSSION: Because production equaled planned output, and fixed costs equaled the budgeted amount, fixed overhead was not over- or under-applied. Also, planned fixed overhead equaled the actual amount. Thus, no fixed overhead variances had to be accounted for. Osawa applied $600,000 of fixed overhead, or $3 per unit ($600,000 ÷ 200,000 units), to its output. The unit cost of the 80,000 (200,000 – 120,000 sold) units in ending inventory is therefore $33 ($30 VC + $3 FC). Absorption costing net income is computed as follows:

Sales (120,000 units × $40)	$4,800,000
Variable production costs (200,000 units × $30)	$6,000,000
Fixed production costs	600,000
Total production costs (200,000 units)	$6,600,000
Ending inventory (80,000 units × $33)	(2,640,000)
Cost of goods sold	$3,960,000
Gross profit	$ 840,000
Selling and administrative expenses	(400,000)
Operating income	$ 440,000

Answer (A) is incorrect because $200,000 is the operating income under variable costing. Answer (C) is incorrect because $600,000 is the operating income that results from capitalizing $240,000 fixed manufacturing costs and $160,000 of selling and administrative costs (the $160,000 is incorrect as all selling and administrative costs should be expensed). Answer (D) is incorrect because $840,000 is the gross profit under absorption costing, i.e., before selling and administrative expenses.

62. Osawa's operating income for the year using variable costing is

A. $200,000

B. $440,000

C. $800,000

D. $600,000

Answer (A) is correct. *(CMA, adapted)*
REQUIRED: The operating income under variable costing.
DISCUSSION: The contribution margin from manufacturing (sales – variable costs) is $10 ($40 – $30) per unit sold, or $1,200,000 (120,000 units × $10). The fixed costs of manufacturing ($600,000) and selling and administrative costs ($400,000) are deducted from the contribution margin to arrive at an operating income of $200,000. The difference between the absorption income of $440,000 and the $200,000 of variable costing income is attributable to capitalization of the fixed manufacturing costs under the absorption method. Because 40% of the goods produced are still in inventory (80,000 ÷ 200,000), 40% of the $600,000 in fixed costs, or $240,000, was capitalized under the absorption method. That amount was expensed under the variable costing method.
Answer (B) is incorrect because $440,000 is the operating income under absorption costing. Answer (C) is incorrect because $800,000 is the operating income if fixed costs of manufacturing are not deducted. Answer (D) is incorrect because $600,000 is the operating income that results from capitalizing 40% of both fixed manufacturing costs and selling and administrative costs.

63. West Co.'s manufacturing costs for the month just ended were as follows:

Direct materials and direct labor	$700,000
Other variable manufacturing costs	100,000
Depreciation of factory building and manufacturing equipment	80,000
Other fixed manufacturing overhead	18,000

What amount should be considered product cost for external reporting purposes?

   A. $700,000

   B. $800,000

   C. $880,000

   D. $898,000

Answer (D) is correct. *(CPA, adapted)*
   REQUIRED: The product cost for external reporting purposes.
   DISCUSSION: According to GAAP, absorption (full) costing is required for external reporting purposes. Absorption costing includes fixed and variable factory overhead in product cost. Direct materials and direct labor are other elements of product cost. Consequently, the total product cost is $898,000 ($700,000 + $100,000 + $80,000 + $18,000).
   Answer (A) is incorrect because the other variable (presumably overhead) costs and the fixed factory overhead (including depreciation on plant assets) should be inventoried. Answer (B) is incorrect because the depreciation and the other fixed factory overhead are product costs. Answer (C) is incorrect because the other fixed factory overhead is also a product cost.

64. Cay Co.'s fixed manufacturing overhead costs for the month just ended totaled $100,000, and variable selling costs totaled $80,000. Under variable costing, how should these costs be classified?

	Period Costs	Product Costs
A.	$0	$180,000
B.	$80,000	$100,000
C.	$100,000	$80,000
D.	$180,000	$0

Answer (D) is correct. *(CPA, adapted)*
   REQUIRED: The classification of fixed manufacturing overhead and variable selling costs.
   DISCUSSION: Product costs are incurred to produce units of output, and they are expensed when the product is sold. Such costs include direct materials, direct labor, and factory (not general and administrative) overhead. Period costs are charged to expense as incurred because they are not identifiable with a product. Variable (also called direct) costing considers only variable manufacturing costs to be product costs. Fixed manufacturing costs and fixed and variable selling costs are considered period costs and are expensed as incurred. Because fixed manufacturing overhead and variable selling costs are considered general and administrative overhead, they are not product, but period, costs. Thus, the entire $180,000 ($100,000 + $80,000) is classified as period costs.
   Answer (A) is incorrect because the fixed overhead and selling costs are not identifiable with a product. Answer (B) is incorrect because the fixed overhead is not identifiable with a product. Answer (C) is incorrect because the selling costs are not identifiable with a product.

65. During the month just ended, Vane Co. produced and sold 10,000 units of a product. Manufacturing and selling costs incurred were as follows:

Direct materials and direct labor	$400,000
Variable manufacturing overhead	90,000
Fixed manufacturing overhead	20,000
Variable selling costs	10,000

The product's unit cost under variable (direct) costing was

   A. $49

   B. $50

   C. $51

   D. $52

Answer (A) is correct. *(CPA, adapted)*
   REQUIRED: The product's unit cost under direct (variable) costing.
   DISCUSSION: Variable (direct) costing includes variable manufacturing costs only: direct materials, direct labor, and variable manufacturing overhead. Fixed manufacturing overhead and selling expenses are treated as period costs. Hence, the unit cost is $49 [($400,000 + $90,000) ÷ 10,000 units].
   Answer (B) is incorrect because variable selling costs ($1 per unit) of $50 should not be included. Answer (C) is incorrect because unit cost under absorption costing is $51. Answer (D) is incorrect because unit cost under variable (direct) costing does not include fixed manufacturing overhead or variable selling costs.

66. In an income statement prepared as an internal report, total fixed costs normally are shown separately under

	Absorption Costing	Variable Costing
A.	No	No
B.	No	Yes
C.	Yes	Yes
D.	Yes	No

Answer (B) is correct. *(CPA, adapted)*
REQUIRED: The income statement(s) in which total fixed costs are normally shown separately.
DISCUSSION: In a variable-costing income statement, all variable costs are deducted from sales revenue to arrive at the contribution margin. Total fixed costs are then deducted from the contribution margin to determine operating income. In an absorption-costing income statement, fixed factory overhead included in the cost of goods sold is deducted from sales revenue in the calculation of the gross margin. Other fixed costs are among the amounts subtracted from the gross margin to determine operating income.

67. In an income statement prepared using the variable-costing method, fixed factory overhead would

A. Not be used.

B. Be used in the computation of operating income but not in the computation of the contribution margin.

C. Be used in the computation of the contribution margin.

D. Be treated the same as variable factory overhead.

Answer (B) is correct. *(CPA, adapted)*
REQUIRED: The treatment of fixed factory overhead in an income statement based on variable costing.
DISCUSSION: Under the variable-costing method, the contribution margin equals sales minus variable expenses. Fixed selling and administrative costs and fixed factory overhead are deducted from the contribution margin to arrive at operating income. Thus, fixed costs are included only in the computation of operating income.
Answer (A) is incorrect because fixed factory overhead is deducted from the contribution margin to determine operating income. Answer (C) is incorrect because only variable expenses are used in the computation of the contribution margin. Answer (D) is incorrect because variable factory overhead is included in the computation of contribution margin and fixed factory overhead is not.

68. A single-product company prepares income statements using both absorption and variable costing. Manufacturing overhead cost applied per unit produced in Year 2 was the same as in Year 1. The Year 2 variable-costing statement reported a profit, whereas the Year 2 absorption-costing statement reported a loss. A possible explanation for the difference in reported income is that the units produced in Year 2 were

A. Fewer than units sold in Year 2.

B. Fewer than the activity level used for allocating overhead to the product.

C. Greater than the activity level used for allocating overhead to the product.

D. Greater than units sold in Year 2.

Answer (A) is correct. *(CPA, adapted)*
REQUIRED: The circumstances in which variable-costing net income exceeds absorption-costing net income.
DISCUSSION: The sole difference between variable and absorption costing is that the latter applies fixed factory overhead as an inventoriable cost. When sales exceed production, absorption costing recognizes as a cost of goods sold not only the fixed factory overhead of the current period (the amount included for variable-costing purposes) but also the portion of such overhead included in the cost of the units of beginning inventory deemed to have been sold. Thus, variable-costing results in a lower cost of goods sold and a higher net income than absorption-costing when sales exceed production.
Answer (B) is incorrect because under- or over-application of overhead could occur when absorption-costing income exceeds variable-costing income. If production exceeds sales, absorption-costing income will be greater because, regardless of the under- or over-application, some of the overhead that is expensed under variable costing will be inventoried by the absorption-costing method. Answer (C) is incorrect because under- or over-application of overhead could occur when absorption-costing income exceeds variable-costing income. If production exceeds sales, absorption-costing income will be greater because, regardless of the under- or over-application, some of the overhead that is expensed under variable costing will be inventoried by the absorption-costing method. Answer (D) is incorrect because absorption costing results in the higher income when production exceeds sales.

69. In an income statement prepared as an internal report, operating income is normally measured under

	Absorption Costing	Variable Costing
A.	No	Yes
B.	No	No
C.	Yes	No
D.	Yes	Yes

Answer (D) is correct. *(CPA, adapted)*
  REQUIRED: The income statement(s) in which operating income is normally shown separately.
  DISCUSSION: In a variable-costing income statement, all variable costs are deducted from sales revenue to arrive at the contribution margin. Total fixed costs are then deducted from the contribution margin to determine operating income. In an absorption-costing income statement, fixed factory overhead included in the cost of goods sold is deducted from sales revenue in the calculation of the gross margin. Other fixed costs are among the amounts subtracted from the gross margin to determine operating income.

70. In an income statement prepared as an internal report using the variable costing method, variable selling and administrative expenses are

A. Not used.

B. Treated the same as fixed selling and administrative expenses.

C. Used in the computation of operating income but not in the computation of the contribution margin.

D. Used in the computation of the contribution margin.

Answer (D) is correct. *(CPA, adapted)*
  REQUIRED: The treatment of variable selling and administrative expenses in an income statement based on variable costing.
  DISCUSSION: In a variable costing income statement, the contribution margin equals sales minus all variable costs, which include the variable selling and administrative expenses as well as variable manufacturing costs (direct materials, direct labor, and variable factory overhead). Operating income equals the contribution margin minus all fixed costs.
  Answer (A) is incorrect because variable selling and administrative expenses are included in the determination of the contribution margin. Answer (B) is incorrect because fixed selling and administrative expenses are subtracted from the contribution margin to arrive at operation income. Answer (C) is incorrect because variable selling and administrative expenses are used in the computation of the contribution margin.

71. In an income statement prepared as an internal report using the variable (direct) costing method, fixed selling and administrative expenses are

A. Used in the computation of the contribution margin.

B. Used in the computation of operating income but not in the computation of the contribution margin.

C. Treated the same as variable selling and administrative expenses.

D. Not used.

Answer (B) is correct. *(CPA, adapted)*
  REQUIRED: The treatment of fixed selling and administrative expenses in the income statement using the direct (variable) costing method.
  DISCUSSION: In a variable costing income statement, all variable costs are deducted from sales revenue to arrive at the contribution margin. Total fixed costs are then deducted from the contribution margin to determine operating income. Thus, fixed selling and administrative expenses would be used in the computation of operating income but not in the computation of the contribution margin.
  Answer (A) is incorrect because fixed expenses are not used to compute the contribution margin in variable costing. Answer (C) is incorrect because variable costing treats fixed expenses differently from variable expenses. Answer (D) is incorrect because expenses are used in the income statement.

72. A manufacturing company prepares income statements using both absorption and variable costing methods. At the end of a period, actual sales revenues, total gross profit, and total contribution margin approximated budgeted figures, whereas net income was substantially greater than the budgeted amount. There were no beginning or ending inventories. The most likely explanation of the net income increase is that, compared to budget, actual

A. Manufacturing fixed costs had increased.

B. Selling and administrative fixed expenses had decreased.

C. Sales prices and variable costs had increased proportionately.

D. Sales prices had declined proportionately less than variable costs.

Answer (B) is correct. *(CPA, adapted)*
  REQUIRED: Explanation of an increase in actual net income over a budgeted amount.
  DISCUSSION: Both variable and absorption costing income statements exclude fixed selling and administrative expenses from the calculation of gross profit (gross margin) and contribution margin. Since actual sales revenue, total gross profit, and total contribution margin approximated their budgeted amounts, the only item that could have caused an increase in net income without affecting either gross profit or contribution margin would be a decrease in fixed selling and administrative expenses.
  Answer (A) is incorrect because an increase in actual manufacturing fixed costs would have caused a decrease in NI and a decrease in absorption costing gross margin. Answer (C) is incorrect because a proportionate increase in sales prices and variable costs would increase gross margin and gross profit. Answer (D) is incorrect because less of a decline in sales prices than in variable costs would increase gross margin and gross profit.

73. At the end of Killo Co.'s first year of operations, 1,000 units of inventory remained on hand. Variable and fixed manufacturing costs per unit were $90 and $20, respectively. If Killo uses absorption costing rather than variable (direct) costing, the result would be a higher pretax income of

A. $0

B. $20,000

C. $70,000

D. $90,000

Answer (B) is correct. *(CPA, adapted)*

REQUIRED: The increased pretax income resulting from absorption costing.

DISCUSSION: The difference between variable and absorption costing is that variable costing eliminates fixed costs from product inventories. These fixed costs are charged to operating costs during the period in which the costs are incurred under variable costing. Absorption costing charges the fixed costs to the remaining inventory for $20,000 (1,000 × $20). These costs will be recognized during the following period, assuming the inventory is sold. Because variable costing charges the fixed manufacturing costs to the current period, the operating expenses will be $20,000 higher than under absorption costing. Because operating costs would be $20,000 lower using absorption costing, the result would be a higher pretax income of $20,000.

Answer (A) is incorrect because absorption costing results in a higher income. Answer (C) is incorrect because $70,000 charges the difference between fixed and variable costs per unit to current period's income. Answer (D) is incorrect because $90,000 charges the variable costs to current period's income.

74. Using the variable costing method, which of the following costs are assigned to inventory?

	Variable Selling and Administrative Costs	Variable Factory Overhead Costs
A.	Yes	Yes
B.	Yes	No
C.	No	No
D.	No	Yes

Answer (D) is correct. *(CPA, adapted)*

REQUIRED: The costs assigned to inventory.

DISCUSSION: Variable costing charges variable costs, except variable selling, general, and administrative expenses, to inventory. Variable factory overhead is part of the product cost, but fixed factory overhead is treated as an expense of the accounting period.

75. Lynn Manufacturing Co. prepares income statements using both standard absorption and standard variable costing methods. For the month just ended, unit standard costs were unchanged from the previous month. In the month just ended, the only beginning and ending inventories were finished goods of 5,000 units. How would Lynn's ratios using absorption costing compare with those using variable costing?

	Current Ratio	Return on Equity
A.	Same	Same
B.	Same	Smaller
C.	Greater	Same
D.	Greater	Smaller

Answer (D) is correct. *(CPA, adapted)*

REQUIRED: The effect on the current ratio and the return on shareholders' equity of using absorption costing rather than variable costing.

DISCUSSION: Absorption costing includes fixed factory overhead in finished goods inventory. Variable costing does not. Thus, the current ratio is higher under absorption costing. The current ratio equals current assets (including inventory) divided by current liabilities. When production equals sales and costs do not change, the two methods result in the same net income. Because inventory (and therefore retained earnings) is greater under absorption costing, return on equity is smaller than under variable costing.

76. Dowell Co. manufactures a wooden item. Which of the following is included with the inventoriable cost under absorption costing and excluded from the inventoriable cost under variable costing?

A. Cost of electricity used to operate production machinery.

B. Straight-line depreciation on factory equipment.

C. Cost of scrap pieces of lumber.

D. Wages of assembly-line personnel.

Answer (B) is correct. *(CPA, adapted)*
REQUIRED: The cost inventoried under absorption costing but not variable costing.
DISCUSSION: Under variable costing, all direct labor, direct materials, and variable overhead costs are handled in precisely the same manner as in absorption costing. Only fixed factory overhead costs are treated differently. Absorption costing treats fixed factory overhead as a product cost. Variable costing treats variable factory overhead as a product cost but fixed factory overhead as an expense of the accounting period (as are fixed and variable selling, general, and administrative expenses). Straight-line depreciation on factory equipment is an item of fixed factory overhead because it will not vary with output within the relevant range. Accordingly, it will be inventoried under absorption costing and expensed under variable costing.
Answer (A) is incorrect because the cost of electricity used to operate production machinery is a variable factory overhead cost and is therefore treated similarly under absorption and variable costing. Answer (C) is incorrect because scrap is a direct material, so its accounting treatment is not dependent on whether absorption or variable costing is used. Answer (D) is incorrect because the two methods account for direct labor cost in the same way.

77. In its first year of operations, Magna Manufacturers had the following costs when it produced 100,000 units and sold 80,000 units of its only product:

Manufacturing costs:
Fixed	$180,000
Variable	160,000

Selling and administrative costs:
Fixed	90,000
Variable	40,000

How much lower would Magna's net income be if it used variable costing instead of full absorption costing?

A. $36,000

B. $54,000

C. $68,000

D. $94,000

Answer (A) is correct. *(CPA, adapted)*
REQUIRED: The decrease in net income if variable costing is used instead of full absorption costing.
DISCUSSION: Full absorption costing includes fixed manufacturing costs in finished goods inventory. Variable costing treats these costs as period costs. Thus, under full absorption costing, the fixed manufacturing cost is a product cost that must be assigned to the units produced during the period. Fixed manufacturing cost per unit is $1.80 ($180,000 ÷ 100,000 units), so the amount inventoried is $36,000 [(100,000 units produced − 80,000 units sold) × $1.80]. Because this amount would be expensed under variable costing, it equals the excess of pretax full absorption-costing net income over pretax variable-costing net income.
Answer (B) is incorrect because $54,000 assumes that the fixed selling and administrative costs are treated as product costs under full absorption costing. Answer (C) is incorrect because $68,000 equals 20% of total manufacturing costs. Answer (D) is incorrect because $94,000 equals 20% of total costs.

78. Which one of the following considers the impact of fixed overhead costs?

A. Full absorption costing.

B. Marginal costing.

C. Direct costing.

D. Variable costing.

Answer (A) is correct. *(CMA, adapted)*
REQUIRED: The method of costing that considers the impact of fixed overhead costs.
DISCUSSION: Full absorption costing treats fixed manufacturing overhead costs as product costs. Thus, inventory and cost of goods sold include (absorb) fixed manufacturing overhead.
Answer (B) is incorrect because marginal costing considers only the incremental costs of producing an additional unit of product. In most cases, marginal costs are variable costs. Answer (C) is incorrect because direct costing treats only variable costs as product costs. Answer (D) is incorrect because variable costing treats only variable costs as product costs.

Use Gleim's *CPA Test Prep* for interactive testing with over 2,000 additional multiple-choice questions!

STUDY UNIT NINETEEN
PRODUCT COSTING AND RELATED TOPICS

(25 pages of outline)

This study unit is the second of three relating to cost measurement. It addresses the principal methods of accumulating costs and assigning them to products.

19.1 SPOILAGE AND SCRAP

1. **Spoilage** consists of completed products that do not meet quality standards. Because they are defective, they will not fetch the normal selling price.

    a. **Normal spoilage** is an expected part of the production process. It is treated as a product cost and is thus included in CGM.

    b. **Abnormal spoilage** is in excess of what is expected. It is treated as a period cost and is thus charged to a loss account when detection occurs.

2. **Scrap** consists of leftover raw materials after the production process is finished, and is therefore in no sense a completed product like spoilage.

    a. The sale of the normal amount of scrap arising from a manufacturing process is usually recorded as follows:

Cash	$XXX	
Manufacturing overhead control		$XXX

    b. An alternative is

Cash	$XXX	
Miscellaneous revenue		$XXX

    c. In both cases, the effect is to allocate the net cost of the scrap (historical cost – disposal proceeds) to the good units produced. Thus, the total cost of scrap remains in work-in-process control, but overhead that otherwise would have been applied to the good units is reduced by the amount received for the scrap.

        1) If scrap is applicable to a specific job, the realized amounts directly reduce the cost of specific units.

    d. Regardless of the accounting, good units continue to bear at least the costs of scrap that cannot be recovered by its sale.

3. Stop and review! You have completed the outline for this subunit. Study multiple-choice questions 1 through 5 beginning on page 621.

19.2 JOB-ORDER COSTING

1. Job-order costing is concerned with **accumulating costs by specific job**.

    a. This method is appropriate when producing products with individual characteristics or when identifiable groupings are possible, e.g., batches of certain styles or types of furniture.

    b. Units (jobs) should be dissimilar enough to warrant the special record keeping required by job-order costing.

2. The accumulation of costs in a job-order system follows the document flow, whether printed or electronic.

    a. A **sales order** is received from a customer requesting a product or special group of products.

    b. The sales order is approved and a **production order** is issued.

    c. The physical inputs required for the production process are obtained from suppliers.

Raw materials	$XXX	
Accounts payable		$XXX

    d. Production commences and three documents feed cost amounts into the costing system:

        1) **Materials requisition forms** request **direct materials** to be pulled from the warehouse and sent to the production line.

Work-in-process -- Job 1015	$XXX	
Raw materials		$XXX

        2) **Time tickets** track the **direct labor** that workers expend on various jobs.

Work-in-process -- Job 1015	$XXX	
Wages payable		$XXX

        3) These two major components of product cost are charged to work-in-process using the **actual amounts** incurred.

    e. Under job-order costing, the third component, **manufacturing overhead**, is charged using an **estimated rate**.

        1) The application of an estimated overhead rate is necessary under job-order costing because the outputs are customized and the processes vary from period to period.

            a) Contrast this with the treatment of overhead under process costing (item 2.c. in Subunit 19.3) in which actual overhead costs incurred are charged to work-in-process at the end of the period.

        2) As indirect costs are paid throughout the year, they are collected in the **manufacturing overhead control account**.

            a) Note that work-in-process is not affected when actual overhead costs are incurred.

Manufacturing overhead control	$XXX	
Property taxes payable		$XXX
Manufacturing overhead control	$XXX	
Prepaid insurance		$XXX
Manufacturing overhead control	$XXX	
Accumulated depreciation -- factory equipment		$XXX

3) Overhead costs are applied to ("absorbed" by) each job based on a **predetermined overhead application rate** for the year.

    a) At the beginning of the year, an estimate is made of the total amount that will be spent for manufacturing overhead during that year.

    b) This total is divided by the allocation base, such as direct labor hours or machine hours, to arrive at the application rate.

    c) The amount applied equals the number of units of the allocation base used during the period times the application rate.

        i) The credit is to manufacturing overhead applied, a contra-account for manufacturing overhead control.

Work-in-process -- Job 1015	$XXX	
Manufacturing overhead applied		$XXX

    d) By tracking the amounts applied to the various jobs in a separate account, the actual amounts spent on overhead are preserved in the balance of the overhead control account.

        i) In addition, the firm can determine at any time how precise its estimate of overhead costs for the period was by comparing the balances in the two accounts. The closer they are (in absolute-value terms), the better the estimate was.

4) At the **end of the period**, the overhead control and applied accounts are **netted**.

    a) If the result is a **credit**, overhead was **overapplied** for the period. If the result is a **debit**, overhead was **underapplied**.

        i) If the variance is **immaterial**, it can be closed directly to cost of goods sold.

        ii) If the variance is **material**, it should be allocated based on the relative values of work-in-process, finished goods, and cost of goods sold.

  f. The amounts from the input documents are accumulated on **job-cost sheets**. These serve as a subsidiary ledger page for each job.

    1) The total of all job-cost sheets will equal the balance in the general ledger work-in-process account.

3. Output that does not meet the quality standards for salability is considered spoilage.

  a. If the spoilage is the amount expected in the ordinary course of production, it is considered **normal spoilage**.

    1) The accounting treatment is to include normal spoilage as a product cost.

    2) This is accomplished by allowing the net cost of the spoilage to remain in the work-in-process account of the job that generated it.

        a) If the normal spoilage is worthless and must be discarded, no entry is made.

        b) If the normal spoilage can be sold, the entry is:

Spoiled inventory (at fair market value)	$XX	
Work-in-process -- Job 1015		$XX

b. If the spoilage is over and above the amount expected in the ordinary course of production, it is considered **abnormal spoilage**.

    1) The accounting treatment is to highlight abnormal spoilage as a period cost so that management can address the deficiency that caused it.

    2) This is accomplished by charging a loss account for the net cost of the spoilage.

        a) If the abnormal spoilage is worthless and must be discarded, the entry is:

Loss from abnormal spoilage		
(costs up to point of inspection)	$XX	
Work-in-process -- Job 1015		$XX

        b) If the abnormal spoilage can be sold, the entry is:

Spoiled inventory	$XX	
Loss from abnormal spoilage (difference)	XX	
Work-in-process -- Job 1015		
(costs up to point of inspection)		$XX

4. When a job order is completed, all the costs are transferred to finished goods.

Finished goods	$X,XXX	
Work-in-process -- Job 1015		$X,XXX

5. When the output is sold, the appropriate portion of the cost is transferred to cost of goods sold.

Cost of goods sold	$X,XXX	
Finished goods		$X,XXX

6. The following diagram depicts the flow of cost accumulation in a job-order costing system:

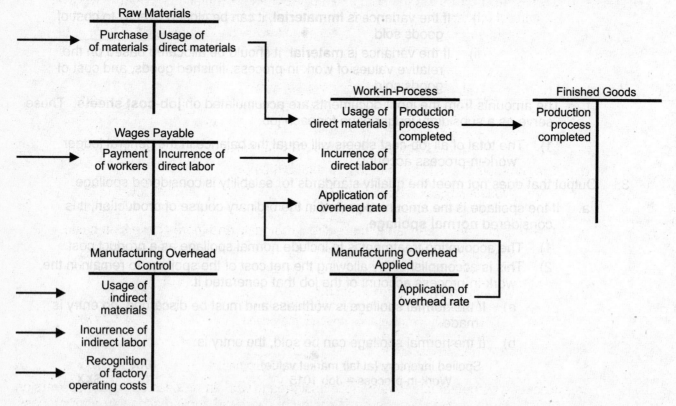

7. Stop and review! You have completed the outline for this subunit. Study multiple-choice questions 6 through 15 beginning on page 623.

19.3 PROCESS COSTING

1. Process cost accounting is used to assign costs to inventoriable goods or services. It is applicable to **relatively homogeneous products** that are mass produced on a continuous basis (e.g., petroleum products, thread, computer monitors).

   a. Where job-order costing uses subsidiary ledgers to keep track of specific jobs, process costing typically has a **work-in-process account for each department** through which the production of output passes.

   b. Process costing is an averaging process that calculates the average cost of all units:

      1) Costs are accumulated for a cost object that consists of a large number of similar units of goods or services;

      2) Work-in-process is stated in terms of equivalent units; and

      3) Unit costs are established.

2. The accumulation of costs under a process costing system is **by department rather than by project**. This reflects the continuous, homogeneous nature of the manufacturing process.

   a. As in job-order costing, the physical inputs required for the production process are obtained from suppliers.

Raw materials	$XXX	
Accounts payable		$XXX

   b. **Direct materials** are used by the first department in the process.

Work-in-process -- Department A	$XXX	
Raw materials		$XXX

   c. **Conversion costs** are the sum of direct labor and manufacturing overhead. The nature of process costing makes this accounting treatment more efficient (the implications of this for the calculation of unit quantities are covered in item 4. on page 603).

Work-in-process -- Department A	$XXX	
Wages payable (direct and indirect labor)		$XXX
Manufacturing supplies (indirect materials)		XXX
Property taxes payable		XXX
Prepaid insurance		XXX
Accumulated depreciation -- factory equipment		XXX

   d. The products move from one department to the next.

Work-in-process -- Department B	$XXX	
Work-in-process -- Department A		$XXX

   e. The second department adds more direct materials and more conversion costs.

Work-in-process -- Department B	$XXX	
Raw materials		$XXX

Work-in-process -- Department B	$XXX	
Wages payable (direct and indirect labor)		$XXX
Manufacturing supplies (indirect materials)		XXX
Property taxes payable		XXX
Prepaid insurance		XXX
Accumulated depreciation -- factory equipment		XXX

   f. Because manufacturing overhead is assigned to work-in-process as part of conversion costs, there is rarely an overhead control or overhead applied account under process costing, and the issue of over- or underapplied overhead does not arise.

      1) The exception is when a standard costing system is used. Under standard costing, a predetermined overhead rate (as in job-order costing) is used to assign overhead costs.

g. When processing is finished in the last department, all the costs are transferred to finished goods.

Finished goods	$X,XXX	
Work-in-process -- Department B		$X,XXX

h. As products are sold, the costs are transferred to cost of goods sold.

Cost of goods sold	$X,XXX	
Finished goods		$X,XXX

3. The following diagram depicts the flow of cost accumulation in a process costing system:

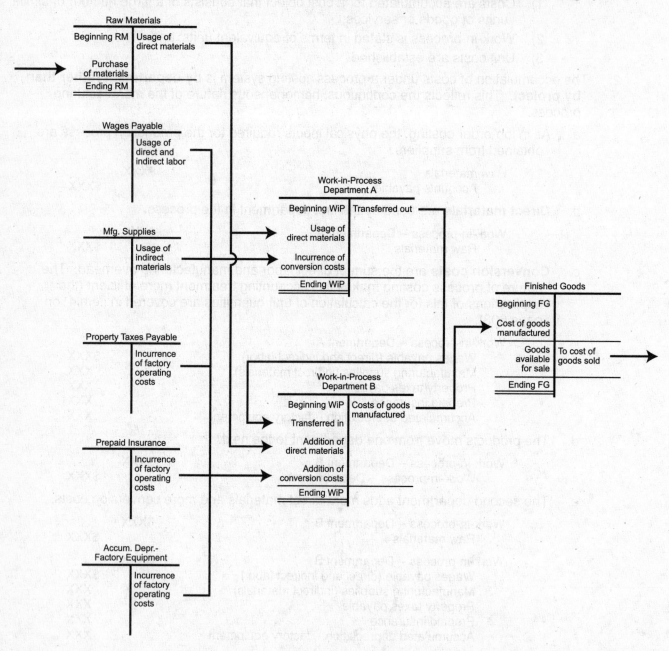

4.   Some units remain unfinished at the end of the period. For each department to account adequately for the costs attached to its unfinished units, the units must be restated in terms of equivalent units of production.

   a.   **Equivalent units of production (EUP)** is the number of complete goods that could have been produced using the inputs consumed during the period.

      1)   The EUP conversion is a two-phase process: First, the **equivalent units** are determined; second, the **per-unit cost** is calculated.

      2)   The two calculations are made separately for direct materials and conversion costs (transferred-in costs are by definition 100% complete). Conversion costs are assumed to be uniformly incurred.

   b.   Two methods of calculating EUP are in common use: weighted-average and FIFO.

      1)   Under the **weighted-average method**, units in beginning work-in-process inventory are treated as if they were started and completed during the current period. Beginning work-in-process is therefore not included in the EUP calculation.

      2)   Under the **first-in, first-out (FIFO) method**, units in beginning work-in-process inventory are part of the EUP calculation. The calculation is thus more complex than weighted-average but tends to be more accurate.

   c.   EXAMPLE: A department of a manufacturing concern is preparing its cost reports for the month.

      1)   The first step is to prepare a quantity schedule:

	Units	Completed for Direct Materials	Completed for Conversion Costs
Beginning work-in-process	2,000	80%	40%
Units started during period	8,000		
Units to account for	10,000		
Units transferred to next department	9,000		
Ending work-in-process	1,000	90%	70%
Units accounted for	10,000		

      2)   The costs to be allocated are presented in this table:

	Direct Materials	Conversion Costs
Beginning work-in-process	$25,000	$10,000
Added during the month	55,000	50,000

      3)   The next step is to calculate the equivalent units of production. This table illustrates the different outcomes of applying the two methods. Note that beginning work-in-process plays no role in the weighted-average computation but is backed out under FIFO.

	Weighted-Average		FIFO	
	Direct Materials	Conversion Costs	Direct Materials	Conversion Costs
Units transferred to next department	9,000	9,000	9,000	9,000
Add: ending work-in-process FUP				
Direct materials: 1,000 units × 90%	900		900	
Conversion costs: 1,000 units × 70%		700		700
Total completed units			9,900	9,700
Less: beginning work-in-process EUP				
Direct materials: 2,000 units × 80%			(1,600)	
Conversion costs: 2,000 units × 40%				(800)
Equivalent units of production	9,900	9,700	8,300	8,900

4) Once the equivalent units have been calculated, the per-unit costs under each of the two methods can be derived.

a) Under the **weighted-average** method, **all direct materials and conversion costs** are averaged in, both those incurred in the current period and those in beginning work-in-process.

Direct materials: $\dfrac{\$25,000 + \$55,000}{9,900 \text{ EUP}}$ = $ 8.08

Conversion costs: $\dfrac{\$10,000 + \$50,000}{9,700 \text{ EUP}}$ = $ 6.19

Total unit cost under weighted-average $14.27

b) Under the **FIFO** method, **only the costs incurred in the current period** are included in the calculation.

Direct materials: $\dfrac{\$55,000}{8,300 \text{ EUP}}$ = $ 6.63

Conversion costs: $\dfrac{\$50,000}{8,900 \text{ EUP}}$ = $ 5.62

Total unit cost under first-in, first-out $12.24

5. Stop and review! You have completed the outline for this subunit. Study multiple-choice questions 16 through 35 beginning on page 626.

19.4 OVERHEAD COSTS AND NORMAL COSTING

1. Whenever overhead is to be allocated, as in job-order costing and activity-based costing, an appropriate **allocation base** must be chosen.

a. In traditional cost accounting, allocation bases include direct labor hours, direct labor cost, machine hours, materials cost, and units of production.

b. The crucial quality of an allocation base is that it be a **cost driver** of the costs in the pool to be allocated.

1) Recall that a cost driver must capture a **cause-and-effect relationship** between the cost being allocated and the cost object to which the costs are being attached.

2) Overhead is usually allocated to products based upon the **level of activity**.

a) For example, if overhead is largely made up of machine maintenance, the activity base may be machine hours.

b) In capital-intensive industries, the amount of overhead will probably be related more to machine hours than to either direct labor hours or direct labor cost.

c) In labor-intensive industries, overhead is usually allocated on a labor activity base.

i) If more overhead is incurred by the more highly skilled and paid employees, the overhead rate should be based upon direct labor cost rather than direct labor hours.

3) Overhead is usually not allocated on the basis of units produced because of the lack of a cause-and-effect relationship.

a) When only one product is manufactured, this method may be acceptable because all costs are to be charged to the single product.

2. The **predetermined overhead application rate** equals budgeted overhead divided by the budgeted activity level (measure of capacity).

    a. The **numerator** of the calculation is the total amount of manufacturing overhead that must be allocated for the period, i.e., the sum of indirect materials, indirect labor, depreciation, factory insurance, etc.

        1) The **denominator** is the allocation base.

    b. Inevitably, the overhead amounts applied throughout the year will vary from the amount actually incurred, which is only determinable once the job is complete.

        1) This variance is called **over- or underapplied overhead**.

        2) Overapplied overhead (a credit balance in overhead) results when product costs are overstated because the

            a) Activity level was higher than expected, or
            b) Actual overhead costs were lower than expected.

        3) Underapplied overhead (a debit balance in overhead) results when product costs are understated because the

            a) Activity level was lower than expected, or
            b) Actual overhead costs were higher than expected.

        4) Over- and underapplied overhead is subject to one of two treatments:

            a) If the variance is **immaterial**, it can be closed directly to cost of goods sold.

If overapplied:		
Manufacturing overhead applied	$XXX	
Cost of goods sold		$XXX

If underapplied:		
Cost of goods sold	$XXX	
Manufacturing overhead applied		$XXX

            b) If the variance is **material**, it should be allocated based on the relative values of work-in-process, finished goods, and cost of goods sold.

If overapplied:		
Manufacturing overhead applied (balance)	$XXX	
Work-in-process (overapplied amount × allocation %)		$XXX
Finished goods (overapplied amount × allocation %)		XXX
Cost of goods sold (overapplied amount × allocation %)		XXX
Manufacturing overhead control (balance)		XXX

If underapplied:		
Manufacturing overhead applied (balance)	$XXX	
Work-in-process (underapplied amount × allocation %)	XXX	
Finished goods (underapplied amount × allocation %)	XXX	
Cost of goods sold (underapplied amount × allocation %)	XXX	
Manufacturing overhead control (balance)		$XXX

3. During times of low production, per-unit overhead charges will skyrocket. This leads to higher product costs during years of lower production and to **distortions in the financial statements**.

    a. EXAMPLE: A manufacturing firm is expecting the following units of production and sales over a three-year period. Note that production is expected to fluctuate but sales are expected to be even:

	Year 1	Year 2	Year 3	Totals
Production	10,000	6,000	8,000	24,000
Sales	7,000	7,000	7,000	21,000

Variable overhead costs are calculated at $1 per unit, and fixed overhead is projected to remain constant over the period:

	Year 1	Year 2	Year 3	Totals
Variable overhead cost	$10,000	$ 6,000	$ 8,000	$24,000
Fixed overhead cost	20,000	20,000	20,000	60,000
Total overhead cost	$30,000	$26,000	$28,000	$84,000

Next, the overhead application rate for each year is calculated.

Year 1	Year 2	Year 3
Estimated total overhead / Estimated production		
$\dfrac{\$30,000}{10,000} = \$3.00$	$\dfrac{\$26,000}{6,000} = \$4.33$	$\dfrac{\$28,000}{8,000} = \$3.50$

These fluctuations in the applied overhead rate will lead to fluctuations in unit cost:

	Year 1	Year 2	Year 3
Direct materials	$ 3.00	$ 3.00	$ 3.00
Direct labor	4.00	4.00	4.00
Manufacturing overhead	3.00	4.33	3.50
Total overhead cost	$10.00	$11.33	$10.50

The comparative income statements make clear the distorting effect:

	Year 1	Year 2	Year 3	Totals
Production:				
From Year 1	7,000	3,000		
From Year 2		4,000	2,000	
From Year 3			5,000	
Expected unit sales	7,000	7,000	7,000	
Expected selling price	× $12	× $12	× $12	
Total expected sales	$84,000	$84,000	$84,000	$252,000
Cost of goods sold:				
From Year 1	$70,000	$30,000		
From Year 2		45,333	$22,667	
From Year 3			52,500	
Total expected CGS	$70,000	$75,333	$75,167	$220,500
Gross margin	$14,000	$ 8,667	$ 8,833	$ 31,500

Large fluctuations in gross margin are reported during a period when there was no fluctuation at all in the company's underlying cost structure.

b. To prevent these distortions in the financial statements, **normal costing** derives the overhead application rate by looking at several years at a time, not just one.

   1) EXAMPLE: Instead of using a different overhead application rate for each year, the company uses a single average figure for the period.

      a) The company expects to produce 24,000 units over three years.

      b) Dividing the fixed overhead of $20,000 for each year by an average of 8,000 units per year yields a fixed overhead application rate of $2.50.

      c) The new total overhead application rate per unit is $3.50 ($1.00 variable cost + $2.50 fixed cost).

      d) The new per-unit cost for all three years is thus $10.50 ($3.00 direct materials + $4.00 direct labor + $3.50 overhead application rate).

      e) The revised income statements prepared using a normalized overhead rate reveal the smoothing effect on gross margin:

	Year 1	Year 2	Year 3	Totals
Production:				
From Year 1	7,000	3,000		
From Year 2		4,000	2,000	
From Year 3			5,000	
Expected unit sales	7,000	7,000	7,000	
Expected selling price	× $12	× $12	× $12	
Total expected sales	$84,000	$84,000	$84,000	$252,500
Cost of goods sold:				
From Year 1	$73,500	$31,500		
From Year 2		42,000	$21,000	
From Year 3			52,500	
Total expected CGS	$73,500	$73,500	$73,500	$220,500
Gross margin	$10,500	$10,500	$10,500	$ 31,500

c. **Extended normal costing** applies the use of a normalized rate to direct costs as well as to manufacturing overhead.

d. The following table summarizes the use of rates in the three costing methods described:

	Actual Costing	Normal Costing	Extended Normal Costing
Direct Materials	Actual	Actual	Budgeted
Direct Labor	Actual	Actual	Budgeted
Manufacturing Overhead	Actual	Budgeted	Budgeted

4. Stop and review! You have completed the outline for this subunit. Study multiple-choice questions 36 through 38 beginning on page 633.

19.5 ACTIVITY-BASED COSTING (ABC)

1. **Activity-based costing (ABC)** is a response to the significant increase in the incurrence of indirect costs resulting from the rapid advance of technology.

   a. ABC is a **refinement of an existing costing system** (job-order or process)

      1) Under a traditional (volume-based) costing system, overhead is simply dumped into a single cost pool and spread evenly across all end products.

      2) Under ABC, indirect costs are attached to activities which are then rationally allocated to end products.

   b. ABC may be used by manufacturing, service, or retailing entities.

2. The inaccurate averaging or spreading of indirect costs over products or service units that use different amounts of resources is called **peanut-butter costing**.

   a. Peanut-butter costing results in **product-cost cross-subsidization**, the condition in which the miscosting of one product causes the miscosting of other products.

   b. The peanut-butter effect of using a **traditional (i.e., volume-based) costing system** can be summarized as follows:

      1) Direct labor and direct materials are traced to products or service units.

      2) A single pool of indirect costs (overhead) is accumulated for a given organizational unit.

      3) Indirect costs from the pool are assigned using an allocative (rather than a tracing) procedure, such as using a single overhead rate for an entire department, e.g., $3 of overhead for every direct labor hour.

         a) The effect is an averaging of costs that may result in significant inaccuracy when products or service units do not use similar amounts of resources.

3. EXAMPLE: The effect of product-cost cross-subsidization can be illustrated as follows:

   a. A company produces two similar products.

      1) Both products require one unit of raw material and one hour of direct labor. Raw materials costs are $20 per unit, and direct labor is $70 per hour.

   b. During the month just ended, the company produced 1,000 units of Product A and 100 units of Product B. Manufacturing overhead for the month totaled $20,000.

   c. Using direct labor hours as the overhead allocation base, per-unit costs and profits are calculated as follows:

	Product A	Product B	Total
Raw materials	$ 14,000	$ 1,400	
Direct labor	70,000	7,000	
Overhead {$20,000 × [$70,000 ÷ ($70,000 + $7,000)]}	18,182		
Overhead {$20,000 × [$7,000 ÷ ($70,000 + $7,000)]}		1,818	
Total costs	$102,182	$ 10,218	$112,400
Selling price	$ 119.99	$ 139.99	
Cost per unit	(102.18)	(102.18)	
Profit per unit	$ 17.81	$ 37.81	

d. The company's management accountants have determined that overhead consists almost entirely of production line setup costs and that the two products require equal setup times. Allocating overhead on this basis yields vastly different results.

	Product A	Product B	Total
Raw materials	$14,000	$ 1,400	
Direct labor	70,000	7,000	
Overhead ($20,000 × 50%)	10,000		
Overhead ($20,000 × 50%)		10,000	
Total costs	$94,000	$18,400	$112,400
Selling price	$119.99	$139.99	
Cost per unit	(94.00)	(184.00)	
Profit (loss) per unit	$ 25.99	$ (44.01)	

e. Rather than the comfortable profit the company believed it was making on both products using peanut-butter costing, it becomes clear that the company is losing money on every unit of Product B that it sells. The high-volume Product A has been heavily subsidizing the setup costs for the low-volume Product B.

4. The example beginning on the previous page assumed a single component of overhead for clarity. In reality, overhead is made up of many components.

    a. The **peanut-butter effect** of traditional overhead allocation is illustrated in the following diagram:

Overhead Allocation in a Traditional (Volume-Based) Cost Accumulation System

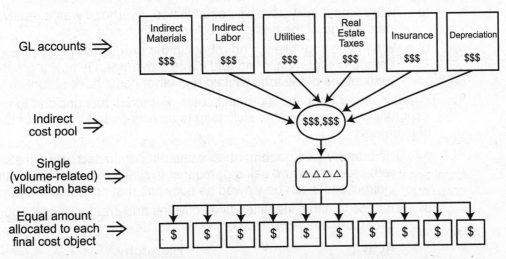

5. Volume-based systems were appropriate throughout the decades when direct costs were the bulk of manufacturing costs. With **increasing automation**, however, overhead became an ever greater percentage of the total. ABC was developed to deal with this increasing complexity of overhead costs.

    a. **Volume-based systems**, as illustrated above, involve:

        1) Accumulating costs in **general ledger accounts** (utilities, taxes, etc.)
        2) Using a **single cost pool** to combine the costs in all the related accounts
        3) Selecting a **single driver** to use for the entire indirect cost pool
        4) Allocating the indirect cost pool to **final cost objects**

    b. **Activity-based systems**, by contrast, involve:

        1) Identifying organization **activities** that constitute overhead
        2) Assigning the costs of **resources** consumed by the activities
        3) Assigning the costs of the activities to **final cost objects**

6. **Step 1 – Activity Analysis**

   a. An **activity** is a set of work actions undertaken within the entity, and a **cost pool** is established for each activity.

   b. Activities are classified in a **hierarchy** according to the level of the production process at which they take place.

      1) **Unit-level activities** are performed for each unit of output produced. Examples are using direct materials and using direct labor.

      2) **Batch-level activities** occur for each group of outputs produced. Examples are materials ordering, materials handling, and production line setup.

      3) **Product-sustaining** (or service-sustaining) **activities** support the production of a particular product (or service), irrespective of the level of production. Examples are product design, engineering changes, and testing.

      4) **Facility-sustaining activities** concern overall operations and therefore cannot be traced to products at any point in the production process. Examples are accounting, human resources, maintenance of physical plant, and safety/security arrangements.

   c. EXAMPLE: Fabulous Foundry uses a job-order system to accumulate costs for the custom pipe fittings of all sizes that it produces.

      1) Since the 1950s, Fabulous has accumulated overhead costs in six general ledger accounts (indirect materials, indirect labor, utilities, real estate taxes, insurance, and depreciation), combined them into a single indirect cost pool, and allocated the total to its products based on machine hours.

         a) At the time this system was established, overhead was a relatively small percentage of the foundry's total manufacturing costs.

         b) With increasing reliance on robots in the production process and computers for monitoring and control, overhead is now a greater percentage of the total while direct labor costs have shrunk.

      2) To obtain better data about product costs, Fabulous has decided to refine its job-order costing system by switching to activity-based costing for the allocation of overhead.

         a) The foundry's management accountants conducted extensive interviews with production and sales personnel to determine how the incurrence of indirect costs can be viewed as activities that consume resources.

         b) The accountants identified five activities and created a cost pool for each to capture the incurrence of indirect costs:

Activity	Hierarchy
Product design	Product-sustaining
Production setup	Batch-level
Machining	Unit-level
Inspection & testing	Unit-level
Customer maintenance	Facility-sustaining

7. **Step 2 – Assign Resource Costs to Activities**

    a.   Once the activities are designated, the next step in enacting an ABC system is to **assign the costs of resources** to the activities. This is termed **first-stage allocation**.

    b.   **Identifying resource costs** is not the simple matter it is in volume-based overhead allocation (where certain GL accounts are designated for combination into a single cost pool).

        1)   A **separate accounting system** may be necessary to track resource costs separately from the general ledger.

    c.   Once the resources have been identified, resource drivers are designated to allocate resource costs to the activity cost pools.

        1)   **Resource drivers** are measures of the resources consumed by an activity.

    d.   EXAMPLE: Fabulous Foundry's management accountants identified the following resources used by its indirect cost processes:

Resource	Driver
Computer processing	CPU cycles
Production line	Machine hours
Materials management	Hours worked
Accounting	Hours worked
Sales & marketing	Number of orders

8. **Step 3 – Allocate Activity Cost Pools to Final Cost Objects**

    a.   The final step in enacting an ABC system is **allocating the activity cost pools** to final cost objects. This is termed **second-stage allocation**.

    b.   Costs are reassigned to final-stage (or, if intermediate cost objects are used, next-stage) cost objects on the basis of activity drivers.

        1)   **Activity drivers** are measures of the demands made on an activity by next-stage cost objects, such as the number of parts in a product used to measure an assembly activity.

        2)   EXAMPLE: Fabulous Foundry's management accountants have designated these drivers to associate with their corresponding activities:

Activity	Driver
Product design	Number of products
Production setup	Number of setups
Machining	Number of units produced
Inspection & testing	Number of units produced
Customer maintenance	Number of orders

9. The differences between traditional overhead allocation and activity-based costing are illustrated in the following diagram:

Indirect Cost Assignment in an Activity-Based Costing System

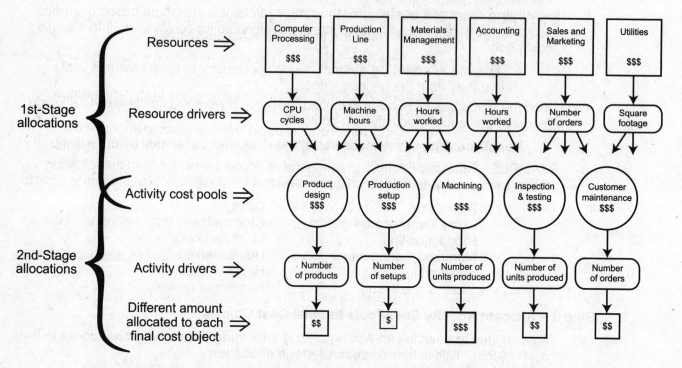

10. **Drivers** (both resource and activity) must be chosen on the basis of a **cause-and-effect relationship** with the resource or activity cost being allocated, not simply on the basis of a high positive correlation.

    a. A **cost object** may be a job, product, process, activity, service, or anything else for which a cost measure is desired.

    b. **Intermediate cost objects** receive temporary accumulations of costs as the cost pools move from their originating points to the final cost objects.

        1) For example, work-in-process is an intermediate cost object, and finished salable goods are final cost objects.

11. Stop and review! You have completed the outline for this subunit. Study multiple-choice questions 39 through 43 beginning on page 634.

19.6 BACKFLUSH COSTING AND JIT INVENTORY

1. **Backflush costing** is often used by firms that have adopted a **just-in-time (JIT)** production philosophy.

    a. A JIT system **treats carrying inventory as a nonvalue-adding activity**.

        1) Hence, components are made available just in time to be used in the production process.

        2) Backflush costing **complements JIT** because it simplifies costing.

    b. A traditional system tracks costs as they are incurred (sequential tracking), but backflush costing delays recording of some cost information.

        1) Backflush costing treats the detailed recording of inventory data as a nonvalue-adding activity.

2) **Work-in-process is usually eliminated**, journal entries to inventory accounts may be delayed until the time of product completion or even the time of sale, and standard costs are used to assign costs to units when journal entries are made, that is, to "flush" costs out of the system to the points at which inventories remain.

c. Backflush costing works well with JIT systems because of the simplification of production, which is reflected in the use of **manufacturing cells**.

     1) These cells are groups of machines and workers producing a given type of product.

     2) Each worker can operate and maintain the machines, perform set-up activities, make quality inspections, and move work-in-process within the cell.

     3) The result is **less need for central support departments**, placement of materials and tools close to the point of use, savings of space, and greater production flexibility.

     4) A further benefit is that a JIT system allows for identification of more direct costs and therefore minimizes overhead allocations.

         a) For the same reason, backflush costing also complements activity-based costing (ABC).

d. **One variation of backflush costing** records raw materials inventory at standard cost when it is purchased.

     1) Because materials arrive just in time for processing, an entry to a separate materials inventory account is unnecessary.

Raw and in-process inventory	$XXX	
Materials price variance (dr. or cr.)	XXX	
Accounts payable		$XXX

     2) Conversion costs (direct labor and overhead) are recorded when incurred at their actual amounts.

Conversion costs	$XXX	
Salaries and wages payable, etc.		$XXX

     3) The entry for the transfer to finished goods is where backflush costing gets its name. Because costs have not been accumulated sequentially during production, these costs must be "flushed out" once production is complete.

Finished goods (standard cost)	$XXX	
Raw and in-process inventory (standard cost)		$XXX
Conversion costs (standard cost)		XXX

         a) This one entry summarizes the effect of all the sequential entries of a traditional costing system that do not get made in backflush costing.

     4) After a count, raw and in-process inventory is adjusted for the materials efficiency variance (debit or credit).

         a) This variance is recorded for the difference between actual usage and standard usage for the amount of goods finished.

     5) The under- or overapplied conversion costs (debit conversion costs applied and credit conversion costs control) are usually closed to cost of goods sold instead of being prorated because the amounts tend to be small.

     6) The final entry is the same as under a traditional costing system.

Cost of goods sold	$XXX	
Finished goods		$XXX

e. **A greater departure from traditional methods** is to recognize the sale but not the completion of units.

1) In this variation of backflush costing, only one inventory account is used (inventory control) instead of two (raw and in-process inventory and finished goods).

2) The entry at the time of the acquisition of direct materials is:

Inventory control	$XXX	
Materials price variance (dr. or cr.)	XXX	
Accounts payable		$XXX

3) As described in d.2) on the previous page, actual conversion costs are debited to a control account.

4) Under this method, no finished goods inventory is carried at all.

Cost of goods sold	$XXX	
Inventory control		$XXX
Conversion costs		XXX

5) As described in d.5) on the previous page, under- or overapplied conversion costs are recognized by debiting conversion costs applied and crediting conversion costs control with, typically, a debit or credit to cost of goods sold.

6) All conversion costs are period costs in this version of backflush costing.

7) If recognition of a direct materials efficiency variance is desired, a physical count is made, and the difference between what is on hand and what should be on hand is the variance for which inventory is adjusted.

f. **Another possibility** is to eliminate entries to a materials inventory account altogether.

1) Accordingly, finished goods are debited when completed (with credits to accounts payable, etc., and to overhead applied) and credited when sold, but no other inventory entries are made.

g. **Yet another variation** of backflush costing records costs (direct materials, direct labor, and overhead) directly in cost of goods sold.

1) At the end of the period, the standard costs of the ending work-in-process and finished goods inventories are flushed back from cost of goods sold (debit WIP and FG, credit CGS).

h. Backflush costing may undervalue inventory and is therefore **inconsistent with GAAP** except when the difference is not material or an adjustment is made. Another criticism is that the lack of sequential tracking leaves an inadequate audit trail.

2. Stop and review! You have completed the outline for this subunit. Study multiple-choice questions 44 through 47 beginning on page 636.

19.7 JOINT PRODUCT AND BY-PRODUCT COSTING

1. When two or more separate products are produced by a common manufacturing process from a common input, the outputs from the process are **joint products**.

a. **Joint (common) costs** are those costs incurred up to the point where the products become separately identifiable, called the split-off point.

1) Joint costs include direct materials, direct labor, and manufacturing overhead. Because they are not separately identifiable, they must be allocated to the individual joint products.

2) EXAMPLE: Crude oil can be refined into multiple salable products. All costs incurred in getting the crude oil to the distilling tower are joint costs.

b. At the **split-off point**, the joint products acquire separate identities. Costs incurred after split-off are separable costs.

   1) **Separable costs** can be identified with a particular joint product and allocated to a specific unit of output.

   2) EXAMPLE: Once crude oil had been distilled into asphalt, fuel oil, diesel fuel, kerosene, and gasoline, costs incurred in further refining and distributing these individual products are separable costs.

2. Several methods are available to **allocate joint costs**. These can be grouped into two approaches.

   a. A **physical measure-based approach** employs a physical measure such as volume, weight, or a linear measure.

      1) The **physical-unit method** allocates joint production costs to each product based on its relative proportion of the measure selected.

      2) EXAMPLE: A refinery processes 1,000 barrels of crude oil and incurs $100,000 of processing costs. The process results in the following outputs. Under the physical unit method, the joint costs up to split-off are allocated as follows:

Asphalt	$100,000 × (300 barrels ÷ 1,000 barrels) =	$ 30,000
Fuel oil	$100,000 × (300 barrels ÷ 1,000 barrels) =	30,000
Diesel fuel	$100,000 × (200 barrels ÷ 1,000 barrels) =	20,000
Kerosene	$100,000 × (100 barrels ÷ 1,000 barrels) =	10,000
Gasoline	$100,000 × (100 barrels ÷ 1,000 barrels) =	10,000
		$100,000

      3) The physical-unit method's simplicity makes it appealing, but it does not match costs with the individual products' revenue-generating potential.

   b. A **market-based approach** assigns a proportionate amount of the total cost to each product on a quantitative basis.

      1) These allocations are performed using the entire production run for an accounting period, not units sold. This is because the joint costs were incurred on all the units produced, not just those sold.

      2) Three major methods of allocation are available under this approach.

      3) The **sales-value split-off method** is based on the relative sales values of the separate products at split-off.

         a) EXAMPLE: The refinery estimates that the five outputs can sell for the following prices at split-off:

Asphalt	300 barrels @ $ 60/barrel =	$ 18,000
Fuel oil	300 barrels @ $180/barrel =	54,000
Diesel fuel	200 barrels @ $160/barrel =	32,000
Kerosene	100 barrels @ $ 80/barrel =	8,000
Gasoline	100 barrels @ $180/barrel =	18,000
		$130,000

The total expected sales value for the entire production run at split-off is thus $130,000. Multiply the total joint costs to be allocated by the proportion of the total expected sales of each product:

Asphalt	$100,000 × ($18,000 ÷ $130,000) =	$ 13,846
Fuel oil	$100,000 × ($54,000 ÷ $130,000) =	41,538
Diesel fuel	$100,000 × ($32,000 ÷ $130,000) =	24,616
Kerosene	$100,000 × ($ 8,000 ÷ $130,000) =	6,154
Gasoline	$100,000 × ($18,000 ÷ $130,000) =	13,846
		$100,000

4) The **estimated net realizable value (NRV) method** also allocates joint costs based on the relative market values of the products.

    a)   The significant difference is that, under the estimated NRV method, all separable costs necessary to make the product salable are added in before the allocation is made.

    b)   EXAMPLE: The refinery estimates final sales prices as follows:

Asphalt	300 barrels @ $ 70/barrel =	$ 21,000
Fuel oil	300 barrels @ $200/barrel =	60,000
Diesel fuel	200 barrels @ $180/barrel =	36,000
Kerosene	100 barrels @ $ 90/barrel =	9,000
Gasoline	100 barrels @ $190/barrel =	19,000
		$145,000

From these amounts, separable costs are deducted:

Asphalt	$21,000 – $1,000=	$ 20,000
Fuel oil	$60,000 – $1,000=	59,000
Diesel fuel	$36,000 – $1,000=	35,000
Kerosene	$ 9,000 – $1,000=	7,000
Gasoline	$19,000 – $1,000=	17,000
		$138,000

The total final sales value for the entire production run is thus $138,000. Multiply the total joint costs to be allocated by the proportion of the final expected sales of each product:

Asphalt	$100,000 × ($20,000 ÷ $138,000) =	$ 14,493
Fuel oil	$100,000 × ($59,000 ÷ $138,000) =	42,754
Diesel fuel	$100,000 × ($35,000 ÷ $138,000) =	25,362
Kerosene	$100,000 × ($ 7,000 ÷ $138,000) =	5,072
Gasoline	$100,000 × ($17,000 ÷ $138,000) =	12,319
		$100,000

5) The **constant gross-margin percentage NRV method** is based on allocating joint costs so that the gross-margin percentage is the same for every product.

    a)   There are three steps under this method:

        i)   Determine the overall gross-margin percentage.

        ii)   Subtract the appropriate gross margin from the final sales value of each product to calculate total costs for that product.

        iii)   Subtract the separable costs to arrive at the joint cost amount.

    b)   EXAMPLE: The refinery uses the same calculation of expected final sales price as under the estimated NRV method:

Asphalt	300 barrels @ $ 70/barrel =	$ 21,000
Fuel oil	300 barrels @ $200/barrel =	60,000
Diesel fuel	200 barrels @ $180/barrel =	36,000
Kerosene	100 barrels @ $ 90/barrel =	9,000
Gasoline	100 barrels @ $190/barrel =	19,000
		$145,000

The final sales value for the entire production run is thus $145,000. From this total the joint costs and total separable costs are deducted to arrive at a total gross margin for all products:

$$145,000 - $100,000 - $7,000 = $38,000$$

The gross margin percentage can then be derived:

$$38,000 \div $145,000 = 26.21\%$$

Deduct gross margin from each product to arrive at a cost of goods sold:

Asphalt	$21,000 – ($21,000 × 26.21%) =	$ 15,497
Fuel oil	$60,000 – ($60,000 × 26.21%) =	44,276
Diesel fuel	$36,000 – ($36,000 × 26.21%) =	26,565
Kerosene	$ 9,000 – ($ 9,000 × 26.21%) =	6,641
Gasoline	$19,000 – ($19,000 × 26.21%) =	14,021
		$107,000

Deduct the separable costs from each product to arrive at the allocated joint costs:

Asphalt	$15,497 – $1,000 =	$ 14,497
Fuel oil	$44,276 – $1,000 =	43,276
Diesel fuel	$26,566 – $1,000 =	25,565
Kerosene	$ 6,641 – $2,000 =	4,641
Gasoline	$14,021 – $2,000 =	12,021
		$100,000

3. **By-products** are one or more products of relatively small total value that are produced simultaneously from a common manufacturing process with products of greater value and quantity.

   a. The first question that must be answered in regard to by-products is: Do the **benefits** of further processing and bringing them to market **exceed the costs**?

Selling price	$x,xxx
Less: additional processing costs	(xxx)
Less: selling costs	(xxx)
Net realizable value	**$x,xxx**

   1) If the **net realizable value** is zero or negative, the by-products should be discarded as scrap.

   b. Once the decision is made to proceed with further processing, two more questions must be answered to determine the **proper accounting treatment** for by products:

   1) Will the net realizable value of the by-products be **material** enough to warrant recognizing them as inventory on the **balance sheet**?

   2) Will the expected proceeds from the sale of the by-products be reported as **revenue** or as a reduction to **cost of goods**?

   c. If the by-products are **material**, they are recognized at the **time of production** and recorded in a separate inventory account, as in this example:

Finished goods inventory – Asphalt (net manufacturing costs)	$xx,xxx	
Finished goods inventory – Fuel oil (net manufacturing costs)	xx,xxx	
Finished goods inventory – Diesel fuel (net manufacturing costs)	xx,xxx	
Finished goods inventory – Kerosene (net manufacturing costs)	xx,xxx	
Finished goods inventory – Gasoline (net manufacturing costs)	xx,xxx	
By-product inventory – Sludge (estimated net realizable value)	x,xxx	
Work-in-process (total manufacturing costs for period)		$xxx,xxx

   1) The amount of miscellaneous revenue (or reduction to cost of goods sold) reported is the **entire estimated net realizable value** of the by-products generated during the period.

      a) This treatment is justifiable when a ready market for the by-products is available.

   2) Because revenue (or cost of goods sold) was affected at the time of production, these accounts are unaffected when the by-products are sold.

Cash	$x,xxx	
By-product inventory – Sludge		$x,xxx

d. If the by-products are **immaterial**, they are not recognized until the **time of sale** and are thus not recorded on the balance sheet.

1) The amount of miscellaneous revenue (or reduction to cost of goods sold) reported is the **actual proceeds** from the sale of the by-products.

e. Regardless of the timing of their recognition in the accounts, by-products usually do not receive an allocation of joint costs because the cost of this accounting treatment ordinarily exceeds the benefit.

4. The decision to **sell or process further** is made based on whether the incremental revenue to be gained by further processing exceeds the incremental cost thereof.

a. The joint cost of the product is irrelevant because it is a sunk cost.

5. Stop and review! You have completed the outline for this subunit. Study multiple-choice questions 48 through 63 beginning on page 637.

19.8 SERVICE COST ALLOCATION

1. **Service (support) department costs** are considered part of overhead (indirect costs). Thus, they cannot feasibly be traced to cost objects and therefore must be allocated to the operating departments that use the services.

a. When service departments also render services to each other, their costs may be allocated to each other before allocation to operating departments.

2. Four criteria are used to allocate costs.

a. **Cause and effect** should be used if possible because of its objectivity and acceptance by operating management.

b. **Benefits received** is the most frequently used alternative when a cause-and-effect relationship cannot be determined.

1) However, it requires an assumption about the benefits of costs, for example, that advertising which promotes the company but not specific products was responsible for increased sales by the various divisions.

c. **Fairness** is sometimes mentioned in government contracts but appears to be more of a goal than an objective allocation base.

d. **Ability to bear** (based on profits) is usually unacceptable because of its dysfunctional effect on managerial motivation.

3. **Three methods** of service department allocation are in general use.

a. The **direct method** is the simplest.

1) The direct method allocates service department costs directly to the producing departments without regard for services rendered by service departments to each other.

2) Service department costs are allocated to production departments based on an allocation base appropriate to each service department's function.

3) EXAMPLE:

a) A company has the following service department costs and allocation bases:

Service Department	Costs to Be Allocated	Allocation Base
Information Technology	$120,000	CPU cycles
Custodial Services	40,000	Floor space
Total	$160,000	

b) The production departments have the following preallocation costs and allocation base amounts:

Production Department	Preallocation Costs	CPU Cycles Used	%	Floor Space in Sq. Ft.	%
Department A	$300,000	60,000,000	62.5%	56,000	70.0%
Department B	200,000	36,000,000	37.5%	24,000	30.0%
Totals	$500,000	96,000,000	100.0%	80,000	100.0%

c) The direct method allocates the service department costs to the production departments as follows:

	Service Departments		Production Departments		
	Information Technology	Custodial Services	Department A	Department B	Total
Totals before allocation	$120,000	$40,000	$300,000	$200,000	$660,000
Allocate IT (62.5%, 37.5%)	(120,000)		75,000	45,000	0
Allocate Custodial (70.0%, 30.0%)		(40,000)	28,000	12,000	0
Totals after allocation	$ 0	$ 0	$403,000	$257,000	$660,000

b. The **step** or **step-down method** allocates some of the costs of services rendered by service departments to each other.

1) The step method derives its name from the procedure involved: The service departments are allocated in order, from the one that provides the most service to other service departments down to the one that provides the least.

2) EXAMPLE:

a) The services that each service department provides the other must be ascertained:

Service Department	CPU Cycles Used	%	Floor Space in Sq. Ft.	%
Information Technology	196,000,000	98.0%	20,000	80.0%
Custodial Services	4,000,000	2.0%	5,000	20.0%
Totals	200,000,000	100.0%	25,000	100.0%

b) Looking just at reciprocal service department activity, custodial services provides 20% of its services to information technology, but IT only provides 2% of its services to custodial. Thus, custodial will be allocated first.

c) The next step is to determine the relative proportions of the three departments that will receive the first allocation (the second allocation will only be distributed to the two production departments, whose allocation bases were determined under the direct method beginning on the previous page).

Allocate Custodial Services:	Floor Space in Sq. Ft.	%
To Department A	56,000	56.0%
To Department B	24,000	24.0%
To Information Technology	20,000	20.0%
Totals	100,000	100.0%

d) The step-down allocation is performed as follows:

	Service Departments		Production Departments		
	Custodial Services	Information Technology	Department A	Department B	Total
Totals before allocation	$40,000	$120,000	$300,000	$200,000	$660,000
Allocate Custodial (20.0%, 56.0%, 24.0%)	(40,000)	8,000	22,400	9,600	0
Totals after first allocation	$ 0	$128,000	$322,400	$209,600	$660,000
Allocate IT (62.5%, 37.5%)		(128,000)	80,000	48,000	0
Totals after allocation	$ 0		$402,400	$257,600	$660,000

c. The **reciprocal method** is the most complex and the most theoretically sound of the three methods. It is also known as the simultaneous solution method, cross allocation method, matrix allocation method, or double distribution method.

1) The reciprocal method recognizes services rendered by all service departments to each other.

2) EXAMPLE:

a) The reciprocal method requires calculating the allocation base amounts for information technology, i.e., the service department that was not allocated to the other service department under the step method.

	CPU Cycles	
Allocate Information Technology:	Used	%
To Department A	60,000,000	60.0%
To Department B	36,000,000	36.0%
To Custodial Services	4,000,000	4.0%
Totals	100,000,000	100.0%

b) Use linear algebra to calculate fully reciprocated information technology costs (FRITC) and fully reciprocated custodial services costs (FRCSC):

FRITC = Preallocation IT costs (FRCSC × Portion of custodial effort used by IT)
= $120,000 (FRCSC × 20%)

FRCSC = Preallocation custodial costs (FRITC × Portion of IT effort used by custodial)
= $40,000 (FRITC × 4%)

c) These algebraic equations can be solved simultaneously.

$$
\begin{aligned}
FRITC &= \$120,000 + (FRCSC \times 20\%) \\
&= \$120,000 + \{[\$40,000 + (FRITC \times 4\%)] \times 20\%\} \\
&= \$120,000 + [(\$40,000 + .04FRITC) \times .2] \\
&= \$120,000 + \$8,000 + .008FRITC \\
.992FRITC &= \$128,000 \\
FRITC &= \$129,032
\end{aligned}
$$

$$
\begin{aligned}
FRCSC &= \$40,000 + (FRITC \times 4\%) \\
&= \$40,000 + (\$129,032 \times .04) \\
&= \$40,000 + \$5,161 \\
&= \$45,161
\end{aligned}
$$

d) The reciprocal allocation is performed as follows:

	Service Departments		Production Departments		
	Custodial Services	Information Technology	Department A	Department B	Total
Totals before allocation	$40,000	$120,000	$300,000	$200,000	$ 660,000
Allocate Custodial Services	(45,161)				(45,161)
(20.0%, 56.0%, 24.0%)		9,032	25,290	10,839	45,161
Allocate Information Technology		(129,032)			(129,032)
(4.0%, 60.0%, 36.0%)	5,161		77,419	46,452	129,032
Totals after allocation	$ 0	$ 0	$402,710	$257,290	$ 660,000

4. Some service department cost allocation methods involve a **dual-rate method**, i.e., variable costs from a service department allocated using one rate and fixed costs allocated using another. The examples in this section employed a single rate.

5. Stop and review! You have completed the outline for this subunit. Study multiple-choice questions 64 through 66 beginning on page 643.

QUESTIONS

19.1 Spoilage and Scrap

1. During the month just ended, Delta Co. experienced scrap, normal spoilage, and abnormal spoilage in its manufacturing process. The cost of units produced includes

A. Scrap, but not spoilage.

B. Normal spoilage, but neither scrap nor abnormal spoilage.

C. Scrap and normal spoilage, but not abnormal spoilage.

D. Scrap, normal spoilage, and abnormal spoilage.

Answer (C) is correct. *(CPA, adapted)*
REQUIRED: The accounting for scrap and spoilage.
DISCUSSION: One method of accounting for scrap is to credit a revenue account for the net amount realized or expected to be realized. An alternative is to credit factory overhead control (or WIP for a specific job if the scrap relates only to that job). In the first case, the costs of scrap remain in WIP. In the second case, the amounts realized indirectly reduce the costs of all units. However, if scrap is applicable to a specific job, the realized amounts directly reduce the cost of specific units. Regardless of the accounting, good units continue to bear at least the costs of scrap that cannot be recovered by its sale. The net cost of normal spoilage is likewise included in the cost of good units. But the cost of abnormal spoilage is credited to WIP, with debits to a loss account and to an account that records the disposal value. Thus, good units do not bear the costs of abnormal spoilage.
Answer (A) is incorrect because good units bear the cost of normal spoilage. Answer (B) is incorrect because good units bear the cost of scrap. Answer (D) is incorrect because good units do not bear the cost of abnormal spoilage.

2. Hoyt Co. manufactured the following units:

Salable	5,000
Unsalable (normal spoilage)	200
Unsalable (abnormal spoilage)	300

Manufacturing costs totaled $99,000. What amount should Hoyt debit to finished goods?

A. $90,000

B. $93,600

C. $95,400

D. $99,000

Answer (B) is correct. *(CPA, adapted)*
REQUIRED: The amount of debit to finished goods.
DISCUSSION: Normal spoilage occurs under normal operating conditions and should be treated as a product cost. However, abnormal spoilage is not expected to occur and should be treated as a period cost because of its unusual nature. Consequently, the cost of abnormal spoilage is removed from the manufacturing costs based on the relative number of units spoiling abnormally. Thus, the amount debited to finished goods is $93,600 {$99,000 – [300 ÷ (5,000 + 200 + 300) × $99,000]}.
Answer (A) is incorrect because $90,000 excludes the cost due to normal spoilage. Answer (C) is incorrect because $95,400 excludes the cost due to normal spoilage and includes the cost due to abnormal spoilage. Answer (D) is incorrect because $99,000 includes the cost of abnormal spoilage.

3. The sale of scrap from a manufacturing process usually is recorded as a(n)

A. Decrease in factory overhead control.

B. Increase in factory overhead control.

C. Decrease in finished goods control.

D. Increase in finished goods control.

Answer (A) is correct. *(CPA, adapted)*
REQUIRED: The usual accounting for a sale of scrap.
DISCUSSION: The sale of the normal amount of scrap arising from a manufacturing process is usually recorded by debiting cash or a receivable and crediting factory overhead control. The effect is to allocate the net cost of the scrap (historical cost – disposal proceeds) to the good units produced. Thus, the total cost of scrap remains in work-in-process control, but overhead that otherwise would have been applied to the good units is reduced by the amount received for scrap.
Answer (B) is incorrect because factory overhead control is credited for the amounts realized upon sale. Answer (C) is incorrect because crediting finished goods would not allocate the disposal value to all good units. Answer (D) is incorrect because amounts received from the sale of scrap reduce the costs inventoried.

4. Spoilage from a manufacturing process was discovered during an inspection of work in process. In a process costing system, the cost of the spoilage would be added to the cost of the good units produced if the spoilage is

	Abnormal	Normal
A.	No	Yes
B.	No	No
C.	Yes	Yes
D.	Yes	No

Answer (A) is correct. *(CPA, adapted)*
REQUIRED: The kind(s) of spoilage added to the cost of good units in a process-costing system.
DISCUSSION: Normal spoilage is the spoilage that occurs under normal operating conditions. It is essentially uncontrollable in the short run. Normal spoilage arises under efficient operations and is treated as a product cost. Abnormal spoilage is spoilage that is not expected to occur under normal, efficient operating conditions. Because of its unusual nature, abnormal spoilage is typically treated as a loss in the period in which it is incurred.
Answer (B) is incorrect because normal spoilage is a product cost. Answer (C) is incorrect because abnormal spoilage is a period cost. Answer (D) is incorrect because normal, not abnormal, spoilage is a product cost.

5. In its production process, Hern Corp., which does not use a standard cost system, incurred total production costs for the month of $900,000, of which Hern attributed $60,000 to normal spoilage and $30,000 to abnormal spoilage. Hern should account for this spoilage as

A. Period cost of $90,000.

B. Inventoriable cost of $90,000.

C. Period cost of $60,000 and inventoriable cost of $30,000.

D. Inventoriable cost of $60,000 and period cost of $30,000.

Answer (D) is correct. *(CPA, adapted)*
REQUIRED: The proper accounting for spoilage.
DISCUSSION: Normal spoilage arises under efficient operating conditions and is therefore a product cost. Abnormal spoilage is not expected to occur under efficient operating conditions. It is accounted for as a period cost. Thus, the normal spoilage of $60,000 is an inventoriable cost, and the abnormal spoilage of $30,000 is a period cost.
Answer (A) is incorrect because normal spoilage is inventoried. Answer (B) is incorrect because abnormal spoilage is not inventoried. Answer (C) is incorrect because normal spoilage is an inventoriable cost, and abnormal spoilage is not.

19.2 Job-Order Costing

6. Jonathan Manufacturing adopted a job-costing system. For the current year, budgeted cost driver activity levels for direct labor hours and direct labor costs were 20,000 and $100,000, respectively. In addition, budgeted variable and fixed factory overhead costs were $50,000 and $25,000, respectively. Actual costs and hours for the year were as follows:

Direct labor hours	21,000
Direct labor costs	$110,000
Machine hours	35,000

For a particular job, 1,500 direct-labor hours were used. Using direct-labor hours as the cost driver, what amount of overhead should be applied to this job?

    A. $3,214

    B. $5,357

    C. $5,625

    D. $7,500

Answer (C) is correct. *(CPA, adapted)*
    REQUIRED: The overhead applied using direct-labor hours as the cost driver.
    DISCUSSION: To apply overhead to the job, both variable and fixed overhead must be properly allocated using standard rates and direct-labor hours as the cost driver. The pertinent information given for this year's budget includes direct-labor hours of 20,000 and the budgeted variable and fixed factory overhead of $50,000 and $25,000, respectively. The variable overhead cost per direct labor hour is $2.50 ($50,000 ÷ 20,000 DLH), and the fixed overhead per direct labor hour is $1.25 ($25,000 ÷ 20,000 DLH). Thus, the total standard overhead cost per direct labor hour is $3.75. The total overhead to be applied is $5,625 (1,500 DLH × $3.75).
    Answer (A) is incorrect because $3,214 is based on actual total machine hours for the year. Answer (B) is incorrect because $5,357 is based on actual total direct labor hours for the year. Answer (D) is incorrect because $7,500 [1,500 DLH × ($100,000 ÷ $20,000)] is the standard direct labor cost applied.

7. In a job-order cost system, the use of direct materials previously purchased usually is recorded as an increase in

    A. Work-in-process control.

    B. Factory overhead control.

    C. Factory overhead applied.

    D. Stores control.

Answer (A) is correct. *(CPA, adapted)*
    REQUIRED: The account increased by the use of direct materials already on hand.
    DISCUSSION: The purchase of direct materials requires a debit to (an increase in) direct materials inventory (stores control). This account is credited and work-in-process control is debited when direct materials are issued to a production department.
    Answer (B) is incorrect because factory overhead control is debited (increased) when indirect, not direct, materials are issued. Answer (C) is incorrect because factory overhead applied is increased (credited) only when overhead is charged to work-in-process at a predetermined rate based on an appropriate activity base. Answer (D) is incorrect because stores control is increased when direct materials are purchased.

8. Under Pick Co.'s job-order costing system, manufacturing overhead is applied to work-in-process using a predetermined annual overhead rate. During the month just ended, Pick's transactions included the following:

Direct materials issued to production	$ 90,000
Indirect materials issued to production	8,000
Manufacturing overhead incurred	125,000
Manufacturing overhead applied	113,000
Direct labor costs	107,000

Pick had neither beginning nor ending work-in-process inventory. What was the cost of jobs completed during the month?

    A. $302,000

    B. $310,000

    C. $322,000

    D. $330,000

Answer (B) is correct. *(CPA, adapted)*
    REQUIRED: The cost of jobs completed.
    DISCUSSION: Given no beginning or ending work-in-process, the cost of jobs completed equals the sum of direct materials, direct labor, and manufacturing overhead applied. Indirect materials costs are charged to overhead control and are not included in the amount transferred from work-in-process to finished goods. The difference between overhead incurred and overhead applied, if material, is allocated among finished goods, cost of goods sold, and ending work-in-process ($0 in this case). Hence, the cost of jobs completed was $310,000 ($90,000 + $113,000 + $107,000).
    Answer (A) is incorrect because $302,000 results from subtracting indirect materials from the cost of jobs completed. Answer (C) is incorrect because $322,000 is based on overhead incurred. Answer (D) is incorrect because $330,000 includes indirect materials and overhead incurred.

9. Birk Co. uses a job-order cost system. The following debits (credit) appeared in Birk's work-in-process account for the month just ended:

Date	Description	Amount
1	Balance	$ 4,000
31	Direct materials	24,000
31	Direct labor	16,000
31	Factory overhead	12,800
31	To finished goods	(48,000)

Birk applies overhead to production at a predetermined rate of 80% of direct labor cost. Job No. 5, the only job still in process at month end, has been charged with direct labor of $2,000. What was the amount of direct materials charged to Job No. 5?

A. $3,000

B. $5,200

C. $8,800

D. $24,000

Answer (B) is correct. *(CPA, adapted)*
   REQUIRED: The dollar value of direct materials in ending work-in-process.
   DISCUSSION: Total debits to WIP are $56,800 ($4,000 + $24,000 + $16,000 + $12,800). Given a credit of $48,000 for finished goods, EWIP is $8,800 ($56,800 – $48,000). Of this amount, $2,000 is direct labor and $1,600 ($2,000 × 80%) is overhead. Hence, the amount of direct materials charged to Job No. 5 was $5,200 ($8,800 – $2,000 – $1,600).
   Answer (A) is incorrect because $3,000 is a random figure. Answer (C) is incorrect because $8,800 is the total EWIP credit. Answer (D) is incorrect because $24,000 is the debit for direct materials during the month.

10. A direct labor overtime premium should be charged to a specific job when the overtime is caused by the

A. Increased overall level of activity.

B. Customer's requirement for early completion of the job.

C. Management's failure to include the job in the production schedule.

D. Management's requirement that the job be completed before the annual factory vacation closure.

Answer (B) is correct. *(CPA, adapted)*
   REQUIRED: The circumstances in which a direct labor overtime premium should be charged to a specific job.
   DISCUSSION: A direct labor overtime premium equals the excess of the overtime pay rate over the regular rate, multiplied by total overtime hours. It is ordinarily considered an indirect cost, charged to overhead, and thereby allocated to all jobs. The reason is that the association of an overhead premium with a specific job may be attributable solely to random scheduling. Accordingly, the incurrence of the premium is usually regarded as a function of an abnormally large production volume, that is, as a condition affecting all jobs. However, if the premium directly results from the demands of a specific job, it should be charged as a direct cost to that job.
   Answer (A) is incorrect because an overtime premium arising from increased overall activity is an indirect cost charged to overhead. Answer (C) is incorrect because management's scheduling omission is a random factor. In such a case, the overtime premium is not caused by the demands of the specific job omitted. Answer (D) is incorrect because assuming all jobs are to be completed prior to the closing, no specific job is the cause of the premium.

11. In a traditional job-order cost system, the issue of indirect materials to a production department increases

A. Stores control.

B. Work-in-process control.

C. Factory overhead control.

D. Factory overhead applied.

Answer (C) is correct. *(CPA, adapted)*
   REQUIRED: The account increased when indirect materials are issued to a production department.
   DISCUSSION: As overhead is incurred, factory overhead control is debited and accounts payable, supplies, etc., are credited. When overhead is applied, work-in-process is debited and factory overhead applied is credited. The difference between the debited and credited amounts is over- or underapplied overhead.
   Answer (A) is incorrect because stores control decreases (i.e., is credited). Answer (B) is incorrect because work-in-process increases (with a debit) when overhead is applied. Answer (D) is incorrect because factory overhead applied increases (with a credit) when overhead is applied, not when it is incurred.

12. A job-order cost system uses a predetermined factory overhead rate based on expected volume and expected fixed cost. At the end of the year, underapplied overhead might be explained by which of the following situations?

	Actual Volume	Actual Fixed Costs
A.	Greater than expected	Greater than expected
B.	Greater than expected	Less than expected
C.	Less than expected	Greater than expected
D.	Less than expected	Less than expected

Answer (C) is correct. *(CPA, adapted)*
REQUIRED: The situations resulting in underapplied overhead.
DISCUSSION: If too little fixed overhead is applied at the predetermined rate (expected fixed cost ÷ expected volume), the result is underapplied overhead (actual factory overhead exceeds overhead applied). If the actual and expected fixed costs are the same, but the actual volume is less than the expected (denominator) volume, overhead will be underapplied. If the actual volume equals expected volume, but actual fixed costs exceed the expected (numerator) fixed costs, overhead is likewise underapplied.
Answer (A) is incorrect because, if actual volume is greater than expected, overhead may be overapplied. Answer (B) is incorrect because, if actual volume is greater than expected or actual fixed costs are less than expected, overhead may be overapplied. Answer (D) is incorrect because, if actual fixed costs are less than expected, overhead may be overapplied.

13. In a job cost system, manufacturing overhead is

	An Indirect Cost of Jobs	A Necessary Element in Production
A.	No	Yes
B.	No	No
C.	Yes	Yes
D.	Yes	No

Answer (C) is correct. *(CPA, adapted)*
REQUIRED: The nature of factory overhead.
DISCUSSION: Factory overhead consists of indirect manufacturing costs that cannot be traced to specific units but are necessarily incurred as part of the production process. Examples are depreciation, utilities expense, insurance, and supervisors' salaries. Factory overhead is usually allocated to products based upon the level of activity during the period, e.g., direct labor hours or machine hours.
Answer (A) is incorrect because factory overhead is an indirect cost. Answer (B) is incorrect because factory overhead is both an indirect cost and necessary to production. Answer (D) is incorrect because factory overhead is necessary to production.

14. Mason Co. uses a job-order cost system and applies manufacturing overhead to jobs using a predetermined overhead rate based on direct-labor dollars. The rate for the current year is 200% of direct-labor dollars. This rate was calculated last year and will be used throughout the current year. Mason had one job, No. 150, in process at the beginning of the month with raw materials costs of $2,000 and direct-labor costs of $3,000. During the month, raw materials and direct labor added to jobs were as follows:

	No. 150	No. 151	No. 152
Raw materials	$ --	$4,000	$1,000
Direct labor	1,500	5,000	2,500

Actual manufacturing overhead for the month was $20,000. During the month, Mason completed Job Nos. 150 and 151. For the month, manufacturing overhead was

A. Overapplied by $4,000.

B. Underapplied by $7,000.

C. Underapplied by $2,000.

D. Underapplied by $1,000.

Answer (C) is correct. *(CPA, adapted)*
REQUIRED: The under- or overapplied manufacturing overhead.
DISCUSSION: Mason incurred direct-labor costs of $9,000 ($1,500 Job 150 + $5,000 Job 151 + $2,500 Job 152). Hence, overhead applied was $18,000 ($9,000 × 200%). The amount underapplied was $2,000 ($20,000 actual OH – $18,000).
Answer (A) is incorrect because overhead would have been overapplied by $4,000 if the direct-labor costs in beginning work-in-process had been treated as incurred during the month. Answer (B) is incorrect because overhead would have been underapplied by $7,000 if Job 152 had been ignored. Answer (D) is incorrect because overhead would have been underapplied by $1,000 if the direct-labor costs in beginning work-in-process had been treated as incurred during the month and if Job 152 had been ignored.

15. The completion of goods is recorded as a decrease in work-in-process control when using

	Job-Order Costing	Process Costing
A.	Yes	No
B.	Yes	Yes
C.	No	Yes
D.	No	No

Answer (B) is correct. *(CPA, adapted)*
REQUIRED: The costing system(s) in which work-in-process control is decreased when goods are completed.
DISCUSSION: The cost flow among accounts in process costing is similar to that for job-order costing. Both use the basic general ledger accounts, for example, materials control, work-in-process control, factory overhead control, finished goods control, and cost of goods sold. Consequently, each system credits (decreases) work-in-process control and debits (increases) finished goods control when goods are completed.
Answer (A) is incorrect because process costing credits work-in-process control when goods are completed. Answer (C) is incorrect because job-order costing credits work-in-process control when goods are completed. Answer (D) is incorrect because job-order and process costing systems credit work-in-process control when goods are completed.

19.3 Process Costing

16. Black, Inc. employs a weighted-average method in its process costing system. Black's work-in-process inventory on June 30 consists of 40,000 units. These units are 100% complete with respect to materials and 60% complete with respect to conversion costs. The equivalent unit costs are $5.00 for materials and $7.00 for conversion costs. What is the total cost of the June 30 work-in-process inventory?

A. $200,000

B. $288,000

C. $368,000

D. $480,000

Answer (C) is correct. *(CPA, adapted)*
REQUIRED: The total cost of work-in-process given equivalent-unit data.
DISCUSSION: Because the weighted-average method of process costing is used, no distinction is made between current-period and prior-period costs. Given 40,000 physical units that are 100% complete with regard to materials, the equivalent-unit cost of materials is $200,000 [(40,000 × 100%) × $5]. Given also that these units are 60% complete with regard to conversion costs, the equivalent-unit cost of conversion is $168,000 [(40,000 × 60%) × $7]. The total cost of work-in-process given equivalent-unit data is therefore $368,000 ($200,000 + $168,000).
Answer (A) is incorrect because $200,000 is the materials cost. Answer (B) is incorrect because $288,000 is based on the assumption that the work-in-process also is 60% complete with regard to materials. Answer (D) is incorrect because $480,000 is based on the assumption that conversion also is 100% complete.

17. During the current year, the following manufacturing activity took place for a company's products:

Beginning work-in-process, 70% complete	10,000 units
Units started into production during the year	150,000 units
Units completed during the year	140,000 units
Ending work-in-process, 25% complete	20,000 units

What was the number of equivalent units produced using the first-in, first-out method (FIFO)?

A. 138,000

B. 140,000

C. 145,000

D. 150,000

Answer (A) is correct. *(CPA, adapted)*
REQUIRED: The equivalent units produced using the first-in, first-out method.
DISCUSSION: The FIFO method considers only the work done in the current period in calculating equivalent units of production (EUP). The EUP needed to complete beginning work-in-process (BWIP) equal 3,000 [10,000 units × (100% – 70%)]. The EUP for units started and completed equal 130,000 [(140,000 units completed – 10,000 units in BWIP) × 100%]. The EUP for units in ending work-in-process (EWIP) equal 5,000 (20,000 units × 25%). Hence, total EUP equal 138,000.
Answer (B) is incorrect because 140,000 is the number of physical units completed. Answer (C) is incorrect because 145,000 is the number of EUP based on the weighted-average assumption. Answer (D) is incorrect because 150,000 is the number of physical units started.

Questions 18 and 19 are based on the following information.

A sporting goods manufacturer buys wood as a direct material for baseball bats. The Forming Department processes the baseball bats, and the bats are then transferred to the Finishing Department where a sealant is applied. The Forming Department began manufacturing 10,000 "Casey Sluggers" during the month of May. There was no beginning inventory.

Costs for the Forming Department for the month of May were as follows:

Direct materials	$33,000
Conversion costs	17,000
Total	$50,000

A total of 8,000 bats were completed and transferred to the Finishing Department; the remaining 2,000 bats were still in the forming process at the end of the month. All of the Forming Department's direct materials were placed in process, but, on average, only 25% of the conversion cost was applied to the ending work-in-process inventory.

18. The cost of the units transferred to the Finishing Department is

A. $50,000

B. $40,000

C. $53,000

D. $42,400

Answer (D) is correct. *(CMA, adapted)*
REQUIRED: The cost of the units transferred to the Finishing Department.
DISCUSSION: The total equivalent units for materials equals 10,000 because all materials for the ending work-in-process had already been added to production. Hence, the materials cost per unit was $3.30 ($33,000 ÷ 10,000). For conversion costs, the total equivalent units equals 8,500 [8,000 completed + (2,000 in EWIP × 25%)]. Thus, the conversion cost was $2.00 per unit ($17,000 ÷ 8,500). The total cost transferred was therefore $42,400 [8,000 units × ($3.30 + $2.00)].
Answer (A) is incorrect because a portion of the total costs is still in work-in-process. Answer (B) is incorrect because $40,000 assumes that work-in-process is 100% complete as to conversion costs. Answer (C) is incorrect because $53,000 exceeds the actual costs incurred during the period. Given no beginning inventory, the amount transferred out cannot exceed the costs incurred during the period.

19. The cost of the work-in-process inventory in the Forming Department at the end of May is

A. $10,000

B. $2,500

C. $20,000

D. $7,600

Answer (D) is correct. *(CMA, adapted)*
REQUIRED: The cost of the work-in-process inventory.
DISCUSSION: The equivalent units for materials equal 10,000 (8,000 + 2,000) because the work-in-process is 100% complete as to materials. Thus, dividing the $33,000 by 10,000 units results in a unit cost for materials of $3.30. The equivalent units for conversion costs equal 8,500 units [8,000 + (2,000 units × .25)]. Dividing the $17,000 of conversion costs by 8,500 equivalent units results in a unit cost of $2 per bat, and the total cost of goods transferred out is $5.30, consisting of $3.30 for materials and $2 for conversion costs. Multiplying $5.30 by the 8,000 bats completed results in a total transfer of $42,400. Consequently, the cost of the ending work-in-process must have been $7,600 ($50,000 total costs incurred − $42,400).
Answer (A) is incorrect because $10,000 assumes that work-in-process inventory is 100% complete as to conversion costs. Answer (B) is incorrect because $2,500 assumes that work-in-process inventory is 100% complete as to conversion costs and that 500 bats are in inventory. Answer (C) is incorrect because $20,000 assumes that work-in-process is 100% complete as to conversion costs and that 6,000 units were transferred out.

Questions 20 through 26 are based on the following information.

Rebel Corporation uses a process-costing system. Products are manufactured in a series of three departments. The following data relate to Department Two for the month of February:

Beginning work-in-process (70% complete)	10,000 units
Goods started in production	80,000 units
Ending work-in-process (60% complete)	5,000 units

The beginning work-in-process was valued at $66,000, consisting of $20,000 of transferred-in costs, $30,000 of materials costs, and $16,000 of conversion costs. Materials are added at the beginning of the process; conversion costs are added evenly throughout the process. Costs added to production during February were

Transferred-in	$16,000
Materials used	88,000
Conversion costs	50,000

All preliminary and final calculations are rounded to two decimal places.

20. Under the weighted-average method, how much conversion cost did Rebel Corporation transfer out of Department Two during February?

A. $69,259

B. $63,750

C. $66,000

D. $64,148

Answer (B) is correct. *(Publisher, adapted)*
REQUIRED: The conversion cost transferred out under the weighted-average method.
DISCUSSION: For conversion costs, the equivalent-unit calculation under the weighted-average method is as follows:

Beginning WIP	10,000 units × 100% =	10,000
Started and completed	75,000 units × 100% =	75,000
Ending WIP	5,000 units × 60% =	3,000
		88,000

The conversion costs consisted of $16,000 in beginning inventory and $50,000 incurred during the month, for a total of $66,000. Unit conversion cost is therefore $.75 ($66,000 ÷ 88,000 EU). Thus, the total conversion cost transferred was $63,750 [(10,000 units in BWIP + 80,000 units started – 5,000 units in EWIP) × $.75].
Answer (A) is incorrect because $69,259 results from using the equivalent units calculated under FIFO (81,000) in determining the unit conversion cost under the weighted-average method. Answer (C) is incorrect because $66,000 equals the total conversion costs to be accounted for. Answer (D) is incorrect because $64,148 is the conversion cost transferred out under a FIFO assumption.

21. Under the weighted-average method, how much materials cost did Rebel Corporation transfer out of Department Two during February?

A. $88,000

B. $93,500

C. $111,350

D. $112,500

Answer (C) is correct. *(Publisher, adapted)*
REQUIRED: The materials cost transferred out under the weighted-average method.
DISCUSSION: For materials, the equivalent-unit calculation under the weighted-average method is

Beginning WIP	10,000 units × 100% =	10,000
Started and completed	75,000 units × 100% =	75,000
Ending WIP	5,000 units × 100% =	5,000
		90,000

The materials costs consisted of $30,000 in beginning inventory and $88,000 incurred during the month, for a total of $118,000. The equivalent unit cost of materials is therefore $1.31 ($118,000 ÷ 90,000 EU). Total materials cost transferred is $111,350 (85,000 units transferred × $1.31).
Answer (A) is incorrect because $88,000 is the materials costs incurred during the month. Answer (B) is incorrect because $93,500 results from using a unit cost based on the FIFO method. Answer (D) is incorrect because $112,500 is the materials cost transferred out under FIFO.

22. Under the weighted-average method, what is the total of equivalent units for Rebel's transferred-in costs for the month?

A. 75,000 units.

B. 80,000 units.

C. 81,000 units.

D. 90,000 units.

Answer (D) is correct. *(Publisher, adapted)*
REQUIRED: The equivalent units for transferred-in costs under the weighted-average method.
DISCUSSION: The equivalent units for transferred-in costs are calculated in the same way as those for materials added at the beginning of the process. The equivalent-unit calculation under the weighted-average method is

Beginning WIP	10,000 units × 100% =	10,000
Started and completed	75,000 units × 100% =	75,000
Ending WIP	5,000 units × 100% =	5,000
		90,000

Answer (A) is incorrect because 75,000 units is the amount started and completed during the month; it ignores the impact of inventories. Answer (B) is incorrect because 80,000 units is based on the FIFO method. Answer (C) is incorrect because 81,000 units is based on the equivalent units for conversion costs calculated under the FIFO method.

23. Assume that the company uses the first-in, first-out (FIFO) method of inventory valuation. Under FIFO, how much conversion cost did Rebel Corporation transfer out of Department Two during February?

A. $63,750

B. $64,360

C. $66,000

D. $74,500

Answer (B) is correct. *(Publisher, adapted)*
REQUIRED: The conversion cost transferred out under the FIFO method.
DISCUSSION: For conversion costs, the equivalent-unit calculation under the FIFO method is

Beginning WIP	10,000 units × 30% =	3,000
Started and completed	75,000 units × 100% =	75,000
Ending WIP	5,000 units × 60% =	3,000
		81,000

The conversion cost includes $16,000 in beginning inventory, all of which would have been transferred out. The $50,000 incurred during the month is divided by the 81,000 equivalent units to arrive at a unit cost for the current period of $.62. Given that 78,000 equivalent units (85,000 physical units transferred out – 7,000 EU in BWIP completed in the prior period) of current-period production were completed and transferred, the total conversion cost transferred out was $64,360 [$16,000 BWIP + (78,000 FIFO EU × $.62)].
Answer (A) is incorrect because $63,750 is based on the weighted-average method. Answer (C) is incorrect because $66,000 equals total conversion costs incurred. Answer (D) is incorrect because $74,500 is based on the weighted-average unit cost per equivalent unit.

24. Assuming Rebel uses the FIFO method of inventory valuation, conversion costs included in the ending work-in-process inventory equal

A. $1,860

B. $2,250

C. $3,100

D. $5,500

Answer (A) is correct. *(Publisher, adapted)*
REQUIRED: The conversion cost included in ending inventory under the FIFO method.
DISCUSSION: The FIFO unit conversion cost for the current period is $.62. Moreover, ending work-in-process consists of 3,000 equivalent units of conversion cost (5,000 physical units × 60%). Accordingly, the conversion cost in the ending work-in-process inventory consists of $1,860 (3,000 EU × $.62) of current-period cost. The conversion cost incurred in the prior period and attached to the beginning work-in-process inventory is deemed to have been transferred out.
Answer (B) is incorrect because $2,250 is based on the weighted-average method. Answer (C) is incorrect because $3,100 is based on the equivalent units for materials. Answer (D) is incorrect because $5,500 is the amount of materials cost in the ending work-in-process inventory.

25. Refer to the information on the preceding page(s). Assume that the company uses the first-in, first-out (FIFO) method of inventory valuation. Under FIFO, how much materials cost did Rebel Corporation transfer out of Department Two during February?

A. $88,000

B. $111,350

C. $112,500

D. $114,615

Answer (C) is correct. *(Publisher, adapted)*
REQUIRED: The materials cost transferred out under the FIFO method.
DISCUSSION: For materials, the equivalent-unit calculation under the FIFO method is

Beginning WIP	10,000 units × 0% =	0
Started and completed	75,000 units × 100% =	75,000
Ending WIP	5,000 units × 100% =	5,000
		80,000

The materials cost includes $30,000 in beginning inventory, all of which would have been transferred out. The $88,000 incurred during the month is divided by the 80,000 equivalent units to arrive at a unit cost for the current period of $1.10. Thus, given that 75,000 equivalent units (85,000 physical units transferred out – 10,000 EU in BWIP completed in the prior period) of current-period production were completed and transferred, total materials cost transferred out equals $112,500 [$30,000 BWIP + (75,000 FIFO EU × $1.10)].
Answer (A) is incorrect because $88,000 is the amount of materials costs incurred during the month. Answer (B) is incorrect because $111,350 is based on the weighted-average method. Answer (D) is incorrect because $114,615 is based on the equivalent units for conversion costs.

26. Refer to the information on the preceding page(s). Assuming the company uses the FIFO method of inventory valuation, what amount of materials cost is included in Rebel's ending work-in-process inventory?

A. $1,860

B. $3,300

C. $5,500

D. $6,450

Answer (C) is correct. *(Publisher, adapted)*
REQUIRED: The materials cost left in ending work-in-process inventory under FIFO.
DISCUSSION: The unit cost of materials under FIFO is $1.10. Because the 5,000 units in ending work-in-process inventory are 100% complete as to materials, its materials cost consists of $5,500 (5,000 EU × $1.10) of current-period costs. Materials costs incurred in the prior period and attached to the beginning work-in-process inventory are deemed to have been transferred out.
Answer (A) is incorrect because $1,860 is the amount of conversion costs. Answer (B) is incorrect because $3,300 assumes that materials are added proportionately throughout the process. Answer (D) is incorrect because $6,450 is based on the unit cost under the weighted-average method.

27. Yarn Co.'s inventories in process were at the following states of completion at the end of the month:

No. of Units	Percent Complete
100	90%
50	80%
200	10%

Equivalent units of production amounted to

A. 150

B. 180

C. 330

D. 350

Answer (A) is correct. *(CPA, adapted)*
REQUIRED: The EUP given the number of units and their percentage of completion.
DISCUSSION: The equivalent units of production are calculated as shown below.

100 units × 90% complete	90
50 units × 80% complete	40
200 units × 10% complete	20
Equivalent units	150

Answer (B) is incorrect because 180 results from incorrectly summing the percentages. Answer (C) is incorrect because 330 results from incorrectly summing the unweighted units and the percentages. Answer (D) is incorrect because 350 results from incorrectly summing the units without weighting them.

28. A process costing system was used for a department that began operations in January. Approximately the same number of physical units, at the same degree of completion, were in work-in-process at the end of both January and February. Monthly conversion costs are allocated between ending work-in-process and units completed. Compared with the FIFO method, would the weighted-average method use the same or a greater number of equivalent units to calculate the monthly allocations?

Equivalent Units for Weighted Average Compared with FIFO	
January	February
A. Same	Same
B. Greater number	Greater number
C. Greater number	Same
D. Same	Greater number

Answer (D) is correct. *(CPA, adapted)*
  REQUIRED: The comparison of equivalent units calculated under the FIFO and weighted-average methods.
  DISCUSSION: The weighted-average method calculates equivalent units by adding the equivalent units in EWIP to the total of all units completed during the period, regardless of when they were started. The FIFO method determines equivalent units by subtracting the work done on the BWIP in the prior period from the weighted-average total. If the number of equivalent units in BWIP is zero, as it was for the month of January, the two methods produce the same result. Otherwise, the weighted-average computation is greater.
  Answer (A) is incorrect because the weighted-average method calculates the greater number of equivalent units except when the number of equivalent units in BWIP is zero. Answer (B) is incorrect because both the FIFO and the weighted-average methods produce the same result for the first month of operations. Answer (C) is incorrect because the weighted-average total is greater for February and the same for January.

29. The following information pertains to Lap Co.'s Palo Division for the month just ended:

	Number of Units	Cost of Materials
Beginning work-in-process	15,000	$ 5,500
Started during the month	40,000	18,000
Units completed	42,500	
Ending work-in-process	12,500	

All materials are added at the beginning of the process. Using the weighted-average method, the cost per equivalent unit for materials is

A. $0.59

B. $0.55

C. $0.45

D. $0.43

Answer (D) is correct. *(CPA, adapted)*
  REQUIRED: The cost per equivalent unit for materials using the weighted-average method.
  DISCUSSION: The weighted-average method does not distinguish between work done in the previous period and that done in the current period. Consequently, given that materials are added at the start of the process, the total equivalent units equal 55,000 (42,500 units completed + 12,500 units in EWIP), the total cost of materials is $23,500, and the cost per equivalent unit for materials is $0.43 (rounded).
  Answer (A) is incorrect because $0.59 results from deducting the units in BWIP from the total equivalent units. Answer (B) is incorrect because $0.55 equals cost divided by units completed. Answer (C) is incorrect because $0.45 is based on the FIFO method.

30. In computing the current period's manufacturing cost per equivalent unit of production (EUP), the FIFO method of process costing considers current period costs

A. Only.

B. Plus cost of beginning work-in-process (BWIP) inventory.

C. Less cost of beginning work-in-process (BWIP) inventory.

D. Plus cost of ending work-in-process (EWIP) inventory.

Answer (A) is correct. *(CPA, adapted)*
  REQUIRED: The computation of cost per equivalent unit assuming FIFO.
  DISCUSSION: An equivalent unit of production is a set of inputs required to manufacture one physical unit. Calculating equivalent units for each factor of production facilitates measurement of output and cost allocation when work-in-process exists. Under the FIFO assumption, only current-period costs are allocated between cost of goods manufactured and ending work in process because FIFO maintains beginning inventory costs completely separable from current-period costs. Although both the BWIP and EWIP are required to compute EUP, the cost per EUP considers only current period costs.
  Answer (B) is incorrect because, under FIFO, only current-period costs are considered. Answer (C) is incorrect because, under FIFO, neither beginning nor ending costs are added or deducted. Answer (D) is incorrect because no cost amounts other than those incurred in current period are included in the FIFO calculation.

31. In process 2, material G is added when a batch is 60% complete. Ending work-in-process units, which are 50% complete, would be included in the computation of equivalent units for

	Conversion Costs	Material G
A.	Yes	No
B.	No	Yes
C.	No	No
D.	Yes	Yes

Answer (A) is correct. *(CPA, adapted)*
    REQUIRED: The computation(s) of equivalent units that will include ending work-in-process.
    DISCUSSION: Conversion costs (direct labor and factory overhead) are the costs of transforming direct materials into finished products. If EWIP is 50% complete, it is presumably 50% complete as to conversion costs (all costs other than direct materials). But if material G is added only at the 60% point, no equivalent units of G have been produced. Thus, EWIP is included in the computation of equivalent units of conversion costs but not material G.
    Answer (B) is incorrect because EWIP is included in the computation for conversion costs but not material G. Answer (C) is incorrect because EWIP is included in the computation for conversion costs. Answer (D) is incorrect because EWIP is not included in the computation of equivalent units of material G.

32. A department adds material at the beginning of a process and identifies defective units when the process is 40% complete. At the beginning of the period, there was no work in process. At the end of the period, the number of work-in-process units equaled the number of units transferred to finished goods. If all units in ending work in process were 66% complete, then ending work in process should be allocated

A. 50% of all normal defective unit costs.

B. 40% of all normal defective unit costs.

C. 50% of the material costs and 40% of the conversion costs of all normal defective unit costs.

D. None of the normal defective unit costs.

Answer (A) is correct. *(CPA, adapted)*
    REQUIRED: The normal spoilage costs allocated to EWIP.
    DISCUSSION: Inspection occurs when the units are 40% complete. Hence, EWIP, which is 66% complete, contains good units only. Because normal spoilage attaches to good units, and the units transferred to finished goods equal those in EWIP, the normal defective unit costs should be allocated 50% to EWIP and 50% to finished goods.
    Answer (B) is incorrect because EWIP contains 50% of the good units produced. Answer (C) is incorrect because EWIP should be allocated 50% of all normal spoilage costs. Answer (D) is incorrect because normal spoilage costs should be allocated to EWIP if it contains inspected units.

33. Forming Department is the first of a two-stage production process. Spoilage is identified when the units complete the forming process. Costs of spoiled units are assigned to units completed and transferred to the second department in the period spoilage is identified. The following concerns Forming's conversion costs:

	Units	Conversion Costs
Beginning work-in-process		
(50% complete)	2,000	$10,000
Units started during month	8,000	75,500
Spoilage-normal	500	
Units completed & transferred	7,000	
Ending work-in-process		
(80% complete)	2,500	

What was Forming's weighted-average conversion cost transferred to the second department?

A. $59,850

B. $64,125

C. $67,500

D. $71,250

Answer (C) is correct. *(CPA, adapted)*
    REQUIRED: The conversion costs transferred to the second production department.
    DISCUSSION: Under the weighted-average method, total equivalent units include the equivalent units transferred and the equivalent units in ending work-in-process. Because normal spoilage costs attach to the good output, the transferred costs equal the costs of both the good units and the spoiled units. Total conversion costs under the weighted-average method are $85,500 ($10,000 BWIP + $75,500 May costs). Total equivalent units are 9,500 [7,000 good units transferred + (2,500 uninspected units in EWIP × 80%) + 500 completed units spoiled]. Accordingly, the conversion cost per equivalent unit is $9 ($85,500 ÷ 9,500), and total costs transferred are $67,500 [(7,000 good units transferred + 500 completed units spoiled) × $9].
    Answer (A) is incorrect because $59,850 equals 7,000 units times $8.55 ($85,500 ÷ 10,000 units). Answer (B) is incorrect because $64,125 equals 7,500 units times $8.55 ($85,500 ÷ 10,000 units). Answer (D) is incorrect because $71,250 results from not calculating equivalent units for spoilage in determining unit conversion cost. It equals $9.50 times 7,500 units.

34. The Cutting Department is the first stage of Mark Company's production cycle. BWIP for this department was 80% complete as to conversion costs. EWIP was 50% complete. Conversion costs in the Cutting Department for the month just ended were as follows:

	Units	CC
Beginning WIP	25,000	$ 22,000
Units started and costs incurred during the month	135,000	143,000
Units completed and transferred to next department during the month	100,000	

Using the FIFO method, what was the conversion cost of ending WIP in the Cutting Department?

- A. $22,000
- B. $33,000
- C. $39,000
- D. $78,000

Answer (C) is correct. *(CPA, adapted)*
    REQUIRED: The FIFO conversion cost of EWIP.
    DISCUSSION: Under the FIFO method, EUP for a period include only the work done that period and exclude any work done in a prior period. The total of conversion cost EUP for the period is calculated below.

	Units	Work Done in Current Period	CC (EUP)
BWIP	25,000	20%	5,000
Started & completed	75,000	100%	75,000
EWIP	60,000	50%	30,000
Total EUP			110,000

The total of the conversion costs for the period is given as $143,000. Dividing by total EUP of 110,000 gives a unit cost of $1.30. Thus, the conversion cost of the EWIP inventory is $39,000 (30,000 EUP in EWIP × $1.30).
    Answer (A) is incorrect because $22,000 is the BWIP. Answer (B) is incorrect because $33,000 equals the unit conversion cost for the preceding period [$22,000 ÷ (25,000 × 80%)] times 30,000 EUP. Answer (D) is incorrect because $78,000 equals $1.30 times 60,000 units.

35. Kerner Manufacturing uses a process cost system to manufacture laptop computers. The following information summarizes operations relating to laptop computer model #KJK20 during the quarter ending March 31:

	Units	Direct Materials
WIP inventory, January 1	100	$70,000
Started during the quarter	500	
Completed during the quarter	400	
WIP inventory, March 31	200	
Costs added during the quarter		$750,000

Beginning work-in-process inventory was 50% complete for direct materials. Ending work-in-process inventory was 75% complete for direct materials. Using the FIFO method, what were the equivalent units of production with regard to materials for March?

- A. 450
- B. 500
- C. 550
- D. 600

Answer (B) is correct. *(CPA, adapted)*
    REQUIRED: The equivalent units of materials under FIFO.
    DISCUSSION: Under the FIFO method, equivalent units are determined based only on work performed during the current period. They include work performed to complete BWIP, work on units started and completed during the period, and work done on EWIP. Thus, total FIFO equivalent units of materials are

BWIP	100 units	×	50% =		50
Started and completed (400 – 100 in BWIP)	300 units	×	100% =		300
EWIP	200 units	×	75% =		150
Total equivalent units					500

    Answer (A) is incorrect because 450 units omits the 50 equivalent units of work on BWIP during the current period. Answer (C) is incorrect because 550 units is based on the weighted-average method. Answer (D) is incorrect because 600 units equals the sum of the physical units completed plus the physical units in BWIP.

19.4 Overhead Costs and Normal Costing

36. In a process cost system, the application of factory overhead usually is recorded as an increase in

- A. Cost of goods sold.
- B. Work-in-process inventory control.
- C. Factory overhead control.
- D. Finished goods inventory control.

Answer (B) is correct. *(CPA, adapted)*
    REQUIRED: The account in which the application of factory overhead is recorded in a process costing system.
    DISCUSSION: The principal distinction between process costing and job-order costing systems is that the latter use subsidiary WIP and finished goods ledgers to account for separate jobs. However, the same general ledger accounts are used in both systems, and cost flow among accounts is also the same. Both systems increase work-in-process control to record applied overhead.
    Answer (A) is incorrect because CGS is debited when finished goods are sold. Answer (C) is incorrect because factory overhead control is debited when actual factory overhead is incurred. Answer (D) is incorrect because finished goods control is debited when goods are completed.

37. In developing a predetermined factory overhead application rate for use in a process costing system, which of the following could be used in the numerator and denominator?

	Numerator	Denominator
A.	Actual factory overhead	Actual machine hours
B.	Actual factory overhead	Estimated machine hours
C.	Estimated factory overhead	Actual machine hours
D.	Estimated factory overhead	Estimated machine hours

38. The following were among Gage Co.'s costs during the month just ended:

Normal spoilage	$ 5,000
Freight out	10,000
Excess of actual manufacturing costs over standard costs	20,000
Standard manufacturing costs	100,000
Actual prime manufacturing costs	80,000

Gage's actual manufacturing overhead was

A. $40,000

B. $45,000

C. $55,000

D. $120,000

19.5 Activity-Based Costing (ABC)

39. What is the normal effect on the numbers of cost pools and allocation bases when an activity-based cost (ABC) system replaces a traditional cost system?

	Cost Pools	Allocation Bases
A.	No effect	No effect
B.	Increase	No effect
C.	No effect	Increase
D.	Increase	Increase

Answer (D) is correct. *(CPA, adapted)*
REQUIRED: The possible numerator and denominator of a predetermined factory overhead rate.
DISCUSSION: The predetermined factory overhead rate is calculated by dividing the estimated factory overhead (the numerator) by the estimated amount of the activity base (the denominator). The latter may be direct labor hours, direct labor dollars, machine hours, or some other reasonable base.
Answer (A) is incorrect because actual amounts of factory overhead and machine hours are not known. Answer (B) is incorrect because estimated factory overhead must be used in the numerator. Answer (C) is incorrect because estimated machine hours must be used in the denominator.

Answer (A) is correct. *(CPA, adapted)*
REQUIRED: The actual manufacturing overhead.
DISCUSSION: Factory (manufacturing) overhead consists of all costs other than direct materials and direct labor that are associated with the manufacturing process. Prime costs are direct materials and direct labor. Because the excess of actual manufacturing costs over standard costs is $20,000, and the standard costs are $100,000, the actual manufacturing costs are $120,000. However, because $80,000 of these costs are prime costs, the remainder is factory overhead. Thus, actual manufacturing overhead is $40,000 ($120,000 – $80,000).
Answer (B) is incorrect because $45,000 includes normal spoilage twice. Answer (C) is incorrect because $55,000 includes normal spoilage and freight out twice. Answer (D) is incorrect because $120,000 is the actual manufacturing costs including prime costs.

Answer (D) is correct. *(CPA, adapted)*
REQUIRED: The normal effect on the numbers of cost pools and allocation bases when an activity-based cost (ABC) system replaces a traditional cost system.
DISCUSSION: In an activity-based system, cost allocation is more precise than in traditional systems because activities rather than functions or departments are defined as cost objects. This structure permits allocation to more cost pools and the identification of a cost driver specifically related to each activity. A cost driver is a factor that causes a change in the cost pool for a particular activity. Thus, an ABC system uses more cost pools and allocation bases than a traditional system.
Answer (A) is incorrect because, under direct costing, both the number of cost pools and the number of drivers used to allocate them will increase. Answer (B) is incorrect because the greater number of cost pools will require a great number of drivers. Answer (C) is incorrect because increasing the number of drivers would be pointless without increasing the number of cost pools.

40. In an activity-based costing (ABC) system, cost reduction is accomplished by identifying and eliminating

	All Cost Drivers	Nonvalue-Adding Activities
A.	No	No
B.	Yes	Yes
C.	No	Yes
D.	Yes	No

Answer (C) is correct. *(CPA, adapted)*
REQUIRED: The item(s), if any, identified and eliminated when reducing costs in an ABC system.
DISCUSSION: An ABC system determines activities associated with the incurrence of costs and then accumulates a cost pool for each activity. It then identifies the cost driver for each activity. A cost driver is a factor that causes a change in the cost pool for a particular activity. Activities that do not add value to the product are identified and eliminated to the extent possible. A clear understanding of what causes a cost (the cost driver) helps eliminate the nonvalue-adding activities. However, all cost drivers cannot be eliminated.
Answer (A) is incorrect because one of the principal goals of ABC is to eliminate nonvalue-adding activities. Answer (B) is incorrect because no organization can eliminate cost drivers; they are inherent in doing business. Answer (D) is incorrect because nonvalue-adding activities are unnecessary and therefore are targeted for elimination under ABC.

41. Which of the following is true about activity-based costing?

A. It should not be used with process or job-order costing.

B. It can be used only with process costing.

C. It can be used only with job-order costing.

D. It can be used with either process or job-order costing.

Answer (D) is correct. *(CPA, adapted)*
REQUIRED: The true statement about activity-based costing.
DISCUSSION: Activity-based costing may be used by manufacturing, service, or retailing entities and in job-order or process costing systems.
Answer (A) is incorrect because activity-based costing is a complement to both job-order and process costing. Answer (B) is incorrect because activity-based costing is a means of assigning overhead costs; thus, it can be used with job-order costing as well. Answer (C) is incorrect because activity-based costing may be used to allocate manufacturing overhead with either process or job-order costing.

42. Nile Co.'s cost allocation and product costing procedures follow activity-based costing principles. Activities have been identified and classified as being either value-adding or nonvalue-adding as to each product. Which of the following activities, used in Nile production process, is nonvalue-adding?

A. Design engineering activity.

B. Heat treatment activity.

C. Drill press activity.

D. Raw materials storage activity.

Answer (D) is correct. *(CPA, adapted)*
REQUIRED: The nonvalue-adding activity under activity-based costing.
DISCUSSION: In an ABC system, cost allocation is more precise than in traditional systems because activities rather than functions or departments are defined as cost objects. This structure permits allocation to more cost objects and the identification of a cost driver specifically related to each activity. A cost driver is a factor that causes a change in the cost pool for a particular activity. ABC provides for better cost control as well as for more precise cost allocation. Some activities may prove to be unnecessary (not add value). An example of a nonvalue-adding activity is raw materials storage. A clear understanding of what causes a cost may facilitate reduction of the cost driver and therefore the cost.
Answer (A) is incorrect because design engineering activities are value-adding activities. Answer (B) is incorrect because heat treatment activities relate directly to product quality and thus add value. Answer (C) is incorrect because drill press activities add value, since they are inherent in the product's manufacture.

43. A basic assumption of activity-based costing (ABC) is that

A. All manufacturing costs vary directly with units of production.

B. Products or services require the performance of activities, and activities consume resources.

C. Only costs that respond to unit-level drivers are product costs.

D. Only variable costs are included in activity cost pools.

Answer (B) is correct.   *(CPA, adapted)*
REQUIRED: The basic assumption of ABC.
DISCUSSION: ABC identifies activities needed to provide products or services, assigns costs to those activities, and then reassigns costs to the products or services based on their consumption of activities. ABC helps to manage costs by providing more detailed analyses of costs than traditional methods. It also facilitates cost reduction by determining which activities do and do not add value to the product or service.
Answer (A) is incorrect because ABC does not assume that units produced is a cost driver for all manufacturing costs. Answer (C) is incorrect because activities and their drivers may be classified as unit-level, batch-level, product-level, and facility-level. The first three levels pertain to specific products or services. Thus, costs at these levels are accurately assignable to those products or services. Furthermore, although facility-level activities do not pertain to specific products or services, organizations that apply ABC customarily assign them to products or services to obtain a full-absorption cost suitable for external financial reporting in accordance with GAAP. Answer (D) is incorrect because ABC recognizes that some fixed costs are product costs.

19.6 Backflush Costing and JIT Inventory

44. Backflush costing is most likely to be used when

A. Management desires sequential tracking of costs.

B. A just-in-time production philosophy has been adopted.

C. The company carries significant amounts of inventory.

D. Actual production costs are debited to work-in-process.

Answer (B) is correct.   *(Publisher, adapted)*
REQUIRED: The true statement about backflush costing.
DISCUSSION: Backflush costing is often used with a JIT system because it minimizes the effort devoted to accounting for inventories. It delays much of the accounting for production costs until the completion of production or even the sale of goods. Backflush costing is most appropriate when inventories are low or when the change in inventories is minimal, that is, when most production costs for a period flow into cost of goods sold.
Answer (A) is incorrect because traditional systems track costs as units pass through each step of production. Answer (C) is incorrect because backflush costing is inconsistent with the full-costing requirement of GAAP. The larger the inventories or the change therein, the greater the discrepancy. Moreover, larger inventories require more detailed information. Answer (D) is incorrect because backflush costing eliminates the work-in-process account.

45. Key Co. changed from a traditional manufacturing operation with a job-order costing system to a just-in-time operation with a backflush costing system. What are the expected effects of these changes on Key's inspection costs and recording detail of costs tracked to jobs in process?

	Inspection Costs	Detail of Costs Tracked to Jobs
A.	Decrease	Decrease
B.	Decrease	Increase
C.	Increase	Decrease
D.	Increase	Increase

Answer (A) is correct.   *(CPA, adapted)*
REQUIRED: The effects of changing to a JIT operation with backflush costing.
DISCUSSION: In a JIT system, materials go directly into production without being inspected. The assumption is that the vendor has already performed all necessary inspections. The minimization of inventory reduces the number of suppliers, storage costs, transaction costs, etc. Backflush costing eliminates the traditional sequential tracking of costs. Instead, entries to inventory may be delayed until as late as the end of the period. For example, all product costs may be charged initially to cost of sales, and costs may be flushed back to the inventory accounts only at the end of the period. Thus, the detail of cost accounting is decreased.
Answer (B) is incorrect because, with less raw materials inventory, the detail of costs tracked to jobs will decrease as well. Answer (C) is incorrect because inspection costs also will decrease as a result of greater reliance on the supplier. Answer (D) is incorrect because, under a just-in-time inventory management system, both inspection costs and the detail of costs tracked to jobs decrease.

46. Which changes in costs are most conducive to switching from a traditional inventory ordering system to a just-in-time ordering system?

	Cost per Purchase Order	Inventory Unit Carrying Costs
A.	Increasing	Increasing
B.	Decreasing	Increasing
C.	Decreasing	Decreasing
D.	Increasing	Decreasing

Answer (B) is correct. *(CPA, adapted)*
   REQUIRED: The changes in costs most conducive to switching to a just-in-time ordering system.
   DISCUSSION: A JIT system is intended to minimize inventory. Thus, if inventory carrying costs are increasing, a JIT system becomes more cost effective. Moreover, purchases are more frequent in a JIT system. Accordingly, a decreasing cost per purchase order is conducive to switching to a JIT system.
   Answer (A) is incorrect because switching to a JIT system is more appropriate when ordering costs decrease. Answer (C) is incorrect because switching to a JIT system offers fewer incentives when carrying costs decrease. Answer (D) is incorrect because switching to a JIT system should be considered when ordering costs decrease.

47. Which of the following is not a typical characteristic of a just-in-time (JIT) production environment?

   A. Lot sizes equal to one.

   B. Insignificant setup times and costs.

   C. Push-through system.

   D. Balanced and level workloads.

Answer (C) is correct. *(CPA, adapted)*
   REQUIRED: The item not typically a characteristic of a just-in-time (JIT) production environment.
   DISCUSSION: In a JIT system, minimization of inventory is a goal because many inventory-related activities are nonvalue-added. Moreover, it is a pull system; items are pulled through production by current demand, not pushed through by anticipated demand. Thus, one operation produces only what is needed by the next operation, and components and raw materials arrive just in time to be used. To implement this approach and to eliminate waste, the factory is reorganized to permit what is often called lean production. Plant layout in a JIT/lean production environment is arranged by manufacturing cells. Cells are sets of machines, often grouped in semicircles, that produce a given product or product type. Each worker must be able to operate all machines and, possibly, to perform support tasks, such as setup activities, preventive maintenance, movement of work-in-process within the cell, and quality inspection. In a pull system, workers might often be idle if they were not multi-skilled. Hence, central support departments are reduced or eliminated, space is saved, fewer and smaller factories may be required, and materials and tools are brought close to the point of use. Manufacturing cycle time and setup time are also reduced. As a result, on-time delivery performance and response to changes in markets are enhanced, and production of custom goods in small lots is feasible.
   Answer (A) is incorrect because, under a JIT/lean production system, production of custom goods in small lots becomes more feasible. Answer (B) is incorrect because reduced setup times and costs are benefits of JIT/lean production. Answer (D) is incorrect because balanced and level workloads become easier to maintain in a JIT/lean production environment.

19.7 Joint Product and By-Product Costing

48. In joint-product costing and analysis, which one of the following costs is relevant when deciding the point at which a product should be sold to maximize profits?

   A. Separable costs after the split-off point.

   B. Joint costs to the split-off point.

   C. Sales salaries for the period when the units were produced.

   D. Purchase costs of the materials required for the joint products.

Answer (A) is correct. *(CMA, adapted)*
   REQUIRED: The cost relevant to deciding when a joint product should be sold.
   DISCUSSION: Joint products are created from processing a common input. Joint costs are incurred prior to the split-off point and cannot be identified with a particular joint product. As a result, joint costs are irrelevant to the timing of sale. However, separable costs incurred after the split-off point are relevant because, if incremental revenues exceed the separable costs, products should be processed further, not sold at the split-off point.
   Answer (B) is incorrect because joint costs have no effect on the decision as to when to sell a product. Answer (C) is incorrect because sales salaries for the production period do not affect the decision. Answer (D) is incorrect because purchase costs are joint costs.

Questions 49 and 50 are based on the following information.

Petro-Chem, Inc. is a small company that acquires high-grade crude oil from low-volume production wells owned by individuals and small partnerships. The crude oil is processed in a single refinery into Two Oil, Six Oil, and impure distillates. Petro-Chem does not have the technology or capacity to process these products further and sells most of its output each month to major refineries. There were no beginning inventories of finished goods or work-in-process on November 1. The production costs and output of Petro-Chem for November are shown in the next column.

Crude oil acquired and placed in production	$5,000,000
Direct labor and related costs	2,000,000
Manufacturing overhead	3,000,000

Production and sales

- Two Oil, 300,000 barrels produced; 80,000 barrels sold at $20 each.
- Six Oil, 240,000 barrels produced; 120,000 barrels sold at $30 each.
- Distillates, 120,000 barrels produced and sold at $15 per barrel.

49. The portion of the joint production costs assigned to Two Oil based upon the relative sales value of output is

A. $4,800,000

B. $4,000,000

C. $2,286,000

D. $2,500,000

Answer (B) is correct. *(CMA, adapted)*
REQUIRED: The joint production costs assigned to Two Oil based on relative sales value.
DISCUSSION: The total production costs incurred are $10,000,000, consisting of crude oil of $5,000,000, direct labor of $2,000,000, and overhead of $3,000,000. The total value of the output is as follows:

Two Oil (300,000 × $20)	$ 6,000,000
Six Oil (240,000 × $30)	7,200,000
Distillates (120,000 × $15)	1,800,000
Total sales value	$15,000,000

Because Two Oil composes 40% of the total sales value ($6,000,000 ÷ $15,000,000), it will be assigned 40% of the $10,000,000 of joint costs, or $4,000,000.
Answer (A) is incorrect because $4,800,000 is the amount that would be assigned to Six Oil. Answer (C) is incorrect because $2,286,000 is based on the relative sales value of units sold. Answer (D) is incorrect because $2,500,000 is based on the physical quantity of barrels sold.

50. The portion of the joint production costs assigned to Six Oil based upon physical output is

A. $3,636,000

B. $3,750,000

C. $1,818,000

D. $7,500,000

Answer (A) is correct. *(CMA, adapted)*
REQUIRED: The joint production costs assigned to Six Oil based on physical output.
DISCUSSION: The total production costs incurred are $10,000,000, consisting of crude oil of $5,000,000, direct labor of $2,000,000, and overhead of $3,000,000. The total physical output was 660,000 barrels, consisting of 300,000 barrels of Two Oil, 240,000 barrels of Six Oil, and 120,000 barrels of distillates. Thus, the allocation (rounded) is $3,636,000 {$10,000,000 × [240,000 ÷ (300,000 + 240,000 + 120,000)]}.
Answer (B) is incorrect because $3,750,000 is based on the physical quantity of units sold, not units produced. Answer (C) is incorrect because $1,818,000 is the amount that would be assigned to distillates. Answer (D) is incorrect because Six Oil does not compose 75% of the total output in barrels.

51. Mighty, Inc. processes chickens for distribution to major grocery chains. The two major products resulting from the production process are white breast meat and legs. Joint costs of $600,000 are incurred during standard production runs each month, which produce a total of 100,000 pounds of white breast meat and 50,000 pounds of legs. Each pound of white breast meat sells for $2 and each pound of legs sells for $1. If there are no further processing costs incurred after the split-off point, what amount of the joint costs would be allocated to the white breast meat on a relative sales value basis?

A. $120,000

B. $200,000

C. $400,000

D. $480,000

Answer (D) is correct. *(CPA, adapted)*
REQUIRED: The joint costs allocated to a product based on relative sales value.
DISCUSSION: Given no additional processing costs, white breast meat has a sales value of $200,000 (100,000 pounds × $2), and legs have a sales value of $50,000 (50,000 pounds × $1). Thus, the joint costs allocated to white breast meat based on relative sales value is $480,000 [$600,000 × ($200,000 ÷ $250,000)].
Answer (A) is incorrect because $120,000 is the amount allocated to legs. Answer (B) is incorrect because $200,000 is the sales value of white breast meat. Answer (C) is incorrect because $400,000 is the amount allocated to white breast meat by volume.

52. A company manufactures two products, X and Y, through a joint process. The joint (common) costs incurred are $500,000 for a standard production run that generates 240,000 gallons of X and 160,000 gallons of Y. X sells for $4.00 per gallon, while Y sells for $6.50 per gallon. If there are no additional processing costs incurred after the split-off point, what is the amount of joint cost for each production run allocated to X on a physical-quantity basis?

A. $200,000

B. $240,000

C. $260,000

D. $300,000

Answer (D) is correct. *(CPA, adapted)*
REQUIRED: The joint cost for each production run allocated to X on a physical-quantity basis.
DISCUSSION: The company produces products X and Y in each production run at a joint cost of $500,000. No additional processing costs are incurred. To allocate the common cost on a physical-quantity basis means to distribute the costs based on each product's pro-rata share of the total units produced. A production run produces 240,000 gallons of product X and 160,000 gallons of product Y, resulting in 400,000 total units. Thus, product X is allocated $300,000 of the cost [$500,000 × (240,000 ÷ 400,000)]. Product Y is allocated $200,000 [$500,000 × (160,000 ÷ 400,000)].
Answer (A) is incorrect because $200,000 is the joint cost allocated to Y. Answer (B) is incorrect because $240,000 is the joint cost allocated to X on a relative sales value basis. Answer (C) is incorrect because $260,000 is the joint cost allocated to Y on a relative sales value basis.

53. Mig Co., which began operations in the month just ended, produces gasoline and a gasoline by-product. The following information is available pertaining to sales and production for the month:

Total production costs to split-off point	$120,000
Gasoline sales	270,000
By-product sales	30,000
Gasoline ending inventory	15,000
Additional by-product costs:	
Marketing	$10,000
Production	15,000

Mig accounts for the by-product at the time of production. What was Mig's cost of sales for gasoline and the by-product?

	Gasoline	By-Product
A.	$105,000	$25,000
B.	$115,000	$15,000
C.	$108,000	$37,000
D.	$100,000	$0

Answer (D) is correct. *(CPA, adapted)*
REQUIRED: The cost of sales for both the gasoline and the by-product.
DISCUSSION: If the by-product is accounted for at the time of production, by-product inventory is recorded at its selling price (or NRV in this case, given separable by-product costs) because by-products usually do not receive an allocation of joint costs. Thus, the by-product's cost of sales is zero. Assuming sales of the by-product reduced joint costs, the cost of sales of the gasoline was $100,000 ($120,000 cost to split-off – $30,000 sales of the by-product + $25,000 additional by-product costs – $15,000 EI).
Answer (A) is incorrect because $105,000 is the result of subtracting the ending gasoline inventory from total production costs to split-off point, and $25,000 equals the additional by-product costs. Answer (B) is incorrect because $115,000 ignores the $15,000 ending inventory. Answer (C) is incorrect because allocating joint costs to by-products based on relative sales value is not cost effective, and by-product cost of sales should be zero.

54. For purposes of allocating joint costs to joint products, the sales price at point of sale, reduced by cost to complete after split-off, is assumed to be equal to the

    A. Total costs.

    B. Joint costs.

    C. Sales price minus a normal profit margin at point of sale.

    D. Net sales value at split-off.

Answer (D) is correct. *(CPA, adapted)*
    REQUIRED: The assumption about the sales price at point of sale, reduced by cost to complete after split-off.
    DISCUSSION: The relative sales value method is the most frequently used method to allocate joint costs to joint products. It allocates joint costs based upon the products' proportion of total sales revenue. For joint products salable at the split-off point, the relative sales value is the selling price at split-off. However, if further processing is needed, the relative sales value is approximated by subtracting the additional anticipated processing costs from the final sales value to arrive at the estimated net sales value at split-off.
    Answer (A) is incorrect because total costs include the cost to complete after split-off. Answer (B) is incorrect because joint costs are computed up to the split-off point. Answer (C) is incorrect because the normal profit margin does not necessarily equal the cost to complete after split-off.

Questions 55 and 56 are based on the following information.

A manufacturing company uses a joint production process that produces three products at the split-off point. Joint production costs during April were $720,000. The company uses the sales value method for allocating joint costs. Product information for April was as follows:

	Product		
	R	S	T
Units produced	2,500	5,000	7,500
Units sold	2,000	6,000	7,000
Sales prices:			
At the split-off	$100	$80	$20
After further processing	$150	$115	$30
Costs to process after split-off	$150,000	$150,000	$100,000

55. Assume that all three products are main products and that they can be sold at the split-off point or processed further, whichever is economically beneficial to the company. What is the total cost of Product S in April if joint cost allocation is based on sales value at split-off?

    A. $375,000

    B. $390,000

    C. $510,000

    D. $571,463

Answer (C) is correct. *(CIA, adapted)*
    REQUIRED: The total cost of Product S in April.
    DISCUSSION: Total sales value at split-off is $800,000 [(2,500 × $100) + (5,000 × $80) + (7,500 × $20)]. Product S accounts for 50% (5,000 × $80 = $400,000) of the sales value and therefore $360,000 (50% × $720,000) of the joint costs. The total cost of Product S is $510,000 ($360,000 allocated costs + $150,000 differential costs).
    Answer (A) is incorrect because $375,000 is the total cost of R. Answer (B) is incorrect because $390,000 is based on the physical units method of allocating the joint costs. Answer (D) is incorrect because $571,463 uses the sales value at split-off based on actual sales.

56. Assume that Product T is treated as a by-product and that the company accounts for the by-product at net realizable value as a reduction of joint cost. Assume also that Products S and T must be processed further before they can be sold. What is the total cost of Product R in April if joint cost allocation is based on net realizable values?

A. $220,370

B. $370,370

C. $374,630

D. $595,000

Answer (A) is correct. *(CIA, adapted)*
  REQUIRED: The total cost of Product R for April.
  DISCUSSION: The net realizable value (NRV) method is an appropriate method of allocation when products cannot be sold at split-off. Further processing of R, which is salable at split-off, is not economical because the cost ($150,000) exceeds the benefit [2,500 units × ($150 – $100) = $125,000]. Thus, R's NRV is $250,000 (2,500 units × $100 price at split-off). However, S and T must be processed further. S's NRV is $425,000 [(5,000 units × $115) – $150,000], and T's NRV is $125,000 [(7,500 units × $30) – $100,000]. Given that the NRV of T is a reduction of joint cost, the total joint cost to be allocated is therefore $595,000 ($720,000 – $125,000 NRV of T). Accordingly, based on the NRV method, the joint cost allocated to R is $220,370 {$595,000 allocable joint cost × [$250,000 R's NRV ÷ ($250,000 R's NRV + $425,000 S's NRV)]}. Because further processing of R is uneconomical, the total cost of R is $220,370.
  Answer (B) is incorrect because $370,370 includes additional processing costs. Answer (C) is incorrect because $374,630 is the joint cost allocated to S. Answer (D) is incorrect because $595,000 is the allocable joint cost.

57. In accounting for by-products, the value of the by-product may be recognized at the time of

	Production	Sale
A.	Yes	Yes
B.	Yes	No
C.	No	No
D.	No	Yes

Answer (A) is correct. *(CPA, adapted)*
  REQUIRED: The timing of recognition of by-products.
  DISCUSSION: Practice with regard to recognizing by-products in the accounts is not uniform. The most cost-effective method for the initial recognition of by-products is to account for their value at the time of sale as a reduction in the joint cost or as a revenue. The alternative is to recognize the net realizable value at the time of production, a method that results in the recording of by-product inventory.
  Answer (B) is incorrect because by-products may also be initially recognized at the time of sale. Answer (C) is incorrect because by-products may be initially recognized at the time of sale or at the time of production. Answer (D) is incorrect because by-products may also be recorded in the accounts when produced.

58. Actual sales values at the split-off point for joint products Y and Z are not known. For purposes of allocating joint costs to products Y and Z, the relative sales value at split-off method is used. An increase in the costs beyond split-off occurs for Product Z, while those of Product Y remain constant. If the selling prices of finished products Y and Z remain constant, the percentage of the total joint costs allocated to Product Y and Product Z will

A. Decrease for Product Y and Product Z.

B. Decrease for Product Y and increase for Product Z.

C. Increase for Product Y and Product Z.

D. Increase for Product Y and decrease for Product Z.

Answer (D) is correct. *(CPA, adapted)*
  REQUIRED: The effect on the allocation of joint costs, given an increase in separable costs beyond split-off for one product.
  DISCUSSION: The actual sales values of products Y and Z at the split-off point are not known. However, these values may be approximated by calculating the estimated net realizable values (final sales values – separable costs). Assuming constant selling prices and increasing costs for product Z, the net realizable value at split-off for Z must necessarily be decreasing. The relative sales value method allocates joint costs in accordance with the ratio of each joint product's sales value at split-off to the total sales value at split-off for all joint products. Therefore, the costs allocated to Z must be decreasing, while the costs allocated to Y are increasing.
  Answer (A) is incorrect because the costs allocated to Y are increasing. Answer (B) is incorrect because the costs allocated to Z must be decreasing, while the costs allocated to Y are increasing. Answer (C) is incorrect because the costs allocated to Z are decreasing.

59. The following information pertains to a by-product called Moy:

Sales for the month	5,000 units
Selling price per unit	$6
Selling costs per unit	$2
Processing costs	$0

Inventory of Moy was recorded at net realizable value when produced in the previous month. No units of Moy were produced in the month just ended. What amount should be recognized as profit on Moy's sales?

A. $0

B. $10,000

C. $20,000

D. $30,000

Answer (A) is correct. *(CPA, adapted)*
REQUIRED: Profit on by-products sold at net realizable value (NRV).
DISCUSSION: Net realizable value is selling price less selling and disposal costs, which means there is no (zero) profit when sold. If valued at NRV less normal profit, normal profit is recognized at the point of sale.
Answer (B) is incorrect because $10,000 is the total selling costs. Answer (C) is incorrect because $20,000 is the NRV of the product sold. Answer (D) is incorrect because $30,000 is the total sales.

60. Kode Co. manufactures a major product that gives rise to a by-product called May. May's only separable cost is a $1 selling cost when a unit is sold for $4. Kode accounts for May's sales by deducting the $3 net amount from the cost of goods sold of the major product. There are no inventories. If Kode were to change its method of accounting for May from a by-product to a joint product, what would be the effect on Kode's overall gross margin?

A. No effect.

B. Gross margin increases by $1 for each unit of May sold.

C. Gross margin increases by $3 for each unit of May sold.

D. Gross margin increases by $4 for each unit of May sold.

Answer (B) is correct. *(CPA, adapted)*
REQUIRED: The effect on gross margin of treating a product as a joint product rather than a by-product.
DISCUSSION: Gross margin is the difference between sales and the cost of goods sold. Deducting the $3 net amount from cost of goods sold does not have the same effect on overall gross margin as recording the $4 sales revenue and deducting the $1 cost. In the latter case, the $1 unit selling cost is not deducted in arriving at the gross margin. Thus, gross margin increases by $1 for each unit of May sold.
Answer (A) is incorrect because there is no effect on net income (not gross margin). Answer (C) is incorrect because $3 is the amount net income increases using either by-product or joint-product costing. Answer (D) is incorrect because $4 is the increase in sales when switching to joint-product from by-product costing.

61. A processing department produces joint products Ajac and Bjac, each of which incurs separable production costs after split-off. Information concerning a batch produced at a $60,000 joint cost before split-off follows:

Product	Costs	Separable Sales Value
Ajac	$ 8,000	$ 80,000
Bjac	22,000	40,000
	$30,000	$120,000

What is the joint cost assigned to Ajac if costs are assigned using the relative net realizable value?

A. $16,000

B. $40,000

C. $48,000

D. $52,000

Answer (C) is correct. *(CPA, adapted)*
REQUIRED: The joint cost assigned to Ajac if costs are assigned based on relative NRV.
DISCUSSION: The NRV of Ajac is $72,000 ($80,000 – $8,000), and the NRV of Bjac is $18,000 ($40,000 – $22,000). Thus, the joint cost assigned to Ajac if costs are assigned based on relative NRV is $48,000 {$60,000 × [$72,000 ÷ ($72,000 + $18,000)]}.
Answer (A) is incorrect because $16,000 results from allocating joint costs on the basis of separable costs. Answer (B) is incorrect because $40,000 ignores the separable costs. Answer (D) is incorrect because $52,000 equals the joint cost minus the separable costs of Ajac.

62. One hundred pounds of raw material W is processed into 60 pounds of X and 40 pounds of Y. Joint costs are $135. X is sold for $2.50 per pound, and Y can be sold for $3.00 per pound or processed further into 30 pounds of Z (10 pounds are lost in the second process) at an additional cost of $60. Each pound of Z can then be sold for $6.00. What is the effect on profits of further processing product Y into product Z?

A. $60 increase.

B. $30 increase.

C. No change.

D. $60 decrease.

Answer (C) is correct. *(CPA, adapted)*
REQUIRED: The effect on profits of further processing of a product.
DISCUSSION: The joint costs of $135 do not vary with the option chosen. Without further processing of product Y, revenue equals $270 [(60 lbs × $2.50) + (40 lbs × $3.00)], and net revenue equals $135 ($270 – $135). If product Y is processed further into product Z, revenue equals $330 [(60 lbs × $2.50) + (30 lbs × $6.00)]. This additional processing is at an incremental cost of $60, resulting in net revenue of $135 ($330 – $135 – $60). Hence, further processing results in no increase or decrease in net revenue.
Answer (A) is incorrect because the additional cost of $60 must be considered in evaluating the profit effect of processing product Y into product Z. Answer (B) is incorrect because a greater sales amount is obtained by processing product Y into product Z with an additional cost of $60, creating the same profit under each process. Answer (D) is incorrect because the profit effect is the same whether or not product Y is processed into product Z.

63.

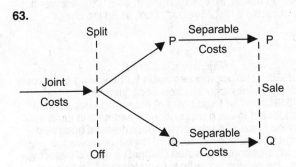

The diagram represents the production and sales relationships of joint products P and Q. Joint costs are incurred until split-off; then separable costs are incurred in refining each product. Market values of P and Q at split-off are used to allocate joint costs. If the market value of P at split-off increases and all other costs and selling prices remain unchanged, then the gross margin of

	P	Q
A.	Increases	Decreases
B.	Increases	Increases
C.	Decreases	Decreases
D.	Decreases	Increases

Answer (D) is correct. *(CPA, adapted)*
REQUIRED: The effects on the gross margins of joint products if the market value of one product at split-off increases while other costs and prices are constant.
DISCUSSION: The allocation of joint costs to P and Q is in accordance with their relative sales values at split-off. If P's market value at split-off increases, its allocation of joint costs will increase and Q's will decrease. Given that other costs and final selling prices are constant, P's gross margin (final sales revenue – cost of goods sold, which includes the allocation of joint costs) decreases and Q's increases.
Answer (A) is incorrect because P's gross margin decreases and Q's increases. Answer (B) is incorrect because P's gross margin decreases. Answer (C) is incorrect because Q's gross margin increases.

19.8 Service Cost Allocation

64. In allocating factory service department costs to producing departments, which one of the following items would most likely be used as an activity base?

A. Units of product sold.

B. Salary of service department employees.

C. Units of electric power consumed.

D. Direct materials usage.

Answer (C) is correct. *(CMA, adapted)*
REQUIRED: The item most likely used as an activity base when allocating factory service department costs.
DISCUSSION: Service department costs are considered part of factory overhead and should be allocated to the production departments that use the services. A basis reflecting cause and effect should be used to allocate service department costs. For example, the number of kilowatt hours used by each producing department is probably the best allocation base for electricity costs.
Answer (A) is incorrect because making allocations on the basis of units sold may not meet the cause-and-effect criterion. Answer (B) is incorrect because the salary of service department employees is the cost allocated, not a basis of allocation. Answer (D) is incorrect because making allocations on the basis of materials usage may not meet the cause-and-effect criterion.

65. Parat College allocates support department costs to its individual schools using the step method. Information for the month just ended is as follows:

	Support Departments	
	Maintenance	Power
Costs incurred	$99,000	$54,000

Service percentages provided to:

	Maintenance	Power
Maintenance	-	10%
Power	20%	-
School of Education	30%	20%
School of Technology	50%	70%
	100%	100%

What is the amount of support department costs allocated to the School of Education?

A. $40,500

B. $42,120

C. $46,100

D. $49,125

66. The fixed costs of the service department should be allocated to each production department based on

A. Actual short-run use based on predetermined rates.

B. Actual short-run units based on actual rates.

C. The service department's expected costs of long-run capacity.

D. The service department's actual costs based on actual use of services.

Answer (C) is correct. *(CPA, adapted)*
REQUIRED: The amount of costs allocated.
DISCUSSION: The step method allocates service costs to other service departments as well as to production departments but does not provide for reciprocal allocations. In this case, the process should begin with Maintenance because it has the higher total costs and it provides a higher percentage of services to the other service department. However, once these costs are allocated, no Power costs will be allocated to Maintenance. They are allocated as follows:

	M	P	SE	ST
Usage of M	--	20%	30%	50%
Usage of P	10%	--	20%	70%
Allocation of M	$(99,000)	$19,800	$29,700	$49,500
		54,000		
Allocation of P		(73,800)	16,400	57,400
			$46,100	

Answer (A) is incorrect because $40,500 equals 30% of $99,000 plus 20% of $54,000. Answer (B) is incorrect because the step method results in an allocation of $46,100. Answer (D) is incorrect because $49,125 results from using the direct method.

Answer (C) is correct. *(Publisher, adapted)*
REQUIRED: The appropriate basis for allocating fixed costs of service departments to production departments.
DISCUSSION: The fixed costs of the service department should be allocated to each production department in lump-sum amounts on the basis of each service department's budgeted costs of long-term capacity to serve. This basis allows the production departments to develop (budget) a certain capacity needed from the service department and to agree on the assessment of costs. Analysis of actual results permits evaluation of the service department's ability to provide the estimated volume of service.

Answer (A) is incorrect because fixed costs are independent of short-run use. Answer (B) is incorrect because a short-run base is inappropriate for allocating fixed costs on long-run capacity. Answer (D) is incorrect because allocating the service department's actual costs based on actual use of services transfers any efficiencies or inefficiencies of the service department to the production departments.

Use Gleim's *CPA Test Prep* for interactive testing with over 2,000 additional multiple-choice questions!

STUDY UNIT TWENTY
STANDARD COSTS AND VARIANCE ANALYSIS

(22 pages of outline)

This study unit is the last of three relating to cost measurement. A standard cost is an estimate of what a cost should be under normal operating conditions based on accounting and engineering studies. Standard costs are used to control actual costs. Comparing actual and standard costs permits evaluation of managerial performance.

20.1 STATIC AND FLEXIBLE BUDGETING

1. One of the **uses of a budget** is to communicate to employees what an organization's **operational and strategic goals** are. The budget quantifies the operational steps that ultimately lead to achievement of the strategic goals.

    a. A budget is useless without a performance evaluation system to monitor progress toward the budget's objectives.

        1) The measures in any performance evaluation system must therefore be directly related to the organization's strategic and operational goals.

        2) The system must give timely feedback so that managers can take corrective action.

    b. These are aspects of a **management-by-objectives (MBO)** system. MBO requires the establishment of specific, measurable goals and the provision of ongoing feedback.

2. **Variance analysis** is the foundation of any performance evaluation system based on a budget.

    a. Variances are the calculated differences between the amounts budgeted and the amounts actually incurred (or, in the case of revenues, earned).

        1) On the cost side, a **favorable variance** occurs when actual costs are less than standard; an **unfavorable variance** occurs when actual costs are greater than standard.

        2) On the revenue side, a **favorable variance** occurs when actual revenues are greater than budgeted; an **unfavorable variance** occurs when actual revenues are less than budgeted.

    b. Variance analysis enables **management-by-exception**, the practice of giving attention primarily to significant deviations from expectations (whether favorable or unfavorable). When a variance occurs, management is signaled that corrective action may be needed.

        1) Attending to operations not performing within expected limits is likely to yield the best ratio of the benefits of investigation to costs.

    c. The significance of variances depends not only on their amount but also on their direction, frequency, and trend. Moreover, persistent variances may indicate that standards need to be reevaluated.

3. Variances usually **do not appear on the financial statements** of a firm. They are recorded in the ledger accounts but are only used for managerial control.

   a. **Immaterial variances** are customarily closed to cost of goods sold or income summary.

   b. **Material variances** may be prorated. A simple approach is to allocate the total net variance to work-in-process, finished goods, and cost of goods sold based on the balances in those accounts.

4. A crucial part of variance analysis is the **assignment of responsibility**.

   a. The performance measures on which managers are judged should be directly related to the factors that drive the element being measured, e.g., cost drivers and revenue drivers.

   b. The goal is to assign responsibility for variances to those most likely to have information that will enable management to find solutions.

      1) A manager who does not control an activity may nevertheless be the individual who is best informed about it. Thus, a purchasing agent may be in the best position to explain price variances even though (s)he cannot control them.

   c. The constructive approach is to promote learning and continuous improvement in manufacturing operations, not to assign blame. However, information about variances may be useful in evaluating managers' performance.

5. **Algebraic conventions** make the calculation of input variances simpler.

   a. AQ = Actual quantity of inputs consumed   SQ = Standard quantity of inputs consumed
      AP = Actual price of inputs consumed   SP = Standard price of inputs consumed

   b. When analyzing costs, **subtracting actual from budget** always results in a favorable variance being a positive number.

6. The **starting point** for variance analysis is the **static (master) budget**. The static budget is management's best estimate about sales, production levels, and costs for the upcoming period.

   $$\text{Static budget} = (\text{Standard quantity} \times \text{Standard price}) = (SQ \times SP)$$

   a. After the end of the period, the **actual results** of revenues earned, output produced, and costs incurred can be compiled.

   $$\text{Actual results} = (\text{Actual quantity} \times \text{Actual price}) = (AQ \times AP)$$

   b. The **static budget variance** is the **total variance to be explained**.

   $$\text{Static budget variance} = \text{Static budget} - \text{Actual results}$$
   $$= (SQ \times SP) - (AQ \times AP)$$

      1) Note that the static budget variance **holds neither quantity nor price constant**. The total variance to be explained consists of the difference in both elements.

   c. EXAMPLE: A manufacturer's production process uses a single direct material, and the planned consumption was 100 pounds costing $10 per pound last month. The total budgeted for raw materials cost was therefore $1,000 (100 pounds × $10).

      1) At month end, it was determined that the company used only 80 pounds of raw material but had to pay $12.50 per pound for it. Total cost of raw materials was therefore $1,000 (80 pounds × $12.50).

      2) The static budget variance for direct materials was $0 ($1,000 static budgeted cost – $1,000 actual cost incurred).

7. Variance analysis becomes much more meaningful when the static budget variance is decomposed into its two component variances. In order to do this, the flexible budget must be prepared.

    a. **Flexible budgeting** captures the complexity of the relationships among input, output, and resource prices.

        1) **Three major variables** in the production process are the quantity of inputs consumed, the price paid for inputs, and the quantity of outputs produced. A difference in any one of these renders the static budget less useful.

    b. The **flexible budget** consists of the costs that **should have been** incurred given the actual level of production achieved. It is calculated as follows:

        Flexible budget = Actual number of outputs produced (AO)
                         × Standard number of inputs per unit of output (SI/O)
                         × Standard price per unit of input (SP)

        1) The product of the first two elements of this equation makes up the **"expected" quantity (EQ) of inputs**.

        Expected quantity = (AO × SI/O)

    c. EXAMPLE: The company planned to produce 90 units of output during the month. Since 100 pounds of raw material were budgeted for this level of output, the standard input usage per unit of output was 1.1111 (100 pounds ÷ 90 outputs).

        1) The actual level of production for the month was 94 units.

            a) The expected quantity of direct materials was thus 104.4434 units (94 outputs × 1.1111).

            b) The flexible budget was thus $1,044 (104.4434 units × $10).

        2) In other words, given its standard cost for raw materials, the company would have expected to spend $1,044, not $1,000, to produce 94 units of output.

8. The two component variances of the static budget variance can now be derived.

    a. The **sales volume variance** reveals how the number of inputs codified in the master budget before the period began compares to the inputs that should have been used given the achieved level of output (holding price constant).

        1) A more accurate name for this variance, therefore, would be production volume variance.

        Sales volume variance = Static budget − Flexible budget

        2) The formula can be simplified algebraically as follows:

        Sales volume variance = Static budget − Flexible budget
                              = (SQ × SP) − (EQ × SP)
                              = (SQ − EQ) × SP

        3) EXAMPLE: The company planned to spend only $1,000 on direct materials during the month but, given its standard cost and actual level of production, would have expected to spend $1,044.

            a) Therefore, the company experienced an unfavorable sales volume variance of $44 on direct materials ($1,000 static budget − $1,044 flexible budget).

b. The **flexible budget variance** reveals how both the price paid for inputs and the quantity of inputs consumed compares to the price and quantity that should have been paid and consumed given the actual level of output.

1) What was codified in the master budget is not relevant to this side of the calculation.

Flexible budget variance = Flexible budget – Actual results

2) The formula is stated algebraically as follows:

Flexible budget variance = (EQ × SP) – (AQ × AP)

3) EXAMPLE: The company actually spent $1,000 on direct materials during the month, but, given its standard cost and actual level of production, would have expected to spend $1,044.

   a) Therefore, the company experienced a favorable flexible budget variance of $44 on direct materials ($1,044 flexible budget – $1,000 actual cost incurred).

c. By definition, the sales volume and flexible budget variances **net to the static budget variance**.

Static budget variance = Sales volume variance + Flexible budget variance
= $44 F + $44 U
= $0

9. The relationships between the budget amounts and the resulting variances can be depicted graphically as follows:

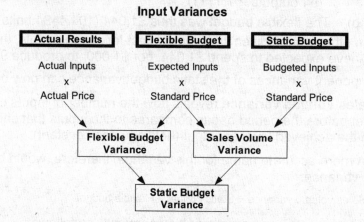

a. Note that **expected quantity** is derived by **combining an actual component and a standard component**.

b. This model can be **applied to any of the three variable inputs** to the production process (direct materials, direct labor, and variable overhead).

1) Fixed overhead is dealt with slightly differently, as discussed in item 4. in Subunit 4.

10. Overview Example of Manufacturing Variance Analysis

a.   A pet products manufacturer is beginning its budgeting cycle for the upcoming month, and the company projects that it will produce 700 tons of dog food.

    1)   The company combines three different raw materials in its production process and so uses a weighted-average standard cost for calculating its direct materials budget.

      Static Budget:

Direct materials	1,000 tons used × $54 per ton	$54,000

    2)   The company employs workers at three different skill levels and so uses a weighted-average standard rate for calculating its direct labor budget.

      Static Budget:

Direct labor	900 hours spent × $17 per hour	$15,300

    3)   The application rates for the two components of manufacturing overhead can only be calculated after selecting an appropriate allocation base for each.

      a)   Management chooses machine hours as the driver for variable overhead. Total variable overhead costs for the period are projected to be $9,600, and total machine usage is projected to be 200 hours.

        Static Budget Driver:

Variable overhead	$9,600 total ÷ 200 machine hours	$48 per machine hour

      b)   Management also chooses machine hours as the driver for fixed overhead as well. Total fixed overhead costs for the period are projected to be $8,000.

        Static Budget Driver:

Fixed overhead	$8,000 total ÷ 200 machine hours	$40 per machine hour

b.   During the month, the company experienced different market conditions from those expected. Only 660 tons of dog food were produced, and actual input usage was as follows:

Actual Results:

Direct materials	1,078 tons used × $50 per ton	$53,900
Direct labor	880 hours spent × $16 per hour	$14,080
Variable overhead	Actual costs incurred	$ 9,702
Fixed overhead	Actual costs incurred	$ 9,496

c.   The static budget variance for each of these elements can now be derived:

	Actual Results	Static Budget Variances		Static Budget
Direct materials	$53,900	$ 100	F	$54,000
Direct labor	14,080	1,220	F	15,300
Variable overhead	9,702	(102)	U	9,600
Fixed overhead	9,496	(1,496)	U	8,000
Total	$87,178	$ (278)	U	$86,900

    1)   The company did better than planned in its outlays for materials and labor but worse than planned for both components of overhead.

      a)   These results only report the difference between actual costs and the master budget in absolute terms. They reveal nothing about how the prices of inputs or the level of production varied from what was planned for at the time the master budget was prepared.

d. To enable further analysis, the flexible budget amounts must be calculated.

1) The flexible budget for direct materials consists of the actual number of outputs produced, times the standard input per ton of output, times the standard price for the input.

a) As noted on the previous page, the company actually produced only 660 tons of dog food instead of the 700 projected.

b) The standard input quantity per unit of output can be derived from the static budget (1,000 tons standard input ÷ 700 tons budgeted output = 1.42857 tons in per ton out).

Flexible Budget:
Direct materials   660 tons produced × 1.42857 × $54 per ton $50,914

2) Likewise, the flexible budget for direct labor consists of the actual number of outputs produced, times the standard input per ton of output, times the standard price for the input.

a) The standard input quantity per unit of output can be derived from the static budget (900 hours standard input ÷ 700 tons budgeted output = 1.28571 hours spent per ton out).

Flexible Budget:
Direct labor   660 tons produced × 1.28571 × $17 per hour $14,426

3) The flexible budget for variable overhead consists of the actual number of outputs produced, times the budgeted number of allocation-base units per ton of output, times the budgeted allocation rate.

a) The standard allocation-base driver per unit of output can be derived from the static budget (200 machine hours standard input ÷ 700 tons output budgeted = 0.28571 machine hours per ton out).

Flexible Budget:
Variable overhead   660 tons produced × 0.28571 × $48 per machine hour $9,051

4) The flexible budget amount for fixed overhead is identical to the static budget. This is because fixed costs are by their nature unchanging over the relevant range.

Flexible Budget:
Fixed overhead   Same as static budget $8,000

e. The static budget variance for each of the inputs can now be decomposed into the flexible budget variance and the sales volume variance.

	Actual Results	Flexible Budget Variances		Flexible Budget	Sales Volume Variances		Static Budget
Direct materials	$53,900	$(2,986)	U	$50,914	$3,086	F	$54,000
Direct labor	14,080	346	F	14,426	874	F	15,300
Variable overhead	9,702	(651)	U	9,051	549	F	9,600
Fixed overhead	9,496	(1,496)	U	8,000	----		8,000
Total	$87,178	$(4,787)	U	$82,391	$4,509	F	$86,900

1) The situation is obviously more complex than the static budget variances alone reveal.

2) For instance, the **small total variance in direct materials** was caused by (a) the amount that "should" have been spent being substantially **lower** than what was originally planned on and (b) the amount actually spent being substantially **higher** than what "should" have been spent.

11. Stop and review! You have completed the outline for this subunit. Study multiple-choice questions 1 through 7 beginning on page 667.

20.2 DIRECT MATERIALS VARIANCES

1. The **flexible budget variance** portion of the total variance for any of the three variable production inputs (direct materials, direct labor, and variable overhead) can be **subdivided** into two component variances.

    a. In the case of direct materials, the two components are the price variance and the quantity (also called the efficiency or usage) variance.

    b. The **materials price variance** is a pure measure of how much the actual price paid for inputs deviated from the standard (holding quantity constant).

$$\text{Materials price variance} = AQ \times (SP - AP)$$

        1) EXAMPLE: The materials price variance for the month is calculated as follows:

$$
\begin{aligned}
\text{Materials price variance} &= AQ \times (SP - AP) \\
&= 1{,}078 \text{ tons used} \times (\$54 \text{ per ton} - \$50 \text{ per ton}) \\
&= \mathbf{\$4{,}312\ F}
\end{aligned}
$$

    c. The **materials quantity variance** measures how efficiently direct materials were used given the actual level of production (holding price constant).

$$\text{Materials quantity variance} = (EQ - AQ) \times SP$$

        1) EXAMPLE: The materials quantity variance for the month is calculated as follows:

$$
\begin{aligned}
\text{Materials quantity variance} &= (EQ - AQ) \times SP \\
&= [(660 \text{ tons produced} \times 1.42857) - 1{,}078 \text{ tons}] \times \$54 \text{ per ton} \\
&= (942.8562 \text{ tons} - 1{,}078 \text{ tons}) \times \$54 \text{ per ton} \\
&= \mathbf{\$7{,}298\ U}
\end{aligned}
$$

        2) The calculations are confirmed by the fact that the net of the two equals the flexible budget variance.

$$
\begin{aligned}
\text{Materials flexible budget variance} &= \text{Price variance} + \text{Quantity variance} \\
&= \$4{,}312 + (-\$7{,}298) \\
&= \mathbf{\$2{,}986\ U}
\end{aligned}
$$

    d. Conceptually, the price and quantity (rate and efficiency in the case of direct labor) variances can be thought of as resulting from the insertion into the schematic of a **"third" budget amount**, consisting of the actual inputs used times the standard price.

        1) The algebraic formulas can be restated in terms of the budget amounts

$$
\begin{aligned}
\text{Materials price variance} &= AQ \times (SP - AP) \\
&= (AQ \times SP) - (AQ \times AP) \\
&= \text{"Third" budget} - \text{Actual results}
\end{aligned}
$$

$$
\begin{aligned}
\text{Materials quantity variance} &= (EQ - AQ) \times SP \\
&= (EQ \times SP) - (AQ \times SP) \\
&= \text{Flexible budget} - \text{"Third" budget}
\end{aligned}
$$

2)   These relationships can be depicted graphically as follows:

Materials and Labor Variances

Actual Results	Third Budget	Flexible Budget	Static Budget
Actual Inputs x Actual Price	Actual Inputs x Standard Price	Expected Inputs x Standard Price	Budgeted Inputs x Standard Price

Materials Price /
Labor Rate
Variance

Mat. Quantity /
Labor Efficiency
Variance

Flexible Budget
Variance

Sales Volume
Variance

Static Budget
Variance

2.   The interpretation of **unfavorable materials variances** is straightforward.

    a.   An **unfavorable price variance** means that the actual price paid for inputs was higher than expected.

    b.   An **unfavorable quantity variance** means that the actual number of inputs consumed was higher than expected.

        1)   An unfavorable materials quantity variance is usually caused by waste, shrinkage, or theft. It may be the responsibility of the production department supervisor because the excess usage occurred while the materials were under that person's supervision.

3.   **Favorable materials variances** are more ambiguous.

    a.   A **favorable price variance** could be caused by the purchasing manager dealing effectively with the company's suppliers.

        1)   Unfortunately, the purchasing manager could also engineer a favorable price variance for him/herself by contracting for a quantity discount on materials that results in the company carrying excess inventory.

        2)   Alternatively, the purchasing manager could have bought from the low bidder without regard for the quality of the materials.

    b.   A **favorable quantity variance** is also subject to varying interpretations.

        1)   A favorable materials quantity variance indicates that the workers either have been unusually efficient or are producing lower-quality products with less than the standard quantity of materials.

            a)   A favorable quantity variance, therefore, may suggest that costs have been reduced at the expense of product quality.

    c.   These aspects of variance analysis emphasize the point that variances cannot be interpreted in isolation. No variance by itself is either "good" or "bad" news.

4.   Stop and review! You have completed the outline for this subunit. Study multiple-choice questions 8 through 13 beginning on page 669.

20.3 DIRECT LABOR VARIANCES

1. As with direct materials, the **flexible budget variance** portion of the total variance for direct labor can be **subdivided** into two component variances.

   a. In the case of direct labor, the two components are the rate variance and the efficiency variance.

   b. The **labor rate variance** is a pure measure of how much the actual price paid for labor deviated from the standard (holding hours worked constant).

   Labor rate variance = AQ × (SP – AP)

   1) EXAMPLE: The labor rate variance for the month is calculated as follows:

   Labor rate variance = AQ × (SP – AP)
   = 880 hours spent × ($17.00 per hour – $16.00 per hour)
   = **$880 F**

   c. The **labor efficiency variance** measures how efficiently direct labor was employed given the actual level of production (holding the wage rate constant).

   Labor efficiency variance = (EQ – AQ) × SP

   1) EXAMPLE: The labor rate variance for the month is calculated as follows:

   Labor efficiency variance = (EQ – AQ) × SP
   = [(660 tons output × 1.28571) – 880 hours] × $17.00 per hour
   = (848.5686 – 880 hours) × $17.00 per hour
   = **$534 U**

   2) The calculations are confirmed by the fact that the net of the two equals the flexible budget variance.

   Labor flexible budget variance = Rate variance + Efficiency variance
   = $880 F + $534 U
   = **$346 F**

   d. Once again, it is helpful to conceive of the rate and efficiency variances as resulting from the insertion of a "third" budget, consisting of the actual hours worked times the standard wage.

   1) These relationships can be depicted algebraically as follows:

   Labor rate variance = (AQ × SP) – (AQ × AP)
   = "Third" budget – Actual results

   Labor efficiency variance = (EQ × SP) – (AQ × SP)
   = Flexible budget – "Third" budget

2. The interpretation of **unfavorable labor variances** is straightforward.

   a. An **unfavorable rate variance** means that the actual wages paid for labor were higher than expected.

   b. An **unfavorable efficiency variance** means that the actual number of hours worked was higher than expected.

   1) An unfavorable labor efficiency variance may be caused by workers taking unauthorized work breaks. It may also be caused by production delays resulting from materials shortages or inferior materials.

3.   **Favorable labor variances** are more ambiguous.

    a.   A **favorable rate variance** could be caused by the company securing a good contract with the union.

        1)   Unfortunately, the shift supervisor could also engineer a favorable price variance for him/herself by scheduling employees of insufficient skill level. They have lower wages but may be unable to produce products of the proper level of quality.

    b.   A **favorable efficiency variance** is also subject to varying interpretations.

        1)   A favorable labor efficiency variance indicates that the workers either have been unusually efficient or are producing lower-quality products with less than sufficient attention.

            a)   A favorable efficiency variance, therefore, may suggest that costs have been reduced at the expense of product quality.

    c.   As with direct materials, labor variances cannot be interpreted in isolation. No variance by itself is either "good" or "bad" news.

4.   Stop and review! You have completed the outline for this subunit. Study multiple-choice questions 14 through 17 beginning on page 670.

20.4 OVERHEAD VARIANCES

1.   As with direct materials and direct labor, the static budget variance for variable overhead can be subdivided into two component variances (the variances for fixed overhead are described in item 4. on page 656).

    a.   The **variable overhead flexible budget variance** reports how much actual variable overhead costs deviated from what was expected given the actual level of production.

        1)   In other words, the variable overhead flexible budget variance is the **amount of over- or underapplied variable overhead**.

        2)   Obviously, actual overhead costs for the period can simply be totaled to prepare for variance calculation. If an "actual rate" is desired, this total can be divided by the actual number of allocation-base units expended.

    b.   The **variable overhead sales volume variance** reports how much variable overhead costs that were expected given the actual level of production (i.e., the amount applied) deviated from what was planned for when the master budget was prepared.

2.   Likewise, the flexible budget variance for variable overhead can be subdivided into two component variances. The spending and efficiency variances are analogous to the price/rate and quantity/efficiency variances for materials and labor, respectively.

    a.   The **variable overhead spending variance** measures how much the "actual" overhead rate deviated from the standard (holding the driver level constant).

$$\text{Variable OH spending variance} = AQ \times (SP - AP)$$
$$= (AQ \times SP) - (AQ \times AP)$$
$$= (AQ \times SP) - \text{Actual costs incurred}$$

        1)   EXAMPLE: The variable OH spending variance for the month is calculated as follows:

$$\text{Variable OH spending variance} = (AQ \times SP) - \text{Actual costs incurred}$$
$$= (198 \text{ machine hours spent} \times \$48 \text{ per hour}) - \$9,702 \text{ actual costs}$$
$$= \$9,504 - \$9,702$$
$$= \mathbf{\$198 \ U}$$

b.   The **variable overhead efficiency variance** measures the "efficiency" with which the allocation base was used (holding the application rate constant).

Variable OH efficiency variance = (EQ − AQ) × SP

1)   EXAMPLE: The variable OH efficiency variance for the month is calculated as follows:

Variable OH efficiency variance = (EQ − AQ) × SP
= [(660 tons output × 0.28571) − 198 machine hours] × $48
= (188.5685 − 198) × $48
= **$453 U**

2)   The calculations are confirmed by the fact that the net of the two equals the flexible budget variance.

Variable OH flexible budget variance = Spending variance + Efficiency variance
= $198 U + $453 U
= **$651 U**

c.   The similarity of the variable overhead variances to the price/rate and quantity/efficiency variances for materials and labor can be seen in the following diagram:

Variable Overhead Variances

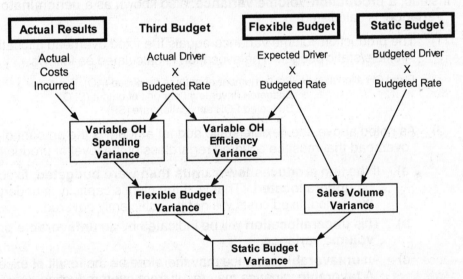

3.   **Variable overhead variances** do not directly measure production performance as materials and labor variances do.

a.   A **variable overhead spending variance** measures the accuracy of the estimates used to derive the application rate.

1)   Multiple indirect costs are pooled in variable overhead (indirect materials, indirect labor, utilities, etc.). Explaining this variance, **favorable or unfavorable**, would require detailed information about each of these costs.

b.   A **variable overhead efficiency variance** indicates a deviation in the efficiency of the allocation base for variable overhead.

1)   Machine hours are a commonly used driver for variable overhead. An **unfavorable** variance could be caused by:

a)   Obsolete machinery
b)   Improper machine maintenance
c)   Lack of training in proper use of machines
d)   Jobs poorly scheduled

4.   The **fixed portion of the total overhead variance** also has two components, but they are not combined.

   a.   Just as with variable overhead, the **fixed overhead spending variance** is derived by comparing the actual costs incurred with the flexible budget.

   1)   This variance is caused by an unexpected change in the amount of fixed costs, such as a sudden increase in factory insurance or the penalty-free cancelation of an equipment lease.

   2)   EXAMPLE: The fixed OH spending variance for the month is calculated as follows:

   Fixed OH spending variance = Flexible/Static budget − Actual costs incurred
   = $8,000 − $9,496
   = **$1,496 U**

   3)   Note that fixed overhead has **no efficiency variance**, due to the fact that the **flexible and static budget amounts** for fixed overhead are the **same**.

   a)   This is because fixed costs are, by their nature, unchanging within the relevant range of the budgeting cycle. The same amount of fixed costs must be covered regardless of machine usage or output level.

   b.   Instead, a **production-volume variance**, also known as a **denominator-level variance**, is calculated.

   1)   The production volume variance equals the fixed overhead allocation minus the flexible/static budget. The allocation is calculated as follows:

   Fixed OH allocation = Actual number of outputs produced (AO)
   × Budgeted driver level per unit of output (SI/O)
   × Budgeted FOH application rate (SP)

   2)   As noted above, the flexible/static budget amount is the amount of fixed overhead that must be covered regardless of the level of production.

   a)   If the firm **produces fewer units than were budgeted**, fixed overhead will be **underallocated**. That is, if the plant's capacity is underutilized during the period, fixed costs will not be sufficiently covered.

   b)   This **underallocation** will be indicated by an **unfavorable production-volume variance**.

   c)   An **unfavorable** variance may therefore be the result of excess capacity. A **favorable** variance may result from overproduction.

   3)   EXAMPLE: The fixed OH production-volume variance is calculated as follows:

   Fixed OH production-volume variance = Fixed OH allocated − Flexible/Static budget
   = (660 tons output × 0.28571 × $40 per hour) − $8,000
   = $7,543 − $8,000
   = **$457 U**

c. The fixed overhead variances can be depicted graphically as follows:

Fixed Overhead Variances

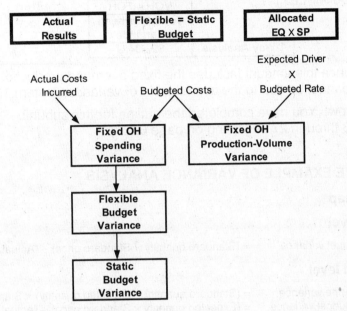

5. **Integrated overhead variance analysis** combines the variable and fixed portions of the overhead variance to allow simplified scrutiny.

a. **Four-way** overhead variance analysis includes all four intermediate variances calculated on pages 654–656.

1) EXAMPLE:

4-Way Analysis	Spending	Efficiency	Production-Volume
Variable	$198 U	$453 U	--
Fixed	$1,496 U	--	$457 U

b. **Three-way** overhead variance analysis combines the variable and fixed spending variances into a single spending variance and reports the other two variances separately.

1) EXAMPLE:

	VOH + FOH	VOH	FOH
	Spending	Efficiency	Production-Volume
3-Way Analysis	$1,694 U	$453 U	$457 U

c. **Two-way** overhead variance analysis combines the spending and efficiency variances into a flexible budget variance and reports the production-volume variance separately.

1) EXAMPLE:

	VOH + FOH	FOH
	Flexible Budget	Production-Volume
2-Way Analysis	$2,147 U	$457 U

2) The flexible budget variance in 2-way analysis is also called the **controllable variance**. It is the portion of the total not attributable to the production-volume variance.

d. **One-way** overhead variance analysis combines all the overhead variances into a single amount.

1) EXAMPLE:

	VOH + FOH
	Total Overhead Variance
1-Way Analysis	$2,604 U

2) Since this amount includes the fixed overhead production-volume variance, it cannot be tied to the overall table of variances in item 10.e. in Subunit 1.

6. Stop and review! You have completed the outline for this subunit. Study multiple-choice questions 18 through 27 beginning on page 672.

20.5 COMPREHENSIVE EXAMPLE OF VARIANCE ANALYSIS

1. **Formula Recap**

    a. **First level**

Static budget variance	= (Standard quantity × Standard price) − (Actual quantity × Actual price)

    b. **Second level**

Sales volume variance	= (Standard quantity − Expected quantity) × Standard price
Flexible budget variance	= (Expected quantity × Standard price) − (Actual quantity × Actual price)

    c. **Third level**

Price / rate variance	= Actual quantity × (Standard price − Actual price)
Quantity / efficiency variance	= (Expected quantity − Actual quantity) × Standard price

2. **Situation**

	BUDGET			ACTUAL
OUTPUT	1,000 units			1,020 units
DIRECT MATERIALS	Carbon	150,000 units @ $1.00		233,333.3 units @ $1.90
	Chromium	150,000 units @ $1.00		233,333.3 units @ $1.90
	Copper	300,000 units @ $3.00		233,333.3 units @ $1.90
DIRECT LABOR	68,000 hours @ $7.00 per hour			65,000 hours @ $7.20
OVERHEAD	Variable:	$6.00 per direct labor hour		$396,000
	Fixed:	$2.00 per direct labor hour		$130,000

3. Use this worksheet as an aid in deriving the variances.

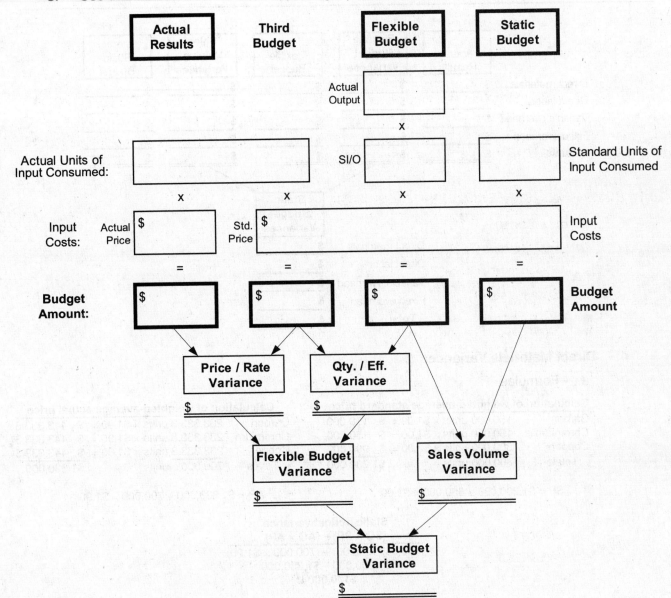

Master Variances

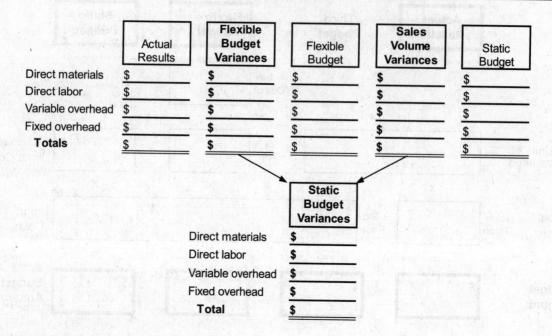

	Actual Results	Flexible Budget Variances	Flexible Budget	Sales Volume Variances	Static Budget
Direct materials	$	$	$	$	$
Direct labor	$	$	$	$	$
Variable overhead	$	$	$	$	$
Fixed overhead	$	$	$	$	$
Totals	$	$	$	$	$

Static Budget Variances

Direct materials	$
Direct labor	$
Variable overhead	$
Fixed overhead	$
Total	$

4.   Direct Materials Variances

a.   Formulas

Calculation of weighted-average standard price

Carbon	150,000 units × $1.00 =	$ 150,000
Chromium	150,000 units × $1.00 =	$ 150,000
Copper	300,000 units × $3.00 =	$ 900,000
Totals	600,000 units	$1,200,000

$$SP = \$1,200,000 \div 600,000 = \$2.00$$

Calculation of weighted-average actual price

Carbon	233,333.3 units × $1.90 =	$ 443,333.3
Chromium	233,333.3 units × $1.90 =	$ 443,333.3
Copper	233,333.3 units × $1.90 =	$ 443,333.3
Totals	700,000 units	$1,330,000

$$AP = \$1,330,000 \div 700,000 = \$1.90$$

Static budget variance
$$(SQ \times SP) - (AQ \times AP)$$
$$(600,000 \times \$2.00) - (700,000 \times \$1.90)$$
$$\$1,200,000 - \$1,330,000$$
$130,000 U

Calculation of expected quantity

$$SI/O = \text{Budgeted inputs} \div \text{Budgeted outputs}$$
$$= 600,000 \text{ units} \div 1,000 \text{ units}$$
$$= 600$$
$$EQ = \text{Actual outputs} \times SI/O$$
$$= 1,020 \text{ units} \times 600$$
$$= 612,000$$

Flexible budget variance
$$(EQ \times SP) - (AQ \times AP)$$
$$(612,000 \times \$2.00) - (700,000 \times \$1.90)$$
$$\$1,224,000 - \$1,330,000$$
$106,000 U

Sales volume variance
$$(SQ - EQ) \times SP$$
$$(600,000 - 612,000) \times \$2.00$$
$$-12,000 \times \$2.00$$
$24,000 U

Materials price variance
$$AQ \times (SP - AP)$$
$$700,000 \times (\$2.00 - \$1.90)$$
$$700,000 \times \$.10$$
$70,000 F

Materials quantity variance
$$(EQ - AQ) \times SP$$
$$(612,000 - 700,000) \times \$2.00$$
$$-88,000 \times \$2.00$$
$176,000 U

b. Diagram

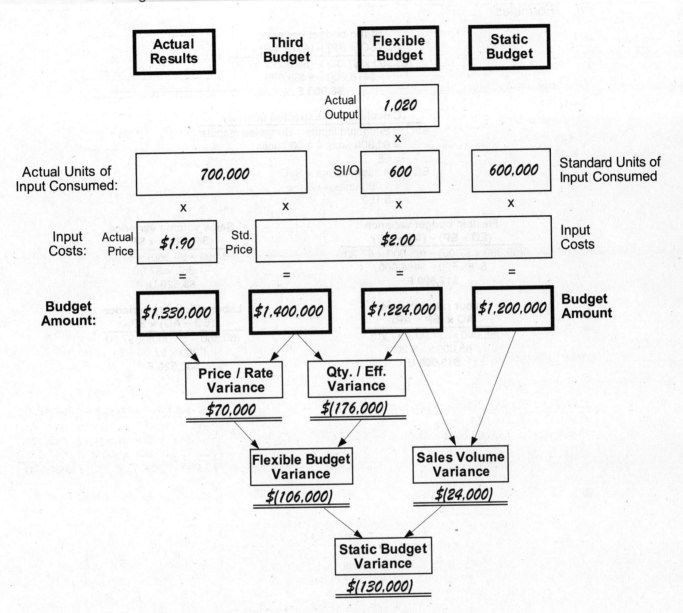

5.   **Direct Labor Variances**

    a.   Formulas

Static budget variance
(SQ × SP) – (AQ × AP)

$(68,000 × \$7.00) – (65,000 × \$7.20)$
$\$476,000 – \$468,000$
\$8,000 F

Calculation of expected quantity

SI/O = Budgeted inputs ÷ Budgeted outputs
     = 68,000 units ÷ 1,000 units
     = 68
EQ = Actual outputs × SI/O
     = 1,020 units × 68
     = 8,160

Flexible budget variance	**Sales volume variance**
(EQ × SP) – (AQ × AP)	**(SQ – EQ) × SP**
$(69,360 × \$7.00) – (65,000 × \$7.20)$	$(68,000 – 69,360) × \$7.00$
$\$485,520 – \$468,000$	$-1,360 × \$7.00$
\$17,520 F	**\$9,520 U**
Labor rate variance	**Labor efficiency variance**
AQ × (SP – AP)	**(EQ – AQ) × SP**
$65,000 × (\$7.00 – \$7.20)$	$(69,360 – 65,000) × \$7.00$
$65,000 × -\$.20$	$4,360 × \$7.00$
\$13,000 U	**\$30,520 F**

b.   Diagram

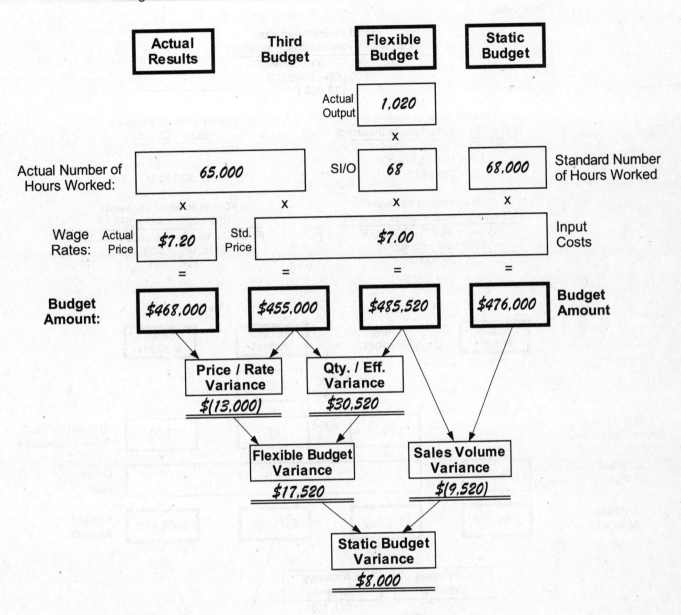

6.   **Variable Overhead Variances**

a.   Formulas

Static budget variance
(SQ × SP) – Actual costs incurred
(68,000 × $6.00) – $396,000
$408,000 – $396,000
$12,000 F

Flexible budget variance
(EQ × SP) – Actual costs incurred
(69,360 × $6.00) – $396,000
$416,160 – $396,000
$20,160 F

Sales volume variance
(SQ – EQ) × SP
(68,000 – 69,360) × $6.00
–1,360 × $6.00
$8,160 U

VOH spending variance
(AQ × SP) – Actual costs incurred
(65,000 × $6.00) – $396,000
$390,000 – $396,000
$6,000 U

VOH efficiency variance
(EQ × SP) – AQ × SP)
(69,360 × $6.00) – (65,000 × $6.00)
$416,160 – $390,000
$26,160 F

b.   Diagram

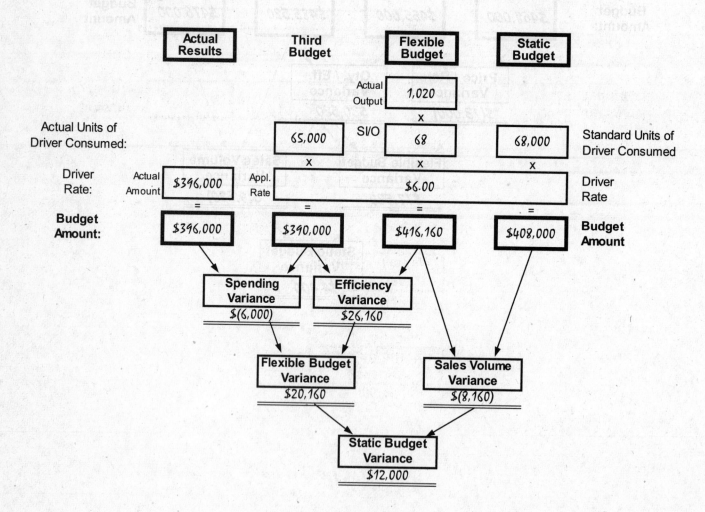

7. **Fixed Overhead Variances**

   a. Formulas

Static budget variance	Sales volume variance
(SQ × SP) – Actual costs incurred	(EQ – SQ) × SP
(68,000 × $2.00) – $130,000	(69,360 – 68,000) × $2.00
$136,000 – $130,000	1,360 × $2.00
$6,000 F	**$2,720 F**

   b. Diagram

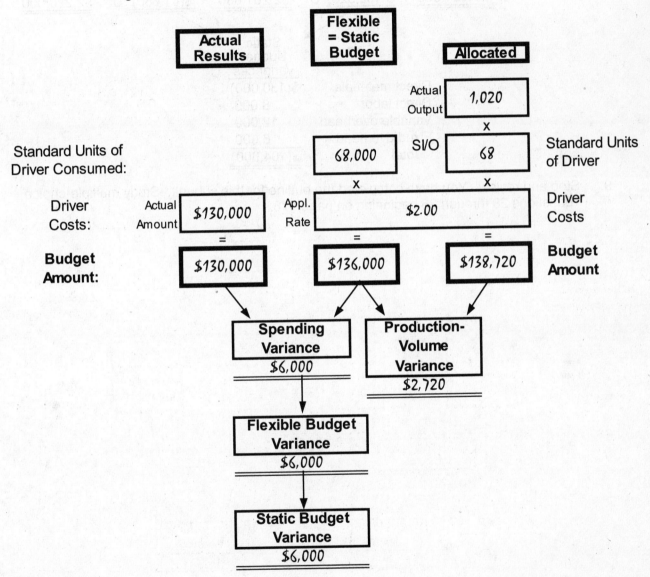

8.   The individual variances can be combined in a single schedule.

	Actual Results	Flexible Budget Variances		Flexible Budget	Sales Volume Variances		Static Budget
Direct materials	$1,330,000	$(106,000)	U	$1,224,000	$(24,000)	U	$1,200,000
Direct labor	468,000	17,520	F	485,520	(9,520)	U	476,000
Variable overhead	396,000	20,160	F	416,160	(8,160)	U	408,000
Fixed overhead	130,000	6,000	F	136,000	----		136,000
Total	$2,324,000	$ (62,320)	U	$2,261,680	$(41,680)	U	$2,220,000

	Static Budget Variances
Direct materials	$(130,000)
Direct labor	8,000
Variable overhead	12,000
Fixed overhead	6,000
Total	$(104,000)

9.   Stop and review! You have completed the outline for this subunit. Study multiple-choice questions 28 through 36 beginning on page 676.

QUESTIONS

20.1 Static and Flexible Budgeting

1. A difference between standard costs used for cost control and budgeted costs

A. Can exist because standard costs must be determined after the budget is completed.

B. Can exist because standard costs represent what costs should be, whereas budgeted costs represent expected actual costs.

C. Can exist because budgeted costs are historical costs, whereas standard costs are based on engineering studies.

D. Cannot exist because they should be the same amounts.

Answer (B) is correct. *(CMA, adapted)*
REQUIRED: The true statement about the difference between standard costs and budgeted costs.
DISCUSSION: Standard costs are predetermined, attainable unit costs. Standard cost systems isolate deviations (variances) of actual from expected costs. One advantage of standard costs is that they facilitate flexible budgeting. Accordingly, standard and budgeted costs should not differ when standards are currently attainable. However, in practice, budgeted (estimated actual) costs may differ from standard costs when operating conditions are not expected to reflect those anticipated when the standards were developed.
Answer (A) is incorrect because standard costs are determined independently of the budget. Answer (C) is incorrect because budgeted costs are expected future costs, not historical costs. Answer (D) is incorrect because budgeted and standard costs should in principle be the same, but in practice they will differ when standard costs are not expected to be currently attainable.

2. The best basis upon which cost standards should be set to measure controllable production inefficiencies is

A. Engineering standards based on ideal performance.

B. Normal capacity.

C. Recent average historical performance.

D. Engineering standards based on attainable performance.

Answer (D) is correct. *(CMA, adapted)*
REQUIRED: The best basis upon which cost standards should be set.
DISCUSSION: Standards must be accepted by those who will carry them out if they are to have maximum effectiveness. Subordinates should believe that standards are both fair and achievable; otherwise they may tend to sabotage, ignore, or circumvent them. Standard costs are often based on the results of time and motion studies, or other types of engineering standards.
Answer (A) is incorrect because employees may not cooperate with standards based on ideal performance; attainable standards are usually better for motivational purposes. Answer (B) is incorrect because normal capacity may not be sufficient to control production inefficiencies. Answer (C) is incorrect because historical performance may not always be a guide to future performance, and standards should be based on anticipated future conditions.

3. In connection with a standard cost system being developed by Flint Co., the following information is being considered with regard to standard hours allowed for output of one unit of product:

	Hours
Average historical performance for the past 3 years	1.85
Production level to satisfy average consumer demand over a seasonal time span	1.60
Engineering estimates based on attainable performance	1.50
Engineering estimates based on ideal performance	1.25

To measure controllable production inefficiencies, what is the best basis for Flint to use in establishing standard hours allowed?

A. 1.25

B. 1.50

C. 1.60

D. 1.85

Answer (B) is correct. *(CPA, adapted)*
REQUIRED: The best basis for establishing standard hours allowed.
DISCUSSION: A standard cost system separates the expected cost from the actual cost. Thus, deviations from expected results are identified on a routine basis. The best standards are based on attainable performance so that any deviation will denote inefficiencies that deserve review and have a reasonable probability of responding to management attention. Attainable standards also motivate employees. Thus, the engineering estimate based on attainable performance, 1.50, is the best basis for establishing standard hours allowed.
Answer (A) is incorrect because ideal standards are seldom attainable. Answer (C) is incorrect because standard hours should be lower than the production level to satisfy average customer demand. Answer (D) is incorrect because average historical performance standard hours are higher than the attainable standard.

4. A standard-cost system may be used in

A. Job-order costing but not process costing.

B. Either job-order costing or process costing.

C. Process costing but not job-order costing.

D. Neither process costing nor job-order costing.

Answer (B) is correct. *(CPA, adapted)*
REQUIRED: The cost accumulation system(s) that may use standard costing.
DISCUSSION: A standard-cost system costs the product at standard (predetermined) costs and compares expected with actual cost. This comparison allows deviations (i.e., variances) from expected results to be identified and investigated. A standard-cost system can be used in both job-order and process-costing systems to isolate variances.

5. The following direct labor information pertains to the manufacture of product Glu:

Time required to make one unit	2 direct labor hours
Number of direct workers	50
Number of productive hours per week, per worker	40
Weekly wages per worker	$500
Workers' benefits treated as direct labor costs	20% of wages

What is the standard direct labor cost per unit of product Glu?

A. $30

B. $24

C. $15

D. $12

Answer (A) is correct. *(CPA, adapted)*
REQUIRED: The standard direct labor cost per unit.
DISCUSSION: The hourly wage per worker is $12.50 ($500 ÷ 40 hrs.). The direct labor cost per hour is $15 [$12.50 × (1.0 + benefits equal to 20% of wages)]. Consequently, the standard direct labor cost per unit is $30 ($15 × 2 hrs.).
Answer (B) is incorrect because the weekly wages and benefits per worker ($500 × 1.2) should be divided by 40 hours per week, not by 50 workers. Answer (C) is incorrect because $15.00 is the DL cost per hour. Two DL hours are required per unit. Answer (D) is incorrect because the weekly wages and benefits per worker ($500 × 1.2) should be divided by 40 hours per week, not by 50 workers. Furthermore, 2 DL hours are required per unit.

6. Companies in what type of industry may use a standard cost system for cost control?

	Mass Production Industry	Service Industry
A.	Yes	Yes
B.	Yes	No
C.	No	No
D.	No	Yes

Answer (A) is correct. *(CPA, adapted)*
REQUIRED: The types of industry that may use a standard cost system.
DISCUSSION: A standard cost system costs output at a predetermined unit amount. It is applicable to both job-order and process costing systems and to service as well as mass production industries. For example, a standard labor cost may be developed for the labor involved in a service activity.

7. When a manager is concerned with monitoring total cost, total revenue, and net profit conditioned upon the level of productivity, an accountant would normally recommend

	Flexible Budgeting	Standard Costing
A.	Yes	Yes
B.	Yes	No
C.	No	Yes
D.	No	No

Answer (A) is correct. *(CPA, adapted)*
REQUIRED: The technique(s) for monitoring cost, revenue, and profit given different levels of activity.
DISCUSSION: A flexible budget is a set of static budgets prepared in anticipation of varying levels of activity. It permits evaluation of actual results when actual and expected production differ. Setting cost standards facilitates preparation of a flexible budget. For example, a standard unit variable cost is useful in determining the total variable cost for a given output.
Answer (B) is incorrect because standard costing should also be recommended. Answer (C) is incorrect because flexible budgeting is also appropriate. Answer (D) is incorrect because flexible budgeting and standard costing should be used.

20.2 Direct Materials Variances

8. To meet its monthly budgeted production goals, Acme Mfg. Co. planned a need for 10,000 widgets at a price of $20 per widget. Acme's actual units were 11,200 at a price of $18.50 per widget. What amount reflected Acme's price variance?

A. $7,200 unfavorable.

B. $15,000 favorable.

C. $16,800 favorable.

D. $16,800 unfavorable.

Answer (C) is correct. *(CPA, adapted)*
REQUIRED: The materials price variance.
DISCUSSION: The materials price variance is a pure measure of how much the actual price paid for inputs deviated from the standard (holding quantity constant). The formula is: $AQ \times (SP - AP)$. Thus, the price variance is equal to $16,800 [11,200 units $\times$ ($20 – $18.50)]. It is favorable because the actual price is less than the standard price.
Answer (A) is incorrect because $7,200 unfavorable is the total (static budget) direct materials variance. Answer (B) is incorrect because $15,000 favorable results from improperly using the standard, not the actual, quantity. Answer (D) is incorrect because $16,800 unfavorable results from reversing the subtraction of the actual and standard price.

9. Virgil Corp. uses a standard cost system. In May, Virgil used 17,500 pounds of materials at a cost of $70,000. The materials usage variance was $2,500 unfavorable and the quantity of materials expected given the level of May production was 17,000 pounds. What was the materials price variance for May?

A. $17,500 favorable.

B. $17,500 unfavorable.

C. $15,000 favorable.

D. $15,000 unfavorable.

Answer (A) is correct. *(CPA, adapted)*
REQUIRED: The materials price variance.
DISCUSSION: The materials usage (also called the quantity or efficiency) variance measures how efficiently direct materials were used given the actual level of production (holding price constant). The formula is: $(EQ - AQ) \times SP$. Substituting the given information about quantities allows the standard price to be calculated:

$$(EQ - AQ) \times SP = \$2,500 \ U$$
$$(17,000 - 17,500) \times SP = \$2,500 \ U$$
$$(- 500) \times SP = \$2,500 \ U$$
$$SP = \$5.00$$

Once the standard price is known, the materials price variance can be calculated:

$$AQ \times (SP - AP) = \$17,500 \times (\$5.00 - \$4.00)$$
$$= 17,500 \times \$1.00$$
$$= \$17,500 \ F$$

Answer (B) is incorrect because the variance is favorable. Answer (C) is incorrect because $15,000 F is the flexible budget variance. Answer (D) is incorrect because the materials price variance is favorable.

10. Tower Company planned to produce 3,000 units of its single product, Titactium, during November. The standard specifications for one unit of Titactium include 6 pounds of materials at $.30 per pound. Actual production in November was 3,100 units of Titactium. Tower's accountant computed a favorable materials price variance of $380 and an unfavorable materials quantity variance of $120. Based on these variances, the accountant could conclude that

A. More materials were purchased than were used.

B. More materials were used than were produced.

C. The actual cost of materials was less than the standard cost.

D. The actual usage of materials was less than the standard allowed.

Answer (C) is correct. *(CMA, adapted)*
REQUIRED: The implications of a favorable materials price variance with an unfavorable materials quantity variance.
DISCUSSION: The materials price variance is a pure measure of how much the actual price paid for inputs deviated from the standard (holding quantity constant). It equals the actual quantity of materials consumed times the difference between the actual and standard unit prices. Hence, a favorable materials price variance means that materials were purchased at a price less than the standard price.
Answer (A) is incorrect because no variance relates quantity purchased to quantity used. Answer (B) is incorrect because it is a nonsense answer. Answer (D) is incorrect because the unfavorable quantity variance indicates that more materials were used than allowed by the standards.

11. Carr Co. had an unfavorable materials usage variance of $900. What amounts of this variance should be charged to each department?

	Purchasing	Warehousing	Manufacturing
A.	$0	$0	$900
B.	$0	$900	$0
C.	$300	$300	$300
D.	$900	$0	$0

Answer (A) is correct. *(CPA, adapted)*
REQUIRED: The amount of materials usage variance charged to each department.
DISCUSSION: The material usage (also called the quantity or efficiency) variance is typically influenced most by activities within the production (manufacturing) department. Thus, the entire variance should be charged to the manufacturing department.

12. The standard direct materials cost to produce a unit of Lem is 4 meters of materials at $2.50 per meter. During the month just ended, 4,200 meters of materials costing $10,080 were purchased and used to produce 1,000 units of Lem. What was the flexible budget variance for materials for the month?

A. $400 favorable.

B. $420 favorable.

C. $80 unfavorable.

D. $500 unfavorable.

Answer (C) is correct. *(CPA, adapted)*
REQUIRED: The flexible budget variance.
DISCUSSION: The actual amount spent on direct materials is given as $10,800. The flexible budget equals the actual units of output (1,000) times the standard inputs per unit of output (4 meters) times the standard unit price ($2.50). The flexible budget variance, calculated as the flexible budget minus the actual results, is therefore $80 unfavorable [(1,000 × 4 × $2.50) – $10,080)].
Answer (A) is incorrect because $400 favorable results from improperly using the expected quantity rather than the actual quantity. Answer (B) is incorrect because $420 favorable is the price variance. Answer (D) is incorrect because $500 unfavorable is the quantity variance.

13. Herald Corporation manufactures greeting cards. It purchases paper monthly to be used in its production process. In December, Herald used 200 reams of paper when the budgeted amount for the month was 180 reams. The standard price budgeted for each ream of paper is $30, but the actual price on the purchase date was $35 per ream. What is Herald's direct materials quantity variance for December?

A. $1,600 unfavorable.

B. $1,000 unfavorable.

C. $700 unfavorable.

D. $900 unfavorable.

Answer (A) is correct. *(Publisher, adapted)*
REQUIRED: The direct materials static budget variance.
DISCUSSION: The static budget variance is the total variance to be explained for the period. It is calculated as the static budget minus the actual results. In Herald's case, the static budget consists of the budgeted level of materials usage (180 reams) times the standard price ($30 per ream), and the actual results consist of the actual level of usage (200 reams) times the actual price ($35 per ream). The static budget variance is thus (180 × $30) – (200 × $35) = $5,400 – $7,000 = $1,600 unfavorable.
Answer (B) is incorrect because $1,000 unfavorable is the price variance. Answer (C) is incorrect because $700 is the result of multiplying the actual price by the difference between the actual and standard quantities. Answer (D) is incorrect because $900 is the result of multiplying the standard quantity by the difference between the actual price and the standard price.

20.3 Direct Labor Variances

14. Normal Company produced 600 units of one of its products last year. The standard for labor hours allowed was 2 hours per unit at a standard rate of $6 per hour. Actual hours worked amounted to 1,230 hours. The labor rate variance was $246 unfavorable. What was the actual labor cost for the period?

A. $7,134

B. $7,200

C. $7,380

D. $7,626

Answer (D) is correct. *(Publisher, adapted)*
REQUIRED: The amount of actual labor costs for the period.
DISCUSSION: The labor rate variance is the difference between the "third" budget and the actual results. The formula is (AQ × SP) – (AQ × AP). The actual amount spent on labor can thus be derived as follows:

$$(AQ \times SP) - \text{Actual results} = \$246 \text{ U}$$
$$(1{,}230 \text{ hours} \times \$6.00) - \text{Actual results} = \$246 \text{ U}$$
$$- \text{Actual results} = \$246 \text{ U} - \$7{,}380$$
$$\text{Actual results} = \$7{,}626$$

The information provided about the actual level of output and the standard hours per unit of output is irrelevant; these data are important to the calculation of the expected quantity, which plays no role in the determination of the rate variance.
Answer (A) is incorrect because $7,134 results from improperly using a favorable rate variance. Answer (B) is incorrect because $7,200 is the flexible budget. Answer (C) is incorrect because $7,380 is the "third" budget, that is, the actual hours times the standard rate.

15. The static budget for the month of May was for 9,000 units with direct materials at $15 per unit. Each unit of output requires one unit of direct material. Direct labor was budgeted at 45 minutes per unit for a total of $81,000. Actual output for the month was 8,500 units with $127,500 in direct materials and $77,775 in direct labor expense. The direct labor standard of 45 minutes was maintained throughout the month. Variance analysis of the performance for the month of May would show a(n)

A. Favorable materials usage variance of $7,500.

B. Favorable direct labor static budget variance of $3,225.

C. Unfavorable materials efficiency variance of $7,500.

D. Favorable direct labor rate variance of $17,250.

Answer (B) is correct. *(CMA, adapted)*
REQUIRED: The result of variance analysis based on a flexible budget for direct labor and materials.
DISCUSSION: The static budget for direct labor is given as $81,000, and the actual amount spent on labor is given as $77,775. The static budget variance for direct labor is therefore $3,225 favorable ($81,000 – $77,775).

Answer (A) is incorrect because $7,500 favorable is the sales volume variance for direct materials. Answer (C) is incorrect because the materials efficiency (usage) variance is favorable. Answer (D) is incorrect because $17,250 favorable is the direct labor sales volume variance.

16. A company produces widgets with budgeted standard direct materials of 2 pounds per widget at $5 per pound. Standard direct labor was budgeted at 0.5 hour per widget at $15 per hour. The actual usage in the current year was 25,000 pounds and 3,000 hours to produce 10,000 widgets. What were the direct materials quantity and the direct labor efficiency variances?

	Direct Materials Quantity	Direct Labor Efficiency
A.	Indeterminable	$30,000 favorable
B.	Indeterminable	$30,000 unfavorable
C.	$25,000 unfavorable	$30,000 favorable
D.	$25,000 favorable	$30,000 unfavorable

Answer (C) is correct. *(CPA, adapted)*
REQUIRED: The direct materials quantity and direct labor efficiency variances.
DISCUSSION: The quantity/efficiency variance is the flexible budget minus the "third" budget. The formula for both materials and labor is $(EQ – AQ) \times SP$. The calculations are thus as follows:

Direct Materials Quantity:

$(EQ – AQ) \times SP$
= [(10,000 units output × 2 standard pounds DM per unit of output) – 25,000 pounds used] × $5.00
= (20,000 pounds – 25,000 pounds) × $5.00
= –5,000 pounds × $5.00
= $25,000 unfavorable

Direct Labor Efficiency:

$(EQ – AQ) \times SP$
= [(10,000 units output × 0.5 standard hour DL per unit of output) – 3,000 hours worked] × $15.00
= (5,000 hours – 3,000 hours) × $15.00
= 2,000 hours × $15.00
= $30,000 favorable

Answer (A) is incorrect because the expected quantity can be calculated from the information given, making both variances determinable. Answer (B) is incorrect because the expected quantity can be calculated from the information given, making both variances determinable. Answer (D) is incorrect because the materials variance is unfavorable and the labor variance is favorable.

17. Yola Co. manufactures one product with a standard direct labor cost of 4 hours at $12.00 per hour. During the month just ended, 1,000 units were produced using 4,100 hours at $12.20 per hour. The unfavorable direct labor efficiency variance was

A. $1,220

B. $1,200

C. $820

D. $400

Answer (B) is correct.   *(CPA, adapted)*
REQUIRED: The amount of unfavorable direct labor efficiency variance.
DISCUSSION: The direct labor efficiency variance measures how efficiently labor was employed given the actual level of production (holding the wage rate constant). It is calculated as the flexible budget minus the "third" budget. The formula is: $(EQ - AQ) \times SP$. For Yola, the calculation is thus

$(EQ - AQ) \times SP$
$= [(1{,}000 \text{ units output} \times 4 \text{ standard pounds DL per unit of output}) - 4{,}100 \text{ hours worked}] \times \$12.00$
$= (4{,}000 \text{ hours} - 4{,}100 \text{ hours}) \times \$12.00$
$= -100 \text{ hours} \times \$12.00$
$= \$1{,}200 \text{ unfavorable}$

Note that the actual cost of labor is not relevant to this calculation.
     Answer (A) is incorrect because $1,220 uses the actual labor price. Answer (C) is incorrect because $820 is the labor rate variance. Answer (D) is incorrect because $400 is the difference between the direct labor efficiency variance and the cost difference ($.20) times the standard hours.

20.4 Overhead Variances

18. Variable overhead is applied on the basis of standard direct labor hours. If, for a given period, the direct labor efficiency variance is unfavorable, the variable overhead efficiency variance will be

A. Favorable.

B. Unfavorable.

C. Zero.

D. The same amount as the labor efficiency variance.

Answer (B) is correct.   *(CMA, adapted)*
REQUIRED: The effect on the variable overhead efficiency variance.
DISCUSSION: If variable overhead is applied to production on the basis of direct labor hours, both the variable overhead efficiency variance and the direct labor efficiency variance will be calculated on the basis of the same number of hours. If the labor efficiency variance is unfavorable, the overhead efficiency variance also will be unfavorable because both variances are based on the difference between standard and actual labor hours worked.
     Answer (A) is incorrect because both efficiency variances are based on the same number of hours worked. Thus, if one is unfavorable, the other will also be unfavorable. Answer (C) is incorrect because the variable overhead efficiency variance will be unfavorable. Answer (D) is incorrect because the amount of the variances will be different depending on the amount of the costs anticipated and actually paid.

19. If overhead is applied on the basis of units of output, the variable overhead efficiency variance will be

A. Zero.

B. Favorable, if output exceeds the budgeted level.

C. Unfavorable, if output is less than the budgeted level.

D. A function of the direct labor efficiency variance.

Answer (A) is correct.   *(CMA, adapted)*
REQUIRED: The effect on the variable overhead efficiency variance.
DISCUSSION: The variable overhead efficiency variance equals the product of the variable overhead application rate and the difference between the standard input for the actual output and the actual input. Hence, the variance will be zero if variable overhead is applied on the basis of units of output because the difference between actual and standard input cannot be recognized.

20. The following information pertains to Roe Co.'s manufacturing operations during the month just ended:

Standard direct labor hours per unit	2
Actual direct labor hours	10,500
Number of units produced	5,000
Standard variable overhead per standard direct labor hour	$3
Actual variable overhead	$28,000

Roe's unfavorable variable overhead efficiency variance for the month was

- A. $0
- B. $1,500
- C. $2,000
- D. $3,500

Answer (B) is correct. *(CPA, adapted)*
REQUIRED: The amount of unfavorable variable overhead efficiency variance.
DISCUSSION: The overhead efficiency variance is the standard price times the difference between the actual and standard hours. The standard price for variable overhead is $3 per direct labor hour. The actual direct labor hours are 10,500. The standard labor hours are 10,000 (5,000 units × 2 hours per unit). Thus, the variable overhead efficiency variance is $1,500 [3 × (10,500 – 10,000)]. The variance is unfavorable because actual hours exceeded standard hours.
Answer (A) is incorrect because an unfavorable variable overhead efficiency variance exists. Answer (C) is incorrect because $2,000 is the difference between the actual overhead and the overhead rate applied to the standard hours. Answer (D) is incorrect because $3,500 is the spending variance.

21. Which of the following standard costing variances would be least controllable by a production supervisor?

- A. Overhead volume.
- B. Overhead efficiency.
- C. Labor efficiency.
- D. Material usage.

Answer (A) is correct. *(CPA, adapted)*
REQUIRED: The variance least controllable by a production supervisor.
DISCUSSION: The volume variance measures the effect of not operating at the budgeted activity level. This variance can be caused by, for example, insufficient sales or a labor strike. These events are out of the production supervisor's control. Thus, the volume variance is the least controllable by a production supervisor.
Answer (B) is incorrect because the overhead efficiency variance is wholly attributable to variable overhead. Answer (C) is incorrect because the efficiency of employees affects the labor efficiency variance. Answer (D) is incorrect because the material usage variance is typically influenced most by activities within the production department.

22. Under the two-variance method for analyzing overhead, which of the following variances consists of both variable and fixed overhead elements?

	Flexible Budget Variance	Production-Volume Variance
A.	Yes	Yes
B.	Yes	No
C.	No	No
D.	No	Yes

Answer (B) is correct. *(CPA, adapted)*
REQUIRED: The variance(s), if any, including both fixed and variable O/H elements.
DISCUSSION: In two-way analysis, the two components are the flexible budget variance (VOH spending variance + VOH efficiency variance + FOH spending variance) and the production-volume variance (a fixed overhead variance, also called the denominator-level variance). Consequently, only the flexible budget variance contains both fixed and variable elements.
Answer (A) is incorrect because the production-volume variance refers only to fixed overhead. Answer (C) is incorrect because the flexible budget variance contains both variable and fixed overhead elements. Answer (D) is incorrect because the flexible budget variance contains both variable and fixed overhead elements; also, the production-volume variance refers only to fixed overhead.

23. During the month just ended, a department's three-variance overhead standard costing system reported unfavorable spending and production-volume variances. The activity level selected for allocating overhead to the product was based on 80% of practical capacity. If 100% of practical capacity had been selected instead, how would the reported unfavorable spending and production-volume variances be affected?

	Spending Variance	Production-Volume Variance
A.	Increased	Unchanged
B.	Increased	Increased
C.	Unchanged	Increased
D.	Unchanged	Unchanged

24. Which of the following variances would be useful in calling attention to a possible short-term problem in the control of overhead costs?

	Spending Variance	Production-Volume Variance
A.	No	No
B.	No	Yes
C.	Yes	No
D.	Yes	Yes

25. Under the three-variance method for analyzing manufacturing overhead, which of the following is affected when the actual level of output for the period differs from the budgeted level?

	Spending Variance	Efficiency Variance	Production-Volume Variance
A.	Yes	Yes	Yes
B.	No	Yes	Yes
C.	No	No	Yes
D.	No	No	No

Answer (C) is correct. *(CPA, adapted)*
   REQUIRED: The effects on unfavorable spending and production-volume variances of increasing the budgeted activity level.
   DISCUSSION: In three-way analysis, the spending variance is the combination of the variable and fixed overhead spending variances. Because variable unit costs are assumed to be constant within a relevant range, the variable O/H application rate is constant within that range. Accordingly, the product of the actual input and the standard variable O/H rate does not change when the denominator volume increases. The production-volume variance (fixed O/H applied based on the standard input allowed for the actual output – budgeted fixed O/H) is unfavorable when budgeted fixed O/H exceeds fixed O/H applied. The application rate equals budgeted fixed O/H divided by the budgeted activity level. If the denominator increases, the rate and the amount applied decrease. Consequently, an unfavorable volume variance will increase when the denominator level increases.

Answer (C) is correct. *(CPA, adapted)*
   REQUIRED: The variance(s) useful for controlling overhead costs.
   DISCUSSION: The production-volume variance, also called the denominator-level variance, is the difference between total budgeted overhead at the standard input allowed for actual output and total overhead absorbed (applied). The difference is attributable solely to the difference between budgeted fixed overhead and the fixed overhead applied. However, the spending variance is simply a price variance for factory overhead. Consequently, it is the spending variance, not the production-volume variance, that would be useful in calling attention to short-term problems in the control of overhead costs.
   Answer (A) is incorrect because the spending variance is actually a price variance. Answer (B) is incorrect because the spending variance, not the production-volume variance, would be useful for controlling overhead costs. Answer (D) is incorrect because the production-volume variance would not point out problems regarding the control of costs.

Answer (B) is correct. *(Publisher, adapted)*
   REQUIRED: The item(s), if any, used in the computation of the variance.
   DISCUSSION: The actual level of output is used in the calculation of the "expected" driver activity level, that is, the amount of the driver that the firm "should" have consumed given the achieved level of production. The expected quantity is used to derive the variable overhead flexible budget (a component of the efficiency variance) and the allocated fixed overhead (a component of the production-volume variance). The expected driver level plays no role in the calculation of either the variable or fixed overhead spending variance.

26. Jones, a department manager, exercises control over the department's costs. Following is selected information relating to the department for the month just ended:

Variable factory overhead

Budgeted based on expected hours	$80,000
Budgeted based on actual hours	87,000
Actual costs incurred	85,000

Fixed factory overhead

Budgeted	25,000
Actual	27,000
Applied	28,000

In a three-way analysis of variance, the department's unfavorable spending variance was

A. $7,000

B. $5,000

C. $2,000

D. $0

Answer (D) is correct. *(CPA, adapted)*
REQUIRED: The amount of unfavorable spending variance.
DISCUSSION: The overhead spending variance in 3-way analysis is the combined spending variances for variable and fixed overhead. The variable spending variance is the difference between the budget based on actual hours (the "third" budget) and the actual costs incurred ($87,000 – $85,000 = $2,000 favorable). The fixed spending variance is the difference between the flexible/static budget and the actual costs incurred ($25,000 – $27,000 = $2,000 unfavorable). The sum of these two variances yields a combined spending variance of $0.
Answer (A) is incorrect because $7,000 unfavorable is the variable overhead efficiency variance. Answer (B) is incorrect because $5,000 unfavorable is the variable overhead flexible budget variance. Answer (C) is incorrect because $2,000 unfavorable is the fixed overhead spending variance.

27. Baby Frames, Inc. evaluates manufacturing overhead in its factory by using variance analysis. The following information applies to the month just ended:

	Actual	Budgeted
Number of frames manufactured	19,000	20,000
Variable overhead costs	$4,100	$2 per direct labor hour
Fixed overhead costs	$22,000	$20,000
Direct labor hours	2,100 hours	0.1 hour per frame

What is the fixed overhead spending variance?

A. $1,000 favorable.

B. $1,000 unfavorable.

C. $2,000 favorable.

D. $2,000 unfavorable.

Answer (D) is correct. *(CPA, adapted)*
REQUIRED: The fixed overhead spending variance.
DISCUSSION: The fixed overhead spending variance or budget variance is the difference between actual fixed manufacturing overhead costs and the amount budgeted. The fixed overhead spending variance is thus $2,000 unfavorable ($20,000 – $22,000).
Answer (A) is incorrect because $1,000 favorable is the reverse of the production-volume variance. Answer (B) is incorrect because $1,000 unfavorable is the production-volume variance. Answer (C) is incorrect because actual costs exceed budgeted costs, causing the $2,000 variance to be unfavorable.

20.5 Comprehensive Example of Variance Analysis

Questions 28 through 31 are based on the following information.

Ardmore Enterprises uses a standard cost system in its small appliance division. The standard cost of manufacturing one unit of Zeb is as follows:

Direct Materials – 60 pounds at $1.50 per pound	$ 90
Direct Labor – 3 hours at $12 per hour	36
Variable Overhead – 3 hours at $8 per DL hour	24
Total standard variable cost per unit	$150

The budgeted fixed overhead is $27,000 per month. During May, Ardmore produced 1,650 units of Zeb compared with a normal capacity of 1,800 units. The actual cost per unit was as follows:

Direct Materials (purchased and used) –	
58 pounds at $1.65 per pound	$ 95.70
Direct Labor – 3.1 hours at $12.40 per hour	38.44
Variable Overhead – $39,930 for 1,650 units	24.20
Total actual variable cost per unit	$158.34

28. Ardmore's total direct materials quantity variance for May is

A. $14,355 favorable.

B. $14,355 unfavorable.

C. $4,950 favorable.

D. $4,950 unfavorable.

Answer (C) is correct. *(CMA, adapted)*
REQUIRED: The direct materials quantity variance.
DISCUSSION: The direct materials quantity (efficiency, usage) variance measures how efficiently direct materials were used given the actual level of production (holding price constant). It is calculated as the flexible budget minus the "third" budget. The formula is: $(EQ - AQ) \times SP$. For Ardmore, the calculation is thus

$(EQ - AQ) \times SP$
$= [(1{,}650 \text{ units output} \times 60 \text{ standard pounds DM}$
$\quad \text{per unit of output}) - (1{,}650 \text{ units output} \times 58$
$\quad \text{actual pounds DM per unit of output})] \times \$1.50$
$= (99{,}000 \text{ pounds} - 95{,}700 \text{ pounds}) \times \$1.50$
$= 3{,}300 \text{ pounds} \times \$1.50$
$= \$4{,}950 \text{ favorable}$

Answer (A) is incorrect because $14,355 is the amount of the direct materials price variance. Answer (B) is incorrect because $14,355 unfavorable is the direct materials price variance. Answer (D) is incorrect because a favorable variance exists. The expected quantity exceeded the actual quantity.

29. Ardmore's direct materials price variance for May is

A. $14,355 unfavorable.

B. $14,850 unfavorable.

C. $14,355 favorable.

D. $14,850 favorable.

Answer (A) is correct. *(CMA, adapted)*
REQUIRED: The direct materials price variance.
DISCUSSION: The direct materials price variance is a pure measure of how much the actual price paid for inputs deviated from the standard (holding quantity constant). It is calculated as the "third" budget minus the actual results. The formula is: $AQ \times (SP - AP)$. For Ardmore, the calculation is thus

$AQ \times (SP - AP) = (1{,}650 \text{ units output} \times 58 \text{ actual pounds DM}$
$\quad \text{per unit of output}) \times (\$1.50 - \$1.65)$
$= 95{,}700 \text{ pounds} \times (-\$0.15)$
$= \$14{,}355 \text{ unfavorable}$

Answer (B) is incorrect because $14,850 is based on the standard unit quantity, not the actual quantity. Answer (C) is incorrect because the price variance is unfavorable. The actual price is greater than the standard price. Answer (D) is incorrect because the variance is unfavorable, and $14,850 is based on the standard unit quantity.

30. Ardmore's direct labor rate variance for May is

    A. $1,980 unfavorable.

    B. $0

    C. $2,046 unfavorable.

    D. $2,046 favorable.

Answer (C) is correct. *(CMA, adapted)*
    REQUIRED: The direct labor rate variance.
    DISCUSSION: The direct labor rate variance is a pure measure of how much the actual price paid for labor deviated from the standard (holding hours worked constant). It is calculated as the "third" budget minus the actual results. The formula is: AQ × (SP – AP). For Ardmore, the calculation is thus

$$AQ \times (SP - AP) = (1{,}650 \text{ units output} \times 3.1 \text{ actual hours DL per unit of output}) \times (\$12.00 - \$12.40)$$
$$= 5{,}115 \text{ hours} \times (-\$0.40)$$
$$= \$2{,}046 \text{ unfavorable}$$

    Answer (A) is incorrect because $1,980 unfavorable is the labor efficiency variance. Answer (B) is incorrect because direct labor does have a rate variance. Answer (D) is incorrect because $2,046 favorable results from reversing the order of subtraction of the standard and actual rates.

31. Ardmore's flexible budget variance for flexible overhead for May is

    A. $330 unfavorable.

    B. $990 favorable.

    C. $1,320 unfavorable.

    D. $1,320 favorable.

Answer (A) is correct. *(CMA, adapted)*
    REQUIRED: The flexible budget variable overhead variance.
    DISCUSSION: The flexible budget variable overhead variance is the difference between actual variable overhead costs incurred and the flexible budget amount. The flexible budget variance for variable overhead is determined in the same manner as that for materials and labor. It is calculated as the flexible budget minus the actual costs incurred. Ardmore's driver for variable overhead is direct labor hours. The formula for the flexible budget variance is: (EQ × SP) – Actual costs incurred. For Ardmore, the calculation is thus

$$(EQ \times SP) - \text{Actual costs incurred})$$
$$= [(1{,}650 \text{ units output} \times 3 \text{ DL driver hours per unit of output}) \times \$8.00] - \$39{,}930$$
$$= \$39{,}600 - \$39{,}930$$
$$= \$330 \text{ unfavorable}$$

    Answer (B) is incorrect because $990 favorable is the variable overhead spending variance. Answer (C) is incorrect because $1,320 unfavorable is the variable overhead efficiency variance. Answer (D) is incorrect because $1,320 favorable results from reversing the order of subtraction of the variable overhead efficiency variance.

Questions 32 through 36 are based on the following information.

Water Control Systems manufactures pumps and uses a standard cost system. The standard factory overhead costs per water pump are based on direct labor hours and are as follows:

Variable overhead (4 hours at $8/hour)	$32
Fixed overhead (4 hours at $5/hour)	20
Total overhead cost per unit	$52

The following additional information is available for the month of November:

- 22,000 pumps were produced although 25,000 had been scheduled for production.
- 94,000 direct labor hours were worked at a total cost of $940,000.
- The standard direct labor rate is $9 per hour.
- The standard direct labor time per unit is 4 hours.
- Variable overhead costs were $740,000.
- Fixed overhead costs were $540,000.

32. Water Control Systems' fixed overhead spending variance for November was

A. $40,000 unfavorable.

B. $70,000 unfavorable.

C. $60,000 unfavorable.

D. $100,000 unfavorable.

Answer (A) is correct. *(CMA, adapted)*
REQUIRED: The fixed overhead spending variance.
DISCUSSION: The fixed overhead spending variance equals the flexible/static budget minus the actual costs incurred (the flexible and static budgets for fixed overhead are identical because the same amount of fixed costs must be covered regardless of the level of production). Since the static budget called for the production of 25,000 pumps, each pump takes 4 hours of direct labor (the fixed overhead driver), and fixed overhead is budgeted at the rate of $5 per DL hour, the flexible/static budget is $500,000 (25,000 pumps × $5 × 4 hours). Actual fixed overhead costs incurred amounted to $540,000. Thus, the fixed overhead spending variance was $40,000 unfavorable ($500,000 – $540,000).
Answer (B) is incorrect because $70,000 unfavorable is the difference between actual fixed overhead and the product of the standard rate and the actual direct labor hours. Answer (C) is incorrect because $60,000 unfavorable is the production-volume variance. Answer (D) is incorrect because $100,000 unfavorable results from improperly combining the spending and production-volume variances.

33. Water Control Systems' variable overhead spending variance for November was

A. $60,000 favorable.

B. $12,000 favorable.

C. $48,000 unfavorable.

D. $36,000 unfavorable.

Answer (B) is correct. *(CMA, adapted)*
REQUIRED: The variable overhead spending variance.
DISCUSSION: The spending variance for variable overhead is determined in the same manner as the price variance for materials and the rate variance for labor. It measures the accuracy of the estimates used to derive the application rate. It is calculated as the "third" budget minus the actual costs incurred. For Water Control Systems, the calculation is thus

"Third" budget – Actual
    costs incurred   = (AQ × SP) – Actual costs incurred
                     = (94,000 DL driver hours worked × $8) – $740,000
                     = $752,000 – $740,000
                     = $12,000 favorable

Answer (A) is incorrect because $60,000 favorable is the static budget variance. Answer (C) is incorrect because $48,000 unfavorable is the efficiency variance. Answer (D) is incorrect because $36,000 unfavorable is the flexible budget variance.

34. Water Control Systems' variable overhead efficiency variance for November was

A. $48,000 unfavorable.

B. $60,000 favorable.

C. $96,000 favorable.

D. $36,000 unfavorable.

Answer (A) is correct. *(CMA, adapted)*
REQUIRED: The variable overhead efficiency variance.
DISCUSSION: The efficiency variance for variable overhead is determined in the same manner as the quantity variance for materials and the efficiency variance for labor. It measures the efficiency with which the allocation base was used (holding the application rate constant). It is calculated as the flexible budget minus the "third" budget. For Water Control Systems, the calculation is thus

$(EQ - AQ) \times SP$
= [(22,000 pumps produced × 4 standard DL hours per pump) − 94,000 actual DL hours] × $8
= (88,000 hours − 94,000 hours) × $8
= −6,000 pounds × $8
= $48,000 unfavorable

Answer (B) is incorrect because $60,000 favorable is the static budget variance. Answer (C) is incorrect because $96,000 favorable is the sales volume variance. Answer (D) is incorrect because $36,000 unfavorable is the flexible budget variance.

35. Water Control Systems' direct labor rate variance for November was

A. $54,000 unfavorable.

B. $94,000 unfavorable.

C. $40,000 unfavorable.

D. $148,000 unfavorable.

Answer (B) is correct. *(CMA, adapted)*
REQUIRED: The direct labor rate variance.
DISCUSSION: The direct labor rate variance is a pure measure of how much the actual price paid for labor deviated from the standard (holding hours worked constant). It is calculated as the "third" budget minus the actual results. For Water Control Systems, the calculation is thus

"Third" budget −
Actual results   = (AQ × SP) − $940,000
= (94,000 hours worked × $9) − $940,000
= $846,000 − $940,000
= $94,000 unfavorable

Answer (A) is incorrect because $54,000 unfavorable is the efficiency variance. Answer (C) is incorrect because $40,000 unfavorable is the static budget variance. Answer (D) is incorrect because $148,000 unfavorable is the flexible budget variance.

36. Water Control Systems' direct labor efficiency variance for November was

A. $108,000 favorable.

B. $148,000 unfavorable.

C. $40,000 unfavorable.

D. $54,000 unfavorable.

Answer (D) is correct. *(CMA, adapted)*
REQUIRED: The direct labor efficiency variance.
DISCUSSION: The direct labor efficiency variance measures how efficiently labor was employed given the actual level of production (holding the wage rate constant). It is calculated as the flexible budget minus the "third" budget. The formula is: [(EQ − AQ) × SP]. For Water Control Systems, the calculation is thus

$(EQ - AQ) \times SP$
= [(22,000 pumps produced × 4 standard DL hours per pump) − 94,000 actual DL hours] × $9
= (88,000 hours − 94,000 hours) × $9
= −6,000 pounds × $9
= $54,000 unfavorable

Answer (A) is incorrect because $108,000 favorable is the sales volume variance. Answer (B) is incorrect because $148,000 unfavorable is the flexible budget variance. Answer (C) is incorrect because $40,000 unfavorable is the static budget variance between actual hours.

Use Gleim's *CPA Test Prep* for interactive testing with over 2,000 additional multiple-choice questions!

REVIEW CHECKLIST
BUSINESS

Your objective is to prepare to pass this section of the CPA exam. It is **not** to do a certain amount of work or spend a certain amount of time with this book or other CPA review material/courses. Rather, you **must**

1. Understand the CPA exam thoroughly -- study *CPA Review: A System for Success* and the Introduction in this book.

2. Understand the subject matter in the 20 study units in this book. The list of subunits in each of the 20 study units (presented below and on the following page) should bring to mind core concepts, basic rules, principles, etc.

3. If you have not already done so, prepare a 1- to 2-page summary of each study unit for your final review just before you go to the exam (do not bring notes into the examination room).

Study Unit 1: Proprietorships and General Partnerships

1.1 Sole Proprietorships
1.2 General Partnerships
1.3 Joint Ventures

Study Unit 2: Noncorporate Limited Liability Entities

2.1 Limited Partnerships
2.2 Limited Liability Partnerships (LLPs)
2.3 Limited Liability Companies (LLCs)

Study Unit 3: Corporations: Formation, Powers, and Financing

3.1 Definition
3.2 Formation
3.3 Powers of a Corporation
3.4 Financing

Study Unit 4: Corporations: Governance and Fundamental Changes

4.1 Governance
4.2 Fundamental Corporate Changes

Study Unit 5: Microeconomics

5.1 Demand, Supply, and Equilibrium
5.2 Elasticity
5.3 Market Structures

Study Unit 6: Macroeconomics

6.1 Three Principal Issues in Macroeconomics
6.2 Domestic Output, National Income, and Price Levels
6.3 Business Cycles
6.4 Fiscal Policy
6.5 Monetary Policy

Study Unit 7: International Trade

7.1 Advantages of International Trade
7.2 Trade Barriers
7.3 Foreign Currency Rates and Markets
7.4 Balance of Payments

Study Unit 8: Working Capital Policy and Management

8.1 Financial Management
8.2 Cash Management
8.3 Marketable Securities Management
8.4 Receivables Management
8.5 Short-Term Credit
8.6 Inventory and Supply Chain Management

Study Unit 9: Long-Term Capital Financing

9.1 Sources of Long-Term Financing
9.2 Optimal Capitalization and Cost of Capital
9.3 Dividend Policy
9.4 Ranking Investment Proposals

Study Unit 10: Risk Management and Profitability

10.1 Types of Risk
10.2 Risk Measurement
10.3 Portfolio Management
10.4 Derivative Financial Instruments
10.5 Ratios
10.6 Limitations of Ratio Analysis

Study Unit 11: Information Technology I

11.1 Role of Business Information Systems
11.2 Risks Associated with Business Information Systems
11.3 Roles and Responsibilities within the IT Function
11.4 Systems Development and Design

Study Unit 12: Information Technology II

12.1 Hardware
12.2 Software
12.3 Networks
12.4 Internet and Intranet

Study Unit 13: Information Technology III

13.1 Operating Systems
13.2 Security
13.3 Types of Data Files
13.4 Nature of Binary Data Storage
13.5 File Organization and Access Methods

INDEX

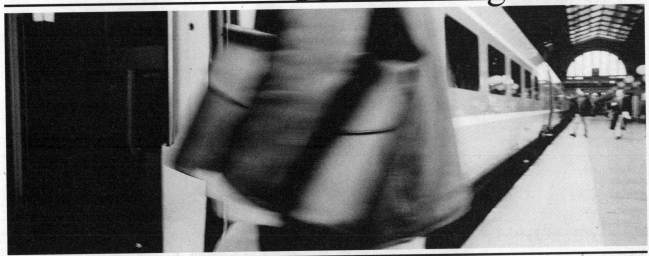

The GLEIM CPA System Works!

GLEIM
KNOWLEDGE
TRANSFER
SYSTEMS®

CPA

COMPLETE GLEIM CPA SYSTEM

All 4 sections, including Gleim Online, books*, *Test Prep CD-Rom*, *Test Prep for Pocket PC*, Audio CDs, plus bonus book bag.

Also available by exam section @ $274.95 (does not include book bag).

*Fifth book: *CPA Review: A System for Success*

☐ $989.95

$_____

CMA

COMPLETE GLEIM CMA SYSTEM

Includes: Gleim Online, books*, *Test Prep CD-Rom*, *Test Prep for Pocket PC*, Audio CDs, plus bonus book bag.

Also available by exam part @ $213.95 (does not include book bag).

*Fifth book: *CMA Review: A System for Success*

☐ CMA $739.95

$_____

CIA

COMPLETE GLEIM CIA SYSTEM

Includes: Gleim Online, books*, *Test Prep CD-Rom*, *Test Prep for Pocket PC*, Audio CDs, plus bonus book bag.

Also available by exam part @ $224.95 (does not include book bag).

*Fifth book: *CIA Review: A System for Success*

☐ $824.95

$_____

EA

GLEIM EA REVIEW SYSTEM

Includes: Gleim Online, books, *Test Prep CD-Rom*, *Test Prep for Pocket PC*, Audio CDs, plus bonus book bag.

Also available by exam part @ $224.95 (does not include book bag).

☐ $629.95

$_____

EQE

"THE GLEIM SERIES" EXAM QUESTIONS AND EXPLANATIONS

Includes: 5 books and *Test Prep CD-Rom*.

Also available by part @ $29.95.

☐ $112.25

$_____

Contact
GLEIM PUBLICATIONS
for further assistance:

gleim.com
800.874.5346
sales@gleim.com

SUBTOTAL $_____
Complete your
order on the
next page

GLEIM PUBLICATIONS, INC.

P. O. Box 12848   Gainesville, FL 32604

TOLL FREE: 800.874.5346
LOCAL: 352.375.0772
FAX: 352.375.6940
INTERNET: gleim.com
E-MAIL: sales@gleim.com

Customer service is available (Eastern Time):

8:00 a.m. - 7:00 p.m., Mon. - Fri.

9:00 a.m. - 2:00 p.m., Saturday

Please have your credit card ready,
or save time by ordering online!

SUBTOTAL (from previous page)	$_____
Add applicable sales tax for shipments within Florida.	_____
Shipping (nonrefundable)	25.00
TOTAL	$_____

Fax or write for prices/instructions on shipments outside the 48 contiguous states, or simply order online.

NAME (please print) _____

ADDRESS _____ Apt. _____
(street address required for UPS)

CITY _____ STATE _____ ZIP _____

____ MC/VISA/DISC ____ Check/M.O.   Daytime Telephone (____)_____

Credit Card No. _____ - _____ - _____ - _____

Exp. ____/____   Signature _____
    Month / Year

E-mail address _____

1. We process and ship orders daily, within one business day over 98.8% of the time. Call by 3:00 pm for same day service.
2. Please PHOTOCOPY this order form for others.
3. No CODs. Orders from individuals must be prepaid.
4. Gleim Publications, Inc. guarantees the immediate refund of all resalable texts and unopened software and audios if returned within 30 days. Applies only to items purchased direct from Gleim Publications, Inc. Our shipping charge is nonrefundable.
5. Components of specially priced package deals are nonrefundable.

Prices subject to change without notice.
12/07

For updates and other important information, visit our website.

GLEIM
KNOWLEDGE
TRANSFER
SYSTEMS®

Please forward your suggestions, corrections, and comments concerning typographical errors, etc., to **Irvin N. Gleim • c/o Gleim Publications, Inc. • P.O. Box 12848 • University Station • Gainesville, Florida • 32604.** Please include your name and address so we can properly thank you for your interest.

1. _____

2. _____

3. _____

4. _____

5. _____

6. _____

7. _____

8. _____

9. _____

10. _____

706

CPA Review: Business Environment and Concepts, 2008 Edition, First Printing -- Please complete and mail to us pages 705 and 706 the week following the CPA exam. The information requested on these pages is in full compliance with the AICPA's policy on candidate disclosure of exam information.

11. _____

12. _____

13. _____

14. _____

15. _____

16. _____

17. _____

18. _____

Remember, for superior service: Mail, email, or fax questions about our materials.
Telephone questions about orders, prices, shipments, or payments.

Name: _____

Address: _____

City/State/Zip: _____

Telephone: Home: _____ Work: _____ Fax: _____

Email: _____